WITHDRAWN
Wilmette Public Library

WILMETTE PUBLIC LIBRARY
1242 WILMETTE AVE.
WILMETTE, IL 60091
847-256-5025

Historic Documents
of 2016

Sara Miller McCune founded SAGE Publishing in 1965 to support the dissemination of usable knowledge and educate a global community. SAGE publishes more than 1000 journals and over 800 new books each year, spanning a wide range of subject areas. Our growing selection of library products includes archives, data, case studies and video. SAGE remains majority owned by our founder and after her lifetime will become owned by a charitable trust that secures the company's continued independence.

Los Angeles | London | New Delhi | Singapore | Washington DC | Melbourne

Historic Documents
of 2016

Heather Kerrigan, Editor

WILMETTE PUBLIC LIBRARY

FOR INFORMATION:

CQ Press

An Imprint of SAGE Publications, Inc.

2455 Teller Road

Thousand Oaks, California 91320

E-mail: order@sagepub.com

SAGE Publications Ltd.

1 Oliver's Yard

55 City Road

London EC1Y 1SP

United Kingdom

SAGE Publications India Pvt. Ltd.

B 1/I 1 Mohan Cooperative Industrial Area

Mathura Road, New Delhi 110 044

India

SAGE Publications Asia-Pacific Pte. Ltd.

3 Church Street

#10-04 Samsung Hub

Singapore 049483

SAGE Editor: Laura Notton

Editor: Heather Kerrigan

Managing Editor: Linda Fecteau Grimm

Contributors: Brian Beary

Melissa Feinberg

Linda Fecteau Grimm

Robert Howard

Megan Howes

Heather Kerrigan

Production Editor: Andrew Olson

Copy Editor: Deanna Noga

Typesetter: C&M Digitals (P) Ltd.

Proofreader: Talia Greenberg

Indexer: Karen Wiley

Cover Designer: Michael Dubowe

Marketing Manager: Kate Brummitt

Copyright © 2017 by CQ Press, an Imprint of SAGE Publications, Inc. CQ Press is a registered trademark of Congressional Quarterly Inc.

All rights reserved. No part of this book may be reproduced or utilized in any form or by any means, electronic or mechanical, including photocopying, recording, or by any information storage and retrieval system, without permission in writing from the publisher.

Printed in the United States of America

ISBN 978-1-5063-7500-7

ISSN 0892-080X

This book is printed on acid-free paper.

17 18 19 20 21 10 9 8 7 6 5 4 3 2 1

973
Co

Contents

JANUARY

Secretary of State John Kerry from January 16, 2016, following the plan's implementation; and a joint statement from EU High Representative Federica Mogherini and Iranian Foreign Minister Javad Zarif from January 16, 2016, about the plan's implementation.

FEBRUARY

MARCH

APRIL

MAY

JUNE

JULY

A statement from July 10, 2016, by United Nations Secretary-General
Ban Ki-moon on renewed fighting in South Sudan; a July 10, 2016,
statement from the UN Security Council on the violence in South
Sudan; a July 27, 2016, press release from the United Nations on the
cholera outbreak in South Sudan; an August 3, 2016, press release from
the United Nations on the humanitarian crisis in South Sudan; and a
press release from the Ethiopian Ministry of Foreign Affairs on
September 30, 2016, announcing the border demarcation agreement.

Remarks by President Barack Obama at a memorial service for the
Dallas police officers on July 12, 2016; remarks by Obama from
July 17, 2016, during a press conference about the Baton Rouge
shooting; the U.S. Circuit Court for Baltimore City, Maryland's ruling
from July 18, 2016, in the case of *State of Maryland vs. Brian Rice*; and
the executive summary from the U.S. Department of Justice's report
on its investigation into the Baltimore City Police Department, released
on August 10, 2016.

A July 16, 2016, statement from the Turkish Ministry of Foreign
Affairs on the coup attempt in Turkey; a July 25, 2016, statement
from the Turkish government regarding a meeting at the presidential
complex on the coup attempt; and a press release from the Turkish
Armed Forces on July 27, 2016, detailing the attempted coup.

The executive summary of the World Anti-Doping Agency's report from
July 18, 2016, in which it outlined the findings of its independent-person
investigation into Russian doping allegations; a statement by Russian President
Vladimir Putin from July 18, 2016, responding to the World Anti-Doping
Agency's investigation; the International Olympic Committee (IOC) Executive
Board's July 24, 2016, decision on Russian athletes' participation in the 2016
Olympic Games; and IOC President Thomas Bach's remarks at the games'
opening and closing ceremonies on August 5 and August 21, 2016.

Excerpts of a White House press briefing on July 25, 2016, in which Press
Secretary Josh Earnest answered questions about the Democratic National

Committee hack; and a press release issued by U.S. Chief Information Officer Tony Scott and Special Assistant to the President and Cybersecurity Coordinator Michael Daniel from September 8, 2016, announcing the first federal chief information security officer.

AUGUST

SEPTEMBER

NOVEMBER

DECEMBER

Thematic Table of Contents

GOVERNMENT AND POLITICS

HEALTH AND SOCIAL SERVICES

INTERNATIONAL AFFAIRS
AFRICA

INTERNATIONAL AFFAIRS
ASIA

INTERNATIONAL AFFAIRS
CANADA

INTERNATIONAL AFFAIRS
EUROPE

INTERNATIONAL AFFAIRS
LATIN AMERICA AND THE CARIBBEAN

INTERNATIONAL AFFAIRS
MIDDLE EAST

INTERNATIONAL AFFAIRS
RUSSIA AND THE FORMER SOVIET UNION

INTERNATIONAL AFFAIRS
GLOBAL ISSUES

NATIONAL SECURITY AND TERRORISM

RIGHTS, RESPONSIBILITIES, AND JUSTICE

List of Document Sources

CONGRESS

EXECUTIVE DEPARTMENTS, AGENCIES, FEDERAL OFFICES, AND COMMISSIONS

INTERNATIONAL GOVERNMENTAL ORGANIZATIONS

INTERNATIONAL NONGOVERNMENTAL ORGANIZATIONS

JUDICIARY

NONGOVERNMENTAL ORGANIZATIONS

NON-U.S. GOVERNMENTS

U.S. STATE AND LOCAL GOVERNMENTS

WHITE HOUSE AND THE PRESIDENT

Preface

The closely watched, impassioned U.S. presidential election, the impeachment of Brazil's and South Korea's first female presidents, major milestones in human spaceflight and space exploration, ISIL-affiliated attacks across Europe and the Middle East, the "Panama Papers" scandal, tensions between U.S. law enforcement and black communities, the historic "Brexit" referendum, political unrest and humanitarian concerns in Sudan and the Democratic Republic of the Congo, strides in global efforts to combat climate change, and Supreme Court decisions on immigration, abortion, and voting district apportionment are just a few of the topics of national and international significance chosen for discussion in *Historic Documents of 2016*. This edition marks the forty-fourth volume of a CQ Press project that began with *Historic Documents of 1972*. This series allows students, librarians, journalists, scholars, and others to research and understand the most important domestic and foreign issues and events of the year through primary source documents. To aid research, many of the lengthy documents written for specialized audiences have been excerpted to highlight the most important sections. The official statements, news conferences, speeches, special studies, and court decisions presented here should be of lasting public and academic interest.

Historic Documents of 2016 opens with an "Overview of 2016," a sweeping narrative of the key events and issues of the year, which provides context for the documents that follow. The balance of the book is organized chronologically, with each article comprising an introduction and one or more related documents on a specific event, issue, or topic. Often an event is not limited to a particular day. Consequently, readers will find that some events include multiple documents that may span several months. Their placement in the book corresponds to the date of the first document included for that event. The event introductions provide context and an account of further developments during the year. A thematic table of contents (page xvii) and a list of documents organized by source (page xxi) follow the standard table of contents and assist readers in locating events and documents.

As events, issues, and consequences become more complex and far-reaching, these introductions and documents yield important information and deepen understanding about the world's increasing interconnectedness. As memories of current events fade, these selections will continue to further understanding of the events and issues that have shaped the lives of people around the world.

How to Use This Book

Each of the sixty entries in this edition consists of two parts: a comprehensive introduction followed by one or more primary source documents. The articles are arranged in chronological order by month. Articles with multiple documents are placed according to the date of the first document. There are several ways to find events and documents of interest:

By date: If the approximate date of an event or document is known, browse through the titles for that month in the table of contents. Alternatively, browse the tables of contents that appear at the beginning of each month's articles.

By theme: To find a particular topic or subject area, browse the thematic table of contents.

By document type or source: To find a particular type of document or document source, such as the White House or Congress, review the list of document sources.

By index: The index allows researchers to locate references to specific events or documents as well as entries on the same or related subjects.

An online edition of this volume, as well as an archive going back to 1972, is available and offers advance search and browse functionality.

Each article begins with an introduction. This feature provides historical and intellectual contexts for the documents that follow. Documents are reproduced with the original spelling, capitalization, and punctuation of the original or official copy. Ellipsis points indicate textual omissions (unless they were present in the documents themselves indicating pauses in speech), and brackets are used for editorial insertions within documents for text clarification. The excerpting of Supreme Court opinions has been done somewhat differently from other documents. In-text references and citations to laws and other cases have been removed when not part of a sentence to improve the readability of opinions. In those documents, readers will find ellipses used only when sections of narrative text have been removed.

Full citations appear at the end of each document. If a document is not available on the Internet, this too is noted. For further reading on a particular topic consult the "Other Historic Documents of Interest" section at the end of each article. These sections provide cross-references for related articles in this edition of *Historic Documents* as well as in previous editions. References to articles from past volumes include the year and page number for easy retrieval.

Overview of 2016

In the United States, 2016 was characterized by events surrounding the presidential election that pitted former secretary of state Hillary Clinton against businessman Donald Trump. The candidates waged campaigns that were focused more on the wrongdoings of the opponent rather than on the candidate's own plans for the country. Ultimately, Trump was victorious in the Electoral College, despite Clinton winning the popular vote. The year also saw the resurgence of the gun control debate in Congress after forty-nine were killed in a nightclub in Orlando, Florida, by an individual who had been investigated for links to terrorism. As in years past, 2016 came to a close without any action on the issue at the federal level. President Barack Obama used his last year in office to deliver on many of the promises he had made during the previous seven years, many of which were related to climate change and protecting the environment. For the first time, the United States ratified an international climate change agreement (the United States was previously only a signatory to the Kyoto Protocol) that seeks to limit the worldwide temperature increase during the current century to less than 2° C above pre-industrial levels. With the full backing of the United States, the Paris Agreement was believed by many in the international community to have more force than previous climate pacts.

Internationally, the Islamic State of Iraq and the Levant (ISIL) dominated headlines as it carried out numerous attacks in Europe and the Middle East. A North Atlantic Treaty Organization (NATO)–led coalition struggled to combat the group's ongoing insurgence, and many countries, including the United States, committed additional troops and carried out more airstrikes in Iraq and Syria to stop the terrorist organization. ISIL's power continued to force civilians to flee their homes, and many of these individuals sought shelter in Europe. The growing number of refugees arriving on the continent, and ongoing ISIL attacks, fueled the rise of nationalist sentiments that resulted in right-wing political groups growing in popularity in nations such as France, Germany, the United Kingdom (UK), and the Netherlands. In a surprising turn of events, UK voters opted to leave the European Union (EU), in part because of its border policies that allowed refugees to relocate across the continent. South American nations also experienced unrest in 2016. Brazil's first female president was impeached while the nation struggled with multifaceted challenges including widespread economic distress, a Zika virus outbreak, and preparing for the Olympics. In neighboring Colombia, the government reached an historic peace agreement with the Revolutionary Armed Forces of Colombia (FARC) to end a fifty-year-long civil war. That agreement was rejected by voters and had to be rewritten in a way that ensured FARC rebels would face greater responsibility for their actions. In Africa, both South Sudan and the Democratic Republic of the Congo (DRC) experienced power struggles at the highest levels of government that resulted in mass unrest and protests leading to the deaths of hundreds of civilians.

DOMESTIC ISSUES

States and Localities in the National Spotlight

Although public attention was largely focused throughout 2016 on the contentious presidential election, states and localities across the country found their way into the spotlight. In January, federal and local states of emergency were declared in Flint, Michigan, a city on the outskirts of Detroit, because the water supply had become undrinkable due to elevated levels of lead. The problem began when the city changed water sources in 2014, but failed to follow federal guidelines and introduce a corrosion inhibitor to the water to stop the city's aging water pipes from corroding. Prior to the declarations, some city residents who drank the water experienced abdominal pain, sudden hair loss, and rashes. In response to the crisis, Michigan's governor and the federal government pledged millions to provide safe drinking water to residents and upgrade the city's infrastructure. State and congressional investigations into the crisis revealed negligence on the part of officials at many levels, who were in turn fired from their positions.

In North Carolina, then-governor Pat McCrory signed into law the Public Facilities Privacy & Security Act on March 23. The bill had two primary functions: to require those in public facilities to use the restroom, locker room, or other similar facility that corresponds with their gender at birth rather than the gender with which the individual identifies, and to overturn an LGBT antidiscrimination order passed in the city of Charlotte and further prevent other municipalities from implementing similar laws. Negative response to the bill was swift, and it even drew a lawsuit from the federal Justice Department. In late April, McCrory used his executive authority to implement changes to the law that he said would help clarify its meaning and allay concerns that had been raised about whether the state was discriminating against transgender individuals. The changes did not lift the ban on municipal action, nor did it remove the public facility regulations. It instead called for the maintenance of "common sense gender specific . . . facilities in government buildings and schools" and struck the word *biological* from the law, raising questions about how sexual identity would be defined. The bathroom bill, as it became known, was a key issue in the North Carolina gubernatorial election, which resulted in McCrory's defeat by the state's attorney general, Roy Cooper, a Democrat.

President Obama's Final Year in Office

President Barack Obama began his last year in office with a State of the Union address about the importance of moving America forward and looking to the future. While he did not provide the traditional laundry list of plans for the year, it was clear that he also did not intend to become a lame-duck president. Despite the attention focused on the 2016 state and federal elections, President Obama was able to make progress on a number of his long-term promises, although most of his action came through executive order rather than Congress.

In September, Obama stood with Chinese President Xi Jinping to ratify the Paris climate agreement, a successor to the Kyoto Protocol and viewed by many as a necessary step toward limiting global climate change. Combating rising temperatures was a focal point for the president throughout his eight years in office, and he worked diligently to secure policies like the Clean Power Plan, an Environmental Protection Agency policy aimed at reducing carbon emissions from power plants. The ratification of the Paris Agreement by the United States and China led many other nations to quickly sign onto the plan, which required that nations implement greenhouse gas–reducing plans of action that had been submitted to the United Nations Framework Convention on Climate Change. The Paris Agreement entered into force during the first week of November, just days before the U.S. presidential election.

One month before Inauguration Day, President Obama used his executive authority to ban drilling on hundreds of millions of acres of federal land in the Arctic and Atlantic Oceans. Although the move would not impact leases that were already in place, it would put offshore areas along most of the eastern seaboard off limits for oil and gas exploration. Also in the final month of his presidency, Obama designated 1.6 million acres of land in Nevada and Utah as national monuments. Such designation prohibits mining and drilling on the land and brought the total amount of lands protected during his presidency to 550 million acres.

Congress refused to move forward on a number of the president's proposals, most notably to vote on his nominee to replace Supreme Court Justice Antonin Scalia, who died in February. Obama nominated Merrick Garland, a chief judge for the United States Court of Appeals for the District of Columbia Circuit, despite a promise from Senate Republican leadership that it would not consider any nominee put forth by Obama, arguing that in a presidential election year, it would be more appropriate to let the next president choose a justice to fill Scalia's seat. The inaction in the Senate left the Supreme Court with only eight members, four of whom generally vote liberal and four conservative, causing deadlocks on a number of cases.

Gun Violence

In 2014 and 2015, public debate over police overreach reached a fever pitch when a number of unarmed black men were shot by police during separate incidents across the country. The ire some in the public felt for police carried on into 2016 when three Baltimore officers accused of being involved in the death of twenty-five-year-old Freddie Gray, who died while in police custody, were acquitted. A fourth officer's trial had already resulted in a hung jury in December 2015, and prosecutors ultimately dropped all remaining charges in July after determining that convictions would be unlikely in any future trials. Following the acquittals and decision not to pursue additional trials, the U.S. Justice Department released a report on the Baltimore Police Department that indicated it has a history of disproportionately targeting African Americans for stops, searches, arrests, and use of excessive force.

Shortly before the acquittals in Baltimore, two other African American men were killed by police in Minneapolis and Baton Rouge. At a July 7 gathering in Dallas organized by Black Lives Matter to protest the deaths of these individuals, five police officers assigned to protect the gathering were killed and seven others were wounded. The suspected shooter, Micah Xavier Johnson, a twenty-five-year-old African American Army veteran, was eventually killed by police. Only ten days later, three officers were killed and two others wounded near a Baton Rouge police station. The targeting of police officers led to changes to policing practices across the country aimed at pairing officers and providing them with additional security.

On June 12, the worst mass shooting in American history occurred at the Pulse night-club in Orlando, Florida, where forty-nine people plus the shooter were killed. The venue was frequented by those in the LGBTQ community, leading President Obama to label the event as not just a terror attack but also a hate crime. The shooting raised questions among some in Congress about the necessity of ensuring greater restrictions on gun ownership. Omar Mateen, the Pulse shooter, had been investigated twice for ties to terror groups and had for a time been on a terror watch list. Had Mateen still been on the list at the time he purchased the weapons, the Justice Department would have been immediately alerted. Two weeks after the shooting, on June 23, Rep. John Lewis, D-Ga., led a sit-in on the floor of the House of Representatives calling on House leadership to "bring common-sense gun control legislation" for a vote on the floor. Senate Democrats had one week earlier held a twelve-hour filibuster in support of four gun control measures before the body, most of which would prevent those on terror watch lists from buying a gun, but all four bills ultimately failed. Although the sit-in drew 170 participants and gained traction across social media when it was live-streamed, by the close of 2016, Congress had failed to pass any gun control legislation.

U.S. PRESIDENTIAL ELECTION

The U.S. presidential primary season kicked off in earnest in 2015, with nineteen candidates vying for the Republican nomination and five for the Democratic nomination. After the March Super Tuesday primaries, the top candidates emerged as former secretary of state Hillary Clinton on the Democratic side and businessman Donald Trump for the Republicans. The two formally secured their party's nominations during conventions in July, but the events, typically meant to display party unity, were not without controversy. In the days leading up to the Democratic convention in Philadelphia, a Democratic National Committee e-mail leak indicated that the party chair, Rep. Debbie Wasserman Schultz, D-Fla., worked to secure a Clinton victory throughout the primary process, instead of maintaining neutrality as is expected. The scandal forced the ouster of Wasserman Schultz from her party leadership position. The situation provided even more fuel for delegates of Clinton's main primary opponent, Sen. Bernie Sanders, I-Vt., who had to be stopped through a diligent effort by the Sanders campaign from walking out in protest of Clinton's nomination. On the Republican side, a group of delegates bound to vote for Trump attempted to implement a rules change that would allow them to unbind themselves from the requirement to vote on behalf of the candidate their state had chosen. After fifteen hours of debate, the rules committee rejected the proposal. A petition was put forth by delegates protesting the requirement to vote with their state, but it was not recognized by the presiding officer who, despite protests coming from the floor of the convention, pushed through the rules by unanimous consent. The Colorado delegation walked out in protest.

Clinton and Trump frequently traded barbs on the campaign trail, but they came face-to-face for three debates in the two months leading up to Election Day. Moderators often struggled to keep the candidates on topic, because they sniped at each other for personal and professional missteps. Trump focused primarily on Clinton's handling of the 2012 Benghazi attack on U.S. government facilities that resulted in the deaths of four Americans, including Ambassador Chris Stevens; the private e-mail server Clinton used during her time as secretary of state; and the sexual assault claims made against Clinton's husband, former president Bill Clinton. Clinton's attacks revolved around Trump's treatment of women—most notably the recording of the candidate insinuating that he is able to sexually assault women because he is famous—as well as his views on Muslims and immigrants, and the temperament of his supporters, whom she classified as racist xenophobes.

Clinton had a comfortable lead in the polls heading into late October, but on October 28, Federal Bureau of Investigation (FBI) director James Comey sent a letter to Congress indicating that the department was looking into Clinton's e-mail from her time as secretary of state, separate from those that had been previously investigated that resulted in no charges being filed. The letter appeared to give fuel to the Trump campaign, and on November 8, the first president without public or military service was elected. Trump took 304 electoral votes to Clinton's 227, while Clinton became the fifth candidate in history to win the popular vote but lose the electoral vote. Electors attempted to unbind themselves ahead of the December convening of the Electoral College to officially cast ballots for president. The delegates were unsuccessful in their attempts at the courts, and ultimately more delegates defected from Clinton than from Trump during the final vote.

President-elect Trump began to assemble his transition team in late November, and reports immediately began surfacing that there was turmoil within Trump's staff. The president was also criticized for not having the proper team in place both prior to and immediately following his election, raising concerns that he might not be fully prepared to take office in January 2017. Among his first key picks, Trump brought in some of his children to fill top advisory roles on the transition team; Reince Priebus, former chair of the Republican National Committee, was named to the chief of staff position; and Stephen Bannon, former executive of the right-wing *Breitbart News*, was named chief strategist and senior counselor. Trump's first choices to fill cabinet positions included Sen. Jeff Sessions, R-Ala., to take on the role of attorney general; Rep. Mike Pompeo, R-Kans., to take over as director of the Central Intelligence Agency (CIA); and Lt. Gen. Michael Flynn to fill the role of national security adviser. Trump's cabinet quickly became the wealthiest in U.S. history, leading to criticism from the left that while Trump had promised to "drain the swamp" of Washington elite serving in government, he was instead filling it with New York's elite. Trump himself had to release a plan to avoid conflicts of interest in his position as president that were related to his business holdings. This primarily included resigning from his positions within the Trump Organization and transferring his assets into a trust that would be managed by his sons. The move did little to allay the concerns of those who thought the president may run afoul of ethics rules.

A major story during the 2016 election was the rise of fake news and the difficulty people had discerning fact from falsehoods distributed by left- or right-leaning organizations, in part due to the frequent sharing of these "news" articles on social media. These sources of information were lent credibility by the American public, and in particular young adults who rely on social media outlets for their news, and Facebook and Google became two of the first Internet companies to come forward and announce that they would make an effort to begin screening links to determine whether the information came from a credible source or was from a potentially questionable, nonmainstream media outlet. The impact of these stories reached a fever pitch in December when U.S. intelligence agencies revealed they had been conducting an assessment that indicated that a misinformation campaign was waged specifically against Clinton and was perpetrated by Russian intelligence officials. According to the CIA, the attempts to influence the presidential election included the hacking of DNC servers that resulted in the release of Wasserman

Schultz's e-mail. Russia denied any such action, but the reports resulted in the decision of the Obama administration to place additional sanctions on some Russian intelligence services, businesses, and individuals. The Trump campaign dismissed the concerns, but the questions about Russian involvement in Trump's election continued into 2017.

FEDERAL COURT DECISIONS

Throughout 2016, federal courts at all levels issued rulings on cases that had wide-ranging impact. For example, on April 4, in one of its first rulings released for the year, the Court dealt with the principle of "one person, one vote" and who should be included in the count to create equal voting districts within a state. The Court's decision in *Evenwel v. Abbott* struck down the challenge to the current method of apportionment—which uses U.S. Census data containing number of total people—that argued that only voting-eligible individuals should be counted in the district drawing rather than all people.

On May 16, the Supreme Court ruled for the fourth time on the 2010 Affordable Care Act (ACA), this time in the case of *Zubik v. Burwell* that challenged the law's provision that employers be required to provide free contraceptive coverage as part of any health care plan offered to employees. The petitioners, all nonprofit religious organizations, argued that, while they were provided a method to opt-out of the requirement, the opt-out itself violated their religious liberty. In a unanimous decision, the Court sent the case back to the lower courts, stating that it "expresses no view on the merits of the case."

On June 27, the Supreme Court overturned a Texas law that required abortion clinics to have specific building standards, such as hallways as wide as those in hospitals, and to employ only doctors with admitting privileges at a nearby hospital. The law placed such stringent restrictions on abortion providers that all but a handful of clinics in the state would be forced to close. In its decisive 5–3 ruling in *Whole Woman's Health v. Hellerstedt* the Court relied on the "undue burden" standard that has been infrequently used by recent Courts. The case was expected to have an impact on not only abortion providers in Texas, but also states across the country that had put in place similar restrictions on requirements for abortion clinics.

Just a few days earlier, on June 23, 2016, the Supreme Court deadlocked on *United States v. Texas*, a case that challenged the legality of President Obama's Deferred Action for Parents of Americans (DAPA) program that allowed an estimated five million illegal immigrants to remain, at least temporarily, in the United States without the fear of deportation and also provided them with the ability to work legally. Due to the death of Justice Antonin Scalia in February, the Court only had eight members, and a tie in the case left in place the lower court's ruling against DAPA.

At the federal district court level, privacy concerns were among the hot-button issues early in the year, and on February 16, the U.S. District Court for the Central District of California issued a court order that would require Apple to assist the FBI in accessing the iPhone of 2015 San Bernardino County shooter Syed Farook. The FBI asserted that information contained in the shooter's iPhone may reveal others involved in the attack that killed fourteen people and the whereabouts of the shooter between the time of the attack and when he was found and killed by police. Apple refused to comply, arguing that doing so would set a dangerous precedent and put consumer privacy at risk. On February 19, the Justice Department filed a motion to force Apple to comply, to which Apple responded by filing an appeal restating its decision not to assist further in unlocking the phone, but the motion was dropped in March after the Justice Department found a third party that could assist with unlocking the phone.

Perhaps the most widely followed case of 2016 was that of the Dakota Access Pipeline, an oil pipeline that would cross multiple states in the Midwest, but which crossed within a half mile of the Standing Rock Sioux tribe's reservation in North Dakota. The tribe opposed the building of the pipeline, arguing that it impacted sacred land, and thousands gathered on the reservation to protest the ongoing construction of the pipeline. The tribe filed multiple lawsuits against the Army Corps of Engineers, the federal agency tasked with providing permits for pipeline construction, citing federal laws that prohibit building on such cultural lands. On September 9, a court ruled against the tribe, noting that the Corps had made the attempts required under the law to work with the tribe to reach a resolution. That same day, multiple federal departments announced that the completion of the pipeline near the reservation would be put on hold until the full impact could be determined and another possible route explored. Ultimately, on February 9, 2017, construction went ahead after the federal government provided the building permits for project completion.

FOREIGN AFFAIRS

Peace Talks and Ceasefires in Syria

As the Syrian civil war dragged on into its sixth year, the United Nations convened a new round of peace talks between the government of Syrian President Bashar al-Assad and opposition groups calling for major reforms. The goals of the negotiations, which began on February 1, 2016, were to secure a ceasefire agreement and to develop a plan for establishing a transitional government and holding new elections. In an indication of how the talks would proceed over the coming months, the Syrian High Negotiations Committee—representing several opposition groups—withdrew from the initial round of talks, citing a new government-led offensive north of Aleppo. Two subsequent rounds of talks failed to result in an agreement.

With talks faltering, the United States and Russia worked to establish a ceasefire agreement to ease hostilities and allow the delivery of humanitarian aid to war-torn areas. Implemented on February 27, the agreement appeared to be effective for about a month before it began unraveling amid government air strikes near Aleppo. The ceasefire collapsed by the summer, and a second ceasefire announced in September lasted for barely a week. The second ceasefire's failure, and Russia's purported support of a government bombing campaign in Aleppo, prompted the United States to withdraw from bilateral talks.

In November, the Syrian government intensified its efforts to retake the opposition-held eastern portion of Aleppo, trapping an estimated 100,000 rebels and civilians in an increasingly smaller area of the city with dwindling supplies. The quickly deteriorating humanitarian situation drew international calls for an agreement to allow aid deliveries and safe passage out of Aleppo for those stuck in the city. With the breakdown of multilateral talks and the United States' decreased involvement in diplomatic efforts to resolve the conflict, Russia and Turkey stepped in to negotiate a deal that eventually allowed all civilians and fighters to leave the city and returned Aleppo to government control by December 22.

The retaking of Aleppo was widely viewed as a turning point in the conflict; however, the war was far from over: fighting between rebel groups and government forces continued outside of Aleppo, particularly around the Syrian capital of Damascus. A new round of negotiations in January 2017—this time sponsored by Russia, Turkey, and Iran—resulted in a partial ceasefire agreement, and further trilateral and UN-mediated talks were planned for later in the year.

International Community Responds to ISIL Attacks

The Islamic State of Iraq and the Levant (ISIL) continued to target Western countries with terrorist attacks throughout 2016, including France and Belgium. In March, bombs went off in Brussels's Zaventem airport, followed by an explosion at the Maalbeek metro station near the city's center. The attacks killed thirty-two civilians and injured more than 300 people. In July, a truck drove through a crowd that had gathered to watch Bastille Day fireworks in Nice, France, killing more than 80 people and wounding more than 300. ISIL claimed responsibility for both the Brussels and Nice attacks, stating that it had targeted Belgium because of the country's ongoing involvement in offensives against ISIL in Iraq and Syria. ISIL was also believed to have orchestrated a June attack against Turkey's Atatürk airport in Istanbul. The incident began as a shooting but ended when the three attackers detonated suicide vests. More than 40 civilians were killed, and at least 200 were wounded.

Following these attacks, Western governments increased security at airports, transit hubs, and population centers. French President François Hollande extended a state of emergency that had been in place since November 2015, and pledged to increase attacks against ISIL in Iraq and Syria. Turkish officials conducted a series of raids in which thirty people were arrested; of those, thirteen were charged with affiliation with a terrorist organization, homicide, and endangering the unity of the state. In the United States, President Obama committed to send additional special forces to Syria to support the fight against ISIL, as well as deploy 600 troops to Iraq, where the Iraqi military was attempting to retake Mosul from the terrorist group. Coalition airstrikes against ISIL also continued, and international officials called for increased coordination of efforts to combat the organization.

Europe Challenged by Ongoing Influx of Refugees

Hundreds of thousands of refugees and economic migrants continued to make the dangerous Mediterranean Sea crossing into Europe in 2016. More than 5,000 migrants drowned throughout the year, due largely to smugglers overcrowding passengers into increasingly flimsy vessels. An agreement between the European Union (EU) and Turkey to increase border controls attempted to stem the flow of refugees traveling to Greece and other European countries via an Eastern Mediterranean route, but migrants simply shifted their travels to a Southern Mediterranean route, arriving in Italy instead.

The public was initially sympathetic to the migrants' plight, particularly those fleeing the civil war in Syria, but this sentiment gave way to growing anxiety and fear about what their arrival may bring as Islamic terrorist attacks continued to target European countries. The governments of Italy and Greece were criticized for not requiring migrants to remain in their territories until their asylum claims were processed, as was German Chancellor Angela Merkel, who announced in August 2016 that Germany would receive asylum claims from Syrians even if they had first arrived in the EU via another country. Despite European officials' efforts to strengthen border controls and share the burden of incoming refugees more evenly, the public remained skeptical of migrants and adopted an increasingly negative view of Muslims. These perceptions fueled an uptick in support for anti-immigrant political parties, which appears likely to influence the outcome of 2017 elections in France, Germany, and the Netherlands.

"Brexit" Vote Stuns European Union

After more than forty years of United Kingdom (UK) membership in the EU, Britons shocked the world and sent financial markets reeling by voting in a June 2016 referendum to leave the union. The relationship between the EU and the UK had become increasingly strained, with Britons objecting to the EU's growing lawmaking powers, treaties that increased integration among EU countries, and the influx of immigrants fueled by the acceptance of new EU members and the global refugee crisis. Prime Minister David Cameron's Conservative Party was particularly hostile to the EU, and, despite his support for remaining in the union, Cameron was the one who called for the referendum to appease Eurosceptics within the party.

The referendum campaign was highly contentious and polarizing, with immigration playing a central role in the debate, particularly amid mounting terrorism concerns and ongoing ISIL attacks. Those favoring continued EU membership emphasized the favorable economic agreements and business opportunities the UK benefited from as an EU member. Polls had predicted the Stronger In campaign would win a narrow victory, but when results were tallied, Vote Leave won by a margin of roughly 4 percent. Notably, majorities in Scotland and Northern Ireland voted to remain in the EU, while majorities in England and Wales voted to leave. Scottish officials subsequently raised the possibility of holding a new independence referendum, while Northern Ireland has demanded the opportunity to reunify with the Republic of Ireland in the south, which intends to remain part of the EU.

Cameron announced his resignation the day after the vote, leading to a frantic scramble within the Conservative Party to find a new leader. Theresa May was eventually selected as the party's new leader and the new prime minister. Although May quietly supported the Stronger In side, she made it clear after taking office that she would push forward with "Brexit." May has yet to invoke Article 50 of the EU Treaty, which outlines a procedure and two-year timeline for EU member countries to leave the bloc if they wish. This must be done before the UK can negotiate a new relationship with the EU.

Political Change in South America

South American countries faced several political and social challenges in 2016, particularly in Brazil, which was experiencing its worst economic recession since the 1930s. As Brazil's economy faltered, dozens of politicians were implicated in a wide-reaching scandal known as Operation Car Wash, through which they had received kickbacks from construction companies that won building contracts with state-owned oil company Petrobras. Adding to the country's political turmoil, Brazil's Tribunal de Contas da União ruled in October 2015 that President Dilma Rousseff had violated the country's fiscal responsibility law by delaying the repayment of loans received from state banks to cover budget shortfalls in 2014. Lawmakers in Brazil's Chamber of Deputies and Senate voted to begin impeachment proceedings against Rousseff in the spring of 2016, and the Senate voted to remove her from office at the end of August. Rousseff insisted she had been the victim of a "parliamentary coup" and asked the Supreme Federal Tribunal to annul the decision, but the court rejected her appeal.

While Rousseff's impeachment trial moved forward, Brazil was also making final preparations to host the 2016 Summer Olympics in Rio de Janeiro. Concerns about rising crime, cost overruns, construction delays, and pollution plagued Brazil ahead of the games—issues made more challenging by national and local economic struggles. Thousands of Brazilians living in Rio's *favelas*, or slums, were evicted to make room for Olympics-related construction projects, and many protested the government's spending of billions of dollars on the games instead of on needed social programs. In addition, the mosquito-borne Zika virus continued to spread across Brazil and to at least sixty other countries and territories. Declared a Public Health Emergency of International Concern by the World Health Organization in February 2016, the virus has been linked to microcephaly and other birth defects, and its spread led some to call for the Olympics to be postponed or canceled. However, the games began as scheduled on August 5 and were the first to be held in South America. They were also the first to feature a team of refugees who competed under the Olympic flag. The games largely proceeded without incident, and were described by International Olympic Committee president Thomas Bach as "marvelous."

In neighboring Venezuela, opponents of President Nicolas Maduro initiated a recall referendum against him, with the goal of removing the president from office before the end of the year to force new elections. Venezuela was in the midst of a staggering economic crisis that was widely attributed to mismanagement and corruption within the country's Socialist government and led to chronic shortages of food, medicine, and basic items that left many Venezuelans eating only once per day. Blaming Maduro for the country's failing economy, his political opponents submitted a petition calling for a referendum to Venezuela's National Electoral Council in May 2016. Despite having more than enough valid signatures, the council suspended the referendum effort in October, citing findings that several thousand of the signatures collected were fraudulent. Hundreds of thousands of Venezuelans protested the council's decision, and opposition lawmakers agreed to open impeachment proceedings against the president. The Vatican stepped in to mediate talks between the two sides; however, the talks faltered in November after government officials did not attend meetings with the opposition.

In Colombia, the government announced that it had reached an historic peace agreement with the Revolutionary Armed Forces of Colombia (FARC) to end the country's more than fifty-year-long civil war. In addition to establishing a total ceasefire between the FARC—the primary guerilla group involved in the war—and the government, the agreement provided a path for FARC members to disarm and reintegrate into Colombian society, with reparations to be made for victims of the conflict. While the agreement was hailed as a major achievement by many in the international community, Colombians were divided over the terms of the deal, with many feeling that there should be tougher consequences for the FARC. Colombians were given an opportunity to vote on the deal during a nationwide referendum held in October, and despite polls showing the agreement would be approved in a landslide, voters rejected the deal by a margin of less than 1 percent. The government and the FARC announced a new peace agreement in November that had been revised to satisfy the opposition, but this time, the agreement was not put to a referendum. The Colombian Congress approved the deal on November 30. For his work on the agreement, the Colombian president was awarded the Nobel Peace Prize for 2016.

Instability in Africa

Violence and political unrest shaped developments in South Sudan and the Democratic Republic of the Congo (DRC) in 2016. Fighting between rival groups loyal to South Sudan President Salva Kiir, leader of the People's Liberation Movement, and First Vice President Riek Machar, head of the People's Liberation Movement in Opposition, broke out in July, resulting in the deaths of an estimated 300 people and prompting another 42,000 South Sudanese to seek refuge. A ceasefire was declared several days after the violence began, and Machar fled the country shortly thereafter. Despite pledging to return to South Sudan by October to resume implementation of a 2015 peace agreement between the two parties, Machar had not returned by the end of the year. Meanwhile, the summer skirmishes further weakened the country's already struggling economy and deepened its humanitarian crisis, with the UN estimating that more than half the population needed aid and one in three children was at risk of starvation.

With DRC President Joseph Kabila's second term ending in December 2016, the country was set to hold a presidential election in November. However, Kabila's allies in parliament, the Constitutional Court, and the Independent Electoral Commission acted to postpone the election and extend Kabila's time in office, claiming that the government needed more time to prepare for the vote. Thousands of Congolese protested the delays. A government crackdown on the demonstrations resulted in the deaths of more than 50 Congolese and wounded more than 140 others, drawing sanctions against Congolese officials from the United States and the EU. On the last day of the year, following talks mediated by the National Episcopal Conference of Congo, the ruling and opposition political parties agreed to hold an election by the end of 2017, with Kabila remaining in power until that time.

In October, three African countries—Burundi, South Africa, and Gambia—announced, in rapid succession, their withdrawal from the International Criminal Court (ICC). Two of the three countries were being investigated by the ICC at the time: Burundi for alleged human rights abuses; South Africa for refusing to execute an arrest warrant issued by the ICC against Sudan's President Omar al-Bashir. The tribunal's critics observed that every individual to have faced an ICC trial has been African, and that nine of the ten ongoing ICC investigations are Africa-focused.

—Heather Kerrigan and Linda Fecteau Grimm

January

State and Federal Officials Respond to Flint Water Crisis

JANUARY 5 AND 16, AND MARCH 15 AND 17, 2016

Flint, Michigan, an impoverished city outside Detroit with a population of around 100,000, landed in the national spotlight in early 2016. A state of emergency was issued at both the state and federal levels when the city's water supply became unsafe to drink due to elevated levels of lead. It was quickly discovered that when Flint changed its water supply, the city failed to follow federal guidelines because it did not introduce a corrosion inhibitor to the water to stop the breakdown of the city's water pipes. Failure to do so increased toxin levels in adults and children and led to the filing of charges against a number of state and local officials.

FLINT CHANGES ITS WATER SOURCE AND BLOOD TOXINS RISE

In April 2014, Flint changed its water source from the Detroit Water and Sewerage Department, which pulls its supply from Lake Huron and the Detroit River, to the Flint River. The adjustment was meant to be a cost-saving measure for the city, which, through its partnership with the Karegnondi Water Authority (KWA), had planned to install a new pipeline that would run from Lake Huron to Flint. When the city made the switch, it failed to add corrosion inhibitors that are mandatory for all drinking water systems. This oversight resulted in the breakdown of the city's aging water pipes, which ultimately leached lead into the water supply. Residents of Flint quickly began complaining of strange odors coming from their taps and outbreaks of rashes after using the water. Despite the complaints, city officials and water system representatives continued to tell residents that the water was safe to use and drink.

Within weeks of the switch, Flint residents began filling medical clinics with complaints of abdominal pain, sudden hair loss, and persistent rashes. Blood tests revealed elevated levels of neurotoxin, a heavy metal that can cause a number of health problems, including cognitive damage in children and kidney damage in adults. One city resident, Lee-Anne Walters, was ignored by city officials and the Michigan Department of Environmental Quality (MDEQ) when she raised concerns about the discolored water and health issues her family had been experiencing. She was connected by an Environmental Protection Agency (EPA) official to scientists at Virginia Tech who focus on public health crises. Walters worked with the scientists in Virginia, collecting water samples and sending them to a lab for testing. Walters's water had a lead level that tested between 300 parts per billion (ppb) and 13,000 ppb. According to the EPA, an acceptable level is 15 ppb, while the safest level is zero. There are many water systems across the United States that have had elevated levels of lead, but none were as high as that of Flint. When the university's findings were presented to city leaders, residents were quickly told to stop drinking the water without a filter. Between the time when the city changed its water supply to the

Flint River to when residents were warned to stop drinking it, eighteen months had elapsed. In October 2015, the city reverted back to its old water supply from the Detroit Water and Sewerage Department.

STATE OF EMERGENCY DECLARED

Flint had been under a local emergency declaration since December 14, 2015, and on January 5, Michigan Governor Rick Snyder issued a state of emergency for the city and Genesee County. According to the governor's declaration, the move was made "due to the ongoing health and safety issues caused by lead in the city of Flint's drinking water." By declaring a state of emergency, Snyder was able to release state funds and emergency assistance for the city. It also opened the possibility that Snyder could request help from the Federal Emergency Management Agency (FEMA). "The health and welfare of Flint residents is a top priority, and we're committed to a coordinated approach with resources from state agencies to address all aspects of this situation," Snyder said in the declaration. Snyder was criticized for issuing the declaration too late, but the governor's office stated that it had to receive a formal request for a declaration from Genesee County before such an order could be released. The governor also argued that he took action as soon as he became aware of elevated levels of toxins in the blood of Flint's residents.

Less than two weeks later, on January 16, President Barack Obama signed a federal declaration of a state of emergency for the city of Flint. This action authorized FEMA to "coordinate all disaster relief efforts which have the purpose of alleviating the hardship and suffering caused by the emergency." FEMA would be able to provide a maximum $5 million for up to ninety days for supplies for those affected by the water crisis, including filters and clean bottled water. Although Snyder requested that the president declare a disaster in Flint rather than an emergency, federal law prohibited the president from doing so because the water crisis was manmade. Such a declaration would have allowed for more federal aid to be provided to the city, which it desperately needed given Governor Snyder's estimate that it would cost $767 million to replace the entirety of Flint's water infrastructure.

RESPONSE TO THE WATER CRISIS

After the state of emergency was declared, bottled water, filters, and water test kits flooded into Flint from across the country. Federal and state funds offered to aid those impacted by the crisis were slow to reach Flint residents because the state worked with city officials to determine how the funds could best be spent now, while also ensuring that longer-term assistance would be available. Because of the ongoing crisis, FEMA agreed to a request from Governor Snyder to extend its disaster assistance beyond mid-April—when the state of emergency was intended to expire—to ensure that additional bottled water and other much-needed supplies could continue to be provided.

Snyder issued a formal apology to the citizens of Flint on January 19 during his State of the State address. While outlining his pledge to fix the problem, and announcing the deployment of National Guard members to aid the city, the governor stated, "To you, the people of Flint, I say tonight as I have before: I am sorry and I will fix it." The statement was followed by $28 million to Flint for medical care, infrastructure upgrades, and supplies for those affected by the crisis. In late February, the governor signed an additional $30 million budget bill for the city of Flint, which would give credits of up to 65 percent to those customers who had paid for the contaminated water. Calling the move "just one more step" to improve the Flint water system and the lives of its residents, Snyder said the specific purpose of this bill was to "give relief to the city of Flint for water that they shouldn't have to pay for." In June, the governor signed a new budget bill, which included another $165 million for Flint infrastructure upgrades and further credits for those who had been paying their water bills.

President Obama made a visit to Flint in May, during which he took a drink of filtered Flint water and told residents that they should feel safe to drink their filtered water. "If you're using a filter . . . then Flint water at this point is drinkable," the president said, while adding that there was still need to replace the city's water infrastructure. Obama told parents to "be angry," but "not [to] somehow communicate to our children here in this city that they're going to be saddled with problems for the rest of their lives, because they will not. They'll do just fine." He added, "Kids rise to the expectations that we set for them." Obama went on to indicate his belief that there was no one related to this crisis who made a conscious effort to harm Flint's residents. But, he added, "I do think there's a larger issue that we have to acknowledge, because I do think that part of what contributed to this crisis was a broader mindset, a bigger attitude, a corrosive attitude that exists in our politics and exists in too many levels of our government. And it's a mindset that believes that less government is the highest good no matter what."

INVESTIGATIONS INTO THE WATER CRISIS

Following the federal and state issuance of states of emergency, one Flint city official, two MDEQ officials, and EPA Great Lakes regional director Susan Hedman all resigned their positions. One MDEQ official was fired.

In March 2016, the House Committee on Oversight and Government Reform convened a hearing on Flint's water crisis to determine why it took city officials so long to act and why warning signs were ignored. The hearing focused heavily on a June 2015 report from the EPA that indicated that there were extremely high lead levels at one Flint resident's home and noted that corrosion control was never added to the water. There was a six-month gap between when this report was released and when Flint began adding the corrosion chemicals to its water supply. The scientists who initially released the report were reprimanded for sharing it with the residents of Flint who had high levels of lead in their water.

Hedman told the House Committee that she had limited options to force Flint to add corrosion control to its water. She said that the EPA first learned that the city had failed to add corrosion inhibitors in April 2015, and at that time immediately began encouraging the city and state to add the chemicals. "I don't think anyone at the EPA did anything wrong, but I do believe we could have done more," she told the committee. Committee members pushed back, arguing that there is a provision in the Safe Drinking Water Act that states that when a city or state does not take action to prevent drinking water contamination that presents "an imminent and substantial endangerment" the EPA can step in to "take such actions as [it] may deem necessary in order to protect the health of such persons." Ted Lieu, D-Calif., called the EPA's actions "negligence bordering on deliberate indifference." Hedman used the latter portion of her testimony to shore up her reputation, saying, "I resigned, in part, because of the false allegations about me that were published in early January—which EPA was unable to correct on the record before they began to damage the Agency's ability to perform critical work in Flint." She added that, contrary to media reports, she "did not sit on the sidelines" and "did not downplay any concerns raised by EPA scientists or apologize for any memos they wrote."

EPA administrator Gina McCarthy also appeared before the House Committee on March 17, and was highly critical of both the state of Michigan and the EPA itself. "While EPA did not cause the lead problem, in hindsight, we should not have been so trusting of the State for so long when they provided us with overly simplistic assurances of technical compliance rather than substantive responses to our growing concerns." She said that the EPA was now attempting to provide assistance wherever possible, including acting as a technical adviser for the city as it continues to make decisions about its water system. She also announced that she had asked the EPA's inspector general to investigate failures within the federal agency to recognize and respond to the Flint crisis and requested a separate investigation into whether MDEQ was capable of following and implementing the requirements of the federal Safe Drinking Water Act. McCarthy also said that she would be working with Congress to review and revise the federal Lead and Copper rule. In his own testimony before the House Committee, Governor Snyder called on revisions to the federal Lead and Copper Rule to ensure that what occurred in Flint does not happen elsewhere. "The American people deserve rules that make sense and professionals to enforce them who know that health and safety are urgent matters. I can make sure that happens in Michigan," the governor said.

In late June, the state attorney general, Bill Schuette, sued two companies—Veolia North America and Lockwood, Andrews & Newman (LAN)—that had been awarded contracts to advise the city both prior to and after its switch to water from the Flint River. The companies denied that they were negligent in their duties or that they had failed to point out problems with the water and the pipes. In a statement, LAN said that Schuette "blatantly mischaracterized the role of LAN's service to Flint." The two companies had already been sued separately by Flint residents. The cases have not yet been settled.

Charges were filed against three MDEQ employees, three Michigan Department of Health and Human Services employees, and a former city water plant operator for involvement in the water crisis that included misconduct, conspiracy to tamper with evidence, tampering with evidence, treatment violation, willful neglect of office, and monitoring violations. The six cases were consolidated for the preliminary hearing on August 9, and on September 15, one of the Michigan Department of Health and Human Services defendants pleaded no contest and agreed to testify against the other five. Additionally, in late October, a state court ruled that residents of Flint could sue the state of Michigan for their decisions that led to the water crisis. Another four individuals were charged in late December for their role in the water crisis, including two former emergency managers and two water plant officials. All four were charged with felonies of false pretenses and conspiracy.

Impact of the Flint Water Crisis

A Centers for Disease Control and Prevention (CDC) analysis of 7,000 children conducted in June 2016 revealed that lead levels in the blood of Flint's children spiked after the city began using water from the Flint River and that children who drank that water had a 50 percent higher risk of dangerous levels of lead in the blood. After the change back to the old water supply, "the percentage of children under 6 years with elevated blood lead levels returned to levels seen before the water switch took place," according to the CDC. The CDC noted, however, that many children had lead in their blood prior to the change in water supply. "Most inner city kids and children in other settings have lead levels that are detectable in their blood," said Patrick Breysse, director of the CDC's National Center for Environmental Health. However, the CDC cautioned, there is no safe level of lead for children because it kills developing brain cells and can lead to lower IQ scores and behavioral disorders. Some studies have suggested that lead in the blood is linked to disorders, delinquency, and criminal behavior, and it can be deadly in very high doses.

According to the National Resources Defense Council, Flint is not the only city with high levels of toxic chemicals in its water. There are more than 5,000 other water systems across the country (out of 152,000) that are in violation of the EPA's Lead and Copper Rule, which is aimed at keeping these toxins out of drinking water. Together, these water systems serve more than 18 million Americans. According to the NRDC, "[t]hese violations include failures to properly test the water for lead or conditions that could result in lead contamination, failures to report contamination to state officials or the public, and failures to treat the water appropriately to reduce corrosion." The NRDC added, "Sometimes, public water systems fail to properly monitor their water . . . so violations are not recorded and reported." The group says that significant investment in the nation's water infrastructure over the next twenty-five years—to the tune of $1 trillion—is needed to fix these ongoing issues. McCarthy hinted at the necessity of ensuring water systems across the country are repaired or replaced, especially in low-income areas where the infrastructure is most likely to be severely underfunded. "We need to start having a serious conversation about how we advance the technologies and investments necessary to deliver clean water to American families," McCarthy said.

—Heather Kerrigan

Following is a January 5, 2016, press release from Governor Rick Snyder declaring a state of emergency in the Flint water crisis; a January 16, 2016, press release from the White House announcing the declaration of a federal state of emergency; the text of the testimonies before Congress by former and current EPA administrators on March 15 and 17, 2016; and the text of a testimony by Governor Snyder before Congress on March 17, 2016.

Governor Snyder Declares State of Emergency

January 5, 2016

Gov. Rick Snyder today declared a state of emergency for Genesee County due to the ongoing health and safety issues caused by lead in the city of Flint's drinking water.

By declaring a state of emergency, Snyder has made available all state resources in cooperation with local response and recovery operations. The declaration authorizes the Michigan State Police, Emergency Management and Homeland Security Division (MSP/EMHSD) to coordinate state efforts.

"The health and welfare of Flint residents is a top priority and we're committed to a coordinated approach with resources from state agencies to address all aspects of this situation," Snyder said. "Working in full partnership with the Flint Water Advisory Task Force, all levels of government and water quality experts, we will find both short-term and long-term solutions to ensure the health and safety of Flint residents."

In addition to the emergency declaration, Snyder activated the State Emergency Operations Center to coordinate state response and recovery activities. State agencies will report to the center to coordinate resources, assess the situation and begin providing assets to assist with local relief operations.

"Our staff recognizes the urgency of this situation and is already working closely with local officials," said Capt. Chris A. Kelenske, Deputy State Director of Emergency Management and Homeland Security and commander of the MSP/EMHSD. "We will continue to collaborate with state, city and county leaders to coordinate relief efforts, streamline communication and use all available resources to help residents."

On Jan. 4, Genesee County declared a "local state of emergency," which activated local emergency response and recovery plans. By requesting a governor's declaration, the county has determined local resources are insufficient to address the situation and state assistance is required to protect public health, safety and property to lessen or avert the threat of a crisis.

The city of Flint has been under a local emergency declaration since Dec. 14, 2015.

The SEOC is the emergency operations center for the state of Michigan. Located in Lansing, the center is overseen by the MSP/EMHSD and coordinates response and recovery efforts by state agencies and local government. The SEOC is staffed by members of state agencies and other partners for decision making and information coordination during disasters or emergencies in the state of Michigan.

SOURCE: State of Michigan. Office of Governor Rick Snyder. "Gov. Snyder Declares Emergency for Genesee County." January 5, 2016. www.michigan.gov/snyder/0,4668,7-277-57577_57657-372653--,00.html.

President Obama Signs Michigan Emergency Declaration

January 16, 2016

The President today, in response to a request from the Governor submitted on January 14, 2016, declared that an emergency exists in the State of Michigan and ordered federal aid to supplement state and local response efforts due to the emergency conditions in the area affected by contaminated water.

The President's action authorizes the Department of Homeland Security, Federal Emergency Management Agency (FEMA), to coordinate all disaster relief efforts which have the purpose of alleviating the hardship and suffering caused by the emergency on the local population, and to provide appropriate assistance for required emergency measures, authorized under Title V of the Stafford Act, to save lives and to protect property and public health and safety, and to lessen or avert the threat of a catastrophe in Genesee County.

Specifically, FEMA is authorized to identify, mobilize, and provide at its discretion, equipment and resources necessary to alleviate the impacts of the emergency. Emergency protective measures, limited to direct federal assistance, will be provided at 75 percent federal funding. This emergency assistance is to provide water, water filters, water filter cartridges, water test kits, and other necessary related items for a period of no more than 90 days.

Additionally, the President offered assistance in identifying other Federal agency capabilities that could support the recovery effort but do not require an emergency declaration under the Stafford Act.

W. Craig Fugate, Administrator, Federal Emergency Management Agency (FEMA), Department of Homeland Security, named David G. Samaniego as the Federal Coordinating Officer for federal recovery operations in the affected area.

SOURCE: The White House. "President Obama Signs Michigan Emergency Declaration." January 16, 2016. https://obamawhitehouse.archives.gov/the-press-office/2016/01/16/president-obama-signs-michigan-emergency-declaration.

Former EPA Regional Administrator Testifies before Congress on Flint Water Crisis

March 15, 2016

[Footnotes have been omitted.]

Good morning, Mr. Chairman, Ranking Member Cummings and distinguished Members of the Committee. I'm Susan Hedman, the former EPA Region 5 Administrator. Thank you for this opportunity to testify about my role in EPA's response to the Flint water crisis—and the reasons that I decided to resign.

I first learned that Flint was not implementing corrosion control treatment on June 30, 2015—approximately fourteen months after the City started using Flint River water that was not treated with orthophosphate. The very next day I offered technical assistance to Flint's Mayor—assistance from EPA experts on lead and drinking water distribution systems. The following week, we issued our first statement encouraging Flint residents to contact their water utility for lead testing and providing information about limiting exposure to lead in tap water.

On July 21st, three weeks after I first learned about this problem, the Michigan Department of Environmental Quality (MDEQ) agreed with EPA's recommendation to require Flint to implement corrosion control as soon as possible—a recommendation that my staff had been making since late April, when they first found out that corrosion control was not being implemented.

That should have solved the problem—but it did not. During the weeks and months that followed, MDEQ was slow to deliver on the agreement we reached on July 21st and the City of Flint was hampered by a lack of institutional capacity and resources.

EPA responded in the only we could: by working within the cooperative federalism framework of the Safe Drinking Water Act. That framework assigns legal primacy to states to implement drinking water regulations and gives EPA the job of setting standards and providing technical assistance. So, in keeping with that framework, we provided technical support to the State and the City—to implement corrosion control and to provide the assistance that Flint residents needed to limit their exposure to lead.

Most of the time, this cooperative federalism model works well—even in a crisis. In fact, it worked exactly the way it's supposed to work when the Toledo water crisis occurred in 2014. But, as we all know, it did not work in Flint.

Consequently, EPA was forced to evaluate the enforcement tools available under the Safe Drinking Water Act, which are more limited than the enforcement provisions in other federal environmental statutes. And, while I used the threat of enforcement action to motivate the State and City to move forward, we found that the enforcement options available to us were of limited utility last fall, due to the unique circumstances of this case.

In the end, with the help of the EPA Task Force, corrosion control was finally implemented—and testing now indicates that the protective coating that prevents lead from leaching into tap water is being restored.

That's the good news.

The bad news is that this problem should never have happened in the first place, and I need to remind you: EPA had nothing at all to do with that.

Finally, I'd like to say a few words about my resignation:

I resigned, in part, because of the false allegations about me that were published in early January—which EPA was unable to correct on the record before they began to damage the Agency's ability to perform critical work in Flint. By the third week of January, I was widely portrayed in the media as someone who ". . . sat on the sidelines during the crisis . . . and . . . downplayed concerns raised by an E.P.A. scientist about lead in the water."

That's completely untrue. My testimony today and the material in Appendices Two and Three make clear that I did not sit on the sidelines and I did not downplay any concerns raised by EPA scientists or apologize for any memos they wrote—in fact, I repeatedly asked for a final memo about lead in a form that EPA could publicly release. And, when MDEQ attacked a Region 5 scientist by calling him a "rogue employee," I immediately called the MDEQ Director to complain—and in a subsequent call with the MDEQ Director and the Governor's staff, I made it clear that the scientist is a valued member of the Region 5 Water Division team—and I made it even clearer when I subsequently appointed the scientist to EPA's Flint Task Force.

There wasn't time for these explanations in January—in the wake of all the emergency declarations. Flint residents had lost trust in governmental institutions—and the false allegations about me gave the people of Flint less reason to trust EPA.

On the day I resigned, I sent a note to Administrator McCarthy saying: "In light of the allegations that have been made about me . . . and the time it will take to set the record straight, I think this is the best course of action to ensure the effectiveness of EPA's response to the Flint water crisis and to make sure that Flint residents get the help that they deserve."

That was one reason for my resignation, but there was another: quite simply, this tragedy happened on my watch.

I did not make the catastrophic decision to provide drinking water without corrosion control treatment; I did not vote to cut funding for water infrastructure or for EPA;

And I did not design the imperfect statutory framework that we rely on to keep our drinking water safe. But I was the Regional Administrator when this crisis occurred.

Having spent my entire adult life as an advocate for environmental and public health issues—and much of that time representing citizen groups—I knew that only one thing mattered to Flint residents: the water wasn't safe to drink.

What happened in Flint, should not have happened anywhere in [the] United States—and I was horrified that it happened in my region, the Great Lakes Region. I thought—and still think—that resigning was the honorable thing to do.

Although I have left government service—I have not stopped worrying about the people of Flint. I am very encouraged to see that the corrosion control treatment that was implemented in December is re-coating the pipes and that the water may soon be safe to drink. I am even more encouraged to read that there is growing Congressional support for funding to replace lead service lines in Flint and to fund water infrastructure throughout the country. I'd like to close by asking all of you to support that legislation—and, more generally, to support the long overdue investments that are needed in this nation's water infrastructure.

Thank you for this opportunity to testify. I welcome any questions.

[The appendices included with the testimony have been omitted.]

SOURCE: House Committee on Oversight and Government Reform. "Testimony of Susan Hedman." March 15, 2016. https://oversight.house.gov/wp-content/uploads/2016/03/Hedman-Statement-3-15-Flint-Water-II.pdf.

EPA Administrator Testifies before Congress Regarding Flint Water Crisis

March 17, 2016

Good morning, Mr. Chairman, Ranking Member Cummings, distinguished Members of the Committee. Thank you for the opportunity to testify about EPA's response to the drinking water crisis in Flint, Michigan.

I want to start by saying what happened in Flint should not have happened and can never happen again. The crisis we're seeing was the result of a state-appointed emergency manager deciding that the City would stop purchasing treated drinking water and instead switch to an untreated source to save money. The State of Michigan approved that decision, and did so without requiring corrosion control treatment. Without corrosion control, lead from pipes, fittings and fixtures can leach into the drinking water. These decisions resulted in Flint residents being exposed to dangerously high levels of lead.

Under the Safe Drinking Water Act, Congress gives states the primary responsibility to enforce drinking water rules for the nation's approximately 152,000 water systems, but EPA has oversight authority. Typically, EPA has a strong relationship with states under the Act. But looking back on Flint, from day one, the state provided our regional office with confusing, incomplete and incorrect information. Their interactions with us were intransigent, misleading and contentious. As a result, EPA staff were unable to understand the potential scope of the lead problem until a year after the switch and had insufficient information to indicate a systemic lead problem until mid-summer of 2015.

While EPA did not cause the lead problem, in hindsight, we should not have been so trusting of the State for so long when they provided us with overly simplistic assurances of technical compliance rather than substantive responses to our growing concerns. Although EPA regional staff repeatedly urged the Michigan Department of Environmental Quality, or MDEQ, to address the lack of corrosion control, we missed the opportunity late last summer to quickly get EPA's concerns on the public's radar screen.

Since October, EPA has been providing technical advice to the City. Additionally, an EPA response team of scientists, water quality experts, community involvement coordinators, and support staff has been on the ground every day since late January. EPA's efforts are part of a broader Federal response to the community, led by the Department of Health and Human Services. The EPA team has visited hundreds of homes and collected thousands of samples to assess the City's water system. We're encouraged by these test results, but our enhanced efforts with Flint will continue until the system is fully back on track.

We've also been engaging Flint residents—visiting places of worship, schools, libraries, community centers, and senior living facilities—to hear their concerns and share information.

I have also taken several concrete steps at the agency to address some of the systemic issues raised during this crisis. I directed a review of MDEQ and its ability to implement the Safe Drinking Water Act. I called on EPA's inspector general to investigate EPA's response to the Flint crisis. I issued an EPA-wide elevation memo encouraging staff to raise issues of concern to managers and managers to be welcoming of staff concerns and questions. I also recently sent letters to every governor and every state environmental and health commissioner in the country asking them to work with EPA on infrastructure investments, transparency, technology, oversight, risk assessment, and public education. And I have asked the states to join EPA in taking action to strengthen our safe drinking water programs, to ensure drinking water programs are working for our communities. Additionally, we are actively working on revisions to the Lead and Copper Rule.

While the contours of this situation are unique, the underlying circumstances that allowed it to happen are not. As a country, we have a systemic problem of underinvestment in "environmental justice" communities. Not only are these underserved populations more vulnerable to the health impacts of pollution, but they often lack the tools and resources to do something about it. That's what stacks the deck against a city like Flint. That's what creates an environment where a crisis like this can happen.

There are many missteps along the way that can tip the scales toward a crisis. In many areas across our country, water infrastructure is aging, it is antiquated, and it is severely underfunded—particularly in low-income communities, which may have the most difficulty securing traditional funding through rate increases or municipal bonds. This threatens citizens' access to safe drinking water. We need to start having a serious conversation about how we advance the technologies and investments necessary to deliver clean water to American families.

I'm personally committed to doing everything possible to make sure a crisis like this never happens again. But EPA can't do it alone. We need the cooperation of our colleagues at every level of Government and beyond. Thank you and I look forward to answering your questions.

Source: House Committee on Oversight and Government Reform. "Testimony of Gina McCarthy Administrator U.S. Environmental Protection Agency Before the Committee on Oversight and Government Reform." March 17, 2016. https://oversight.house.gov/wp-content/uploads/2016/03/McCarthy-EPA-Statement-3-17-Flint-III-1.pdf.

Governor Snyder Testifies before Congress on Flint Water Crisis

March 17, 2016

Chairman Chaffetz, Ranking Member Cummings, and Members of the Committee. Thank you for the opportunity to speak with you today about the crisis in Flint and the actions we are taking to ensure that nothing like this ever happens again.

Let me be blunt. This was a failure of government at all levels. Local, state, and federal officials—we all failed the families of Flint.

This is not about politics or partisanship. I am not going to point fingers or shift blame; there is plenty of that to share, and neither will help the people of Flint.

Not a day or night goes by that this tragedy doesn't weigh on my mind . . . the questions I should have asked . . . the answers I should have demanded . . . how I could have prevented this. That's why I am so committed to delivering permanent, long-term solutions and the clean, safe drinking water that every Michigan citizen deserves.

Today, I will report what we've done, what we're doing, and what we will do to deliver real results and real relief for the families of Flint.

But before going through the facts, I want to express my profound gratitude for the help and heroism of Professor Marc Edwards, Dr. Mona Hanna-Attisha, and Flint resident LeeAnne Walters. They were among the first to sound the alarm about the failures of government and the crisis afflicting the Flint community.

Here are the facts.

From the day the City of Flint began using the Flint River as an interim water supply on April 25, 2014—and repeatedly after that—the state Department of Environmental Quality assured us that Flint's water was safe.

It wasn't. A water expert at the federal EPA, tried to raise an alarm in February 2015, and he was silenced.

It was on October 1, 2015, that I learned that our state experts were wrong. Flint's water had dangerous levels of lead.

On that day, I took immediate action.

First, we quickly reconnected to the Detroit water supply to begin sealing the damaged pipes.

Second, I ordered the immediate distribution of water filters and extensive blood-level testing in schools and homes to identify those at the highest risk so they received healthcare, nutrition and additional support.

Third, we deployed $67 million to address both short-term needs and long-term solutions.

Our focus, and our priority, is on both short-term health and long-term safety. This includes diagnostic testing, nurse visits and environmental assessments in the home to treat any children with high lead levels.

That is only the beginning.

Right now we are in the appropriations process for an additional $165 million to deliver permanent, long-term solutions. I urge Congress to pass the bipartisan bill for aiding Flint immediately so we can further protect the health and safety of Flint families. From identifying every pipe that must be replaced to long-term medical support, we are working with local leaders like Mayor Karen Weaver and our representatives here in Washington to deliver the assistance our citizens deserve.

We are also holding those who failed accountable. And we are being open with the public about how these failures came about—including releasing my emails and my staff's emails relating to this water crisis.

And we are in the process of publicly releasing relevant documents from the state agencies involved, so that the people have an open, honest assessment of what happened and what we're doing to fix it.

We also began a thorough investigation of what went wrong. We have uncovered systemic failures at the Michigan DEQ. The fact is, bureaucrats created a culture that valued technical compliance over common sense—and the result was that lead was leaching into residents' water.

That's why I am committed to a complete and comprehensive change in state government that puts public health and safety first. And it's why I called for a thorough investigation of the Michigan Department of Health and Human Services by the auditor general and the inspector general.

We are taking responsibility and taking action in Michigan, and that is absolutely essential here in Washington, too. Inefficient, ineffective, and unaccountable bureaucrats at the EPA allowed this disaster to continue unnecessarily.

I am glad to be sitting next to the Administrator from the EPA, because all of us must acknowledge our responsibility and be held accountable. I do want to thank Miguel del Toral, a water specialist at the EPA, who spoke up early about the crisis. Tragically, his superiors at the EPA told local leaders in Flint to ignore his call for action.

The truth is, there are many communities with potentially dangerous lead problems. And if the DEQ and EPA do not change . . . and if the dumb and dangerous federal lead and copper rule is not changed . . . then this tragedy will befall other American cities. Professor Edwards has been sounding this alarm for years. I look forward to joining with him to address this failure of government.

I am grateful to have been elected to serve the people of Michigan. I understand their anger. I've been humbled by this experience. And I'm going to make Flint and every community in Michigan a better place to live. We have a lot to learn, and a lot to do.

I close with a simple plea. . . . Partner with me in fixing this—not just for the people of Flint, but for people all over the country. Ranking Member Cummings is right. This is America, and this never should have happened. The American people deserve rules that make sense and professionals to enforce them who know that health and safety are urgent matters. I can make sure that happens in Michigan. You can make sure it happens for every American.

Thank you, and I look forward to your questions.

SOURCE: House Committee on Oversight and Government Reform. "Examining Federal Administration of the Safe Drinking Water Act in Flint, Michigan, Part 3." March 17, 2016. https://oversight.house.gov/wp-content/uploads/2016/03/Governor-Snyder-Testimony-1.pdf.

OTHER HISTORIC DOCUMENTS OF INTEREST

FROM PREVIOUS HISTORIC DOCUMENTS

Response to North Korean Hydrogen Bomb Test

JANUARY 6, FEBRUARY 7, MARCH 2, AND JULY 6, 2016

Throughout 2016, the North Korean government continued to flout the international community's efforts to restrict its nuclear program by conducting a series of ballistic missile and nuclear tests, including the country's purported detonation of an underground hydrogen bomb in January. The ongoing tests prompted a new round of sanctions by the UN Security Council and the United States and fueled increased speculation and concern about North Korea's nuclear capability expansion.

NORTH KOREA'S NUCLEAR AMBITIONS

North Korea revealed that it had a secret nuclear weapons program in October 2002, and it withdrew from the Nuclear Non-Proliferation Treaty, an international agreement that seeks to stop the spread of nuclear weapons, the following year. This prompted Japan, South Korea, China, Russia, and the United States to initiate Six-Party talks with the North Korean government to persuade officials to abandon the country's nuclear program in exchange for economic aid and security guarantees. North Korea announced its first test of a nuclear device in 2006, leading the UN Security Council to impose its first package of sanctions against North Korea and ban the country from activities related to its ballistic missile program.

In 2009, North Korea launched a long-range rocket, which it claimed was intended to put a peaceful communications satellite into space, but the United States and several other countries accused the government of using the launch to test long-range missile technologies. The UN Security Council subsequently condemned the launch and promised to strengthen its sanctions. North Korea responded by withdrawing from the Six-Party talks, expelling international inspectors and restarting its nuclear plants, which the government had agreed to dismantle in 2007. In a further provocation, North Korea conducted its second underground nuclear test later that year. Its third nuclear test was not completed until 2013. North Korea relies on outdated technology and techniques to develop its weapons program, and most of its rocket and missile tests have failed.

Since 2006, the international community has typically responded to North Korea's nuclear activities by implementing various sanctions. These efforts have not been a particularly effective deterrent, in part because the UN Security Council does not enforce them thoroughly and North Korea has found creative ways to avoid them. China's relationship with North Korea is also a complicating factor. China opposes North Korea's nuclear weapons program, but has traditionally resisted harsh sanctions or efforts to address its reported human rights abuses, largely because the two countries maintain a significant trade relationship. In addition, China's border with North Korea is a known point of entry for smuggled goods, with some of this trade allegedly run by, or involving kickbacks to, North Korea's Communist Party and military officials.

HYDROGEN BOMB TEST

On January 6, 2016, state-controlled Korean Central News Agency (KCNA) announced that North Korea had completed its first successful underground test of a hydrogen bomb, a weapon that is significantly more powerful than an atomic bomb. According to the televised report, the test had involved a "miniaturized" hydrogen bomb and was a demonstration of North Korea's growing nuclear power. The television anchor declared, "It is our legal right as a sovereign nation to own hydrogen bomb for justice as we stand against the U.S., which is the culprit of invasion and who is looking for every opportunity to attack us with its vast pool of murderous nuclear weapons."

North Korean leader Kim Jong-un claimed in December 2015 that the country had developed a hydrogen bomb, but most in the international community were skeptical, and no independent organization has been able to confirm that the January exercise tested a hydrogen bomb. The U.S. Geological Survey and the Comprehensive Nuclear-Test-Ban Treaty Organization both detected unusual seismic activity in the northeastern part of North Korea, where the country has conducted previous nuclear tests, but reported that the magnitude of the quakes was not large enough to indicate that a hydrogen bomb had been detonated.

Despite questions about the claim's credibility, the international community reacted swiftly and with great alarm. South Korean President Park Geun-hye called the test "an act that threatens our lives and future," and UN Secretary-General Ban Ki-moon condemned the act "unequivocally," saying that it was "profoundly destabilizing for regional security and seriously undermines international non-proliferation efforts." A statement from the UN Security Council indicated that members would begin considering "further significant measures" in response to the test.

One month after the purported hydrogen bomb test, North Korea announced its launch of an "Earth observation satellite" into space. Both the U.S. Defense Department and the South Korean Defense Ministry confirmed the launch and that the satellite appeared to have reached space. North Korea had reportedly warned various maritime and airspace authorities that it planned to launch a rocket between February 7 and February 14. Various analysts and government officials speculated that the launch was a disguised test of the technology needed to deliver an intercontinental ballistic missile, or ICBM, which is launched into space before turning back to Earth to bomb its target. The launch's success, and its proximity to January's test, amplified international concerns over North Korea's progress in developing nuclear weapons, and the UN Security Council called an emergency meeting.

NEW SANCTIONS IMPOSED

In response to North Korea's actions, the UN Security Council unanimously approved new sanctions against the country on March 2. Widely described as the toughest sanctions yet imposed on North Korea, the measures included a requirement that all countries inspect all cargo received from or going to North Korea for the presence of contraband items. Previous sanctions only required countries to inspect cargo if they had reasonable suspicion that it included black market goods. The new sanctions also require countries to expel North Korean diplomats if they violate sanctions or assist others in their circumvention, allow members to deny North Korean planes access to their countries if the aircraft is carrying contraband items, and prevent members and their citizens from providing training to North Koreans that "could contribute to the proliferation of sensitive nuclear activities or the development of nuclear-weapon delivery systems." All weapons trade and the sale or supply of aviation fuel to North Korea is prohibited, and the lists of sanctioned individuals and banned goods were expanded. The same day, U.S. officials announced that the Treasury and State Departments had sanctioned five North Korean government entities, including the National Defense Commission, and a dozen individuals for their involvement in the country's nuclear and weapons programs. These sanctions froze any assets under U.S. jurisdiction held by these entities and individuals and prohibited Americans from conducting business with them.

The United States continued to take punitive action against North Korea following the satellite launch. In June, the Treasury Department designated North Korea a "primary money laundering concern" and issued a notice of proposed rulemaking that recommended "prohibiting covered U.S. financial institutions from opening or maintaining correspondent accounts with North Korean financial institutions, and prohibiting the use of U.S. correspondent accounts to process transactions for North Korean financial institutions." Treasury officials alleged that North Korea uses its financial system to engage in money laundering and procure equipment for nuclear and ballistic missile programs, in addition to other illicit business ventures. Other U.S. officials have accused North Korea of trafficking in narcotics and using counterfeit dollars.

On July 6, the Treasury Department announced its imposition of sanctions against Kim—marking the first time he was personally targeted with sanctions—as well as fifteen other individuals and entities responsible for censorship and serious human rights abuses within the country. The announcement coincided with the State Department's release of a report detailing human rights concerns in North Korea and identifying officials who had allegedly been involved in censorship, extrajudicial killings, forced labor, arbitrary arrests, forced disappearances, and torture. "With these efforts, we aim to send a signal to all government officials who might be responsible for human rights abuses, including prison camp managers and guards, interrogators, and defector chasers, with the goal of changing their behavior," said John Kirby, State Department spokesperson. Analysts suggested that the new sanctions demonstrated an escalated effort by the United States to further isolate North Korea and pressure it to return to multilateral negotiations around its nuclear program, similar to the approach used to encourage Iran's participation in nuclear talks. Officials acknowledged that the sanctions were unlikely to have a significant impact on Kim but might be effective against low- or mid-level officials.

Tests Continue

North Korea appeared unfazed by the new sanctions and conducted seven missile tests between March and April. In June, North Korea fired two intermediate-range missiles from its east coast. U.S. and South Korean officials later confirmed that one missile had flown just 93 miles before falling into the sea, while the other had traveled nearly 250 miles. On July 9, just a few days after the United States released its human rights report and one day after the United States and South Korea announced their planned deployment of the Terminal High Altitude Area Defense (THAAD) missile defense system against North Korean attacks, North Korea fired a ballistic missile from a submarine. The test was unsuccessful, because the missile fell into the water shortly after launch. However, the test raised fresh concerns over the country's nuclear program, because submarine-launch capabilities could enable North Korea to deploy a missile without having to develop the long-range technology otherwise needed to reach locations in the United States. Submarine-launched ballistic missiles are also harder to detect, meaning a target may have less warning of an impending attack and can evade the THAAD system. Only six countries currently have this capability, including the United States, Russia, and China.

Three days later, the South Korean Joint Chiefs of Staff reported that North Korea fired three more missiles off its east coast. They believed these were short-range missiles because they traveled between 310 and 370 miles. According to KCNA, the test was conducted "under the simulated conditions of making preemptive strikes" in the part of South Korea where the THAAD system would be based.

Tests continued into August, with North Korea firing a submarine-launched ballistic missile toward Japan on August 24. It was the first missile to reach Japan's air defense identification zone, which is designated airspace in which a country seeks to locate, identify, and control the presence of aircraft as a national security measure. Officials and analysts said that, given the distance this missile traveled, the test was evidence that North Korea's weapons technology and capabilities were progressing. "This poses a grave threat to Japan's security, and is an unforgivable act that damages regional peace and stability markedly," said Japanese Prime Minister Shinzo Abe. The UN Security Council pledged to "closely monitor the situation and take further significant measures in line with the Council's previously expressed determination."

North Korea proceeded to conduct its fifth underground nuclear test on September 9. Based on seismic activity, South Korea's Meteorological Administration estimated that the device had the explosive power of 10 kilotons—nearly twice the power of the bomb tested in January. For comparison, the two atomic bombs dropped on Japan during World War II had the power of 15 and 21 kilotons, respectively.

At the time of writing, the UN Security Council had declined to impose additional sanctions on North Korea for its continued weapons tests, though it continued to issue statements condemning the country's actions.

—Linda Fecteau Grimm

Following is a statement from UN Secretary-General Ban Ki-moon from January 6, 2016, in response to North Korea's nuclear test; a UN Security Council statement from February 7, 2016, in response to North Korea's satellite launch; sanctions issued by the UN Security Council on March 2, 2016, against North Korea; and a report from the U.S. State Department from July 6, 2016, on human rights abuses and censorship in North Korea.

UN Secretary-General on North Korea's Nuclear Test

January 6, 2016

The underground nuclear test announced by the Democratic People's Republic of Korea (DPRK) on 6 January is deeply troubling. This test once again violates numerous

Security Council resolutions despite the united call by the international community to cease such activities. It is also a grave contravention of the international norm against nuclear testing.

This act is profoundly destabilising for regional security and seriously undermines international non-proliferation efforts. I condemn it unequivocally.

I demand the DPRK cease any further nuclear activities and meet its obligations for verifiable denuclearization.

We are monitoring and assessing developments in close coordination with the concerned international organisations—including the Comprehensive Nuclear-Test-Ban Treaty Organization—and interested parties.

Thank you.

SOURCE: Office of United Nations Secretary-General Ban Ki-moon. "Secretary-General's statement on the Nuclear Test announced by the Democratic People's Republic of Korea." January 6, 2016. http://www .un.org/sg/en/content/sg/statement/2016-01-06/secretary-generals-statement-nuclear-test-announced-democratic.

UN Security Council on North Korea Missile Launch

February 7, 2016

The following Security Council press statement was issued today by Council President Rafael Darío Ramírez Carreño (Venezuela):

The members of the Security Council held urgent consultations to address the serious situation arising from the launch using ballistic missile technology conducted by the Democratic People's Republic of Korea (DPRK) on 7 February 2016.

The members of the Security Council strongly condemned this launch. The members of the Security Council underscored that this launch, as well as any other DPRK launch that uses ballistic missile technology, even if characterized as a satellite launch or space launch vehicle, contributes to the DPRK's development of nuclear weapon delivery systems and is a serious violation of Security Council resolutions. . . .

The members of the Security Council restated their intent to develop significant measures in a new Security Council resolution in response to the nuclear test conducted by the DPRK on 6 January 2016, in grave violation of the DPRK's international obligations.

The members of the Security Council also recalled that they have previously expressed their determination to take "further significant measures" in the event of another DPRK launch. . . .

The members of the Security Council expressed their commitment to continue working toward a peaceful, diplomatic and political solution to the situation leading to the denuclearization of the Korean Peninsula.

SOURCE: United Nations. "Security Council Press Statement on Democratic People's Republic of Korea Long-Range Launch." February 7, 2016. http://www.un.org/press/en/2016/sc12234.doc.htm.

DOCUMENT   *UN Security Council Resolution 2270*

March 2, 2016

The Security Council . . .

Acting under Chapter VII of the Charter of the United Nations, and taking measures under its Article 41,

1. *Condemns* in the strongest terms the nuclear test conducted by the DPRK on 6 January 2016 in violation and flagrant disregard of the Council's relevant resolutions, and further *condemns* the DPRK's launch of 7 February 2016, which used ballistic missile technology and was in serious violation of resolutions 1718 (2006), 1874 (2009), 2087 (2013), and 2094 (2013);

2. *Reaffirms* its decisions that the DPRK shall not conduct any further launches that use ballistic missile technology, nuclear tests, or any other provocation, and shall suspend all activities related to its ballistic missile program and in this context re-establish its pre-existing commitments to a moratorium on missile launches, and *demands* that the DPRK immediately comply fully with these obligations;

3. *Reaffirms* its decisions that the DPRK shall abandon all nuclear weapons and existing nuclear programs in a complete, verifiable and irreversible manner, and immediately cease all related activities;

4. *Reaffirms* its decision that the DPRK shall abandon all other existing weapons of mass destruction and ballistic missile programs in a complete, verifiable and irreversible manner;

5. *Reaffirms* that, pursuant to paragraph 8 (c) of resolution 1718 (2006), all Member States shall prevent any transfers to the DPRK by their nationals or from their territories, or from the DPRK by its nationals or from its territory, of technical training, advice, services or assistance related to the provision, manufacture, maintenance or use of nuclear-related, ballistic missile-related or other weapons of mass destruction-related items, materials, equipment, goods and technology. . . .

6. *Decides* that the measures in paragraph 8 (a) of resolution 1718 (2006) shall also apply to all arms and related materiel. . . .

7. *Affirms* that the obligations imposed in paragraphs 8 (a), 8 (b) and 8 (c) of resolution 1718 (2006), as extended by paragraphs 9 and 10 of resolution 1874 (2009), apply with respect to the shipment of items to or from the DPRK for repair, servicing, refurbishing, testing, reverse-engineering, and marketing, regardless of whether ownership or control is transferred. . . .

8. *Decides* that the measures imposed in paragraphs 8 (a) and 8 (b) of resolution 1718 (2006) shall also apply to any item, except food or medicine, if the State determines that such item could directly contribute to the development of the DPRK's operational capabilities of its armed forces. . . .

9. *Recalls* that paragraph 9 of resolution 1874 (2009) requires States to prohibit the procurement from the DPRK of technical training, advice, services or assistance related to the provision, manufacture, maintenance or use of arms and related materiel. . . .

12. *Affirms* that "economic resources," as referred to in paragraph 8 (d) of resolution 1718 (2006), includes assets of every kind. . . .

13. *Decides* that if a Member State determines that a DPRK diplomat, governmental representative, or other DPRK national acting in a governmental capacity, is working on behalf or at the direction of a designated individual or entity, or of an individual or entities assisting in the evasion of sanctions or violating the provisions of resolutions 1718 (2006), 1874 (2009), 2087 (2013), 2094 (2013) or this resolution, then the Member State shall expel the individual from its territory. . . .

14. *Decides* that, if a Member State determines that an individual who is not a national of that State is working on behalf of or at the direction of a designated individual or entity or assisting the evasion of sanctions or violating the provisions of resolutions 1718 (2006), 1874 (2009), 2087 (2013), 2094 (2013) or this resolution, then Member States shall expel the individual from their territories. . . .

15. *Underscores* that, as a consequence of implementing the obligations imposed in paragraph 8 (d) of resolution 1718 (2006) and paragraphs 8 and 11 of resolution 2094 (2013), all Member States shall close the representative offices of designated entities and prohibit such entities, as well as individuals or entities acting for or on their behalf, directly or indirectly, from participating in joint ventures or any other business arrangements. . . .

16. *Notes* that the DPRK frequently uses front companies, shell companies, joint ventures and complex, opaque ownership structures for the purpose of violating measures imposed in relevant Security Council resolutions, and, in this regard, *directs* the Committee, with the support of the Panel, to identify individuals and entities engaging in such practices. . . .

17. *Decides* that all Member States shall prevent specialized teaching or training of DPRK nationals within their territories or by their nationals of disciplines which could contribute to the DPRK's proliferation sensitive nuclear activities or the development of nuclear weapon delivery systems. . . .

18. *Decides* that all States shall inspect the cargo within or transiting through their territory, including in their airports, seaports and free trade zones, that has originated in the DPRK, or that is destined for the DPRK, or has been brokered or facilitated by the DPRK or its nationals, or by individuals or entities acting on their behalf or at their direction, or entities owned or controlled by them, or by designated individuals or entities, or that is being transported on DPRK flagged aircraft or maritime vessels, for the purposes of ensuring that no items are transferred in violation of resolutions. . . .

19. *Decides* that Member States shall prohibit their nationals and those in their territories from leasing or chartering their flagged vessels or aircraft or providing crew services to the DPRK, and *decides* that this prohibition shall also apply with respect to any designated individuals or entities, any other DPRK entities, any other individuals or entities whom the State determines to have assisted in the evasion of sanctions or in violating the provisions of resolutions. . . .

20. *Decides* that all States shall prohibit their nationals, persons subject to their jurisdiction and entities incorporated in their territory or subject to their jurisdiction from registering vessels in the DPRK, obtaining authorization for a vessel to use the DPRK flag, and from owning, leasing, operating, providing any vessel classification, certification or associated service, or insuring any vessel flagged by the DPRK. . . .

21. *Decides* that all States shall deny permission to any aircraft to take off from, land in or overfly, unless under the condition of landing for inspection, their territory, if they

have information that provides reasonable grounds to believe that the aircraft contains items the supply, sale, transfer or export of which is prohibited by resolutions. . . .

22. *Decides* that all Member States shall prohibit the entry into their ports of any vessel if the Member State has information that provides reasonable grounds to believe the vessel is owned or controlled, directly or indirectly, by a designated individual or entity, or contains cargo the supply, sale, transfer or export of which is prohibited by resolutions. . . .

24. *Decides* that the DPRK shall abandon all chemical and biological weapons and weapons-related programs. . . .

29. *Decides* that the DPRK shall not supply, sell or transfer, directly or indirectly, from its territory or by its nationals or using its flag vessels or aircraft, coal, iron, and iron ore, and that all States shall prohibit the procurement of such material from the DPRK by their nationals, or using their flag vessels or aircraft, and whether or not originating in the territory of the DPRK, and *decides* that this provision shall not apply with respect to:

(a) Coal that the procuring State confirms on the basis of credible information has originated outside the DPRK and was transported through the DPRK solely for export from the Port of Rajin (Rason). . . .

(b) Transactions that are determined to be exclusively for livelihood purposes. . . .

30. *Decides* that the DPRK shall not supply, sell or transfer, directly or indirectly, from its territory or by its nationals or using its flag vessels or aircraft, gold, titanium ore, vanadium ore, and rare earth minerals. . . .

31. *Decides* that all States shall prevent the sale or supply, by their nationals or from their territories or using their flag vessels or aircraft, of aviation fuel, including aviation gasoline, naptha-type jet fuel, kerosene-type jet fuel, and kerosene-type rocket fuel, whether or not originating in their territory, to the territory of the DPRK. . . .

32. *Decides* that the asset freeze imposed by paragraph 8 (d) of resolution 1718 (2006) shall apply to all the funds, other financial assets and economic resources outside of the DPRK that are owned or controlled, directly or indirectly, by entities of the Government of the DPRK or the Worker's Party of Korea, or by individuals or entities acting on their behalf or at their direction, or by entities owned or controlled by them, that the State determines are associated with the DPRK's nuclear or ballistic missile programs or other activities prohibited by resolutions. . . .

33. *Decides* that States shall prohibit in their territories the opening and operation of new branches, subsidiaries, and representative offices of DPRK banks, *decides* further that States shall prohibit financial institutions within their territories or subject to their jurisdiction from establishing new joint ventures and from taking an ownership interest in or establishing or maintaining correspondent relationships with DPRK banks, unless such transactions have been approved by the Committee in advance, and *decides* that States shall take the necessary measures to close such existing branches, subsidiaries and representative offices, and also to terminate such joint ventures, ownership interests and correspondent banking relationships. . . .

34. *Decides* that States shall prohibit financial institutions within their territories or subject to their jurisdiction from opening new representative offices or subsidiaries, branches or banking accounts in the DPRK. . . .

35. *Decides* that States shall take the necessary measures to close existing representative offices, subsidiaries or banking accounts in the DPRK within ninety days, if the State

concerned has credible information that provides reasonable grounds to believe that such financial services could contribute to the DPRK's nuclear or ballistic missile programs, or other activities prohibited. . . .

36. *Decides* that all States shall prohibit public and private financial support from within their territories or by persons or entities subject to their jurisdiction for trade with the DPRK . . . where such financial support could contribute to the DPRK's nuclear or ballistic missile programs. . . .

39. *Reaffirms* the measures imposed in paragraph 8 (a) (iii) of resolution 1718 (2006) regarding luxury goods, and *clarifies* that the term "luxury goods" includes, but is not limited to, the items specified in Annex V of this resolution;

40. *Calls upon* all States to report to the Security Council within ninety days of the adoption of this resolution, and thereafter upon request by the Committee, on concrete measures they have taken in order to implement effectively the provisions of this resolution. . . .

41. *Calls* upon all States to supply information at their disposal regarding non-compliance with the measures imposed in resolutions 1718 (2006), 1874 (2009), 2087 (2013), 2094 (2013) or this resolution;

42. *Encourages* all States to examine the circumstances of previously reported sanctions violations, particularly the items seized or activities prevented pursuant to the relevant resolutions, so as to assist in ensuring full and appropriate implementation of these resolutions. . . .

43. *Directs* the Committee to respond effectively to violations of the measures decided in resolutions 1718 (2006), 1874 (2009), 2087 (2013), 2094 (2013), and this resolution. . . .

48. *Underlines* that measures imposed by resolutions 1718 (2006), 1874 (2009), 2087 (2013), 2094 (2013) and this resolution are not intended to have adverse humanitarian consequences for the civilian population of the DPRK or to affect negatively those activities, including economic activities and cooperation, that are not prohibited. . . .

50. *Reaffirms* its support to the Six Party Talks, *calls* for their resumption, and *reiterates* its support for the commitments set forth in the Joint Statement of 19 September 2005 issued by China, the DPRK, Japan, the Republic of Korea, the Russian Federation, and the United States, including that the goal of the Six-Party Talks is the verifiable denuclearization of the Korean Peninsula in a peaceful manner, that the United States and the DPRK undertook to respect each other's sovereignty and exist peacefully together, and that the Six Parties undertook to promote economic cooperation, and all other relevant commitments;

51. *Affirms* that it shall keep the DPRK's actions under continuous review and is prepared to strengthen, modify, suspend or lift the measures as may be needed in light of the DPRK's compliance, and, in this regard, expresses its determination to take further significant measures in the event of a further DPRK nuclear test or launch;

52. *Decides* to remain seized of the matter.

[Annexes 1–4 have been omitted and list individuals, entities, vessels, and luxury goods subject to the sanctions.]

Source: United Nations. "Resolution 2270 (2016)." March 2, 2016. http://www.un.org/en/ga/search/view_doc.asp?symbol=S/RES/2270(2016).

State Department Report on Human Rights Abuses and Censorship in North Korea

July 6, 2016

. . . The Government of the Democratic People's Republic of Korea (DPRK or North Korea) continues to commit serious human rights abuses, including extrajudicial killings, enforced disappearances, arbitrary arrests and detention, forced labor, and torture. Many of these abuses are committed in the country's political prison camps (*kwanliso*), which hold an estimated 80,000–120,000 prisoners, including children and family members of the accused. The government also maintains an extensive system of forced labor through its rigid controls over workers, and restricts the exercise of freedoms of expression, peaceful assembly, association, religion or belief, and movement.

There are no independent media in the country; all media are strictly censored and no deviation from the official government line is tolerated. The government allows no editorial freedom; all stories are centrally directed and reviewed to ensure that they are in line with the state ideology. The government also controls academic and cultural content. Authorities prohibit listening to foreign media broadcasts and take steps to jam foreign radio broadcasts. . . .

This report details aspects of the human rights situation in North Korea and the conduct of relevant persons, including those responsible for the commission of serious human rights abuses and censorship in the DPRK. . . .

National Defense Commission: . . . According to the COI, since the accession of Kim Jong Un, there has been an increase in the number of executions of senior officials that "seem to have political purposes," which the COI described as appearing to be linked to his consolidation of power. In certain instances, the executions were carried out in secret after the individuals were forcibly disappeared. . . .

Per its mandate and in practice, the National Defense Commission exercised direct authority over entities responsible for some of the most pervasive and notorious human rights abuses in the DPRK, including those described below; the ministry of state security, ministry of public security, and the Korean People's Army all reported directly to it, and these ministries' respective ministers all sat on the commission. . . .

Organization and Guidance Department of the Korean Worker's Party (OGD): . . . The OGD is also instrumental in implementing the DPRK's censorship policies. When a party official deviates from the official message in public remarks, the OGD will dispatch an official to monitor a self-criticism session. The OGD will also step in and assume oversight responsibilities over organizations undergoing party audits to inspect for ideological discipline.

The OGD also had a role in the disappearance of Pak Nam Gi, the former Director of the Finance and Planning Department, according to a report by the now deceased former 1st Director of the OGD Ri Je Gang.

Ministry of State Security (AKA State Security Department): . . . According to the COI report, the Ministry of State Security is implicated in "widespread gross human rights violations," including those involving torture and cruel, inhuman, and degrading treatment, deliberate starvation, and sexual violence. It is the lead agency investigating political crimes and administering the country's network of political prison camps. . . . According to defector testimony and satellite imagery, within the camps, summary executions and other cruel extrajudicial punishments are commonplace. Additionally, according to extensive testimony, prisoners in these prison camps are subject to brutal treatment, torture, sexual violence, and forced abortions, and many succumb to starvation and disease.

The ministry also plays a role in censorship through the enforcement of laws banning foreign media. . . . Bureau 27 . . . is responsible for modifying television equipment to receive only approved North Korean channels and blocking television channels from the Republic of Korea (ROK), Russia, and China. The bureau also carries out surprise inspections in homes to investigate whether individuals have modified their radios or televisions, watched foreign DVDs or used foreign flash drives and uses monitoring equipment to identify individuals who use Chinese SIM cards.

Ministry of People's Security: . . . According to the COI, the Ministry of People's Security is involved in gross violations of human rights. The correctional bureau within the ministry previously operated one of the country's political prison camps (Camp 18) and continues to operate the majority of the country's labor camps (*kyohwaso*) and other detention/interrogation facilities. Torture and other forms of abuse are reportedly employed regularly as tools of control in these camps.

Defectors have also reported the ministry regularly uses torture and other forms of abuse to extract confessions, including techniques involving sexual violence, hanging individuals from the ceiling for extended periods of time, prolonged periods of exposure, and severe beatings . . .

Propaganda and Agitation Department (PAD): . . . Within the department, the Publication and Broadcasting Department controls all media content, including content used on television, in newspapers and on the radio. According to the COI report, this sub-agency distributes a "monthly plan for publication and report," which directs content for the month, and all media outlets are required to build their work plan from it. . . .

Reconnaissance General Bureau (RGB): . . . The RGB has reportedly been involved with kidnapping and extrajudicial assassinations that span decades. According to HRNK, the Operations Department of the Korean Workers' Party, the predecessor to RGB, was responsible for abducting South Korean and Japanese citizens. Moreover, the RGB has been associated with multiple assassination attempts, including the 1968 attempt on ROK President Park Chung-hee, the 1983 attempted assassination of ROK President Chun Doo-hwan that left 21 dead, and the 2010 attempt on high-ranking DPRK defector Hwang Jang-yeop.

[Annex A has been omitted and contains an abbreviated list of individuals and entities named in the report.]

Source: U.S. State Department Bureau of Democracy, Human Rights, and Labor. "Report on Human Rights Abuses and Censorship in North Korea." July 6, 2016. http://www.state.gov/j/drl/rls/259366.htm.

OTHER HISTORIC DOCUMENTS OF INTEREST

FROM PREVIOUS *HISTORIC DOCUMENTS*

State of the Union Address and Republican Response

JANUARY 12, 2016

On January 12, 2016, President Barack Obama delivered the final State of the Union address of his presidency before a joint session of Congress. Often, the goal of a final State of the Union is for a president to cement his legacy, and, as such, President Obama's speech offered few policy proposals. He spent the bulk of his less than one-hour long speech focusing on America's potential and taking pointed jabs at the Republican presidential contenders. "It's easier to be cynical; to accept that change isn't possible, and politics is hopeless, and to believe that our voices and actions don't matter," he said, adding, "but if we give up now, then we forsake a better future." The president faced a low approval rating of 45 percent heading into the speech and also found himself up against a hotly contested presidential primary and an even further divided political climate.

Republican South Carolina Governor Nikki Haley delivered the Republican response to the president's speech. Haley had been a star of the Republican Party and gained even greater national prominence in 2015 for her handling of the Charleston church shooting that killed nine and for spearheading the removal of the Confederate flag from statehouse grounds. Haley's speech was focused on how the Republican Party should position itself following the Obama presidency, including a return to issues such as Second Amendment rights and ending the Affordable Care Act.

DOMESTIC POLICY

Ahead of the president's speech, the White House announced that it would be "non-traditional," but offered no details about what that might mean. In the opening lines of the speech, the president made clear that meant he would be more casual than usual, and his speech contained few of the moving, climactic moments it has in the past. He even opened with a joke. "For this final one, I'm going to try to make it shorter. I know some of you are antsy to get back to Iowa," Obama said. "I've been there. I'll be shaking hands afterwards if you want some tips."

Contrary to past speeches, the president spent little time focusing on his key domestic policies. He said from the outset that he wanted his final address to "just talk about next year. I want to focus on the next 5 years, the next 10 years, and beyond. I want to focus on our future." But, the president said, he would continue pushing in his final year in office for work on issues including immigration, gun control, equal pay, helping those with drug addictions, and raising the minimum wage.

Obama spoke about the recovery from the Great Recession, noting that the country has created more than 14 million new jobs, cut unemployment in half, and is "in the middle of the longest streak of private sector job creation in history." But, he said, there is still work ahead of the country to ensure a stronger middle class and to lift more families out of poverty. However, he cautioned in an attack of then–Republican presidential contender Donald Trump, "Anyone claiming that America's economy is in decline is peddling fiction." Obama said that to continue the nation's current economic trajectory, he would welcome a discussion about how to further increase growth by ensuring that tax cuts do not only benefit the wealthiest Americans and finding ways to help small businesses grow.

Obama praised Republican Speaker of the House Paul Ryan for urging bipartisanship, and throughout the various themes in his speech, President Obama pled for better politics. "It's one of the few regrets of my presidency—that the rancor and suspicion between the parties has gotten worse instead of better," Obama said. He went on to note, in a nod to the presidential primary, "Democracy does require basic bonds of trust between its citizens. It doesn't work if we think the people who disagree with us are all motivated by malice, or that our political opponents our unpatriotic. . . . Our public life withers when only the most extreme voices get attention."

Obama encouraged the nation to continue focusing on moving forward, despite what some presidential contenders might be saying. "America has been through big changes before—wars and depression, the influx of immigrants, workers fighting for a fair deal, and movements to expand civil rights," the president said. "Each time there have been those who told us to fear the future; who claimed we could slam the brakes on change, promising to restore past glory if we just got some group or idea that was threatening America under control. And each time, we overcame those fears." He added, "Such progress is not inevitable. It is the result of choices we make together."

The longest portion of the president's speech was dedicated to climate change. He praised the December 2015 Paris climate agreement and demanded further action on emissions. And he took aim at those who doubt the existence of climate change. "Look, if anybody still wants to dispute the science around climate change, have at it. You'll be pretty lonely, because you'll be debating our military, most of America's business leaders, the majority of the American people, almost the entire scientific community, and 200 nations around the world who agree it's a problem and intend to solve it," Obama said.

Noting that 2015 was the warmest year on record, and calling for greater investments in clean energy, Obama asked the audience why the country shouldn't become the producer and provider of the clean energy that the entire world will use in the future. Current investments in solar power have saved "Americans tens of millions of dollars a year on their energy bills and employs more Americans than coal in jobs that pay better than average," Obama said. He added that this shift in focus to clean energy has cut American imports of oil by almost 60 percent and helped reduce carbon pollution. The president called on Congress to continue investing in these growth areas rather than subsidizing the past.

FOREIGN AFFAIRS

The president's remarks on foreign affairs focused primarily on the rhetoric being shared on the presidential campaign trail that America's enemies continue to get stronger and that attacks are imminent because America has failed to invest enough in its military to fight terrorism around the world. "The United States is the most powerful nation on Earth. Period. It's not even close," Obama said. "We spend more on our military than the next eight nations combined. Our troops are the finest fighting force in the history of the world." He continued, "No nation attacks us directly, or our allies, because they know that's the path to ruin." Obama cautioned that those saying that we cannot fight the

Islamic State of Iraq and the Levant (ISIL) or that the United States has become embroiled in World War III are spreading "the kind of propaganda they use to recruit." Obama also spoke directly to those who have criticized him for not referring to ISIL-linked attacks as "radical Islamic terrorism," saying that the terrorist group is not representative of an entire religion and that "we just need to call them what they are: killers and fanatics who have to be rooted out, hunted down, and destroyed."

In calling for increased military action against ISIL, Obama said that the United States has continued to lead a coalition of more than sixty countries that advise and train local forces, conduct counterterrorism operations, and carry out airstrikes that have killed key leaders and wiped out ISIL infrastructure. But Obama also called for calculated action against ISIL and other terrorist organizations around the world. "We also can't try to take over and rebuild every country that falls into crisis. That's not leadership; that's a recipe for quagmire, spilling American blood and treasure that ultimately weakens us. It's the lesson of Vietnam, of Iraq. And we should have learned it by now," he said. The smarter solution, the president said, is to work with our allies as well as the countries impacted by growing terrorist activity. America must "make sure other countries pull their own weight," he said. Obama said that the policies currently in place in nations such as Afghanistan and Syria protect American interests while also strengthening the region. "American leadership . . . is not a choice between ignoring the rest of the world—except when we kill terrorists—or occupying and rebuilding whatever society is unraveling. Leadership means a wise application of military power and rallying the world behind causes that are right. It means seeing our foreign assistance as part of our national security, not something separate, not charity."

GOVERNOR HALEY DELIVERS REPUBLICAN RESPONSE

The choice of Governor Haley, South Carolina's first Indian American governor, to give the response raised speculation that she might be considered as a vice presidential nominee. Haley opened her speech speaking about the historic election of President Obama that brought hope to millions, but criticizing him for falling "far short of his soaring words." She said the president has left the nation with a weak economy and "the most dangerous terrorist threat our nation has seen since September 11th."

Haley chided both Democrats and Republicans in her speech for raising the rancor and negative political discourse and for failing to keep America moving forward in a positive direction. "We need to be honest with each other and with ourselves: While Democrats in Washington bear much responsibility for the problems facing America today, they do not bear it alone. There is more than enough blame to go around," she said. "We as Republicans need to own that truth. We need to recognize our contributions to the erosion of the public trust in America's leadership. We need to accept that we've played a role in how and why our government is broken." She added, "Some people think that you have to be the loudest voice in the room to make a difference. That is just not true. Often, the best thing we can do is turn down the volume. When the sound is quieter, you can actually hear what someone is saying. And that can make a world of difference."

Haley also used her own background to call for immigration reform. "My story," she said, "is really not much different from millions of other Americans. Immigrants have been coming to our shores for generations to live the dream that is America. They wanted better for their children than for themselves." She noted that Republicans do not want open borders, but they do want to ensure that all immigrants are properly vetted before entering the country.

Haley ended her speech by calling on Americans to recognize and celebrate their differences rather than making attacks on each other based on race and religion, especially in light of the rhetoric used by some on the campaign trail. She said that citizens and government leaders should take a cue from how everyone came together after the Charleston church shooting. "Our state was struck with shock, pain, and fear. But our people would not allow hate to win. We didn't have violence, we had vigils. We didn't have riots, we had hugs," Haley said. Speaking of certain presidential contenders, Haley said, "We live in a time of threats like few others in recent memory. During anxious times, it can be tempting to follow the siren call of the angriest voices. We must resist that temptation."

—Heather Kerrigan

Following is the text of President Barack Obama's State of the Union address delivered before a joint session of Congress on January 12, 2016; and the Republican response delivered by South Carolina Governor Nikki Haley, also on January 12, 2016.

DOCUMENT

President Obama's Final State of the Union Address

January 12, 2016

Thank you. Mr. Speaker, Mr. Vice President, Members of Congress, my fellow Americans: Tonight marks the eighth year that I've come here to report on the State of the Union. And for this final one, I'm going to try to make it a little shorter. I know some of you are antsy to get back to Iowa. [*Laughter*] I've been there. I'll be shaking hands afterwards if you want some tips. [*Laughter*]

Now, I understand that because it's an election season, expectations for what we will achieve this year are low. But, Mr. Speaker, I appreciate the constructive approach that you and other leaders took at the end of last year to pass a budget and make tax cuts permanent for working families. So I hope we can work together this year on some bipartisan priorities like criminal justice reform and helping people who are battling prescription drug abuse and heroin abuse. So, who knows, we might surprise the cynics again.

But tonight I want to go easy on the traditional list of proposals for the year ahead. Don't worry, I've got plenty—[*laughter*]—from helping students learn to write computer code to personalizing medical treatments for patients. And I will keep pushing for progress on the work that I believe still needs to be done: fixing a broken immigration system, protecting our kids from gun violence, equal pay for equal work, paid leave, raising the minimum wage. All these things still matter to hard-working families. They're still the right thing to do. And I won't let up until they get done.

But for my final address to this Chamber, I don't want to just talk about next year. I want to focus on the next 5 years, the next 10 years, and beyond. I want to focus on our future.

We live in a time of extraordinary change, change that's reshaping the way we live, the way we work, our planet, our place in the world. It's change that promises amazing medical breakthroughs, but also economic disruptions that strain working families. It promises this education for girls in the most remote villages, but also connects terrorists plotting an ocean away. It's change that can broaden opportunity or widen inequality. And whether we like it or not, the pace of this change will only accelerate.

America has been through big changes before: wars and depression, the influx of new immigrants, workers fighting for a fair deal, movements to expand civil rights. Each time, there have been those who told us to fear the future; who claimed we could slam the brakes on change; who promised to restore past glory if we just got some group or idea that was threatening America under control. And each time, we overcame those fears. We did not, in the words of Lincoln, adhere to the "dogmas of the quiet past." Instead, we thought anew and acted anew. We made change work for us, always extending America's promise outward, to the next frontier, to more people. And because we did, because we saw opportunity with a—where others saw peril, we emerged stronger and better than before.

What was true then can be true now. Our unique strengths as a nation—our optimism and work ethic, our spirit of discovery, our diversity, our commitment to rule of law— these things give us everything we need to ensure prosperity and security for generations to come.

In fact, it's in that spirit that we have made progress these past 7 years. That's how we recovered from the worst economic crisis in generations. That's how we reformed our health care system and reinvented our energy sector. That's how we delivered more care and benefits to our troops coming home and our veterans. That's how we secured the freedom in every State to marry the person we love.

But such progress is not inevitable. It's the result of choices we make together. And we face such choices right now. Will we respond to the changes of our time with fear, turning inward as a nation, turning against each other as a people? Or will we face the future with confidence in who we are, in what we stand for, in the incredible things that we can do together?

So let's talk about the future and four big questions that I believe we as a country have to answer, regardless of who the next President is or who controls the next Congress. First, how do we give everyone a fair shot at opportunity and security in this new economy? Second, how do we make technology work for us and not against us, especially when it comes to solving urgent challenges like climate change? Third, how do we keep America safe and lead the world without becoming its policeman? And finally, how can we make our politics reflect what's best in us and not what's worst?

Let me start with the economy and a basic fact: The United States of America right now has the strongest, most durable economy in the world. We're in the middle of the longest streak of private sector job creation in history. More than 14 million new jobs, the strongest 2 years of job growth since the 1990s, an unemployment rate cut in half. Our auto industry just had its best year ever. That's just part of a manufacturing surge that's created nearly 900,000 new jobs in the past 6 years. And we've done all this while cutting our deficits by almost three-quarters.

Anyone claiming that America's economy is in decline is peddling fiction. Now, what is true—and the reason that a lot of Americans feel anxious—is that the economy has been changing in profound ways, changes that started long before the great recession hit, changes that have not let up.

Today, technology doesn't just replace jobs on the assembly line, but any job where work can be automated. Companies in a global economy can locate anywhere, and they face tougher competition. As a result, workers have less leverage for a raise. Companies have less loyalty to their communities. And more and more wealth and income is concentrated at the very top.

All these trends have squeezed workers, even when they have jobs, even when the economy is growing. It's made it harder for a hard-working family to pull itself out of poverty, harder for young people to start their careers, tougher for workers to retire when they want to. And although none of these trends are unique to America, they do offend our uniquely American belief that everybody who works hard should get a fair shot.

For the past 7 years, our goal has been a growing economy that also works better for everybody. We've made progress, but we need to make more. And despite all the political arguments that we've had these past few years, there are actually some areas where Americans broadly agree.

We agree that real opportunity requires every American to get the education and training they need to land a good-paying job. The bipartisan reform of No Child Left Behind was an important start, and together, we've increased early childhood education, lifted high school graduation rates to new highs, boosted graduates in fields like engineering. In the coming years, we should build on that progress, by providing pre-K for all and offering every student the hands-on computer science and math classes that make them job-ready on day one. We should recruit and support more great teachers for our kids.

And we have to make college affordable for every American. No hard-working student should be stuck in the red. We've already reduced student loan payments by—to 10 percent of a borrower's income. And that's good. But now we've actually got to cut the cost of college. Providing 2 years of community college at no cost for every responsible student is one of the best ways to do that, and I'm going to keep fighting to get that started this year. It's the right thing to do.

But a great education isn't all we need in this new economy. We also need benefits and protections that provide a basic measure of security. It's not too much of a stretch to say that some of the only people in America who are going to work the same job, in the same place, with a health and retirement package for 30 years are sitting in this Chamber. [*Laughter*] For everyone else, especially folks in their forties and fifties, saving for retirement or bouncing back from job loss has gotten a lot tougher. Americans understand that at some point in their careers, in this new economy, they may have to retool, they may have to retrain. But they shouldn't lose what they've already worked so hard to build in the process.

That's why Social Security and Medicare are more important than ever. We shouldn't weaken them, we should strengthen them. And for Americans short of retirement, basic benefits should be just as mobile as everything else is today. That, by the way, is what the Affordable Care Act is all about. It's about filling the gaps in employer-based care so that when you lose a job or you go back to school or you strike out and launch that new business, you'll still have coverage. Nearly 18 million people have gained coverage so far. And in the process, health care inflation has slowed. And our businesses have created jobs every single month since it became law.

Now, I'm guessing we won't agree on health care anytime soon, but—[*laughter*]—a little applause back there. [*Laughter*] Just a guess. But there should be other ways parties can work together to improve economic security. Say a hard-working American loses his job. We shouldn't just make sure that he can get unemployment insurance, we should make sure that program encourages him to retrain for a business that's ready to hire him. If that new job doesn't pay as much, there should be a system of wage insurance in place so that he can still pay his bills. And even if he's going from job to job, he should still be able to save for retirement and take his savings with him. That's the way we make the new economy work better for everybody.

I also know Speaker Ryan has talked about his interest in tackling poverty. America is about giving everybody willing to work a chance, a hand up. And I'd welcome a serious discussion about strategies we can all support, like expanding tax cuts for low-income workers who don't have children.

But there are some areas where—we just have to be honest—it has been difficult to find agreement over the last 7 years. And a lot of them fall under the category of what role the Government should play in making sure the system's not rigged in favor of the wealthiest and biggest corporations. And it's an honest disagreement, and the American people have a choice to make.

I believe a thriving private sector is the lifeblood of our economy. I think there are outdated regulations that need to be changed. There is redtape that needs to be cut. [*Applause*] There you go! Yes! See? But after years now of record corporate profits, working families won't get more opportunity or bigger paychecks just by letting big banks or big oil or hedge funds make their own rules at everybody else's expense. Middle class families are not going to feel more secure because we allowed attacks on collective bargaining to go unanswered. Food stamp recipients did not cause the financial crisis; recklessness on Wall Street did. Immigrants aren't the principal reason wages haven't gone up; those decisions are made in the boardrooms that all too often put quarterly earnings over long-term returns. It's sure not the average family watching tonight that avoids paying taxes through offshore accounts. [*Laughter*]

The point is, I believe that in this new economy, workers and startups and small businesses need more of a voice, not less. The rules should work for them. And I'm not alone in this. This year, I plan to lift up the many businesses who have figured out that doing right by their workers or their customers or their communities ends up being good for their shareholders. And I want to spread those best practices across America. That's part of a brighter future.

In fact, it turns out many of our best corporate citizens are also our most creative. And this brings me to the second big question we as a country have to answer: How do we reignite that spirit of innovation to meet our biggest challenges?

Sixty years ago, when the Russians beat us into space, we didn't deny Sputnik was up there. [*Laughter*] We didn't argue about the science or shrink our research and development budget. We built a space program almost overnight. And 12 years later, we were walking on the Moon.

Now, that spirit of discovery is in our DNA. America is Thomas Edison and the Wright Brothers and George Washington Carver. America is Grace Hopper and Katherine Johnson and Sally Ride. America is every immigrant and entrepreneur from Boston to Austin to Silicon Valley, racing to shape a better future. That's who we are.

And over the past 7 years, we've nurtured that spirit. We've protected an open Internet and taken bold new steps to get more students and low-income Americans online. We've launched next-generation manufacturing hubs and online tools that give an entrepreneur everything he or she needs to start a business in a single day. But we can do so much more.

Last year, Vice President Biden said that with a new moonshot, America can cure cancer. Last month, he worked with this Congress to give scientists at the National Institutes of Health the strongest resources that they've had in over a decade. Well—so tonight I'm announcing a new national effort to get it done. And because he's gone to the mat for all of us on so many issues over the past 40 years, I'm putting Joe in charge of mission control. For the loved ones we've all lost, for the families that we can still save, let's make America the country that cures cancer once and for all. What do you say, Joe? Let's make it happen.

Now, medical research is critical. We need the same level of commitment when it comes to developing clean energy sources. Look, if anybody still wants to dispute the science around climate change, have at it. [*Laughter*] You will be pretty lonely, because you'll be debating our military, most of America's business leaders, the majority of the American people, almost the entire scientific community, and 200 nations around the world who agree it's a problem and intend to solve it. But even if the planet wasn't at stake, even if 2014 wasn't the warmest year on record—until 2015 turned out to be even hotter—why would we want to pass up the chance for American businesses to produce and sell the energy of the future? Listen, 7 years ago, we made the single biggest investment in clean energy in our history. Here are the results. In fields from Iowa to Texas, wind power is now cheaper than dirtier, conventional power. On rooftops from Arizona to New York, solar is saving Americans tens of millions of dollars a year on their energy bills and employs more Americans than coal in jobs that pay better than average. We're taking steps to give homeowners the freedom to generate and store their own energy, something, by the way, that environmentalists and Tea Partiers have teamed up to support. And meanwhile, we've cut our imports of foreign oil by nearly 60 percent and cut carbon pollution more than any other country on Earth. Gas under 2 bucks a gallon ain't bad either. [*Laughter*]

Now we've got to accelerate the transition away from old, dirtier energy sources. Rather than subsidize the past, we should invest in the future, especially in communities that rely on fossil fuels. We do them no favor when we don't show them where the trends are going. And that's why I'm going to push to change the way we manage our oil and coal resources so that they better reflect the costs they impose on taxpayers and our planet. And that way, we put money back into those communities and put tens of thousands of Americans to work building a 21st-century transportation system.

Now, none of this is going to happen overnight. And yes, there are plenty of entrenched interests who want to protect the status quo. But the jobs we'll create, the money we'll save, the planet we'll preserve—that is the kind of future our kids and our grandkids deserve. And it's within our grasp.

Now, climate change is just one of many issues where our security is linked to the rest of the world. And that's why the third big question that we have to answer together is how to keep America safe and strong without either isolating ourselves or trying to nation-build everywhere there's a problem.

Now, I told you earlier all the talk of America's economic decline is political hot air. Well, so is all the rhetoric you hear about our enemies getting stronger and America getting weaker. Let me tell you something: The United States of America is the most powerful nation on Earth. Period. [*Applause*] Period. It's not even close. [*Applause*] It's not even close. It's not even close. We spend more on our military than the next eight nations combined. Our troops are the finest fighting force in the history of the world. [*Applause*] All right. No nation attacks us directly, or our allies, because they know that's the path to ruin. Surveys show our standing around the world is higher than when I was elected to this office, and when it comes to every important international issue, people of the world do not look to Beijing or Moscow to lead. They call us. So I think it's useful to level set here, because when we don't, we don't make good decisions.

Now, as someone who begins every day with an intelligence briefing, I know this is a dangerous time. But that's not primarily because of some looming superpower out there, and it's certainly not because of diminished American strength. In today's world, we're threatened less by evil empires and more by failing states.

The Middle East is going through a transformation that will play out for a generation, rooted in conflicts that date back millennia. Economic headwinds are blowing in from a Chinese economy that is in significant transition. Even as their economy severely contracts, Russia is pouring resources in to prop up Ukraine and Syria, client states that they saw slipping away from their orbit. And the international system we built after World War II is now struggling to keep pace with this new reality. It's up to us, the United States of America, to help remake that system. And to do that well, it means that we've got to set priorities. Priority number one is protecting the American people and going after terrorist networks. Both Al Qaida and now ISIL pose a direct threat to our people, because in today's world, even a handful of terrorists who place no value on human life, including their own, can do a lot of damage. They use the Internet to poison the minds of individuals inside our country. Their actions undermine and destabilize our allies. We have to take them out.

But as we focus on destroying ISIL, over-the-top claims that this is world war III just play into their hands. Masses of fighters on the back of pickup trucks, twisted souls plotting in apartments or garages, they pose an enormous danger to civilians; they have to be stopped. But they do not threaten our national existence. That is the story ISIL wants to tell. That's the kind of propaganda they use to recruit. We don't need to build them up to show that we're serious, and we sure don't need to push away vital allies in this fight by echoing the lie that ISIL is somehow representative of one of the world's largest religions. We just need to call them what they are: killers and fanatics who have to be rooted out, hunted down, and destroyed.

And that's exactly what we're doing. For more than a year, America has led a coalition of more than 60 countries to cut off ISIL's financing, disrupt their plots, stop the flow of terrorist fighters, and stamp out their vicious ideology. With nearly 10,000 airstrikes, we're taking out their leadership, their oil, their training camps, their weapons. We're training, arming, and supporting forces who are steadily reclaiming territory in Iraq and Syria.

If this Congress is serious about winning this war and wants to send a message to our troops and the world, authorize the use of military force against ISIL. Take a vote. [*Applause*] Take a vote. But the American people should know that with or without congressional action, ISIL will learn the same lessons as terrorists before them. If you doubt America's commitment—or mine—to see that justice is done, just ask Usama bin Laden. Ask the leader of Al Qaida in Yemen, who was taken out last year, or the perpetrator of the Benghazi attacks, who sits in a prison cell. When you come after Americans, we go after you. And it may take time, but we have long memories, and our reach has no limits.

Our foreign policy has to be focused on the threat from ISIL and Al Qaida, but it can't stop there. For even without ISIL, even without Al Qaida, instability will continue for decades in many parts of the world: in the Middle East, in Afghanistan and parts of Pakistan, in parts of Central America, in Africa and Asia. Some of these places may become safe havens for new terrorist networks. Others will just fall victim to ethnic conflict or famine, feeding the next wave of refugees. The world will look to us to help solve these problems, and our answer needs to be more than tough talk or calls to carpet-bomb civilians. That may work as a TV sound bite, but it doesn't pass muster on the world stage.

We also can't try to take over and rebuild every country that falls into crisis, even if it's done with the best of intentions. That's not leadership; that's a recipe for quagmire, spilling American blood and treasure that ultimately will weaken us. It's the lesson of Vietnam; it's the lesson of Iraq. And we should have learned it by now.

Now, fortunately there is a smarter approach: a patient and disciplined strategy that uses every element of our national power. It says America will always act, alone if necessary, to protect our people and our allies, but on issues of global concern, we will mobilize the world to work with us and make sure other countries pull their own weight. That's our approach to conflicts like Syria, where we're partnering with local forces and leading international efforts to help that broken society pursue a lasting peace. That's why we built a global coalition, with sanctions and principled diplomacy, to prevent a nuclear-armed Iran. And as we speak, Iran has rolled back its nuclear program, shipped out its uranium stockpile, and the world has avoided another war.

That's how we stopped the spread of Ebola in West Africa. Our military, our doctors, our development workers—they were heroic; they set up the platform that then allowed other countries to join in behind us and stamp out that epidemic. Hundreds of thousands, maybe a couple million, lives were saved.

That's how we forged a Trans-Pacific Partnership to open markets and protect workers and the environment and advance American leadership in Asia. It cuts 18,000 taxes on products made in America, which will then support more good jobs here in America. With TPP, China does not set the rules in that region, we do. You want to show our strength in this new century? Approve this agreement. Give us the tools to enforce it. It's the right thing to do.

Let me give you another example. Fifty years of isolating Cuba had failed to promote democracy. It set us back in Latin America. That's why we restored diplomatic relations, opened the door to travel and commerce, positioned ourselves to improve the lives of the Cuban people. So if you want to consolidate our leadership and credibility in the hemisphere, recognize that the cold war is over. Lift the embargo.

The point is, American leadership in the 21st century is not a choice between ignoring the rest of the world—except when we kill terrorists—or occupying and rebuilding whatever society is unraveling. Leadership means a wise application of military power and rallying the world behind causes that are right. It means seeing our foreign assistance as a part of our national security, not something separate, not charity.

When we lead nearly 200 nations to the most ambitious agreement in history to fight climate change, yes, that helps vulnerable countries, but it also protects our kids. When we help Ukraine defend its democracy or Colombia resolve a decades-long war, that strengthens the international order we depend on. When we help African countries feed their people and care for the sick, it's the right thing to do, and it prevents the next pandemic from reaching our shores. Right now we're on track to end the scourge of HIV/AIDS. That's within our grasp. And we have the chance to accomplish the same thing with malaria, something I'll be pushing this Congress to fund this year.

That's American strength. That's American leadership. And that kind of leadership depends on the power of our example. That's why I will keep working to shut down the prison at Guantanamo. It is expensive, it is unnecessary, and it only serves as a recruitment brochure for our enemies. There's a better way.

And that's why we need to reject any politics—any politics—that targets people because of race or religion. Let me just say this. This is not a matter of political correctness, this is a matter of understanding just what it is that makes us strong. The world respects us not just for our arsenal, it respects us for our diversity and our openness and the way we respect every faith.

His Holiness Pope Francis told this body from the very spot that I'm standing on tonight that "to imitate the hatred and violence of tyrants and murderers is the best way to take their place." When politicians insult Muslims, whether abroad or our fellow citizens, when a mosque is vandalized or a kid is called names, that doesn't make us safer. That's not telling it what—telling it like it is. It's just wrong. It diminishes us in the eyes of the world. It makes it harder to achieve our goals. It betrays who we are as a country. "We the People." Our Constitution begins with those three simple words, words we've come to recognize mean all the people, not just some; words that insist we rise and fall together, that that's how we might perfect our Union. And that brings me to the fourth and maybe most important thing that I want to say tonight.

The future we want—all of us want—opportunity and security for our families, a rising standard of living, a sustainable, peaceful planet for our kids—all that is within our reach. But it will only happen if we work together. It will only happen if we can have rational, constructive debates. It will only happen if we fix our politics.

A better politics doesn't mean we have to agree on everything. This is a big country: different regions, different attitudes, different interests. That's one of our strengths too. Our Founders distributed power between States and branches of government and expected us to argue, just as they did, fiercely, over the size and shape of government, over commerce and foreign relations, over the meaning of liberty and the imperatives of security.

But democracy does require basic bonds of trust between its citizens. It doesn't work if we think the people who disagree with us are all motivated by malice. It doesn't work if we think that our political opponents are unpatriotic or trying to weaken America. Democracy grinds to a halt without a willingness to compromise or when even basic facts are contested or when we listen only to those who agree with us. Our public life withers when only the most extreme voices get all the attention. And most of all, democracy breaks down when the average person feels their voice doesn't matter, that the system is rigged in favor of the rich or the powerful or some special interest.

Too many Americans feel that way right now. It's one of the few regrets of my Presidency: that the rancor and suspicion between the parties has gotten worse instead of better. I have no doubt, a President with the gifts of Lincoln or Roosevelt might have better bridged the divide, and I guarantee, I'll keep trying to be better so long as I hold this office.

But, my fellow Americans, this cannot be my task—or any President's—alone. There are a whole lot of folks in this Chamber, good people, who would like to see more cooperation, would like to see a more elevated debate in Washington, but feel trapped by the imperatives of getting elected, by the noise coming out of your base. I know; you've told me. It's the worst kept secret in Washington. And a lot of you aren't enjoying being trapped in that kind of rancor.

But that means if we want a better politics—and I'm addressing the American people now—if we want a better politics, it's not enough just to change a Congressman or change a Senator or even change a President. We have to change the system to reflect our better selves.

I think we've got to end the practice of drawing our congressional districts so that politicians can pick their voters and not the other way around. Let a bipartisan group do it.

I believe we've got to reduce the influence of money in our politics so that a handful of families or hidden interests can't bankroll our elections. And if our existing approach to campaign finance reform can't pass muster in the courts, we need to work together to find a real solution. Because it's a problem. And most of you don't like raising money. [*Laughter*] I know. I've done it.

We've got to make it easier to vote, not harder. We need to modernize it for the way we live now. This is America: We want to make it easier for people to participate. And over the course of this year, I intend to travel the country to push for reforms that do just that. But I can't do these things on my own. Changes in our political process—in not just who gets elected, but how they get elected—that will only happen when the American people demand it. It depends on you. That's what's meant by a government of, by, and for the people.

What I'm suggesting is hard. It's a lot easier to be cynical; to accept that change is not possible and politics is hopeless and the problem is, all the folks who are elected don't care; and to believe that our voices and our actions don't matter. But if we give up now, then we forsake a better future. Those with money and power will gain greater control over the decisions that could send a young soldier to war or allow another economic disaster or roll back the equal rights and voting rights that generations of Americans have fought, even died, to secure. And then, as frustration grows, there will be voices urging us to fall back into our respective tribes, to scapegoat fellow citizens who don't look like us or pray like us or vote like we do or share the same background.

We can't afford to go down that path. It won't deliver the economy we want. It will not produce the security we want. But most of all, it contradicts everything that makes us the envy of the world.

So, my fellow Americans, whatever you may believe, whether you prefer one party or no party, whether you supported my agenda or fought as hard as you could against it, our collective futures depends on your willingness to uphold your duties as a citizen. To vote. To speak out. To stand up for others, especially the weak, especially the vulnerable, knowing that each of us is only here because somebody, somewhere, stood up for us. We need every American to stay active in our public life—and not just during election time—so that our public life reflects the goodness and the decency that I see in the American people every single day.

It is not easy. Our brand of democracy is hard. But I can promise that a little over a year from now, when I no longer hold this office, I will be right there with you as a citizen, inspired by those voices of fairness and vision, of grit and good humor and kindness, that have helped America travel so far. Voices that help us see ourselves not, first and foremost, as Black or White or Asian or Latino, not as gay or straight, immigrant or native born, not Democrat or Republican, but as Americans first, bound by a common creed. Voices Dr. King believed would have the final word: voices of "unarmed truth and unconditional love."

And they're out there, those voices. They don't get a lot of attention; they don't seek a lot of fanfare; but they're busy doing the work this country needs doing. I see them everywhere I travel in this incredible country of ours. I see you, the American people. And in your daily acts of citizenship, I see our future unfolding.

I see it in the worker on the assembly line who clocked extra shifts to keep his company open and the boss who pays him higher wages instead of laying him off. I see it in the dreamer who stays up late at night to finish her science project and the teacher who comes in early, maybe with some extra supplies that she bought because she knows that that young girl might someday cure a disease.

I see it in the American who served his time, made bad mistakes as a child, but now is dreaming of starting over. And I see it in the business owner who gives him that second chance. The protester determined to prove that justice matters and the young cop walking the beat, treating everybody with respect, doing the brave, quiet work of keeping us safe.

I see it in the soldier who gives almost everything to save his brothers, the nurse who tends to him till he can run a marathon, the community that lines up to cheer him on. It's the son who finds the courage to come out as who he is and the father whose love for that son overrides everything he's been taught.

I see it in the elderly woman who will wait in line to cast her vote as long as she has to, the new citizen who casts his vote for the first time, the volunteers at the polls who believe every vote should count. Because each of them, in different ways, know how much that precious right is worth.

That's the America I know. That's the country we love: clear eyed, big hearted, undaunted by challenge. Optimistic that unarmed truth and unconditional love will have the final word. That's what makes me so hopeful about our future. I believe in change because I believe in you, the American people. And that's why I stand here as confident as I have ever been that the state of our Union is strong.

Thank you. God bless you. God bless the United States of America. Thank you.

SOURCE: Executive Office of the President. "Address Before a Joint Session of Congress on the State of the Union." January 12, 2016. *Compilation of Presidential Documents* 2016, no. 00012 (January 12, 2016). http://www.gpo.gov/fdsys/pkg/DCPD-201600012/pdf/DCPD-201600012.pdf.

DOCUMENT

Governor Haley Delivers Republican Response to the State of the Union

January 12, 2016

Good evening.

I'm Nikki Haley, Governor of the great state of South Carolina.

I'm speaking tonight from Columbia, our state's capital city. Much like America as a whole, ours is a state with a rich and complicated history, one that proves the idea that each day can be better than the last.

In just a minute, I'm going to talk about a vision of a brighter American future. But first I want to say a few words about President Obama, who just gave his final State of the Union address.

Barack Obama's election as president seven years ago broke historic barriers and inspired millions of Americans. As he did when he first ran for office, tonight President Obama spoke eloquently about grand things. He is at his best when he does that.

Unfortunately, the President's record has often fallen far short of his soaring words.

As he enters his final year in office, many Americans are still feeling the squeeze of an economy too weak to raise income levels. We're feeling a crushing national debt, a health care plan that has made insurance less affordable and doctors less available, and chaotic unrest in many of our cities.

Even worse, we are facing the most dangerous terrorist threat our nation has seen since September 11th, and this president appears either unwilling or unable to deal with it.

Soon, the Obama presidency will end, and America will have the chance to turn in a new direction. That direction is what I want to talk about tonight.

At the outset, I'll say this: you've paid attention to what has been happening in Washington, and you're not naive.

Neither am I. I see what you see. And many of your frustrations are my frustrations.

A frustration with a government that has grown day after day, year after year, yet doesn't serve us any better. A frustration with the same, endless conversations we hear over and over again. A frustration with promises made and never kept.

We need to be honest with each other, and with ourselves: while Democrats in Washington bear much responsibility for the problems facing America today, they do not bear it alone. There is more than enough blame to go around.

We as Republicans need to own that truth. We need to recognize our contributions to the erosion of the public trust in America's leadership. We need to accept that we've played a role in how and why our government is broken.

And then we need to fix it.

The foundation that has made America that last, best hope on earth hasn't gone anywhere. It still exists. It is up to us to return to it.

For me, that starts right where it always has: I am the proud daughter of Indian immigrants who reminded my brothers, my sister and me every day how blessed we were to live in this country.

Growing up in the rural south, my family didn't look like our neighbors, and we didn't have much. There were times that were tough, but we had each other, and we had the opportunity to do anything, to be anything, as long as we were willing to work for it.

My story is really not much different from millions of other Americans. Immigrants have been coming to our shores for generations to live the dream that is America. They wanted better for their children than for themselves. That remains the dream of all of us, and in this country we have seen time and again that that dream is achievable.

Today, we live in a time of threats like few others in recent memory. During anxious times, it can be tempting to follow the siren call of the angriest voices. We must resist that temptation.

No one who is willing to work hard, abide by our laws, and love our traditions should ever feel unwelcome in this country.

At the same time, that does not mean we just flat out open our borders. We can't do that. We cannot continue to allow immigrants to come here illegally. And in this age of terrorism, we must not let in refugees whose intentions cannot be determined.

We must fix our broken immigration system. That means stopping illegal immigration. And it means welcoming properly vetted legal immigrants, regardless of their race or religion. Just like we have for centuries.

I have no doubt that if we act with proper focus, we can protect our borders, our sovereignty and our citizens, all while remaining true to America's noblest legacies.

This past summer, South Carolina was dealt a tragic blow. On an otherwise ordinary Wednesday evening in June, at the historic Mother Emanuel church in Charleston, twelve faithful men and women, young and old, went to Bible study.

That night, someone new joined them. He didn't look like them, didn't act like them, didn't sound like them. They didn't throw him out. They didn't call the police. Instead, they pulled up a chair and prayed with him. For an hour.

We lost nine incredible souls that night.

What happened after the tragedy is worth pausing to think about.

Our state was struck with shock, pain, and fear. But our people would not allow hate to win. We didn't have violence, we had vigils. We didn't have riots, we had hugs.

We didn't turn against each other's race or religion. We turned toward God, and to the values that have long made our country the freest and greatest in the world.

We removed a symbol that was being used to divide us, and we found a strength that united us against a domestic terrorist and the hate that filled him.

There's an important lesson in this. In many parts of society today, whether in popular culture, academia, the media, or politics, there's a tendency to falsely equate noise with results.

Some people think that you have to be the loudest voice in the room to make a difference. That is just not true. Often, the best thing we can do is turn down the volume. When the sound is quieter, you can actually hear what someone else is saying. And that can make a world of difference.

Of course that doesn't mean we won't have strong disagreements. We will. And as we usher in this new era, Republicans will stand up for our beliefs.

If we held the White House, taxes would be lower for working families, and we'd put the brakes on runaway spending and debt.

We would encourage American innovation and success instead of demonizing them, so our economy would truly soar and good jobs would be available across our country.

We would reform education so it worked best for students, parents, and teachers, not Washington bureaucrats and union bosses.

We would end a disastrous health care program, and replace it with reforms that lowered costs and actually let you keep your doctor.

We would respect differences in modern families, but we would also insist on respect for religious liberty as a cornerstone of our democracy.

We would recognize the importance of the separation of powers and honor the Constitution in its entirety. And yes, that includes the Second and Tenth Amendments.

We would make international agreements that were celebrated in Israel and protested in Iran, not the other way around.

And rather than just thanking our brave men and women in uniform, we would actually strengthen our military, so both our friends and our enemies would know that America seeks peace, but when we fight wars we win them.

We have big decisions to make. Our country is being tested.

But we've been tested in the past, and our people have always risen to the challenge. We have all the guidance we need to be safe and successful.

Our forefathers paved the way for us.

Let's take their values, and their strengths, and rededicate ourselves to doing whatever it takes to keep America the greatest country in the history of man. And woman.

Thank you, good night, and God bless.'

SOURCE: Office of Speaker of the House Paul Ryan. "Full Text: Gov. Nikki Haley Delivers the Republican Address to the Nation." January 12, 2016. http://www.speaker.gov/press-release/full-text-gov-nikki-haley-delivers-republican-address-nation.

OTHER HISTORIC DOCUMENTS OF INTEREST

FROM THIS VOLUME

FROM PREVIOUS *HISTORIC DOCUMENTS*

Iranian Nuclear Deal Takes Effect

JANUARY 16, 2016

In July 2015, representatives from the United States, China, France, Germany, Russia, the United Kingdom, and Iran signed the Joint Comprehensive Plan of Action (JCPOA), an agreement through which Iran pledged to significantly limit its nuclear activities in return for international sanctions relief. The result of nearly two years of negotiations, the JCPOA required Iran to meet certain milestones in the reduction of its nuclear capabilities before United Nations (UN), U.S., and European sanctions could be lifted. In January 2016, the International Atomic Energy Agency (IAEA) confirmed that Iran had met its obligations as outlined in the agreement and that the JCPOA could now take full effect. The United States, UN, and European Union (EU) accordingly began removing the sanctions that had been used as the primary tool for restricting Iran's nuclear program for approximately twenty years. At the same time, the United States announced the completion of a prisoner exchange with Iran—a deal that officials said became possible through the increased contact and intense nuclear negotiations with Iran.

Both the JCPOA's implementation and the prisoner exchange were denounced by Republican lawmakers and presidential candidates as actions that put the United States' national security at risk and placed misguided trust in Iran. These criticisms were amplified following revelations that the United States made a cash payment to Iran after the prisoner exchange. With presidential elections planned in both the United States and Iran, and frustrations in some quarters that the benefits of sanctions relief were not being felt quickly enough, the JCPOA's future is in question.

THE JOINT COMPREHENSIVE PLAN OF ACTION

Western countries have long suspected that Iran has been attempting to build nuclear weapons in violation of the Nuclear Non-Proliferation Treaty, despite Iranian officials' insistence that their nuclear program has only peaceful goals. By signing the JCPOA, Iran reaffirmed that it would not seek, develop, or acquire any nuclear weapons.

Under the agreement, Iran retained the ability to enrich uranium, but can only maintain a 300kg stockpile of low-enriched uranium for the next fifteen years, as opposed to the 10,000kg it had at the time the agreement was signed. The JCPOA also limits the number of centrifuges Iran can operate at its Fordow and Natanz facilities to roughly 6,000, and either prohibits their use for uranium enrichment or allows only for low-enriched uranium production. All other centrifuges, totaling approximately 13,500, are to be placed in storage until the agreement expires.

Additionally, the agreement limits Iran's nuclear-related research and development activities over the next eight years, after which time the country will be allowed to resume some activities. Iran also agreed to convert its Fordow facility into a nuclear, physics, and technology center and to redesign the heavy water research reactor at its Arak facility to support only "peaceful nuclear research." Other key provisions included Iran's commitment to allow the IAEA to have a long-term presence in Iran and monitor its implementation of these measures, marking a sharp change in the country's history of attempting to conceal its nuclear activities.

In return, once the IAEA verified Iran's compliance with the JCPOA, all previous UN Security Council resolutions relating to Iran's nuclear program would be terminated and the EU and United States would lift some of their sanctions.

IMPLEMENTATION DAY AND LIFTING OF SANCTIONS

On January 16, 2016, IAEA director-general Yukiya Amano submitted a report to the IAEA Board of Governors and the UN Security Council verifying that Iran had implemented its nuclear-related commitments as specified in the JPOA, as confirmed by IAEA inspectors on the ground in Iran. "This paves the way for the IAEA to begin verifying and monitoring Iran's nuclear-related commitments under the agreement, as requested by the U.N. Security Council and authorised by the IAEA Board," Amano said, adding that "Iran will start to provisionally implement the Additional Protocol to its Safeguards Agreement with the IAEA."

U.S. secretary of state John Kerry said that the United States would immediately lift select sanctions and remarked on the deal's significance, noting that the current level of enriched uranium present in Iran is roughly 2 percent of what it had been before the agreement was reached and that Iran had removed two-thirds of its centrifuges. "To get to this point. . . . Iran has undertaken significant steps that many—and I do mean many—people doubted would ever come to pass," Kerry said. "And that should be recognized, even though the full measure of this achievement can only be realized by assuring continued full compliance in the coming years." Kerry added that officials were confident that it would take Iran at least one year to reverse the steps it had taken to scale back its nuclear program and generate enough material for a nuclear weapon, and offered assurances that the United States would "remain vigilant in verifying Iran's compliance."

In a joint statement, EU high representative Federica Mogherini and Iranian foreign minister Javad Zarif announced that UN sanctions related to Iran's nuclear program had been lifted and that "the EU has confirmed that the legal framework providing for the lifting of its nuclear-related economic and financial sanctions is effective." The pair hailed the use of diplomacy, stating, "This achievement clearly demonstrates that with political will, perseverance, and through multilateral diplomacy, we can solve the most difficult issues and find practical solutions that are effectively implemented."

The sanctions lifted by the United States as a result of Iran's compliance with the JCPOA were mostly secondary sanctions, or those that apply to non-U.S. individuals and other countries doing business with Iran. For example, the United States will no longer sanction non-U.S. individuals who engage in financial transactions with Iran's government, central bank, or financial institutions; are a part of or engage with Iran's energy and shipping sectors; or are engaged in trading gold and precious metals with Iran. In addition, the United States lifted its ban on the import of Iranian pistachios, caviar, and carpets, and agreed to stop attempting to limit Iran's crude oil sales. U.S. companies would also now be allowed to sell commercial aircraft and parts to Iran. Four hundred Iranians and others were removed from the United States' list of sanctioned individuals, though another 200 names remain on the list for reasons including terrorism, human rights abuses, involvement in the Syrian or Yemeni civil wars, or having ties to Iran's ballistic missile program.

By comparison, the EU now allows Iranian banks to open locations in EU member states and will permit the transfer of money between the EU and Iran without requiring special authorization or notification. EU member states are allowed to import and sell Iranian oil and gas, trade gold and precious metals with Iran, and trade naval equipment and ship building technology with Iran. Also, cargo flights from Iran can now access airports in EU member states.

The lifting of sanctions also allows Iran to rejoin the international banking system, and the country was expected to receive between $50 billion and $100 billion once its assets (mostly from past oil sales) were unfrozen.

In the United States, Republican lawmakers were quick to decry the agreement's implementation and the lifting of sanctions. "As the president himself has acknowledged, Iran is likely to use this cash infusion—more than $100 billion in total—to finance terrorists," said House Speaker Paul Ryan, R-Wis. "A bipartisan majority in the House voted to reject this deal in the first place, and we will continue to do everything possible to prevent a nuclear Iran." The fifteen Republican presidential candidates were highly critical of the agreement, describing it in terms including "deeply flawed, and short sighted," "a historic mistake," and "one of America's worst diplomatic failures."

Lawmakers' concerns over the JCPOA also manifested in a legislative effort to block Boeing's efforts to broker a deal to sell and lease passenger jets to Iran Air, the government-owned airline. Lawmakers speculated that the aircraft could be used in ways that would support the Iranian Revolutionary Guard Corps, which remains under U.S. sanction, or Bashar al-Assad's government in Syria. Rep. Peter Roskam, R-Ill., proposed two amendments to a financial services appropriations bill to prevent the sale. The House voted to approve the bill with Roskam's amendments on July 7. The bill was pending in the Senate at the time of this writing.

U.S.–IRAN PRISONER EXCHANGE CONTROVERSY

January 16 was also the day that the U.S. State Department announced the release of five Americans as part of a prisoner exchange with Iran. In exchange for these prisoners, the United States released seven Iranians who had either been charged with or convicted of breaking U.S. embargos, and another fourteen Iranians were removed from international wanted lists. According to Kerry, negotiations surrounding the prisoner exchange were not directly related to the JCPOA negotiations, though he noted that "the pace and the progress of the humanitarian talks accelerated in light of the relationships forged and the diplomatic channels unlocked over the course of the nuclear talks."

The prisoner exchange became a political flashpoint in early August, after the *Wall Street Journal* reported that the Obama administration had made a $400 million payment to Iran and sent the money in coordination with the prisoners' release. The payment was reportedly the initial installment of a $1.7 billion settlement the administration had reached with Iran in a dispute over a failed arms deal signed shortly before the Iranian Revolution in 1979. Republicans jumped on the news, claiming the money amounted to a "ransom" payment. Administration officials denied there was any connection between the money and the prisoners' release. "As we've made clear, the negotiations over the settlement of an outstanding claim . . . were completely separate from the discussions about returning our American citizens home," said State Department spokesperson John Kirby.

Some lawmakers expressed concerns that the money would be used to fund groups such as Hezbollah, which the United States has designated as a terrorist organization, and the Syrian government. Some also proposed legislation to prevent the administration from making future cash payments to Iran, with one bill calling for the White House to publicly release details of the $400 million payment.

Then, on August 18, the State Department confirmed that the United States made the $400 million payment conditional upon the American prisoners' release and departure from Iran. "We deliberately leveraged that moment to finalize these outstanding issues nearly simultaneously," said Kirby. "With concerns that Iran may renege on the prisoner release, given unnecessary delays regarding persons in Iran who could not be located as well as, to be quite honest, mutual mistrust between Iran and the United States, we of course sought to retain maximum leverage until after American citizens were released."

Republicans claimed that Kirby's confirmation was essentially an admission that the United States had paid a ransom to Iran, including then–Republican presidential nominee Donald Trump, who said the president had "put every American traveling overseas, including our military personnel, at greater risk of being kidnapped."

Iranian Nuclear Scientist Executed

Iran's execution on August 7 of Shahram Amiri, a nuclear scientist accused of cooperating with U.S. intelligence agencies, drew further attention to the country's nuclear program and U.S.–Iran relations. Iran accused the United States of abducting Amiri after he disappeared in 2009 while on a religious pilgrimage to Mecca. In a series of YouTube videos released in June 2010, Amiri claimed to have been kidnapped and tortured by the CIA, but then escaped. The following month, Amiri surfaced at the Pakistani Embassy in Washington, D.C., and said he wanted to return to Iran. At that point, then–Secretary of State Hillary Clinton confirmed that Amiri had been in the United States "of his own free will and he is free to go." U.S. officials reported that Amiri had been a CIA informant for several years while he lived in Iran and had provided information about the country's nuclear program. Following Amiri's return to Iran, the government initially claimed that Amiri had in fact served as a double agent and arrested him shortly thereafter. "Shahram Amiri was hanged for revealing the country's top secrets to the enemy," said Gholam-Hossein Mohseni-Eje'i, a spokesperson for the Iranian Justice Ministry.

The Future of the JCPOA

There is some doubt about the future viability of the JCPOA. Various Iranian officials have complained that the United States has delayed the removal of economic sanctions and that the country is not getting relief quickly enough. U.S. officials maintain that they have fully complied with the JCPOA and that uncertainty among the international business community was the cause of Iran's delayed sanctions relief. Iranian president Hassan Rouhani has in turn claimed that the U.S. Treasury Department has not provided sufficient clarity around remaining sanctions to encourage businesses to engage with Iran.

In addition, Donald Trump has repeatedly criticized the JCPOA throughout his presidential campaign and suggested he would "rip up" the deal if elected, though a campaign adviser later said Trump would instead seek to renegotiate the deal. By contrast, Hillary Clinton has said she will "vigorously enforce the nuclear deal" and that her approach to Iran will be "to distrust and verify." President Rouhani is also facing reelection in June 2017 and is likely to face conservative challengers who are opposed to negotiating with the United States and believe that the deal provided too many concessions.

—Linda Fecteau Grimm

Following is the IAEA's report from January 16, 2016, verifying Iran's compliance with the Joint Comprehensive Plan of Action; public remarks from U.S. secretary of state John Kerry from January 16, 2016, following the plan's implementation; and a joint statement from EU high representative Federica Mogherini and Iranian foreign minister Javad Zarif from January 16, 2016, about the plan's implementation.

IAEA Issues Report on Iran's JCPOA Compliance

January 16, 2016

[All footnotes have been omitted.]

Verification and Monitoring in the Islamic Republic of Iran in light of United Nations Security Council Resolution 2231 (2015)

Report by the Director General

1. The Board of Governors has authorized the Director General to implement the necessary verification and monitoring of the Islamic Republic of Iran's (Iran's) nuclear-related commitments as set out in the Joint Comprehensive Plan of Action (JCPOA), and report accordingly, for the full duration of those commitments in light of United Nations Security Council (Security Council) resolution 2231 (2015).

2. This report to the Board of Governors and in parallel to the Security Council is to confirm that the Agency has verified that Iran has taken the actions specified in paragraphs 15.1–15.11 of Annex V of the JCPOA.

3. The Agency has verified and confirms that, as of 16 January 2016, Iran:

Arak Heavy Water Research Reactor (15.1)

    i. was not pursuing the construction of the existing IR-40 Reactor (Arak Heavy Water Research Reactor) based on its original design (JCPOA, Annex I–Nuclear-related measures, para. 3);

    ii. had removed the existing calandria from the IR-40 Reactor (para. 3);

    iii. had rendered the calandria inoperable by filling the openings in it with concrete, such that the Agency was able to verify that the calandria is not usable for a future nuclear application (para. 3);

iv. was not producing or testing natural uranium pellets, fuel pins or fuel assemblies specifically designed for the support of the IR-40 Reactor as originally designed (para. 10);

v. had stored under continuous Agency monitoring all existing natural uranium pellets and fuel assemblies for the IR-40 Reactor (para. 10);

vi. had modified the fuel production process line at the Fuel Manufacturing Plant at Esfahan such that it cannot be used for the fabrication of fuel for the IR-40 Reactor as originally designed (para. 10);

Heavy Water Production Plant (15.2)

i. had no more than 130 metric tonnes of nuclear grade heavy water or its equivalent in different enrichments (para. 14);

ii. had informed the Agency about the inventory and the production of the Heavy Water Production Plant (HWPP) and was allowing the Agency to monitor the quantities of Iran's heavy water stocks and the amount of heavy water produced at the HWPP (para. 15);

Enrichment Capacity (15.3)

i. had no more than 5060 IR-1 centrifuges installed at the Fuel Enrichment Plant (FEP) at Natanz in no more than 30 of the cascades in the configurations of the operating units at the time the JCPOA was agreed (para. 27);

ii. was not enriching uranium above 3.67% U–235 (para. 28) at any of its declared nuclear facilities;

iii. had removed and stored in Hall B of FEP, under Agency continuous monitoring, all excess centrifuges and infrastructure not associated with the 5060 IR-1 centrifuges in FEP (para. 29), including all IR-2m centrifuges (para. 29.1), UF_6 pipework, and UF_6 withdrawal equipment from one of the withdrawal stations that was not in service at the time the JCPOA was agreed (para. 29.2);

Centrifuge Research and Development (15.4)

i. was not accumulating enriched uranium through its enrichment research and development (R&D) activities and its enrichment R&D with uranium was not being conducted using centrifuges other than IR-4, IR-5, IR-6 and IR-8 centrifuges (para. 32);

ii. was not conducting mechanical testing on more than two single centrifuges of type IR-2m, IR-4, IR-5, IR-6, IR-6s, IR-7 and IR-8 (para. 32);

iii. was not building or testing, with or without uranium, types of centrifuge other than those specified in the JCPOA (para. 32);

iv. had removed all of the centrifuges from the 164-machine IR-2m cascade and the 164-machine IR-4 cascade at PFEP and placed them in storage in Hall B of FEP in Natanz under Agency continuous monitoring (paras 33 and 34);

v. was testing centrifuges installed at PFEP within the limits set out in the JCPOA i.e. a single IR-4 machine (para. 35), a 10-machine IR-4 cascade (para. 35), a single IR-5 machine (para. 36), a single IR-6 machine and its intermediate cascades (para. 37);

vi. had yet to start testing its single IR-8 centrifuge (para. 38);

vii. had recombined the streams from the R&D cascades at PFEP through the use of welded pipework in a manner that precludes the withdrawal of the enriched and depleted uranium material produced (para. 39);

viii. was, in relation to its declared nuclear facilities, testing centrifuges using uranium only at PFEP and conducting all mechanical testing of centrifuges only at PFEP and the Tehran Research Centre (para. 40);

ix. had removed to Hall B of FEP in Natanz under Agency continuous monitoring all centrifuges at PFEP, except those needed for testing as described in the relevant paragraphs above, and those in Cascade 1 at PFEP; had rendered inoperable Cascade 1 by, inter alia, removing the rotors, injecting epoxy resin into the pipework and removing the electrical systems (para. 41);

x. had stored all the IR-1 centrifuges previously installed in Cascade 6 at PFEP, and their associated infrastructure, in Hall B of FEP in Natanz under Agency continuous monitoring (para. 41); and was keeping the space in this line empty for R&D (para. 41);

xi. was maintaining the cascade infrastructure for testing single centrifuges and small and intermediate cascades in two R&D lines (nos. 2 and 3); and had adapted two other R&D lines (nos. 4 and 5) through the requisite removal of existing infrastructure (para. 42);

Fordow Fuel Enrichment Plant (15.5)

i. was not conducting any uranium enrichment or related R&D at the Fordow Fuel Enrichment Plant (FFEP) (para. 45);

ii. had removed all nuclear material from FFEP (para. 45);

iii. was maintaining no more than 1044 IR-1 centrifuges at FFEP, which were all in one wing (para. 46);

iv. had modified for the production of stable isotopes two of the cascades at FFEP that had never experienced UF_6 by removing the connection to the UF_6 feed main header; and had moved cascade UF_6 pipework to storage in Fordow under continuous Agency monitoring (para. 46.1);

v. was maintaining two cascades in an idle state and two cascades spinning, and had removed pipework that enables crossover tandem connections for these four cascades (para. 46.2);

vi. had removed from the aforementioned wing two other cascades by removing the IR-1 centrifuges and associated cascade UF_6 pipework (para. 47.1);

vii. had removed from the other wing of FFEP all IR-1 centrifuges and related uranium enrichment infrastructure, including pipework, and feed and withdrawal stations (para. 48.1);

Other Aspects of Enrichment (15.6)

i.   had provided the Agency with Iran's long-term enrichment and R&D enrichment plan which is to be part of Iran's initial declaration described in Article 2 of the Additional Protocol (para. 52);

ii. had provided the Agency with a template for describing different centrifuge types (IR-1, IR-2m, IR-4, IR-5, IR-6, IR-6s, IR-7, IR-8) and associated definitions that have been agreed with JCPOA participants (para. 54);

iii. had agreed with the JCPOA participants a procedure for measuring IR-1, IR-2m and IR-4 centrifuge performance data (para. 55);

Uranium Stocks and Fuels (15.7)

i.   had a stockpile of no more than 300 kg of UF_6 enriched up to 3.67% U–235 (or the equivalent in different chemical forms), as a result of either down-blending to natural uranium, or sale and delivery out of Iran (para. 57);

ii. had fabricated into fuel plates for the Tehran Research Reactor, transferred out of Iran or diluted to an enrichment level of 3.67% U–235 or less, all uranium oxide enriched to between 5% and 20% U–235 (para. 58);

Centrifuge Manufacturing (15.8)

i.   was not producing IR-1 centrifuges to replace damaged or failed machines, as its stock of such centrifuges was in excess of 500 (para. 62);

Transparency Measures (15.9)

i.   had completed the modalities and facility-specific arrangements to allow the Agency to implement all transparency measures provided for in Annex I of the JCPOA (see para. 4 below);

Additional Protocol and Modified Code 3.1 (15.10)

i.   had notified the Agency pursuant to paragraph 64, Section L of Annex I of the JCPOA that, effective on Implementation Day, Iran will provisionally apply the Additional Protocol to its Safeguards Agreement in accordance with Article 17(b) of the Additional Protocol (para. 64);

ii. had notified the Agency pursuant to paragraph 65, Section L of Annex I of the JCPOA that, effective on Implementation Day, Iran will fully implement the modified Code 3.1 of the Subsidiary Arrangements to Iran's Safeguards Agreement as long as the Safeguards Agreement remains in force (para. 65);

Centrifuge Component Manufacturing Transparency (15.11)

i.   had provided to the Agency an initial inventory of all existing centrifuge rotor tubes and bellows and permitted the Agency to verify this inventory by item counting and numbering, and through containment and surveillance (para. 80.1); and

ii. had declared to the Agency all locations and equipment that are used for the production of centrifuge rotor tubes or bellows and permitted the Agency to implement continuous monitoring of this equipment (para. 80.2).

4. In addition, the Agency also confirms that, as of 16 January 2016, Iran:

Modern Technologies and Long-Term Presence of the Agency

a) had permitted the Agency to use on-line enrichment measurement devices and electronic seals which communicate their status within nuclear sites to Agency inspectors (para. 67.1);

b) had facilitated the automated collection of Agency measurement recordings registered by installed measurement devices (para. 67.1);

c) had made the necessary arrangements to allow for a long-term Agency presence, including issuing long-term visas, as well as by providing proper working space for the Agency at nuclear sites and, with best efforts, at locations near nuclear sites in Iran (para. 67.2);

Transparency Related to Uranium Ore Concentrate

a) had permitted the Agency to monitor through measures agreed with Iran, including containment and surveillance, that all uranium ore concentrate (UOC) produced in Iran or obtained from any other source is transferred to the Uranium Conversion Facility in Esfahan (para. 68);

b) had provided the Agency with all information necessary to enable the Agency to verify the production of UOC and the inventory of UOC produced in Iran or obtained from any other source (para. 69); and

Transparency Related to Enrichment

a) had permitted the Agency to have regular access to relevant buildings at Natanz, including all of FEP and PFEP, and daily access upon request (para. 71).

SOURCE: International Atomic Energy Agency. "Verification and Monitoring in the Islamic Republic of Iran in light of United Nations Security Council Resolution 2231 (2015)." January 16, 2016. http://www .iaea.org/sites/default/files/gov-inf-2016-1.pdf.

Secretary Kerry Remarks on Implementation of Iranian Nuclear Agreement

DOCUMENT

January 16, 2016

Good evening, everybody. Thank you very much for your patience. And I apologize for the fact that I can't stay to take questions, which I would like to do. But we are operating under some very tight constraints on the rest period the law allows for our pilots, because of some of the delays. So as a result, I need to get to the airport and get on the plane. But I will make a statement before doing so, and I hope it will cover much of what you're concerned about.

This evening, we are really reminded once again of diplomacy's power to tackle significant challenges. And thanks to years of hard work and committed dialogue, we have made vital breakthroughs related to both the nuclear negotiation and a separate long-term diplomatic effort. I'm very happy to say that as we speak, we have received confirmation that five Americans who had been unjustly detained in Iran have been released from custody. And they should be on their way home to their families before long—shortly.

The President will have more to say about their release later. But I can tell you one thing: While the two tracks of negotiations were not directly related—and they were not—there is no question that the pace and the progress of the humanitarian talks accelerated in light of the relationships forged and the diplomatic channels unlocked over the course of the nuclear talks. And certainly in the time since we reached an agreement last July, there was a significant pickup in that dialogue.

We have also reached a critical and auspicious milestone on the nuclear issue as well. Today, more than four years after I first traveled to Oman at the request of President Obama to discreetly explore whether the kind of nuclear talks that we ultimately entered into with Iran were even possible, after more than two and a half years of intense multilateral negotiations, the International Atomic Energy Agency has now verified that Iran has honored its commitments to alter—and in fact, dismantle—much of its nuclear program in compliance with the agreement that we reached last July. . . .

To get to this point, ladies and gentlemen, Iran has undertaken significant steps that many—and I do mean many—people doubted would ever come to pass. And that should be recognized, even though the full measure of this achievement can only be realized by assuring continued full compliance in the coming years. In return for the steps that Iran has taken, the United States and the EU will immediately lift nuclear-related sanctions, expanding the horizon of opportunity for the Iranian people. And I have even tonight, before coming over here, signed a number of documents over those sanctions that the State Department has jurisdiction over in order to effect that lifting.

In the words of the agreement itself, today—January 16th, 2016—we have reached implementation day. Today marks the moment that the Iran nuclear agreement transitions from an ambitious set of promises on paper to measurable action in progress. Today, as a result of the actions taken since last July, the United States, our friends and allies in the Middle East, and the entire world are safer because the threat of a nuclear weapon has been reduced. Today we can confidently say that each of the pathways that Iran had toward enough fissile material for a nuclear weapon has been verifiably closed down.

That begins with the uranium path. . . . Iran has now reduced that stockpile to less than 300 kilograms, sending the rest of it out on a ship which has gone to Russia to be processed there. That means that their current level of enriched uranium is 2 percent of what it was before we completed the agreement, and the rest is shipped out of the country.

Iran has also removed a full two thirds of its centrifuges from nuclear facilities, along with the infrastructure that supported them. . . .

The second path open to Iran was the plutonium path. . . . Iran has now begun the process of modifying the entire Arak reactor so that it will only be used for peaceful purposes. It has removed the reactor's core and filled it with cement, ensuring that it can be never used again.

Finally, the third path—the most troubling path, in many respects—was the potential for Iran to pursue enough fissile material for a weapon covertly, using a facility not publicly declared. . . . Today, the IAEA has put in place every one of the extensive transparency and verification measures called for in the agreement. . . .

So today, Iran would need far more than one covert facility in order to try to break out. It would need to develop an entire covert supply chain, from start to finish—which experts around the world agree is not possible without early detection.

As I said, the steps that Iran has taken to fully implement the nuclear agreement have fundamentally altered the country's nuclear program. Two years ago we assessed that Iran's breakout time, the amount of time it took to go from producing fissile—enriched uranium to have enough for one bomb—that amount of time has gone from two to three months, where it was; now, today we are confident that—based on the reductions in its stockpile, reductions in its centrifuges—it would take Iran at least a year to try to break out of the agreement, kick out the inspectors, accumulate the amount of fissile material needed for a single bomb.

And if Iran ever did decide to do that, because of the steps that are in this agreement, we would know it almost immediately, and we would have enough time to respond accordingly.

Let me underscore: Verification remains, as it always has been, the backbone of this agreement. We welcome that Iran has followed through on the promises that it made. It has kept its word. And we will continue to do the same. But we will also remain vigilant in verifying Iran's compliance every hour of every day in the years ahead. . . .

The hard work will continue, no question. And the tough politics surrounding this issue in many countries, including the United States and Iran—that's obviously not going to get easier overnight. But the fact is that today marks the first day of a safer world, one where we believe it is possible to remain safer for years to come, and particularly with the compliance of this agreement.

I think we have also proven once again why diplomacy has to always be our first choice, and war our last resort. And that is a very important lesson to reinforce. We have approached this challenge that the—with the firm belief that exhausting diplomacy before choosing war is an imperative. And we believe that today marks the benefits of that choice.

Thank you. [*Applause.*]

SOURCE: U.S. State Department. "Remarks on Implementation Day." January 16, 2016. https://2009-2017
.state.gov/secretary/remarks/2016/01/251336.htm.

 ## European Union–Iran Joint Statement on Iranian Nuclear Deal

January 16, 2016

Today, we have reached Implementation Day of the Joint Comprehensive Plan of Action (JCPOA). Ever since Adoption Day, we worked hard and showed mutual commitment and collective will to finally bring the JCPOA to implementation. Today, six months after finalisation of the historic deal, the International Atomic Energy Agency (IAEA) has verified that Iran has implemented its nuclear related commitments under the JCPOA.

As Iran has fulfilled its commitments, today, multilateral and national economic and financial sanctions related to Iran's nuclear programme are lifted in accordance with the JCPOA. The EU and E3+3 countries, consisting of the People's Republic of China, the Republic of France, the Federal Republic of Germany, the Russian Federation, the United Kingdom of Great Britain and Northern Ireland, and the United States of America, and Iran will also cooperate in the field of peaceful uses of nuclear energy, in the framework of the JCPOA.

UN sanctions related to Iran's nuclear programme are lifted. United Nations Security Council resolution 2231 (2015), which endorsed the JCPOA, will from now onwards, together with the Treaty on the Non-Proliferation of Nuclear Weapons (NPT), be the sole international legal framework related to Iran's nuclear activities. . . .

The EU has confirmed that the legal framework providing for the lifting of its nuclear-related economic and financial sanctions is effective. The United States today is ceasing the application of its nuclear-related statutory sanctions on Iran, including terminating relevant Executive Orders and licensing of certain activities, as specified in the JCPOA. The EU and the United States have issued relevant guidelines on the details of sanctions which have been lifted thus facilitating international engagement in Iran's economic development. As foreseen, we will continue to thoroughly monitor and oversee the full and effective implementation of the JCPOA, exactly as agreed on 14 July 2015, through the Joint Commission, consisting of the E3+3 and Iran, and coordinated by the High Representative of the Union for Foreign Affairs and Security Policy. On its side, the IAEA is entrusted with the responsibility for the monitoring and verification of the JCPOA as well as of Iran's obligations as a Party to Non-Proliferation Treaty and its safeguards agreement and the provisional application of its Additional Protocol. . . .

All sides remain firmly convinced that this historic deal is both strong and fair, and that it meets the requirements of all; its proper implementation will be a key contribution to improved regional and international peace, stability and security.

This achievement clearly demonstrates that with political will, perseverance, and through multilateral diplomacy, we can solve the most difficult issues and find practical solutions that are effectively implemented. This is an encouraging and strong message that the international community must keep in mind in our efforts to make the world a safer place.

Source: European External Action Service. "Joint Statement by EU High Representative Federica Mogherini and Iranian Foreign Minister Javad Zarif." January 16, 2016. https://eeas.europa.eu/headquarters/headquarters-homepage/2991_en.

Other Historic Documents of Interest

From previous Historic Documents

February

Health Organizations Respond as Zika Virus Spreads

FEBRUARY 1, MARCH 8, AND AUGUST 1, 2016

Early in 2016, governments and public health organizations found themselves facing a new global threat: the growing reach and impact of the Zika virus. Called the "mystery disease" when it first appeared in Brazil, the virus has been linked to microcephaly and other congenital defects as well as neurological disorders. Zika's effects and rapid spread to dozens of countries and territories prompted the World Health Organization (WHO) to declare it a Public Health Emergency of International Concern (PHEIC). With no vaccine available, officials around the world focused on preventive measures and issued a variety of travel and other advisories for pregnant women and those living in Zika-affected areas.

A HISTORY OF ZIKA OUTBREAKS

Zika was first detected in humans in Uganda and Tanzania in 1952. It is believed that the virus spread from Africa to Asia in the 1960s, and then to the South Pacific. The virus's spread did not attract significant attention at that time, primarily because it remained in regions where other diseases with more severe effects, such as dengue, were present. Also, many people living in regions exposed to the virus tended to be immune from Zika, which limited its impact.

The Zika virus is primarily transmitted by infected mosquitos in the *Aedes* genus, specifically *Aedes aegypti* and *Aedes albopictus* mosquitos. To date, most infections are caused by bites from the *Aedes aegypti* mosquito, which is prevalent in tropical climates and is the same mosquito that may carry dengue, yellow fever, and chikungunya. People infected with the Zika virus may have symptoms such as mild fever, skin rash, conjunctivitis, muscle and joint pain, or headaches, typically lasting two to seven days, though roughly 80 percent of those infected do not exhibit any symptoms.

The first large Zika outbreak was reported on the Island of Yap in 2007. The outbreak only lasted for six months, but 73 percent of the island's residents were infected. Then, in 2013, an outbreak occurred in French Polynesia, a collection of more than 100 islands in the South Pacific. During that outbreak, doctors confirmed forty-two cases of Guillain-Barré Syndrome, a rare disease in which the immune system attacks the peripheral nervous system and can lead to paralysis in severe cases. This unusually high number of Guillain-Barré diagnoses provided doctors with the first indication of the Zika virus's potential neurological effects.

From the South Pacific, the virus spread to South America, with Brazil reporting the first confirmed Zika infection in May 2015. Brazilian scientists believe that fans traveling to the country for the 2014 World Cup may have brought the disease with them. French scientists at the Pasteur Institute have alternatively suggested that the virus arrived later in

2014 during the Va'a World Sprint canoe race, in which teams from several Polynesian islands competed.

Zika quickly spread throughout Brazil, and doctors began identifying links between the virus and other disorders as they diagnosed patients. Doctors first reported an association between Zika and Guillain-Barré in July 2015. In October, doctors began reporting an association between Zika and microcephaly, a condition in which a baby's brain stops growing and the child is born with a head that is much smaller than those of babies of the same age and sex. Babies born with microcephaly often experience developmental challenges as they grow, although some children may develop normally.

Doctors in the Brazilian state of Pernambuco identified a surge in the number of babies born with this disorder whose mothers had been infected with Zika. Approximately nine infants are diagnosed with microcephaly in Pernambuco each year, but by November 2015, nearly 650 babies had been born with this defect. Nearly 4,000 suspected cases of microcephaly were reported in Brazil between October 2015 and January 2016. It has since been determined that Zika can cause a severe form of microcephaly. Zika has also been linked to blindness, deafness, seizures, and other congenital defects. While researchers are still studying how Zika does this, it is known that the virus can be transmitted from pregnant women to their fetus through the placenta and that the virus attacks fetal nerve cells, some of which develop into the brain.

Brazilian officials declared a health emergency in November 2015, while the number of infected grew. The virus has since spread exponentially. According to the Centers for Disease Control and Prevention (CDC), as of October 2016, sixty countries and territories have reported mosquito-borne transmission of Zika, including nearly every country in South and Central America. On March 20, the WHO confirmed that the same strain of Zika identified in Brazil had been found in Cape Verde, marking the first time that the strain linked to neurological disorders was in Africa. On July 1, officials in Guinea-Bissau confirmed several cases of Zika in its Bijagos Archipelago, prompting concerns that the virus would soon arrive on the African mainland. On July 29, the Florida State Department of Health announced that four cases of locally transmitted Zika had been found in the state. Roughly one month later, the first local Zika cases were confirmed in Singapore.

As the virus continued to spread, medical professionals determined that Zika may also be transmitted sexually, though the vast majority of cases are still from mosquito bites. As of June 2016, all known cases of sexual transmission were man to woman or man to man, leading health organizations to recommend that men who have been to Zika-infected areas use contraception for eight weeks to six months after their travel, depending on whether they have symptoms. Researchers are also investigating the possibility that Zika could be transmitted through blood transfusion after Brazil reported a number of Zika cases that appear to be linked to blood donors.

There is currently no vaccine for Zika, and treatment typically includes rest, fluid intake, and the use of common pain and fever medications. Organizations including the CDC and WHO have recommended a number of preventive measures for those living in or visiting areas where Zika is present, including wearing pants and long-sleeve shirts to cover the body; using air conditioning, when possible, as well as window and door screens; sleeping under mosquito nets; using insect repellent containing DEET or similar substances; and eliminating standing water, which provides a breeding ground for mosquitos.

GLOBAL RESPONSE

Governments and health officials quickly began responding to the Zika virus's spread. Between December 2015 and January 2016, officials in Brazil, Ecuador, Colombia, Jamaica, and El Salvador advised women living in Zika-affected areas to postpone pregnancy for periods ranging from six months to several years. Such guidance was criticized by women living in these countries and women's rights and health advocates, who argued variously that the advice was unrealistic given religious and cultural norms and lack of access to sufficient contraceptive methods, or that it ran contrary to the law. In El Salvador, for instance, abortion is illegal in all circumstances. On February 5, the UN High Commissioner for Human Rights urged Latin American governments to reconsider their policies restricting abortion and contraception. This drew criticism from the Vatican, which called it "an illegitimate response" to Zika. However, Pope Francis later remarked that "avoiding pregnancy is not an absolute evil," which some interpreted as an admission that contraceptive use would be acceptable as a means of preventing the further spread of Zika.

The CDC issued its first Zika-related travel warning on January 15, advising pregnant women to consider postponing travel to Brazil and thirteen other countries and territories. The United Kingdom, Japan, Ireland, South Korea, New Zealand, Malaysia, Singapore, the Philippines, and the European Union issued similar travel warnings early in 2016. In Brazil, the National Biosafety Committee approved the release of genetically modified male *Aedes aegypti* mosquitos that would transmit a self-limiting gene to their female mates, causing offspring to die before reaching adulthood. While this technique had previously been used to combat Zika, dengue, and chikungunya, it is also controversial because some environmental groups claim that eradicating a species of mosquito could disrupt the ecosystem. The committee's January decision was followed by Brazil's February deployment of 60 percent of its armed forces to 350 municipalities to talk to residents about the risks of Zika and educate them about prevention methods.

On February 1, WHO director-general Dr. Margaret Chan convened a meeting of the organization's Emergency Committee to discuss the spread of Zika and the severity of the health threat posed by the disease. Consisting of eighteen experts and advisers, the committee advised Dr. Chan that the cases of microcephaly and neurological disorders identified in Brazil constituted an "extraordinary event" and posed a public health threat to other parts of the world. Following the meeting, at the advice of the committee, Dr. Chan issued a statement declaring Zika to be a PHEIC. The statement also called for a coordinated international effort to "improve surveillance, the detection of infections, congenital malformations, and neurological complications, to intensify the control of mosquito populations, and to expedite the development of diagnostic tests and vaccines to protect people at risk, especially during pregnancy." Notably, the statement did not recommend restrictions on travel or trade. The WHO also activated its Zika Virus Disease Incident Management System, through which the WHO reviews existing risk assessments, increasing surveillance of the disease, assessing testing capabilities, and supporting community engagement and risk communications in priority countries.

Dr. Chan convened a second Emergency Committee meeting on March 8. The committee agreed that Zika continued to be a PHEIC and offered a series of new recommendations, including that pregnant women should be advised against traveling to areas with Zika and should be informed of practices to prevent getting Zika from a sexual partner while pregnant. The committee added that "[p]regnant women who have been exposed to

Zika virus should be counselled and followed for birth outcomes based on the best available information and national practice and policies." The committee agreed to maintain Zika's designation as an international public health emergency during its subsequent meetings in June and September and continued to provide guidance for travelers to and those living in Zika-affected areas.

On May 6, UN Secretary-General Ban Ki-moon announced the creation of the UN Zika Response Multi-Partner Trust Fund. Contributions to the fund are used to directly support the WHO's Zika Strategic Response Framework and "finance critical unfunded priorities in the response to the Zika outbreak." The same day, Major League Baseball announced its decision to move a series of games scheduled to be played in Puerto Rico to Miami, after several players expressed concerns about the possibility of contracting Zika while in Puerto Rico. Similar concerns were raised ahead of the 2016 Summer Olympics, hosted in Rio de Janeiro, Brazil. Some called for the games to be canceled or postponed, though this was not supported by the WHO or the Pan American Health Organization (PAHO). Dr. Marcos Espinal, director of PAHO's Zika response, said the two organizations expected "very little circulation of mosquitos and virus in Brazil in August" and did not think the games should be canceled. Instead, WHO and PAHO issued guidance to athletes and travelers on prevention measures. Local authorities in Brazil spent the months leading up to the Olympics fumigating Rio de Janeiro and monitoring standing water in the city for mosquito larvae. Despite these measures, ten athletes withdrew from the games, citing Zika concerns. According to the WHO, as of September 2, no athletes or visitors reported Zika infections during or after the Olympic games.

Following the identification of locally spread Zika cases in Florida, the CDC issued its first-ever guidance for travel within the continental United States. Officials said that the area of concern was limited to one square mile in Miami's Wynwood neighborhood, and the CDC's recommendations applied to those who traveled to or lived in the area on or after June 15—the earliest known date that the patients could have been infected. The CDC also announced that it was sending an emergency response team to Florida to help with disease response, at the state's request, and public health personnel started going door to door to survey neighborhood residents and collect blood and urine samples.

Other developments within the United States included the Food and Drug Administration's (FDA) guidance on August 26 that all blood and blood components donated in the United States and its territories should be tested for the Zika virus. On September 28, Congress approved $1.1 billion in funding to help combat Zika, after months of contentious and partisan debate. President Barack Obama had requested $1.9 billion in emergency federal funding in February, but Republicans and Democrats had disagreed on the language of the bill authorizing this funding. In particular, Democrats objected to Republicans' inclusion of a measure that would defund Planned Parenthood. The final bill did not include this language.

Vaccine Clinical Trials

A host of pharmaceutical companies and researchers began working to develop a Zika vaccine in 2016. Inovio Pharmaceuticals launched the first clinical trial of a vaccine in late July, after receiving approval from the FDA in June. Phase One of the trial will test the vaccine's safety and side effects; Phase Two will examine vaccine efficacy. The National Institutes of Health's National Institute of Allergy and Infectious Diseases (NIAID) started a clinical trial of another vaccine on August 3. Data from the initial phases of these clinical trials is not expected until 2017, and it is likely that the earliest an approved vaccine could be available to consumers is 2018.

—Linda Fecteau Grimm

Following is a statement from WHO director-general Dr. Margaret Chan on February 1, 2016, following the first International Health Regulations Emergency Committee meeting on the Zika virus; a press release from the WHO on March 8, 2016, following the Emergency Committee's second meeting on the Zika virus; and a press release from the CDC on August 1, 2016, following the confirmation of local Zika transmission in Florida.

WHO Statement on
Emergency Zika Meeting

February 1, 2016

I convened an Emergency Committee, under the International Health Regulations, to gather advice on the severity of the health threat associated with the continuing spread of Zika virus disease in Latin America and the Caribbean. The Committee met today by teleconference.

In assessing the level of threat, the 18 experts and advisers looked in particular at the strong association, in time and place, between infection with the Zika virus and a rise in detected cases of congenital malformations and neurological complications.

The experts agreed that a causal relationship between Zika infection during pregnancy and microcephaly is strongly suspected, though not yet scientifically proven. All agreed on the urgent need to coordinate international efforts to investigate and understand this relationship better.

The experts also considered patterns of recent spread and the broad geographical distribution of mosquito species that can transmit the virus.

The lack of vaccines and rapid and reliable diagnostic tests, and the absence of population immunity in newly affected countries were cited as further causes for concern.

After a review of the evidence, the Committee advised that the recent cluster of microcephaly cases and other neurological disorders reported in Brazil, following a similar cluster in French Polynesia in 2014, constitutes an "extraordinary event" and a public health threat to other parts of the world.

In their view, a coordinated international response is needed to minimize the threat in affected countries and reduce the risk of further international spread.

Members of the Committee agreed that the situation meets the conditions for a Public Health Emergency of International Concern.

I have accepted this advice.

I am now declaring that the recent cluster of microcephaly cases and other neurological disorders reported in Brazil, following a similar cluster in French Polynesia in 2014, constitutes a Public Health Emergency of International Concern.

A coordinated international response is needed to improve surveillance, the detection of infections, congenital malformations, and neurological complications, to intensify the control of mosquito populations, and to expedite the development of diagnostic tests and vaccines to protect people at risk, especially during pregnancy.

The Committee found no public health justification for restrictions on travel or trade to prevent the spread of Zika virus.

At present, the most important protective measures are the control of mosquito populations and the prevention of mosquito bites in at-risk individuals, especially pregnant women.

Source: World Health Organization. "WHO Director-General summarizes the outcome of the Emergency Committee regarding clusters of microcephaly and Guillain-Barré syndrome." February 1, 2016. http://www.who.int/mediacentre/news/statements/2016/emergency-committee-zika-microcephaly/en.

WHO Convenes Second Emergency Meeting on Zika and Its Effects

DOCUMENT

March 8, 2016

The second meeting of the Emergency Committee (EC) convened by the Director-General under the International Health Regulations (2005) (IHR 2005) regarding clusters of microcephaly cases and other neurological disorders in some areas affected by Zika virus was held by teleconference on 8 March 2016, from 13:00 to 16:45 Central European Time.

The WHO Secretariat briefed the Committee on action in implementing the Temporary Recommendations issued by the Director-General on 1 February 2016, and on clusters of microcephaly and Guillain-Barré Syndrome (GBS) that have had a temporal association with Zika virus transmission. The Committee was provided with additional data from observational, comparative and experimental studies on the possible causal association between Zika virus infection, microcephaly and GBS.

The following States Parties provided information on microcephaly, GBS and other neurological disorders occurring in the presence of Zika virus transmission: Brazil, Cabo Verde, Colombia, France, and the United States of America.

The Committee noted the new information from States Parties and academic institutions in terms of case reports, case series, 1 case control study (GBS) and 1 cohort study (microcephaly) on congenital abnormalities and neurologic disease in the presence of Zika virus infection. It reinforced the need for further work to generate additional evidence on this association and to understand any inconsistencies in data from countries. The Committee advised that the clusters of microcephaly cases and other neurological disorders continue to constitute a Public Health Emergency of International Concern (PHEIC), and that there is increasing evidence that there is a causal relationship with Zika virus.

The Committee provided the following advice to the Director-General for her consideration to address the PHEIC, in accordance with IHR (2005).

Microcephaly, other neurological disorders and Zika virus

- Research into the relationship between new clusters of microcephaly, other neurological disorders, including GBS, and Zika virus, should be intensified.

- Particular attention should be given to generating additional data on the genetic sequences and clinical effect of different Zika virus strains, studying the neuropathology of microcephaly, conducting additional case-control and cohort studies in other and more recently infected settings, and developing animal models for experimental studies.

- Research on the natural history of Zika virus infection should be expedited, including on the rates of asymptomatic infection, the implications of asymptomatic infection, particularly with respect to pregnancy, and the persistence of virus excretion.

- Retrospective and prospective studies of the rates of microcephaly and other neurological disorders should be conducted in other areas known to have had Zika virus transmission but where such clusters were not observed.

- Research should continue to explore the possibility of other causative factors or co-factors for the observed clusters of microcephaly and other neurological disorders.

- To facilitate this research and ensure the most rapid results:
  - surveillance for microcephaly and GBS should be standardized and enhanced, particularly in areas of known Zika virus transmission and areas at risk,
  - work should begin on the development of a potential case definition for "congenital Zika infection",
  - clinical, virologic and epidemiologic data related to the increased rates of microcephaly and/or GBS, and Zika virus transmission, should be rapidly shared with the World Health Organization to facilitate international understanding of the these events, to guide international support for control efforts, and to prioritize further research and product development.

SURVEILLANCE

- Surveillance for and notification of Zika virus infection should be enhanced with the dissemination of standard case definitions and diagnostics to areas of transmission and at-risk areas; newly infected areas should undertake the vector control measures outlined below.

VECTOR CONTROL

- Vector surveillance, including the determination of mosquito vector species and their sensitivity to insecticides, should be enhanced to strengthen risk assessments and vector control measures.

- Vector control measures and appropriate personal protective measures should be aggressively promoted and implemented to reduce the risk of exposure to Zika virus.

- Countries should strengthen vector control measures in the long term and the Director-General of WHO should explore the use of IHR mechanisms, and consider bringing this to a forthcoming World Health Assembly, as means to better engage countries on this issue.

RISK COMMUNICATION

- Risk communication should be enhanced in countries with Zika virus transmission to address population concerns, enhance community engagement, improve reporting, and ensure application of vector control and personal protective measures.

- These measures should be based on an appropriate assessment of public perception, knowledge and information; the impact of risk communication measures should be rigorously evaluated to guide their adaptation and improve their impact.

- Attention should be given to ensuring women of childbearing age and particularly pregnant women have the necessary information and materials to reduce risk of exposure.

- Information on the risk of sexual transmission, and measures to reduce that risk, should be available to people living in and returning from areas of reported Zika virus transmission.

CLINICAL CARE

- Pregnant women who have been exposed to Zika virus should be counselled and followed for birth outcomes based on the best available information and national practice and policies.

- In areas of known Zika virus transmission, health services should be prepared for potential increases in neurological syndromes and/or congenital malformations.

TRAVEL MEASURES

- There should be no general restrictions on travel or trade with countries, areas and/or territories with Zika virus transmission.

- Pregnant women should be advised not [to] travel to areas of ongoing Zika virus outbreaks; pregnant women whose sexual partners live in or travel to areas with Zika virus outbreaks should ensure safe sexual practices or abstain from sex for the duration of their pregnancy.

- Travellers to areas with Zika virus outbreaks should be provided with up to date advice on potential risks and appropriate measures to reduce the possibility of exposure to mosquito bites and, upon return, should take appropriate measures, including safe sex, to reduce the risk of onward transmission.

- The World Health Organization should regularly update its guidance on travel with evolving information on the nature and duration of risks associated with Zika virus infection.

- Standard WHO recommendations regarding vector control at airports should be implemented in keeping with the IHR (2005). Countries should consider the disinsection of aircraft.

RESEARCH & PRODUCT DEVELOPMENT

- The development of new diagnostics for Zika virus infection should be prioritized to facilitate surveillance and control measures, and especially the management of pregnancy.

- Research, development and evaluation of novel vector control measures should be pursued with particular urgency.

- Research and development efforts should also be intensified for Zika virus vaccines and therapeutics in the medium term.

Based on this advice the Director-General declared the continuation of the Public Health Emergency of International Concern (PHEIC). The Director-General endorsed the Committee's advice and issued them as Temporary Recommendations under IHR (2005). The Director-General thanked the Committee Members and Advisors for their advice.

SOURCE: World Health Organization. "WHO statement on the 2nd meeting of IHR Emergency Committee on Zika virus and observed increase in neurological disorders and neonatal malformations." March 8, 2016. http://www.who.int/mediacentre/news/statements/2016/2nd-emergency-committee-zika/en.

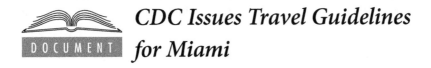

CDC Issues Travel Guidelines for Miami

DOCUMENT

August 1, 2016

New assessments of mosquito populations and test results this past weekend by Florida public health officials, as part of a community survey in the Miami neighborhood where several Zika infections were recently confirmed, have found persistent mosquito populations and additional Zika infections in the same area. This information suggests that there is a risk of continued active transmission of Zika virus in that area. As a result, CDC and Florida are issuing travel, testing and other recommendations for people who traveled to or lived in the Florida-designated areas on or after June 15, 2016, the earliest known date that one of the people could have been infected with Zika. At Florida's request, CDC is also sending a CDC Emergency Response Team (CERT) with experts in Zika virus, pregnancy and birth defects, vector control, laboratory science, and risk communications to assist in the response. Two CDC team members are already on the ground in Florida, three more will arrive today, and three more on Tuesday, August 2.

CDC recommends:

- Pregnant women not travel to the identified area.

- Pregnant women and their partners living in this area should consistently follow steps to prevent mosquito bites and sexual transmission of Zika.

- Pregnant women who traveled to this area on or after June 15, 2016, should talk with their healthcare provider and should be tested for Zika.

- Pregnant women without symptoms of Zika who live in or frequently travel to this area should be tested for Zika virus infection in the first and second trimesters of pregnancy.

- Male and female sexual partners of pregnant women who live in or who have traveled to this area should consistently and correctly use condoms or other barriers against infection during sex or abstain from sex for the duration of the pregnancy.

- All pregnant women in the United States who live in or travel to an area with active Zika virus transmission, or who have sex with a partner who lives in or traveled to an area with active Zika virus transmission without using condoms or other barrier methods to prevent infection should be assessed for possible Zika virus exposure during each prenatal care visit and tested according to CDC guidance.

- Women and men who traveled to this area wait at least 8 weeks before trying for a pregnancy; men with symptoms of Zika wait at least 6 months before trying for a pregnancy.

- Women and men who live in or frequently travel to this area who do not have signs or symptoms consistent with Zika virus disease and are considering pregnancy should consider the risks associated with Zika virus infection, and may wish to consult their healthcare provider to help inform their decisions about timing of pregnancy.

- Anyone with possible exposure to Zika virus and symptoms of Zika should be tested for Zika.

"We work closely with Florida to gather and analyze new information every day. With the new information that there are active mosquitoes still in the area and additional Zika infections, we conclude that pregnant women should avoid this area—and make every effort to prevent mosquito bites if they live or work there," said CDC Director Tom Frieden, M.D., M.P.H. "We apply the same criteria within and outside of the United States, and are working closely with the State of Florida and Miami health departments to provide preventive services, including mosquito control."

CDC continues to encourage everyone living in areas with *Aedes aegypti* and *Aedes albopictus* mosquitoes, especially pregnant women and women planning to become pregnant, to protect themselves from mosquito bites. Apply insect repellent, such as those containing DEET or other EPA-approved products, to uncovered skin, wear long-sleeved shirts and long pants, use or repair screens on windows and doors, use air conditioning when available, and remove standing water where mosquitoes lay eggs.

"We continue to work closely with Florida public health officials to investigate the infections identified in Miami and to intensify mosquito control efforts to reduce the risk of additional infections," said Lyle R. Petersen, M.D., M.P.H., incident manager for CDC's Zika Response and director, Division of Vector-Borne Diseases. "Florida officials are experienced in this type of work, and together we are working to protect pregnant women from the potentially devastating effects of this virus."

Based on the confirmation of local Zika transmission in Florida, CDC has updated its Interim Zika Response Plan (CONUS and HI) and has released the Zika Community Action Response Toolkit (Z-CART) to help states with risk communication and community engagement when local transmission is identified. . . .

SOURCE: Centers for Disease Control and Prevention. "CDC issues travel guidance related to Miami neighborhood with active Zika spread." August 1, 2016. http://www.cdc.gov/media/releases/2016/p0801-zika-travel-guidance.html.

OTHER HISTORIC DOCUMENTS OF INTEREST

FROM PREVIOUS *HISTORIC DOCUMENTS*

- World Health Organization on Infectious Diseases, *1996*, p. 303

Syria Peace Talks Begin

FEBRUARY 4 AND 22, MARCH 24, AND APRIL 28, 2016

With the Syrian civil war about to enter its fifth year, the United Nations (UN) and foreign ministers from nearly twenty countries came together at the end of 2015 to push for a new round of peace talks between the government of Syrian President Bashar al-Assad and the opposition groups calling for major government reforms. Set to begin in early 2016, the Geneva III talks aimed to achieve what a prior round of negotiations had failed to accomplish: agreement on a cessation of hostilities and a plan to establish a transitional government and hold new elections.

CIVIL WAR ESCALATES

The Syrian conflict began in March 2011, when residents of one Syrian city protested the torture of students who had been accused of making antigovernment graffiti. Assad ordered the police to crack down on the protestors, a response that spurred widespread demonstrations by Syrians demanding government reform and an end to violence against protestors. The conflict between the government and demonstrators grew increasingly violent during the remainder of the year, with the skyrocketing number of civilian casualties and growing humanitarian crisis prompting the UN to declare that the country was embroiled in a civil war.

The government opposition, which is comprised of various rebel groups, gained momentum in 2012 when it began to take control of various Syrian cities. It also began receiving support from countries including Saudi Arabia, fueling the government's efforts to undermine the opposition's legitimacy by claiming it is a front for the Gulf states and Western countries. The ongoing conflict has since drawn in numerous international players, with Turkey, Saudi Arabia, Qatar, the United States, the UK, and France supporting the opposition, and Russia, Iran, and Hezbollah backing Assad and his government. At least 250,000 people have been killed since the conflict began, and the war has also contributed to the international refugee crisis. According to the UN High Commissioner for Refugees, more than 10 million Syrians have either fled the country or have been displaced internally.

The first attempt to resolve the Syrian conflict diplomatically took place in January and February 2014, when the UN sponsored the Geneva II talks. Involving foreign ministers from nearly forty nations, the negotiations lasted for two weeks, but delegates were unable to reach a consensus and questioned the likelihood that future negotiations would be held. The talks underscored a clear divide between the two sides. The Syrian government wanted negotiations to focus on combatting "terrorists"—a term it broadly applies to all opposition groups, not just extremist organizations. The opposition wants to focus on forming a transitional government that does not include Assad or any of his associates who have been involved in the civil war, a subject that is a nonstarter with the government. Further complicating efforts to resolve the conflict peacefully, moderate opposition rebel groups often fight alongside groups such as the al-Nusra Front, an al Qaeda affiliate that the UN had designated as a terrorist organization.

The Geneva III Talks Begin

As the Syrian conflict dragged on, a group of eighteen countries and the European Union came together to form the International Syria Support Group (ISSG) in the fall of 2015. The group represents interests on both sides of the conflict—with members including the United States, Russia, Iran, and Saudi Arabia—and met in October and November to discuss the possibility of reviving peace talks. At the conclusion of the ISSG's November meeting in Vienna, the group agreed to support and implement a ceasefire and the need to convene a new round of negotiations as soon as possible. The group set a target date of January 1, 2016, for the talks to begin and created a framework for the negotiations. They also agreed that the talks' primary goals would be to establish a transitional government and set a process and schedule for drafting a new constitution within six months and holding new elections within eighteen months. A UN Security Council resolution approved in December 2015 formalized this agreement and set a deadline of August 1 for forming a transitional government and determining a constitutional plan.

On February 1, 2016, the UN announced that the Geneva III talks had begun. Negotiations were to involve delegations representing the Syrian government and the Syrian High Negotiations Committee (HNC), a Saudi-backed coalition representing several opposition groups, including the National Coalition of Syrian Revolution and Opposition Forces, which had represented the opposition during the Geneva II talks. Groups regarded as terrorist organizations, including the Islamic State of Iraq and the Levant (ISIL) and the al-Nusra Front, were not invited to participate.

Notably, the government and the HNC only agreed to participate in proximity talks, meaning that Staffan de Mistura, UN Special Envoy to Syria, held separate meetings with each delegation. The HNC did not commit to joining the talks until the Friday before they were scheduled to start, saying it would not continue participating in negotiations unless there was an end to violence and opposition prisoners were freed. "If there [is] no progress on the ground, we are leaving," said Monzer Makhous, a member of the HNC delegation.

The first round of the Geneva III talks lasted only two days. On the same day that the talks began, the government launched an offensive to take control of the region north of Aleppo, one of the world's oldest cities and Syria's largest city before the war began. Aleppo is divided between the government-controlled west and the opposition-held east and has been wrought by some of the war's most intense and devastating fighting. As a result of this latest offensive, the HNC withdrew from the negotiations and de Mistura announced on February 3 that the talks would be suspended. The HNC claimed that the government offensive was being supported by Russian air strikes, and U.S. and French officials blamed Russia for destabilizing the negotiations. Russia had begun conducting air strikes in Syria in September 2015, saying that it was targeting terrorist organizations. However, U.S. officials said that the majority of Russian attacks hit Western-backed rebel groups in an effort to prop up Assad's government. In announcing the talks' suspension, de Mistura insisted that they had not failed and would resume on February 25. He also called for a ceasefire agreement, stating that "when the Geneva talks actually start, in parallel there should be the beginning of a serious discussion around ceasefires."

Conference Supporting Syria and the Region

The day after talks were suspended, the UN, UK, Germany, Kuwait, and Norway cohosted the fourth Conference Supporting Syria and the Region in London. The conference's primary goal was to obtain pledges from the international community to support humanitarian aid efforts to help those affected by the civil war. More than $7 billion had been raised by the first three conferences, and the 2016 conference secured pledges of more than $12 billion. Roughly half that amount was pledged for 2016, while the remainder has been committed to support longer-term aid efforts between 2017 and 2020.

Ceasefire Agreement Reached

On February 12, the ISSG agreed to seek a cessation of hostilities in Syria and to accelerate deliveries of humanitarian aid. The group established a Ceasefire Taskforce cochaired by the United States and Russia, which was charged with reaching an agreement within one month. It was agreed that ISIL and other designated terrorist groups would be excluded from the ceasefire, to allow the United States and Russia to continue fighting those organizations. This created some concern that Russia would be allowed to continue its air strikes against moderate opposition groups, since Russia claimed it was targeting terrorists. Indeed, opposition groups said they would not accept a ceasefire if it did not put an end to the Russian attacks.

The United States and Russia announced the adoption of a final ceasefire agreement in a joint statement released on February 22. The cessation of hostilities was to take effect at midnight Damascus time on February 27 and was "to be applied to those parties to the Syrian conflict that have indicated their commitment to and acceptance of its terms." The ceasefire was endorsed by a UN Security Council resolution on February 26, with the council demanding that all parties to the ceasefire fulfill their commitments, that member states use their influence to help ensure commitments were met, and that humanitarian agencies be provided immediate access to Syria.

The ceasefire appeared to be effective in its first month. Officials reported a significant reduction in violence and that some humanitarian aid had been delivered, although not enough. However, the ceasefire agreement had essentially unraveled by the summer, after government air strikes near Aleppo killed dozens of people, destroyed several medical clinics, and cut off the last remaining supply route to the city's rebel-held eastern neighborhoods. The HNC accused the government and its supporters of "repeated, systematic and deliberate violations" of the ceasefire agreement.

Geneva III Talks Resume

Before the ceasefire collapsed, the UN and de Mistura were able to bring both sides back to the negotiating table in March. Proximity talks resumed on March 14 and adjourned on March 24. At their conclusion, de Mistura released a paper detailing "commonalities that exist between the two negotiating parties." The paper did not "constitute in any way a framework document or a negotiating text" but was provided to the two sides to consider ahead of the next round of talks. The document summarized the talks' results to date, covering topics such as the rejection of terrorism and foreign interference in Syria, refugees' right of return, and the political transition of power.

A second round of talks began on April 13; however, the HNC withdrew from the talks after five days to demonstrate its "displeasure and concern" over the deteriorating ceasefire agreement—including a recent government air offensive against rebel groups in the north—and a worsening humanitarian situation. New fighting broke out between government forces and Syrian Kurdish militias on April 21, the same day de Mistura reported that humanitarian aid had only reached about 560,000 people out of the roughly 4 million believed to be in need of assistance. The United States had also expressed concerns that Russia was beginning to position artillery around Aleppo in advance of a new government effort to retake the area. De Misutra urged the ISSG to come together to save the negotiations, and said he planned to continue the talks "at the technical level" through their scheduled conclusion on April 27.

On May 17, foreign ministers from the United States, Russia, Europe, and the Middle East met in Vienna to discuss the Syrian situation. The group issued a warning that if the government continued to violate the terms of the ceasefire, then they would lose the protection the agreement provided. The group also directed the UN World Food Programme to begin air dropping food, medicine, and water to areas under siege on June 1 if either the government or the opposition continued to block humanitarian aid delivery. However, the group did not set a new date for peace talks to resume.

PARLIAMENTARY ELECTIONS HELD

Parallel with the second round of talks, the Syrian government held parliamentary elections on April 13. Opposition groups boycotted the election, and voting only took place in government-controlled areas of Syria. Opposition groups and Western officials said the election was illegitimate and out of line with the UN Security Council resolution calling for elections after an eighteen-month transition period. The government claimed that the election's timing complied with Syria's constitution, and Russian officials backed the vote, arguing that a legal or political vacuum should be avoided while peace talks are ongoing. Assad's Ba'ath party and its political allies won 200 of the 250 parliamentary seats up for election.

A NEW CEASEFIRE

On September 10, Russian foreign minister Sergey Lavrov and U.S. secretary of state John Kerry announced that they had reached a new ceasefire agreement. The deal called for the withdrawal of government forces around Aleppo to allow humanitarian aid to reach communities in need, and required Russia to work with the Syrian air force to end the attacks on antigovernment positions that had killed many civilians. The United States was charged with getting the moderate opposition groups to separate themselves from al-Nusra. If the government was able to respect the ceasefire for a week, the United States and Russia would establish a joint coordination unit and conduct air strikes against agreed-upon targets.

The new ceasefire barely lasted a week. On September 17, the United States confirmed that an American airstrike in Syria had accidentally killed government troops, but that it had been an accident—the pilots thought they were hitting ISIL targets. The Syrian government claimed it was not a mistake and called it "a very serious and flagrant aggression." Two days later, the Syrian military declared an end to the ceasefire and began conducting intense air strikes in rebel-held parts of Aleppo and other locations. A UN convoy carrying food, medicine, and other supplies was also attacked by multiple airstrikes.

Peace in Jeopardy

The United States withdrew from bilateral talks with Russia on October 3, following the second ceasefire's failure and Russia's purported support of a Syrian Air Force bombing campaign in Aleppo. Russia responded by withdrawing from a post–Cold War arms control agreement, under which the United States and Russia had each agreed to dispose of 34 tons of plutonium. Russian officials also said they would not stop their airstrikes because they were trying to prevent "black flags"—(a reference to ISIL) from flying over Damascus.

Kerry insisted that the United States was "not giving up on the Syrian people" or "abandoning the pursuit of peace," but the United States' withdrawal from the talks places the possibility of reaching a peaceful resolution to the civil war in greater jeopardy. The Geneva III negotiations did not resume before the end of the year, and attempts to secure even temporary or region-specific ceasefires have met with little success. Meanwhile, the government's aggressive campaign to retake Aleppo continues, with residents of its eastern neighborhoods facing the constant threat of airstrikes and dwindling supplies of food and water.

—Linda Fecteau Grimm

Following are UN Secretary-General Ban Ki-moon's opening remarks at the Conference Supporting Syria and the Region from February 4, 2016; a joint statement from U.S. and Russian officials from February 22, 2016, to announce a ceasefire agreement; UN special envoy Staffan de Mistura's paper from March 24, 2016, on points of commonalities in the Geneva III talks; and a UN summary of the second round of Geneva III talks from April 28, 2016.

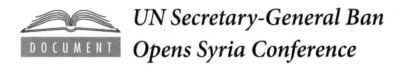

UN Secretary-General Ban
Opens Syria Conference

February 4, 2016

Your Excellency Prime Minister David Cameron,
Your Excellency Chancellor Angela Merkel,
Your Excellency Sheikh Sabah Ahmad Al-Jaber Al-Sabah,
Prime Minister Erna Solberg,
Your Majesties and Royal Highnesses,
Distinguished Heads of State and Government,
Honorable Ministers,
Excellencies,
Ladies and gentlemen,

Thank you for being here.

This is the fourth time we have come together to show our solidarity with the people of Syria and the region. . . .

The crisis in Syria is about to enter its sixth year. The international community bears a heavy responsibility for failing to end it.

We all hope that the efforts guided by my Special Envoy Staffan de Mistura would yield progress. But the temporary pause in the shows just how deep and difficult the divisions are.

It is deeply disturbing that the initial steps of the talks have been undermined by the continuous lack of sufficient humanitarian access, and by a sudden increase of aerial bombings and military activities within Syria. The focus on the people of Syria is also being lost amid petty procedural matters. . . .

These latest political developments add even greater urgency to our efforts here today to ease the suffering of millions of Syrian men, women and children.

We are here today with three objectives.

First, to meet the enormous humanitarian needs—at least $7 billion for this year alone, twice as much as last year. . . .

Second, to lay foundations for long-term international support. Even if, by some miracle, the conflict ends tomorrow, the enormous humanitarian and development needs will continue for years and even decades. The United Nations stands to lead and coordinate this effort.

Syrian and other refugees need the chance to work and provide for their families. Today, let us commit to getting all Syrian children into school, within months, not years. Offering hope is the best way to slow the exodus of educated Syrians and prevent the radicalization of a lost generation.

Third, we are here to find ways to protect civilians. All sides in this conflict are committing human rights abuses of a shocking scale and depravity. . . . We must end sieges and bring food to starving people. . . .

The situation is not sustainable. We cannot go on like this. There is no military solution. Only political dialogue, inclusive political dialogue, will rescue the Syrian people from their intolerable suffering. . . .

Today, let us change the narrative. Let us, by and with our solidarity and generosity, and compassionate leadership, bring true hope to the people of Syria and the region.

Thank you.

SOURCE: Office of United Nations Secretary-General Ban Ki-moon. "Opening remarks to the Conference Supporting Syria and the Region." February 4, 2016. http://www.un.org/sg/en/content/sg/speeches/2016-02-04/opening-remarks-conference-supporting-syria-and-region#.V2xepdIrLX4.

U.S.–Russian Joint Statement on Syrian Cessation of Hostilities

February 22, 2016

The United States of America and the Russian Federation, as co-chairs of the International Syria Support Group (ISSG) and seeking to achieve a peaceful settlement of the Syrian crisis with full respect for the fundamental role of the United Nations, are fully determined to provide their strongest support to end the Syrian conflict and establish conditions for a successful Syrian-led political transition process, facilitated by the UN. . . .

In this regard, and in furtherance of the February 11th decisions of the ISSG, the United States and Russia, as co-chairs of the ISSG and ISSG Ceasefire Task Force, announce the adoption on February 22, 2016, of the Terms for a Cessation of Hostilities in Syria attached as an Annex to this statement, and propose that the cessation of hostilities commence at 00:00 (Damascus time) on February 27, 2016. The cessation of hostilities is to be applied to those parties to the Syrian conflict that have indicated their commitment to and acceptance of its terms. Consistent with UN Security Council Resolution 2254 and the statements of the ISSG, the cessation of hostilities does not apply to "Daesh", "Jabhat al-Nusra", or other terrorist organizations designated by the UN Security Council.

Any party engaged in military or para-military hostilities in Syria, other than "Daesh", "Jabhat al-Nusra", or other terrorist organizations designated by the UN Security Council will indicate to the Russian Federation or the United States, as co-chairs of the ISSG, their commitment to and acceptance of the terms for the cessation of hostilities by no later than 12:00 (Damascus time) on February 26, 2016. In order to implement the cessation of hostilities in a manner that promotes stability and protects those parties participating in it, the Russian Federation and the United States are prepared to work together to exchange pertinent information (e.g., aggregated data that delineates territory where groups that have indicated their commitment to and acceptance of the cessation of hostilities are active, and a focal point for each side, in order to ensure effective communication) and develop procedures necessary for preventing parties participating in the cessation of hostilities from being attacked by Russian Armed Forces, the U.S.-led Counter ISIL Coalition, the Armed Forces of the Syrian government and other forces supporting them, and other parties to the cessation of hostilities. Military actions, including airstrikes, of the Armed Forces of the Syrian Arab Republic, the Russian Armed Forces, and the U.S.-led Counter ISIL Coalition will continue against ISIL, "Jabhat al-Nusra," and other terrorist organizations designated by the UN Security Council. The Russian Federation and United States will also work together, and with other members of the Ceasefire Task Force, as appropriate and pursuant to the ISSG decision of February 11, 2016, to delineate the territory held by "Daesh," "Jabhat al-Nusra" and other terrorist organizations designated by the UN Security Council, which are excluded from the cessation of hostilities. . . .

The United States and Russia are prepared, in their capacities as co-chairs of the Ceasefire Task Force and in coordination with other members of the ISSG Ceasefire Task Force as appropriate, to develop effective mechanisms to promote and monitor compliance with the ceasefire both by the governmental forces of the Syrian Arab Republic and other forces supporting them, and the armed opposition groups. To achieve this goal and to promote an effective and sustainable cessation of hostilities, the Russian Federation and the United States will establish a communication hotline and, if necessary and appropriate, a working group to exchange relevant information after the cessation of hostilities has gone into effect. . . .

The United States and the Russian Federation together call upon all Syrian parties, regional states and others in the international community to support the immediate cessation of violence and bloodshed in Syria and to contribute to the swift, effective and successful promotion of the UN-facilitated political transition process in accordance with U.N. Security Council Resolution 2254, the February 11 Statement of the ISSG, the 2015 Vienna statements of the ISSG, and the 2012 Geneva Communiqué.

[An annex listing the terms of the ceasefire has been omitted.]

Source: U.S. State Department. "Joint Statement of the United States and the Russian Federation, as Co-Chairs of the ISSG, on Cessation of Hostilities in Syria." February 22, 2016. https://2009-2017.state.gov/r/pa/prs/ps/2016/02/253115.htm.

UN Special Envoy Paper on Syria

March 24, 2016

EXPLANATORY NOTE

... During the course of talks the Special Envoy noted that certain commonalities existed between the two sides in relation to their respective visions of what a future of [the] Syrian state might look like.... The paper is a useful guide as to the commonalties that exist[] between the two negotiating parties. It is not an agreed paper of the two negotiating parties. It does not constitute in any way a framework document or a negotiating text and shall not be put before the UN Security Council or the ISSG unless specifically authorised by both sides. Instead, the Special Envoy has invited each of the two negotiating parties to take away the paper to examine whether it accurately captures points of convergence if not consensus....

ESSENTIAL PRINCIPLES OF A POLITICAL SOLUTION IN SYRIA

... The sides confirm that a political settlement is the only way to peace. Towards this end the parties recognize the following essential principles as the foundation for a future Syrian state that meets the aspirations of the Syrian people:

1. Respect for the sovereignty, independence, unity and territorial integrity of Syria. No part of the national territory shall be ceded. ...

2. The principles of sovereign equality and non-intervention shall apply, in conformity with the UN Charter. The Syrian people alone shall determine the future of their country by democratic means, through the ballot box, and have the exclusive right to choose their own political, economic and social system without external pressure or interference.

3. Syria shall be a democratic, non-sectarian state based on citizenship and political pluralism, the representation of all components of Syrian society, the rule of law, the independence of the judiciary, equal rights, non-discrimination, human rights and fundamental freedoms, transparency, accountability and the principles of national reconciliation and social peace.

4. ... Acts of revenge against individuals or groups shall not be tolerated. There shall be no discrimination against, and full protection of, all national, ethnic, religious, linguistic and cultural identities. ...

5. Women shall enjoy equality of rights and representation in all institutions and decision-making structures at a level of at least 30 per cent during the transition and thereafter.

6. As per Security Council resolution 2254 (2015), the political transition in Syria shall include mechanisms for credible, inclusive and non-sectarian governance, a schedule and process for drafting a new constitution and free and fair elections

pursuant to the new constitution, administered under supervision by the United Nations, to the satisfaction of the governance and to the highest international standards of transparency and accountability, with all Syrians, including members of the diaspora, eligible to participate.

7. Such governance shall ensure an environment of stability and calm during the transition, offering safety and equal chances to political actors to establish themselves and campaign in the forthcoming elections and participate in public life.

8. Continuity and reform of state institutions and public services, along with measures to protect the public infrastructure and private property, shall ensure stability in accordance with international standards, principles of good governance and human rights. . . .

9. Syria categorically rejects terrorism and strongly opposes terrorist organizations and individuals identified by the UN Security Council and will engage in a national endeavour, in international partnership, to defeat terrorism and to address the causes of terrorism. . . .

10. Syrians are committed to rebuilding a strong and unified national army, also through the disarmament and integration of members of armed groups supporting the transition and the new constitution. . . . There shall be no intervention by foreign fighters on Syrian soil.

11. All refugees and internally displaced people wishing it shall be enabled to return safely to their homes with national and international support and in line with international protection standards. Those arbitrarily detained shall be released and the fate of the disappeared, kidnapped or missing shall be resolved.

12. There shall be reparations, redress, care, and restitution of rights and property lost for those who have suffered loss or injury in consequence of the conflict. . . .

SOURCE: United Nations Office at Geneva. "UN Special Envoy's Paper on Points of Commonalities." March 24, 2016. http://www.unog.ch/unog/website/news_media.nsf/(httpPages)/8E6FDF778A229D66 C1257F800066B7EE?OpenDocument.

Summary on UN-Facilitated Syrian Peace Talks

DOCUMENT

APRIL 28, 2016

This paper sets out an account of developments and the work plan executed by the UN Special Envoy during the round of UN facilitated Intra-Syrian Talks held in Geneva between 13–27 April 2016.

AGENDA

The work plan for this round of Talks was based upon the agenda as set by Security Council resolution 2254 (2015), which provides for, within the target of six months, the establishment of a credible, inclusive, and non-sectarian governance, the setting of a schedule and process for drafting a constitution, and further expresses support for the holding of free and fair elections. Prior to the beginning of this round of Talks, the Special Envoy informed the participants that the round would focus on political transition and governance, in accordance with the exclusive mandate given to him by the Security Council. . . .

The participants were further informed on 15 April 2016 that the Special Envoy intended to hold four sessions on four central issues of transition, namely:

- The functions and powers of the institution, or institutions, of governance established to carry through the political transition

- The method of establishing the institution, or institutions, of governance through mutual consent and the decision-making process

- The relationship of the transitional institutions with the overall institutions of the state

- The process of moving on from political transition to a permanent, new constitution and eventually to new elections. . . .

The response of the participants

During the course of this round of Talks the participants set out their visions of political transition including in relation to governance.

In the course of seven formal proximity sessions, the Government of Syria delegation offered its vision of a political transition, including a mechanism of governance leading up to the enactment of a new constitution for Syria. The Government Representative confirmed that such a mechanism consisted of the establishment of a Broad-Based National Unity Government, which included members of the government, opposition, independents, and others, and is formed on the basis of consensus. . . .

Prior to this round, the opposition HNC delegation had begun to elaborate upon its vision of a political transition through the submission of a significant number of substantive papers that focused on the establishment and functions of a Transitional Governing Body with full executive and legislative powers during the transition. That vision was further defined during the course of this round of Talks. . . .

Commonalities on political transition

The present round of Talks confirmed that substantial differences exist between the two negotiating parties on their visions of the transition as well as on the interpretation of resolution 2254 (2015). Notwithstanding this, a number of points of commonalities on political transition have emerged. . . . Such points of commonalities include:

- That a Syrian-led and Syrian-owned political transition is necessary in order to end the conflict in Syria

- That any political transition will be overseen by a new, credible and inclusive transitional governance which will replace the present governance arrangements

- That the transitional governance will be responsible for protecting Syria's independence, territorial integrity and unity in accordance with the principles of national sovereignty and non-interference in internal affairs

- That the transitional governance will ensure an environment of stability, calm and safety during the transition so that equal opportunities are available to all, including political actors, to establish themselves, campaign in the forthcoming elections and public life

- That the transitional governance will ensure the continuity and improvement and reform of ministries, institutions and other public service entities during the transition

- That the transitional governance could include members of the present government and the opposition, independents and others

- That women shall enjoy equality of rights and representation in all institutions and decision-making structures during the transition

- That all Security Council resolutions on combatting terrorism will be implemented during the transition

- That Syria requires a new constitution and that a key responsibility of the transitional governance will be to oversee the drafting of this constitution by Syrians

- That the current preferred method for endorsement of the new constitution is by popular referendum

- That the parties foresee free and fair elections being held pursuant to the new constitution at the conclusion of the transitional period

- That human rights and fundamental freedoms must be guaranteed during the transition

- That acts of revenge or discrimination against individuals or groups shall not be tolerated, and that all Syrian citizens are equal and shall be fully protected during the transition

- That as part of the transition, reparations, redress and care should be provided for those who have suffered loss or injury

- That any governance shall be agreed upon in UN facilitated Intra-Syrian Talks on the basis of mutual consent

The Special Envoy takes the view that in time these initial commonalities can begin to form a basis for an agreement on political transition between the two parties.

FUNDAMENTAL ISSUES FOR A VIABLE TRANSITION

Further detail on practical aspects of how a viable transition will be created is required from the parties. There is also a need to determine how the respective visions of the two negotiating parties conform to the requirements of resolution 2254 for a credible, inclusive and non-sectarian governance. . . . The two sides will accordingly have to go deeper into their vision of political transition concerning the structure, functions, operational rules, entities, membership, selection, roles and responsibility of any new transitional governance arrangement, as well as how it relates to other state institutions during and after transition. The two sides will also need to set out the practical priorities of any transitional governance beyond that of drafting a new constitution, as well as how to sequence and deal with the fundamental issues listed in Annex 1. . . .

Furthermore, if the two sides are to go into these issues in further detail, each party will need to give up its insistence that it will not provide further detail on its vision of transition until the other accepts from the outset its own ascribed governance mechanism. Accordingly, nothing as a matter of principle should be excluded from the negotiations.

PROCESS DESIGN OF THE TALKS GOING FORWARD

The ultimate aim of the UN facilitated Talks remains to bring the two sides to a position of direct negotiations. . . . Going forward the Special Envoy is likely to invite the parties to engage in technical sessions with OSE experts both during and between rounds of the Intra-Syrian Talks in Geneva. . . .

Additionally, it is likely that the Special Envoy shall hold a range of civil society and women focused consultations both during and between rounds of the Talks to ensure that the broadest possible spectrum of views of Syrian stakeholders and independents are also fed into the formal negotiations over a political transition. The Special Envoy may also seek to identify a set of practical implementing benchmarks for transition so as to ensure that any political vision agreed by mutual consent results in concrete benefits on the ground for ordinary Syrians.

CESSATION OF HOSTILITIES AND HUMANITARIAN ACCESS

The political track will continue to be impacted by the urgent situation on the ground inside of Syria. . . . The increasing violence and the need for safe and unhindered humanitarian access to besieged and hard-to-reach areas necessitate urgent action by the International Syria Support Group in order to create a conducive environment for the next round of Intra-Syrian Talks. . . .

The Special Envoy has repeatedly made clear that if Talks about a political transition are to be viable then they must be accompanied by tangible and visible benefits to the Syrian people on the ground. It is also for this reason that the Special Envoy has requested the co-chairs of the ISSG to call another ISSG meeting at ministerial level.

[An annex detailing issues concerning a viable transition of power has been omitted.]

SOURCE: United Nations Office at Geneva. "Mediator's Summary of the 13–27 April Round of UN Facilitated Intra-Syrian Talks." April 28, 2016. http://www.unog.ch/unog/website/news_media.nsf/(httpPages)/F37F7E194B2AF1B7C1257FA30027E636?OpenDocument.

OTHER HISTORIC DOCUMENTS OF INTEREST

FROM PREVIOUS *HISTORIC DOCUMENTS*

Scientists Prove the Theory of Relativity

FEBRUARY 11, 2016

In February 2016, a group of more than 1,000 scientists from around the globe announced that they had observed gravitational waves for the first time in history. The Laser Interferometer Gravitational-Wave Observatory (LIGO) team's discovery was heralded as proof of Albert Einstein's theory of general relativity—proof that scientists had been actively seeking for more than fifty years. The observation of gravitational waves, and the development of technologies sensitive enough to detect them, presents scientists with new tools and opportunities to further explore our universe and deepen our understanding of gravity.

THE QUEST TO PROVE EINSTEIN'S THEORY

Published in 1915, Einstein's theory of general relativity was revolutionary in that it challenged the concepts of Newtonian physics that had prevailed within the scientific community for more than 200 years. Isaac Newton theorized that all objects in the universe are innately attracted to each other by gravity, though he did not explain how that attraction occurs. Newton also stated that gravity only acts on space, not time. This means that the passage of time will remain consistent, regardless of gravity's effects on an object. Guided by Isaac Newton's laws of physics, scientists held that space and time were separate dimensions.

By contrast, Einstein posited that space and time are not two separate dimensions and that time is relative, meaning that forces such as gravity and speed can impact the passage of time. Einstein's theory of general relativity combined space and time into a four-dimensional model known as space-time, and argued that the effect of gravity is produced when matter and energy distort the fabric of space-time. Gravity's warping of space-time causes light and matter to follow a curved path through space, which explains why the planets orbit the sun in ellipses. A cosmic disturbance could also cause space-time to stretch, collapse, and even jiggle, which would create ripples of gravity known as gravitational waves. The gravitational waves would then compress space in one direction, and stretch it in another, as they traveled through space, much like a ripple effects the surface of a pond.

Einstein's theory also predicted various phenomena that would occur as a result of space-time distortions and gravitational pull. For example, the theory predicted that two black holes orbiting each other in space would lose energy through the emission of gravitational waves. As they lost energy, the black holes would gradually move toward each other over the course of billions of years, gaining speed as they grew closer so that they would be traveling at nearly one-half the speed of light by the time they collided. This collision would create a single, more massive black hole, and a portion of the combined black holes' mass would be converted into energy that would be emitted in a burst of gravitational waves.

Scientists attempted to test Einstein's theory and its predictions, but had little success in proving its concepts. Astrophysicist Arthur Eddington announced in 1919 that he had verified the theory's prediction that starlight would be deflected when passing near the surface of the sun through observations conducted during solar eclipses, but this was the only support for Einstein's theory found over several decades. In the 1960s, advances in satellite and radar technology created new opportunities for scientists to conduct more precise experiments. Joseph Weber claimed the first discovery of gravitational waves in 1969, but his results could not be replicated by other scientists and his findings were largely discredited. Then, in 1974, Joseph Taylor and Russell Hulse discovered a pulsar orbiting a neutron star. (Neutron stars are incredibly dense objects that are formed when a giant star collapses. Pulsars are a type of neutron star that regularly emits radio waves and other electromagnetic radiation in pulses.) By timing the pulsar's emissions, Taylor and Hulse determined that the two stars were losing energy and growing closer together at the rate that would be expected if the stars were radiating gravitational waves. The two received the Nobel Prize in Physics in 1993 for their discovery and the opportunity it represented to further test Einstein's theory of general relativity.

Building LIGO

Also in the 1960s, a number of scientists began studying the potential use of interferometers (devices that use the interference of two beams of laser light to make very precise distance measurements) to detect gravitational waves. Three of these scientists, MIT's Rainer Weiss and Caltech's Kip Thorne and Ronald Drever, formed a LIGO steering committee in the 1980s in response to pressure from the National Science Foundation to combine their institutions' respective work on interferometers.

Due to several organizational challenges, leadership changes, and difficulties in securing funding, construction of the LIGO detectors did not begin until 1994. Two detector sites were selected: one in Livingston, Louisiana, and another in Hanford, Washington. The LIGO detectors were designed to observe the collisions of neutron stars, which scientists hypothesized would behave similarly to black holes when colliding and would produce gravitational waves, though at a higher pitch than black holes. A two-and-a-half mile L-shaped interferometer was built at each site, with a mirror positioned at the end of each of the interferometer's arms. A laser light split into two beams that travel back and forth down the arms measures the distance between the two mirrors. According to Einstein's theory, a gravitational wave passing by the detector should cause the distance between the mirrors to change by a tiny amount. Although the detectors were very sensitive, only the most massive and violent cosmic events would be big enough to register.

While LIGO is led by Caltech and MIT, the detectors' operation is an international effort. The National Science Foundation is LIGO's largest funder, with additional financial support provided by the Max Planck Society in Germany, the United Kingdom's Science and Technology Facilities Council, and the Australian Research Council. Data from the detectors is analyzed by members of the LIGO Scientific Collaboration, a group comprised of more than 1,000 scientists from over ninety universities in fifteen countries, and the VIRGO Collaboration, a team of more than 250 physicists and engineers from nineteen different European research groups.

Construction was completed in 1999, and the detectors began their first observational run in 2002. The LIGO team did not report any findings for the first eight years, and researchers concluded that the interferometers were barely sensitive enough to detect gravitational waves. Over the next five years, the detectors underwent a major upgrade that enhanced their sensitivity and enabled them to probe a larger portion of the universe.

A Historic Discovery

The gravitational waves were detected by LIGO on September 14, 2015, during the upgraded interferometers' first observational run and amid the centennial celebration of Einstein's theory of general relativity. The LIGO team's public announcement of the discovery coincided with their publication of a report in *Physical Review Letters*, which presented their findings in detail. Based on their calculations, the team determined that the waves had been produced by the collision of two black holes, which they estimated were roughly 29 and 36 times the sun's mass. The collision took place 1.3 billion years ago and created gravitational waves containing 50 times more power than all the stars in the universe combined. Shortly before the black holes collided, they circled each other at a rate of 250 times per second. The team determined that the gravitational waves grew stronger as the black holes approached each other, and that once the new black hole had been created, it vibrated briefly before going quiet. They also estimated that the new black hole has a mass that is equivalent to sixty-two suns. Despite these vast sizes, the collision only moved the LIGO detectors' mirrors four one-thousandths of a proton's diameter. In addition to these observations, the team released a brief recording of the sound the black holes made when they collided, noting that the sound's frequency was too low to be from the collision of neutron stars. Taken together, these findings conformed to the theory of general relativity's predictions for black holes and were celebrated as proof of Einstein's theory.

"With this discovery, we humans are embarking on a marvelous new quest: the quest to explore the warped side of the universe—objects and phenomena that are made from warped space-time," said Kip Thorne. "Colliding black holes and gravitational waves are our first beautiful examples."

On June 15, the LIGO team announced a second gravitational wave detection. That detection, observed on December 25, 2015, was also determined to be the result of two black holes colliding. "The second discovery means the first discovery was not a one-off, 'we got lucky,' kind of thing," LIGO Laboratory Executive Director David Reitze said in an interview with Space.com. "If I could encapsulate what the second discovery means . . . it's that LIGO is for real."

Looking Farther into Space

LIGO's success in detecting gravitational waves presents a new opportunity for scientists to study cosmic objects that are too dim to be seen by telescopes, including black holes and neutron stars. Measuring gravitational waves could help scientists learn more about how these bodies manipulate gravity and the makeup of their interiors. "It's not just that we're checking on a theory," said Ira Thorpe, a NASA astrophysicist. "The real important part of this is it gives us a completely new tool for understanding our Universe."

The LIGO team will next work to increase the detectors' sensitivity in hopes that the interferometers may be able to detect and measure black holes that are more than 100 times larger than the sun's mass and farther from Earth. A third detector called Virgo, which has been in operation in Italy since 2003, was scheduled to become a part of the LIGO effort in 2016. Japan is building a detector that is expected to be operational in 2019, and India has also expressed interest in building a detector. With these additional detectors deployed, the LIGO team will be able to search different parts of the universe for cosmic events and gravitational waves.

Additionally, NASA and the European Space Agency are currently exploring opportunities for space-based gravitational wave measurement through their joint LISA Pathfinder mission. Establishing an observatory in space would eliminate some of the disturbances that could interfere with measurements on Earth, such as vibrations from construction sites or subway trains, or the planet's own motion. The LISA Pathfinder spacecraft was launched in December 2015 and is currently testing some of the technologies needed to build detectors in space. A paper published in *Physical Review Letters* in June 2016 shared the results of the spacecraft's initial experiments, reporting that the test results had exceeded expectations and that the technology was close to achieving the precision needed for a full-scale observatory. Such an observatory "would achieve essentially all of the ultimate science goals," said Thorpe. "That's amazing in itself, and data from this mission will help us build on an already impressive foundation."

—Linda Fecteau Grimm

Following is a press release from the Laser Interferometer Gravitational-Wave Observatory on February 11, 2016, following the observatory's detection of gravitational waves.

LIGO Detects Gravitational Waves

February 11, 2016

LIGO Opens New Window on the Universe with Observation of Gravitational Waves from Colliding Black Holes

For the first time, scientists have observed ripples in the fabric of spacetime called gravitational waves, arriving at the earth from a cataclysmic event in the distant universe. This confirms a major prediction of Albert Einstein's 1915 general theory of relativity and opens an unprecedented new window onto the cosmos.

Gravitational waves carry information about their dramatic origins and about the nature of gravity that cannot otherwise be obtained. Physicists have concluded that the detected gravitational waves were produced during the final fraction of a second of the merger of two black holes to produce a single, more massive spinning black hole. This collision of two black holes had been predicted but never observed.

The gravitational waves were detected on September 14, 2015 at 5:51 a.m. Eastern Daylight Time (09:51 UTC) by both of the twin Laser Interferometer Gravitational-wave Observatory (LIGO) detectors, located in Livingston, Louisiana, and Hanford, Washington, USA. The LIGO Observatories are funded by the National Science Foundation (NSF), and were conceived, built, and are operated by Caltech and MIT. The discovery, accepted for publication in the journal Physical Review Letters, was made by the LIGO Scientific Collaboration (which includes the GEO Collaboration and the Australian Consortium for

Interferometric Gravitational Astronomy) and the Virgo Collaboration using data from the two LIGO detectors.

Based on the observed signals, LIGO scientists estimate that the black holes for this event were about 29 and 36 times the mass of the sun, and the event took place 1.3 billion years ago. About 3 times the mass of the sun was converted into gravitational waves in a fraction of a second—with a peak power output about 50 times that of the whole visible universe. By looking at the time of arrival of the signals—the detector in Livingston recorded the event 7 milliseconds before the detector in Hanford—scientists can say that the source was located in the Southern Hemisphere.

According to general relativity, a pair of black holes orbiting around each other lose energy through the emission of gravitational waves, causing them to gradually approach each other over billions of years, and then much more quickly in the final minutes. During the final fraction of a second, the two black holes collide into each other at nearly one-half the speed of light and form a single more massive black hole, converting a portion of the combined black holes' mass to energy, according to Einstein's formula $E = mc^2$. This energy is emitted as a final strong burst of gravitational waves. It is these gravitational waves that LIGO has observed.

The existence of gravitational waves was first demonstrated in the 1970s and 80s by Joseph Taylor, Jr., and colleagues. Taylor and Russell Hulse discovered in 1974 a binary system composed of a pulsar in orbit around a neutron star. Taylor and Joel M. Weisberg in 1982 found that the orbit of the pulsar was slowly shrinking over time because of the release of energy in the form of gravitational waves. For discovering the pulsar and showing that it would make possible this particular gravitational wave measurement, Hulse and Taylor were awarded the Nobel Prize in Physics in 1993.

The new LIGO discovery is the first observation of gravitational waves themselves, made by measuring the tiny disturbances the waves make to space and time as they pass through the earth.

"Our observation of gravitational waves accomplishes an ambitious goal set out over 5 decades ago to directly detect this elusive phenomenon and better understand the universe, and, fittingly, fulfills Einstein's legacy on the 100th anniversary of his general theory of relativity," says Caltech's David H. Reitze, executive director of the LIGO Laboratory.

The discovery was made possible by the enhanced capabilities of Advanced LIGO, a major upgrade that increases the sensitivity of the instruments compared to the first generation LIGO detectors, enabling a large increase in the volume of the universe probed—and the discovery of gravitational waves during its first observation run. The US National Science Foundation leads in financial support for Advanced LIGO. Funding organizations in Germany (Max Planck Society), the U.K. (Science and Technology Facilities Council, STFC) and Australia (Australian Research Council) also have made significant commitments to the project. Several of the key technologies that made Advanced LIGO so much more sensitive have been developed and tested by the German UK GEO collaboration. Significant computer resources have been contributed by the AEI Hannover Atlas Cluster, the LIGO Laboratory, Syracuse University, and the University of Wisconsin–Milwaukee. Several universities designed, built, and tested key components for Advanced LIGO: The Australian National University, the University of Adelaide, the University of Florida, Stanford University, Columbia University of the City of New York, and Louisiana State University.

"In 1992, when LIGO's initial funding was approved, it represented the biggest investment the NSF had ever made," says France Córdova, NSF director. "It was a big risk. But the National Science Foundation is the agency that takes these kinds of risks. We support fundamental science and engineering at a point in the road to discovery where that path is anything but clear. We fund trailblazers. It's why the U.S. continues to be a global leader in advancing knowledge."

LIGO research is carried out by the LIGO Scientific Collaboration (LSC), a group of more than 1000 scientists from universities around the United States and in 14 other countries. More than 90 universities and research institutes in the LSC develop detector technology and analyze data; approximately 250 students are strong contributing members of the collaboration. The LSC detector network includes the LIGO interferometers and the GEO600 detector. The GEO team includes scientists at the Max Planck Institute for Gravitational Physics (Albert Einstein Institute, AEI), Leibniz Universität Hannover, along with partners at the University of Glasgow, Cardiff University, the University of Birmingham, other universities in the United Kingdom, and the University of the Balearic Islands in Spain.

"This detection is the beginning of a new era: The field of gravitational wave astronomy is now a reality," says Gabriela González, LSC spokesperson and professor of physics and astronomy at Louisiana State University.

LIGO was originally proposed as a means of detecting these gravitational waves in the 1980s by Rainer Weiss, professor of physics, emeritus, from MIT; Kip Thorne, Caltech's Richard P. Feynman Professor of Theoretical Physics, emeritus; and Ronald Drever, professor of physics, emeritus, also from Caltech.

"The description of this observation is beautifully described in the Einstein theory of general relativity formulated 100 years ago and comprises the first test of the theory in strong gravitation. It would have been wonderful to watch Einstein's face had we been able to tell him," says Weiss.

"With this discovery, we humans are embarking on a marvelous new quest: the quest to explore the warped side of the universe—objects and phenomena that are made from warped spacetime. Colliding black holes and gravitational waves are our first beautiful examples," says Thorne.

Virgo research is carried out by the Virgo Collaboration, consisting of more than 250 physicists and engineers belonging to 19 different European research groups: 6 from Centre National de la Recherche Scientifique (CNRS) in France; 8 from the Istituto Nazionale di Fisica Nucleare (INFN) in Italy; 2 in The Netherlands with Nikhef; the Wigner RCP in Hungary; the POLGRAW group in Poland; and the European Gravitational Observatory (EGO), the laboratory hosting the Virgo detector near Pisa in Italy.

Fulvio Ricci, Virgo Spokesperson, notes that, "This is a significant milestone for physics, but more importantly merely the start of many new and exciting astrophysical discoveries to come with LIGO and Virgo."

Bruce Allen, managing director of the Max Planck Institute for Gravitational Physics (Albert Einstein Institute), adds, "Einstein thought gravitational waves were too weak to detect, and didn't believe in black holes. But I don't think he'd have minded being wrong!"

"The Advanced LIGO detectors are a tour de force of science and technology, made possible by a truly exceptional international team of technicians, engineers, and scientists," says David Shoemaker of MIT, the project leader for Advanced LIGO. "We are very proud that we finished this NSF-funded project on time and on budget."

At each observatory, the two-and-a-half-mile (4-km) long L-shaped LIGO interferometer uses laser light split into two beams that travel back and forth down the arms (four-foot diameter tubes kept under a near-perfect vacuum). The beams are used to monitor the distance between mirrors precisely positioned at the ends of the arms.

According to Einstein's theory, the distance between the mirrors will change by an infinitesimal amount when a gravitational wave passes by the detector. A change in the lengths of the arms smaller than one-ten-thousandth the diameter of a proton (10–19 meter) can be detected.

"To make this fantastic milestone possible took a global collaboration of scientists—laser and suspension technology developed for our GEO600 detector was used to help make Advanced LIGO the most sophisticated gravitational wave detector ever created," says Sheila Rowan, professor of physics and astronomy at the University of Glasgow.

Independent and widely separated observatories are necessary to determine the direction of the event causing the gravitational waves, and also to verify that the signals come from space and are not from some other local phenomenon.

Toward this end, the LIGO Laboratory is working closely with scientists in India at the Inter-University Centre for Astronomy and Astrophysics, the Raja Ramanna Centre for Advanced Technology, and the Institute for Plasma to establish a third Advanced LIGO detector on the Indian subcontinent. Awaiting approval by the government of India, it could be operational early in the next decade. The additional detector will greatly improve the ability of the global detector network to localize gravitational-wave sources.

"Hopefully this first observation will accelerate the construction of a global network of detectors to enable accurate source location in the era of multi-messenger astronomy," says David McClelland, professor of physics and director of the Centre for Gravitational Physics at the Australian National University.

SOURCE: Laser Interferometer Gravitational-Wave Observatory at Caltech. "Gravitational Waves Detected 100 Years After Einstein's Prediction." February 11, 2016. http://www.ligo.caltech.edu/news/ligo20160211.

OTHER HISTORIC DOCUMENTS OF INTEREST

FROM THIS VOLUME

- NASA Announces Milestones in Human Spaceflight and Space Exploration, p. 150

FROM PREVIOUS *HISTORIC DOCUMENTS*

- New Horizons Spacecraft Reaches Pluto, *2015*, p. 384
- NASA Announces Successful Orbiting of Dwarf Planet, *2015*, p. 120
- European Space Agency Successfully Lands Spacecraft on Comet, *2014*, p. 541
- NASA's *Voyager 1* Reaches Interstellar Space, *2013*, p. 423

Senate Leadership Refuses to Consider Supreme Court Nominee

FEBRUARY 13 AND MARCH 16, 2016

The death of U.S. Supreme Court justice Antonin Scalia in February 2016 amid a contentious election season ignited a partisan dispute over the process of selecting his successor. Republican lawmakers united behind the viewpoint that the next president should make the nomination, and so they refused to consider President Barack Obama's nominee. With Republicans and Democrats entrenched in their respective positions, the Supreme Court was left with eight justices for the remainder of its 2015 term and the start of its 2016–2017 term.

A Vacancy on the Highest Court

On February 13, Supreme Court Justice Antonin Scalia was found dead at a resort he was visiting in west Texas. Appointed to the Court in 1986 by President Ronald Reagan and unanimously confirmed by the Senate, Scalia was the longest serving member of the current Court at the time of his death. He was among the Court's conservative contingent of justices and largely adhered to the originalism theory of constitutional interpretation, meaning that he tried to apply the understanding of those who drafted and ratified the Constitution to its modern interpretation. Widely regarded as one of the Court's most influential members, Scalia wrote noteworthy opinions that included the majority in *District of Columbia v. Heller*, which held that the Second Amendment protects the individual right to bear arms. Scalia was known for his strong critiques of vague laws and Court opinions that did not provide clear guidance, either to lower courts or Americans who may run afoul of the law, as well as for his scathing dissents and creative use of language. In a statement marking Scalia's death, Obama described the justice as "a brilliant legal mind with an energetic style, incisive wit, and colorful opinions," as well as "a larger-than-life presence" on the Court.

Political wrangling over the selection of Scalia's successor began almost immediately following his death. Obama said that he planned "to fulfill [his] constitutional responsibilities to nominate a successor in due time" and called on the Senate "to give that person a fair hearing and a timely vote." However, Senate Majority Leader Mitch McConnell, R-Ky., said the Senate would not consider Obama's nominee and that the soon-to-be-elected next president should fill Scalia's seat. McConnell reaffirmed this position during a press conference on February 23, during which he told reporters, "I can now confidently say the view shared by virtually everybody in my conference, is that the nomination should be made by the president the people elect in the election that's underway right now." McConnell added that if the current situation were reversed, and a Republican president had nominated a justice during an election year, a Senate controlled by the Democrats would not confirm the president's nominee. Senate Judiciary Committee Chair Chuck Grassley, R-Iowa, echoed McConnell's statements, saying that his committee would not move forward with confirmation hearings. Several Republicans also said they would not even follow the customary procedure of meeting with Obama's eventual nominee, because there was no point in meeting the nominee if the Senate was not going to proceed with confirmation.

The Nomination of Merrick Garland

After evaluating a shortlist of potential candidates, Obama announced his nomination of Merrick Garland to the Supreme Court on March 16. Garland, sixty-three years old, had been a chief judge on the U.S. Circuit Court of Appeals for the District of Columbia since 2013. He was appointed to that court by President Bill Clinton in 1997 and was confirmed by a Senate vote of 76 to 23. Garland's early legal career included clerkships for a judge on the U.S. Court of Appeals for the Second Circuit and for Supreme Court Justice William Brennan. He was a partner at major law firm Arnold & Porter before leaving private practice to become the assistant U.S. attorney for the District of Columbia and then the deputy assistant attorney general for the Department of Justice's Criminal Division. Garland also served as the principal associate deputy attorney general, during which time he oversaw the prosecution of Timothy McVeigh and Terry Nichols for the 1995 Oklahoma City bombing as well as the government's response to the Unabomber and the Montana Freeman.

Obama emphasized Garland's moderate record and the bipartisan support he received for his appointment to the Second Circuit in his announcement. "I've selected a nominee who is widely recognized not only as one of America's sharpest legal minds, but someone who brings to his work a spirit of decency, modesty, integrity, even-handedness, and excellence," he said. "These qualities, and his long commitment to public service, have earned him the respect and admiration of leaders from both sides of the aisle." Obama added that during his two terms as president, Garland's name had frequently been mentioned in conversations with both Republicans and Democrats as someone who would be a good Supreme Court nominee. Obama urged lawmakers to avoid playing partisan politics with Garland's nomination. "I have fulfilled my constitutional duty. Now it's time for the Senate to do theirs," he said. "Presidents do not stop working in the final year of their term. Neither should a Senator."

Later that day, McConnell issued a statement reiterating that the Senate would not consider Garland, but would "appropriately revisit the matter when it considers the qualifications of the nominee the next President nominates, whoever that might be." He also accused Obama of not actually wanting to see Garland's nomination confirmed, but wanting to "politicize it for purposes of the election." House Speaker Paul Ryan, R-Wis., offered his support for McConnell's decision. "This has never been about who the nominee is. It is about a basic principle," he said. Even Republicans who had voted to confirm Garland in 1997 expressed opposition to hearing his nomination, claiming their concern was with the process, not the person. Senate Minority Leader Harry Reid, D-Nev., expressed optimism that "cooler heads will prevail" and that "sensible Republicans will provide Judge Garland with the fair treatment that a man of his stature and qualifications deserves." The presidential candidates' responses to the nomination were also sharply divided along party lines, with Democrats arguing that Garland was a strong candidate and his nomination should be heard, while Republicans backed the Senate leadership's position.

The Partisan Debate

Generally, Republican lawmakers argued that since Scalia's successor would influence the Court over the course of a generation, Americans should be given an opportunity to vote for the president who would select the new justice. As McConnell said, not filling the vacant seat until after the election would ensure voters "have a voice in this momentous decision." Democrats countered that Americans' voices had already been heard on this matter when they elected and reelected Obama.

Republicans also pointed to statements made by Reid and Sen. Chuck Schumer, D-N.Y., that they said lent credence to their position. Republicans cited Reid's past statements that the Senate is "not a rubber stamp" for the executive branch and that the Constitution does not require the Senate to give presidential nominees a vote. Republicans also highlighted Schumer's statements reflecting the senator's critique of former president George W. Bush's judicial nominees, and his assertion that he would "do everything in my power" to prevent more of Bush's nominees from being confirmed.

Republicans also frequently cited the "Biden Rule" to defend their position. The origin of this so-called rule was a 1992 floor speech given by Vice President Joe Biden when he was a senator and the chair of the Senate Judiciary Committee. During that speech, Biden described a hypothetical situation in which President George H. W. Bush would be faced with a Supreme Court vacancy six months before the election. Biden said that going through the confirmation process during a contentious presidential election was "not fair to the president, to the nominee, or to the Senate itself." However, Biden also stated that the confirmation process should only be delayed until after the election, not until the new president took office.

Speaking at Georgetown University Law School on March 24, Biden challenged the notion of the Biden Rule, saying it was "ridiculous" and that "it doesn't exist." He said that all nominees received a hearing during his tenure as Senate Judiciary chair, which was proof that the rule did not exist. Biden also noted that Republicans did not share another portion of his floor speech, in which he said that the consideration of such election-year nominations should move forward if the president had consulted with the Senate and chosen a moderate nominee. Biden—and Obama—argued that the president had taken those exact steps in selecting Merrick Garland. "No one is suggesting individual senators have to vote yes; voting no is always an option," Biden said. "But deciding in advance to turn your back before the president even names a nominee is not an option the Constitution leaves open. It's quite frankly an abdication of duty, and one that has been never happened in our history." Republicans pounced on Biden's Georgetown remarks as hypocritical and accused him of selective memory, claiming that while he was a senator he refused to hold hearings for dozens of Bush nominees to lower courts and had voted against a procedural motion to allow an up or down vote on Samuel Alito's nomination.

In some instances, the Thurmond Rule was also used to bolster Republicans' position. The rule is named for the late senator Strom Thurmond, R-S.C., who led the Senate's effort in 1968 to block President Lyndon Johnson's nomination of Justice Abe Fortas to serve as chief justice. The Thurmond Rule similarly maintains that a high-level judicial nominee should not be confirmed in the months preceding an election and says that the opposition party can refuse to allow votes on the nomination. Important note: neither the Biden Rule nor the Thurmond Rule are written or legally binding rules. In fact, there is no Senate rule stating that a presidential nominee should not be considered until after an election.

The lack of a ninth justice on the Court creates the potential for a tied decision. In these situations, the lower court's ruling in a case is affirmed, but no national precedent is set. Without a national precedent, the application of the law in question may not be uniform across the country if different appellate courts rule differently on the same legal issues, which could in turn create significant confusion and legal ambiguity. Democrats and their supporters pointed to these concerns, arguing that major cases coming before the Supreme Court on issues including immigration, women's health, and voting rights may go unresolved unless a ninth justice was quickly confirmed.

A NOMINEE IN LIMBO

Republicans continued to maintain their position that Garland's nomination should not move forward, despite several public opinion polls showing that roughly half the country did not support them. A Monmouth University poll released in late March, for example, found that 53 percent of Americans thought the Senate should consider a president's nomination to the Court, even at the end of his term, and that 77 percent—including 62 percent of Republicans—thought the Senate was "playing politics" with the Court vacancy. An April *Wall Street Journal*/NBC poll found that 52 percent of Americans wanted the Senate to vote on Garland's nomination in 2016, and that the number of Republicans who favored waiting for a new president to pick Scalia's replacement had decreased by 13 percent since a similar poll was taken in March.

In July, Garland's became the longest pending Supreme Court nomination in U.S. history. Democrats attempted another public push to put pressure on the Republicans and persuade them to start the confirmation process in September, to little effect. Some Republicans appeared to take a firmer stance on judicial nominations, including Sen. John McCain, R-Ariz., who suggested on a Philadelphia talk radio program that if Hillary Clinton were elected, Republicans would unite to block any of her Supreme Court nominees. A McCain spokesperson later said that the senator would "of course, thoroughly examine the record of any Supreme Court nominee put before the Senate and vote for or against that individual based on their qualifications." Comments by other Republicans suggested that Garland's nomination could move forward after the election. In October, as polling data indicated that Clinton was leading in the presidential race, Sen. Jeff Flake, R-Ariz., reiterated his position that if Clinton won, the Senate should consider Garland's nomination during a lame duck session.

—Linda Fecteau Grimm

Following is a statement from President Barack Obama from February 13, 2016, on the death of Justice Antonin Scalia; remarks by Obama from March 16, 2016, announcing his nomination of Merrick Garland to the Supreme Court; and a statement from Senate Majority Leader Mitch McConnell on March 16, 2016, in response to the president's nomination.

DOCUMENT

President Obama Remarks on Death of Justice Scalia

February 13, 2016

Good evening, everybody. For almost 30 years, Justice Antonin "Nino" Scalia was a larger-than-life presence on the Bench: a brilliant legal mind with an energetic style, incisive wit, and colorful opinions.

He influenced a generation of judges, lawyers, and students and profoundly shaped the legal landscape. He will no doubt be remembered as one of the most consequential judges and thinkers to serve on the Supreme Court. Justice Scalia dedicated his life to the cornerstone of our democracy: the rule of law. Tonight we honor his extraordinary service to our Nation and remember one of the towering legal figures of our time.

Antonin Scalia was born in Trenton, New Jersey, to an Italian immigrant family. After graduating from Georgetown University and Harvard Law School, he worked at a law firm and taught law before entering a life of public service. He rose from Assistant Attorney General for the Office of Legal Counsel to the judge on the DC Circuit Court to Associate Justice of the Supreme Court.

A devout Catholic, he was the proud father of nine children and grandfather to many loving grandchildren. Justice Scalia was both an avid hunter and an opera lover, a passion for music that he shared with his dear colleague and friend, Justice Ruth Bader Ginsberg. Michelle and I were proud to welcome him to the White House, including in 2012 for a state dinner for Prime Minister David Cameron. And tonight we join his fellow Justices in mourning this remarkable man.

Obviously, today is a time to remember Justice Scalia's legacy. I plan to fulfill my constitutional responsibilities to nominate a successor in due time. There will be plenty of time for me to do so and for the Senate to fulfill its responsibility to give that person a fair hearing and a timely vote. These are responsibilities that I take seriously, as should everyone. They're bigger than any one party. They are about our democracy. They're about the institution to which Justice Scalia dedicated his professional life and making sure it continues to function as the beacon of justice that our Founders envisioned.

But at this moment, we most of all want to think about his family, and Michelle and I join the Nation in sending our deepest sympathies to Justice Scalia's wife Maureen and their loving family, a beautiful symbol of a life well lived. We thank them for sharing Justice Scalia with our country.

God bless them all, and God bless the United States of America.

SOURCE: The White House. "Remarks by the President on the Passing of the U.S. Supreme Court Justice Antonin Scalia." February 13, 2016. https://obamawhitehouse.archives.gov/the-press-office/2016/02/13/remarks-president-passing-us-supreme-court-justice-antonin-scalia.

President Obama Nominates Chief Judge Garland

March 16, 2016

Good morning. Everybody, please have a seat.

Of the many powers and responsibilities that the Constitution vests in the Presidency, few are more consequential than appointing a Supreme Court Justice, particularly one to succeed Justice Scalia, one of the most influential jurists of our time. . . .

So this is not a responsibility that I take lightly. It's a decision that requires me to set aside short-term expediency and narrow politics so as to maintain faith with our Founders and, perhaps more importantly, with future generations. That's why, over the past several weeks,

I've done my best to set up a rigorous and comprehensive process. I've sought the advice of Republican and Democratic Members of Congress. We've reached out to every member of the Senate Judiciary Committee, to constitutional scholars, to advocacy groups, to bar associations, representing an array of interests and opinions from all across the spectrum.

And today, after completing this exhaustive process, I've made my decision. I've selected a nominee who is widely recognized not only as one of America's sharpest legal minds, but someone who brings to his work a spirit of decency, modesty, integrity, even-handedness, and excellence. These qualities, and his long commitment to public service, have earned him the respect and admiration of leaders from both sides of the aisle. He will ultimately bring that same character to bear on the Supreme Court, an institution in which he is uniquely prepared to serve immediately.

Today I am nominating Chief Judge Merrick Brian Garland to join the Supreme Court. Now, in law enforcement circles and the in the legal community at large, Judge Garland needs no introduction. But I'd like to take a minute to introduce Merrick to the American people, whom he already so ably serves. . . .

Merrick graduated magna cum laude from Harvard Law, and the early years of his legal career bear all the traditional marks of excellence. He clerked for two of President Eisenhower's judicial appointees: first for a legendary judge on the Second Circuit, Judge Henry Friendly, and then for Supreme Court Justice William Brennan. Following his clerkships, Merrick joined a highly regarded law firm, with a practice focused on litigation and pro bono representation of disadvantaged Americans. Within 4 years, he earned a partnership, the dream of most lawyers. But in 1989, just months after that achievement, Merrick made a highly unusual career decision. He walked away from a comfortable and lucrative law practice to return to public service.

Merrick accepted a low-level job as a Federal prosecutor in President George H.W. Bush's administration, took a 50-percent pay cut, traded in his elegant partner's office for a windowless closet that smelled of stale cigarette smoke. This was a time when crime here in Washington had reached epidemic proportions, and he wanted to help. And he quickly made a name for himself, going after corrupt politicians and violent criminals.

His sterling record as a prosecutor led him to the Justice Department, where he oversaw some of the most significant prosecutions in the 1990s, including overseeing every aspect of the Federal response to the Oklahoma City bombing. In the aftermath of that act of terror, when 168 people, many of them small children, were murdered, Merrick had one evening to say goodbye to his own young daughters before he boarded a plane to Oklahoma City. And he would remain there for weeks. He worked side by side with first responders, rescue workers, local and Federal law enforcement. He led the investigation and supervised the prosecution that brought Timothy McVeigh to justice. . . .

It's no surprise then, that soon after his work in Oklahoma City, Merrick was nominated to what's often called the second highest court in the land, the DC Circuit Court. During that process, during that confirmation process, he earned overwhelming bipartisan praise from Senators and legal experts alike. Republican Senator Orrin Hatch, who was then chairman of the Senate Judiciary Committee, supported his nomination. Back then, he said, "In all honesty, I would like to see one person come to this floor and say one reason why Merrick Garland does not deserve this position." He actually accused fellow Senate Republicans trying to obstruct Merrick's confirmation of "playing politics with judges." And he has since said that Judge Garland would be a "consensus nominee" for the Supreme Court who "would be very well supported by all sides," and there would be "no question" Merrick would be confirmed with bipartisan support.

Now, ultimately, Merrick was confirmed to the DC Circuit, the second highest court in the land, with votes from a majority of Democrats and a majority of Republicans. Three years ago, he was elevated to Chief Judge. And in his 19 years on the DC Circuit, Judge Garland has brought his trademark diligence, compassion, and unwavering regard for the rule of law to his work.

On a Circuit Court known for strong-minded judges on both ends of the spectrum, Judge Garland has earned a track record of building consensus as a thoughtful, fairminded judge who follows the law. He's shown a rare ability to bring together odd couples, assemble unlikely coalitions, persuade colleagues with wide-ranging judicial philosophies to sign on to his opinions.

And this record on the bench speaks, I believe, to Judge Garland's fundamental temperament: his insistence that all views deserve a respectful hearing; his habit, to borrow a phrase from former Justice John Paul Stevens, "of understanding before disagreeing" and then disagreeing without being disagreeable. It speaks to his ability to persuade, to respond to the concerns of others with sound arguments and airtight logic. As his former colleague on the DC Circuit and our current Chief Justice of the Supreme Court, John Roberts, once said, "Any time Judge Garland disagrees, you know you're in a difficult area."

At the same time, Chief Judge Garland is more than just a brilliant legal mind. He's someone who has a keen understanding that justice is about more than abstract legal theory; more than some footnote in a dusty casebook. . . . He understands the way law affects the daily reality of people's lives in a big, complicated democracy and in rapidly changing times. And throughout his jurisprudence runs a common thread: a dedication to protecting the basic rights of every American; a conviction that in a democracy, powerful voices must not be allowed to drown out the voices of everyday Americans.

To find someone with such a long career of public service, marked by complex and sensitive issues, to find someone who just about everyone not only respects, but genuinely likes, that is rare. And it speaks to who Merrick Garland is, not just as a lawyer, but as a man.

People respect the way he treats others, his genuine courtesy and respect for his colleagues and those who come before his court. They admire his civic-mindedness: mentoring his clerks throughout their careers, urging them to use their legal training to serve their communities, setting his own example by tutoring a young student at a Northeast DC elementary school each year for the past 18 years. They're moved by his deep devotion to his family. . . .

I said I would take this process seriously, and I did. I chose a serious man and an exemplary judge, Merrick Garland. Over my 7 years as President, in all my conversations with Senators from both parties in which I asked their views on qualified Supreme Court nominees—and this includes the previous two seats that I had to fill—the one name that has come up repeatedly, from Republicans and Democrats alike, is Merrick Garland.

Now, I recognize that we have entered the political season—or perhaps, these days it never ends—a political season that is even noisier and more volatile than usual. I know that Republicans will point to Democrats who have made it hard for Republican Presidents to get their nominees confirmed. And they're not wrong about that. There's been politics involved in nominations in the past. Although it should be pointed out that, in each of those instances, Democrats ultimately confirmed a nominee put forward by a Republican President.

I also know that because of Justice Scalia's outsized role on the Court and in American law and the fact that Americans are closely divided on a number of issues before the Court, it is tempting to make this confirmation process simply an extension of our divided politics, the squabbling that's going on in the news every day. But to go down that path would be wrong. It would be a betrayal of our best traditions and a betrayal of the vision of our founding documents.

At a time when our politics are so polarized, at a time when norms and customs of political rhetoric and courtesy and comity are so often treated like they're disposable, this is precisely the time when we should play it straight and treat the process of appointing a Supreme Court Justice with the seriousness and care it deserves. Because our Supreme Court really is unique. It's supposed to be above politics. It has to be. And it should stay that way.

To suggest that someone as qualified and respected as Merrick Garland doesn't even deserve a hearing, let alone an up-or-down vote, to join an institution as important as our Supreme Court, when two-thirds of Americans believe otherwise, that would be unprecedented.

To suggest that someone who has served his country with honor and dignity, with a distinguished track record of delivering justice for the American people, might be treated, as one Republican leader stated, as a political "piñata," that can't be right.

Tomorrow Judge Garland will travel to the Hill to begin meeting with Senators, one on one. I simply ask Republicans in the Senate to give him a fair hearing and then an up-or-down vote. If you don't, then it will not only be an abdication of the Senate's constitutional duty, it will indicate a process for nominating and confirming judges that is beyond repair. It will mean everything is subject to the most partisan of politics—everything. It will provoke an endless cycle of more tit-for-tat and make it increasingly impossible for any President, Democrat or Republican, to carry out their constitutional function. The reputation of the Supreme Court will inevitably suffer. Faith in our justice system will inevitably suffer. And our democracy will ultimately suffer as well.

I have fulfilled my constitutional duty. Now it's time for the Senate to do theirs. Presidents do not stop working in the final year of their term. Neither should a Senator. . . .

I hope they're fair. That's all. I hope they are fair. As they did when they confirmed Merrick Garland to the DC Circuit, I ask that they confirm Merrick Garland now to the Supreme Court so that he can take his seat in time to fully participate in its work for the American people this fall. He is the right man for the job. He deserves to be confirmed. I could not be prouder of the work that he has already done on behalf of the American people. He deserves our thanks, and he deserves a fair hearing. . . .

[Merrick Garland's statement has been omitted.]

Source: Executive Office of the President. "Remarks on the Nomination of Merrick B. Garland To Be a United States Supreme Court Associate Justice." March 16, 2016. *Compilation of Presidential Documents* 2016, no. 00154 (March 16, 2016). http://www.gpo.gov/fdsys/pkg/DCPD-201600154/pdf/DCPD-201600154.pdf.

Senator McConnell on Supreme Court Nomination

March 16, 2016

U.S. Senate Majority Leader Mitch McConnell made the following remarks on the Senate floor today following the President's announcement of his nomination of Judge Merrick Garland to the United States Supreme Court:

"The next justice could fundamentally alter the direction of the Supreme Court and have a profound impact on our country, so of course the American people should have a say in the Court's direction.

"It is a President's constitutional right to nominate a Supreme Court justice and it is the Senate's constitutional right to act as a check on a President and withhold its consent.

"As Chairman Grassley and I declared weeks ago, and reiterated personally to President Obama, the Senate will continue to observe the Biden Rule so that the American people have a voice in this momentous decision.

"The American people may well elect a President who decides to nominate Judge Garland for Senate consideration. The next President may also nominate someone very different. Either way, our view is this: Give the people a voice in the filling of this vacancy.

"Let me remind colleagues what Vice President Biden said when he was Judiciary Chairman here in the Senate:

> 'It would be our pragmatic conclusion that once the political season is under way, and it is, action on a Supreme Court nomination must be put off until after the election campaign is over. That is what is fair to the nominee and is central to the process. Otherwise, it seems to me . . . we will be in deep trouble as an institution. Others may fret that this approach would leave the Court with only eight members for some time, but as I see it . . . the cost of such a result—the need to reargue three or four cases that will divide the Justices four to four—are quite minor compared to the cost that a nominee, the President, the Senate, and the Nation would have to pay for what would assuredly be a bitter fight, no matter how good a person is nominated by the President . . .'

"Consider that last part. Then-Senator Biden said that the cost to the nation would be too great no matter who the President nominates. President Obama and his allies may now try to pretend this disagreement is about a person, but as I just noted, his own Vice President made clear it's not. The Biden Rule reminds us that the decision the Senate announced weeks ago remains about a principle, not a person.

"It seems clear that President Obama made this nomination not with the intent of seeing the nominee confirmed but in order to politicize it for purposes of the election—which is the type of thing then–Senate Judiciary Chairman Biden was concerned about. The Biden Rule underlines that what the President has done with this nomination would be unfair to any nominee, and more importantly the rule warns of the great costs the President's action could carry for our nation.

"Americans are certain to hear a lot of rhetoric from the other side in the coming days, but here are the facts they'll keep in mind:

- The current Democratic Leader said the Senate is not a rubber stamp, and he noted that the Constitution does not require the Senate to give presidential nominees a vote.

- The incoming Democratic Leader did not even wait until the final year of George W. Bush's term to essentially tell the Senate not to consider any Supreme Court nominee the President sent.

- The 'Biden Rule' supports what the Senate is doing today, underlining that what we're talking about is a principle not a person.

"So here's our view. Instead of spending more time debating an issue where we can't agree, let's keep working to address the issues where we can.

"We just passed critical bipartisan legislation to help address the heroin and prescription opioid crisis in our country. Let's build on that success. Let's keep working together to get our economy moving again and make our country safer, rather than endlessly debating an issue where we don't agree.

"As we continue working on issues like these, the American people are perfectly capable of having their say on this issue. So let's give them a voice. The Senate will appropriately revisit the matter when it considers the qualifications of the nominee the next President nominates, whoever that might be."

SOURCE: Office of Majority Leader Mitch McConnell. "McConnell on Supreme Court Nomination." March 16, 2016. http://www.mcconnell.senate.gov/public/index.cfm/pressreleases?ID=50492600-6758-4FC2-928D-302FAB54BEA8.

OTHER HISTORIC DOCUMENTS OF INTEREST

FROM THIS VOLUME

United Nations Report on Afghanistan Casualties; United States Adjusts Its Military Strategy

FEBRUARY 14 AND JULY 6, 2016

In February, the United Nations Assistance Mission in Afghanistan (UNAMA) released its annual report detailing the situation on the ground in Afghanistan. The report noted that more Afghan civilians were killed or injured in 2015 than in any other year since 2009, when the United Nations first began tracking this information. A majority of the casualties were caused by Taliban forces. In response to the ongoing crisis in Afghanistan, President Barack Obama announced that the United States would slow its withdrawal of support and counter-terrorism troops and would leave 8,400 troops in Afghanistan through the end of his term in January 2017. The president indicated his belief that such a move would not only help further stabilize the country by better equipping Iraqi security forces with the training they needed, but would also give his successor the opportunity to start from a position of strength.

UN FEBRUARY REPORT

In its February 2016 release, UNAMA reported 11,002 casualties—including 3,545 deaths and 7,457 injuries—in 2015. These casualties were concentrated in northeastern and central Afghanistan, specifically around Kunduz and Kabul. Overall, the total number of casualties was up 4 percent from 2014, which equated to 4 percent fewer deaths but 9 percent more injuries. More than 60 percent of the casualties were attributed to anti-government groups, a decrease of 10 percent from 2014. President Ashraf Ghani's government said in a statement that the decreasing number of casualties caused by the Taliban had little to do with the group slowing its insurgency, but that it should rather be attributed to the hundreds of thousands of Afghans fleeing their homes in conflict zones. UNAMA report noted that while the Taliban stated throughout 2015 that "civilian protection was one of their core objectives," they "continued to cause the majority of civilian casualties and to conduct attacks in locations with a high likelihood of causing civilian harm."

Another 14 percent of the casualties were attributed to Afghan security forces, an increase from 12 percent in 2014, and foreign militaries were responsible for 2 percent of all civilian casualties. Half the casualties caused by foreign militaries occurred during the U.S. airstrike on a *Médecins Sans Frontières* (MSF) hospital in Kunduz province in October 2015. Progovernment armed groups were responsible for 1 percent of all casualties.

The largest number of casualties in 2015 was caused by ground engagements between pro- and antigovernment groups, followed by IEDs, and then suicide and complex attacks in which suicide bombers detonate themselves and then gunmen follow on suicide missions. The UNAMA report noted that targeted attacks and abductions rose in 2015, and that many of those attacks were aimed at the Shia Hazara minority. The highest one-day casualty toll occurred on August 7, 2015, when two suicide attacks in Kabul killed 42 civilians and injured 313. Although Ghani's government blamed the attack on the Taliban, the terrorist organization denied any involvement. Of note, many international aid organizations and the United Nations (UN) believed that the number of total civilian casualties in Afghanistan was likely understated because the UN has a strict policy for how casualties are counted and verified.

In response to the report, Nicholas Haysom, the special representative for Afghanistan and head of UNAMA, said, "The real cost we are talking about in these figures is measured in the maimed bodies of children, the communities who have to live with loss, the grief of colleagues and relatives, the families who have to make do without a breadwinner, the parents who grieve for lost children, the children who grieve for lost parents . . . these are the real consequences of the attacks described in this report." While Haysom noted that a peace agreement is desperately needed in the region, he called for "those parties engaged in the conflict, who have it within their power to reduce the number of civilian casualties, to commit to taking every step that will avoid harm and injury to civilians." Zeid Ra'ad al-Hussein, the UN High Commissioner for Human Rights, added, "The people of Afghanistan continue to suffer brutal and unprincipled attacks that are forbidden under international law." He continued, "This is happening with almost complete impunity."

UN REPORT RECOMMENDATIONS

In its February report, UNAMA made a number of recommendations to help slow the increase in civilian casualties. The group called on antigovernment elements to stop targeting civilians and also asked that the Afghan government and international forces do more to ensure their targeted strikes are not directed toward civilian areas. The UN encouraged all groups to stop using mortars, rockets, grenades, and IEDs, and to ensure that hospitals, clinics, and schools were neither attacked nor used for military purposes. The government of Afghanistan was called on to "investigate all allegations of violations of international humanitarian and human rights law and human rights abuses by Afghan national security forces and pro-Government armed groups," and the UN also asked that the government do more to ensure the disbanding of all progovernment armed groups that are not overseen by the Afghan government.

UNAMA also used the report to renew its call for an independent investigation to be conducted into the October 2015 airstrike that hit an MSF hospital. The United States has argued that it inadvertently struck the hospital, but reports from those on the ground indicate that they repeatedly informed the coalition that the hospital was being attacked, but that the airstrikes continued anyway. The UNAMA report asked for those responsible for the attack to be investigated and for those "reasonably suspected to have engaged in war crimes with the requisite intent should be prosecuted by a legally constituted tribunal, with due regard for the rights of the accused."

In response to the growing number of calls from the United Nations, MSF, and other international bodies, the United States released a report in April 2016 on its investigation into the Kunduz airstrike, and said the "tragic accident resulted from a combination of unintentional human errors and equipment failures." In a June report, however, UNAMA further questioned whether the U.S. investigation was carried out with utmost impartiality and said that the findings "are *prima facie* grounds to warrant further investigation into whether United States personnel committed war crimes." The report went on to indicate that the findings released by the United States never "addressed the issue of criminal liability for recklessness in the commission of war crimes, nor criminal liability under the United States Uniform Code of Military Justice." By the close of 2016, President Obama continued to reject calls for a secondary investigation, despite receiving a petition from MSF with hundreds of thousands of signatures.

FURTHER U.S. TROOP ADJUSTMENTS

Since removing a majority of their troops from Afghanistan in 2009, U.S. forces have acted primarily in counterterrorism and noncombat support and training roles, aided by coalition troops. A majority of NATO troops left the region in 2014, which was followed by a subsequent increase in violence perpetrated by the Taliban. Increasing violence in the years following the troop drawdown forced President Obama to continuously readjust his timeframe for full withdrawal of troops from Afghanistan. The 2016 UNAMA reports on civilian deaths in Afghanistan served as another call to action for the United States.

In July, President Obama announced that instead of decreasing the number of support troops in Afghanistan to 5,500 by the end of 2016, he would instead leave 8,400 troops in the country through the end of his administration. This, Obama said, "will allow us to continue to provide tailored support to help Afghan forces continue to improve." Obama said that his decision "also sends a message to the Taliban and all those who have opposed Afghanistan's progress. You have now been waging war against the Afghan people for many years. You've been unable to prevail. Afghan security forces continue to grow stronger." In his speech announcing the change in the troop status, President Obama added that the slowing of the drawdown would give his predecessor, who would take office in January 2017, greater flexibility in determining how the U.S. mission in Afghanistan would proceed.

INCREASING CASUALTIES

In July, UNAMA reported that the number of casualties during the first half of 2016 had reached a record high, with 1,601 killed and 3,565 wounded. By the end of September, this number had risen to 2,562 dead and 5,835 wounded, a 1 percent decrease from the same time period in 2015. The increasing insurgency was specifically aimed at toppling the U.S.-backed government, and the deadliest fighting took place in Kabul. "Every single casualty documented in this report—people killed while praying, working, studying, fetching water, recovering in hospitals—every civilian casualty represents a failure of commitment and should be a call to action for parties to the conflict to take meaningful, concrete steps to reduce civilians' suffering and increase protection," said Tadamichi Yamamoto, who took over as head of UNAMA in June. "Platitudes not backed by meaningful action ring hollow over time. History and the collective memory of the Afghan people will judge leaders of all parties to this conflict by their actual conduct," he added.

In mid-2016, the United Nations announced that total civilian casualties had reached 63,934 since January 1, 2009, with approximately one-third of that number killed. Al Hussein, the UN High Commissioner for Human Rights, said, "The violations laid bare in this report set in motion a cascade of potential human rights abuses that stretch from Afghanistan to the Mediterranean and beyond, as so many Afghans are driven to seek refuge abroad, taking enormous risks." He continued, "Parties to the conflict must cease the deliberate targeting of civilians and the use of heavy weaponry in civilian-populated areas. There must be an end to the prevailing impunity enjoyed by those responsible for civilian casualties—no matter who they are."

Also in its October report, UNAMA noted that the targeting of health facilities, schools, and sites that provide humanitarian aid has risen and that ground engagements caused more than half of all casualties during the first nine months of the year. In the first nine months of 2016 there was a 42 percent increase in the number of casualties caused by progovernment forces, and civilian casualties caused by aerial strikes by progovernment forces rose 72 percent. A third of those casualties were caused by international military forces. Yamamoto said of the findings that "increased fighting in densely populated areas makes it imperative for parties to take immediate steps to ensure all feasible precautions are being taken to spare civilians from harm."

IMPACT ON WOMEN AND CHILDREN

In its February report, the UN highlighted the growing level of violence aimed at women and children. According to the report, every fourth victim in 2015 was a child, while every tenth was a woman. The report marked a 14 percent increase in the number of child casualties and a 37 percent increase in the number of women casualties over 2014. "In 2015, the conflict caused extreme harm to the civilian population, with particularly appalling consequences for children. Unprecedented numbers of children were needlessly killed and injured last year," said Danielle Bell, the human rights director for UNAMA. "Other children suffered the loss of parents, and increasingly their mothers, sisters, and female role models," she added.

According to UNAMA, child casualties in Afghanistan have risen every year since 2013. In October 2016, UNAMA reported another rise in the number of children killed and wounded. During the first six months of 2016, there were 2,461 child casualties, of which 639 were deaths, a 15 percent increase over the first nine months of 2015. Children were most frequently affected by unexploded ordinances, explosive devices that do not detonate when originally intended.

—Heather Kerrigan

Following is a report released on February 14, 2016, by the United Nations Assistance Mission in Afghanistan noting that 2015 was the deadliest year for civilians in Afghanistan since 2009; and a statement by President Barack Obama on July 6, 2016, on the U.S. military strategy in Afghanistan.

DOCUMENT *UNAMA Report on Afghanistan*

February 14, 2016

[All maps, photos, graphics, footnotes, and pull quotes have been omitted.]

[The Mandate and Methodology sections have been omitted.]

EXECUTIVE SUMMARY

In 2015, the conflict in Afghanistan continued to cause extreme harm to the civilian population, with the highest number of total civilian casualties recorded by UNAMA since 2009. Following increases in 2013 and 2014, civilian deaths and injuries from conflict-related violence increased by four per cent compared with 2014. Between 1 January and 31 December 2015, UNAMA documented 11,002 civilian casualties (3,545 civilian deaths and 7,457 injured), marking a four per cent decrease in civilian deaths and a nine per cent increase in civilians injured. Since UNAMA began systematically documenting civilian casualties on 1 January 2009 up to 31 December 2015, UNAMA recorded 58,736 civilian casualties (21,323 deaths and 37,413 injured).

This report documents the immediate harm to the civilian population of Afghanistan from conflict related violence in 2015. The consequences of the armed conflict, and the related violations of human rights and international humanitarian law accompanying it, went far beyond the tragic loss of life and physical injury. Throughout 2015, conflict-related violence destroyed homes, livelihoods and property, displaced thousands of families and restricted the freedom of civilians to access to education, health and other services. Moreover, the short and long-term effects of growing insecurity, weakened civilian protection and lack of respect for human rights and international humanitarian law will continue long beyond these immediate impacts. Generations of people in Afghanistan suffer the physical and mental effects of the conflict, receiving little or no support from Government institutions.

Conflict-related violence increasingly harmed the most vulnerable: in 2015, one in 10 civilian casualties was a woman and one in four was a child. While overall civilian casualties increased by four per cent in 2015, the mission documented a 37 per cent increase in women casualties (1,246 women casualties, comprising 333 deaths and 913 injured) and a 14 per cent increase in child casualties (2,829 comprising 733 deaths and 2,096 injured).

Ground engagements between parties to the conflict continued to cause the highest number of total civilian casualties (deaths and injured), followed by improvised explosive devices (IEDs) and suicide and complex attacks. Ground engagements killed the most civilians, followed by targeted and deliberate killings.

The rise in overall civilian casualties in 2015 mainly stemmed from increases in complex and suicide attacks and targeted and deliberate killings by Anti-Government Elements, increasing civilian casualties caused by Pro-Government Forces during ground engagements and aerial operations, and rising numbers of civilians caught in crossfire between the parties to the conflict, most notably in Kunduz province.

ATTRIBUTION OF RESPONSIBILITY FOR CIVILIAN CASUALTIES

UNAMA attributed 62 per cent of all civilian casualties to Anti-Government Elements and 17 per cent to Pro-Government Forces (14 per cent to Afghan national security forces, two per cent to international military forces and one per cent to pro-Government armed groups). Seventeen per cent of all civilian casualties resulted from ground engagements between Anti-Government Elements and Afghan national security forces not be attributed to one specific party. Four per cent of civilian casualties resulted from unattributed explosive remnants of war.

Anti-Government Elements

Between 1 January and 31 December 2015, UNAMA documented 6,859 civilian casualties (2,315 deaths and 4,544 injured) from operations and attacks carried out by all Anti-Government Elements, a 10 per cent decrease from 2014. The decrease resulted from fewer civilian casualties attributed to Anti-Government Elements from IEDs and ground engagements. However, UNAMA documented a 16 per cent increase in civilian casualties attributed to Anti-Government Elements from complex and suicide attacks, and a 27 per cent increase in civilian casualties from targeted killings, which became the second leading cause of civilian deaths in 2015.

Consistent with trends documented in the UNAMA 2015 Midyear Report on Protection of Civilians in Armed Conflict, civilian casualties attributed to Anti-Government Elements during ground engagements decreased by 38 per cent while civilian casualties from IEDs decreased by 20 per cent compared to 2014. The reduction in civilian casualties from IEDs results from a combination of factors, including increased counter-IED efforts by Afghan national security forces and potential improvements in targeting practices by Anti-Government Elements. Additionally, it should be noted that in 2014, UNAMA documented high numbers of civilian casualties around the presidential and run-off elections of April and June 2014. Of key relevance, the decrease in civilian casualties from Anti-Government Elements should also be seen against the fact that the number of unattributed civilian casualties from ground engagements rose significantly.

Pro-Government Forces

Pro-Government Forces—in particular Afghan security forces—continued to cause increasing numbers of civilian casualties in 2015. UNAMA documented 1,854 civilian casualties (621 deaths and 1,233 injured) caused by Pro-Government Forces, a 28 per cent increase compared to 2014. Consistent with trends documented in the UNAMA 2015 Midyear Report on Protection of Civilians in Armed Conflict, the majority of civilian casualties caused by Pro-Government Forces occurred during ground engagements, primarily from the use of indirect and explosive weapons such as artillery, mortars, rockets and grenades. UNAMA notes that the increase in civilian casualties attributed to Afghan security forces is likely a result of the significant growth of security operations conducted by Afghan security forces since taking primary responsibility for security throughout Afghanistan.

Reversing declines documented in previous years, civilian casualties from aerial operations conducted by both international military forces and Afghan security forces increased by 83 per cent in 2015, causing 296 civilian casualties (149 deaths and 147 injured). Offensive air-to-ground strikes carried out by Afghan security forces caused nearly half (43 per cent) of all civilian casualties from aerial operations. Civilian casualties from Afghan security forces' aerial operations tripled in the second half of 2015 compared to the first semester. UNAMA notes that this increase should also be viewed in the context of the security transition and the growing ability of Afghan security forces to employ close air support without relying on international military forces.

Civilian Casualties not Attributed to a Specific Party

Of the 11,002 civilian casualties documented by UNAMA 493 civilian deaths and 1392 injured (1,885 civilian casualties)—17 per cent—could not be attributed to one specific party. The vast majority of these casualties resulted from ground engagements between Anti-Government Elements and Pro-Government Forces.

This represents a 90 per cent increase compared to 2014 and largely resulted from fighting in Kunduz city between 28 September and 13 October for which UNAMA could not attribute the casualties to one party to the conflict.

GROUND ENGAGEMENTS

Ground engagements remained the leading cause of civilian casualties, causing 4,137 casualties (1,116 deaths and 3,021 injured) in 2015, an increase of 15 per cent. Just under half of these casualties—44 per cent (1,834 casualties, 472 deaths and 1,362 injured)—resulted from ground engagements—mainly crossfire—between Anti-Government Elements and Pro-Government Forces but could not be attributed to a specific party.

As noted, civilian casualties solely attributed to Anti-Government Elements during ground engagements decreased and casualties solely attributed to Pro-Government Forces increased.

OBSERVATIONS

In 2015, parties to the conflict failed to ensure the safety of civilians in exchange for military, territorial or political gains. While Taliban and other Anti-Government Elements remained responsible for the majority of civilian casualties, UNAMA documented a reduction in casualties caused by certain tactics employed by such groups—including both ground engagements and IEDs. Anti-Government Elements continued to carry out suicide and complex attacks in populated areas with obvious disregard for civilians living in the vicinity of their targets—and in many cases without regard to the civilian nature of the targets.

In 2015, Anti-Government Elements (Taliban and other armed opposition groups) focused on challenging Government control of territory, seizing more district administrative centres and holding them for longer than in previous years. They briefly captured Kunduz city, the first provincial capital since the fall of the Taliban regime in 2001. Anti-Government Elements focused on population centres (cities, towns, and large villages)—simultaneously challenging Government control of such centres while carrying out regular, deadly suicide attacks in major cities, particularly Kabul. Taliban claimed responsibility for more than half of the suicide and complex attacks resulting in civilian casualties.

Throughout 2015, Taliban repeatedly stated that civilian protection was one of their core objectives yet continued to cause the majority of civilian casualties and to conduct attacks in locations with a high likelihood of causing civilian harm. Although they publicly admitted to causing civilian casualties in two claims of responsibility, they understated the actual impact on civilians. Taliban claimed that only a few civilians were "slightly wounded" although the two attacks killed four civilians and wounded 42 others.

The Government struggled to adequately secure and protect territory and populations as the country underwent simultaneous political, security and economic transitions. The convergence of the trends above combined with these transitions placed civilians increasingly at risk. In 2015, Taliban forces captured 24 district centres, compared to four in 2014, forcing Afghan security forces to fight on multiple fronts simultaneously. Four of the 24 districts remained under Taliban control at the end of 2015. The losses of Afghan regular forces weakened their ability to protect the civilian population, leading to a loss in public confidence in the Government.

In their response to the intensification of attacks carried out by Anti-Government Elements, Afghan security forces and international military forces both caused increasing harm to the civilian population. UNAMA notes concern that Afghan security forces often relied on heavy or explosive weapons defensively or as weapons of first resort.

Following record battlefield casualties of Afghan security forces (more than 12,000 casualties in 2015), branches of the Government began arming pro-Government armed groups and supporting "national uprising movements" while simultaneously pledging to disarm such groups, raising serious concerns for human rights protection in 2016 and beyond. 2015 also bore witness to the operational emergence of more extreme Anti-Government Elements groups, including Islamic State of Iraq and the Levant (ISIL) or Daesh, that brought with it a dangerous and new, though geographically limited, threat to the population.

On 1 January 2015, international military forces transitioned from a combat mission to a train, assist and advise mission. Despite the formal end of the NATO/ISAF mission, international military forces continued to provide direct military support for their Afghan counterparts: as fighting intensified, international forces continued to be drawn into direct combat situations. In addition, the emergence of new Anti-Government Elements, including ISIL or Daesh affiliated groups and a fracturing of Taliban following the revelation of the death of Mullah Omar, as well as resurgent pro-Government armed groups in parts of the country, further complicated efforts to ensure civilian protection.

The increase in civilian casualties in 2015 was concentrated in two regions, northeastern and central Afghanistan. Although certain trends, such as the rise in targeted and deliberate killings of civilians and the increase in civilian casualties from airstrikes proved consistent across the country, UNAMA documented decreased civilian casualties in all other regions. This included a six per cent decrease in the southern region, which nonetheless continued to suffer the highest number of civilian casualties followed by the northeastern and central regions.

In the northeast, civilian casualties doubled in 2015 compared with 2014, due to repeated fighting in and around Kunduz city. Following advances in April and June 2015, on 28 September, Taliban launched an attack on and captured Kunduz city, sparking more than two weeks of urban fighting that continued until 13 October, when they formally announced their withdrawal from the city and Afghan security forces regained control. The vast majority of civilian casualties resulted from ground fighting between Taliban fighters and Afghan security forces, although UNAMA documented civilian casualties from targeted or deliberate killings, parallel justice punishments and aerial operations, including the United States airstrike on the Médecins Sans Frontières (MSF) hospital on 3 October.

In the central region, notably in Kabul city, complex and suicide attacks caused an 18 per cent increase in civilian casualties. For example, two suicide attacks in Kabul city on 7 August caused 355 civilian casualties (43 deaths and 312 injured)—the highest number of civilians killed and injured in one day since UNAMA began systematically recording civilian casualties in 2009.

Following trends documented in the UNAMA 2014 Midyear and Annual Reports on Protection of Civilians in Armed Conflict, women and child casualties continued to increase at a higher rate than the general population in 2015. Women casualties accounted for 11 per cent of all civilian casualties (up from nine per cent in 2014) while children accounted for 26 per cent of all civilian casualties (up from 24 per cent in 2014).

The thousands of civilians killed and injured from conflict-related violence in 2015 reflects [sic] the changing nature of the conflict and the continued failure of parties to the conflict to protect civilians from harm. UNAMA reiterates that international humanitarian law requires all parties to the conflict to take meaningful measures to protect the civilian population from conflict-related harm, including measures to ensure accountability for violations of international humanitarian and human rights law, and compensation and support for affected civilians.

In this context, UNAMA once again calls on all parties to the conflict to take concrete actions to prevent civilian casualties, in compliance with their obligations under international humanitarian law, in order to significantly reduce civilian casualties in 2016. Anti-Government Elements in particular must stop conducting complex and suicide attacks against civilian targets and carrying out attacks using explosive devices of any kind in civilian-populated areas. Anti-Government Elements must immediately cease the deliberate killing of civilians and stop using illegal, indiscriminate pressure plate IEDs.

All parties, including Afghan security forces, must take all feasible precautions to prevent civilian casualties in their military operations, and cease the use of heavy, indirect fire, and explosive weapons in civilian-populated areas.

UNAMA reinforces its call for all parties to the conflict to ensure accountability for those armed forces and individuals deliberately, indiscriminately or negligently killing and injuring civilians.

UNAMA offers the following recommendations to the parties to the conflict to support their efforts to protect civilians and civilian communities, prevent civilian casualties, and uphold their obligations under international humanitarian law and international human rights law.

RECOMMENDATIONS

Anti-Government Elements

In compliance with obligations under international humanitarian law:

- Cease the deliberate targeting of civilians and civilian locations, in particular, aid workers, civilian Government officials, journalists, human rights defenders, judges and prosecutors and places of worship and culture; apply a definition of 'civilian(s)' that is consistent with international humanitarian law.

- Cease the use of IEDs, particularly in indiscriminate and disproportionate complex and suicide attacks, in all areas frequented by civilians, and stop using illegal pressure-plate IEDs.

- Cease firing mortars, rockets and grenades from and into civilian-populated areas.

- Enforce statements by Taliban leadership that prohibit attacks against civilians and in civilian-populated areas; implement directives ordering Taliban members to prevent and avoid civilian casualties and hold accountable those members who target, kill or injure civilians.

- Uphold statements by Taliban leadership regarding the human rights of women and girls in areas under Taliban influence; cease attacks and threats against girls' education, teachers and the education sector in general.

- Ensure that fighters do not use schools, hospitals, clinics and other protected sites for military purposes, and cease all attacks and threats against healthcare workers, including polio vaccinators and polio vaccination campaigns.

GOVERNMENT OF AFGHANISTAN

- Cease the use of mortars, rockets, grenades, other indirect weapons, and aerial attacks in civilian-populated areas. Develop and implement clear tactical directives, rules of engagement and other procedures in relation to the use of explosive weapons and armed aircraft.

- Finalize the national policy on civilian casualty mitigation backed by an action plan with concrete objectives to prevent civilian casualties in the conduct of hostilities, and ensure the establishment of a dedicated entity within the Government to investigate all incidents of conflict-related harm to civilians.

- Immediately disband and disarm all armed groups, militias and 'national uprising movements'.

- Investigate all allegations of violations of international humanitarian and human rights law and human rights abuses by Afghan national security forces and pro-Government armed groups; prosecute and punish those found responsible, as required under Afghan and international law, and dismantle patronage networks that enable impunity.

- Ensure that victims of violations have effective remedy; strengthen procedures for compensation to women and families of civilians killed and injured in conflict-related violence; and raise public awareness of procedures to obtain compensation and access to basic services.

- Prioritize the further capacity development of Afghan national security forces to command, control and effectively conduct counter-IED operations and IED-disposal, including exploitation. Dedicate all necessary resources to ensure the full implementation of the national counter-IED strategy.

- Immediately cease the use of schools, hospitals and clinics for military purposes, and ensure respect for medical facilities as neutral facilities.

INTERNATIONAL MILITARY FORCES

- Conduct an independent, impartial, transparent and effective investigation of the airstrike on the MSF hospital and make the findings public. Ensure accountability for those responsible. States with jurisdiction over personnel involved in this incident must ensure that individuals responsible for authorizing and carrying out this attack are investigated subject to a prompt, effective, independent, impartial and transparent process. Individuals reasonably suspected to have engaged in war crimes with the requisite intent should be prosecuted by a legally constituted tribunal, with due regard for the rights of the accused. Appropriate steps should be taken to ensure compensation.

- Review current targeting protocols, operational policies and pre-engagement targeting criteria to prevent attacks against civilian locations, including hospitals.

- Ensure transparent post-operation reviews and investigations following allegations of civilian casualties on operations involving international security or intelligence forces, especially regarding UAV strikes and search operations; take appropriate steps to ensure accountability, compensation and better operational practice.

- Support the Government of Afghanistan to develop and implement a national policy on civilian casualty mitigation in the conduct of hostilities.

- Continue to provide training, resources and related support to Afghan national security forces beyond 2016 at the policy and operational level and expand to the tactical level, noting in particular the need for appropriate protocols, training and civilian casualty mitigation measures in relation to use of indirect fire weapons and armed aircraft.

- Continue support to Afghan national security forces to command, control and effectively conduct counter-IED operations and IED-disposal, including exploitation, in 2016 and beyond.

[The remainder of the report, further outlining the information in the Executive Summary, has been omitted.]

Source: United Nations Assistance Mission in Afghanistan. "Annual Report 2015: Protection of Civilians in Armed Conflict." February 14, 2016. http://unama.unmissions.org/sites/default/files/poc_annual_report_2015_final_14_feb_2016.pdf.

President Obama on Afghanistan Troop Strategy

DOCUMENT

July 6, 2016

Good morning, everybody.

More than 14 years ago, after Al Qaida attacked our nation on 9/11, the United States went to war in Afghanistan against these terrorists and the Taliban that harbored them. Over the years—and thanks to heroic efforts by our military, our intelligence community, our diplomats, and our development professionals—we pushed Al Qaida out of its camps, helped the Afghan people topple the Taliban and helped them establish a democratic government. We dealt crippling blows to the Al Qaida leadership. We delivered justice to Usama bin Laden. And we trained Afghan forces to take responsibility for their own security.

And given that progress, a year and a half ago, in December 2014, America's combat mission in Afghanistan came to a responsible end. Compared to the 100,000 troops we once had there, today, fewer than 10,000 remain. And compared to their previous mission—helping to lead the fight—our forces are now focused on two narrow missions: training and advising Afghan forces and supporting counterterrorist operations against the remnants of Al Qaida as well as other terrorist groups, including ISIL. In short, even as we've maintained a relentless case against those who are threatening us, we are no longer engaged in a major ground war in Afghanistan.

But even these narrow missions continue to be dangerous. Over the past year and a half, 38 Americans—military and civilian—have lost their lives in Afghanistan on behalf of our security. And we honor their sacrifice. We stand with their families in their grief and in their pride. And we resolve to carry on the mission for which they gave their last full measure of devotion.

This is also not America's mission alone. In Afghanistan, we're joined by 41 allies and partners, a coalition that contributes more than 6,000 troops of their own. We have a partner in the Afghan Government and the Afghan people, who support a long-term strategic partnership with the United States. And in fact, Afghans continue to step up. For the second year now, Afghan forces are fully responsible for their own security. Every day, nearly 320,000 Afghan soldiers and police are serving and fighting, and many are giving their lives to defend their country.

To their credit—and in the face of a continued Taliban insurgency and terrorist networks—Afghan forces remain in control of all the major population centers, provincial capitals, major transit routes and most district centers. Afghan forces have beaten back attacks, and they've pushed the Taliban out of some areas. And meanwhile, in another milestone, we recently removed the leader of the Taliban, Akhtar Mohammad Mansur.

Nevertheless, the security situation in Afghanistan remains precarious. Even as they improve, Afghan security forces are still not as strong as they need to be. With our help, they're still working to improve critical capabilities such as intelligence, logistics, aviation, and command and control. At the same time, the Taliban remains a threat. They have gained ground in some cases. They've continued attacks and suicide bombings, including in Kabul. Because the Taliban deliberately target innocent civilians, more Afghan men, women, and children are dying. And often overlooked in the global refugee crisis, millions of Afghans have fled their homes and many have been fleeing their country.

Now, as President and Commander in Chief, I've made it clear that I will not allow Afghanistan to be used as safe haven for terrorists to attack our Nation again. That's why I constantly review our strategy with my national security team, including our commanders in Afghanistan. In all these reviews, we're guided by the facts—what's happening on the ground—to determine what's working and what needs to be changed. And that's why, at times, I've made adjustments, for example, by slowing the drawdown of our forces and, more recently, by giving U.S. forces more flexibility to support Afghan forces on the ground and in the air. And I strongly believe that it is in our national security interest—especially after all the blood and treasure we've invested in Afghanistan over the years—that we give our Afghan partners the very best opportunity to succeed.

Upon taking command of coalition forces this spring, General Nicholson conducted a review of the security situation in Afghanistan and our military posture. It was good to get a fresh set of eyes. And based on the recommendation of General Nicholson, as well as Secretary Carter and Chairman Dunford, and following extensive consultations with my national security team, as well as Congress and the Afghan Government and our international partners, I'm announcing an additional adjustment to our posture.

Instead of going down to 5,500 troops by the end of this year, the United States will maintain approximately 8,400 troops in Afghanistan into next year, through the end of my administration. The narrow missions assigned to our forces will not change. They remain focused on supporting Afghan forces and going after terrorists. But maintaining our forces at this specific level, based on our assessment of the security conditions and the strength of Afghan forces, will allow us to continue to provide tailored support to help Afghan forces continue to improve. From coalition bases in Jalalabad and Kandahar, we'll be able to continue supporting Afghan forces on the ground and in the air. And we continue supporting critical counterterrorism operations.

Now, in reaffirming the enduring commitment of the United States to Afghanistan and its people, the decision I'm making today can help our allies and partners align their own commitments. As you know, tomorrow I depart for the NATO summit in Warsaw, where I'll meet with our coalition partners and Afghan President Ghani and Chief Executive Abdullah. Many of our allies and partners have already stepped forward with commitments of troops and funding so that we can keep strengthening Afghan forces through the end of this decade. The NATO summit will be an opportunity for more allies and partners to affirm their contributions, and I'm confident they will, because all of us have a vital interest in the security and stability of Afghanistan.

My decision today also sends a message to the Taliban and all those who have opposed Afghanistan's progress. You have now been waging war against the Afghan people for many years. You've been unable to prevail. Afghan security forces continue to grow stronger. And the commitment of the international community, including the United States, to Afghanistan and its people will endure. I will say it again: The only way to end this conflict and to achieve a full drawdown of foreign forces from Afghanistan is through a lasting political settlement between the Afghan Government and the Taliban. That's the only way. And that is why the United States will continue to strongly support an Afghan-led reconciliation process and why we call on all countries in the region to end safe havens for militants and terrorists.

Finally, today's decision best positions my successor to make future decisions about our presence in Afghanistan. In January, the next U.S. President will assume the most solemn responsibility of the Commander in Chief: the security of the United States and the safety of the American people. The decision I'm making today ensures that my successor has a solid foundation for continued progress in Afghanistan as well as the flexibility to address the threat of terrorism as it evolves.

So, in closing, I want to address directly what I know is on the minds of many Americans, especially our troops and their families who have borne a heavy burden for our security. When we first sent our forces into Afghanistan 14 years ago, few Americans imagined we'd be there—in any capacity—this long. As President, I focused our strategy on training and building up Afghan forces. It has been continually my belief that it is up to Afghans to defend their country. Because we have emphasized training their capabilities, we've been able to end our major ground war there and bring 90 percent of our troops back home.

But even as we work for peace, we have to deal with the realities of the world as it is. And we can't forget what's at stake in Afghanistan. This is where Al Qaida is trying to regroup. This is where ISIL continues to try to expand its presence. If these terrorists succeed in regaining areas and camps where they can train and plot, they will attempt more attacks against us. And we cannot allow that to happen. I will not allow that to happen.

This September will mark 15 years since the attacks of 9/11. And once more, we'll pause to remember the lives we lost, Americans and peoples from around the world. We'll stand with their families, who still grieve. We'll stand with survivors, who still bear the scars of that day. We'll thank the first responders who rushed to save others. And perhaps most importantly, we'll salute our men and women in uniform—our 9/11 generation—who have served in Afghanistan and beyond for our security. We'll honor the memory of all those who've made the ultimate sacrifice, including more than 2,200 American patriots who have given their lives in Afghanistan. As we do, let's never forget the progress their service has made possible.

Afghanistan is not a perfect place. It remains one of the poorest countries in the world. It is going to continue to take time for them to build up military capacity that we sometimes take for granted. And given the enormous challenges they face, the Afghan people will need the partnership of the world, led by the United States, for many years to come. But with our support, Afghanistan is a better place than it once was. Millions of Afghan children—boys and girls—are in school. Dramatic improvements in public health have saved the lives of mothers and children. Afghans have cast their ballots in democratic elections and seen the first democratic transfer of power in their country's history. The current National Unity Government continues to pursue reforms—including record revenues last year—to strengthen their country and, over time, help decrease the need for international support.

That Government is a strong partner with us in combating terrorism. That's the progress we've helped make possible. That's the progress that our troops have helped make possible, and our diplomats and our development personnel. That's the progress we can help sustain, in partnership with the Afghan people and our coalition partners. And so I firmly believe the decision I'm announcing today is the right thing to do: for Afghanistan, for the United States, and for the world.

May God bless our troops and all who serve to protect us. May God bless the United States of America.

SOURCE: Executive Office of the President. "Remarks on United States Military Strategy in Afghanistan." July 6, 2016. *Compilation of Presidential Documents* 2016, no. 00450 (July 6, 2016). http://www.gpo.gov/fdsys/pkg/DCPD-201600450/pdf/DCPD-201600450.pdf.

OTHER HISTORIC DOCUMENTS OF INTEREST

FROM PREVIOUS *HISTORIC DOCUMENTS*

Apple and Microsoft Respond to Government Orders Seeking Access to Consumer Data

FEBRUARY 16 AND 25, MARCH 28, AND APRIL 14, 2016

Consumer privacy and data security issues were raised early in 2016 in the United States as Apple challenged a government order to unlock an iPhone that belonged to Syed Farook, who, along with his wife, killed fourteen people and injured twenty-two others in the 2015 San Bernardino County shooting. Shortly after Apple's case captured the public's attention, Microsoft announced it was suing the U.S. Justice Department for the right to inform customers under investigation that the government had asked the company to turn over their digital information. Both legal disputes reflect technology companies' lingering concerns about protecting customers' privacy and desire to promote greater transparency around government requests for consumer data following the 2013 revelation of several top-secret intelligence-gathering programs operated by the National Security Agency. Since then, many technology companies have increased the security of their devices, software, and online platforms, particularly by using encryption technologies. Government officials claim that encryption makes it more difficult for law enforcement and intelligence agencies to anticipate and prevent terrorist attacks and to solve cases because it limits their access to suspects' data.

Attempt to Unlock an iPhone

The FBI retrieved Farook's iPhone during a search of the shooters' home and car. The phone had been issued by San Bernardino County, for whom Farook worked as a public health inspector, and the FBI believed that the data it contained may reveal whom the perpetrators may have contacted before the shootings and where they had gone in the time between the attack and when they were killed in a shootout with police. However, unencrypted copies of the phone's data, which had been backed up to the iCloud, had not been updated since October, and the county's attempt—at the government's request—to reset Farook's iCloud password and obtain November and December data through the cloud was unsuccessful. The FBI then turned to Apple, saying it could not access the phone's encrypted data without the company's assistance. At issue was an iPhone feature that requires users to enter a four-digit passcode to unlock the device and gain full access to data stored on the phone. After ten unsuccessful login attempts, the phone erases a key that can be used to decrypt the user's data, thus rendering all information on the phone inaccessible.

On February 16, in response to an application from the U.S. government, Magistrate Judge Sheri Pym of the U.S. District Court for the Central District of California issued a court order compelling Apple to provide "reasonable technical assistance" to allow the

FBI to access and search the iPhone. Specifically, the order called for Apple to devise a technical solution that would allow the FBI to try an unlimited number of passwords to unlock the phone, and would also remove the time delay mandated by Apple's operating system in between failed password attempts. The order acknowledged that a technical solution that could achieve these things might not be viable and asked Apple to respond within five business days if that were the case.

APPLE RESPONDS TO THE FBI

Apple refused to comply with the court order. In a letter to Apple customers published on February 16, CEO Tim Cook described the order as "chilling" and "dangerous" and claimed it had implications "far beyond the legal case at hand." The FBI, Cook wrote, "wants us to make a new version of the iPhone operating system, circumventing several important security features, and install it on an iPhone recovered during the investigation. In the wrong hands, this software—which does not exist today—would have the potential to unlock any iPhone in someone's physical possession." The letter explained that Apple had "done everything that is both within our power and within the law" to help the FBI, including by providing data that was in the company's possession to the FBI at the bureau's request. But now, the letter continued, "the U.S. government has asked us for something we simply do not have, and something we consider too dangerous to create."

Apple argued that acceding to the FBI's request would set a dangerous legal precedent that could be used to compel Apple and other companies to develop software for surveillance purposes without consumers' knowledge. In addition, the company cited concerns that hackers, foreign intelligence agencies, and authoritarian governments could obtain the software Apple created to unlock Farook's phone, thus compromising the security of every iPhone and putting consumers' privacy at risk worldwide. Cook's letter to customers also noted Apple's belief that the court order was the result of government "overreach" because officials were relying on an overly broad interpretation of the All Writs Act to compel the company's cooperation. The act authorizes federal courts to issue "all writs necessary or appropriate in aid of their respective jurisdictions and agreeable to the usages and principles of law." The FBI countered that it only wanted software that could be used to unlock Farook's phone and that accessing his data was crucial to the ongoing investigation. "The San Bernardino litigation isn't about trying to set a precedent or send any kind of message. It is about the victims and justice," said FBI director James Comey. "Fourteen people were slaughtered and many more had their lives and bodies ruined. We owe them a thorough and professional investigation under law."

Several civil liberties groups weighed in on the dispute, echoing Apple's concerns. "This isn't just about one iPhone, it's about all of our software and all of our digital devices, and if this precedent gets set it will spell digital disaster for the trustworthiness of everyone's computers and mobile phones," said Kevin Bankston, director of New America's Open Technology Institute. Alex Abdo, a staff attorney for the ACLU, described the case as an "unprecedented power-grab" by the government, stating, "We would all be more secure if the government ended this reckless effort."

On February 19, the Justice Department filed a motion to force Apple to comply with the District Court's order. Prosecutors wrote in the filing that Apple's refusal to comply "appears to be based on its concern for its business model and public brand marketing strategy." Apple executives, including Cook, told various news outlets that the company had cooperated with the FBI in the months preceding the court order and had attempted several solutions in coordination with FBI agents. The company filed an "application for relief" in opposition to the court order on February 25, and filed an appeal on March 2, stating that it would not develop code to unlock the phone. Apple's filings were supported by seventeen amicus briefs submitted by entities ranging from organizations such as the ACLU and Electronic Frontier Foundation to major technology companies and competitors, including Microsoft, Google, Intel, and AT&T. The Justice Department responded to Apple's appeal on March 10, arguing that the agency's request for assistance had been "modest" because it only applied to one iPhone and accusing Apple of making false arguments. Apple responded in turn by claiming that the Justice Department did not have the authority to force the company to comply with the order, adding that "the [country's] Founders would be appalled."

A hearing in the case was scheduled for March 22, but was postponed at the government's request. The Justice Department said it had found a third party who could unlock the iPhone, though it did not name the company. On March 28, the Justice Department reported that it had accessed the data it needed on the iPhone and submitted a filing asking the District Court to drop the case. This news raised some questions about the security of Apple devices, given that an unknown third party could hack into the iPhone. Apple's lawyers said the company would want to know how the FBI and third party were able to circumvent the passcode feature, but the FBI declined to share that information. "The FBI purchased the method from an outside party so that we could unlock the San Bernardino device. We did not, however, purchase the rights to technical details about how the method functions, or the nature and extent of any vulnerability upon which the method may rely in order to operate," said Amy Hess, executive assistant director of the FBI's Science and Technology Branch.

Although the government dropped its case, the issue is far from resolved. In a letter unsealed in federal court in February, a lawyer for Apple disclosed that the Justice Department was seeking the company's assistance to unlock at least nine other iPhones and that the company was challenging the government's arguments in seven of those cases. In response, Melanie Newman, a Justice Department spokesperson, said, "It remains a priority for the government to ensure that law enforcement can obtain crucial digital information to protect national security and public safety, either with cooperation from relevant parties, or through the court system when cooperation fails. We will continue to pursue all available options for this mission, including seeking the cooperation of manufacturers and relying upon the creativity of both the public and private sectors."

MICROSOFT AND THE ELECTRONIC COMMUNICATIONS PRIVACY ACT

Roughly two weeks after the Justice Department dropped its case against Apple, Microsoft filed a suit against the agency with the U.S. District Court for the Western District of Washington, claiming that it was violating the Constitution by preventing Microsoft from informing its customers about government requests for their e-mail and other information stored in the cloud. The case centered on the government's increasing use of the Electronic Communications Privacy Act (ECPA) to investigate data stored on remote servers, or the cloud. The ECPA allows the government to prevent companies from disclosing data requests if the government has "reason to believe" that such disclosure could be detrimental to an investigation. A judge must grant the government authority to prevent companies from disclosing to customers that they are being investigated.

Brad Smith, Microsoft's president and chief legal officer, told the Associated Press that the company decided to sue the Justice Department following a case in which Microsoft tried to contest one nondisclosure ECPA order, and in response the government threatened to hold the company in contempt. Smith said the incident prompted the company to review the number of ECPA orders it had received. According to Microsoft's complaint, filed on April 14, over the past eighteen months "federal courts have issued nearly 2,600 secrecy orders silencing Microsoft from speaking about warrants and other legal process seeking Microsoft customers' data; of those, more than two-thirds contained no fixed end date." The complaint alleged that the government's increased requests for online data and greater secrecy around those requests had "combined to undermine confidence in the privacy of the cloud and have impaired Microsoft's right to be transparent with its customers, a right guaranteed by the First Amendment." Microsoft further argued that the government's gag orders violated the Fourth Amendment, which protects against unreasonable search and seizure. The complaint also accused the government of exploiting the transition to cloud computing "as a means of expanding its power to conduct secret investigations." However, this transition "does not alter the fundamental constitutional requirement that the government must—with few exceptions—give notice when it searches and seizes the private information or communications of individuals or businesses."

Smith acknowledged in a public blog post that "there are times when secrecy around a government warrant is needed. This is the case, for example, when disclosure of the government's warrant would create a real risk of harm to another individual or when disclosure would allow people to destroy evidence and thwart an investigation." But, he wrote, "based on the many secrecy orders we have received, we question whether these orders are grounded in specific facts that truly demand secrecy. To the contrary, it appears that the issuance of secrecy orders has become too routine."

Microsoft called on the Justice Department to adopt a new policy for secrecy orders. If it did not, Congress should amend the ECPA in a way that contains clearer limitations on secrecy. Congress had already begun considering ECPA reforms earlier in 2016, with a bill earning House approval in late April. However, this bill has yet to move forward in the Senate.

Dozens of amicus briefs have been filed on Microsoft's behalf, including those by technology companies, privacy advocates, news organizations, and private companies representing a broad range of industries. The Justice Department has filed a motion to dismiss the case, arguing that Microsoft does not have standing to challenge all ECPA gag orders at once, instead of naming a specific order and injury caused by said order. At the time of writing, Microsoft's case was pending before the U.S. District Court for the Western District of Washington.

—Linda Fecteau Grimm

Following is a court order from the U.S. District Court for the Central District of California from February 16, 2016, directing Apple to assist the FBI; Apple's motion to vacate the order, filed on February 25, 2016; the U.S. government's filing from March 28, 2016, in which it requested that the order be vacated; and an excerpt from Microsoft's lawsuit against the Justice Department, filed on April 14, 2016.

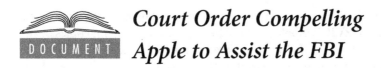

Court Order Compelling
Apple to Assist the FBI

February 16, 2016

United States District Court for the Central District of California Eastern Division

In the Matter of the Search of Apple iPhone Seized During the Execution of a Search Warrant on a Black Lexus 15300, California License plate #KGD203

No. ED 15-0451M
~~Proposed~~ Order Compelling Apple, Inc. to Assist Agents in Search

This matter is before the Court pursuant to an application pursuant to the All Writs Act, 28 U.S.C. § 1651, by Assistant United States Attorneys Tracy Wilkison and Allen Chiu, requesting an order directing Apple Inc. ("Apple") to assist law enforcement agents in enabling the search of a digital device seized in the course of a previously issued search warrant in this matter.

For good cause shown, IT IS HEREBY ORDERED that:

1. Apple shall assist in enabling the search of a cellular telephone, Apple make: iPhone 5C, Model: A1532, P/N:MGFG2LL/A, S/N:FFMNQ3MTG2DJ, IMEI:358820052301412, on the Verizon Network, (the "SUBJECT DEVICE") pursuant to a warrant of this Court by providing reasonable technical assistance to assist law enforcement agents in obtaining access to the data on the SUBJECT DEVICE.

2. Apple's reasonable technical assistance shall accomplish the following three important functions: (1) it will bypass or disable the auto-erase function whether or not it has been enabled; (2) it will enable the FBI to submit passcodes to the SUBJECT DEVICE for testing electronically via the physical device port, Bluetooth, Wi-Fi, or other protocol available on the SUBJECT DEVICE; and (3) it will ensure that when the FBI submits passcodes to the SUBJECT DEVICE, software running on the device will not purposefully introduce any additional delay between passcode attempts beyond what is incurred by Apple hardware.

3. Apple's reasonable technical assistance may include, but is not limited to: providing the FBI with a signed iPhone Software file, recovery bundle, or other Software Image File ("SIF") that can be loaded onto the SUBJECT DEVICE. . . . The SIF will be coded by Apple with a unique identifier of the phone so that the SIF would only load and execute on the SUBJECT DEVICE. . . .

4. If Apple determines that it can achieve the three functions stated above in paragraph 2, as well as the functionality set forth in paragraph 3, using an alternate technological means from that recommended by the government, and the government concurs, Apple may comply with this Order in that way.

5. Apple shall advise the government of the reasonable cost of providing this service.

6. Although Apple shall make reasonable efforts to maintain the integrity of data on the SUBJECT DEVICE, Apple shall not be required to maintain copies of any user data as a result of the assistance ordered herein. All evidence preservation shall remain the responsibility of law enforcement agents.

7. To the extent that Apple believes that compliance with this Order would be unreasonably burdensome, it may make an application to this Court for relief within five business days of receipt of the Order.

Dated: February 16, 2016

Sheri Pym
United States Magistrate Judge

SOURCE: U.S. Justice Department. "No. ED 15-0451M Order Compelling Apple, Inc. to Assist Agents in Search." February 16, 2016. http://www.justice.gov/usao-cdca/file/825001/download.

DOCUMENT *Apple Motion to Vacate Court Order*

February 25, 2016

[Footnotes have been omitted.]

United States District Court for the Central District of California Eastern Division

In the Matter of the Search of Apple iPhone Seized During the Execution of a Search Warrant on a Black Lexus 15300, California License plate #KGD203

ED No. ED 16-10 (SP)
  Apple Inc's Motion to Vacate Order Compelling Apple Inc. to Assist Agents in Search, and Opposition to Government's Motion to Compel Assistance
  Apple Inc. ("Apple"), by and through its counsel of record, hereby files this Motion to Vacate the Order Compelling Apple Inc. to Assist Agents in Search, and Opposition to the Government's Motion to Compel Assistance.
  This Motion and Opposition is based upon the attached memorandum of points and authorities, the attached declarations of Nicola T. Hanna, Lisa Olle, and Erik Neuenschwander and exhibits, the files and records in this case, and such further evidence and argument as the Court may permit.

Dated: February 25, 2016

Respectfully submitted,
GIBSON, DUNN & CRUTCHER LLP

INTRODUCTION

This is not a case about one isolated iPhone. Rather, this case is about the Department of Justice and the FBI seeking through the courts a dangerous power that Congress and the American people have withheld: the ability to force companies like Apple to undermine the basic security and privacy interests of hundreds of millions of individuals around the globe. The government demands that Apple create a back door to defeat the encryption on the iPhone, making its users' most confidential and personal information vulnerable to hackers, identity thieves, hostile foreign agents, and unwarranted government surveillance. The All Writs Act, first enacted in 1789 and on which the government bases its entire case, "does not give the district court a roving commission" to conscript and commandeer Apple in this manner. *Plum Creek Lumber Co. v. Hutton*, 608 F.2d 1283, 1289 (9th Cir. 1979). In fact, no court has ever authorized what the government now seeks, no law supports such unlimited and sweeping use of the judicial process, and the Constitution forbids it.

Since the dawn of the computer age, there have been malicious people dedicated to breaching security and stealing stored personal information. Indeed, the government itself falls victim to hackers, cyber-criminals, and foreign agents on a regular basis, most famously when foreign hackers breached Office of Personnel Management databases and gained access to personnel records, affecting over 22 million current and former federal workers and family members. In the face of this daily siege, Apple is dedicated to enhancing the security of its devices, so that when customers use an iPhone, they can feel confident that their most private personal information—financial records and credit card information, health information, location data, calendars, personal and political beliefs, family photographs, information about their children—will be safe and secure. To this end, Apple uses encryption to protect its customers from cyber-attack and works hard to improve security with every software release because the threats are becoming more frequent and sophisticated. Beginning with iOS 8, Apple added additional security features that incorporate the passcode into the encryption system. It is these protections that the government now seeks to roll back by judicial decree.

There are two important and legitimate interests in this case: the needs of law enforcement and the privacy and personal safety interests of the public. In furtherance of its law enforcement interests, the government had the opportunity to seek amendments to existing law, to ask Congress to adopt the position it urges here. But rather than pursue new legislation, the government backed away from Congress and turned to the courts, a forum ill-suited to address the myriad competing interests, potential ramifications, and unintended consequences presented by the government's unprecedented demand. And more importantly, by invoking "terrorism" and moving ex parte behind closed courtroom doors, the government sought to cut off debate and circumvent thoughtful analysis.

The order demanded by the government compels Apple to create a new operating system—effectively a "back door" to the iPhone—that Apple believes is too dangerous to build. Specifically, the government would force Apple to create new software with functions to remove security features and add a new capability to the operating system to attack iPhone encryption, allowing a passcode to be input electronically. This would make it easier to unlock the iPhone by "brute force," trying thousands or millions of passcode combinations with the speed of a modern computer. In short, the government wants to compel Apple to create a crippled and insecure product. Once the process is created, it provides an avenue for criminals and foreign agents to access millions of iPhones. And once developed for our government, it is only a matter of time before foreign governments demand the same tool.

The government says: "Just this once" and "Just this phone." But the government knows those statements are not true; indeed the government has filed multiple other applications for similar orders, some of which are pending in other courts. And as news of this Court's order broke last week, state and local officials publicly declared their intent to use the proposed operating system to open hundreds of other seized devices—in cases having nothing to do with terrorism. If this order is permitted to stand, it will only be a matter of days before some other prosecutor, in some other important case, before some other judge, seeks a similar order using this case as precedent. Once the floodgates open, they cannot be closed, and the device security that Apple has worked so tirelessly to achieve will be unwound without so much as a congressional vote. As Tim Cook, Apple's CEO, recently noted: "Once created, the technique could be used over and over again, on any number of devices. In the physical world, it would be the equivalent of a master key, capable of opening hundreds of millions of locks—from restaurants and banks to stores and homes. No reasonable person would find that acceptable." Declaration of Nicola T. Hanna ("Hanna Decl."), Ex. D [Apple Inc., *A Message to Our Customers* (Feb. 16, 2016)].

Despite the context of this particular action, no legal principle would limit the use of this technology to domestic terrorism cases—but even if such limitations could be imposed, it would only drive our adversaries further underground, using encryption technology made by foreign companies that cannot be conscripted into U.S. government service—leaving law-abiding individuals shouldering all of the burdens on liberty, without any offsetting benefit to public safety. Indeed, the FBI's repeated warnings that criminals and terrorists are able to "go dark" behind end-to-end encryption methods proves this very point. See Hanna Decl. Ex. F [FBI, Operational Technology, *Going Dark Issue* (last visited Feb. 23, 2016) ("FBI, Going Dark")].

Finally, given the government's boundless interpretation of the All Writs Act, it is hard to conceive of any limits on the orders the government could obtain in the future. For example, if Apple can be forced to write code in this case to bypass security features and create new accessibility, what is to stop the government from demanding that Apple write code to turn on the microphone in aid of government surveillance, activate the video camera, surreptitiously record conversations, or turn on location services to track the phone's user? Nothing.

As FBI Director James Comey expressly recognized:

> Democracies resolve such tensions through robust debate. . . . It may be that, as a people, we decide the benefits [of strong encryption] outweigh the costs and that there is no sensible, technically feasible way to optimize privacy and safety in this particular context, or that public safety folks will be able to do their job well enough in the world of universal strong encryption. Those are decisions Americans should make, but I think part of my job is [to] make sure the debate is informed by a reasonable understanding of the costs.

Hanna Decl. Ex. G [James Comey, *Encryption, Public Safety, and "Going Dark,"* Lawfare (July 6, 2015, 10:38 AM) ("Comey, *Going Dark*")]; *see also* Hanna Decl. Ex. H [James Comey, *We Could Not Look the Survivors in the Eye if We Did Not Follow This Lead,* Lawfare (Feb. 21, 2016, 9:03 PM) ("Comey, *Follow This Lead*")] (reiterating that the tension between national security and individual safety and privacy "should not be resolved by the FBI, which investigates for a living[, but rather] . . . by the American people. . . .").

The government, by seeking an order mandating that Apple create software to destabilize the security of the iPhone and the law-abiding citizens who use it to store data touching on every facet of their private lives, is not acting to inform or contribute to the debate; it is seeking to avoid it.

Apple strongly supports, and will continue to support, the efforts of law enforcement in pursuing justice against terrorists and other criminals—just as it has in this case and many others. But the unprecedented order requested by the government finds no support in the law and would violate the Constitution. Such an order would inflict significant harm—to civil liberties, society, and national security—and would preempt decisions that should be left to the will of the people through laws passed by Congress and signed by the President. Accordingly, the Court should vacate the order and deny the government's motion to compel.

[Sections 2 through 4, containing background on issues relevant to the case and more detailed arguments supporting Apple's motion, have been omitted, as have the declarations of Nicola T. Hanna, Lisa Olle, and Erik Neuensch.]

SOURCE: U.S. District Court for the Central District of California Eastern Division. "ED No. ED 16-10 (SP) Apple Inc's Motion to Vacate Order Compelling Apple Inc. to Assist Agents in Search, and Opposition to Government's Motion to Compel Assistance." February 25, 2016.

DOCUMENT   *Justice Department Case Status Report*

March 28, 2016

United States District Court for the Central District of California Eastern Division

In the Matter of the Search of Apple iPhone Seized During the Execution of a Search Warrant on a Black Lexus 15300, California License Plate #KGD203

ED No. CM 16-10 (SP)
Government's Status Report

Applicant United States of America, by and through its counsel of record, the United States Attorney for the Central District of California, hereby files this status report called for by the Court's order issued on March 21, 2016. (CR 199.)

The government has now successfully accessed the data stored on Farook's iPhone and therefore no longer requires the assistance from Apple Inc. mandated by Court's Order Compelling Apple Inc. to Assist Agents in Search dated February 16, 2016.

Accordingly, the government hereby requests that the Order Compelling Apple Inc. to Assist Agents in Search dated February 16, 2016 be vacated.

Dated: March 28, 2016

Respectfully submitted,
Eileen M. Decker
United States Attorney

Patricia A. Donohue
Assistant United States Attorney
Chief, National Security Division

Tracy L. Wilkison
Assistant United States Attorney

Attorneys for Applicant
United States of America

SOURCE: U.S. Justice Department. "ED No. CM 16-10 (SP) Government's Status Report." March 28, 2016. http://www.justice.gov/usao-cdca/file/836311/download.

DOCUMENT *Microsoft ECPA Complaint*

April 14, 2016

[The following content has been excerpted from Microsoft's lawsuit against the U.S. Justice Department and provides a summary of the company's arguments in the case.]

United States District Court Western District of Washington at Seattle

Microsoft Corporation, Plaintiff,

v.

The United States Department of Justice, and Loretta Lynch, in her official capacity as Attorney General of the United States, Defendants.

Complaint for Declaratory Judgment

Microsoft Corporation ("Microsoft") alleges as follows.

INTRODUCTION

1. Microsoft brings this case because its customers have a right to know when the government obtains a warrant to read their emails, and because Microsoft has a right to tell them. Yet the Electronic Communications Privacy Act ("ECPA") allows courts to order Microsoft to keep its customers in the dark when the government seeks their email content or other private information, based solely on a "reason to believe" that disclosure might hinder an investigation.

Nothing in the statute requires that the "reason to believe" be grounded in the facts of the particular investigation, and the statute contains no limit on the length of time such secrecy orders may be kept in place. 18 U.S.C. § 2705(b). Consequently, as Microsoft's customers increasingly store their most private and sensitive information in the cloud, the government increasingly seeks (and obtains) secrecy orders under Section 2705(b). This statute violates both the Fourth Amendment, which affords people and businesses the right to know if the government searches or seizes their property, and the First Amendment, which enshrines Microsoft's rights to talk to its customers and to discuss how the government conducts its investigations—subject only to restraints narrowly tailored to serve compelling government interests. People do not give up their rights when they move their private information from physical storage to the cloud. Microsoft therefore asks the Court to declare that Section 2705(b) is unconstitutional on its face.

2. Before the digital age, individuals and businesses stored their most sensitive correspondence and other documents in file cabinets and desk drawers. As computers became prevalent, users moved their materials to local computers and on-premises servers, which continued to remain within the user's physical possession and control. In both eras, the government had to give notice when it sought private information and communications, except in the rarest of circumstances.

3. Cloud computing has spurred another profound change in the storage of private information. Today, individuals increasingly keep their emails and documents on remote servers owned by third parties, i.e., in the cloud. . . . But the transition to the cloud does not alter the fundamental constitutional requirement that the government must—with few exceptions—give notice when it searches and seizes the private information or communications of individuals or businesses.

4. The government, however, has exploited the transition to cloud computing as a means of expanding its power to conduct secret investigations. As individuals and business have moved their most sensitive information to the cloud, the government has increasingly adopted the tactic of obtaining the private digital documents of cloud customers not from the customers themselves, but through legal process directed at online cloud providers like Microsoft. At the same time, the government seeks secrecy orders under 18 U.S.C. § 2705(b) to prevent Microsoft from telling its customers (or anyone else) of the government's demands. These secrecy orders generally assert that abiding by the centuries-old requirement of seeking evidence directly from its owner would jeopardize the government's investigation. Most of the time, these secrecy orders prohibit notification for unreasonably long (or even unlimited) periods of time, which Section 2705(b) permits whenever a court has "reason to believe" any of several adverse consequences might otherwise ensue—including any time notice would "seriously jeopardiz[e] an investigation or unduly delay[] a trial."

5. Over the past 18 months, federal courts have issued nearly 2,600 secrecy orders silencing Microsoft from speaking about warrants and other legal process seeking Microsoft customers' data; of those, more than two-thirds contained no fixed end date. (In fact, of the twenty-five secrecy orders issued to Microsoft by judges

in this District, none contained a time limit.) These twin developments—the increase in government demands for online data and the simultaneous increase in secrecy—have combined to undermine confidence in the privacy of the cloud and have impaired Microsoft's right to be transparent with its customers, a right guaranteed by the First Amendment.

6. There may be exceptional circumstances when the government's interest in investigating criminal conduct justifies an order temporarily barring a provider from notifying a customer that the government has obtained the customer's private communications and data. But Section 2705(b) sweeps too broadly. That antiquated law (passed decades before cloud computing existed) allows courts to impose prior restraints on speech about government conduct—the very core of expressive activity the First Amendment is intended to protect—even if other approaches could achieve the government's objectives without burdening the right to speak freely. The statute sets no limits on the duration of secrecy orders, and it permits prior restraints any time a court has "reason to believe" adverse consequences would occur if the government were not allowed to operate in secret. Under the statute, the assessment of adverse consequences need not be based on the specific facts of the investigation, and the assessment is made only at the time the government applies for the secrecy order, with no obligation on the government to later justify continued restraints on speech even if circumstances change because, for instance, the investigation is closed or the subject learns of it by other means. It also permits those restraints based on the application of purely subjective criteria, such as a finding that notice would "jeopardiz[e] an investigation" in unspecified ways or "unduly delay a trial." Section 2705(b) is therefore facially overbroad under the First Amendment, since it does not require the government to establish that the continuing restraint on speech is narrowly tailored to promote a compelling interest.

7. The statute also violates the Constitution's protection against unreasonable searches and seizures. The Fourth Amendment's requirement that government engage only in "reasonable" searches necessarily includes a right for people to know when the government searches or seizes their property. See Wilson v. Arkansas, 514 U.S. 927, 934 (1995). For example, if the government comes into a person's home to seize her letters from a desk drawer or computer hard drive, that person in almost all circumstances has the right to notice of the government's intrusion. The same is true when the government executes a search of a business to seize emails from the business's on-site server. But Section 2705(b) subjects Microsoft's cloud customers to a different standard merely because of how they store their communications and data: the statute provides a mechanism for the government to search and seize customers' private information without notice to the customer, based upon a constitutionally insufficient showing. In so doing, Section 2705(b) falls short of the intended reach of Fourth Amendment protections, which do not depend on the technological medium in which private "papers and effects" are stored.

8. For these reasons, Microsoft asks the Court to declare that Section 2705(b) is unconstitutional on its face. . . .

PRAYER FOR RELIEF

Microsoft prays for an Order and Judgment:

(a) Declaring that 18 U.S.C. § 2705(b) is facially unconstitutional under the First Amendment;

(b) Declaring that 18 U.S.C. § 2705(b) is facially unconstitutional under the Fourth Amendment; and

(c) Granting such other and further equitable or legal relief as the Court deems proper.

DATED this 14th day of April, 2016.   Davis Wright Tremaine LLP [et. al]
Attorneys for Microsoft Corporation

SOURCE: United States District Court for the Western District of Washington. Microsoft v. United States Department of Justice. Complaint for Declaratory Judgment. April 14, 2016. http://ia601503.us.archive .org/34/items/gov.uscourts.wawd.229935/gov.uscourts.wawd.229935.1.0.pdf.

OTHER HISTORIC DOCUMENTS OF INTEREST

FROM PREVIOUS *HISTORIC DOCUMENTS*

March

RNC and DNC Leaders Remark on Super Tuesday; Trump and Clinton Accept Nominations

---

MARCH 1, AND JULY 21 AND 29, 2016

The campaign for president began in earnest in the summer of 2015 when the Republican contenders held their first debate; the Democrats followed in October. What began as a field of nineteen Republican and five Democratic candidates was quickly narrowed to four by early 2016: Republicans Donald Trump and Sen. Ted Cruz, R-Tex., and Democrats Sen. Bernie Sanders, I-Vt., and former secretary of state Hillary Clinton. Generally seen as the turning point in any primary, Super Tuesday on March 1, 2016, made clear that there was a slim likelihood that any hopeful would surpass the delegates that had been earned by Trump and Clinton. Despite some suspense about whether delegates would attempt to unbind themselves during the convention, it was ultimately Trump who accepted the Republican Party nomination, and Clinton accepted the Democratic nomination.

SUPER TUESDAY ARRIVES

March 1, 2016, was designated as Super Tuesday because it is the day on which the most states hold their primaries and caucuses. The Republicans held primaries in twelve states, while the Democrats had primaries in eleven states. American Samoa and Democrats Abroad also held their Democratic caucuses on March 1. A total of 1,460 delegates were up for grabs, 865 for Democrats and 595 for Republicans, or 22 percent of all delegates. The Democratic contests would also feature 150 "superdelegates" who were free to vote based on their personal preference at the Democratic convention.

In the Republican primaries, Trump won seven states (Alabama, Arkansas, Georgia, Massachusetts, Tennessee, Vermont, and Virginia), Cruz won three states (Alaska, Oklahoma, and Texas), and Sen. Marco Rubio, R-Fla., won the state of Minnesota. RNC Chair Reince Priebus celebrated the record number of Republicans who voted in the primary in a statement released on March 1, saying that it indicates "the country is ready for change after eight years of failed leadership from President Obama." Noting the decrease in Democratic turnout, Priebus said, "Democrats are saddled with two fundamentally flawed candidates destined to fail in a general election" and that their race has "become a race to the far left."

During a victory speech, Trump told supporters Super Tuesday was "our biggest night" and that he now considered himself "the presumptive nominee," despite still needing approximately 300 more delegates. Trump also attacked Clinton, who had days earlier responded to Trump's assertion that she was playing the woman card. Clinton said, "If fighting for women's health care and paid family leave and equal pay is playing the woman card, then deal me in." In his victory speech, Trump said, "The only card she has is the women's card," adding, "She has got nothing else going. Frankly, if Hillary Clinton were a man, I don't think she would get 5 percent of the vote." Trump went on to add his opinion that Clinton failed to win support from women. While Trump was already focusing on the general election and honing his attacks of Clinton, his opponents Cruz and Rubio were thinking about the upcoming states that they would be more likely to win, particularly their home states of Texas and Florida, respectively. Trump ultimately became the party's presumptive nominee on May 3 after all remaining candidates dropped out of the race.

For the Democrats, Clinton won seven states (Alabama, Arkansas, Georgia, Massachusetts, Tennessee, Texas, and Virginia), and her rival, Sanders, won four states (Colorado, Minnesota, Oklahoma, and Vermont). In her statement on the Super Tuesday results, DNC chair Rep. Debbie Wasserman Schultz, D-Fla., focused on Trump's continued victories, saying it was "hard to imagine an erratic and irrational demagogue" would become president. She added that the Republican Party has continued to alienate Americans with economic policies that favor only the wealthiest Americans, while the two Democratic challengers "offered smart and substantive visions for moving our country forward." In her victory speech, Clinton, who was about 400 delegates shy of the nomination, said, "We will unify our party to win this election and build an America where we can all rise together, an America where we lift each other up instead of tearing each other down." Sanders, who had vowed to stay in the race until the convention, reasserted his position that he would stay until "the last vote is cast" so that he could "fight for a progressive party platform" when the party held its convention in Philadelphia in July.

REPUBLICANS CONVENE IN CLEVELAND

From July 18–21, 2016, the Republicans held their presidential convention in Cleveland, Ohio. A number of prominent Republicans declined to attend the convention in light of Trump's divisive rhetoric, including former presidents George W. Bush and George H. W. Bush, Sen. John McCain, former Massachusetts Governor and 2012 presidential nominee Mitt Romney, and Ohio Governor and 2016 presidential contender John Kasich. In addition, a number of companies, including Apple, UPS, JPMorgan Chase, Ford, and Wells Fargo, refused to sponsor the convention.

There were a total of 2,472 delegates at the convention, of which 1,237, a simple majority, would be required to choose the party's nominee for president and vice president. Trump already had enough delegates heading into the convention; however, there were many questions raised by delegates leading up to the convention regarding whether they were legally bound to support the candidate for which their state had voted. A month before the convention, a group called Delegates Unbound had formed in an effort to convince delegates that they could cast a vote for whichever presidential candidate they wished. The group put forth a proposal before the convention's rules committee, which met a week before the convention, to add a "conscience clause" to the rules that would allow Trump delegates to unbind themselves. After fifteen hours of debate, the committee rejected the proposal and instead included a rule specifically requiring delegates to vote based on the result of their state's primary or caucus. Delegates Unbound took their fight to the convention and attempted to wrangle support to force a roll call vote on the convention rules. The petition required to call such a vote, which had to include the signatures of a majority of delegates from ten states, was submitted the morning of July 18. The petition was not recognized by the presiding officer, who instead forced through the rules by unanimous consent, despite the protests occurring on the floor. Reportedly, the RNC and Trump campaign, in an effort to stop a floor fight, encouraged enough delegates to remove their support of the petition so that it could be declared invalid. The Colorado delegation walked out in protest.

Trump was ultimately nominated on the first ballot with nearly 70 percent of delegates voting for him, the lowest number since the 1976 Republican convention. Indiana Governor Mike Pence was then nominated as the vice presidential candidate. The first night of the convention featured a speech by Trump's wife, Melania, who was heavily criticized for plagiarizing portions of a speech given by Michelle Obama at the 2008 Democratic National Convention. Trump himself spoke on the last night of the convention to accept the nomination and was introduced by his daughter Ivanka, who, along with Trump's other children who spoke throughout the convention, sought to paint him in a softer, more humanizing light. In his speech, Trump portrayed a nation in turmoil. "Our convention occurs at a moment of crisis for our nation. The attacks on our police, and the terrorism in our cities, threaten our very way of life. Any politician who does not grasp this danger is not fit to lead our country," Trump said, adding that "[t]he crime and violence that today afflicts our nation will soon . . . come to an end. Beginning on January 20th, 2017, safety will be restored."

Trump attempted to portray himself as the law and order candidate who would also be a voice for working Americans. According to Trump, "Nobody knows the system better than me, which is why I alone can fix it." Before outlining his vision for America, Trump focused on his opponent and her time as secretary of state, accusing her of being responsible for the rise of the Islamic State of Iraq and the Levant (ISIL) and instability in the Middle East. "This is the legacy of Hillary Clinton: Death. Destruction and terrorism and weakness." Throughout his speech, Trump frequently attacked the current administration and Secretary Clinton for poor judgment that left America on the brink of collapse. The crowd intermittently shouted, "Lock her up" throughout the speech, in reference to Clinton's e-mail scandal, to which Trump responded, "Let's defeat her."

Trump devoted the bulk of his convention acceptance remarks to focal points for his administration, but stopped short of providing details on how he would accomplish many of his goals. Trump promised to protect the nation from terrorism, eliminate crime from America's inner cities, reform the tax code, promote energy growth, provide school choice for all students, protect gun rights, and add new jobs and wealth. Trump argued that he would use "the greatest businesspeople of the world" to rewrite trade deals—both those currently in effect and those in the negotiation phases. One of the candidate's most controversial proposals to build a wall along the U.S.–Mexico border also made its way into the speech, with Trump indicating that the wall would help stop illegal immigration and the crime that comes with it. Trump also promised to "appoint justices to the United States Supreme Court who will uphold our laws and our Constitution."

DEMOCRATS SELECT CLINTON

The week following the Republican convention, the Democratic Party held its nominating event in Philadelphia from July 25–28. Although Clinton went into the convention with enough delegates to be selected as the nominee, Sanders stuck to his promise to his supporters that he would not concede until the votes were counted at the convention. Ultimately, Clinton was chosen as the nominee on the first ballot on July 26 with 59.7 percent of the vote to Sanders's 39.2 percent. A poignant moment came during the roll call vote when Sanders's brother, a delegate in the Democrats Abroad contingent, cast the group's delegates for Sanders. Sen. Tim Kaine, D-Va., was subsequently chosen as the vice presidential nominee.

Much like the Republican convention, the Democrats were unable to escape controversy. In the days leading up to the convention, e-mail from the Democratic National Committee were leaked, and they indicated that the party's leader, Representative Schultz, had been biased toward Clinton. Schultz was ultimately forced to resign as chair of the committee and was replaced by Rep. Marcia Fudge, D-Ohio, as convention chair. There was some talk ahead of the convention, and even on its first day, that Sanders supporters would walk out in protest of Clinton's nomination, but it never came to fruition. In his speech, Sanders called on his supporters to recognize not the loss but rather the work they had done to force the party to accept a more progressive platform that adopted many of the ideas that Sanders had focused on throughout the primaries. A text message ahead of Clinton's speech to supporters from the Sanders campaign explained that Clinton's supporters had been respectful while Sanders spoke and "as a courtesy to Bernie, our campaign would greatly appreciate it if you would extend the same respect during Secretary Clinton's speech." Although Sanders was successful in stopping his supporters from walking out en masse, some held signs of protest while Clinton spoke to accept the nomination, including those reading "No More War" and "No TPP."

Clinton, who had long been panned for an inability to connect with audiences and a cold, calculated demeanor, used the speeches on the first three nights of the convention to paint herself as someone who has long fought for the rights of women and children, and who has worked hard to ensure that every American achieves his or her full potential. Clinton delivered her speech and accepted her nomination on the final night of the convention, making history as the first female candidate nominated by a major political party. "Tonight we've reached a milestone in our nation's march toward a more perfect union," Clinton said, adding that "even more important than the history we make tonight is the history we will write together in the years ahead."

Clinton focused her speech on her belief that the promise in America could never be fully realized if Trump were elected. "He wants to divide us from the rest of the world, and from each other," Clinton said, adding, "He's betting that the perils of today's world will blind us to its unlimited promise." Trump, Clinton said, "wants us to fear the future and fear each other." Instead, Clinton invited those listening to "join us" and promised to work across the aisle for the American people. "In my first 100 days, we will work with both parties to pass the biggest investment in new, good-paying jobs since World War II. Jobs in manufacturing, clean energy, technology and innovation, small business, and infrastructure. If we invest in infrastructure now, we'll not only create jobs today, but lay the foundation for the jobs of the future."

Clinton's speech stuck to key Democratic priorities, including an economy that focuses on building the middle class and lifting people out of poverty, immigration reform, clean energy policies that focus on reducing climate change, expanding Social Security, gun control, and defeating ISIL. In a nod to Sanders's supporters, Clinton said that she would partner with the senator to "make college tuition-free for the middle class and debt-free for all." The Democratic nominee also spoke of her desire to nominate a Supreme Court justice who would "get money out of politics and expand voting rights, not restrict them."

Clinton lobbed harsh criticisms at Trump throughout her speech, saying that "a man you can bait with a tweet is not a man we can trust with nuclear weapons." Speaking directly to Trump's campaign slogan "Make America Great Again," Clinton said, "In the end, it comes down to what Donald Trump doesn't get: America is great because America is good."

—Heather Kerrigan

Following are statements from the RNC and DNC regarding Super Tuesday results, both released on March 1, 2016; the text of the speech given by Donald Trump on July 21, 2016, after accepting the nomination as the Republican presidential nominee; and the text of a speech delivered by Hillary Clinton upon accepting the Democratic presidential nomination on July 29, 2016.

RNC Chair Reince Priebus on Super Tuesday Results

March 1, 2016

While Democrats have seen turnout drop across the board, the record number of Republicans who have gone to the polls in each state shows the country is ready for change after eight years of failed leadership from President Obama. Democrats simply aren't being energized by Hillary Clinton's calculated campaign to maintain the status quo or Bernie Sanders' fringe calls for a socialist "revolution."

The Democrat Primary has become a race to the far left between an embattled front-runner facing an FBI investigation and a self-avowed socialist who continues to win states and outraise the Clinton machine. At the end of the day, Democrats are saddled with two fundamentally flawed candidates destined to fail in a general election and a message that isn't resonating or in line with the majority of Americans.

Source: Republican National Committee. "RNC Statement on Super Tuesday." March 1, 2016. https://gop.com/rnc-statement-on-super-tuesday.

DNC Chair Wasserman Schultz on Super Tuesday

March 1, 2016

As expected, tonight Donald Trump continued to tighten his grip on the Republican nomination. The GOP establishment can try to run away from him, but they were the architects of the ugly and divisive politics that are fueling his rise. Tonight's results mean that a man who wavers on whether or not to disavow the KKK is one step closer to becoming the Republican Party's standard-bearer. It's hard to imagine an erratic and irrational demagogue like Donald Trump picking Supreme Court justices.

Furthermore, the Republican Party's obsession with economically devastating tax cuts for the few at the very top, and their constant obstructionism, have alienated the vast majority of Americans. It's becoming clearer every day that we must elect a Democrat as the 45th President of the United States to keep Republicans from dragging our country backward.

As results continue to come in from across the country, I want to congratulate both of our Democratic presidential candidates and their campaigns for their hard work engaging and energizing voters throughout the Super Tuesday states. Bernie Sanders and Hillary Clinton have campaigned directly on the issues that matter most to the American people. They've offered smart and substantive visions for moving our country forward, and they continue to show that they have the right priorities and the temperament to serve as commander in chief.

SOURCE: Democratic National Committee. "DNC Chair Statement on Super Tuesday." March 1, 2016. http://www.democrats.org/Post/709.

DOCUMENT *Trump Accepts Republican Nomination*

July 21, 2016

[Footnotes have been omitted.]

Friends, delegates and fellow Americans: I humbly and gratefully accept your nomination for the presidency of the United States.

Who would have believed that when we started this journey on June 16, last year, we—I say we because we are a team—would have received almost 14 million votes, the most in the history of the Republican party?

And that the Republican Party would get 60 percent more votes than it received eight years ago. Who would have believed it? The Democrats on the other hand, received 20 percent fewer votes than they got four years ago, not so good.

Together, we will lead our party back to the White House, and we will lead our country back to safety, prosperity, and peace. We will be a country of generosity and warmth. But we will also be a country of law and order.

Our convention occurs at a moment of crisis for our nation. The attacks on our police, and the terrorism in our cities, threaten our very way of life. Any politician who does not grasp this danger is not fit to lead our country.

Americans watching this address tonight have seen the recent images of violence in our streets and the chaos in our communities. Many have witnessed this violence personally. Some have even been its victims.

I have a message for all of you: The crime and violence that today afflicts our nation will soon—and I mean very soon come to an end. Beginning on January 20th 2017, safety will be restored.

The most basic duty of government is to defend the lives of its citizens. Any government that fails to do so is a government unworthy to lead.

It is finally time for a straightforward assessment of the state of our nation. I will present the facts plainly and honestly. We cannot afford to be so politically correct anymore.

So if you want to hear the corporate spin, the carefully-crafted lies, and the media myths—the Democrats are holding their convention next week. Go there.

But here, at our convention, there will be no lies. We will honor the American people with the truth, and nothing else.

These are the facts:

Decades of progress made in bringing down crime are now being reversed by this administration's rollback of criminal enforcement.

Homicides last year increased by 17% in America's fifty largest cities. That's the largest increase in 25 years.

In our nation's capital, killings have risen by 50 percent. They are up nearly 60 percent in nearby Baltimore.

In the president's hometown of Chicago, more than 2,000 have been the victims of shootings this year alone. And almost 4,000 have been killed in the Chicago area since he took office.

The number of police officers killed in the line of duty has risen by almost 50 percent compared to this point last year.

Nearly 180,000 illegal immigrants with criminal records, ordered deported from our country, are tonight roaming free to threaten peaceful citizens.

The number of new illegal immigrant families who have crossed the border so far this year already exceeds the entire total of 2015.

They are being released by the tens of thousands into our communities with no regard for the impact on public safety or resources.

One such border-crosser was released and made his way to Nebraska. There, he ended the life of an innocent young girl named Sarah Root. She was 21 years old and was killed the day after graduating from college with a 4.0 grade point average. Her killer was then released a second time, and he is now a fugitive from the law. I've met Sarah's beautiful family. But to this administration, their amazing daughter was just one more American life that wasn't worth protecting. One more child to sacrifice on the altar of open borders.

What about our economy? Again, I will tell you the plain facts that have been edited out of your nightly news and your morning newspaper:

Nearly four in 10 African-American children are living in poverty, while 58% of African-American youth are now not employed.

2 million more Latinos are in poverty today than when the president took his oath of office eight years ago.

Another 14 million people have left the workforce entirely.

Household incomes are down more than $4,000 since the year 2000. That is 16 years ago.

Our trade deficit in goods reached—think of this—our trade deficit is $800 hundred billion dollars. Think of that. $800 billion last year alone. We will fix that.

The budget is no better. President Obama has almost doubled our national debt to more than $19 trillion, and growing.

Yet, what do we have to show for it? Our roads and bridges are falling apart, our airports are in third world condition, and 43 million Americans are on food stamps.

Now let us consider the state of affairs abroad. Not only have our citizens endured domestic disaster, but they have lived through one international humiliation after another. One after another.

We all remember the images of our sailors being forced to their knees by their Iranian captors at gunpoint. This was just prior to the signing of the Iran deal, which gave back to Iran $150 billion and gave us absolutely nothing. It will go down in history as one of the worst deals ever negotiated.

Another humiliation came when President Obama drew a red line in Syria and the whole world knew it meant absolutely nothing.

In Libya, our consulate, the symbol of American prestige around the globe was brought down in flames.

America is far less safe and the world is far less stable than when Obama made the decision to put Hillary Clinton in charge of America's foreign policy. I am certain it is a decision he truly regrets.

Her bad instincts and her bad judgment, something pointed out by Bernie Sanders are what caused the disasters unfolding today. Let's review the record.

In 2009, pre-Hillary, ISIS was not even on the map. Libya was stable. Egypt was peaceful. Iraq had seen a big reduction in violence. Iran was being choked by sanctions. Syria was somewhat under control.

After four years of Hillary Clinton, what do we have? ISIS has spread across the region and the entire world. Libya is in ruins, and our ambassador and his staff were left helpless to die at the hands of savage killers. Egypt was turned over to the radical Muslim Brotherhood, forcing the military to retake control. Iraq is in chaos. Iran is on the path to nuclear weapons. Syria is engulfed in a civil war and a refugee crisis that now threatens the West. After 15 years of wars in the Middle East, after trillions of dollars spent and thousands of lives lost, the situation is worse than it has ever been before.

This is the legacy of Hillary Clinton: Death, destruction and terrorism and weakness.

But Hillary Clinton's legacy does not have to be America's legacy. The problems we face now—poverty and violence at home, war and destruction abroad—will last only as long as we continue relying on the same politicians who created them. A change in leadership is required to produce a change in outcomes.

Tonight, I will share with you for action for America. The most important difference between our plan and that of our opponents, is that our plan will put America first. Americanism, not globalism, will be our credo.

As long as we are led by politicians who will not put America first, then we can be assured that other nations will not treat America with respect. The respect that we deserve. The American people will come first once again.

First, my plan will begin with safety at home which means safe neighborhoods, secure borders, and protection from terrorism. There can be no prosperity without law and order.

On the economy, I will outline reforms to add millions of new jobs and trillions in new wealth that can be used to rebuild America.

A number of these reforms that I will outline tonight will be opposed by some of our nation's most powerful special interests. That is because these interests have rigged our political and economic system for their exclusive benefit. Believe me. It is for their benefit. For their benefit.

Big business, elite media and major donors are lining up behind the campaign of my opponent because they know she will keep our rigged system in place. They are throwing money at her because they have total control over every single thing she does. She is their puppet, and they pull the strings. That is why Hillary Clinton's message is that things will never change. Never ever.

My message is that things have to change and they have to change right now. Every day I wake up determined to deliver a better life for the people all across this nation that had been ignored, neglected and abandoned.

I have visited the laid-off factory workers, and the communities crushed by our horrible and unfair trade deals. These are the forgotten men and women of our country, and they are forgotten, but they will not be forgotten long. These are people who work hard but no longer have a voice. I am your voice.

I have embraced crying mothers who have lost their children because our politicians put their personal agendas before the national good.

I have no patience for injustice. No tolerance for government incompetence. When innocent people suffer, because our political system lacks the will, or the courage, or the basic decency to enforce our laws, or worse still, has sold out to some corporate lobbyist for cash I am not able to look the other way. And I won't look the other way.

And when a Secretary of State illegally stores her emails on a private server, deletes 33,000 of them so the authorities can't see her crime, puts our country at risk, lies about it in every different form and faces no consequence—I know that corruption has reached a level like never ever before in our country.

When the FBI director says that the Secretary of State was "extremely careless" and "negligent" in handling our classified secrets, I also know that these terms are minor compared to what she actually did. They were just used to save her from facing justice for her terrible, terrible crimes.

In fact, her single greatest accomplishment may be committing such an egregious crime and getting away with it, especially when others who have been far less have paid so dearly.

When that same Secretary of State rakes in millions of dollars trading access and favors to special interests and foreign powers, I know the time for action has come.

I have joined the political arena so that the powerful can no longer beat up on people that cannot defend themselves.

Nobody knows the system better than me, which is why I alone can fix it. I have seen firsthand how the system is rigged against our citizens, just like it was rigged against Bernie Sanders. He never had a chance.

But his supporters will join our movement, because we will fix his biggest issue: Trade deals that strip our country of jobs and the distribution of wealth in the country.

Millions of Democrats will join our movement, because we are going to fix the system so it works fairly and justly for each and every American.

In this cause, I am proud to have at my side the next Vice President of the United States: Governor Mike Pence of Indiana. And a great guy. We will bring the same economic success to America that Mike brought Indiana, which is amazing. He is a man of character and accomplishment. He is the right man for the job.

The first task for our new administration will be to liberate our citizens from the crime and terrorism and lawlessness that threatens their—our communities.

America was shocked to its core when our police officers in Dallas were so brutally executed. Immediately after Dallas, we have seen continued threats and violence against our law enforcement officials. Law officers have been shot or killed in recent days in Georgia, Missouri, Wisconsin, Kansas, Michigan and Tennessee.

On Sunday, more police were gunned down in Baton Rouge, Louisiana. Three were killed, and three were very badly injured. An attack on law enforcement is an attack on all Americans.

I have a message to every last person threatening the peace on our streets and the safety of our police: When I take the oath of office next year, I will restore law and order to our country.

I will work with, and appoint, the best prosecutors and law enforcement officials in the country to get the job properly done. In this race for the White House, I am the law and order candidate.

The irresponsible rhetoric of our president, who has used the pulpit of the presidency to divide us by race and color, has made America a more dangerous environment than frankly, I have ever seen and anybody in this room has ever watched or seeing.

This administration has failed America's inner cities. Remember, it has failed America's inner cities. It's failed them on education. It's failed them on jobs. It's failed them on crime. It's failed them in every way and on every single level.

When I am president, I will work to ensure that all of our kids are treated equally, and protected equally. Every action I take, I will ask myself: Does this make life better for young Americans in Baltimore, Chicago, Detroit, and Ferguson who have really come in every way, have the same right to live out their dreams as any other child in America?

To make life safe in America, we must also address the growing threats from outside the country. We are going to defeat the barbarians of ISIS. And we are going to defeat them bad.

Once again, France is the victim of brutal Islamic terrorism. Men, women and children viciously mowed down. Lives ruined. Families ripped apart. A nation in mourning. The damage and devastation that can be inflicted by Islamic radicals has been proven over and over. At the World Trade Center, at an office party in San Bernardino, at the Boston Marathon, and a military recruiting center in Chattanooga, Tennessee. And many other locations.

Only weeks ago, in Orlando, Florida, 49 wonderful Americans were savagely murdered by an Islamic terrorist. This time, the terrorist targeted LGBTQ community.

No good. And we're going to stop it. As your president, I will do everything in my power to protect our LGBTQ citizens from the violence and oppression of a hateful foreign ideology. Believe me. And I have to say as a Republican, it is so nice to hear you cheering for what I just said. Thank you.

To protect us from terrorism, we need to focus on three things.

We must have the best, absolutely the best, gathering of intelligence anywhere in the world. The best.

We must abandon the failed policy of nation-building and regime change that Hillary Clinton pushed in Iraq, Libya, in Egypt, and Syria.

Instead, we must work with all of our allies who share our goal of destroying ISIS and stamping out Islamic terrorism and doing it now, doing it quickly. We're going to win. We're going to win fast. This includes working with our greatest ally in the region, the state of Israel.

Recently I have said that NATO was obsolete. Because it did not properly cover terror. And also that many of the member countries were not paying their fair share. As usual, the United States has been picking up the cost. Shortly thereafter, it was announced that NATO will be setting up a new program in order to combat terrorism. A true step in the right direction.

Lastly, and very importantly, we must immediately suspend immigration from any nation that has been compromised by terrorism until such time as proven vetting mechanisms have been put in place. We don't want them in our country.

My opponent has called for a radical 550 percent increase—think of this, this is not believable, but this is what is happening—a 550 percent increase in Syrian refugees on top of existing massive refugee flows coming into our country already under the leadership of president Obama.

She proposes this despite the fact that there's no way to screen these refugees in order to find out who they are or where they come from. I only want to admit individuals into our country who will support our values and love our people. Anyone who endorses violence, hatred or oppression is not welcome in our country and never ever will be.

Decades of record immigration have produced lower wages and higher unemployment for our citizens, especially for African-American and Latino workers. We are going to have an immigration system that works, but one that works for the American people.

On Monday, we heard from three parents whose children were killed by illegal immigrants Mary Ann Mendoza, Sabine Durden, and my friend Jamiel Shaw. They are just three brave representatives of many thousands who have suffered so greatly.

Of all my travels in this country, nothing has affected me more, nothing even close than the time I have spent with the mothers and fathers who have lost their children to violence spilling across our borders, which we can solve. We have to solve it. These families have no special interests to represent them. There are no demonstrators to protect them and none too protest on their behalf.

My opponent will never meet with them, or share in their pain. Believe me. Instead, my opponent wants sanctuary cities. But where was sanctuary for Kate Steinle? Where was sanctuary for the children of Mary Ann, Sabine and Jamiel? Is so sad to even be talking about this. We can solve it so quickly. Where was sanctuary for all the other Americans who have been so brutally murdered, and who have suffered so horribly? These wounded American families have been alone. But they are not alone any longer.

Tonight, this candidate and this whole nation stand in their corner to support them, to send them our love, and to pledge in their honor that we will save countless more families from suffering the same awful fate.

We are going to build a great border wall to stop illegal immigration, to stop the gangs and the violence, and to stop the drugs from pouring into our communities.

I have been honored to receive the endorsement of America's Border Patrol agents, and will work directly with them to protect the integrity of our lawful, lawful, immigration system.

By ending catch-and-release on the border, we will stop the cycle of human smuggling and violence. Illegal border crossings will go down. We will stop it. It will not be happening very much anymore. Believe me.

Peace will be restored by enforcing the rules for the millions who overstay their visas, our laws will finally receive the respect they deserve.

Tonight, I want every American whose demands for immigration security have been denied and every politician who has denied them to listen very closely to the words I am about to say: On January 20 of 2017, the day I take the oath of office, Americans will finally wake up in a country where the laws of the United States are enforced.

We are going to be considerate and compassionate to everyone. But my greatest compassion will be for our own struggling citizens.

My plan is the exact opposite of the radical and dangerous immigration policy of Hillary Clinton. Americans want relief from uncontrolled immigration. Which is what we have now. Communities want relief. Yet Hillary Clinton is proposing mass amnesty, mass immigration, and mass lawlessness.

Her plan will overwhelm your schools and hospitals, further reduce your jobs and wages, and make it harder for recent immigrants to escape from the tremendous cycle of poverty they are going through right now and make it almost impossible for them to join the middle class.

I have a different vision for our workers. It begins with a new, fair trade policy that protects our jobs and stands up to countries that cheat—of which there are many.

It's been a signature message of my campaign from day one, and it will be a signature feature of my presidency from the moment I take the oath of office. I have made billions of dollars in business making deals. Now I'm going to make our country rich again. Using the greatest businesspeople of the world, I'm going to turn our bad trade agreements into great trade agreements.

America has lost nearly-one third of its manufacturing jobs since 1997, following the enactment of disastrous trade deals supported by bill and Hillary Clinton. Remember, it was Bill Clinton who signed NAFTA, one of the worst economic deals ever made by our country. Or frankly, any other country. Never ever again.

I am going to bring our jobs back our jobs to Ohio and Pennsylvania and New York and Michigan and all of America and I am not going to let companies move to other countries, firing their employees along the way, without consequences. Not going to happen anymore.

My opponent, on the other hand, has supported virtually every trade agreement that has been destroying our middle class. She supported NAFTA, and she supported China's entrance into the world trade organization. Another one of her husband's colossal mistakes and disasters. She supported the job killing trade deal with South Korea. She supported the Trans-Pacific Partnership which will not only destroy our manufacturing but it will make America subject to the rulings of foreign governments. And it is not going to happen.

I pledge to never sign any trade agreement that hurts our workers, or that diminishes our freedom and Independence. We will never ever sign bad trade deals. America first again. American first.

Instead, I will make individual deals with individual countries. No longer will we enter into these massive transactions with many countries that are thousands of pages long and which no one from our country even reads or understands. We are going to enforce all trade violations against any country that cheats. This includes stopping China's outrageous theft of intellectual property, along with their illegal product dumping, and their devastating currency manipulation. They are the greatest that ever came about, they are the greatest currently manipulators ever.

Our horrible trade agreements with China, and many others, will be totally renegotiated. That includes renegotiating NAFTA to get a much better deal for America and will walk away if we don't get that kind of a deal. Our country is going to start building and making things again.

Next comes the reform of our tax laws, regulations and energy rules. While Hillary Clinton plans a massive, and I mean massive, tax increase, I have proposed the largest tax reduction of any candidate who has run for president this year, Democrat or Republican. Middle-income Americans will experience profound relief, and taxes will be greatly simplified for everyone. I mean everyone.

America is one of the highest-taxed nations in the world. Reducing taxes will cause new companies and new jobs to come roaring back into our country. Believe me. It will happen and it will happen fast.

Then we are going to deal with the issue of regulation, one of the greatest job killers of them all. Excessive regulation is costing our country as much as $2 trillion a year, and we will end and it very quickly.

We are going to lift the restrictions on the production of American energy. This will produce more than $20 trillion in job-creating economic activity over the next four decades.

My opponent, on the other hand, wants to put the great miners and steelworkers of our country out of work and out of business. That will never happen with Donald J trump as president. Our steelworkers and are miners are going back to work again.

With these new economic policies, trillions of dollars will start flowing into our country. This new wealth will improve the quality of life for all Americans. We will build the roads, highways, bridges, tunnels, airports, and the railways of our tomorrow. This, in turn, will create millions of more jobs.

We will rescue kids from failing schools by helping their parents send them to a safe school of their choice. My opponent would rather protect education bureaucrats than serve American children. That is what she is doing and that is what she has done.

We will repeal and replace disastrous Obamacare. You will be able to choose your own doctor again.

And we will fix TSA at the airports, which is a total disaster. Thank you.

We are going to work with all of our students who are drowning in debt to take the pressure off these young people just starting out in their adult lives. Tremendous problems.

We will completely rebuild our depleted military. And the countries that we protecting at a massive cost to us will be asked to pay their fair share.

We will take care of our great veterans like they have never been taken care of before. My just-released 10 point plan has received tremendous better support. We will guarantee those who serve this country will be able to visit the doctor or hospital of their choice without waiting five days in a line and dying.

My opponent dismissed the VA scandal, one more sign of how out of touch she really is.

We are going to ask every department head and government to provide a list of wasteful spending projects that we can eliminate in my first 100 days. The politicians have talked about this for years, but I'm going to do it.

We are also going to appoint justices to the United States Supreme Court who will uphold our laws and our constitution. The replacement of our beloved Justice Scalia will be a person of similar views, principles and judicial philosophies. Very important. This will be one of the most important issues decided by this election.

My opponent wants to essentially abolish the 2nd Amendment. I, on the other hand, received the early and strong endorsement of the National Rifle Association. And will protect the right of all Americans to keep their families safe.

At this moment, I would like to thank the evangelical community because, I will tell you what, the support they have given me—and I'm not sure I totally deserve it—has been so amazing. And has been such a big reason I'm here tonight. They have much to contribute to our policies.

Yet our laws prevent you from speaking your mind from your own pulpits. An amendment, pushed by Lyndon Johnson, many years ago, threatens religious institutions with a loss of their tax-exempt status if they openly advocate their political views. Their voice has been taken away. I will work hard to repeal that language and to protect free speech for all Americans.

We can accomplish these great things and so much more. All we need to do is start believing in ourselves a in our country again. Start believing. It is time to show the whole world that America is back, bigger and better and stronger than ever before.

In this journey, I'm so lucky to have at my side my wife Melania and my wonderful children Don, Ivanka, Eric, Tiffany, and Barron: You will always be my greatest source of pride and joy. And by the way, Melania and Ivanka, did they do a job?

My dad, Fred Trump, was the smartest and hardest working man I ever knew. I wonder sometimes what he'd say if he were here to see this tonight. It's because of him that I learned, from my youngest age, to respect the dignity of work and the dignity of working people.

He was a guy most comfortable in the company of bricklayers, carpenters, and electricians and I have a lot of that in me also. I love those people.

Then there's my mother, Mary. She was strong, but also warm and fair-minded. She was a truly great mother. She was also one of the most honest and charitable people I have ever known, and a great, great judge of character. She could pick them out from anywhere.

To my sisters, Mary Anne and Elizabeth, my brother Robert and my late brother Fred, I will always give you my love. You are most special to me. I have loved my life in business.

But now, my sole and exclusive mission is to go to work for our country, to go to work for you. It is time to deliver a victory for the American people. We don't win anymore, but we are going to start winning again. But to do that, we must break free from the petty politics of the past.

America is a nation of believers, dreamers, and strivers that is being led by a group of censors, critics, and cynics. Remember: All of the people telling you can't have the country you want, are the same people, that would not stand, I mean they said Trump does not have a chance of being here tonight, not a chance, the same people. We love defeating those people, don't we? Love it.

No longer can we rely on those same people. In the media and politics who, will say anything to keep a rigged system in place. Instead, we must choose to believe in America.

History is watching us now. It's we don't have much time. We don't have much time. It's waiting to see if we will rise to the occasion, and if we will show the whole world that America is still free and independent and strong.

I am asking for your support tonight so that I can be year champion in the White House. And I will be a champion. Your champion.

My opponent asks her supporters to recite a three-word loyalty pledge. It reads: "I'm with her."

I choose to recite a different pledge. My pledge reads: "I'm with you the American people."

I am your voice. So to every parent who dreams for their child, and every child who dreams for their future, I say these words to you tonight: I'm with you, and I will fight for you, and I will win for you.

To all Americans tonight, in all our cities and towns, I make this promise:

We will make America strong again.
We will make America proud again.

We will make America safe again.
And we will make America great again!
God bless you and goodnight! I love you!

SOURCE: Donald J. Trump Campaign Website. "Donald J. Trump Republican Nomination Acceptance Speech." July 21, 2016. https://assets.donaldjtrump.com/DJT_Acceptance_Speech.pdf.

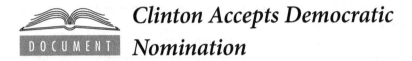

Clinton Accepts Democratic Nomination

July 29, 2016

Thank you. Thank you so much. Thank you. Thank you all so much. Thank you. Thank you. Thank you all very, very much. Thank you for that amazing welcome. Thank you all for the great convention that we've had.

And, Chelsea, thank you. I am so proud to be your mother and so proud of the woman you've become. Thank you for bringing Marc into our family and Charlotte and Aidan into the world.

And, Bill, that conversation we started in the law library 45 years ago, it is still going strong.

That conversation has lasted through good times that filled us with joy and hard times that tested us. And I've even gotten a few words in along the way. On Tuesday night, I was so happy to see that my explainer-in-chief is still on the job. (Applause.) I'm also grateful to the rest of my family and to the friends of a lifetime.

For all of you whose hard work brought us here tonight and to those of you who joined this campaign this week, thank you. What a remarkable week it's been. We heard the man from Hope, Bill Clinton; and the man of hope, Barack Obama. America is stronger because of President Obama's leadership, and I am better because of his friendship.

We heard from our terrific Vice President, the one and only Joe Biden. He spoke from his big heart about our party's commitment to working people as only he can do.

And First Lady Michelle Obama reminded us that our children are watching and the president we elect is going to be their president, too.

And for those of you out there who are just getting to know Tim Kaine, you—you will soon understand why the people of Virginia keep promoting him from city council and mayor, to governor, and now Senator. And he will make our whole country proud as our vice president.

And I want to thank Bernie Sanders. Bernie. Bernie, your campaign inspired millions of Americans, particularly the young people who threw their hearts and souls into our primary. You put economic and social justice issues front and center, where they belong.

And to all of your supporters here and around the country, I want you to know I have heard you. Your cause is our cause. Our country needs your ideas, energy, and passion. That is the only way we can turn our progressive platform into real change for America. We wrote it together. Now let's go out and make it happen together.

My friends, we've come to Philadelphia, the birthplace of our nation, because what happened in this city 240 years ago still has something to teach us today. We all know the story, but we usually focus on how it turned out, and not enough on how close that story came to never being written at all. When representatives from 13 unruly colonies met just down the road from here, some wanted to stick with the king, and some wanted to stick it to the king.

The revolution hung in the balance. Then somehow they began listening to each other, compromising, finding common purpose. And by the time they left Philadelphia, they had begun to see themselves as one nation. That's what made it possible to stand up to a king. That took courage. They had courage. Our founders embraced the enduring truth that we are stronger together.

Now America is once again at a moment of reckoning. Powerful forces are threatening to pull us apart. Bonds of trust and respect are fraying. And just as with our founders, there are no guarantees. It truly is up to us. We have to decide whether we will all work together so we can all rise together. Our country's motto is *e pluribus unum*: out of many, we are one. Will we stay true to that motto?

Well, we heard Donald Trump's answer last week at his convention. He wants to divide us from the rest of the world and from each other. He's betting that the perils of today's world will blind us to its unlimited promise. He's taken the Republican Party a long way from "Morning in America" to "Midnight in America." He wants us to fear the future and fear each other.

Well, a great Democratic President, Franklin Delano Roosevelt, came up with the perfect rebuke to Trump more than eighty years ago, during a much more perilous time: "The only thing we have to fear is fear itself."

Now we are clear-eyed about what our country is up against, but we are not afraid. We will rise to the challenge, just as we always have. We will not build a wall. Instead, we will build an economy where everyone who wants a good job can get one. And we'll build a path to citizenship for millions of immigrants who are already contributing to our economy. We will not ban a religion. We will work with all Americans and our allies to fight and defeat terrorism.

Yet, we know there is a lot to do. Too many people haven't had a pay raise since the crash. There's too much inequality, too little social mobility, too much paralysis in Washington, too many threats at home and abroad.

But just look for a minute at the strengths we bring as Americans to meet these challenges. We have the most dynamic and diverse people in the world. We have the most tolerant and generous young people we've ever had. We have the most powerful military, the most innovative entrepreneurs, the most enduring values—freedom and equality, justice and opportunity. We should be so proud that those words are associated with us. I have to tell you, as your Secretary of State, I went to 112 countries. When people hear those words, they hear America.

So don't let anyone tell you that our country is weak. We're not. Don't let anyone tell you we don't have what it takes. We do. And most of all, don't believe anyone who says, "I alone can fix it." Yes. Those were actually Donald Trump's words in Cleveland. And they should set off alarm bells for all of us. Really? "I alone can fix it? Isn't he forgetting troops on the front lines, police officers and firefighters who run toward danger, doctors and nurses who care for us? Teachers who change lives, entrepreneurs who see possibilities in every problem, mothers who lost children to violence and are building a movement to keep other kids safe? He's forgetting every last one of us. Americans don't say, "I alone fix can it." We say, "We'll fix it together."

And remember. Remember. Our founders fought a revolution and wrote a Constitution so America would never be a nation where one person had all the power. 240 years later, we still put our faith in each other. Look at what happened in Dallas. After the assassinations of five brave police officers, Police Chief David Brown asked the community to support his force, maybe even join them. And do you know how the community responded? Nearly 500 people applied in just 12 days.

That's how Americans answer when the call for help goes out. 20 years ago, I wrote a book called It Takes a Village. And a lot of people looked at the title and asked, what the heck do you mean by that? This is what I mean. None of us can raise a family, build a business, heal a community, or lift a country totally alone. America needs every one of us to lend our energy, our talents, our ambition to making our nation better and stronger. I believe that with all my heart. That's why "Stronger Together" is not just a lesson from our history, it's not just a slogan for our campaign, it's a guiding principle for the country we've always been, and the future we're going to build.

A country where the economy works for everyone, not just those at the top. Where you can get a good job and send your kids to a good school no matter what ZIP Code you live in. A country where all our children can dream, and those dreams are within reach. Where families are strong, communities are safe, and, yes, where love trumps hate. That's the country we're fighting for. That's the future we're working toward. And so, my friends, it is with humility, determination, and boundless confidence in America's promise that I accept your nomination for president of the United States.

Now, sometimes the people at this podium are new to the national stage. As you know, I'm not one of those people. I've been your first lady, served eight years as a senator from the great state of New York. Then I represented all of you as Secretary of State. But my job titles only tell you what I've done. They don't tell you why. The truth is, through all these years of public service, the service part has always come easier to me than the public part. I get it that some people just don't know what to make of me. So let me tell you.

The family I'm from, well, no one had their name on big buildings. My families were builders of a different kind, builders in the way most American families are. They used whatever tools they had, whatever God gave them, and whatever life in America provided, and built better lives and better futures for their kids.

My grandfather worked in the same Scranton lace mill for 50 years because he believed that if he gave everything he had, his children would have a better life than he did. And he was right. My dad, Hugh, made it to college. He played football at Penn State and enlisted in the Navy after Pearl Harbor. When the war was over he started his own small business, printing fabric for draperies. I remember watching him stand for hours over silkscreens. He wanted to give my brothers and me opportunities he never had, and he did.

My mother, Dorothy, was abandoned by her parents as a young girl. She ended up on her own at 14, working as a housemaid. She was saved by the kindness of others. Her first grade teacher saw she had nothing to eat at lunch, and brought extra food to share the entire year. The lesson she passed on to me years later stuck with me: No one gets through life alone. We have to look out for each other and lift each other up. And she made sure I learned the words from our Methodist faith: "Do all the good you can, for all the people you can, in all the ways you can, as long as ever you can."

So I went to work for the Children's Defense Fund, going door to door in New Bedford, Massachusetts on behalf of children with disabilities who were denied the chance to go to school. Remember meeting a young girl in a wheelchair on the small back porch of her house. She told me how badly she wanted to go to school. It just didn't seem possible in those days. And I couldn't stop thinking of my mother and what she'd gone through as a child. It became clear to me that simply caring is not enough. To drive real progress, you have to change both hearts and laws. You need both understanding and action.

So we gathered facts. We build a coalition. And our work helped convince Congress to ensure access to education for all students with disabilities. It's a big idea, isn't it? Every kid with a disability has the right to go to school. But how do you make an idea like that real? You do it step by step, year by year, sometimes even door by door. My heart just swelled when I saw Anastasia Somoza representing millions of young people on this stage because we changed our law to make sure she got an education.

So it's true. I sweat the details of policy, whether we're talking about the exact level of lead in the drinking water in Flint, Michigan the number of mental health facilities in Iowa, or the cost of your prescription drugs. Because it's not just a detail if it's your kid, if it's your family. It's a big deal. And it should be a big deal to your president, too.

After the four days of this convention, you've seen some of the people who've inspired me, people who let me into their lives and became a part of mine, people like Ryan Moore and Lauren Manning. They told their stories Tuesday night. I first met Ryan as a 7-year-old. He was wearing a full body brace that must have weighed 40 pounds because I leaned over to lift him up. Children like Ryan kept me going when our plan for universal health care failed, and kept me working with leaders of both parties to help create the Children's Health Insurance Program that covers eight million kids in our country. Lauren Manning, who stood here with such grace and power, was gravely injured on 9/11.

It was the thought of her, and Debbie Stage. John who you saw in the movie, and John Dolan and Joe Sweeney and all the victims and survivors, that kept me working as hard as I could in the Senate on behalf of 9/11 families and our first responders who got sick from their time at Ground Zero. I was thinking of Lauren, Debbie, and all the others ten years later in the White House Situation Room, when President Obama made the courageous decision that finally brought Osama bin Laden to justice.

And in this campaign I've met many more people who motivate me to keep fighting for change, and with your help, I will carry all of your voices and stories with me to the White House. And you heard from Republicans and Independents who are supporting our campaign. Well, I will be a president for Democrats, Republicans, Independents, for the struggling, the striving, the successful, for all those who vote for me and for those who don't. For all Americans together.

Tonight, we've reached a milestone in our nation's march toward a more perfect union: the first time that a major party has nominated a woman for president. Standing here as my mother's daughter, and my daughter's mother, I'm so happy this day has come. I'm happy for grandmothers and little girls and everyone in between. I'm happy for boys and men—because when any barrier falls in America, it clears the way for everyone. After all, when there are no ceilings, the sky's the limit. So let's keep going until every one of the 161 million women and girls across America has the opportunity she deserves to have. But even more important than the history we make tonight is the history we will write together in the years ahead. Let's begin with what we're going to do to help working people in our country get ahead and stay ahead.

Now, I don't think President Obama and Vice President Biden get the credit they deserve for saving us from the worst economic crisis of our lifetimes. Our economy is so much stronger than when they took office. Nearly 15 million new private sector jobs. Twenty million more Americans with health insurance. And an auto industry that just had its best year ever.

Now, that's real progress. But none of us can be satisfied with the status quo. Not by a long shot. We're still facing deep-seated problems that developed long before the recession and have stayed with us through the recovery. I've gone around the country talking to working families. And I've heard from many who feel like the economy sure isn't working for them. Some of you are frustrated—even furious. And you know what? You're right. It's not yet working the way it should.

Americans are willing to work—and work hard. But right now, an awful lot of people feel there is less and less respect for the work they do. And less respect for them, period. Democrats, we are the party of working people. But we haven't done a good enough job showing we get what you're going through, and we're going to do something to help.

So tonight I want to tell you how we will empower Americans to live better lives. My primary mission as president will be to create more opportunity and more good jobs with rising wages right here in the United States. From my first day in office to my last. Especially in places that for too long have been left out and left behind. From our inner cities to our small towns, from Indian country to coal country. From communities ravaged by addiction to regions hollowed out by plant closures.

And here's what I believe. I believe America thrives when the middle class thrives. I believe our economy isn't working the way it should because our democracy isn't working the way it should. That's why we need to appoint Supreme Court justices who will get money out of politics and expand voting rights, not restrict them. And if necessary, we will pass a constitutional amendment to overturn Citizens United.

I believe American corporations that have gotten so much from our country should be just as patriotic in return. Many of them are, but too many aren't. It's wrong to take tax breaks with one hand and give out pink slips with the other. And I believe Wall Street can never, ever be allowed to wreck Main Street again.

And I believe in science. I believe that climate change is real and that we can save our planet while creating millions of good-paying clean energy jobs.

I believe that when we have millions of hardworking immigrants contributing to our economy, it would be self-defeating and inhumane to try to kick them out. Comprehensive immigration reform will grow our economy and keep families together—and it's the right thing to do.

So whatever party you belong to, or if you belong to no party at all, if you share these beliefs, this is your campaign.

If you believe that companies should share profits, not pad executive bonuses, join us. If you believe the minimum wage should be a living wage, and no one working full-time should have to raise their children in poverty, join us.

If you believe that every man, woman, and child in America has the right to affordable health care, join us! If you believe that we should say no to unfair trade deals; that we should stand up to China; that we should support our steelworkers and autoworkers and homegrown manufacturers, then join us.

If you believe we should expand Social Security and protect a woman's right to make her own heath care decisions, then join us. And yes, yes, if you believe that your working mother, wife, sister, or daughter deserves equal pay join us. That's how we're going to make sure this economy works for everyone, not just those at the top.

Now, you didn't hear any of this, did you, from Donald Trump at his convention. He spoke for 70-odd minutes—and I do mean odd. And he offered zero solutions. But we already know he doesn't believe these things. No wonder he doesn't like talking about his plans. You might have noticed, I love talking about mine.

In my first 100 days, we will work with both parties to pass the biggest investment in new, good-paying jobs since World War II. Jobs in manufacturing, clean energy, technology and innovation, small business, and infrastructure. If we invest in infrastructure now, we'll not only create jobs today, but lay the foundation for the jobs of the future.

And we will also transform the way we prepare our young people for those jobs. Bernie Sanders and I will work together to make college tuition-free for the middle class and debt-free for all. We will also—we will also liberate millions of people who already have student debt. It's just not right that Donald Trump can ignore his debts, and students and families can't refinance their debts.

And something we don't say often enough: Sure, college is crucial, but a four-year degree should not be the only path to a good job. We will help more people learn a skill or practice a trade and make a good living doing it. We will give small businesses, like my dad's, a boost, make it easier to get credit. Way too many dreams die in the parking lots of banks. In America, if you can dream it, you should be able to build it.

And we will help you balance family and work. And you know what, if fighting for affordable child care and paid family leave is playing the "woman card," then deal me in.

Now—now, here's the other thing. Now, we're not only going to make all of these investments. We're going to pay for every single one of them. And here's how. Wall Street, corporations, and the super-rich are going to start paying their fair share of taxes. This is—this is not because we resent success, but when more than 90 percent of the gains have gone to the top 1 percent, that's where the money is. And we are going to follow the money. And if companies take tax breaks and then ship jobs overseas, we'll make them pay us back. And we'll put that money to work where it belongs: creating jobs here at home.

Now, I imagine that some of you are sitting at home thinking, well, that all sounds pretty good, but how are you going to get it done? How are you going to break through the gridlock in Washington? Well, look at my record. I've worked across the aisle to pass laws and treaties and to launch new programs that help millions of people. And if you give me the chance, that's exactly what I'll do as President.

But then—but then I also imagine people are thinking out there, but Trump, he's a businessman. He must know something about the economy. Well, let's take a closer look, shall we? In Atlantic City, 60 miles from here, you will find contractors and small businesses who lost everything because Donald Trump refused to pay his bills. Now, remember what the President said last night. Don't boo. Vote.

But think of this. People who did the work and needed the money, not because he couldn't pay them, but because he wouldn't pay them, he just stiffed them. And you know that sales pitch he's making to be president: put your faith in him, and you'll win big? That's the same sales pitch he made to all those small businesses. Then Trump walked away and left working people holding the bag.

He also talks a big game about putting America first. Well, please explain what part of America First leads him to make Trump ties in China, not Colorado; Trump suits in Mexico, not Michigan; Trump furniture in Turkey, not Ohio; Trump picture frames in India, not Wisconsin. Donald Trump says he wants to make America great again. Well, he could start by actually making things in America again.

Now, the choice we face in this election is just as stark when it comes to our national security.

Anyone—anyone reading the news can see the threats and turbulence we face. From Baghdad and Kabul, to Nice and Paris and Brussels, from San Bernardino to Orlando, we're dealing with determined enemies that must be defeated. So it's no wonder that people are anxious and looking for reassurance, looking for steady leadership, wanting a leader who understands we are stronger when we work with our allies around the world and care for our veterans here at home. Keeping our nation safe and honoring the people who do that work will be my highest priority.

I'm proud that we put a lid on Iran's nuclear program without firing a single shot. Now we have to enforce it, and we must keep supporting Israel's security. I'm proud that we shaped a global climate agreement. Now we have to hold every country accountable to their commitments, including ourselves. And I'm proud to stand by our allies in NATO against any threat they face, including from Russia.

I've laid out my strategy for defeating ISIS. We will strike their sanctuaries from the air and support local forces taking them out on the ground. We will surge our intelligence so we detect and prevent attacks before they happen. We will disrupt their efforts online to reach and radicalize young people in our country. It won't be easy or quick, but make no mistake we will prevail.

Now Donald Trump—Donald Trump says, and this is a quote, "I know more about ISIS than the generals do." No, Donald, you don't.

He thinks—he thinks he knows more than our military because he claimed our armed forces are "a disaster." Well, I've had the privilege to work closely with our troops and our veterans for many years, including as a Senator on the Armed Services Committee. And I know how wrong he is. Our military is a national treasure. We entrust our commander-in-chief to make the hardest decisions our nation faces: decisions about war and peace, life and death. A president should respect the men and women who risk their lives to serve our country, including—including Captain Khan and the sons of Tim Kaine and Mike Pence, both Marines. So just ask yourself: Do you really think Donald Trump has the temperament to be commander-in-chief? Donald Trump can't even handle the rough-and-tumble of a presidential campaign. He loses his cool at the slightest provocation—when he's gotten a tough question from a reporter, when he's challenged in a debate, when he sees a protestor at a rally. Imagine, if you dare imagine, imagine him in the Oval Office facing a real crisis. A man you can bait with a tweet is not a man we can trust with nuclear weapons.

I can't put it any better than Jackie Kennedy did after the Cuban Missile Crisis. She said that what worried President Kennedy during that very dangerous time was that a war might be started—not by big men with self-control and restraint, but by little men, the ones moved by fear and pride.

America's strength doesn't come from lashing out. It relies on smarts, judgment, cool resolve, and the precise and strategic application of power. And that's the kind of commander-in-chief I pledge to be.

And if we're serious about keeping our country safe, we also can't afford to have a president who's in the pocket of the gun lobby. I'm not here to repeal the Second Amendment. I'm not here to take away your guns. I just don't want you to be shot by someone who shouldn't have a gun in the first place.

We will work tirelessly with responsible gun owners to pass common-sense reforms and keep guns out of the hands of criminals, terrorists, and all others who would do us harm.

For decades, people have said this issue was too hard to solve and the politics too hot to touch. But I ask you: How can we just stand by and do nothing? You heard, you saw, family members of people killed by gun violence on this stage. You heard, you saw family members of police officers killed in the line of duty because they were outgunned by criminals. I refuse to believe we can't find common ground here. We have to heal the divides in our country, not just on guns but on race, immigration, and more.

And that starts with listening, listening to each other, trying as best we can to walk in each other's shoes. So let's put ourselves in the shoes of young black and Latino men and women who face the effects of systemic racism and are made to feel like their lives are disposable. Let's put ourselves in the shoes of police officers, kissing their kids and spouses goodbye every day and heading off to do a dangerous and necessary job. We will reform our criminal justice system from end to end, and rebuild trust between law enforcement and the communities they serve. And we will defend—we will defend all our rights: civil rights, human rights, and voting rights; women's rights and workers' rights; LGBT rights and the rights of people with disabilities. And we will stand up against mean and divisive rhetoric wherever it comes from.

For the past year, many people made the mistake of laughing off Donald Trump's comments, excusing him as an entertainer just putting on a show. They thought he couldn't possibly mean all the horrible things he says, like when he called women "pigs" or said that an American judge couldn't be fair because of his Mexican heritage, or when he mocks and mimics a reporter with a disability, or insults prisoners of war—like John McCain, a hero and a patriot who deserves our respect.

Now, at first, I admit, I couldn't believe he meant it, either. It was just too hard to fathom, that someone who wants to lead our nation could say those things, could be like that. But here's the sad truth: There is no other Donald Trump. This is it. And in the end, it comes down to what Donald Trump doesn't get: America is great because America is good.

So enough with the bigotry and the bombast. Donald Trump's not offering real change. He's offering empty promises. And what are we offering? A bold agenda to improve the lives of people across our country—to keep you safe, to get you good jobs, to give your kids the opportunities they deserve.

The choice is clear, my friends. Every generation of Americans has come together to make our country freer, fairer, and stronger. None of us ever have or can do it alone. I know that at a time when so much seems to be pulling us apart, it can be hard to imagine how we'll ever pull together. But I'm here to tell you tonight—progress is possible. I know. I know because I've seen it in the lives of people across America who get knocked down and get right back up.

And I know it from my own life. More than a few times, I've had to pick myself up and get back in the game. Like so much else in my life, I got this from my mother too. She never let me back down from any challenge. When I tried to hide from a neighborhood bully, she literally blocked the door. "Go back out there," she said. And she was right. You have to stand up to bullies. You have to keep working to make things better, even when the odds are long and the opposition is fierce.

We lost our mother a few years ago, but I miss her every day. And I still hear her voice urging me to keep working, keep fighting for right, no matter what. That's what we need to do together as a nation. And though "we may not live to see the glory," as the song from the musical Hamilton goes, "let us gladly join the fight." Let our legacy be about "planting seeds in a garden you never get to see."

That's why we're here, not just in this hall, but on this Earth. The Founders showed us that, and so have many others since. They were drawn together by love of country, and the selfless passion to build something better for all who follow. That is the story of America. And we begin a new chapter tonight.

Yes, the world is watching what we do. Yes, America's destiny is ours to choose. So let's be stronger together, my fellow Americans. Let's look to the future with courage and confidence. Let's build a better tomorrow for our beloved children and our beloved country. And when we do, America will be greater than ever.

Thank you and may God bless you and the United States of America.

SOURCE: Hillary Clinton Campaign Website. "Remarks at the Democratic National Convention." July 29, 2016. http://www.hillaryclinton.com/speeches/remarks-at-the-democratic-national-convention.

OTHER HISTORIC DOCUMENTS OF INTEREST

FROM THIS VOLUME

FROM PREVIOUS *HISTORIC DOCUMENTS*

NASA Announces Milestones in Human Spaceflight and Space Exploration

MARCH 2, MAY 10, AND JULY 5, 2016

The National Aeronautics and Space Administration (NASA) marked a number of firsts in manned spaceflight and space exploration in 2016. From celebrating the return of the first American astronaut to complete a year-long mission in space, to discovering hundreds of new planets and beginning the first in-depth exploration of Jupiter, NASA's achievements present new opportunities to study our solar system and the broader universe and will inform the agency's efforts to send astronauts to Mars and beyond.

THE ONE-YEAR MISSION

On March 1, American astronaut Scott Kelly and Russian cosmonaut Mikhail Kornienko returned to Earth after spending 340 days aboard the International Space Station (ISS) to complete NASA and Roscosmos's joint One-Year Mission. Double the length of NASA's typical manned space flights, the mission made Kelly the first American to spend a year in space continuously, and also set a new record for total days spent in space—520—by a U.S. astronaut.

The mission was part of NASA's Human Research Program, which works to identify the best methods and technologies for supporting safe and productive human space travel. The program was developed in 2004, because NASA shifted its focus to exploring more distant parts of the solar system and sending manned spacecraft on longer missions, with the ultimate goal of traveling to Mars and beyond. NASA has set a goal of sending a manned spacecraft to Mars in the 2030s, and it is expected to take approximately one year to make the round trip from Earth to Mars. Human Research Program scientists study all aspects of human space travel, from making space food appetizing and ensuring sufficient astronaut nutrition, to the risks of exposure to radiation and other environmental factors over such an extended timeframe.

After arriving at ISS with fellow crewmember and cosmonaut Gennady Padalka in March 2015, Kelly and Kornienko participated in nearly 400 studies and experiments designed to assess the medical, psychological, and biomedical challenges of long-duration spaceflight and inform strategies for mitigating these challenges. Some effects of spaceflight on the human body are well known. For example, astronauts' faces typically swell due to fluid collection and swollen tissue in their head, which in turn puts pressure on their optic nerves and makes it more difficult to see. Astronauts also tend to lose bone and muscle mass while in space because their bodies are not bearing the weight of a person walking in an environment with gravity. However, these effects and how long it may take for an astronaut to recover from them have not been studied over an extended period of time. With the One-Year Mission, NASA sought to collect data about the long-term effects of weightlessness, isolation, radiation, stress on astronauts' bodies, and the amount of time needed to recover from these effects. The tests Kelly and Kornienko underwent included cognition tests, sleep monitoring, neuromapping studies, and journaling analyses to assess their behavioral health; studies of their physical performance, with a focus on bone, muscle, and cardiovascular health; a test to determine whether long-duration spaceflight puts astronauts at a higher risk of atherosclerosis; vision tests; and studies of how they interacted with the ISS environment. The men also tested some of the countermeasures that NASA has designed to reduce health risks and help preserve astronauts' physical and mental well-being during future missions of a similar duration. These included a pair of pants that is designed to pull fluids back down to astronauts' legs, techniques for measuring intracranial pressure, and a flight-compatible strategy for monitoring astronauts' immune systems that involves the collection of blood, urine, and saliva samples.

In addition to its extended length, the One-Year Mission was unique because it involved what NASA dubbed the "Twins Study." Kelly's twin brother, Mark, a retired NASA astronaut, participated in ten of the same studies as Scott, but on Earth. As twins with the same genetic makeup, the Kelly brothers presented an opportunity for scientists to compare the effects of two different environments on the body, down to the cellular level. NASA suggested that this first-of-its-kind study could lead to the development of personalized countermeasures for individual astronauts, since researchers would be using techniques employed in personalized medicine to study the twins' responses. The twins participated in tests that explored how spaceflight may cause changes to organs such as the heart, muscles, and brain; effects of spaceflight on perception, reasoning, decision making, and alertness; dietary differences between the twins and stressors to determine how these factors affect organisms in the twins' guts; how certain genes may be turned on and off as a result of spaceflight; and how radiation, confinement, and other environmental factors cause changes in proteins and metabolites.

Other assignments completed during the mission included testing a new instrument designed to study dark matter and the network capabilities required to operate multiple spacecraft simultaneously. Kelly also conducted three space walks during the mission to perform various upgrade, maintenance, and repair tasks.

NASA continued to collect data on Kelly and Kornienko for at least one year after the date of their return to assess their recovery and potential long-term effects. Many of the samples the men collected while in space will remain on the ISS until a cargo flight can deliver them to Earth.

New Planets Discovered

NASA followed Kelly and Kornienko's return with an announcement on May 10 that its Kepler mission had verified the existence of 1,284 new planets—the largest single finding of planets in history. The discovery came after scientists analyzed images captured by the Kepler space telescope in July 2015. The telescope had identified 4,302 potential planets as it surveyed 150,000 stars in a portion of our galaxy, searching for planets in or near the habitable zone of those stars.

NASA scientists used an automated statistical computation to determine the likelihood that each identified body was an actual planet. The application of this process to such a large group of potential planets was also a first, because similar techniques had only been used on smaller subgroups of planet candidates until that point. Using this computation, scientists found that 1,284 of the bodies found by Kepler had a greater than 99 percent probability of being a planet. NASA reported that another 1,327 candidates were likely to be planets, but would need to be studied further before a final determination could be made since they did not meet the minimum 99 percent probability. Among the verified planets were roughly 550 bodies that, based on their size, scientists hypothesized could be rocky like Earth. Nine of these orbited within their sun's habitable zone, meaning they were far enough from the sun that liquid water could potentially pool on the surface. NASA confirmed in June that the new planets also included the youngest exoplanet ever found. Roughly the size of Neptune, the planet is estimated to be 5 to 10 million years old.

Launched on March 6, 2009, the Kepler telescope is designed to capture what NASA calls the "discrete signals" of faraway planets. These signals are decreases in a planet's brightness, which are observed when the planet passes in front of its star. Capturing these signals enables scientists to identify potential planets, and Kepler is equipped to study those planets' orbits, the properties of the stars they orbit, and the makeup of the planetary systems that are identified.

The Kepler telescope is currently conducting its second mission, which began in 2014. During its first mission, which ended in 2012, the telescope found nearly 5,000 planet candidates, of which more than 1,000 were confirmed. This included Kepler's discovery of the first near-Earth-size planet orbiting a sun's habitable zone, which was verified in the summer of 2015. Named Kepler-452b, it is the smallest planet yet found in the habitable zone of a star similar to our sun, though it is larger than Earth. "We can think of Kepler-452b as an older, bigger cousin to Earth, providing an opportunity to understand and reflect upon Earth's evolving environment," said Jon Jenkins, the Kepler data analysis lead at NASA's Ames Research Center. "It's awe-inspiring to consider that this planet has spent 6 billion years in the habitable zone of its star; longer than Earth. That's substantial opportunity for life to arise, should all the necessary ingredients and conditions for life exist on this planet."

With its second discovery, Kepler has identified a total of 2,325 new planets since its launch, out of a total of 3,200 new planets found to date. As planets are verified, scientists will seek to detect light directly from the planet and obtain a light spectrum that will help them determine what kind of atmosphere the planet has, which in turn will provide clues about whether the planet has life.

Juno Orbits Jupiter

NASA celebrated another milestone in space exploration on July 5, when its Juno spacecraft entered Jupiter's orbit after nearly five years of traveling around our solar system. Launched on August 5, 2011, the Juno mission seeks to study Jupiter and collect information about the planet's interior and how it was formed. Scientists also believe that Jupiter holds clues to understanding the solar system's origin and evolution because Jupiter is comprised of the same gases as the nebula (a giant cloud of gas and dust) that collapsed to form the solar system. The Juno spacecraft's nine science instruments are designed to examine whether Jupiter has a solid core, map the planet's magnetic field, measure substances in the planet's deep atmosphere, and collect observations about the planet's auroras.

Juno project manager Rick Nybakken described the spacecraft's entry into orbit as "a big step and the most challenging remaining in our mission plan." Juno is scheduled to complete thirty-six orbits around Jupiter. The first two orbits will take the spacecraft about fifty-three days to complete, after which an engine burn will be conducted to move Juno into a fourteen-day orbit. Due to the planet's rotation, the spacecraft will pass over a different section of Jupiter during each of its orbits.

The first in-orbit photo of Jupiter was received from Juno on July 10, during the spacecraft's first orbit, and showed atmospheric features such as the Great Red Spot as well as three of Jupiter's four largest moons. Juno completed its first close flyby of the planet on August 27, traveling roughly 2,600 miles above Jupiter's clouds. This flyby produced the first photos of Jupiter's north pole, which was revealed to be bluer than the rest of the planet and lacking the bands typically seen on Jupiter. NASA also found indications that Jupiter's clouds cast shadows, suggesting that the clouds were at a higher altitude than other planetary features. Juno also captured the first images of Jupiter's southern aurora on this flyby as well as radio signals emitted by the aurora, which were later converted into audio and released as an eerie sound clip.

The Juno mission is scheduled to end in February 2018, at which point the spacecraft will effectively self-destruct by flying into the planet.

—Linda Fecteau Grimm

Following is a press release from NASA on March 2, 2016, following astronaut Scott Kelly's return to Earth; a press release from NASA on May 10, 2016, announcing the Kepler mission's verification of new planets; and a press release from NASA on July 5, following the Juno spacecraft's insertion into Jupiter's orbit.

Scott Kelly Returns to Earth
after One-Year Mission

March 2, 2016

NASA astronaut and Expedition 46 Commander Scott Kelly and his Russian counterpart Mikhail Kornienko returned to Earth Tuesday after a historic 340-day mission aboard the International Space Station. They landed in Kazakhstan at 11:26 p.m. EST (10:26 a.m. March 2 Kazakhstan time).

Joining their return trip aboard a Soyuz TMA-18M spacecraft was Sergey Volkov, also of the Russian space agency Roscosmos, who arrived on the station Sept. 4, 2015. The crew touched down southeast of the remote town of Dzhezkazgan.

"Scott Kelly's one-year mission aboard the International Space Station has helped to advance deep space exploration and America's Journey to Mars," said NASA Administrator Charles Bolden. "Scott has become the first American astronaut to spend a year in space, and in so doing, helped us take one giant leap toward putting boots on Mars."

During the record-setting One-Year mission, the station crew conducted almost 400 investigations to advance NASA's mission and benefit all of humanity. Kelly and Kornienko specifically participated in a number of studies to inform NASA's Journey to Mars, including research into how the human body adjusts to weightlessness, isolation, radiation and the stress of long-duration spaceflight. Kelly's identical twin brother, former NASA astronaut Mark Kelly, participated in parallel twin studies on Earth to help scientists compare the effects of space on the body and mind down to the cellular level.

One particular research project examined fluid shifts that occur when bodily fluids move into the upper body during weightlessness. These shifts may be associated with visual changes and a possible increase in intracranial pressure, which are significant challenges that must be understood before humans expand exploration beyond Earth's orbit. The study uses the Russian Chibis device to draw fluids back into the legs while the subject's eyes are measured to track any changes. NASA and Roscosmos already are looking at continuing the Fluid Shifts investigation with future space station crews.

The crew took advantage of the unique vantage point of the space station, with an orbital path that covers more than 90 percent of Earth's population, to monitor and capture images of our planet. They also welcomed the arrival of a new instrument to study the signature of dark matter and conducted technology demonstrations that continue to drive innovation, including a test of network capabilities for operating swarms of spacecraft.

Kelly and Kornienko saw the arrival of six resupply spacecraft during their mission. Kelly was involved in the robotic capture of two NASA-contracted cargo flights—SpaceX's Dragon during the company's sixth commercial resupply mission and Orbital ATK's Cygnus during the company's fourth commercial resupply mission. A Japanese cargo craft and three Russian resupply ships also delivered several tons of supplies to the station.

Kelly ventured outside the confines of the space station for three spacewalks during his mission. The first included a variety of station upgrade and maintenance tasks, including routing cables to prepare for new docking ports for U.S. commercial crew spacecraft. On a second spacewalk, he assisted in the successful reconfiguration of an ammonia cooling system and restoration of the station to full solar power-generating capability. The third spacewalk was to restore functionality to the station's Mobile Transporter system.

Including crewmate Gennady Padalka, with whom Kelly and Kornienko launched on March 27, 2015, 13 astronauts and cosmonauts representing seven different nations (the United States, Russia, Italy, Japan, Denmark, Kazakhstan and England) lived aboard the space station during the yearlong mission.

With the end of this mission, Kelly now has spent 520 days in space, the most among U.S. astronauts. Kornienko has accumulated 516 days across two flights, and Volkov has 548 days on three flights.

Expedition 47 continues operating the station, with NASA astronaut Tim Kopra in command. Kopra, Tim Peake of ESA (European Space Agency) and Yuri Malenchenko of Roscosmos will operate the station until the arrival of three new crew members in about two weeks. NASA astronaut Jeff Williams and Russian cosmonauts Alexey Ovchinin and Oleg Skripochka are scheduled to launch from Baikonur, Kazakhstan, on March 18.

The International Space Station is a convergence of science, technology and human innovation that enables us to demonstrate new technologies and make research breakthroughs not possible on Earth. It has been continuously occupied since November 2000 and, since then, has been visited by more than 200 people and a variety of international and commercial spacecraft. The space station remains the springboard to NASA's next giant leap in exploration, including future missions to an asteroid and Mars.

SOURCE: National Aeronautics and Space Administration. "NASA Astronaut Scott Kelly Returns Safely to Earth after One-Year Mission." March 2, 2016. http://www.nasa.gov/press-release/nasa-astronaut-scott-kelly-returns-safely-to-earth-after-one-year-mission.

NASA Announces Largest Collection of Planets Ever Discovered

May 10, 2016

NASA's Kepler mission has verified 1,284 new planets—the single largest finding of planets to date.

"This announcement more than doubles the number of confirmed planets from Kepler," said Ellen Stofan, chief scientist at NASA Headquarters in Washington. "This gives us hope that somewhere out there, around a star much like ours, we can eventually discover another Earth."

Analysis was performed on the Kepler space telescope's July 2015 planet candidate catalog, which identified 4,302 potential planets. For 1,284 of the candidates, the probability of being a planet is greater than 99 percent—the minimum required to earn the status of "planet." An additional 1,327 candidates are more likely than not to be actual planets, but they do not meet the 99 percent threshold and will require additional study. The remaining 707 are more likely to be some other astrophysical phenomena. This analysis also validated 984 candidates previously verified by other techniques.

"Before the Kepler space telescope launched, we did not know whether exoplanets were rare or common in the galaxy. Thanks to Kepler and the research community, we now know there could be more planets than stars," said Paul Hertz, Astrophysics Division director at NASA Headquarters. "This knowledge informs the future missions that are needed to take us ever-closer to finding out whether we are alone in the universe."

Kepler captures the discrete signals of distant planets—decreases in brightness that occur when planets pass in front of, or transit, their stars—much like the May 9 Mercury transit of our sun. Since the discovery of the first planets outside our solar system more than two decades ago, researchers have resorted to a laborious, one-by-one process of verifying suspected planets.

This latest announcement, however, is based on a statistical analysis method that can be applied to many planet candidates simultaneously. Timothy Morton, associate research scholar at Princeton University in New Jersey and lead author of the scientific paper published in The Astrophysical Journal, employed a technique to assign each Kepler candidate a planet-hood probability percentage—the first such automated computation on this scale, as previous statistical techniques focused only on sub-groups within the greater list of planet candidates identified by Kepler.

"Planet candidates can be thought of like bread crumbs," said Morton. "If you drop a few large crumbs on the floor, you can pick them up one by one. But, if you spill a whole bag of tiny crumbs, you're going to need a broom. This statistical analysis is our broom."

In the newly-validated batch of planets, nearly 550 could be rocky planets like Earth, based on their size. Nine of these orbit in their sun's habitable zone, which is the distance from a star where orbiting planets can have surface temperatures that allow liquid water to pool. With the addition of these nine, 21 exoplanets now are known to be members of this exclusive group.

"They say not to count our chickens before they're hatched, but that's exactly what these results allow us to do based on probabilities that each egg (candidate) will hatch into a chick (bona fide planet)," said Natalie Batalha, co-author of the paper and the Kepler mission scientist at NASA's Ames Research Center in Moffett Field, California. "This work will help Kepler reach its full potential by yielding a deeper understanding of the number of stars that harbor potentially habitable, Earth-size planets—a number that's needed to design future missions to search for habitable environments and living worlds."

Of the nearly 5,000 total planet candidates found to date, more than 3,200 now have been verified, and 2,325 of these were discovered by Kepler. Launched in March 2009, Kepler is the first NASA mission to find potentially habitable Earth-size planets. For four years, Kepler monitored 150,000 stars in a single patch of sky, measuring the tiny, telltale dip in the brightness of a star that can be produced by a transiting planet. In 2018, NASA's Transiting Exoplanet Survey Satellite will use the same method to monitor 200,000 bright nearby stars and search for planets, focusing on Earth and Super-Earth-sized.

Ames manages the Kepler missions for NASA's Science Mission Directorate in Washington. The agency's Jet Propulsion Laboratory in Pasadena, California, managed Kepler mission development. Ball Aerospace & Technologies Corporation operates the flight system, with support from the Laboratory for Atmospheric and Space Physics at the University of Colorado in Boulder.

SOURCE: National Aeronautics and Space Administration. "NASA's Kepler Mission Announces Largest Collection of Planets Ever Discovered." May 10, 2016. http://www.nasa.gov/press-release/nasas-kepler-mission-announces-largest-collection-of-planets-ever-discovered.

DOCUMENT *Juno Spacecraft Orbits Jupiter*

July 5, 2016

After an almost five-year journey to the solar system's largest planet, NASA's Juno spacecraft successfully entered Jupiter's orbit during a 35-minute engine burn. Confirmation that the burn had completed was received on Earth at 8:53 pm. PDT (11:53 p.m. EDT) Monday, July 4.

"Independence Day always is something to celebrate, but today we can add to America's birthday another reason to cheer—Juno is at Jupiter," said NASA Administrator Charlie Bolden. "And what is more American than a NASA mission going boldly where no spacecraft has gone before? With Juno, we will investigate the unknowns of Jupiter's massive radiation belts to delve deep into not only the planet's interior, but into how Jupiter was born and how our entire solar system evolved."

Confirmation of a successful orbit insertion was received from Juno tracking data monitored at the navigation facility at NASA's Jet Propulsion Laboratory (JPL) in Pasadena, California, as well as at the Lockheed Martin Juno operations center in Denver. The telemetry and tracking data were received by NASA's Deep Space Network antennas in Goldstone, California, and Canberra, Australia.

"This is the one time I don't mind being stuck in a windowless room on the night of the Fourth of July," said Scott Bolton, principal investigator of Juno from Southwest Research Institute in San Antonio. "The mission team did great. The spacecraft did great. We are looking great. It's a great day."

Preplanned events leading up to the orbital insertion engine burn included changing the spacecraft's attitude to point the main engine in the desired direction and then increasing the spacecraft's rotation rate from 2 to 5 revolutions per minute (RPM) to help stabilize it.

The burn of Juno's 645-Newton Leros-1b main engine began on time at 8:18 p.m. PDT (11:18 p.m. EDT), decreasing the spacecraft's velocity by 1,212 mph (542 meters per second) and allowing Juno to be captured in orbit around Jupiter. Soon after the burn was completed, Juno turned so that the sun's rays could once again reach the 18,698 individual solar cells that give Juno its energy.

"The spacecraft worked perfectly, which is always nice when you're driving a vehicle with 1.7 billion miles on the odometer," said Rick Nybakken, Juno project manager from JPL. "Jupiter orbit insertion was a big step and the most challenging remaining in our mission plan, but there are others that have to occur before we can give the science team members the mission they are looking for."

Over the next few months, Juno's mission and science teams will perform final testing on the spacecraft's subsystems, final calibration of science instruments and some science collection.

"Our official science collection phase begins in October, but we've figured out a way to collect data a lot earlier than that," said Bolton. "Which when you're talking about the single biggest planetary body in the solar system is a really good thing. There is a lot to see and do here."

Juno's principal goal is to understand the origin and evolution of Jupiter. With its suite of nine science instruments, Juno will investigate the existence of a solid planetary core, map Jupiter's intense magnetic field, measure the amount of water and ammonia in the deep atmosphere, and observe the planet's auroras. The mission also will let us take a giant step forward in our understanding of how giant planets form and the role these titans played in putting together the rest of the solar system. As our primary example of a giant planet, Jupiter also can provide critical knowledge for understanding the planetary systems being discovered around other stars.

The Juno spacecraft launched on Aug. 5, 2011, from Cape Canaveral Air Force Station in Florida. JPL manages the Juno mission for NASA. Juno is part of NASA's New Frontiers Program, managed at NASA's Marshall Space Flight Center in Huntsville, Alabama, for the agency's Science Mission Directorate. Lockheed Martin Space Systems in Denver built the spacecraft. The California Institute of Technology in Pasadena manages JPL for NASA.

SOURCE: National Aeronautics and Space Administration. "NASA's Juno Spacecraft in Orbit Around Mighty Jupiter." July 5, 2016. www.nasa.gov/press-release/nasas-juno-spacecraft-in-orbit-around-mighty-jupiter.

OTHER HISTORIC DOCUMENTS OF INTEREST

FROM PREVIOUS *HISTORIC DOCUMENTS*

President Obama on Historic Visits to Cuba and Hiroshima

MARCH 21 AND MAY 27, 2016

In 2016, President Barack Obama made historic trips to Cuba and Hiroshima, a nation and a city, respectively, that had not been visited by a sitting U.S. president in decades. In Cuba, President Obama celebrated the reopening of diplomatic ties with the island nation and spoke of the ongoing progress being made toward normalizing the relationship between the U.S. and Cuba. In Hiroshima (Obama visited only briefly while traveling for a Group of 7 meeting), the focus was on peace in the world and the further nonproliferation of nuclear weapons. Both of Obama's visits were panned by critics who felt the president was attempting to placate two former enemies of the United States.

Obama Meets with Cuban Leaders

When Obama landed in Cuba in March 2016, he became the first sitting president to visit the country since prior to 1959, when Fidel Castro overthrew the U.S.-friendly regime of Fulgencio Batista. President Obama was there to mark the ongoing effort to normalize relations with the Cuban government, which began two years earlier through a series of secret talks that led to agreements allowing Americans to travel to Cuba (with limitations); reopening of the Cuban embassy in Washington, D.C., and the U.S. embassy in Havana; and laying the groundwork for the lifting of the economic embargo on Cuba.

During his visit, the president and his family toured the streets of Havana's old town, and Obama and his advisers met with Raúl Castro to discuss trade and other activities that were anticipated to begin again as the two countries continued to repair their relationship. The most controversial part of Obama's trip came when he met with political dissidents. Ahead of his trip, Obama said he would carry out that meeting regardless of the opinion of the Cuban government, and, shortly before Obama's arrival, many members of one Cuban antigovernment group, Ladies in White, were arrested. Obama held his meeting on March 22 with activists and opposition leaders for nearly two hours at the U.S. embassy in Havana. "All of the individuals around this table have shown extraordinary courage. They have spoken out on behalf of the issues that they care deeply about," Obama said of those in the meeting, noting that their presence highlights the importance of American leaders listening to the broad spectrum of Cuban people to ensure their needs and desires help shape U.S. policy in Cuba.

Obama and Castro held a joint press conference on March 21 to mark the visit, and topics included in the two leaders' speeches and those addressed by the media ranged from human rights to the trade embargo. Obama said that he came to Cuba "to bury the last remnant of the Cold War in the Americas." He continued, "It is time for us to look forward to the future together—a future of hope." The president explained that the actions necessary for fully normalizing relations "won't be easy, and there will be setbacks. It will take time. But my time here in Cuba renews my hope and my confidence in what the Cuban people will do. We can make this journey as friends, and as neighbors, and as family—together." Obama promised during his remarks that he would fully lift the trade embargo on Cuba, but did not give a deadline for doing so because it requires the approval of Congress, and Republicans have continued to oppose it, believing that it gives a free pass to the communist-run government.

Castro focused primarily on the work toward reestablishing diplomatic and economic ties, saying that the efforts are "beneficial not only for Cuba and the United States, but also for our hemisphere at large." Castro devoted a significant portion of his remarks to the lifting of the economic embargo. "We recognize the position of President Obama and his administration against the blockade and his repeated appeals to Congress to have it removed," Castro said, while calling the president's efforts "insufficient." Castro said that he had discussed with Obama other methods that might be taken to lift some of the economic restrictions. "The blockade stands as the most important obstacle to our economic development and the well-being of the Cuban people," Castro said. Castro also defended Cuba's human rights record. "We defend human rights, in our view civil, political, economic, social, and cultural rights are indivisible, interdependent, and universal." Castro was asked by one member of the media present at the press conference why Cuba has political prisoners. In response, Castro asked, "What political prisoners? Give me a name or names. After this meeting is over, you can give me a list of political prisoners, and if we have those political prisoners, they will be released before tonight ends." This exchange was met by a flood of responses on Twitter of the names of those thought to be held by the state.

Fidel Castro, the former leader of Cuba and Raúl's older brother, made only one official statement ahead of Obama's visit, saying, "I don't trust in the United States' policy, nor have I exchanged a word with them." Castro penned an article in the Communist Party newspaper *Granma* a week after Obama's visit. "We don't need the empire to give us anything," he wrote, and went on to note what Castro considered to be abuses committed by the United States against Cuba, including the Bay of Pigs invasion and the long-standing trade embargo.

PRESIDENT OBAMA VISITS HIROSHIMA

In late May, President Obama made another historic visit, this time to Hiroshima, Japan, where seventy-one years earlier the United States had dropped a nuclear bomb during World War II. Obama had committed to making this visit before the end of his presidency during a trip to Japan in 2009. He was accompanied on his visit by Japanese Prime Minister Shinzo Abe—who would reciprocate the visit in December by visiting Pearl Harbor—and the two delivered remarks and laid wreaths at Peace Memorial Park, nearby ground zero for the bomb explosion that killed at least 140,000. Ahead of his visit, the White House made clear that the president would focus on reconciliation, not responsibility over the war and the bomb. Ben Rhodes, Obama's communications adviser, said that the president would "not revisit the decision to use the atomic bomb at the end of World War II. Instead, he will offer a forward-looking vision focused on our shared future."

"Death fell from the sky and the world was changed," Obama said in his opening remarks. "Why do we come to this place, to Hiroshima? We come to ponder the terrible force unleashed in the not-so-distant past. We come to mourn the dead including over

100,000 Japanese men, women, and children, thousands of Koreans, a dozen Americans held prisoner," he added. Recognizing that "mankind possesses the means to destroy itself," Obama said, "We may not eliminate mankind's capacity to do evil . . . but among those nations like my own that hold nuclear stockpiles, we must have the courage to escape the logic of fear and pursue a world without them." Abe echoed those remarks. "This tragedy must not be allowed to occur again," the Japanese president said, adding, "We are determined to realize a world free of nuclear weapons."

Obama did not offer an apology for the United States' attack seven decades earlier during his remarks. Although some Japanese victim organizations had called for an apology, polls taken in Japan before the visit indicated that there was no longer a belief among the Japanese public at large that an apology was necessary. Similarly, U.S. veteran groups argued against the necessity of apology. Obama instead offered sympathy. "Mere words cannot give voice to such suffering," he said. The bombing of Hiroshima has long been controversial. Some believe that dropping the bomb on Hiroshima, and another on Nagasaki days later, came at a time when Japan was already planning to surrender, while others believe it hastened the end of the war. Japan ultimately surrendered nine days after the Hiroshima bombing.

During his visit, the president met with survivors of the blast. One of the most poignant moments came when Obama hugged a seventy-nine-year-old survivor, Shigeaki Mori, who had for decades searched for the families of twelve American airmen who died in the bombing while they were being held as prisoners of war. Obama said that Mori had "sought out the families of Americans who were killed here because he believed their loss was equal to his own."

In closing his speech, Obama said, "Those who died, they are like us. Ordinary people understand this, I think. They do not want more war. They would rather that the wonder of science be focused on improving life and not eliminating it. . . . The world was forever changed here, but today the children of this city will go through their day in peace. . . . That is a future we can choose, a future in which Hiroshima and Nagasaki are known not as the dawn of atomic warfare but as the start of our own moral awakening."

CRITICISM OF OBAMA VISITS

President Obama's visit to Cuba was widely panned in the United States by those who believe the Cuban government has not yet done enough to provide greater freedoms to its citizens, specifically those who speak out against the government. "President Obama promised to extend a hand to dictators if they were willing to unclench their fists—that has not happened in Cuba," said Rep. Ileana Ros-Lehtinen, R-Fla. Sen. Ted Cruz, R-Tex., a Republican presidential candidate, wrote in a column for *Politico* that Obama had "chosen to legitimize the corrupt and oppressive Castro regime with his presence on the island." President Obama, however, continued to defend his trip, noting his belief that as the United States and Cuba continue to work together to overcome a number of issues, it will slowly help to bring about democratic reforms. "The more that U.S. businesses are engaged there, the more Americans that visit and the more Cuban Americans that visit their families, the more likely we will see the changes we are hoping for," Obama said.

In general, peace groups celebrated Obama's trip to Hiroshima. Criticism of the visit was led by those arguing that President Obama's rhetoric in Japan did not match his actions at home. "His administration has proposed the largest increase in spending on nuclear weapons and their delivery systems in recent history—$1 trillion over 30 years," said Paul Kawika Martin, senior director for policy and political affairs of Peace Action, the country's largest grassroots peace organization. A Pentagon census of the current stockpile of U.S. nuclear weapons confirms this finding. No other president in the post–Cold War world has reduced the U.S. nuclear stockpile less than Obama.

—Heather Kerrigan

Following is the text of President Barack Obama's press conference in Havana with Cuban leader Raúl Castro on March 21, 2016; and the text of President Obama's remarks in Hiroshima with Japanese Prime Minister Shinzo Abe on May 27, 2016.

President Obama's Press Conference with Raúl Castro

March 21, 2016

President Castro. Mr. President Barack Obama, we are pleased to welcome you on this, the first visit of a President of the United States of America to our country in 88 years. We have observed that in the 15 months that have passed since the decision was made to establish our diplomatic relations, we have obtained concrete results. We were able to resume direct postal exchanges, and we signed an agreement to resume commercial flights.

We have signed two memorandums of understanding on the protection of the environment and maritime areas and another one to secure the safety of sea navigation. Today another one will be signed on cooperation in the area of agriculture. At the moment, another set of bilateral instruments are being negotiated to cooperate in such areas as counternarcotics, the safety of commerce and travelers, and health. About this last issue, we have agreed to deepen our cooperation in the prevention and treatment of transmissible diseases such as Zika and nontransmissible chronic diseases, cancer included.

This cooperation is beneficial not only for Cuba and the United States, but also for our hemisphere at large. Following the decisions made by President Obama to modify the application of some aspects of the blockade, Cuban enterprises and their American counterparts are working to identify possible commercial operations that could materialize in the still restrictive framework of existing regulations.

The fact is that some have already materialized, especially in the area of telecommunications, an area in which our country already has a program designed on the basis of its priorities and the necessary technological sovereignty, one that can secure the appropriate use and the service of national interests.

Progress has also been made toward the acquisition of medicines, medical material, and equipment for power generation and environmental protection, these among others. Much more could be done if the U.S. blockade were lifted.

We recognize the position of President Obama and his administration against the blockade and his repeated appeals to Congress to have it removed. The most recent measures adopted by his administration are positive, but insufficient. I have the opportunity to discuss with the President other steps that we think could be taken in order to remove restrictions that remain in force and make a significant contribution to the debunking of the blockade. This is essential because the blockade remains in force and because it contains discouraging elements and intimidating effects and extraterritorial outreach. I put forward to the President some examples on this, showing their negative consequences for both Cuba and other countries.

The blockade stands as the most important obstacle to our economic development and the well-being of the Cuban people. That's why its removal will be of the essence to normalize bilateral relations. And actually, it will also bring benefits to the Cuban émigrés who wish the best for their families and their country. In order to move forward towards normalization, it will also be necessary to return the territory illegally occupied by Guantanamo naval base.

Since they stand as the two main obstacles, these issues were again dealt with in the editorial ran on March 9 by the official newspaper of the Communist Party of Cuba and again only 4 days ago in the press conference offered by our Foreign Minister Bruno Rodriguez, both pieces extensively reported by the media.

Other policies should also be abolished for normal relations to develop between the United States and Cuba. No one should intend to have the Cuban people renounce the destiny it chose in freedom and sovereignty, the same for which it has made enormous sacrifices.

We also discussed international issues, particularly those that could have an impact on regional peace and stability. We had thought to discuss other issues, but we did not have enough time. I had planned to raise our concern over the destabilization some are trying to promote in Venezuela, something which we consider to be counterproductive to the overall situation in the continent. I did not have the chance to raise it with him; I'm raising it here.

Likewise, we talked about the ongoing peace process in Colombia and the efforts to put an end to that conflict. There are profound differences between our countries that will not go away. Since we hold different concepts on many subjects such as political systems, democracy, the exercise of human rights, social justice, international relations, and world peace and stability.

We defend human rights. In our view, civil, political, economic, social, and cultural rights are indivisible, interdependent, and universal. Actually, we find it inconceivable that a government does not defend and ensure the right to health care, education, social security, food provision and development, equal pay, and the rights of children. We oppose political manipulation and double standards in the approach to human rights.

Cuba has much to say and show on this issue. That is why I have reiterated to the President our willingness to continue moving forward with the dialogue on this matter that was already initiated.

On December 17, 2014, as we announced the decision to reestablish diplomatic relations, I said that we should learn the art of coexisting with our differences in a civilized manner. In my remarks to Parliament on July 15, 2015, I said changing everything that needs to be changed is the sovereign and exclusive concern of Cubans. The revolutionary Government is willing to advance toward normalization of relations, for it is convinced that both countries can coexist and cooperate in a civilized manner and for the mutual benefit regardless of existing and future differences and thus contribute to peace, security, stability, development, and equity in our continent and around the world.

Today I reaffirmed that we should exercise the art of civilized coexistence, which involves accepting and respecting differences and preventing these from becoming the center of our relationship. We should instead promote links that can benefit both our countries and peoples while focusing on those things that bring us closer and not on those that pull us apart. We agree that a long and complex path still lies ahead. But what is most important is that we have started taking the first steps to build a new type of relationship, one that has never existed between Cuba and the United States.

Actually, destroying a bridge can be an easy and quick undertaking. However, its solid reconstruction can prove a lengthy and challenging endeavor. After four failed attempts and giving proof of her will and perseverance, on September 2, 2013, American swimmer Diane Nyad managed to cross the Florida Straits, swimming without an antishark cage to protect her.

For that exploit of conquering the geographical distance between our two countries—it was for that exploit that on August 30, 2014, as the national anthems of Cuba and the United States were played, she was presented with the Order of Sport Merits, a decoration awarded by the State Council. Such feat carries a powerful message, one that should serve as an example to our bilateral relations. For it confirms that if she could do it, then we can do it too.

To President Obama, I reiterate our appreciation for his visit and the willingness of the Government of Cuba to continue moving forward in the forthcoming months, for the well-being of our peoples and countries. Thank you very much.

President Obama. Buenas tardes. President Castro, to you, the Cuban Government, and the Cuban people, thank you for the welcome that you have extended to me, to my family, and to my delegation. For more than half a century, the sight of a U.S. President here in Havana would have been unimaginable. But this is a new day—*es un nuevo día*—between our two countries.

. . . With your indulgence, Mr. President, I want to go just briefly off topic because during this weekend, I received news that one of our outstanding United States Armed Servicemembers, Marine Staff Sergeant Louis F. Cardin of Temecula, California, was killed in northern Iraq as we assisted the Iraqi Government in dealing with ISIL, the terrorist organization there. And I just wanted to give my thoughts and prayers to the family there and those who have been injured. It's a reminder that even as we embark on this historic visit, there are U.S. Armed Servicemembers who are sacrificing each and every day on behalf of our freedom and our safety. So I'm grateful to them.

. . . My wife Michelle and I brought our daughters—and by the way, they don't always want to go with us; they're teenagers now. They have friends at home, and they have things to do, but they wanted to come to Cuba because they understood, and we wanted to show them, the beauty of Cuba and its people. We were moved by the Cubans who received us yesterday, smiling and waving, as we drove in from the airport. We were grateful for the opportunity to experience Old Havana and some excellent Cuban food. Our visit to the Cathedral was a reminder of the values that we share, of the deep faith that sustains so many Cubans and Americans. And it also gave me an opportunity to express my gratitude to Cardinal Ortega, who, along with His Holiness Pope Francis, did so much to support the improved relations between our governments. This morning I was honored to pay tribute to José Martí, not only his role in Cuban independence, but the profound words that he wrote and spoke in support of liberty and freedom everywhere.

I bring with me the greetings and the friendship of the American people. In fact, I'm joined on this trip by nearly 40 Members of Congress, Democrats and Republicans. This is the largest such delegation of my Presidency, and it indicates the excitement and interest in America about the process that we've undertaken. These Members of Congress recognize that our new relationship with the Cuban people is in the interest of both nations. I'm also joined by some of America's top business leaders and entrepreneurs because we're ready to pursue more commercial ties, which create jobs and opportunity for Cubans and Americans alike.

And I'm especially pleased that I'm joined on this trip by so many Cuban Americans. For them and for the more than 2 million proud Cuban Americans across the United States, this is a moment filled with great emotion. Ever since we made it easier to travel between our countries, more Cuban Americans are coming home. And for many, this is a time of new hope for the future.

So, President Castro, I want to thank you for the courtesy and the spirit of openness that you've shown during our talks. At our meeting in Panama last year, you said that we're willing to discuss every issue, and everything is on the table. So, with your understanding, my statement will be a little longer than usual.

President Castro always jokes with me about how long Castro brothers' speeches can be. But I'm going to actually go a little longer than you probably today, with your indulgence. We have a half a century of work to catch up on.

Our growing engagement with Cuba is guided by one overarching goal: advancing the mutual interests of our two countries, including improving the lives of our people, both Cubans and Americans. That's why I'm here. I've said consistently, after more than five very difficult decades, the relationship between our governments will not be transformed overnight. We continue, as President Castro indicated, to have some very serious differences, including on democracy and human rights. And President Castro and I have had very frank and candid conversations on these subjects.

The United States recognizes progress that Cuba has made as a nation, its enormous achievements in education and in health care. And perhaps most importantly, I affirmed that Cuba's destiny will not be decided by the United States or any other nation. Cuba is sovereign and rightly has great pride. And the future of Cuba will be decided by Cubans, not by anybody else.

At the same time, as we do wherever we go around the world, I made it clear that the United States will continue to speak up on behalf of democracy, including the right of the Cuban people to decide their own future. We'll speak out on behalf of universal human rights, including freedom of speech and assembly and religion. Indeed, I look forward to meeting with and hearing from Cuban civil society leaders tomorrow.

But as you heard, President Castro has also addressed what he views as shortcomings in the United States around basic needs for people and poverty and inequality and race relations. And we welcome that constructive dialogue as well, because we believe that when we share our deepest beliefs and ideas with an attitude of mutual respect, that we can both learn and make the lives of our people better.

Now, part of normalizing relations means that we discuss these differences directly. So I'm very pleased that we've agreed to hold our next U.S.–Cuba human rights dialogue here in Havana this year. And both of our countries will welcome visits by independent United Nations experts as we combat human trafficking, which we agree is a profound violation of human rights.

Even as we discuss these differences, we share a belief that we can continue to make progress in those areas that we have in common. President Castro, you said in Panama that "we might disagree on something today on which we would agree tomorrow." And that's certainly been the case over the past 15 months and the days leading up to this visit. And today I can report that we continue to move forward on many fronts when it comes to normalizing relations.

We're moving ahead with more opportunities for Americans to travel to Cuba and interact with the Cuban people. Over the past year, the number of Americans coming here has surged. Last week, we gave approval for individual Americans to come here for educational travel. U.S. airlines will begin direct commercial flights this year. With last week's port security announcement, we've removed the last major hurdle to resuming cruises and ferry service. All of which will mean even more Americans visiting Cuba in the years ahead and appreciating the incredible history and culture of the Cuban people.

We're moving ahead with more trade. With only 90 miles between us, we're natural trading partners. Other steps we took last week—allowing the U.S. dollar to be used more widely with Cuba, giving Cubans more access to the dollar in international transactions, and allowing Cubans in the U.S. to earn salaries—these things will do more to create opportunities for trade and joint ventures. We welcome Cuba's important announcement that it plans to end the 10-percent penalty on dollar conversions here, which will open the door to more travel and more commerce. And these steps show that we're opening up to one another.

With this visit, we've agreed to deepen our cooperation on agriculture to support our farmers and our ranchers. This afternoon I'll highlight some of the new commercial deals being announced by major U.S. companies. And just as I continue to call on Congress to lift the trade embargo, I discussed with President Castro the steps we urge Cuba to take to show that it's ready to do more business, which includes allowing more joint ventures and allowing foreign companies to hire Cubans directly.

We're moving ahead with our efforts to help connect more Cubans to the Internet and the global economy. Under President Castro, Cuba has set a goal of bringing Cubans online. And we want to help. At this afternoon's entrepreneurship event, I'll discuss additional steps we're taking to help more Cubans learn, innovate, and do business online. Because in the 21st century, countries cannot be successful unless their citizens have access to the Internet.

We're moving ahead with more educational exchanges. Thanks to the generous support of the Cuban American community, I can announce that my 100,000 Strong in the Americas initiative will offer new opportunities for university students to study abroad: more Americans at Cuban schools and more Cubans at U.S. schools. And going forward, educational grants and scholarships will be available to Cuban students. And in partnership with the Cuban Government, we'll offer more English language training for Cuban teachers, both in Cuba and online.

Now, even as Cubans prepare for the arrival of the Rolling Stones—[laughter]—we're moving ahead with more events and exchanges that bring Cubans and Americans together as well. We all look forward to tomorrow's matchup between the Tampa Bay Rays and the Cuban National Team.

And more broadly, we're moving ahead with partnerships in health, science, and the environment. Just as Cubans and American medical teams have worked together in Haiti against cholera and in West Africa against Ebola—and I want to give a special commendation to Cuban doctors who volunteered and took on some very tough assignments to save lives in West Africa in partnership with us and other nations; we very much appreciate the work that they did—our medical professionals will now collaborate in new areas, preventing the spread of viruses like Zika and leading new research into cancer vaccines. Our governments will also work together to protect the beautiful waters of this region that we share.

And as two countries threatened by climate change, I believe we can work together to protect communities at our low-lying coasts. And we're inviting Cuba to join us and our Caribbean and Central American partners at this spring's regional energy summit in Washington.

And finally, we're moving ahead with our closer cooperation on regional security. We're working to deepen our law enforcement coordination, especially against narcotraffickers that threaten both of our peoples. I want to thank President Castro and the Cuban Government for hosting peace talks between the Colombian Government and the FARC. And we remain optimistic that Colombians can achieve a lasting and just peace. And although we did not have an extensive discussion of Venezuela, we did touch on the subject. And I believe that the whole region has an interest in a country that is addressing its economic challenges, is responsive to the aspirations of its people, and is a source of stability in the region. That is, I believe, an interest that we should all share.

So again, President Castro, I want to thank you for welcoming me. I think it's fair to say that the United States and Cuba are now engaged across more areas than any time during my lifetime. And with every passing day, more Americans are coming to Cuba, more U.S. businesses and schools and faith groups are working to forge new partnerships with the Cuban people. More Cubans are benefiting from the opportunities that this travel and trade bring.

As you indicated, the road ahead will not be easy. Fortunately, we don't have to swim with sharks in order to achieve the goals that you and I have set forth. As you say here in Cuba, *echar para adelante.* Despite the difficulties, we will continue to move forward. We're focused on the future.

And I'm absolutely confident that if we stay on this course, we can deliver a better and brighter future for both the Cuban people and the American people.

So *muchas gracias.* Thank you very much.

[The question and answer portion with members of the media has been omitted.]

SOURCE: Executive Office of the President. "The President's News Conference With President Raul Castro Ruz of Cuba in Havana, Cuba." March 21, 2016. *Compilation of Presidential Documents* 2016, no. 00168 (March 21, 2016). http://www.gpo.gov/fdsys/pkg/DCPD-201600168/pdf/DCPD-201600168.pdf.

President Obama Speaks in Hiroshima

May 27, 2016

President Obama. Seventy-one years ago, on a bright, cloudless morning, death fell from the sky, and the world was changed. A flash of light and a wall of fire destroyed a city and demonstrated that mankind possessed the means to destroy itself.

Why do we come to this place, to Hiroshima? We come to ponder a terrible force unleashed in a not-so-distant past. We come to mourn the dead, including over 100,000 Japanese men, women, and children; thousands of Koreans; a dozen Americans held prisoner. Their souls speak to us. They ask us to look inward, to take stock of who we are and what we might become.

It is not the fact of war that sets Hiroshima apart. Artifacts tell us that violent conflict appeared with the very first man. Our early ancestors, having learned to make blades from flint and spears from wood, used these tools not just for hunting, but against their own kind. On every continent, the history of civilization is filled with war, whether driven by scarcity of grain or hunger for gold, compelled by nationalist fervor or religious zeal. Empires have risen and fallen. Peoples have been subjugated and liberated. And at each juncture, innocents have suffered, a countless toll, their names forgotten by time.

The World War that reached its brutal end in Hiroshima and Nagasaki was fought among the wealthiest and most powerful of nations. Their civilizations had given the world great cities and magnificent art. Their thinkers had advanced ideas of justice and harmony and truth. And yet the war grew out of the same base instinct for domination or conquest that had caused conflicts among the simplest tribes, an old pattern amplified by new capabilities and without new constraints. In the span of a few years, some 60 million people would die: men, women, children no different than us, shot, beaten, marched, bombed, jailed, starved, gassed to death.

There are many sites around the world that chronicle this war: memorials that tell stories of courage and heroism; graves and empty camps that echo of unspeakable depravity. Yet in the image of a mushroom cloud that rose into these skies, we are most starkly reminded of humanity's core contradiction; how the very spark that marks us as a species—our thoughts, our imagination, our language, our tool-making, our ability to set ourselves apart from nature and bend it to our will—those very things also give us the capacity for unmatched destruction.

How often does material advancement or social innovation blind us to this truth. How easily we learn to justify violence in the name of some higher cause. Every great religion promises a pathway to love and peace and righteousness, and yet no religion has been spared from believers who have claimed their faith as a license to kill. Nations arise, telling a story that binds people together in sacrifice and cooperation, allowing for remarkable feats, but those same stories have so often been used to oppress and dehumanize those who are different.

Science allows us to communicate across the seas and fly above the clouds, to cure disease and understand the cosmos. But those same discoveries can be turned into ever-more efficient killing machines.

The wars of the modern age teach this truth. Hiroshima teaches this truth. Technological progress without an equivalent progress in human institutions can doom us. The scientific revolution that led to the splitting of an atom requires a moral revolution as well.

That is why we come to this place. We stand here, in the middle of this city, and force ourselves to imagine the moment the bomb fell. We force ourselves to feel the dread of children confused by what they see. We listen to a silent cry. We remember all the innocents killed across the arc of that terrible war and the wars that came before and the wars that would follow.

Mere words cannot give voice to such suffering, but we have a shared responsibility to look directly into the eye of history and ask what we must do differently to curb such suffering again. Someday the voices of the *hibakusha* will no longer be with us to bear witness. But the memory of the morning of August 6, 1945, must never fade. That memory allows us to fight complacency. It fuels our moral imagination. It allows us to change.

And since that fateful day, we have made choices that give us hope. The United States and Japan forged not only an alliance, but a friendship that has won far more for our people than we could ever claim through war. The nations of Europe built a Union that replaced battlefields with bonds of commerce and democracy. Oppressed peoples and nations won liberation. An international community established institutions and treaties that worked to avoid war and aspire to restrict and roll back and ultimately eliminate the existence of nuclear weapons.

Still, every act of aggression between nations, every act of terror and corruption and cruelty and oppression that we see around the world shows, our work is never done. We may not be able to eliminate man's capacity to do evil, so nations—and the alliances that we've formed—must possess the means to defend ourselves. But among those nations like my own that hold nuclear stockpiles, we must have the courage to escape the logic of fear and pursue a world without them.

We may not realize this goal in my lifetime. But persistent effort can roll back the possibility of catastrophe. We can chart a course that leads to the destruction of these stockpiles. We can stop the spread to new nations and secure deadly materials from fanatics.

And yet that is not enough. For we see around the world today how even the crudest rifles and barrel bombs can serve up violence on a terrible scale. We must change our mindset about war itself: to prevent conflict through diplomacy and strive to end conflicts after they've begun; to see our growing interdependence as a cause for peaceful cooperation and not violent competition; to define our nations not by our capacity to destroy, but by what we build.

And perhaps above all, we must reimagine our connection to one another as members of one human race. For this, too, is what makes our species unique. We're not bound by genetic code to repeat the mistakes of the past. We can learn. We can choose. We can tell our children a different story: one that describes a common humanity, one that makes war less likely and cruelty less easily accepted.

We see these stories in the *hibakusha*: the woman who forgave a pilot who flew the plane that dropped the atomic bomb, because she recognized that what she really hated was war itself; the man who sought out families of Americans killed here, because he believed their loss was equal to his own.

My own Nation's story began with simple words: All men are created equal and endowed by our Creator with certain unalienable rights, including life, liberty, and the pursuit of happiness. Realizing that ideal has never been easy, even within our own borders, even among our own citizens.

But staying true to that story is worth the effort. It is an ideal to be strived for, an ideal that extends across continents and across oceans. The irreducible worth of every person, the insistence that every life is precious, the radical and necessary notion that we are part of a single human family—that is the story that we all must tell.

That is why we come to Hiroshima. So that we might think of people we love: the first smile from our children in the morning, the gentle touch from a spouse over the kitchen table, the comforting embrace of a parent. We can think of those things and know that those same precious moments took place here 71 years ago. Those who died, they are like us. Ordinary people understand this, I think. They do not want more war. They would rather that the wonders of science be focused on improving life and not eliminating it.

When the choices made by nations, when the choices made by leaders, reflect this simple wisdom, then the lesson of Hiroshima is done.

The world was forever changed here. But today, the children of this city will go through their day in peace. What a precious thing that is. It is worth protecting and then extending to every child. That is the future we can choose, a future in which Hiroshima and Nagasaki are known not as the dawn of atomic warfare, but as the start of our own moral awakening.

Prime Minister Abe. Last year, at the 70th anniversary of the end of war, I visited the United States and made a speech as Prime Minister of Japan at a joint meeting of the U.S. Congress. That war deprived many American youngsters of their dreams and futures. Reflecting upon such harsh history, I offered my eternal condolences to all the American souls that were lost during World War II. I expressed gratitude and respect for all the people in both Japan and the United States who have been committed to reconciliation for the past 70 years.

Seventy years later, enemies who fought each other so fiercely have become friends, bonded in spirit, and have become allies, bound in trust and friendship, deep between us. The Japan–U.S. alliance, which came into the world this way, has to be an alliance of hope for the world.

So I appealed in the speech. One year has passed since then. This time, President Obama, for the first time as leader of the United States, paid a visit to Hiroshima, the city which suffered the atomic bombing. U.S. President witnessing the reality of atomic bombings and renewing his determination for a world free of nuclear weapons, this gives great hope to people all around the world who have never given up their hope for a world without nuclear weapons.

I would like to give a wholehearted welcome to this historic visit, which had been awaited not only by the people of Hiroshima, but also by all the Japanese people. I express my sincere respect to the decision and courage of President Obama. With his decision and courage, we are opening a new chapter to the reconciliation of Japan and the United States and in our history of trust and friendship.

A few minutes ago, together, I and President Obama offered our deepest condolences for all those who lost their lives during World War II and also by the atomic bombings. Seventy-one years ago in Hiroshima and in Nagasaki, a great number of innocent citizens' lives were cost by a single atomic bomb without mercy. Many children and many citizens perished. Each one of them had his or her lifedream and beloved family. When I reflect on this sheer fact, I cannot help, but feel painful grief.

Even today, there are victims who are still suffering unbearably from the bombings. Feeling of those who went through unimaginable tragic experiences, indeed, in this city 71 years ago, it is unspeakable. In their minds, various feelings must have come and gone, but of those, this must be in common: At any place in the world, this tragedy must not be repeated again.

It is the responsibility of us who live in the present to firmly inherit these deep feelings. We are determined to realize a world free of nuclear weapons. No matter how long and how difficult the road will be, it is the responsibility of us who live in the present to continue to make efforts.

Children who were born on that unforgettable day lit the light believing in permanent peace. To make every effort for the peace and prosperity in the world, vowing for this light, this is the responsibility of us all who live in the present. We will definitely fulfill our responsibility.

Together, Japan and the United States will become a light for hope, for the people in the world. Standing in this city, I am firmly determined, together with President Obama. This is the only way to respond to the feelings of the countless spirits: victims of the atomic bombs in Hiroshima and Nagasaki. I am convinced of this.

Source: Executive Office of the President. "Remarks With Prime Minister Shinzo Abe of Japan at Hiroshima Peace Memorial Park in Hiroshima, Japan." May 27, 2016. *Compilation of Presidential Documents* 2016, no. 00357 (May 27, 2016). http://www.gpo.gov/fdsys/pkg/DCPD-201600357/pdf/DCPD-201600357.pdf.

OTHER HISTORIC DOCUMENTS OF INTEREST

FROM PREVIOUS *HISTORIC DOCUMENTS*

International Response to
ISIL-Affiliated Attacks

MARCH 22, APRIL 25, JUNE 28, AND JULY 15, 2016

Throughout the spring and summer of 2016, a number of countries faced attacks perpetrated by the terrorist organization the Islamic State of Iraq and the Levant (ISIL). Airports in Zaventem, Brussels, and Atatürk, Istanbul, were the sites of suicide bombings that killed dozens and injured hundreds, and in France, which had suffered two other major attacks in the previous year, a truck drove through a crowd at a Bastille Day festival in Nice and killed more than eighty. ISIL claimed responsibility for the Brussels and Nice attacks, and it is widely believed by international leaders that the group helped organize and carry out the Atatürk bombing as well. In response to the attacks, Western nations increased their efforts aimed at halting the spread of ISIL in Iraq and Syria. This included additional airstrikes and training for local ground forces; however, no nation committed ground combat troops to the effort.

BRUSSELS AIRPORT BOMBED

In November 2015, Brussels, Belgium, was a hotbed of police activity and the central city was shut down as the masterminds behind the Paris terror attacks that killed 130 were sought out. On March 22, 2016, the nation faced its own tragedy, when two bombs went off in the Zaventem airport and one suicide attack took place at the Maalbeek metro station. Thirty-two civilians and three bombers were killed and more than 300 were injured in the deadliest terrorist attacks in Belgium's history.

According to witnesses, just before 8:00 a.m. local time, shouting was heard in Arabic near the entrance of the airport, before the bombs went off in close succession at both ends of the departure hall. Approximately one hour later, a bomb was detonated inside a train car at the Maalbeek metro station, located in the center of Brussels. Sixteen of the thirty-two killed died in the airport attack, while the other sixteen were killed in the metro bombing. Prime Minister Charles Michel called for "calm and solidarity" in response to the "violent and cowardly" attack, adding that "what we feared has happened." In response to the attack, the Belgium government heightened border security and increased its police presence on public transportation.

ISIL claimed responsibility for the attacks, noting in a statement that they were carried out against Belgium for its ongoing involvement in attacks against ISIL in Iraq and Syria. Many of those who were involved in the attacks belonged to the same terror cell as those who perpetrated the November attack in Paris. There were five bombing suspects in total—Khalid el-Bakaoui, Osama Krayem, Ibrahim el-Bakraoui, Najim Laachraoui, and Mohamed Abrini. The Bakraoui brothers and Laachraoui were killed in the attacks. Krayem and Abrini were arrested on April 8. Another twelve were arrested in relation to the attacks in late March. Local police said that the breakthrough in the investigation came when a taxi driver informed police that he had driven three men with large bags to the airport on the day of the attack and refused to take one of their bags because it was too large to fit in the car. Police went to the address provided by the driver, where they found a bag full of explosives and bomb-making materials.

Istanbul Airport Bombed

Over the past few years, Turkey has faced an increasing number of attacks perpetrated either by ISIL, which controls some of the southeastern border areas that Turkey shares with both Iraq and Syria, or by the Kurdistan Workers' Party (Partiya Karkerên Kurdistanê—PKK), which the government has fought for decades. In early 2016 alone, nearly forty were killed in a car bombing in Ankara, an attack claimed by the PKK, and less than a week later, four were killed by an ISIL suicide bomber in Istanbul. Another twenty-eight died in an attack by a Kurdish group targeting the Turkish military and ten Germans were killed in an ISIL-linked suicide bombing in Istanbul.

On June 28, shortly before 10:00 p.m. local time, three attackers arrived at the entrance of Atatürk airport in Istanbul—one of the world's busiest airports—and began shooting. When police fired back, they detonated suicide vests, two in the international terminal and one in a parking area. More than forty civilians and the three attackers were killed, and more than 200 were injured. Turkish President Recep Tayyip Erdoğan said the attack "shows that terrorism strikes with no regard to faith and values," but that "[d]espite paying a heavy price, Turkey has the power, determination and capacity to continue the fight against terrorism until the end."

Although ISIL did not immediately claim responsibility for the attack, Prime Minister Binali Yildirim was quick to blame the terrorist organization, and U.S. officials said that the use of gunmen in coordination with suicide bombings bore the hallmark of ISIL. In June, the BBC reported that the attackers may have been linked to ISIL, but came from the North Caucuses region in Russia, Uzbekistan, and Kyrgyzstan. In July, Rep. Michael McCaul, R-Tex., chair of the House Committee on Homeland Security, said that Akhmed Chatayev, a Chechen extremist who is an ISIL leader, organized the attack. In late June and early July, thirty were arrested in connection with the attack, following sixteen raids across Turkey. Thirteen of those arrested were charged with affiliation with a terrorist organization, homicide, and endangering the unity of the state. The prime minister said that additional details about those arrested and charged would not be released until the government had completed its "vast inquiry."

Truck Attack in France

At approximately 10:45 p.m. local time, during a July 14 Bastille Day celebration in Nice, France, a truck drove through a crowd gathered to watch fireworks, killing more than 80 and injuring more than 300. Ten of those killed were children. Following the attack, President François Hollande said the nation would "be able to overcome all trials." Hollande said France has "an enemy who is going to continue to strike all the people, all the countries who have freedom as a fundamental value," but that "[n]othing will make us yield in our determination to combat terrorism."

France was the site of a number of terrorist attacks in 2015, leading up to the November 13 attacks in Paris that killed 130. In response to the November attack, President Hollande implemented a state of emergency that allowed French police to conduct searches and raids to root out those who intended to carry out attacks against the nation. Shortly before the attack in Nice, Hollande had announced that he intended to lift the state of emergency; however, Prime Minister Manuel Valls said that it would be extended after the tragedy in Nice. "France has been struck once again in her flesh, on the 14th of July, on the day of our national celebration," Valls said, adding that France will have to "learn to live with terrorism."

The driver in the attack, who jumped out of his truck and fired into the crowd before being killed by police, was Mohamed Lahouaiej-Bouhlel, a thirty-one-year-old man from Tunisia. According to investigators, he was previously unknown to police and had acted alone. ISIL said immediately after the attack that Lahouaiej-Bouhlel was one of their soldiers. A number of arrests were made in connection with the truck attack. Five suspects were charged with helping plan the attack. Three of those, Ramzi A, Mohamed Oualid G, and Chokri C, were charged as accomplices to "murder by a group with terror links." The two others, Enkeldja and Artan, were charged with "breaking the law on weapons in relation to a terrorist group." None of the suspects were previously known to French authorities.

INTERNATIONAL RESPONSE TO THE ATTACKS

Following each attack, Western governments heightened their security measures around airports, transit hubs, and other population centers. Most notably, as it did after the November attack, France again announced that it would ramp up attacks against ISIL in Iraq and Syria. After the event in Nice, Hollande said that additional airstrikes and military training would be provided to aid those fighting ISIL. He did not, however, commit ground troops to the operation.

President Barack Obama also resisted calls to send ground troops to Syria, fearful that the United States would become embroiled in the civil war that had stretched on for five years and led to the deaths of an estimated 250,000. Instead, on April 25, he committed to send an additional 250 special forces to Syria to support the fight against ISIL and join the fifty U.S. troops already there. "These terrorists will learn the same lesson that others before them have, which is: your hatred is no match for our nations, united in defense of our way of life," Obama said during his announcement. The president agreed to send another 600 U.S. troops to assist in the fight against ISIL in September, this time to Iraq, where Iraqi forces were attempting to take back control of Mosul. "These are military forces that will be deployed to intensify the strategy that's in place, to support Iraqi forces as they prepare for an offensive," said White House press secretary Josh Earnest. The United States also continued to participate in coalition airstrikes, which in June, just hours after the Istanbul airport bombing, resulted in the deaths of nearly 250 ISIL fighters and the destruction of at least forty vehicles. It was considered one of the deadliest attacks against the group.

After the attack in Turkey, President Erdoğan called for greater coordination of efforts to combat ISIL. "For terrorist organizations, there is no difference between Istanbul and London, Ankara and Berlin, Izmir and Chicago or Antalya and Rome," he said, adding, "Unless all governments and the entire mankind join forces in the fight against terrorism, much worse things than what we fear to imagine today will come true." President Obama, in a press conference with German chancellor Angela Merkel, noted that the ongoing NATO coalition was making progress and "pushing ISIL back from territory it had controlled." But, he added, "none of us can solve this problem by ourselves," and that all of those involved in the fight "can still do more" to further weaken the group: "In Syria and Iraq, we need more nations contributing to the air campaign. We need more nations contributing trainers to help build up local forces in Iraq. We need more nations to contribute economic assistance to Iraq so it can stabilize liberated areas and break the cycle of violent extremism so that ISIL cannot come back."

—Heather Kerrigan

Following is a statement from the government of Brussels on March 22, 2016, regarding the bombing of the Zaventem airport; President Barack Obama's edited remarks on April 25, 2016, on the U.S. partnership with Europe in fighting ISIL; a June 28, 2016, statement by Turkish President Recep Tayyip Erdoğan on the attack on Istanbul's airport; and a statement by French President François Hollande on the attack in Nice on July 15, 2016.

Brussels Government on Airport Attack

March 22, 2016

This morning, around 8 AM, two explosions occurred in the departure hall of Zaventem airport. The possibility of an attack is currently being investigated.

Regrettably, these explosions have resulted in loss of life. The priority of the authorities and emergency responders is to provide assistance to the victims and secure the area. The Federal Phase of Emergency Planning has been started.

A call centre has been set up to respond to the questions of relatives and passengers: 1771. Everyone is asked to stay away from Zaventem airport.

The OCAM has carried out a new analysis of the threat level, following these explosions. The general level for Belgium is set at level 4, specifically for international railway stations, metro stations, nuclear sites and the Port of Antwerp.

A national security council will be convened later on in the day.

The Belgian government would like to express its greatest support to the victims and their families. . . .

SOURCE: Prime Minister of Belgium. "Statement from the Federal Government." March 22, 2016. http://premier.fgov.be/en/statement-federal-government.

President Obama on Partnering with Europe to Combat ISIL

April 25, 2016

[The portions of President Obama's statement not related to international efforts to combat ISIL have been omitted.]

Right now the most urgent threat to our nations is ISIL, and that's why we're united in our determination to destroy it. And all 28 NATO allies are contributing to our coalition, whether it's striking ISIL targets in Syria and Iraq or supporting the air campaign or training local forces in Iraq or providing critical humanitarian aid. And we continue to make progress, pushing ISIL back from territory that it controlled.

And just as I've approved additional support for Iraqi forces against ISIL, I've decided to increase U.S. support for local forces fighting ISIL in Syria. A small number of American special operations forces are already on the ground in Syria, and their expertise has been critical as local forces have driven ISIL out of key areas. So given the success, I've approved the deployment of up to 250 additional U.S. personnel in Syria, including special forces, to keep up this momentum. They're not going to be leading the fight on the ground, but they will be essential in providing the training and assisting local forces that continue to drive ISIL back.

So make no mistake. These terrorists will learn the same lesson as others before them have, which is: your hatred is no match for our nations united in the defense of our way of life. And just as we remain relentless on the military front, we're not going to give up on diplomacy to end the civil war in Syria, because the suffering of the Syrian people has to end, and that requires an effective political transition.

But this remains a difficult fight, and none of us can solve this problem by ourselves. Even as European countries make important contributions against ISIL, Europe, including NATO, can still do more. So I've spoken to Chancellor Merkel, and I'll be meeting later with the Presidents of France and the Prime Ministers of Great Britain and of Italy. In Syria and Iraq, we need more nations contributing to the air campaign. We need more nations contributing trainers to help build up local forces in Iraq. We need more nations to contribute economic assistance to Iraq so it can stabilize liberated areas and break the cycle of violent extremism so that ISIL cannot come back.

These terrorists are doing everything in their power to strike our cities and kill our citizens, so we need to do everything in our power to stop them. And that includes closing gaps so terrorists can't pull off attacks like those in Paris and Brussels.

Which brings me to one other point. Europeans, like Americans, cherish your privacy. And many are skeptical about governments collecting and sharing information, for good reason. That skepticism is healthy. Germans remember their history of government surveillance; so do Americans, by the way, particularly those who were fighting on behalf of civil rights. So it's part of our democracies to want to make sure our governments are accountable.

But I want to say this to young people who value their privacy and spend a lot of time on their phones: The threat of terrorism is real. In the United States, I've worked to reform our surveillance programs to ensure that they're consistent with the rule of law and upholding our values, like privacy. And by the way, we include the privacy of people outside of the United States. We care about Europeans' privacy, not just Americans' privacy.

But I also, in working on these issues, have come to recognize security and privacy don't have to be a contradiction. We can protect both. And we have to. If we truly value our liberty, then we have to take the steps that are necessary to share information and intelligence within Europe, as well as between the United States and Europe, to stop terrorists from traveling and crossing borders and killing innocent people.

And as today's diffuse threats evolve, our alliance has to evolve. So we're going to have a NATO summit this summer in Warsaw, and I will insist that all of us need to meet our responsibilities, united, together. That means standing with the people of Afghanistan as they build their security forces and push back against violent extremism. It means more ships in the Aegean to shut down criminal networks who are profiting by smuggling desperate families and children.

And that said, NATO's central mission is and always will be our solemn duty: our article 5 commitment to our common defense. That's why we'll continue to bolster the defense of our frontline allies in Poland and Romania and the Baltic States.

So we have to both make sure that NATO carries out its traditional mission, but also to meet the threats of NATO's southern flank. We have to defend the security of every ally. That's why we need to stay nimble and make sure our forces are interoperable and invest in new capabilities like cyberdefense and missile defense. And that's why every NATO member should be contributing its full share—2 percent of GDP—towards our common security, something that doesn't always happen. And I'll be honest, sometimes, Europe has been complacent about its own defense.

SOURCE: Executive Office of the President. "Remarks in Hannover, Germany." April 25, 2016. *Compilation of Presidential Documents* 2016, no. 00663 (April 25, 2016). http://www.gpo.gov/fdsys/pkg/DCPD-201600263/pdf/DCPD-201600263.

President Erdoğan on
Istanbul Airport Attack

June 28, 2016

The statement by President Recep Tayyip Erdoğan on the terror attack that took place at Istanbul Atatürk Airport is as follows:

I strongly condemn the terror attack which took place at Istanbul Atatürk Airport and offer my condolences to the victims' families and our nation. May Allah bless the souls of everyone who lost their lives in this heinous attack.

The attack, which took place during the holy month of Ramadan, shows that terrorism strikes with no regard for faith and values. Nor do terrorists distinguish between their victims.

This attack once again revealed the dark face of terrorist organizations targeting innocent civilians.

It is obvious that this attack does not aim to attain any results but merely aims to produce propaganda material against our country by shedding the blood of and causing pain for innocent civilians.

We urge governments, parliaments, media and civil society organizations around the world, especially in Western countries, to take a firm stand against terrorism.

Despite paying a heavy price, Turkey has the power, determination and capacity to continue the fight against terrorism until the end.

However, I would like to remind that today's attack targeted not only 79 million Turkish citizens but also 7.5 billion human beings around the world.

Due to the treacherous nature of terrorism, the bombs that exploded in Istanbul today could have gone off at any airport in any city around the world.

Make no mistake: For terrorist organizations, there is no difference between Istanbul and London, Ankara and Berlin, Izmir and Chicago or Antalya and Rome.

Unless all government and the entire mankind join forces in the fight against terrorism, much worse things than what we fear to imagine today will come true.

I hope the Atatürk Airport attack will serve as a turning point in the world, particularly for the Western countries, for a joint struggle against terror organizations.

I once again wish Allah's grace upon the victims who lost their lives in this attack and a quick recovery to those injured.

I offer my condolences to our nation.

SOURCE: Presidency of the Republic of Turkey. "Statement by President Recep Tayyip Erdogan on the Terror Attack on Istanbul Atatürk Airport." June 28, 2016. http://www.tccb.gov.tr/en/speeches-statements/558/45540/statement-by-president-recep-tayyip-erdogan-on-the-terror-attack-on-istanbul-ataturk-airport.html.

DOCUMENT

French President Hollande on Attack in Nice

July 15, 2016

Horror . . . Horror has just descended on France once again.

As I speak, 77 people have sadly been killed, including several children, and some 20 people are in a critical condition. It cannot be denied that this was a terrorist attack and, once again, it was an extremely violent one, and it's clear that we must do everything to ensure we can fight the scourge of terrorism.

The driver was shot dead. At this point we don't know whether he had any accomplices, but we're making sure that his identification, which is going to be confirmed, can put us onto any possible leads.

France was hit on its National Day, 14 July, the symbol of freedom, because human rights are denied by the fanatics, and because France is obviously their target.

On behalf of a nation in tears, I express our solidarity with the victims and their families.

All resources are being deployed to help the injured. The White Plan mobilizing all hospitals in the region has been triggered. After Paris in January 2015, then in November last year, along with Saint-Denis, now Nice, in turn, has been hit. The whole of France is under the threat of Islamist terrorism.

So in these circumstances, we must show absolute vigilance and unfailing determination.

Many measures have already been taken. Our legislative arsenal has been strengthened considerably. But because this is the summer season, we must further increase our level of protection.

So I've decided, at the Prime Minister's proposal and together with the ministers concerned—the Defence and Interior Ministers—firstly that we'll maintain Operation Sentinelle at a high level, which enables us to mobilize 10,000 soldiers, in addition to gendarmes and police.

I've also decided to call in operational reserves—i.e. all those who have at some point served under the flag or been in the gendarmerie—to come and help relieve the pressure on the police and gendarmes. We'll be able to deploy them wherever we need them, particularly for border control.

Finally, I have decided that the state of emergency, which was to end on 26 July, will be extended by three months. A bill will be submitted to Parliament by next week.

Nothing will make us yield in our determination to combat terrorism, and we're going to further intensify our strikes in Syria and Iraq. We'll continue to hit those who attack us on our own soil, in their hideouts. I announced this yesterday morning.

A meeting of the Defence Council will be held tomorrow [on 15 July]. It will examine all the measures which we've already taken and which I've just announced. It will therefore enable all the necessary personnel to be deployed on every site and in every town and city where we need protection and vigilance.

Following this Defence Council meeting, I'll go to Nice with the Prime Minister to support the city and its elected representatives in this ordeal and to mobilize all the necessary capabilities.

France is deeply distressed by over this new tragedy. It's horrified by what has just happened, this monstrosity of using a lorry to kill, to deliberately kill dozens of people who had simply come to celebrate 14 July.

France is in tears, it's deeply distressed, but it's strong and will always be stronger— I assure you of that—than the fanatics who seek to attack it today.

SOURCE: French Ministry of Foreign Affairs. "Official Speeches and Statements of July 15, 2016." July 15, 2016. http://basedoc.diplomatie.gouv.fr/exl-doc/FranceDiplomatie/PDF/baen2016-07-15.pdf.

OTHER HISTORIC DOCUMENTS OF INTEREST

FROM PREVIOUS HISTORIC DOCUMENTS

North Carolina Governor Signs Bathroom Bill into Law

MARCH 23 AND MAY 10, 2016

On March 23, 2016, North Carolina Governor Pat McCrory signed into law the Public Facilities Privacy & Security Act. The bill had two primary functions: first, to require those in public facilities to utilize the bathroom, locker room, or other such facility corresponding to their sex assigned at birth, not the one with which they identify, and second, to overturn a LGBT antidiscrimination order passed in Charlotte and prevent local governments from enacting similar policies. While the governor stood by the legislation, public response to what became known as the "bathroom bill" was swift and resulted in the state losing high-profile events, such as the NBA All Star-Game, and drew a lawsuit from the federal Department of Justice.

While public debate continued over North Carolina's law, President Barack Obama's administration issued a directive to public school districts, asking them to allow transgender students to utilize the facilities that correspond with their gender identity. This was quickly met by lawsuits from nearly half the states.

SPECIAL SESSION PASSAGE

House Bill 2 (HB2), the Public Facilities Privacy & Security Act, was passed during a special one-day session called by state House and Senate Republicans. It took less than twelve hours for the bill to be passed by both the House and Senate and for the governor to give it his signature. The House passed the bill 82–26, while the Senate voted 32–0. No Senate Democrats voted on the bill because they walked out in protest prior to the vote being held.

The bill was passed in response to a February 2016 nondiscrimination ordinance in Charlotte that allowed transgender individuals to use the restrooms and locker rooms of the gender with which they identify. The new state law barred transgender individuals from using these facilities in public spaces in accordance with their gender identity and further disallowed any locality in the state from enacting similar LGBT nondiscrimination policies. Upon passage, North Carolina house speaker Tim Moore, a Republican, said that House and Senate leaders were primarily concerned with protecting the privacy of all North Carolina residents when they drafted the bill. "The way the ordinance was written by City Council in Charlotte, it would have allowed a man to go into a bathroom, locker or any changing facility, where women are—even if he was a man. We were concerned. Obviously there is the security risk of a sexual predator, but there is the issue of privacy," Moore added. Lieutenant Governor Dan Forest said that allowing Charlotte's law to remain in the books "would have given pedophiles, sex offenders, and perverts free rein to watch women, boys, and girls undress and use the bathroom." Charlotte Mayor Jennifer Roberts, a Democrat, called the legislation "literally the most anti-LGBT legislation in the country."

RESPONSE TO HB2

Public reaction to the bill was swift. American Civil Liberties Union of North Carolina acting executive director Sarah Preston said, "Rather than expand nondiscrimination laws to protect all North Carolinians, the General Assembly instead spent $42,000 to rush through an extreme bill that undoes all local nondiscrimination laws and specifically excludes gay and transgender people from legal protections." She added, "Legislators have gone out of their way to stigmatize and marginalize transgender North Carolinians by pushing ugly and fundamentally untrue stereotypes that are based on fear and ignorance and not supported by the experiences of more than 200 cities with these protections." In July, the NBA announced that it would not hold its All-Star game in Charlotte as originally planned. "While we recognize that the NBA cannot choose the law in every city, state, and country in which we do business, we do not believe we can successfully host our All-Star festivities in Charlotte in the climate created by HB2," the NBA said in a statement announcing its decision.

In response to the backlash, Governor McCrory issued a statement criticizing the "sports and entertainment elite"—and even the state's attorney general who had publicly criticized the bill—for trying to influence North Carolina's laws and added that "the liberal media have for months misrepresented our laws and maligned the people of North Carolina simply because most people believe boys and girls should be able to use school bathrooms, locker rooms and showers without the opposite sex present." In April, McCrory issued an executive order in an effort to clarify the law's meaning and hit back at some of the public reaction. McCrory said he made the changes "after listening to people's feedback" and arriving at "the conclusion that there is a great deal of misinformation, misinterpretation, confusion, a lot of passion and, frankly, selective outrage and hypocrisy." The executive order did not amend any of the bathroom and changing facility rules and did not lift the ban on municipalities passing their own protections for LGBT individuals. Instead, it called for the maintenance of "common sense gender-specific restroom and locker room facilities in government buildings and schools." The state House and Senate followed the governor's executive order by striking the word *biological* from the law, which left open the question of how sexual identity would be defined. The legislature also increased penalties for those who commit crimes against people in public restrooms. However, the changes did little to placate the law's opponents.

JUSTICE DEPARTMENT LAWSUIT

On May 9, the Justice Department sued North Carolina over its bathroom law, which Attorney General Loretta Lynch referred to as "state-sponsored discrimination." The lawsuit sought to declare HB2 discriminatory under Title VII and Title IX of the Civil Rights Act as well as a violation of the Violence Against Women Act (VAWA). The Justice Department had previously asked the state to stop enactment of the law, but it refused to do so and instead filed its own lawsuit seeking to negate the Justice Department's suit. In announcing the federal suit, Lynch stated, "This action is about a great deal more than bathrooms. This is about the dignity and the respect that we accord our fellow citizens." She added, "You have been told that this law protects vulnerable populations from harm. That is just not the case. What this law does is inflict further indignity for a population that has already suffered far more than its fair share. This law provides no benefit to society, and all it does is harm innocent Americans."

In its filing, the Justice Department argued that both the state and the University of North Carolina were in direct violation of laws that protect minority groups. The Department pointed to a memorandum issued by the president of the university system following the passage of HB2 stating that multiple-occupancy bathroom and changing facilities must be designated for and used by only one biological sex, a move the Justice Department argued was in direct conflict with Title IX of the Civil Rights Act and the VAWA. Similarly, when Governor McCrory issued an executive order implementing HB2, and calling for multiple-occupancy changing and bathroom facilities to be "designated for and only used by persons based on their biological sex," he too was in violation of the Civil Rights Act. According to the Justice Department, "transgender employees of Defendants and other public agencies in North Carolina have suffered and continue to suffer injury, including, without limitation, emotional harm, mental anguish, distress, humiliation, and indignity as a direct and proximate result of Defendants' compliance with and implementation of H.B. 2."

An amicus brief calling for North Carolina's law to be overturned was written by former solicitor general Theodore Olson, who notably litigated California's Proposition 8 case that legalized gay marriage in the state. The brief was signed by sixty-eight major companies, including Apple, Nike, General Electric, and American Airlines. "HB2 is a law that forces transgender persons to deny, disclaim, and conceal their gender identity, particularly whenever they wish to use single-sex restroom facilities on state or local government property," Olson said in a statement. "That so many in the business community are willing to stand up in opposition to HB2 underscores the immeasurable and irreparable harm the law is doing to the transgender community and to North Carolina's economy." A second amicus brief was penned by representatives of states seeking to keep North Carolina's law on the books. The states were primarily those that challenged President Obama's May bathroom directive for public schools. The case of *United States of America v. State of North Carolina* had not been argued as of the end of 2016.

OBAMA ISSUES DIRECTIVE ON SCHOOL BATHROOMS

On May 13, the Obama administration sent a letter to school districts asking them to allow transgender students to use the bathroom and locker room facilities corresponding to the gender with which they identify. Although the request did not carry any legally binding requirements, it was seen as an indication that those districts that chose not to abide by the law could either face lawsuits or loss of federal aid for being viewed as discriminatory. In a statement issued prior to the sending of the letter, John B. King Jr., the secretary of the Department of Education, said, "No student should ever have to go through the experience of feeling unwelcome at school or on a college campus." Furthermore, he said, "We must ensure that our young people know that whoever they are or wherever they come from, they have the opportunity to get a great education in an environment free from discrimination, harassment and violence." After the directive was sent, Attorney General Lynch said that it "gives administrators, teachers, and parents the tools they need to protect transgender students from peer harassment and to identify and address unjust school policies."

The states responded quickly, with eleven filing lawsuits arguing that the directive from the Obama administration "has no basis in law" and would cause "seismic changes in the operations of the nation's school districts." Another ten states filed their own lawsuits in early July. The chief complaint among those seeking an injunction against the Obama administration's directive is that the president is attempting to redefine the word *sex* to include gender identity. Nebraska attorney general Doug Peterson said the Obama decision "circumvents . . . established law by ignoring the appropriate legislative process necessary to change such a law. It also supersedes local school districts' authority to address student issues on an individualized, professional and private basis." Proponents of the law have argued that because the directive is not legally binding, the states filing suit against the administration have no basis in law to do so.

On August 22, a federal judge in Texas temporarily blocked the directive while the state's lawsuit proceeded. The ACLU responded to the decision, noting that it would only serve to further confuse school districts as students returned to class after summer vacation. "Let us make it clear to those districts: your obligations under the law have not changed, and you are still not only allowed but required to treat transgender students fairly," the ACLU said in a statement. As of the close of 2016, the state cases were still making their way through the courts, and many legal experts believe the issue will end up with the U.S. Supreme Court. On October 28, the Supreme Court signaled its willingness to take up the issue when it agreed to hear the case of a transgender student in a Virginia public school district who had been prevented from using the bathroom that conformed to his gender identity. The Court is likely to decide that case in June 2017.

—Heather Kerrigan

Following is the full text of North Carolina House Bill 2, enacted on March 23, 2016; and portions of the Department of Justice lawsuit against the state of North Carolina, filed on May 10, 2016, in opposition to its bathroom bill.

DOCUMENT | *House Bill 2 Becomes Law*

March 23, 2016

AN ACT TO PROVIDE FOR SINGLE-SEX MULTIPLE OCCUPANCY BATHROOM AND CHANGING FACILITIES IN SCHOOLS AND PUBLIC AGENCIES AND TO CREATE STATEWIDE CONSISTENCY IN REGULATION OF EMPLOYMENT AND PUBLIC ACCOMMODATIONS.

Whereas, the North Carolina Constitution directs the General Assembly to provide for the organization and government of all cities and counties and to give cities and counties such powers and duties as the General Assembly deems advisable in Section 1 of Article VII of the North Carolina Constitution; and

Whereas, the North Carolina Constitution reflects the importance of statewide laws related to commerce by prohibiting the General Assembly from enacting local acts regulating labor, trade, mining, or manufacturing in Section 24 of Article II of the North Carolina Constitution; and

Whereas, the General Assembly finds that laws and obligations consistent statewide for all businesses, organizations, and employers doing business in the State will improve intrastate commerce; and

Whereas, the General Assembly finds that laws and obligations consistent statewide for all businesses, organizations, and employers doing business in the State benefit the businesses, organizations, and employers seeking to do business in the State and attracts new businesses, organizations, and employers to the State; Now, therefore,

The General Assembly of North Carolina enacts:

PART I. SINGLE-SEX MULTIPLE OCCUPANCY BATHROOM AND CHANGING FACILITIES

SECTION 1.1. G.S. 115C-47 is amended by adding a new subdivision to read:

"(63) To Establish Single-Sex Multiple Occupancy Bathroom and Changing Facilities. Local boards of education shall establish single-sex multiple occupancy bathroom and changing facilities as provided in G.S. 115C-521.2."

SECTION 1.2. Article 37 of Chapter 115C of the General Statutes is amended by adding a new section to read:

"**§ 115C-521.2. Single-sex multiple occupancy bathroom and changing facilities.**

(a) Definitions. The following definitions apply in this section:

   (1) Biological sex. The physical condition of being male or female, which is stated on a person's birth certificate.

   (2) Multiple occupancy bathroom or changing facility. A facility designed or designated to be used by more than one person at a time where students may be in various states of undress in the presence of other persons. A multiple occupancy bathroom or changing facility may include, but is not limited to, a school restroom, locker room, changing room, or shower room.

   (3) Single occupancy bathroom or changing facility. A facility designed or designated to be used by only one person at a time where students may be in various states of undress. A single occupancy bathroom or changing facility may include, but is not limited to, a single stall restroom designated as unisex or for use based on biological sex.

(b) Single-Sex Multiple Occupancy Bathroom and Changing Facilities. Local boards of education shall require every multiple occupancy bathroom or changing facility that is designated for student use to be designated for and used only by students based on their biological sex.

(c) Accommodations Permitted. Nothing in this section shall prohibit local boards of education from providing accommodations such as single occupancy bathroom or changing facilities or controlled use of faculty facilities upon a request due to special circumstances, but in no event shall that accommodation result in the local boards of education allowing a student to use a multiple occupancy bathroom or changing facility designated under subsection (b) of this section for a sex other than the student's biological sex.

(d) Exceptions. This section does not apply to persons entering a multiple occupancy bathroom or changing facility designated for use by the opposite sex:

(1) For custodial purposes.

(2) For maintenance or inspection purposes.

(3) To render medical assistance.

(4) To accompany a student needing assistance when the assisting individual is an employee or authorized volunteer of the local board of education or the student's parent or authorized caregiver.

(5) To receive assistance in using the facility.

(6) To accompany a person other than a student needing assistance.

(7) That has been temporarily designated for use by that person's biological sex."

SECTION 1.3. Chapter 143 of the General Statutes is amended by adding a new Article to read:

"Article 81.
"Single-Sex Multiple Occupancy Bathroom and Changing Facilities.

"§ 143-760. Single-sex multiple occupancy bathroom and changing facilities.

(a) Definitions. The following definitions apply in this section:

(1) Biological sex. The physical condition of being male or female, which is stated on a person's birth certificate.

(2) Executive branch agency. Agencies, boards, offices, departments, and institutions of the executive branch, including The University of North Carolina and the North Carolina Community College System.

(3) Multiple occupancy bathroom or changing facility. A facility designed or designated to be used by more than one person at a time where persons may be in various states of undress in the presence of other persons. A multiple occupancy bathroom or changing facility may include, but is not limited to, a restroom, locker room, changing room, or shower room.

(4) Public agency. Includes any of the following:

a. Executive branch agencies.

b. All agencies, boards, offices, and departments under the direction and control of a member of the Council of State. c. "Unit" as defined in G.S. 159-7(b)(15).

d. "Public authority" as defined in G.S. 159-7(b)(10).

e. A local board of education.

f. The judicial branch.

g. The legislative branch.

h. Any other political subdivision of the State.

(5) Single occupancy bathroom or changing facility. A facility designed or designated to be used by only one person at a time where persons may be in various states of undress. A single occupancy bathroom or changing facility may include, but is not limited to, a single stall restroom designated as unisex or for use based on biological sex.

(b) Single-Sex Multiple Occupancy Bathroom and Changing Facilities. Public agencies shall require every multiple occupancy bathroom or changing facility to be designated for and only used by persons based on their biological sex.

(c) Accommodations Permitted. Nothing in this section shall prohibit public agencies from providing accommodations such as single occupancy bathroom or changing facilities upon a person's request due to special circumstances, but in no event shall that accommodation result in the public agency allowing a person to use a multiple occupancy bathroom or changing facility designated under subsection (b) of this section for a sex other than the person's biological sex.

(d) Exceptions. This section does not apply to persons entering a multiple occupancy bathroom or changing facility designated for use by the opposite sex:

(1) For custodial purposes.

(2) For maintenance or inspection purposes.

(3) To render medical assistance.

(4) To accompany a person needing assistance.

(4a) For a minor under the age of seven who accompanies a person caring for that minor.

(5) That has been temporarily designated for use by that person's biological sex."

PART II. STATEWIDE CONSISTENCY IN LAWS RELATED TO EMPLOYMENT AND CONTRACTING

SECTION 2.1. G.S. 95-25.1 reads as rewritten:

"§ 95-25.1. Short title and legislative ~~purpose.~~purpose; local governments preempted.

(a) This Article shall be known and may be cited as the "Wage and Hour Act."

(b) The public policy of this State is declared as follows: The wage levels of employees, hours of labor, payment of earned wages, and the well-being of minors are subjects of concern requiring legislation to promote the general welfare of the people of the State without jeopardizing the competitive position of North Carolina business and industry. The General Assembly declares that the general welfare of the State requires the enactment of this law under the police power of the State.

(c) The provisions of this Article supersede and preempt any ordinance, regulation, resolution, or policy adopted or imposed by a unit of local government or other political subdivision of the State that regulates or imposes any requirement upon an employer pertaining to compensation of employees, such as the wage levels of employees, hours of labor, payment of earned wages, benefits, leave, or well-being of minors in the workforce. This subsection shall not apply to any of the following:

(1) A local government regulating, compensating, or controlling its own employees.

(2) Economic development incentives awarded under Chapter 143B of the General Statutes.

(3) Economic development incentives awarded under Article 1 of Chapter 158 of the General Statutes.

(4) A requirement of federal community development block grants.

(5) Programs established under G.S. 153A-376 or G.S. 160A-456."

SECTION 2.2. G.S. 153A-449(a) reads as rewritten:

"(a) Authority. A county may contract with and appropriate money to any person, association, or corporation, in order to carry out any public purpose that the county is authorized by law to engage in. A county may not require a private contractor under this section to abide by any restriction that the county could not impose on all employers in the county, such as paying minimum wage or providing paid sick leave to its employees, regulations or controls on the contractor's employment practices or mandate or prohibit the provision of goods, services, or accommodations to any member of the public as a condition of bidding on a contract.contract or a qualification-based selection, except as otherwise required or allowed by State law."

SECTION 2.3. G.S. 160A-20.1(a) reads as rewritten:

"(a) Authority.—A city may contract with and appropriate money to any person, association, or corporation, in order to carry out any public purpose that the city is authorized by law to engage in. A city may not require a private contractor under this section to abide by any restriction that the city could not impose on all employers in the city, such as paying minimum wage or providing paid sick leave to its employees, regulations or controls on the contractor's employment practices or mandate or prohibit the provision of goods, services, or accommodations to any member of the public as a condition of bidding on a contract.contract or a qualification-based selection, except as otherwise required or allowed by State law."

PART III. PROTECTION OF RIGHTS IN EMPLOYMENT AND PUBLIC ACCOMMODATIONS

SECTION 3.1. G.S. 143-422.2 reads as rewritten:

"§ 143-422.2. Legislative declaration.

(a) It is the public policy of this State to protect and safeguard the right and opportunity of all persons to seek, obtain and hold employment without discrimination or abridgement on account of race, religion, color, national origin, age, biological sex or handicap by employers which regularly employ 15 or more employees.

(b) It is recognized that the practice of denying employment opportunity and discriminating in the terms of employment foments domestic strife and unrest, deprives the State of the fullest utilization of its capacities for advancement and development, and substantially and adversely affects the interests of employees, employers, and the public in general.

(c) The General Assembly declares that the regulation of discriminatory practices in employment is properly an issue of general, statewide concern, such that this Article and other applicable provisions of the General Statutes supersede and preempt any ordinance, regulation, resolution, or policy adopted or imposed by a unit of local government or other political subdivision of the State that regulates or imposes any requirement upon an employer pertaining to the regulation of discriminatory practices in employment, except such regulations applicable to personnel employed by that body that are not otherwise in conflict with State law."

SECTION 3.2. G.S. 143-422.3 reads as rewritten:

"§ 143-422.3. Investigations; conciliations.

The Human Relations Commission in the Department of Administration shall have the authority to receive charges of discrimination from the Equal Employment Opportunity Commission pursuant to an agreement under Section 709(b) of Public Law 88-352, as amended by Public Law 92-261, and investigate and conciliate charges of discrimination. Throughout this process, the agency shall use its good offices to effect an amicable resolution of the charges of discrimination. This Article does not create, and shall not be construed to create or support, a statutory or common law private right of action, and no person may bring any civil action based upon the public policy expressed herein."

SECTION 3.3. Chapter 143 of the General Statutes is amended by adding a new Article to read:

"Article 49B.
"Equal Access to Public Accommodations.

"§ 143-422.10. Short title.

This Article shall be known and may be cited as the Equal Access to Public Accommodations Act.

"§ 143-422.11. Legislative declaration.

(a) It is the public policy of this State to protect and safeguard the right and opportunity of all individuals within the State to enjoy fully and equally the goods, services, facilities, privileges, advantages, and accommodations of places of public accommodation free of discrimination because of race, religion, color, national origin, or biological sex, provided that designating multiple or single occupancy bathrooms or changing facilities according to biological sex, as defined in G.S. 143-760(a)(1), (3), and (5), shall not be deemed to constitute discrimination.

(b) The General Assembly declares that the regulation of discriminatory practices in places of public accommodation is properly an issue of general, statewide concern, such that this Article and other applicable provisions of the General Statutes supersede and preempt any ordinance, regulation, resolution, or policy adopted or imposed by a unit of local government or other political subdivision of the State that regulates or imposes any requirement pertaining to the regulation of discriminatory practices in places of public accommodation.

"§ 143-422.12. Places of public accommodation—defined.

For purposes of this Article, places of public accommodation has the same meaning as defined in G.S. 168A-3(8), but shall exclude any private club or other establishment not, in fact, open to the public.

"§ 143-422.13. Investigations; conciliations.

The Human Relations Commission in the Department of Administration shall have the authority to receive, investigate, and conciliate complaints of discrimination in public accommodations. Throughout this process, the Human Relations Commission shall use its good offices to effect an amicable resolution of the complaints of discrimination. This Article does not create, and shall not be construed to create or support, a statutory or common law private right of action, and no person may bring any civil action based upon the public policy expressed herein."

PART IV. SEVERABILITY

SECTION 4. If any provision of this act or its application is held invalid, the invalidity does not affect other provisions or applications of this act that can be given effect without the invalid provisions or application, and to this end the provisions of this act are severable. If any provision of this act is temporarily or permanently restrained or enjoined by judicial order, this act shall be enforced as though such restrained or enjoined provisions had not been adopted, provided that whenever such temporary or permanent restraining order or injunction is stayed, dissolved, or otherwise ceases to have effect, such provisions shall have full force and effect.

PART V. EFFECTIVE DATE

SECTION 5. This act is effective when it becomes law and applies to any action taken on or after that date, to any ordinance, resolution, regulation, or policy adopted or amended on or after that date, and to any contract entered into on or after that date. The provisions of Sections 2.1, 2.2, 2.3, 3.1, 3.2, and 3.3 of this act supersede and preempt any ordinance, resolution, regulation, or policy adopted prior to the effective date of this act that purports to regulate a subject matter preempted by this act or that violates or is not consistent with this act, and such ordinances, resolutions, regulations, or policies shall be null and void as of the effective date of this act.

In the General Assembly read three times and ratified this the 23rd day of March, 2016.

s/ Daniel J. Forest
President of the Senate

s/ Tim Moore
Speaker of the House of Representatives

s/ Pat McCrory Governor

Approved 9:57 p.m. this 23rd day of March, 2016.

Source: North Carolina General Assembly. Second Extra Session 2016. Session Law 2016–3. "House Bill 2." March 23, 2016. http://www.ncleg.net/sessions/2015e2/bills/house/pdf/h2v4.pdf.

Justice Department Files Suit against North Carolina

May 10, 2016

UNITED STATES DISTRICT COURT
FOR THE MIDDLE DISTRICT OF NORTH CAROLINA

UNITED STATES OF AMERICA, Plaintiff,

v.

STATE OF NORTH CAROLINA; PATRICK MCCRORY, in his official capacity as Governor of North Carolina; NORTH CAROLINA DEPARTMENT OF PUBLIC SAFETY; UNIVERSITY OF NORTH CAROLINA; and BOARD OF GOVERNORS OF THE UNIVERSITY OF NORTH CAROLINA, Defendants

Case No. 1:16-cv-425

COMPLAINT PRELIMINARY STATEMENT

1.   The United States files this complaint challenging a provision of North Carolina law requiring public agencies to deny transgender persons access to multiple-occupancy bathrooms and changing facilities consistent with their gender identity.

2.   As set forth below, Defendants' compliance with and implementation of Part I of North Carolina Session Law 2016-3, House Bill 2 ("H.B. 2"), which was enacted and became effective on March 23, 2016, constitutes a pattern or practice of employment

discrimination on the basis of sex in violation of Title VII of the Civil Rights Act of 1964, as amended, 42 U.S.C. § 2000e, *et seq.* ("Title VII"); discrimination on the basis of sex in an education program receiving federal funds in violation of Title IX of the Education Amendments of 1972, 20 U.S.C. § 1681, *et seq.* ("Title IX"), and its implementing regulations, 28 C.F.R. Part 54 (2000), 34 C.F.R. Part 106 (2010); and discrimination on the basis of sex and gender identity in programs receiving federal funds in violation of the Violence Against Women Reauthorization Act of 2013 ("VAWA"), 42 U.S.C. § 13925(b)(13).

[The Jurisdiction and Venue and Defendants sections have been omitted.]

FACTUAL ALLEGATIONS

Enactment of H.B. 2

11. On March 23, 2016, the North Carolina legislature convened a special session for the purpose of passing H.B. 2.

12. H.B. 2 mandates, *inter alia*, that all "[p]ublic agencies . . . require multiple occupancy bathrooms or changing facilities . . . be designated for and only used by individuals based on their biological sex." H.B. 2 defines "biological sex" as "[t]he physical condition of being male or female, which is stated on a person's birth certificate." H.B. 2 further defines "public agencies" to include, among other entities, the state executive, judicial and legislative branches, including the University of North Carolina system.

13. H.B. 2 was enacted in direct response to Ordinance 7056 passed by the City Council in Charlotte, North Carolina (the "Charlotte Ordinance"), which permitted transgender individuals to use facilities corresponding to their gender identity by prohibiting discrimination based on "gender identity" in places of public accommodation.

14. Governor McCrory and North Carolina legislators made explicit public statements indicating that they proposed, passed, and signed H.B. 2 to overturn the Charlotte Ordinance and to ensure transgender individuals would not be permitted to access bathrooms and other facilities consistent with their gender identity in schools and other public agencies.

15. Prior to the passage of the Charlotte Ordinance in February 2016, Governor McCrory told members of the Charlotte City Council that the Ordinance could "create major public safety issues by putting citizens in possible danger from deviant actions by individuals taking improper advantage of a bad policy." Governor McCrory went on to explain that the "action of allowing a person with male anatomy, for example, to use a female restroom or locker room will most likely cause immediate State legislative intervention which I would support as governor."

16. When State Representative Dan Bishop introduced H.B. 2, he stated that "[a] small group of far-out progressives should not presume to decide for us all that a cross-dresser's liberty to express his gender nonconformity trumps the right of women and girls to peace of mind."

17. The bill passed both houses on March 23, 2016—the same day it was introduced. Governor McCrory signed the bill that night. H.B. 2 took effect immediately.

18. Following the conclusion of the special session, Senate President Phil Berger stated on his website, "[t]he North Carolina Senate voted unanimously Wednesday [March 23, 2016] to stop a radical and illegal Charlotte City Council ordinance allowing men into public bathrooms and locker rooms with young girls and women." Senator Berger characterized

the Charlotte Ordinance as "dangerous" and claimed that it "created a loophole that any man with nefarious motives could use to prey on women and young children."

19. Lieutenant Governor Dan Forest stated that the Charlotte Ordinance "would have given pedophiles, sex offenders, and perverts free rein to watch women, boys, and girls undress and use the bathroom."

Defendants' Compliance with and Implementation of H.B. 2 and the United States' Response

20. On April 5, 2016, following the enactment of H.B. 2, Defendant University of North Carolina's President, Margaret Spellings, issued a Memorandum to all Chancellors in the University of North Carolina system, titled "Guidance—Compliance with the Public Facilities Privacy & Security Act." The Memorandum directed Chancellors that "University institutions must require every multiple-occupancy bathroom and changing facility to be designated for and used only by persons based on their biological sex."

21. As a federal funding agency, when the Department of Justice has reason to question a funding recipient's compliance with Title IX, it gives notice of non-compliance and attempts to secure the recipient's compliance through voluntary means.

22. On April 8, 2016, the United States sent a letter to President Spellings seeking information to determine whether the University was complying with federal law.

23. In a response dated April 13, 2016, President Spellings affirmed that "the University is specifically covered by H.B. 2 and is required as a public agency to comply with its applicable portions, including the provisions related to multiple-occupancy bathrooms and changing facilities."

24. On April 12, 2016, Governor McCrory issued Executive Order 93, implementing H.B. 2 and affirming that "every multiple occupancy restroom, locker room or shower facility located in a cabinet agency must be designated for and only used by persons based on their biological sex."

25. Access to bathrooms and changing facilities on the University of North Carolina campus are covered by the non-discrimination mandates of Title IX and VAWA.

26. Access to bathrooms and changing facilities operated by Defendant North Carolina Department of Public Safety and its sub-recipients are covered by the non-discrimination mandate of VAWA.

27. Access to bathrooms and changing facilities in the workplace at public agencies in the State of North Carolina is a term, condition and privilege of employment and, therefore, is covered by the non-discrimination mandate of Title VII.

28. In letters dated May 4, 2016, the United States notified all Defendants, including the University of North Carolina, that the United States had determined they were not in compliance with Title VII, Title IX, and/or VAWA, based on their compliance with and implementation of provisions of H.B. 2 that are irreconcilable with federal law. The United States requested that Defendants immediately agree not to comply with those provisions of H.B. 2, ensure that transgender persons were entitled to use multiple-occupancy bathrooms and changing facilities consistent with their gender identity as required by federal law, and retract any statements to the contrary. The United States advised Defendants that it would take enforcement action under the above statutes if such compliance with federal law was not demonstrated.

29. As of the filing of this Complaint, no Defendant has taken steps to achieve that compliance.

Gender Identity and Its Relationship to Sex

30. Individuals are typically assigned a sex on their birth certificate solely on the basis of the appearance of the external genitalia at birth. Additional aspects of sex (for example, chromosomal makeup) typically are not assessed and considered at the time of birth, except in cases of infants born with ambiguous genitalia.

31. An individual's "sex" consists of multiple factors, which may not always be in alignment. Among those factors are hormones, external genitalia, internal reproductive organs, chromosomes, and gender identity, which is an individual's internal sense of being male or female.

32. For individuals who have aspects of their sex that are not in alignment, the person's gender identity is the primary factor in terms of establishing that person's sex. External genitalia are, therefore, but one component of sex and not always determinative of a person's sex.

33. Although there is not yet one definitive explanation for what determines gender identity, biological factors, most notably sexual differentiation in the brain, have a role in gender identity development.

34. Transgender individuals are individuals who have a gender identity that does not match the sex they were assigned at birth. A transgender man's sex is male and a transgender woman's sex is female.

35. A transgender individual may begin to assert a gender identity inconsistent with their sex assigned at birth at any time from early childhood through adulthood. The decision by transgender individuals to assert their gender identity publicly is a deeply personal one that is made by the individual, often in consultation with family, medical and health care providers, and others.

36. Gender identity is innate and external efforts to change a person's gender identity can be harmful to a person's health and well-being.

37. Gender identity and transgender status are inextricably linked to one's sex and are sex-related characteristics.

38. Most states authorize changing the sex marker on one's birth certificate, but the requirements for doing so vary and are often onerous. Specifically, many states require surgical procedures. At least one state does not allow persons to change the sex marker on their birth certificates.

39. Individuals born in North Carolina must have proof of certain surgeries, such as "sex reassignment surgery," in order to change the sex marker on their birth certificates. N.C. Gen. Stat. § 130A-118(b)(4).

40. Surgery related to gender transitioning is generally unavailable to children under age 18.

41. In addition, the great majority of transgender individuals do not have surgery as part of their gender transition. Determinations about such surgery are decisions about medical care made by physicians and patients on an individual basis. For some, health-related conditions or other medical criteria counsel against invasive surgery. For others, the high cost of surgical procedures, which are often excluded from health insurance coverage, present an insurmountable barrier.

42. Standards of medical care for surgery related to gender transitioning generally advise that transgender individuals present consistent with their gender identity on a day-to-day basis across all settings of life, including in bathrooms and changing facilities at school and at work, for a significant time period prior to undergoing surgery.

Impact of H.B. 2 on Transgender Individuals in North Carolina

43. H.B. 2 requires public agencies to follow a facially discriminatory policy of treating transgender individuals, whose gender identity may not match their birth certificates, differently from similarly situated non-transgender individuals.

44. Because of Defendants' compliance with and implementation of H.B. 2, non-transgender employees of Defendants and of other public agencies in North Carolina may access bathrooms and changing facilities that are consistent with their gender identity in their places of work, while transgender employees may not access bathrooms and changing facilities that are consistent with their gender identity.

45. Defendants' compliance with and implementation of H.B. 2 stigmatizes and singles out transgender employees, results in their isolation and exclusion, and perpetuates a sense that they are not worthy of equal treatment and respect.

46. Upon information and belief, transgender employees of Defendants and other public agencies in North Carolina have suffered and continue to suffer injury, including, without limitation, emotional harm, mental anguish, distress, humiliation, and indignity as a direct and proximate result of Defendants' compliance with and implementation of H.B. 2.

47. Because of the compliance with and implementation of H.B. 2 by Defendants University of North Carolina and Board of Governors of the University of North Carolina, individuals who are not transgender may access campus bathrooms and changing facilities that are consistent with their gender identity, while individuals who are transgender may not access campus bathrooms and changing facilities that are consistent with their gender identity.

48. The compliance with and implementation of H.B. 2 by Defendants University of North Carolina and Board of Governors of the University of North Carolina stigmatizes and singles out transgender individuals, results in their isolation and exclusion, and perpetuates a sense that they are not worthy of equal treatment and respect.

49. Upon information and belief, transgender individuals seeking access to the University of North Carolina campus have suffered and continue to suffer injury, including, without limitation, emotional harm, mental anguish, distress, humiliation, and indignity as a direct and proximate result of compliance with and implementation of H.B. 2.

50. Because of the compliance with and implementation of H.B. 2 by Defendants North Carolina Department of Public Safety, University of North Carolina, and Board of Governors of the University of North Carolina, individuals who are not transgender may access bathrooms and changing facilities that are consistent with their gender identity in covered facilities, while individuals who are transgender may not access bathrooms and changing facilities that are consistent with their gender identity.

51. The compliance with and implementation of H.B. 2 by Defendants North Carolina Department of Public Safety, University of North Carolina, and Board of Governors of the University of North Carolina stigmatizes and singles out transgender individuals seeking access to covered facilities, results in their isolation and exclusion, and perpetuates a sense that they are not worthy of equal treatment and respect.

52. Upon information and belief, transgender individuals seeking access to covered facilities have suffered and continue to suffer injury, including, without limitation, emotional harm, mental anguish, distress, humiliation, and indignity as a direct and proximate result of compliance with and implementation of H.B. 2.

CLAIMS FOR RELIEF

COUNT I

Violation of Title VII of the Civil Rights Act of 1964 ("Title VII")
42 U.S.C. § 2000e, *et seq.*

(Against All Defendants)

53. As alleged in this Complaint, Defendants State of North Carolina, North Carolina Department of Public Safety, University of North Carolina, and Board of Governors of the University of North Carolina are engaged in, and continue to engage in, a pattern or practice of sex discrimination in the terms, conditions, and privileges of employment against their transgender employees in violation Title VII.

54. As alleged in this Complaint, Defendants State of North Carolina and Governor McCrory have engaged in a pattern or practice of resistance to the full enjoyment of employment rights under Title VII by implementing and requiring compliance with policies and practices that require public agencies to discriminate against their transgender employees based on sex in the terms, conditions, and privileges of employment in violation of Title VII.

COUNT II

Violation of Title IX of the Education Act Amendments of 1972 ("Title IX")
20 U.S.C. § 1681, *et seq.*

(Against Defendants University of North Carolina and Board of Governors of the University of North Carolina)

55. As alleged in this Complaint, Defendants University of North Carolina and Board of Governors of the University of North Carolina are discriminating on the basis of sex in violation of Title IX.

COUNT III

Violation of the Violence Against Women Reauthorization Act of 2013 ("VAWA")
42 U.S.C. § 13925(b)(13)
(Against Defendants North Carolina Department of Public Safety,
University of North Carolina, and Board of Governors of the
University of North Carolina)

56. As alleged in this Complaint, Defendants North Carolina Department of Public Safety, University of North Carolina, and Board of Governors of the University of North Carolina are discriminating on the basis of sex and gender identity, in violation of VAWA.

PRAYER FOR RELIEF

WHEREFORE, the United States respectfully requests that this Court:

A. Declare that, by complying with and implementing H.B. 2's provisions that apply to multiple-occupancy bathrooms or changing facilities, Defendants discriminate on the basis of sex in violation of Title VII;

B. Declare that, by complying with and implementing H.B. 2's provisions that apply to multiple-occupancy bathrooms or changing facilities, Defendants University of North Carolina and Board of Governors of the University of North Carolina discriminate on the basis of sex in violation of Title IX;

C. Declare that, by complying with and implementing H.B. 2's provisions that apply to multiple-occupancy bathrooms or changing facilities, Defendants North Carolina Department of Public Safety, University of North Carolina, and Board of Governors of the University of North Carolina discriminate on the basis of sex and gender identity in violation of VAWA;

D. Issue a preliminary and permanent injunction to prevent further violations of federal law; and

E. Grant such additional relief as the needs of justice may require. Dated: May 9, 2016

Respectfully submitted,

Vanita Gupta

Principal Deputy Assistant Attorney General Civil Rights Division

United States Department of Justice

[The list of additional signatories has been omitted.]

Source: U.S. Justice Department. *United States of America v. State of North Carolina.* Case No. 1:16-cv-425. May 10, 2016. http://www.justice.gov/opa/file/849991/download.

OTHER HISTORIC DOCUMENTS OF INTEREST

FROM PREVIOUS *HISTORIC DOCUMENTS*

- President Obama Signs LGBT Employment Protection Executive Order, *2014*, p. 355

April

Mossack Fonseca, International Officials Respond to Leak of "Panama Papers"

APRIL 4 AND 11, AND JUNE 8, 2016

In April 2016, the biggest document leak in journalistic history thrust Panama-based law firm Mossack Fonseca and its clientele into the international media spotlight. Dubbed the "Panama Papers," the leaked documents revealed widespread use of offshore bank accounts and companies by politicians, business leaders, and celebrities worldwide, forcing them and the firm to respond to conflict of interest accusations and allegations of illicit financial activity.

WHISTLEBLOWER LEAKS FILES TO GERMAN NEWSPAPER

In 2015, an anonymous whistleblower contacted reporters at the German newspaper *Süddeutsche Zeitung*, a publication that had previously conducted several investigations into tax evasion and money laundering, and asked if the paper was interested in "data." Over the following months, the whistleblower provided the paper with a total of 11.5 million confidential files in twenty-five different languages from the Panama-based law firm Mossack Fonseca. *Süddeutsche Zeitung*'s reporters spent roughly two months verifying the documents and then turned to the International Consortium of Investigative Journalists (ICIJ) in Washington, D.C., for help with reviewing and analyzing the files' contents. The ICIJ in turn assembled a team of about 400 journalists from more than 100 news organizations in eighty countries to begin processing and developing reports on the information.

In a statement published by *Süddeutsche Zeitung* in May 2016, the whistleblower said he had been motivated by growing income inequality, which he described as "one of the defining issues of our time," and that the documents showed that "massive, pervasive corruption" is the reason why such inequality exists. "Banks, financial regulators, and tax authorities have failed," the statement read. "Decisions have been made that have spared the wealthy while focusing instead on reining in middle- and low-income citizens." The statement added that while "shell companies are not illegal by definition, they are used to carry out a wide array of serious crimes that go beyond evading taxes. I decided to expose Mossack Fonseca because I thought its founders, employees, and clients should have to answer for their roles in these crimes, only some of which have come to light thus far."

"PANAMA PAPERS" REVELATIONS

The first news stories stemming from the leak were published on April 3, 2016, along with roughly 150 of the leaked documents. According to the reports, the documents revealed the names of more than 14,000 clients for whom Mossack Fonseca had created offshore bank accounts or shell companies in so-called "tax havens," such as the British Virgin Islands, Switzerland, and Cyprus, which may have allowed them to avoid taxation. Nearly 215,000 shell companies were identified in the documents, which spanned a nearly forty-year period between 1977 and 2015.

Establishing such offshore companies and accounts is not inherently illegal; however, they tend to draw suspicion due to the secrecy they provide to their owners, which could facilitate illegal activities. National laws and various international agreements require firms that help create companies and bank accounts to determine whether their clients are "politically exposed persons" (government officials or their family members or associates). If they are, the firm is obligated to review the client's activities to ensure they are not engaged in money laundering, tax evasion, or other illicit enterprises.

According to ICIJ, the leaked documents showed that Mossack Fonseca had often failed to follow these legal requirements, and that "in some instances . . . offshore middlemen have protected themselves and their clients by concealing suspect transactions or manipulating official records." On the latter point, ICIJ's specific allegations against Mossack Fonseca included that the firm removed client paperwork and electronic records from its Las Vegas branch to conceal certain activities and that the firm had backdated client documents to provide them with financial advantages.

The news caused a sensation in part because the clients listed in the documents included 143 politicians—and their family members and close associates—from more than fifty countries, as well as business leaders, celebrities, and athletes. Among those named were close associates of Russian President Vladimir Putin, British Prime Minister David Cameron's father, Iceland Prime Minister Sigmundur David Gunnlaugsson, members of the Chinese Communist Party Politburo Standing Committee and President Xi Jinping's relatives, and Argentinian President Mauricio Macri. ICIJ also reported that the list included "at least 33 people and companies blacklisted by the U.S. government because of evidence that they'd been involved in wrongdoing, such as doing business with Mexican drug lords, terrorist organizations like Hezbollah or rogue nations like North Korea and Iran."

Mossack Fonseca issued several statements in response to media reports, the most significant of which was a nearly 3,000-word statement issued on April 4. The statement denied that the firm had been involved in any wrongdoing and provided a point-by-point refutation of specific allegations that had appeared in the media. The statement further maintained that, despite Mossack Fonseca's efforts to correct the record, the media continued to misrepresent the firm's work and relied on stereotypes and conjecture in their reporting. The firm declared that its services "are regulated on multiple levels, often by overlapping agencies, and we have a strong compliance record." The statement noted that "it is legal and common for companies to establish commercial entities in different jurisdictions for a variety of legitimate reasons" and that the firm had always followed international protocols "to assure as is reasonably possible, that the companies we incorporate are not being used for tax evasion, money laundering, terrorist finance, or other illicit purposes." The firm asserted that it conducts "thorough due diligence on all new and prospective clients" and that its employees "are responsible members of the global financial and business community."

This statement and others were published on a separate Mossack Fonseca microsite that was dedicated to responding to the leak and also featured a Frequently Asked Questions document, facts about the firm's work, and case-by-case responses to media reports and requests for information. The firm filed a cease and desist order against the

ICIJ in May to prevent the release of additional documents, arguing that the action was "based on the theft of confidential information and is a violation of the confidentiality agreement between attorney and client." The ICIJ went ahead with its planned release, prompting Mossack Fonseca to threaten further legal action. However, the firm has not yet filed suit.

WORLD LEADERS RESPOND TO ALLEGATIONS

Politicians named, or associated with those named, quickly began responding to the news. In the United Kingdom, Prime Minister David Cameron faced inquiries about his father's hiring of Mossack Fonseca to establish an investment fund in the British Virgin Islands. The opposition Labour Party called for Cameron to share his tax returns and clarify whether he retained any interest in the fund. A spokesperson for Cameron initially stated that these investments were a "private matter" and denied that the prime minister or his family had profited from the fund. Cameron later stated that he and his wife had owned shares in the trust, but sold them off the year before he became prime minister and paid taxes on the dividends received from the sale. Beyond his family's finances, the Panama Papers were also problematic for Cameron because he had positioned himself as a leader of international efforts to combat tax evasion, yet more than half the shell companies listed were registered in British-administered territories and the United Kingdom.

On April 11, Cameron appeared before the House of Commons to "put the record straight." In his statement, Cameron noted that selling his shares of his father's trust was the "simplest and clearest" way for him to avoid a conflict of interest when he became prime minister and reiterated that he had fully followed the House of Commons's rules for registering share holdings. He also spoke about the steps his government had taken to reduce tax evasion and corruption and additional measures that are needed, including creating a new criminal offense for corporations who do not prevent their representatives from criminally facilitating tax evasion. "[I]t is right to tighten the law and change the culture around investment to further outlaw tax evasion and to discourage aggressive tax avoidance," he said. "But as we do so, we should differentiate between schemes designed to artificially reduce tax and those that are encouraging investment."

In Iceland, Prime Minister Sigmundur David Gunnlaugsson faced conflict of interest accusations after the Panama Papers revealed that he and his wife had owned an offshore company established in the Virgin Islands. Gunnlaugsson sold his half of the company to his wife for $1.00 at the end of 2009, before a law took effect that would have required him to declare his involvement in the company as a conflict of interest. The company lost millions of dollars during the 2008 financial crisis and filed a claim for roughly $4 million from three of Iceland's failed banks. The prime minister was involved in negotiating a deal for the banks' claimants. Amid the conflict of interest accusations, Gunnlaugsson asked the deputy prime minister to take over "for an unspecified amount of time," according to a statement from his office.

The Panama Papers also showed that several of Russian President Vladimir Putin's close friends and associates had moved roughly $2 billion through various offshore accounts. One of these friends, cellist Sergei Roldugin, was cited in news reports as being at the center of a plan to hide money from Russian state banks in a complex network of offshore companies. A spokesperson for the Kremlin called the reports "an undisguised paid-for hack job," with Putin claiming that the leak and subsequent accusations were a U.S.-led effort to destabilize Russia. Putin also denied that Roldugin had accumulated substantial wealth and claimed that Roldugin had spent almost all the money he'd earned to buy musical instruments, some of which he had begun donating to government institutions.

Argentinian President Mauricio Macri was shown to have been a director of an offshore company owned by his father, which was dissolved in 2009. Macri had not disclosed his involvement in the company when he completed required asset declarations. A federal prosecutor called for an investigation into Macri's role in the company, though Macri declared he had nothing to hide. Macri's office also stated that the president had never been a shareholder in his father's company and therefore was not required to disclose his involvement.

In China, government officials claimed that the accusations surrounding the Jinping family and Politburo members were unfounded. The government also moved to strip any mentions of the Panama Papers from media reports and blocked related Internet searches.

Amid the ongoing revelations, the Panamanian government sought to defend and distance itself from any allegations of wrongdoing. "We are a country allied in the fight for the transparency of the financial system and we welcome any publication that protects the financial systems of Panama and the world, so that they cannot be used at any time in illicit acts," President Juan Carlos Varela said in a statement. The president noted that since he took office, Panama had taken several steps to transform its financial system and the offering of legal services within the country to help combat illegal activities, including increasing its compliance with international agreements and passing new laws to regulate law firms and real estate businesses as nontraditional financial sectors. Varela also announced that he would create an international panel of experts to explore and propose additional changes to help increase the transparency of Panama's financial sector.

ONGOING INVESTIGATIONS

A series of investigations into the Panama Papers' revelations have been launched across the globe. Shortly after the first news reports were published, Panamanian prosecutors raided Mossack Fonseca's headquarters to search for evidence of criminal activity. A similar raid was conducted by law enforcement officials in San Salvador. The Swiss attorney general announced an investigation into whether Swiss banks participated in any illegal activities related to the financial transactions exposed in the papers, and the U.S. Department of Justice launched a criminal investigation into international tax avoidance schemes. In November, the British Virgin Islands' Financial Services Commission fined Mossack Fonseca $440,000 for eight violations of the islands' anti–money laundering and terrorist financing codes. Officials in the United Kingdom, Canada, India, and Pakistan also began conducting investigations into the companies and individuals named in the Panama Papers. In addition, the European Parliament announced in June the establishment of an inquiry committee to investigate the Panama Papers revelations, with a focus on "alleged contraventions and maladministration in the application by the EU Commission or member states of EU laws on money laundering, tax avoidance, and tax evasion." The committee is expected to present its findings by June 2017.

—Linda Fecteau Grimm

Following is a statement from Mossack Fonseca from April 4, 2016, responding to media reports surrounding the leak of the Panama Papers; a statement from the government of Panama from April 4, 2016, about financial reform efforts and transparency; a statement by British Prime Minister David Cameron before the House of Commons on April 11, 2016, about his finances and the government's efforts to reduce tax evasion and corruption; and a press release from the European Parliament from June 8, 2016, announcing the formation of a Panama Papers inquiry committee.

DOCUMENT

Mossack Fonseca on the Leak of the Panama Papers

April 4, 2016

Recent media reports have portrayed an inaccurate view of the services that we provide and, despite our efforts to correct the record, misrepresented the nature of our work and its role in global financial markets.

These reports rely on supposition and stereotypes, and play on the public's lack of familiarity with the work of firms like ours. The unfortunate irony is that the materials on which these reports are based actually show the high standards we operate under, specifically that:

- we conduct due diligence on clients at the outset of a potential engagement and on an ongoing basis;

- we routinely deny services to individuals who are compromised or who fail to provide information we need in order to comply with "know your client" obligations or when we identify other red flags through our due diligence;

- we routinely resign from client engagements when ongoing due diligence and/ or updates to sanctions lists reveals that a party to a company for which we provide services been either convicted or listed by a sanctioning body;

- we routinely comply with requests from authorities investigating companies or individuals for whom we are providing services; and

- we work with established intermediaries, such as investment banks, accountancies and law firms, as part of the regulated global financial system.

We would like to take this opportunity to address some specific misconceptions about our work and clarify the inaccuracies that are rife in the recent media reports.

We provide company incorporation and related administrative services that are widely available and commonly used worldwide.

Incorporating companies is the normal activity of lawyers and agents around the world. Services such as company formations, registered agent, and others are frequently used and provided in many worldwide jurisdictions, including the United States and the United Kingdom.

Moreover, it is legal and common for companies to establish commercial entities in different jurisdictions for a variety of legitimate reasons, including conducting cross-border mergers and acquisitions, estate planning, personal safety, and restructurings and pooling of investment capital from investors residing in different jurisdictions who want a neutral legal and tax regime that does not benefit or disadvantage any one investor.

Our registered agent and corporate secretarial services are limited to a narrow set of administrative services.

These services are related to facilitating document filings before the authorities and registry of a company's jurisdiction, and helping a company register for taxes and file for licenses, manage patents and trademarks, file tax returns and other documentation.

The resident agent is not involved in managing the business in any way. . . .

Our services are regulated on multiple levels, often by overlapping agencies, and we have a strong compliance record.

Our business is regulated by several different oversight and enforcement agencies, including the Banking Superintendence of Panama and the Intendancy of Non-financial Regulated Services Providers. We are also subject to regulatory oversight and enforcement in all of the other jurisdictions where we incorporate companies. In addition, we have always complied with international protocols such as the Financial Action Task Force (FATF) and, more recently, the U.S. Foreign Account Tax Compliance Act (FATCA) to assure as is reasonably possible, that the companies we incorporate are not being used for tax evasion, money laundering, terrorist finance or other illicit purposes. . . .

We are responsible members of the global financial and business community.

We conduct thorough due diligence on all new and prospective clients that often exceeds in stringency the existing rules and standards to which we and others are bound. . . .

Indeed, the documents cited in the media reports show that we routinely deny services to individuals who are compromised or who fail to provide information we need in order to comply with our KYC and other obligations.

Our due diligence procedures require us to update the information that we have on clients and to periodically verify that no negative results exist in regards to the companies we incorporate and the individuals behind them. Again, the documents cited in the media reports show that we routinely resign from client engagements when ongoing due diligence and updates to sanctions lists reveal that a beneficial owner of a company for which we provide services is compromised.

For 40 years Mossack Fonseca has operated beyond reproach in our home country and other jurisdictions where we have operations. . . .

We operate in jurisdictions with increasingly stringent financial and legal controls.

All of the jurisdictions where we have operations have made significant strides in their efforts to comply with global protocols to prevent abuse of their financial and corporate systems. This includes preventing money laundering, combatting terrorist financing and preventing tax evasion. . . .

We regret any misuse of our services and actively take steps to prevent it.

We regret any misuse of companies that we incorporate or the services we provide and take steps wherever possible to uncover and stop such use. If we detect suspicious activity or misconduct, we are quick to report it to the authorities. Similarly, when authorities approach us with evidence of possible misconduct, we always cooperate fully with them.

[The following paragraphs, containing more detailed responses to specific allegations, have been omitted.]

SOURCE: Mossack Fonseca & Co. "Statement Regarding Recent Media Coverage." April 4, 2016. http://mossfonmedia.com/wp-content/uploads/2016/05/complete_statement.pdf.

Statement by the Government of Panama on Financial Transparency

April 4, 2016

The Government of the Republic of Panama will defend vigorously its international image and its record of reforms unprecedented to do increasingly more solid and transparent financial and legal and services in the country, said today Juan Carlos Varela, President of the Republic.

The President, when approached by the media during the act of sanction of the Colón Free Port Law and the Law amending the Colon Free Zone, reminded that in the first 21 months of his government have taken [sic] unprecedented steps to strengthen the transparency of the financial and legal services of Panama.

"We are a country allied in the fight for the transparency of the financial system and we welcome any publication that protects the financial systems of Panama and the world, so that they cannot be used at any time in illicit acts," said Varela.

The President added that "we will cooperate in whatever is necessary. We are an open country and in these 21 months in office we have taken very specific decisions to transform the financial systems, and legal services and shield them."

The President said that Panama entered the grey list of the Financial Action Task Force (FATF), but the country, in record time[,] was excluded from it after the adoption of important laws that protect the Panamanian financial system from being used by organized crime.

Varela said that "if the challenge is to defend the name of Panama and the financial system that is my job." He said the Vice President and Chancellor, Isabel de Saint Malo de Alvarado[,] and all diplomatic missions were informed of the position of the Government so that they project to the world that this Administration has a permanent fight for transparency.

FACTS

As from January 2016, entered into force new norms limiting the use of bearer shares of Panamanian societies. With these new norms, the societies that have issued bearer shares should deliver them in custody to agents authorized and regulated by financial entities.

In compliance with the commitments with FATF It [sic] was approved Law 23 of 2015, with which measures were taken to strengthen our financial system against money laundering and the financing of terrorism, in accordance with the road map prepared by the Money Laundering Commission with the purpose of bring [sic] our country out from the grey list of FATF.

Additionally, as part of the implementation of monitoring and combating illicit activities, 7 new laws have been approved including new offences as well as the regulation of non-traditional financial sectors such as law firms and real estate business in order to increase transparency and combat the inappropriate use of our financial center.

SOURCE: Government of the Republic of Panama. "The Government will defend image and efforts of Panama on terms of transparency." April 4, 2016. https://www.presidencia.gob.pa/en/Comunicados/The-Government-will-defend-image-and-efforts-of-Panama-on-terms-of-transparency.

Prime Minister Cameron Responds to Panama Papers

April 11, 2016

With permission, Mr Speaker, I would like to make a statement on the Panama Papers.

Dealing with my own circumstances first, yesterday I published all the information in my tax returns not just for the last year, but for the last 6 years.

I have also given additional information about money inherited and given to me by my family, so people can see the sources of income I have.

My salary. The benefit in kind of living in Number 10 Downing Street. The support my wife and I have received as Leader of the Conservative Party. The renting out of our London home. The interest on the savings I have.

Since 2010 I have not owned any shares or any investments.

The publication of a Prime Minister's tax information in this way is unprecedented—but I think it is the right thing to do. . . .

Mr Speaker, let me deal specifically with the shares my wife and I held in an investment fund or unit trust called Blairmore Holdings, set up by my late father.

The fund was registered with the UK's Inland Revenue from the beginning.

It was properly audited and an annual return was submitted to the Inland Revenue every year.

Its share price was listed in the Financial Times.

It wasn't a family trust—it was a commercial investment fund for any investor to buy units in.

UK investors paid all the same taxes as with any other share—including income tax on the dividends every year.

Mr Speaker, there have been some deeply hurtful and profoundly untrue allegations made against my father.

And I want to, if the House will let me, put the record straight.

This investment fund was set up overseas in the first place because it was going to be trading predominantly in dollar securities.

So like very many other commercial investment funds, it made sense to be set up inside one of the main centres of dollar trading.

There are thousands of these investment funds and many millions of people in Britain who own shares, many of whom hold them through investment funds or unit trusts.

Such funds, including those listed outside the UK, are included in the pension funds of local government, most of Britain's largest companies and indeed even some trade unions. . . .

Mr Speaker, one of the country's leading tax lawyers, Graham Aaronson QC[,] has stated unequivocally that this was "a perfectly normal type of collective investment fund." Mr Speaker, this is the man who led the expert study group that developed the General Anti-Abuse Rule, so much debated and demanded in this House, which Parliament finally enacted in 2013.

He also chaired the 1997 examination of tax avoidance by the Tax Law Review Committee.

He has said that it would be—and I quote—"quite wrong to describe the establishment of such funds as 'tax avoidance'" and further that it would—and I quote—"be utterly ridiculous to suggest that establishing or investing in such funds would involve abusive tax avoidance".

That is why getting rid of unit trusts and other such investment funds that are listed overseas has not been part of any Labour policy review[,] any Conservative policy review[,] or any sensible proposals for addressing tax evasion or aggressive tax avoidance.

Now surely—it is said—investors in these funds benefit from them being set up in jurisdictions with low or no taxes.

Again this is a misunderstanding.

Unit trusts do not exist to make profit for themselves but for the holders of the units.

And those holders pay tax.

And if they are UK citizens, they pay full UK taxes.

Mr Speaker, it is right to tighten the law and change the culture around investment to further outlaw tax evasion and to discourage aggressive tax avoidance.

But as we do so, we should differentiate between schemes designed to artificially reduce tax and those that are encouraging investment.

Mr Speaker, this is a government and this should be a country that believes in aspiration and wealth creation.

So we must defend the right of every British citizen to make money lawfully.

Aspiration and wealth creation are not somehow dirty words.

They are the key engines of growth and prosperity in our country and we must always support those who want to own shares and make investments to support their families.

Some people have asked, "If this trust was legitimate, why did you sell your shares in January 2010?"

Mr Speaker, I sold all the shares in my portfolio that year because I didn't want any issues about conflicts of interest.

I did not want anyone to be able to suggest that as Prime Minister I had any other agendas or vested interests.

Selling all my shares was the simplest and clearest way that I could do that.

There are strict rules in this House for the registration of share holdings. I have followed them in full.

The Labour Party has said it will refer me to the Commissioner for Parliamentary Standards.

I have already given her the relevant information and if there is more she believes that I should say, I am very happy to say it.

Mr Speaker, I accept all the criticisms for not responding more quickly to these issues last week. . . .

Mr Speaker, on the issue of inheritance tax, there is an established system in this country.

Far from people being embarrassed about passing things to their children, like wanting to keep a family home within the family[,] I believe it is a natural human instinct and something that should be encouraged.

And as for parents passing money to their children while they are still alive it is something the tax rules fully recognise.

Many parents want to help their children when they buy their first car, get a deposit for their first home or face the costs of starting a family.

It is entirely natural that parents should want to do these things.

And again, it's something that we should not just defend but proudly support.

GOVERNMENT ACTION

Mr Speaker, let me turn to the Panama Papers and the actions that this government is taking to deal with tax evasion, aggressive tax avoidance and international corruption more broadly. . . .

In the last Parliament alone we made an unprecedented 40 tax changes to close loopholes that raised £12 billion.

And in this Parliament we will legislate for more than 25 further measures, forecast to raise £16 billion by 2021. . . .

[T]oday 129 jurisdictions have committed to implementing the international standard for exchange of tax information on request and over 95 jurisdictions have committed to implementing the new global common reporting standard on tax transparency. . . .

And in June this year, Mr Speaker, Britain will become the first country in the G20 to have a public register of beneficial ownership so everyone can see who really owns and controls each company.

This government is also consulting on requiring foreign companies that own property or bid on public contracts also provide their beneficial ownership information.

And we are happy to offer technical support and assistance to any of the devolved administrations also considering these measures.

But as the revelations in the Panama Papers have made clear, we need to go even further.

So Mr Speaker, we are taking 3 additional measures to make it harder for people to hide the proceeds of corruption offshore to make sure that those who smooth the way, can no longer get away with it and to investigate wrongdoing.

But first, let me deal with our Crown Dependencies and our Overseas Territories that function as financial centres.

They have already agreed to exchange taxpayer financial account information automatically—and will begin doing so from this September. . . .

Mr Speaker, today I can tell the House that we have now agreed that they will provide UK law enforcement and tax agencies with full access to information on the beneficial ownership of companies. . . .

For the first time, UK police and law enforcement will be able to see exactly who really owns and controls every company incorporated in these territories. Cayman Islands, British Virgin Islands, Bermuda, Isle of Man, Jersey—the lot.

This is the result of a sustained campaign, building on the progress we made at the G8 in Lough Erne and I welcome the commitment of the governments of these territories to work with us and to implement these arrangements.

And the House should note that this will place our Overseas Territories and Crown Dependencies well ahead of many other similar jurisdictions but also, crucially, ahead of many of our major international partners—including some states in the United States of America.

Next month we will seek to go further still, using our Anti-corruption Summit to encourage consensus not just on exchanging information—but actually on publishing information, putting it in the public domain as we are doing here in the UK.

Because we want everyone with a stake in fighting corruption—from law enforcement, to civil society, to the media—to be able use this data and help us to root out and deter wrongdoing.

Next, we will take another major step forward in dealing with those who facilitate corruption.

Under current legislation it is difficult to prosecute a company that assists with tax evasion.

But we are going to change that.

So we will legislate this year for a new criminal offence to apply to corporations who fail to prevent their representatives from criminally facilitating tax evasion.

Finally, we are providing initial new funding of up to £10 million for a new cross-agency taskforce to swiftly analyse all the information that's been made available from Panama and to take rapid action. . . .

[Concluding remarks have been omitted.]

SOURCE: United Kingdom Prime Minister's Office. "PM Commons Statement on Panama Papers: 11 April 2016." April 11, 2016. http://www.gov.uk/government/speeches/pm-commons-statement-on-panama-papers-11-april-2016.

European Parliament Establishes Panama Papers Inquiry Committee

June 8, 2016

The European Parliament agreed to set up an inquiry committee into the "Panama Papers" revelations, of detailed information on offshore companies and their ultimate beneficiaries, in a vote on Wednesday. The committee is to investigate alleged contraventions and maladministration in the application by the EU Commission or member states of EU laws on money laundering, tax avoidance and tax evasion. It will have 65 members and twelve months to present its report.

The European Parliament Conference of Presidents (EP President and political group leaders), agreed the committee's mandate on Thursday 2 June.

SOURCE: European Parliament. "Parliament sets up 'Panama Papers' inquiry committee." June 8, 2016. © European Union, 2016. http://www.europarl.europa.eu/news/en/news-room/20160603IPR30203/parliament-sets-up-%E2%80%9Cpanama-papers%E2%80%9D-inquiry-committee.

OTHER HISTORIC DOCUMENTS OF INTEREST

FROM THIS VOLUME

- Brazilian President Impeached amid Corruption Scandal, p. 218

FROM PREVIOUS *HISTORIC DOCUMENTS*

- U.S. and Russian Officials Respond to NSA Leaks, *2013*, p. 329
- U.S. Department of State Responds to WikiLeaks, *2010*, p. 596

Supreme Court Rules on Apportionment of Voting Districts

APRIL 4, 2016

On April 4, 2016, the United States Supreme Court delivered a major ruling in *Evenwel v. Abbott* on the meaning of a fundamental constitutional principle of voting rights—that of "one person, one vote." Specifically, the case focused on what "one person" means for the purpose of creating equal voting districts within a state. The Court had never before addressed who should be included in this count. Currently, all fifty states rely on U.S. Census data to create legislative and municipal districts that contain roughly equal numbers of total people. The Supreme Court's unanimous decision left this system in place. The Court rejected the challengers' position that when Texas created equal districts by population, including all people in the count, without regard to whether they were eligible to vote, the state unconstitutionally diluted the challengers' voting power. They argued unsuccessfully that the equal protection provisions of the Constitution require that voting districts equalize voting-eligible populations rather than total population. Justice Ruth Bader Ginsburg, the author of this opinion, concluded, "As history, precedent, and practice demonstrate, it is plainly permissible for jurisdictions to measure equalization by the total population of state and local legislative districts."

ONE PERSON, ONE VOTE

In what is known as the Great Compromise, the Framers of the Constitution provided each state with two senators and allocated House seats based on a state's total population. The idea that voting districts be drawn by total population, and not by populations of voters, was ensconced in Article I, Section 2, of the U.S. Constitution, which dictates that federal congressional districts be apportioned "according to their respective Numbers." For this reason, this case does not involve any federal jurisdictions and only challenges districts drawn by states or municipalities.

The Supreme Court historically has been reluctant to become involved in overseeing the process by which states draw their own legislative districts. This changed in 1964, when the Court, in *Westberry v. Sanders*, invalidated a map of legislative districts in Georgia because some districts had two or three times as many people in them as others. The Court held that the Constitution requires that congressional districts be drawn with equal populations. It was in this case and a series of other landmark decisions in the 1960s that the Court first articulated what has become known as the "one person, one vote" principle, which encapsulates the ideal, rooted in notions of equal protection, that everyone's votes count equally. The *Evenwel* opinion described the cases, read together, as instructing "that jurisdictions must design both congressional and state-legislative districts with equal populations, and must regularly reapportion districts to prevent malapportionment." Today, virtually all state jurisdictions have drawn their political district jurisdictions to hold roughly equal total populations, using figures revised every ten years from the U.S. Census.

The challengers in *Evenwel v. Abbott* did not challenge the "one person, one vote" principle, but rather argued that counting noneligible voters as well as voters when creating equal districts violated their constitutional rights by devaluing their vote. These Texas voters argued that, because they vote in districts with few nonvoters, their vote is not worth as much in their district relative to that of a voter who votes in a district of the same population, but which has fewer overall voters. They further argued that the constitutional principle of equal voting rights requires states to draw districts with equal numbers of voters, not equal total populations.

The conservative political and legal advocacy group that brought the challenge on behalf of the voters, the Project on Fair Representation, was the same group that had brought challenges to the University of Texas's use of affirmative action in admissions, and also brought the case that led the Court to strike a major portion of the Voting Rights Act.

STATUS QUO LEFT IN PLACE

The Supreme Court unanimously turned back the effort to reinterpret the meaning of the "one person, one vote" rule of voting rights. Justice Ginsburg wrote the opinion, joined by Chief Justice John Roberts, and Justices Anthony Kennedy, Stephen Breyer, Sonia Sotomayor, and Elena Kagan. Justices Clarence Thomas and Samuel Alito, while agreeing with the result, wrote separate concurring opinions.

The Equal Protection Clause of the Constitution has been interpreted to grant to each person equal voting power, but, until this case, the Supreme Court had not clarified whether the guarantee was for equality among the same number of people, or whether it guaranteed equality among those who can vote. Justice Ginsburg held that nothing in the Constitution requires states to change from their current system of drawing legislative districts based on total population. "It is," she concludes, "plainly permissible for jurisdictions to measure equalization by the total population of state and local legislative districts." She based this conclusion on a review of the constitutional history, earlier Supreme Court decisions, and long-standing practice.

There is no question that *federal* voting districts must be drawn to equalize total population; this is clearly written in the Constitution. Justice Ginsburg's opinion quoted many Framers underscoring the importance of this principle. Alexander Hamilton, for instance, endorsed apportionment based on total population: "There can be no truer principle than this—that every individual of the community at large has an equal right to the protection of government." The clear intent was to base representation on a count of all inhabitants, even at a time when only white, property-owning men could vote, and slaves were counted as only three-fifths of a person. Debates on this issue after the Civil War made clear that the Equal Protection Clause of the Fourteenth Amendment retained total population as the basis for congressional apportionment. This led Justice Ginsburg to conclude: "It cannot be that the Fourteenth Amendment calls for the apportionment of congressional districts based on total population, but simultaneously prohibits States from apportioning their own legislative districts on the same basis."

Justice Ginsburg's final set of arguments turn on more practical issues. Changing to a standard of voting-eligible population parity, she wrote, would "upset a well-functioning approach to districting that all 50 States and countless local jurisdictions have followed for decades, even centuries." Furthermore, she notes that, when representatives serve a jurisdiction, they "serve all residents, not just those eligible or registered to vote." Children, for example, cannot vote but they may have a strong stake in public education or public benefits. "By ensuring that each representative is subject to requests and suggestions from the same number of constituents," Justice Ginsburg concludes, "total-population apportionment promotes equitable and effective representation."

The unanimous support for the result in this case may be attributable to the fact that it took a limited approach to the issue presented and simply put other, more contentious issues off to be resolved by future cases. The Ginsburg ruling did not give the challengers what they were seeking: a ruling that only voting-eligible populations can be counted in districting. But, at the same time, it stopped short of ruling that the Constitution requires states to rely exclusively on total population counts, as the Obama administration had wanted. Neither did the ruling satisfy those who wanted a ruling that states are free to choose other ways of counting populations for the purposes of redistricting. "We need not and do not resolve whether, as Texas now argues, States may draw districts to equalize voter-eligible population rather than total population," Justice Ginsburg wrote.

Justices Thomas and Alito agreed with the result that states cannot be forced to change how they apportion their voting districts, but neither signed on to the majority decision. Alito used his separate opinion to emphasize the issues that were not completely settled by the Court's decision. He wrote: "Whether a state is permitted to use some measure other than total population is an important and sensitive question that we can consider if and when we have before us a state districting plan that, unlike the current Texas plan, uses something other than total population as the basis for equalizing the size of districts." Justice Thomas went much further, using his lengthy opinion to argue that the Court "has never provided a sound basis for the one-person, one vote principle." In his view, the Constitution grants the states significant leeway over how to apportion their own districts. "There is no single 'correct' method of apportioning state legislatures," he wrote, leaving the states free to choose "total population, eligible voters, or any other nondiscriminatory voter base."

IMPACT OF THE COURT DECISION

This case was highly anticipated and ultimately important because of what it had the potential to do rather than what it did. Had the Court ruled for the challengers, it would have made every state and local legislative map in the United States unconstitutional.

As a practical matter, who gets counted in these districts can have an enormous political impact. Generally, the large, rapidly growing urban areas have the largest percentage of voting-ineligible residents—children, noncitizens, and ex-felons. To render all these nonvoters invisible when drawing political district lines would result in a shifting of political power to the more homogenous and rural parts of the state. Politically, this would lead to a shift of power from more traditionally Democratic urban areas to those that are more Republican and rural. The impact would have been greatest in some of the largest states—Texas, California, New York, New Jersey, Arizona, and Nevada.

Civil rights organizations across the country expressed their support for the result in this case. Kristen Clarke, president of the Lawyers' Committee for Civil Rights Under the Law, praised the decision: "Today's decision renders null and void efforts to marginalize minority communities from having an equal seat at the table in our political process."

This opinion did not shut down the possibility that another case could rise in the future from a state that wanted to change how it sets its political boundaries. The founder of the group that brought the challenge, Edward Blum, expressed his disappointment with the result of the case, but stressed that "the issue of voter equality in the United States is not going to go away. Some Supreme Court cases grow in importance over time, and *Evenwel v. Abbott* may likely be one of those cases."

—Melissa Feinberg

Following is the edited text of the Supreme Court's decision in Evenwel v. Abbott on April 4, 2016, in which the Court ruled unanimously to leave in place the current interpretation of the "one person, one vote" apportionment definition, which allows for the drawing of legislative districts based on total population, rather than only voting-eligible residents.

Evenwel v. Abbott

April 4, 2016

[Syllabus and footnotes have been omitted.]

No. 14–940

Sue Evenwel, et al., appellants

v.

Greg Abbott, Governor of Texas, et al.

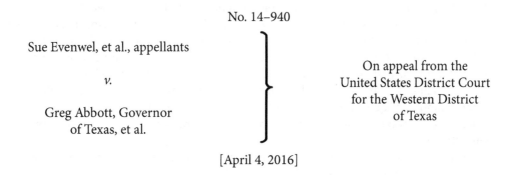

On appeal from the United States District Court for the Western District of Texas

[April 4, 2016]

JUSTICE GINSBURG delivered the opinion of the Court.

Texas, like all other States, draws its legislative districts on the basis of total population. Plaintiffs-appellants are Texas voters; they challenge this uniform method of districting on the ground that it produces unequal districts when measured by voter-eligible population. Voter-eligible population, not total population, they urge, must be used to ensure that their votes will not be devalued in relation to citizens' votes in other districts. We hold, based on constitutional history, this Court's decisions, and longstanding practice, that a State may draw its legislative districts based on total population.

I

[Section I A, outlining the Court's earlier actions in regards to apportionment, has been omitted.]

B

... Appellants Sue Evenwel and Edward Pfenninger live in Texas Senate districts (one and four, respectively) with particularly large eligible- and registered-voter populations. Contending that basing apportionment on total population dilutes their votes in relation to voters in other Senate districts, in violation of the one-person, one-vote principle of the Equal Protection Clause, appellants filed suit in the U. S. District Court for the Western District of Texas. They named as defendants the Governor and Secretary of State of Texas, and sought a permanent injunction barring use of the existing Senate map in favor of a map that would equalize the voter population in each district. ...

II

The parties and the United States advance different positions in this case. As they did before the District Court, appellants insist that the Equal Protection Clause requires jurisdictions to draw state and local legislative districts with equal voter-eligible populations, thus protecting "voter equality," i.e., "the right of eligible voters to an equal vote." Brief for Appellants 14. To comply with their proposed rule, appellants suggest, jurisdictions should design districts based on citizen-voting-age population (CVAP) data from the Census Bureau's American Community Survey (ACS), an annual statistical sample of the U. S. population. Texas responds that jurisdictions may, consistent with the Equal Protection Clause, design districts using any population baseline—including population and voter-eligible population—so long as the choice is rational and not invidiously discriminatory. Although its use of total-population data from the census was permissible, Texas therefore argues, it could have used ACS CVAP data instead. Sharing Texas' position that the Equal Protection Clause does not mandate use of voter-eligible population, the United States urges us not to address Texas' separate assertion that the Constitution allows States to use alternative population baselines, including voter-eligible population. Equalizing total population, the United States maintains, vindicates the principle of representational equality by "ensur[ing] that the voters in each district have the power to elect a representative who represents the same number of constituents as all other representatives." ...

In agreement with Texas and the United States, we reject appellants' attempt to locate a voter-equality mandate in the Equal Protection Clause. As history, precedent, and practice demonstrate, it is plainly permissible for jurisdictions to measure equalization by the total population of state and local legislative districts.

A

We begin with constitutional history. At the time of the founding, the Framers confronted a question analogous to the one at issue here: On what basis should congressional districts be allocated to States? The Framers' solution, now known as the Great Compromise, was to provide each State the same number of seats in the Senate, and to allocate House seats based on States' total populations. "Representatives and direct Taxes," they wrote, "shall be apportioned among the several States which may be included within this Union, *according to their respective Numbers.*" U. S. Const., Art. I, §2, cl. 3 (emphasis added). "It is a fundamental principle of the proposed constitution," James Madison explained in the Federalist Papers, "that as the aggregate number of representatives allotted to the several states, is to be ... founded on the aggregate number of inhabitants; so, the right of choosing this allotted number in each state, is to be exercised by such part of the inhabitants, as the state itself may designate." The Federalist No. 54, p. 284 (G. Carey & J. McClellan eds. 2001). In other words, the basis of *representation* in the House was to include all inhabitants—although slaves were counted as only three-fifths of a person—even though States remained free to deny many of those inhabitants the right to participate in the selection of their representatives. Endorsing apportionment based on total population, Alexander Hamilton declared: "There can be no truer principle than this—that every individual of the community at large has an equal right to the protection of government." 1 Records of the Federal Convention of 1787, p. 473 (M. Farrand ed. 1911).

When debating what is now the Fourteenth Amendment, Congress reconsidered the proper basis for apportioning House seats. ... The product of these debates was §2 of the Fourteenth Amendment, which retained total population as the congressional apportionment base. See U. S. Const., Amdt. 14, §2 ("Representatives shall be apportioned among the several States according to their respective numbers, counting the whole number of persons in each State, excluding Indians not taxed."). ...

Appellants ask us to find in the Fourteenth Amendment's Equal Protection Clause a rule inconsistent with this "theory of the Constitution." But, as the Court recognized in *Westberry*, this theory underlies not just the method of allocating House seats to States; it applies as well to the method of apportioning legislative seats within States.

"The debates at the [Constitutional] Convention," the Court explained, "make at least one fact abundantly clear: that when the delegates agreed that the House should represent 'people,' they intended that in allocating Congressmen the number assigned to each state should be determined solely by the number of inhabitants." 376 U. S., at 13. "While it may not be possible to draw congressional districts with mathematical precision," the Court acknowledged, "that is no excuse for ignoring our Constitution's plain objective of making equal representation for *equal numbers of people* the fundamental goal for the House of Representatives." *Id.*, at 18 (emphasis added). It cannot be that the Fourteenth Amendment calls for the apportionment of congressional districts based on total population, but simultaneously prohibits States from apportioning their own legislative districts on the same basis. ...

[Section B, which speaks of how past Court cases influenced the Court's ruling here, has been omitted.]

C

What constitutional history and our prior decisions strongly suggest, settled practice confirms. Adopting voter-eligible apportionment as constitutional command would upset a well-functioning approach to districting that all 50 States and countless local jurisdictions have followed for decades, even centuries. Appellants have shown no reason for the Court to disturb this longstanding use of total population. See *Walz v. Tax Comm'n of City of New York*, 397 U. S. 664, 678 (1970) ("unbroken practice" followed "openly and by affirmative state action, not covertly or by state inaction, is not something to be lightly cast aside"). As the Framers of the Constitution and the Fourteenth Amendment comprehended, representatives serve all residents, not just those eligible or registered to vote. Nonvoters have an important stake in many policy debates—children, their parents, even their grandparents, for example, have a stake in a strong public-education system—and in receiving constituent services, such as help navigating public-benefits bureaucracies. By ensuring that each representative is subject to requests and suggestions from the same number of constituents, total population apportionment promotes equitable and effective representation. See *McCormick v. United States*, 500 U. S. 257, 272 (1991) ("Serving constituents and supporting legislation that will benefit the district and individuals and groups therein is the everyday business of a legislator.").

In sum, the rule appellants urge has no mooring in the Equal Protection Clause. The Texas Senate map, we therefore conclude, complies with the requirements of the one-person, one-vote principle. Because history, precedent, and practice suffice to reveal the infirmity of appellants' claims, we need not and do not resolve whether, as Texas now argues, States may draw districts to equalize voter-eligible population rather than total population.

* * *

For the reasons stated, the judgment of the United States District Court for the Western District of Texas is

Affirmed.

JUSTICE THOMAS, concurring in the judgment.

. . . I write separately because this Court has never provided a sound basis for the one-person, one-vote principle. For 50 years, the Court has struggled to define what right that principle protects. Many of our precedents suggest that it protects the right of eligible voters to cast votes that receive equal weight. Despite that frequent explanation, our precedents often conclude that the Equal Protection Clause is satisfied when all individuals within a district—voters or not—have an equal share of representation. The majority today concedes that our cases have not produced a clear answer on this point. See *ante,* at 16.

In my view, the majority has failed to provide a sound basis for the one-person, one-vote principle because no such basis exists. The Constitution does not prescribe any one basis for apportionment within States. It instead leaves States significant leeway in apportioning their own districts to equalize total population, to equalize eligible voters, or to promote any other principle consistent with a republican form of government. The majority should recognize the futility of choosing only one of these options. The Constitution leaves the choice to the people alone—not to this Court. . . .

[The remainder of Justice Thomas's concurring opinion has been omitted.]

[The concurring opinion of Justice Alito has been omitted.]

Source: U.S. Supreme Court. *Evenwel v. Abbott.* 578 U.S.___(2016). http://www.supremecourt.gov/opinions/15pdf/14-940_ed9g.pdf.

OTHER HISTORIC DOCUMENTS OF INTEREST

FROM PREVIOUS *HISTORIC DOCUMENTS*

Brazilian President Impeached
amid Corruption Scandal

APRIL 17, MAY 5, AND AUGUST 31, 2016

As Brazil's first female president, Dilma Rousseff made history when she was elected in 2010, boosted by her position as heir apparent to popular incumbent Luiz Inácio Lula da Silva and the country's strong economy. Yet Rousseff's approval rating dwindled as her policies reversed hard-won economic advances made by her predecessors and corruption scandals racked Brazil's political sphere. Accusations that Rousseff used funds from state banks to conceal budget shortfalls in an effort to improve her reelection prospects provided further motivation for an impeachment movement that began in 2015 and culminated in Rousseff's removal from office in 2016.

A Faltering Economy and a Major Political Scandal

Initial calls for Rousseff's impeachment came amid the worst economic recession Brazil had experienced since the 1930s. Rousseff's fiscal policies during her first term failed to maintain the strong economic growth achieved by her two recent predecessors, Luiz Inácio Lula da Silva and Fernando Henrique Cardoso. Following her reelection in 2014, Brazil's already weakened economy was hard hit by the global drop in commodities prices and economic slowdown in China, a key trading partner. Brazil's economy contracted by 4.5 percent in 2015, and was expected to contract by at least another 3.5 percent in 2016. In addition, inflation reached a twelve-year high of 10.7 percent, and unemployment increased to 9 percent in 2015.

Meanwhile, dozens of Brazilian politicians were implicated in a wide-reaching scandal known as Operation Car Wash that involved the state-owned oil company Petrobras. The company became the focus of a $2 billion corruption investigation that began in March 2014, following allegations that Brazil's largest construction companies had overcharged Petrobras for building contracts and then gave portions of the overpayments to Petrobras executives and politicians who were in on the deal. Brazil's attorney general accused Lula da Silva of playing a key role in orchestrating the scandal, and prosecutors claimed that members of the Workers' Party—the party of both Lula da Silva and Rousseff—had partly financed its political campaigns and other expenses using money from the kickbacks.

Prosecutors also alleged that politicians involved in the scandal were using offshore companies to hide their money, or had reinvested the money in expensive art collections or seaside real estate. The 2016 "Panama Papers" leak revealed that at least fifty-seven Brazilians linked to Operation Car Wash had opened 107 offshore companies through the law firm Mossack Fonseca. In addition to the Workers' Party, politicians from six other political parties were named as Mossack Fonseca clients. Brazilian journalists reported that one of the offshore companies was directly linked to Eduardo Cunha, the speaker of the Chamber of Deputies and a vocal critic of Rousseff's, though Cunha denied the allegation. Lula da Silva has also been questioned about some of the shell companies identified in the Panama Papers.

Rousseff served as Petrobras's chair for seven years before becoming president. The Brazilian Social Democracy Party, the main opposition to the Workers' Party, claimed that Rousseff's presidential campaigns were funded with money from the Petrobras scandal. The Workers' Party denies this claim and says that all members' election campaigns have been legally funded. While much of the purported corruption took place while Rousseff was chair, no evidence has yet been found that shows she profited from the scandal.

A Movement to Impeach

By the end of 2015, Rousseff's approval rating had dropped to 10 percent. In March, Brazilians called for Rousseff's impeachment during a series of nationwide protests, and at least twelve petitions for her impeachment had been submitted to the Chamber of Deputies by October, though none had been accepted. (The speaker must accept a petition before impeachment proceedings can begin.)

In addition to dissatisfaction with the country's economic situation and outrage over Operation Car Wash, Rousseff faced accusations that she had used funds from state banks to cover budget shortfalls in 2014. Specifically, she was accused of delaying the repayment of approximately $11.6 billion worth of funding received from state lenders—money that had been used to pay for popular social programs such as unemployment insurance. Rousseff's opponents claimed that Rousseff's budgetary maneuvering was intended to make the country's fiscal state appear stronger than it was, thereby improving her chances for reelection, which she won by a razor-thin margin.

After completing its audit of the government's 2014 accounts, members of Brazil's Tribunal de Contas da União (TCU) issued a unanimous decision in October 2015 that Rousseff had violated the country's fiscal responsibility law. The government denied there had been any irregularities in its accounting. Officials acknowledged the delay in repaying lenders because of limited cash flow at the time, but noted that other administrations had employed the same practice in the past without being found to have broken the law.

The Brazilian Constitution states that any president who breaks fiscal responsibility laws should be impeached and removed from office, meaning that the TCU decision gave Rousseff's opponents the legal standing they needed for an impeachment petition to be accepted. However, the actual influence of the TCU's decision is questionable given widespread speculation that Cunha's personal agenda drove the impeachment process forward. When the calls for Rousseff's impeachment began, Cunha did not pursue the issue, stating that impeachment would be a "backward step for democracy." But he turned against the Workers' Party in August 2015 after he was charged with accepting as much as $40 million in bribes from Petrobras and hiding the money in a Swiss bank account. Cunha accused the party of singling him out among those named in Operation Car Wash to cover up their own corruption. Then, in December, three members of the Workers' Party who sat on the chamber's ethics committee said they would support a full chamber vote on whether Cunha could remain in the legislature while he was under investigation for his involvement in the Petrobras scandal. Shortly thereafter, Cunha accepted a petition to impeach Rousseff.

The perceived relationship between Cunha's actions and the Operation Car Wash investigation fueled claims by Rousseff and her supporters that the impeachment movement was nothing more than a coup, which her opponents were undertaking because she refused to halt the investigation. Sen. Telmário Mota described the impeachment proceedings as "an attempted takeover of power which calls itself impeachment," and said they were "born of revenge, hatred, and revenge." Rousseff's opponents countered by reiterating claims that Rousseff broke fiscal law and blamed her for the country's flailing economy.

IMPEACHMENT PROCEEDINGS BEGIN

After accepting the impeachment petition in December, Cunha assembled a sixty-five-member committee to investigate the accusations against Rousseff and determine whether she should be impeached. On April 6, 2016, the legislator leading the committee's efforts to prepare a report on its investigation recommended that the impeachment proceedings move forward. The committee voted to accept the recommendation on April 11. Before the full chamber voted on impeachment, Rousseff's legal team attempted a last-minute legal challenge, claiming before the Supreme Federal Tribunal (Brazil's highest court) that the committee had considered matters that were irrelevant to the impeachment process and, therefore, the proceedings were illegal. Tribunal justices voted 8–2 against the appeal.

Lawmakers in the Chamber of Deputies voted to begin impeachment proceedings against Rousseff on April 17, after a contentious debate that lasted more than fifty hours. "Let us decide with our vote the future of a country dismantled by a president who, with her arrogance, humiliated the Parliament and governed by turning her back on the people," said Deputy Miguel Haddad, the chamber's minority leader. Rousseff's supporters pledged to continue challenging the impeachment process. "The coup plotters won, but the fight continues," said Deputy José Guimarães.

The impeachment proceedings next moved to the Senate, where lawmakers voted on May 12 to accept the charges against Rousseff and begin her impeachment trial. At that time, Rousseff was suspended as president for a period of 180 days while the trial took place, and Vice President Michel Temer became the interim president. A member of the Brazilian Democratic Movement Party, Temer had been a part of Rousseff's governing coalition, but joined the call for her impeachment in March 2016. Temer was not without his own scandals; he was fined for violating campaign finance limits in May 2016 and faces allegations of illegal ethanol purchasing. Two of Temer's ministers also resigned after he became interim president after leaked recordings suggested that the ministers had attempted to obstruct the Petrobras investigation.

Indeed, many of the politicians involved in the impeachment proceedings faced various corruption allegations. Cunha was removed from his speakership in May 2016 by the Supreme Federal Tribunal in connection with Operation Car Wash. Senate President Renan Calheiros was also suspected of accepting bribes in the Petrobras scandal, in addition to being accused of tax evasion and allowing a lobbyist to pay child support he owed to a woman with whom he had an extramarital affair. According to government watchdog Congress em Foco, half the lawmakers in the Chamber of Deputies are under investigation for graft, fraud, or electoral crimes.

The Senate trial was presided over by the chief justice of the Supreme Federal Tribunal. On August 31, the Senate voted 61–20 to impeach Rousseff and remove her from office. However, the Senate did not pass a separate but related measure banning Rousseff from serving in public office for eight years. Responding to the news, Rousseff remained defiant. "They condemned an innocent person and consummated a parliamentary coup," she said.

"They will have against them a more determined opposition than a coup government can sustain." Rousseff's opponents celebrated the outcome. "Brazil has given itself a new chance, to look to the future and construct an agenda for reform in line with the economic crisis," said Aécio Neves, leader of the Brazilian Social Democracy Party.

Temer Sworn in, Rousseff Files Appeal

Michel Temer was sworn in as president two hours after the Senate vote. "I assume the Presidency of Brazil after a democratic and transparent decision of the National Congress," he said at his swearing in. "The uncertainty has ended. It is time to unite the country. . . ." Temer promised to focus on economic issues while president, pledging to implement austerity measures to help address the country's budget deficit and pursue a constitutional change that would limit spending increases. He will serve out the remainder of Rousseff's term, which ends January 1, 2019.

Rousseff filed an appeal with the Supreme Federal Tribunal on September 1, asking the court to annul the Senate session. Rousseff persisted in her claim that the vote was a coup, and her lawyer argued that the proceedings against her were flawed. The court rejected her appeal on September 8, stating that her case "lacked legal plausibility." The court also noted that "the petitioner's defense had iterative opportunities to refute the prosecution's arguments" including "during the interrogation phase," which lasted more than eleven hours.

Rousseff's impeachment had a quick impact on Brazil's relations with several neighboring countries whose governments had criticized the effort. Brazil and Venezuela recalled each other's ambassadors, and Brazil ordered its envoys to Bolivia and Ecuador to return home. Some legal experts and political analysts have also raised concerns about the impeachment's impact on Brazil's domestic politics. "This will set a very dangerous precedent for democracy in Brazil, because from now on, any moment that we have a highly unpopular president, there will be pressure to start an impeachment process," said Lincoln Secco, a history professor at the University of São Paulo.

—Linda Fecteau Grimm

Following are press releases from the Brazilian House of Deputies from April 17 and May 5, 2016, announcing the results of the House and Senate votes to impeach President Dilma Rousseff; a statement by Rousseff from August 31, 2016, responding to the Senate vote; and Michel Temer's remarks from his swearing-in ceremony on August 31, 2016, which have all been translated from Portuguese to English.

DOCUMENT

House of Deputies Votes to Initiate Impeachment Process

April 17, 2016

With the votes of 367 deputies in favor, 137 opposed, and 7 abstaining, the chamber of the House of Deputies approved the impeachment articles and authorized the Federal

Senate to judge the president of the Republic, Dilma Rousseff, for the crime of breach of duty. The deputies Pompeo de Mattos (PDT-RS), Vinicius Gurgel (PR-AP), Beto Salame (PP-PA), Gorete Pereira (PR-CE), Sebastiao Oliveira (PR-PE), Mario Negromonte Jr (PP-BA) and CACA Leao (PP-BA) abstained from the voting.

The session was tense and tumultuous from the beginning. Each of the votes of the 511 deputies—Anibal Gomes (PMDB-CE) and Clarissa Garotinho (PR-RJ) being absent—was marked by acclamations on either side. The 342nd vote, the minimum required to guarantee judgment in the Senate, was celebrated to the point of exhaustion by the impeaching faction, which had the support of 22 parties. Only Psol, PT, and PCdoB did not vote in favor of the restriction of president Dilma.

The voting lasted about six hours, but the whole process of discussion and voting on impeachment, which began on Friday the 15th, lasted almost 53 hours.

In the Senate

It appears now that the recommendation to investigate President Dilma Rousseff will proceed to the Federal Senate. Once there, a special commission will be formed to decide whether or not to ratify a request for opening an investigation. If approved by 41 senators, the president will be removed from office and judged by the Senate. Ultimately, a conviction, requiring the approval of two-thirds of the House (54 senators), would remove Dilma from office and make her ineligible for eight years.

Repercussions

The majority of the leaders in favor of impeachment have referred to not only the accusations against the president, but the fact that she is not able to govern because of the lack of support from the Congress and the people. "There is no corner in this country where one can discern on the face of the people any sign of hope. Let us decide with our vote the future of a country dismantled by a president who, with her arrogance, humiliated the Parliament and governed by turning her back on the people," criticized the minority leader, Deputy Miguel Haddad (PSDB-SP).

The president of the special commission that approved the request to open impeachment proceedings, Deputy Rogerio Rosso (PSD-DF), affirmed that the challenge now is to seek a reunification of a people so divided. "Beginning tomorrow, every political leader, every party leader will need to set aside his personal agenda so that we can overcome the crisis," he said.

The leader of the government, Deputy Jose Guimarães (CE), declared that an impeachment would not be the solution. "The removal of President Dilma Rousseff is not the way to solve Brazilian problems." He questioned whether the vice president, Michel Temer, should also be removed, along with other governors who made the same fiscal maneuvers which weigh against Dilma.

Executive Orders and Accelerators

According to the approved report, one of the infractions of President Dilma Rousseff would be the issuing of supplemental orders without the authorization of the Legislature and in non-conformity with an article of the Budgetary Law, which links costs with the accomplishment of the fiscal plan. Deputy Jovair Arantes (PTB-PE), rapporteur of the material for the special commission, asserts that without a revision of the approved fiscal plan, the Administration cannot, of its own accord, issue such orders, falling back on a draft bill or a Provisional Measure. "In this approach, all of these regulations cited in the censure, independent of the method utilized, would be proved to be of no legislative authority," says the rapporteur's text.

Regarding the use of fiscal "accelerators," the only analysis was of the use of resources of the Bank of Brazil to pay benefits under the "Harvest Plan." The government delayed transfers to the bank, which paid the farmers with its own funds. This delay has been interpreted by the Federal Court of Accounts (TCU) as comprising an irregular credit operation. By compromising the fiscal health of the country, asserts Jovair Arantes, the government puts democracy at risk rather than watching over the financial and economic stability of the country. "The breaking of fiscal rules and the lack of transparency in this area signals a deterioration of public funds and, in the end, the risk of the insolvency of the country," he said in the report.

DEFENSE

All of the accusations were rebutted by the Attorney General, Jose Eduardo Cardozo, who acted in defense of President Dilma Rousseff. According to him, there are no facts in the report that prove that the president intentionally committed acts that threaten the country.

In addition, both the executive orders and the delay of transfers, according to Cardozo, are common in all administrations and were considered to be crimes only because of a change in interpretation by the Federal Court of Accounts. "This procedure was requested by other powers, including the same TCU, which asked the Chief Executive for the supplemental order. Why? Because the TCU allowed this, because the TCU said this was possible," he asserted during the defense before the full House. "Suddenly, the TCU changed its opinion. And when the TCU changed, the government stopped handing down orders. Where then, is the bad faith?"

Just before the final voting, the leader of the House, Deputy Jose Guimarães (CE), admitted defeat, but reasserted that the general public is with the government. "The coup leaders won, but the fight continues. We will bar the process in the Senate. The Senate will correct this act of the coup."

The leader emphasized that the decision of the House in favor of impeachment is an assault against democratic law, and an insult against 54 million people who voted for President Dilma Rousseff. He believes that the vice president, Michel Temer, is not in a position to lead the country and "the process of impeachment was conducted by people without ethics."

SOURCE: House of Deputies of Brazil. "House authorizes initiation of the process of impeachment of Dilma with 367 votes in favor and 137 against." April 17, 2016. Translated from Portuguese by Barry Mathews for SAGE Publishing. http://www2.camara.leg.br/camaranoticias/noticias/POLITICA/507325-CAMARA-AUTORIZA-INSTAURACAO-DE-PROCESSO-DE-IMPEACHMENT-DE-DILMA-COM-367-VOTOS-A-FAVOR-E-137-CONTRA.html.

Senate Votes to Begin Impeachment Proceedings, Suspend Rousseff

May 5, 2016

The Senate Plenary approved, shortly after 6:30 this Thursday (the 12th), the opening of the process against President Dilma Rousseff for the crime of breach of duty. Dilma is accused of violating fiscal regulations in 2015. Of the 78 senators present at the session, which started yesterday morning, 55 were in favor of the pro-impeachment report of Senator Antonio Anastasia (PSDB-MG), rapporteur of the indictment in the special commission. Another 22 voted against. There were two absent, and the president of the Senate, Renan Calheiros, did not vote.

Verification of How Each Senator Voted

With the approval of the indictment, the president will be removed from office for a maximum term or 180 days in accordance with Constitutional rules. During this period, the vice president Michel Temer will assume the presidency. . . .

The Trial Phase

Starting now, the phase of discovery of the impeachment process begins, when there is an analysis of the evidence presented by the defense and the prosecution. Witnesses and specialists may be called by the senators, who also will have the right to ask for expert testimony and hearings in addition to analyzing the documents on which to base a decision.

All of this work will be accomplished, first of all, by a special commission presided over by Senator Raimundo Lira (PMDB-PB) and authored by Senator Anastasia. Lira has said that this Wednesday he intends to complete this part of the process in less than the expected 180 days. . . .

Temporary Removal

The last senator to speak before the voting last Thursday, Antonio Anastasia, reaffirmed his support of impeachment and called attention to the opening of alternative credit without the authorization of Congress and the so-called "fiscal accelerators" as reasons for the opening of the process against Dilma. He reminded, on the other hand, that this removal from office is provisional. "This removal does not come to pass at the whim of the Senate, the commission, or the report writers. It comes to pass expressly from the Constitution. Accordingly, it is a command arising from the constituent residents," he stated.

"Historical Injustice"

The government had a final opportunity to defend itself, by means of the attorney general, Jose Eduardo Cardozo. Cardozo said that Dilma Rousseff did not commit the crime of breach of duty, and calls the process of impeachment a "coup."

"It is a coup, with the right of defense, presumably to simulate legitimacy. That is what is happening in this process. They are right now condemning an honest and innocent woman. They are right now using a judicial pretext to accuse the president of the Republic, legitimately elected, of acts which all of the prior governments practiced. They are committing a historic injustice," he declared.

According to Cardozo, all of the methods singled out in the report were taken by the government in conformity with the spending laws before a change in interpretation by the Federal Court of Accounts (TCU) on the subject. He charged in addition that the process of impeachment started as revenge against the government by Eduardo Cunha, who was removed as president of the House.

The current president, Renan Calheiros, stated that the process in the Senate was conducted with "impartiality," but that history, "open and disinterested," will allow for diverse interpretations of the event.

Renan called for meeting of the Senate leadership at 4 p.m. this Thursday along with the president of the Federal Supreme Court, Ricardo Lewandowski, who will assume the presidency of the process of impeachment of Dilma.

Source: House of Deputies of Brazil. "Senate approves opening of process of impeachment and removal of Dilma for 180 days." May 5, 2016. Translated from Portuguese by Barry Mathews for SAGE Publishing. http://www2.camara.leg.br/camaranoticias/noticias/POLITICA/508623-SENADO-APROVA-ABERTURA-DE-PROCESSO-DE-IMPEACHMENT-E-AFASTA-DILMA-POR-180-DIAS.html.

Rousseff's Statement on Impeachment Vote

August 31, 2016

In a statement shortly after the Federal Senate approved the impeachment this Thursday (the 31st), the former President Dilma Rousseff declared that the senators shredded the Federal Constitution, because she did not commit the crime of breach of duty.

"They condemned an innocent person and consummated a parliamentary coup. With the approval of my removal now assured, the politicians that seek desperately to escape the arm of Justice will take the power accumulated by the defeated in the last four elections," she charged.

Dilma added that the national progressive project she represented was interrupted by a powerful force she called "conservative and reactionary." She criticized the press and predicted setbacks in the social agenda: "With the help of a factious press, they will capture the institutions of the State to put them in the service of the most radical liberal economy and of social retrogression."

She repeated her defense and characterized her exit from the presidency as a coup: "The coup is against the social movements and partnerships and is against those who fight for rights in all their accepted forms: right to work and the protection of workers; right to a just retirement; right to housing and land; right to education, health, and culture; right of youth to fulfill their own ambitions; rights of blacks, Indians, the LGBT population, women; right to demonstrate, without repression."

Dilma Rousseff also asserted that the new government would be confronted with a fierce opposition. "They will have against them a more determined opposition than a coup government can sustain." And she added, "I hope that we know how to unite in defense of the common causes of all progressives, independent of party affiliation or political persuasion. I propose that we all fight together against regression, against the conservative agenda, against the extinction of rights, for the national good, and for the establishment of a fullness of democracy."

The former president did not rule out her return. "At this time, I do not say goodbye to you. I am certain that I can say: until a little later. Either I, or others, will continue the process."

Dilma Rousseff finished by stating that, from now on, she will fight indefatigably to continue to build a better Brazil.

SOURCE: House of Deputies of Brazil. "Dilma speaks after approval of impeachment and says that the senators shredded the Constitution." August 31, 2016. Translated from Portuguese by Barry Mathews for SAGE Publishing. http://www2.camara.leg.br/camaranoticias/noticias/POLITICA/515695-DILMA-DISCURSA-APOS-APROVACAO-DO-IMPEACHMENT-E-DIZ-QUE-SENADORES-RASGARAM-A-CONSTITUICAO.html.

Michel Temer, Brazilian Lawmakers Remark on Swearing In

August 31, 2016

In a quick ceremony in the Senate Plenary, Michel Temer was sworn in as president of the Republic on Wednesday after the impeachment of former president Dilma Rousseff. Surrounded by supportive ministers and politicians, Temer observed the required protocols of office, such as the signing of the terms of office and the oath.

"I promise to maintain, defend, and follow the Constitution, observe the laws, promote the general welfare of the Brazilian people, sustain the Union, the integrity and the independence of Brazil."

In the first ministerial meeting after taking office, Temer refuted the label of "coup" given by the opposition and asked that the base of allied parties remain united. On radio and TV networks, he made a pronouncement to say that "the worst has passed," and that it is time to unite "to make a better country." Temer cited measures that he has taken or plans to take to reduce unemployment, the national debt, and the breakdown of retirement programs.

"I assume the Presidency of Brazil after a democratic and transparent decision of the National Congress. The uncertainty has ended. It is time to unite the country. I will emphasize the foundations of our government: administrative efficiency, recovery of growth, creation of jobs, legal safeguards, expansion of social programs, and pacification of the country. To guarantee the payment of retirees, we need to reform social security. Our mission is to show the entrepreneurs and investors from all over the world our willingness to provide good business opportunities that will bring jobs to Brazil. We must modernize labor laws: open bargaining is an advance in these areas."

All of these themes will have to pass the scrutiny of Congress. The leader of the government, Deputy Andre Moura, of the PSC (Sergipe), said that a proposal for reform of the retirement programs should be sent in October, while a labor bill should be ready by the end of the year. Moura guaranteed that, regardless of size, the political base will remain united to confront the opposition and approve those proposals of interest to the country.

"I disagree with the statement of the opposition that this is not a legitimate government. It's a government just as legitimate as it was before, especially since the president, Michel Temer, was also elected with more than 54 million votes. And now the market is reacting in a positive way, investors want to come back to Brazil with confidence. I have no doubt that we will continue so that we can resume the statistics of growth, fight against 12 million unemployment, the high rate of inflation and of recession, and high interest rates. Of course important measures will have to be approved here in the House, such as the PEC [constitutional amendment], which limits public spending and the question of reforms in retirement programs and the workplace."

The leader of the PT, Deputy Afonso Florence, reaffirmed that the Temer government is illegitimate and announced the focus of the party in anticipation of the presidential elections in 2018.

"We will continue to oppose, in defense of the economic, labor, and social achievements of our people. This is a government that does not have the vote or legitimacy. There was not breach of duty (by Dilma): it is a coup. And we will renew the fight for the victory of the legitimacy of Brazilian government, through the popular sovereignty, the popular vote, through direct elections. To do this, we will fight for direct elections for the presidency of the Republic."

The Network took a neutral position in relation to the Temer government. Deputy Miro Teixeira, of the Rio de Janeiro Network and the politician with the largest number of bills in the House, independently spoke in expectation of a fight against corruption, and said how he intends to comport himself before the new government.

"I will examine every bill as soon as it arrives. If it manages to close the tap of corruption in Brazil, provides money to solve the problems of health and education, and puts thieves in jail."

Deputy Antonio Imbassahy, a supporter of the Temer government and leader of the PSDB, put responsibility on the opposition, particularly the PT.

"Now a new hope, a new setting, with the perspective that the country will manage to overcome this crisis. I hope that the opposition, that governed this country until very recently, knows of their responsibility and the consequences. I understand that they should have matured."

Source: House of Deputies of Brazil. "Michel Temer takes office as president of the Republic in congressional ceremony." August 31, 2016. Translated from Portuguese by Barry Mathews for SAGE Publishing. http://www2.camara.leg.br/camaranoticias/radio/materias/RADIOAGENCIA/515698-MICHEL-TEMER-TOMA-POSSE-COMO-PRESIDENTE-DA-REPUBLICA-EM-CERIMONIA-NO-CONGRESSO.html.

OTHER HISTORIC DOCUMENTS OF INTEREST

FROM THIS VOLUME

FROM PREVIOUS HISTORIC DOCUMENTS

May

Supreme Court Sends Affordable Care Act Case Back to Lower Courts

MAY 16, 2016

Since its passage, the Affordable Care Act (ACA)—the Obama administration's signature health care legislation, informally referred to as "Obamacare"—has been the subject of intense litigation. Legal challenges to numerous aspects of the law have made it all the way to the highest court in the country. In past cases, the Supreme Court has upheld some of the law's most significant components, including the individual mandate and health care subsidies, while it has ruled against the Medicaid expansion.

On May 16, 2016, the Supreme Court released its fourth opinion in *Zubik v. Burwell* to address a religious freedom challenge to the law's mandate that employers include no-cost contraceptive coverage as part of their employees' health insurance plans. The challengers to this mandate were religious nonprofits arguing that, even though the law included an opt-out provision for employers who assert religious objections, the very act of triggering this opt-out is enough to make them complicit in "sinful" behavior in violation of their religious liberty. The Supreme Court side-stepped resolving the issues and instead took the highly unusual step of requesting supplemental briefings from the parties after oral argument to determine the possibility of reaching an accommodation that could resolve the outstanding issues between them. Based on answers to these questions, the Court, in a unanimous, unsigned opinion, sent the cases back to the appellate courts to help the parties reach resolution, stressing emphatically that "the Court expresses no view on the merits of the cases." This outcome led many commentators to speculate that the Court, operating with only eight members since the death of Justice Antonin Scalia, had deadlocked on the central issues.

THE SUPREME COURT AND THE CONTRACEPTION MANDATE

In 2011, the Department of Health and Human Services (HHS) promulgated rules to implement the ACA requirement that the cost of contraceptives must be covered by all employee health plans. These rules specifically exempted houses of worship from the requirement, but did not exempt religiously affiliated nonprofit organizations, such as hospitals, universities, schools, and social service organizations, because such organizations, employing thousands of people, were considered less likely to limit employment to members of the same religious faith.

The contraceptive coverage mandate sparked dozens of lawsuits and lower court decisions. In 2014, the first case to deal with its implications reached the Supreme Court. In *Burwell v. Hobby Lobby*, a narrowly divided Court held that the contraceptive mandate violates the religious rights of certain privately held for-profit corporations whose owners have religious objections to contraceptives. The decision was based on the Religious Freedom Restoration Act (RFRA), which states that no federal law may "substantially burden a person's exercise of religion even if the burden results from a rule of general applicability," unless the government has "a compelling governmental interest" and the law is the "least restrictive means of furthering" that interest. In the *Hobby Lobby* case, the Court noted the exemption that the rules provided to houses of worship as proof that the government could craft an accommodation to more narrowly tailor the statute to avoid violations of religious rights.

In the following years, HHS made several changes to the rules to try to accommodate religious objections while still ensuring contraceptive coverage. It added what the Obama administration described as an "easy" opt-out provision for religiously affiliated nonprofit organizations. If such organizations submit a form notifying their insurance providers or HHS that they object on religious grounds to providing the required coverage, then the responsibility for providing contraceptive coverage shifts to the private insurance company.

Dozens of religious nonprofits, including faith-based hospitals, religiously affiliated schools, and service organizations, filed federal lawsuits in courts around the country arguing that even filing out the form necessary to opt-out of the mandate imposes a substantial religious burden in violation of the RFRA. Notifying the government of their objection and triggering the government to arrange other coverage for contraceptives, the parties argued, made them "complicit" in behavior that they regard as sinful. Furthermore, any fines they incurred for failure to comply with the law would be substantial.

All but one of the appellate courts to hear the issues dismissed the nonprofits' complaints, finding that the government offers an acceptable work around, sufficient to protect their rights. Typical of these opinions was the one issued by the U.S. Court of Appeals for the D.C. Circuit, which emphasized how minimal the requirement is: "All plaintiffs must do to opt out is express what they believe and seek what they want via a letter or two-page form." Once these religious nonprofits opt out, the opinion continued, they "are excused from playing any role in the provision of contraception services, and they remain free to condemn contraception in the clearest terms." But the one appellate court to rule the opposite way, the U.S. Court of Appeals for the Eighth Circuit, took a different view of the issues. This court focused on whether the nonprofits "have a sincere religious belief that their participation in the accommodation process makes them morally and spiritually complicit in providing abortifacient coverage." If they believe it does, the court concluded, it "is not for us to dispute."

In November 2015, the Supreme Court accepted the appeal and consolidated the cases into the single case, *Zubik v. Burwell*. The issue presented in the case was whether the opt-out provision for the religious nonprofits violated the RFRA by substantially burdening their religious practice. The parties themselves described the issues more colorfully. Solicitor General Donald B. Verrilli Jr. described the central issue in the government petition to the Court as whether the RFRA "entitles petitioners not only to opt out of providing contraceptive coverage themselves but also to prevent the government from arranging for third parties to provide separate coverage to the affected women." By contrast, Noel Francisco, a lawyer for one of the petitioners, described the issue in his papers as "whether the government can commandeer petitioners and their health plans as vehicles for delivering abortifacient and contraceptive coverage in violation of their religion."

SUPREME COURT SENDS THE ISSUE BACK TO THE LOWER COURTS

None of the issues presented in the case were resolved. After hearing oral arguments in the case, the Supreme Court did something very unusual; it asked the parties to submit new briefs addressing the possibility of finding a compromise. Specifically, the Court asked the parties "whether contraceptive coverage could be provided to petitioners' employees, through petitioners' insurance companies, without any such notice from petitioners?" According to the Court, the government confirmed that this would be feasible to modify the exemption while still "ensuring that the affected women receive contraceptive coverage seamlessly," and the religious organizations who were suing the government expressed agreement that they could accept a solution where they "need to do nothing more than contract for a plan that does not include coverage for some or all forms of contraception" even if this resulted in their employees receiving free contraceptive coverage from that same insurance company.

These answers in the supplemental papers convinced the Court that a compromise was still possible and led it to issue a *per curiam* decision—that is, an unsigned decision reached unanimously and collectively. In just over two pages, the Court sent the cases back to the various federal appellate courts where they originated, with directions to work harder to reach agreement. "We anticipate," the Court wrote, "that the Courts of Appeals will allow the parties sufficient time to resolve any outstanding issues between them." The goal, the opinion made clear, is for the parties to come to "an approach going forward that accommodates petitioners' religious exercise while at the same time ensuring that women covered by petitioners' health plans 'receive full and equal health coverage, including contraceptive coverage.'" The Court emphasized that it "expresses no view on the merits of the cases," not whether the opt-out substantially burdened the petitioners' religious exercise, whether the government has a compelling interest, or whether the regulations are the least restrictive way possible to serve that interest.

Justice Sonia Sotomayor wrote a brief concurring opinion, joined by Justice Ruth Bader Ginsburg, strongly emphasizing that the ruling expresses "no view on the merits" of the cases. She mentioned that lower courts have, in the past, ignored similarly explicit disclaimers, and she cautioned that "the Courts of Appeals should not make the same mistake." She made clear her view that the Court's opinion does not endorse the petitioners' arguments that they must be able to provide their employees with contraceptive coverage through a completely "separate policy, with a separate enrollment process." Not only are there numerous legal and practical obstacles to creating this kind of separate process, but making women affirmatively opt for this coverage would, she wrote, would "impose precisely the kind of barrier to the delivery of preventive services that Congress sought to eliminate."

The nature of this decision led many commentators to theorize that the Court had tied 4–4 on the underlying issues and that this resolution reflected a compromise among the justices. That the Court sidestepped the opportunity to resolve these issues illustrated to some that the Court, short a member, was sliding toward paralysis. The practical impact of the order was that the earlier decisions made by the appellate courts, most of which were in favor of the government, were vacated and the ultimate legal resolution of the issues was still up in the air. To head off the possibility that the thousands of employees of the suing companies would risk losing their coverage, the Court was clear that, by filing the lawsuits, the petitioners had, in effect, given the requisite notice to be exempted from the contraceptive mandate, and the government could go ahead and provide full contraceptive coverage to the employees through their insurance companies. At the same time, the Court was clear that the nonprofit petitioners may not be penalized by the government for failure to provide the necessary notice.

Everyone Claims Partial Victory

Immediately after the ruling, Mark Rienzi, senior counsel at The Becket Fund for Religious Liberty, which represented the Little Sisters of the Poor, one of the groups that sued over providing employees with contraceptive coverage, hailed the Court's action as "a game-changer" and "a huge win for the Little Sisters, religious liberty, and all Americans." He further characterized the government's responses to the Supreme Court as a "concession that it could deliver these services without the Little Sisters," and emphasized that the decision "eliminated all of the wrong decisions from the lower courts and protected the Little Sisters from government fines."

Supporters of the ACA were similarly confident that they would ultimately prevail. Gretchen Borchelt, vice president for reproductive rights and health at the National Women's Law Center, expressed some disappointment that the issues were not resolved once and for all by the Court, but stressed that "eight of nine Circuit Courts of Appeals have already upheld women's access to birth control no matter where they work. We are confident that the government's birth control accommodation once again will prevail." Louise Melling, deputy legal director of the American Civil Liberties Union, was encouraged because "the opinion states clearly the need for women to receive full and equal coverage."

How and when the issues will ultimately be settled is still undetermined. The Court's opinion did not rush the lower courts, but instead instructed them to "allow the parties sufficient time to resolve any outstanding issues between them." And Justice Sotomayor noted that these courts "remain free to reach the same conclusion or a different one on each of the questions presented by these cases." What is clear is that the issue of religious accommodation, particularly the question of what counts as a substantial religious burden, will not go away and will extend beyond the issue in this particular case. Future cases regarding religious-based challenges to government protections for the LGBT community are likely. By way of example of the kinds of cases that could arise in the future, within a month of the ruling in *Zubik*, HHS banned the recipients of funds such as Medicare and Medicaid reimbursements from discriminating on the basis of gender identity and included no explicit religious exemptions, although it referenced that it would not be applied in ways to violate the RFRA.

—Melissa Feinberg

Following is the full text of the Supreme Court's per curiam *decision in* Zubik v. Burwell *on May 16, 2016, in which the court vacated a court of appeals ruling on whether religious institutions other than churches should be exempt from the Affordable Care Act mandate to provide contraceptive coverage to employees and sent the case back to the courts of appeal for reconsideration.*

DOCUMENT   *Zubik v. Burwell*

May 16, 2016

Nos. 14–1418, 14–1453,
14–1505, 15–35, 15–105,
15–119, and 15–191

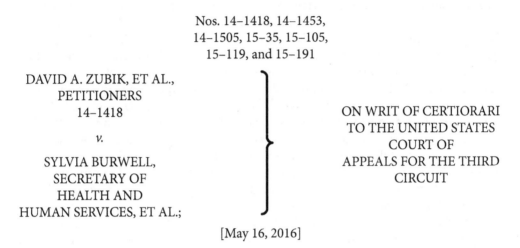

DAVID A. ZUBIK, ET AL.,
PETITIONERS
14–1418

v.

SYLVIA BURWELL,
SECRETARY OF
HEALTH AND
HUMAN SERVICES, ET AL.;

ON WRIT OF CERTIORARI
TO THE UNITED STATES
COURT OF
APPEALS FOR THE THIRD
CIRCUIT

[May 16, 2016]

PER CURIAM.

Petitioners are primarily nonprofit organizations that provide health insurance to their employees. Federal regulations require petitioners to cover certain contraceptives as part of their health plans, unless petitioners submit a form either to their insurer or to the Federal Government, stating that they object on religious grounds to providing contraceptive coverage. Petitioners allege that submitting this notice substantially burdens the exercise of their religion, in violation of the Religious Freedom Restoration Act of 1993, 107 Stat. 1488, 42 U. S. C. §2000bb *et seq.*

Following oral argument, the Court requested supplemental briefing from the parties addressing "whether contraceptive coverage could be provided to petitioners' employees, through petitioners' insurance companies, without any such notice from petitioners." *Post,* p. ___.Both petitioners and the Government now confirm that such an option is feasible. Petitioners have clarified that their religious exercise is not infringed where they "need to do nothing more than contract for a plan that does not include coverage for some or all forms of contraception," even if their employees receive cost-free contraceptive coverage from the same insurance company. Supplemental Brief for Petitioners 4. The Government has confirmed that the challenged procedures "for employers with insured plans could be modified to operate in the manner posited in the Court's order while still ensuring that the affected women receive contraceptive coverage seamlessly, together with the rest of their health coverage." Supplemental Brief for Respondents 14–15.

In light of the positions asserted by the parties in their supplemental briefs, the Court vacates the judgments below and remands to the respective United States Courts of Appeals for the Third, Fifth, Tenth, and D. C. Circuits. Given the gravity of the dispute and the substantial clarification and refinement in the positions of the parties, the parties on remand should be afforded an opportunity to arrive at an approach going forward that accommodates petitioners' religious exercise while at the same time ensuring that women covered by petitioners' health plans "receive full and equal health coverage, including contraceptive coverage." *Id.*, at 1. We anticipate that the Courts of Appeals will allow the parties sufficient time to resolve any outstanding issues between them.

The Court finds the foregoing approach more suitable than addressing the significantly clarified views of the parties in the first instance. Although there may still be areas of disagreement between the parties on issues of implementation, the importance of those areas of potential concern is uncertain, as is the necessity of this Court's involvement at this point to resolve them. This Court has taken similar action in other cases in the past. See, *e.g., Madison County* v. *Oneida Indian Nation of N. Y.*, 562 U. S. 42, 43 (2011) (*per curiam*) (vacating and remanding for the Second Circuit to "address, in the first instance, whether to revisit its ruling on sovereign immunity in light of [a] new factual development, and—if necessary—proceed to address other questions in the case consistent with its sovereign immunity ruling"); *Kiyemba* v. *Obama*, 559 U. S. 131, 132 (2010) (*per curiam*) (vacating and remanding for the D. C. Circuit to "determine, in the first instance, what further proceedings in that court or in the District Court are necessary and appropriate for the full and prompt disposition of the case in light of the new developments"); *Villarreal* v. *United States*, 572 U. S. ___ (2014) (vacating and remanding to the Fifth Circuit "for further consideration in light of the position asserted by the Solicitor General in his brief for the United States").

The Court expresses no view on the merits of the cases. In particular, the Court does not decide whether petitioners' religious exercise has been substantially burdened, whether the Government has a compelling interest, or whether the current regulations are the least restrictive means of serving that interest.

Nothing in this opinion, or in the opinions or orders of the courts below, is to affect the ability of the Government to ensure that women covered by petitioners' health plans "obtain, without cost, the full range of FDA approved contraceptives." *Wheaton College* v. *Burwell*, 573 U. S. ___, ___ (2014) (slip op., at 1). Through this litigation, petitioners have made the Government aware of their view that they meet "the requirements for exemption from the contraceptive coverage requirement on religious grounds." *Id.*, at ___ (slip op., at 2). Nothing in this opinion, or in the opinions or orders of the courts below, "precludes the Government from relying on this notice, to the extent it considers it necessary, to facilitate the provision of full contraceptive coverage" going forward. *Ibid.* Because the Government may rely on this notice, the Government may not impose taxes or penalties on petitioners for failure to provide the relevant notice.

The judgments of the Courts of Appeals are vacated, and the cases are remanded for further proceedings consistent with this opinion.

It is so ordered.

JUSTICE SOTOMAYOR, with whom JUSTICE GINSBURG joins, concurring.

I join the Court's *per curiam* opinion because it expresses no view on "the merits of the cases," "whether petitioners' religious exercise has been substantially burdened," or "whether the current regulations are the least restrictive means of serving" a compelling governmental interest. *Ante*, at 4–5. Lower courts, therefore, should not construe either today's *per curiam* or our order of March 29, 2016, as signals of where this Court stands. We have included similarly explicit disclaimers in previous orders. See, *e.g., Wheaton College* v. *Burwell*, 573 U. S. ___ (2014) ("[T]his order should not be construed as an expression of the Court's views on the merits"). Yet some lower courts have ignored those instructions. See, *e.g., Sharpe Holdings, Inc.,* v. *Department of Health and Human Servs.,* 801 F. 3d 927, 944 (CA8 2015) ("[I]n *Wheaton College, Little Sisters of the Poor,* and *Zubik,* the Supreme Court approved a method of notice to HHS that is arguably less onerous than [existing regulations] yet permits the government to further its interests. Although the Court's orders were not final rulings on the merits, they at the very least collectively constitute a signal that less restrictive means exist by which the government may further its interests"). On remand in these cases, the Courts of Appeals should not make the same mistake.

I also join the Court's opinion because it allows the lower courts to consider only whether existing or modified regulations could provide seamless contraceptive coverage "'to petitioners' employees, through petitioners' insurance companies, without any . . . notice from petitioners.'" *Ante,* at 3. The opinion does not, by contrast, endorse the petitioners' position that the existing regulations substantially burden their religious exercise or that contraceptive coverage must be provided through a "separate policy, with a separate enrollment process." Supp. Brief for Petitioners 1; Supp. Reply Brief for Petitioners 5. Such separate contraceptive-only policies do not currently exist, and the Government has laid out a number of legal and practical obstacles to their creation. See Supp. Reply Brief for Respondents 3–4. Requiring standalone contraceptive-only coverage would leave in limbo all of the women now guaranteed seamless preventive-care coverage under the Affordable Care Act. And requiring that women affirmatively opt into such coverage would "impose precisely the kind of barrier to the delivery of preventive services that Congress sought to eliminate." *Id.,* at 6.

Today's opinion does only what it says it does: "afford[s] an opportunity" for the parties and Courts of Appeals to reconsider the parties' arguments in light of petitioners' new articulation of their religious objection and the Government's clarification about what the existing regulations accomplish, how they might be amended, and what such an amendment would sacrifice. *Ante,* at 4. As enlightened by the parties' new submissions, the Courts of Appeals remain free to reach the same conclusion or a different one on each of the questions presented by these cases.

Source: U.S. Supreme Court. *Zubik v. Burwell.,* 578 U.S. ___ (2016). http://www.supremecourt.gov/opinions/15pdf/14-1418_8758.pdf.

Other Historic Documents of Interest

From this volume

- Donald Trump Elected U.S. President, p. 612

From previous *Historic Documents*

- Supreme Court Upholds Affordable Care Act Subsidies, *2015,* p. 293
- Supreme Court Rules on Affordable Care Act Birth Control Mandate, *2014,* p. 286
- Supreme Court Rules on Affordable Care Act, *2012,* p. 292
- Health Care Reform Signed into Law, *2010,* p. 83

Nigerian Officials on the Rescue of the Chibok Schoolgirls

MAY 19 AND 20, AND OCTOBER 19, 2016

On the evening of April 14, 2014, more than 200 teenage girls were kidnapped from a school in Nigeria's northeastern Borno state by the Islamic extremist group Boko Haram. The girls, aged sixteen to eighteen, were taken into the Sambisa Forest, a known terrorist refuge, where many were believed to have been sold as child brides to Boko Haram fighters. Fifty-seven managed to escape shortly after their capture, but it would be another two years before any of the other captured girls were located. Despite the freeing of twenty-three girls in May and October 2016, the Nigerian government and military remain unsure of the whereabouts of the remainder of the girls, as well as their status, and it has been reported that some have died or were killed in captivity.

ATTEMPTS TO FREE THE CAPTURED GIRLS

Boko Haram (translated as "Western education is sinful") claimed responsibility for the kidnapping one month after the attack, and the group's leader, Abubakar Shekau, threatened to sell the girls into slavery. He later requested that the Nigerian government release Boko Haram hostages in exchange for the girls, which the government refused to do. In the weeks following the kidnapping, there was significant confusion about the number of girls who were still missing, which ranged from 8 to 219, the latter of which is believed to be the most accurate estimate.

Then-President Goodluck Jonathan was hesitant to publicly acknowledge the kidnapping, and the lagging response of his government led to numerous protests against the government and gave rise to the international social media campaign #BringBackOurGirls. The government announced in mid-October 2014 that, after months of negotiation, it had reached an agreement with Boko Haram leaders to release the girls. The truce, however, never came to fruition. Instead, the Nigerian army, a largely untrained and ill-equipped fighting force, conducted a number of operations to root out Boko Haram insurgents and free hundreds of kidnapped women and girls throughout 2015, but none of these efforts uncovered the whereabouts of the Chibok schoolgirls.

NEW PRESIDENT PROMISES TO FREE THE GIRLS

Due in part to his failure to free the missing schoolgirls, Jonathan lost his reelection bid in 2015 to General Muhammadu Buhari, who campaigned on a platform of ending the terrorist insurgency and finding the Chibok girls. After his victory, Buhari declared, "[W]hen my new Administration takes office . . . we will do everything we can to defeat Boko Haram. We will act differently than the government we replace." In October 2015, Buhari set the end of the year as the deadline for defeating Boko Haram, but noted earlier that he would not declare the group defeated until after the schoolgirls had been rescued. Despite that, in a December 24 interview with the BBC, Buhari said that the group had been "technically defeated," sparking intense criticism and protests from the Chibok families and their supporters.

In January 2016, Buhari ordered a new investigation be conducted into the 2014 kidnapping, specifically looking at the events surrounding the abductions and the lack of action on the part of Jonathan's government. "The unfortunate incident happened before this government came into being. What have we done since we assumed office? We re-organized the military, removed all the service chiefs, and ordered the succeeding service chiefs to deal decisively with the Boko Haram insurgency," Buhari said, according to his spokesperson Garba Shehu. Buhari added that the investigation would be coupled with the retraining and re-equipping of Nigerian soldiers to better prepare them to fight the terrorist group. Buhari also announced his willingness to negotiate for the release of the schoolgirls and other hostages being held by Boko Haram. However, international analysts were skeptical that the group would come to the table after it aligned itself with the Islamic State of Iraq and the Levant (ISIL) in early 2015. Indeed, talks with Boko Haram broke down many times through late 2015 and into 2016, at one point because lead Boko Haram negotiators were killed.

TWENTY-THREE CHIBOK GIRLS FOUND

On May 2, during a patrol by a local militia, one of the schoolgirls, Amina Ali, was rescued with her four-month-old child. A second Chibok girl, Serah Luka, was found on May 19 during a raid that killed thirty-five Boko Haram fighters and led to the rescue of another ninety-seven women and children being held by the group; none of the ninety-seven were Chibok girls. When Ali was freed, President Buhari told his citizens to "rest assured that this administration will continue to do all it can to rescue the remaining Chibok girls who are still in Boko Haram captivity." He added his belief that Ali's education would "definitely be a priority for the federal government. . . . Amina must be enabled to go back to school. No girl in Nigeria should be put through the brutality of forced marriage. Every girl has the right to an education and a life choice."

Buhari's government worked at length to negotiate the release of more of the schoolgirls, and to find Boko Haram insurgents, with the help of U.S. and British special forces. On October 13, twenty-one of the kidnapped girls were released. "The release of the girls, in a limited number, is the outcome of negotiations between the administration and Boko Haram brokered by the International Red Cross and the Swiss government. The negotiations will continue," said Shehu. Preliminary reports indicated that in return for the girls Buhari gave up four Boko Haram prisoners, which the Nigerian minister of information and culture denied. "This is not a swap," said Lai Mohammed. "It is a release, the product of painstaking negotiations and trust on both sides." It is believed that the breakthrough in negotiations was aided by a splintering of Boko Haram into separate factions after ISIL imposed a new leader on the terrorist group in September, while the former leader has continued to insist that he is in charge. During a reception for the twenty-one Chibok girls, Buhari promised to "redouble efforts to ensure that we fulfill our pledge of bringing the remaining girls back home."

Later in October, the Boko Haram faction that released the twenty-one girls said it was holding another eighty-three and would be willing to negotiate with the Nigerian government to secure their release. By the close of 2016, no additional hostages had been freed, and questions abound about the status of the remaining girls. According to media reports, when she was rescued Ali informed the military that six of the kidnapped schoolgirls had died in captivity. Boko Haram also claimed that some of the girls were killed or injured by government airstrikes.

—Heather Kerrigan

Following are two statements from the Nigerian military—on May 19 and 20, 2016—regarding the rescue of two Chibok schoolgirls; and a speech delivered by Nigerian President Muhammadu Buhari on October 19, 2016, upon meeting with the twenty-one rescued Chibok girls.

Nigerian Military Remarks on Rescued Chibok Schoolgirl

May 19, 2016

The rescued Chibok school girl, Amina Ali, was airlifted by Nigeria Air Force Super Puma aircraft from Damboa to Maiduguri alongside her baby and supposed husband, Mohammed Hayatu.

Prior to that they were examined at Air Force medical facility and were found to be stable and normal blood pressure was observed.

Thereafter, she was released to the Operation LAFIYA DOLE headquarters for further investigation and handing over.

After preliminary investigation, the rescued girl and her baby has been handed over to Borno State Governor, His Excellency, Honourable Kashim Shetima, at Government house, Maiduguri this evening by the Acting General Officer Commanding 7 Division, Brigadier General Victor Ezugwu in a brief ceremony. It is believed that she will be brought to Abuja tomorrow along with her parents to meet with Mr President. Meanwhile, the supposed husband is undergoing further investigation at Joint Intelligence Centre. It should be noted that Mohammed Hayatu is well treated in line with Operation LAFIYA DOLE Rules of Engagement regarding insurgents who voluntarily surrender to the military.

SOURCE: Nigerian Army. "Rescued Chibok Girl Handed Over to Borno State Governor." May 19, 2016. http://www.army.mil.ng/rescued-chibok-girl-handed-over-to-borno-state-governor.

Nigerian Army on Rescue of Second Chibok Schoolgirl

May 20, 2016

At about 11.00am yesterday, Thursday, 19th May 2016, troops of 231 Battalion, 331 Artillery Regiment (AR), Detachment of Armed Forces Special Forces (AFSF) 2, Explosive Ordinance (EOD) Team and Civilian Vigilante group of Buratai, conducted clearance operations at Shettima Aboh, Hong and Biladdili general area in Damboa Local Government Area of Borno State.

During the operations, the troops killed 35 Boko Haram terrorists and recovered several arms and ammunitions and other items.

In addition, they rescued 97 women and children held captives by the Boko Haram terrorists. We are glad to state that among those rescued is a girl believed to be one of the Chibok Government Secondary School girls that were abducted on 14th April 2014 by the Boko Haram terrorists.

Her name is Miss Serah Luka, who is number 157 on the list of the abducted school girls. She is believed to be the daughter of Pastor Luka. During debriefing the girl revealed that she was a JSS1 student of the school at the time they were abducted. She further added that she hails from Madagali, Adamawa State.

She averred that she reported at the school barely two months and one week before her unfortunate abduction along with other girls over two years ago.

She added that there [were three other] girls who fled from Shettima Aboh when the troops invaded the area earlier today which led to their rescue.

She is presently receiving medical attention at the medical facility of Abogo Largema Cantonment, Biu, Borno State.

Thank you for your kind and usual cooperation.

Colonel Sani Kukasheka Usman

Acting Director Army Public Relations

SOURCE: Nigerian Army. "Another Chibok School Girl Rescued." May 20, 2016. http://www.army.mil.ng/another-chibok-school-girl-rescued.

President Buhari Meets Freed Chibok Girls

DOCUMENT

October 19, 2016

My dear children. This is a happy moment for me and for all Nigerians. I welcome you back to freedom. It is a moment your parents, the Nation and the International Community have been eagerly waiting for, since your abduction on 14th April 2014.

We must from the onset, thank Almighty God for this day that 21 of the Chibok girls have again breathed the air of freedom and are reunited with their parents. We are equally prayerful, that God in his infinite mercies and benevolence will see to it that the girls remaining in captivity will be freed and returned to us soonest.

All Nigerians recall, sadly the night of 14th April 2014, 276 young female Nigerian students were abducted from the Government Secondary School in Chibok Borno State by the Boko Haram.

Fortunately, 57 of the kidnapped school girls were able to escape, leaving 219 in captivity. One of the abducted girls, Amina Ali was found in May 2016. And today we are here celebrating the freedom and return of another 21 girls that regained freedom on Thursday 13th October. We are equally as hopeful as we are praying, that the remaining girls will be freed and returned to us without further delay.

The release of these 21 girls followed a series of negotiations between Government and the Boko Haram group, brokered by our friends both local and International. Since this Administration assumed office, we have been working towards the safe release of the girls. The Nigerian DSS, Military and other Security Agencies have spared no effort to secure our girls. These 21 girls are the manifestation of our doggedness and commitments to the release and return of the Chibok girls.

While joining their parents to rejoice and praise the Almighty, we shall redouble efforts to ensure that we fulfill our pledge of bringing the remaining girls back home. Already, the credible first step has been taken and Government will sustain the effort until all the remaining girls return safely[.]

These 21 girls will be given adequate and comprehensive medical, nutritional and psychological care and support. The Federal Government will rehabilitate them, and ensure that their reintegration back to the Society is done as quickly as possible.

Aside from rescuing them, we are assuming the responsibility for their personal, educational and professional goals and ambitions in life. Obviously, it is not late for the girls to go back to school and continue the pursuit of their studies.

These dear daughters of ours have seen the worst that the world has to offer. It is now time for them to experience the best that the world can do for them. The Government and all Nigerians must encourage them to achieve their desired ambitions.

The Federal Government appreciates the patience and understanding of the parents of all the abducted Chibok girls. We equally thank Nigerians and the International Community for their support and prayers, and for never losing confidence in our ability to secure the safe release of our girls.

Once again, I congratulate the 21 released girls, their parents, the Chibok Community[,] the security agencies and all Nigerians on this day of delight and rejoicing.

Thank You

SOURCE: Office of the President. Federal Republic of Nigeria. "President Buhari's remarks at the reception for 21 Chibok School girls at the State House, Abuja." October 19, 2016. http://www.statehouse.gov.ng/index.php/news/speeches/2765-president-buhari-s-remarks-at-the-reception-for-21-chibok-school-girls-at-the-state-house-abuja.

OTHER HISTORIC DOCUMENTS OF INTEREST

FROM PREVIOUS HISTORIC DOCUMENTS

June

U.S. Officials Remark on Changes to Military Personnel Policies

JUNE 8 AND 30, 2016

Several long-debated changes to military personnel policies were implemented during President Barack Obama's administration, including the repeal of "Don't Ask, Don't Tell" and the opening of combat roles to women. Expanding upon these changes, the U.S. Defense Department announced in June 2016 that transgender individuals could begin serving openly in the military and could undergo gender transition treatment while enlisted. At the same time, lawmakers in Congress sought to institute a requirement that women register for the Selective Service, given their new ability to serve in combat roles.

Congress Seeks to Extend Selective Service Requirement to Women

In spring 2016, both the House and Senate began deliberating the fiscal year 2017 National Defense Authorization Act (NDAA), including a provision that would require women to register for the Selective Service, also known as the draft. Rep. Duncan Hunter, R-Calif., first proposed adding this measure to the House's version of the NDAA in April. Sen. John McCain, R-Ariz., introduced the Senate version of the NDAA, with the requirement that women register for the draft. Opening floor debate on the bill on June 8, Senator McCain remarked, "[A]fter months of rigorous oversight, a large bipartisan majority on the Armed Services Committee agreed that there is simply no further justification to limit selective service registration to men. That is not just my view, but the view of every single one of our military service chiefs, including the Army Chief of Staff and the Commandant of the Marine Corps."

The U.S. military has been comprised entirely of volunteers since 1973, but men aged eighteen to twenty-six years old are still required to register for the Selective Service in the event that another draft is needed. Women were not required to register because they were excluded from serving in combat roles in the military. The U.S. Supreme Court upheld the constitutionality of restricting the Selective Service to men in 1981—in response to a legal challenge filed during the Vietnam War—based on the fact that women did not serve in combat.

However, in December 2015, the U.S. Department of Defense announced that all combat roles would be opened to female soldiers. "There will be no exceptions," said Defense Secretary Ash Carter. "They'll be allowed to drive tanks, fire mortars, and lead infantry soldiers into combat. They'll be able to serve as Army Rangers and Green Berets, Navy SEALs, Marine Corps infantry, Air Force parajumpers, and everything else that was previously open only to men." The change in policy opened roughly 220,000 military jobs to women and was a response to a 2012 directive from President Barack Obama, in which he set a deadline for the military to integrate women into all combat roles—or request specific exemptions—by January 2016. Prior to the announcement, the Navy and Air

Force had already made most combat positions open to women and the Army had also begun to integrate its forces, including permitting women to participate in Army Ranger training. The Marine Corps requested an exemption to the policy for infantry and armor positions, but Secretary Carter overruled the request, stating that all branches of the military should operate under a common set of rules. Early in 2016, each branch presented to the Defense Department its plan for integrating women into combat roles, and the Navy began actively recruiting female enlistees, including for the SEALs program.

The decision to allow women to serve in combat roles removed the legal foundation for the Supreme Court's ruling and was the primary argument used in support of requiring women to register for the draft. Those opposed to the requirement, which would apply to women turning eighteen years old in 2018 or later, said more time was needed to consider the policy and to evaluate the draft more broadly, and that it should not be included in "must pass" appropriations legislation.

The issue divided both Democrats and Republicans. Sen. Ted Cruz, R-Tex., said he could not "in good conscience vote to draft our daughters into the military," describing the registration requirement as a "radical change that is attempting to be foisted on the American people." Others viewed the change as an extension of equality for women. "Given where we are today, with women in the military performing virtually all kinds of functions, I personally think it would be appropriate for them to register just like men do," said Senate Majority Leader Mitch McConnell, R-Ky. Some lawmakers called for the draft to be abolished entirely. "It doesn't matter if you're a man, a woman or a houseplant—we need to abolish the Selective Service," said Rep. Peter DeFazio, D-Ore. Yet others argued in favor of its preservation. "Internationally, we are in a very unstable context," said Rep. Steny Hoyer, D-Md. "Therefore, it may well make sense to continue to have a pool available . . . in the event that we need to, in very rapid order, ramp up the number of folks in the armed forces."

The measure was ultimately stripped from the final version of the bill that passed the House of Representatives on May 18, but the Senate retained the requirement in its version of the bill, passed on June 14, leaving the issue to be resolved in conference committee. Following the objections of Republicans in both chambers, the provision was not included in the final bill filed by the conference committee on November 30. Instead, lawmakers included a provision calling for a review of the Selective Service system to assess whether a draft is still a realistic and cost-effective option for the military.

Pentagon Allows Transgender Troops to Serve Openly

The Defense Department announced another policy change on June 30, declaring that transgender individuals currently enlisted in the military could begin serving openly and that "service members may no longer be involuntarily separated, discharged, or denied reenlistment solely on the basis of gender identity." Prior to the announcement, transgender service members were discharged if discovered, similar to how homosexual individuals had been discharged prior to the repeal of "Don't Ask, Don't Tell." Secretary Carter's limitation of discharge-related decision-making authority to higher-ranking commanders in July 2015 had made it more difficult for transgendered troops to be discharged, but they still faced this risk if they came out.

The Defense Department stated that its shift in policy would be phased in over a year-long period, to allow time to develop specific guidelines, training, and other policies to support the change. Enlisted service members can begin serving openly, effective immediately. By October 1, 2016, each military branch must begin providing "medically necessary care and treatment to transgender service members" through the Military Health System, as directed by Defense Department–developed medical protocols. These protocols will include a process by which service members may transition gender while enlisted. Troops are required to get a diagnosis from a military medical provider stating that gender transition is medically necessary before the process can begin. Once the individual has fully transitioned, they will be required to follow the standards for their "preferred gender," including using the bathroom, shower, and housing facilities designated for that gender.

By July 1, 2017, the Defense Department will finalize plans and conduct training for all members of the military on the policy change, develop implementation guidance for commanders, and revise all related regulations and forms. At that time, enlistment will be open to other transgender individuals, provided that they meet the military's accession standards. Initially, the policy will require interested individuals to have "completed any medical treatment that their doctor has determined is necessary in connection with their gender transition, and to have been stable in their preferred gender for eighteen months, as certified by their doctor, before they can enter the military."

A study group comprised of military leaders, Defense Department medical and personnel experts, transgender service members, outside medical experts, advocacy groups, and the RAND Corporation spent nearly one year working to develop the policy. According to a study commissioned by the Defense Department and conducted by the RAND Corporation, there are an estimated 1,320 to 6,630 transgender individuals among the active duty military, which has a total population of 1.3 million troops. Of those transgendered individuals, the RAND Corporation estimated roughly 30 to 140 would seek hormone treatment, and another 25 to 130 would seek gender transition surgery.

"This is the right thing to do for our people and for the force," said Secretary Carter. "We're talking about talented Americans who are serving with distinction or who want the opportunity to serve. We can't allow barriers unrelated to a person's qualifications prevent us from recruiting and retaining those who can best accomplish the mission."

The announcement was received with mixed feedback from lawmakers, interest groups, and those who had served in the military. Chair of the House Armed Services Committee Rep. Mac Thornberry, R-Tex., described the change as "the latest example of the Pentagon and the President prioritizing politics over policy." Tony Perkins, president of the conservative Family Research Council, claimed that the president was focusing on fighting "culture wars" instead of "real wars against the enemies of our nation." Others applauded the announcement. "This is about equality, about civil rights . . . about recognizing the decency of human beings, that we are all equal and that gender is not a barrier to service," said Capt. Sage Fox, an Army Reserve officer who transitioned genders. Aaron Belkin, founder and executive director of the PALM Center, which had advocated for allowing transgender individuals to serve openly, said it was "an amazing, historic event" that meant people "can serve without having to lie about who they are" and could receive the medical care they needed.

The policy will be reviewed by July 1, 2018, and will be updated to reflect the most relevant medical information, as well as lessons learned from the first two years of the policy's implementation.

—Linda Fecteau Grimm

Following are remarks by Sen. John McCain, R-Ariz., on June 8, 2016, opening the Senate floor debate on the National Defense Authorization Act; and a press release from the U.S. Department of Defense from June 30, 2016, announcing that transgender individuals will now be allowed to serve openly in the military.

DOCUMENT

Sen. John McCain Remarks on the FY2017 NDAA

June 8, 2016

U.S. Senator John McCain (R-AZ), Chairman of the Senate Armed Services Committee, delivered the following remarks today on the Senate Floor opening debate on the National Defense Authorization Act for Fiscal Year 2017:

"It is my pleasure to rise with my friend and colleague from Rhode Island to speak about the National Defense Authorization Act for Fiscal Year 2017. For 54 consecutive years, Congress has passed this vital piece of legislation, which provides our military service members with the resources, equipment, and training they need to defend the nation. The NDAA is one of few bills in Congress that continues to enjoy bipartisan support year after year. That's a testament to this legislation's critical importance to our national security, and the high regard with which it is held by the Congress.

"Last month, the Senate Armed Services Committee voted 23–3 to approve the NDAA, an overwhelming vote that reflects the Committee's proud tradition of bipartisan support for the brave men and women of our Armed Forces.

"I want to thank the Committee's Ranking Member, the Senator from Rhode Island, for his months of hard work on the NDAA. It has been a pleasure to work with him on this legislation. And I remain appreciative of the thoughtfulness and bipartisan spirit with which he approaches our national security. He is a great partner.

"I also want to thank the Majority Leader, the Senator from Kentucky, for his commitment to bringing the NDAA to the Senate floor on time and without delay. It is a testimony to his leadership that the Senate will once again consider this bill in regular order with an open amendment process.

"I am tremendously proud of the Armed Services Committee's work on this legislation. This year's NDAA is the most significant piece of defense reform legislation in 30 years. It includes major reforms to the Department of Defense that can help our military to rise to the challenge of a more dangerous world.

"The NDAA contains major updates to the Pentagon's organization to prioritize innovation and improve the development and execution of defense strategy. . . .

"Among the many military personnel policy provisions in the NDAA, there is one that has already attracted some controversy. That, of course, is the provision in the NDAA that requires women to register for selective service to the same extent as men beginning in 2018. Earlier this year, the Department of Defense lifted the ban on women serving in ground combat units. And after months of rigorous oversight, a large bipartisan majority on the Armed Services Committee agreed that there is simply no further justification to limit selective service registration to men. That is not just my view, but the view of every single one of our military service chiefs, including the Army Chief of Staff and the Commandant of the Marine Corps.

"There will likely be further debate on this issue. And as it unfolds, we must never forget that women have served honorably in our military for years. They've filled critical roles in every branch of our military. Some have served as pilots, like Martha McSally who flew combat missions in Afghanistan. Some served as logisticians, like Senator Joni Ernst, who ran convoys into Iraq. Others have served as medics, intelligence officers, nuclear engineers, boot camp instructors, and more. Many of these women have served in harms' way. And many women have made the ultimate sacrifice, including 160 killed in Afghanistan and Iraq. . . .

"We must not let them down. As we move forward with consideration of the NDAA, I stand ready to work with my colleagues on both sides of the aisle to pass this important legislation and give our military the resources they need and deserve."

SOURCE: Office of U.S. Senator John McCain. "Remarks by SASC Chairman John McCain Opening Debate on the National Defense Authorization Act for FY17." June 8, 2016. http://www.mccain.senate .gov/public/index.cfm/floor-statements?ID=8586EB52-2B08-4C25-A537-254F045CE68D.

Defense Department Announces New Policy for Transgender Service Members

June 30, 2016

Secretary of Defense Ash Carter today announced that transgender individuals will now be able to openly serve in the U.S. armed forces.

The DoD policy announced today also establishes a construct by which service members may transition gender while serving, sets standards for medical care and outlines responsibilities for military services and commanders to develop and implement guidance, training and specific policies in the near and long-term.

"This is the right thing to do for our people and for the force," Carter said. "We're talking about talented Americans who are serving with distinction or who want the opportunity to serve. We can't allow barriers unrelated to a person's qualifications prevent us from recruiting and retaining those who can best accomplish the mission."

The policy will be phased in during a one-year period. Effective immediately, service members may no longer be involuntarily separated, discharged or denied reenlistment solely on the basis of gender identity. Service members currently on duty will be able to serve openly.

Not later than October 1, 2016, DoD will create and distribute a commanders' training handbook, medical protocol and guidance for changing a service member's gender in the Defense Eligibility Enrollment System (DEERS). At this point, the services will be required to provide medically necessary care and treatment to transgender service members according to the medical protocol and guidance, and may begin changing gender markers in DEERS. Prior to October 1, 2016, requests for medical treatment will be handled on a case-by-case basis consistent with the spirit of the Directive Type Memorandum and the DoD Instruction issued today.

Over the course of the next year, the Department will finalize force training plans and implementation guidance, revise regulations and forms, and train the force, including commanders, human resources specialists, recruiters and service members. Acting Under Secretary of Defense for Personnel and Readiness Peter Levine will work with the military services to monitor and oversee this effort.

At one year, the services will begin allowing transgender individuals to join the armed forces, assuming they meet accession standards. In addition, an otherwise-qualified individual's gender identity will not be considered a bar to admission to a military service academy, or participation in the Reserve Officers' Training Corps or any other accession program if the individual meets the new criteria.

The full policy must be completely implemented no later than July 1, 2017.

To support service members, medical professionals and commanders during the implementation period, the DoD has set up a central coordination cell which will serve as a central point of contact for technical questions and concerns. The coordination cell is made up of legal experts, policy experts and medical professionals familiar with the issue.

SOURCE: U.S. Defense Department. "Secretary of Defense Ash Carter Announces Policy for Transgender Service Members." June 30, 2016. http://www.defense.gov/News/News-Releases/News-Release-View/Article/821675/secretary-of-defense-ash-carter-announces-policy-for-transgender-service-members.

OTHER HISTORIC DOCUMENTS OF INTEREST

FROM PREVIOUS *HISTORIC DOCUMENTS*

Federal Officials Remark on Gun Violence and Regulation

JUNE 12, 22, AND 27, 2016

Following a spate of mass shootings in 2015, the year 2016 saw yet more violence, including the worst mass shooting in modern American history, which occurred on June 12 when fifty were killed inside the Pulse nightclub in Orlando, Florida. The incident renewed calls for gun control legislation and led to a sit-in on the floor of the United States House of Representatives led by Democratic congressman John Lewis of Georgia. A number of attempts were made in the Senate to pass bills directed specifically at ending the ability of those on the Federal Bureau of Investigation's (FBI) terrorist watch list to acquire guns, but all failed. By the end of 2016, Congress had not passed any legislation pertaining to gun ownership, and while the Supreme Court took up the issue, its ruling would not impact current law.

PULSE NIGHT CLUB SHOOTING

On June 12, Pulse, a gay nightclub in Orlando, Florida, was the site of the worst mass shooting in modern American history. Shortly after 2:00 a.m. local time, Omar Mateen, a twenty-nine-year-old of Afghan descent, arrived at Pulse, exchanged gunfire with the bouncer, and then entered the club, where he began shooting with an automatic Sig Sauer MCX semi-automatic rifle and a 9mm Glock pistol. Many club-goers admitted after the event that when they first heard the shots, they thought it was from the music. But when the DJ turned it down, the more than 300 people in the club scattered. Some hid in bathrooms and under the DJ stand, while others attempted to reach the exits. At 2:09 a.m., Pulse posted on its Facebook page, "Everyone get out of pulse and keep running." Shortly thereafter, Mateen's shooting spree, which killed forty-nine and injured more than fifty, ended with the taking of thirty hostages.

Local police and a SWAT team attempted to negotiate with Mateen by phone for the release of the hostages for nearly three hours until 5:00 a.m., at which point they decided to enter the building. A controlled explosion and armored vehicle were used to breach a wall to allow the SWAT team to enter the building. Hostages quickly escaped, and at 5:53 a.m., a heavily armed Mateen was killed by police.

Speaking from the White House following the shooting, President Barack Obama said, "We stand with the people of Orlando, who have endured a terrible attack on their city. Although it's still early in the investigation, we know enough to say that this was an act of terror and an act of hate. And as Americans, we are united in grief, in outrage, and in resolve to defend our people." The president also criticized the inaction across government to limit access to the kinds of weapons Mateen had used. "This massacre is . . . a further reminder of how easy it is for someone to get their hands on a weapon that lets them shoot people in a school or in a house of worship or in a movie theater or in a nightclub. And we have to decide if that's the kind of country we want to be. And to actively do nothing is a decision as well."

Immediately following the attack, questions arose about Mateen's motives and whether he was linked to any terror group. Mateen had called 911 from Pulse multiple times during the shooting and pledged his allegiance to the Islamic State of Iraq and the Levant (ISIL). Police would later reveal that he had been investigated for terrorist ties in 2013 and 2014 after coworkers reported comments he made about having family ties to al Qaeda. Both cases were closed after no significant findings were made. After the Pulse shooting, the CIA opened a similar investigation but found no direct, credible links between Mateen and any terror group. On July 26, the Senate Homeland Security and Governmental Affairs Committee requested additional information from the Justice Department on why Mateen had been removed from a terror watch list in 2014. (Mateen was initially added to the list after the 2013 investigation.) The letter sent by Sen. Ron Johnson, R-Wis., stated that had Mateen still been on the terror watch list in early June 2016 when he purchased the weapons used in the shooting, the Justice Department would have been alerted and could have acted potentially to prevent the attack. The committee further requested a review of the guidelines governing the watch list to determine if they are stringent enough to ensure the safety of the American people.

CONGRESSIONAL GUN CONTROL SIT-IN

On June 23, less than two weeks after the Pulse nightclub shooting, Democratic members of Congress took an unusual measure to demand House action on gun control: They conducted a sit-in on the House floor. Representative Lewis began the sit-in with a speech stating, "We have lost hundreds and thousands of innocent people to gun violence. . . . And what has this body done, Mr. Speaker? Nothing. Not one thing. We have turned deaf ears to the blood of the innocent and the concerns of our nation." Noting that bipartisan efforts have been "pushed aside" and that "reason is criticized" in the debate over gun control, Lewis called on the leadership of the House to "bring common-sense gun control legislation to the House Floor. Give us a vote! Let us vote! We came here to do our jobs! We came here to work! The American people are demanding action." Before taking his seat in the well of the House, Lewis said, "Sometimes you have to do something out of the ordinary. Sometimes you have to make a way out of no way. . . . The time to act is now. We will be silent no more."

In the week prior to the sit-in, after a twelve-hour filibuster by Democrats, the Senate voted on four different measures for gun control, mostly aimed at restricting those on terror watch lists from buying a gun, and they all failed. Although the overarching idea had bipartisan support, senators could not agree on whether they should allow the attorney general to ban the sale to those on the watch lists or whether the courts should be given the opportunity to weigh in. The slim chance at enacting any change in Congress was a bill brought by Sen. Susan Collins, R-Maine, that would allow the attorney general to ban the sale of guns to anyone on two specific FBI terrorist watch lists, which amounted to an estimated 2,700 individuals. That bill, too, ultimately failed. Even it if had passed, House Speaker Paul Ryan, R-Wis., said he would only consider bringing the bill for a vote on the House floor if it received significant support in the Senate.

The sit-in drew 170 legislators and lasted more than twenty-four hours, even through an unrelated procedural vote and a middle-of-the-night Republican attempt to adjourn the House for the July 4 recess. During the procedural vote, the Democrats who sat in the well of the House shouted, "No bill, no break!" and "Shame, shame, shame!" The sit-in was overwhelmingly criticized by Republicans, including Senator Collins, who said that the "sit-in on the House side . . . made it partisan, and I've worked very hard to keep this bipartisan." The event was a social media frenzy, with Democrats sharing the proceedings, including speeches on Americans killed by gun violence, by livestreaming from their phones because the House cameras had been cut off (House cameras are only permitted to carry official proceedings). There was little expectation that the sit-in would change the course of the House on gun control, and recent attempts at enacting measures that have bipartisan support have shown that neither party has the votes to change current U.S. gun laws. By the close of 2016, no headway was made in either house of Congress on gun control legislation.

Supreme Court Upholds Domestic Violence Gun Ban; Newtown Families Sue Gun Manufacturers

In June, the Supreme Court released a ruling in *Voisine v. United States* brought by two men in Maine who had been convicted of violating federal gun laws because they possessed weapons after being convicted on misdemeanor domestic abuse charges. The men argued that because their domestic abuse offenses did not have violent intent, but rather were committed recklessly, they should not be subject to the gun ban.

The Court ultimately ruled 6–2 to uphold the ban on gun ownership by those convicted of domestic abuse, even if the abuse case was a misdemeanor offense. In a twelve-page opinion authored by Justice Elena Kagan, the majority asserted that the gun ban, enacted two decades earlier, was meant to "prohibit domestic abusers convicted under run-of-the-mill misdemeanor assault and battery laws from possessing guns." Excluding misdemeanors, the majority argued, would "substantially undermine the provision's design."

Although not one of the Court's more highly anticipated rulings in 2016, the case was notable because, for the first time in ten years, Justice Clarence Thomas asked a number of questions from the bench during the February hearings on the case. The concern addressed by Thomas echoed that of those who brought the case—that misdemeanor domestic abuse charges, often those when a person acted recklessly in the heat of the moment, can result in the loss of gun ownership privileges for life. In his nineteen-page dissent, Thomas asserted that the Court treats "no other constitutional right so cavalierly." Thomas was joined in his dissent in part by Justice Sonia Sotomayor, who agreed that Congress should have written the gun ban law in a more specific way if the intent was to cover misdemeanor offenses.

In a separate case involving gun use and ownership, ten of the families of those killed during the Newtown, Connecticut, shooting at Sandy Hook Elementary School in 2012 brought a lawsuit against the maker, distributor, and seller of the Bushmaster AR-15 rifle, which had been used in the shooting. The families argued in the suit that the weapon should not have been made available to the general public and that the defendants were negligent in allowing its sale outside of the military because it had reasonable cause to believe it could be used to kill a large number of individuals. The defendants filed a separate motion to have the case thrown out, arguing that federal law—specifically the Protection of Lawful Commerce in Arms Act—protects gun manufacturers from the crimes committed with their products, but the motion was denied in April and the case was allowed to proceed. In June, Connecticut Superior Court judge Barbara Bellis dismissed the lawsuit, stating, "Based on the clear intent of Congress to narrowly define the 'negligent entrustment' exception, Adam Lanza's use of the firearm is the only actionable use. Accordingly, the plaintiffs have not alleged that any of the defendants' entrustees 'used' the firearm within the confines of PLCAA's definition of the term. To the contrary, the plaintiffs have alleged facts that place them directly in the category of victims to which Congress knowingly denied relief." The families appealed the case to the Connecticut Supreme Court, which agreed on December 1 to accept the lawsuit.

—Heather Kerrigan

Following is a statement by President Barack Obama on June 12, 2016, on the mass shooting at Orlando's Pulse nightclub; a June 22, 2016, statement delivered on the House floor by Rep. John Lewis, D-Ga., on the need for congressional action on gun control; and the syllabus from the Supreme Court's decision in Voisine v. United States, *in which the Court ruled 6–2 on June 27, 2016, to uphold the ban on gun ownership by those convicted of domestic abuse.*

President Obama Remarks on Mass Shooting in Orlando

June 12, 2016

Today, as Americans, we grieve the brutal murder—a horrific massacre—of dozens of innocent people. We pray for their families, who are grasping for answers with broken hearts. We stand with the people of Orlando, who have endured a terrible attack on their city. Although it's still early in the investigation, we know enough to say that this was an act of terror and an act of hate. And as Americans, we are united in grief, in outrage, and in resolve to defend our people.

I just finished a meeting with FBI Director Comey and my homeland security and national security advisers. The FBI is on the scene and leading the investigation, in partnership with local law enforcement. I've directed that the full resources of the Federal Government be made available for this investigation.

We are still learning all the facts. This is an open investigation. We've reached no definitive judgment on the precise motivations of the killer. The FBI is appropriately investigating this as an act of terrorism. And I've directed that we must spare no effort to determine what—if any—inspiration or association this killer may have had with terrorist groups. What is clear is that he was a person filled with hatred. Over the coming days, we will uncover why and how this happened, and we will go wherever the facts lead us.

This morning I spoke with my good friend, Orlando Mayor Buddy Dyer, and I conveyed to him the deepest condolences of the American people. This could have been any one of our communities. So I told Mayor Dyer that whatever help he and the people of Orlando need, they are going to get it. As a country, we will be there for the people of Orlando today, tomorrow, and for all the days to come.

We also express our profound gratitude to all the police and first responders who rushed to harm's way. Their courage and professionalism saved lives, and kept the carnage from being even worse. It's the kind of sacrifice that our law enforcement professionals make every single day for all of us, and we can never thank them enough.

This is an especially heartbreaking day for all our friends—our fellow Americans—who are lesbian, gay, bisexual, or transgender. The shooter targeted a nightclub where people came together to be with friends, to dance and to sing, and to live. The place where they were attacked is more than a nightclub; it is a place of solidarity and empowerment where people have come together to raise awareness, to speak their minds, and to advocate for their civil rights.

So this is a sobering reminder that attacks on any American—regardless of race, ethnicity, religion, or sexual orientation—is an attack on all of us and on the fundamental values of equality and dignity that define us as a country. And no act of hate or terror will ever change who we are or the values that make us Americans.

Today marks the most deadly shooting in American history. The shooter was apparently armed with a handgun and a powerful assault rifle. This massacre is therefore a further reminder of how easy it is for someone to get their hands on a weapon that lets them shoot people in a school or in a house of worship or a movie theater or in a nightclub. And we have to decide if that's the kind of country we want to be. And to actively do nothing is a decision as well.

In the coming hours and days, we'll learn about the victims of this tragedy: their names, their faces, who they were, the joy that they brought to families and to friends, and the difference that they made in this world. Say a prayer for them, and say a prayer for their families: that God give them the strength to bear the unbearable; and that He give us all the strength to be there for them and the strength and courage to change. We need to demonstrate that we are defined more—as a country—by the way they lived their lives than by the hate of the man who took them from us.

As we go together, we will draw inspiration from heroic and selfless acts: friends who helped friends, took care of each other, and saved lives. In the face of hate and violence, we will love one another. We will not give in to fear or turn against each other. Instead, we will stand united, as Americans, to protect our people, and defend our Nation, and to take action against those who threaten us.

May God bless the Americans we lost this morning, may He comfort their families, and may God continue to watch over this country that we love. Thank you.

SOURCE: Executive Office of the President. "Remarks on the Shootings in Orlando, Florida." June 12, 2016. *Compilation of Presidential Documents* 2016, no. 00396 (June 12, 2016). http://www.gpo.gov/fdsys/pkg/DCPD-201600396/pdf/DCPD-201600396.pdf.

DOCUMENT

Rep. John Lewis Calls for Gun Control Legislation

June 22, 2016

Congressman John Lewis (GA) spoke on the House Floor this morning to condemn Congressional inaction to mass shootings and gun violence in the United States.

He made this statement and led a sit-in against the inaction of Congress on this crisis of violence:

"On occasion, Mr. Speaker, I have had what I call an executive session with myself.

"For months, even for years, through several sessions of Congress, I wondered what will bring this body to take action. What will finally make Congress do what is right, what is just, what the people of this country have been demanding, and what is long overdue?

"We have lost hundreds and thousands of innocent people to gun violence. Tiny, little children. Babies. Students and teachers. Mothers and fathers. Sisters and brothers. Daughters and sons. Friends and neighbors.

"And what has this body done, Mr. Speaker? NOTHING. Not one thing. We have turned deaf ears to the blood of the innocent and the concerns of our nation. We are blind to a crisis. Mr. Speaker, where is the heart of this body? Where is our soul? Where is our moral leadership? Where is our courage?

"Those who work on bipartisan solutions are pushed aside. Those who pursue common-sense improvements are beaten down. Reason is criticized. Obstruction is praised.

"Newtown, Aurora, Charleston, Orlando. What is the tipping point? Are we blind? Can we see? How many more mothers, how many more fathers need to shed tears of grief before we do something?

"We were elected to lead, Mr. Speaker. We must be headlights, and not taillights. We cannot continue to stick our heads in the sand and ignore the reality of mass gun violence in our nation. Deadly mass shootings are becoming more and more frequent. Mr. Speaker, this is a fact. It is not an opinion. We must remove the blinders. The time for silence and patience is long gone.

"We are calling on the leadership of the House to bring common-sense gun control legislation to the House Floor. Give us a vote! Let us vote! We came here to do our jobs! We came here to work! The American people are demanding action.

"Do we have the courage? Do we have raw courage to make at least a down-payment on ending gun violence in America? We can no longer wait. We can no longer be patient. So today, we come to the well of the House to dramatize the need for action. Not next month, not next year, but now—today!

"Sometimes you have to do something out of the ordinary. Sometimes you have to make a way out of no way. We have been too quiet for too long. There comes a time when you have to say something, when you have to make a little noise. When you have to move your feet. And this is the time. Now is the time to get in the way. The time to act is now. We will be silent no more. The time for silence is over. Thank you, Mr. Speaker."

SOURCE: Representative John Lewis. "Rep. John Lewis on the Need for Congress to Act Now on Gun Violence and Mass Shootings." June 22, 2016. https://johnlewis.house.gov/media-center/press-releases/rep-john-lewis-need-congress-act-now-gun-violence-and-mass-shootings.

Supreme Court Rules on Gun Ownership for Domestic Abusers

June 27, 2016

Syllabus

Voisine et al. v. United States

Certiorari to the United States Court of Appeals for the First Circuit

No. 14-10154

Argued February 29, 2016—Decided June 27, 2016

In an effort to "close [a] dangerous loophole" in the gun control laws, *United States v. Castleman*, 572 U. S. ___, ___, Congress extended the federal prohibition on firearms possession by convicted felons to persons convicted of a "misdemeanor crime of domestic violence," 18 U. S. C. §922(g)(9). Section 921(a)(33)(A) defines that phrase to include a misdemeanor under federal, state, or tribal law, committed against a domestic relation that necessarily involves the "use . . . of physical force." In *Castleman*, this Court held that a knowing or intentional assault qualifies as such a crime, but left open whether the same was true of a reckless assault.

Petitioner Stephen Voisine pleaded guilty to assaulting his girlfriend in violation of §207 of the Maine Criminal Code, which makes it a misdemeanor to "intentionally, knowingly or recklessly cause[ ] bodily injury" to another. When law enforcement officials later investigated Voisine for killing a bald eagle, they learned that he owned a rifle. After a background check turned up Voisine's prior conviction under §207, the Government charged him with violating §922(g)(9). Petitioner William Armstrong pleaded guilty to assaulting his wife in violation of a Maine domestic violence law making it a misdemeanor to commit an assault prohibited by §207 against a family or household member. While searching Armstrong's home as part of a narcotics investigation a few years later, law enforcement officers discovered six guns and a large quantity of ammunition. Armstrong was also charged under §922(g)(9). Both men argued that they were not subject to §922(g)(9)'s prohibition because their prior convictions could have been based on reckless, rather than knowing or intentional, conduct and thus did not quali[f]y as misdemeanor crimes of domestic violence. The District Court rejected those claims, and each petitioner pleaded guilty. The First Circuit affirmed, holding that "an offense with a *mens rea* of recklessness may qualify as a 'misdemeanor crime of violence' under §922(g)(9)." Voisine and Armstrong filed a joint petition for certiorari, and their case was remanded for further consideration in light of *Castleman*. The First Circuit again upheld the convictions on the same ground.

Held: A reckless domestic assault qualifies as a "misdemeanor crime of domestic violence" under §922(g)(9). Pp. 4–12.

(a) That conclusion follows from the statutory text. Nothing in the phrase "use . . . of physical force" indicates that §922(g)(9) distinguishes between domestic assaults committed knowingly or intentionally and those committed recklessly.

Dictionaries consistently define the word "use" to mean the "act of employing" something. Accordingly, the force involved in a qualifying assault must be volitional; an involuntary motion, even a powerful one, is not naturally described as an active employment of force. See *Castleman*, 572 U. S., at ___. But nothing about the definition of "use" demands that the person applying force have the purpose or practical certainty that it will cause harm, as compared with the understanding that it is substantially likely to do so. Nor does *Leocal v. Ashcroft*, 543 U. S. 1, which held that the "use" of force excludes accidents. Reckless conduct, which requires the conscious disregard of a known risk, is not an accident: It involves a deliberate decision to endanger another. The relevant text thus supports prohibiting petitioners, and others with similar criminal records, from possessing firearms. Pp. 5–8.

(b) So too does the relevant history. Congress enacted §922(g)(9) in 1996 to bar those domestic abusers convicted of garden-variety assault or battery misdemeanors— just like those convicted of felonies—from owning guns. Then, as now, a significant majority of jurisdictions—34 States plus the District of Columbia—defined such misdemeanor offenses to include the reckless infliction of bodily harm. In targeting those laws, Congress thus must have known it was sweeping in some persons who had engaged in reckless conduct. See, e.g., *United States v. Bailey*, 9 Pet. 238, 256. Indeed, that was part of the point: to apply the federal firearms restriction to those abusers, along with all others, covered by the States' ordinary misdemeanor assault laws.

Petitioners' reading risks rendering §922(g)(9) broadly inoperative in the 35 jurisdictions with assault laws extending to recklessness. Consider Maine's law, which criminalizes "intentionally, knowingly or recklessly" injuring another. Assuming that statute defines a single crime, petitioners' view that §921(a)(33)(A) requires at least a knowing *mens rea* would mean that no conviction obtained under that law could qualify as a "misdemeanor crime of domestic violence." *Descamps v. United States*, 570 U. S. ___, ___. In *Castleman*, the Court declined to construe §921(a)(33)(A) so as to render §922(g)(9) ineffective in 10 States. All the more so here, where petitioners' view would jeopardize §922(g)(9)'s force in several times that many. Pp. 8–11.

778 F. 3d 176, affirmed.

KAGAN, J., delivered the opinion of the Court, in which ROBERTS, C. J., and KENNEDY, GINSBURG, BREYER, and ALITO, JJ., joined. THOMAS, J., filed a dissenting opinion, in which SOTOMAYOR, J., joined as to Parts I and II.

SOURCE: United States Supreme Court. *Voisine v. United States*. Syllabus. 579 U.S.__(2016). http://www .supremecourt.gov/opinions/15pdf/14-10154_19m1.pdf.

OTHER HISTORIC DOCUMENTS OF INTEREST

FROM THIS VOLUME

FROM PREVIOUS *HISTORIC DOCUMENTS*

Federal Court Upholds
Net Neutrality Order

JUNE 14, 2016

The Federal Communications Commission's (FCC) adoption of the 2015 Open Internet Order—and particularly its reclassification of broadband Internet as a telecommunications service—prompted several broadband Internet providers and the trade associations that represent them to file lawsuits challenging the FCC's authority to reclassify broadband services and the legality of the new regulations promoting net neutrality. Among these lawsuits was *USTelecom v. FCC*, filed by USTelecom before the U.S. Court of Appeals for the District of Columbia Circuit. The court ruled in June 2016 that the FCC did in fact have the authority to reclassify broadband and upheld all portions of the order.

OPEN INTERNET ORDER OF 2015

The FCC adopted its latest Open Internet Order on February 26, 2015. Portions of the commission's previous Open Internet Order, issued in 2010, had been vacated by the U.S. Court of Appeals for the District of Columbia Circuit in the case of *Verizon v. FCC*. With its 2015 order, the FCC sought to reinstate open Internet rules that followed the legal roadmap provided by the court's ruling.

The most notable provision of the 2015 rules reclassified broadband Internet as a telecommunications service under Title II of the Communications Act. This reclassification meant that broadband was considered an essential public utility, which gives the FCC more power to regulate it. In a nod to concerns raised by providers that such a reclassification would lead to burdensome regulations that could impede investment and growth, the FCC's order said that twenty-seven of Title II's provisions—and more than 700 regulations adopted under the title—would not apply to broadband. For example, broadband providers will not be subject to utility-style rate regulations under the new rules. The order also applied open Internet rules to both fixed and mobile broadband service for the first time.

In addition, the 2015 order prohibited broadband providers from blocking access to legal content, applications, or nonharmful devices; impairing or degrading lawful Internet traffic on the basis of content, applications, or nonharmful devices; and creating fast lanes that favor some lawful Internet traffic over other, lawful Internet traffic. A general conduct rule stated that providers cannot "unreasonably interfere with or unreasonably disadvantage" consumers' ability to access and use lawful content, applications, services or devices, or edge providers' ability to make lawful content, applications, services, or devices available to consumers. Other measures required broadband providers to disclose promotional rates, fees, surcharges, and data caps in a consistent format, as well as any network management practices that could affect customers' service.

Consumer groups, free speech advocates, and open Internet supporters praised the order as protecting consumer rights and preserving access to the Internet. Providers and telecom industry groups claimed that the commission had overstepped its authority and that the new rules were unnecessary. Others also expressed a concern that the Communications Act (passed in 1934) was too outdated to be applied to modern technologies. Several companies and organizations filed lawsuits in 2015 to challenge these rules, including USTelecom.

USTelecom v. FCC

USTelecom filed its lawsuit in federal court on March 23, 2015. The suit included several other petitioners, such as CenturyLink, AT&T, the American Cable Association, CTIA—The Wireless Association, and NCTA—The Internet & Television Association. The petitioners argued that the FCC had improperly classified broadband as a telecommunications service, and that it lacked the authority to do so. They also claimed that the FCC's 2014 notice of proposed rulemaking seeking public comment on the order failed to provide sufficient notification about the coming reclassification and related rules and that mobile broadband should be considered separately from fixed broadband services due to the shared nature of mobile networks. Furthermore, the suit alleged that some of the FCC's rules violated providers' First Amendment rights. Eleven amicus briefs were filed in support of the petitioners, while fourteen amicus briefs were filed in support of the FCC and the new rules. In July 2015, the court rejected USTelecom's request to partly suspend implementation of the rules while they were being legally challenged, and oral arguments were heard in December 2015.

The court issued its ruling in the case on June 14, 2016. In a 2–1 decision among the three-judge panel, the court upheld the FCC's order in full, affirming that the FCC did have the authority to reclassify broadband as a telecommunications service under Title II and that the commission had done so properly. As the majority opinion stated, content from edge providers such as Netflix and YouTube had "transformed nearly every aspect of our lives" and broadband providers offer services that can be defined as telecommunications services. The court also ruled that the order should apply to both wired and wireless Internet, noting mobile broadband's ubiquity and that consumers do not see a difference between these services since their devices automatically switch between the two. In addition, the court found that broadband providers are acting as "mere conduits for the messages of others, not as agents exercising editorial discretion," do not "speak" or exercise editorial control, and therefore do not receive First Amendment protections. Writing for the dissent, Judge Stephen Williams described the FCC's rules as an "unreasoned patchwork" that would discourage competition in the broadband industry.

FCC Chair Tom Wheeler welcomed the ruling as validation of the FCC's efforts to preserve the open Internet. "Today's ruling . . . ensures the internet remains a platform for unparalleled innovation, free expression and economic growth," Wheeler said in a statement. "After a decade of debate and legal battles, today's ruling affirms the Commission's ability to enforce the strongest possible internet protections—both on fixed and mobile networks—that will ensure the internet remains open, now and in the future."

USTelecom and its fellow petitioners are expected to file an appeal in hopes of bringing their case before the U.S. Supreme Court. "We have always expected this issue to be decided by the Supreme Court, and we look forward to participating in that appeal," said David McAtee, general counsel for AT&T. Others have encouraged Congress's intervention. "While this is unlikely the last step in this decade-long debate over internet regulation, we urge bipartisan leaders in Congress to renew their efforts to craft meaningful legislation that can end ongoing uncertainty, promote network investment and protect consumers," said NCTA in a statement.

First Regulations Issued under Open Internet Order

Shortly before USTelecom filed its suit, on March 10, the FCC released a proposed set of privacy rules for Internet service providers (ISPs), marking its first major regulatory action since it adopted the Open Internet Order. As proposed, the rules sought clear disclosures from providers on how data about consumers' online browsing and other activities may be collected, as well as increased data security. The rules would also prevent ISPs from sharing virtually any consumer data with noncommunications partners without consumers' permission, including nonsensitive data.

The FCC said its reclassification of broadband as a telecommunications service compelled it to establish privacy rules for ISPs, but providers argued that the Federal Trade Commission was already enforcing strong consumer privacy protections, and that the FCC's measures were unnecessary. The FCC relaxed its proposed rules in October only to require ISPs to obtain consumer approval to share sensitive information with third parties. These revised rules were adopted by the FCC on October 27.

—Linda Fecteau Grimm

Following is the decision of the U.S. Court of Appeals for the District of Columbia Circuit from June 14, 2016, in the case of USTelecom v. FCC.

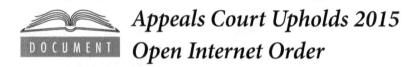

Appeals Court Upholds 2015 Open Internet Order

June 14, 2016

Argued December 4, 2015   Decided June 14, 2016
No. 15-1063

UNITED STATES TELECOM ASSOCIATION, ET AL.,
PETITIONERS

v.

FEDERAL COMMUNICATIONS COMMISSION AND UNITED STATES OF AMERICA,
RESPONDENTS

INDEPENDENT TELEPHONE & TELECOMMUNICATIONS ALLIANCE, ET AL.,
INTERVENORS

TATEL and SRINIVASAN, Circuit Judges: For the third time in seven years, we confront an effort by the Federal Communications Commission to compel internet openness—commonly known as net neutrality—the principle that broadband providers must treat all internet traffic the same regardless of source. . . . The Commission then promulgated the order at issue in this case—the 2015 Open Internet Order—in which it reclassified broadband service as a telecommunications service, subject to common carrier regulation under Title II of the Communications Act. The Commission also exercised its statutory authority to forbear from applying many of Title II's provisions to broadband service and promulgated five rules to promote internet openness. Three separate groups of petitioners, consisting primarily of broadband providers and their associations, challenge the Order, arguing that the Commission lacks statutory authority to reclassify broadband as a telecommunications service, that even if the Commission has such authority its decision was arbitrary and capricious, that the Commission impermissibly classified mobile broadband as a commercial mobile service, that the Commission impermissibly forbore from certain provisions of Title II, and that some of the rules violate the First Amendment. For the reasons set forth in this opinion, we deny the petitions for review. . . .

I.

Understanding the issues raised by the Commission's current attempt to achieve internet openness requires familiarity with its past efforts to do so, as well as with the history of broadband regulation more generally.

A.

Much of the structure of the current regulatory scheme derives from rules the Commission established in its 1980 Computer II Order. The Computer II rules distinguished between "basic services" and "enhanced services." Basic services, such as telephone service, offered "pure transmission capability over a communications path that is virtually transparent in terms of its interaction with customer supplied information." In re Amendment of Section 64.702 of the Commission's Rules and Regulations ("Computer II"), 77 F.C.C. 2d 384, 420 ¶ 96 (1980). Enhanced services consisted of "any offering over the telecommunications network which is more than a basic transmission service," for example, one in which "computer processing applications are used to act on the content, code, protocol, and other aspects of the subscriber's information," such as voicemail. Id. at 420 ¶ 97. The rules subjected basic services, but not enhanced services, to common carrier treatment under Title II of the Communications Act. Id. at 387 ¶¶ 5–7. Among other things, Title II requires that carriers "furnish . . . communication service upon reasonable request," 47 U.S.C. § 201(a), engage in no "unjust or unreasonable discrimination in charges, practices, classifications, regulations, facilities, or services," id. § 202(a), and charge "just and reasonable" rates, id. § 201(b).

The Computer II rules also recognized a third category of services, "adjunct-to-basic" services: enhanced services, such as "speed dialing, call forwarding, [and] computer-provided directory assistance," that facilitated use of a basic service. See In re Implementation of the Non-Accounting Safeguards ("Non-Accounting Safeguards Order"), 11 FCC Rcd. 21,905, 21,958 ¶ 107 n.245 (1996). Although adjunct-to-basic services fell within the definition of enhanced services, the Commission nonetheless treated them as basic because of their role in facilitating basic services. See Computer II, 77 F.C.C. 2d at 421 ¶ 98 (explaining that the Commission would not treat as an enhanced service those services used to "facilitate [consumers'] use of traditional telephone services").

Fifteen years later, Congress, borrowing heavily from the Computer II framework, enacted the Telecommunications Act of 1996, which amended the Communications Act. The Telecommunications Act subjects a "telecommunications service," the successor to basic service, to common carrier regulation under Title II. 47 U.S.C. § 153(51) ("A telecommunications carrier shall be treated as a common carrier under [the Communications Act] only to the extent that it is engaged in providing telecommunications services."). By contrast, an "information service," the successor to an enhanced service, is not subject to Title II. The Telecommunications Act defines a "telecommunications service" as "the offering of telecommunications for a fee directly to the public, or to such classes of users as to be effectively available directly to the public, regardless of the facilities used." Id. § 153(53). It defines telecommunications as "the transmission, between or among points specified by the user, of information of the user's choosing without change in the form or content of the information as sent and received." Id. § 153(50). An information service is an "offering of a capability for generating, acquiring, storing, transforming, processing, retrieving, utilizing, or making available information via telecommunications." Id. § 153(24). The appropriate regulatory treatment therefore turns on what services a provider offers to the public: if it offers telecommunications, that service is subject to Title II regulation.

Tracking the Commission's approach to adjunct-to-basic services, Congress also effectively created a third category for information services that facilitate use of a telecommunications service. The "telecommunications management exception" exempts from information service treatment—and thus treats as a telecommunications service—"any use [of an information service] for the management, control, or operation of a telecommunications system or the management of a telecommunications service." Id. . . .

II.

In the Open Internet Order, the Commission determined that broadband service satisfies the statutory definition of a telecommunications service: "the offering of telecommunications for a fee directly to the public." 47 U.S.C. § 153(53). In accordance with Brand X, the Commission arrived at this conclusion by examining consumer perception of what broadband providers offer. 2015 Open Internet Order, 30 FCC Rcd. at 5750 ¶ 342. In Brand X, the Supreme Court held that it was "consistent with the statute's terms" for the Commission to take into account "the end user's perspective" in classifying a service as "information" or "telecommunications." 545 U.S. at 993. Specifically, the Court held that the Commission had reasonably concluded that a provider supplies a telecommunications service when it makes a "'stand-alone' offering of telecommunications, i.e., an offered service that, from the user's perspective, transmits messages unadulterated by computer processing." Id. at 989. In the Order, the Commission concluded that consumers perceive broadband service both as a standalone offering and as providing telecommunications. See 2015 Open Internet Order, 30 FCC Rcd. at 5765 ¶ 365. These conclusions about consumer perception find extensive support in the record and together justify the Commission's decision to reclassify broadband as a telecommunications service. . . .

With respect to its first conclusion—that consumers perceive broadband as a standalone offering—the Commission explained that broadband providers offer two separate types of services: "a broadband Internet access service," id. at 5750 ¶ 341, which provides "the ability to transmit data to and from Internet endpoints," id. at 5755 ¶ 350; and "'add-on' applications, content, and services that are generally information services," id. at

5750 ¶ 341, such as email and cloud-based storage programs, id. at 5773 ¶ 376. It found that from the consumer's perspective, "broadband Internet access service is today sufficiently independent of these information services that it is a separate offering." Id. at 5757–58 ¶ 356.

In support of its conclusion, the Commission pointed to record evidence demonstrating that consumers use broadband principally to access third-party content, not email and other add-on applications. "As more American households have gained access to broadband Internet access service," the Commission explained, "the market for Internet-based services provided by parties other than broadband Internet access providers has flourished." Id. at 5753 ¶ 347. Indeed, from 2003 to 2015, the number of websites increased from "approximately 36 million" to "an estimated 900 million." Id. By one estimate, two edge providers, Netflix and YouTube, "account for 50 percent of peak Internet download traffic in North America." Id. at 5754 ¶ 349. . . .

The Commission found, moreover, that broadband consumers not only focus on the offering of transmission but often avoid using the broadband providers' add-on services altogether, choosing instead "to use their high-speed Internet connections to take advantage of competing services offered by third parties." 2015 Open Internet Order, 30 FCC Rcd. at 5753 ¶ 347. For instance, two third-party email services, Gmail and Yahoo! Mail, were "among the ten Internet sites most frequently visited during the week of January 17, 2015, with approximately 400 million and 350 million visits respectively." Id. at 5753 ¶ 348. Some "even advise consumers specifically not to use a broadband provider-based email address[] because a consumer cannot take that email address with them if he or she switches providers." Id. . . .

Petitioners assert numerous challenges to the Commission's decision to reclassify broadband. Finding that none has merit, we uphold the classification. . . .

III.

Having thus rejected petitioners' arguments against reclassification, we turn to US Telecom's challenges to the Commission's regulation of interconnection arrangements—arrangements that broadband providers make with other networks to exchange traffic in order to ensure that their end users can access edge provider content anywhere on the internet. Broadband providers have such arrangements with backbone networks, as well as with certain edge providers, such as Netflix, that connect directly to broadband provider networks. In the Order, the Commission found that regulation of interconnection arrangements was necessary to ensure broadband providers do not "use terms of interconnection to disadvantage edge providers" or "prevent[] consumers from reaching the services and applications of their choosing." 2015 Open Internet Order, 30 FCC Rcd. at 5694 ¶ 205. . . .

As authority for regulating interconnection arrangements, the Commission relied on Title II. "Broadband Internet access service," it explained, "involves the exchange of traffic between . . . . broadband provider and connecting networks," since "[t]he representation to retail customers that they will be able to reach 'all or substantially all Internet endpoints' necessarily includes the promise to make the interconnection arrangements necessary to allow that access." Id. at 5693–94 ¶ 204. Because the "same data is flowing between the end user and edge consumer," the end user necessarily experiences any discriminatory treatment of the edge provider, the Commission reasoned, making interconnection "simply derivative of" the service offered to end users. Id. at 5748–49 ¶ 339.

As a result, the Commission concluded that it could regulate interconnection arrangements under Title II as a component of broadband service. Id. at 5686 ¶ 195. It refrained, however, from applying the General Conduct Rule or any of the bright-line rules to interconnection arrangements because, given that it "lack[ed] [a] background in practices addressing Internet traffic exchange," it would be "premature to adopt prescriptive rules to address any problems that have arisen or may arise." Id. at 5692–93 ¶ 202. Rather, it explained that interconnection disputes would be evaluated on a case-by-case basis under sections 201, 202, and 208 of the Communications Act. See id. at 5686–87 ¶ 195. US Telecom presents two challenges to the Commission's decision to regulate interconnection arrangements under Title II, one procedural and one substantive. We reject both. . . .

IV.

We now turn to the Commission's treatment of mobile broadband service, i.e., high-speed internet access for mobile devices such as smartphones and tablets. As explained above, the Commission permissibly found that mobile broadband—like all broadband—is a telecommunications service subject to common carrier regulation under Title II of the Communications Act. We address here a second set of provisions that pertain to the treatment of mobile broadband as common carriage.

Those provisions, found in Title III of the Communications Act, segregate "mobile services" into two, mutually exclusive categories: "commercial mobile services" and "private mobile services." 47 U.S.C. § 332(c). Providers of commercial mobile services—mobile services that are, among other things, available "to the public" or "a substantial portion of the public"—are subject to common carrier regulation. Id. § 332(c)(1), (d)(1). Providers of private mobile services, by contrast, "shall not . . . be treated as [] common carrier[s]." Id. § 332(c)(2).

In 2007, the Commission initially classified mobile broadband as a private mobile service. At the time, the Commission considered mobile broadband a "nascent" service. 2007 Wireless Order, 22 FCC Rcd. at 5922 ¶ 59. In the 2015 Order we now review, the Commission found that, "[i]n sharp contrast to 2007," the "mobile broadband marketplace has evolved such that hundreds of millions of consumers now use mobile broadband to access the Internet." 2015 Open Internet Order, 30 FCC Rcd. at 5785 ¶ 398. The Commission thus concluded that "today's mobile broadband Internet access service, with hundreds of millions of subscribers," is not a "private" mobile service "that offer[s] users access to a discrete and limited set of endpoints." Id. at 5788–89 ¶ 404. Rather, "[g]iven the universal access provided today and in the foreseeable future by and to mobile broadband and its present and anticipated future penetration rates in the United States," the Commission decided to "classify[] mobile broadband Internet access as a commercial mobile service" subject to common carrier regulation. Id. at 5786 ¶ 399; see generally id. at 5778–88 ¶¶ 388–403. . . .

We reject mobile petitioners' arguments and find that the Commission's reclassification of mobile broadband as a commercial mobile service is reasonable and supported by the record. . . .

V.

Having upheld the Commission's reclassification of broadband services, both fixed and mobile, we consider next Full Service Network's challenges to the Commission's decision to forbear from applying portions of the Communications Act to those services. Section 10 of the Communications Act provides that the Commission "shall forbear from applying any regulation or any provision" of the Communications Act to a telecommunications service or carrier if three criteria are satisfied: (1) "enforcement of such regulation or provision is not necessary to ensure that" the carrier's practices "are just and reasonable and are not unjustly or unreasonably discriminatory," 47 U.S.C. § 160(a)(1); (2) "enforcement of such regulation or provision is not necessary for the protection of consumers," id. § 160(a)(2); and (3) "forbearance from applying such provision or regulation is consistent with the public interest," id. § 160(a)(3). Under the third criterion, "the Commission shall consider whether forbearance . . . will promote competitive market conditions, including the extent to which such forbearance will enhance competition among providers of telecommunications services." Id. § 160(b). Thus, section 10 imposes a mandatory obligation upon the Commission to forbear when it finds these conditions are met. . . .

In the Order, the Commission decided to forbear from numerous provisions of the Communications Act. 2015 Open Internet Order, 30 FCC Rcd. at 5616 ¶ 51. Full Service Network raises both procedural and substantive challenges to the Commission's forbearance decision. None succeeds.

VI.

We turn next to petitioners' challenges to the particular rules adopted by the Commission. As noted earlier, the Commission promulgated five rules in the Order: rules banning (i) blocking, (ii) throttling, and (iii) paid prioritization, 2015 Open Internet Order, 30 FCC Rcd. at 5647 ¶ 110; (iv) a General Conduct Rule, id. at 5660 ¶ 136; and (v) an enhanced transparency rule, id. at 5669–82 ¶¶ 154–85. Petitioners Alamo and Berninger (together, Alamo) challenge the anti-paid-prioritization rule as beyond the Commission's authority. US Telecom challenges the General Conduct Rule as unconstitutionally vague. We reject both challenges. . . .

A.

In its challenge to the anti-paid-prioritization rule, petitioner Alamo contends that, even with reclassification of broadband as a telecommunications service, the Commission lacks authority to promulgate such a rule under section 201(b) of Title II and section 303(b) of Title III. The Commission, however, grounded the rules in "multiple, complementary sources of legal authority"—not only Titles II and III, but also section 706 of the Telecommunications Act of 1996 (now codified at 47 U.S.C. § 1302). Id. at 5720–21 ¶¶ 273–74. As to section 706, this court concluded in Verizon that it grants the Commission independent rulemaking authority. 740 F.3d at 635–42. . . . Consequently, we reject Alamo's challenges to the Commission's section 706 authority and to the anti-paid-prioritization rule.

B.

The Due Process Clause "requires the invalidation of laws [or regulations] that are impermissibly vague." *FCC v. Fox Television Stations, Inc.*, 132 S. Ct. 2307, 2317 (2012). US Telecom argues that the General Conduct Rule falls within that category. We disagree.

The General Conduct Rule forbids broadband providers from engaging in conduct that "unreasonably interfere[s] with or unreasonably disadvantage[s] (i) end users' ability to select, access, and use broadband Internet access service or the lawful Internet content, applications, services, or devices of their choice, or (ii) edge providers' ability to make lawful content, applications, services, or devices available to end users." 2015 Open Internet Order, 30 FCC Rcd. at 5660 ¶ 136. . . .

The degree of vagueness tolerable in a given statutory provision varies based on "the nature of the enactment." Hoffman Estates, 455 U.S. at 498. Thus, "the Constitution is most demanding of a criminal statute that limits First Amendment rights." *DiCola v. FDA*, 77 F.3d 504, 508 (D.C. Cir. 1996). The General Conduct Rule does not implicate that form of review because it regulates business conduct and imposes civil penalties. In such circumstances, "regulations will be found to satisfy due process so long as they are sufficiently specific that a reasonably prudent person, familiar with the conditions the regulations are meant to address and the objectives the regulations are meant to achieve, would have fair warning of what the regulations require." *Freeman United Coal Mining Co. v. Federal Mine Safety & Health Review Commission*, 108 F.3d 358, 362 (D.C. Cir. 1997). . . . That standard is met here. . . .

VII.

We finally turn to Alamo and Berninger's First Amendment challenge to the open internet rules. Having upheld the FCC's reclassification of broadband service as common carriage, we conclude that the First Amendment poses no bar to the rules. . . .

B.

Alamo argues that the open internet rules violate the First Amendment by forcing broadband providers to transmit speech with which they might disagree. We are unpersuaded. . . . Common carriers have long been subject to nondiscrimination and equal access obligations akin to those imposed by the rules without raising any First Amendment question. Those obligations affect a common carrier's neutral transmission of others' speech, not a carrier's communication of its own message. . . .

Because the constitutionality of each of the rules ultimately rests on the same analysis, we consider the rules together. The rules generally bar broadband providers from denying or downgrading end-user access to content and from favoring certain content by speeding access to it. In effect, they require broadband providers to offer a standardized service that transmits data on a nondiscriminatory basis. Such a constraint falls squarely within the bounds of traditional common carriage regulation. . . .

VIII.

For the foregoing reasons, we deny the petitions for review.

So ordered.

SOURCE: U.S. Court of Appeals District of Columbia Circuit. *United State Telecom Association, Et Al, Petitioners v. Federal Communications Commission and United States of America, Respondents.* June 14, 2016. http://www.cadc.uscourts.gov/internet/opinions.nsf/3F95E49183E6F8AF85257FD200505A3A/$file/15-1063-1619173.pdf.

OTHER HISTORIC DOCUMENTS OF INTEREST

Supreme Court Rules on Obama Administration Immigration Program

JUNE 23, 2016

In late 2015, a federal court in Texas blocked the implementation of an executive order issued by President Barack Obama that would temporarily exempt certain long-term undocumented immigrants from the threat of deportation and provide those immigrants temporarily with the ability to work legally. Agreeing to hear this appeal put the Supreme Court at the heart of one of the most contentious arenas in American politics—illegal immigration—during a heated presidential election campaign where the issue was front and center. The executive action challenged in this case came after years of frustrating political gridlock in Congress and was characterized by the Obama administration as a necessary enforcement policy, while its opponents described it as an unconstitutional power grab by the executive branch. The Supreme Court agreed to hear the case, and when the decision in *United States v. Texas* was released on June 23, 2016, it was only nine words long: "The judgment is affirmed by an equally divided Court." A deadlocked Court, rendered ineffectual by its unfilled seat, was unable to reach and resolve the legal issues, leaving the lower court's ruling against the executive action as the final word. The terseness of the Supreme Court's words belied the vast impact of the decision. The estimated five million immigrants who hoped to find a reprieve through the program, if only temporarily, from the constant threat of deportation, would continue to live with that fear. Former solicitor general Walter Dellinger said to the *New York Times*, "Seldom have the hopes of so many been crushed by so few words."

CONGRESS AND THE PRESIDENT DEADLOCK ON IMMIGRATION REFORM

When President Obama came into office he had hoped to make fixing what he described as a "broken" immigration system part of his legacy. He campaigned on promises to secure the border, crack down on the hiring of undocumented immigrants, and provide a path to citizenship and to legal work for the estimated eleven million undocumented immigrants living in the United States. In June 2013, the possibility of such immigration reform seemed possible. Due in large part to the work of the Senate's "Gang of Eight," a bipartisan bill for comprehensive immigration reform passed the Senate by an overwhelming margin of 68–32. Senate Bill 744—known as the Border Security, Economic Opportunity, and Immigration Modernization Act—included provisions to provide millions of undocumented immigrants with a path to citizenship as well as make it easier for companies to attract necessary workers from around the world and the most extensive investment ever made in border security. The Republican-controlled House refused to consider the bill or any other immigration reform, thus ending any hope for a comprehensive overhaul of immigration laws.

Because of congressional inaction, in November 2014, President Obama held a prime-time televised address to announce two major reforms of immigration policy, collectively referred to as the Immigration Accountability Executive Actions. The first reform was an expansion of an existing rule called the Deferred Action for Childhood Arrivals (DACA), a policy first introduced by the Obama administration in June 2012 that provided a two-year shield from deportation and work permits for undocumented immigrants who were under age sixteen when they were brought to the United States and who meet several other standards. The expanded DACA would have now granted a three-year deferment and would have been available to more immigrants. The second reform was a new initiative called the Deferred Action for Parents of Americans and Lawful Permanent Residents (DAPA). Under DAPA's program, the president authorized the Department of Homeland Security to defer for three years the deportation of those undocumented immigrants who have been in the United States since 2010, have not committed any serious crimes, and have children who are citizens or legal permanent residents. These two initiatives sought to collectively provide temporary relief from the fear of deportation to an estimated five million immigrants, keep families together, and contribute to the economy through increased productivity and tax revenue.

While only Congress can pass laws, the authority for DAPA and the expanded DACA rested, the Obama administration argued, on the executive branch's authority to exercise discretion in the enforcement and prosecution of immigration cases, including the power to defer deportation. Given the limited resources available, it is necessary to prioritize which undocumented immigrants to deport, and this, the administration urged, falls within the enforcement authority of the executive. Past presidents have also granted temporary relief from deportation; for instance, in 1987, then-President Ronald Reagan ordered that 200,000 Nicaraguan asylum seekers be exempted from deportation and granted work visas. In 1990, President George H. W. Bush put in place the Family Fairness Program, an executive order deferring the deportation of the spouses and children of immigrants who had been granted citizenship by an earlier immigration law.

The President's Immigration Orders and the Federal Courts

Within hours of the new orders' announcement, Sheriff Joe Arpaio of Maricopa County, Arizona, filed a lawsuit in Washington, D.C., challenging the president's plan to defer deportations. His lawsuit was quickly dismissed by the federal court in a decision that was upheld unanimously by the D.C. Circuit Court of Appeals. A few weeks later, however, Texas and twenty-five other states sued the Obama administration in a federal district court in Texas for failing to enforce the nation's immigration laws. They argued that the president had overstepped his authority with these orders and that they had standing to sue because the new policy would lead to increased costs for the states from a new class of people eligible to apply for state-subsidized drivers' licenses. On February 16, 2015, Judge Andrew Hanen of the U.S. District Court for the Southern District of Texas granted a temporary injunction, blocking the enactment of both DAPA and the expanded DACA nationwide. Judge Hanen did not rest his ruling on constitutional issues, but instead on a finding that the immigration policy was not a general statement of policy, but rather a substantive rule subject to the requirements of the Administrative Procedure Act, which would have required the administration to hold notice-and-comment rulemaking before enacting the policy.

The government appealed the lower court ruling to the Fifth Circuit Court of Appeals, where, on November 9, 2015, a divided three-judge panel affirmed the injunction and ordered the case back to the district court for trial. The court accepted the lower court's decision that the cost of issuing drivers' licenses to aliens is sufficient to give Texas standing to bring the case and that the administration violated rulemaking requirements of the Administrative Procedure Act. The court also rejected the administration's argument that DAPA was a form of "prosecutorial discretion" necessary for a government with limited resources and that must set priorities for its enforcement of deportation rules. Instead, the Fifth Circuit characterized the rule as providing a positive benefit—that of "lawful presence"—specifically not provided by the Immigration and Nationalization Act. Providing such a benefit, the court found, is much more than nonenforcement and was outside the authority of the executive branch.

The Supreme Court Rules on the President's Immigration Action

On January 19, 2016, the Supreme Court agreed to hear the appeal from the Fifth Circuit opinion. The issues briefed for the Court included whether Texas and the other states had standing to sue the federal government and whether the government should have submitted the deportation deferral programs for a mandatory public notice-and-comment period. The lower courts had answered both these questions affirmatively. The parties also briefed the question of whether, as the Fifth Circuit found, the programs violated the federal immigration law. Finally, the Supreme Court asked the parties to add a constitutional argument to their briefs—specifically, whether the challenged executive actions changed the immigration law in such a way as to violate the constitutional requirement in Article II, Section 3, that the president "take care that the laws be faithfully executed." The lower courts had not addressed the constitutional issue.

Court watchers eagerly waited for what they anticipated would be a major Court ruling on the scope of presidential power. Then, on February 16, 2016, Justice Antonin Scalia died and the Senate refused to act on a new nominee during the last year of the Obama administration, leaving an empty seat on the Supreme Court. When the Court released its decision on *Texas v. United States*, it had deadlocked, 4–4. The legal impact of an evenly split Court is that the ruling of the lower court is simply affirmed, with no Court opinion of any precedential impact. In this case, the Court of Appeals ruling that blocked the implementation of the president's plan is left in effect. Because the lower court cases had not involved the original DACA program, it was not affected by the outcome of the case. But the injunction halting the expanded DACA and DAPA stands.

Reaction to the Court's Ruling

President Obama spoke from the White House shortly after word came from the Court. He expressed frustration, but vowed to continue a policy of placing top priority on deporting violent criminals rather than longtime residents who had never broken the law and had stable family relationships in the United States. "Today's decision," he said, "is frustrating to those who seek to grow our economy and bring a rationality to our immigration system, and to allow people to come out of the shadows and lift this perpetual cloud on them." Thinking of those affected, he said, "I think it is heartbreaking for the millions of immigrants who've made their lives here, who've raised families here, who hoped for the opportunity to work, pay taxes, serve in our military, and more fully contribute to this country we all love in an open way." He also described the Court ruling as a vivid reminder of the consequences of the Senate Republicans' refusal to consider his nominee, Judge Merrick B. Garland, to fill the vacancy on the Supreme Court, describing them as "willfully preventing the Supreme Court from being fully staffed and functioning as our founders intended."

In a statement released after the ruling, Ken Paxton, the Texas attorney general who led the coalition of twenty-six states challenging the president's program, said, "Today's decision keeps in place what we have maintained from the very start: One person, even a president, cannot unilaterally change the law. This is a major setback to President Obama's attempts to expand executive power and a victory for those who believe in the separation of powers and the rule of law." Similarly, House Speaker Paul Ryan, R-Wis., described the ruling as a "win" both for Congress and the constitutional separation of powers.

The ruling, coming in the months before a presidential election, highlighted the importance of the election, not only for the future of the Supreme Court with an open seat to be filled and several aged justices, but also for the ongoing contentious issue of immigration. The Democratic nominee, Hillary Rodham Clinton, supported the president's executive actions, and said that, if elected, she would seek to expand them and propose comprehensive immigration reform within the first 100 days in office. The Republican nominee, and eventual winner of the election, Donald J. Trump, called for building a wall along the Mexican border and deporting all illegal immigrants. He reacted to the Court ruling by saying that it "blocked one of the most unconstitutional actions ever undertaken by a president."

—Melissa Feinberg

Following is the full text of the Supreme Court's decision in United States v. Texas *on June 23, 2016, in which a divided Court affirmed the lower court's decision to block President Barack Obama's immigration program; and President Barack Obama's statement on June 23, 2016, responding to the Supreme Court's decision.*

DOCUMENT *United States v. Texas*

June 23, 2016

No. 15–674

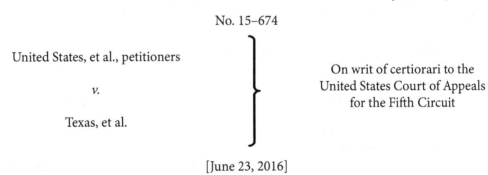

United States, et al., petitioners

v.

Texas, et al.

On writ of certiorari to the
United States Court of Appeals
for the Fifth Circuit

[June 23, 2016]

PER CURIAM.

The judgment is affirmed by an equally divided Court.

SOURCE: U.S. Supreme Court. *United States v. Texas.* 579 U.S.__(2016). http://www.supremecourt.gov/opinions/15pdf/15-674_jhlo.pdf.

President Obama Responds to Supreme Court Ruling

June 23, 2016

Good morning, everybody. I wanted to say a few words on two of the cases the Supreme Court spoke on today.

First, in the affirmative action case, I'm pleased that the Supreme Court upheld the basic notion that diversity is an important value in our society and that this country should provide a high-quality education to all our young people, regardless of their background. We are not a country that guarantees equal outcomes, but we do strive to provide an equal shot to everybody. And that's what was upheld today.

Second, one of the reasons why America is such a diverse and inclusive nation is because we're a nation of immigrants. Our Founders conceived of this country as a refuge for the world. And for more than two centuries, welcoming wave after wave of immigrants has kept us youthful and dynamic and entrepreneurial. It has shaped our character, and it has made us stronger.

But for more than two decades now, our immigration system, everybody acknowledges, has been broken. And the fact that the Supreme Court wasn't able to issue a decision today doesn't just set the system back even further, it takes us further from the country that we aspire to be.

Just to lay out some basic facts that sometimes get lost in what can be an emotional debate. Since I took office, we've deployed more border agents and technology to our southern border than ever before. That has helped cut illegal border crossings to their lowest levels since the 1970s. It should have paved the way for comprehensive immigration reform. And in fact, as many of you know, it almost did. Nearly 70 Democrats and Republicans in the Senate came together to pass a smart, commonsense bill that would have doubled the border patrol and offered undocumented immigrants a pathway to earn citizenship if they paid a fine, paid their taxes, and played by the rules.

Unfortunately, Republicans in the House of Representatives refused to allow a simple yes-or-no vote on that bill. So I was left with little choice but to take steps within my existing authority to make our immigration system smarter, fairer, and more just.

Four years ago, we announced that those who are our lowest priorities for enforcement—diligent, patriotic young DREAMers who grew up pledging allegiance to our flag—should be able to apply to work here and study here and pay their taxes here. More than 730,000 lives have been changed as a result. These are students, they're teachers, they're doctors, they're lawyers. They're Americans in every way but on paper. And fortunately, today's decision does not affect this policy. It does not affect the existing DREAMers.

Two years ago, we announced a similar, expanded approach for others who are also low priorities for enforcement. We said that if you've been in America for more than 5 years, with children who are American citizens or legal residents, then you, too, can come forward, get right with the law, and work in this country temporarily, without fear of deportation. Both were the kinds of actions taken by Republican and Democratic Presidents over the past half-century. Neither granted anybody a free pass. All they did was focus our enforcement resources—which are necessarily limited—on the highest priorities: convicted criminals, recent border crossers, and threats to our national security.

Now, as disappointing as it was to be challenged for taking the kind of actions that other administrations have taken, the country was looking to the Supreme Court to resolve the important legal questions raised in this case. Today the Supreme Court was unable to reach a decision. This is part of the consequence of the Republican failure so far to give a fair hearing to Mr. Merrick Garland, my nominee to the Supreme Court. It means that the expanded set of commonsense deferred action policies—the ones that I announced 2 years ago—can't go forward at this stage, until there is a ninth justice on the Court to break the tie.

Now, I know a lot of people are going to be disappointed today, but it is important to understand what today means. The deferred action policy that has been in place for the last 4 years is not affected by this ruling. Enforcement priorities developed by my administration are not affected by this ruling. This means that the people who might have benefited from the expanded deferred action policies—long-term residents raising children who are Americans or legal residents—they will remain low priorities for enforcement. As long as you have not committed a crime, our limited immigration enforcement resources are not focused on you.

But today's decision is frustrating to those who seek to grow our economy and bring a rationality to our immigration system and to allow people to come out of the shadows and lift this perpetual cloud on them. I think it is heartbreaking for the millions of immigrants who've made their lives here, who've raised families here, who hoped for the opportunity to work, pay taxes, serve in our military, and more fully contribute to this country we all love in an open way.

So where do we go from here? Most Americans—including business leaders, faith leaders, and law enforcement, Democrats and Republicans and Independents—still agree that the single best way to solve this problem is by working together to pass commonsense, bipartisan immigration reform.

That is obviously not going to happen during the remainder of this Congress. We don't have a Congress that agrees with us on this. Nor do we have a Congress that's willing to do even its most basic of jobs under the Constitution, which is to consider nominations. Republicans in Congress currently are willfully preventing the Supreme Court from being fully staffed and functioning as our Founders intended. And today's situation underscores the degree to which the Court is not able to function the way it's supposed to.

The Court's inability to reach a decision in this case is a very clear reminder of why it's so important for the Supreme Court to have a full Bench. For more than 40 years, there's been an average of just over 2 months between a nomination and a hearing. I nominated Judge Merrick Garland to the Supreme Court more than 3 months ago. But most Republicans so far have refused [t]o—to even meet with him. They are allowing partisan politics to jeopardize something as fundamental as the impartiality and integrity of our justice system. And America should not let it stand.

This is an election year. And during election years, politicians tend to use the immigration issue to scare people with words like "amnesty" in hopes that it will whip up votes. Keep in mind that millions of us, myself included, go back generations in this country, with ancestors who put in the painstaking effort to become citizens. And we don't like the notion that anyone might get a free pass to American citizenship. But here's the thing. Millions of people who have come forward and worked to get right with the law under this policy, they've been living here for years too, in some cases, even decades. So leaving the broken system the way it is, that's not a solution. In fact, that's the real amnesty. Pretending we can deport 11 million people or build a wall without spending tens of billions of dollars of taxpayer money is abetting what is really just factually incorrect. It's not going to work. And it's not good for this country. It's a fantasy that offers nothing to help the middle class, and it demeans our tradition of being both a nation of laws and a nation of immigrants.

In the end, it is my firm belief that immigration is not something to fear. We don't have to wall ourselves off from those who may not look like us right now or pray like we do or have a different last name. Because being an American is about something more than that. What makes us America is our shared commitment to an ideal that all of us are created equal, all of us have a chance to make of our lives what we will. And every study shows that whether it was the Irish or the Poles or the Germans or the Italians or the Chinese or the Japanese or the Mexicans or the Kenyans—[laughter]—whoever showed up, over time, by a second generation, third generation, those kids are Americans. They do look like us, because we don't look one way. We don't all have the same last names, but we all share a creed, and we all share a commitment to the values that founded this Nation. That's who we are. And that is what I believe most Americans recognize.

So here's the bottom line. We've got a very real choice that America faces right now. We will continue to implement the existing programs that are already in place. We're not going to be able to move forward with the expanded programs that we wanted to move forward on, because the Supreme Court was not able to issue a ruling at this stage. And now we've got a choice about who we're going to be as a country, what we want to teach our kids, and how we want to be represented in Congress and in the White House.

We're going to have to make a decision about whether we are a people who tolerate the hypocrisy of a system where the workers who pick our fruit or make our beds never have the chance to get right with the law or whether we're going to give them a chance, just like our forebears had a chance, to take responsibility and give their kids a better future.

We're going to have to decide whether we're a people who accept the cruelty of ripping children from their parents' arms or whether we actually value families and keep them together for the sake of all of our communities.

We're going to have to decide whether we're a people who continue to educate the world's brightest students in our high schools and universities, only to then send them away to compete against us, or whether we encourage them to stay and create new jobs and new businesses right here in the United States.

These are all the questions that voters now are going to have to ask themselves and are going to have to answer in November. These are the issues that are going to be debated by candidates across the country, both congressional candidates as well as the Presidential candidates. And in November, Americans are going to have to make a decision about what we care about and who we are.

I promise you this though: Sooner or later, immigration reform will get done. Congress is not going to be able to ignore America forever. It's just—it's not a matter of if, it's a matter of when. And I can say that with confidence because we've seen our history. We get these spasms of politics around immigration and fear-mongering, and then our traditions and our history and our better impulses kick in. That's how we all ended up here. Because I guarantee you, at some point, every one of us has somebody in our background who people didn't want coming here, and yet here we are.

And that's what's going to happen this time. Now, the question is, do we do it in a smart, rational, sensible way, or we just keep on kicking the can down the road? I believe that this country deserves an immigration policy that reflects the goodness of the American people. And I think we're going to get that. Hopefully, we're going to get that in November.

All right. I'll take two questions.

Q. Mr. President—

The President. Two questions. Go ahead.

Immigration Policy

Q. Thank you. Realistically, what do you see is the risk of deportation for these more than 4 million people? I mean, you say we can't deport 11 million. This is 4 million, and there's a chunk of time here before something else——

The President. Well, let me just be very clear. What was unaffected by today's ruling—or lack of a ruling—is the enforcement priorities that we've put in place. And our enforcement priorities that have been laid out by Secretary Jeh Johnson at the Department of Homeland Security are pretty clear: We prioritize criminals, we prioritize gangbangers, we prioritize folks who have just come in. What we don't do is to prioritize people who have been here a long time, who are otherwise law abiding, who have roots and connections in their communities. And so those enforcement priorities will continue.

The work that we've done with the DREAM Act kids, those policies remain in place. So what this has prevented us from doing is expanding the scope of what we've done with the DREAM Act kids. Keep in mind though that even that was just a temporary measure. All it was doing was basically saying to these kids, you can have confidence that you are not going to be deported, but it does not resolve your ultimate status. That is going to require congressional action.

So although I'm disappointed by the lack of a decision today by the Supreme Court, a deadlock, this does not substantially change the status quo, and it doesn't negate what has always been the case, which is if we're really going to solve this problem effectively, we've got to have Congress pass a law.

I have pushed to the limits of my executive authority. We now have to have Congress act. And hopefully, we're going to have a vigorous debate during this election—this is how democracy is supposed to work—and there will be a determination as to which direction we go in.

As I said, over the long term, I'm very confident about the direction this country will go in, because we've seen this in the past. But—if we hadn't seen it in the past, America would look very different than it looks today. But whether we're going to get this done now, soon, so that this does not continue to be this divisive force in our politics and we can get down to the business of all pulling together to create jobs and educate our kids and protect ourselves from external threats and do the things that we need to do to ensure a better future for the next generation, that's going to be determined in part by how voters turn out and who they vote for in November.

All right. One more question. Go ahead, Mike [Mike Dorning, *Bloomberg News*].

**Immigration Policy/The President's
Executive Authority/Judicial Confirmation Process**

Q. Two practical, going-forward questions. Number one, is this going to—are you going to be able to do anything more at all for immigrants going forward in terms of executive action before the election of the next President? And number two, do you in any way take this as some Republicans have presented this, as a slap at your use of executive authority, this tie vote? And will this in any way circumscribe how aggressively or forcefully you use executive authority in the remainder of your time in office?

The President. Okay. I—on the specifics of immigration, I don't anticipate that there are additional executive actions that we can take. We can implement what we've already put in place that is not affected by this decision. But we have to follow now what has been ruled on in the Fifth Circuit because the Supreme Court could not resolve the issue.

And we're going to have to abide by that ruling until an election and a confirmation of a ninth justice of the Supreme Court so that they can break this tie. Because we've always said that we are going to do what we can lawfully through executive action, but we can't go beyond that. And we've butted up about as far as we can on this particular topic.

It does not have any impact on, from our perspective, on the host of other issues that we're working on, because each one of these issues has a different analysis and is based on different statutes or different interpretations of our authority.

So, for example, on climate change, that's based on the Clean Air Act and the EPA and previous Supreme Court rulings, as opposed to a theory of prosecutorial discretion that, in the past, has—every other President has exercised. And the Supreme Court wasn't definitive one way or the other on this. I mean, the problem is, they don't have a ninth justice. So that will continue to be a problem.

With respect to the Republicans, I think what it tells you is, is that if you keep on blocking judges from getting on the bench, then courts can't issue decisions. And what that means is, then, you're going to have the status quo frozen, and we're not going to be able to make progress on some very important issues.

Now, that may have been their strategy from the start. But it's not a sustainable strategy. And it's certainly a strategy that will be broken by this election, unless their basic theory is, is that we will never confirm judges again. Hopefully, that's not their theory, because that's not how our democracy is designed.

The President's Executive Authority

Q. But you reject their portrayal of this as a chastisement of you for your use of executive authority?

The President. It was a one-word opinion that said, we can't come up with a decision. I think that would be a little bit of a stretch, yes. Maybe the next time they can—if we have a full Court issuing a full opinion on anything, then we take it seriously. This we have to abide by, but it wasn't any kind of value statement or a decision on the merits on these issues.

All right? Thank you, guys.

SOURCE: Executive Office of the President. "Remarks on the Supreme Court's Decisions Regarding Affirmative Action and Immigration and an Exchange With Reporters." June 23, 2016. *Compilation of Presidential Documents* 2016, no. 00419 (June 23, 2016). http://www.gpo.gov/fdsys/pkg/DCPD-201600419/pdf/DCPD-201600419.pdf.

OTHER HISTORIC DOCUMENTS OF INTEREST

Britons Vote to Exit the
European Union

JUNE 24 AND 28, AND JULY 13, 2016

In a move that rocked the foundations of the European Union (EU) and sent shockwaves reverberating around the world, the British people on June 23, 2016, decided that the United Kingdom should leave the EU. The referendum result—52 percent to 48 percent—was a surprise because polls in the days leading up to the vote indicated that the side favoring remaining in the union would secure a narrow win against the side seeking to leave.

UK Prime Minister David Cameron, who had called the referendum and campaigned to remain, immediately resigned following the vote. Within a month, Cameron was replaced, both as prime minister and Conservative Party leader, by Theresa May. The win for the "Brexit," as it was called—an amalgam of "Britain" and "exit"—was a stunning victory for the populist UK Independence Party, founded in the 1990s, which harbors this singular goal. The outcome also widened existing divisions within the UK because majorities of Scottish and Northern Irish voters voted to remain, while majorities in England and Wales voted to leave.

BRITAIN AND THE EU

When the EU's forerunner, the European Economic Community (EEC), was established in 1957 by the Treaty of Rome, the UK was not one of the six founding member countries, but shortly afterward it applied to join. After a decade where its membership was vetoed by France, eventually in 1973 the UK acceded to the free trade bloc. Britain did not have a referendum on whether to join, although in 1975 it had one to remain in it, which passed with 67 percent voting in favor.

Over the course of four decades of membership, the UK grew to have an increasingly uneasy relationship with the bloc. This was partly because the EEC, or the EU as it was renamed in 1992 under the Maastricht Treaty, continually accrued more lawmaking powers in diverse fields, including on environmental protection and workers' rights. When in the 1990s the EU adopted its own currency, the euro, the UK opted to maintain its use of the pound. Within Britain, the political party most hostile to the EU was the Conservative Party, where a strong Eurosceptic wing emerged opposed to further integration, albeit mostly without success because the EU proceeded to conclude several pro-integration treaties.

The EU also continued to grow in membership, enlarging from the original six countries to reach twenty-eight after Croatia joined in 2013. The addition of ten countries from Central and Eastern Europe in the early 2000s led to an influx of more than a million immigrants from these states to the UK, causing significant societal tensions. By 2016, net inward migration to the UK—from EU and non-EU countries—stood at about 330,000 per year.

Largely to appease his party's Eurosceptic wing, in 2013 Cameron pledged that, if reelected, he would hold a referendum where the British people would be given a choice between remaining a member of the EU or leaving it. In the 2015 UK parliamentary elections, Cameron led the Conservatives to victory, winning a slim overall majority. He quickly moved to negotiate with his EU partners some revisions to the founding treaties, the essence of which was to grant the UK an opt-out from further EU integration. Cameron pushed for these concessions in the belief that they would be enough to persuade the British people to vote to stay inside the EU. With the treaty adjustments finalized in February 2016, he set June 23 as the date for a referendum on EU membership.

BRITONS HEAD TO THE POLLS

The referendum campaign was extremely contentious and polarizing. Immigration was a flashpoint, with the side opting to leave, known as Vote Leave, alleging that EU membership had stretched the UK's public services to a breaking point. The campaign also claimed that the £350 million the UK contributed to the EU budget each week would be redirected to the National Health Service if the UK left the union. The side pushing to remain, known as Stronger In, stressed favorable economic arguments and leaned heavily on the business community, most of whom advocated staying in the EU. Illustrating how heated the debate became, a Stronger In campaigner, Labour Party parliamentarian Jo Cox, was shot and stabbed to death in the street on June 16 by a man who shouted "Britain first!" as he killed her.

As results trickled in on the evening of June 23, the Vote Leave side inched ahead, buoyed by a strong performance in most of England apart from London. The final result was 51.9 percent for leaving and 48.1 percent for remaining, with a turnout of 71.8 percent. In contrast to much of the rest of England, the London metropolitan area voted heavily—60–40 percent—to remain, and the city of London, the small inner-city area that forms the heart of the UK financial services industry, voted 75–25 percent to remain.

Speaking from outside 10 Downing Street the morning after the vote, Prime Minister Cameron announced his resignation. He justified having called the referendum in the first place, saying, "We not only have a parliamentary democracy, but on questions about the arrangements for how we are governed, there are times when it is right to ask the people themselves, and that is what we have done." He added, "The British people have voted to leave the European Union and their will must be respected."

Looking to the future of Brexit negotiations with the EU, he stressed the "need to involve the full engagement of the Scottish, Welsh, and Northern Ireland governments." Cameron said, "I was clear about my belief that Britain is stronger, safer, and better off inside the EU . . . but the British people have made a very clear decision to take a different path, and as such I think the country requires fresh leadership to take it in this direction." It would be his successor, not Cameron himself, who would launch the exit negotiations, he said. That would require invoking Article 50 of the EU Treaty, the clause that outlines a procedure and two-year timeline for EU member countries to leave the bloc if they wish.

Financial markets reacted negatively to these dramatic developments. Within hours, the British pound had lost 10 percent of its value against the dollar, and one main credit rating agency downgraded the UK's credit rating. In a bid to stave off economic recession, the Bank of England in August lowered interest rates from 0.5 percent to 0.25 percent.

EUROPEAN PARLIAMENT DEBATE BECOMES HEATED

Five days after the referendum, the European Parliament, the EU's lawmaking arm, held an emotionally charged debate on the referendum result. EU Council representative Jeanine Hennis-Plasschaert said that June 23 would go down in history as a "day that shook the UK and the EU." She said that since its foundation in 1957, the EU had reunited East and West Europe and brought peace, diversity, and strength. "Why [did] the people [give] their live[s] in Ukraine, carrying a blue banner with golden stars, why do people from Africa and Asia leave their families in rickety boats to reach our shores? It is because of the fundamental values that bind us," she said. While mounting a spirited defense of the EU, she acknowledged the rise of Euroscepticism, noting "the sentiments of a large part of the British voters are shared in many other EU member states."

Speaking on behalf of the EU Commission (the EU's executive arm) was its president, Jean-Claude Juncker. Responding to jeers from European Parliament members from the UK Independence Party, Juncker turned to them and said, "To some extent I'm really surprised you are here. You are fighting for the exit. The British people voted in favor of the exit. Why are you here?" Juncker, who will be a lead negotiator for the EU in the Brexit talks, insisted that no negotiations could take place until the UK invokes Article 50: "No notification, no negotiation."

Nigel Farage, leader of the UK Independence Party, also spoke. "When I came here 17 years ago and said that I wanted to lead a campaign to get Britain to leave the European Union, you all laughed at me. Well I have to say, you're not laughing now, are you?" he said. Farage called the outcome "a seismic result not just for British politics, for European politics, but perhaps even for global politics too," adding, "we want our country back . . . we want to be an independent, self-governing normal nation." He gave a diagnosis of what he believed fueled Eurosceptic sentiment. "The biggest problem you've got and the main reason the UK voted the way that it did is because you have, by stealth, by deception, without ever telling the truth to the rest of the peoples of Europe, imposed upon them a political union," he said.

Marine Le Pen, leader of the National Front party from France who, along with Farage, is a leading Eurosceptic voice, called the vote "by far the most important historic event known by our continent since the fall of the Berlin Wall." Le Pen hailed it as a "victory for democracy" because it proved that the EU was not irreversible. On the other side, a leading advocate for further EU integration, Belgium's Guy Verhofstadt, denounced the "lies" that he said the campaign to leave had used. Verhofstadt cited as examples the claim that Turkey was on the verge of joining the EU, and that £350 million extra would be spent on the National Health Service post-Brexit, a claim that the day after the referendum Farage admitted was a mistake. Verhofstadt called for "immediate invocation" of Article 50, saying it was necessary to "end what I call the toxic climate that has been created since Thursday of last week."

NEW PRIME MINISTER VOWS TO PROCEED WITH BREXIT

It looked as though no one was prepared either for the referendum outcome or Cameron's sudden resignation. There followed a scramble in the Conservative Party to elect a new leader and prime minister. The initial frontrunner was Boris Johnson, the colorful former mayor of London who played a decisive role in the Vote Leave campaign. But Johnson's leadership bid was thwarted by his erstwhile political campaign ally, Michael Gove, who announced his own candidacy. That move effectively split their support in two, and both failed to advance beyond the preliminary stages.

The race was whittled down to two candidates, Theresa May and Andrea Leadsom. May had supported the Stronger In side, but played no active role in the campaign, whereas Leadsom was a prominent figure on the Vote to Leave side. May was a veteran in British politics, with nearly two decades of experience as a parliamentarian and serving as home secretary for the previous six years. By comparison, Leadsom was a relative rookie and was also widely seen as a less steady figure. For example, at one point, Leadsom said that it would be a disaster for the economy if the UK were to leave the EU, only later to switch allegiances entirely and campaign for Vote Leave. May's low profile in the campaign served her well; post-referendum, she was perceived as someone capable of reunifying and healing a still-reeling party.

In early July, Leadsom made a gaffe by appearing to suggest in a newspaper interview that her experience as a mother put her in a better position to lead than someone without children. (May is married but does not have children.) Shortly afterward, Leadsom quit the leadership race and announced her support for May. On July 13, having been invited by Queen Elizabeth to form a government, May become the UK's seventy-sixth prime minister.

May made clear there would be no turning back from Brexit. "As we leave the European Union, we will forge a bold new positive role for ourselves in the world," she said in her first statement as prime minister. She indicated a desire to reunify the country in the wake of a campaign that had exposed and exacerbated regional divisions. Noting the party's official name is the Conservative and Unionist Party, she said, "That word 'unionist' is very important to me."

Being only the second woman to occupy the post, comparisons were drawn with the UK's first female prime minister, Margaret Thatcher, who held office from 1979 to 1990. Both came from fairly modest families, and grew up in mid-sized towns in England, and both from a young age were Conservative Party activists who rose through the ranks. However, May had some socially liberal edges, for instance backing Cameron's successful effort to legalize same-sex marriage. While Thatcher was an ardent and outspoken opponent of EU integration, May developed a more nuanced view of the EU.

Comparisons were also drawn between May and another prominent female leader of a major European country, German chancellor Angela Merkel. Both women were the daughters of Protestant clergymen: May's father an Anglican vicar, Merkel's a Lutheran pastor. Both earned reputations among their peers as serious-minded, hardworking pragmatists and "safe pairs of hands" who could be trusted with the reins of power.

In appointing her cabinet, May chose a mix of Vote Leave and Stronger In supporters. However, she gave the jobs most closely connected to the upcoming Brexit negotiation to prominent Vote Leave campaigners. Thus, Johnson was appointed as Foreign Secretary, David Davis was given the new position of Brexit Secretary, and Liam Fox was made International Trade Secretary, and the press quickly labeled this trio "The Three Brexiteers." May announced that she would invoke Article 50 by the end of March 2017, putting the UK on course to leave the EU by March 2019. May ruled out holding an early election, signifying that she would be the one steering the country toward that course, the next election not being due to take place until 2020.

UK POLITICAL SHAKEUP

The Brexit referendum outcome caused a shakeup across the UK political spectrum. Jeremy Corbyn, leader of Labour, the main opposition party, faced a rebellion from his fellow parliamentarians. A majority called on him to resign, accusing him of giving lackluster support for the Stronger In side, which they said was a contributing factor to the outcome. Corbyn survived their challenge because the wider party membership had the final say, and 61.8 percent of them supported him in a vote in September.

First minister of the devolved Scottish government, Nicola Sturgeon, announced tentative plans to hold a new referendum on Scottish independence if Scotland is forced to leave the EU. Sturgeon's Scottish National Party was one of the main drivers behind a Scottish independence referendum in 2014, which failed when 55 percent of voters opted to remain in the UK. In the Brexit vote, 62 percent of Scots voted to remain in the EU.

In Northern Ireland, the largest party representing Irish Catholics, Sinn Féin, demanded a "border poll" where Northern Irish voters would be offered the choice of reunifying with the Republic of Ireland in the south. The Republic intends to remain part of the EU. Such a referendum looks unlikely to occur given opposition from Northern Ireland's Protestant Unionist parties, and from both the Irish and UK governments. Meanwhile, political leaders in Wales, while generally supporting the UK's exit, began demanding that Wales have a say in the Brexit negotiations.

In November, the UK's High Court handed down a ruling that could constrain the British government somewhat in the Brexit negotiations. The Court ruled that the British Parliament was required to give consent for Article 50 to be invoked, thus allowing the exit talks to begin. The UK government had argued in the case that it had the authority to invoke Article 50 unilaterally.

The UK government is concerned that the UK Parliament, most of whose members were in favor of remaining in the EU during the campaign, will impose detailed terms and conditions as the price for giving their approval to launch the talks. The Court case was brought by Gina Miller, a Guyana-born investment manager based in London. While she supported the Stronger In side in the referendum, Miller told the Court that she did not seek to overturn the result, rather to affirm the sovereignty of the British Parliament. The government appealed to the High Court, which is expected to make a final ruling in early 2017.

FUTURE OF UK–EU RELATIONS UNCERTAIN

With a UK exit from the EU looking likely, speculation has begun about what kind of future relationship the country will have with the EU post-Brexit. The UK would be the first entire country to leave the bloc. The nearest precedent is Greenland, which forms part of Denmark, an EU member state, but which left the EU in 1985 following a referendum.

Those who want the UK to stay as close as possible to the EU point to the example of Norway, which is fully integrated into the EU single market but which is not an EU member. But detractors of this model have noted that Norway has to implement most EU regulations despite having no say in writing them—and is required to allow citizens of EU countries to immigrate to Norway if they wish. Another possible model is Switzerland, which is not an EU member or part of the EU single market but has gained good access to it through various bilateral agreements. A looser option again would be for the UK to sign a free trade agreement with the EU as other major trade partners as Canada and South Korea have done.

However, before any of these options can be pursued, the terms of the Brexit will need to be negotiated. Article 50 gives a bit of a negotiating advantage to the remaining EU member states because, once triggered, the UK by default will leave after two years, even if no post-exit agreement is in place by then. The twenty-seven remaining member states can extend that two-year deadline, but must agree unanimously to do so.

The danger posed for the UK is the possibility that the Brexit talks could stall and the clock runs out with no deal, causing Britain to lose its privileged access to the EU single market. This so-called "hard Brexit" scenario is feared especially by Britain's business community. A hard Brexit is also a difficult prospect for more than a million UK citizens who live in other EU countries—mostly in France, Ireland, and Spain—and 1.6 million citizens of other EU countries who live in the UK. Without a Brexit deal in place, a shadow will be cast over their legal status in their adoptive countries. Meanwhile, UK nationalists have the opposite fear, specifically that a "soft Brexit" agreement will be cobbled together that still binds the UK to follow some EU rules. At this point, either scenario looks equally plausible.

—Brian Beary

Following is the text of a speech delivered by British Prime Minister David Cameron on June 24, 2016, remarking on the outcome of the EU referendum; a speech by European parliament member Nigel Farage of Great Britain on June 28, 2016, on the EU referendum; and a July 13, 2016, statement by incoming British prime minister Theresa May, marking her assumption of duties.

Prime Minister Cameron on the EU Referendum

DOCUMENT

June 24, 2016

The country has just taken part in a giant democratic exercise—perhaps the biggest in our history. Over 33 million people—from England, Scotland, Wales, Northern Ireland and Gibraltar—have all had their say.

We should be proud of the fact that in these islands we trust the people with these big decisions.

We not only have a parliamentary democracy, but on questions about the arrangements for how we are governed, there are times when it is right to ask the people themselves, and that is what we have done.

The British people have voted to leave the European Union and their will must be respected.

I want to thank everyone who took part in the campaign on my side of the argument, including all those who put aside party differences to speak in what they believed was the national interest.

And let me congratulate all those who took part in the Leave campaign—for the spirited and passionate case that they made.

The will of the British people is an instruction that must be delivered. It was not a decision that was taken lightly, not least because so many things were said by so many different organisations about the significance of this decision.

So there can be no doubt about the result.

Across the world people have been watching the choice that Britain has made. I would reassure those markets and investors that Britain's economy is fundamentally strong.

And I would also reassure Brits living in European countries, and European citizens living here, that there will be no immediate changes in your circumstances. There will be no initial change in the way our people can travel, in the way our goods can move or the way our services can be sold.

We must now prepare for a negotiation with the European Union. This will need to involve the full engagement of the Scottish, Welsh and Northern Ireland governments to ensure that the interests of all parts of our United Kingdom are protected and advanced.

But above all this will require strong, determined and committed leadership.

I am very proud and very honoured to have been Prime Minister of this country for 6 years.

I believe we have made great steps, with more people in work than ever before in our history, with reforms to welfare and education, increasing people's life chances, building a bigger and stronger society, keeping our promises to the poorest people in the world, and enabling those who love each other to get married whatever their sexuality.

But above all restoring Britain's economic strength, and I am grateful to everyone who has helped to make that happen.

I have also always believed that we have to confront big decisions—not duck them.

That's why we delivered the first coalition government in 70 years to bring our economy back from the brink. It's why we delivered a fair, legal and decisive referendum in Scotland. And why I made the pledge to renegotiate Britain's position in the European Union and hold a referendum on our membership, and have carried those things out.

I fought this campaign in the only way I know how—which is to say directly and passionately what I think and feel—head, heart and soul.

I held nothing back.

I was absolutely clear about my belief that Britain is stronger, safer and better off inside the European Union, and I made clear the referendum was about this and this alone—not the future of any single politician, including myself.

But the British people have made a very clear decision to take a different path, and as such I think the country requires fresh leadership to take it in this direction.

I will do everything I can as Prime Minister to steady the ship over the coming weeks and months, but I do not think it would be right for me to try to be the captain that steers our country to its next destination.

This is not a decision I have taken lightly, but I do believe it is in the national interest to have a period of stability and then the new leadership required.

There is no need for a precise timetable today, but in my view we should aim to have a new Prime Minister in place by the start of the Conservative party conference in October.

Delivering stability will be important and I will continue in post as Prime Minister with my Cabinet for the next 3 months. The Cabinet will meet on Monday.

The Governor of the Bank of England is making a statement about the steps that the Bank and the Treasury are taking to reassure financial markets. We will also continue taking forward the important legislation that we set before Parliament in the Queen's Speech. And I have spoken to Her Majesty the Queen this morning to advise her of the steps that I am taking.

A negotiation with the European Union will need to begin under a new Prime Minister, and I think it is right that this new Prime Minister takes the decision about when to trigger Article 50 and start the formal and legal process of leaving the EU.

I will attend the European Council next week to explain the decision the British people have taken and my own decision.

The British people have made a choice. That not only needs to be respected—but those on the losing side of the argument, myself included, should help to make it work.

Britain is a special country.

We have so many great advantages.

A parliamentary democracy where we resolve great issues about our future through peaceful debate.

A great trading nation, with our science and arts, our engineering and our creativity respected the world over.

And while we are not perfect, I do believe we can be a model of a multi-racial, multi-faith democracy, where people can come and make a contribution and rise to the very highest that their talent allows.

Although leaving Europe was not the path I recommended, I am the first to praise our incredible strengths. I have said before that Britain can survive outside the European Union, and indeed that we could find a way.

Now the decision has been made to leave, we need to find the best way, and I will do everything I can to help.

I love this country—and I feel honoured to have served it.

And I will do everything I can in future to help this great country succeed.

SOURCE: United Kingdom Prime Minister's Office. "EU referendum outcome: PM statement, 24 June 2016." June 24, 2016. http://www.gov.uk/government/speeches/eu-referendum-outcome-pm-statement-24-june-2016.

Nigel Farage Speaks to the EU Parliament on the Brexit Vote

June 28, 2016

[All statements from the meeting not delivered by Farage have been omitted.]

Mr President, isn't it funny? When I came here 17 years ago and said that I wanted to lead a campaign to get Britain to leave the European Union, you all laughed at me. Well I have to say, you're not laughing now, are you? And the reason you are so upset, the reason you are so angry, has been perfectly clear from all the angry exchanges this morning: you, as a political project, are in denial. You are in denial that your currency is failing. You are in denial. . . .

[Murmurs of protest]

Well, just look at the Mediterranean. No, no, as a policy to impose poverty on Greece and the rest of the Mediterranean you have done very well, and you are in denial over Mrs. Merkel's call last year for as many people as possible to cross the Mediterranean into the European Union, which has led to massive divisions between countries and within countries. But the biggest problem you have got, and the main reason the United Kingdom voted the way that it did, is that you have, by stealth, by deception, without ever telling the truth to the British or the rest of the peoples of Europe, imposed upon them a political union. You have imposed upon them a political union, and when the people in 2005 in the Netherlands and France voted against that political union, when they rejected the Constitution, you simply ignored them and brought the Lisbon Treaty in through the back door.

[Applause from certain quarters]

What happened last Thursday was a remarkable result. It was indeed a seismic result, not just for British politics, for European politics, but perhaps even for global politics, too, because what the little people did, what the ordinary people did, the people who have been oppressed over the last few years and seen their living standards go down, they rejected the multinationals. They rejected the merchant banks, they rejected big politics, and they said, actually, we want our country back. We want our fishing waters back, we want our borders back, we want to be an independent, self-governing normal nation, and that is what we have done and that is what must happen. And in doing so, we now offer a beacon of hope to democrats across the rest of the European continent. I will make one prediction this morning: the United Kingdom will not be the last Member State to leave the European Union.

So the question is: what we do next? Now it is up to the British Government to invoke Article 50 and I have to say that I do not think we should spend too long in doing it. I totally agree, Mr Juncker, that the British people have voted. We need to make sure that it happens. But what I would like to see is a grown-up and sensible attitude to how we negotiate a different relationship.

[Cries of disapproval]

Now I know that virtually none of you have ever done a proper job in your lives. . . .

[Protests and catcalls]

. . . or worked in business, or worked in trade, or indeed ever created a job. But listen. Just listen. . . .

[The interjection of the presiding member has been omitted.]

You are quite right, Mr Schulz, UKIP used to protest against the establishment, and now the establishment protests against UKIP, so something has happened here. Let us listen to some simple pragmatic economics. We, between us, between your countries and my country, do an enormous amount of business in goods and services. That trade is mutually beneficial to both of us. That trade matters. If you were to decide to cut off your noses to spite your faces and to reject any idea of a sensible trade deal, the consequences would be far worse for you than it would be for us.

[Murmurs of disapproval]

Even no deal is better for the United Kingdom than the current rotten deal that we have got. But if we were to move to a position where tariffs were reintroduced on products like motor cars, then hundreds of thousands of German workers would risk losing their jobs. So why don't we just be pragmatic, sensible, grown-up, realistic and let's cut between us a sensible tariff-free deal, and thereafter recognise that the United Kingdom will be your friend, that we will trade with you, we will cooperate with you, we will be your best friends in the world, but do it sensibly and allow us to go off and pursue our global ambitions and future.

[Applause and loud catcalls]

SOURCE: European Parliament. "Outcome of the referendum in the United Kingdom (debate)." June 28, 2016. http://www.europarl.europa.eu/sides/getDoc.do?pubRef=-%2f%2fEP%2f%2fTEXT%2bCRE%2b2 0160628%2bITEM-004%2bDOC%2bXML%2bV0%2f%2fEN&language=EN.

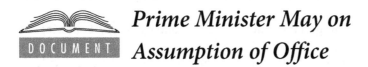

Prime Minister May on Assumption of Office

July 13, 2016

I have just been to Buckingham Palace, where Her Majesty The Queen has asked me to form a new government, and I accepted.

In David Cameron, I follow in the footsteps of a great, modern Prime Minister. Under David's leadership, the government stabilised the economy, reduced the budget deficit, and helped more people into work than ever before.

But David's true legacy is not about the economy but about social justice. From the introduction of same-sex marriage, to taking people on low wages out of income tax altogether; David Cameron has led a one-nation government, and it is in that spirit that I also plan to lead.

Because not everybody knows this, but the full title of my party is the Conservative and Unionist Party, and that word 'unionist' is very important to me.

It means we believe in the Union: the precious, precious bond between England, Scotland, Wales and Northern Ireland. But it means something else that is just as important; it means we believe in a union not just between the nations of the United Kingdom but between all of our citizens, every one of us, whoever we are and wherever we're from.

That means fighting against the burning injustice that, if you're born poor, you will die on average 9 years earlier than others.

If you're black, you're treated more harshly by the criminal justice system than if you're white.

If you're a white, working-class boy, you're less likely than anybody else in Britain to go to university.

If you're at a state school, you're less likely to reach the top professions than if you're educated privately.

If you're a woman, you will earn less than a man. If you suffer from mental health problems, there's not enough help to hand.

If you're young, you'll find it harder than ever before to own your own home.

But the mission to make Britain a country that works for everyone means more than fighting these injustices. If you're from an ordinary working class family, life is much harder than many people in Westminster realise. You have a job but you don't always have job security. You have your own home, but you worry about paying a mortgage. You can just about manage but you worry about the cost of living and getting your kids into a good school.

If you're one of those families, if you're just managing, I want to address you directly.

I know you're working around the clock, I know you're doing your best, and I know that sometimes life can be a struggle. The government I lead will be driven not by the interests of the privileged few, but by yours.

We will do everything we can to give you more control over your lives. When we take the big calls, we'll think not of the powerful, but you. When we pass new laws, we'll listen not to the mighty but to you. When it comes to taxes, we'll prioritise not the wealthy, but you. When it comes to opportunity, we won't entrench the advantages of the fortunate few. We will do everything we can to help anybody, whatever your background, to go as far as your talents will take you.

We are living through an important moment in our country's history. Following the referendum, we face a time of great national change.

And I know because we're Great Britain, that we will rise to the challenge. As we leave the European Union, we will forge a bold new positive role for ourselves in the world, and we will make Britain a country that works not for a privileged few, but for every one of us.

That will be the mission of the government I lead, and together we will build a better Britain.

SOURCE: United Kingdom Prime Minister's Office. "Theresa May delivered her first statement as Prime Minister in Downing Street." July 13, 2016. www.gov.uk/government/speeches/statement-from-the-new-prime-minister-theresa-may.

OTHER HISTORIC DOCUMENTS OF INTEREST

FROM PREVIOUS *HISTORIC DOCUMENTS*

- Scotland Votes Against Independence, *2014*, p. 458

Supreme Court Rejects Texas Abortion Law

JUNE 27, 2016

On June 27, 2016, in a decisive 5–3 opinion, the United States Supreme Court in *Whole Woman's Health v. Hellerstedt* overturned a Texas law that contained restrictions on abortion providers so strict that their implementation would lead to the closure of all but seven facilities in the state. While the state of Texas had argued that the law was necessary to protect women's health and safety, the petitioners had countered that the law merely increased the burdens on women seeking abortions but did not provide any health benefits. The Court, in an opinion written by Justice Stephen Breyer, agreed with those challenging the law, finding that it "provides few, if any health benefits for women, poses a substantial obstacle to women seeking abortions and constitutes an 'undue burden' on their constitutional right to do so." This was the first time the high court used the "undue burden" standard to strike down an abortion law since the language appeared in a plurality opinion in a 1992 case. Giving new teeth to this language could likely have immediate and broad implications nationwide because more than two dozen states have in recent years passed restrictions on abortion providers similar to the Texas law at issue in this case.

LEGAL RESTRICTIONS ON PROVIDERS OF ABORTIONS

The modern Supreme Court history of abortion begins in 1973 with *Roe v. Wade*, the landmark case that first held that a constitutionally protected privacy right encompasses a woman's decision to have an abortion. It was not an absolute right, but had to be balanced by legitimate state interests in protecting women's health and the potentiality of human life, an interest that grew stronger in the third trimester. The next important case to wrestle with the abortion issue came in 1983 in *City of Akron v. Akron Center for Reproductive Health*. In this case, the Court articulated a new test in the context of abortion decisions, writing that "if the particular regulation does not 'unduly burden' the fundamental right, then our evaluation of that regulation is limited to our determination that the regulation rationally relates to a legitimate state purpose." This standard was next relied on in 1992 with *Planned Parenthood v. Casey*, where a plurality of the Court struck down a Pennsylvania law requiring a married woman seeking an abortion to notify her spouse. The *Casey* Court found the spousal notification unconstitutional because it placed an "undue burden" on married women seeking abortions. At the same time, however, it upheld requirements for parental consent, informed consent, and a twenty-four-hour waiting period, finding no similar "undue burden." The Supreme Court has not struck down an abortion restriction under this standard, or any other standard, since this 1992 case.

In recent years, opponents of abortion, unable to overturn *Roe v. Wade* but achieving significant success in state legislative contests, have adopted a strategy of supporting legislation that makes it much more difficult to obtain abortions either by trying to dissuade women from having abortions—specifically by mandating waiting periods, requiring transvaginal sonograms, provisioning graphic consent materials, and passing more stringent regulations for abortion providers than required for other more risky medical procedures. In July 2013, Texas passed House Bill 2, despite a televised eleven-hour filibuster by Texas state senator Wendy Davis. The law was comprised of two provisions relating to the regulation of abortion providers. The first was a new requirement that all physicians performing or inducing an abortion must have active admitting privileges at a hospital within thirty miles. The second provision required all abortion facilities to meet the standards adopted for ambulatory surgical centers. The law survived an initial legal challenge.

In April 2014, a group of abortion providers filed a new lawsuit challenging these two provisions as being in violation of the Constitution's Fourteenth Amendment, as interpreted by the *Casey* case. The district court held a four-day bench trial and concluded that the two provisions would cause "the closing of almost all abortion clinics in Texas" and thereby create a constitutionally "impermissible obstacle as applied to all women seeking a previability abortion" by "restricting access to previously available legal facilities." The district court issued a statewide injunction barring the enforcement of both provisions of the Texas law. On appeal, the Fifth Circuit Court of Appeals reversed the district court, finding that the law was constitutional. On November 13, 2015, the Supreme Court granted a *writ of certiorari* to review the Fifth Circuit's decision.

Oral arguments on the case were heard on March 2, 2016. Many news commentators wrote about the scathing questioning of Texas solicitor general Scott Keller by Justice Ruth Bader Ginsburg, particularly when he argued that the many women who would live far from the few remaining Texas abortion clinics would not be unduly burdened because they could access clinics across the state border in New Mexico, a state that has more lenient standards. This was an argument that the Fifth Circuit had found compelling. Justice Ginsburg, however, probed, "So if your argument is right, then New Mexico is not an available way out for Texas, because Texas says: To protect our women, we need these things. But send them off to New Mexico," to clinics with more lenient standards, "and that's perfectly all right." "Well," Ginsburg concluded, with just a hint of pique in her voice, "if that's all right for the women in the El Paso area, why isn't it right for the rest of the women in Texas?"

Texas Law an "Undue Burden" on Abortion Rights

Justice Breyer wrote the majority opinion in this case, joined by Justices Anthony Kennedy, Ginsburg, Sonia Sotomayor, and Elena Kagan. The case, decided 5–3, was unaffected by the absence of the late justice Antonin Scalia, who would likely have sided with the dissenters and, therefore, not changed the outcome. Justice Breyer quoted *Casey* when describing the standard by which courts must evaluate laws impacting abortion: "Unnecessary health regulations that have the purpose or effect of presenting a substantial obstacle to a woman seeking an abortion impose an undue burden on the right." The Constitution, he wrote, requires that courts consider both the burdens a law imposes on abortion access and the benefits the laws confer. He then evaluated the two provisions of the Texas law separately.

First, the opinion discussed the "admitting-privileges" requirement that Texas asserted was necessary to protect women who have complications during an abortion procedure. It replaced an earlier requirement that the abortion doctors have a "working relationship" with a doctor who has admitting privileges. Looking first to any benefits conferred by this law, the Court cited the findings of fact made by the trial court. Before the new law was passed, abortions in Texas were "extremely safe with particularly low rates of serious complications and virtually no deaths." To the extent that complications requiring hospitalization arise, they mostly would do so in the days after an abortion, not on the spot. "In the rare case" of a serious complication at the clinic, it would necessitate emergency hospitalization, so "the quality of care that the patient receives is not affected by whether the abortion provider has admitting privileges at the hospital." Nothing in the record, the opinion concludes, shows that the admitting-privileges requirement advanced the state interest in protecting women's health. Then the decision turned to the burdens imposed by the requirement. Briefs filed by hospital organizations explained that hospitals do not make privileges available based on just the skill of the practitioner, but rather, condition them on "reaching a certain number of admissions a year." Because abortion is considered a safe procedure in comparison to other medical procedures—for example, the El Paso clinic performed 17,000 abortions over ten years without a single emergency hospitalization—doctors performing them would not be able to obtain the law's required privileges. In fact, the number of clinics providing abortion services in Texas dropped in half shortly after this provision began to be enforced because they were unable to find providers with the necessary privileges. The Court wrote that the closures "meant fewer doctors, longer waiting times, and increased crowding." The number of women who would face more than a 300-mile roundtrip drive to get an abortion grew from approximately 100,000 to over 900,000—enough, the Court found, to support the conclusion of undue burden.

The Court similarly rejected the "surgical-center" requirement of the Texas law, with its specified corridor widths and other building features, finding support for the district court's opinion that "[m]any of the building standards mandated by the act and its implementing rules have such a tangential relationship to patient safety in the context of abortion as to be nearly arbitrary." Indeed, the Court noted evidence that many procedures that are significantly riskier than abortions can be legally performed outside such surgical centers. Childbirth itself is fourteen times more likely than abortion to result in death; colonoscopies have a mortality rate ten times higher than that of abortion; liposuction is 28 percent more likely to result in death. Yet Texas does not require that they be performed in surgical centers. Not only did the Court find no benefit to the law, it found that it placed a "substantial obstacle in the path of women seeking an abortion." The parties to the lawsuit all agreed that the enforcement of this requirement would reduce the number of abortion facilities in Texas to seven or eight, and all located in the larger cities. Quoting the district court's findings, Justice Breyer wrote that the argument that these few surviving centers "could meet the demand of the entire State stretches credulity."

Having found no evidence that either provision of the Texas law protects the health of women, and evidence that the law has led to dramatic closures of all but a few abortion providers, the Court concluded that it places "an undue burden" on women's constitutional right to seek an abortion.

Justice Clarence Thomas wrote a dissenting opinion expressing his objection that the majority "reimagines the undue-burden standard" for evaluating abortion regulations, replacing it with a "benefits-and-burdens balancing test" that it applies in a way, he wrote, "that will surely mystify lower courts for years to come." Justice Samuel Alito also wrote a dissent rooted primarily in procedural objections and was joined by Chief Justice John Roberts and Justice Thomas. He objected to the majority's conclusion that the Texas regulations had led to the closing of the clinics, arguing that other factors may have influenced the closures such as the withdrawal of state funds, declining demand for abortion, and retirements of doctors. He was also less willing to discredit the benefit of the law, which, he wrote, "was one of many enacted by States in the wake of the Kermit Gosnell scandal, in which a physician who ran an abortion clinic in Philadelphia was convicted for the first-degree murder of three infants who were born alive and for the manslaughter of a patient." Justice Breyer responded to this argument in the majority opinion: "Gosnell's behavior was terribly wrong. But there is no reason to believe that an extra layer of regulation would have affected that behavior."

IMPACT OF THE DECISION

Reaction to the decision was predictably mixed. President Barack Obama issued a statement applauding the decision and emphasizing his ongoing commitment to "women's health, including protecting a woman's access to safe, affordable health care and her right to determine her own future." Opponents of abortion rights found the decision disappointing. Tony Perkins, President of the Family Research Council, recommitted that his organization "will continue our work to protect women and children from the predatory abortion industry."

In Texas, the decision prevented further planned closings of abortion facilities, leaving the state with nineteen open clinics. Some of the clinics that had already closed may reopen, although not immediately.

Beyond Texas, the decision is likely to have a broad impact nationwide because roughly half the states have in place laws like those at issue in this case, including the requirements for hospital-admitting privileges and surgical-center facilities, and many of the laws in these states have been subject to ongoing legal challenges. The day after the Court released its opinion, it rejected appeals from Wisconsin and Mississippi, which were seeking review of lower court judgments blocking the enforcement of their states' admitting-privileges requirements. Moreover, now that a majority of the Supreme Court has shown a willingness to balance the benefits of abortion regulations against the real-world impact those regulations have on the availability and safety of abortions, it is likely that this new test will lead to challenges of other abortion regulations, including, for example, prohibitions on telemedicine for nonsurgical abortions that involve the dispensing of abortifacient drugs and requirements on abortion providers to allow state inspectors access to patient records.

—Melissa Feinberg

Following is the edited text of the Supreme Court's ruling in Whole Woman's Health v. Hellerstedt, *in which the Court ruled 5–3 to overturn a Texas abortion law.*

DOCUMENT *Whole Woman's Health v. Hellerstedt*

June 27, 2016

[Tables and footnotes have been omitted.]

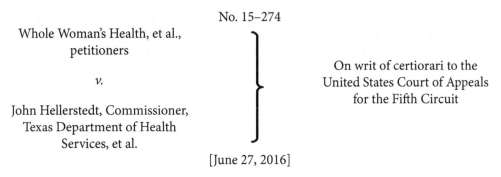

No. 15–274

Whole Woman's Health, et al.,
petitioners

v.

John Hellerstedt, Commissioner,
Texas Department of Health
Services, et al.

On writ of certiorari to the
United States Court of Appeals
for the Fifth Circuit

[June 27, 2016]

JUSTICE BREYER delivered the opinion of the Court.

In *Planned Parenthood of Southeastern Pa. v. Casey*, 505 U. S. 833, 878 (1992), a plurality of the Court concluded that there "exists" an "undue burden" on a woman's right to decide to have an abortion, and consequently a provision of law is constitutionally invalid, if the "*purpose or effect*" of the provision "*is to place a substantial obstacle* in the path of a woman seeking an abortion before the fetus attains viability." (Emphasis added.) The plurality added that "[u]nnecessary health regulations that have the purpose or effect of presenting a substantial obstacle to a woman seeking an abortion impose an undue burden on the right." *Ibid.*

We must here decide whether two provisions of Texas' House Bill 2 violate the Federal Constitution as interpreted in *Casey*. The first provision, which we shall call the "*admitting-privileges requirement*," says that "[a] physician performing or inducing an abortion . . . must, on the date the abortion is performed or induced, have active admitting privileges at a hospital that . . . is located not further than 30 miles from the location at which the abortion is performed or induced." Tex. Health & Safety Code Ann. §171.0031(a) (West Cum. Supp. 2015).

This provision amended Texas law that had previously required an abortion facility to maintain a written protocol "for managing medical emergencies and the transfer of patients requiring further emergency care to a hospital." 38 Tex. Reg. 6546 (2013).

The second provision, which we shall call the "*surgical center requirement*," says that "the minimum standards for an abortion facility must be equivalent to the minimum standards adopted under [the Texas Health and Safety Code section] for ambulatory surgical centers." Tex. Health & Safety Code Ann. §245.010(a).

We conclude that neither of these provisions confers medical benefits sufficient to justify the burdens upon access that each imposes. Each places a substantial obstacle in the path of women seeking a previability abortion, each constitutes an undue burden on abortion access, *Casey, supra,* at 878 (plurality opinion), and each violates the Federal Constitution. Amdt. 14, §1.

[Sections I and II, covering the background of the case and earlier Court rulings on the matter, have been omitted.]

III

Undue Burden—Legal Standard

We begin with the standard, as described in *Casey*. We recognize that the "State has a legitimate interest in seeing to it that abortion, like any other medical procedure, is performed under circumstances that insure maximum safety for the patient." *Roe v. Wade*, 410 U. S. 113, 150 (1973). But, we added, "a statute which, while furthering [a] valid state interest, has the effect of placing a substantial obstacle in the path of a woman's choice cannot be considered a permissible means of serving its legitimate ends." *Casey*, 505 U. S., at 877 (plurality opinion). Moreover, "[u]nnecessary health regulations that have the purpose or effect of presenting a substantial obstacle to a woman seeking an abortion impose an undue burden on the right." *Id.*, at 878. . . .

[The remainder of the section, containing additional information on the Court of Appeals's findings, has been omitted.]

IV

Undue Burden—Admitting-Privileges Requirement

Turning to the lower courts' evaluation of the evidence, we first consider the admitting-privileges requirement. Before the enactment of H. B. 2, doctors who provided abortions were required to "have admitting privileges *or* have a working arrangement with a physician(s) who has admitting privileges at a local hospital in order to ensure the necessary back up for medical complications." Tex. Admin. Code, tit. 25, §139.56 (2009) (emphasis added). The new law changed this requirement by requiring that a "physician performing or inducing an abortion . . . must, on the date the abortion is performed or induced, have active admitting privileges at a hospital that . . . is located not further than 30 miles from the location at which the abortion is performed or induced." Tex. Health & Safety Code Ann. §171.0031(a). The District Court held that the legislative change imposed an "undue burden" on a woman's right to have an abortion. We conclude that there is adequate legal and factual support for the District Court's conclusion.

The purpose of the admitting-privileges requirement is to help ensure that women have easy access to a hospital should complications arise during an abortion procedure. Brief for Respondents 32–37. But the District Court found that it brought about no such health-related benefit. The court found that "[t]he great weight of evidence demonstrates that, before the act's passage, abortion in Texas was extremely safe with particularly low rates of serious complications and virtually no deaths occurring on account of the procedure." 46 F. Supp. 3d, at 684. Thus, there was no significant health-related problem that the new law helped to cure.

The evidence upon which the court based this conclusion included, among other things . . .

- Expert testimony stating that "it is extremely unlikely that a patient will experience a serious complication at the clinic that requires emergent hospitalization" and "in the rare case in which [one does], the quality of care that the patient receives is not affected by whether the abortion provider has admitting privileges at the hospital."

- Expert testimony stating that in respect to surgical abortion patients who do suffer complications requiring hospitalization, most of these complications occur in the days after the abortion, not on the spot. See *id.*, at 382; see also *id.*, at 267.

- Expert testimony stating that a delay before the onset of complications is also expected for medical abortions, as "abortifacient drugs take time to exert their effects, and thus the abortion itself almost always occurs after the patient has left the abortion facility." *Id.*, at 278.

- Some experts added that, if a patient needs a hospital in the day or week following her abortion, she will likely seek medical attention at the hospital nearest her home. See, *e.g.*, *id.*, at 153.

We have found nothing in Texas' record evidence that shows that, compared to prior law (which required a "working arrangement" with a doctor with admitting privileges), the new law advanced Texas' legitimate interest in protecting women's health.

We add that, when directly asked at oral argument whether Texas knew of a single instance in which the new requirement would have helped even one woman obtain better treatment, Texas admitted that there was no evidence in the record of such a case. See Tr. of Oral Arg. 47. . . .

At the same time, the record evidence indicates that the admitting-privileges requirement places a "substantial obstacle in the path of a woman's choice." *Casey*, 505 U. S., at 877 (plurality opinion). The District Court found, as of the time the admitting-privileges requirement began to be enforced, the number of facilities providing abortions dropped in half, from about 40 to about 20. 46 F. Supp. 3d, at 681. . . .

Other evidence helps to explain why the new requirement led to the closure of clinics. We read that other evidence in light of a brief filed in this Court by the Society of Hospital Medicine. That brief describes the undisputed general fact that "hospitals often condition admitting privileges on reaching a certain number of admissions per year." Returning to the District Court record, we note that, in direct testimony, the president of Nova Health Systems, implicitly relying on this general fact, pointed out that it would be difficult for doctors regularly performing abortions at the El Paso clinic to obtain admitting privileges at nearby hospitals because "[d]uring the past 10 years, over 17,000 abortion procedures were performed at the El Paso clinic [and n]ot a single one of those patients had to be transferred to a hospital for emergency treatment, much less admitted to the hospital." App. 730. In a word, doctors would be unable to maintain admitting privileges or obtain those privileges for the future, because the fact that abortions are so safe meant that providers were unlikely to have any patients to admit. . . .

In our view, the record contains sufficient evidence that the admitting-privileges requirement led to the closure of half of Texas' clinics, or thereabouts. Those closures meant fewer doctors, longer waiting times, and increased crowding. Record evidence also supports the finding that after the admitting-privileges provision went into effect, the "number of women of reproductive age living in a county . . . more than 150 miles from a provider increased from approximately 86,000 to 400,000 . . . and the number of women living in a county more than 200 miles from a provider from approximately 10,000 to 290,000." 46 F. Supp. 3d, at 681. We recognize that increased driving distances do not always constitute an "undue burden." But here, those increases are but one additional burden, which, when taken together with others that the closings brought about, and when viewed in light of the virtual absence of any health benefit, lead us to conclude that the record adequately supports the District Court's "undue burden" conclusion. . . .

V

Undue Burden—Surgical-Center Requirement

The second challenged provision of Texas' new law sets forth the surgical-center requirement. Prior to enactment of the new requirement, Texas law required abortion facilities to meet a host of health and safety requirements. . . .

H. B. 2 added the requirement that an "abortion facility" meet the "minimum standards . . . for ambulatory surgical centers" under Texas law. §245.010(a) (West Cum. Supp. 2015). The surgical-center regulations include, among other things, detailed specifications relating to the size of the nursing staff, building dimensions, and other building requirements. . . .

There is considerable evidence in the record supporting the District Court's findings indicating that the statutory provision requiring all abortion facilities to meet all surgical center standards does not benefit patients and is not necessary. The District Court found that "risks are not appreciably lowered for patients who undergo abortions at ambulatory surgical centers as compared to nonsurgical center facilities." The court added that women "will not obtain better care or experience more frequent positive outcomes at an ambulatory surgical center as compared to a previously licensed facility." And these findings are well supported.

The record makes clear that the surgical-center requirement provides no benefit when complications arise in the context of an abortion produced through medication. That is because, in such a case, complications would almost always arise only after the patient has left the facility. See *supra*, at 23; App. 278. The record also contains evidence indicating that abortions taking place in an abortion facility are safe—indeed, safer than numerous procedures that take place outside hospitals and to which Texas does not apply its surgical-center requirements. The total number of deaths in Texas from abortions was five in the period from 2001 to 2012, or about one every two years (that is to say, one out of about 120,000 to 144,000 abortions). Nationwide, childbirth is 14 times more likely than abortion to result in death, *ibid.*, but Texas law allows a midwife to oversee childbirth in the patient's own home. Colonoscopy, a procedure that typically takes place outside a hospital (or surgical center) setting, has a mortality rate 10 times higher than an abortion (the mortality rate for liposuction, another outpatient procedure, is 28 times higher than the mortality rate for abortion). Medical treatment after an incomplete miscarriage often involves a procedure identical to that involved in a nonmedical abortion, but it often takes place outside a hospital or surgical center. . . . These facts indicate that the surgical-center provision imposes "a requirement that simply is not based on differences" between abortion and other surgical procedures "that are reasonably related to" preserving women's health, the asserted "purpos[e] of the Act in which it is found."

Moreover, many surgical-center requirements are inappropriate as applied to surgical abortions. Requiring scrub facilities; maintaining a one-way traffic pattern through the facility; having ceiling, wall, and floor finishes; separating soiled utility and sterilization rooms; and regulating air pressure, filtration, and humidity control can help reduce infection where doctors conduct procedures that penetrate the skin. App. 304. But abortions typically involve either the administration of medicines or procedures performed through the natural opening of the birth canal, which is itself not sterile. See *id.*, at 302–303. Nor do provisions designed to safeguard heavily sedated patients (unable to help themselves) during fire emergencies, see Tex. Admin. Code, tit. 25, §135.41; App. 304, provide any help to abortion patients, as abortion facilities do not use general anesthesia or deep sedation, *id.,* at 304–305. Further, since the few instances in which serious complications do arise following an abortion almost always require hospitalization, not treatment at a surgical center, surgical-center standards will not help in those instances either.

The upshot is that this record evidence, along with the absence of any evidence to the contrary, provides ample support [for] the District Court's conclusion that "[m]any of the building standards mandated by the act and its implementing rules have such a tangential relationship to patient safety in the context of abortion as to be nearly arbitrary." 46 F. Supp. 3d, at 684. That conclusion, along with the supporting evidence, provides sufficient support for the more general conclusion that the surgical-center requirement "will not [provide] better care or . . . more frequent positive outcomes." *Ibid.* The record evidence thus supports the ultimate legal conclusion that the surgical-center requirement is not necessary.

At the same time, the record provides adequate evidentiary support for the District Court's conclusion that the surgical-center requirement places a substantial obstacle in the path of women seeking an abortion. The parties stipulated that the requirement would further reduce the number of abortion facilities available to seven or eight facilities, located in Houston, Austin, San Antonio, and Dallas/Fort Worth. See App. 182–183. In the District Court's view, the proposition that these "seven or eight providers could meet the demand of the entire State stretches credulity." 46 F. Supp. 3d, at 682. We take this statement as a finding that these few facilities could not "meet" that "demand". . . .

Unlike the Court of Appeals, we hold that the record provides adequate support for the District Court's finding. . . .

For another thing, common sense suggests that, more often than not, a physical facility that satisfies a certain physical demand will not be able to meet five times that demand without expanding or otherwise incurring significant costs. . . . Courts are free to base their findings on commonsense inferences drawn from the evidence. And that is what the District Court did here. . . .

More fundamentally, in the face of no threat to women's health, Texas seeks to force women to travel long distances to get abortions in crammed-to-capacity super facilities. Patients seeking these services are less likely to get the kind of individualized attention, serious conversation, and emotional support that doctors at less taxed facilities may have offered. Healthcare facilities and medical professionals are not fungible commodities. Surgical centers attempting to accommodate sudden, vastly increased demand, see 46 F. Supp. 3d, at 682, may find that quality of care declines. Another commonsense inference that the District Court made is that these effects would be harmful to, not supportive of, women's health. See *id.,* at 682–683.

Finally, the District Court found that the costs that a currently licensed abortion facility would have to incur to meet the surgical-center requirements were considerable, ranging from $1 million per facility (for facilities with adequate space) to $3 million per facility (where additional land must be purchased). *Id.,* at 682. This evidence supports the conclusion that more surgical centers will not soon fill the gap when licensed facilities are forced to close.

We agree with the District Court that the surgical center requirement, like the admitting-privileges requirement, provides few, if any, health benefits for women, poses a substantial obstacle to women seeking abortions, and constitutes an "undue burden" on their constitutional right to do so.

[Section VI, containing additional arguments made by Texas but which the Court deemed nonpersuasive, has been omitted.]

* * *

For these reasons the judgment of the Court of Appeals is reversed, and the case is remanded for further proceedings consistent with this opinion.

It is so ordered.

[The concurring opinion of Justice Ginsburg has been omitted.]

JUSTICE THOMAS, dissenting.

Today the Court strikes down two state statutory provisions in all of their applications, at the behest of abortion clinics and doctors. That decision exemplifies the Court's troubling tendency "to bend the rules when any effort to limit abortion, or even to speak in opposition to abortion, is at issue." *Stenberg v. Carhart*, 530 U. S. 914, 954 (2000) (Scalia, J., dissenting). As JUSTICE ALITO observes, see post (dissenting opinion), today's decision creates an abortion exception to ordinary rules of res judicata, ignores compelling evidence that Texas' law imposes no unconstitutional burden, and disregards basic principles of the severability doctrine. I write separately to emphasize how today's decision perpetuates the Court's habit of applying different rules to different constitutional rights—especially the putative right to abortion.

To begin, the very existence of this suit is a jurisprudential oddity. Ordinarily, plaintiffs cannot file suits to vindicate the constitutional rights of others. But the Court employs a different approach to rights that it favors. So in this case and many others, the Court has erroneously allowed doctors and clinics to vicariously vindicate the putative constitutional right of women seeking abortions.

This case also underscores the Court's increasingly common practice of invoking a given level of scrutiny—here, the abortion-specific undue burden standard—while applying a different standard of review entirely. Whatever scrutiny the majority applies to Texas' law, it bears little resemblance to the undue-burden test the Court articulated in Planned Parenthood of Southeastern Pa. v. Casey, 505 U. S. 833 (1992), and its successors. Instead, the majority eviscerates important features of that test to return to a regime like the one that Casey repudiated.

Ultimately, this case shows why the Court never should have bent the rules for favored rights in the first place. Our law is now so riddled with special exceptions for special rights that our decisions deliver neither predictability nor the promise of a judiciary bound by the rule of law.

[The body of Justice Thomas's dissent has been omitted.]

***

Today's decision will prompt some to claim victory, just as it will stiffen opponents' will to object. But the entire Nation has lost something essential. The majority's embrace of a jurisprudence of rights-specific exceptions and balancing tests is "a regrettable concession of defeat—an acknowledgement that we have passed the point where 'law,' properly speaking, has any further application." Scalia, The Rule of Law as a Law of Rules, 56 U. Chi. L. Rev. 1175, 1182 (1989). I respectfully dissent.

JUSTICE ALITO, with whom THE CHIEF JUSTICE and JUSTICE THOMAS join, dissenting.

The constitutionality of laws regulating abortion is one of the most controversial issues in American law, but this case does not require us to delve into that contentious dispute. Instead, the dispositive issue here concerns a workaday question that can arise in any case no matter the subject, namely, whether the present case is barred by res judicata. As a court of law, we have an obligation to apply such rules in a neutral fashion in all cases, regardless of the subject of the suit. If anything, when a case involves a controversial issue, we should be especially careful to be scrupulously neutral in applying such rules.

The Court has not done so here. On the contrary, determined to strike down two provisions of a new Texas abortion statute in all of their applications, the Court simply disregards basic rules that apply in all other cases.

Here is the worst example. Shortly after Texas enacted House Bill 2 (H. B. 2) in 2013, the petitioners in this case brought suit, claiming, among other things, that a provision of the new law requiring a physician performing an abortion to have admitting privileges at a nearby hospital is "facially" unconstitutional and thus totally unenforceable. Petitioners had a fair opportunity to make their case, but they lost on the merits in the United States Court of Appeals for the Fifth Circuit, and they chose not to petition this Court for review. The judgment against them became final. *Planned Parenthood of Greater Tex. Surgical Health Servs. v. Abbott*, 951 F. Supp. 2d 891 (WD Tex. 2013), aff'd in part and rev'd in part, 748 F. 3d 583 (CA5 2014) (Abbott).

Under the rules that apply in regular cases, petitioners could not relitigate the exact same claim in a second suit. As we have said, "a losing litigant deserves no rematch after a defeat fairly suffered, in adversarial proceedings, on an issue identical in substance to the one he subsequently seeks to raise." *Astoria Fed. Sav. & Loan Assn. v. Solimino*, 501 U. S. 104, 107 (1991).

In this abortion case, however, that rule is disregarded. The Court awards a victory to petitioners on the very claim that they unsuccessfully pressed in the earlier case. The Court does this even though petitioners, undoubtedly realizing that a rematch would not be allowed, did not presume to include such a claim in their complaint. The Court favors petitioners with a victory that they did not have the audacity to seek.

Here is one more example: the Court's treatment of H. B. 2's "severability clause." When part of a statute is held to be unconstitutional, the question arises whether other parts of the statute must also go. If a statute says that provisions found to be unconstitutional can be severed from the rest of the statute, the valid provisions are allowed to stand. H. B. 2 contains what must surely be the most emphatic severability clause ever written. This clause says that every single word of the statute and every possible application of its provisions is severable. But despite this language, the Court holds that no part of the challenged provisions and no application of any part of them can be saved. Provisions that are indisputably constitutional—for example, provisions that require facilities performing abortions to follow basic fire safety measures—are stricken from the books. There is no possible justification for this collateral damage.

The Court's patent refusal to apply well-established law in a neutral way is indefensible and will undermine public confidence in the Court as a fair and neutral arbiter.

[The body of Justice Alito's dissent has been omitted.]

When we decide cases on particularly controversial issues, we should take special care to apply settled procedural rules in a neutral manner. The Court has not done that here.

I therefore respectfully dissent.

Source: U.S. Supreme Court. *Whole Woman's Health v. Hellerstedt.* 579 U.S.___(2016). http://www.supremecourt.gov/opinions/15pdf/15-274_p8k0.pdf.

OTHER HISTORIC DOCUMENTS OF INTEREST

FROM PREVIOUS *HISTORIC DOCUMENTS*

- FDA on Approval of the Plan B Emergency Contraceptive Drug, *2006*, p. 466
- GAO on the FDA's Handling of the "Morning-After" Pill, *2005*, p. 814
- President, Federal Courts on Partial Birth Abortion, *2003*, p. 995

President Obama Signs PROMESA into Law

JUNE 30, 2016

Puerto Rico continued to face a severe financial crisis in 2016, and defaulted on its debt payments. Following several failed attempts to approve debt relief legislation, Congress passed, and President Barack Obama signed into law, a bipartisan bill that will allow the commonwealth to restructure its debt with oversight from a federally appointed fiscal board.

PUERTO RICO'S BALLOONING DEBT

Puerto Rico's financial crisis is generally attributed to several factors. In 2006, Congress repealed a federal tax credit that exempted U.S. companies from paying taxes on income originated in U.S. territories and had encouraged many mainland businesses to establish a presence on the island. Once this incentive was removed, many of these companies withdrew from Puerto Rico. High corporate taxes on domestic businesses had discouraged the development of Puerto Rican–based companies, meaning that the local market was not able to fill the economic void left by the departing mainland companies. Puerto Ricans lost their jobs or left the commonwealth to find employment, further reducing the island's tax revenue. This led to a period of economic contraction that drove up government deficits. Additionally, Puerto Rico has relied heavily on deficit financing and the issuance of various bonds to keep its government running. All of Puerto Rico's bonds are exempt from federal, state, and local taxes, making them particularly attractive to investors. Between 2006 and 2013, the commonwealth enjoyed a significant and steady demand for its bonds, which enabled the government to continue borrowing and spending beyond its means. However, the more bonds Puerto Rico issued, the more interest payments it had to make to more bond holders, and interest rates increased in 2013 amid declining investor confidence.

By 2015, Puerto Rico accumulated approximately $72 billion in debt, mostly in the form of municipal bonds. Lacking sufficient resources to repay its creditors, the commonwealth defaulted on its debt on August 3. In December, the government announced that it would also default on a debt payment due in January 2016, and a third default occurred in May 2016.

Throughout 2015, Puerto Rican officials and their mainland supporters called for an agreement that would enable the commonwealth to declare bankruptcy under Chapter 9 of the U.S. Bankruptcy Code and restructure its debt in the same manner as U.S. states. Most Republican lawmakers did not support this proposal. They argued that alternative options were available and claimed that allowing Puerto Rico to declare bankruptcy would hurt U.S. investors because nearly 60 percent of the commonwealth's debt is held in Americans' retirement accounts. Investment fund managers also opposed extending Chapter 9 to Puerto Rico because it would violate the terms of investors' bond agreements and impose unanticipated risk on bond holders.

Lawmakers made several attempts to pass a legislative solution in 2015. Puerto Rico's Resident Commissioner Pedro Pierluisi introduced a bill in February 2015 that would permit some parts of the commonwealth's government to declare bankruptcy, but the bill did not make it out of committee. The Obama administration released its own proposal for handling Puerto Rico's financial crisis in October, calling on Congress to give the commonwealth a mechanism for restructuring all its debt, in addition to providing independent fiscal oversight of the commonwealth's recovery plan, reforming Puerto Rico's Medicaid program, and enabling Puerto Ricans to qualify for the Earned Income Tax Credit. Sen. Orrin Hatch, R-Utah, and Rep. Sean Duffy, R-Wis., each proposed debt relief legislation in December, but neither bill passed.

THE PUERTO RICO OVERSIGHT, MANAGEMENT, AND ECONOMIC STABILITY ACT

On May 18, 2016, Representative Duffy introduced the Puerto Rico Oversight, Management, and Economic Stability Act, or PROMESA. The bill granted Puerto Rico the ability to restructure $70 billion of its debt and placed a hold on creditor lawsuits. PROMESA also established a seven-member fiscal oversight board—to be appointed by congressional leaders and President Obama—with the power to force Puerto Rico to balance its budget, negotiate with creditors, and restructure debt. Additionally, the bill allowed the federal minimum wage to be lowered to $4.25 per hour for Puerto Rican workers aged twenty-four or younger and established expedited procedures for approving "critical" energy and infrastructure projects that could help boost the commonwealth's economy.

While both Republican and Democratic lawmakers voiced support for PROMESA, the bill faced significant opposition from Puerto Rico's creditors, who argued that it would cause their investments to lose value. An advertising campaign reportedly backed by these creditors also claimed that American taxpayers would be paying for a bailout of Puerto Rico, which lawmakers refuted. "This bill won't cost taxpayers a dime—not a dime," said Senate Majority Leader Mitch McConnell, R-Ky.

Several Puerto Rican civil society organizations opposed PROMESA's creation of an oversight board, arguing that it would supersede the will of the Puerto Rican people. In June, a coalition comprised of these groups sent an open letter to U.S. senators, urging them to oppose the bill. "Puerto Ricans want a move towards full self-government not a limitation of democracy," they wrote. "They want to see an end to the colonial rule, not its perpetuation." Sen. Bernie Sanders, I-Vt., was among the lawmakers who expressed similar concerns. "This legislation strips away the most important powers of the democratically elected officials of Puerto Rico, the governor, the legislature, and the municipal governments as well," he said.

The Obama administration pressed Congress to pass PROMESA ahead of Puerto Rico's next debt payment deadline on July 1, when the commonwealth was supposed to make a $1.9 billion payment. The House passed PROMESA on June 9, and the Senate passed the bill on June 29. Upon signing the bill into law on June 30, President Obama acknowledged that PROMESA was not going "to solve all the problems that Puerto Rico faces," but he said it was an "important first step on the path of creating more stability, better services, and greater prosperity over the long term." Governor Padilla welcomed the bill's passage. "Today we take back our country," he said in a statement. However, he also recognized the bill's imperfections, telling a Puerto Rican radio station, "We have to take the good with the bad, and while I may not agree with a control board, this is a way to restructure our debt and move our country forward." Shortly after PROMESA's signing, Governor Padilla issued an executive order authorizing the suspension of payments on the commonwealth's general obligation bonds.

OVERSIGHT BOARD APPOINTED

On August 31, President Obama announced the appointment of four Republicans and three Democrats to the fiscal oversight board. Per PROMESA's provisions, six board members were selected from candidate lists provided by House Speaker Paul Ryan, R-Wis.; House Minority Leader Nancy Pelosi, D-Calif.; Senator McConnell; and Senate Minority Leader Harry Reid, D-Nev., while the seventh was appointed at Obama's discretion. Governor Padilla also serves on the board, but is not allowed to vote.

The board held its first meeting on September 30, during which it officially requested a fiscal plan for the commonwealth from Governor Padilla. The governor's draft plan, presented at the board's October meeting, forecast a budget gap as high as $59 billion over the next ten years. While the plan included some proposals for revenue-generating measures to make up this difference, it mostly relied on reducing repayment to bondholders. The board set a target date of January 31, 2017, to certify a final fiscal plan.

—Linda Fecteau Grimm

Following are remarks made by President Barack Obama on June 30, 2016, upon signing the Puerto Rico Oversight, Management, and Economic Stability Act.

President Obama Remarks on Signing the PROMESA Act

June 30, 2016

[The following has been excerpted from the president's remarks at the signing of the FOIA Improvement and PROMESA Acts.]

The second piece of legislation relates to the crisis that we're seeing in Puerto Rico. We've got millions of our fellow citizens in Puerto Rico who have been suffering under one of the worst financial crises, fiscal crises in memory. And as a consequence of the inability for them to restructure their debt, you've seen hospitals unable to operate, ambulances shutting down, basic services shutting down, and government workers not being paid. It has brought enormous hardship to Puerto Rico.

Through some amazing work by our Treasury Department, our legislative staff, and a bipartisan effort in both the House and the Senate, we finally have legislation that at least is going to give Puerto Rico the capacity, the opportunity to get out from under this lingering uncertainty with respect to their debt and start stabilizing government services and to start growing again.

It's not, in and of itself, going to be sufficient to solve all the problems that Puerto Rico faces, but it is a [*sic*] important first step on the path of creating more stability, better services, and greater prosperity over the long term for the people of Puerto Rico.

So I want to thank all four leaders in Congress for the hard work in getting this to my desk. And I want to let the people of Puerto Rico know that although there's still some tough work that we're going to have to do to dig Puerto Rico out of the hole that it's in, this indicates how committed my administration is to making sure that they get the help they need. And it's not going to stop here; we've got to keep on working to figure out how we promote the long-term growth and sustainability that's so desperately needed down there. But the people of Puerto Rico need to know that they're not forgotten, that they're part of the American family. And Congress's responsiveness to this issue—even though this is not a perfect bill—at least moves us in the right direction.

[The president signed the bill.]

Okay, thank you very much, everybody.

SOURCE: Executive Office of the President. "Remarks on Signing the FOIA Improvement Act of 2016 and the Puerto Rico Oversight, Management, and Economic Stability Act." June 30, 2016. *Compilation of Presidential Documents* 2016, no. 0440 (June 30, 2016). http://www.gpo.gov/fdsys/pkg/DCPD-201600440/pdf/DCPD-201600440.pdf.

OTHER HISTORIC DOCUMENTS OF INTEREST

FROM PREVIOUS *HISTORIC DOCUMENTS*

■ American and Puerto Rican Leaders Remark on Island Nation's Default, *2015*, p. 537

July

Renewed Fighting in South Sudan; Continuation of Border Negotiations

JULY 10 AND 27, AUGUST 3, AND SEPTEMBER 30, 2016

Five years after gaining its independence from Sudan, South Sudan was again the site of renewed fighting by rival armed groups that killed hundreds. The clashes in and around the capital city of Juba resulted in calls from the United Nations for the country's neighbors to take action and send more troops to support the UN peacekeeping mission in the fledgling country. Although the clashes lasted only days, it was a reminder that the country has a number of ongoing challenges that must be resolved if it is to continue on its path toward stable governance and instill a lasting peace. Simmering tensions throughout the summer and fall of 2016 forced many South Sudanese to flee their homes for refugee camps in neighboring nations, and the lack of humanitarian aid eventually resulted in a cholera outbreak.

The July conflict was followed by ongoing border demarcation negotiations between Sudan and South Sudan. After their acrimonious split in 2011, the two countries had committed to draw a formal border that would require reaching agreements on which nation held control over oil- and mineral-rich lands. By the close of 2016, the boundary had not been finalized.

REBEL GROUPS CLASH

Although the split from Sudan in 2011 was expected to bring about the end of decades of violence in the region between the predominantly Christian South Sudan and predominantly Muslim Sudan, it only exposed the deeper rifts that existed between rival factions within South Sudan's population. Those long-simmering tensions appeared again the evening of July 7, when a skirmish broke out at a checkpoint during a disagreement between soldiers loyal to President Salva Kiir, who heads the Sudan People's Liberation Movement (SPLM), and those who back First Vice President Riek Machar, founder and head of the Sudan People's Liberation Movement in Opposition (SPLM-IO). The violence spilled over into the following day, and major clashes broke out near the presidential compound where Kiir and Machar were meeting.

The conflict between supporters of Kiir—who belongs to the nation's largest ethnic group, the Dinka—and Machar—who belongs to the second-largest ethnic group, the Nuer—dates back to 2013, when Machar was accused by Kiir of plotting to overthrow his government. Machar, who at that time served as first vice president, was fired from his position along with the rest of the president's cabinet. Civil war broke out between the Dinka and Neur ethnic groups. According to the United Nations, the rival militias terrorized neighborhoods across South Sudan by rounding up citizens, dividing them among ethnic lines, and then massacring those of the opposite sect. Tens of thousands were killed and more than three million displaced in the violence; of note, aid groups operating in the nation put the number killed much lower. Although a peace agreement was signed by Kiir and Machar in August 2015, which included Machar's reinstatement as first vice president, tensions have continued to fester because the elements of the peace deal have not yet been fully implemented, most notable of which is the integration and demobilization of forces on both sides of the conflict. The failure of the government to carry out all aspects of the peace agreement is thought to be due to a lack of trust between Kiir and Machar's supporters.

The violence that ensued after July 7 is widely thought to be linked to one of two causes. Some believed that a Facebook post by the nation's ambassador to Kenya, a Machar supporter, led Machar supporters to attack the presidential palace. The post incorrectly stated that Machar was being detained by Kiir, when in fact the two were holding a meeting. Others believed that those killed at the checkpoint on July 7 were targeted for their support of Machar, causing his followers to take up arms against Kiir. However, statements from each side accuse the other of being the first to arouse renewed violence.

CEASEFIRE IMPLEMENTED

The United Nations, which stationed 12,000 peacekeepers in South Sudan since the country gained independence, called on the warring factions immediately to cease the violence and further asked that the neighboring nations of Ethiopia, Uganda, Kenya, the Democratic Republic of the Congo, and the Central African Republic prepare to begin taking in refugees. "I am shocked and appalled by the heavy fighting that is currently taking place in Juba," said UN Secretary-General Ban Ki-moon. "This senseless violence is unacceptable and has the potential of reversing the progress made so far in the peace process." After attacks against UN compounds in South Sudan resulted in the deaths of at least two peacekeepers, the Security Council issued a statement urging "an immediate end to the fighting by all concerned" and "demanded that President Kiir and First Vice President Machar do their utmost to control their respective forces" to "urgently end the fighting and prevent the spread of violence." The General Assembly further called on the UN Security Council to issue an arms embargo against South Sudan. The body attempted to do so in December but fell two votes short of approving a measure that included both an arms embargo and targeted sanctions.

Those in the Kiir government called for peace. "Our people have suffered so much, they don't need any more suffering even for a minute. This is a call to our generals in both armies that they should ceasefire immediately," said Minister of Mining Taban Deng. On July 11, Kiir called for a ceasefire. Presidential spokesperson Ateny Wek Ateny announced, "All the commanders of [Kiir's] forces are directed to cease any hostility and abide by the order and control their forces," adding that the president was "determined to carry on his partnership with Riek Machar." Machar followed the president's ceasefire request, stating, "The president has declared a unilateral ceasefire. I want to reciprocate the declaration of unilateral ceasefire." By the morning of July 12, it appeared that the order was holding.

According to the United Nations, 42,000 fled during the days of violence, with approximately 7,000 seeking refuge in UN compounds around the country. An estimated 300 were killed.

FIRST VICE PRESIDENT FLEES SOUTH SUDAN

Shortly after the ceasefire was declared, Machar fled the capital city of Juba, and later the nation, for the Democratic Republic of the Congo, despite calls from President Kiir for his return to continue the implementation of the 2015 peace agreement. Because of Machar's ongoing refusal to return, in his absence, Kiir temporarily appointed Minister Deng as first vice president. Machar immediately called for Deng's dismissal from his party, the SPLM-IO, and from his position as Minister of Mining. Deng did not step down, but instead announced his intent only to hold the seat until Machar's return. "If the man comes back . . . I will gladly step aside if that could bring peace to South Sudan," Deng said.

In late September, Machar, who was moved to North Sudan's capital of Khartoum and later to South Africa for medical treatments, issued a call on behalf of his SPLM-IO to take up arms against Kiir's government. According to Machar, the Kiir government had been targeting SPLM-IO forces. Kiir's spokesperson, Ateny, responded to Machar's comments, saying, "Riek Machar . . . will never have anything better to offer to the people of South Sudan apart from war," adding, "We have reached the conclusion that we are not going to go back to war. We are not going to give anybody war because the people of South Sudan deserve more than war. They deserve peace, something better than war."

Stephen Par Kuol, a senior member of the SPLM-IO, denied that the party wished to incite more violence but that it must confront the "violent, ethnocentric regime of Salva Kiir." Kuol added that Deng's appointment was illegal per the terms of the 2015 peace agreement, which binds Kiir and Machar to work together as president and first vice president, or both would be forced to leave their positions. In October, Machar pledged to return to South Sudan and called on regional leaders to help the country develop "a political process which will bring about peace again, and the resuscitation of the peace agreement, and the reconstitution of the transitional government of national unity." By the end of the year, neither Machar nor his closest supporters had returned to Juba and remained in a SPLM-IO stronghold in Pagak, South Sudan. According to Machar's troops, they were not given flight clearance by Kiir's government, and Machar refused to fly ahead of his forces, while the Kiir government argues that Machar is attempting to bring more of his troops into the capital than allowed under the 2015 peace agreement.

HUMANITARIAN CRISIS DEEPENS

A month after the ceasefire, South Sudan found itself reeling from yet another crisis. The economy had already been struggling as ongoing violence made other nations wary of trade with South Sudan, and the July fighting stopped shipments of goods from crossing into the country, which increased inflation to 835 percent and further pushed up prices on food and other goods. According to the United Nations, as of August 2016, more than half the population in the country required humanitarian assistance, and one in three children was at risk of starvation. "I am extremely concerned as the humanitarian crisis in South Sudan continues to deepen and spread, causing untold devastation to so many innocent [people]," said Eugene Owusu, the UN's humanitarian coordinator for South Sudan. The newly appointed First Vice President Deng called the nation's humanitarian crisis "appalling" and asked UN member states not to forget the ongoing crisis in South Sudan. "The difference between failure and success is very narrow," Deng said, while highlighting some of the work that the Kiir government is doing to ensure safe passage of humanitarian aid.

The lack of access to adequate food, humanitarian aid, and sanitary living spaces allowed a cholera epidemic to spread across the capital city of Juba and into other parts of the nation. The World Health Organization (WHO), which established treatment camps around the country, said that 4.4 million South Sudanese were in need of health assistance, and by late July only $4.3 million of the necessary $17.5 million funds had been raised to address ongoing health crises. "We have this opportunity to save, improve, and protect the health of millions of people before it gets worse," said Dr. Abdulmumini Usman, the WHO's Country Representative for South Sudan. "WHO is committed to containing the cholera outbreak in South Sudan but, without urgent funding, we cannot implement most of the planned interventions." By the end of the year, the UN reported 3,359 cases of the disease and sixty-one deaths.

Despite the end of the July clashes, forces loyal to both Kiir and Machar continued to patrol the streets, putting citizens at risk when they left their homes or the UN compounds to seek food. The desperate situation across the South Sudan forced many to cross into neighboring countries, where refugee camps have been established by the United Nations. More than 900,000 were thought to have fled the country between December 2013 and August 2016, primarily to Uganda, Kenya, and the Democratic Republic of the Congo. However, these camps have struggled to keep up with the influx of citizens from South Sudan and food stores have been looted, making food shortages common.

DEMARCATION NEGOTIATIONS CONTINUE

As a condition of South Sudan's independence, its leaders were required to reach an agreement with North Sudan on the demarcation of the border between the two nations. The countries agreed to open negotiations on drawing the border in 2012, and in 2015 agreed to the technical details of their demarcation meetings. At that time, the boundary was based on a colonial border first set in 1956 when Sudan gained independence from Great Britain. This demarcation, however, was not drawn precisely and is not noted completely on most maps. The border also runs in disputed lands, including oil- and mineral-rich areas, thus making the task more difficult for the Joint Boundary Commission (JBC), the group tasked with drawing the border.

The JBC convened from September 26 to 29, 2016, in sessions mediated by the African Union. At that time, the JBC agreed to form a committee that would be responsible for developing and proposing the final demarcation of the border, adopting a budget, and setting future meeting dates. The group was further able to conclude that the nations should have a soft border that would allow nomadic communities to traverse between the two nations. The two countries met again from November 30 to December 2, 2016, in Addis Ababa, under the auspices of the African Union, and concluded only with an agreement that the two countries should act expeditiously to finalize the border demarcation. While the two nations were unable to finalize the demarcation by the end of 2016, the agreements established in the fall and winter were hailed as major steps forward for two groups that have long been at odds with each other.

—Heather Kerrigan

Following is a statement from July 10, 2016, by the United Nations Secretary-General, Ban Ki-moon, on renewed fighting in South Sudan; a July 10, 2016, statement from the UN Security Council on the violence in South Sudan; a July 27, 2016, press release from the United Nations on the cholera outbreak in South Sudan; an August 3, 2016, press release from the United Nations on the humanitarian crisis in South Sudan; and a press release from the Ethiopian Ministry of Foreign Affairs on September 30, 2016, announcing the border demarcation agreement.

UN Secretary-General Responds to Fighting in South Sudan

July 10, 2016

I am shocked and appalled by the heavy fighting that is currently taking place in Juba. I strongly urge President Kiir and First Vice-President Riek Machar to do everything within their power to de-escalate the hostilities immediately and to order their respective forces to disengage and withdraw to their bases. This senseless violence is unacceptable and has the potential of reversing the progress made so far in the peace process.

United Nations compounds and protection of civilians sites in Juba have been caught in the cross-fire. I am deeply frustrated that despite commitments by South Sudan's leaders, fighting has resumed. They must take decisive action to regain control of the security situation in Juba; prevent the spread of violence to other parts of the country; guarantee the safety and security of civilians, United Nations and other personnel; and genuinely commit themselves to the full implementation of the peace agreement.

The United Nations Mission in South Sudan continues to protect displaced civilians and engage all stakeholders in order to end the fighting and restore security.

SOURCE: United Nations Secretary-General. "Statement by the Secretary-General on South Sudan." July 10, 2016. http://www.un.org/sg/en/content/sg/statement/2016-07-10/statement-secretary-general-south-sudan.

UN Security Council Remarks on Violence in South Sudan

July 10, 2016

The following Security Council press statement was issued today by Council President Koro Bessho (Japan):

The members of the Security Council condemned in the strongest terms the escalation of fighting in Juba, South Sudan, that started on 7 July. The members of the Security Council expressed particular shock and outrage at the attacks on United Nations compounds and protection of civilians sites in Juba. The members of the Security Council condemned in the strongest terms all attacks and provocations against civilians and the United Nations. They expressed their condolences and sympathies to the families of Chinese and Rwandan peacekeepers who were killed or injured in the attacks. They emphasized the need for United Nations protection of civilians sites and United Nations personnel to remain secure.

The members of the Security Council urged an immediate end to the fighting by all concerned and demanded that President Salva Kiir and First Vice-President Riek Machar do their utmost to control their respective forces, urgently end the fighting and prevent the spread of violence and genuinely commit themselves to the full and immediate implementation of the peace agreement, including the permanent ceasefire and redeployment of military forces from Juba.

The members of the Security Council reminded all parties, including Government security forces, of the civilian character of the protection of civilians sites in South Sudan. The members of the Security Council stressed that attacks against civilians and United Nations premises and personnel may constitute war crimes and they emphasized the importance of transparent investigations into these crimes and that those involved must be held accountable and could be potentially subject to sanctions as authorized under resolution 2206 (2015) for actions that threaten the peace, security or stability of South Sudan.

The members of the Security Council encouraged countries in the region, the African Union Peace and Security Council and the Inter-Governmental Authority on Development to continue firmly engaging with South Sudanese leaders to address the crisis.

The members of the Security Council expressed their support for the United Nations Mission in South Sudan (UNMISS). The members of the Security Council expressed their readiness to consider enhancing UNMISS to better ensure that UNMISS and the international community can prevent and respond to violence in South Sudan. The members of the Security Council encouraged States in the region to prepare to provide additional troops in the event the Council so decides. In the interim, the members of the Security Council stressed the need for UNMISS to make full use of its authority to use all necessary means to protect civilians.

SOURCE: United Nations. "Security Council Press Statement on Escalation of Fighting in Juba, South Sudan." July 10, 2016. http://www.un.org/press/en/2016/sc12441.doc.htm.

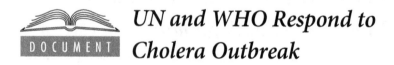

UN and WHO Respond to Cholera Outbreak

July 27, 2016

The United Nations and its partners are rushing to ramp up support for South Sudan's fight to contain a cholera outbreak through measures, including an oral vaccination campaign to reach over 14,000 people and the creation of treatment and rehydration centres.

Across the country, 271 cholera cases have been reported, including 14 deaths since 12 July 2016.

"Cholera is an acute diarrhoeal disease that causes massive loss of body fluids and can be deadly within hours if not adequately treated," Dr. Abdulmumini Usman, Country Representative of the World Health Organization (WHO) for South Sudan, said in a press release.

WHO is taking all the necessary control measures to support the Ministry of Health to respond to the situation urgently, and put an end to this outbreak, he added.

With the conditions favourable for transmission of cholera due to increased population displacement, overcrowding, poor hygiene and sanitation, this outbreak could further exacerbate an already weak health system which is also battling malnutrition, measles and malaria.

"The risk of further spread of diseases is a major concern. With the coming rains, it is realistic to expect an increase in malaria and water-borne diseases. Consequently, we can expect medical needs to increase in an environment where WHO and partners are already working hard to keep up with existing health needs," says Dr. Abdulmumini.

A National Cholera Taskforce, comprising the Ministry of Health, WHO, the UN Children's Fund (UNICEF), Médecins Sans Frontières (MSF) and other partners, has been activated and is providing oversight and coordination for the response to the cholera outbreak.

Treatment centre, rehydration points established

WHO, with support from partners, has established a cholera treatment centre capable of treating 100 patients at Juba Teaching Hospital, while strengthening disease surveillance and comprehensive disease investigation, including following up on people who may have come into contact with the disease.

To improve access to timely rehydration, UNICEF supported the establishment of eight oral rehydration points.

WHO, along with the Ministry of Health and partners, was set to launch an oral cholera vaccination campaign from Tuesday at various sites including communities in Gorom and Giada and special populations such as internally displaced people in Tomping, in order to reach over 14,000 people.

Additionally, WHO and partners are supporting social mobilization and community engagement activities. The media is currently airing cholera prevention messages and a toll-free phone line to report cholera cases has been activated.

WHO and partners have delivered supplies including tents and cholera kits that provide treatment for 400 people. To improve case detection and treatment of cholera, WHO has also distributed cholera preparedness and response guidelines.

More funds needed

With 4.4 million people in need of health assistance, funding is urgently needed to respond to the rising needs. The South Sudan Humanitarian Response Plan launched earlier this year requests $110 million, of which $31.3 million, or 29 per cent, has been received.

Of this amount, WHO requires $17.5 million for this year, of which only $4.3 million has been received.

"We have this opportunity to save, improve and protect the health of millions of people before it gets worse," said Dr. Abdulmumini. "WHO is committed to containing the cholera outbreak in South Sudan but, without urgent funding, we cannot implement most of the planned interventions. We need donors and partners to urgently fund our operations."

SOURCE: United Nations News Centre. "UN rushes to ramp up support for South Sudan's battle against cholera outbreak." July 27, 2016. http://www.un.org/apps/news/story.asp?NewsID=54566#.WJm_uhjMwRF.

UN Condemns Violence against Humanitarian Workers

August 3, 2016

United Nations Under-Secretary-General for Humanitarian Affairs and Emergency Relief Coordinator, Stephen O'Brien, concluded his three-day mission to South Sudan today, calling for all parties to uphold their responsibilities to protect civilians, amidst fresh fighting that has displaced tens of thousands of people in multiple locations across the country.

"The people of this country have suffered far too much, and for far too long," said USG O'Brien. "I am outraged by the heinous acts of violence that have been committed against civilians, including by members of the armed forces, and call for swift and decisive action to halt these abuses and bring the perpetrators to account."

The humanitarian situation in South Sudan is catastrophic. More than half of the population—some 6.1 million people—are in need of humanitarian assistance. An estimated 4.8 million people are severely food insecure across the country, with a quarter of a million children facing severe acute malnutrition. Forced displacement remains a defining feature of the crisis, with some 1.6 million people internally displaced, and more than 900,000 having fled to neighbouring countries, including more than 60,000 who fled to Uganda in July alone. Protection of civilians is a paramount concern, with extensive reports received of rape and other forms of sexual violence during recent fighting, including in Juba and Wau.

"My visit to Wau and Aweil was heart-wrenching," said the Emergency Relief Coordinator. "The women I met in both locations told me that it is a daily struggle to keep themselves and their children alive, one for fear of violence, the other due to hunger."

So far this year, aid workers have reached more than 2.8 million people with assistance and protection. However, the Humanitarian Response Plan for 2016 is only 40 per cent funded, leaving a gap of US$765 million. More funding is urgently required for the scale-up of the response across the country.

Humanitarians from the UN and non-governmental organizations are ready to do so, but the resources are needed now. Moreover, violence against aid workers and assets remains prevalent in South Sudan, as evidenced by the looting of vital humanitarian warehouses during and after the fighting in Juba. Since December 2013, at least 57 aid workers have been killed in South Sudan, including one killed during the recent conflict in Juba. Many more are still missing.

"Despite the daily challenges they face, aid workers across South Sudan—particularly NGOs on the frontlines of humanitarian action—are working tirelessly and courageously to bring desperately needed relief to people in need," said Mr. O'Brien. "I categorically condemn all attacks against aid workers and assets and call on all those in leadership positions to step up and take action against these wholly unacceptable incidents. It is imperative that humanitarian organizations are granted free, safe, and unhindered humanitarian access, to reach all people in need, wherever they are."

During his three-day visit, Mr. O'Brien met with humanitarian partners and Government officials, and visited people affected by the crisis in Juba, Wau and Aweil. In his meetings, the Emergency Relief Coordinator stressed that, "We humanitarians are here in South Sudan to save lives and for no other reason. Our task and our demand by the

UN and beyond is to impartially meet the urgent and severe humanitarian and protection needs of the millions of suffering people in this country."

SOURCE: United Nations Office of the Coordination of Humanitarian Affairs. "UN Humanitarian Chief Condemns Violence Against Civilians and Aid Workers in South Sudan." August 3, 2016. http://reliefweb.int/sites/reliefweb.int/files/resources/SouthSudan_USG_O_Brien_condemns_violence_against_civilians_and_aid_workers.pdf.

Sudan and South Sudan Complete Additional Border Demarcation Work

September 30, 2016

The sixth Joint Border Commission meeting between Sudan and South Sudan that ended on Thursday last week (September 29) in Addis Ababa, provided new momentum to speed up the remaining issues between them and consolidate their bilateral relations in different ways. The four-day meeting, held under the auspices of the African Union, was a milestone of significance opening a new chapter as the two sides signed a number of documents regarding border demarcation.

The documents approved by the Joint Border Commission covered various topics, including the list of procedural provisions of the Commission, a list of the terms of reference for the Joint Technical Team, the border line demarcation budget and work plan, and the report of the outcome of the sixth meeting. The official Sudan news agency, SUNA, added that it was agreed that the Joint Border Commission would hold its seventh meeting in Addis Ababa in November.

This round of the joint Border Commission was co-chaired by Sudan's Al-Rasheed Haroun, State Minister at the Presidency and South Sudan's Michael Makuei, Minister of Information. Mr. Makuei said subsequently that the South Sudan delegation had signed all the documents agreed in the meeting and said firmly that the Commission was a right course moving ahead in addressing border issues. State Minister Al-Rasheed Haroun also emphasized his commitment to resolve any remaining issues at the next meeting of the joint commission due in November, 2016.

The endorsement of the documents by both parties marks a new stage in the implementation of the Cooperation Agreements signed between Sudan and South Sudan in September 2012 under the auspices of the AU High-Level Implementation Panel (AUHIP). The undisputed areas of the border between the two countries have not been demarcated since South Sudan's independence five years ago. Talks between the two sides over delimitation of the disputed areas which make up about 20% of the border, are continuing. These disputed and claimed areas of the border include Abyei, the 14-Mile area, Joudat Al-Fakhar, Jebel al-Migainais, Kaka, and KafiaKingi enclave (Hofrat al-Nahas).

The two countries signed a series of cooperation agreements on various fields of common interest ranging from oil, citizenship rights, security issues, and banking to border trade in September 2012. In March 2013, they signed an implementation matrix to turn their cooperation agreements into action. Little progress has been made since then. Now, this latest round of talks, in addition to the endorsement of demarcation documents, represents an encouraging step towards fast-tracking implementation of the cooperation agreements, demarcation, and delimitation of the remaining disputed boundary areas.

SOURCE: Federal Democratic Republic of Ethiopia Ministry of Foreign Affairs. "Sudan and South Sudan endorse border demarcation documents." September 30, 2016. http://www.mfa.gov.et/-/sudan-and-south-sudan-endorse-border-demarcation-documents.

OTHER HISTORIC DOCUMENTS OF INTEREST

FROM PREVIOUS *HISTORIC DOCUMENTS*

- ■ President of South Sudan on Nation's Independence, *2011*, p. 447

President Obama Responds to Police Shootings; Officers Acquitted in Freddie Gray Case

JULY 12, 17, AND 18, AND AUGUST 10, 2016

In 2014 and 2015, a spate of incidents involving the deaths of unarmed African American men at the hands of police sparked a divisive national conversation about race and racism in America as well as policing practices and use of force. The national dialogue reached a fever pitch in 2016 following two shootings that targeted local law enforcement and killed eight police officers in Dallas, Texas, and Baton Rouge, Louisiana. Both attacks were carried out by African American men motivated by anger over the shootings of other black men. The conversation was also shaped by ongoing legal proceedings against officers charged in the death of Freddie Gray, a black Baltimore man who sustained fatal injuries while in police custody in April 2015. In the wake of these events, public officials called for unity and understanding, while police departments adopted new strategies to better protect their officers.

DALLAS OFFICERS SHOT

On July 7, 2016, hundreds of demonstrators gathered for a peaceful march through downtown Dallas to protest the deaths of Alton Sterling and Philando Castile. Sterling was shot and killed by officers two days earlier in Baton Rouge. He was selling CDs and DVDs outside a convenience store when a homeless man approached and persistently asked Sterling for money. Sterling showed the man his gun in an attempt to dissuade him, which led the man to call the police. Police tackled Sterling, then shot him several times after he had been restrained. The officers later said they thought Sterling was reaching for a gun before they shot him. The following day, Philando Castile was pulled over by cops in Falcon Heights, Minnesota, for a broken taillight. Castile informed the officer that he had a firearm before reaching for—and stating that he was getting—his wallet. The officer shot Castile multiple times. Castile's fiancée was also in the car and live-streamed the moments after the shooting on Facebook.

The Dallas protest was organized by Black Lives Matter, a movement that began as a Twitter hashtag following the 2012 shooting of Trayvon Martin, an unarmed black teenager. It has since grown to comprise thirty-eight local chapters that have organized protests around the country. The group states that it is "rooted in the experiences of Black people in this country who actively resist our dehumanization" and "is a call to action and a response to the virulent anti-Black racism that permeates our society."

At the Dallas demonstration just before 9:00 p.m., Micah Xavier Johnson, a twenty-five-year-old African American Army veteran, began shooting at officers assigned to protect the gathering. Officers Lorne Aherns, Michael Smith, Michael Krol, Patrick Zamarripa, and Brent Thompson were killed, and another seven officers were wounded, in what became the deadliest single incident for law enforcement since September 11, 2001. Johnson was eventually cornered in the El Centro Community College building, where a standoff with police ensued. Johnson reportedly told negotiators that he was upset about the recent shootings of black men and wanted to kill white people, especially white police officers. He said that more officers were going to be hurt and that bombs were planted all over downtown Dallas. (Police did not find any explosives when they swept the area.) After hours of unsuccessful negotiations, police exchanged gunfire with Johnson before sending a bomb robot carrying an explosive device toward Johnson's location and detonating the device. Johnson was killed in the explosion.

A vigil honoring the victims was held in Dallas on July 8, and a memorial service took place on July 12. Former president George W. Bush and President Barack Obama spoke at the service. In his remarks, Obama observed that "the overwhelming majority of police officers do an incredibly hard and dangerous job fairly and professionally," but also that "centuries of racial discrimination . . . didn't simply vanish with the end of lawful segregation" and that "no institution is entirely immune" from the bias that remains. He encouraged protestors and those in law enforcement to try to understand each other. "With an open heart, we can abandon the overheated rhetoric and the oversimplification that reduces whole categories of our fellow Americans, not just to opponents, but to enemies," he said.

The Fraternal Order of Police criticized Obama's response and called for the shooting to be investigated as a hate crime. William Johnson, executive director for the National Association of Police Organizations, blamed the Obama administration for appeasing those who attacked police and declared that "a war on cops" was underway. These sentiments echoed those expressed by Blue Lives Matter, a movement formed by police officers and their families to counter what they perceive as "the vilification of law enforcement" and "to change these wrongs to law enforcement and once again shed positive light on America's heroes to help boost morale and gain society's much needed support." In a blog post the day after the shooting, the group wrote, "With a president dividing with political fervor and a media ruthlessly hunting for ratings, we have lost 5 heroes. . . . All in the name of what? A racially fueled hate group? Terrorists?" The father of one of the fallen officers filed a lawsuit against Black Lives Matter and others, including Al Sharpton, the New Black Panthers Party, and the National Action Network, claiming that Johnson was acting as an agent for those organizations and individuals. Black Lives Matter condemned the shooting.

A few days after the shooting, Dallas police chief David Brown told protestors that if they wanted to improve the Dallas Police Department, they should join it. "Serve your communities. We're hiring," he said. "Get off that protest line and put an application in. We'll put you in your neighborhood and we will help you resolve some of the problems you're protesting about." Brown's call to action appeared to work: the department received 467 applications between July 8 and July 20—a 344 percent increase over the same period in June.

POLICE AMBUSHED IN BATON ROUGE

On July 17, two days after Alton Sterling's funeral, Officers Montrell Jackson, Matthew Gerald, and Brad Garafola were killed and three other officers were wounded in an attack about a mile from the police station in Baton Rouge. Around 8:40 a.m., police received a call about a "suspicious person walking down Airline Highway with an assault rifle." When police arrived at the scene, they were ambushed by Gavin Long, a twenty-nine-year-old former Marine from Kansas City. Long was killed in a gunfight with police and SWAT team members following the attack.

A week before the shooting occurred, the Louisiana State Police announced it had received threats against the Baton Rouge police. Following the incident, state police superintendent Col. Michael Edmonson said that there was "no doubt whatsoever that these officers were intentionally targeted and assassinated" by Long. Based on surveillance footage, officials reported that Long appeared to be searching for police officers, and they noted that he ignored civilians in the area of the shooting. Long also recorded and posted a video online prior to the incident in which he said, "Zero have been successful just over simple protesting. . . . You gotta fight back."

Louisiana Governor John Bel Edwards condemned the "absolutely unspeakable heinous attack," as did Quinyetta McMillon, mother of Alton Sterling's son. "We are disgusted by the despicable act of violence today that resulted in the shooting deaths of members of the Baton Rouge law enforcement," she said. Obama recognized the officers for their service and mourned their loss during a press conference about the shooting. He declared that "attacks on police are an attack on all of us and the rule of law that makes society possible." Obama acknowledged that the country's divisions "are not new" and are sometimes amplified by social media and the twenty-four-hour news cycle. He also directed a portion of his remarks at those running for office in the 2016 election. "I know we're about to enter a couple of weeks of conventions where our political rhetoric tends to be more overheated than usual," he said. "And that is why it is so important that everyone—regardless of race or political party or profession, regardless of what organizations you are a part of—everyone right now focus on words and actions that can unite this country rather than divide it further." A memorial service for the slain officers was held in Baton Rouge on July 28.

In the aftermath of both shootings, police departments across the country began to adjust policing practices to provide increased protection for officers. This included mandating that officers conduct patrols in pairs. While previously a standard practice, many departments limited patrols to one officer amid budget cuts and staffing limitations. The Baltimore Police Department began requiring two police cars to respond to all calls, while the Los Angeles Police Department temporarily shifted staff to provide more assistance to those on patrol and increased the number of helicopters flying over the city. Several departments also moved to increase security around antipolice protests and demonstrations.

THE FREDDIE GRAY CASE

While the nation reacted to the killings of police officers and black men alike, legal proceedings against the officers involved in the Freddie Gray case continued in Baltimore. Gray, a twenty-five-year-old black man, died on April 19, 2015, due to injuries sustained while in police custody. According to police, Gray ran away "unprovoked" from three officers who tried to approach him on April 12. The police said they suspected Gray was "immediately involved or had been recently involved in criminal activity" and pursued him, apprehending Gray a couple of blocks away. Gray was shackled and handcuffed and loaded into the back of a police van, but not secured by a seat belt. Gray was unresponsive when they arrived at the police station. The police said they called for medical help about a half hour after returning to the station, but Gray's family alleged they waited at least an hour. Gray died from severe neck injuries a week later, and the medical examiner ruled his death a homicide. Baltimore erupted in mostly peaceful protests following Gray's death, but protest turned to rioting, looting, and arson the day of Gray's funeral. City officials imposed a curfew and Maryland Governor Larry Hogan summoned the National Guard.

The six officers involved in the incident were charged with second-degree depraved-heart murder or manslaughter, reckless endangerment, and misconduct in office. Prosecutors claimed the officers had acted unreasonably and disregarded their training and orders when they did not secure Gray with a seat belt and did not seek medical help quickly. All officers pleaded not guilty. Their attorneys argued that the cops had acted reasonably and professionally and had nothing to do with Gray's death, which they described as a tragic accident.

Each of the officers faced a trial. The first, held in December 2015 for Officer William Porter, ended with a hung jury and was declared a mistrial. Lt. Brian Rice and Officers Edward Nero and Ceasar Goodson were acquitted by Judge Barry Williams during bench trials in May, June, and July 2016. Determining that convictions were unlikely in the remaining trials, prosecutors dropped all charges on July 27. Baltimore State's Attorney Marilyn Mosby defended her decision to bring the charges considering the medical examiner's findings and said the outcome of the cases showed "an inherent bias that is a direct result of when police police themselves." Gene Ryan, president of the Baltimore Fraternal Order of Police, decried Mosby's comments as "outrageous and uncalled for and simply untrue," adding that "justice has been done." Police Commissioner Kevin Davis called the decision to drop charges a "wise one" and urged Baltimoreans "to direct our emotions in a constructive way to reduce violence and strengthen citizen partnerships." The six officers now face administrative reviews and possible discipline.

Two weeks after the charges were dropped, the U.S. Justice Department released the findings of its investigation into the Baltimore Police Department's policing practices, which the department initiated in May 2015. The investigation found "reasonable cause to believe that the Baltimore City Police Department engages in a pattern or practice of conduct that violates the First and Fourth Amendments of the Constitution as well as federal anti-discrimination laws." The department went on to state that "BPD makes stops, searches, and arrests without the required justification; uses enforcement strategies that unlawfully subject African Americans to disproportionate rates of stops, searches, and arrests; uses excessive force; and retaliates against individuals for their constitutionally-protected expression." City officials agreed to work with the Justice Department on a plan to address the issues identified by the investigation, including by investing in technology and infrastructure that would allow for more effective monitoring of officer activity and by making changes to policies, training, and data collection practices to ensure officers' actions comply with the law. The police department is expected to reach out to and involve the community in the development of its plan. "We have begun this journey to reform long-standing issues in many real, tangible ways," said Davis. "DOJ's findings will serve to solidify our road map."

—Linda Fecteau Grimm

Following are remarks by President Barack Obama at a memorial service for the Dallas police officers on July 12, 2016; remarks by Obama from July 17, 2016, during a press conference about the Baton Rouge shooting; the U.S. Circuit Court for Baltimore City, Maryland's ruling from July 18, 2016, in the case of State of Maryland vs. Brian Rice; *and the executive summary from the U.S. Department of Justice's report on its investigation into the Baltimore City Police Department, released on August 10, 2016.*

President Obama Speaks at Memorial Service for Dallas Police Officers

DOCUMENT

July 12, 2016

Thank you very much. . . . Scripture tells us that in our sufferings there is glory, "because we know that suffering produces perseverance; perseverance, character; and character, hope." Now, sometimes, the truths of these words are hard to see. Right now those words test us. Because the people of Dallas—people across the country—are suffering.

We're here to honor the memory, and mourn the loss, of five fellow Americans; to grieve with their loved ones, to support this community, to pray for the wounded, and to try and find some meaning amidst our sorrow. . . .

Like police officers across the country, these men and their families shared a commitment to something larger than themselves. They weren't looking for their names to be up in lights. They'd tell you the pay was decent, but wouldn't make you rich. They could have told you about the stress and long shifts, and they'd probably agree with Chief Brown when he said that cops don't expect to hear the words "thank you" very often, especially from those who need them the most.

No, the reward comes in knowing that our entire way of life in America depends on the rule of law; that the maintenance of that law is a hard and daily labor; that in this country, we don't have soldiers in the streets or militias setting the rules. Instead, we have public servants—police officers—like the men who were taken away from us.

And that's what these five were doing last Thursday when they were assigned to protect and keep orderly a peaceful protest in response to the killing of Alton Sterling of Baton Rouge and Philando Castile of Minnesota. They were upholding the constitutional rights of this country.

For a while, the protest went on without incident. And despite the fact that police conduct was the subject of the protest, despite the fact that there must have been signs or slogans or chants with which they profoundly disagreed, these men and this department did their jobs like the professionals that they were. . . .

And then, around 9 o'clock, the gunfire came. Another community torn apart. More hearts broken. More questions about what caused, and what might prevent, another such tragedy.

I know that Americans are struggling right now with what we've witnessed over the past week. First, the shootings in Minnesota and Baton Rouge and the protests, then the targeting of police by the shooter here, an act not just of demented violence, but of racial hatred. All of it's left us wounded and angry and hurt. It's as if the deepest faultlines of our democracy have suddenly been exposed, perhaps even widened. And although we know that such divisions are not new—though they've surely been worse in even the recent past—that offers us little comfort.

Faced with this violence, we wonder if the divides of race in America can ever be bridged. We wonder if an African American community that feels unfairly targeted by police, and police departments that feel unfairly maligned for doing their jobs, can ever understand each other's experience. We turn on the TV or surf the Internet, and we can watch positions harden and lines drawn, and people retreat to their respective corners, and politicians calculate how to grab attention or avoid the fallout. We see all this, and it's hard not to think sometimes that the center won't hold and that things might get worse.

I understand. I understand how Americans are feeling. But, Dallas, I'm here to say we must reject such despair. I'm here to insist that we are not as divided as we seem. And I know that because I know America. I know how far we've come against impossible odds. I know we'll make it because of what I've experienced in my own life, what I've seen of this country and its people—their goodness and decency—as President of the United States. And I know it because of what we've seen here in Dallas, how all of you, out of great suffering, have shown us the meaning of perseverance and character and hope. . . .

In the aftermath of the shooting, we've seen Mayor Rawlings and Chief Brown, a White man and a Black man with different backgrounds, working not just to restore order and support a shaken city, a shaken department, but working together to unify a city with strength and grace and wisdom. And in the process, we've been reminded that the Dallas Police Department has been at the forefront of improving relations between police and the community. The murder rate here has fallen. Complaints of excessive force have been cut by 64 percent. The Dallas Police Department has been doing it the right way. And so, Mayor Rawlings and Chief Brown, on behalf of the American people, thank you for your steady leadership, thank you for your powerful example. We could not be prouder of you.

These men, this department, these—this is the America I know. And today, in this audience, I see people who have protested on behalf of criminal justice reform grieving alongside police officers. I see people who mourn for the five officers we lost, but also weep for the families of Alton Sterling and Philando Castile. In this audience, I see what's possible when we recognize that we are one American family, all deserving of equal treatment, all deserving of equal respect, all children of God. That's the America I know. . . .

We know that the overwhelming majority of police officers do an incredibly hard and dangerous job fairly and professionally. They are deserving of our respect and not our scorn. And when anyone, no matter how good their intentions may be, paints all police as biased or bigoted, we undermine those officers we depend on for our safety. And as for those who use rhetoric suggesting harm to police, even if they don't act on it themselves, well, they not only make the jobs of police officers even more dangerous, but they do a disservice to the very cause of justice that they claim to promote.

We also know that centuries of racial discrimination—of slavery and subjugation and Jim Crow—they didn't simply vanish with the end of lawful segregation. They didn't just stop when Dr. King made a speech or the Voting Rights Act and the Civil Rights Act were signed. Race relations have improved dramatically in my lifetime. Those who deny it are dishonoring the struggles that helped us achieve that progress.

But we know—but, America, we know that bias remains. We know it. Whether you are Black or White or Hispanic or Asian or Native American or of Middle Eastern descent, we have all seen this bigotry in our own lives at some point. We've heard it at times in our own homes. If we're honest, perhaps we've heard prejudice in our own heads and felt it in our own hearts. We know that. And while some suffer far more under racism's burden, some feel to a far greater extent discrimination's sting; although most of us do our best to guard against it and teach our children better, none of us is entirely innocent. No institution is entirely immune. And that includes our police departments. We know this.

And so when African Americans from all walks of life, from different communities across the country, voice a growing despair over what they perceive to be unequal treatment; when study after study shows that Whites and people of color experience the criminal justice system differently so that if you're Black you're more likely to be pulled over or searched or arrested, more likely to get longer sentences, more likely to get the death penalty for the same crime; when mothers and fathers raise their kids right and have "the talk" about how to respond if stopped by a police officer—"yes, sir," "no, sir"—but still fear that something terrible may happen when their child walks out the door, still fear that kids being stupid and not quite doing things right might end in tragedy—when all this takes place more than 50 years after the passage of the Civil Rights Act, we cannot simply turn away and dismiss those in peaceful protest as troublemakers or paranoid. We can't simply dismiss it as a symptom of political correctness or reverse racism. To have your experience denied like that, dismissed by those in authority, dismissed perhaps even by your White friends and coworkers and fellow church members again and again and again, it hurts. Surely, we can see that, all of us.

We also know what Chief Brown has said is true: That so much of the tensions between police departments and minority communities that they serve is because we ask the police to do too much and we ask too little of ourselves. As a society, we choose to underinvest in decent schools. We allow poverty to fester so that entire neighborhoods offer no prospect for gainful employment. We refuse to fund drug treatment and mental health programs. We flood communities with so many guns that it is easier for a teenager to buy a Glock than get his hands on a computer or even a book, and then we tell the police, "You're a social worker, you're the parent, you're the teacher, you're the drug counselor." We tell them to keep those neighborhoods in check at all costs and do so without causing any political blowback or inconvenience. . . .

I confess that sometimes I, too, experience doubt. I've been to too many of these things. I've seen too many families go through this. But then I am reminded of what the Lord tells Ezekiel. "I will give you a new heart," the Lord says, "and put a new spirit in you. I will remove from you your heart of stone and give you a heart of flesh."

That's what we must pray for, each of us: a new heart. Not a heart of stone, but a heart open to the fears and hopes and challenges of our fellow citizens. That's what we've seen in Dallas these past few days. That's what we must sustain.

Because with an open heart, we can learn to stand in each other's shoes and look at the world through each other's eyes so that maybe the police officer sees his own son in that teenager with a hoodie who's kind of goofing off, but not dangerous; and the teenager, maybe the teenager will see in the police officer the same words and values and authority of his parents.

With an open heart, we can abandon the overheated rhetoric and the oversimplification that reduces whole categories of our fellow Americans, not just to opponents, but to enemies. With an open heart, those protesting for change will guard against reckless language going forward, look at the model set by the five officers we mourn today, acknowledge the progress brought about by the sincere efforts of police departments like this one in Dallas, and embark on the hard but necessary work of negotiation, the pursuit of reconciliation.

With an open heart, police departments will acknowledge that, just like the rest of us, they are not perfect; that insisting we do better to root out racial bias is not an attack on cops, but an effort to live up to our highest ideals. And I understand, these protests—I see them—they can be messy. Sometimes, they can be hijacked by an irresponsible few. Police can get hurt. Protestors can get hurt. They can be frustrating. . . .

With an open heart, we can worry less about which side has been wronged and worry more about joining sides to do right. Because the vicious killer of these police officers, they won't be the last person who tries to make us turn on one other. . . .

America does not ask us to be perfect. Precisely because of our individual imperfections, our Founders gave us institutions to guard against tyranny and ensure no one is above the law; a democracy that gives us the space to work through our differences and debate them peacefully, to make things better, even if it doesn't always happen as fast as we'd like. America gives us the capacity to change.

But as the men we mourn today—these five heroes—knew better than most, we cannot take the blessings of this Nation for granted. Only by working together can we preserve those institutions of family and community, rights and responsibilities, law and self-government that is the hallmark of this Nation. For, it turns out, we do not persevere alone. Our character is not found in isolation. Hope does not arise by putting our fellow man down, it is found by lifting others up.

And that's what I take away from the lives of these outstanding men. The pain we feel may not soon pass, but my faith tells me that they did not die in vain. I believe our sorrow can make us a better country. I believe our righteous anger can be transformed into more justice and more peace. Weeping may endure for a night, but I'm convinced joy comes in the morning. We cannot match the sacrifices made by Officers Zamarripa and Ahrens, Krol, Smith, and Thompson, but surely we can try to match their sense of service. We cannot match their courage, but we can strive to match their devotion.

May God bless their memory. May God bless this country that we love.

SOURCE: Executive Office of the President. "Remarks at a Memorial Service for Victims of the Shootings in Dallas, Texas." July 12, 2016. *Compilation of Presidential Documents* 2016, no. 00461 (July 12, 2016). http://www.gpo.gov/fdsys/pkg/DCPD-201600461/pdf/DCPD-201600461.pdf.

President Obama Remarks on the Shooting of Police Officers in Baton Rouge

DOCUMENT

July 17, 2016

Good afternoon, everybody. As all of you know now, this morning three law enforcement officers in Baton Rouge were killed in the line of duty. Three others were wounded. One is still in critical condition.

As of right now, we don't know the motive of the killer. We don't know whether the killer set out to target police officers or whether he gunned them down as they responded to a call. Regardless of motive, the death of these three brave officers underscores the danger that police across the country confront every single day. And we as a nation have to be loud and clear that nothing justifies violence against law enforcement. Attacks on police are an attack on all of us and the rule of law that makes society possible. . . .

Most of all, our hearts go out to the families who are grieving. Our prayers go out to the officer who is still fighting for his life. This has happened far too often. And I've spent a lot of time with law enforcement this past week. . . . And I know whenever this happens, wherever this happens, you feel it. Your families feel it. But what I want you to know today is the respect and the gratitude of the American people for everything that you do for us.

And 5 days ago, I traveled to Dallas for the memorial service of the officers who were slain there. I said that that killer would not be the last person who tries to make us turn on each other. Nor will today's killer. It remains up to us to make sure that they fail. That decision is all of ours: the decision to make sure that our best selves are reflected across America, not our worst—that's up to us.

We have our divisions, and they are not new. Around-the-clock news cycles and social media sometimes amplify these divisions, and I know we're about to enter a couple of weeks of conventions where our political rhetoric tends to be more overheated than usual.

And that is why it is so important that everyone—regardless of race or political party or profession, regardless of what organizations you are a part of—everyone right now focus on words and actions that can unite this country rather than divide it further. We don't need inflammatory rhetoric. We don't need careless accusations thrown around to score political points or to advance an agenda. We need to temper our words and open our hearts, all of us. . . . And it is up to all of us to make sure we are part of the solution and not part of the problem.

Someone once wrote, "A bullet need happen only once, but for peace to work, we need to be reminded of its existence again and again and again."

My fellow Americans, only we can prove, through words and through deeds, that we will not be divided. And we're going to have to keep on doing it "again and again and again." That's how this country gets united. . . . And that's the best way for us to honor the sacrifice of the brave police officers who were taken from us this morning.

May God bless them and their families, and may God bless the United States of America. Thank you very much.

SOURCE: Executive Office of the President. "Remarks on the Shooting of Law Enforcement Officers in Baton Rouge, Louisiana." July 17, 2016. *Compilation of Presidential Documents* 2016, no. 00471 (July 17, 2016). http://www.gpo.gov/fdsys/pkg/DCPD-201600471/pdf/DCPD-201600471.pdf.

DOCUMENT   *State of Maryland vs. Brian Rice*

July 18, 2016

THE COURT: The court will issue it's [*sic*] ruling.

The State has charged the defendant with Involuntary Manslaughter, Reckless Endangerment and Misconduct in Office. As the finder of fact, and in determining the outcome of the charges, the court must be guided by the law that pertains to the pending charges.

In order to convict the defendant of involuntary manslaughter, the State must prove that the defendant acted in a grossly negligent manner and that this grossly negligent conduct caused the death of Freddie Gray.

In order to convict the defendant of reckless endangerment, the State must prove that the defendant engaged in conduct that created a substantial risk of death or serious physical injury to another; that a reasonable person would not have engaged in that conduct and that the defendant acted recklessly.

Finally, in order to convict the defendant of misconduct in office the State must prove that the defendant was a public officer, that the defendant acted in his official capacity and that the defendant corruptly failed to do an act required by the duties of his office.

The State has the burden of proving, beyond a reasonable doubt, each and every element of the crimes charged. If the State fails to meet that burden for any element of any of the charged offenses, this court is constitutionally required to find the defendant not guilty of that crime. . . .

The State alleges that the failure to seat belt Mr. Gray, combined with his injuries that he suffered while in the van resulting in his death, constitute Involuntary Manslaughter. In order to convict the defendant of involuntary manslaughter the State must prove that the defendant acted in a grossly negligent manner; and that this grossly negligent conduct caused the death of Mr. Gray.

The term "grossly negligent" means that the defendant, while aware of the risk, acted in a manner that created a high risk to, and showed a reckless disregard for, human life. The evidence shows that Mr. Gray, while in the custody of the police at stop 1, was yelling as he entered the wagon. The evidence also shows that after Mr. Gray was place[d] in the wagon at stop 1, the defendant had a meeting with Officers Miller and Nero who were on the scene at stop 1 and had the initial interaction with Mr. Gray.

The court was not provided any evidence concerning what, if anything[,] the officers told the defendant about Mr. Gray's behavior and actions at stop 1. What is in evidence is that the defendant, during the discussion, made the decision to have Mr. Gray shackled and transported to the Western District instead of Central Booking. There are a number of possibilities the court could entertain, some that are innocent and some that are not. However, the burden of proof rests with the State, and the court's imaginings do not serve as a substitute for evidence.

At stop 2, Mr. Gray was removed from the wagon, recuffed, shackled and placed in the wagon without being seat-belted by the defendant. . . .

With the individuals in the area, having ordered Mr. Gray to Mount and Baker to switch cuffs, a decision was made to place shackles on him. The court does not know why that decision was made. . . . The State would have court to simply infer that it was for reasons that were criminal. In that vein, the State also seeks to have this court find that the failure to seatbelt, under the circumstances, was grossly negligent—not a mistake, not an error in judgment, but a grossly negligent act, that effectively, on its face should rise to the level of wanton and abandoned indifference to human life required to meet the standard of gross criminal negligence.

Based on the evidence presented, the court does not make that finding. Furthermore, this court does not find that the State has proven that the defendant was aware that the failure to seatbelt created a risk of death or serious physical injury to Mr. Gray under the facts presented. The State presented no evidence to this court concerning the defendant's training or knowledge concerning the issue of death or serious physical injury occurring in police transport vehicles. Even had that information been available and presented, this court would note that the State produced no evidence that the defendant, had he had been aware of the danger, consciously disregarded the risk when he did not seatbelt Mr. Gray. Finally, even if the court found that the failure to seatbelt Mr. Gray was grossly negligent conduct, which again the court does not, the State failed to prove beyond a reasonable doubt that the failure of the defendant to seatbelt Mr. Gray at stop 2 was the conduct that caused the death of Mr. Gray. For those reasons the court finds the defendant not guilty on the charge of Involuntary Manslaughter.

The State alleges that the failure of the defendant to seat belt Mr. Gray once he was placed back in the wagon at stop 2 rises to the level of reckless endangerment. In order to convict the defendant of reckless endangerment, the State must prove that the defendant engaged in conduct that created a substantial risk of death or serious physical injury to another. That a reasonable person would not have engaged in that conduct and that the defendant acted recklessly.

The defendant acted recklessly if he was aware that his conduct created a risk of death or serious physical injury to another and then he consciously disregarded that risk.

Reckless endangerment focuses on the actions of the defendant and whether or not his conduct created a substantial risk of death or injury to another. The crime occurs when the actions are found to be unreasonable under the circumstances presented. It does not focus on the end result which can be, and in this case was, charged as a separate crime. That crime was Involuntary Manslaughter.

Since again the conduct is the failure to seatbelt Mr. Gray, the analysis is similar to the analysis for Involuntary Manslaughter except there is no need for the court to determine whether the failure to seatbelt led to the death of Mr. Gray.

Md. Code Crim. Law, Section 3-204(a)(1) states that a person may not recklessly engage in conduct that creates a substantial risk of death or serious physical injury to another. However, Section 3-204(c)(1) states that (a)(1) does not apply to conduct involving the use of a motor vehicle as defined in Section 11-135 of the Transportation Article. Section 11-135 defines a motor vehicle as a vehicle that is self-propelled.

This Court finds that a police wagon or van constitutes a motor vehicle and that the reckless endangerment statute would prohibit prosecution of conduct arising from the use of a motor vehicle in this case, a police transport wagon. This court finds that the Reckless Endangerment charge should fail as a matter of law because the alleged reckless conduct is failing to seat belt Mr. Gray in a vehicle.

In order for the defendant's failure to seatbelt Mr. Gray to rise to the level of reckless conduct and create a risk of death or serious physical injury, there has to be some use and movement of the vehicle. The simple placement of a person in a vehicle that is not used, without seat-belting him, cannot and does not constitute a crime.

Therefore, the alleged misconduct on the defendant's part for failure to seatbelt would not fall within the conduct proscribed by this statute. Nevertheless, the court will review Reckless Endangerment solely in the context of the failure to seat belt.

Again, the State has failed to show that the defendant was aware, not that he should have been aware, but that he was aware that his conduct created a risk of death or serious physical injury. The State also failed to show that the defendant, even if he was aware of the risk, consciously disregarded that risk. So even looking at this charge solely on the issue of failing to seatbelt Mr. Gray, this court finds that the State has failed to meet the burden required and the verdict on the charge of Reckless Endangerment is not guilty.

This court finds that the State has failed to prove that the defendant's failure to seat belt Mr. Gray, under the circumstances presented at stop 2, was unreasonable. Given that the State did not charge the defendant with failing to render medical aid, and the State's failure to show that the defendant's failure to seatbelt Mr. Gray was grossly negligent, there is no need the for this court to assess the medical evidence and testimony presented at trial in reference to the charges. . . .

Finally, there is the misconduct charge stemming from the stop on Mount and Baker. The State alleges that the defendant failed to ensure Mr. Gray's safety when the defendant failed to secure him with a seatbelt during the process of Mr. Gray being transported in a police vehicle while in police custody. In order to convict the defendant the State must prove that the defendant was a public officer, that he acted in his official capacity[,] and that he corruptly failed to do an act required by the duties of his office.

There is no question that elements one and two of the misconduct charge are met since the defendant was a public officer acting in his capacity as a law enforcement officer on the day of Mr. Gray's arrest.

The State asserts the defendant failed to do an act required by his office, and that failure to act is corrupt behavior that warrants a conviction for misconduct.

While this court has already determined that the defendant is not guilty of reckless endangerment based on the facts presented, the court still must determine whether the State has provided sufficient evidence to prove beyond a reasonable doubt that the defendant corruptly failed to do an act that is required by the duties of his office. The comments to the Maryland Pattern Jury Instructions note that the committee chose not to define or explain "corrupt" or "corruptly" believing that the words communicate their meaning better than a definition would. A review of relevant case law shows that a police officer corruptly fails to do an act required by the duties of his office if he willfully fails or willfully neglects to perform the duty. A willful failure or willful neglect is one that is intentional, knowing and deliberate. A mere error in judgment is not enough to constitute corruption, but corruption does not require that the public official acted for any personal gain or benefit.

The court is satisfied that pursuant to General Order K-14, the defendant had a duty to assess whether or not to seatbelt Mr. Gray in the back of the van. While this court notes there is a duty to assess, the State retains the burden to present evidence that the defendant corruptly failed to follow his duty, not that the defendant [made] a mistake, and not that the defendant made an error in judgment. Rather, the State bears the burden to show that the defendant corruptly failed to follow his duty. The law is clear that the standard for the State to secure a criminal conviction is higher than mere civil negligence.

The State did not offer the defendant's academy records or training records into evidence. The court is mindful of the fact that as a discovery sanction, the State was precluded from presenting certain documents into evidence and that those documents may or may not have been relevant to the defendant's training concerning seat-belting a prisoner in a transport wagon. But again, the inability to present that evidence was based on a discovery violation by the State and the State must bear responsibility for its failure to provide discovery.

The State's choice not to, or inability to, produce such evidence would leave the court to merely assume facts, which of course, it cannot do.

In order for there to be a conviction the State must show not simply that the defendant failed to do an act required by the duties of his office but that the defendant corruptly failed to do an act required by the duties of his office. Here the duty stems from K-14, a Baltimore City Police Department General Order. The commission of a crime is not, and cannot be, simply equated to failure to follow a general order of the police department. The court notes that the duty does not stem from a federal, state or local statute or law. Case law makes it abundantly clear that a violation of a general order may be an indicator that there is a violation of criminal law, but failing to seatbelt a detainee in a transport wagon is not inherently criminal conduct. More must be proven for a conviction. As stated at the outset, the burden is on the State to prove the elements of each charge. It is not the defendant's job to disprove the allegations.

Here, the failure to seatbelt may have been a mistake or it may have been bad judgement, but without showing more than has been presented to the court concerning the failure to seatbelt and the surrounding circumstances, the State has failed to meet its burden to show that the actions of the defendant rose above mere civil negligence. What the court cannot do, based on the evidence presented, is find that that the defendant's failure to seatbelt Mr. Gray, based on all that went on at Mount and Baker, rose to the level of corruptly failing to do an act required.

For all the reasons stated, this court finds that the State has failed to meet its burden of proving that the defendant is guilty beyond a reasonable doubt of misconduct in office. Therefore the verdict is not guilty on all counts. This court is in recess.

SOURCE: U.S. Circuit Court for Baltimore City, Maryland. "State of Maryland vs. Brian Rice, Defendant." July 18, 2016. http://www.baltimorecitycourt.org/wp-content/uploads/2016/05/Rice-7-18-16-Ruling.pdf.

Executive Summary of the Department of Justice Report on Baltimore Police Department

August 10, 2016

[All footnotes have been omitted.]

Today, we announce the outcome of the Department of Justice's investigation of the Baltimore City Police Department (BPD). After engaging in a thorough investigation, initiated at the request of the City of Baltimore and BPD, the Department of Justice concludes that there is reasonable cause to believe that BPD engages in a pattern or practice of conduct that violates the Constitution or federal law. BPD engages in a pattern or practice of:

(1) making unconstitutional stops, searches, and arrests;

(2) using enforcement strategies that produce severe and unjustified disparities in the rates of stops, searches and arrests of African Americans;

(3) using excessive force; and

(4) retaliating against people engaging in constitutionally-protected expression.

This pattern or practice is driven by systemic deficiencies in BPD's policies, training, supervision, and accountability structures that fail to equip officers with the tools they need to police effectively and within the bounds of the federal law. . . .

We recognize the challenges faced by police officers in Baltimore and other communities around the country. Every day, police officers risk their lives to uphold the law and keep our communities safe. Investigatory stops, arrests, and force—including, at times, deadly force—are all necessary tools used by BPD officers to do their jobs and protect the safety of themselves and others. Providing policing services in many parts of Baltimore is particularly challenging, where officers regularly confront complex social problems rooted in poverty, racial segregation and deficient educational, employment and housing opportunities. Still, most BPD officers work hard to provide vital services to the community.

The pattern or practice occurs as a result of systemic deficiencies at BPD. The agency fails to provide officers with sufficient policy guidance and training; fails to collect and analyze data regarding officers' activities; and fails to hold officers accountable for misconduct. BPD also fails to equip officers with the necessary equipment and resources they need to police safely, constitutionally, and effectively. Each of these systemic deficiencies contributes to the constitutional and statutory violations we observed. . . .

UNCONSTITUTIONAL STOPS, SEARCHES, AND ARRESTS

BPD's legacy of zero tolerance enforcement continues to drive its policing in certain Baltimore neighborhoods and leads to unconstitutional stops, searches, and arrests. Many BPD supervisors instruct officers to make frequent stops and arrests—even for minor offenses and with minimal or no suspicion—without sufficient consideration of whether this enforcement strategy promotes public safety and community trust or conforms to constitutional standards. These instructions, coupled with minimal supervision and accountability for misconduct, lead to constitutional violations.

- Stops. BPD officers recorded over 300,000 pedestrian stops from January 2010–May 2015, and the true number of BPD's stops during this period is likely far higher due to under-reporting. These stops are concentrated in predominantly African-American neighborhoods and often lack reasonable suspicion.

    o BPD's pedestrian stops are concentrated on a small portion of Baltimore residents. BPD made roughly 44 percent of its stops in two small, predominantly African-American districts that contain only 11 percent of the City's population. Consequently, hundreds of individuals—nearly all of them African American—were stopped on at least 10 separate occasions from 2010–2015. Indeed, seven African-American men were stopped more than 30 times during this period.

    o BPD's stops often lack reasonable suspicion. Our review of incident reports and interviews with officers and community members found that officers regularly approach individuals standing or walking on City sidewalks to detain and question them and check for outstanding warrants, despite lacking reasonable suspicion to do so. Only 3.7 percent of pedestrian stops resulted in officers issuing a citation or making an arrest. And, as noted below, many of those arrested based upon pedestrian stops had their charges dismissed upon initial review by either supervisors at BPD's Central Booking or local prosecutors.

- Searches. During stops, BPD officers frequently pat-down or frisk individuals as a matter of course, without identifying necessary grounds to believe that the person is armed and dangerous. And even where an initial frisk is justified, we found that officers often violate the Constitution by exceeding the frisk's permissible scope. We likewise found many instances in which officers strip search individuals without legal justification. In some cases, officers performed degrading strip searches in public, prior to making an arrest, and without grounds to believe that the searched individuals were concealing contraband on their bodies.

- Arrests. We identified two categories of common unconstitutional arrests by BPD officers: (1) officers make warrantless arrests without probable cause; and (2) officers make arrests for misdemeanor offenses, such as loitering and trespassing, without providing the constitutionally-required notice that the arrested person was engaged in unlawful activity.

o Arrests without probable cause: from 2010–2015, supervisors at Baltimore's Central Booking and local prosecutors rejected over 11,000 charges made by BPD officers because they lacked probable cause or otherwise did not merit prosecution. Our review of incident reports describing warrantless arrests likewise found many examples of officers making unjustified arrests. In addition, officers extend stops without justification to search for evidence that would justify an arrest. These detentions—many of which last more than an hour—constitute unconstitutional arrests.

o Misdemeanor arrests without notice: BPD officers arrest individuals standing lawfully on public sidewalks for "loitering," "trespassing," or other misdemeanor offenses without providing adequate notice that the individuals were engaged in unlawful activity. Indeed, officers frequently invert the constitutional notice requirement. While the Constitution requires individuals to receive pre-arrest notice of the specific conduct prohibited as loitering or trespassing, BPD officers approach individuals standing lawfully on sidewalks in front of public housing complexes or private businesses and arrest them unless the individuals are able to "justify" their presence to the officers' satisfaction.

DISCRIMINATION AGAINST AFRICAN AMERICANS

BPD's targeted policing of certain Baltimore neighborhoods with minimal oversight or accountability disproportionately harms African-American residents. Racially disparate impact is present at every stage of BPD's enforcement actions, from the initial decision to stop individuals on Baltimore streets to searches, arrests, and uses of force. These racial disparities, along with evidence suggesting intentional discrimination, erode the community trust that is critical to effective policing.

- BPD disproportionately stops African-American pedestrians. Citywide, BPD stopped African-American residents three times as often as white residents after controlling for the population of the area in which the stops occurred. In each of BPD's nine police districts, African Americans accounted for a greater share of BPD's stops than the population living in the district. And BPD is far more likely to subject individual African Americans to multiple stops in short periods of time. In the five and a half years of data we examined, African Americans accounted for 95 percent of the 410 individuals BPD stopped at least 10 times. One African American man in his mid-fifties was stopped 30 times in less than 4 years. Despite these repeated intrusions, none of the 30 stops resulted in a citation or criminal charge.

- BPD also stops African American drivers at disproportionate rates. African Americans accounted for 82 percent of all BPD vehicle stops, compared to only 60 percent of the driving age population in the City and 27 percent of the driving age population in the greater metropolitan area.

- BPD disproportionately searches African Americans during stops. BPD searched African Americans more frequently during pedestrian and vehicle stops, even though searches of African Americans were less likely to discover contraband. Indeed, BPD officers found contraband twice as often when searching white individuals compared to African Americans during vehicle stops and 50 percent more often during pedestrian stops.

- African Americans similarly accounted for 86 percent of all criminal offenses charged by BPD officers despite making up only 63 percent of Baltimore residents.
  - o Racial disparities in BPD's arrests are most pronounced for highly discretionary offenses: African Americans accounted for 91 percent of the 1,800 people charged solely with "failure to obey" or "trespassing"; 89 percent of the 1,350 charges for making a false statement to an officer; and 84 percent of the 6,500 people arrested for "disorderly conduct." Moreover, booking officials and prosecutors decline charges brought against African Americans at significantly higher rates than charges against people of other races, indicating that officers' standards for making arrests differ by the race of the person arrested.
  - o We also found large racial disparities in BPD's arrests for drug possession. While survey data shows that African Americans use drugs at rates similar to or slightly exceeding other population groups, BPD arrested African Americans for drug possession at five times the rate of others.

BPD deployed a policing strategy that, by its design, led to differential enforcement in African-American communities. But BPD failed to use adequate policy, training and accountability mechanisms to prevent discrimination, despite longstanding notice of concerns about how it polices African-American communities in the City. BPD has conducted virtually no analysis of its own data to ensure that its enforcement activities are non-discriminatory, and the Department misclassifies or otherwise fails to investigate specific complaints of racial bias. Nor has the Department held officers accountable for using racial slurs or making other statements exhibiting racial bias. In some cases, BPD supervisors have ordered officers to specifically target African Americans for stops and arrests. These failures contribute to the large racial disparities in BPD's enforcement that undermine the community's trust in the fairness of the police. BPD leadership has acknowledged that this lack of trust inhibits their ability to forge important community partnerships.

USE OF CONSTITUTIONALLY EXCESSIVE FORCE

Our review of investigative files for all deadly force cases from 2010 until May 1, 2016, and a random sample of over eight hundred non-deadly force cases reveals that BPD engages in a pattern or practice of excessive force. Deficiencies in BPD's policies, training, and oversight of officers' force incidents have led to the pattern or practice of excessive force that we observed. We identified several recurring issues with BPD's use of force:

- First, BPD uses overly aggressive tactics that unnecessarily escalate encounters, increase tensions, and lead to unnecessary force, and fails to de-escalate encounters when it would be reasonable to do so. Officers frequently resort to physical force when a subject does not immediately respond to verbal commands, even where the subject poses no imminent threat to the officer or others. These tactics result from BPD's training and guidance.

- Second, BPD uses excessive force against individuals with mental health disabilities or in crisis. Due to a lack of training and improper tactics, BPD officers end up in unnecessarily violent confrontations with these vulnerable individuals. BPD provides less effective services to people with mental illness and intellectual disabilities by failing to account for these disabilities in officers' law enforcement actions, leading to unnecessary and excessive force being used against them. BPD has failed to make reasonable modifications in its policies, practices, and procedures to avoid discriminating against people with mental illness and intellectual disabilities.

- Third, BPD uses unreasonable force against juveniles. These incidents arise from BPD's failure to use widely-accepted tactics for communicating and interacting with youth. Instead, officers interacting with youth rely on the same aggressive tactics they use with adults, leading to unnecessary conflict.

- Fourth, BPD uses unreasonable force against people who present little or no threat to officers or others. Specifically, BPD uses excessive force against (1) individuals who are already restrained and under officers' control and (2) individuals who are fleeing from officers and are not suspected of serious criminal offenses.

  o Force used on restrained individuals: we found many examples of BPD officers using unreasonable force on individuals who were restrained and no longer posed a threat to officers or the public.

  o Force used on fleeing suspects: BPD officers frequently engage in foot pursuits of individuals, even where the fleeing individuals are not suspected of violent crimes. BPD's foot pursuit tactics endanger officers and the community, and frequently lead to officers using excessive force on fleeing suspects who pose minimal threat. BPD's aggressive approach to foot pursuits extends to flight in vehicles.

  We also examined BPD's transportation of detainees, but were unable to make a finding due to a lack of available data. We were unable to secure reliable records from either BPD or the jail regarding injuries sustained during transport or any recordings. Nonetheless, we found evidence that BPD: (1) routinely fails to properly secure arrestees in transport vehicles; (2) needs to continue to update its transport equipment to protect arrestees during transport; (3) fails to keep necessary records; and (4) must implement more robust auditing and monitoring systems to ensure that its transport policies and training are followed.

- Our concerns about BPD's use of excessive force are compounded by BPD's ineffective oversight of its use of force. Of the 2,818 force incidents that BPD recorded in the nearly six-year period we reviewed, BPD investigated only ten incidents based on concerns identified through its internal review. Of these ten cases, BPD found only one use of force to be excessive.

Retaliation for Activities Protected by the First Amendment

BPD violates the First Amendment by retaliating against individuals engaged in constitutionally protected activities. Officers frequently detain and arrest members of the public for engaging in speech the officers perceive to be critical or disrespectful. And BPD officers use force against members of the public who are engaging in protected speech. BPD has failed to provide officers with sufficient guidance and oversight regarding their interactions with individuals that implicate First Amendment protections, leading to the violations we observed.

INDICATIONS OF GENDER BIAS IN SEXUAL ASSAULT INVESTIGATIONS

Although we do not, at this time, find reasonable cause to believe that BPD engages in gender-biased policing in violation of federal law, the allegations we received during the investigation, along with our review of BPD files, suggests that gender bias may be affecting BPD's handling of sexual assault cases. We found indications that officers fail to meaningfully investigate reports of sexual assault, particularly for assaults involving women with additional vulnerabilities, such as those who are involved in the sex trade. Detectives fail to develop and resolve preliminary investigations; fail to identify and collect evidence to corroborate victims' accounts; inadequately document their investigative steps; fail to collect and assess data, and report and classify reports of sexual assault; and lack supervisory review. We also have concerns that officers' interactions with women victims of sexual assault and with transgender individuals display unlawful gender bias.

DEFICIENT POLICIES, TRAINING, SUPERVISION, AND ACCOUNTABILITY

BPD's systemic constitutional and statutory violations are rooted in structural failures. BPD fails to use adequate policies, training, supervision, data collection, analysis, and accountability systems, has not engaged adequately with the community it polices, and does not provide its officers with the tools needed to police effectively.

- BPD lacks meaningful accountability systems to deter misconduct. The Department does not consistently classify, investigate, adjudicate, and document complaints of misconduct according to its own policies and accepted law enforcement standards. Instead, we found that BPD personnel discourage complaints from being filed, misclassify complaints to minimize their apparent severity, and conduct little or no investigation. As a result, a resistance to accountability persists throughout much of BPD, and many officers are reluctant to report misconduct for fear that doing so is fruitless and may provoke retaliation. The Department also lacks adequate civilian oversight—its Civilian Review Board is hampered by inadequate resources, and the agency's internal affairs and disciplinary process lacks transparency.

- Nor does BPD employ effective community policing strategies. The Department's current relationship with certain Baltimore communities is broken. As noted above, some community members believe that the Department operates as if there are "two Baltimores" in which the affluent sections of the City receive better services than its impoverished and minority neighborhoods. This fractured relationship exists in part because of the Department's legacy of zero tolerance enforcement, the failure of many BPD officers to implement community policing principles, and the Department's lack of vision for engaging with the community.

- BPD fails to adequately supervise officers through policy guidance and training. Until recently, BPD lacked sufficient policy guidance in critical areas, such as bias-free policing and officers' use of batons and tasers. In other areas, such as its policy governing "stop and frisk," BPD policy conflicts with constitutional requirements. The Department likewise lacks effective training on important areas, such as scenario-based training for use of force, an adequate Field Training program; and supervisory or leadership training.

- BPD also fails to collect data on a range of law enforcement actions, and even when it collects data, fails to store it in systems that are capable of effective tracking and analysis. Partly as a result, the BPD does not use an effective early intervention system to detect officers who may benefit from additional training or guidance to ensure that they do not commit constitutional and statutory violations.

- In addition, BPD fails to adequately support its officers with adequate staffing and material resources. The Department lacks effective strategies for staffing, recruitment and retention, forcing officers to work overtime after long shifts, lowering morale, and leading to officers working with deteriorated decision-making skills. Moreover, BPD lacks adequate technology infrastructure and tools that are common in many similar-sized law enforcement agencies, such as in-car computers. These technology deficits create inefficiencies for officers and inhibit effective data collection and supervision. The City must invest in its police department to ensure that officers have the tools they need to properly serve the people of Baltimore.

Notwithstanding our findings, we are heartened by the support for police reform throughout BPD[,] the City, and the broader Baltimore community. Based on the cooperation and spirit of engagement we witnessed throughout our investigation, we are optimistic that we will be able to work with the City, BPD, and the diverse communities of Baltimore to address the issues described in our findings and forge a court-enforceable agreement to develop enduring remedies to the constitutional and statutory violations we found. Indeed, although much work remains, BPD has already begun laying the foundation for reform by self-initiating changes to its policies, training, data management, and accountability systems.

To that end, the Department of Justice and the City have entered into an Agreement in Principle that identifies categories of reforms the parties agree must be taken to remedy the violations of the Constitution and federal law described in this report. Both the Justice Department and the City seek input from all communities in Baltimore on the reforms that should be included in a comprehensive, court-enforceable consent decree to be negotiated by the Justice Department and the City in the coming months, and then entered as a federal court order.

As we have seen in jurisdictions across America, it is possible for law enforcement agencies to enhance their effectiveness by promoting constitutional policing and restoring community partnerships. Strengthening community trust in BPD will not only increase the effectiveness of BPD's law enforcement efforts, it will advance officer and public safety in a manner that serves the entire Baltimore community. Together with City officials and the people of Baltimore, we will work to make this a reality.

SOURCE: U.S. Justice Department. "Investigation of the Baltimore City Police Department." August 10, 2016. http://www.justice.gov/opa/file/883366/download.

OTHER HISTORIC DOCUMENTS OF INTEREST

Turkish Leaders Respond to Attempted Coup

JULY 16, 25, AND 27, 2016

A small faction of Turkey's military tried to overthrow the country's government on July 15, 2016, in a coup attempt that quickly failed. The plot received little support from the Turkish public and was unable to take control of major military or government installations. In response, President Recep Tayyip Erdoğan swiftly cracked down on any opposition to his government and promised to bring to justice those who had orchestrated the attempt to subvert his government. The July coup attempt was the fourth in Turkey to be led by the military since 1960, and each time the military faction involved reasserted its belief that it is the defender of democracy and secularism and that it is the military's responsibility to intervene in political dealings when it feels that those principles are being attacked.

MILITARY COUP ATTEMPT

In the late evening of July 15, a small fraction of Turkey's armed forces attempted to overthrow the government of President Recep Tayyip Erdogan, who at the time was out of the country on vacation. The coup began at approximately 11:00 p.m. local time, when the military faction, which called itself the Peace at Home Council, stopped traffic over two of Istanbul's bridges and used military helicopters to bomb police headquarters. The Peace at Home Council declared via state-run media that it had seized power from Erdoğan in an effort to protect democracy in Turkey. The coup plotters also announced a curfew, marshal law, and the preparation of a new constitution that would respect democracy, secularism, and reinstate Turkey's position on the global stage. "Turkish armed forces seized the rule of the country completely with the aim of reinstalling the constitutional order, democracy, human rights and freedoms, to make rule of law pervade again, to re-establish the ruined public order," the Peace at Home Council announced. Those supporting the coup raided television stations in an attempt to bar Erdoğan's government from broadcasting its control over the situation and shot at those who came out to protest the coup. The coup gained little support, however. Even the main opposition parties to Erdoğan's government protested the coup attempt. "This country has suffered a lot from coups," said Kemal Kiliçdaroğlu, leader of the main secular opposition party, the Republican People's Party (CHP). "It should be known that the CHP fully depends on the free will of the people as indispensable of our parliamentary democracy."

Turkish Prime Minister Binali Yildirim took to the airwaves to reassert the government's control of the country. "Some people illegally undertook an illegal action outside of the chain of command," Yildirim said, adding, "The government elected by the people remains in charge. This government will only go when the people say so." From an undisclosed location, Erdoğan spoke to the Turkish citizenry via FaceTime. "There is no power higher than the power of the people," he said, rejecting the notion that those carrying out the coup were doing so in the name of democracy. The president quickly returned to Turkey and spoke again from Ataturk Airport the morning of July 16. "A minority within the armed forces has unfortunately been unable to stomach Turkey's unity," he said, adding, "What is being perpetrated is a rebellion and a treason. They will pay a heavy price for their treason to Turkey." Erdoğan called on his supporters to take to the streets and protest the attempt to overthrow his government.

Coup Quickly Unravels

According to reporters inside the country, Turkey's National Intelligence Organization had discovered on July 15 that a coup was being plotted, thereby forcing those leading the effort to launch their plans in an uncoordinated manner earlier than expected. Shortly after the coup began, one of its leaders was executed, causing further chaos among the Peace at Home Council. Without strong centralized control and any public support, the group was unable to execute those activities that are the hallmark of a successful coup attempt, namely capturing or killing key leaders and taking control of the media.

The coup lasted only hours, and those involved began to surrender early in the morning of July 16. The military headquarters were quickly retaken by the government, and Gen. Umit Guler, commander of the First Army, verified that the nation's military did "not support this movement comprised of a small group within our ranks." According to the state-run Anadolu Agency news network, 200 Turkish soldiers surrendered to police the day after the coup attempt, and quickly thereafter, 1,500 thought to be linked to the attempt were arrested. In the end, more than 300 people were killed, approximately half of whom were the instigators of the coup attempt.

Two days later, Erdoğan formally addressed the nation at a rally for Turkish unity. "July 15 showed our friends that this country isn't just strong against political, economic and diplomatic attacks, but against military sabotage as well. It showed that it will not fall, it will not be derailed," Erdoğan said. "Those wringing their hands on that night hoping for Turkey to fall woke up the next day to realize their work was much harder than they thought."

The Turkish Armed Forces released a statement on July 27 after conducting an investigation into the attempted coup. Their findings indicated that only 1.5 percent of their ranks participated in the attempt, which "clearly demonstrates that a vast majority of Turkish military strongly opposed the heinous attack." The statement also went on to accuse those involved as being part of the Gülen movement, considered to be a terrorist group by the Turkish government. The Gülen movement derives its name from Fethullah Gülen, a U.S.-based cleric who has been in self-exile since 1980. Gülen was a well-respected *imam* when he lived in Turkey and is still considered a spiritual leader among his followers. Gülen's teachings promote education, hard work, modesty, and altruism. His followers have opened hundreds of schools, many of which attract Turkey's middle class, and they have also taken positions within the government. Gülen was accused of attempting to overthrow the government during a military coup in 1980, after which he fled the country.

Fallout

Thousands of soldiers, police, judges, teachers, and government employees were suspended, detained, or investigated after the coup. An estimated 32,000 were formally arrested, and due to the large volume, the nation was forced to release inmates to make space in its prisons. Erdoğan promised to overhaul Turkey's military, starting with the arrest of more than 150 generals and admirals, and also raised the possibility of reinstating the death penalty, which was outlawed in 2004 as a prerequisite to Turkey's attempt to gain membership to the European Union (EU). Turkey is party to the European Convention on Human Rights, which disallows the use of the death penalty, and EU leaders were quick to let the Turkish leader know that reinstating the death penalty would spell the end of ongoing negotiations to admit Turkey to the EU. Although it was not reinstated by the end of 2016, Turkey's president and prime minister continued to state publicly that it would be put before parliament and would be used as a "limited measure." Use of the death penalty, they argued, was in line with the will of the Turkish people.

As part of the ongoing efforts to root out those responsible for or supporting the coup, Erdoğan declared a three-month state of emergency to allow the government to act against those responsible for the coup by conducting raids and arresting those thought to be connected to the plot. The declaration included the suspension of a portion of the European Convention on Human Rights, although, as a signatory, Turkey could not refuse any of those arrested a fair trial and could not torture anyone for information on the plot. The state of emergency was extended for another three months in early October, and Erdoğan expressed his expectation that the measure could be implemented for more than a year, which raised concerns among his opponents in parliament about additional coup attempts.

Erdoğan's crackdown in Turkey was met by calls for calm from the West. While the United States expressed support for the country's democratically elected government, it called on Erdoğan to proceed with caution. Erdoğan, in turn, decried the lack of support he received from the nation's greatest NATO ally. On July 29, Erdoğan accused the head of U.S. Central Command of "taking the side of coup plotters instead of thanking this state for defeating the coup attempt," something the United States has strongly denied. Erdoğan went on to say, "Not a single person has come to give condolences either from the European Union . . . or from the West. . . . Those countries or leaders who are not worried about Turkey's democracy, the lives of our people, its future—while being so worried about the fate of the putschists—cannot be our friends."

Erdoğan publicly accused Gülen of orchestrating the coup, but Gülen denied any involvement in the uprising. Erdoğan called Gülen's followers "simply the visible tools of the threat against our country. We know that this game, this scenario, is far beyond their league." The Turkish leader called on President Barack Obama to extradite Gülen as quickly as possible, while Gülen called for the United States to "reject any effort to abuse the extradition process to carry out political vendettas." President Obama requested solid proof of Gülen's involvement and refused to hastily agree to the demand, noting that "America's governed by rules of law, and those are not ones that the president of the United States or anybody else can just set aside for the sake of expediency." In a statement, Gülen said of the extradition request, "[A]s someone who suffered under multiple military coups during the past five decades, it is especially insulting to be accused of having any link to such an attempt." By the close of 2016, Gülen had not been extradited, despite warnings from the Turkish government that failure to do so would result in growing anti-American sentiment.

—Heather Kerrigan

Following is a July 16, 2016, statement from the Turkish Ministry of Foreign Affairs on the coup attempt in Turkey; a July 25, 2016, statement from the Turkish

*government regarding a meeting at the presidential complex on the coup attempt;
and a press release from the Turkish Armed Forces on July 27, 2016, detailing the
attempted coup.*

Turkish Government Responds to Coup Attempt

July 16, 2016

The situation unfolded in Turkey was a coup attempt to overthrow the democratically-elected government. This attempt was foiled by the Turkish people in unity and solidarity. Our President and Government are in charge. Turkish Armed Forces was not involved in the coup attempt in its entirety. It was conducted by a clique within the Armed Forces and received a well-deserved response from our nation.

SOURCE: Republic of Turkey Ministry of Foreign Affairs. Turkish Consulate General in Houston. "Statement By Turkish Mfa Regarding Coup Attempt." July 16, 2016. http://houston.cg.mfa.gov.tr/ShowAnnouncement.aspx?ID=308616.

Erdoğan Holds Meeting on Coup

July 25, 2016

In the reception, which took place at the invitation of President Recep Tayyip Erdoğan at the Presidential Complex on 25 July 2016 with the participation of Chairman of the Justice and Development Party and Prime Minister Binali Yıldırım, Chairman of the Republican People's Party Kemal Kılıçdaroğlu and Chairman of the Nationalist Movement Party Devlet Bahçeli, July 15 coup attempt was discussed and views were exchanged on the process to come.

President Erdoğan thanked the party leaders for the open and clear stance they displayed in support of democracy, freedoms and the rule of law against the coup on the night of July 15, stressing that this spirit of unity and solidarity is our biggest source of power to overcome every kind of problem. President Erdoğan said the heroic deeds of the nation, who took to the streets and squares leaving aside differences of political opinion, and of our security forces, who carried out the instructions given to them, will never be forgotten. The fight against the Fetullah Terrorist Organization (FETO), the PKK and other security threats will be continued with determination. President Erdoğan also briefed the leaders on incidents that took place on the night of July 15 and in its aftermath.

President Erdoğan listened to chairmen's views on the coup attempt and the future steps that should be taken. In the reception, steps to be taken for the freedom, the security and the welfare of our nation—who united around the principles of the rule of law and democracy—the state of emergency, security measures, works related to the constitution, and economic policies were evaluated. It was underscored that a resolute fight shall be waged against terrorist organizations like the FETO and the PKK, which are working to take over and demolish the state, and that it is of vital importance to take necessary measures to prevent the repetition of any incident similar to the July 15 coup attempt. The importance of cooperation between all political parties on the handling of the investigation into the July 15 coup attempt and the management of the process of state of emergency with utmost care was emphasized. In the reception, a consensus was reached on the effective use of dialogue mechanisms to find permanent solutions to common problems.

President Erdoğan said that Turkey would become stronger at the end of this process and thanked the chairmen for visiting the Presidential Complex and defending democracy.

SOURCE: Presidency of the Republic of Turkey. "Statement by Presidential Spokesperson Ambassador Ibrahim Kalin on the Meeting at the Presidential Complex." July 25, 2016. http://www.tccb.gov.tr/en/spokesperson/1696/49841/statement-by-presidential-spokesperson-ambassador-ibrahim-kalin-on-the-meeting-at-the-presidential-complex.html.

Turkish Armed Forces on Attempted Coup

DOCUMENT

July 27, 2016

Turkish Armed Forces (TAF) announced that 8 thousand 651 staff took part in the coup attempt. The statement of TAF noted that this figure accounted for 1.5 percent of the current number of Turkish Armed Forces personnel.

According to the statement of Turkish Armed Forces (TAF), 8 thousand 651 military personnel took part in the coup attempt of July 15 perpetrated by Gülenist Terrorist Organization (FETÖ). This amounts to 1.5 percent of the current number of Turkish Armed Forces personnel.

The statement added that 35 planes, 37 helicopters, 74 tanks, and three ships of the Turkish Armed Forces were used during the coup attempt of FETÖ.

Following are highlights from the statement of Turkish General Staff regarding the coup attempt of July 15:

- A total of 246 armoured vehicles including 74 tanks were used during the coup attempt.

- 1.5 percent of the Turkish Armed Forces personnel took part in the coup attempt.

- Coup plotters used 35 planes and 37 helicopters.

- 3 ships and 3 thousand 992 small arms were used.

- Coup plotters are FETÖ terrorists in military uniforms.

- 8 thousand 651 personnel took part in the coup attempt.

- A total of 1,676 non-commissioned officers and soldiers, and 1,214 military students, joined the coup attempt.

The statement of TAF said the following:

"Turkish Armed Forces identified the personnel involved in the coup attempt of July 15 perpetrated by members of the illegal Gülenist Terrorist Organization nestled in TAF and dressed in military uniforms as well as the state-owned weaponry and equipment used by them.

The investigation revealed that there were a total of 8,651 members of illegal Gülenist Terrorist Organization (1,676 non-commissioned officers and soldiers, and 1,214 military students) in military uniforms acting against our nation, values, particularly the Turkish Grand National Assembly as well as all other institutions, and that this figure accounted for 1.5 percent of the current number of TAF personnel, which clearly demonstrates that a vast majority of Turkish military strongly opposed the heinous attack."

SOURCE: Republic of Turkey Office of the Prime Minister. "TAF Releases Statement on Coup Attempt." July 27, 2016. http://www.byegm.gov.tr/english/agenda/taf-releases-statement-on-coup-attempt/97821.

OTHER HISTORIC DOCUMENTS OF INTEREST

FROM PREVIOUS HISTORIC DOCUMENTS

- Turkish President Remarks on Party's Election Victory, *2015*, p. 559

Rio de Janeiro Hosts 2016 Olympic Games; Officials Respond to Russian Athlete Doping Scandal

---

JULY 18 AND 24, AUGUST 5 AND 21, 2016

The International Olympic Committee's (IOC) 2009 designation of Rio de Janeiro as the host city for the 2016 Summer Olympics was celebrated in Brazil as a major win for the country. Yet as the games approached, Brazil faced a growing economic and political crisis, and reports of rising crime, cost overruns, construction delays, and polluted waterways—in addition to the Zika outbreak—raised concerns about whether the country would be ready to host the games, and even led some to question if the games should be canceled or postponed. At the same time, revelations of a state-sponsored doping program thrust Russia and its athletes into the spotlight and prompted calls for the Russian Olympic team to be banned from the 2016 games.

A "Perfect Storm" of Challenges

Brazil weathered the 2008 international financial crisis better than other countries, and when the IOC named Rio as the 2016 Olympic Games' host city, the country was enjoying an economic boom and implementing a series of new social programs designed to address poverty and crime. But in the years preceding the games, Brazil's economy suffered from the global drop in commodities prices and China's economic slowdown. Brazil's economy contracted, sending inflation and unemployment soaring in 2015 and 2016 as social programs and salaries for public workers were cut. Brazil was also reeling from a widespread corruption scandal after an investigation that began in May 2014 revealed that dozens of its politicians had accepted kickbacks from construction companies that overcharged the state-owned oil company for building contracts. In addition, President Dilma Rousseff was in the midst of impeachment proceedings, facing accusations that she used funds from state banks to hide budget shortfalls prior to her reelection in 2014. Beginning in May 2016, Rousseff was suspended from office while her trial took place and Vice President Michel Temer became the interim president. Further complicating Brazil's Olympic preparations was the outbreak of the Zika virus, which is linked to microcephaly and other congenital defects, and had been spreading quickly through Brazil since the first confirmed infection was reported in May 2015. While some called for the games to be canceled or postponed due to the Zika threat, international health organizations did not support this and instead issued infection prevention guidance for those traveling to Rio. This did not stop at least ten athletes from withdrawing from the Olympics, citing Zika concerns.

A host of other challenges plagued Brazil ahead of the games, many of which were directly connected to the national and local economic struggles. The government pledged during the bidding process to clean up the heavily polluted Guanabara Bay and other Rio waterways where some aquatic events would be held. However, the government lacked sufficient funds to complete cleanup efforts and fell short of its promise to treat 80 percent of the sewage found in the water before the Olympics. As of July 2016, reports indicated that raw sewage was still seeping into some waterways. Construction of a ten-mile subway line connecting the Olympic Park to hotels and competition sites in Ipanema and Copacabana suffered continued delays, providing limited time for safety testing, and cost nearly twice as much as originally estimated. Thousands of Brazilians who live in Rio's *favelas*, or slums, were forcibly evicted to make room for Olympics-related construction projects and were in some cases moved far away from their jobs and children's schools. The government responded to criticisms from human rights organizations by arguing that those who were moved were now living in much better accommodations and that the infrastructure improvements the city was making would benefit all Brazilians. The state of athlete accommodations was also called into question in July, when the Australian Olympic team said its athletes and staff would stay at hotels instead of the Athlete's Village for at least two days due to electrical and plumbing problems.

Ensuring the security of athletes and visitors was also a prime concern for Rio. Several Spanish and Australian athletes reported being robbed at gunpoint in the spring, and a New Zealand athlete was reportedly kidnapped and robbed by police. In June, armed men stormed a Rio hospital that was among the medical facilities recommended for use by Olympics visitors to free a known drug trafficker. A wave of gun battles between law enforcement officials and drug traffickers were reported throughout the summer, and in late June, human body parts washed up on a beach near where volleyball competitions would be held. Olympics organizers deployed approximately 85,000 police and soldiers to provide security during the games.

Brazil budgeted roughly $14 billion to pay for Olympic stadiums, transportation improvements, an Olympic Village, security and logistics, and other preparations. By June, it was estimated that Brazil would end up paying closer to $20 billion to host the games. Organizers struggled to find the funds to cover cost overruns and made several cuts to try to save money, including paring down the opening and closing ceremonies, reducing the number of volunteers to be trained to help visitors, constructing temporary tents instead of more permanent venues in some locations, and simplifying athletes' accommodations. In mid-June, the governor of the state of Rio de Janeiro declared a state of "public calamity," saying that Rio was bankrupt and would not be able to meet its commitments without financial assistance. The federal government authorized an emergency loan worth $850 million in response.

The day the games began, thousands of Brazilians gathered in Rio to protest the government and the billions it had spent on the Olympics. "We love sports in our city, but our city needs other things like better schools, better hospitals, free access to education," said one protestor. Commenting on the city's Olympics preparations, Mario Andrada, a spokesperson for the Rio 2016 Olympic Committee, said, "We were surprised by a perfect storm of a political crisis married with an intense economic crisis. Usually it's one or the other, but we have both, and they're both very intense."

Russian Athletes Doping Scandal

As Brazil contended with these challenges, a separate scandal was unfolding that shook confidence in the international athletics community's anti-doping governance and the integrity of the Olympics themselves.

In 2010, former Russian Anti-Doping Agency (RUSADA) employee Vitaly Stepanov began sending more than 200 e-mails to the World Anti-Doping Agency (WADA) claiming that RUSADA was engaged in the systemic doping of Russian athletes. WADA launched an investigation into Stepanov's claims in 2015, with a focus on Russia's track and field programs, and released its findings in November 2015. WADA confirmed that Russian officials and lab workers had covered up positive test results and that some athletes had used false identities to avoid testing, paid to cover up positive tests, or bribed anti-doping authorities. As a result of WADA's report, and at its recommendation, the International Association of Athletics Federations (IAAF) provisionally suspended Russian track and field athletes from all international competitions.

In May 2016, further details about Russia's doping program emerged from interviews given by Dr. Grigory Rodchenkov, the former director of Russia's anti-doping laboratory, to documentary filmmaker Bryan Fogel. Rodchenkov claimed that dozens of Russian competitors in the 2014 Sochi Olympics had been part of a government-run doping program, at least fifteen of whom won medals. Rodchenkov said he developed a three-drug mix of banned substances that he combined with alcohol and gave to the Ministry of Sport, which then gave the drugs to Russian athletes. He said he worked with anti-doping experts and members of the Russian intelligence service each night during the Sochi games to replace athletes' tainted urine samples with clean urine that had been collected months before. Rodchenkov and his team reportedly did their work in a storage space located next to the anti-doping lab's sample collection room. One team member would pass tainted samples from the collection room to the storage space through a small hole in the wall that was hidden during the day. Clean samples were passed back through the same hole. Rodchenkov estimated that his team replaced about 100 tainted urine samples over the course of the games. Russian minister of sport Vitaly Mutko said Rodchenkov's allegations were "a continuation of the information attack on Russian sport."

The IOC asked WADA to investigate Rodchenkov's claims immediately, and the group engaged Canadian professor Richard H. McLaren to conduct an independent review of the allegations. WADA released McLaren's findings on July 18. The report exposed "a modus operandi of serious manipulation of the doping control process" in the lab created for the Sochi games and in a Moscow lab that operated before and after the games. It confirmed that the doping program was directed by the Ministry of Sport, that it extended beyond track and field programs, and that RUSADA and some members of the Russian Olympic Committee were also involved. McLaren found evidence that Russia manipulated the anti-doping process for the Sochi games, in addition to the 2013 IAAF World Championships in Moscow and the 2013 World University Games in Kazan, and took measures to circumvent the anti-doping process of the 2012 Olympic Games in London. Based on these findings, WADA recommended that the IOC and International Paralympic Committee (IPC) consider banning all Russian athletes from the Olympic and Paralympic Games. (Russian track and field athletes had already been banned pursuant to an IAAF decision announced on June 17.)

In a statement responding to WADA's report, Russian President Vladimir Putin claimed that all Russian athletes had undergone anti-doping tests overseen by the United Kingdom's Anti-Doping Agency and other anti-doping laboratories abroad within the past six months. He questioned the legitimacy of the allegations against the Russian team, stating that they were "based on information given by one single person, an individual with a notorious reputation." Putin argued that the U.S. Anti-Doping Agency and other groups who supported banning all Russian athletes from the Olympics were being hasty in their judgment and suggested the United States may even have set the tone and content of

WADA's report. Putin also compared the situation to the 1980s, when Western countries boycotted the Moscow Olympics because of the presence of Soviet troops in Afghanistan; Russia reciprocated by boycotting the Los Angeles Games. "Today, we see a dangerous return to this policy of letting politics interfere with sport," Putin said. "Yes, this intervention takes different forms today, but the essence remains the same; to make sport an instrument for geopolitical pressure and use it to form a negative image of countries and peoples. The Olympic movement, which is a tremendous force for uniting humanity, once again could find itself on the brink of division." Putin added that the officials WADA said were involved in the scandal would be temporarily removed from their positions and that Russia was conducting its own investigation.

On July 24, the IOC Executive Board issued its decision on whether Russian athletes should be permitted to participate in the 2016 Olympic Games. The board chose not to issue a blanket ban for all Russian athletes; instead, it said that each athlete must meet a certain set of conditions before they could compete. The IOC's decision largely relied on the various International Sports Federations to verify each athlete's anti-doping record and identify eligible athletes, though it stated that no athlete implicated in WADA's report could compete in the games and that Russia could not enter any athlete who had ever been sanctioned for doping even if they had served their sanction. The IOC further declared that any athlete accepted to the games would be subject to additional "out-of-competition testing" and that if the athlete did not participate in this testing they would be withdrawn from the Olympics.

The IPC did not follow the IOC's lead. Instead, the IPC announced on August 7 the immediate suspension of the Russian Paralympic Committee "due to its inabilities to fulfill its IPC membership responsibilities and obligations," namely, compliance with the IPC Anti-Doping Code and World Anti-Doping Code. This in turn meant that no Russian athletes would be permitted to compete in the 2016 Paralympic Games, scheduled to begin on September 7. Russia appealed the IPC's decision to the Court of Arbitration for Sport, which denied the appeal on August 23, stating that the IPC's decision was "proportionate in the circumstances."

As of August 6, some 271 Russian athletes were cleared to compete in the Rio games. The full Russian team would have comprised 398 competitors.

The Games Begin

The 2016 Olympic Games began on August 5, ended on August 21, and were the first to be hosted in South America. Speaking at the opening ceremony, IOC President Thomas Bach commended Brazil on its efforts to prepare for the games. "You have transformed the wonderful city of Rio de Janeiro into a modern metropolis and made it even more beautiful," he said. "Our admiration is even greater because you managed this at a very difficult time in Brazilian history."

For the first time, due to the ongoing migrant crisis and violent conflicts in some countries, the IOC allowed a refugee team to compete in the games under the Olympic flag. Comprised of ten athletes from Syria, South Sudan, Ethiopia, and the Democratic Republic of the Congo, the refugee team was greeted with a standing ovation as members entered the Olympic stadium, and Bach extended a special welcome. "You are sending a message of hope to all the many millions of refugees around the globe," he said.

Over the next sixteen days, more than 11,000 athletes from 207 countries competed in 306 events across 28 sports. Golf and rugby were among the sports featured in the games, after having been removed from Olympics programming more than ninety years prior. Competitors set ninety-one Olympic records and twenty-seven world records during the games. Teams from the United States, Great Britain, and China won the most medals; Russia came in fourth place in the medal standings, winning fifty-six medals. The games largely proceeded without incident, and Bach hailed them as "marvelous Olympic Games in the 'marvelous city'" in his remarks at the games' closing ceremony.

The next Olympic Games will take place in Pyeongchang, South Korea, in the winter of 2018. The next summer Olympic Games will be held in Tokyo, Japan, in 2020.

—Linda Fecteau Grimm

Following are the executive summary of the World Anti-Doping Agency's report from July 18, 2016, in which it outlined the findings of its independent-person investigation into Russian doping allegations; a statement by Russian President Vladimir Putin from July 18, 2016, responding to the World Anti-Doping Agency's investigation; the International Olympic Committee (IOC) Executive Board's July 24, 2016, decision on Russian athletes' participation in the 2016 Olympic Games; and IOC President Thomas Bach's remarks at the games' opening and closing ceremonies on August 5 and August 21, 2016.

Executive Summary of WADA Investigation into Russian Doping Scandal

July 18, 2016

Key Findings

1. The Moscow Laboratory operated, for the protection of doped Russian athletes, within a State-dictated failsafe system, described in the report as the Disappearing Positive Methodology.

2. The Sochi Laboratory operated a unique sample swapping methodology to enable doped Russian athletes to compete at the Games.

3. The Ministry of Sport directed, controlled and oversaw the manipulation of [athletes'] analytical results or sample swapping, with the active participation and assistance of the FSB, CSP, and both Moscow and Sochi Laboratories.

This Report will explain these key findings.

[1.1 Introduction has been omitted.]

1.2 Creation and Terms of Reference of the Independent Investigation into Sochi and Other Allegations

On 19 May 2016 the World Anti-Doping Agency (WADA) announced the appointment of an Independent Person (IP) to conduct an investigation of the allegations made by the former Director of the Moscow Laboratory, Dr. Grigory Rodchenkov ("Dr. Rodchenkov"). Professor Richard H. McLaren, law professor at Western University, Canada; CEO of McLaren Global Sport Solutions Inc.; counsel to McKenzie Lake Lawyers, LLP and long standing CAS arbitrator, was appointed as the IP to investigate.

Professor Richard McLaren was previously a member of WADA's three-person Independent Commission (IC), led by founding WADA President Richard W. Pound QC, which exposed widespread doping in Russian Athletics. Working independently as the IP, Professor Richard McLaren was supported by a multi-disciplinary team. He has significant experience in the world of international sports law, including having conducted many international investigations related to doping and corruption.

"The Terms of Reference directed the IP to establish whether:

1. *There has been manipulation of the doping control process during the Sochi Games, including but not limited to, acts of tampering with the samples within the Sochi Laboratory.*

2. *Identify the modus operandi and those involved in such manipulation.*

3. *Identify any athlete that might have benefited from those alleged manipulations to conceal positive doping tests.*

4. *Identify if this Modus Operandi was also happening within Moscow Laboratory outside the period of the Sochi Games.*

5. *Determine other evidence or information held by Grigory Rodchenkov."*

Throughout the course of his mandate, the IP has personally reviewed all evidence gathered by his independent investigative team.

This Report was prepared from the collective work of the IP's investigative team. The investigative process is outlined and the many significant aspects that were studied and analyzed ultimately provide evidence for findings of fact.

The third paragraph of the IP's mandate, identifying athletes who benefited from the manipulations, has not been the primary focus of the IP's work. The IP investigative team has developed evidence identifying dozens of Russian athletes who appear to have been involved in doping. The compressed timeline of the IP investigation did not permit compilation of data to establish an anti-doping rule violation. The time limitation required the IP to deem this part of the mandate of lesser priority. The IP concentrated on the other four directives of the mandate.

The highly compressed timeline has meant that the IP investigative team has had to be selective in examining the large amount of data and information available to it. This Report reflects the work of the IP but it must be recognised that we have only skimmed the surface of the extensive data available. In doing so, then IP has only made Findings in this Report that meet the standard of beyond a reasonable doubt. WADA must decide if the IP investigative team should continue its work in respect of reviewing all of its material in relation to specific athletes and examining the remaining material it has.

1.3 Summary of the Evidence Gathering Process

The IP was appointed to lead this investigation to ensure an unbiased and independent examination of the evidence and from which all stakeholders could have confidence in the reporting of careful, thorough and balanced assessment of proven facts. The IP relied and built upon the work previously done by the Independent Commission (IC).

The IP conducted a number of witness interviews and reviewed thousands of documents, employed cyber analysis, conducted cyber and forensic analysis of hard drives, urine sample collection bottles and laboratory analysis of individual athlete samples.

The IP has gathered and reviewed as much evidence as could be accessed in the limited 57 day time frame in which this Report was required to be completed. More evidence is becoming available by the day but a cut-off had to be implemented in order to prepare the Report.

This Report contains evidence that the IP considers to be established beyond a reasonable doubt. There is more data that needs to be further analysed but does not affect the factual findings in this Report.

The mandate was not limited to just the published allegations. The IP examined other evidence of what was transpiring in the Moscow Laboratory before and after the period of the Sochi Games. The scope of the IP's work to establish the cover up of doping included looking into and reporting on any other information or evidence that materialized throughout the course of the investigation.

The investigation has established the Findings set out in this Report beyond a reasonable doubt. . . .

1.4 Witnesses

Dr. Rodchenkov's public statements triggered the creation of the IP investigation. He cooperated with the investigation, agreeing to multiple interviews and providing thousands of documents electronically or in hard copy. The IP has concluded that in the context of the investigation he has been truthful with the IP. . . . Vitaly Stepanov, a former employee of RUSADA did not participate in the investigation but the IP did review the allegations he made.

There were other witnesses who came forward on a confidential basis. They were important to the work of the IP investigation in that they provided highly credible cross-corroboration of evidence both viva voce and documentary that the IP had already secured. I have promised not to name these individuals, however I do want to thank them for their assistance, courage and fortitude in coming forward and sharing information and documents with the IP.

The IP did not seek to interview persons living within the Russian Federation. This includes government officials. My experience on the IC was such that individuals who were identified to give interviews were fearful of speaking to the IC. I did not seek to meet with government officials and did not think it necessary having already done so with the IC with little benefit to that investigation. I also received, unsolicited, an extensive narrative with attachments from one important government representative described in this Report. In the short time of 57 days that I was given to conduct this IP investigation it was simply not practical and I deemed such interviewing would not be helpful based on my experience with the IC.

1.5 Findings of IC and Relationship to IP Investigation

The IC uncovered a system within Russia for doping athletes directed by senior coaching officials of Russian athletics. That was accomplished by the corruption of Doping Control Officers ("DCO") working under the direction of RUSADA. The coaches were also able to achieve their objectives of doping athletes under their direction by knowing the wash out periods for various performance enhancing drugs ("PED"). They would be assisted in that regard by various informed medical personnel. The coaches were using the well-known and tried system of doping with anabolic steroids without understanding that what they were accomplishing with the PEDs program. This was starting to show up in the Athlete Biological Passport ("ABP"), which was legally recognized in 2011 but not well understood in Russian sporting circles for at least another full year. As the problem became more acute, the corruption of both Russian and international Athletics officials was used as a method of slowing down and otherwise distorting the reporting of positive results by use of the ABP. All of what has just been described is documented in the two IC reports of November 2015 and January 2016.

What the IP investigation adds to the bigger picture is how the WADA accredited laboratory was controlled by the state and acted as the failsafe mechanism to cover up doping. If all other steps were unsuccessful in covering up or manipulating the doping control system then the laboratory's role was to make an initial finding of a positive result disappear. With the additional evidence available to the IP, this Report provides facts and proof beyond that of the IC and describes a larger picture of Russian doping activity and the sports involved beyond merely Athletics.

1.6 Overall Outcomes of the Independent Investigation

Upon embarking on its investigation the IP quickly found a wider means of concealing positive doping results than had been publically [sic] described for Sochi.

The Sochi Laboratory urine sample swapping scheme was a unique standalone approach to meet a special set of circumstances. Behind this lay a greater systematic scheme operated by the Moscow Laboratory for false reporting of positive samples supported by what the IP termed the disappearing positive methodology. What emerged from all the investigative sources was a simple but effective and efficient method for direction and control under the Deputy Minister of Sport to force the Laboratory to report any positive screen finding as a negative analytical result. The disappearing positive!

The Disappearing Positive Methodology was used as a State directed method following the very abysmal medal count by the Russian Olympic athletes participating in the 2010 Winter Olympic Games in Vancouver. At that time, Sochi had already been designated as the next Winter Olympic venue. A new Deputy Minister of Sport, Yuri Nagornykh, was appointed in 2010 by Executive Order of then Prime Minister, Vladimir Putin. Nagornykh, also a member of the Russian Olympic Committee ("ROC"), reports to the Minister of Sport, Vitaly Mutko. Minister Mutko has continuously held this appointment since the Presidential Order of President Medvedev in May 2008. He is also the chairman of the organising committee for the 2018 FIFA World Cup in Russia and is a member of the FIFA Executive Committee.

Deputy Minister Nagornykh was critical to the smooth running of the Disappearing Positive Methodology. Representing the State, he was advised of every positive analytical finding arising in the Moscow Laboratory from 2011 onwards. Nagornykh, as the Deputy Minister of Sport, decided who would benefit from a cover up and who would not be protected.

In total violation of the WADA International Standard for Laboratories ("ISL") all analytical positives appearing on the first sample screen at the Moscow laboratory were reported up to the Deputy Minister after the athlete's name had been added to the information to be supplied. The order would come back from the Deputy Minister "SAVE" or "QUARANTINE".

If the order was a SAVE the laboratory personnel were required to report the sample negative in WADA's Anti-Doping Management System ("ADAMS"). Then the laboratory personnel would falsify the screen result in the Laboratory Information Management System ("LIMS") to show a negative laboratory result. The athlete benefited from the cover up determined and directed by the Deputy Minister of Sport and could continue to compete dirty.

The Disappearing Positive Methodology worked well to cover up doping except at international events where there were independent observers such as the IAAF World Championships held in Moscow in 2013 and the Winter Olympics and Paralympics in Sochi in 2014.

Through the efforts of the FSB, a method for surreptitiously removing the caps of tamper evident sample bottles containing the urine samples of doped Russian athletes had been developed for use at Sochi. The IP has developed forensic evidence that establishes beyond a reasonable doubt some method was used to replace positive dirty samples during the Sochi Games. The bottle opening method was used again in December 2014 to cover up some dirty samples, which WADA had advised would be removed from the Moscow Laboratory for further analysis.

Unlike the method used during the Sochi Games, the Disappearing Positive Methodology was in operation at IAAF World Championships ("IAAF Championships"). The IP also has evidence that sample swapping occurred after the IAAF Championships in respect of positive samples.

The IP investigation, assisted by forensic experts, has conducted its own experiments and can confirm, without any doubt whatsoever, that the caps of urine sample bottles can be removed without any evidence visible to the untrained eye. Indeed, this was demonstrated in front of Professor Richard McLaren. As will be noted later in this report, evidence of tampering could be detected on bottle caps from Sochi and the December 2014 sample seizure by WADA with the use of microscopic technology.

The fundamental building block of the Sochi scheme was in place. The FSB was intricately entwined in the scheme to allow Russian athletes to compete while dirty. The FSB developed a method to surreptitiously open the urine bottles to enable sample swapping. This keystone step cleared the way for the development of a clean urine bank as a source from which to draw urine samples for swapping. The coordinating role for this aspect of the State run system was that of Irina Rodionova. Rodionova currently sits as the Deputy Director of the Center of Sports Preparation of National Teams of Russia ("CSP") (in Russian "ЦСП"), which is a subordinate organisation of the Russian Ministry of Sport. She was a staff member of the Russian Olympic Committee ("ROC") during the Sochi 2014 Games as the head of the Monitoring and Management of Medical Anti-doping Programs Department and also on the ROC staff for the London 2012 Games as the head of the Medical and Research Department.

Athletes, on instruction, would collect what were thought to be clean urine samples outside of the wash out periods for any PEDs they were using. Rodionova would receive these samples from athletes and arrange for their freezer storage at the CSP. Dr. Rodchenkov would test some of these clean urine samples to ensure they were in fact not positive.

Once the clean urine bank was fully populated by the chosen athletes, the samples were then secretly transported by the FSB from Moscow to the FSB storage freezer in the FSB building located next to the Sochi Laboratory. The bank of clean urine sat in storage awaiting the swapping program at Sochi when required.

The swapping occurred largely as described in The New York Times article. Dr. Rodchenkov provided credible evidence that the A and B bottles would pass through the "mouse hole" from the aliquoting room inside the secure perimeter of the Sochi Laboratory into an adjacent operations room, outside the secure perimeter. From there, FSB officer Evgeny Blokhin would take the B bottles and leave the operations room. In the meantime, clean urine from the athletes who had given their sample at a Sochi doping control venue would be withdrawn from the freezer at the FSB building and brought over to the operations room to complete its thawing there. The B sample bottle would be returned to the operations room by FSB Blokhin, open and with the cap removed. The dirty urine disposed of and replaced by clean urine would be put in the A and B bottles. The stopper replaced in the A bottle and the B bottle cap screwed back into place; the bottles would be passed back through the mouse hole thereby reentering the secure perimeter of the laboratory aliquoting room ready for clinical bench work the following morning.

Dr. Rodchenkov's role in the sample swapping scheme included ensuring that the substituted sample was manipulated to match as closely as possible the Specific Gravity (SG) indicated on the original Doping Control Form ("DCF") taken at the Sochi venue. This adjustment was accomplished by adding table salt to raise the clean urine SG or distilled water to dilute the clean urine sample so as to closely match the SG number on the DCF.

The veracity of Dr. Rodchenkov's statements to The New York Times article is supported by the forensic analysis of the IP which included laboratory analysis of the salt content of samples selected by the investigative team. The London WADA accredited Laboratory, at the request of the IP, advised that of the forensically representative samples tested, 6 had salt contents higher than what should be found in urine of a healthy human. The forensic examination for marks and scratches within the bottle caps confirmed that they had been tampered with. Both findings support the evidence of Dr. Rodchenkov.

The Sochi sample swapping methodology was a unique situation, required because of the presence of the international community in the Laboratory. It enabled Russian athletes to compete dirty while enjoying certainty that their anti-doping samples would be reported clean. Following the Winter Olympics, the scheme to cover up State sponsored doping returned to the Disappearing Positive Methodology described previously.

The first ARD documentary aired in early December of 2014. The concerns of the international sporting community led to the appointment of the IC, one of the Commissioners of whom was subsequently to become the IP. In connection with the creation of the IC, but not by way of direction of the IC, Dr. Olivier Rabin from WADA asked the Moscow laboratory to prepare for a visit during which the samples stored in the laboratory would be packed up and shipped out of the country for storage and further analysis.

The anxiety level of personnel in the laboratory rose because of the pending WADA visit. The Disappearing Positive Methodology was used during the summer of 2014. As a consequence, Dr. Rodchenkov knew that he would have dirty B samples from that period. A number of dirty samples had been collected and reported as negative, and were stored in the laboratory. The solution to the problem in part was to destroy thousands of samples obtained and stored prior to 10 September 2014, being the minimal 90-day period of storage as prescribed under the ISL. However, the massive destruction of samples only got rid of part of the problem. Still to be dealt with were the samples between 10 September 2014 and 10 December 2014.

Dr Rodchenkov prepared a schedule of 37 athletes whose samples were potentially a problem if another accredited laboratory were to analyze them. A meeting was held with Deputy Minister Nagornykh in which the jeopardy of the laboratory was discussed were something not done to deal with the selected samples. The upshot of that meeting was that Deputy Minister Nagornykh resolved to call in the "magicians". That night the FSB visited the laboratory and the next day sample bottles were in the laboratory without their caps. The IP found that these samples all had negative findings recorded on ADAMS.

The IP forensic examination of these bottles found evidence of scratches and marks confirmed tampering. A urine examination of 3 of the samples showed that the DNA was not that of the athlete involved.

[The remainder of the report, Chapters 2–7, has been omitted.]

SOURCE: World Anti-Doping Agency. "The Independent Person Report." July 18, 2016. http://www .wada-ama.org/sites/default/files/resources/files/20160718_ip_report_newfinal.pdf.

President Vladimir Putin Responds to World Anti-Doping Agency Report

July 18, 2016

President of Russia Vladimir Putin: Recent events and the tense atmosphere that has formed around international sport and the Olympic movement involuntarily recall the situation in the early 1980s. Back then, many Western countries, citing the deployment of Soviet troops in Afghanistan, boycotted the Moscow Olympics. Four years later, the Soviet Union retaliated by boycotting the Los Angeles Olympics, using the pretext of an allegedly insufficient level of security for the Soviet team. The result was that many Soviet and American athletes and athletes from other countries were caught up in this campaign of reciprocal boycotts and lost the chance to add their names to world sporting history. Their years of long and hard effort and training were in vain. In short, people had their dreams broken and became hostages of political confrontation. The Olympic movement found itself in a serious crisis and faced divisions within. Later, some of the political figures of that era on both sides admitted that this had been a mistake.

Today, we see a dangerous return to this policy of letting politics interfere with sport. Yes, this intervention takes different forms today, but the essence remains the same; to make sport an instrument for geopolitical pressure and use it to form a negative image of countries and peoples. The Olympic movement, which is a tremendous force for uniting humanity, once again could find itself on the brink of division.

Today, so-called "doping scandals" are the method used, attempts to apply sanctions for detected cases of doping to all athletes, including those who are "clean", supposedly to protect their interests. But unlike in the 1980s, athletes undergo very strict and comprehensive anti-doping tests during competition and during the entire training process. Over the last 6 months, all Russian athletes have undergone anti-doping tests on WADA's recommendations, with the tests overseen by the UK Anti-Doping Agency and other anti-doping laboratories abroad.

The accusations against Russia's athletes are based on information given by one single person, an individual with a notorious reputation. Criminal charges were opened against him in 2012 for violating anti-doping laws, but there was not enough evidence against him at that moment and the case was dropped. On June 17 this year, following his allegations of involvement in using banned substances and information from Russian athletes concerning extortion, a criminal case was reopened against him in connection with the new circumstances that had come to light. One of his close relatives, who used to work under his direction, has already been convicted in Russia for illegal trade in anabolic steroids. The question arises as to how much trust we can place in arguments based solely on the allegations of people of this kind, and how much weight can such allegations have.

The US Anti-Doping Agency (USADA) and several anti-doping agencies in other countries, without waiting for the official publication of the World Anti-Doping Agency's commission, have hastened to demand that the entire Russian team be banned from taking part in the Rio de Janeiro Olympics.

What is behind this haste? Is it an attempt to create the needed media atmosphere and apply pressure? We have the impression that the USADA experts had access to what is an unpublished report at the very least, and have set its tone and even its content themselves. If this is the case, one country's national organisation is again trying to dictate its will to the entire world sports community.

The officials named in the commission's report as directly involved will be temporarily removed from their posts until a full investigation is complete. But to be able to make a final decision on these officials' responsibility, we ask the WADA commission to provide fuller and more objective fact-based information so that Russia's law enforcement and investigative agencies can use it in their investigation. We can guarantee that their work will be seen through to its conclusion and that all subsequent measures will be taken in full to prevent violation of Russian law and ensure that our country fulfils its international obligations.

We have always taken the clear position that there is no place for doping in sport. It endangers athletes' health and lives and discredits fair sporting competition. We are consistent in eliminating this scourge, improve our national laws in this area, and cooperate openly with the relevant international organisations and the International Olympic Committee. We are unfailing in meeting our obligations.

Russia is well aware of the Olympic movement's immense significance and constructive force, and shares in full the Olympic movement's values of mutual respect, solidarity, fairness, and the spirit of friendship and cooperation.

This is the only way to preserve the Olympic family's unity and ensure international sport's development in the interest of bringing peoples and cultures closer together. Russia is open to cooperation on achieving these noble goals.

SOURCE: Office of the President of Russia. "Statement in response to the report by the World Anti-Doping Agency." July 18, 2016. http://en.kremlin.ru/events/president/news/52537.

International Olympic Committee Decision on Russian Athletes' Participation in 2016 Olympics

July 24, 2016

I.

The IOC Executive Board (EB) has today further studied the question of the participation of Russian athletes in the Olympic Games Rio 2016. In its deliberations, the IOC EB was guided by a fundamental rule of the Olympic Charter to protect clean athletes and the integrity of sport.

The study included the discussion of the World Anti-Doping Agency (WADA)'s Independent Person (IP) Report by Prof. Richard McLaren; the decision of the Court of Arbitration for Sport (CAS) on 21 July 2016 concerning the rules of the International Association of Athletics Federations (IAAF); as well as the Olympic Charter and the World Anti-Doping Code.

Given the urgency of the situation, with the Olympic Games Rio 2016 starting in 12 days, and the athletes' entry process already underway, the IOC EB had to take a preliminary decision with regard to the participation of Russian athletes in Rio de Janeiro. Prof. McLaren states in his report that it "fulfils partially the mandate of the Independent Person". This is why the IOC supports his request to continue and finalise his work. On the other hand, this situation leads to an urgency for the IOC which does not allow it sufficient time for hearings for affected athletes, officials and organisations.

The IOC EB has given the Russian Olympic Committee (ROC) the opportunity to present the case of the Russian athletes and the ROC. This was done by Mr Alexander Zhukov, ROC President, at the beginning of the EB telephone conference, which he left immediately following his presentation.

During his presentation, Mr. Zhukov explained that the Russian Federation and the ROC guarantee full cooperation with all international organisations to shed light on the issue in every respect. He also guaranteed that the ROC commits to a complete and comprehensive restructuring of the Russian anti-doping system. In this context, he stressed that the ROC is committed to clean sport and would work towards guaranteeing clean sport in Russia.

He further stated that all Russian athletes selected for the Olympic Games Rio 2016 have been tested over the last six months by foreign anti-doping agencies. Samples were taken by foreign doping control officers and the samples analysed in foreign laboratories. Russian athletes who participated in different competitions in all sports have submitted more than 3,000 doping samples. The vast majority of the results were negative.

The IOC EB discussed the status of the ROC. In this respect, it took note of the fact that the IP Report made no findings against the ROC as an institution.

The IOC EB took note of a letter dated 23 July 2016 from the International Shooting Sport Federation (ISSF). In this letter the ISSF confirms having received from WADA information about the three "disappearing samples" concerning shooting. The ISSF states that these three samples had been entered, at the time they were reported, into WADA's ADAMS Results Management System as positives, and all the result management procedures have already been followed.

On the basis of the Findings of the IP Report, all Russian athletes seeking entry to the Olympic Games Rio 2016 are considered to be affected by a system subverting and manipulating the anti-doping system. The IP Report indicates that, due to "the highly compressed timeline", the IP has "only skimmed the surface of the extensive data available". The IOC EB therefore came to the conclusion that this view cannot be restricted only to athletes from the 20 Olympic summer sports mentioned in the IP Report.

Under these exceptional circumstances, Russian athletes in any of the 28 Olympic summer sports have to assume the consequences of what amounts to a collective responsibility in order to protect the credibility of the Olympic competitions, and the "presumption of innocence" cannot be applied to them. On the other hand, according to the rules of natural justice, individual justice, to which every human being is entitled, has to be applied. This means that each affected athlete must be given the opportunity to rebut the applicability of collective responsibility in his or her individual case.

After deliberating, the IOC EB decided:

1. The IOC will not accept any entry of any Russian athlete in the Olympic Games Rio 2016 unless such athlete can meet the conditions set out below.

2. Entry will be accepted by the IOC only if an athlete is able to provide evidence to the full satisfaction of his or her International Federation (IF) in relation to the following criteria:

   - The IFs*, when establishing their pool of eligible Russian athletes, to apply the World Anti-Doping Code and other principles agreed by the Olympic Summit (21 June 2016).

   - The absence of a positive national anti-doping test cannot be considered sufficient by the IFs.

   - The IFs should carry out an individual analysis of each athlete's anti-doping record, taking into account only reliable adequate international tests, and the specificities of the athlete's sport and its rules, in order to ensure a level playing field.

   - The IFs to examine the information contained in the IP Report, and for such purpose seek from WADA the names of athletes and National Federations (NFs) implicated. Nobody implicated, be it an athlete, an official, or an NF, may be accepted for entry or accreditation for the Olympic Games.

   - The IFs will also have to apply their respective rules in relation to the sanctioning of entire NFs.

3. The ROC is not allowed to enter any athlete for the Olympic Games Rio 2016 who has ever been sanctioned for doping, even if he or she has served the sanction.

4. The IOC will accept an entry by the ROC only if the athlete's IF is satisfied that the evidence provided meets conditions 2 and 3 above and if it is upheld by an expert from the CAS list of arbitrators appointed by an ICAS Member, independent from any sports organisation involved in the Olympic Games Rio 2016.

5. The entry of any Russian athlete ultimately accepted by the IOC will be subject to a rigorous additional out-of-competition testing programme in coordination with the relevant IF and WADA. Any non-availability for this programme will lead to the immediate withdrawal of the accreditation by the IOC.

Beyond these decisions, the IOC EB reaffirmed the provisional measures already taken on 19 July 2016. They remain in place until 31 December 2016, and will be reviewed by the EB in December 2016.

Additional sanctions and measures may be imposed by the IOC following the final report of the IP and due legal procedure by the IOC Disciplinary Commission established on 19 July 2016 under the chairmanship of Mr Guy Canivet (Vice-Chair of the IOC Ethics Commission, former member of the French Constitutional Court and President of the French Cour de Cassation) and the IOC EB.

The IOC EB reaffirms its serious concerns about the obvious deficiencies in the fight against doping. The IOC thus emphasises again its call to WADA to fully review their anti-doping system. The IOC will make its contribution to this review by proposing measures for clearer responsibilities, more transparency, better supervision procedures and more independence.

* The IAAF has already established its eligibility pool with regard to Russian athletes.

II.

The IOC EB further studied the request by the Russian track and field athlete, Mrs Iuliia Stepanova, to compete in the Olympic Games Rio 2016 as a "neutral athlete". Since Mrs Stepanova declined to compete as a member of the ROC Team, the IOC EB had to consider the question of whether an exception to the rules of the Olympic Charter is possible and appropriate. Since this request has important ethical aspects, the IOC EB had asked the IOC Ethics Commission for its advice. The Ethics Commission has heard Mrs Stepanova and IAAF and ROC representatives.

Mrs Stepanova is basing her request on her role as "whistle-blower" with regard to the manipulation of the anti-doping system and corruption involving the WADA-accredited Moscow Anti-Doping Laboratory, the All-Russia Athletic Federation (ARAF) and the IAAF. The Ethics Commission applauds the contribution of Mrs Stepanova to the fight against doping. It put this contribution into the perspective of Mrs Stepanova's own long implication, of at least five years, in this doping system and the timing of her whistle-blowing, which came after the system did not protect her any longer following a positive test for which she was sanctioned for doping for the first time.

After a careful evaluation of the arguments, the Ethics Commission gave the following advice to the IOC EB:

"While it is true that Mrs Stepanova's testimony and public statements have made a contribution to the protection and promotion of clean athletes, fair play and the integrity and authenticity of sport, the Rules of the Olympic Charter related to the organisation of the Olympic Games run counter to the recognition of the status of neutral athlete. Furthermore, the sanction to which she was subject and the circumstances in which she denounced the doping practices which she had used herself, do not satisfy the ethical requirements for an athlete to enter the Olympic Games."

The IOC EB accepted the advice of the IOC Ethics Commission, also taking into consideration its above-mentioned decision not to allow any Russian athlete who has ever been sanctioned for doping to participate in the Olympic Games Rio 2016. Therefore, the IOC will not enter Mrs Stepanova as a competitor in the Olympic Games Rio 2016.

However, the IOC EB would like to express its appreciation for Mrs Stepanova's contribution to the fight against doping and to the integrity of sport. Therefore the IOC invites Mrs Stepanova and her husband to the Olympic Games Rio 2016. Furthermore, the IOC is ready to support Mrs Stepanova so that she can continue her sports career and potentially join a National Olympic Committee.

SOURCE: International Olympic Committee. "Decision of the IOC Executive Board Concerning the Participation of Russian Athletes in the Olympic Games Rio 2016." July 24, 2016. http://www.olympic .org/news/decision-of-the-ioc-executive-board-concerning-the-participation-of-russian-athletes-in-the-olympic-games-rio-2016.

Olympics Opening Ceremony Remarks
by IOC President Thomas Bach

August 5, 2016

Boa noite, cariocas,
Boa noite, Brasil,

Dear fellow Olympians,

Distingués représentants des autorités brésiliennes,
Votre Excellence, Monsieur le Secrétaire général des Nations Unies, Ban Ki-moon,
Excellences,
Monsieur le Président du comité d'organisation des Jeux Olympiques Rio 2016, mon cher
collègue et ami Carlos Nuzman,
Chers amis olympiques du monde entier,

Bienvenue aux Jeux de la XXXIe Olympiade Rio 2016.

This is the moment of the *cidade maravilhosa*. The first-ever Olympic Games in South America will go from Brazil to the entire world. The Organising Committee, Brazilian authorities at all levels, and all Brazilians can be very proud tonight. With the Olympic Games as catalyst you have achieved in just seven years what generations before you could only dream of. You have transformed the wonderful city of Rio de Janeiro into a modern metropolis and made it even more beautiful.

Our admiration is even greater because you managed this at a very difficult time in Brazilian history. We have always believed in you.

Votre passion pour le sport et votre joie de vivre nous inspirent. Célébrons ensemble ces Jeux
Olympiques dans ce grand pays, le Brésil.

The best ambassadors of this Olympic Spirit à la Brazil are the many thousands of volunteers. *Muito obrigado, voluntários!*

We are living in a world of crises, mistrust and uncertainty.

Here is our Olympic answer:

The ten thousand best athletes in the world, competing with each other, at the same time living peacefully together in one Olympic Village, sharing their meals and their emotions.

In this Olympic world there is one universal law for everybody. In this Olympic world we are all equal. In this Olympic world we see that the values of our shared humanity are stronger than the forces which want to divide us.

So I call upon you, the Olympic athletes: Respect yourself, respect each other, respect the Olympic Values which make the Olympic Games unique for you and for the entire world.

We are living in a world where selfishness is gaining ground, where certain people claim to be superior to others.

Here is our Olympic answer:

In the spirit of Olympic solidarity and with the greatest respect, we welcome the Refugee Olympic Team.

Dear refugee athletes: you are sending a message of hope to all the many millions of refugees around the globe. You had to flee from your homes because of violence, hunger or just because you were different. Now with your great talent and human spirit you are making a great contribution to society.

In this Olympic world we do not just tolerate diversity. In this Olympic world we welcome you as an enrichment to our "Unity in Diversity."

There are millions of people around the world who contribute in different ways to make our world a better place through sport. To honour such outstanding personalities who put sport at the service of humanity, the International Olympic Committee has created a unique distinction, which we award for the first time now. . . .

And now let us all celebrate together Olympic Games à la Brazil.

SOURCE: International Olympic Committee. "Speech on the Occasion of the Opening Ceremony." August 5, 2016. https://stillmed.olympic.org/media/Document%20Library/OlympicOrg/News/President-speech-Rio-2016-Opening-Ceremony/President-speech-Rio-2016-Opening-Ceremony.pdf.

DOCUMENT

Olympics Closing Ceremony Remarks by IOC President Thomas Bach

August 21, 2016

Muito obrigado, cariocas!
Parabéns, Brasil!

Dear fellow Olympians,

Monsieur le Président du comité d'organisation des Jeux Olympiques Rio 2016, mon cher collègue et ami Carlos Nuzman,
Distingués représentants des autorités brésiliennes,
Chers amis olympiques du monde entier,
Nós te amamos, brasileiros! . . .

Thank you to all the volunteers. Your smiles have warmed our hearts. *Valeu, voluntários!*

Thank you to all the Olympic athletes! You have amazed the world with your incredible performances.

You have shown us all the power of sport to unite the world. By competing in friendship and respect, by living in harmony under one roof in one Olympic Village, you are sending a powerful message of peace to the whole world. Together, we can go further. Together, we can aim higher. United in our diversity, we are stronger.

Thank you, dear Refugee Athletes. You have inspired us with your talent and human spirit. You are a symbol of hope to the millions of refugees in the world. We will continue to stay at your side after these Olympic Games.

We arrived in Brazil as guests. Today we depart as your friends. You will have a place in our hearts forever.

Estes foram Jogos Olímpicos maravilhosos, na cidade maravilhosa!

These were marvellous Olympic Games in THE marvellous city!

These Olympic Games are leaving a unique legacy for generations to come. History will talk about a Rio de Janeiro before and a much better Rio de Janeiro after the Olympic Games.

The International Olympic Committee would like to honour the people who made this outstanding success happen. 110 years ago, the founder of the Modern Olympic Games, Pierre de Coubertin, created a unique award—the Olympic Cup.

Tonight this Olympic Cup goes to: *os cariocas!*

The IOC has invited six of you to accept this Olympic Cup.

After sixteen glorious Olympic days, I now have to perform my last official duty here in Rio de Janeiro:

I declare the Games of the XXXI Olympiad closed. In accordance with tradition, I call upon the youth of the world to assemble four years from now in Tokyo, Japan, to celebrate with us the Games of the XXXII Olympiad.

SOURCE: International Olympic Committee. "Speech on the Occasion of the Closing Ceremony." August 21, 2016. https://stillmed.olympic.org/media/Document%20Library/OlympicOrg/News/President-speech-Rio-2016-Closing-Ceremony/President-speech-Rio-2016-Closing-Ceremony.pdf.

OTHER HISTORIC DOCUMENTS OF INTEREST

FROM THIS VOLUME

FROM PREVIOUS *HISTORIC DOCUMENTS*

First Federal CISO Installed; U.S. Officials Respond to Democratic National Committee Hacks

JULY 25 AND SEPTEMBER 8, 2016

The 2016 hack of the Democratic National Committee's (DNC) computer system and allegations that the Russian government was behind the attack fed growing concerns over the United States' cybersecurity. Amid these concerns, President Barack Obama continued his efforts to strengthen the security of the federal government's networks and technology infrastructure, including by naming the first federal Chief Information Security Officer (CISO).

DEMOCRATIC NATIONAL COMMITTEE HACKED

In mid-June, DNC officials reported that the organization's system had been hacked and that hackers had not only accessed the DNC's opposition research on presidential candidate Donald Trump but had also read committee staff e-mail and chats. The DNC reassured donors that no financial or personal information had been accessed or taken.

DNC leaders reportedly learned of the hack in late April, after their information technology team noticed some unusual activity on the committee's computer network. The DNC quickly hired CrowdStrike, a cybersecurity firm, to help identify the hackers. Based on its analysis, the company determined that two hacker groups working for the Russian government were responsible for the attack. One group accessed and took opposition research on Trump, and the other monitored the DNC's e-mail and chat communications. These groups were dubbed "Fancy Bear" and "Cozy Bear," respectively, by CrowdStrike. The company suspected the hackers accessed the DNC's network through "spearfishing" e-mail sent to staff that were made to look as though they were sent by a colleague or trusted source but contained a link or attachment that installed malicious software on computers when clicked, thereby creating an entry point for hackers. CrowdStrike said it believed Fancy Bear worked for the GRU, Russia's military intelligence service, and speculated that Cozy Bear may have worked for Russia's Federal Security Service. Cozy Bear is believed to have been involved in the 2014 hacking of the unclassified e-mail systems of the White House, U.S. State Department, and Joint Chiefs of Staff, and CrowdStrike said that both groups are suspected of hacking public and private entities in the United States and several other countries. At least three other cybersecurity firms independently confirmed CrowdStrike's findings, reporting that the malware and servers used by the hackers were consistent with those used by Fancy Bear and Cozy Bear in prior attacks.

Russian officials denied any involvement in the hack. "I absolutely rule out the possibility that the government or government agencies were involved in this," said Dmitry Peskov, a spokesperson for President Vladimir Putin. German Klimenko, an adviser to

Putin, suggested the hack was the result of DNC carelessness. "Usually these kinds of leaks take place not because hackers broke in, but, as any professional will tell you, because someone simply forgot the password or set the simple password 123456," he said.

LEAKED DOCUMENTS RILE DEMOCRATIC PARTY, PRESIDENTIAL CAMPAIGN

The day after the DNC announced the hack, an individual calling itself Guccifer 2.0 claimed responsibility. Guccifer said it was a Romanian hacker without strong political leanings, which appeared to call Russia's involvement into question. However, experts were not convinced that Guccifer was Romanian or even a single person. Notably, Guccifer had difficulty conversing in Romanian when tested.

Guccifer soon began releasing various DNC documents and e-mail messages to the press, including files related to controversial donors, opposition research conducted on Trump as well as former vice presidential candidate and Alaska Governor Sarah Palin, databases of donor names and contact information, and documents outlining Democrats' strategy for the 2016 election. These leaks were followed by WikiLeaks' publication on July 22 of nearly 20,000 DNC e-mails, which it described as "part one of our new Hillary Leaks series." The e-mail were sent by DNC officials including Communications Director Luis Miranda, National Finance Director Jordan Kaplan, and Finance Chief of Staff Scott Comer, among others, between January 2015 and May 25, 2016. Guccifer 2.0 claimed to have provided the e-mail to WikiLeaks.

The content of the e-mail was politically embarrassing for the DNC, particularly those related to the presidential campaign of Sen. Bernie Sanders, I-Vt. In some exchanges, DNC staff appeared to discuss how to weaken Sanders's campaign, including by encouraging people to ask him about his faith at campaign events and press him about whether he was Jewish or an atheist. Other messages revealed frustrations among some staff over Sanders's refusal to abandon his campaign, particularly once it became clear that former secretary of state Hillary Clinton was going to be the party's nominee. Another e-mail appeared to show a Clinton campaign attorney advising the DNC on how to resolve a dispute between the two campaigns over fundraising for state parties. Sanders had claimed that Clinton's campaign was not doing its fair share of fundraising. The attorney advised the DNC to put out a statement saying Sanders's claims were not true. In yet another e-mail, DNC chair Debbie Wasserman Schultz, D-Fla., called Sanders campaign manager Jeff Weaver "a damn liar" after he criticized the Nevada Democratic Party for how it ran its primary.

The leaks prompted an outcry among Sanders's supporters and threatened the Democratic Party's efforts to unite members behind Clinton with only three days until the Democratic National Convention. Sanders's supporters claimed that the e-mail showed what they had been saying all along—the Democratic Party favored Clinton as a candidate and had acted on that bias. More than 1,000 of them marched in Philadelphia, Pennsylvania, the location of the Democrats' convention, in protest. Sanders called the e-mail an "outrage" and said that Wasserman Schultz should step down as DNC chair. "The party leadership must also always remain impartial in the presidential nominating process, something which did not occur in the 2016 race," he said.

Facing mounting pressure from her party, Wasserman Schultz announced her resignation on July 24, the day before the convention began. "I know that electing Hillary Clinton as our next president is critical for America's future," she said in a statement. "Going forward, the best way for me to accomplish those goals is to step down as party chair at the end of this convention." Wasserman Schultz initially planned to open and close the convention and speak to the delegates, but she abandoned those plans after being confronted by protestors at a breakfast for the Florida delegation. Donna Brazile, a DNC vice chair, was named the interim chair through the election. The DNC apologized to Sanders on July 25. "On behalf of everyone at the DNC, we want to offer a deep and sincere apology to Senator Sanders, his supporters, and the entire Democratic Party for the inexcusable remarks made over email," the statement read. A week later, the DNC announced that CEO Amy Dacey, CFP Brad Marshall, and Miranda were leaving the organization.

Amid these changes in DNC leadership, the Clinton campaign began to suggest that Russia was attempting to influence the outcome of the presidential election with the hack and subsequent leak of DNC documents. Clinton campaign manager Robby Mook said on ABC's *This Week* that "experts are telling us that Russian state actors broke into the DNC, stole these emails, [and are] releasing these emails for the purpose of helping Donald Trump." He also noted that Trump favored warmer relations with Russia. When asked on the same program whether there were any ties between the Trump campaign and Russia, Trump campaign chair Paul Manafort responded, "No, there are not. That's absurd. And, you know, there's no basis to it." Trump fueled questions about his potential connection to Russia when he said, "Russia, if you're listening, I hope you're able to find the 30,000 emails that are missing" during a press conference. Trump later said the comment, a reference to e-mail from Clinton's tenure as secretary of state, was "sarcastic" and denied accusations that he was inviting a foreign government to interfere with the election. Trump further speculated that the hack had been faked by the DNC in an effort to damage his campaign and claimed that the e-mail showed the Democrats' primary election system was "rigged."

Metadata from the leaked e-mail indicated that the documents passed through Russian computers before they were released. The Federal Bureau of Investigation (FBI) announced an investigation into the hack on July 25. "A compromise of this nature is something we take very seriously, and the FBI will continue to investigate and hold accountable those who pose a threat in cyberspace," it said in a statement. When asked during a press conference if the White House believed Russia was behind the attack, Press Secretary Josh Earnest demurred, stating, "We know that there are a variety of actors, both state and criminal, who are looking for vulnerabilities in the cybersecurity of the United States, and that includes Russia. But as it relates to this situation . . . the FBI is going to lead a careful investigation, and if there is a decision that's made to release information about conclusions that have been reached about the attribution of this attack, then it's likely that the FBI would be the first one to make that announcement." Earnest also said he did not believe Obama had discussed the hacking incident with Putin.

A few days later, officials disclosed that the Democratic Congressional Campaign Committee (DCCC) had also been hacked. Guccifer 2.0 and WikiLeaks continued to publish documents from both the DNC and DCCC through the summer and into the fall.

Federal CISO Named in Obama Administration Cybersecurity Push

The DNC hack was one of several incidents that fed concerns over cybersecurity and potential cyber-attacks against the United States, including a major security breach at the Office of Personnel Management (OPM) in 2015. In two separate hacks, personnel data for more than 4 million current and former federal government employees were stolen and records from the background investigations of more than 21 million current, former, and prospective government employees and contractors were stolen. OPM Director Katherine Archuleta resigned, and U.S. chief information officer Tony Scott launched a thirty-day Cybersecurity Sprint to prompt federal agencies to begin taking immediate steps to increase the security of federal information and networks. The Obama administration, which had already taken a number of actions to bolster national cybersecurity, took further action on this issue in 2016.

On September 8, Scott and Special Assistant to the President and Cybersecurity Coordinator Michael Daniel announced the installation of retired brigadier general Gregory Touhill as the nation's first federal CISO. In this newly created position, Touhill is responsible for driving cybersecurity policy, planning, and implementation across the federal government. He also works with a team from the Office of Management and Budget (OMB) to conduct "periodic cyberstat reviews with federal agencies to insure that implementation plans are effective and achieve the desired outcomes." In addition to Touhill's appointment, Scott and Daniel announced that Grant Schneider, the National Security Council's (NSC) director for cybersecurity policy, would serve as the acting deputy CISO. "Strong cybersecurity depends on robust policies, secure networks and systems and, importantly, a cadre of highly skilled cybersecurity talent," said Scott and Daniel in their joint release. "[T]he CISO will play a central role in helping to ensure the right set of policies, strategies, and practices are adopted across agencies and keeping the Federal Government at the leading edge of 21st century cybersecurity."

Creating the federal CISO position was one of several measures called for in Obama's Cybersecurity National Action Plan, announced in February 2016. According to the White House, the plan "takes near-term actions and puts in place a long-term strategy to enhance cybersecurity awareness and protections, protect privacy, maintain public safety as well as economic and national security, and empower Americans to take better control of their digital security." The Obama administration took several additional steps to begin implementing this plan in 2016, including by establishing the Commission on Enhancing National Cybersecurity. Comprised of twelve "top strategic, business, and technical thinkers from outside of Government," the commission is charged with recommending actions the federal government can take in the next ten years to strengthen cybersecurity in both the public and private sectors. The administration also proposed creating a $3.1 billion Information Technology Modernization Fund that would help modernize government IT and replace technology that is difficult to maintain and secure. Additionally, a Federal Cybersecurity Workforce Strategy was developed to "grow the pipeline of highly skilled cybersecurity talent entering federal service, and retain and better invest in the talent already in public service."

The Cybersecurity National Action Plan built on the Obama administration's previous actions to address cybersecurity concerns. These included the administration's 2015 implementation of a Cybersecurity Strategy and Implementation Plan for the federal civilian government, which seeks to identify cybersecurity gaps and priorities and make recommendations for addressing those issues. A 2014 Executive Order created the BuySecure initiative to give American consumers more tools to help secure their personal financial information and to improve the security of the government's electronic payment systems. Congress also acted to bolster cybersecurity when it passed the Cybersecurity Act in

December 2015, which makes it easier for private companies to share information about cyber threats among themselves and with the government, among other measures.

—Linda Fecteau Grimm

Following are excerpts of a White House press briefing on July 25, 2016, in which Press Secretary Josh Earnest answered questions about the Democratic National Committee hack; and a press release issued by U.S. chief information officer Tony Scott and Special Assistant to the President and Cybersecurity Coordinator Michael Daniel from September 8, 2016, announcing the first federal chief information security officer.

Press Secretary Josh Earnest Responds to the DNC Hack

July 25, 2016

[The following text related to the DNC hacking has been excerpted from the full press briefing transcript.]

Q. . . . Does the President feel that what we're seeing the last couple days in the party hurts the party's unity, heading into the general? Does he think the emails show favoritism by the DNC towards Clinton during the primary? And does he have any thoughts on who should be the next leader of the Democratic Party?

MR. EARNEST: . . . There are plenty of people who are in Philadelphia who can speak to the current state of our party and the current efforts to organize our party for success in the general election, and I'll let them speak to that. . . .

As it relates to the situation at the, the President has been clear about a couple of things. The first is he deeply appreciates what Congresswoman Wasserman Schultz has done during her five-year-plus tenure at the Democratic National Committee. She took the helm at the DNC at a critically important time in President Obama's career. She had to, on a pretty short turnaround, work to prepare the DNC for the general election in 2012. And obviously the President won that reelection campaign with more than 50 percent of the vote. He's the first President since Eisenhower to both be elected and reelected with more than 50 percent of the vote. And that certainly speaks to some of Congresswoman Wasserman Schultz's skills because the apparatus at the DNC was an important part of that effort.

So that's the first thing. And I think the President conveyed that appreciation in the context of the statement that we issued last night. What's also true, and what's been true for some time, is that the President believes that the leadership at the DNC is something that should be determined by the party nominee. The ability of the party apparatus and the Democratic nominee's campaign working effectively together will be important to our success in the fall. And so as the leader of the party, that's the President's interest. So he's long said that it's the party nominee that should make the decisions about the leadership of the DNC. And he certainly has been unequivocal in his support for Secretary Clinton, the presumptive nominee, and her ability to make that decision.

Q. Does he think Wasserman Schultz was fair to Sanders in the primary?

MR. EARNEST: Listen, I'm not going to get into the content of the email. Obviously there are plenty of people with plenty of opinions about that, and I know that Senator Sanders, himself, spoke to this a little bit yesterday and certainly in those comments he indicated his unwavering support for Secretary Clinton.

Q. Turning to the investigation into this hack that the FBI is now leading, after the Sony hack, you were all relatively quick to point the finger at North Korea. Are you prepared at this point to say anything about whether Russia was involved in this hack and whether it may have been an attempt by a foreign state to try and sway the election towards Donald Trump?

MR. EARNEST: . . . [L]et's go back to the Sony situation back in late 2014. There was a careful and intensive law enforcement investigation into that hack. Obviously it generated lots of headlines. And an assessment was reached by a variety of national security agencies, including the FBI, that the actor involved was clear and the impact that it would have on the investigation to release the conclusions that they'd reached about the attribution would be beneficial.

So those are two separate determinations that have to be reached. Ultimately those conclusions will be reached by these national security agencies who are focused on the national security of the United States and the successful completion of the investigation.

So I know that there's been a lot of public reporting about this particular matter and I know that there are some private sector entities that have conducted their own investigations and even released their own reports on these investigations. I'm not in a position to speak to the veracity of what conclusions have been reached by private sector entities. At this point, it's my responsibility to protect the ability of the FBI and other national security agencies to do their work, to conduct these investigations and to follow the facts where they lead.

So if there's a decision that is made by our national security professionals to release additional information about what they've learned in the context of this investigation, it seems likely, as was the case in 2014, that they will be the first to release that information.

So the FBI has put out a statement indicating that they are investigating this situation, and the President and his team obviously have made cybersecurity a top priority. We know that there are a variety of actors, both state and criminal, who are looking for vulnerabilities in the cybersecurity of the United States, and that includes Russia. But as it relates to this situation, we're going to conduct—the FBI is going to lead a careful investigation, and if there is a decision that's made to release information about conclusions that have been reached about the attribution of this attack, then it's likely that the FBI would be the first one to make that announcement. . . .

Q. How does the President or you feel about what was in those emails that were leaked?

MR. EARNEST: Well, listen, I have very little insight into the inner workings of the Democratic National Committee, so I'll refer you to the DNC and the Clinton campaign to describe the content of those emails and what it says about the operations of the DNC. . . .

Q. So you don't have a feeling on whether that was—whether it seemed to be an attempt to undermine Bernie Sanders while this was going on?

MR. EARNEST: Again, I can't speak to the veracity of the emails. I'd refer you to the DNC.

Q. And what role did the President play in Wasserman Schultz stepping down? Did he want that to happen? And I know the conversation happened afterwards, but how did the President make his feeling known in the process?

MR. EARNEST: . . . [T]he President's view is that the Democrat at the top of the ticket in the fall is the one who should make decisions about the leadership of the DNC. It's been the President's view for quite some time. The President obviously had that prerogative when he was running in 2008. The President had that prerogative when he was at the top of the ticket in 2012. But his name is not on the ballot in 2016. . . .

So, ultimately, the Clinton campaign had to determine what they believed was in the best interest of their campaign and the best interest of the party. And that's what they did. The substance of the phone call yesterday was simply the President taking the opportunity to express his appreciation to Congresswoman Wasserman Schultz for her service to the country and to the party. And he certainly continues to be enthusiastic about her reelection campaign—he endorsed her earlier this year. And he believes that the people of South Florida have been remarkably well-served by having her represent their interests in the United States Congress, and he believes they'll—as he said in his statement that we issued earlier this spring—he made clear that he supports her reelection. . . .

Q. Has the President spoken with President Putin about that hack, or have other high-level administration officials spoken with Russian officials about this hack?

MR. EARNEST: I'm not aware that the President has mentioned any of these reports to President Putin in their conversations. I know the issue of cybersecurity is one that President Obama has prioritized, and I feel confident that at one point or another, that issue has come up in his previous conversations with President Putin. But I'm not aware that this particular incident, or the reports of this particular incident have been a subject of conversation between President Obama and President Putin.

Q. Do you have a sense of the motive for this attack? And would it possibly have been to interfere with the electoral process?

MR. EARNEST: Well, as the FBI conducts their investigation, they certainly would be looking to ascribe some responsibility for this breach, and, in doing so, I'm sure they will consider potential motives.

Q. You don't—the administration doesn't have an opinion on that at this point?

MR. EARNEST: Again, this particular situation is still being investigated by the FBI, and I just don't want to do anything that would make their—or say anything that would make their investigation more complicated than it already is.

Q. Have you said anything to the Russian government at this point about, hey, we don't think it's kosher for you to interfere in our political process? . . .

MR. EARNEST: Well, again, I'm not aware of any communication like that at least from the White House, in part because this is the subject of an ongoing FBI investigation. But I'm not aware of a message like that being sent.

Q. You mentioned two criteria that the administration examined in deciding to reveal that North Korea was the source of the Sony leak. One was clarity of evidence, and the other was a determination by the intelligence agencies that it was beneficial to the United States to release that information. In this case, would there be other criteria you would consider? And would that decision be shaped by the possibility that this would be an attempt to interfere with the U.S. electoral process?

MR. EARNEST: Well, listen, what I can tell you is that this investigation will be guided by the facts and not by the political implications, or potential political implications. The FBI and other national security agencies are focused on this, and they have experts that they can use to examine this situation. And they will use that expertise and they will follow the facts where they lead to reach conclusions, and then they will determine, based on broader policy implications, how much of that they can discuss publicly.

So this is a process that is ongoing. And again, there's just not that much that I can say about it as the President's spokesperson that doesn't risk potentially interfering or some- how making their investigation even more complicated than it already is.

Q. . . . Looking at it, looking at the way it's played out, do you think [Wasserman Schultz] and the DNC have been fair to Bernie Sanders, as you, as astute political observers, can determine from the outside?

MR. EARNEST: Well, listen, I think what is true is that there are going to be people with intense passions with a variety of points of view. And given the fact that I don't have much insight into the inner workings of the DNC beyond what I guess what we've all read in the—

Q. —what we all saw.

MR. EARNEST: Yes, based on what we've all read in the newspaper, that's given plenty of people an opportunity to develop their own perspective and, in some cases, share their point of view. I just don't have much insight into the inner workings of the DNC, particu- larly over the course of this campaign.

So I'll let other people make up their own minds on this. But what is true is that Senator Sanders himself has indicated that even in light of all this news and some of these emails, his support for Secretary Clinton hasn't changed. . . .

Q. And lastly this—just slightly different than what people have asked before, but not too distant. Is the President happy that he kept Ms. Schultz in charge of the DNC up through this point—

MR. EARNEST: Congresswoman Wasserman Schultz has done—

Q. —through this primary process?

MR. EARNEST: Look, the President believes that Congresswoman Wasserman Schultz, over the course of the last five years that she was leading the DNC, did an excellent job. And again, I think the results speak for themselves in terms of the President's success in winning reelection with more than a majority of the vote. Obviously the DNC made an important contribution to that effort.

And Congresswoman Wasserman Schultz has also been responsible for leading the party through a competitive Democratic primary process. And the prospects—again, based on the—there are many people, publicly, who have taken a look at the election and have concluded that the Democratic Party is in good shape in the general election. And certainly the condition of the Democratic Party is something that Congresswoman Wasserman Schultz deserves credit for.

I would just add that there's nobody who thinks that being the chair of a national party is an easy job, or is a job where a whole bunch of people come up to you and say thank you. And having worked for two previous DNC chairs directly, I can speak first-hand to that. So it's not just that Congresswoman Wasserman Schultz served for five years; it's not just that she did an excellent job both in helping the President get reelected but also in positioning the party for success in 2016; it's that this is a job that's really hard and is subject to a lot of intense criticism. . . .

Q. Was there a meeting here at the White House over the weekend regarding the DNC hack?

MR. EARNEST: Well, I know that there have been some reports about national security officials discussing this breach. I don't have any specific meetings to tell you about. What I can tell you is that it shouldn't be a surprise that there are national security officials that meet on a regular basis here at the White House to discuss cybersecurity. The President has made that a top priority and obviously the cybersecurity, both the public sector but also private sector, entities is important to our national security. And this is something that is discussed frequently by national security officials across the government, but including here at the White House. . . .

Q. You outlined that it's going to be a very deliberate process, and you can't say whether or not officially that Russia is behind this. But the Clinton campaign is being pretty direct in attributing this attack to Russia. Do you think they're jumping the gun?

MR. EARNEST: Well, they're not the only ones that have been pretty direct. I know that a number of your news organizations have been quite direct in drawing that link. And there are also some private sector—at least one high-profile private sector group that's issued a report drawing that link in rather bright lines. . . . I'd refer you to that company or to the DNC or the Clinton campaign about those conclusions. Right now, the United States government is conducting an investigation to formulate our own conclusions about this situation, and I just don't want to get ahead of their investigation from here. . . .

Q. Josh, I mean the thing that's different is it wouldn't be unprecedented for Russia to hack the administration. They recently have hacked unclassified systems at State and the White House, and that's been acknowledged. When it comes to this particular thing, though, this seems a different level to be directly interfering in an election. . . . Can you explain how you're thinking of this?

MR. EARNEST: I actually don't believe, at least from here, we have been direct about ascribing any attribution for the other breaches that you mentioned, including at the State Department and here at the White House. . . . We take those matters quite seriously, and the fact that I'm unwilling to talk in much detail about this situation is not an indication that somehow the administration or our national security agencies take this lightly. In fact, I think it might be an indication of just how seriously we treat this matter that I don't want to say something that could, as a representative of the White House and as a spokesperson for the President, that would make this investigation even more complicated than it already is. . . .

SOURCE: The White House. "Press Briefing by Press Secretary Josh Earnest, 7/25/16." July 25, 2016. https://obamawhitehouse.archives.gov/the-press-office/2016/07/25/press-briefing-press-secretary-josh-earnest-72516.

Announcement of the First Federal Chief Information Security Officer

September 8, 2016

In February, President Obama announced a Cybersecurity National Action Plan (CNAP) that takes a series of short-term and long-term actions to improve our cybersecurity posture within the Federal Government and across the country. The CNAP builds upon a comprehensive series of actions over the last nearly eight years that have fundamentally shifted the way we approach security in the digital age and raised the level of cybersecurity across the country.

Over the last year alone we've made significant progress. For example, we've:

- established the Commission on Enhancing National Cybersecurity, consisting of top strategic, business, and technical thinkers from outside the government to make critical recommendations on actions that can be taken over the next decade to strengthen cybersecurity in both the public and private sectors while protecting privacy and public safety;

- proposed legislation to establish a $3.1 billion Information Technology Modernization Fund (ITMF) to modernize government IT and retire and replace legacy IT that is difficult to secure and expensive to maintain;

- directed implementation of a Cybersecurity Strategy and Implementation Plan (CSIP) for the Federal civilian government as well as the first-ever Federal Cybersecurity Workforce Strategy to identify, recruit, develop, retain, and expand the pipeline of the best, brightest, and most diverse cybersecurity talent for Federal service and for our Nation.

While we've seen progress, and as the President has made clear on many occasions, there's much more to do. That's why today we are proud to announce Brigadier

General (retired) Gregory J. Touhill as the first Federal Chief Information Security Officer (CISO).

A key feature of the CNAP is creation of the first CISO to drive cybersecurity policy, planning, and implementation across the Federal Government. General Touhill is currently the Deputy Assistant Secretary for Cybersecurity and Communications in the Office of Cybersecurity and Communications (CS&C) at the Department of Homeland Security (DHS), where he focuses on the development and implementation of operational programs designed to protect our government networks and critical infrastructure. In his new role as Federal CISO, Greg will leverage his considerable experience in managing a range of complex and diverse technical solutions at scale with his strong knowledge of both civilian and military best practices, capabilities, and human capital training, development and retention strategies. Greg will lead a strong team within OMB who have been at the forefront of driving policy and implementation of leading cyber practices across federal agencies, and is the team that conducts periodic cyberstat reviews with federal agencies to insure that implementation plans are effective and achieve the desired outcomes.

In addition to the naming the first Federal CISO, we are also proud to announce Grant Schneider as the Acting Deputy CISO. In creating the CISO role, and looking at successful organizational models across government, it became apparent that having a career role partnered with a senior official is not only the norm but also provides needed continuity over time. Grant currently serves as the Director for Cybersecurity Policy on the National Security Council staff at the White House where he focuses on development and oversight of cybersecurity policies to protect government data, networks, and systems, and brings over 20 years of technical skills to the role.

Strong cybersecurity depends on robust policies, secure networks and systems and, importantly, a cadre of highly skilled cybersecurity talent. Building on the Cybersecurity Workforce Strategy to identify, recruit, and retain top talent, the CISO will play a central role in helping to ensure the right set of policies, strategies, and practices are adopted across agencies and keeping the Federal Government at the leading edge of 21st century cybersecurity.

SOURCE: The White House. "Announcing the First Federal Chief Information Security Officer." September 8, 2016. http://www.whitehouse.gov/blog/2016/09/08/announcing-first-federal-chief-information-security-officer.

OTHER HISTORIC DOCUMENTS OF INTEREST

FROM THIS VOLUME

- RNC and the DNC Leaders Remark on Super Tuesday; Trump and Clinton Accept Nominations, p. 127
- CIA and FBI Release Findings on Russian Involvement in U.S. Election, p. 511
- Donald Trump Elected U.S. President, p. 612

FROM PREVIOUS *HISTORIC DOCUMENTS*

- FBI and North Korea Respond to Sony Hack, *2014*, p. 637

August

United Nations, Haitian Government Respond to Cholera Epidemic and Hurricane Matthew

AUGUST 19, OCTOBER 5, AND NOVEMBER 4, 2016

Late in the 2016 hurricane season, the first Category 5 hurricane in the Atlantic in nearly a decade made landfall on the small Caribbean island nation of Haiti. The damage was catastrophic: Hurricane Matthew inflicted nearly $2 billion in damage, killed hundreds of Haitians, washed away entire towns and villages, and left over a million more people food insecure. However, the full extent of the destruction would remain unknown until the following days and weeks. In remote mountain towns and coastal villages, relief workers found a county ravaged not just by the storm, but also by the resurgence of cholera, a deadly bacterial infection. Since 2010, Haiti had fought against a cholera epidemic, which began when waste from infected United Nations (UN) peacekeepers, who were sent to rebuild following the 2010 earthquake, entered local water supplies. Following six years of denial and silence, and after mounting international and public pressure, the UN acknowledged its role in, and issued a rare public apology for, sparking and spreading the cholera epidemic. While relief efforts continued, the UN pledged to eliminate cholera from the island, citing its "moral responsibility" to assist the impoverished nation and to compensate victims of the epidemic.

From Tropical Wave to Category 5 Hurricane, Preparation for Hurricane Matthew

In late September 2016, a tropical wave emerged in the warm waters off the coast of Africa. Just over one week later, the wave, now a tropical storm, rapidly intensified as it tracked across the Caribbean Sea, growing into a Category 5 hurricane. People across the Caribbean, Central and South America, and the southeast United States braced for impact.

Originally forecast to pass to the southwest of Haiti, the storm unexpectedly turned eastward, threatening to bisect the island nation. Days before its scheduled landfall, the Haitian government upgraded its warning to a hurricane watch, activated its National Emergency Operations Center, and halted all coastal shipping. In an address to the nation, provisional President Jocelerme Privert called on residents on outlying islands and in poorly constructed homes to evacuate to the mainland.

Despite the early warnings, the impoverished island nation was largely unprepared to deal with a large-scale natural disaster. The government maintained only 576 shelters, with a collective capacity of 90,000 people, for all of southern Haiti. Residents refused to leave their homes, and many were unaware that a deadly storm bore down on them. Municipalities lacked adequate supplies, including clean drinking water, causing authorities to ask citizens in more secure housing to take in vulnerable neighbors. In total, the government prepared 1,300 shelters with a total capacity of 340,000 people, well below the amount needed to adequately prepare the population threatened by the storm's path.

While the Haitian government prepared for impact, nongovernmental and nonprofit groups readied aid workers to assist in the aftermath. The poorest county in the Western hemisphere, Haiti appealed for coordinated help from humanitarian aid groups, wealthier neighbor countries, and international organizations. The Haitian embassy in Washington, D.C., strongly encouraged "a coordinated and strategic approach" from response groups and asked each to work with local organizations and institutions "to prevent misused time and resources." In total, more than 18,000 volunteers and members of the UN Disaster Assessment and Coordination, international relief organizations such as the Red Cross and Save the Children, municipal committees, and local emergency services readied to assist in the aftermath of Hurricane Matthew.

LANDFALL, DESTRUCTION, AND DISEASE

On the morning of October 4, 2016, Hurricane Matthew made landfall in southwest Haiti near the town of Les Anglais. Despite weakening to a Category 4, Matthew was the largest disaster to hit the country since the catastrophic 2010 earthquake. Winds of nearly 145 miles per hour flattened homes and power lines, heavy rainfall between twenty to forty inches sparked flash floods and inundated city centers, and a nearly ten-foot surge washed away buildings and flooded much of the Tiburon Peninsula. Nationwide, the hurricane severely damaged or destroyed hundreds of thousands of homes, including 90 percent of those along the southern coast. Entire cocoa and coffee plantations and food stores were swept away. In all, Matthew inflicted an estimated $1.89 billion in damage and left nearly one-fifth of the Haitian population, or 1.4 million people, in need of humanitarian assistance and food insecure. The Center for Disaster Management and Risk Reduction Technology estimated that approximately 1,600 Haitians were killed by the storm; however, the official government casualty count stands at 546.

The Grand'Anse Department in southwest Haiti was the hardest hit. High winds destroyed power lines and communication towers, throwing the region into darkness and isolating residents from relief efforts. Crops and livestock were destroyed. The capital of the department, Jérémie, lost 80 percent of its buildings and remained cut off from outside aid for four days. Families who did survive were ripped apart. Save the Children reported that at least 2,000 children who were separated from their parents or living in orphanages were evacuated in the days following the hurricane.

Yet the storm's full destruction was unknown until aid workers made their way into the coastal towns and mountain villages. There, officials found areas ravaged not only by rainfall, mudslides, and floodwater, but also by cholera, a highly infectious and deadly intestinal bacterial disease. Cholera is caused when contaminated food or water is ingested and inflicts uncontrollable diarrhea, vomiting, and dehydration. Though easily treatable, the disease is extremely deadly. Nearly 50 percent of victims who do not get adequate rehydration therapy die.

Although Haiti had battled a cholera epidemic since 2010, Hurricane Matthew's destruction offered the disease new opportunities to spread. More than 1,300 new cases were reported following the storm, which destroyed thirty-four cholera treatment centers nationwide, including roughly three-fourths of relief facilities in the south. Floods caused by waves and high winds spread dirty water over the mountains, contaminating rivers and drinking supplies. Clean water, hard to find long before the storm, was now in even greater demand.

UN Role in Spreading Cholera

Cholera first arrived at the island nation six years prior by the same international aid workers now dispatched to help rebuild Haiti following Hurricane Matthew. In response to the devastating 2010 earthquake, the UN sent international aid workers and peacekeepers from across the globe to establish health clinics, protect those stranded, and help rebuild vital public infrastructures. Of these peacekeepers, 454 arrived directly from Nepal, where a cholera outbreak was flourishing at the time. Later investigations indicated that some of these peacekeepers were infected and uncovered that the base that housed them lacked appropriate sewage infrastructure and waste disposal procedures, which allowed waste to leak into nearby waterways.

The deadly disease spread quickly, sustained by lack of clean water and an inadequate initial response from the Haitian government and the UN. Haiti's rudimentary sanitation and health practices, untreated water, and poor hygiene offered the disease a foothold. Compounding the issue, the UN could not raise the necessary funds from its member countries to address the epidemic, while a lack of proper administrative oversight crippled response systems. As such, the cholera eradication program failed to stem the rising infection rates, and sanitation projects dried up in their infancy from a lack of funds.

By the time Hurricane Matthew struck, the UN had not completed a single major sanitation project established in the wake of the 2010 epidemic; other efforts, such as pilot wastewater processing plants, withered due to a lack of donor funds. Most distressing, internal auditors found that peacekeepers continued to release waste into public canals as late as 2014, four years after the epidemic began. In the six years between the deadly earthquake and Hurricane Matthew, the cholera epidemic killed nearly 10,000 Haitians and infected more than 800,000 others, according to official accounts. Some research has suggested that the death toll could be far higher.

A "Moral Responsibility" to Help

While the UN struggled to battle the epidemic on the ground, its leadership refused to acknowledge the source of the disease or claim any responsibility. Despite a class action lawsuit filed in October 2013 in the U.S. District Court for the Southern District of New York in connection with the outbreak, the UN denied any fault and rejected calls to compensate the victims. However, medical reports, outside investigations, and public inquiries from member countries' governing bodies, including the United States Congress, forced the UN to more accurately and publicly assess its role in sparking the epidemic.

In particular, a scathing report from Philip Alston, an independent UN human rights adviser, placed the spotlight back on the international organization's role in and response to the cholera outbreak. Alston lambasted the UN's years of silence and denial, stating in the confidential report sent to UN Secretary-General Ban Ki-moon—later leaked to *The New York Times*—that the epidemic "would not have broken out but for the actions of the United Nations."

Alston described the UN's Haiti cholera policy as "morally unconscionable, legally indefensible, and politically self-defeating," and argued that it "upholds a double standard according to which the U.N. insists that member states respect human rights, while rejecting any such responsibility for itself." The entire UN system was at fault, Alston argued. "As the magnitude of the disaster became known, key international officials carefully avoided acknowledging that the outbreak had resulted from discharges from the camp."

Faced with mounting international pressure, the UN renewed its call to fight the epidemic and promised to compensate those harmed. Ban issued a statement in which he said he "deeply regrets the terrible suffering the people of Haiti have endured as a result of the cholera epidemic" and described the UN's "moral responsibility" to help Haiti overcome the epidemic and build proper water, sanitation, and health systems. Following Hurricane Matthew, the secretary-general went a step further, issuing a rare public apology for the international organization's role in the spread of the disease. Speaking before the General Assembly in December, Ban said the UN is "profoundly sorry about our role" and admitted that it "simply did not do enough with regard to the cholera outbreak and its spread in Haiti."

CONTINUED RESPONSE EFFORTS

Despite the horrific loss of property and life, the Haitian government restored order and basic services over the next few weeks. Schools reopened within two weeks of landfall, while repair crews restored roads and communications systems. At the same time, international organizations including the World Health Organization (WHO) treated those affected, while others such as the Pan American Health Organization monitored and mitigated the spread of the disease. The UN, among other efforts, transferred $8 million to UNICEF to further programs to stem the spread of disease and established the UN Haiti Cholera Response Multi-Partner Trust Fund, which managed and provided resources dedicated to fighting cholera.

Despite the urgent response from international humanitarian groups, calls to help rebuild Haiti continue. According to the WHO, Haiti still requires assistance in five priority areas: access to health services, increased early detection systems, protective environmental health measures, rapid and effective response to cholera outbreaks, and logistical support for humanitarian assistance. The UN has echoed these concerns, while also pledging to eradicate the deadly disease from the island nation.

—Robert Howard

Following is a statement from UN secretary-general Ban Ki-moon from August 19, 2016, about Haiti's cholera epidemic and UN prevention efforts; a press release issued by the Embassy of Haiti in Washington, D.C., on October 5, 2016, about the nation's hurricane relief efforts; and a press release issued by UNICEF on November 4, 2016, describing the organization's efforts to help rebuild Haiti.

UN Secretary-General Statement on the Cholera Epidemic in Haiti

August 19, 2016

The Secretary-General notes yesterday's decision of the United States Court of Appeals for the Second Circuit, which upheld the immunity of the Organization from legal proceedings in the case of *Georges et al v. United Nations et. al*, in accordance with the UN Charter and other international treaties.

The Secretary-General deeply regrets the terrible suffering the people of Haiti have endured as a result of the cholera epidemic. The United Nations has a moral responsibility to the victims of the cholera epidemic and for supporting Haiti in overcoming the epidemic and building sound water, sanitation and health systems.

Sustained efforts by national authorities and the international community have contributed to a 90 per cent reduction in the number of cases since the peak in 2011. However, eliminating cholera from Haiti will take the full commitment of the Haitian Government and the international community and, crucially, the resources to fulfill our shared duty.

The Secretary-General is actively working to develop a package that would provide material assistance and support to those Haitians most directly affected by cholera. These efforts must include, as a central focus, the victims of the disease and their families. The United Nations also intends to intensify its support to reduce, and ultimately end, the transmission of cholera, improve access to care and treatment and address the longer-term issues of water, sanitation and health systems in Haiti.

Despite repeated appeals, these efforts have been seriously underfunded, and severe and persistent funding shortfalls remain. The Secretary-General urges Member States to demonstrate their solidarity with the people of Haiti by increasing their contributions to eliminate cholera and provide assistance to those affected.

For decades, the United Nations has stood by the Haitian people, supporting them in their quest for democracy and the strengthening of their institutions and helping to rebuild the nation after the tragic earthquake of 2010. The Secretary-General and the United Nations as a whole are determined to continue this support, honour the people of Haiti and help them usher in a more peaceful and prosperous future.

SOURCE: United Nations Secretary-General. "Statement attributable to the Spokesman for the Secretary-General on Haiti." August 19, 2016. http://www.un.org/sg/en/content/sg/statement/2016-08-19/statement-attributable-spokesman-secretary-general-haiti.

Embassy of Haiti Statement on Hurricane Matthew Recovery Efforts

October 5, 2016

On October 4, 2016, a category 4 storm landed in Haiti dumping rain and scouring the land with maximum sustained winds of 145 miles per hour. While this natural disaster has left crops, homes and bridges severely damaged, there have been few casualties. Five storm-related deaths have been reported. As of now, the country is in a period of assessing the full impact and damage caused by this hostile visitor. The government of Haiti, in partnership with civil society organizations, has taken concrete steps to address the urgent needs on the ground.

The next few days will be critical to the recovery process of the nation. It is expected that many will want to engage and take initiatives towards recovery and relief efforts. The state of Haiti strongly encourages all individuals who are in the process of organizing specific responses and action plans, to work with the local organizations and institutions in Haiti. To prevent misused time and resources, a coordinated and strategic approach is highly advised.

The Embassy of Haiti has made itself available to provide guidance, current developments and recent updates. We encourage all who wish to assist to connect with the Embassy of Haiti in Washington DC. . . .

SOURCE: Embassy of the Republic of Haiti in Washington, D.C. "The Embassy of Haiti's Statement on Hurricane Matthew Recovery Efforts." October 5, 2016. http://www.haiti.org/the-embassy-of-haitis-statement-on-hurricane-matthew-recovery-efforts.

UNICEF Reports More than 600,000 Haitian Children Still in Need of Aid

November 4, 2016

One month after Hurricane Matthew pummeled Haiti, nearly 600,000 children remain in need of humanitarian assistance, stalked by disease, hunger and malnutrition, UNICEF said today.

"One month after the hurricane, life for more than half a million children in Haiti is still far from back to normal," said Marc Vincent, UNICEF Representative in Haiti. "Too many children are still homeless, hungry, out of school and in danger. We are scaling up our response and are determined to help as many of them as possible as fast as we can."

Taking stock of the situation of children since the Category 4 storm flattened buildings and destroyed livelihoods, UNICEF said there have been at least 1,000 suspected cholera cases among children in the past month. Out of 219 cholera treatment centres in the country, 18 have been damaged in the worst-hit departments of Grand'Anse and South, further complicating efforts to contain the disease.

Total destruction of crops and loss of food-stocks and livestock in some of the worst affected areas have left over 800,000 people in need of immediate food assistance and more than 112,000 children at risk of acute malnutrition.

An estimated 50,000 children have been left homeless and are staying in temporary shelters. Another 3,500 children living in institutions need help accessing nutrition, water and sanitation services.

Up to 80 per cent of hospitals and health centres in Grand'Anse have lost their roofs. An additional seven health centres in Grand'Anse, four in South and three in Nippes are no longer operational.

More than 700 schools have been affected and about 86 schools have been used as temporary shelters, causing school disruption for at least 150,000 children.

UNICEF is working with national and other partners to provide basic assistance to the most vulnerable children. Joint actions so far include:

- Providing 100,000 people a day with safe water;

- Supporting a cholera vaccination campaign that will be launched next week to immunize up to 900,000 people;

- Providing cholera prevention kits that contain water purification tablets, soap and oral rehydration salts. Between 100 and 200 kits are distributed every day;

- Delivering an integrated package of services to prevent and treat malnutrition among children under five as well as pregnant and breastfeeding mothers living in the hurricane affected areas;

- Replenishing vaccines and restoring the cold chain so that routine immunization can resume in the health centers that are still operational and in mobile clinics;

- Distributing emergency medical supplies to 18 health centers;

- Setting up mobile child friendly spaces where vulnerable children and families can receive psychosocial support, and training 60 volunteers to staff them;

- Repairing 130 schools and distributing school-in-a-box and early childhood development kits so that children can resume their learning as soon as possible.

UNICEF requires over $23 million through the end of the year to meet children's humanitarian needs following the hurricane, including for the cholera response.

SOURCE: United Nations International Children's Emergency Fund. "Hurricane Matthew one month on: More than 600,000 children still in need of aid—UNICEF." November 4, 2016. http://www.unicef.org/media/media_93040.html.

OTHER HISTORIC DOCUMENTS OF INTEREST

FROM PREVIOUS *HISTORIC DOCUMENTS*

Colombia and FARC Reach
Historic Peace Deal

AUGUST 24, OCTOBER 5 AND 28, 2016

For more than fifty years, the Colombian government has been engaged in a civil war involving leftist guerilla and far-right paramilitary groups that has killed thousands, displaced millions, and fueled the country's drug trade. After three previous efforts to secure peace failed, the government reached an historic peace agreement with the Revolutionary Armed Forces of Colombia (FARC), one of the primary guerilla groups involved in the conflict, in 2016. Heralded as a victory for peace, the agreement was surprisingly rejected by Colombian voters, despite projections indicating it would be approved by overwhelming margins. The referendum result pushed the government and the FARC back to the negotiating table to develop a revised agreement that addressed the opposition's concerns.

A DECADES-OLD CONFLICT

Inspired by the Cuban Revolution of the 1950s, leftist groups in Colombia began to form guerilla organizations and challenge the government, claiming that the government's neglect of rural areas had led to poverty and highly concentrated land ownership among the wealthy. The FARC and the National Liberation Army (ELN) are the two primary organizations involved in the conflict, of which the FARC has arguably been the most visible. Beginning as a rural peasant movement based in a mountainous region of Colombia, the FARC evolved into the armed wing of the Colombian Communist Party and declared itself dedicated to overturning systemic social inequality in the country.

Colombia's lack of a strong central government with a widespread presence created an opportunity for the leftists' insurgency to take hold. Both the FARC and the ELN began conducting attacks across the country, destroying villages and infrastructure, as well as killing, raping, and kidnapping civilians. In response, wealthy landowners organized to protect themselves from attack, forming a right-wing paramilitary organization known as the United Self Defense Force of Colombia (AUC). In addition to carrying out attacks against the leftists, the AUC was responsible for numerous attacks against civilians, including the Mapiripán Massacre, in which at least thirty civilians were killed. All three groups are strongly connected to the drug trade in Colombia, which is a major source country for cocaine and heroin. Drug trafficking provided an important source of funding for the groups' activities; Colombian defense minister Juan Carlos Pinzón estimated in October 2012 that the FARC alone made roughly $2.4 billion to $3.5 billion per year from the drug trade.

Roughly 220,000 Colombians have been killed and more than 5 million have been internally displaced because of the conflict. The government also estimates that more than 25,000 Colombians have gone missing or disappeared since the conflict began. Three attempts to negotiate peace were made by the government, the last of which took place between 1998 and 2002 under President Andrés Pastrana. The government designated a demilitarized zone in which peace negotiations could take place, but the FARC used the area as a base for launching attacks, holding hostages, and growing coca for cocaine production. Additionally, the FARC continued its insurgent activities, which included hijacking a commercial airliner and kidnapping a Colombian senator. These actions prompted Pastrana to call off the talks and order the military to retake the designated area; they also contributed to Colombians' disillusionment with the peace process and support for adopting a hardline stance against the FARC.

SANTOS ADMINISTRATION ANNOUNCES PEACE TALKS

In August 2012, President Juan Manuel Santos announced that the government and the FARC had been engaged in exploratory peace talks since 2011, and that these talks had produced an agreed-upon framework for formal negotiations. Observers of the conflict suggested that the timing was right for new talks, given both the government's and the FARC's respective circumstances.

The FARC had weakened considerably since Pastrana left office, due in part to actions taken by President Álvaro Uribe, Pastrana's successor. Uribe implemented a policy of democratic security that combined counterterrorism and counternarcotics tactics in an effort to weaken the guerilla groups and regain control over the country. At the time, estimates indicated the FARC controlled as much as 40 percent of Colombia's territory and the government appeared to be on the verge of collapse due to pressure from the guerillas. In 2003, with U.S. support, Uribe sent troops into parts of Colombia's rural south where the FARC was particularly strong. The military reduced the FARC's fighting force, recaptured land, and confiscated the group's cocaine processing equipment. Five years later the FARC was dealt several blows: the group's supreme leader and founder died of a heart attack; the government killed the FARC's second in command; a third member of the group's seven-person ruling secretariat was killed by his security guard; and the government rescued fifteen longtime hostages. Santos, previously Uribe's defense minister, also made strides against the FARC early in his administration, including killing the FARC's new leader and top military commander in 2010. Additionally, estimates placed the FARC's fighting force at about half the size it was at the height of the conflict, while the Colombian military had doubled in size. Despite these gains, analysts believed the government would not be able to overcome the FARC with force, in part because the group's remaining fighters are spread across terrain that would make a military operation difficult. Amid these realities, the FARC's third leader, Rodrigo Londoño Echeverri, reached out to the government in 2011 to explore possible talks.

Formal negotiations began in Norway in October 2012 before moving to Havana. The FARC was the only group included in the negotiations. Uribe reached a peace deal with the AUC in 2003, and the group was disbanded in 2006. The Santos administration began preliminary peace talks with the ELN in June 2014, but formal negotiations did not begin until February 2017, after the ELN met the government's preconditions of releasing hostages and ending kidnappings. (The FARC met these conditions in the first half of 2012.)

AGREEMENT REACHED, COLOMBIANS VOTE

After more than thirty rounds of talks over nearly four years, the Colombian government and the FARC reached a peace agreement on August 24, 2016. A total ceasefire between the government and the FARC, agreed to in June as part of the negotiations, went into effect five days later.

Among the agreement's key provisions was a stipulation that FARC members would abandon their camps and relocate to twenty-three protected "transitional local zones for normalization" and eight camps scattered across the country. Once they entered the zones, members would surrender all weapons to United Nations (UN) arms inspectors over the course of a six-month period. The agreement also allowed for the FARC to become a national political party, with a guaranteed minimum of five seats in the Senate and in the Chamber of Representatives, and provided special protections for those participating in the party. These security measures were a nod to the 1980s, when the FARC previously tried to establish its own political party, the Patriotic Union. Many party members were elected at the local and national levels in 1986 and 1988, but were targeted by assassination attempts. More than 3,000 party members were killed, prompting the FARC to withdraw from politics and resume its militancy.

The Colombian government agreed to establish a "transitional justice" system through which FARC fighters would be granted amnesty or pardon for certain offenses and reduced sentences for others, as long as they met certain conditions:

> In order to access the special treatment provided for in the Justice component of the [Integral System of Truth, Justice, Reparation and Non-Repetition], it is necessary to provide full truth, to provide reparation to victims, and to guarantee non-repetition. To provide full truth means to report (when the elements for this are available), in a comprehensive and detailed manner the conduct and the circumstances of its commission, as well as the information necessary and sufficient to assign responsibilities, to ensure the satisfaction of the rights of the victims to reparation and non-repetition.

The agreement went on to state that per international humanitarian law, Colombia could grant widespread amnesty at the end of hostilities, and that "rebels who belong to organizations that have signed a final peace agreement . . . will be granted the broadest amnesty possible." However, while the Colombian Constitution permits amnesties or pardons for "the crime of rebellion and other political and related crimes," those suspected of committing crimes against humanity, genocide, war crimes, and other serious offenses would not be eligible for amnesty or pardon.

Additionally, the agreement established a comprehensive program of reparations for victims of the conflict, including psychosocial rehabilitation programs, land restitution programs, a commitment to find and return displaced persons, and mechanisms to enable the FARC and others to contribute to victim reparations. The agreement also covered the reincorporation of the FARC's child fighters into society, prioritizing their access to health care and education and extending the same benefits provided to victims of the conflict. Furthermore, the government committed to investing billions of dollars in long-term rural development projects designed to provide greater access to land, improve infrastructure, and "promote an equitable relationship between rural and urban areas."

The agreement was officially signed in Havana on September 26. "What we sign today is a declaration from the Colombian people before the world that we are tired of war . . . that we don't accept violence as the means of defending ideas," said Santos. On behalf of the FARC, Londoño asked for Colombians' forgiveness for "all of the pain that we have caused during this war," adding, "let no one doubt that we will now pursue politics without weapons." The agreement was welcomed by world leaders, including those in attendance at the signing ceremony. "Today, Colombians are bidding farewell to decades of flames, and sending up a bright flare of hope that illuminates the entire world," said UN Secretary-General Ban Ki-moon. U.S. secretary of state John Kerry also praised the deal, pledging that the United States would provide nearly $400 million to support its implementation. He noted that the United States would not remove the FARC from its list of designated foreign terrorist organizations, but that it would consider removal after implementation began. The European Union's (EU) foreign policy chief, Federica Mogherini, announced that the EU would remove the FARC from its list of terrorist groups, stating the removal would allow the EU "to support the post-conflict programme" and would "be of benefit to all Colombians." Santos would later receive the Nobel Peace Prize for "his resolute efforts to bring the country's more than 50-year long civil war to an end."

Not all Colombians, however, were united behind the peace agreement. Opponents, led by Uribe, argued that the agreement was too lenient. While not opposed to peace, they felt that the agreement should be renegotiated, with tougher consequences for the FARC. For victims of the conflict and their families, the provisions extending amnesty or allowing FARC members to be pardoned were particularly controversial. "With these agreements, there is neither justice nor truth for the victims," said Uribe, who also called Santos a traitor.

As promised by Santos at the start of formal talks, Colombians had an opportunity to vote for or against the deal during a nationwide referendum on October 1. Polling data suggested that the deal would be approved in a landslide, with an estimated 70 percent or more of the public casting votes in its favor. To help shore up support, Santos asked his cabinet to travel across the country to meet with Colombians and explain the tenets of the agreement to them. The FARC also attempted to improve its perception among the public, meeting with families of victims at the sites of FARC-led massacres to ask forgiveness and detonating roughly 1,400 pounds of explosives and military ordnance in the presence of UN observers.

In a surprising turn, Colombians rejected the agreement by a narrow margin of 50.2 percent against to 49.8 percent in favor. Santos was quick to accept and respond to the result, assuring the public that the ceasefire agreement would remain in effect and pledging to meet with the opposition and the negotiating team to determine how to move forward. "I won't give up," he promised. Londoño reiterated the FARC's commitment to peace and declared that "peace will triumph."

A NEW DEAL

On November 11, the government and the FARC announced that they had reached a revised peace agreement, which was signed on November 24. More than fifty changes were made to the original agreement to satisfy the opposition. This included a requirement that the FARC declare and hand over all assets, which would be used to compensate conflict victims. The revised agreement also banned the FARC from running for elected office in newly created districts that are in former conflict zones, although the group could still form a political party and run for office once they disarm. Additionally, a ten-year time limit was established for the transitional justice system, and the revised agreement exposed more FARC fighters to criminal prosecution and jail sentences.

Uribe and his supporters called for another referendum on the revised agreement, but Santos said that since the opposition had already been consulted and many of their requested changes made, Congress should be able to speak for the Colombian people and decide whether to ratify the deal. Congress approved the agreement on November 30 by a unanimous vote after opponents in both chambers walked out in protest. They claimed they were not given enough time to review or comment on the changes. Others said the changes were only cosmetic and that harsher sentences were still needed for FARC rebels who committed crimes.

Congress must now pass various legislation to begin implementing the agreement, including legislation to set up the transitional justice system. On December 13, Colombia's Constitutional Court ruled in favor of a request by the Santos administration for fast-track authority, which enables the president to seek expedited congressional approval for laws and constitutional changes needed to implement the agreement. The Court also affirmed that Congress had the "democratic legitimacy" to approve the deal without holding another referendum. The first piece of legislation likely to be taken up by Congress is an amnesty bill that would free approximately 2,000 FARC rebels from jail and protect them from arrest as they begin moving into the UN-run zones and camps. FARC leaders have said they will not begin to disarm until this amnesty bill is passed.

—Linda Fecteau Grimm

Following are excerpts from the text of the peace agreement reached by the Colombian government and the FARC on August 24, 2016; a transcript of a U.S. State Department background briefing from October 5, 2016, on the Colombian peace process; and a communiqué from Colombia's Commission on Peace from October 28, 2016.

DOCUMENT   *Final FARC Peace Agreement*

August 24, 2016

[The Preamble has been omitted.]

INTRODUCTION

After more than a half century of confrontation, the National Government and FARC-EP have agreed to put a definitive end to the internal armed conflict.

In the first place, the termination of the armed conflict will signify the end of the enormous suffering the conflict has caused. Millions of Colombians are victims of forced displacement, hundreds of thousands are dead, and tens of thousands are missing, not to mention the large amount of the population that has been affected in one way or another across the country, including: women, children, adolescents, rural communities, indigenous peoples, Afro-Colombians, Blacks, *palenqueras*, *Raizals* and *Roms*, political parties, social and union movements, and economic labor unions, among others. We don't want even one more victim in Colombia.

Secondly, the end of the conflict will signify the beginning of a new chapter in our history. It is about starting a new phase of transition that contributes to a larger integration of our territories, a greater social inclusion—especially of those who have lived at the margin of development and have endured the conflict—and strengthening our democracy so that it spreads across the nation and assures that social conflicts are negotiated through institutional channels, with full guarantees for those who participate in politics.

It deals with creating a stable and long-lasting peace, with the participation of all Colombians. With that intent, to put an end once and for all to the historic cycles of violence and to establish a basis of peace, we agreed upon the points of the Agenda of the General Accord of August 2012, which the present Accord puts into practice.

The Accord is comprised of a series of accords that nevertheless constitutes an indissoluble whole, because they are permeated by the same focus on rights, so that the measures agreed upon here contribute to the realization of Colombians' constitutional rights; by the same distinguishing focus on race, to guarantee that the implementation bears in mind racial, ethnic, and cultural diversity, and that they adopt measures for the poorest and most vulnerable populations and groups, especially children, women, the disabled, and victims; and especially by the same territorial focus.

The territorial focus in the Accord means to recognize and bear in mind the necessities, characteristics, and distinctive economic, cultural, and social features of the regions and communities, guaranteeing socio-environmental sustainability; and to be able to implement the different parts of a comprehensive and coordinated method, with active citizen participation. The implementation will be carried out over the regions and territories, with the participation of regional authorities and different sectors of society.

Citizen participation is the foundation of all of the accords that make up the Final Accord. Society's overall participation in the construction of peace, and in particular the planning, execution, and monitoring of plans and programs in the regions, is also a guarantee of transparency.

Additionally, the participation and dialogue between the different sectors of society contribute to the building of confidence and the promotion of a culture of tolerance, respect, and general coexistence that is the objective of all of the accords. Decades of conflict have opened gaps of distrust at society's interior, especially in the regions most affected by the conflict. Breaking those barriers requires making room for diverse citizen participation and spaces that promote the acknowledgment of victims, the acknowledgment and establishment of responsibilities, and in general, the acknowledgment by all of society of what occurred and of the necessity of making the most of the opportunity for peace.

As a result, the Colombian government and FARC-EP, with the intent to further consolidate the basis upon which peace and national reconciliation will be built, once the referendum is completed, will bring together all of the political parties, political and social movements, and all of the intense strength of the country to reach a great NATIONAL POLITICAL ACCORD aimed at defining the reforms and institutional agreements necessary to deal with the challenges that peace demands, setting in motion a new framework of political and social coexistence.

*

The Final Accord contains the following points, with their corresponding accords, that hope to contribute to the transformations necessary to establish the bases of a stable and long-lasting peace.

Point 1 contains the accord "Integrated Rural Reform," that will contribute to the structural transformation of the countryside, closing the breaches between the countryside and the city and creating conditions of well-being and *buen vivir* for the rural population. The "Integrated Rural Reform" should integrate the regions, contribute to eradicating poverty, promote equality, and secure the full benefit of citizens' rights.

Point 2 contains the accord "Political Participation: Opening Democracy to Build Peace." The construction and consolidation of peace, in the time of the end of the conflict, requires a democratic expansion that allows the emergence of new strengths in the political scene to enrich the debate and deliberation around the profound national problems and, that way, strengthen the pluralism and therefore the representation of the different views and concerns of the society, with the due guarantees for participation and political inclusion.

The implementation of the Final Accord will especially contribute to the expansion and deepening of democracy when it will involve the relinquishment of arms and the banishment of violence as a method of political action for all Colombians so as to move to a scene in which democracy prevails, with full guarantees for those who participate in politics, and in that way will open new spaces for participation.

Point 3 contains the accord "Bilateral and Definitive Ceasefire and End of Hostilities and Relinquishment of Arms," which targets the definitive termination of offensive actions between the Public Force and FARC-EP (and hostilities in general) and any planned action in the rules that govern the Ceasefire, including the affectation of the population, and in this way create the conditions for the initiation of the implementation of the Final Accord and the relinquishment of arms and to prepare the institution and the country for the reincorporation of FARC-EP into civilian life.

It also contains the accord "Reintegration of FARC-EP into civilian life—economic, social, and political—according to their interests." To establish the bases for the building of a stable and long-lasting peace requires the effective reintegration of FARC-EP into the social, economic, and political life of the country. The reintegration ratifies the agreement of FARC-EP to close the chapter of internal conflict, become a valid player within democracy, and decidedly contribute to the consolidation of peaceful cohabitation, non-repetition, and to transform the conditions that have facilitated the persistence of violence in the country.

Point 3 also includes the accord on "Guarantees of safety and fight against the criminal organizations responsible for homicides and massacres (or those attempted) against defenders of human rights, social movements or political movements, including the criminal organizations that have been referred to as successors of paramilitarism and their support systems, and the pursuit of criminal behaviors that threaten the implementation of the accords and the construction of peace." To fulfill this purpose, the accord includes measures like the National Political Pact; the National Committee on Safety Guarantees; the Special Investigation Unit; the Elite Body in the National Police; the Integral Security System for the Practice of Politics; the Integral Program of Security and Protection for the Communities and Organizations in the Territories; and the Measures of Prevention and Fight against Corruption.

Point 4 contains the accord "Solution to the Problem of Illicit Drugs." In order to create peace it is necessary to find a definitive solution to the problem of illicit drugs, including the cultivation of illicit use and the production and commercialization of illicit drugs. To this end, a new vision is promoted that gives a different and differentiated treatment to the phenomenon of consumption, to the problem of illicit use of crops, and to organized crime associated with drug trafficking, ensuring a general focus on human rights and public health, differentiated and gendered.

Point 5 contains the accord "Victims." From the Exploratory Conference of 2012, we agree that the compensation of victims should be at the center of each accord. The accord creates the Comprehensive System of Truth, Justice, Reparation, and Non-Repetition, that contributes to the fight against impunity combining judicial mechanisms that permit the investigation and penalty of the grave human rights violations and serious infractions of the International Humanitarian Law, with the supplementary extrajudicial mechanisms that contribute to the elucidation of the truth of what happened, the search for missing loved ones, and the reparation of damages caused to people, to groups, and to entire territories.

The Integral System is composed by the Commission for the Elucidation of Truth, Cohabitation, and Non-Repetition; the Special Unit for the Search for People Reported Missing in the context and reason of the armed conflict; the Special Jurisdiction for Peace; the Measures for Integral Reparation for the Building of Peace; and the Guarantees of Non-Repetition.

Point 6 contains the accord "Mechanisms of implementation and verification" in which is created a "Commission of implementation, monitoring, and verification of the Final Peace Accord and the resolution of differences," integrated for representatives of the National Government and FARC-EP with the purpose, among others, of monitoring the components of the Accord and verifying their compliance, serving as an instance for the resolution of differences, and the momentum and follow-up of the legislative implementation.

In addition, it creates an accompanying mechanism for the international community to contribute in a variety of ways to guaranteeing the implementation of the Final Accord, and in the verification process to set up a model with an integrated international component for the countries that during the process have had the role of guarantors and companions and two international spokespeople, all of them supported in the technical capacity of the project of the Kroc Institute for International Peace Studies at the University of Notre Dame in the United States.

*

The delegations of the National Government and FARC-EP reiterate our profound gratitude to all of the victims, social and human rights organizations, communities including ethnic groups, women's organizations, farmers, youth, academics, entrepreneurs, the Church and communities of faith, and in general to the citizens who actively participated and through their suggestions contributed to the Final Accord. With their participation we will reach the building of a stable and long-lasting peace.

[Sections 1 and 2, which outline a comprehensive rural reform program and measures designed to strengthen democracy and promote citizen participation in politics, respectively, have been omitted.]

3. End of the Conflict

3.1 Accord on Bilateral and Definitive Ceasefire and End of Hostilities and Relinquishment of Arms between the National Government and FARC-EP

The government of the Republic of Colombia (National Government) and the *Fuerzas Armadas Revolucionarias de Colombia-Ejército del Pueblo* (FARC-EP), in development of sub-points 1: Bilateral and Definitive Ceasefire and End of Hostilities and 2: Relinquishment of Arms, of Point 3, End of the Conflict, of the General Accord for the Termination of the Conflict and the Building of a Stable and Long-Lasting Peace, signed in the city of La Habana, Cuba, the 26th of August 2012, agree:

The National Government, in compliance with and on the terms agreed on in Point 2: Political Participation: Opening Democracy to Build Peace," reaffirm their commitment to the implementation of measures that lead to a full political and citizen participation of all political and social sectors, including measures to guarantee the citizens' mobilization and participation in public interest, as well as to facilitate the formation of new parties and political movements with the due guarantees of participation, in safe conditions.

Likewise, the National Government reaffirms its commitment to what was agreed upon in Points 3.4 and 3.6 of Point 3 End of the Conflict, among which is the creation of a new Integral Security System for the Practice of Politics, in the terms agreed on in Point 2 Political Participation, as part of a modern, qualitatively new concept of security which, in the context of the end of the conflict, is founded on respect for human dignity, the promotion and respect of human rights, and the defense of the democratic values, in particular in the protection of the rights and liberties of those who practice politics, especially those who, after the end of the armed confrontation, will become a political movement and therefore must be recognized and treated as such.

In addition, the National Government and FARC-EP express their commitment to contribute to the emergence of a new culture that outlaws the use of weapons in the exercise of politics and to work together to achieve a national consensus of all political, economic, and social sectors, we commit ourselves to an exercise of politics in which the values of democracy, the free exercise of ideas and civilized debate come first; in which there is no room for intolerance and persecution for political reasons. This commitment is part of the guarantees of non-repetition of the acts that contributed to the armed confrontation between Colombians for political reasons.

Finally, the National Government and FARC-EP commit themselves to the accomplishment of what is agreed upon in the matter of the *Cese al fuego y de hostilidades bilateral y definitivo* (CFHBD) and *Dejación de Armas* (DA), for which they will draw up a roadmap containing the mutual commitments so that no later than 180 days after the signing of the Final Accord, the process of relinquishing of arms will have ended.

[The details contained in 3.1.1–3.1.7 have been omitted.]

3.2 Reintegration of FARC-EP into civilian life—economically, socially, and politically—in accordance with their interests

The delegates of the Government of the Republic of Colombia (the National Government) and the *Fuerzas Armadas Revolucionarias de Colombia-Ejército del Pueblo* (FARC-EP) consider that:

To lay the groundwork for the construction of a stable and long-lasting peace requires the effective reintegration of FARC-EP to the social, economic, and political life of the country. The process of reintegration ratifies the commitment of FARC-EP to contribute to the termination of the armed conflict, become upstanding political subjects and decisively contribute to the consolidation of national reconciliation, peaceful coexistence, non-repetition, and to transform the conditions that have allowed the origin and persistence of violence in the national territory. For FARC-EP it is a step of confidence in Colombian society and particularly in the State, insofar as it is expected that everything agreed upon in the set of accords that make up the Final Accord will be effectively implemented in the agreed terms.

The reintegration into civilian life will be a process of integral and sustainable character, exceptional and transitional, which will consider the interests of the FARC-EP community in the process of reintegration, of their members and their families, aimed at strengthening the social fabric in the territories, at the coexistence and reconciliation among those who inhabit them; additionally, to the deployment and development of productive activity and of local democracy. The reintegration of FARC-EP is based on the recognition of individual freedom and the free exercise of the individual rights of each member of FARC-EP who is now in the process of reintegration. The characteristics of the reintegration of this accord are complementary to the accords already agreed upon. The process of reintegration will have in all of its components a differential approach and a gender perspective, with emphasis on women's rights.

In accordance with the provisions of the *Acuerdo Jurisdicción Especial para la Paz* (JEP), with respect to those persons belonging to rebel organizations who have signed the peace accord with the government, for the purpose of reintegration, the criminal offense convictions of the Tribunal for Peace placed by ordinary or disciplinary justice shall be effectively suspended until such time as the convictions have been dealt with by the Special Jurisdiction for Peace within its power.

3.2.1 Political reintegration

The transition of FARC-EP, from organizing in arms to a new party or political movement, which enjoys the rights and fulfills the obligations and proper duties of the constitutional order, is a necessary condition for the end of the armed conflict, the building of a stable and long-lasting peace, and, in general, for the strengthening of democracy in Colombia. To this end, necessary guarantees and conditions that facilitate the creation and operation of a new party or political movement that emerges from the transition of FARC-EP to legal political activity will be adopted, following the signing of the Final Accord and the relinquishment of arms.

In consideration of the above and in development of the political component of the reintegration of FARC-EP to civilian life, according to their interests, as provided for in the General Accord, the following special rules are agreed upon:

3.2.1.1. Guarantees for the new party or political movement

- **Legal status**

At the signing of the Final Accord, the National Electoral Council will process the application for registration submitted by the political grouping of citizens in offices whose purpose is to promote the creation of the future party or political movement that arises from the transition of FARC-EP to legal political life.

After the process of relinquishing arms, the plenipotentiaries of FARC-EP in the Table of Conversations will appear before the National Electoral Council and formally register the decision of their transformation into a political party or movement, the constitutional act, their statutes, code of ethics, the ideological platform and the appointment of its directors. By virtue of this formal act, the political party or movement, with the name it adopts, will be recognized for all purposes and on equal terms as a political party or movement with legal status, for which the National Government will lay out the regulatory reforms that may occur.

The political party or movement thus recognized shall comply with the requirements for the maintenance of legal status and shall be subject to the same grounds for loss established for other parties and political movements, in accordance with the Constitution and the law, except for the accreditation of a number of affiliates, the submission to electoral ceremonies and obtaining a voting threshold, during the time between the date of registration and July 19, 2026.

- **Financing and technical assistance**

- **Operation**

As a measure to facilitate the transition of FARC-EP into legal political activity, the party or political movement that they form will receive annually, between the date of registration and July 19, 2026, a sum equivalent to 10% per year of the budgetary appropriation for the functioning of political parties and movements.

On the other hand, in order to contribute to financing the dissemination and divulgation of its ideological and programmatic platform, an annual 5% of the budget appropriation will be allocated to the functioning of political parties and movements between the date of registration and July 19, 2022.

The above amounts will not affect the amount to be distributed by the Fund for the other parties and political movements with legal status.

The Government will encourage international cooperation to support, with due transparency, the development of infrastructure necessary for the constitution and initial operation of the new party of political movement that arises from the transition of FARC-EP into legal political activity as well as for the training of its leaders.

- **Election campaigns**

The campaigns of candidates for the Presidency and the Senate of the Republic registered by the party or political movement that arises from the transition of FARC-EP into legal political activity to participate in the 2018 and 2022 elections will have predominantly state funding in accordance with the following rules: i) In the case of presidential campaigns, state funding will be recognized that corresponds with to [sic] the candidates who meet the requirements of law, in accordance with provisions applicable to such campaigns; ii) In the case of campaigns to the Senate, anticipated state funding will be received equivalent to 10% of the expenditure limit set by the electoral authority; iii) prior state financing will not be subject to repayment, provided that the resources allocated have been destined to the purposes established in the law.

- **Media access**

The party or political movement that arises from the transition of FARC-EP to legal political activity will have access to spaces in the media under the same conditions as other parties and political movements with legal status, in accordance with the application of the current rules.

- **Security**

The new political movement, its leaders, and militants, will have special security guarantees in the Framework of the Comprehensive Security System for the Exercise of the Policy agreed in section 2.1.2.1., such as those agreed to in section 3.4.

3.2.1.2. Political representation

a. Congress of the Republic

After the signing of the Final Accord and after the relinquishment of FARC-EP arms, and in order to facilitate transition to legal politics and to secure a stage for the promotion of its ideological platform, the National Government will implement the constitutional and legal reforms necessary to ensure, through a provisional formula, the political representation in the Congress of the Republic of the new party or political movement, during two constitutional periods counted from July 20, 2018:

- It may register single lists of its own candidates or in coalition with other parties and/or political movements with legal status for the ordinary district of the Senate of the Republic and for each of the ordinary territorial districts in which the House of Representatives is elected.

- These lists will compete on equal terms in accordance with the ordinary rules by the totality of the seats that are chosen in each circumscription. In the Senate, a minimum of 5 seats is guaranteed, including those obtained in accordance with ordinary rules. For this purpose, the House of Representatives will allocate a seat to each one of the 5 lists that obtain the majority of votes and that have not obtained a seat.

From the effective date of the Final Accord, the political grouping constituted with the objective of promoting the creation of a future party or political movement that arises from the transition of FARC-EP into legal political life, will appoint 3 spokespersons in each of the houses (Senate and House of Representatives), who must be citizens in exercise, exclusively to participate in the debate on draft constitutional or legal reforms that are handled through the Special Legislative Procedure for Peace referred to in the Legislative Act 01 of 2016. These spokespersons should be summoned to all sessions in which draft legislative or legislative acts are discussed and may intervene during the legislative process with the same powers as the delegates, save for the vote. The requirements for performance of your work will be defined with the Ministry of the Interior.

b. Participation in the National Electoral Council

The political party or movement that arises from the transition of FARC-EP to legal political activity may temporarily designate a delegate to the National Electoral Council, who will have a voice but no vote, and may participate in the deliberations of that party conglomerate.

c. Reforms of the democratic opening to build peace

The implementation of the reforms agreed upon in the Accord on "Political Participation: Opening Democracy to Build Peace" is a necessary condition to guarantee a sustainable process of reintegration of FARC-EP into political civilian life. Under the procedure established in Legislative Act 01 of 2016, priority will be given to the presentation and approval of the Statute of the Opposition and the reform of the electoral system.

3.2.2 Economic and social reintegration

3.2.2.1 Organization for collective economic and social reintegration In order to promote a process of collective economic reintegration, FARC-EP will form an organization of social economy and solidarity, called Common Social Economies—ECOMUN. This entity will have national coverage and may have territorial sections. Current members of FARC-EP can voluntarily join this entity. The government will facilitate the legal formalization of ECOMUN through the financing of legal and technical advice, the definition of an expedited and extraordinary procedure for its constitution.

3.2.2.2 Center for Political Thinking and Training The political grouping of citizens in exercise whose purpose is to promote the creation of the future political party or movement that emerges from the transition of FARC-EP to legal political activity will form a Center of thought and political formation, an institution without the intention of profit, which will aim to advance studies and social research, as well as design and advance programs. For this purpose it may hold agreements with public and private entities and international cooperation. For the operation of the Center, the National Government will allocate, from the general budget of the nation, an annual amount equal to that allocated for the dissemination and divulgation of the aforementioned ideological and program platform, until July 19, 2022.

3.2.2.3 Institutional organization—National Council of Reintegration The *Consejo Nacional de la Reincorporación* (CNR), composed of two (2) members of the Government and two (2) of the FARC-EP, will be created, with the task of defining activities, establishing the timetable, and advancing the follow-up of the reintegration, according to the terms agreed on with the government. There will be Territorial Councils of Reintegration equally represented in terms and conditions and with the functions defined by the CNR. These Councils will be organized at the signing of the Final Accord. The CNR may invite institutions, social organizations, or international organizations for the development of their functions.

3.2.2.4 Accreditation and Transition to legality Upon the arrival of the *Zonas Veredales Transitorias de Normalización* (ZVTN) and the *Puntos Transitorios de Normalización* (PTN), the FARC-EP, through a delegate expressly designated for this purpose, will deliver to the National Government a list of all FARC-EP members. This list will be received and accepted by the National Government in good faith, in accordance with the principle of legitimate expectations, without prejudice to the corresponding verifications. In the construction of this list FARC-EP is responsible for the veracity and accuracy of the information contained therein. The Government will provide the necessary facilities for the construction of the lists in the prison centers and will contribute the information available to them in the different institutions of the State.

For the purposes of accreditation, once FARC-EP delivers the list of all members of its organization, the National Government will begin the process of reviewing and contrasting the information contained in it. Their observations will be presented to the FARC, and if not taken into account, a joint dispute settlement mechanism will be established for the review of those cases. The foregoing without prejudice to the acceptance of the other persons included in the list on which no observations are submitted.

As a result of FARC-EP's commitment to end the conflict, to lay down their weapons, to not use them again, to comply with the accord and to move to civilian life; once the members of FARC-EP have left their weapons and ratified the commitment of the organization, will receive their respective accreditation by the National Government based on the list delivered by FARC-EP.

The accreditation will be based on the road map that the Government and FARC-EP agree upon to transition the legality of the members of FARC-EP.

The National Government will receive and accept the definitive list, by means of a formal administrative act, no later than D + 180, without prejudice to previous accreditations that must be made in compliance with the roadmap agreed for the purpose, subsequent accreditations as agreed upon in the framework of the JEP. Exceptionally and after justification, FARC-EP will include or exclude people from the list. The names included will be subject to verification by the National Government.

The final list will include all of the members of FARC-EP whether or not they are deprived of their liberty.

This accreditation is necessary to accede to the measures agreed for FARC-EP in the Final Accord, without prejudice to what was established in the accord to create the Special Jurisdiction for Peace.

3.2.2.5 Reintegration for minors who have left FARC-EP camps   Minors who have left the FARC-EP camps since the beginning of the peace talks, as well as those who leave until the end of the process of the relinquishment of arms, will be subject to special attention and protection measures. The framework of the Monitoring Commission will be discussed and will include the guiding principles that will be applicable to minors and the guidelines for the design of the Special Program in accordance with Joint Communiqué No. 70 of May 15, 2016 to ensure the restitution of their rights with a differential approach, prioritizing their access to health and education. These minors will be granted all the rights, benefits, and provisions established for the victims of the conflict in the Victims' Law 1448 of 2011 and prioritize their family reunification when possible, as well as their definitive location in their communities of origin or in others of similar characteristics, always taking into account the best interest of the child. The monitoring of these programs will be carried out by the National Council of Reintegration.

3.2.2.6 Identification of needs of the economic and social reintegration process

a. **Socioeconomic census:**
Within sixty (60) days of the start of the ZVTN, a socioeconomic census will be conducted to provide the information required to facilitate the process of full reintegration of FARC-EP into civilian life as a community and as individuals. The CNR will define the content of the Census, its form of application, and the safekeeping and good use of the information. The accomplishment of the census will be entrusted to the National University of Colombia.

b. **Identification of sustainable productive programs and projects**
Based on the results of the census, the possible productive programs and projects will be identified in order to link the largest possible number of men and women currently

belonging to FARC-EP. Participation in programs and projects for environmental protection and humanitarian demining will receive special attention.

c. Development and implementation of sustainable productive programs and projects

Each member of FARC-EP in the process of reintegration will have the one-time right to an economic backing to undertake an individual or collective productive project, for the sum of 8 million pesos.

- **Programs and projects with ECOMUN**

A one-time Fund will be set up for the execution of programs and projects for the process of economic and social reintegration through ECOMUN, the viability of which will be verified by the CNR. The resources corresponding to the people who decide to participate in collective projects that have been identified and made feasible, will be transferred by the National Government to ECOMUN, no later than thirty (30) days after the feasibility of each project. The value of the fund will depend on the total number of allowances for today's FARC-EP members who have opted for this option. For its administration, ECOMUN will be a fiduciary charge.

- **Individual Projects**

To the members of FARC-EP in the process of reintegration who wish to undertake productive projects or housing individually, and have verified their viability by the CNR, the National Government will allocate the sum mentioned above once.

3.2.2.7. Guarantees for a sustainable economic and social reintegration

- **Basic income**

Each of the men and women now belonging to FARC-EP from the termination of the ZVTN and for twenty-four (24) months will receive a monthly basic income equal to 90% of the SMMLV, provided they do not have a contractual link that generates income.

Subsequent to this term, a monthly allowance will be granted in accordance with the regulations that are issued for that effect, and not less than the one that was in force, provided that the beneficiary proves that he has continued his educational route in function of the reintegration purposes. For the above, the Government will constitute a fiduciary charge. For its part, ECOMUN will provide its members with advice and support in the process of selecting educational entities.

- **Single standardization assignment**

Each of the men and women now belonging to FARC-EP, at the time of the termination of the ZVTN, will receive a single standardization allowance equal to 2 million pesos.

- **Social Security**

The amounts corresponding to payments for social security in health and pensions, in accordance with current regulations for those who are not linked to remunerated activities, will be guaranteed by the National Government, which will be a fiduciary charge for payments during 24 months. ECOMUN, for its part, will advise its members in the selection of social security institutions providing these services.

- **Social plans or programs**

According to the results of the socioeconomic census, the plans or programs necessary to attend to the fundamental and integral rights of the population subject to this agreement, such as formal (basic and secondary, technical and technological, university) and education for work and human development, as well as for the validation and homologation of knowledge and understanding; housing; culture, recreation, and sport; protection and recovery of the environment; psychosocial accompaniment; reunification of families, extended families, and older adults, including measures to protect and care for the children of members of FARC-EP in the process of reintegration.

The actions and measures of each one of the programs that can begin their execution will be defined by the beginning of the process of relinquishment of arms in the ZVTN.

Such programs shall be guaranteed by the National Government in the terms and duration defined by the CNR.

The identification of projects and mechanisms that allow access to housing, including self-construction projects, will deserve priority treatment and will receive special attention and support from the Government.

- **Pedagogy for Peace**

The FARC-EP will appoint three spokespersons each for ZVTN and PTN, of the ten members of FARC-EP authorized to mobilize at the municipal level, to advance peace education work in the councils of the respective municipality. In the case of departmental assemblies, such work shall be carried out after the CNR has concluded its consultations with the respective assemblies and governors.

3.2.2.8. Other resources for economic reintegration projects

The economic resources provided by international cooperation, the private sector, foundations, and multilateral organizations for the economic reintegration projects of FARC-EP members into civilian life, as well as the technical cooperation resources for these projects, will not diminish the amounts referred to in the preceding paragraphs, i.e., increase the economic resources made available by the National Government for the implementation of the reintegration agreement.

[Sections 3.4 and 4–6 have been omitted. They establish an agreement on security guarantees and the fight against criminal organizations, measures for combating illicit drug use, a system for victim reparations, a Special Jurisdiction for Peace, and mechanisms for implementing and verifying the agreement. The Protocols and Annexes have also been omitted.]

Source: Office of the High Commissioner for Peace. "Full text of the Final Agreement for the Ending of Conflict and the Construction of a Stable and Lasting Peace." August 24, 2016. Translated by SAGE Publishing. http://www.altocomisionadoparalapaz.gov.co/procesos-y-conversaciones/Paginas/Texto-completo-del-Acuerdo-Final-para-la-Terminacion-del-conflicto.aspx.

State Department Background
Briefing on the Colombia Peace Process

October 5, 2016

SENIOR STATE DEPARTMENT OFFICIAL: Thank you very much. I'll just make some brief opening remarks and then open this to questions.

As everyone knows, the October 2nd plebiscite resulted in a majority vote for the no campaign. It's about a 51,000 vote difference between the two sides, and the turnout was about 37 percent. President Santos immediately recognized and accepted the results of the plebiscite, as do all of the international community, and recognize and respect the views of the Colombian people on this. Nobody in the plebiscite voted for resuming the war. That's the good news. And President Santos has made it clear that he is open to and seeks a dialogue with those who voted no as well as those who didn't vote at all, to see if he can build a new national consensus that will allow for a final peace settlement.

Both the FARC and the government reiterated their desire to maintain the current ceasefire. The UN monitoring and verification mission is still in place and playing the role that was intended to do so. The FARC and the government continue to cooperate in removing land mines and searching for the remains of disappeared to be returned to their relatives, cooperating in the return of child soldiers, cooperating in crop substitution and anti-narcotics, all of which are called for under the agreement. Secretary Kerry has been in touch with President Santos and reiterated strong U.S. support for the peace process. Obviously, Colombia is divided about the best terms on which to end this war through negotiations, because it's not divided on the desire to end this war through negotiations. So it's obviously up to Colombians to try to come to some new consensus that will allow the peace process to be finalized, and the United States stands ready to help that effort in any way the Colombian Government wishes us to do so. . . .

QUESTION: Just curious to know, since you're in Havana, what's your gauge of how willing or not the FARC are to reopen negotiations. Obviously, you saw the comment from Timochenko that the agreement is done and it's actually not a—it's only a political problem, but legally the referendum had—should have no legal impact. I'm curious to know whether you see any wiggle room on the part of the FARC. And also, what about that argument? I mean, is the accord legally binding even though it failed the referendum?

SENIOR STATE DEPARTMENT OFFICIAL: That last question is up for the Colombian constitutional scholars to determine, but the president of the republic has made it clear he respects the results of the referendum. And after all, he called for it and said he would abide by the results. So the legal issues are secondary to that democratic and political commitment. The FARC spent four and a half years negotiating an agreement, they signed it at Cartagena, they thought that it would be ratified. And obviously, they're facing a profoundly changed circumstance. I think they are aware of the new political reality in Colombia. They certainly made some constructive statements about maintaining the ceasefire, about continuing to use words to seek political goals, not weapons. Obviously, they have to consider what the options are. But they have made it clear they want the peace process to continue, and they want to negotiate a settlement to the war. So we'll have to see how their position evolves, and obviously it will depend on what suggestions are made in terms of clarifying the agreement, if any such suggestions are made. . . .

QUESTION: I was wondering—you already know what Uribe or Uribismo wants from the FARC. They have made it clear that they want them to spend actual time in jail and they would not have political recognition nor the possibility to run for public office. Do you think that's something that the FARC would go with?

SENIOR STATE DEPARTMENT OFFICIAL: Well, I don't—I think it is premature to ascribe a set of proposals to the CD until they speak for themselves. They're committed to this dialogue, I believe, and that *(inaudible)* attempt to build a consensus. But I don't want to speculate about what positions they may or may not take in that conversation. . . .

QUESTION: Thank you. Hi, [Senior State Department Official]. I wonder if you could tell us what exactly the Obama Administration is doing in order to get this process back on track. Has there been—have there been or will there be conversations with President Uribe? Is the United States attempting to play a part in inter-Colombian—leaving out the FARC for a minute—attempts to get this to reach some kind of consensus that would allow them to move forward? Has anybody been in touch with President Uribe?

SENIOR STATE DEPARTMENT OFFICIAL: The United States was invited by President Santos several years ago to become engaged in the process. That's why we are engaged. We're not there by our own volition. And President Santos has continued to ask us to try to be helpful where we can. And we've maintained a regular dialogue through our embassy's Ambassador Whitaker with senior members of the Centro Democratico Party.

Both Ambassador Whitaker and I met with President Uribe during the process, not in the most recent weeks, but certainly have kept our open dialogue with him. As I said, Secretary of State Kerry spoke with President Santos yesterday morning and reiterated U.S. support for the process. I met in Havana this morning and yesterday with the government's negotiating team, with the FARC, with the special envoy from Norway and Jean Arnault, the head of the UN MVM—the monitoring and verification mission. And we'll continue, at the government's request, to talk to parties where it might be helpful and to share our views and play a constructive role. . . .

QUESTION: Is the problem right now for both sides trying to figure out how to craft a revision of the plan that could pass muster in a plebiscite? Is that the immediate problem? Or do you see that they're having to go back and restart all of the negotiations and take the chance that the population may vote against a revision of the deal?

SENIOR STATE DEPARTMENT OFFICIAL: I don't think anybody in Colombia is talking about going back, starting brand new and not taking advantage of many of the things that were negotiated that have broad national support. I mentioned four of them— cooperation on removing landmines from the countryside; releasing child soldiers, which has already begun in *(inaudible)*; helping provide crop substitution and for coca production; recovering the remains of disappeared Colombians from the war and reuniting them with their families.

But what the plebiscite clearly revealed was that while Colombians desperately want to see an end to violence and have, I think, appreciated the fact that the war has really been dormant for the last two years under the unilateral ceasefire, they are deeply divided about the terms on which they would settle a final peace agreement. And so what I think the government has said it is doing is to reach out to all voices and all sectors inside the country, including those who opposed the agreement, to listen to their views about why they took the stance they had and see whether their concerns can be addressed, and see whether a new national consensus can be built that would allow for the agreement to go forward. Whether there'd be a second plebiscite or not is not an issue that has been discussed and is probably not really germane at this point in the process. . . .

QUESTION: Okay. My question is: Is there any indication that the United States millions-dollar aid to Colombia may be affected after the peace deal was rejected? Thank you.

SENIOR STATE DEPARTMENT OFFICIAL: Well, there's no discussions at this point within the government about the President's request for assistance to Colombia and it's not worth speculating on. Our hope is that the peace accord will go forward with a broad mass of support within the country, and the United States wants to be supportive of the implementation in areas that we have talked about in the past. . . .

SOURCE: U.S. State Department. "Background Briefing on the Colombia Peace Process." October 5, 2016. https://2009-2017.state.gov/r/pa/prs/ps/2016/10/262835.htm.

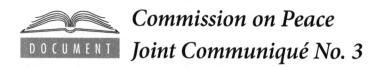

Commission on Peace
Joint Communiqué No. 3

October 28, 2016

The Delegations of the National Government and the FARC-EP, after meetings held in Havana with guarantor countries, would like to inform the public that:

1. We confirm that the Final Agreement for the Completion of Conflict and the Construction of a Stable and Lasting Peace, signed on September 26, 2016, contains the necessary reforms and measures to lay the foundations for peace and to guarantee an end to the armed conflict.

2. In the development of what was agreed in the Joint Communiqué last October 7, we have analyzed the proposals for adjustments and clarifications of the Final Agreement that different sectors of society have put to the consideration of the Delegations of the National Government and the FARC-EP in charge of creating the new agreement.

3. The proposals are being discussed with care. Many of them have been incorporated into the texts of the new agreement.

4. Quickly and promptly, we will continue listening to a number of significant and diverse organizations and national figures who have come forward in one way or another, even those who abstained from voting in the plebiscite, looking for peace and reconciliation for Colombians.

5. We will continue to carry out this work next Thursday, November 3, with the objective of promptly having a new definitive agreement. Both delegations positively noted that all of this discussion is possible thanks to the fact that for the first time in our recent history, peace is an essential focus of citizen reflection, leaving behind the past of war.

6. Taking into consideration that the president of the Republic is invested with constitutional authority to bring forth peace, we trust his efforts to do so.

7. We thank the guarantor countries, Cuba and Norway, the accompanying countries, Venezuela and Chile, and the international community for their continued support of our work for reconciliation. Likewise, we extend our gratitude to all the citizens who have given their proposals and expressed support for the Delegations of the National Government and the FARC-EP with the aim of building peace.

Delegations of the National Government and the FARC-EP

Source: Office of the High Commissioner for Peace. "Joint Communique No 3." October 28, 2016. Translated by SAGE Publishing. http://www.altocomisionadoparalapaz.gov.co/procesos-y-conversaciones/documentos-y-comunicados-conjuntos/Paginas/Comunicado-Conjunto-No-03-28-de-octubre-de-2016.aspx.

Other Historic Documents of Interest

From this volume

■ Colombian President Awarded Nobel Peace Prize, p. 673

From previous *Historic Documents*

■ Uribe on Inauguration as President of Colombia, *2002*, p. 571
■ General Accounting Office on Colombia Aid Program, *2000*, p. 841

September

U.S. and Chinese Presidents Remark on Ratification of Paris Climate Agreement

SEPTEMBER 3 AND NOVEMBER 17, 2016

An effort to replace the Kyoto Protocol, an international agreement to reduce greenhouse gas emissions to control climate change, had been in the works long before the agreement was set to expire in 2012. That year, those who were party to the negotiations passed an extension of Kyoto to 2020, while work on a replacement continued. Concerns preventing a new climate-governing document primarily revolved around what enforcement mechanism a new agreement would have, how developing nations would be treated, and what requirements should be placed on each country, specifically the world's largest greenhouse gas emitters, the United States and China. In December 2015, the United Nations Framework Convention on Climate Change (UNFCCC) negotiated the Paris Agreement, which was hailed by the climate change community as a necessary first step in reducing or reversing the effects of rising global temperatures. The effectiveness of the agreement rested on ratification by the United States and China, and the two nations came together to do so on September 3, 2016. The Paris Agreement entered into force in early November.

COP21 CONFERENCE AIMS TO REPLACE KYOTO

In December 2015, nearly 200 nations participated in the 21st Conference of the Parties (COP21) to the UNFCCC. The conference, held in Paris, relied on decades of international climate change negotiations to reach an historic agreement to replace the 1997 Kyoto Protocol. The Paris Agreement, as it became known, is expected to significantly reduce greenhouse gas emissions in an effort to combat consistently rising global temperatures. However, the agreement could not go into effect until it was ratified by fifty-five countries that together make up at least 55 percent of global emissions.

An initial signing ceremony was held on April 22, 2016, but the document was left unsigned by major contributors to global emissions, most notably the United States and China, who account for nearly 18 percent and 20 percent, respectively, of total global emissions. Those who criticized the Kyoto Protocol agree that it was unable to have the force intended because the United States signed but never ratified the agreement and was therefore not subject to the emissions regulations.

U.S. opponents of controlling greenhouse gas emissions have long argued that any effort at reduction in the United States would be outweighed by increasing emissions in China. President Barack Obama, who campaigned on clean energy, thus made it his goal to bring China into the fold to position the two nations as drivers of global action on climate change. In spite of opposition, led primarily by Republicans in Congress and major energy companies, in November 2014, President Obama and Chinese President Xi Jinping announced a joint agreement to limit greenhouse gas emissions to curb climate change. The nonbinding pact was seen internationally as a step toward securing agreement on what ultimately became the Paris Agreement.

UNITED STATES, CHINA RATIFY PARIS AGREEMENT

The negotiations between the United States and China peaked on September 3, 2016, when the presidents of the two countries stood together to announce that they would ratify the Paris Agreement and commit themselves to the emission goals they had outlined the previous year. In announcing the agreement, President Obama said that the commitment was ahead of schedule, which would likely mean that the Paris Agreement could enter into force earlier than anticipated. "We have a saying in America that you need to put your money where your mouth is," President Obama said. "And when it comes to combating climate change, that's what we're doing, both the United States and China. We're leading by example. As the world's two largest economies and two largest emitters, our entrance into this agreement continues the momentum of Paris and should give the rest of the world confidence—whether developed or developing countries—that a low-carbon future is where the world is heading." The president admitted that the ratification of the Paris Agreement was just one step toward combating climate change, but that the United States would continue to work with its international partners, and specifically China, to address the crisis.

President Xi, on reaching an agreement with the United States to ratify the Paris Agreement, said, "I have said many times that green mountains and clear water are as good as mountains of gold and silver. To protect the environment is to protect productivity and to improve the environment is to boost productivity." Xi added that the rapidly industrializing nation would "unwaveringly pursue sustainable development" and "make China a beautiful country with blue sky, green vegetation and clear rivers, so that our people will enjoy life in a livable environment and the ecological benefits created by economic development." For its part, under the agreement China will be required to cut its carbon emissions by 60 percent to 65 percent of 2005 levels by 2030. In addition, it would be required to draw 20 percent of its energy from non-fossil fuel sources by 2030.

Whether the United States will be able to uphold the requirements of the Paris Agreement remains in question. Twenty-seven states had sued the Obama administration in late 2015 to block implementation of the Clean Power Plan, which seeks to reduce carbon emissions from power plants and which would be a major piece of the U.S. effort to cut greenhouse gas emissions under the Paris Agreement. The suit alleges that the regulations of the plan place an undue burden on the states and represents federal overreach on an issue that should fall primarily to the states because of how energy decisions are made based on market conditions. The Supreme Court in February 2016 stayed implementation of the plan pending further judicial review, and the case was referred to an appellate court that heard oral arguments in late September 2016. As of this writing, the appellate court has not yet ruled on the issue. Of note, most of those states party to the lawsuit were set to meet Clean Power Plan standards by the end of 2016.

Also of concern for supporters of the Paris Agreement is questioning by congressional Republicans regarding President Obama's legal authority to use his executive power to sign the Paris Agreement, instead of referring it for the "advice and consent" of the Senate. The Obama administration argued that the Paris Agreement is not a treaty that would fall under the purview of the Senate, but is rather akin to those nonbinding international agreements that have been put in force by executive authority.

PARIS AGREEMENT ENTERS INTO FORCE

With the signatures of the United States and China, it was widely believed that other nations would quickly ratify the Paris Agreement. "Today's announcement is the strongest signal yet that what we agreed in Paris will soon be the law of the land," said Mattlan Zackhras, the minister-in-assistance to the president of the Marshall Islands. "With the two biggest emitters ready to lead, the transition to a low-emissions, climate-resilient global economy is now irreversible," he added. Prior to the United States and China signing the agreement, only twenty-four nations had ratified it, accounting for only 1.08 percent of global emissions, while 180 had signed it. As expected, other large emitters quickly came on board after September 3, including Brazil, France, India, Mexico, Saudi Arabia, and Canada. On October 5, the agreement reached the required threshold, and it officially entered into force on November 4. In a joint statement, UNFCCC executive secretary Patricia Espinosa and President of COP22 Salaheddine Mezouar called the agreement "undoubtedly a turning point in the history of common human endeavor, capturing the combined political, economic and social will of governments, cities, regions, citizens, business and investors to overcome the existential threat of unchecked climate change." Once the agreement went into force, nations were bound by their emissions reduction plans that were submitted in 2015 prior to the Paris Agreement being finalized. All nations signatory to the agreement would also maintain a commitment to keep global temperature rises to below 2°C above preindustrial levels, but strive to limit it to 1.5°C. Nations will be expected to review their progress every five years. Much like its predecessor, the Paris Agreement has no enforcement authority to penalize those nations that do not follow through on their emission reduction plans.

Three days after the agreement went into force, representatives from around the world convened for the two-week COP22, the aim of which was to recommit nations to the Paris Agreement and carve a path forward. The conference was put on uncertain footing one day after its opening when Donald Trump, someone who in 2012 called global warming a hoax and who on the campaign trail promised to pull U.S. support from the climate pact, won the U.S. presidential election. Climate change experts have expressed concern that without the full backing and efforts put forth by the United States, it is unlikely that other large nations—specifically China—will follow through on their own greenhouse gas reduction efforts. "If the U.S. won't, why should developing nations cut their emissions?" asked John Sterman, a professor of system dynamics at the Massachusetts Institute of Technology. After Trump's victory, French President François Hollande called the Paris Agreement "irreversible," adding that "the United States, the largest economic power in the world, the second largest greenhouse gas emitter, must respect the commitments it has undertaken." UN Secretary-General Ban Ki-moon, after speaking with Trump by phone, told COP22 delegates that the new president would "make a fast and wise decision" on how to proceed under the Paris Agreement. Secretary of State John Kerry, who addressed the conference after Trump's victory, said ahead of his remarks that he could not speak to what the next administration might do with regard to the Paris Agreement, adding that he knew there was strong support for the agreement among the American public. "No one should doubt the overwhelming majority of Americans who know climate change is occurring and are committed to addressing it," Kerry said.

Throughout the COP22 conference, parties to the Paris Agreement more fully developed their emission strategies. Developing nations, which were promised $100 billion per year under the Paris Agreement to support their emissions activities without hampering their development, said they would "strive to lead" a transition to becoming 100 percent renewable. Larger nations, such as the United States, Canada, and Germany, published their final plans for cutting emissions by upwards of 80 percent by 2050; the United States and Canada's levels would be cut from 2005 emissions levels, while Germany's would be marked from 1990 levels.

At the conclusion of COP22, those in attendance issued the Marrakech Action Proclamation to affirm the commitment to and implementation of the Paris Agreement. "This momentum is irreversible—it is being driven not only by governments, but by science, business and global action of all types at all levels," the proclamation reads. "Our task now is to rapidly build on that momentum together, moving forward purposefully to reduce greenhouse gas emissions and to foster adaptation efforts, thereby benefiting and supporting the 2030 Agenda for Sustainable Development and its Sustainable Development Goals." By the time the meeting ended, 111 nations had ratified the Paris Agreement.

—Heather Kerrigan

Following are remarks by U.S. President Barack Obama on September 3, 2016, upon ratification of the Paris Climate Change Agreement; a joint statement issued on September 3, 2016, by the leaders of the United States and China on the climate change signing; and a November 17, 2016, proclamation from the United Nations Framework Convention on Climate Change COP22 meeting.

President Obama on Ratification of Paris Climate Agreement

September 3, 2016

[President Obama made his remarks during a meeting with President Xi Jinping of China and Secretary-General Ban Ki-moon of the United Nations. His remarks were joined in progress.]

We are here together because we believe that for all the challenges that we face, the growing threat of climate change could define the contours of this century more dramatically than any other challenge.

One of the reasons I ran for this office was to make sure that America does its part to protect this planet for future generations. Over the past 7½ years, we've transformed the United States into a global leader in the fight against climate change. But this is not a fight that any one country, no matter how powerful, can take alone. That's why last December's Paris Agreement was so important. Nearly 200 nations came together as a strong, enduring framework to set the world on a course to a low-carbon future. And someday, we may see this as the moment that we finally decided to save our planet.

There are no shortage of cynics who thought the agreement would not happen. But they missed two big things: The investments that we made to allow for incredible innovation in clean energy, and the strong, principled diplomacy over the course of years that we were able to see pay off in the Paris Agreement. The United States and China were central to that effort. Over the past few years, our joint leadership on climate has been one of the most significant drivers of global action.

In 2014, President Xi and I stood together in Beijing to announce landmark climate targets for our two countries to meet. That announcement set us on the road to Paris by jumpstarting an intense diplomatic effort to put other countries on the same course. In 2015, we stood together in Washington to lay out additional actions our two countries would take, along with a roadmap for ultimately reaching a strong agreement in Paris. This year, in 2016, we meet again to commit formally to joining the agreement ahead of schedule, creating the prospect that the agreement might enter into force ahead of schedule as well.

The United States and China are taking that step today, as our two nations formally join the Paris Agreement. Of course, we could not have done this extraordinary work without the strong support of the Secretary-General of the United Nations, Mr. Ban Ki-moon, who has been an outstanding leader on this issue as well.

Now, just as I believe the Paris Agreement will ultimately prove to be a turning point for our planet, I believe that history will judge today's efforts as pivotal. For the agreement to enter into force, as has already been stated, 55 countries representing 55 percent of global emissions must formally join. Together, the U.S. and China represent about 40 percent of global emissions. So today we are moving the world significantly closer to the goal that we have set.

We have a saying in America that you need to put your money where your mouth is. And when it comes to combating climate change, that's what we're doing, both the United States and China. We're leading by example. As the world's two largest economies and two largest emitters, our entrance into this agreement continues the momentum of Paris and should give the rest of the world confidence—whether developed or developing countries—that a low-carbon future is where the world is heading.

Of course, the Paris Agreement alone won't solve the climate crisis. But it does establish an enduring framework that enables countries to ratchet down their carbon emissions over time and to set more ambitious targets as technology advances. That means full implementation of this agreement will help delay or avoid some of the worst consequences of climate change and pave the way for more progress in the coming years. This is the single best chance that we have to deal with a problem that could end up transforming this planet in a way that makes it very difficult for us to deal with all the other challenges that we may face.

President Xi and I intend to continue working together in the months ahead to make sure our countries lead on climate. Three years ago, in California, we first resolved to work together to secure a global agreement to phase down the use of super pollutants known as HFCs, and we're now just 6 weeks away from final negotiations. We also have the chance to reach a global agreement to curb emissions from the global airline industry, one that actually has the support of industry. And today we're putting forward roadmaps to get both negotiations done this year.

On each of these issues, the United States and China have now developed a significant record of leadership on one of the most important issues of our time. Our teams have worked together and developed a strong relationship that should serve us very well. And despite our differences on other issues, we hope that our willingness to work together on this issue will inspire greater ambition and greater action around the world.

Yes, diplomacy can be difficult, and progress on the world stage can be slow. But together, we're proving that it is possible. And I was reflecting before we came in here with Secretary-General Ban Ki-moon about the meeting that we had in Copenhagen in my first year of my Presidency, which was quite chaotic. And I think it is fair to say that if you had looked at the outcome of that meeting, the prospects of us being here today, the prospects of a Paris Agreement seemed very far away. And yet here we are, which indicates that where there's a will and there's a vision—and where countries like China and the United States are prepared to show leadership and to lead by example—it is possible for us to create a world that is more secure, more prosperous, and more free than the one that was left for us.

So to all of you that have participated in this extraordinary effort, thank you very much. Thank you to President Xi. Thank you to the Secretary-General.

SOURCE: Executive Office of the President. "Remarks Announcing the United States Formal Entry Into the United Nations Framework Convention on Climate Change Paris Agreement in Hangzhou, China." September 3, 2016. *Compilation of Presidential Documents* 2016, no. 00556 (September 3, 2016). http://www.gpo.gov/fdsys/pkg/DCPD-201600556/pdf/DCPD-201600556.pdf.

U.S. and Chinese Presidents Remark on Signing of Climate Change Agreement

September 3, 2016

1. President Barack Obama and President Xi Jinping have forged a historic partnership between the United States and China to lead in combatting climate change. From the Sunnylands meeting in 2013, to the landmark November 2014 Joint Announcement on Climate Change and the September 2015 and March 2016 Joint Presidential Statements on Climate Change, leadership by the United States and China has galvanized global action to build a green, low-carbon, and climate-resilient world and was a major contributor to achieving the historic Paris Agreement. Climate change has formed a central pillar of the bilateral relationship between the two countries. Both sides are committed to implementing the three presidential joint statements on climate change and will continue to deepen and broaden bilateral climate change cooperation, building on the concrete progress and productive outcomes achieved thus far.

2. Today, the United States and China deposited with United Nations Secretary-General Ban Ki-moon their respective instruments to join the Paris Agreement, marking a significant contribution towards the early entry into force of the Paris Agreement. The two Presidents call on all other Parties to the United Nations Framework Convention on Climate Change to join the Paris Agreement as early as possible with the expectation of the Agreement's entry into force this year. The Presidents further express their continued commitment to work together and with others to promote the full implementation of the Paris Agreement. The

United States and China will formulate and publish their respective strategies for mid-century, low-greenhouse gas emission development. The United States will release its strategy in 2016, and China will do so as early as possible. The two countries agree to hold a series of technical exchanges on the formulation of such strategies, beginning this year.

3.   The United States and China are committed to working bilaterally and with other countries to advance the post-Paris negotiation process and to achieve successful outcomes this year in related multilateral fora. The United States and China commit to work together and with others to reach agreement this year on an ambitious and comprehensive HFC amendment to the Montreal Protocol, including an early first reduction step and early freeze date for Article 2 and Article 5 Parties respectively and an ambitious phase-down schedule, with increased and adequate financial support from Article 2 Parties to help Article 5 Parties with their implementation. The United States and China also intend to work together on critical research regarding the safe use of flammable alternatives and commit to collaborate on enhanced domestic action to reduce use of HFCs, improve efficiency standards, support policies to transform the air conditioning market, and remain active participants in the Clean Energy Ministerial's Advanced Cooling Challenge.

4.   The two sides welcome the decision of the ICAO Council to forward to the ICAO Assembly its recommended Resolution on a global market-based measure to address carbon emissions from international aviation. Recognizing the important role of international aviation in addressing climate change, the United States and China support the ICAO Assembly to reach consensus on a global market-based measure this October, and expect to be early participants in such measure.

5.   The two Presidents celebrate the achievements of the U.S.–China Climate Change Working Group (CCWG) and U.S.–China Clean Energy Research Center (CERC) in recent years and commit to further enhance bilateral cooperation on climate change under these and other frameworks. They welcome the success of the U.S.–China Climate-Smart/Low-Carbon Cities Summits in 2015 and 2016 and look forward to the next summit, to be held in Boston, the United States, in 2017, as well as the next Clean Energy Ministerial to be hosted by China in 2017.

6.   The United States and China commit to continue taking ambitious domestic action to further promote the transition towards green, low-carbon and climate-resilient economies both domestically and internationally.

7.   In the United States' power sector, a five-year extension of production and investment tax credits for wind and solar energy will deploy roughly 100GW of renewable energy over the next 5 years, and the United States has paused new coal leasing on federal lands, while undertaking a comprehensive review of the federal coal program, which makes up roughly 40% of United States coal supply. In the transportation sector, the United States has finalized efficiency standards for heavy-duty vehicles, which will reduce more than 1 billion tons of carbon pollution over

the life of the program. In the building sector, the United States is on track to finalize 20 additional efficiency standards for appliances and equipment by the end of the year, which will contribute to achieving its goal of cutting 3 billion metric tons of carbon pollution from such standards. With respect to non-CO2 emissions, the United States finalized this year measures to reduce domestic HFCs and methane from the oil and gas and landfill sectors.

8. China is making great efforts to advance ecological civilization and promote green, low-carbon, climate resilient and sustainable development. During the 13th Five-Year Period (2016–2020), China will lower its carbon dioxide per unit of GDP and energy consumption per unit of GDP by 18% and 15% respectively, increase the share of non-fossil fuels in primary energy consumption to 15% and increase the forest stock volume by 1.4 billion cubic meters, as concrete and crucial steps towards implementing its nationally determined contribution. China will continue its efforts to increase energy efficiency in industries, transportation and buildings, promote green power dispatch to accelerate the development of renewable energy, start in 2017 its national emission trading system and phase down the production and consumption of HFCs. China will also promote low-carbon development of transportation by developing standard modern transportation equipment and energy-efficient, environmentally-friendly means of transport.

9. Internationally, as part of an ongoing commitment to strengthen low-carbon policies, in 2015 the United States worked with other OECD member countries to adopt new OECD guidelines to limit export finance for overseas coal-fired power plants. The United States also remains committed with other developed countries to the goal of jointly mobilizing 100 billion US dollars per year by 2020 to address the needs of developing countries in the context of meaningful mitigation and adaptation action. This funding will come from a wide variety of sources, public and private, bilateral and multilateral, including alternative sources of finance. China is taking concrete steps to strengthen green and low-carbon policies and regulations with a view to strictly controlling public investment flowing into projects with high pollution and carbon emissions both domestically and internationally.

SOURCE: Executive Office of the President. "Joint Statement—United States–China Climate Change Cooperation Outcomes." September 3, 2016. *Compilation of Presidential Documents* 2016, no. 00558 (September 3, 2016). http://www.gpo.gov/fdsys/pkg/DCPD-201600558/pdf/DCPD-201600558.pdf.

COP22 Meeting Issues Proclamation on Paris Agreement

November 17, 2016

We, Heads of State, Government, and Delegations, gathered in Marrakech, on African soil, for the High-Level Segment of the 22nd Session of the Conference of the Parties to the United Nations Framework Convention on Climate Change, the 12th Session of the Conference of the Parties serving as the Meeting of the Parties to the Kyoto Protocol, and the 1st Session of the Conference of the Parties serving as the Meeting of the Parties to the Paris Agreement, at the gracious invitation of His Majesty the King of Morocco, Mohammed VI, issue this proclamation to signal a shift towards a new era of implementation and action on climate and sustainable development.

Our climate is warming at an alarming and unprecedented rate and we have an urgent duty to respond.

We welcome the Paris Agreement, adopted under the Convention, its rapid entry into force, with its ambitious goals, its inclusive nature and its reflection of equity and common but differentiated responsibilities and respective capabilities, in the light of different national circumstances, and we affirm our commitment to its full implementation.

Indeed, this year, we have seen extraordinary momentum on climate change worldwide, and in many multilateral fora. This momentum is irreversible—it is being driven not only by governments, but by science, business and global action of all types at all levels.

Our task now is to rapidly build on that momentum, together, moving forward purposefully to reduce greenhouse gas emissions and to foster adaptation efforts, thereby benefiting and supporting the 2030 Agenda for Sustainable Development and its Sustainable Development Goals.

We call for the highest political commitment to combat climate change, as a matter of urgent priority.

We call for strong solidarity with those countries most vulnerable to the impacts of climate change, and underscore the need to support efforts aimed to enhance their adaptive capacity, strengthen resilience and reduce vulnerability.

We call for urgently raising ambition and strengthening cooperation amongst ourselves to close the gap between current emissions trajectories and the pathway needed to meet the long-term temperature goals of the Paris Agreement.

We call for an increase in the volume, flow and access to finance for climate projects, alongside improved capacity and technology, including from developed to developing countries.

We the Developed Country Parties reaffirm our USD $100 billion mobilization goal.

We call for all Parties to strengthen and support efforts to eradicate poverty, ensure food security and to take stringent action to deal with climate change challenges in agriculture.

We, unanimously, call for further climate action and support, well in advance of 2020, taking into account the specific needs and special circumstances of developing countries, the least developed countries and those particularly vulnerable to the adverse impacts of climate change.

We who are Parties to the Kyoto Protocol encourage the ratification of the Doha Amendment.

We, collectively, call on all non-state actors to join us for immediate and ambitious action and mobilization, building on their important achievements, noting the many initiatives and the Marrakech Partnership for Global Climate Action itself, launched in Marrakech.

The transition in our economies required to meet the objectives of the Paris Agreement provides a substantial positive opportunity for increased prosperity and sustainable development.

The Marrakech Conference marks an important inflection point in our commitment to bring together the whole international community to tackle one of the greatest challenges of our time.

As we now turn towards implementation and action, we reiterate our resolve to inspire solidarity, hope and opportunity for current and future generations.

SOURCE: United Nations Framework Convention on Climate Change. "Marrakech Action Proclamation for Our Climate and Sustainable Development." November 17, 2016. http://unfccc.int/files/meetings/ marrakech_nov_2016/application/pdf/marrakech_action_proclamation.pdf.

OTHER HISTORIC DOCUMENTS OF INTEREST

FROM PREVIOUS *HISTORIC DOCUMENTS*

Philippine President Declares State of Emergency; U.S. Officials Comment on Philippine Relations amid Drug War

SEPTEMBER 7 AND 26, 2016

The 2016 election of President Rodrigo Duterte in the Philippines marked the beginning of an aggressive antidrug campaign in which thousands of suspected drug users and dealers were killed without trial by law enforcement and vigilantes. Drawing condemnations from human rights organizations and the United Nations, the campaign also resulted in strained relations with the United States, a longtime Philippine ally. At the same time, Duterte's government was fighting persistent terrorist threats from the insurgent group Abu Sayyaf, which prompted the president to declare an ongoing state of emergency.

DUTERTE LAUNCHES ANTIDRUG WAR

Duterte pledged during his presidential campaign to fight aggressively against the Philippine drug trade, stating that he would kill "100,000 criminals" and would end crime and corruption in the first six months of his presidency. In his inaugural State of the Nation address on July 25, 2016, Duterte declared that his war on drugs "will not stop until the last drug lord . . . and the last pusher have surrendered or are put either behind bars or below the ground, if they so wish." He also claimed that there were more than 3.7 million drug addicts in the country.

Duterte's assertions about the severity of the drug crisis conflict with statistics from the government's own Dangerous Drugs Board, which found in a 2015 survey that about 1.8 million Filipinos use drugs. Roughly a third of those individuals had only used drugs once in the previous thirteen months, and fewer than half had used crystal meth, which government officials most often cite as the cause of high crime rates. According to the United Nations Office on Drugs and Crime, at its highest, the Philippines had a 2.35 percent prevalence rate for amphetamine usage among those aged fifteen to sixty-four. By comparison, the United States had a prevalence rate of 2.20 percent among this same population. Prevalence of illicit opioid and cocaine use is also significantly lower in the Philippines than in the United States and Australia. Some speculated that, by using inflated statistics, Duterte was attempting to feed a moral panic around drugs and justify his hardline stance against drug users and dealers. Filipino officials did not appear to be troubled by Duterte's use of data. "He just exaggerates it so we will know that the problem is very big," Wilkins Villanueva, the Metro Manila regional director for the Philippine Drug Enforcement Agency, told Reuters. "The implication is that we have to work hard to solve the problem and we have to work hard so that . . . occasional drug users do not turn into regular drug users."

Duterte's promised crackdown began shortly after he took office on June 30, prompting a rash of killings of suspected drug dealers and users by both police and vigilantes. Duterte encouraged all Filipinos to assist in the fight against crime and drugs during a nationally televised address, urging them to shoot and kill drug dealers who resisted arrest and promising to award medals to those who did. He also promised to pay bounties to those who provided drug dealers, "dead or alive." Duterte pledged to protect police officers who killed suspects, as well. "Do your duty, and if in the process you kill 1,000 persons because you were doing your duty, I will protect you," he told them during an event in July. To help finance his antidrug campaign, Duterte cut the country's health budget by 25 percent and reduced spending in other areas including agriculture, labor, employment, and foreign affairs.

According to a report by *Time Magazine*, the Philippine National Police (PNP) were providing lists of suspected drug users and dealers to the leaders of the country's *barangays*, or villages. Community leaders were then expected to endorse the lists and add names to them, without needing to provide evidence. Once named on a list, Filipinos faced the risk of death at the hands of vigilantes and arrest or lethal police action, or they could surrender to the authorities. Those who surrendered were required to sign a waiver saying they would never again use drugs and then participate in either a community or private rehabilitation program. Thousands of arrests made because of the drug war further strained the Philippines' already crowded prisons. In mid-August, for example, the Quezon City Jail held more than 4,000 inmates, despite being built to hold only 800.

According to the PNP, as of November 2016, roughly 5,000 people had been killed since the antidrug effort began in July. Approximately 2,000 of those Filipinos were killed by police, while the remaining 3,000 were killed by vigilantes. Another 730,000 Filipinos surrendered to the government.

The widespread killings have been condemned by human rights groups such as Amnesty International and Human Rights Watch, and UN and U.S. officials have also been critical of Duterte's war on drugs. "Claims to fight illicit drug trade do not absolve the Government from its international legal obligations and do not shield State actors or others from responsibility for illegal killings," said Agnes Callamard, the UN special rapporteur on summary executions. Callamard added that Duterte had basically given citizens "a license to kill" by promising rewards for those who turn in drug dealers dead or alive. U.S. State Department spokesperson Mark Toner said the United States was "deeply concerned" about the reports of extrajudicial killings and urged Duterte to ensure law enforcement followed international "human rights norms."

Duterte has responded sharply to such criticisms from the international community. He threatened to withdraw from the UN and form a new international organization with China and African countries, calling the UN "inutile" and "stupid," and questioned the effectiveness of its work in the Philippines. Duterte also criticized the UN and the United States for their inability to address ongoing conflicts such as the Syrian Civil War and suggested that the killings of black men by U.S. police may also constitute human rights violations.

Duterte faced a challenge from Philippine Senator Leila de Lima, the head of the Senate Committee on Justice and Human Rights, as well. De Lima called for an investigation into the killings shortly after Duterte took office and led a two-day joint hearing on the subject with the Committee on Public Order and Dangerous Drugs in August. De Lima was vilified by the president's supporters for calling the hearing, and Duterte launched his own smear campaign against her, claiming that she was paid by drug dealers and had an affair with her driver. The Senate removed de Lima from her leadership position in September and replaced her with a Duterte supporter, Senator Richard Gordon, who said the committee would no longer discuss extrajudicial killings. In addition, the House of Representatives launched an investigation into de Lima's tenure at the Department of Justice—specifically, allegations that she accepted bribes from drug lords and allowed them to continue dealing drugs from prison. De Lima said the evidence against her was fabricated.

Killings continued through the end of 2016, but Duterte suspended his war on drugs in January 2017 after antinarcotics officers kidnapped and killed a South Korean businessman. Duterte apologized to South Korea, and the Philippine Senate began investigating the man's death.

WHITE HOUSE CANCELS DUTERTE MEETING

Duterte's drug war and the United States' response have strained relations between the two allies. President Barack Obama was scheduled to meet with Duterte during a summit of the Association of Southeast Asian Nations in Laos the week of September 5, but the White House canceled the meeting and said Obama would meet with South Korean President Park Guen-hye instead. The decision followed Duterte's demand that human rights concerns not be discussed during the meeting with Obama and remarks that "plenty will be killed" in his antidrug campaign. He also blamed the United States for causing the Philippines' drug problems (the Philippines were a U.S. colony from 1898 to 1946). Speaking at a press briefing on September 7, Ben Rhodes, the U.S. deputy national security adviser for strategic communications, said that "given the focus of attention on President Duterte's comments leading into the meetings here, we felt that it did not create a constructive environment for a bilateral meeting." Rhodes added that he expected the "close cooperation" between the two countries to continue and that the United States would support antinarcotic efforts, but he wanted "to make sure that they're consistent with the rule of law and due process."

Duterte responded by issuing a statement that he regretted that his words "came across as a personal attack on the U.S. president," and he looked forward to "ironing out differences arising out of national priorities and perceptions, and working in mutually responsible ways for both countries." Since the canceled meeting, Duterte has continued to take actions that have added to tensions with the United States. In October, Duterte threatened to end joint U.S.–Philippine military exercises, though he reversed his position and allowed the drills to proceed as planned in November. He also threatened to annul a 2014 defense pact between the two countries that allows the United States to deploy troops to Philippine bases to help balance China's influence in the region and to establish stronger relations with Russia and China.

The Philippines has historically relied on U.S. support for its claims in territory disputes with China in the South China Sea. Some defense analysts suggest ongoing disputes could push Duterte to take a less antagonistic stance with the United States. U.S.–Philippine relations began to warm when Donald Trump was elected president in late 2016. Neither Trump nor his nominee for secretary of state, Rex Tillerson, have condemned the drug war–related killings or said the United States will interfere.

STATE OF EMERGENCY DECLARED IN THE PHILIPPINES

While Duterte's drug war raged, his government also combatted terrorist threats from Abu Sayyaf, a jihadist organization based in the southern Philippines. The group grew out of a separatist insurgency and seeks to establish an independent Islamic state. In addition to bombings and assassinations, the group has carried out kidnappings and demanded ransoms. In some instances, Abu Sayyaf has beheaded male victims whose ransoms were not paid, as well as those who do not believe in Islam. Duterte has pledged to "destroy" Abu Sayyaf and has sent the military to conduct operations against the group in the regions where it is based.

On September 2, an explosion in Davao City's Roxas night market killed fourteen people. Abu Sayyaf later claimed responsibility for the attack, stating that it was a "call for unity" among Islamic guerilla fighters. Two days later, Duterte signed a proclamation declaring a state of emergency "on account of lawless violence." The proclamation cited as reasons for the state of emergency "abductions, hostage-takings and murder of innocent civilians, bombing of power transmission facilities, highway robberies and extortions, attacks on military outposts, assassinations [of] media people and mass jailbreaks" in Mindanao, the island where Davao City is located, as well as government intelligence on "credible threats of further terror attacks and other similar acts in other parts of the country, including metropolitan areas." Duterte said he was not declaring martial law and that the writ of habeas corpus would not be suspended, but that more soldiers and police would be deployed and more security checkpoints would be established. Presidential Communications Office assistant secretary Kristian Ablan said the proclamation "technically took effect today and remains in force until lifted by the President."

Duterte issued a memorandum on September 7 that provided guidelines for the military and PNP "to undertake all necessary measures to suppress any and all forms of lawless violence in Mandanao and prevent the spread and escalation thereof elsewhere in the country." Among its provisions, the memorandum called for the deployment of additional security forces, the police, and military to "intensify their local and transnational intelligence operations" against those suspected of or responsible for committing or conspiring to commit acts of violence, and the Department of Justice to coordinate with law enforcement to ensure quick investigations and prosecutions of those arrested for committing violence. The memorandum stated that "at all times, the constitutional rights of every individual shall be respected" and that "no civil or political rights are suspended," though it also outlined situations in which warrantless arrests would be permitted. A second memorandum was issued on September 26, which extended the original guidelines to the Philippine Coast Guard. That memorandum called for additional personnel to be deployed in ports, harbors, and major coastal areas and for the PCG to "intensify its activities related to the enforcement and maintenance of maritime safety and security to prevent or suppress lawless violence at sea."

At the time of writing, the state of emergency was still in effect.

—Linda Fecteau Grimm

Following is a memorandum issued by Philippine President Rodrigo Duterte on September 7, 2016, providing guidance to the armed forces and police on measures for suppressing violence during the state of emergency; the transcript of a press briefing conducted by White House press secretary Josh Earnest and Deputy

National Security Adviser for Strategic Communications Ben Rhodes on September 7, 2016, about the United States' decision to cancel a meeting with Duterte and U.S.-Philippine relations; and a memorandum issued by Duterte on September 26, 2016, extending this guidance to include the Philippine Coast Guard.

Philippine President Issues Violence Suppression Guidelines for Armed Forces and Police

DOCUMENT

September 7, 2016

Office of the President
Of the Philippines
Malacañang

PROVIDING GUIDELINES FOR THE ARMED FORCES OF THE PHILIPPINES AND THE PHILIPPINE NATIONAL POLICE IN THE IMPLEMENTATIONS OF MEASURES TO SUPPRESS AND PREVENT LAWLESS VIOLENCE.

WHEREAS, on 04 September 2016 President Rodrigo Roa Duterte promulgated Proclamation No. 55 declaring a state of national emergency on account of lawless violence in Mindanao and calling out the Armed Forces of the Philippines (AFP) and the Philippine National Police (PNP) to undertake all necessary measures to suppress any and all forms of lawless violence in Mindanao and prevent the spread and escalation thereof elsewhere in the country;

WHEREAS, there is a need for an effective and expeditious implementation of the President's directive in order to prevent further loss of innocent lives and destruction of property and bring the whole country back to a state of complete normalcy as quick as possible;

WHEREAS, to ensure respect and protection of the fundamental civil and political rights of our citizens, there is also a need to define and delimit the measures that the AFP and PNP can undertake during the state of lawless violence.

NOW, THEREFORE, I, SALVADOR C. MEDIALDEA, by the authority and order of the President, do hereby promulgate the following directives and guidelines to be observed during the subsistence of a state of lawless violence;

SECTION 1. The Department of National Defense (DND) and the Department of Interior and Local Government (DILG) shall coordinate the immediate deployment of additional forces of the AFP and the PNP to suppress lawless violence and acts of terror in Mindanao and prevent such violence from spreading and escalating elsewhere in the country. To the extent possible, the DND and the DILG shall deploy AFP and PNP personnel on major streets and thoroughfares, as well as near crowded places such as malls and train stations, in order to increase troop and military visibility for deterrence and quick-response purposes, without causing undue alarm to the general public.

SECTION 2. The AFP and the PNP shall intensify their local and transnational intelligence operations against individuals or groups suspected of, or responsible for, committing or conspiring to commit acts of lawless violence in the Philippines, and may draw on budgetary funds duly appropriated for this purpose.

SECTION 3. The Department of Justice (DOJ) shall closely coordinate with the PNP and other law-enforcement agencies for the prompt investigation and prosecution of all individuals or groups apprehended for committing, or conspiring to commit, acts of lawless violence.

SECTION 4. All local government units are enjoined to give their full support and utmost cooperation to ensure the effective implementation of this Memorandum Order.

SECTION 5. At all times, the constitutional rights of every individual shall be respected and given due regarded by the AFP and the PNP in the implementation of this Memorandum Order. No civil or political rights are suspended during the existence of a state of lawless violence.

In particular, no warrantless arrests shall be effected unless the situation falls under any of the following circumstances, among others:

(i) when the person to be arrested has committed, is actually committing, or is attempting to commit an offense in the presence of the arresting officer;

(ii) when an offense has just been committed and the arresting officer has personal knowledge of facts indicating that the person to be arrested has committed the offense;

(iii) when the person to be arrested is a prisoner who escaped from a penal establishment or place where he is serving final judgment or temporarily confined with his case is pending;

(iv) when the person arrested, or to be arrested, has voluntarily waived his rights against warrantless arrests.

Similarly, existing rules and jurisprudence shall be strictly observed in effecting warrantless searches and seizures, such as in the following instances:

(i) when the person to be searched has consented to the search or has voluntarily waived his right against warrantless searches and seizures.

(ii) as an incident to a lawful arrest and the search is made contemporaneous to the arrest and within a permissible area of search;

(iii) search of vessels and aircraft for violation of immigration and customs laws;

(iv) search of automobiles at borders of "constructive" borders for violation of immigration or smuggling laws;

(v) where the objects and effects to be seized are in plain view;

(vi) stop-and-frisk situations; and

(vii) search arising from exigent and emergency circumstances.

In the case of police/military checkpoints, inspection shall be limited to a request to roll down vehicle windows, search for things in plain view only, and production of identification and vehicle registration papers. No further intrusive actions shall be taken, such as demanding the opening of trucks or lids or asking person(s) on board to step out, unless the subject individual consents or agrees thereto.

In stop-and-frisk situations, search shall be limited to light patting on the outer garments of the subject individual to detect the possession of weapons or similar effects.

SECTION 6. Any AFP/PNP personnel found violating any of the foregoing constitutional rights shall be held administratively and civilly/criminally liable therefor.

SECTION 7. This Memorandum Order shall take effect immediately.

By Order of the President:
(Sgd.) SALVADOR C. MEDIALDEA
Executive Secretary

SOURCE: Office of the President of the Philippines. "Memorandum Order No. 3, s. 2016." September 7, 2016. http://www.gov.ph/2016/09/07/memorandum-order-no-3-s-2016.

Press Briefing by Press Secretary Josh Earnest and Deputy National Security Adviser for Strategic Communications Ben Rhodes

September 7, 2016

MR. EARNEST: Good evening, everybody. It's nice to see you all. Obviously this will be the—one of the briefings that we'll do on the trip. I don't think we have anything at the top, so I think we'll just go to straight to your questions for the sake of efficiency. Who wants to get us started?

Q. I wanted to ask about the cancellation of the meeting with Duterte. The President said yesterday this wasn't going to affect our long-term relationship with the Philippines, but how is that the case if the President and the head of this other—our ally are essentially in a war of words with each other? And the office of the Philippine leader said that the decision to cancel the meeting was mutual. Is that the case, or did the U.S. basically inform them that this was not happening?

MR. RHODES: Well, look, first of all, the nature of our alliance with the Philippines has been and remains rock solid. We have incredibly close working relationships with the government of the Philippines on issues related to disaster response, maritime security, diplomatic coordination on issues related to the South China Sea; economic, commercial and people-to-people ties. So I think people should certainly expect that our very close working relationship with the Philippines is going to be enduring. And in fact, we continue to consult closely at a variety of levels, and in fact, I think Chairman Dunford has even been in the Philippines recently, if not today, for a chiefs of defense meeting.

With respect to the bilateral meeting, I think it was our judgment that given the focus of attention on President Duterte's comments leading into the meetings here, we felt that that did not create a constructive environment for a bilateral meeting. All of the attention, frankly, was on those comments and, therefore, not on the very substantive agenda that we have with the Philippines. So, again, given that focus, we felt that it wasn't the right time to have a bilateral meeting between the two Presidents. And that's something that we discussed with officials from the government of the Philippines last night.

Going forward, I would expect our close cooperation to continue, and where we also have differences, we'll continue to speak to those. And as President Obama said, for any country in the world, not just the Philippines, we'll certainly support very robust counternarcotic efforts, but we also want to make sure that they're consistent with the rule of law and due process. . . .

Q. Back on the meeting with Duterte. You said that it was your judgment that given the focus on his comments that you decided not to do the meeting. So are you saying that it wasn't the content of what he said that you found objectionable. . . .

MR. RHODES: Well, look, I think the two are fundamentally interrelated. So certainly the nature of those comments was not constructive, and therefore there was an enormous amount of tension on this series of statements by President Duterte. And again, given the important issues that we have, having a meeting where all we were going to discuss was a series of comments, frankly, did not strike us as the most constructive way to approach a bilateral meeting.

At the same time, we also knew that we could have a very important meeting with President Park of the Republic of Korea at a time when we just recently had an additional provocation from North Korea. So we had a lot of business to do with President Park, and we had a constructive meeting with her today.

But, again, we remain in contact with Filipino officials, and our close alliance relationship obviously continues and will going forward. . . .

Q. Is there any chance at all that President Obama would have kind of like an informal pull-aside or informal chat with President Duterte on the sidelines of these summits . . . ? And secondly, how concerned is the White House that this spat, whatever you want to call it, could have an impact and push the Philippines into sort of China's arms?

MR. RHODES: So I would expect that the President will see President Duterte in the course of those summits. We have an ASEAN meeting, we have an East Asia Summit meeting. He tends to interact with all the leaders at those events. So I would not expect a formal bilateral meeting, but I think he'll have an opportunity to interact with him, as with all leaders.

With respect to the South China Sea, we've sustained very close cooperation with the Philippines over the course of the transition to the new government there on those issues. So, first of all, we've supported the outcome of the arbitral ruling because we believe that international legal processes are the way to resolve these issues. We have a very close partnership with the Philippines on maritime security issues and continue to provide them with assistance in that space. We have a recently agreed-upon access agreement as it relates to bases in the Philippines. . . .

Frankly, where we've had differences with President Duterte has related more to our concerns that there needs to be a clear commitment to due process and the rule of law as it relates to some of the internal security efforts that had been undertaken there. On the alliance issues, we'll continue to work closely with them. . . .

As it relates to China, we welcome efforts by the Philippines to engage in a dialogue with China. Our position has always been that we're not picking a winner in terms of claims; that we want to see basic international principles upheld, including the peaceful resolution of disputes consistent with international law. What we don't want to see is these claims resolved through force or coercion. So we don't want to see a bigger nation forcing a smaller nation to accept their will. However, if the Philippines can reach a mutual understanding with China, or any of the claimants can reach a peaceful resolution to these disputes consistent with international law, then we believe that would be a constructive development. And, in fact, we've encouraged all ASEAN countries who are claimants to engage in dialogue, and we've encouraged ASEAN as a collective to support these basic sets of international principles. . . .

Q. Do you see this as a trend of anti-Americanism in the Philippines? And are you concerned about some of the things Duterte has said about perhaps getting a little closer to the Chinese, putting the court ruling aside?

MR. RHODES: So, each time we've seen comments like that, I think we've expressed concern. We were certainly concerned about the comments that related to our ambassador. I think that, again, what we are focused on here is whether or not comments like that on the eve of a meeting, and comments that related to a very substantive difference that we have raised consistently as it relates to due process, that those comments were going to prevent us from having the right environment to have a serious, productive discussion.

In terms of anti-Americanism, I think if you look at the views of the people of the Philippines, they're overwhelmingly in favor of the alliance. They're overwhelmingly positive about the United States. Frankly, we've come a long way from a number of years ago when there was a greater degree of anti-American sentiment. I think we've built trust with the people of the Philippines. President Obama has invested a lot in that relationship. I think he's very well thought of in the Philippines. The fact that we're able to conclude a basing access agreement I think signaled that we're in a new chapter in our relationship. . . .

What we want is an effective working relationship, though, so our hope is that there's an effort that is continued to be made by the government of the Philippines to have the right tone for our discussions to be productive going forward.

Q. Do you want an apology?

MR. RHODES: I think it's their determination as to how they address his comments. We've noted the statements that they've made over the course of the day. I think we'd welcome efforts to set a positive tone for the discussions between our leaders. At the same time, the working relationships continue to be very strong in the relevant ministries and throughout our diplomatic and military channels. So none of these comments have affected the basic cooperation that takes place on a day to day basis with the Philippines. . . .

Oh and again on China, look, we don't—we have no concerns about there being positive relations between our allies and China. In fact, when our allies have constructive relations with China, it contributes to stability broadly in the Asia Pacific. We do have concerns about circumstances where China or any other nation may seek to coerce another country. So if the government of the Philippines is engaged in a dialogue with China about South China Sea claims or other issues, that's consistent with the type of diplomatic resolutions we seek here.

Frankly, what nobody has an interest in is there to be an escalation or a conflict over these issues. We do take the position on the arbitral ruling that this is legally binding and that claims should be resolved under international law. And China is party to the U.N. convention on the law of the sea, and so therefore we believe that they and other countries should respect that ruling as final and binding. . . .

Q. A couple questions. Just to be clear, the Philippine government I believe suggested that there would be some sort of rescheduling of this meeting. . . . But is there any date set for them to actually meet before President Obama leaves office, perhaps during UNGA? . . .

MR. RHODES: . . . On the Philippines, again, I think they'll see each other at the summit, as the President will see leaders over the course of tomorrow's dinner and the meetings the following day. We do not have a formal bilateral meeting scheduled. We don't anticipate a formal bilateral meeting. I do think it's the case that—we're not indicating that we'll never speak to the President of the Philippines, we just don't think that this is the right environment after the series of comments. . . .

SOURCE: Office of the White House Press Secretary. "Press Briefing by Press Secretary Josh Earnest and Deputy National Security Advisor for Strategic Communications Ben Rhodes." September 7, 2016. http://www.whitehouse.gov/the-press-office/2016/09/07/press-briefing-press-secretary-josh-earnest-and-deputy-national-security.

Violence Suppression Guidelines Expanded and Extended to Philippine Coast Guard

DOCUMENT

September 26, 2016

Office of the President
Of the Philippines
Malacañang

MEMORANDUM ORDER NO. 04

EXPANDING THE APPLICATION OF MEMORANDUM ORDER NO. 3 (s.2016) TO THE PHILIPPINE COAST GUARD AND PROVIDING ADDITIONAL GUIDELINES

IN THE IMPLEMENTATION OF MEASURES TO SUPPRESS AND PREVENT LAWLESS VIOLENCE

WHEREAS, on 05 September 2016, the Executive Secretary, by the authority and order of the President, and pursuant to Presidential Proclamation No. 55 (s.2016), promulgated Memorandum Order No. 03 providing guidelines for the AFP and the PNP in the implementation of measures to suppress and prevent any and all forms of lawless violence in Mindanao and prevent the spread and escalation thereof elsewhere in the country;

WHEREAS, there is a need for a comprehensive implementation of the President's directive to prevent further loss of innocent lives and destruction of property in the entire Philippine territory including the country's maritime jurisdiction, with due respect for and protection of the fundamental civil and political rights of our citizens;

WHEREAS, Republic Act (RA) No. 9993, otherwise known as the Philippine Coastguard Law of 2009, and its Implementing Rules and Regulations (IRR) established the Philippine Coast Guard (PCG) as an armed and uniformed service attached to the Department of Transportation (DoTr) and tasked, among others, to assist in the enforcement of laws on firearms and explosives, controlled chemicals, transnational crimes, and other laws within the maritime jurisdiction of the Philippines; and

WHEREAS, Section 27, Chapter 9, Title Ill, Book Ill of Executive Order No. 292, otherwise known as the "Administrative Code of 1987," empowers the Executive Secretary to implement presidential directives, orders and decisions;

NOW, THEREFORE, I, SALVADOR C. MEDIALDEA, by the authority and order of the President, do hereby promulgate the following additional directives and guidelines to be observed during the subsistence of a state of national emergency on account of lawless violence in Mindanao:

SECTION 1. Consistent with its mandate and powers under RA No. 9993 and its IRR, the PCG shall be subject to the same directives addressed to the Armed Forces of the Philippines and the Philippine National Police under Sections 1, 2, 5, and 6 of Memorandum Order No. 03 (s.2016), and is hereby ordered to comply strictly therewith.

Additional PCG units and personnel to increase visibility and security shall immediately be deployed in all Philippine ports, harbors, and major coastal areas.

SECTION 2. With due regard to the constitutional rights of every individual, the PCG shall intensify its activities related to the enforcement and maintenance of maritime safety and security to prevent or suppress lawless violence at sea including, among others, the:

    (i)   inspection of all merchant ships and vessels to ensure compliance with safety standards, rules and regulations;

    (ii) surveillance and inspection of persons, vessels and watercrafts navigating within the maritime jurisdiction of the Philippines, and suspected of committing, or conspiring to commit, an offense in the Philippines;

    (iii) control and flow of traffic of vessels within the maritime jurisdiction of the Philippines;

    (iv) marshaling of passenger-laden vessels nationwide; and

(v) maintenance, in coordination with the Maritime Industry Authority, of a unified numbering system for all Philippine-registered vessels, watercrafts and water conveyances that are not covered by the International Maritime Organization numbering system.

SECTION 3. The PCG shall strictly enforce maritime security communications protocol to enhance detection of any threat to maritime safety and security.

SECTION 4. The Department of Justice shall closely coordinate with the PCG and other law-enforcement agencies for the prompt investigation and prosecution of all individuals or groups apprehended for committing, or conspiring to commit, acts of lawless violence.

SECTION 5. All government agencies and local government units are directed to assist the PCG to ensure the effective implementation of this Memorandum Order, consistent with their respective mandates and functions.

SECTION 6. The DoTr is hereby directed to supervise and coordinate the PCG's compliance with the foregoing directives.

SECTION 7. This Memorandum Order shall take effect immediately.

26 September 2016.
By Order of the President:

(Sgd.) SALVADOR C. MEDIALDEA
Executive Secretary

Source: Office of the President of the Philippines. "Memorandum Order No. 4, s. 2016." September 26, 2016. http://www.gov.ph/2016/09/26/memorandum-order-no-4-s-2016.

OTHER HISTORIC DOCUMENTS OF INTEREST

FROM PREVIOUS *HISTORIC DOCUMENTS*

Circuit Court Rules on Construction of the Dakota Access Pipeline

SEPTEMBER 9, 2016

Throughout the summer and fall of 2016, thousands gathered at the Standing Rock Sioux reservation in North Dakota to protest the proposed construction of an oil pipeline within a half mile of the tribe's land. Those demonstrating argued that the initial refusal of the government to withhold permits from the pipeline's developer amounted to another land grab perpetrated against Native Americans. Despite receiving the necessary permits to move forward, the pipeline project was put on hold when the Army Corps of Engineers, as encouraged by multiple federal departments, decided to conduct additional reviews of the land to determine whether the pipeline would impact Standing Rock Sioux cultural lands. On February 9, 2017, drilling near the Standing Rock Sioux reservation resumed, after the federal government provided the permits for the project to be completed.

DAKOTA ACCESS PIPELINE

The Dakota Access Pipeline is intended to carry oil approximately 1,200 miles from North Dakota to Illinois. Once complete, the pipeline would carry 470,000 barrels of crude oil each day, an amount that could eventually reach 570,000 barrels per day as production at sites around the Midwest ramps up. The pipeline is believed to be more cost effective than carrying this crude oil from North Dakota to Illinois by rail. Supporters argue that the pipeline will create 8,000 to 12,000 jobs and will be a boon for tax revenue.

According to the developer, Energy Transfer Partners, the $3.8 billion project is nearly 90 percent complete. The part that has not yet been finished, due to a federal decision temporarily halting the project, traverses Lake Oahe, less than a half mile from the Standing Rock Sioux reservation. The pipeline project was initially intended to cross under the Missouri River near Bismarck, North Dakota; however, there was concern that an oil spill would ruin Bismarck's water supply, and so the exact direction of the pipeline was moved to a different portion of the river nearby the Standing Rock Sioux's land.

Opposition to construction of the pipeline has largely been led by the Standing Rock Sioux tribe. It first started a protest camp, Sacred Stone Camp, near the proposed pipeline site in April 2016. Since then, 200 tribes have pledged their support for the effort of the Standing Rock Sioux and thousands have come from around the country to take part in the protest, from military veterans to celebrities to politicians. While the Native American protestors have committed to remaining unarmed and peaceful, police have accused protestors of throwing makeshift bombs. Police have responded to the protests by utilizing pepper spray, rubber bullets, and hoses, despite the freezing cold temperatures, to disperse the demonstrators to no avail. A private security company hired by Energy Transfer Partners was accused of using attack dogs against the protestors, and police arrested dozens for rioting and criminal trespassing. Opponents of the pipeline unable to take part in the demonstrations used Facebook's "check-in" feature to falsely note their location as the Standing Rock Sioux reservation. The move was thought by protestors to confuse police about the number who would be demonstrating, but police have claimed that they were not using the social media page to track protestors.

STANDING ROCK SIOUX FILE LAWSUIT

To build the Dakota Access Pipeline, Energy Transfer Partners was required to receive siting approval from any states it would cross. It received approval from South Dakota and Illinois in 2015 and from North Dakota and Iowa in early 2016. The developers were also required to seek federal approval for specific portions of the pipeline. These approvals came from the Army Corps of Engineers, which verifies that the pipeline would not disturb wetlands or waterways as prohibited under the Rivers and Harbors Act and the Clean Water Act. It also needed approval from the U.S. Fish and Wildlife Service (USFWS) to ensure, under the National Wildlife Refuge System Administration Act, that wildlife refuges would not be impacted. In June 2016, the USFWS gave the pipeline developer a "finding of no significant impact." One month later, the Army Corps of Engineers gave the final go-ahead to the project by granting a general permit called Nationwide Permit 12, which authorized development of those portions of the pipeline that are under the Army Corps of Engineers' jurisdiction.

Under the National Historic Preservation Act (NHPA), prior to granting such permits, the Army Corps of Engineers is required to consult any Native American tribes about sites of cultural or religious significance that might be impacted by a project resulting from the granting of a permit. On July 27, the Standing Rock Sioux filed a lawsuit against the Army Corps of Engineers, asking for declaratory and injunctive relief. The tribe alleged that it was not properly consulted by the Army Corps of Engineers, and that, as such, the Army Corps did not properly comply with the NHPA when issuing the permits. In their filing, the Standing Rock Sioux argued that because the pipeline would run within a half mile of the boundary of its reservation, a spill would have a significant impact on the land and water on which the tribe relies. Furthermore, the pipeline would pass through areas considered sacred by the Standing Rock Sioux, including burial grounds. On August 4, the Standing Rock Sioux filed a second case, this time seeking a preliminary injunction for withdrawal of the verifications provided by the Army Corps to Energy Transfer Partners. In this second filing, the tribe only alleged that the Army Corps of Engineers had erred in not compiling with the NHPA and did not press its environmental concerns. On September 4, the tribe filed a third case, this time an emergency motion for a temporary restraining order to stop construction near its land.

On September 9, U.S. District Judge James E. Boasberg ruled on the second filing by the Standing Rock Sioux, that which dealt with the preliminary injunction requested based on the alleged failure of the Army Corps of Engineers to adhere to the provisions of the NHPA. The ruling documents attempts made by the Army Corps of Engineers to consult with the Standing Rock Sioux and the tribe's responses on a variety of issues. Ultimately, the judge denied preliminary injunction, noting that "the Corps has likely complied with the NHPA and that the Tribe has not shown it will suffer injury that would be prevented by any injunction the Court could issue." In response to the decision, Dave Archambault II, chair of the Standing Rock Sioux, said the tribe would not be deterred by the decision: "We are guided by prayer, and we will continue to fight for our people. We will not rest until our lands, people, waters, and sacred places are permanently protected from this destructive pipeline."

DAKOTA ACCESS PIPELINE SUSPENDED

Following the ruling of Judge Boasberg not to grant preliminary injunction, the Department of Justice, Department of the Army, and Department of the Interior instructed Energy Transfer Partners to halt construction on twenty miles of the pipeline both east and west of Lake Oahe. "We appreciate the District Court's opinion on the U.S. Army Corps of Engineers' compliance with the National Historic Preservation Act. However, important issues raised by the Standing Rock Sioux Tribe and other tribal nations and their members regarding the Dakota Access pipeline specifically, and pipeline-related decision-making generally, remain," the group said in a press release. According to the announcement, authorization for further construction would be put on hold until additional research could be conducted to determine the potential impact of the pipeline to cultural and religious lands. In praising the nonviolent protest efforts used by the Standing Rock Sioux and their supporters, the group said it is "incumbent on all of us to develop a path forward that serves the broadest public interest." The announcement also called for further discussion on how issues of infrastructure development should proceed in the future to take into account concerns of Native American tribes.

On December 4, the Army Corps of Engineers announced that it would temporarily suspend the Dakota Access Pipeline project to conduct further analysis and possibly determine a new site for the pipeline. In its announcement, the Corps said it would "not grant an easement to cross Lake Oahe at the proposed location based on the current record." Upon hearing of the delay, the leader of the Lakota, Dakota, and Nakota Nations, Chief Arvol Looking Horse, Keeper of the Sacred White Buffalo Calf Pipe, said to supporters gathered at the reservation, "People have said that this is a make it or break it, and I guess we made it." He also asked protesters to leave, noting that there would likely be no further action on the pipeline until the administration of President-elect Donald Trump was installed in January 2017. On January 18, two days before Trump's inauguration, the Army Corps of Engineers published a Notice of Intent in the *Federal Register* announcing that it would put together an Environmental Impact statement on the current proposed crossing at Lake Oahe. Energy Transfer Partners responded by filing a motion in federal court requesting permission to continue constructing the pipeline.

On January 24, 2017, just days after taking office, President Trump signed permits for the Dakota Access Pipeline and Keystone XL pipeline projects to move ahead, noting that they would be "subject to terms and conditions negotiated by us." He further issued an executive memorandum directing the Corps to consider changing its December decision and to withdraw its Notice of Intent. The Standing Rock Sioux, noting that it will not be deterred from its fight, said it would "vigorously pursue legal action" if the new administration stopped the Army Corps of Engineers' review. "To abandon the [environmental impact statement] would amount to a wholly unexplained and arbitrary change based on the President's personal views and, potentially, personal investments," the tribe said in a statement.

On January 31, Sen. John Hoeven, R-N.D., announced that the acting secretary of the Army "has directed the Army Corps of Engineers to proceed with the easement needed to complete the Dakota Access Pipeline." Protestors vowed not to let construction continue, but on February 9, 2017, drilling began under Lake Oahe. The Standing Rock Sioux filed for another temporary restraining order and said in a statement, "This administration has expressed utter and complete disregard for not only our treaty and water rights, but the environment as a whole." Legal experts believe it is unlikely that the tribe will be victorious in court.

—Heather Kerrigan

Following is the excerpted opinion in the case of Standing Rock Sioux Tribe v. U.S. Army Corps of Engineers, *in which the D.C. District Court ruled on September 9, 2016, to deny the request of the Standing Rock Sioux Tribe to stop construction of the Dakota Access Pipeline; and a joint statement from the Departments of Justice, Army, and Interior, also on September 9, 2016, responding to the ruling.*

Court Issues Opinion on Construction of Dakota Access Pipeline

September 9, 2016

Standing Rock Sioux Tribe, et al., Plaintiffs

v.

U.S. Army Corps of Engineers, et al., Defendants

Civil Action No. 16-1534 (JEB)

MEMORANDUM OPINION

"Since the founding of this nation, the United States' relationship with the Indian tribes has been contentious and tragic. America's expansionist impulse in its formative years led to the removal and relocation of many tribes, often by treaty but also by force." *Cobell v. Norton,* 240 F.3d 1081, 1086 (D.C. Cir. 2001). This case also features what an American Indian tribe believes is an unlawful encroachment on its heritage. More specifically, the Standing Rock Sioux Tribe has sued the United States Army Corps of Engineers to block the operation of Corps permitting for the Dakota Access Pipeline (DAPL). The Tribe fears that construction of the pipeline, which runs within half a mile of its reservation in North and South Dakota, will destroy sites of cultural and historical significance. It has now filed a Motion for Preliminary Injunction, asserting principally that the Corps flouted its duty to engage in tribal consultations under the National Historic Preservation Act (NHPA) and that irreparable harm will ensue. After digging through a substantial record on an expedited basis, the Court cannot concur. It concludes that the Corps has likely complied with the NHPA and that the Tribe has not shown it will suffer injury that would be prevented by any injunction the Court could issue. The Motion will thus be denied.

I. Background

DAPL is a domestic oil pipeline designed to move over a half-billion gallons of crude oil across four states daily. The oil enters the pipeline in North Dakota, crosses South Dakota and Iowa, and winds up in Patoka, Illinois, nearly 1,200 miles later. Although the route does not actually cross the Standing Rock reservation, it runs within a half-mile of it.

A project of this magnitude often necessitates an extensive federal appraisal and permitting process. Not so here. Domestic oil pipelines, unlike natural-gas pipelines, require no general approval from the federal government. In fact, DAPL needs almost no federal permitting of any kind because 99% of its route traverses private land.

One significant exception, however, concerns construction activities in federally regulated waters at hundreds of discrete places along the pipeline route. The Corps needed to permit this activity under the Clean Water Act or the Rivers and Harbors Act—and sometimes both. For DAPL, accordingly, it permitted these activities under a general permit known as Nationwide Permit 12. The Tribe alleges that the Corps violated multiple federal statutes in doing so, including the National Environmental Policy Act (NEPA) and the National Historic Preservation Act (NHPA). In its Complaint, the Tribe asserts that this DAPL permitting threatens its environmental and economic well-being, as well as its cultural resources.

Despite this broad lawsuit, however, the Standing Rock Sioux now seek a preliminary injunction only on the alleged violation of the NHPA. That statute encompasses sites of cultural or religious significance to Indian tribes and requires that federal agencies consult with tribes prior to issuing permits that might affect these historic resources. The Tribe claims that the Corps did not fulfill this obligation before permitting the DAPL activities. It bears noting that the Tribe does not press its environmental claims under NEPA here. Nor does it seek a preliminary injunction to protect itself from the potential environmental harms that might arise from having the pipeline on its doorstep. Instead, it asserts only that pipeline-construction activities—specifically, the grading and clearing of land—will cause irreparable injury to historic or cultural properties of great significance.

The statutes and permitting scheme involved in this Motion are undeniably complex. The Court first sets forth the operation of the NHPA, which the Tribe asserts was violated. It next explains the Clean Water Act and the Rivers and Harbors Act, under which the Corps permitted the DAPL activities. Subsequent sections lay out the factual and legal proceedings that have taken place thus far.

[Section A providing background information on the National Historic Preservation Act, Section B discussing the Clean Water Act, and Section C on the Rivers and Harbors Act have been omitted.]

D. Factual History

The Standing Rock Sioux Tribe is a federally recognized American Indian Tribe with a reservation spanning the border between North and South Dakota. See ECF No. 1 (Complaint), ¶ 1. The sweep of the Tribe's historic and cultural connection to the Great Plains, however, extends beyond these modern reservation boundaries. *Id.*, ¶¶ 7–8. A successor to the Great Sioux Nation, the Tribe's ancestors once lived, loved, worshipped, and mourned "[w]herever the buffalo roamed." ECF No. 6-2 (Declaration of Jon Eagle, Sr.), ¶ 24. These people created stone alignments, burial cairns, and other rock features throughout the area to conduct important spiritual rituals related to the rhythms of their daily life. See ECF No. 14–1 (Declaration of Tim Mentz, Sr.), ¶ 3; Eagle Decl., ¶¶ 20, 25. Along the region's waterways in particular, the prevalence of these artifacts reflects water's sacred role in their deeply held spiritual beliefs. See Eagle Decl., ¶ 25. Today, the Standing Rock Sioux continue to honor these practices and cherish the connection they have to their ancestors through these sites. *Id.*

One place of particular significance to the Tribe lies at the traditional confluence of the Missouri and Cannonball Rivers. *Id.*, ¶¶ 11–12; ECF No. 6–1 (Declaration of Dave Archambault II), ¶ 12. The ancestors to the Standing Rock Sioux gathered in this location to peacefully trade with other tribes. See Mentz Decl., ¶ 36. They also considered the perfectly round stones shaped by the meeting of these two great rivers to be sacred. See Eagle Decl., ¶ 11. Mighty natural forces, however, no longer hone these stones. *Id.* In 1958, the Corps dredged and altered the course of the Cannonball River to construct a dam. *Id.* As a result, a large man-made lake known as Lake Oahe now covers the confluence. *Id.*

The Tribe nevertheless continues to use the banks of the Missouri River for spiritual ceremonies, and the River, as well as Lake Oahe, plays an integral role in the life and recreation of those living on the reservation. *Id.* Naturally, then, the Tribe was troubled to learn in late 2014 that a new pipeline was being planned that would cross the Missouri River under Lake Oahe about a half-mile north of the reservation. See Archambault Decl., ¶¶ 8–12. This was, of course, DAPL3—a 1,172-mile crude-oil pipeline poised to wind its way from the Bakken oil fields near Stanley, North Dakota, to refineries and terminals in Patoka, Illinois.

The conflict that has arisen since this revelation is, to say the least, factually complex. To ease digestion of the relevant information, the Court first describes how Dakota Access chose the pipeline route. It then lays out the facts surrounding the Corps' permitting and concurrent Section 106 process for the project. These following summaries admittedly contain significant detail and may try the reader's patience. The Court nonetheless believes such a narrative is necessary because a key question here is whether the Corps engaged in sufficient consultation with the Tribe under Section 106.

1. *DAPL*

In the summer of 2014, Dakota Access crafted the route that brought DAPL to Standing Rock's doorstep. See ECF No. 22, Exh. B (Declaration of Monica Howard), ¶¶ 2–3. The plotted course almost exclusively tracked privately held lands and, in sensitive places like Lake Oahe, already-existing utility lines. As only 3% of the work needed to build the pipeline would ever require federal approval of any kind and only 1% of the pipeline was set to affect U.S. waterways, the pipeline could proceed largely on the company's timeline.

Dakota Access nevertheless also prominently considered another factor in crafting its route: the potential presence of historic properties. *Id.* Using past cultural surveys, the company devised DAPL's route to account for and avoid sites that had already been identified as potentially eligible for or listed on the National Register of Historic Places. *Id.*, ¶¶ 2–4. With that path in hand, in July 2014, the company purchased rights to a 400-foot corridor along its preliminary route to conduct extensive new cultural surveys of its own. *Id.*, ¶ 3. These surveys eventually covered the entire length of the pipeline in North and South Dakota, and much of Iowa and Illinois. *Id.*, ¶ 8. Professionally licensed archaeologists conducted Class II cultural surveys, which are "focused on visual reconnaissance of the ground surface in settings with high ground visibility." *Id.* In some places, however, the same archaeologists carried out more intensive Class III cultural surveys, which involve a "comprehensive archaeological survey program" requiring both surface visual inspection and shovel-test probes of fixed grids to "inventory, delineate, and assess" historic sites. *Id.* These latter surveys required coordination with and approval by State Historic Preservation Officers. *Id.*

Where this surveying revealed previously unidentified historic or cultural resources that might be affected, the company mostly chose to reroute. *Id.*, ¶¶ 4–6. In North Dakota, for example, the cultural surveys found 149 potentially eligible sites, 91 of which had stone features. *Id.*, ¶ 5. The pipeline workspace and route was modified to avoid all 91 of these stone features and all but 9 of the other potentially eligible sites. *Id.* By the time the company finally settled on a construction path, then, the pipeline route had been modified 140 times in North Dakota alone to avoid potential cultural resources. *Id.*, ¶ 6. Plans had also been put in place to mitigate any effects on the other 9 sites through coordination with the North Dakota SHPO. *Id.*, ¶ 13. All told, the company surveyed nearly twice as many miles in North Dakota as the 357 miles that would eventually be used for the pipeline. *Id.*, ¶ 12.

The company also opted to build its new pipeline along well-trodden ground wherever feasible. See ECF No. 22–1 (Declaration of Joey Mahmoud), ¶¶ 18, 24, 40. Around Lake Oahe, for example, the pipeline will track both the Northern Border Gas Pipeline, which was placed into service in 1982, and an existing overhead utility line. *Id.*, ¶ 18. In fact, where it crosses Lake Oahe, DAPL is 100% adjacent to, and within 22 to 300 feet from, the existing pipeline. *Id.* Dakota Access chose this route because these locations had "been disturbed in the past—both above and below ground level—making it a 'brownfield crossing location.'" *Id.*, ¶ 19. This made it less likely, then, that new ground disturbances would harm intact cultural or tribal features. *Id.*

Around the time the cultural survey work began, Dakota Access took its plan public. See Howard Decl., ¶ 12. On September 30, 2014, it met with the Standing Rock Sioux Tribal Council to present the pipeline project as part of a larger community-outreach effort. *Id.*, ¶ 22. Personnel from Dakota Access also spoke with the Tribe's Historic Preservation Officer (THPO), Waste' Win Young, several times over the course of the next month. *Id.*, ¶¶ 23–27. At one related meeting, a DAPL archaeologist answered questions about the proposed survey work and invited input from Young on any areas that might be of particular tribal interest. *Id.*, ¶¶ 25–28. The company agreed as well to send the centerline files from its cultural survey to her for review, and did so on November 13. *Id.*, ¶ 28. It never received any response from Young. *Id.*

2. Entry of Corps

Based on the current record, the Corps appears to have had little involvement in Dakota Access's early planning. The one exception is a June 2014 meeting between the two parties to discuss the company's plan to build a pipeline through the region. See ECF No. 21-18 (Declaration of Martha Chieply), ¶ 8. At this meeting, the Corps informed the company about its permitting requirements and explained the importance of tribal coordination for any actions taken under its jurisdiction. *Id.* There is no indication that the company sought to secure any permitting or that it presented the Corps with a specific proposed route for DAPL at this time. *Id.* This conclusion is consistent with the record evidence that Dakota Access was still buying up the necessary right-of-ways for the pipeline surveys in July 2014. See Howard Decl., ¶ 3; Mahmoud Decl., ¶ 40.

The writing was on the wall, however, that many DAPL permitting requests would eventually land in the Corps inbox. The Corps' Tribal Liaison, Joel Ames, accordingly, tried to set up a meeting with THPO Young beginning around September 17, 2014, without success. See ECF No. 21-17 (Declaration of Joel Ames), ¶¶ 5–6; see also ECF No. 21, Exh. 9 (Corps Tribal Consultation Spreadsheet) at 1 (documenting five attempts by Ames to coordinate a meeting with Young in September 2014). On October 2, other Corps personnel also sought to hold an arranged meeting with the Tribal Council and Dakota Access on the Standing Rock reservation. See Chiefly Decl., ¶ 9. But when the Corps timely arrived for the meeting, Tribal Chairman David Archambault told them that the conclave had started earlier than planned and had already ended. Id. Ames nevertheless continued to reach out to Young to try to schedule another meeting throughout the month of October. See Ames Decl., ¶¶ 5–6. When the new meeting was finally held at the reservation on November 6, though, DAPL was taken off the agenda because Young did not attend. Id., ¶ 7.

3. Soil-Bore Testing at Lake Oahe

The Corps' North Dakota office also received the first request for DAPL permitting around this time and launched a formal NHPA Section 106 consultation as a result. See ECF No. 21-19 (Declaration of Richard Harnois), ¶ 5. This solitary preconstruction request from Dakota Access sought permitting only to conduct preliminary soil-bore testing at the Lake Oahe site, not to actually begin any construction. Id., ¶ 12. Dakota Access needed to conduct these tests to determine whether it could subsequently use its preferred method of Horizontal Directional Drilling at the crossing. Id. HDD—which the company plans to use on all land subject to the RHA or owned by the Corps—allows for "construction across a sensitive area without excavation of a trench by installing the pipeline through a drilled hole significantly below the conventional depth of a pipeline." Howard Decl., ¶ 7. This particular test involved drilling just seven holes of 4-inch diameter with an estimated 10 feet of impact on areas around the holes. See Harnois Decl., Exhs. 1–2. Access to and from the sites, moreover, would take place on existing roads. Id.

As a first cut, the Corps reviewed extensive existing cultural surveys both within and outside the Lake Oahe project area to determine whether the work might affect cultural resources. Id. Then, on October 24, the Corps sent out a letter to tribes, including the Standing Rock Sioux, with information about the proposed work and maps documenting the known cultural sites that the Corps had already identified. Id., ¶ 6; see id., Exh. 1. These included sites that the Corps considered to be outside the projected area of effect. Id., ¶ 6. In addition, the letter requested that any party interested in consulting on the matter reply within thirty days. Id. No response was received from the Tribe. Id. The Corps did receive responses from other tribes and the North Dakota SHPO, which it considered. Id., ¶ 7. After granting an extra three weeks for additional responses, on December 18 the Corps made an initial determination of "No Historic Properties Affected" for the soil-bore testing. Id., ¶¶ 7–11.

The Corps mailed out this decision in a Determination of Effect letter to the North Dakota SHPO and all affected tribes on the same day. Id., ¶ 11. The letter explained that the Corps had concluded that no historic properties would be affected by the tests and clarified that a previous "not eligible" determination had already been made for a nearby site that would also not be affected by the work. Id. The Corps also emailed Young again the next day to seek possible dates for a January 2015 meeting with the Tribe to discuss

DAPL. See Tribal Consultation Sheet at 1 (documenting email on December 19, 2014). No response is in the record.

On February 12, 2015, having still heard nothing from the Tribe, Corps Senior Field Archaeologist Richard Harnois emailed Young again to solicit comments on the narrow issue of the soil-bore testing. See Harnois Decl., ¶¶ 13–14. Again, no reply. *Id.* Around this same time, Young informed the Corps' Tribal Liaison, Ames, at an unrelated regulatory meeting that she did not need to consult with the Corps at the moment as she was currently working directly with Dakota Access. See Ames Decl., ¶ 8; see also Tribal Consultation Sheet at 1 (documenting contact). As a result, on February 18, the Corps granted the PCN authorization under NWP 12 for the limited exploratory soil-bore testing requested by Dakota Access. See Harnois Decl., ¶¶ 13–14. . . .

. . . several weeks later, on March 2, 2015, the Corps finally received a letter from Young expressing concerns over sites that might be affected by the bore testing. *Id.*, ¶ 15. The letter was dated on the same day that the Corps had green-lighted the work. *Id.* In particular, Young mentioned the North Cannonball Village Site, which was almost a half-mile from the closest "area of potential effect" boundary set by the Corps. *Id.* The letter further requested Class III and other cultural surveys under tribal monitoring before the testing, and tribal monitoring during both the testing and any later pipeline construction. . . .

4. PCN Authorizations

In the meantime, Dakota Access initiated efforts on December 29, 2014, to secure five additional PCN authorizations under NWP 12 for pipeline-construction work in North Dakota. . . .

While discussions between Dakota Access and the Corps were ongoing, the Corps also sent a form letter to Young on February 17, informing her that it was now considering 55 PCN requests across its offices for DAPL. See ECF No. 6, Exh. 5. The letter went on to explain that the majority of the pipeline work would occur in uplands that were not subject to Corps jurisdiction, but the Corps would need to permit crossings at the Missouri, James, Big Sioux, Des Moines, Mississippi, and Illinois Rivers. *Id.* The letter, moreover, noted that Dakota Access was conducting cultural surveys along the entire route. *Id.* Finally, the Corps requested that the Tribe let it "know if you have any knowledge or concerns regarding cultural resources . . . you would like the Corps to consider" and asked whether it wanted to consult on the project. *Id.* A response was requested prior to March 30 "to help facilitate a timely Section 106 review." *Id.* The Corps also attached the current proposed alignment provided by Dakota Access for the pipeline and contact information for various Corps staff involved in facilitating tribal consultations. *Id.*

On the date of the deadline to respond, Ames and Young exchanged emails, but the content of this exchange is not in the record. See Tribal Consultation Sheet at 8. Young did, however, formally respond on April 8. See ECF No. 6, Exh. 7. In her response this time, she acknowledged receipt of the Corps' February 17 letter about the 55 construction-related PCNs. *Id.* at 1. . . . Young informed the Corps that the Tribe opposed "any kind of oil pipeline construction through our ancestral lands," in part because the potential dredging would take place where "human remains of relatives of current . . . tribal members" were present. *Id.* at 3. Young ultimately closed, though, by reiterating that the Tribe "look[ed] forward to participation in a full tribal consultation process" once it commenced. *Id.* On the same day, Corps personnel and Standing Rock Archaeologist Dr. Kelly Morgan discussed future pipeline realignments over the phone. See Tribal Consultation Sheet at 7.

5. *Summer of 2015*

Relations between the Tribe and Corps did not improve in the summer of 2015. Ames attempted to speak with Young about the project in June, but she informed him via email that she was on an extended leave of absence until July 27. *Id.* at 8; see Ames Decl., ¶ 9. Ames was unable to determine whether anyone was empowered to act on the Tribe's behalf in her absence. See Ames Decl., ¶ 9. On July 22, Corps Operations Manager Eric Stasch also sent a letter to Standing Rock describing the planned use of HDD for the Oahe crossing. See Harnois Decl., ¶ 16; see also *id.*, Exh. 3. In his letter, Stasch provided details about the areas of potential effects and explained that the Corps would consider the work a federal undertaking despite its location on private land. See id., Exh. 3 at 1–2. The letter went on to say that Dakota Access's cultural surveys had identified an additional cultural site within the proposed preparation and staging area for this work. *Id.* at 2. Finally, the letter requested a response within thirty days if the Tribe wished to consult on this particular crossing and indicated that consultations about other pipeline crossings would happen separately. *Id.* at 2–3. Attached to the letter were current and previous survey information, as well as general and detailed project maps illustrating the location and nature of the Lake Oahe crossing and recorded cultural resources. See Harnois Decl., ¶ 16.

In August, the Tribe responded with two letters of its own . . . The first, sent on August 19 from Chairman Archambault to Colonel Cross—the Corps' Commander and District Engineer for the Omaha District—described the Chairman's frustration in not being contacted earlier in regard to DAPL. . . . Archambault invited Cross to the reservation to discuss the matter and provided contact information for his administrative assistant to arrange the visit. *Id.* The very same day, Ames emailed Archambault's assistant in an attempt to schedule a meeting, but without success. . . . The second letter responded directly to Stasch's offer to consult on the Lake Oahe crossing. . . . In it, Young again reiterated that the Section 106 consultation run by the Corps had failed to respond to concerns raised by the Tribe in their February letters about the soil-bore testing prior to the completion of that work. *Id.* She further expressed her frustration in being excluded from the Dakota Access surveying despite company promises to include tribal monitors, and she reiterated her concern that sites might be overlooked or damaged unless the Standing Rock Sioux participated in surveying. *Id.* In closing, Young again said the Tribe looked forward to participating in "future consultation prior to any work being completed . . . [and] to playing a primary role in any and all survey work and monitoring." *Id.* at 2.

The Corps responded in at least three ways to the Tribe over the next month. . . .

On the same day as Stasch's letter, Harnois also emailed Standing Rock Archaeologist Morgan to invite her to participate in the "working level, on-the-ground site visit of the proposed DAPL Oahe Crossing." *Id.*, ¶ 23. This sparked an email exchange between the two on logistics and dates. *Id.* The very next day, however, Morgan emailed the Corps to back out of the visit. *Id.*, Exh. 4. In an attached letter, she explained that "after careful consideration the [Standing Rock] THPO has determined that it is in the best interest of the THPO to decline participation in the site visits and walking the project corridor's [area of projected effects] at this time until government-to-government consultation has occurred for this project per Section 106 requirements as requested by the Standing Rock Sioux

Tribe." *Id.* By this she seemed to mean that the Corps needed to first hold the previously requested meeting between Chairman Archambault and Colonel Henderson. *Id.* Despite the Tribe's withdrawal, the Corps ultimately proceeded to hold the onsite visit with the North Dakota SHPO. See Harnois Decl., ¶ 26.

About a week later, the Tribe sent another letter, this time from Young to Colonel Henderson. See ECF No. 6, Exh. 11 (Letter from Young to Henderson on Sept. 28, 2015). In this letter, Young noted her concern "about the lack of consultation prior to the start of archaeological surveys." *Id.* at 1. She further indicated that the Tribe had "received no correspondence prior to the soil bore hole testing," which she then characterized as evidence that "the Corps is attempting to circumvent the Section 106 process." *Id.* Citing the potential for "irreparable damage to . . . known sites," she complained about the Tribe's "exclusion of tribal participation up to this point" from the identification efforts and Section 106 process. *Id.* In addition, she indicated that the Tribe believed "the entire length of the DAPL [is] one project under the . . . [RHA], as well as" the CWA, and that the Corps was trying to avoid "federalization." *Id.* at 2.

6. Fall of 2015

In the fall, the Corps responded by redoubling its efforts to meet with the Tribe. . . . The Corps, moreover, documented ten different attempts to contact the Tribe over the course of the [*sic*] October to speak about the project. See Tribal Consultation Sheet at 14.

Then, in November, the Corps twice invited the Tribe to a general tribal meeting in Sioux Falls, South Dakota, scheduled for December 8 to 9. . . . Five tribes attended this meeting. *Id.*, ¶ 18. Standing Rock did not. *Id.* At the meeting, the Corps made sure that the tribes had copies of the cultural surveys, and the group agreed to reconvene on January 25, 2016, to discuss any issues they found with those surveys. *Id.* Around the time of this meeting, the Corps also independently looked through these cultural surveys and other route maps to determine whether any additional DAPL crossings might have the potential to affect historic properties. See ECF No. 21-18, Exh. 16. The Corps concluded that only the James River crossing (PCN #4) raised any concerns; no others triggered the need for a PCN under General Condition 20. *Id.*

During this tribal gathering, Morgan sent a letter to the Corps, indicating that the Tribe was "still interested in formal consultation on the proposed" pipeline despite its decision not to attend. See ECF No. 6, Exh. 12 (Letter from Morgan to Chieply on Dec. 8, 2015) at 1. The Tribe yet again noted that it had not received a response from the Corps about the concerns it had raised in regard to the bore testing. . . . Morgan further indicated that the Tribe looked forward to playing a primary role in any surveying or monitoring and explained that it would refuse to participate in tribal meetings until Colonel Henderson came to their reservation to meet with them first. . . .

Again, the Corps appears to have taken action in response to the Tribe's demands. . . .

On December 8, the Corps released a draft EA for the project, which contained a request for comment by January 8, 2016. . . .

7. 2016

The Tribe provided timely and extensive comments to the draft EA in letters on January 8 and March 24, 2016. . . . In these comments, Archambault asserted that the Corps had failed to consult on the identification of cultural sites important to the Tribe . . . He explained the importance of such consultations by, in part, describing tribal "oral traditions and historical records" that recorded the presence of known sites and burials in the direct path of the pipeline. *Id.* (counting "at least 350 known sites within the project corridor in North Dakota alone"); see also *id.* at 4 (indicating that Draft EA misrepresented Tribe's position in October 2014 meeting thanks to false impression from Dakota Access). As a result, he concluded that those outside the Tribe could not properly identify these sites. . . .

The Section 106 process between the Corps and Tribe finally picked up steam in the spring of 2016. From January to May, there were no fewer than seven meetings between the two entities. . . . Perhaps most significantly, Morgan met with the Corps to express specific concerns about tribal burial sites at the James River crossing (PCN # 4). See Harnois Decl., ¶ 24. Based on the information she provided, the Corps verified the presence of cultural resources at the site and successfully instructed Dakota Access to move the pipeline alignment to avoid them. *Id.*

. . . Indeed, in March, Archambault acknowledged that the Corps had recently made strides toward righting the Section 106 ship and indicated he felt this particular onsite visit was productive at identifying new stones, graves, burial sites, and earthen lodges that needed to be considered by the Corps. . . .

The improved relationship, however, had its limits. In the spring, the Corps worked with Dakota Access to offer consulting tribes an opportunity to conduct cultural surveys at PCN locations where the private landowner would permit them. See Chieply Decl., ¶ 28. This included 7 of the 11 sites in North and South Dakota. *Id.* Three tribes took the opportunity, and it paid off. See ECF No. 22, Exh. C (Declaration of Michelle Dippel) ¶ 28. The Upper Sioux Community identified areas of tribal concern at three PCN sites, and Dakota Access agreed to additional avoidance measures at all of them. *Id.* At one of these sites, the tribal surveyors and the Iowa SHPO declared a site eligible for listing on the National Registry that had not previously been identified on Dakota Access's surveys. . . .

Standing Rock took a different tack. The Tribe declined to participate in the surveys because of their limited scope. See Chieply Decl., ¶ 29. Instead, it urged the Corps to redefine the area of potential effect to include the entire pipeline and asserted that it would send no experts to help identify cultural resources until this occurred. . . .

On April 22, Harnois made a Determination of Effect for the site and emailed it to the consulting parties. *Id.*, ¶ 33; see also ECF No. 6, Exh. 43. In it, Harnois described the project, explained the location, and discussed data on 41 potential historic sites in detail. *Id.* He concluded that one of the sites identified, 32MOx0570, was "not eligible" for listing and that the project overall had "no historic properties subject to effect." *Id.* Four days later, the North Dakota SHPO concurred with his determination via email. . . .

On July 25, 2016, it issued an EA finding of "no significant impact" and verified all 204 PCN locations under NWP 12. See ECF No. 6, Exhs. 33–36; Ames Decl., ¶ 36. The PCNs, however, contained additional restrictions. See ECF No. 6, Exhs. 33–36. Most importantly, they instituted a "Tribal Monitoring Plan" that requires Dakota Access to allow tribal monitors at all PCN sites when construction is occurring. *Id.* Dakota Access immediately notified the tribes of its intent to begin construction at the PCN sites within five to seven days. See ECF No. 6, Exh. 49 (Letter from Dippel to Upper Sioux).

* * *

In summary, the Corps has documented dozens of attempts it made to consult with the Standing Rock Sioux from the fall of 2014 through the spring of 2016 on the permitted DAPL activities. These included at least three site visits to the Lake Oahe crossing to assess any potential effects on historic properties and four meetings with Colonel Henderson.

E. Procedural History and Recent Activities

Two days after the Corps issued the PCN authorizations, Standing Rock filed this suit against it under the Administrative Procedure Act, 5 U.S.C. § 701 *et seq.*, asserting in part that the Corps had violated its obligation under the NHPA prior to issuing the permitting for DAPL-related construction along the entire pipeline route. The Tribe then filed, on August 4, 2016, this Motion for Preliminary Injunction to mandate a withdrawal of this permitting. The next day, Dakota Access intervened in the action in support of the Corps. See ECF No. 7 (Dakota Access Motion to Intervene). . . .

At the Motion hearing, Dakota Access revealed that most of the construction associated with DAPL is, in fact, already complete. Because only 3% of the pipeline is subject to federal permitting, Dakota Access has always been free to proceed with the vast majority of the construction, which will occur on private land. In fact, 48% of the pipeline had already been cleared, graded, trenched, piped, backfilled, and reclaimed. . . .

Nine days after the hearing, on Friday, September 2, the Tribe filed a supplemental declaration by Tim Mentz, the Tribe's former Tribal Historic Preservation Officer and a member of the Standing Rock Sioux Tribe. See ECF No. 29-1 (Supplemental Declaration of Tim Mentz, Sr.). In the declaration, Mentz explained that he had been invited by a land-owner to conduct cultural surveys on private land along the DAPL route that had already been cleared for pipeline construction. . . .

Mentz, over the course of several days beginning on August 30, avers that he surveyed this private land around the pipeline right-of-way. *Id.,* ¶ 6. During these surveys, he observed several rock cairns and other sites of cultural significance inside the 150-foot corridor staked for DAPL construction. *Id.,* ¶¶ 7–11. He was, however, confined in his actual surveying to those areas immediately adjacent to the pipeline right-of-way and did not enter the corridor itself.

Id. Mentz documented the presence of several sites that he believed to be of great cultural note nearby. . . .

The next day, on Saturday, September 3, Dakota Access graded this area. See ECF No. 30 (Emergency Motion for Temporary Restraining Order). On September 4, both the Tribe and the Cheyenne River Sioux Tribe filed for a Temporary Restraining Order on any additional construction work at the site described by Mentz—i.e., the length of the pipeline route for approximately two miles west of Highway 1806 in North Dakota—and for any additional construction work on the pipeline within 20 miles on either side of Lake Oahe, until the Court ruled on this Motion for Preliminary Injunction. *Id.* The Corps responded that it would not oppose the restraining order while awaiting this decision.

Dakota Access, not surprisingly, hotly contested Mentz's version of events in its opposition to the TRO motion. In a map of the area, the company sought to demon-strate that many of the sites documented by Mentz were in fact well outside the pipeline route. See ECF No. 34 (Response to TRO) at 6–8. The rest, according to Dakota Access, were directly over the existing Northern Border Natural Gas Pipeline that runs through the area and thus could not have been historic artifacts. *Id.* at 6. The company instead alleges that the route of the pipeline in this area proves its point: it twists and turns to avoid the finds that Mentz documented adjacent to the pipeline and thus demonstrates that Dakota Access did purposefully shift the route to avoid any sites of cultural significance in its planning phase. *Id.* The Court acknowledges that the map provided by the company does seem to indicate that the pipeline curves to accommodate the cultural sites. *Id.* at 7.

This Court held a TRO hearing on September 6, the first business day after that motion was filed. Without making factual determinations about the truth of Mentz's observations, the Court was able to obtain Dakota Access's agreement not to perform any construction activities within 20 miles east of Lake Oahe and within about two miles west of the Lake, as it had already ceased such operations while awaiting the Court's preliminary-injunction ruling. The Court otherwise denied the TRO. This current Opinion now issues on a highly expedited basis.

II. Legal Standard

"[I]njunctive relief" is "an extraordinary remedy that may only be awarded upon a clear showing that the plaintiff is entitled to such relief." *Winter v. Nat. Res. Def. Advisory Council, Inc.*, 555 U.S. 7, 22 (2008). "A plaintiff seeking a preliminary injunction must establish [1] that he is likely to succeed on the merits, [2] that he is likely to suffer irreparable harm in the absence of preliminary relief, [3] that the balance of equities tips in his favor, and [4] that an injunction is in the public interest." . . .

Whether a sliding-scale analysis still exists or not, courts in our Circuit have held that "if a party makes no showing of irreparable injury, the court may deny the motion for injunctive relief without considering the other factors." *Dodd v. Fleming*, 223 F. Supp. 2d 15, 20 (D.D.C. 2002) (citing *CityFed Fin. Corp. v. Office of Thrift Supervision*, 58 F.3d 738, 747 (D.C. Cir. 1995)). Likewise, a failure to show a likelihood of success on the merits alone is sufficient to defeat a preliminary-injunction motion. *Ark. Dairy Co-op Ass'n, Inc. v. USDA*, 573 F.3d 815, 832 (D.C. Cir. 2009) (citing *Apotex, Inc. v. FDA*, 449 F.3d 1249, 1253 (D.C. Cir. 2006)). It follows, then, that the Court may deny a motion for preliminary injunction, without further inquiry, upon finding that a plaintiff is unable to show *either* irreparable injury or a likelihood of success on the merits. Here, Standing Rock fails on both grounds.

III. Analysis

The Corps gave the go-ahead, under NWP 12, for DAPL's construction activities in federally regulated waters at hundreds of discrete places along its nearly 1,200-mile route. In seeking a preliminary injunction, the Tribe contends that the Corps, in doing so, shirked its responsibility to first engage in the tribal consultations required by the NHPA. Because DAPL construction is ongoing, the Tribe further asserts that sites of great significance will likely be damaged or destroyed unless this Court pumps the brakes now. It also contends that the balance of harms and the public interest favor its position.

Defendants rejoin that preliminary-injunctive relief is inappropriate both because the Corps has satisfied its obligations under the NHPA—in other words, the Tribe is unlikely to succeed on the merits of its NHPA claim—and because the Tribe has failed to show that any harm will befall it in the absence of an injunction. As the Court agrees on both points, it need not consider the final two factors—balance of harms and the public interest—to deny the Motion. It now discusses the merits and the harm separately.

A. Likelihood of Success on the Merits

Although the Tribe's legal theory is not entirely clear, the Court believes it can infer four separate arguments that the Corps' permitting of DAPL was unlawful. First, the Standing Rock Sioux assert that the Corps violated the NHPA when it promulgated NWP 12 without a Section 106 process. Next, they contend that, even if the Corps could defer site-specific Section 106 consultations when promulgating NWP 12, it violated the NHPA by permitting DAPL-related activities at some federally regulated waters without a Section 106 determination. Third, the Tribe maintains that, even where the Corps did conduct a Section 106 process, it unlawfully narrowed the scope of its review to only those areas around the permitted activity, as opposed to the entire pipeline. Finally, the Tribe urges that the Section 106 process at the PCN sites was inadequate because the quality of the consultations was deficient. None of these claims appears likely to succeed on the merits at this stage.

1. NWP 12

Although many DAPL-related construction activities in federally regulated waters occurred or will occur at places where the Corps did not require a PCN verification, such activities nevertheless required approval from the Corps under the CWA or RHA. That approval was provided on a general level when the Corps re-promulgated NWP 12 in 2012. Because these activities thus were "permitted" by a federal agency, they fall within the NHPA's definition of a federal "undertaking." See 54 U.S.C. § 300320; 36 C.F.R. § 800.16(y). As federal undertakings, they triggered the Corps' NHPA duty to consider, *prior* to the issuance of the permit, their effects on properties of cultural or historic significance. See 54 U.S.C. § 306108 ("[P]rior to the issuance of any license, [the federal agency] shall take into account the effect of the undertaking on any historic property."). According to the Tribe, the Corps did not fulfill this obligation because NWP 12 was issued without any tribal consultations.

As an initial matter, the Tribe's assertion that the Corps did not engage in *any* NHPA consultations prior to promulgating NWP 12 is false. Before issuing NWP 12, the Corps, in November 2009, sent an early notification to tribes, including Standing Rock, containing information pertaining to its proposed NWPs. See ECF No. 21, Exh. 14 (Letter from Ruchs to Brings Plenty on Nov. 9, 2009). The letter contained a graphic depiction of the types of activities that were most often authorized by nationwide permits in the Omaha District. *Id.* In addition, in 2010, the Corps proceeded to hold "listening sessions and workshops" with tribes to discuss their concerns related to the proposed nationwide permits. See ECF No. 21, Exh. 13 (Tribal Information Fact Sheet). In March 2010, the Corps contacted Standing Rock personally to discuss the permits and any additional regional conditions that the Tribe thought might need to be included to protect their cultural resources. See Chieply Decl., ¶ 5.

Then, on February 10, 2011, the Corps sent a letter to the Standing Rock Sioux Tribal Chairman and THPO Young, notifying them of its plan to publish a proposal in the Federal Register to reissue NWP 12. See ECF No. 21, Exh. 13 (Letter from Ruchs to Murphy on Feb. 10, 2011). Attached to the letter, the Corps provided a description of the proposed NWP 12, as well as a draft of the current Omaha District regional conditions that would apply to the permit. *Id.* The Corps requested that the Tribe "consider this letter our invitation to begin consultation on the proposal to reissue the NWPs." *Id.* It went on to say that the Corps "look[s] forward to consulting with you on a government-to-government basis on this issue" and requested that the Tribe notify the Corps if it was "interested in consulting." *Id.* The Corps further committed to provide a "Corps representative at consultation and fact-finding meetings" and to "fully consider any information you wish to provide." *Id.* In an email on March 9, 2011, the Corps followed up on the offer. See Chieply Decl., ¶ 7. The Corps also seems to have conducted district-level tribal listening sessions and workshops. See Tribal Information Fact Sheet at 1. There is no indication in the record that the Tribe responded to the Corps' invitation to consult, but was ignored. The Tribe, in fact, concedes that it did not participate in the notice-and-comment for NWP 12 at all. See Reply at 2. When it actually promulgated NWP 12, moreover, the Corps included a section on its compliance with the NHPA, noting that GC 20 "requires consultation for activities that have the *potential* to cause effects to historic properties" prior to those activities' proceeding under the general permit. See ECF No 6, Exh. 1 (Nationwide Permit 12 Decision Document) at 10 (emphasis added).

To the extent that the Tribe now seeks in this Motion to launch a belated facial attack against NWP 12, then, it is unlikely to succeed. The Corps made a reasonable effort to discharge its duties under the NHPA prior to promulgating NWP 12, given the nature of the general permit. Cf. *Sierra Club v. Bostick*, 787 F.3d 1043, 1047, 1057 (10th Cir. 2015) (holding Corps permissibly interpreted CWA "to allow partial deferral of minimal-impacts analysis" because of "the difficulty of predicting the impact of activities allowed under nationwide permits").

Without definite knowledge of the specific locations that would require permitting in the future, it is hard to ascertain what else the Corps might have done, before issuing a general permit, to discharge its NHPA duties. In other words, the Corps, when it promulgated NWP 12, had no knowledge of DAPL or its proposed route. The CWA and RHA plainly allow the Corps to do just what it did here: preauthorize a group of similar activities that, alone and combined, have minimal impact on navigable waterways. This Court cannot conclude that the Corps does not have the ability to promulgate these general permits at all. As a result, the Corps' effort to speak with those it thought might be concerned was sufficient to discharge its NHPA obligations.

This conclusion is reinforced by the limited scale and scope of the federally sanctioned activities at issue. The Advisory Council's regulations provide that the "agency official should plan consultations appropriate to the scale of the undertaking and the scope of the Federal involvement." 36 C.F.R. § 800.4(a). Here, the scope of the Corps' involvement was limited. It never had the ability, after all, to regulate the entire construction of a pipeline. Congress has decided that no general federal regulation applies to domestic oil pipelines. In addition, the scale of the federally permitted undertaking here is narrow. The CWA and RHA regulate, as relevant here, only certain limited construction activities in waterways. The CWA, moreover, restricts the use of general permits to an even narrower subset of these already limited activities in waterways. The Corps can only authorize discharges that have a *minimal* impact on the jurisdictional waterway through a general permit. See 33 U.S.C. § 1344(e). In other words, NWP 12, by definition, can authorize only that regulated conduct that will have little effect on the regulated waterway in the first place. Given these restrictions, the Corps' decision to promulgate NWP 12 after the effort to consult that it made here was reasonable.

The Tribe responds that the Corps was instead required to work out a "programmatic agreement" with any tribe that might one day be affected by the activities permitted under NWP 12. See Mot. at 22–23. A programmatic agreement is an "agreement to govern the implementation of a particular program or the resolution of adverse effects from certain complex project situations or multiple undertakings" that is negotiated by the Advisory Council and the permitting agency. See 36 C.F.R. § 800.14(b). On this score, Standing Rock is certainly right that the Corps could have pursued a programmatic agreement to fulfill its NHPA duties, as it did in 2004 with several tribes in regard to the Missouri Basin. See ECF No. 6, Exh. 4 (Programmatic Agreement). But the Advisory Council does not make the pursuit of a programmatic agreement mandatory. See 36 C.F.R. § 800.14(b) ("The Advisory Council and the agency official *may* negotiate a programmatic agreement.") (emphasis added). The Court thus cannot conclude that a PA was the *only* avenue available to the Corps to fulfill its duties under the NHPA. There is, indeed, no indication that such a requirement would even be feasible for a nationwide permitting scheme given the sheer number of possible consulting parties. Nor could the Corps have complied with the full Advisory Council process, which is clearly designed for project-specific determinations. As a result, it was reasonable for the Corps to engage in a general process at the time it promulgated NWP 12 and to defer site-specific NHPA determinations to a later time.

2. NWP 12 Applied at Non-PCN Sites

The Tribe next argues that NWP 12's operation is unlawful because the Corps makes no site-specific Section 106 determination for numerous generally permitted activities—i.e., non-PCN sites. In particular, it claims that GC 20 improperly delegates authority to the *permittee* to assess whether its activities will have a potential effect on historic properties. To refresh the reader, GC 20 requires that "[i]n cases where the district engineer determines that the activity may affect [NHPA] properties . . . , the activity is not authorized, until the requirements of Section 106 of the [NHPA] have been satisfied." 77 Fed. Reg at 10,284. The Advisory Council, too, seems to concur that, in individual cases of permitting under NWP 12, Section 106 is not satisfied where the Corps itself does not make a site-specific determination about whether a permitted activity has the potential to affect historic properties. See ECF No. 6, Exh. 50 at 1–2. As the Tribe and the Advisory Council read GC 20, the Corps never considers whether an individual activity will have the potential to affect historic sites unless the permittee decides that it might and, accordingly, seeks a PCN. The Corps, in turn, responds that it does consider itself to retain the authority and responsibility under GC 20 to determine whether permitted activity has the potential to damage historic properties. See Corps Opp. at 13–14.

Standing Rock and the Advisory Council make a good argument. It is possible that the Corps' permitting under NWP 12 would be arbitrary and capricious where it relies completely on the unilateral determination of a permittee that there is no potential cultural resource that will be injured by its permitted activity. Fortunately, this Court need not decide that issue because that is not how the Corps interpreted and applied GC 20 to DAPL. In this case, the Corps looked at reports and maps of the pipeline to determine which jurisdictional crossings had the potential to affect historic properties. See Chieply Decl., Exh. 16 at 1; see also *id.*, Exh. 15 at 1. These extensive maps reflected cultural surveys conducted by licensed archaeologists (sometimes with SHPO participation). See Howard Decl., ¶¶ 4–10; see, e.g., ECF No. 6, Exh. 44. The Corps ultimately concluded that only 204 of the jurisdictional crossings triggered either GC 20 or some other concern that would require a PCN verification. See Chieply Decl., Exh. 16 at 1.

The Court must review that determination under the Administrative Procedure Act's deferential standard. See 5 U.S.C. § 706(2)(a). Under this standard, the Tribe bears the burden to demonstrate that the agency action was unlawful, arbitrary or capricious, or not in accordance with the law. See *Kleppe v. Sierra Club*, 427 U.S. 390, 412 (1976). Plaintiff has not done so here. At no point has the Tribe clearly pointed this Court to a specific non-PCN activity—i.e., crossings the Corps permitted—where there is evidence that might indicate that cultural resources would be damaged. The Tribe instead focuses on the potential impact to cultural resources elsewhere along the pipeline. But to show the Corps' determination was unreasonable, Standing Rock needs to offer more than vague assertions that some places in the Midwest around some bodies of water may contain some sacred sites that could be affected. For example, if the Corps had not required a PCN verification for a site like Lake Oahe (assuming it was not subject to the RHA), to which the Tribe has shown it has important historic and cultural connections, this Court might well find unreasonable the Corps' determination that construction at the site would have no potential to cause negative effects to these resources. Without such a specific showing involving a site within the Corps' jurisdiction, however, the Court can find no ground at this juncture to hold that the Corps' considered judgment—based as it was on its expertise, the activity involved, extensive cultural surveys, and additional research—was unreasonable. The Tribe has had more than a year to come up with evidence that the Corps acted unreasonably in permitting even a single jurisdictional activity without a PCN, and it has not done so. As a result, it has not met its burden here.

3. Scope of Section 106 Process at PCN Sites

The Tribe next asserts that the Corps' Section 106 process was deficient even at those places where it *did* in fact require a PCN notification. Here, again, Standing Rock largely focuses its efforts on a sweeping claim that the Corps was obligated in permitting this narrow activity—i.e., certain construction activities in U.S. waterways—to consider the impact on potential cultural resources from the construction of the *entire* pipeline. In particular, the Tribe contends that the NHPA requires such an analysis because the statute defines the potential effect of an undertaking to include the indirect effects of the permitted activity on historic properties.

This argument, however, misses the mark. In its regulations concerning compliance with the adverse-effects analysis required by the NHPA, the Corps determined that entire pipelines need not be considered part of the analyzed areas. Rather, only construction activity in the federally regulated waterways—the direct effect of the undertaking—and in uplands around the federally regulated waterways—the indirect effect of the undertaking— [r]equires analysis. See 33 C.F.R. pt. 325, app. C, § 1(g)(i). This Circuit has held just such an approach to be reasonable in the context of a challenge brought under a similar "stop, look, and listen" provision in NEPA, and these two statutes are often treated similarly. See, e.g., *Karst Envtl. Educ. & Prot., Inc. v. EPA*, 475 F.3d 1291, 1294–95 (D.C. Cir. 2007) ("Because of the 'operational similarity' between NEPA and NHPA, both of which impose procedural obligations on federal agencies after a certain threshold of federal involvement, courts treat 'major federal actions' under NEPA similarly to 'federal undertakings' under NHPA."). Specifically, this Circuit held that where a federal easement and CWA permitting encompassed only five percent of the length of a pipeline, "the federal government was not required to conduct NEPA analysis of the entirety of the . . . pipeline, including portions not subject to federal control or permitting." *Sierra Club v. U.S. Army Corps of Eng'rs*, 803 F.3d 31, 34–35 (D.C. Cir. 2015). Other Circuits have held the same. See *Bostick*, 787 F.3d at 1051–54 (holding Corps was not required to prepare NEPA analysis of entire pipeline when verifying NWPs for 485-mile oil pipeline crossing over 2,000 waterways); *Winnebago Tribe of Neb. v. Ray*, 621 F.2d 269, 272–73 (8th Cir. 1980) (concluding same for electric utility line). The Tribe offers no persuasive argument as to why the facts here demand a different conclusion. As a result, this Court cannot conclude here that a federal agency with limited jurisdiction over specific activities related to a pipeline is required to consider all the effects of the *entire* pipeline to be the indirectly or directly foreseeable effects of the narrower permitted activity.

The Corps' decision in this regard is also entitled to deference under the APA as it falls squarely within the expertise of the Corps, not the Advisory Council, to determine the scope of the effects of construction activities at U.S. waterways. See *Bldg. & Constr. Trades Dep't v. Brock*, 838 F.2d 1258, 1266 (D.C. Cir. 1988) (holding courts must be especially deferential to an agency's determination within an area in which it has "special expertise"). The Tribe, moreover, fails to provide any evidence that would call the Corps' technical judgment in this regard into question. See 33 C.F.R. pt. 325, app. C, § 1(g)(i) (explaining that for linear crossings, the "permit area shall extend in either direction from the crossing to that point at which alternative alignments leading to a reasonable alternative locations for the crossing can be considered and evaluated"). The Tribe contends instead, without evidence, that the entire pipeline must be the indirect effect of the permitted activity because the pipeline cannot feasibly avoid all federally regulated water crossings. In other words, no permitting means no pipeline. The Court cannot say on this record, however, that the Tribe is right. In fact, as DAPL's own construction demonstrates, the use of technology such as HDD can at least sometimes avoid the Corps' jurisdiction at federally regulated waters by eliminating the need for the discharge of dredge or fill material.

The limited nature of the Corps' jurisdiction, in fact, reinforces the reasonableness of the its [*sic*] decision not to consider the effects of the entire pipeline on historic properties before issuing the DAPL permitting. "[W]here an agency has no ability to prevent a certain effect due to its limited statutory authority over the relevant actions, the agency['s action] cannot be considered a legally relevant 'cause' of the effect." *Dep't of Transp. v. Public Citizen*, 541 U.S. 752, 770 (2004). Section 106 analysis is designed only to "discourage[e] federal agencies from ignoring preservation values in projects they initiate, approve funds for or otherwise control." *Lee v. Thornburgh*, 877 F.2d 1053, 1056 (D.C. Cir. 1989). That section does not require that the Corps consider the effects of actions over which it has no control and which are far removed from its permitting activity. The Corps here ultimately determined that the route taken by the pipeline through private lands, up to a certain point approaching a federally regulated waterway, is driven by factors that have little to do with the discrete activities that the Corps needs to permit. The Court cannot conclude otherwise on this record. As such, it cannot hold the Corps' decision arbitrary, capricious, or otherwise unlawful.

4. Sufficiency of Consultations

Plaintiff's last point on the merits is that the Corps failed to offer it a reasonable opportunity to participate in the Section 106 process as to the narrow scope of the construction activity that the Corps did consider to be an effect of the permitted waterway activities. The factual proceedings recited in exhaustive detail in Section I.D., *supra*, tell a different story. The Corps has documented dozens of attempts to engage Standing Rock in consultations to identify historical resources at Lake Oahe and other PCN crossings. To the reader's relief, the Court need not repeat them here. Suffice it to say that the Tribe largely refused to engage in consultations. It chose instead to hold out for more—namely, the chance to conduct its own cultural surveys over the entire length of the pipeline.

In fact, on this record, it appears that the Corps exceeded its NHPA obligations at many of the PCN sites. For example, in response to the Tribe's concerns about burial sites at the James River crossing, the Corps verified that cultural resources indeed were present and instructed Dakota Access to move the pipeline to avoid them. Dakota Access did so. See Ames Decl., ¶ 24. Furthermore, the Corps took numerous trips to Lake Oahe with members of the Tribe to identify sites of cultural significance. See *Summit Lake Paiute Tribe of Nevada v. U.S. Bureau of Land Mgmt.*, 496 F. App'x 712, 715 (9th Cir. 2012) (not reported) (holding four visits with a tribe to site constituted sufficient consultation for resolution of adverse effects). Colonel Henderson also met with the Tribe no fewer than four times in the spring of 2016 to discuss their concerns with the pipeline. Ultimately, the Corps concluded that no sites would be affected by the DAPL construction at Lake Oahe, and the State Historic Preservation Officer who had visited that site concurred. The Corps' effort to consult the Tribe on this site—the place that most clearly implicated the Standing Rock Sioux's cultural interests—sufficed under the NHPA.

Contact, of course, is not consultation, and "consultation with one tribe doesn't relieve the [agency] of its obligation to consult with any other tribe." *Quechan Tribe of Fort Yuma Indian Reservation v. U.S. Dep't of Interior*, 755 F. Supp. 2d 1104, 1112, 1118 (S.D. Cal. 2010). But this is not a case about empty gestures. As noted in Section I.D., supra, and the examples just above, the Corps and the Tribe engaged in meaningful exchanges that in some cases resulted in concrete changes to the pipeline's route. "This is not a case like Quechan Tribe, where a tribe entitled to consultation actively sought to consult with an agency and was not afforded the opportunity." *Wilderness Soc'y. v. Bureau of Land Mgmt.*, 526 F. App'x 790, 793 (9th Cir. May 28, 2013) (not reported).

The Tribe nevertheless asserts that the Corps' failure to include it in the early cultural surveys rendered the permitting unlawful for at least some of the PCN sites. These surveys, however, were not conducted by the Corps or under its direction. Even setting this fact aside, neither the NHPA nor the Advisory Council regulations require that any cultural surveys be conducted for a federal undertaking. The regulations instead demand only that the Corps make a "reasonable and good faith effort" to consult on identifying cultural properties, which "may include background research, consultation, oral history interviews, sample field investigations, and field survey." 36 C.F.R. § 800.4(b)(1). It goes without saying that "'may' means may." *McCreary v. Offner*, 172 F.3d 76, 83 (D.C. Cir. 1999). These regulations contain "no requirement that a good faith effort include all of these things." *Summit Lake Paiute*, 496 F. App'x at 715. The Tribe, then, did not have an absolute right to participate in cultural surveying at every permitted undertaking, as it seems to argue. The Advisory Council regulations direct the agency to "take into account past planning, research, and studies" in making these types of determinations, see 36 C.F.R. § 800.4(b)(1), and that is just what the Corps did here. It gave the Tribe a reasonable and good-faith opportunity to identify sites of importance to it. As a result, the Court must conclude that the Tribe has not shown that it is likely to succeed on the merits of its NHPA claim at this stage.

B. Irreparable Injury

In seeking preliminary-injunctive relief here, the Standing Rock Sioux do not claim that a potential future rupture in the pipeline could damage their reserved land or water. Instead, they point to an entirely separate injury: the likelihood that DAPL's ongoing construction activities—specifically, grading and clearing of land—might damage or destroy sites of great cultural or historical significance to the Tribe. The risk that harm might befall such sites is a matter of unquestionable importance to the Standing Rock people. In the eloquent words of their Tribal Chairman:

> History connects the dots of our identity, and our identity was all but obliterated. Our land was taken, our language was forbidden. Our stories, our history, were almost forgotten. What land, language, and identity remains is derived from our cultural and historic sites. . . . Sites of cultural and historic significance are important to us because they are a spiritual connection to our ancestors. Even if we do not have access to all such sites, their existence perpetuates the connection. When such a site is destroyed, the connection is lost.

Archambault Decl., ¶¶ 6, 15. The tragic history of the Great Sioux Nation's repeated dispossessions at the hands of a hungry and expanding early America is well known. See, e.g., Dee Brown, *Bury My Heart at Wounded Knee* (1970); *United States v. Sioux Nation*, 448 U.S. 371 (1980). The threat that new injury will compound old necessarily compels great caution and respect from this Court in considering the Tribe's plea for intervention.

Although the potential injury may be significant, the Tribe must show that it is probable to occur in the absence of the preliminary injunction it now seeks. See *Winter*, 555 U.S. at 22 ("Issuing a preliminary injunction based only on a possibility of irreparable harm is inconsistent with [the Court's] characterization of injunctive relief as an extraordinary remedy that may only be awarded upon a *clear showing* that the plaintiff is entitled to such relief.") (emphasis added). This is the burden the law imposes for this form of relief. The Court must faithfully and fairly apply that standard in all cases, regardless of how high the stakes or how worthy the cause. After a careful review of the current record, the Court cannot conclude that the Tribe has met it.

To understand Standing Rock's deficit in this regard, it is necessary to first consider the nature of the relief it seeks. The Tribe has not sued *Dakota Access* here for any transgressions; instead, this Motion seeks to enjoin *Corps permitting* of construction activities in discrete U.S. waterways along the pipeline route. Such relief sought cannot stop the construction of DAPL on private lands, which are not subject to any federal law. Indeed, Standing Rock does not point the Court to any law violated by the private contracts that allow for this construction or any federal regulation or oversight of these activities. From the outset, consequently, no federal agency had the ability to prevent DAPL's construction from proceeding on these private lands. At most, the Corps could only have stopped these activities at the banks of a navigable U.S. waterway. An injunction of any unlawful permitting now can, at most, do the same.

The facts previously recited bear this simple conclusion out. Dakota Access, as has been explained, began its construction work on private lands long before it had even secured the Corps permitting that the Tribe now seeks to enjoin. See Mahmoud Decl., ¶ 47. Standing Rock concedes as much. See Mot. at 35; see also Mot. Hearing Tran. at 46

("They started construction months ago, months before the permits were issued."). In many places, this work is already complete. See Mot. Hearing Trans. at 24. There is, moreover, no sign that Dakota Access will pull back from this construction on private land if this Court enjoins the NWP 12 permitting necessary for the 3% of DAPL's route subject to federal jurisdiction. Quite the contrary; the company has indicated that it has little choice but to push ahead in the hopes of meeting contract obligations to deliver oil by January 2017. See, e.g., id. at 40-41; see also Mahmoud Decl., ¶ 51.

The Tribe thus cannot demonstrate that the temporary relief it seeks here—i.e., a preliminary injunction to withdraw permitting by the Corps for dredge or fill activities in federally regulated waters along the DAPL route—can prevent the harm to cultural sites that might occur from this construction on private lands. In other words, Standing Rock cannot show that any harm taking place on private lands removed from the Corps' permitting jurisdiction "will directly result from the action which [it now] seeks to enjoin." *Hunter v. FERC*, 527 F. Supp. 2d 9, 14–15 (D.D.C. 2007) (explaining that to obtain preliminary relief, "the movant must . . . show that 'the alleged harm will directly result from the action which the movant seeks to enjoin'") (quoting *Wisc. Gas Co. v. FERC*, 758 F.2d 669, 674 (D.C. Cir. 1985) (emphasis added)); see also *Buckingham Corp. v. Karp*, 762 F.2d 257, 261 (2d Cir. 1985) ("The purpose of a preliminary injunction is to protect the moving party from irreparable injury during the pendency of the action."). Powerless to prevent these harms given the current posture of the case, the Court cannot consider them likely to occur in the absence of the relief sought here. Put simply, any such harms are destined to ensue whether or not the Court grants the injunction the Tribe desires. As Standing Rock acknowledges, Dakota Access has demonstrated that it is determined to build its pipeline right up to the water's edge regardless of whether it has secured a permit to then build across. See Mot. Hearing Trans. at 46. Like the Corps, this Court is unable to stop it from doing so.

There is a second related problem with the Tribe's claim to irreparable injury, both on the private land and elsewhere along the pipeline. The risk that construction may damage or destroy cultural resources is now moot for the 48% of the pipeline that has already been completed. *Id.* at 24. As the clearing and grading are the "clearest and most obvious" cause of the harm to cultural sites from pipeline construction, *id.* at 18–19, 47 (recognizing that injunction is necessary anywhere not yet cleared "to prevent additional harm or construction until [cultural] surveys can take place"), moreover, the damage has already occurred for the vast majority of the pipeline, with the notable exception of 10% of the route in North Dakota, including at Lake Oahe. Here again, then, the Tribe has not shown for this substantial segment of the pipeline that any *additional* harm is likely to occur to cultural sites absent the preliminary injunction that it now seeks.

Yet a third problem bedevils the Tribe's efforts to enjoin permitting along the entire pipeline route. Plaintiff never defined the boundaries of its ancestral lands vis-à-vis DAPL. Instead, Standing Rock asserts that these lands extend "wherever the buffalo roamed." Even accepting this is true, to find that there is a likelihood that construction might run afoul of a site of cultural significance to the Tribe, this Court must ultimately decide where those culturally significant lands lie. There is at least some evidence in the record that they do not traverse the entirety of DAPL. For example, Jon Eagle, the Tribe's current THPO, indicated prior to this litigation that at least some of the pipeline did not fall within the scope of what he considered ancestral tribal lands. See Chieply Decl., Exh. 14 (Letter from Jon Eagle to Martha Chieply on Mar. 22, 2016) ("*Most* of the DAPL pipeline route crosses

Lakota/Dakota aboriginal land."); see also ECF No. 11–7 (Declaration of H. Frazier). This Court may not enjoin an action that the Corps has authorized by guessing at whether an interest of the Tribe might be affected. Instead, Plaintiff bears the burden to demonstrate that the permitting it seeks to have withdrawn would, in the absence of such relief, likely cause it harm. This it did not do for much of the pipeline.

So what activity remains subject to this Court's injunctive powers? Any *permitted* DAPL activity that the Tribe has shown will likely injure a nearby site of cultural or historic significance to the Standing Rock people. As previously explained, 204 sites were subject to PCN authorizations and thus were clearly permitted by the Corps. Those sites are in play. Other discharges into jurisdictional waters at hypothetical locations along the route, however, may also have been permitted under NWP 12 without a PCN process. But it would be pure speculation based on the current record to determine where such permitting occurred. The Tribe points the Court to no specific crossing of cultural significance that the Corps permitted under NWP 12 without a PCN verification. In fact, many of the pipeline crossings were not permitted by the Corps, sometimes because Dakota Access's use of HDD did not give rise to the dredge or fill activities that trigger federal jurisdiction under the CWA. For example, out of the five places in North Dakota that Dakota Access thought might require a PCN authorization, only three actually needed permitting at all. See Chieply Decl., ¶ 10. Of course, there may be many sites that the Corps permitted under NWP 12 that the Court has missed. But the burden is on the Tribe to indicate why this permitting must be enjoined to prevent an injury likely to occur to it. The Court, again, cannot guess that at some undefined locations there might be harm to the Tribe. It was Standing Rock's burden to point to the specific NWP 12 permitting that was likely to cause it injury. Standing Rock did not do so with regard to the permitting that has occurred outside of the PCN verified locations.

Returning to the 204 PCN sites, the vast majority must be excluded right off the bat. As previously noted, construction at 193 of the 204 PCN has already been completed. See Mot. Hearing Trans. at 24. For those sites, the die is cast. Whatever harms may have occurred from DAPL construction, the Court's intervention to enjoin the permitting now can no longer avoid them. As a result, the Court must deny the Tribe's request for an injunction as to permitting at those sites.

As to the other 11 PCN sites, the Tribe largely neglects to point the Court to any resources that may be affected by permitted activity. Plaintiff seeks to avoid its responsibility to identify a likely injury at these locations by claiming that this failure stems from the Corps' refusal to properly consult in the first place and thus should be excused. See Mot. at 37 n.17. At least with regard to some of these sites, however, the Corps did offer the Tribe the opportunity to visit the sites or even conduct its own surveys, and the Tribe declined to do so. See Chieply Decl., ¶¶ 28–29. The record contains abundant evidence that the Corps also repeatedly sought other input on known cultural sites at these locations, and, in many cases, other tribes conducted site visits to search for any resources likely to be affected by the DAPL work. *Id*. The Tribe cannot now ask the Court to speculate that there would be a likely injury at these places by claiming that it was prevented from assessing these sites.

These sites are also subject to several additional restrictions that make it unlikely that construction will damage or destroy sites of cultural significance to the Tribe. First, the Corps attached restrictions to its PCN authorizations. These restrictions mandate that tribal monitors and archaeologists be allowed at these sites to look for any evidence of previously overlooked resources whenever construction is happening. See ECF No. 6, Exhs. 33–36 (PCN authorizations). GC 21 will also require that Dakota Access stop work until any unanticipated discovery can be evaluated for its historic and cultural significance by the Corps and the SHPO. See NWP 12 at 10,184. Standing Rock, too, will have the right to be involved in that verification process. *Id.* Given all these precautions, and the Tribe's failure to point the Court toward any evidence that a particular resource will be injured by this work, the Court must conclude that Plaintiff has not met its burden to show that irreparable injury is likely to occur without an injunction against this permitting.

And then there was one: Lake Oahe. This is the sole permitting that the Tribe might arguably show is likely to cause harm to cultural or historic sites of significance to it. As previously discussed, Lake Oahe is of undeniable importance to the Tribe, and the general area is demonstrably home to important cultural resources. Even here, though, the Tribe has not met its burden to show that DAPL-related work is likely to cause damage. The Corps and the Tribe conducted multiple visits to the area earlier this year in an effort to identify sites that might be harmed by DAPL's construction. See Eagle Decl., ¶¶ 13–14; Harnois Decl., ¶ 29. While the Tribe identified several previously undiscovered resources during those visits, these sites are located away from the activity required for the DAPL construction. See Harnois Decl., ¶ 29. Ultimately, the Corps considered these findings and determined that they would not be affected by the permitted activity. *Id.*, ¶ 33. Most importantly, the North Dakota SHPO concurred in this opinion after having toured the site as well. See Harnois Decl., ¶ 34.

Several factors unique to the site also support this conclusion. The area around the permitted activity has been subject to previous surveying for other utility projects. See Mahmoud Decl., ¶¶ 18–19. DAPL likewise will run parallel, at a distance of 22 to 300 feet, to an already-existing natural-gas pipeline under the lake. *Id.*; see also Mot. Hearing Tran. at 25. Dakota Access will also use the less-invasive HDD method to run the pipeline, which will require less disturbance to the land around the drilling and bury the pipeline at a depth that is unlikely to damage cultural resources. See Howard Decl., ¶ 7; see also Mahmoud Decl., ¶ 19. Indeed, the Corps concluded that this method would not cause structural impacts at sites away from the direct drilling, and the Tribe presents no evidence to the contrary. See ECF No. 6, Exh. 51 (Omaha District Envtl. Assessment) at 78–79. Any temporary disturbance to the atmospherics around the site, moreover, will not be irreparable as they will be removed once the construction is complete. Finally, like the other PCN sites, there are several protective measures in place to assure that the Tribe and others will be able to monitor the construction activity to protect any previously unidentified resources.

For all of the above reasons, the Tribe has not carried its burden to demonstrate that the Court could prevent damage to important cultural resources by enjoining the Corps' DAPL-related permitting.

IV. CONCLUSION

As it has previously mentioned, this Court does not lightly countenance any depredation of lands that hold significance to the Standing Rock Sioux. Aware of the indignities visited upon the Tribe over the last centuries, the Court scrutinizes the permitting process here with particular care. Having done so, the Court must nonetheless conclude that the Tribe has not demonstrated that an injunction is warranted here. The Court, therefore, will issue a contemporaneous Order denying the Plaintiffs' Motion for Preliminary Injunction.

/s/ James E. Boasberg
JAMES E. BOASBERG
United States District Judge

Date: September 9, 2016

SOURCE: U.S. Government Publishing Office. *Standing Rock Sioux Tribe v. U.S. Army Corps of Engineers.* Case 1:16-cv-01534-JEB. September 9, 2016. http://www.gpo.gov/fdsys/pkg/USCOURTS-dcd-1_16-cv-01534/pdf/USCOURTS-dcd-1_16-cv-01534-0.pdf.

Federal Agencies Issue Joint Statement on Dakota Access Pipeline Ruling

September 9, 2016

"We appreciate the District Court's opinion on the U.S. Army Corps of Engineers' compliance with the National Historic Preservation Act. However, important issues raised by the Standing Rock Sioux Tribe and other tribal nations and their members regarding the Dakota Access pipeline specifically, and pipeline-related decision-making generally, remain. Therefore, the Department of the Army, the Department of Justice, and the Department of the Interior will take the following steps.

The Army will not authorize constructing the Dakota Access pipeline on Corps land bordering or under Lake Oahe until it can determine whether it will need to reconsider any of its previous decisions regarding the Lake Oahe site under the National Environmental Policy Act (NEPA) or other federal laws. Therefore, construction of the pipeline on Army Corps land bordering or under Lake Oahe will not go forward at this time. The Army will move expeditiously to make this determination, as everyone involved—including the pipeline company and its workers—deserves a clear and timely resolution. In the interim, we request that the pipeline company voluntarily pause all construction activity within 20 miles east or west of Lake Oahe.

"Furthermore, this case has highlighted the need for a serious discussion on whether there should be nationwide reform with respect to considering tribes' views on these types of infrastructure projects. Therefore, this fall, we will invite tribes to formal, government-to-government consultations on two questions: (1) within the existing statutory framework, what should the federal government do to better ensure meaningful tribal input into infrastructure-related reviews and decisions and the protection of tribal lands, resources, and treaty rights; and (2) should new legislation be proposed to Congress to alter that statutory framework and promote those goals.

"Finally, we fully support the rights of all Americans to assemble and speak freely. We urge everyone involved in protest or pipeline activities to adhere to the principles of non-violence. Of course, anyone who commits violent or destructive acts may face criminal sanctions from federal, tribal, state, or local authorities. The Departments of Justice and the Interior will continue to deploy resources to North Dakota to help state, local, and tribal authorities, and the communities they serve, better communicate, defuse tensions, support peaceful protest, and maintain public safety.

"In recent days, we have seen thousands of demonstrators come together peacefully, with support from scores of sovereign tribal governments, to exercise their First Amendment rights and to voice heartfelt concerns about the environment and historic, sacred sites. It is now incumbent on all of us to develop a path forward that serves the broadest public interest."

SOURCE: U.S. Justice Department. Office of Public Affairs. "Joint Statement from the Department of Justice, the Department of the Army and the Department of the Interior Regarding Standing Rock Sioux Tribe v. U.S. Army Corps of Engineers." September 9, 2016. http://www.justice.gov/opa/pr/joint-statement-department-justice-department-army-and-department-interior-regarding-standing.

OTHER HISTORIC DOCUMENTS OF INTEREST

FROM PREVIOUS *HISTORIC DOCUMENTS*

Census Bureau Releases Annual Report on Poverty in the United States

SEPTEMBER 13, 2016

In September 2016, the United States Census Bureau released its annual report on the number of Americans living in poverty, along with its supplemental measure of these statistics, designed to take into consideration, among other things, government safety net programs. Both the official and supplemental poverty measures revealed a notable decrease in the number of impoverished Americans from 2014 to 2015. While still higher than it was in 2007 before the recession hit, this decrease in the number of people living in poverty was coupled with an increase in median household income, the first statistically significant increase in this number since 2007.

RATE AND NUMBER OF AMERICANS IN POVERTY DECREASES

Since the end of the recession in 2009, the economy has gradually improved. The unemployment rate, which stood at 10 percent in October 2009, dropped to 4.6 percent in November 2016, its lowest level since 2007, before a slight uptick to 4.7 percent in December 2016. This notable improvement was evidenced in the annual *Income and Poverty in the United States* report, which showed a decrease in the official poverty rate from 14.8 percent in 2014 to 13.5 percent in 2015. Said another way, in 2015, there were 43.1 million Americans living in poverty, 3.5 million less than in 2014.

The 2015 poverty threshold was $24,257 for a family of four, or $12,082 for an individual. Given the decrease in the overall number of individuals in poverty, the demographics of those in poverty also changed. All three Census age groups saw a decline in poverty. For those aged eighteen to sixty-four, the poverty rate decreased from 13.5 percent in 2014 to 12.4 percent, or 24.4 million people, in 2015. Similarly, for those over age sixty-five, the poverty rate fell from 10 percent in 2014 to 8.8 percent in 2015. In 2014, some 21.1 percent of children under age eighteen were in poverty, and that rate decreased to 19.7 percent, or 14.5 million children. Children represented 33.6 percent of those in poverty in 2015.

The poverty rate decreased in three of the four Census regions, but was not statistically different in the Northeast from 2014 to 2015. In the Midwest, the poverty rate fell from 8.7 million individuals to 7.8 million. In the West, the poverty rate was 13.3 percent, or 10.1 million citizens, down from 15.2 percent in 2014. The South continued to have the highest poverty rate at 15.3 percent, or 18.3 million individuals, although this did mark a decrease from 2014's poverty rate of 16.5 percent.

Among racial groups, the poverty rate for non-Hispanic whites remained the lowest at 9.1 percent, or 17.8 million individuals, down from 10.1 percent, or 19.7 million individuals, in 2014. The poverty rate for blacks decreased from 26.2 percent in 2014 to 24.1 percent in 2015, and for Hispanics from 23.6 percent to 21.4 percent. The only racial group that did not mark a statistically significant change from 2014 to 2015 was Asians, who had a poverty rate of 11.4 percent, or 2.1 million people, in 2015.

The number of shared households, those with one or more additional nonhousehold member, spouse, or partner aged eighteen or older—not counting those enrolled in school—was 19.1 percent, or 24.1 million households, in spring 2016. This was not a statistically significant change from the number reported in 2015 of 23.9 million households. The rate of shared households continues to remain well above the 2007, prerecession level of 19.7 million households. According to the Census Bureau, it can be difficult to determine the impact of those living in shared households on the overall poverty rate. For example, young adults aged twenty-five to thirty-four living with their parents in 2016 had an official 2015 poverty rate of 6.8 percent, but if poverty status were determined only based on the income of that individual, the rate would be 39.4 percent.

Median household income was $56,516 in 2015, up 5.2 percent over 2014. This marked the largest single-year increase since the Census Bureau began tracking these data in 1967, but is still 1.6 percent below median income before the recession, when adjusting for inflation. The growth in income is largely due to an increasingly improving job market. According to Trudi Renwick, who oversees publication of the poverty report, 2.4 million more Americans found full-time, year-round employment in 2015 than during the year prior. Many of these jobs were middle-income, as opposed to job growth shortly after the recession, which primarily resulted in low-wage, low-skill jobs being created.

Surprisingly, low-income households—those in the lowest 10 percent—had the largest percentage of gains in medium income of 7.9 percent, while those in the top 10 percent increased only 2.9 percent. While a good sign that the benefits of the improving economy are finally reaching those in the middle and lower end of the income spectrum, Jared Bernstein, an economist at the Center on Budget and Policy Priorities cautioned that "one good year does not reverse decades of stagnation." Growth in median household income was centralized in larger population centers, whereas rural America (those households outside of a metropolitan area as defined by the Census Bureau) experienced a 2 percent decrease in median household income to $44,657.

When the Census Bureau releases its annual figures on income and poverty, it also reports on health insurance coverage. The Census report found that in 2015, some 29 million, or 9.1 percent, of Americans did not have health insurance. This marked a decrease from 10.4 percent, or 33 million, in 2014. The increase in the number of those with health insurance, which now represents more than 90 percent of the population, is due to the implementation of the Affordable Care Act (ACA). According to the Census Bureau, since 2014, when major provisions of the plan were enacted, health insurance coverage has increased 4.3 percent.

Supplemental Report Echoes Improvement

The official Census estimate of poverty does not account for food stamps, cash assistance, tax credits, and a variety of other government support systems, all of which can have a significant impact on the number of Americans considered impoverished. The official estimate also does not account for children under the age of fifteen who are unrelated to anyone in their household. In 2010, the Census released its first supplemental poverty report, which was hailed as a more accurate method for determining the number of Americans living in poverty by taking into account government assistance programs and expenses such as health insurance, child care, housing, job expenses including transportation, and nontraditional children, such as those in foster care.

Released alongside the official poverty rate, the supplemental report recorded a poverty rate of 14.3 percent, higher than the official rate of 13.5 percent, but still lower than the 2014 supplemental rate of 15.3 percent. In 2015, the supplemental report found 45.7 million people in poverty, while the official number was 43.1 million. Poverty rates were lower under the supplemental definition than the official definition for a number of groups, including children, female head-of-household units, blacks, residents of the Midwest, and disabled individuals.

The supplemental poverty report shows the impact of social programs on the number and rate of those in poverty. For example, without Social Security benefits, the overall supplemental poverty rate would have been 8.3 percentage points higher. For those aged sixty-five and older, who are most likely to rely on this government benefit, excluding Social Security from income would triple the number of those in poverty within this age group to 49.7 percent. Looking at other public assistance programs, benefits provided under the Supplemental Nutrition Assistance Program (SNAP) kept 4.6 million people out of poverty.

PRESIDENTIAL CONTENDERS OFFER VARYING ECONOMIC PLANS

The annual Census report was issued less than two months ahead of a contentious presidential election, in which former secretary of state Hillary Clinton and businessman Donald Trump each argued that they had the best plan for lifting millions of Americans out of poverty and into the middle class. President Barack Obama celebrated the report, saying, "We lifted three and a half million people out of poverty, the largest one-year drop in poverty since 1968."

The Republican presidential nominee continued to criticize the president's efforts at improving the economy and seemed to disregard the Census Bureau's findings during a campaign rally after the report's release. "Poverty is beyond belief," he said. "It's time to break up the failed Democratic control over our inner cities, and provide real hope and opportunity to every single community in this nation." Secretary Clinton, in a *New York Times* op-ed, praised the work of the current administration in reducing the poverty rate, and, in a nod to information contained in the official and supplemental reports, noted, "The census report makes clear that when hard-working Americans get a small boost—like food stamps and health insurance thanks to the Affordable Care Act—they can climb out of poverty."

Throughout his campaign, Trump proposed reducing the number of those in poverty by increasing job growth through encouraging more companies to locate to and hire in the United States and promised to create 25 million jobs within the first decade after being elected. This would be coupled with a reduction in the number of tax brackets and loopholes and an increase in some tax incentives, such as a child care tax credit, which tend to favor lower- and middle-income Americans. In contrast, Clinton called for more job training and investment in new energy and technology sectors that would result in higher-paying jobs, as well as the creation of jobs in manufacturing and an increase in the number of small businesses. These training programs and investments in job growth would be paid for by an increase in the tax rate for the wealthiest Americans. Trump declined to reveal how he would pay for his tax breaks and job growth plans.

—Heather Kerrigan

Following are excerpts from the U.S. Census Bureau report on poverty in the United States, released on September 13, 2016; and excerpts from the U.S. Census Bureau supplemental poverty report also released on September 13, 2016.

Census Bureau Report on Poverty in the United States

September 13, 2016

[All portions of the report not corresponding to poverty have been omitted.]

[Tables, graphs, and footnotes, and references to them, have been omitted.]

POVERTY IN THE UNITED STATES

Highlights

- The official poverty rate in 2015 was 13.5 percent, down 1.2 percentage points from 14.8 percent in 2014.

- In 2015 there were 43.1 million people in poverty, 3.5 million less than in 2014.

- The 2015 poverty rate was 1.0 percentage point higher than in 2007, the year before the most recent recession.

- For most demographic groups, 2015 poverty rates and estimates of the number of people in poverty decreased from 2014.

- Between 2014 and 2015, poverty rates decreased for all three major age groups. The poverty rate for children under age 18 dropped 1.4 percentage points, from 21.1 percent to 19.7 percent. Rates for people aged 18 to 64 dropped 1.1 percentage points, from 13.5 percent to 12.4 percent. Poverty rates for people aged 65 and older decreased 1.1 percentage points, from 10.0 percent to 8.8 percent.

Race and Hispanic Origin

For non-Hispanic Whites the poverty rate decreased to 9.1 percent in 2015, down from 10.1 percent in 2014. The number in poverty decreased to 17.8 million, down from 19.7 million. The poverty rate for non-Hispanic Whites was lower than the poverty rates for other racial groups. Non-Hispanic Whites accounted for 61.4 percent of the total population and 41.2 percent of people in poverty.

The poverty rate for Blacks decreased to 24.1 percent in 2015, down from 26.2 percent in 2014. The number in poverty decreased to 10.0 million, down from 10.8 million. For Asians, the 2015 poverty rate and the number in poverty were 11.4 percent and 2.1 million;

neither estimate was statistically different from 2014. The poverty rate decreased for Hispanics to 21.4 percent in 2015, down from 23.6 percent in 2014. The number of Hispanics in poverty decreased to 12.1 million, down from 13.1 million.

Age

In 2015, poverty rates and numbers in poverty declined for all three major age groups. Poverty in 2015 decreased for people aged 18 to 64, to 12.4 percent and 24.4 million, down from 13.5 percent and 26.5 million in 2014. For people aged 65 and older, the 2015 poverty rate declined to 8.8 percent in 2015 from 10.0 percent in 2014, while the number in poverty declined to 4.2 million, down from 4.6 million.

For children under age 18, 19.7 percent and 14.5 million were in poverty in 2015, down from 21.1 percent and 15.5 million in 2014. Children represented 23.1 percent of the total population in 2015 and 33.6 percent of the people in poverty.

Related children are people under age 18 related to the householder by birth, marriage, or adoption, who are not themselves householders or spouses of householders. The poverty rate and the number in poverty for related children under age 18 were 19.2 percent and 14.0 million in 2015, down from 20.7 percent and 15.0 million in 2014. For related children in married-couple families, 9.8 percent and 4.8 million were in poverty in 2015, down from 10.6 percent and 5.2 million in 2014. For related children in families with a female householder, 42.6 percent and 7.9 million were in poverty in 2015, down from 46.5 percent and 8.5 million in 2014. The 2015 poverty estimates for related children in male householder families were 25.9 percent and 1.3 million, not statistically different from 2014.

The poverty rate and the number in poverty for related children under age 6 were 21.0 percent and 4.9 million in 2015, down from 23.5 percent and 5.5 million in 2014. About half (49.5 percent) of related children under age 6 in families with a female householder were in poverty. This was more than four times the rate of their counterparts in married-couple families (10.1 percent).

Sex

In 2015, 12.2 percent of males were in poverty, down from 13.4 percent in 2014. About 14.8 percent of females were in poverty in 2015, down from 16.1 percent in 2014.

Gender differences in poverty rates were more pronounced for those aged 18 to 64. The poverty rate for women aged 18 to 64 was 14.2 percent while the poverty rate for men aged 18 to 64 was 10.5 percent. The poverty rate for women aged 65 and older was 10.3 percent while the poverty rate for men aged 65 and older was 7.0 percent. For children under age 18, the 19.9 percent poverty rate for girls was not statistically different from the 19.5 percent poverty rate for boys.

Nativity

Of all people, 86.5 percent were native born and 13.5 percent were foreign born. The poverty rate and the number in poverty for the native-born population decreased to 13.1 percent and 36.0 million in 2015, down from 14.2 percent and 38.9 million in 2014. Among the foreign-born population, 16.6 percent and 7.2 million lived in poverty in 2015, down from 18.5 percent and 7.8 million in 2014.

Within the foreign-born population in 2015, 46.6 percent were naturalized U.S. citizens, while the remaining were not citizens of the United States. The poverty rate and the number in poverty in 2015 for foreign-born naturalized citizens was 11.2 percent, and 2.3 million, not statistically different from 2014. The poverty rate and the number in poverty for those who were not U.S. citizens decreased in 2015 to 21.3 percent, down from 24.2 percent in 2014. The number in poverty decreased to 4.9 million, down from 5.4 million.

Region

In 2015, the poverty rate and the number in poverty decreased in three of the four regions. The 2015 poverty rate and number in poverty for the Northeast was 12.4 percent and 6.9 million, not statistically different from 2014. In 2015, the Midwest poverty rate declined to 11.7 percent from 13.0 percent in 2014, while the number in poverty decreased to 7.8 million from 8.7 million. For the South, the 2015 poverty rate was 15.3 percent, down from 16.5 percent in 2014, while the number in poverty decreased to 18.3 million from 19.5 million. The poverty rate for the West in 2015 was 13.3 percent, down from 15.2 percent in 2014, while the number in poverty decreased to 10.1 million from 11.4 million. The South had the highest poverty rate in 2015 relative to the other three regions.

Residence

Inside metropolitan statistical areas, the poverty rate was 13.0 percent in 2015, with 35.7 million people in poverty. Among those living outside metropolitan statistical areas, the poverty rate was 16.7 percent in 2015, with 7.4 million people living in poverty.

The 2015 poverty rate for those living inside metropolitan statistical areas but not in principal cities was 10.8 percent. The number of people in poverty was 18.4 million. Among those who lived in principal cities, the 2015 poverty rate was 16.8 percent. The number in poverty was 17.4 million.

Within metropolitan statistical areas, people in poverty were more likely to live in principal cities. In 2015, 37.8 percent of all people living in metropolitan areas lived in principal cities, while 48.6 percent of poor people in metropolitan areas lived in principal cities.

As a result of the 2016 CPS ASEC transition to a new sample design and updated metropolitan statistical area delineations, comparisons from the 2015 ASEC to the 2016 ASEC are not appropriate.

Work Experience

In 2015, 6.3 percent of workers aged 18 to 64 were in poverty, a decline from 6.9 percent in 2014. For those who worked full time, year round, 2.4 percent were in poverty in 2015, down from 3.0 percent in 2014. Those working less than full time, year round had a poverty rate in 2015 of 15.5 percent, which was not statistically different from 2014.

Among those aged 18 to 64 who did not work at least 1 week during the calendar year, the poverty rate decreased to 31.8 percent in 2015 from 33.7 percent in 2014. Those who did not work at least 1 week in 2015 represented 23.8 percent of all people aged 18 to 64, while they made up 61.3 percent of people aged 18 to 64 in poverty.

Disability Status

For people aged 18 to 64 with a disability, the 2015 poverty rate (28.5 percent) and number in poverty (4.4 million) were not statistically different from 2014. For people aged 18 to 64 without a disability, the poverty rate and the number in poverty decreased to 11.0 percent and 20.0 million in 2015, down from 12.3 percent and 22.1 million in 2014.

Among people aged 18 to 64, those with a disability represented 7.7 percent of all people, compared with 17.9 percent of people aged 18 to 64 in poverty.

Educational Attainment

In 2015, 26.3 percent (6.2 millions) of people aged 25 and older without a high school diploma were in poverty, a decline from 28.9 percent (7.1 million) in 2014. The 2015 poverty rate for those with a high school diploma but with no college was 12.9 percent (8.0 million), down from 14.2 percent (8.9 million) in 2014. For those with some college but no degree, 9.6 percent were in poverty in 2015, a decline from 10.2 percent in 2014. The number of these individuals in poverty remained unchanged at 5.6 million in 2015.

Among people with at least a bachelor's degree, 4.5 percent were in poverty in 2015, a decline from 5.0 percent in 2014. The number in poverty decreased to 3.2 million, down from 3.4 million in 2014. People with at least a bachelor's degree in 2015 represented 33.4 percent of all people aged 25 and older, compared with 14.0 percent of people aged 25 and older in poverty.

Families

The poverty rate for families in 2015 was 10.4 percent, representing 8.6 million families, a decline from 11.6 percent and 9.5 million families in 2014.

For married-couple families, the poverty rate decreased to 5.4 percent and the number in poverty decreased to 3.2 million in 2015, down from 6.2 percent and 3.7 million in 2014. The poverty rate and the number in poverty also decreased for families with a female householder to 28.2 percent and 4.4 million in 2015, down from 30.6 percent and 4.8 million in 2014. For families with a male householder, neither the poverty rate nor the number in poverty showed any statistical change between 2014 and 2015. For families with a male householder, 14.9 percent were in poverty in 2015, representing 939,000 families.

Depth of Poverty

Categorizing a person as "in poverty" or "not in poverty" is one way to describe his or her economic situation. The income-to-poverty ratio and measures of income deficit or surplus describe additional aspects of economic well-being. While the poverty rate shows the proportion of people with income below the relevant poverty threshold, the income-to-poverty ratio gauges the depth of poverty and shows how close a family's income is to its poverty threshold. The income-to-poverty ratio is reported as a percentage that compares a family's or an unrelated person's income with the applicable threshold. For example, a family with an income-to-poverty ratio of 125 percent has income that is 25 percent above its poverty threshold.

The income deficit or surplus shows how many dollars a family's or an individual's income is below (or above) their poverty threshold. For those with an income deficit, the measure is an estimate of the dollar amount necessary to raise a family's or a person's income to their poverty threshold.

Ratio of Income to Poverty

. . . . In 2015, 19.4 million people reported family income below one-half of their poverty threshold. They represented 6.1 percent of all people and 45.1 percent of those in poverty. Approximately 17.9 percent of individuals had family income below 125 percent of their threshold, 22.5 percent had family income below 150 percent of their poverty threshold while 31.7 percent had family income below 200 percent of their threshold.

Of the 19.4 million people in 2015 with family income below one-half of their poverty threshold, 6.5 million were children under age 18, 11.6 million were aged 18 to 64, and 1.3 million were aged 65 and older. The demographic makeup of the population differs at varying degrees of poverty. In 2015 children represented:

- 23.1 percent of the overall population.

- 19.7 percent of the people with income above 200 percent of their poverty threshold.

- 28.1 percent of people with income between 100 percent and 200 percent of their poverty threshold.

- 33.6 percent of the population below 50 percent of their poverty threshold.

By comparison, people aged 65 and older represented:

- 14.9 percent of the overall population.

- 15.1 percent of the people with income above 200 percent of their poverty threshold.

- 18.3 percent of the people between 100 percent and 200 percent of their poverty threshold.

- 6.9 percent of people below 50 percent of their poverty threshold.

Income Deficit

The income deficit for families in poverty (the difference in dollars between a family's income and its poverty threshold) averaged $10,118 in 2015, which was not statistically different from the inflation-adjusted 2014 estimate. The average income deficit was larger for families with a female householder ($10,759) than for married-couple families ($9,456).

The average per capita income deficit was also larger for families with a female householder ($3,219) than for married-couple families ($2,501). For unrelated individuals, the average income deficit for those in poverty was $6,873 in 2015. The $6,658 deficit for women was lower than the $7,151 deficit for men.

Shared Households

Shared households are defined as households that include at least one "additional" adult, a person aged 18 or older, who is not the householder, spouse, or cohabiting partner of the householder. Adults aged 18 to 24 who are enrolled in school are not counted as additional adults.

In 2016, the percentage and number of shared households remained higher than in 2007, the year before the most recent recession. In 2007, 17.0 percent of all households were shared households, totaling 19.7 million shared households. In 2016, 19.1 percent of all households were shared households, totaling 24.1 million shared households.

From 2015 to 2016, changes in the percentage and number of shared households were not significant. Changes in the percentage and number of additional adults residing in shared households were also not significant.

In 2016, an estimated 27.2 percent (11.9 millions) of adults aged 25 to 34 were additional adults in someone else's household, representing an increase from 25.8 percent (11.1 million) in 2015. Of young adults aged 25 to 34, 16.0 percent (7.0 million) lived with their parents in 2016, an increase from 15.1 percent (6.5 million) in 2015.

It is difficult to assess the precise impact of household sharing on overall poverty rates. Adults aged 25 to 34 living with their parents in 2016 had an official 2015 poverty rate of 6.8 percent (when the entire family's income is compared with the threshold that includes the young adult as a member of the family). However, if poverty status had been determined using only the young adult's own income, 39.4 percent of those aged 25 to 34 would have been below the poverty threshold for a single person under age 65. However, although 6.6 percent of families including at least one adult child of the householder were in poverty in 2015, the poverty rate for these families would have increased to 12.0 percent if the young adult were not living in the household.

SOURCE: U.S. Census Bureau. "Income and Poverty in the United States: 2015." September 13, 2016. http://www.census.gov/content/dam/Census/library/publications/2016/demo/p60-256.pdf.

DOCUMENT

Census Bureau Report on Supplemental Poverty Measures

September 13, 2016

[All figures, tables (except Table 2), graphics, and references to them, have been omitted.]

[Only the sections related to poverty estimates, poverty rates, and the effect of noncash benefits have been included below.]

POVERTY ESTIMATES FOR 2015: OFFICIAL AND SPM

The measures presented in this study use the 2016 Current Population Survey Annual Social and Economic Supplement (CPS ASEC) income information that refers to calendar year 2015 to estimate SPM resources. These are the same data used for the preparation of official poverty statistics as reported in Proctor, Semega, and Kollar (2016).

The SPM thresholds for 2015 are based on out-of-pocket spending on basic needs (FCSU). Thresholds use 5 years of quarterly data from the CE; the thresholds are produced by the BLS Division of Price and Index Number Research (DPINR). Expenditures on shelter and utilities are determined for three housing tenure groups. The three groups include owners with mortgages, owners without mortgages, and renters. The thresholds used here include the value of Supplemental Nutrition Assistance Program (SNAP) benefits in the measure of spending on food. The American Community Survey (ACS) data on rents paid are used to adjust the SPM thresholds for differences in spending on housing across geographic areas.

The two measures use different units of analysis. The official measure of poverty uses the Census Bureau–defined family that includes all individuals residing together who are related by birth, marriage, or adoption and treats all unrelated individuals over age 14 independently. For the SPM, the family unit includes all related individuals who live at the same address, as well as any coresident unrelated children who are cared for by the family (such as foster children), and any unmarried partners and their children. These units are referred to as SPM Resource Units. Selection of the unit of analysis for poverty measurement implies that members of that unit share income or resources with one another.

SPM thresholds are adjusted for the size and composition of the SPM Resource Unit relative to the two-adult-two-child threshold using an equivalence scale. The official measure adjusts thresholds based on family size, number of children and adults, as well as whether or not the householder is aged 65 or over. The official poverty threshold for a two-adult-two-child family was $24,036 in 2015. The SPM thresholds vary by housing tenure and are higher for owners with mortgages and renters than the official threshold. These two groups comprise about 76 percent of the total population. The official threshold increased by $28 between 2014 and 2015. The changes in the SPM thresholds between 2014 and 2015 were not statistically significant.

SPM resources are estimated as the sum of cash income plus any federal government noncash benefits that families can use to meet their FCSU needs minus taxes (plus tax credits), work expenses, and out-of-pocket medical expenses. The text box summarizes the additions and subtractions for the SPM; descriptions are in the appendix.

POVERTY RATES: OFFICIAL AND SPM

. . . Table 2 shows poverty rates for selected demographic groups. The percentage of the population that was poor using the official measure for 2015 was 13.5 percent (Proctor, Semega, and Kollar, 2016). For this study, including unrelated individuals under age 15 in the universe, the poverty rate was 13.7 percent. The SPM rate was 14.3 percent for 2015, significantly higher than the official rate. While, as noted, SPM poverty thresholds are generally higher than official thresholds, other parts of the measure also contribute to differences in the estimated prevalence of poverty in the United States.

In 2015, 45.7 million people were poor using the SPM definition of poverty, more than the 43.5 million using the official definition of poverty with the adjusted universe. While for most groups, SPM rates were higher than official poverty rates, the SPM shows lower poverty rates for children, individuals living in female householder units, individuals included in new SPM Resource Units, Blacks, renters, those living outside metropolitan

Table 2. Number and Percentage of People in Poverty by Different Poverty Measures: 2015

(Numbers in thousands, margin of error in thousands or percentage points as appropriate. For information on confidentiality protection, sampling error, nonsampling error, and definitions, see www2.census.gov/programs-surveys/cps/techdocs/cpsmar16.pdf)

Characteristic	Number (thousands)	Official**				SPM				Difference	
		Number		Percentage		Number		Percentage		Number	Percentage
		Estimate	Margin of error† (+)	Estimate	Margin of error† (+)	Estimate	Margin of error† (+)	Estimate	Margin of error† (+)	Number	Percent
All people	318,868	43,538	919	13.7	0.3	45,651	901	14.3	0.3	*2,113	*0.7
Sex											
Male	156,205	19,233	467	12.3	0.3	21,385	480	13.7	0.3	*2,152	*1.4
Female	162,664	24,305	542	14.9	0.3	24,266	516	14.9	0.3	–39	Z
Age											
Under 18 years	74,062	14,923	443	20.1	0.6	11,929	375	16.1	0.5	*–2,994	*–4.0
18 to 64 years	197,260	24,414	566	12.4	0.3	27,222	588	13.8	0.3	*2,808	*1.4
65 years and older	47,547	4,201	203	8.8	0.4	6,500	236	13.7	0.5	*2,299	*4.8
Type of Unit											
Married couple	190,108	12,120	534	6.4	0.3	16,920	611	8.9	0.3	*4,800	*2.5
Female householder	65,634	17,373	539	26.5	0.7	16,984	492	25.9	0.7	*–389	*–0.6
Male householder	35,103	5,957	298	17.0	0.8	7,330	333	20.9	0.8	*1,373	*3.9
New SPM unit	28,023	8,088	356	28.9	1.0	4,417	347	15.8	1.2	*–3,670	*–13.1

(Continued)

(Continued)

Characteristic	Number (thousands)	Official**				SPM				Difference	
		Number		Percentage		Number		Percentage		Number	Percentage
		Estimate	Margin of error† (+)	Estimate	Margin of error† (+)	Estimate	Margin of error† (+)	Estimate	Margin of error† (+)	Number	Percent
Race[1] and Hispanic Origin											
White	245,805	28,835	707	11.7	0.3	30,852	711	12.6	0.3	*2,018	*0.8
White, not Hispanic	195,646	17,981	546	9.2	0.3	19,638	555	10.0	0.3	*1,657	*0.8
Black	41,703	10,099	417	24.2	1.0	9,575	421	23.0	1.0	*−524	*−1.3
Asian	18,249	2,086	190	11.4	1.0	2,921	226	16.0	1.2	*836	*4.6
Hispanic (any race)	56,873	12,226	446	21.5	0.8	12,719	479	22.4	0.8	*493	*0.9
Nativity											
Native born	275,798	36,373	805	13.2	0.3	36,328	736	13.2	0.3	−45	Z
Foreign born	43,070	7,165	330	16.6	0.7	9,323	382	21.6	0.8	*2,158	*5.0
Naturalized citizen	20,086	2,258	152	11.2	0.7	3,347	181	16.7	0.9	*1,089	*5.4
Not a citizen	22,984	4,907	285	21.3	1.0	5,976	305	26.0	1.0	*1,069	*4.7
Tenure											
Owner	208,768	15,385	552	7.4	0.3	19,016	605	9.1	0.3	*3,631	*1.7
Owner/mortgage	134,299	6,935	388	5.2	0.3	10,009	467	7.5	0.3	*3,073	*2.3
Owner/no mortgage/ rent free	77,815	9,375	417	12.0	0.5	9,853	414	12.7	0.5	*478	*0.6
Renter	106,754	27,227	695	25.5	0.6	25,789	677	24.2	0.6	−1,438	*−1.3
Residence											
Inside metropolitan statistical areas	274,392	36,065	938	13.1	0.3	39,798	918	14.5	0.3	*3,733	*1.4
Inside principal cities	103,740	17,492	650	16.9	0.6	18,534	701	17.9	0.6	*1,042	*1.0

Characteristic	Number (thousands)	Official** Number Estimate	Official** Number Margin of error[†] (+)	Official** Percentage Estimate	Official** Percentage Margin of error[†] (+)	SPM Number Estimate	SPM Number Margin of error[†] (+)	SPM Percentage Estimate	SPM Percentage Margin of error[†] (+)	Difference Number	Difference Percent
Outside principal cities	170,652	18,573	701	10.9	0.4	21,264	733	12.5	0.4	*2,691	*1.6
Outside metropolitan statistical areas[2]	44,477	7,473	639	16.8	0.8	5,853	528	13.2	0.7	*–1,620	*–3.6
Region											
Northeast	55,879	6,991	391	12.5	0.7	8,004	396	14.3	0.7	*1,012	*1.8
Midwest	67,115	7,934	378	11.8	0.6	7,210	374	10.7	0.6	*–724	*–1.1
South	120,115	18,464	598	15.4	0.5	18,552	602	15.4	0.5	87	0.1
West	75,759	10,148	420	13.4	0.6	11,886	471	15.7	0.6	*1,738	*2.3
Health Insurance Coverage											
With private insurance	214,238	12,462	466	5.8	0.2	18,350	548	8.6	0.3	*5,888	*2.7
With public, no private insurance	75,664	23,552	673	31.1	0.8	19,687	562	26.0	0.6	*–3,864	*–5.1
Not insured	28,966	7,524	318	26.0	0.9	7,614	332	26.3	1.0	90	0.3
Work Experience											
Total 18 to 64 years	197,260	24,414	566	12.4	0.3	27,222	588	13.8	0.3	*2,808	*1.4
All workers	150,229	9,457	297	6.3	0.2	12,478	333	8.3	0.2	*3,021	*2.0
Worked full-time, year-round	105,695	2,537	136	2.4	0.1	4,999	186	4.7	0.2	*2,462	*2.3
Less than full-time, year-round	44,534	6,920	263	15.5	0.6	7,479	273	16.8	0.6	*559	*1.3

(Continued)

(Continued)

Characteristic	Number (thousands)	Official**				SPM				Difference	
		Number		Percentage		Number		Percentage		Number	Percentage
		Estimate	Margin of error† (+)	Estimate	Margin of error† (+)	Estimate	Margin of error† (+)	Estimate	Margin of error† (+)	Number	Percent
Did not work at least 1 week	47,031	14,957	399	31.8	0.7	14,744	404	31.4	0.7	−213	−0.5
Disability Status[3]											
Total 18 to 64 years	197,260	24,414	566	12.4	0.3	27,222	588	13.8	0.3	*2,808	*1.4
With a disability	15,276	4,358	191	28.5	1.1	4,042	184	26.5	1.0	*−316	*−2.1
With no disability	181,069	20,000	526	11.0	0.3	23,101	532	12.8	0.3	*3,101	*1.7

* An asterisk preceding an estimate indicates change is statistically different from zero at the 90 percent confidence level.

** Includes unrelated individuals under the age of 15.

† The margin of error (MOE) is a measure of an estimate's variability. The larger the MOE in relation to the size of the estimate, the less reliable the estimate. The MOE is the estimated 90 percent confidence interval. The MOEs shown in this table are based on standard errors calculated using replicate weights. For more information see 'Standard Errors and Their Use' at www2.census.gov/library/publications/2016/demo/p60-256sa.pdf.

Z Represents or rounds to zero.

[1] Federal surveys give respondents the option of reporting more than one race. Therefore, two basic ways of defining a race group are possible. A group such as Asian may be defined as those who reported Asian and no other race (the race-alone or single-race concept) or as those who reported Asian regardless of whether they also reported another race (the race-alone-or-in-combination concept). This table shows data using the first approach (race alone). The use of the single-race population does not imply that it is the preferred method of presenting or analyzing data. The Census Bureau uses a variety of approaches. Information on people who reported more than one race, such as White and American Indian and Alaska Native or Asian and Black or African American, is available from Census 2010 through American FactFinder. About 2.9 percent of people reported more than one race in Census 2010. Data for American Indians and Alaska Natives, Native Hawaiians and Other Pacific Islanders, and those reporting two or more races are not shown separately.

[2] The 'Outside metropolitan statistical areas' category includes both micropolitan statistical areas and territory outside of metropolitan and micropolitan statistical areas. For more information, see 'About Metropolitan and Micropolitan Statistical Areas' at www.census.gov/population/metro.

[3] The sum of those with and without a disability does not equal the total because disability status is not defined for individuals in the Armed Forces.

SOURCE: U.S. Census Bureau, Current Population Survey, 2016 Annual Social and Economic Supplement.

areas, residents of the Midwest, those covered by only public health insurance, and individuals with a disability. Most other groups had higher poverty rates using the SPM, rather than the official measure. Official and SPM poverty rates for females, individuals born in the United States, residents of the South, the uninsured, and individuals who did not work were not statistically different. Note that poverty rates for those 65 years and over were higher under the SPM compared with the official measure. This partially reflects that the official thresholds are set lower for individuals with householders in this age group, while the SPM thresholds do not vary by age. . . .

The SPM and the Effect of Cash and Noncash Transfers, Taxes, and Other Nondiscretionary Expenses

This section moves away from comparing the SPM with the official measure and looks only at the SPM. This analysis allows one to gauge the effects of taxes and transfers and other necessary expenses using the SPM as the measure of economic well-being.

The official poverty measure takes account of cash benefits from the government, such as Social Security and Unemployment Insurance benefits, Supplemental Security Income (SSI), public assistance benefits, such as Temporary Assistance for Needy Families (TANF), and workers' compensation benefits, but does not take account of taxes or noncash benefits aimed at improving the economic situation of the poor. Besides taking account of cash benefits and necessary expenses, such as MOOP expenses and expenses related to work, the SPM also accounts for taxes and noncash transfers. An important contribution of the SPM is that it allows us to gauge the potential magnitude of the effect of tax credits and transfers on alleviating poverty. We can also examine the effects of nondiscretionary expenses, such as work and MOOP expenses.

Table 5a shows the effect that various additions and subtractions had on the SPM rate in 2015, holding all else the same and assuming no behavioral changes. Additions and subtractions are shown for the total population and by three age groups. Additions shown in the table include cash benefits, also accounted for in the official measure, as well as noncash benefits, included only in the SPM. This allows us to examine the effects of government transfers on poverty estimates. Since child support paid is subtracted from income, we also examine the effect of child support received on alleviating poverty. Child support payments received are counted as income in both the official measure and the SPM. Table 5b shows the same set of additions and subtractions, but shows the number of people affected by removing each element from the SPM, rather than the change in the SPM rate.

Removing one item from the calculation of SPM resources and recalculating poverty rates shows, for example, that without Social Security benefits the SPM rate would have been 8.3 percentage points higher (22.7 percent), rather than 14.3 percent. This means that, without Social Security benefits, an additional 26.6 million people would be living below the poverty line, beyond the 45.7 million people classified as poor with the SPM. Not including refundable tax credits (the EITC and the refundable portion of the child tax credit) in resources, an additional 9.2 million people would have been considered poor, all else constant. On the other hand, removing amounts paid for child support, income and payroll taxes, work-related expenses, and MOOP expenses from the calculation resulted in lower poverty rates.

Without subtracting MOOP expenses from income, the SPM rate would have been 3.5 percentage points lower. In numbers, 11.2 million fewer people would have been classified as poor.

Tables 5a and 5b also show effects for different age groups. In 2015, not accounting for refundable tax credits would have resulted in a 6.5 percentage point increase in the child poverty rate, representing 4.8 million children precluded from poverty by the inclusion of these credits. Not subtracting MOOP expenses from the income of families with children would have resulted in a child poverty rate 3.4 percentage points lower. For the 65 years and over group, SPM rates increased by about 5.7 percentage points with the subtraction of MOOP expenses from income, while Social Security benefits lowered poverty rates by 36.0 percentage points, lifting 17.1 million individuals above the poverty line.

Figure 4 shows the change in the number of people who would have been considered poor by excluding each element in the SPM separately, allowing us to compare the effect of transfers, both cash and noncash, and nondiscretionary expenses on numbers of individuals in poverty, all else equal. Social Security transfers and refundable tax credits had the largest impacts, preventing 26.6 million and 9.2 million individuals, respectively, from falling into poverty. MOOP expenditures contributed the most to increasing the number of individuals in poverty.

Summary

This report provides estimates of the SPM for the United States. The results shown illustrate differences between the official measure of poverty and a poverty measure that takes account of noncash benefits received by families and nondiscretionary expenses that they must pay. The SPM also employs a new poverty threshold that is updated with information on expenditures for FCSU by the BLS. Results showed higher poverty rates using the SPM than the official measure for most groups, with the exception of children who have lower poverty rates using the SPM.

The SPM allows us to examine the effect of taxes and noncash transfers on the poor and on important groups within the poverty population. As such, there are lower percentages of the SPM poverty populations in the very high and very low resource categories than we find using the official measure. Since noncash benefits help those in extreme poverty, there were lower percentages of individuals with resources below half the SPM threshold for most groups. In addition, the effect of benefits received from each program and taxes and other nondiscretionary expenses on SPM rates were examined.

SOURCE: U.S. Census Bureau. "The Supplemental Poverty Measure: 2015." September 13, 2016. www .census.gov/content/dam/Census/library/publications/2016/demo/p60-258.pdf.

OTHER HISTORIC DOCUMENTS OF INTEREST

FROM THIS VOLUME

- State of the Union Address and Republican Response, p. 27
- Clinton and Trump Meet in Second Presidential Debate, p. 546
- Donald Trump Elected U.S. President, p. 612

FROM PREVIOUS *HISTORIC DOCUMENTS*

- Census Bureau Reports on Poverty in the United States, *2015*, p. 439

Wells Fargo CEO, Local and Federal Officials Testify on Banking Scandal

SEPTEMBER 20, 2016

On September 20, 2016, Wells Fargo chair and CEO John Stumpf appeared before the U.S. Senate Committee on Banking, Housing, and Urban Affairs after an investigation by local and federal regulators found that his company misled customers by opening accounts without their consent. For more than four years, Wells Fargo employees created more than two million unauthorized bank and credit card accounts without their customers' permission or knowledge. At the heart of the scandal was a controversial incentive program that compelled employees to open and fund accounts, without notifying customers, to satisfy sales goals and earn money under the bank's incentive-compensation program. Three weeks after testifying, Stumpf resigned his position as CEO amid a class action lawsuit filed by Wells Fargo employees and a Securities and Exchange Commission investigation into the bank's sales tactics.

SALES CULTURE LAYS GROUNDWORK FOR WIDESPREAD FRAUD

Amid heightened regulatory pressure and consumer distrust of large financial institutions as a result of the 2008 financial crisis, many of the nation's largest banks sought to distinguish themselves from competitors. South Dakota–based Wells Fargo saw an opportunity to become a market leader in cross-selling, or selling products and services to existing customers who did not already have them. A common business practice, cross-selling allows a company to generate more revenue from existing customers rather than acquire new customers.

The bank's senior leadership, including Chair and CEO John Stumpf, personally drove the new philosophy. Stumpf pressed retail banking employees to encourage customers to have eight different accounts with the bank, higher than the industry average of six, often repeating the mantra "Eight is great." The bank also established a new sales-incentive program with aggressive goals. However, the goals proved to be extreme. Coupled with a lack of accountability and oversight from senior leadership, it created a perverse incentive environment where retail employees only saw advancement and compensation through aggressive sales tactics and, as government regulators discovered years later, fraud.

To meet new cross-sell quotas, employees relied on a number of fraudulent tactics. In the most common method, known as "pinning," bankers obtained a debit card number and set the personal identification number (PIN) without customer authorization. Then, with the fraudulent account, the banker could enroll a customer in online banking, for which the banker would receive a sales credit. Bankers went so far as to impersonate consumers online, inputting false generic e-mail addresses to ensure that the transaction was completed and that the consumer remained unaware of the activity.

Other methods involved lying directly to customers. Employees falsely told customers that they were unable to get the service they requested unless they signed up for other services, or lied about monthly fees. Many employees told account holders that new accounts did not have monthly fees when they did or said that accounts without monthly fees would carry fees unless the customer signed up for another account. Other methods were less nefarious. Employees described to regulators feeling pressured to recruit family members and friends, spending holiday dinners trying to convince family members to sign up for accounts. Often, employees would wait to open requested accounts until the beginning of the next reporting period, a method known as "sandbagging." As regulators would later discover, these methods were employed throughout the company and, despite being unearthed by a 2013 *Los Angeles Times* investigation, continued to escalate.

State and Federal Regulators Announce Record Penalties

On September 8, 2016, the Consumer Financial Protection Bureau (CFPB), the Los Angeles City Attorney, and the Office of the Comptroller of the Currency (OCC) revealed an investigation into the fraudulent activity and fined the bank $185 million in total, including a record $100 million payable to the CFPB.

The settlement described how Wells Fargo employees created more than 1.5 million bank accounts and submitted applications for 565,443 credit card accounts without customers' knowledge or consent between May 2011 and July 2015. Nearly 14,000 of those accounts incurred more than $400,000 in fees, such as annual fees, overdraft protection fees, and interest charges. Following the initial investigation from federal and state officials, Wells Fargo confirmed that it had terminated 5,300 employees over the previous four years related to the accounts scandal.

CFPB director Richard Cordray called the activity "widespread" and chided the bank's leadership for not holding senior managers accountable. "Wells Fargo employees secretly opened unauthorized accounts to hit sales targets and receive bonuses," Cordray said when announcing the settlement. "Because of the severity of these violations, Wells Fargo is paying the largest penalty the CFPB has ever imposed." The bank agreed to settle the allegations without admitting or denying them. "We regret and take responsibility for any instances where customers may have received a product that they did not request," Wells Fargo said in a statement.

Stumpf Defends Practices before Senate Banking Committee

After the scandal came to light, Republican and Democratic senators on the U.S. Senate Committee on Banking, Housing, and Urban Affairs called Stumpf and the regulators who levied the punishment—Cordray, OCC Comptroller Thomas Curry, and Los Angeles City attorney Michael N. Feuer—to appear before the committee to explain in detail the specifics surrounding the investigation.

The majority of the committee's questioning was reserved for Stumpf. In prepared remarks, the Wells Fargo CEO said he was "deeply sorry" that the bank "failed to fulfill our responsibility to our customers, to our team members, and to the American public." Stumpf continued, apologizing that the bank did not act sooner to stem what he called an "unacceptable activity." However, Stumpf rejected any notion that there were pervasive problems with the senior leadership, or a company-wide culture that encouraged or facilitated fraud. "I do want to make very clear that there was no orchestrated effort, or scheme as some have called it, by the company," Stumpf testified. "We never directed nor wanted our employees, whom we refer to as team members, to provide products and services to customers they did not want or need."

As to the specifics of the allegations, Stumpf defended the original intentions of the programs and outlined steps the company took prior to the enforcement to detect and stem fraudulent activity. Cross-selling, he alleged, indicates and encourages customer loyalty. "Our cross sell strategy is simply another way of saying that we provide our customers a wide variety of products that can satisfy their financial needs." Meanwhile, certain initiatives implemented over the prior five years, according to Stumpf, helped root out and prevent fraud. For example, in 2012, Wells Fargo implemented a Quality-of-Sale Report Card across retail banking designed to "deter and detect misconduct through monitoring of sales patterns that may correlate with unethical behavior." Other methods included reducing sales quotas, strengthening oversight of sales teams, and terminating sales employees who engaged in fraudulent activities.

Senators Criticize Wells Fargo for Lack of Accountability

Senate Banking Committee members were hardly impressed with the CEO's testimony. Members from both parties scoffed at Stumpf, believing he offered little more than platitudes and shirked blame onto low-level, retail employees while heaping top executives with lavish compensation packages.

Sen. Bob Corker, R-Tenn., accused Stumpf of "malpractice" if he does not "clawback" money paid to executives, referring to a tactic in which a corporate board rescinds money already paid to executives. The committee chair, Sen. Richard C. Shelby, R-Ala., questioned how Wells Fargo kept senior managers accountable after the committee revealed that the bank allowed retail banking business manager Carrie Tolstedt, who oversaw the department in which all the problems occurred, to retire at age fifty-six with a compensation package totaling $124.6 million. "Explain to the public: What does accountability look like when an executive departs with millions of dollars?" asked Shelby.

However, the most aggressive questioning came from Sen. Elizabeth Warren, D-Mass. An outspoken consumer advocate and critic of big banks, Warren accused the CEO of "gutless leadership" after Stumpf admitted to not returning any of his compensation or holding any senior manager accountable. In the hearing's most memorable exchange, Warren flatly told the CEO to resign and remarked that he should be investigated criminally. "You should resign," Warren said. "You should give back the money that you gained while this scam was going on, and you should be criminally investigated by the DOJ and the SEC."

Warren, following Corker's line of questioning, also pressed Stumpf on the issue of corporate clawbacks. Stumpf's argument that the decision to rescind compensation rested with the bank's board drew ire from Warren, who pointed out that he was the board's chair. "You keep saying, 'the board, the board,'" she remarked. "You describe them like they are strangers you met in a dark alley. Mr. Stumpf, you are the chairman of the board." Despite being pressed, Stumpf refused to say whether his pay—highest among the top bank executives during the period in question—should be docked.

During the second half of the hearing, lawmakers questioned leaders of three oversight agencies involved in the Wells Fargo scandal. Cordray argued that the fine, the largest in CFPB history, was justified. "Some have said it should be higher," Cordray said. "But it is justified here by the outrageous and abusive nature of these fraudulent practices on such an enormous scale." Curry and Feuer echoed Cordray's assessment. Curry described how "the unsafe and unsound sales practices at the Bank . . . have no place in the federal banking system," while Feuer outlined how his office, through interviews with former employees and customers, discovered that Wells Fargo "victimized consumers" and purposefully kept them in the dark.

CONTINUED INQUIRIES FROM CAPITOL HILL AND GOVERNMENT REGULATORS

Far from satisfying government watchdogs and politicians, Stumpf's testimony fanned the flames. Following the hearing, Sen. Jeff Merkley, D-Ore., called on the Securities and Exchange Commission to examine whether the bank violated the Sarbanes-Oxley Act by failing to stop "widespread fraud." Over the following few days, Senate Democrats asked the U.S. Department of Labor to open an investigation into whether the bank violated the Fair Labor Standards Act and starkly criticized the bank's use of forced arbitration clauses, which some argued kept the scandal hidden from the public and the courts. Later, two former Wells Fargo employees filed a lawsuit against the company, seeking class action status and restitution for improper demotion or firing practices tied to the account scandal.

Days before the Wells Fargo CEO was set to appear before another congressional committee, Wells Fargo announced an internal investigation and corporate clawbacks. Stumpf forwent $41 million worth of promised compensation as well as his usual salary and a bonus, while Tolstedt waived promised compensation worth roughly $19 million. Before members of the House of Representatives Financial Services Committee, Stumpf also announced that the bank would end its controversial sales program two months earlier than previously announced. Despite the measures, investigators continued to press. Senators asked Attorney General Loretta Lynch to investigate the culpability of senior executives, and the SEC opened an investigation into the bank's sales tactics. Three weeks after Stumpf testified before the Senate Banking Committee, he stepped down as CEO.

—Robert Howard

Following are the testimonies given by Wells Fargo chair and CEO John Stumpf, CFPB director Richard Cordray, OCC comptroller Thomas Curry, and Los Angeles City attorney Michael N. Feuer on September 20, 2016, before the Senate Committee on Banking, Housing, and Urban Affairs.

Wells Fargo CEO Testifies before the Senate Committee on Banking, Housing, and Urban Affairs

September 20, 2016

Chairman Shelby, Ranking Member Brown, and Members of the Committee, thank you for inviting me to be with you today. . . .

I am deeply sorry that we failed to fulfill our responsibility to our customers, to our team members, and to the American public. I have been with Wells Fargo through many challenges, none that pains me more than the one we will discuss this morning. I am here to discuss how accounts were opened and products were provided to customers that they did not authorize or want. I am going to explain this morning what happened and what we have done about it. But first, I want to apologize to all Wells Fargo customers. I want to apologize for violating the trust our customers have invested in Wells Fargo. And I want to apologize for not doing more sooner to address the causes of this unacceptable activity.

I do want to make very clear that there was no orchestrated effort, or scheme as some have called it, by the company. We never directed nor wanted our employees, whom we refer to as team members, to provide products and services to customers they did not want or need. It is important to understand that when an employee provides a customer with a product or service that she did not request or authorize, that employee has done something flat wrong. It costs us satisfied customers, and we lose money on these accounts. Wrongful sales practice behavior goes entirely against our values, ethics, and culture and runs counter to our business strategy of helping our customers succeed financially and deepening our relationship with those customers.

That said, I accept full responsibility for all unethical sales practices in our retail banking business, and I am fully committed to doing everything possible to fix this issue, strengthen our culture, and take the necessary actions to restore our customers' trust.

Let me assure you and our customers that Wells Fargo takes allegations of sales practice violations extremely seriously and that we will not rest until the problem is fixed. As I will explain shortly, we are moving to demonstrate once again that Wells Fargo remains the dependable, principled partner that it has been throughout its 164-year history. . . .

Cross Selling Means Deepening Relationships With Customers

A typical American household has multiple financial services and products, and our goal is to have as deep a relationship as we can with those households. Our cross sell strategy is simply another way of saying that we provide our customers a wide variety of products that can satisfy their financial needs. The more products a customer uses, the deeper the relationship of trust and value. Deep relationships with products that are wanted and used are what furthers our business strategy and truly helps our customers to succeed financially.

Retail Banking Has Made Progressive Changes To Detect And Deter Unethical Behavior

Our efforts to detect and deter unethical conduct have progressively evolved over the last five years. . . . For example, in 2011, we piloted our Quality-of-Sale Report Card in California, and it was implemented in 2012 across retail banking. The Quality-of-Sale Report Card was designed to, among other things, deter and detect misconduct through monitoring of sales patterns that may correlate with unethical behavior. . . .

In 2013, the Sales and Service Conduct Oversight Team began its first proactive analysis of "simulated funding" across the retail banking business, reviewing employee-level data around account openings. Let me explain: "simulated funding" is a prohibited practice whereby an employee creates an account for a customer and then funds it in order to make it look as if the customer had funded the account. Based on the original proactive monitoring, our Internal Investigations team began an intensive investigation into simulated funding activity in the Los Angeles and Orange County markets. As a result of these investigations, we terminated team members for sales integrity issues. . . .

Sales-Related Terminations Took Place Over The Course Of 2011–2015

I want to pause for a moment to discuss the issue of terminations. We do not have tolerance for dishonest conduct or behavior inconsistent with our Code of Ethics. It has been reported in the media that Wells Fargo terminated approximately 5,300 individuals after the CFPB's enforcement investigation. Instead, individuals were terminated over time for sales related misconduct as a result of investigations opened from January 1, 2011 through March 7, 2016. In any given year, approximately 100,000 individuals work in our retail bank branches, and we have terminated approximately 1% of that workforce annually for sales practice violations.

Wells Fargo Is Working To Make It Right For Our Customers

Despite all of these efforts, we did not get it right. We should have done more sooner to eliminate unethical conduct and unintended incentives for that conduct to occur. . . .

In August 2015, we began working with a third-party consulting firm, PricewaterhouseCoopers ("PwC"), and asked them to evaluate deposit products, unsecured credit cards, and other services from 2011-2015 to determine whether customers may have incurred financial harm (specifically, fees, other bank charges, and interest) from having been provided an account or service they may not have requested. . . .

Beginning in September 2015 and continuing well into 2016, PwC conducted extensive large-scale data analysis of the more than 82 million deposit accounts and nearly 11 million credit card accounts that we opened during that time frame.

With respect to deposit accounts, PwC focused on identifying transaction patterns that might be consistent with improper conduct. Out of the 82 million deposit accounts, it identified approximately 1.5 million such accounts (or 1.9%) that could have been unauthorized. To be clear, PwC did not find that each of these accounts was unauthorized. Among these accounts, PwC calculated that approximately 100,000 incurred fees in the amount of about $2.2 million.

With respect to credit cards, PwC identified a population of credit cards that had never been activated by the customer nor had other customer transaction activity. . . . PwC calculated that approximately 565,000 consumer cards, or 5.8% of all credit cards opened, had not been activated nor had other customer transaction activity, and approximately 14,000 of these cards had incurred a fee. These fees totaled approximately $400,000. PwC did not find that these cards were unauthorized.

In February 2016, we began the process of remediating the deposit and credit card customers identified above. . . .

Wells Fargo Is Engaged In Multiple Efforts To Take Responsibility For, And Rectify, Our Mistakes

We decided that product sales goals do not belong in our retail banking business. Specifically, as announced last week, we are eliminating all product sales goals for retail banking team members and leaders, including those in branches and retail banking call centers, effective January 1, 2017. We are doing this in order to better align with the additional training, controls, and oversight implemented since 2011 and focus on rewarding excellent customer service rather than product sales.

We have taken, and continue to take, other significant and meaningful steps to prevent unauthorized accounts from being created. These steps include:

- Working closely with our primary regulator, the Office of the Comptroller of the Currency ("OCC"), to strengthen our enterprise oversight of sales conduct risk. We have established an enterprise Sales Conduct Risk Oversight Office, reporting into the Chief Risk Officer, and have regularly responded to numerous inquiries and provided regular briefings to our regulators;

- Creating a new enhanced branch compliance program that will be dedicated to monitoring for sales practice violations by conducting data analytics and frequent branch visits. Results will be reported to the enterprise Sales Conduct Risk Oversight Office;

- Implementing a process whereby, within one hour of opening an account, a customer will receive an email that confirms the opening of the account;

- Revising procedures for credit cards, to require each applicant's documented consent before a credit report is pulled. Consent is manifested by a physical signature or, if the applicant is unable to sign on the PIN pad, by a dual attestation of the banker and the manager or branch designee; and

- To further address possible customer harm, we are contacting all customers with open, inactive credit cards to confirm whether the customer authorized the account. If the customer indicates they did not authorize the card, we will offer to close it (if it is still active) and suppress any bureau inquiry.

I will close by saying again how deeply sorry I am that we failed to live up to our expectations and yours. I also want to take this opportunity to thank our 268,000 team members who come to work every day to serve our customers. Today, I am making a personal commitment to rebuild our customers' and investors' trust, the faith of our team members, and the confidence of the American people.

SOURCE: Senate Committee on Banking, Housing and Urban Affairs. "Testimony of John Stumpf, Chairman and Chief Executive Officer of Wells Fargo & Co. Before the U.S. Senate Committee on Banking, Housing and Urban Affairs." September 20, 2016. http://www.banking.senate.gov/public/_cache/files/18312ce0-5590-4677-b1ab-981b03d1cbbb/3B18AA6E3A96E50C446E2F601B854CF1.092016-stumpf-testimony.pdf.

CFPB Director Remarks on Wells Fargo Banking Scandal

September 20, 2016

Chairman Shelby, Ranking Member Brown, and members of the Committee, thank you for the opportunity to speak with you today. In these brief remarks, I will discuss: (1) what our investigation found about the sales practices at Wells Fargo; (2) what we are seeking to achieve by our Order; and (3) some initial thoughts about what further steps need to be taken to improve the culture and practices of the banking industry.

. . . Our investigations found that, in order to meet sales goals and collect financial bonuses for themselves, employees of the bank created unauthorized deposit and credit card accounts, enrolled consumers in online banking services, and ordered debit cards for consumers, all without their consent or even their knowledge. Some of these practices involved fake email accounts and phony PIN numbers. . . .

The gravity and breadth of the fraud that occurred at Wells Fargo cannot be pushed aside as the stray misconduct of just a few bad apples. As one former federal prosecutor has aptly noted, the stunning nature and scale of these practices reflects instead the consequences of a diseased orchard. As our Order describes, Wells Fargo built and refined an incentive compensation program and implemented sales goals to boost the cross-selling of products, but did so in a way that made it possible for its employees to pursue unfair and abusive sales practices. It appears that the bank did not monitor the program carefully, allowing thousands of employees to game the system and inflate their sales figures to meet their sales targets and claim higher bonuses. Rather than put its customers first, Wells Fargo built and sustained a program where the bank and many of its employees served themselves instead, violating the basic ethics of a banking institution, including the key norm of trust.

Our Order accomplishes several things. First, the kind of detail that we always make it a point to provide in our enforcement orders exposes Wells Fargo's illegal misconduct, including its scale, for all to see for themselves. It has spawned vigorous public scrutiny over the past two weeks that no doubt will continue.

Second, the Order helps answer one question that many of you have asked me from time to time: what does the term "abusive" mean in our governing statute? Although we have been careful in analyzing all the ramifications of that new term, we did not hesitate for one minute to apply it emphatically to what we found here. In this matter, Wells Fargo engaged in abusive conduct toward its customers and consumers. . . .

Third, we have ensured that all consumers who suffered financial harm as a result of these practices will be fully compensated for that harm. Wells Fargo is required to set aside $5 million to cover all of that, and if it turns out to exceed $5 million, the bank will cover that as well.

Fourth, we levied upon Wells Fargo a fine of $100 million, the largest fine by far that the Consumer Bureau has imposed on any financial company to date. Some have said it should have been higher, others have said it should have been lower. All told, the bank will pay $185 million in fines for the illegal actions of these employees. That is a dramatic amount as compared to the actual financial harm to consumers, but it is justified here by the outrageous and abusive nature of these fraudulent practices on such an enormous scale. . . .

Fifth, the Order requires independent consultants to be installed at Wells Fargo to complete all further work on this matter, to ensure that all consumers are fully compensated, and to ensure that changes in the bank's sales practices are fully implemented to ensure that these types of misconduct do not recur. Both the top executives at Wells Fargo and its Board of Directors will be directly engaged in this work. If the independent consultants identify any further issues or concerns, we will address those as well. . . .

This action should serve notice to the entire industry. If sales targets and incentive compensation schemes are implemented in ways that threaten harm to consumers and lead to violations of the law, then banks and other financial companies will be held accountable. . . .

Thank you again to our partners here at this table who worked with us on this important enforcement action. And thank you for this opportunity to testify. I will be happy to answer your questions.

Source: Senate Committee on Banking, Housing and Urban Affairs. "Testimony of Richard Cordray, Director, Consumer Financial Protection Bureau Before the Senate Committee on Banking, Housing, and Urban Affairs." September 20, 2016. http://www.banking.senate.gov/public/_cache/files/98a8db06-fd3b-4f3d-8a43-1b2a9b5b2561/33164C216F154EF9892D0EC31E165735.092016-cordray-testimony.pdf.

OCC Comptroller Testifies on Wells Fargo Banking Scandal

September 20, 2016

[All footnotes have been omitted.]

I. Introduction

Chairman Shelby, Ranking Member Brown, and members of the Committee, thank you for the opportunity to testify today as the Committee reviews matters relating to certain sales practices at Wells Fargo Bank, N.A. (Bank or Wells Fargo). As described below, the Office of the Comptroller of the Currency (OCC) recently took public enforcement actions against Wells Fargo, finding that the Bank engaged in reckless unsafe or unsound banking practices and directing it to take comprehensive corrective action with regard to risk management of its sales practices, reimburse harmed customers, and pay $35 million in civil money penalties (CMPs). . . .

Before discussing the details of our supervisory response, I want to make clear that the unsafe and unsound sales practices at the Bank, including the opening and manipulation of fee-generating customer accounts without the customer's authorization, are completely unacceptable and have no place in the federal banking system. They reflect a lack of effective risk management, a breakdown in controls, and an inappropriate incentive structure. The actions announced on September 8, 2016, are intended to remediate and deter such practices and underscore the importance of robust risk management throughout the federal banking system.

The coordinated and complementary efforts by the OCC and the CFPB make clear to regulated institutions that compliance and safety and soundness go hand in hand.

The actions against the institution hold it accountable, and consistent with our practice in such enforcement matters, the OCC has also initiated a review of individual misconduct and culpability. The OCC may take formal enforcement actions against institution-affiliated parties, including directors, officers, and employees, who violate any law or regulation, engage in unsafe or unsound practices, or breach fiduciary duty. These actions include personal cease and desist orders and CMPs. In addition, the OCC has the authority to remove and prohibit individuals from serving as directors, officers, or employees of federally insured depository institutions if the legal standards for such action are met. Removal and prohibition amount to a lifetime ban on the culpable individual working in the banking industry.

While I believe we have made progress since the financial crisis in fostering healthier cultures at the largest institutions, meaning a commitment to compliance with applicable laws, effective risk management, good governance, and fair treatment of customers, there is clearly more work to do. Regulators and the institutions themselves must be especially vigilant when it comes to practices that can undermine the trust and confidence in financial institutions.

II. OCC SUPERVISION OF THE BANK'S SALES PRACTICES

... In March 2012, the OCC received a small number of complaints from consumers and Bank employees alleging improper sales practices at Wells Fargo, which were forwarded to OCC supervision staff assigned to the Bank, consistent with agency practice at the time. Following these inquiries and a *Los Angeles Times* article in December 2013 regarding the Bank's aggressive sales practices, the examiners initiated a series of meetings with various levels of Bank management, including executive leadership, to evaluate the Bank's activities and actions. The Bank stated that it terminated employees as a result of consumer and internal ethics complaints, and that it was investigating such reports and re-evaluating its oversight of sales practices at the Bank. During this time, the OCC examiners were also reviewing, and meeting with the Bank to discuss, the Bank's development of a corporate risk strategy, risk framework, and implementation plan that included its sales practices.

Between January 2012 and July 2016, the OCC conducted multiple supervisory activities related to Wells Fargo, which included ongoing supervision and targeted examinations through which examiners assessed the Bank's governance and risk management practices related to compliance and operational risk. These activities included assessments of compliance with the OCC's heightened standards requirements that I discuss further below, as well as other regulatory expectations for compliance risk management. These activities also included components that involved assessment of risk management related to sales practices. The supervisory conclusions associated with these activities are summarized below.

[Sections containing further information about the OCC's supervisory activities have been omitted.]

III. NEXT STEPS

While the OCC has made many improvements to our supervisory program in recent years, the actions against Wells Fargo highlight that we must continue our efforts to improve and refine the agency's supervisory program, to sharpen our early warning processes, and to enhance our supervisory capabilities, particularly with respect to our largest, most complex banks. And while the examination and investigation needed to bring comprehensive and coordinated enforcement action against Wells Fargo required deliberation and care, it is critically important that the OCC identify issues and act more quickly. To that end, I have asked the Senior Deputy Comptroller for Enterprise Governance to conduct a review of our actions taken in this matter in order to identify gaps in our supervision and assess any lessons the agency can learn from it.

At the same time, I have directed our examiners to review the sales practices of all the large and midsize banks the OCC supervises and assess the sufficiency of controls with respect to these practices.

[Section IV discussing enhancements made to the OCC's supervisory programs since April 2012 has been omitted.]

V. ADDITIONAL ACTIONS REQUIRED

It is clear from our work and the actions announced on September 8 against the Bank that the misaligned priorities and unacceptable behavior at Wells Fargo resulted in unsafe and unsound practices that led to widespread consumer harm. Issues of incentive compensation are relevant to ensuring behavior aligns with acceptable corporate practice. For those reasons, the OCC strongly supports issuing a final rule on incentive compensation that would address some of the issues I am raising today.

The OCC, along with the Federal Reserve, Federal Deposit Insurance Corporation, the Securities and Exchange Commission, the Federal Housing Finance Agency, and the National Credit Union Administration, issued a proposed rule on incentive-based compensation earlier this year that would apply to financial institutions with total consolidated assets of $1 billion or more. The proposed rule would prohibit incentive-based compensation arrangements that provide excessive compensation and that could lead to material financial loss to a financial institution. A financial institution covered by the proposed rule would not be permitted to provide an incentive-based compensation arrangement unless the arrangement appropriately balanced risk and reward, was compatible with effective risk management and controls, and was supported by effective governance.

The proposed rule also includes specific requirements for incentive-based compensation arrangements at the largest financial institutions, like Wells Fargo, with total consolidated assets of $50 billion or more. The most notable of these is the requirement that larger financial institutions defer a certain percentage (40–60 percent) of the incentive-based compensation they pay to certain senior executive officers and significant risk-takers for a minimum period of time (one to four years). Those deferred amounts would be subject to a forfeiture review by the financial institution if certain triggering events, such as a material risk management or control failure, occurred. Incentive-based compensation paid to these employees would also be subject to claw back for seven years. Additionally, the proposed rule would prohibit larger financial institutions from providing incentive-based compensation based solely on transaction volume or revenue, without regard to transaction quality or compliance with sound risk management. . . .

VI. CONCLUSION

I remain committed to ensuring the OCC completes its review of this matter and takes additional actions to hold the bank and individuals accountable as warranted. Moreover, I will work to foster continuous improvements at the OCC to fulfill our mission. I want to close by expressing my appreciation again for my colleagues at the CFPB and in the L.A. City Attorney's office. Our nation's financial services industry is complex and dynamic. Effective supervision and enforcement requires regulators to work together to achieve a safe and sound banking system that treats customers fairly. I look forward to continued collaboration with my fellow regulators.

SOURCE: Senate Committee on Banking, Housing and Urban Affairs. "Testimony of Thomas J. Curry, Comptroller of the Currency, Before the Committee on Banking, Housing, and Urban Affairs." September 20, 2016. http://www.banking.senate.gov/public/_cache/files/b536fe39-6a01-423c-b2a9-bf47e2617af9/6 A84E268645FE4120535CAE43C198DBC.092016-curry-testimony.pdf.

Los Angeles City Attorney Comments on Banking Scandal before Senate Committee

DOCUMENT

September 20, 2016

Chairman Shelby, Ranking Member Brown, esteemed members of the Committee, thank you for the opportunity to provide testimony on this critical matter.

On a Sunday morning in December, 2013, I was appalled when I opened the *Los Angeles Times* and read an investigative story by Scott Reckard regarding Wells Fargo Bank's sales culture. The story read in part, ***"To meet quotas, employees have opened unneeded accounts for customers, ordered credit cards without customers' permission and forged client signatures on paperwork. Some employees begged family members to open ghost accounts."***

I immediately instructed my staff to investigate to determine if the facts warranted our Office filing an action pursuant to California laws that protect consumers against, and provide relief for, unfair business practices.

Because these laws do not afford my Office pre-litigation subpoena power, our investigation consisted of good old-fashioned detective work. We conducted numerous interviews with former Wells Fargo employees and Wells Fargo consumers, pored over public records, including voluminous court records from wrongful termination lawsuits former employees filed against Wells Fargo, and made use of the consumer complaint databases of the Consumer Financial Protection Bureau and the Federal Trade Commission.

We found that the Bank victimized consumers by opening customer accounts, and issuing credit cards and other products, without authorization. Further, we found that the Bank failed to notify customers that these accounts had been opened without their consent and failed to refund fees incurred by those customers for these unwanted products and services. We found instances in which the Bank made it difficult, if not impossible, for customers to receive accurate and clear information as to how this happened. Many were told that the unauthorized accounts would be closed, only to find later that they were not.

We found that Wells Fargo's business model imposed unrealistic sales quotas that, among other things, incentivized employees to engage in highly aggressive sales practices, creating the conditions for unlawful activity, including opening fee-generating customer accounts, and adding unwanted secondary accounts and products, without customer permission.

Underlying all of this egregious conduct, we found a fundamental breach of trust by the Bank through its misuse of consumers' personal information. We sought to enforce the Bank's obligation to inform its customers that their personal and private information had been accessed by Wells Fargo in order to open unauthorized accounts.

Our 16-month investigation culminated in our May 4, 2015, filing of a civil enforcement action in the name of the People of the State of California, an action that both sought relief for consumers harmed by Wells Fargo's conduct and to end the illegal practices Wells Fargo employed. . . .

Earlier this month, we reached a settlement with Wells Fargo, which, in concert with the settlements reached by the federal regulatory agencies, provides for comprehensive retrospective and prospective remediation and corrective actions, and sends a strong message by imposing a $50 million penalty. Our agreement contains important protections for consumers. It establishes a complaint and mediation system for California consumers harmed by the Bank's practices, and requires Wells Fargo to continue a restitution program for affected customers. Wells Fargo must also alert all its California customers who have consumer or small business checking or savings accounts, credit cards, or unsecured lines of credit, that they should visit their local bank, or call Wells Fargo, to review their accounts, close accounts or discontinue services they do not recognize or want, and resolve any remaining problems. Additionally, every six months for the next two years, Wells Fargo must provide my Office an audit report assessing the Bank's compliance with our agreement, verified under penalty of perjury by an officer or director of the Bank. . . .

There is a sacred trust that consumers put in their financial institutions—a faith that their hard-earned money will be safe and secure, and that their banks' actions will be in the best interests of customers like themselves. Wells Fargo broke that trust. We should all work to assure it never happens again.

SOURCE: Senate Committee on Banking, Housing and Urban Affairs. "Testimony to the U.S. Senate Committee on Banking, Housing and Urban Affairs by the Honorable Michael N. Feuer, Los Angeles City Attorney." September 20, 2016. http://www.banking.senate.gov/public/_cache/files/e5c17a33-d8b0-4e07-8913-a7aaa1ea334c/506BE968E3DBC0673D2DB0B731F45E61.092016-feuer-testimony.pdf.

OTHER HISTORIC DOCUMENTS OF INTEREST

FROM PREVIOUS *HISTORIC DOCUMENTS*

OPEC Takes Action to
Stabilize Oil Prices

SEPTEMBER 28 AND DECEMBER 10, 2016,
AND JANUARY 1, 2017

Throughout the fall of 2016, the Organization of the Petroleum Exporting Countries (OPEC) members, who together account for 40 percent of the global oil supply, negotiated a set of agreements intended to stabilize the price of crude oil and help member states recoup some of the billions of dollars they lost during the prior two years when output rose as demand fell sharply. The move was hailed as a major breakthrough in relations between Saudi Arabia and Iran, the latter of which was allowed to raise its output to account for the economic hit it took from sanctions imposed by the European Union over its nuclear program. The decision was coupled with an agreement from non-OPEC members, most notably Russia, to reduce its output to further increase crude oil prices. Questions remain regarding whether the nations party to the agreement will follow through on their promises to cut production, because similar efforts in the past have resulted in failure to comply.

OPEC Officials Agree to Cut Production

Negotiations to decrease oil production began during a June 2016 OPEC ministers' meeting that sought to find methods to stabilize the oil market. The meeting ended without conclusion because Saudi Arabia, one of the world's largest oil producers, refused to reduce production unless all other nations agreed to do the same. Because of decreasing demand for oil and falling prices, oil revenue in Saudi Arabia has been halved during the past two years. Saudi Arabia depends on its billions of dollars in oil revenue to prop up its economy and had already implemented a number of cost-saving measures in its own country to make up for the budget shortfall it was facing—estimated at $98 billion in 2015. Such measures included curtailing oil and energy subsidies for citizens and the announcement of cuts to public employee salaries. Analysts argued, however, that reduction from Saudi Arabia would likely improve its economic outlook. "This is a case where lower volume from Saudi Arabia will mean higher revenues if prices go up," said Yasser Elguindi, a director at oil consultancy firm Medley Global Advisors.

Discussions about a possible decrease in production continued in September during an unofficial meeting of OPEC members on the sidelines of the International Energy Forum in Algeria. At the time of the impromptu meeting, oil prices had fallen from a height of more than $100 per barrel in mid-2014 to $47 per barrel. In announcing the September meeting, OPEC said that it had been consistently monitoring oil prices worldwide and had been "in constant deliberations with all member states on ways and means to help restore stability and order to the oil market." Furthermore, OPEC argued, the falling prices were temporary, and it noted, "These are more of an outcome resulting from weaker refinery margins, inventory overhang—particularly of product stocks, timing of Brexit, and its impact on the financial futures markets, including that of crude oil."

Reaching an agreement during the September meeting to move OPEC from the "pump at will" stance it had adopted in 2014 would again rely on whether Saudi Arabia could be convinced to reduce its output of 10.7 million barrels per day. Again, Saudi Arabia proposed that it would consider a reduction only if all OPEC and non-OPEC members would do the same. Iran was the primary detractor to such an agreement because it has been hurt economically by sanctions implemented by the European Union (EU) in response to its nuclear program. During negotiations, Iran argued that it should be allowed an exemption from reducing its output while it continues to recover from the lifting of EU sanctions in 2015. Iran's oil production had been stagnant, averaging 3.6 million barrels per day, since the enacting of the sanctions.

After lengthy negotiations, Saudi Arabia relented and agreed to reduce its production by 350,000 barrels per day, while allowing Iran a nominal increase in its production. It was also decided that Nigeria and Libya would not be required to cut back production due to recent oil refinery damage caused by terrorist activities. Under the preliminary deal, which would require final approval at a November 30 all-member meeting, supply from OPEC members would be reduced to somewhere in the range of 32.5 million to 33 million barrels per day, down from 33.4 million barrels per day. The decision effectively reestablished the production ceiling that had been eliminated by OPEC under pressure from member states in 2015. This was the first time in eight years that OPEC member states reached an agreement on cutting production. "OPEC made an exceptional decision today," said Iranian oil minister Bijan Zanganeh. "After two and a half years, OPEC reached consensus to manage the market."

Upon news of the agreement, oil prices surged 5 percent. In addition to requiring final approval at an OPEC ministers' meeting on November 30, finalizing the agreement also rested on encouraging non-OPEC nations to cut their output. A meeting with non-OPEC members was expected to be held on November 28, and analysts believed reaching an agreement would largely rest on the willingness of Russia, which pumped 11.1 million barrels per day in September, up from 400,000 in August, consenting to a large reduction in output.

NOVEMBER MEETING FORMALIZES CUTS

Ahead of the November 30 meeting to formalize the reduction plan, the preliminary agreement looked poised to fall apart. Saudi Arabia declined to attend the November 28 meeting with non-OPEC states, arguing that such a meeting would be pointless until a final decision was reached about reduction in production by OPEC members on November 30. The decision caused the price of oil to fall 4 percent, and the November 28 meeting was canceled and moved to early December. Shortly afterward, Saudi Arabia pulled out of the non-OPEC meeting, Algeria's oil minister traveled to Iran to present its oil minister with a new proposal that would include a 1.1 million barrel per day reduction among OPEC members, coupled with a 600,000-barrel reduction for non-OPEC members. The proposal indicated that OPEC members were not yet prepared simply to agree to the September conditions and that they might instead spend their November 30 meeting rehashing out the details of reduction. The move was seen as an attempt by Saudi Arabia to subvert the earlier efforts and encourage Iran to agree to freeze its production. Saudi oil minister

Khalid al-Falih stated shortly after the meeting between Algeria and Iran that it would make no further concessions, based on a belief that the oil market would eventually stabilize without reductions from Saudi Arabia. "We expect the level of demand to be encouraging in 2017, and the market will reach balance in 2017 even if there is no intervention by OPEC," Falih said.

Given the tension heading into the November 30 meeting, analysts predicted that either no agreement would be reached or the ongoing refusal of Saudi Arabia to cut production could be OPEC's downfall. Ultimately, when OPEC members met on November 30, they agreed to collectively reduce production by 1.2 million barrels per day, if non-OPEC countries would cut their production by 600,000 barrels per day. Combined, this would mark a 2 percent reduction in global oil supply. In what became known as the Vienna Agreement, Saudi Arabia would contribute the greatest reduction, cutting 4.6 percent (approximately 486,000 barrels per day) from production, and Iran was able to maintain its nominal increase. Upon the announcement of the deal, oil prices soared to more than $50 per barrel. After the deal was finalized, Falih said that Saudi Arabia had come to the table prepared to accept a "big hit." He added, "I think it is a good day for the oil markets, it is a good day for the industry and . . . it should be a good day for the global economy. I think it will boost global economic growth."

Indonesia, OPEC's only east-Asian member, decided to leave the organization after refusing to abide by the deal. "The meeting . . . requested for Indonesia to cut around 5 percent of its production, or around 37,000 barrels per day," read a statement from the nation's Energy and Mineral Resources Ministry. "As a net oil importing country, a cut to production capacity would not benefit Indonesia." The nation had been an OPEC member from 1962 until 2009, at which point it became a net importer of crude oil and no longer qualified for full OPEC membership. It had only rejoined OPEC earlier in 2016, as the group's only net crude importer.

Non-OPEC Countries Agree to Reductions

On December 10, leaders from OPEC and non-OPEC nations met to review the terms of the Vienna Agreement. The non-OPEC states agreed to cut production by 558,000 barrels per day, just shy of the 600,000 requested by OPEC. Russia would be responsible for 300,000 barrels per day of that reduction, on the condition that its decrease in production could be gradual and fully in place within six months. This was the first time OPEC and non-OPEC members reached an agreement to limit output since 2001, and marked a turning point in the relationship between Saudi Arabia and Russia, which had only recently restarted negotiations over their oil programs for the first time in fifteen years. According to Falih, the December agreement "cements and prepares us for long-term cooperation."

Production cuts are set to begin on January 1, 2017, and will remain in effect for six months. In late May, OPEC planned to hold another meeting to determine whether the cuts are having their desired impact, and at that point can exercise an option to extend the plan for another six months. The reduction will be monitored based on the number of oil tankers leaving port in member nations. Tracking Russia's oil output will be markedly more difficult because much of its oil is transported by pipeline. A question remains regarding whether Russia will follow through on its agreement because it has failed to cut production in the past and whether other non-OPEC members will consider falling global oil consumption to be their contribution to the agreement rather than an actual reduction in output. Despite the reduction agreement, analysts predict that the oil market will continue to be oversupplied at least until 2018.

—Heather Kerrigan

Following is a press release from the Organization of the Petroleum Exporting Countries (OPEC) on September 28, 2016, summarizing the 17th (Extraordinary) meeting of OPEC members; a speech delivered by the president of OPEC, also on September 28, 2016, about uncertainty in the oil market; a December 10, 2016, OPEC press release on the agreement reached between OPEC and non-OPEC countries to cut oil production; and a copy of the agreement reached by OPEC members and taking effect on January 1, 2017.

DOCUMENT *OPEC Convenes Extraordinary Session*

September 28, 2016

The Conference of the Organization of the Petroleum Exporting Countries (OPEC), following a Consultative Meeting in Algiers, Algeria, resolved to convene an Extraordinary Meeting of the Conference on Wednesday, 28th September 2016 under the Chairmanship of its President, HE Dr. Mohammed Bin Saleh Al-Sada, Qatar's Minister of Energy and Industry and Head of its Delegation.

The Conference expressed its respect and deep appreciation to the President of Algeria, HE Abdelaziz Bouteflika, and to the Prime Minister, HE Abdelmalek Sellal, for hosting the 170th (Extraordinary) Meeting of the OPEC Conference. The Conference, furthermore, acknowledged and thanked HE Noureddine Boutarfa, Algeria's Minister of Energy, for his untiring efforts and support for the ongoing consultations between all parties involved in the preparations for these meetings. At the same time, the Conference also congratulated HE Noureddine Boutarfa, who was attending a Meeting of OPEC Ministers for the first time since his appointment as Algeria's Head of Delegation, and thanked his predecessor in office HE Dr. Salah Khebri, for his contribution to the work of the Organization.

The Conference warmly welcomed Gabon that was attending a Meeting of OPEC Ministers for the first time since officially rejoining the Organization in July, and HE Jabbar Ali Hussein Al-Luiebi, who was also attending a Meeting of the Conference for the first time since his appointment as Iraq's Minister of Oil and Head of its Delegation.

In the last two years, the global oil market has witnessed many challenges, originating mainly from the supply side. As a result, prices have more than halved, while volatility has increased. Oil-exporting countries' and oil companies' revenues have dramatically declined, putting strains on their fiscal position and hindering their economic growth. The oil industry faced deep cuts in investment and massive layoffs, leading to a potential risk that oil supply may not meet demand in the future, with a detrimental effect on security of supply.

The Conference took into account current market conditions and immediate prospects and concluded that it is not advisable to ignore the potential risk that the present stock overhang may continue to weigh negatively well into the future, with a worsening impact on producers, consumers and the industry.

Based on the above observations and analysis, OPEC Member Countries have decided to conduct a serious and constructive dialogue with non-member producing countries, with the objective to stabilize the oil market and avoid the adverse impacts in the short- and medium-term.

The Conference concurs that there is firm and common ground that continuous collaborative efforts among producers, both within and outside OPEC, would help restore the balance and sustainability in the market.

At this juncture, it is foremost to reaffirm OPEC's continued commitment to stable markets, for the mutual interests of producing nations, efficient and secure supplies to the consumers, with a fair return on invested capital for all producers.

The Conference, following the overall assessment of the global oil demand and supply balance presented by the OPEC Secretariat, noted that world oil demand remains robust, while the prospects of future supplies are being negatively impacted by deep cuts in investments and massive layoffs. The Conference, in particular, addressed the challenge of drawing down the excess stock levels in the coming quarters, and noted the drop in United States oil inventories seen in recent weeks.

The Conference opted for an OPEC-14 production target ranging between 32.5 and 33.0 mb/d, in order to accelerate the ongoing drawdown of the stock overhang and bring the rebalancing forward.

The Conference decided to establish a High Level Committee comprising representatives of Member Countries, supported by the OPEC Secretariat, to study and recommend the implementation of the production level of the Member Countries. Furthermore, the Committee shall develop a framework of high-level consultations between OPEC and non-OPEC oil-producing countries, including identifying risks and taking pro-active measures that would ensure a balanced oil market on a sustainable basis, to be considered at the November OPEC Conference.

Finally, the Conference again expressed its deepest appreciation to the Government and to the people of Algeria, and to the authorities of the City of Algiers for their warm hospitality and the excellent arrangements made for the Meeting.

SOURCE: Organization of the Petroleum Exporting Countries. "170th (Extraordinary) Meeting of the OPEC Conference." September 28, 2016. http://www.opec.org/opec_web/en/press_room/3706.htm.

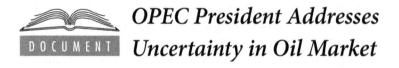

OPEC President Addresses Uncertainty in Oil Market

September 28, 2016

Excellencies,
Good afternoon.

I would like to begin by thanking the Algerian Government and His Excellency Noureddine Boutarfa, Algeria's Minister of Energy, for organizing today's meeting and the

Ministerial of the International Energy Forum. The facilities, the organization, the hospitality, have all been world class.

I feel it is also appropriate to personally welcome His Excellency Noureddine Boutarfa who is attending a meeting of OPEC Ministers for the first time. Your Excellency, in the short period you have been Minister of Energy, you have certainly hit the ground running. Your prominent role in the shuttle diplomacy that has taken place over the last few weeks has been extremely welcome. You have made an enormous contribution in working to make this meeting a success.

I had the privilege of hosting His Excellency Noureddine Boutarfa, as well as His Excellency Mohammad Sanusi Barkindo, OPEC Secretary General, in Doha earlier this month. The meetings we had were extremely open and productive as we discussed the outlook for the oil market, and considered ways that oil producers might respond to the ongoing and future challenges facing the industry.

As OPEC Conference President, I would also like to offer a warm welcome to His Excellency Etienne Dieudonné Ngoubou, Gabon's Minister of Petroleum and Hydrocarbons, and His Excellency Jabbar Ali Hussein Al-Luiebi, Iraq's Minister of Oil, who are attending a meeting of OPEC Ministers for the first time.

Excellencies,

I know everyone here has played an active role in the discussions leading up to this meeting. I would like to thank you all. The efforts to build a consensus have been exemplary, and I very much hope that the constructive, accommodating and encouraging nature of our recent talks carries on today.

I cannot emphasize enough how important it is for us, our Member Countries, OPEC as an Organization, and the oil market, to leave this meeting with a plausible and convincing message. One that shows that OPEC fully understands the current market situation, and is making every effort to deliver the 'sustainable market stability' we all desire.

In this regard, I feel it is important to recall that throughout OPEC's history the Organization has faced numerous challenges. It has been able to overcome these through cooperation and compromise. Through my talks with you all, I feel that there is the same commitment to ensure that we find solutions to come through the current challenges we all face.

Excellencies,

The last time we all met together was at the OPEC Ministerial Conference in Vienna back in June this year.

On 2nd June when we convened, the OPEC Reference Basket stood at just over $45 a barrel. In the period since it has gone both above and below this level. However, thus far in September it has been below $45 a barrel, and today stands in the low 40s. In the meantime, volatility and speculation have remained prevalent in the market.

With regard to global economic growth, the story was somewhat inconsistent and changeable back in June and it remains so today. Our global growth estimate for 2016 has fallen from 3.1 per cent in June to 2.9 per cent today, although for 2017, this is expected to increase to 3.1 per cent.

On the supply side, in June it was anticipated that non-OPEC supply would decline by 740,000 barrels a day in 2016. In the interim, the expected decline has lessened to a contraction of 600,000 barrels a day. Moreover, we also now anticipate non-OPEC supply to grow by 200,000 barrels a day in 2017, against a decline of 100,000 barrels a day when this estimate was first announced in July.

For demand, there has been little change. It remains robust. Global demand is currently anticipated to expand by 1.2 million barrels a day this year, the same level as expected in June. We estimate a similar level of demand growth in 2017.

And from the perspective of stocks, OECD and non-OECD inventories are still very high. In fact, OECD commercial oil stocks are currently little different to the numbers we saw presented in June, at around 340 million barrels above their five-year average.

What this underscores is that there are many uncertainties and the pace of the market readjustment is taking longer than expected. Back in June, the prospects suggested that the market would rebalance by the end of this year or in the first half of 2017. However, there are now serious questions being asked regarding this timeframe, with many agencies and analysts pushing the rebalancing further into the future.

Excellencies,

The market has changed since June and our expectations about the rebalancing process have shifted. It is evident that there is now a greater degree of urgency about ensuring the market returns to balance as quickly as possible.

The last few weeks have seen much talk about how this could be best achieved. I believe there is a common understanding that we need to look at market stabilization measures aimed at reducing the length of the downturn and lessening volatility.

We just need to find an understanding on what measures we can take at this meeting to make it a success, and which will then hopefully lead to a future agreement.

Thank you for your attention.

SOURCE: Organization of the Petroleum Exporting Countries. "Speech by OPEC Conference President." September 28, 2016. www.opec.org/opec_web/en/press_room/3703.htm.

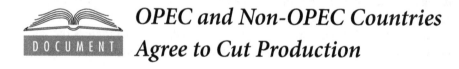

OPEC and Non-OPEC Countries
Agree to Cut Production

December 10, 2016

Following the 'Vienna Agreement' decided upon at the 171st Meeting of the Conference of the Organization of the Petroleum Exporting Countries (OPEC) on 30th November, 2016, Ministers from OPEC met with a number of Ministers from non-OPEC oil producing countries on Saturday, 10th December, at the OPEC Secretariat in Vienna.

The Meeting was jointly chaired by His Excellency Dr. Mohammed Bin Saleh Al-Sada, President of the OPEC Conference and Minister of Energy and Industry of the State of Qatar and His Excellency Alexander Novak, Minister of Energy of the Russian Federation.

The Meeting recalled the rights of peoples and nations to permanent sovereignty over their natural wealth and resources.

The Meeting took into account current oil market conditions and short- to medium-term prospects and recognized the need for joint cooperation of the oil exporting countries, to achieve a lasting stability in the oil market in the interest of oil producers and consumers.

The Meeting noted that OPEC Member Countries met on 30th November 2016 and decided to implement a production adjustment of 1.2 million barrels a day (mb/d), effective from 1st January 2017. The Meeting recorded that OPEC Member Countries, in agreeing to this decision, confirmed their commitment to a stable and balanced oil market and underscored the importance of other oil producing countries joining their efforts.

The Meeting recognized the desire of Azerbaijan, Kingdom of Bahrain, Brunei Darussalam, Equatorial Guinea, Kazakhstan, Malaysia, Mexico, Sultanate of Oman, the Russian Federation, Republic of Sudan, and Republic of South Sudan, as well as other non-OPEC producers, to achieve oil market stability in the interest of all oil producers and consumers. In this regard, the aforementioned countries proposed to adjust their oil production, voluntarily or through managed decline, starting from 1st January 2017 for six (6) months, extendable for another six (6) months, to take into account prevailing market conditions and prospects.

The aforementioned countries and OPEC, convinced of the necessity to jointly cooperate to help stabilize the oil market, reached the following.

- OPEC maintains its decision made on 30th November 2016, whereby arrangements were recorded following the extensive understanding of OPEC's adjustment;

- Azerbaijan, Kingdom of Bahrain, Brunei Darussalam, Equatorial Guinea, Kazakhstan, Malaysia, Mexico, Sultanate of Oman, the Russian Federation, Republic of Sudan, and Republic of South Sudan commit to reduce their respective oil production, voluntarily or through managed decline, in accordance with an accelerated schedule. The combined reduction target was agreed at 558,000 barrels a day for the aforementioned producers;

- That two participating non-OPEC countries shall join the OPEC Ministerial Monitoring Committee, consisting of oil ministers, chaired by Kuwait with the Russian Federation as alternate chair and assisted by the OPEC Secretariat;

- To strengthen their cooperation, including through joint analyses and outlooks, with a view to ensuring a sustainable oil market, for the benefit of producers and consumers; and

- To regularly review at the technical and ministerial levels the status of their cooperation.

Finally, the Meeting expressed its gratitude to the Government and to the people of the Republic of Austria, as well as the authorities of the City of Vienna for their warm hospitality and excellent arrangements made for the Meeting.

SOURCE: Organization of the Petroleum Exporting Countries. "OPEC and non-OPEC Ministerial Meeting." December 10, 2016. http://www.opec.org/opec_web/en/press_room/3944.htm.

OPEC Agreement to Reduce Oil Production

DOCUMENT

January 1, 2017

The global oil market has witnessed a serious challenge of imbalance and volatility pressured mainly from the supply side. It has led to significant investment cuts in the oil industry, which has a direct impact on offsetting the natural depletion of reservoirs and in ensuring security of supply to producers.

Current market conditions are counterproductive and damaging to both producers and consumers, it is neither sustainable nor conducive in the medium- to long-term. It threatens the economies of producing nations, hinders critical industry investments, jeopardizes energy security to meet growing world energy demand, and challenges oil market stability as a whole.

There is a firm and common ground that continuous collaborative efforts among producers, both within and outside OPEC, would complement the market in restoring a global oil demand and supply balance, in particular the drawdown in the stocks overhang, which is currently at a very high level.

At this conjuncture, it is foremost to reaffirm OPEC's continued commitment to stable markets, mutual interests of producing nations, the efficient, economic and secure supply to consumers, and a fair return on invested capital.

Consequently, the recovery of oil market balance could be addressed through dialogue and cooperation among producing countries as a way forward for cohesive, credible, and effective action and implementation. Hence, it is under the principles of good faith that countries participating in today's meeting agree to commit themselves to the following actions:

1. In the fulfilment of the implementation of the Algiers Accord, 171st Ministerial Conference has decided to reduce its production by around 1.2 mb/d to bring its ceiling to 32.5 mb/d, effective 1st of January 2017;

2. The duration of this agreement is six months, extendable for another six months to take into account prevailing market conditions and prospects;

3. To recognize that this Agreement should be without prejudice to future agreements;

4. To establish a Ministerial Monitoring Committee composed of Algeria, Kuwait, Venezuela, and two participating non-OPEC countries, chaired by Kuwait and assisted by the OPEC Secretariat, to closely monitor the implementation of and compliance with this Agreement and report to the Conference;

5. This agreement has been reached following extensive consultations and understanding reached with key non-OPEC countries, including the Russian Federation that they contribute by a reduction of 600 tb/d production.

In testimony of the above-stated the undersigned, authorized by their governments, have signed this Agreement.

SOURCE: Organization of the Petroleum Exporting Countries. "Agreement." January 1, 2017. http://www
.opec.org/opec_web/static_files_project/media/downloads/press_room/OPEC%20agreement.pdf.

OTHER HISTORIC DOCUMENTS OF INTEREST

FROM THIS VOLUME

■ Circuit Court Rules on Construction of the Dakota Access Pipeline, p. 429

FROM PREVIOUS *HISTORIC DOCUMENTS*

■ OPEC Fails to Respond to Falling Oil Prices, *2014*, p. 571

October

Kaine and Pence Engage in Vice Presidential Debate

OCTOBER 4, 2016

On October 4, 2016, Virginia Senator Tim Kaine and Indiana Governor Mike Pence—the Democratic and Republican vice presidential candidates, respectively—took the stage at Longwood University in Farmville, Virginia, in the first and only vice presidential debate of the 2016 campaign. CBS News correspondent Elaine Quijano moderated the debate, which consisted of coverage of both domestic and foreign policy issues. The candidates approached the debate with contrasting strategies. Kaine aggressively pressed Pence to defend controversial statements made by his running mate, Donald Trump, while Pence remained relatively calm, repeatedly sidestepping questions and instead attacking Democratic presidential nominee Hillary Clinton's judgment and President Barack Obama's domestic and foreign policy decisions. The debate underscored the differences between the two tickets, because Pence and Kaine found common ground on few topics, and both sides sought to capitalize on the other's mistakes.

GROUND RULES AND OPENING QUESTIONS

The vice presidential debate pitted Kaine, a popular former governor from a contested swing-state, against Pence, the conservative Indiana governor known for promoting "compassionate conservatism." The two nominees had never shared a stage before, going toe-to-toe at the most high-profile moment of their political careers. The debate lasted ninety minutes and featured nine different segments covering domestic and foreign policy issues. Each segment began with a question posed to both candidates, who each had two minutes to answer. Quijano also inserted follow-up questions to facilitate discussion.

While the debate offered each nominee an opportunity to showcase why they are prepared for the second highest office in the country, both largely focused on representing the top of their ticket instead of themselves (as is common in vice presidential debates). Pence, according to many commentators, needed to defend Donald Trump and his often-controversial comments, while at the same time introducing himself nationally as an even-keeled, reasonable statesman and true conservative. For Kaine, the challenge was to parry tough questions about Clinton's trustworthiness, promote her economic and social agenda, and offer a thorough case against Trump.

A coin flip backstage awarded Kaine with the first answer to the opening question, which focused on the possibility that either candidate may have to serve as president if something happened to his running mate. Kaine touched on his personal and professional experience, drawing on his time as a missionary, a city councilman and mayor, and governor and senator of Virginia, while keeping the focus on Clinton's historic nomination. "My primary role is to be Hillary Clinton's right-hand person and strong supporter as she puts together the most historic administration possible. And I relish that role," he said. In a hint of how the rest of the conversation would unfold, Kaine ended his response by attacking Trump. Noting that he and his wife were the proud parents of a Marine, Kaine remarked that "the thought of Donald Trump as commander-in-chief scares us to death."

Pence similarly touted his upbringing, highlighting his childhood in rural Indiana and his lifelong dream to represent his community in Congress. He also sought to contrast himself and his running mate to the current Democratic administration by positioning Trump as a needed change from the policies of the previous eight years. "We've seen an economy stifled by more taxes, more regulation, a war on coal, and a failing health care reform come to be known as Obamacare, and the American people know that we need to make a change," Pence said.

Contrasting Strategies Shine Throughout

Following the opening salvo, both candidates settled into their respective debate strategies. Kaine forcefully and aggressively pressed Pence to defend controversial statements made by his running mate, directly quoting Trump at times to brand him as an unacceptable choice for president. Pence sidestepped questions and critiques of Trump to attack Clinton's judgment and the previous administration, strategically positioning the Republican ticket as a stark change from the previous eight years.

These respective strategies became apparent after Quijano's second question, one about the trustworthiness and temperament of their running mates. Kaine offered a brief defense of Clinton but pivoted to attack Trump for building his business career, "in the words of one of his own campaign staffers, 'off the backs of the little guy.'" Kaine continued to press this line of attack throughout the debate. Faced with a similar question about Trump's temperament, Pence launched into a critique of the Obama presidency and Clinton's time as secretary of state. "In the wake of Hillary Clinton's tenure as secretary of state, where she was the architect of the Obama administration's foreign policy, we see entire portions of the world, particularly the wider Middle East, literally spinning out of control," Pence argued.

As Pence continued to respond, arguing that Clinton emboldened Russia, Kaine interrupted him with a jab about earlier comments from the Republican ticket praising Russia. "You guys love Russia," Kaine interjected. "You both have said Vladimir Putin is a better leader than the president." The interruption seemingly took Pence aback, as he remarked, "I must have hit a nerve here." Pence continued, refusing to address Kaine's critique or defend Trump's quotes as they were used against him. This exchange exemplified the overall tone of the debate, which saw Kaine forcefully and aggressively interrupt Pence while Pence offered pointed attacks on Clinton and the Obama administration.

Throughout much of the debate, policy specifics took a backseat to personal critiques of both presidential nominees' character and controversies surrounding their candidacies. Kaine prodded at Trump's temperament, judgment, and his refusal to release his tax returns, while Pence hammered Clinton's e-mail controversy and corruption allegations. In a revealing exchange, Kaine recalled Trump's controversial remarks about women, African Americans, Latinos, and Sen. John McCain, R-Ariz., to "talk about the tone that's set from the top." Pence pushed back, arguing that those statements were "small potatoes" when compared to Clinton's remark that half of Mr. Trump's supporters were a "basket of deplorables."

In another exchange, both men attacked each other over their candidates' respective foundations, using each as evidence of corruption and character flaws. Pence first raised the subject by saying that Clinton had engaged in "pay-to-play politics" as secretary of state, citing potential conflicts of interest with the Clinton Foundation. Kaine offered a brief defense that quickly gave way to a broadside attack on Trump, his organization, and his own charity. "The Clinton Foundation is one of the highest-rated charities in the world," Kaine said, before claiming that the Trump Foundation is "putting money into Donald Trump's pockets and into the pockets of his children."

In critiquing his opponent, each vice presidential nominee appeared to reflect their running mate's rhetorical style. Kaine appeared to rely on prepared quips, mirroring Clinton's more cautious approach to speaking on the campaign trail. For example, Kaine sought to brand Pence as Trump's "apprentice," a nod to Trump's reality television show, before asking debate watchers, "Do you want a you're hired President with Hillary Clinton or do you want a you're fired President with Donald Trump?" Pence, on the other hand, seemed less rehearsed, and attacked the Clinton–Kaine ticket for overly scripted lines. After Kaine declared that Trump "can't start a Twitter war with Miss Universe without shooting himself in the foot," Pence suggested that Kaine rehearsed his attack, asking, "Did you work on that one a long time?" before pivoting to an attack on Obama.

At other times, each candidate seemed to borrow the opposing presidential candidate's rhetoric and style. While Trump's inflammatory language was his defining characteristic on the campaign stump, it was Kaine who took a more aggressive tone during the debate, often interrupting and talking over Pence. Similarly, Pence offered a much more measured tone, using a calm demeanor and cordial language to sidestep attacks in a manner reminiscent of Clinton's point-by-point critiques of the Republican ticket and inclusion of robust policy specifics in her campaign speeches. In discussing Syria, for example, Pence offered in moral terms his support for "safe zones" for civilians, an idea backed by Clinton. "But about Aleppo and about Syria, I truly do believe that what America ought to do right now is immediately establish safe zones, so that families and vulnerable families with children can move out of those areas, work with our Arab partners, real time, right now, to make that happen," Pence said, a statement more in line with Clinton than Trump.

RUSSIA AS A FOCAL POINT

Questions around the United States' relationship with Russia were raised early on and at the end of the debate. Pence repeatedly questioned the Obama administration's foreign policy decisions, especially during Clinton's tenure as secretary of state. "The truth of the matter is, the weak and feckless foreign policy of Hillary Clinton and Barack Obama has awakened an aggression in Russia that first appeared a few years ago with their move in Georgia, now their move into Crimea, now their move into the wider Middle East," Pence argued.

Kaine leveraged each mention of Russia to interject questions about the Trump campaign's "shadowy connections with pro-Putin forces," which had long dogged the ticket on the campaign trail. Among the connections were Trump's business ties to Russian banks, his campaign manager's lobbying work for a pro-Russia Ukrainian politician, and Trump's controversial praise for Russian President Vladimir Putin. Kaine also sought to draw a contrast between "dictatorship and leadership," stating that "Vladimir Putin has run his economy into the ground," and adding, "He persecutes LGBT folks and journalists."

Pence denied that Trump had made the statements Kaine quoted and suggested the Virginia senator was simply trying to insult his running mate. "I'm just trying to keep up with the insult-driven campaign on the other side of the table," Pence retorted.

Kaine in turn responded by saying, "Six times tonight I have said to Governor Pence I can't imagine how you can defend your running mate's position," adding that "he is asking everybody to vote for somebody that he cannot defend."

Post-Debate Spin

Following the debate, both sides claimed victory. The Clinton–Kaine campaign tried to shape the post-debate discussion by releasing a video pitting Pence's repeated denial of Trump's most controversial comments against video of Trump making those comments. Republicans saw Pence's calmer, more collected defense of compassionate conservatism as a "strategic reset" of the campaign, following weeks of controversy and stumbles. With just over one month before the election, the debate did little to change the contours of the contentious election but reassured both sides and their supporters that their nominees were up to the second-highest job in the country.

—Robert Howard

Following is a condensed transcript of the vice presidential debate between Virginia Senator Tim Kaine and Indiana Governor Mike Pence on October 4, 2016.

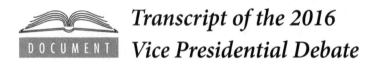

Transcript of the 2016 Vice Presidential Debate

October 4, 2016

[Due to its length, the transcript of the second presidential debate has been excerpted to focus on examples of the candidates' rhetorical and stylistic differences during the debate, as discussed in the headnote.]

... QUIJANO: Senator Kaine, on the campaign trail, you praised Secretary Clinton's character, including her commitment to public service, yet 60 percent of voters don't think she's trustworthy. Why do so many people distrust her? Is it because they have questions about her e-mails and the Clinton Foundation?

KAINE: Elaine, let me tell you why I trust Hillary Clinton. Here's what people should look at as they look at a public servant. Do they have a passion in their life that showed up before they were in public life? And have they held onto that passion throughout their life, regardless of whether they were in office or not, succeeding or failing?

Hillary Clinton has that passion. From a time as a kid in a Methodist youth group in the suburbs of Chicago, she has been focused on serving others with a special focus on empowering families and kids. As a civil rights lawyer in the South, with the Children's Defense Fund, first lady of Arkansas and this country, senator, secretary of state, it's always been about putting others first. And that's a sharp contrast with Donald Trump.

Donald Trump always puts himself first. He built a business career, in the words of one of his own campaign staffers, "off the backs of the little guy." And as a candidate, he started his campaign with a speech where he called Mexicans rapists and criminals, and he has pursued the discredited and really outrageous lie that President Obama wasn't born in the United States.

It is so painful to suggest that we go back to think about these days where an African-American could not be a citizen of the United States. And I can't imagine how Governor Pence can defend the insult-driven selfish "me first" style of Donald Trump.

QUIJANO: Governor Pence, let me ask you, you have said Donald Trump is, quote, "thoughtful, compassionate, and steady." Yet 67 percent of voters feel he is a risky choice, and 65 percent feel he does not have the right kind of temperament to be president. Why do so many Americans think Mr. Trump is simply too erratic?

PENCE: Well, let me—let me say first and foremost that, Senator, you and Hillary Clinton would know a lot about an insult-driven campaign. It really is remarkable. At a time when literally, in the wake of Hillary Clinton's tenure as secretary of state, where she was the architect of the Obama administration's foreign policy, we see entire portions of the world, particularly the wider Middle East, literally spinning out of control. I mean, the situation we're watching hour by hour in Syria today is the result of the failed foreign policy and the weak foreign policy that Hillary Clinton helped lead in this administration and create. The newly emboldened—the aggression of Russia, whether it was in Ukraine or now they're heavy-handed approach . . .

KAINE: You guys love Russia. You both have said . . .

PENCE: . . . their heavy-handed approach.

KAINE: You both have said—you both have said Vladimir Putin is a better leader than the president.

PENCE: Well . . . [crosstalk]

QUIJANO: Well, we're going to get to Russia in just a moment. But I do want to get back to the question at . . .

PENCE: But in the midst—Elaine, thank you. Thank you. Thank you, Senator, I'll . . .

KAINE: These guys have praised Vladimir Putin as a great leader. How can that . . . [crosstalk]

QUIJANO: Yes, and we will get to that, Senator. We do have that coming up here. But in the meantime, the questions . . .

PENCE: Well, Senator, I must have hit a . . . *[crosstalk]* . . . I must have hit a nerve here.

QUIJANO: Why the disconnect?

PENCE: Because at a time of great challenge in the life of this nation, where we've weakened America's place in the world, stifled America's economy, the campaign of Hillary Clinton and Tim Kaine has been an avalanche of insults.

Look, to get to your question about trustworthiness, Donald Trump has built a business through hard times and through good times. He's brought an extraordinary business acumen. He's employed tens of thousands of people in this country.

KAINE: And paid few taxes and lost a billion a year.

[crosstalk]

PENCE: But there's a—there's a reason why people question the trustworthiness of Hillary Clinton. And that's because they're paying attention. I mean, the reality is, when she was secretary of state, Senator, come on. She had a Clinton Foundation accepting contributions from foreign governments.

KAINE: You are Donald Trump's apprentice. Let me talk about this . . . *[crosstalk]*

PENCE: Senator, I think I'm still on my time.

KAINE: Well, I think—isn't this a discussion?

QUIJANO: This is our open discussion.

KAINE: Yeah, let's talk about the state of . . . *[crosstalk]*

PENCE: Well, let me interrupt—let me interrupt you and finish my sentence, if I can.

KAINE: Finish your sentence.

PENCE: The Clinton Foundation accepted foreign contributions from foreign governments and foreign donors while she was secretary of state.

KAINE: OK, now I can weigh in. Now . . .

PENCE: She had a private server . . .

KAINE: Now, I get to weigh in. Now, let me just say this . . .

PENCE: . . . that was discovered . . . *[crosstalk]*

QUIJANO: . . . Senator, you have an opportunity to respond.

PENCE: . . . keep that pay to play process out of the reach of the public. . . .

QUIJANO: Your fellow Republican, Governor Pence, Senator Tim Scott, who is African-American, recently spoke on the Senate floor. He said he was stopped seven times by law enforcement in one year.

KAINE: A U.S. senator.

QUIJANO: He said, "I have felt the anger, the frustration, the sadness, and the humiliation that comes with feeling like you're being targeted for nothing more than being just yourself." What would you say to Senator Scott about his experiences?

PENCE: Well, I have the deepest respect for Senator Scott, and he's a close friend. And what I would say is that we—we need to adopt criminal justice reform nationally. I—I signed criminal justice reform in the state of Indiana, Senator, and we're very proud of it.

I worked when I was Congress on a second chance act. We have got to do a better job recognizing and correcting the errors in the system that do reflect on institutional bias in criminal justice. But what—what—what Donald Trump and I are saying is let's not have the reflex of assuming the worst of men and women in law enforcement. We truly do believe that law enforcement is not a force for racism or division in our country . . .

KAINE: Elaine, can I . . .

QUIJANO: So what would you say to Senator Scott, Governor?

PENCE: Law enforcement in this country is a force for good. They are the—they truly are people that put their lives on the line every single day. But I would—I would suggest to you, what we need to do is assert a stronger leadership at the national level to support law enforcement. You just heard Senator Kaine reject stop-and-frisk. Well, I would suggest to you that the families that live in our inner cities that are besieged by crime . . .

KAINE: Elaine, let me—let me . . .

QUIJANO: Governor, the question is about Senator Scott. What would—what would you tell Senator Scott?

KAINE: Elaine, if I could—if I could jump in. I've heard Senator Scott make that eloquent plea. And look, criminal justice is about respecting the law and being respected by the law. So there is a fundamental respect issue here.

And I just want to talk about the tone that's set from the top. Donald Trump during his campaign has called Mexicans rapists and criminals. He's called women slobs, pigs, dogs, disgusting. I don't like saying that in front of my wife and my mother. He attacked an Indiana-born federal judge and said he was unqualified to hear a federal lawsuit because his parents were Mexican. He went after John McCain, a POW, and said he wasn't [a] hero because he'd been captured. He said African-Americans are living in Hell. And he perpetrated this outrageous and bigoted lie that President Obama is not a U.S. citizen.

If you want to have a society where people are respected and respect laws, you can't have somebody at the top who demeans every group that he talks about. And I just—again, I cannot believe that Governor Pence will defend the insult-driven campaign that Donald Trump has run.

QUIJANO: . . . What would you tell the millions of undocumented immigrants who have not committed violent crimes? Governor Pence?

PENCE: Donald Trump's laid out a plan to end illegal immigration once and for all in this country. We've been talking it to death for 20 years. Hillary Clinton and Tim Kaine want to continue the policies of open borders, amnesty, catch and release, sanctuary cities, all the things that are driving—that are driving wages down in this country, Senator, and also too often with criminal aliens in the country, it's bringing heartbreak.

But I have to tell you, I just—I was listening to the avalanche of insults coming out of Senator Kaine a minute ago.

KAINE: These were Donald's—hold on a second, Governor.

[crosstalk]

. . .

PENCE: Thanks. I forgive you. He says ours is an insult-driven campaign. Did you all just hear that? Ours is an insult-driven campaign?

I mean, to be honest with you, if Donald Trump had said all of the things that you've said he said in the way you said he said them, he still wouldn't have a fraction of the insults that Hillary Clinton leveled when she said that half of our supporters were a basket of deplorables. It's—she said they were irredeemable, they were not American.

I mean, it's extraordinary. And then she labeled one after another "ism" on millions of Americans who believe that we can have a stronger America at home and abroad, who believe we can get this economy moving again, who believe that we can end illegal immigration once and for all. So, Senator, this—this insult-driven campaign, I mean . . .

QUIJANO: Governor . . .

PENCE: That's small potatoes compared to Hillary Clinton . . .

QUIJANO: Senator Kaine?

PENCE: . . . calling half of Donald Trump's supporters a basket of deplorables.

KAINE: Hillary Clinton said something on the campaign trail, and the very next day, she said, you know what, I shouldn't have said that.

PENCE: She said she shouldn't have said half. . . .

QUIJANO: Does the U.S. have a responsibility to protect civilians and prevent mass casualties on this scale, Governor Pence?

PENCE: . . . But about Aleppo and about Syria, I truly do believe that what America ought to do right now is immediately establish safe zones, so that families and vulnerable families with children can move out of those areas, work with our Arab partners, real time, right now, to make that happen.

And secondly, I just have to tell you that the provocations by Russia need to be met with American strength. And if Russia chooses to be involved and continue, I should say, to be involved in this barbaric attack on civilians in Aleppo, the United States of America should be prepared to use military force to strike military targets of the Assad regime to prevent them from this humanitarian crisis that is taking place in Aleppo.

. . . There's a broad range of other things that we ought to do, as well. We ought to deploy a missile defense shield to the Czech Republic and Poland which Hillary Clinton and Barack Obama pulled back on out of not wanting to offend the Russians back in 2009.

QUIJANO: Governor, your two minutes are up.

PENCE: We've just got to have American strength on the world stage. When Donald Trump becomes president of the United States, the Russians and other countries in the world will know they're dealing with a strong American president.

QUIJANO: Senator Kaine?

KAINE: Hillary and I also agree that the establishment of humanitarian zones in northern Syria with the provision of international human aid, consistent with the U.N. Security Council resolution that was passed in February 2014, would be a very, very good idea.

And Hillary also has the ability to stand up to Russia in a way that this ticket does not. Donald Trump, again and again, has praised Vladimir Putin. And it's clear that he has business dealings with Russian oligarchs who are very connected to Putin.

The Trump campaign management team had to be fired a month or so ago because of those shadowy connections with pro-Putin forces. Governor Pence made the odd claim, he said inarguably Vladimir Putin is a better leader than President Obama. Vladimir Putin has run his economy into the ground. He persecutes LGBT folks and journalists. If you don't know the difference between dictatorship and leadership, then you got to go back to a fifth-grade civics class.

I'll tell you what offends me . . .

PENCE: Well, that offended me . . .

KAINE: Governor Pence just said—Governor Pence just said that Donald Trump will rebuild the military. No, he won't. Donald Trump is avoiding paying taxes. The New York Times story—and we need to get this—but the New York Times suggested that he probably didn't pay taxes for about 18 years starting in 1995. Those years included the years of 9/11.

So get this. On 9/11, Hillary Clinton and Donald Trump's hometown was attacked by the worst terrorist attack in the history of the United States. Young men and women—young men and women signed up to serve in the military to fight terrorism. Hillary Clinton went to Washington to get funds to rebuild her city and protect first responders, but Donald Trump was fighting a very different fight. It was a fight to avoid paying taxes so that he wouldn't support the fight against terror.

QUIJANO:	The question was about Aleppo, Senator.
KAINE:	He wouldn't support troops. He wouldn't—he wouldn't support—this is important, Elaine. When a guy running for president will not support the troops, not support veterans, not support teachers, that's really important. . . .
QUIJANO:	We need to talk about Russia. Very quickly, though, Senator, please.
PENCE:	. . . is astonishing to the American people.
KAINE:	Six times tonight, I have said to Governor Pence I can't imagine how you can defend your running mate's position on one issue after the next. And in all six cases, he's refused to defend his running mate.
PENCE:	Well, let's—no, no, don't put words in my mouth.
QUIJANO:	All right.
PENCE:	He's going . . . [crosstalk]
KAINE:	And yet he is asking everybody to vote for somebody that he cannot defend. And I just think that should be underlined.
PENCE:	No, I'm—look . . . [crosstalk]
QUIJANO:	All right, gentlemen, let's talk about Russia. This is a topic that has come up.
PENCE:	I'm very, very happy to defend Donald Trump. If he wants to take these one at a time, I'll take them one at a time.
QUIJANO:	I will give you an opportunity to do that.
KAINE:	More nations should get nuclear weapons. Try to defend that.
PENCE:	Don't put words in my mouth. Well, he never said that, Senator.
KAINE:	He absolutely said it. Saudi Arabia, South Korea, Japan.
PENCE:	Most of the stuffy [sic] you've said, he's never said.
QUIJANO:	Gentlemen, Russia. Russian President Vladimir Putin invaded Ukraine, annexed Crimea, and has provided crucial military support to the Assad regime. What steps, if any, would your administration take to counter these actions? Senator Kaine?
KAINE:	You've got to be tough on Russia. So let's start with not praising Vladimir Putin as a great leader. Donald Trump and Mike Pence have said he's a great leader. And Donald Trump has business . . .
PENCE:	No, we haven't.
KAINE:	. . . has business dealings—has business dealings with Russia that he refuses to disclose. Hillary Clinton has gone toe-to-toe with Russia. She went toe-to-toe with Russia as secretary of state to do the New START

Agreement to reduce Russia's nuclear stockpile. She's had the experience doing it.

She went toe-to-toe with Russia and lodged protests when they went into Georgia. And we've done the same thing about Ukraine, but more than launching protests, we've put punishing economic sanctions on Russia that we need to continue.

Donald Trump, on the other hand, didn't know that Russia had invaded the Crimea. . . .

KAINE: Hillary Clinton has gone toe-to-toe with Russia to work out a deal on New START. She got them engaged on a meaningful way to cap Iran's nuclear weapons program. And yet she stood up to them on issues such as Syria and their invasion of Georgia. You've got to have the ability to do that, and Hillary does.

On the other hand, in Donald Trump, you have somebody who praises Vladimir Putin all the time. America should really wonder about a President Trump, who had a campaign manager with ties to Putin, pro-Putin elements in the Ukraine, who had to be fired for that reason. They should wonder—when Donald Trump is sitting down with Vladimir Putin, is it going to be America's bottom line or is it going to be Donald Trump's bottom line that he's going to be worried about with all of his business dealings?

. . . QUIJANO: Senator, your time is up. Governor?

PENCE: Well, thanks. I'm just trying to keep up with the insult-driven campaign on the other side of the table.

KAINE: You know, I'm just saying facts about your running mate.

PENCE: Yeah.

KAINE: And I know you can't defend.

QUIJANO: Senator, please. This is the governor's two minutes.

PENCE: I'm happy to defend him, Senator. Don't put words in my mouth that I'm not defending him.

KAINE: You're not.

PENCE: I'm happy to defend him. Most of what you said is completely false, and the American people know that. . . .

PENCE: . . . Hillary Clinton and her husband set up a private foundation called the Clinton Foundation. While she was secretary of state, the Clinton Foundation accepted tens of millions of dollars from foreign governments and foreign donors.

Now, you all need to know out there, this is basic stuff. Foreign donors, and certainly foreign governments, cannot participate in the American political process. They cannot make financial contributions. But the Clintons figured out a way to create a foundation where foreign governments and foreign donors could donate millions of dollars. And then we found, thanks to the good work of the Associated Press, that more than half her private meetings when she was secretary of state were given to major donors of the Clinton Foundation. When you talk about all these—all these baseless rumors about Russia and the rest, Hillary Clinton—you asked the trustworthy question at the very beginning—the reason . . .

QUIJANO: Governor, your two minutes are up.

PENCE: . . . the reason the American people don't trust Hillary Clinton is because they are looking at the pay to play politics that she operated with the Clinton Foundation through a private server . . .

QUIJANO: Governor, please.

PENCE: . . . while she's secretary of state.

QUIJANO: Your two minutes are up, Governor.

PENCE: And they're saying enough is enough.

QUIJANO: Senator Kaine?

KAINE: I'm going to talk about the foundation, and then I'll talk about North Korea. So, on the foundation. I am glad to talk about the foundation. The Clinton Foundation is one of the highest-rated charities in the world. It provides AIDS drugs to about 11.5 million people. It helps Americans deal with opioid overdoses. It gets higher rankings for its charity than the American Red Cross does. The Clinton foundation does an awful lot of good work.

Hillary Clinton as secretary of state took no action to benefit the foundation. The State Department did an investigation, and they concluded that everything Hillary Clinton did as secretary of state was completely in the interest of the United States. So the foundation does good work. And Hillary Clinton as secretary of state acted in the interests of the United States.

But let's compare this now with the Trump organization and the Trump Foundation. The Trump organization is an octopus-like organization with tentacles all over the world whose conflict of interests could only be known if Donald Trump would release his tax returns. He's refused to do it.

His sons have said that the organization has a lot of business dealings in Russia. And remember, the Trump organization is not a non-profit. It's putting money into Donald Trump's pockets and into the pockets of his children, whereas the Clinton Foundation is a non-profit and no Clinton family member draws any salary.

PENCE: The Trump Foundation is non-profit.

KAINE: In addition, Donald Trump has a foundation. The foundation was just fined for illegally contributing foundation dollars to a political campaign of a Florida attorney general. They made an illegal contribution, and then they tried to hide it by disguising it to somebody else. And the person they donated to was somebody whose office was charged with investigating Trump University.

This is the difference between a foundation that does good work and a secretary of state who acted in accordance with American interest[s] and somebody who is conflicted and doing work around the world and won't share with the American public what he's doing and what those conflicts are.

QUIJANO: Governor, I will give you 30 seconds to respond, because I know you want to, but, again, I would remind you both this was about North Korea. *[laughter]*

PENCE: Well, [t]hank you. Thank you. The Trump Foundation is a private family foundation. They give virtually every cent in the Trump Foundation to charitable causes.

KAINE: Political contributions?

PENCE: Less than ten cents on the dollar in the Clinton Foundation has gone to charitable causes.

KAINE: A $20,000 portrait of Donald Trump?

PENCE: Less than 10 cents on the dollar of the Clinton Foundation has gone to charitable causes.

KAINE: Ninety percent.

PENCE: It has been a platform for the Clintons to travel the world, to have staff. But honestly, Senator, we would know a lot more about it if Hillary Clinton would just turn over the 33,000 e-mails . . .

QUIJANO: All right, let's turn back to North Korea . . .

PENCE: . . . that she refused to turn over in her private server . . .

QUIJANO: Senator Kaine . . .

PENCE: . . . and we'd have a much better picture of what the Clinton Foundation was about. . . .

QUIJANO: All right, gentlemen, thank you so much.

This concludes the vice presidential debate. My thanks to the candidates, the commission, and to you for watching. Please tune in this Sunday for the second presidential debate at Washington University in St. Louis and the final debate on October 19th at the University of Nevada, Las Vegas.

SOURCE: The American Presidency Project. "Vice Presidential Debate at Longwood University in Farmville, Virginia." October 4, 2016. Online by Gerhard Peters and John T. Woolley, *The American Presidency Project*. http://www.presidency.ucsb.edu/ws/index.php?pid=119012.

OTHER HISTORIC DOCUMENTS OF INTEREST

CIA and FBI Release Findings on Russian Involvement in U.S. Election

OCTOBER 7 AND 16, AND DECEMBER 11 AND 29, 2016

Less than a month after the 2016 presidential campaign concluded, U.S. intelligence agencies revealed a classified investigation into allegations that Russia waged a misinformation and data theft campaign to target Democratic candidate Hillary Clinton and boost Republican candidate Donald Trump. While previous reports from intelligence agencies suggested that the Russian campaign sought to undermine Americans' faith in democracy and the electoral system, the Central Intelligence Agency (CIA) and the Federal Bureau of Investigation (FBI) later concluded that Russia intervened to help Trump win the presidency. Despite mounting evidence, Russian President Vladimir Putin denied the allegations, but President Barack Obama announced several actions in response to the intelligence agencies' findings, including new sanctions against Russian intelligence agencies.

MISINFORMATION, CYBER HACKING TARGET U.S. ELECTION

On November 9, 2016, Clinton called Trump to congratulate him on his electoral victory. Clinton's concession marked the end of an unprecedented presidential campaign, one marked by a deepening partisan divide, eroding trust in democratic institutions, and misleading and false news reports. However, the most lasting—and arguably the most damaging—effect on the election was an alleged misinformation, data theft, and cyber warfare campaign carried out and sponsored by the Russian government.

Months prior, the first cyberattacks designed to influence the presidential campaign surfaced. Hackers breached the Democratic National Committee (DNC) and stole thousands of e-mail and chat logs from DNC officials and the Clinton campaign. Additional hacks targeted Clinton's campaign chair, John Podesta. The U.S. government later discovered that the hackers were sponsored by the Russian government and gained access to the DNC's entire database of opposition research on Trump. The DNC breach was one of several targeting American political organizations, including both presidential campaigns, the Republican National Committee, and the computers of various Republican political action committees.

With the stolen e-mail in hand, the hackers used middlemen to provide the information to WikiLeaks, the controversial international nonprofit organization that publishes secret information, news leaks, and classified media from anonymous sources. WikiLeaks denied Russia was the source of the information, a claim U.S. intelligence agencies disputed. While no illegal activities were discovered in the stolen information, the e-mail revealed efforts within the DNC to help Clinton secure the nomination over her primary rival, Sen. Bernie Sanders, D-Vt. Several DNC officials, including DNC chair Rep. Debbie Wasserman Schultz, D-Fla., resigned following the controversy.

In addition to data theft, it is believed that hackers also sought to undermine Americans' faith in their electoral system and damage Clinton's image through a massive propaganda and misinformation campaign. Anonymous hackers created fake social media accounts to spread false information and conspiracy theories, even going so far as to create fake websites posing as real news outlets. Paid teams of "trolls," or instigators, harassed Democratic supporters, amplified far-right conspiracies, and created new tensions within the U.S. democratic system.

A joint statement from the U.S. Department of Homeland Security (DHS) and the Office of the Director of National Intelligence on October 7 laid out the intelligence community's allegations, stating they were "confident that the Russian Government directed the recent compromises of e-mails from U.S. persons and institutions, including from U.S. political organizations." The statement continued: "These thefts and disclosures are intended to interfere with the U.S. election process. Such activity is not new to Moscow— the Russians have used similar tactics and techniques across Europe and Eurasia, for example, to influence public opinion there. We believe, based on the scope and sensitivity of these efforts, that only Russia's senior-most officials could have authorized these activities."

The agencies maintained, however, that no election systems were at risk of being compromised, stating the intelligence community had determined that "it would be extremely difficult for someone, including a nation-state actor, to alter actual ballot counts or election results by cyber attack or intrusion." The statement concluded by asking state and local election officials to remain vigilant and to work with federal election officials to bolster their cybersecurity defenses.

Despite mounting evidence of Russia's involvement, President Putin repeatedly denied interfering in the election. At a press conference days after U.S. intelligence communities expressed confidence that the Russian government directed the attacks, Putin denied involvement. "I would like to reassure you all, including our American partners and friends: we have no plans to influence the election campaign in the United States," Putin said. He continued, "I will repeat this again: sacrificing Russian–American relations for the sake of internal political events in the U.S. is harmful and counterproductive."

CIA, FBI Report Finds Russia behind Cyber Attacks

One month after the election, news broke that the CIA had concluded in a secret assessment that Russia intervened in the election to help Trump win the presidency. Previously, officials believed Russian hackers merely sought to undermine confidence in the U.S. electoral system. The CIA alleged, however, that Russian operatives went a step further. According to the report, U.S. intelligence agencies identified individuals with known connections to the Russian government who provided WikiLeaks with e-mail stolen from the DNC. The individuals, according to officials briefed on the report, were Russian intelligence officials and middlemen known to the U.S. intelligence community.

The Trump transition team dismissed the findings, questioning instead the integrity of U.S. intelligence agencies. "These are the same people that said Saddam Hussein had weapons of mass destruction," read a statement from the presidential transition team. "The election ended a long time ago in one of the biggest Electoral College victories in history. It's now time to move on and 'Make America Great Again,'" a reference to the

Trump campaign's slogan. The statement largely echoed Trump's continued skepticism around Russian interference in the election. In an interview with *Time* magazine following his victory, Trump remarked, "I don't believe they interfered." Instead, Trump argued, the hacking "could be Russia. And it could be China. And it could be some guy in his home in New Jersey."

On Capitol Hill, Republicans and Democrats alike strongly rebuked Russia for its intervention in the election. Sens. John McCain, R-Ariz., chair of the Senate Committee on Armed Services; Lindsey Graham, R-S.C., member of the Senate Committee on Armed Services; Charles E. Schumer, D-N.Y., Senate minority leader–elect; and Jack Reed, D-R.I., ranking member of the Senate Committee on Armed Services, issued a rare joint statement denouncing Russian involvement. "Recent reports of Russian interference in our election should alarm every American," the statement read. The senators urged politicians to put behind partisan differences to investigate these allegations further. "Democrats and Republicans must work together, and across the jurisdictional lines of the Congress, to examine these recent incidents thoroughly and devise comprehensive solutions to deter and defend against further cyberattacks," they said. "This cannot become a partisan issue. The stakes are too high for our country."

Obama Administration Responds

Two weeks before leaving office, Obama issued an executive order responding to the allegations against Russia. The executive order levied new sanctions on two Russian intelligence services—the Main Intelligence Administration (GRU) and the Federal Security Service (FSB)—as well as four individual GRU officers and three companies that "provided material support to the GRU's cyber operations." Obama also directed the Treasury secretary to designate "two Russian individuals for using cyber-enabled means to cause misappropriation of funds and personal identifying information." In perhaps the highest-profile measure, the U.S. State Department shut down two compounds in Maryland and New York that were used by Russian personnel for intelligence-related purposes and expelled thirty-five Russian intelligence operatives from the country. Finally, Obama directed the DHS and the FBI to release "declassified technical information on Russian civilian and military intelligence service cyber activity, to help network defenders in the United States and abroad identify, detect, and disrupt Russia's global campaign of malicious cyber activities."

The report released by DHS and the FBI following Obama's remarks described the technical details of the tools and infrastructure used by Russian civilian and military intelligence services. Russian intelligence, the report stated, used the outlined methods to "compromise and exploit networks and endpoints associated with the U.S. election, as well as a range of U.S. government, political, and private sector entities." The report expanded on a joint statement issued by the two agencies in October, in which officials described the hacks as an attempt to "interfere" with the U.S. election that is "consistent with the Russian-directed efforts."

Finally, the president reiterated in his statement that these would not be the only measures the U.S. took in retaliation. "We will continue to take a variety of actions at a time and place of our choosing, some of which will not be publicized," the president said. "In addition to holding Russia accountable for what it has done, the United States and friends and allies around the world must work together to oppose Russia's efforts to undermine established international norms of behavior, and interfere with democratic governance."

The White House promised a report to Congress detailing Russia's efforts to interfere in the 2016 election, as well as malicious cyber activity in previous election cycles.

QUESTIONS SURROUNDING RUSSIAN CONNECTIONS CONTINUE INTO TRUMP PRESIDENCY

Despite reports from the intelligence community and retaliatory actions from the Obama administration, questions surrounding Russia's influence in the election lingered into early 2017. Fresh allegations of repeated contact between the Trump campaign and Russian intelligence agents dogged the first month of Trump's presidency. In the most high-profile example of the damaging effects of Russia's intervention, Trump's national security adviser, Michael Flynn, resigned after it was revealed that he discussed the possibility of easing sanctions enacted by Obama with the Russian ambassador following the election and lied about the conversation to Vice President Mike Pence. Flynn's resignation came less than a month after he was appointed and signaled that the lasting impacts of Russian's misinformation and hacking campaign have yet to be fully known.

—Robert Howard

Following is a joint statement from the U.S. Department of Homeland Security and the Office of the Director of National Intelligence from October 7, 2016, on the Russian hacking and election security in the states; excerpts from a press conference on October 16, 2016, in which Russian President Vladimir Putin answered questions about the hacking allegations; a statement by Democratic and Republican senators from December 11, 2016, on Russian interference in the presidential election; and a statement by President Barack Obama from December 29, 2016, announcing new actions taken against Russia in response to its interference.

DOCUMENT

Homeland Security, Director of National Intelligence Statement on Russian Interference, Election Security

October 7, 2016

The U.S. Intelligence Community (USIC) is confident that the Russian Government directed the recent compromises of e-mails from US persons and institutions, including from US political organizations. The recent disclosures of alleged hacked e-mails on sites like DCLeaks.com and WikiLeaks and by the Guccifer 2.0 online persona are consistent with the methods and motivations of Russian-directed efforts. These thefts and disclosures are intended to interfere with the US election process. Such activity is not new to Moscow—the Russians have used similar tactics and techniques across Europe and Eurasia, for example, to influence public opinion there. We believe, based on the scope and sensitivity of these efforts, that only Russia's senior-most officials could have authorized these activities.

Some states have also recently seen scanning and probing of their election-related systems, which in most cases originated from servers operated by a Russian company. However, we are not now in a position to attribute this activity to the Russian Government. The USIC and the Department of Homeland Security (DHS) assess that it would be extremely difficult for someone, including a nation-state actor, to alter actual ballot counts or election results by cyber attack or intrusion. This assessment is based on the decentralized nature of our election system in this country and the number of protections state and local election officials have in place. States ensure that voting machines are not connected to the Internet, and there are numerous checks and balances as well as extensive oversight at multiple levels built into our election process.

Nevertheless, DHS continues to urge state and local election officials to be vigilant and seek cybersecurity assistance from DHS. A number of states have already done so. DHS is providing several services to state and local election officials to assist in their cybersecurity. These services include cyber "hygiene" scans of Internet-facing systems, risk and vulnerability assessments, information sharing about cyber incidents, and best practices for securing voter registration databases and addressing potential cyber threats. DHS has convened an Election Infrastructure Cybersecurity Working Group with experts across all levels of government to raise awareness of cybersecurity risks potentially affecting election infrastructure and the elections process. Secretary Johnson and DHS officials are working directly with the National Association of Secretaries of State to offer assistance, share information, and provide additional resources to state and local officials.

SOURCE: U.S. Homeland Security Department. "Joint Statement from the Department of Homeland Security and Office of the Director of National Intelligence on Election Security." October 7, 2016. http://www.dhs.gov/news/2016/10/07/joint-statement-department-homeland-security-and-office-director-national.

President Vladimir Putin on U.S. Hacking Allegations

October 16, 2016

[The following has been excerpted from the transcript of a press conference during which Putin addressed a variety of topics.]

Question: US Vice President Joseph Biden promised yesterday to send you a message and respond to the hacking that the US blames on Russia . . .

Vladimir Putin: There is nothing surprising about that.

Question: As a matter of fact, it was a threat coming from a very high-ranking official, and if I am not mistaken, it targeted you personally. Do you expect hacking attacks on Russia or some other kinds of attacks?

Vladimir Putin: You can expect anything from our US friends. But was there anything new in what he said? As if we didn't know that US government bodies snoop on and wiretap everyone?

Everyone knows this all too well, there has long been no secret about it and there is sufficient evidence to support this. Billions of dollars are channelled into this activity, with the NSA and the CIA working on it alongside other government bodies. There are both witness accounts and full-fledged confessions.

In fact, they are spying not only on their real or potential enemies, but also on their allies, including the closest ones. We know about so many wiretapping scandals involving top government officials from countries that are allies of the United States, so there is absolutely nothing new here.

The only new thing is that for the first time the US has acknowledged at such a high level, first, that they actually do this, and second that they are making some kind of a threat, which of course is inconsistent with the norms of international dialogue. This is obvious.

Apparently, they are a little bit nervous. The question is why. I think there is a reason. You know, in an election campaign, the current government carefully crafts a pre-election strategy, and any government, especially when seeking re-election, always has unresolved issues. They need to show, to explain to the voters why they remained unresolved. . . .

I'm just saying that there are many problems, and in these conditions, many choose to resort to the usual tactics of distracting voters from their problems.

In my view, this is exactly what we are witnessing. How do you do it? Try to create an enemy and rally the nation against that enemy. Iran and the Iranian nuclear threat did not work well for that. Russia is a more interesting story. In my opinion, this card is being played now.

I said recently at a VTB forum that it is not wise to sacrifice Russian–American relations to solve current internal political problems, because it is destroying international relations in general. . . .

Remark: So we shouldn't see this as a threat?

Vladimir Putin: I just said, anything could happen. With this global surveillance, I assume they do have certain information. That information can be easy to compile.

People can be fed a half-truth or a quarter-truth, or even just a bit of truth diluted in lies, and this information can be used to mislead the public in one country or another. Russia is no exception, we are often the target of these attacks. We already know that.

Question: Mr. President, did you know you are featured in the new episode of the cartoon The Simpsons? You are boosting Trump in it. What is your actual preference? You have been asked many times—Clinton or Trump?

And one more question: the US Vice President said recently that we cannot influence the US election results. Frankly, are we even trying to interfere? Do we even need to?

Vladimir Putin: . . . I would like to reassure you all, including our American partners and friends: we have no plans to influence the election campaign in the United States.

The answer is very simple: we do not know what will happen after the US President is elected. Ms. Clinton chose her aggressive rhetoric and aggressive stance with regard to Russia, and Mr. Trump, on the contrary, is calling for cooperation, at least against terrorism.

We will certainly welcome anyone who wants to work with us, and no, we are not interested in quarrelling constantly with anyone, which only creates threats to oneself and the world, or at the very least makes it harder to achieve the desired results in the fight against terrorism. . . .

I will repeat this again: sacrificing Russian–American relations for the sake of internal political events in the US is harmful and counterproductive. This is not the first time. Look at all the previous election campaigns—it's the same story again and again, as I said.

And then they whisper in our ear: "Just wait it out. This will pass, and things will go back to normal." You know, this is not even funny anymore. But if someone wants a confrontation, it is not our choice. Confrontation means problems. We do not want that. On the contrary, we would like to find common ground and work together to address global challenges facing Russia and the United States and the world. . . .

SOURCE: Office of the President of Russia. "Vladimir Putin Answered Questions from Russian Journalists." October 16, 2016. http://en.kremlin.ru/events/president/news/53103.

Senators' Joint Statement on Russian Interference

December 11, 2016

U.S. Senators John McCain (R-AZ), Chairman of the Senate Committee on Armed Services, Lindsey Graham (R-SC), Member of the Senate Committee on Armed Services, Charles E. Schumer (D-NY), Senate Democratic Leader-elect, and Jack Reed (D-RI), Ranking Member of the Senate Committee on Armed Services released the following joint statement today in response to news reports on the CIA's analysis of Russian interference with the 2016 election:

"For years, foreign adversaries have directed cyberattacks at America's physical, economic, and military infrastructure, while stealing our intellectual property. Now our democratic institutions have been targeted. Recent reports of Russian interference in our election should alarm every American.

"Congress's national security committees have worked diligently to address the complex challenge of cybersecurity, but recent events show that more must be done. While protecting classified material, we have an obligation to inform the public about recent cyberattacks that have cut to the heart of our free society. Democrats and Republicans must work together, and across the jurisdictional lines of the Congress, to examine these recent incidents thoroughly and devise comprehensive solutions to deter and defend against further cyberattacks.

"This cannot become a partisan issue. The stakes are too high for our country. We are committed to working in this bipartisan manner, and we will seek to unify our colleagues around the goal of investigating and stopping the grave threats that cyberattacks conducted by foreign governments pose to our national security."

SOURCE: Senate Committee on Armed Services. "McCain, Graham, Schumer, Reed Joint Statement on Reports That Russia Interfered with the 2016 Election." December 11, 2016. https://www.armed-services.senate.gov/press-releases/mccain-graham-schumer-reed-joint-statement-on-reports-that-russia-interfered-with-the-2016-election.

Obama Responds to Russian Cyber Activity and Harassment

DOCUMENT

December 29, 2016

Today, I have ordered a number of actions in response to the Russian government's aggressive harassment of U.S. officials and cyber operations aimed at the U.S. election. These actions follow repeated private and public warnings that we have issued to the Russian government, and are a necessary and appropriate response to efforts to harm U.S. interests in violation of established international norms of behavior.

All Americans should be alarmed by Russia's actions. In October, my Administration publicized our assessment that Russia took actions intended to interfere with the U.S. election process. These data theft and disclosure activities could only have been directed by the highest levels of the Russian government. Moreover, our diplomats have experienced an unacceptable level of harassment in Moscow by Russian security services and police over the last year. Such activities have consequences. Today, I have ordered a number of actions in response.

I have issued an executive order that provides additional authority for responding to certain cyber activity that seeks to interfere with or undermine our election processes and institutions, or those of our allies or partners. Using this new authority, I have sanctioned nine entities and individuals: the GRU and the FSB, two Russian intelligence services; four individual officers of the GRU; and three companies that provided material support to the GRU's cyber operations. In addition, the Secretary of the Treasury is designating two Russian individuals for using cyber-enabled means to cause misappropriation of funds and personal identifying information. The State Department is also shutting down two Russian compounds, in Maryland and New York, used by Russian personnel for intelligence-related purposes, and is declaring "persona non grata" 35 Russian intelligence operatives. Finally, the Department of Homeland Security and the Federal Bureau of Investigation are releasing declassified technical information on Russian civilian and military intelligence service cyber activity, to help network defenders in the United States and abroad identify, detect, and disrupt Russia's global campaign of malicious cyber activities.

These actions are not the sum total of our response to Russia's aggressive activities. We will continue to take a variety of actions at a time and place of our choosing, some of which will not be publicized. In addition to holding Russia accountable for what it has done, the United States and friends and allies around the world must work together to oppose Russia's efforts to undermine established international norms of behavior, and interfere with democratic governance. To that end, my Administration will be providing a report to Congress in the coming days about Russia's efforts to interfere in our election, as well as malicious cyber activity related to our election cycle in previous elections.

SOURCE: The White House. "Statement by the President on Actions in Response to Russian Malicious Cyber Activity and Harassment." December 29, 2016. https://obamawhitehouse.archives.gov/the-press-office/2016/12/29/statement-president-actions-response-russian-malicious-cyber-activity.

OTHER HISTORIC DOCUMENTS OF INTEREST

FROM THIS VOLUME

International Officials Respond to Unrest in the Democratic Republic of the Congo

OCTOBER 7 AND DECEMBER 12, 2016

The Democratic Republic of the Congo (DRC) was scheduled to hold a presidential election in November 2016, weeks before the conclusion of President Joseph Kabila's second term. However, Kabila's allies in parliament and the Independent National Electoral Commission acted to postpone the election and extend Kabila's time in office. Opposition parties claimed that the delays were an undemocratic attempt to keep Kabila in power, while the government argued more time was needed to make election preparations. Thousands of Congolese protested the delays, prompting a harsh crackdown by government security forces. In response, the United States and the European Union (EU) issued sanctions against Congolese officials involved in suppressing the opposition.

KABILA'S PATH TO THE PRESIDENCY

The DRC's current political environment has been shaped by a history of colonial rule, dictatorship, civil war, and rebellion. In 1965, five years after the DRC gained its independence from Belgium, Joseph-Desiré Mobutu (later known as Mobutu Sese Seko) seized power in a coup and quickly moved to concentrate power in the presidency. Kabila's father, Laurent-Désiré Kabila, led a rebellion against Mobutu, which, with the support of the Rwandan and Ugandan governments, succeeded in ousting the dictator in 1997. Laurent Kabila then became president.

While this power struggle ensured, the DRC also endured a civil war spurred by ethnic strife in the eastern part of the country and a massive influx of Rwandan refugees during the Rwandan genocide. A second rebellion in the late 1990s, also backed by Rwanda and Uganda, challenged Kabila, who received military support from the neighboring countries of Angola, Chad, Namibia, Sudan, and Zimbabwe. Millions of people died during the extended conflict, either while fighting or because of starvation and disease.

Joseph Kabila became the president in January 2001, after his father was assassinated by one of his bodyguards. Kabila was serving as a military commander in the DRC's ongoing conflict at the time and was selected by his father's inner circle—and approved unanimously by the parliament—to take office. Kabila negotiated an agreement for Rwandan forces to withdraw in 2002. Later that year, the Pretoria Accord was signed by all remaining parties to the conflict, ending the war and establishing a national unity government. While the conflict may have officially ended, rebellions are frequent in the eastern part of the country, where various militias control different parts of the territory. Armed groups often terrorize locals to try and gain control of areas containing valuable minerals, such as gold, tin, and copper. The United Nations (UN) maintains a peacekeeping force of about 20,000 troops in the DRC, and most of them are stationed in the east.

The first multiparty elections for the presidency, National Assembly, and provincial legislatures in over forty years took place in 2006, following the approval of a new constitution in 2005. Kabila was elected president and reelected in 2011. The results of the second election were disputed, with independent observers reporting that returns from nearly 2,000 polling stations in areas where Kabila's opponent, Union for Democracy and Social Progress (UDPS) leader Etienne Tshisekedi, enjoyed strong support had been lost and not included in official results. Tshisekedi claimed the results were illegitimate.

AN ELECTION DELAYED

Kabila's second term was set to expire on December 19, 2016, with an election to be held that November. Per the Congolese constitution, Kabila was barred from running for a third term. However, signs that the election would not take place as planned began to emerge early in 2015, when the parliament passed a law requiring a new census be conducted before the next presidential election. This effectively prolonged Kabila's term beyond 2016. The news prompted several days of anti-Kabila demonstrations in Kinshasa and other locations, with some protests devolving into riots and looting. Dozens of protesters were killed by police, who fired live ammunition into the crowds, as well as tear gas. Following the protests, the parliament struck the census requirement from the law, but uncertainty remained about the scheduling of the next election.

Questions about the timing of the election continued in 2016, with the Constitutional Court ruling on May 11 that Kabila could remain in office after his term expired until an election could be organized. Then, on September 17, the Independent National Electoral Commission filed a request with the Constitutional Court to postpone the election. Corneille Nangaa, commission president, claimed that the postponement was needed to provide the commission with enough time to update voter registration lists, although the commission did not propose a new date for the election. At various times preceding the formal request, the commission had argued that the government did not have the money to hold elections, and then that it was "logistically impossible" to hold an election before mid-2018 due to "security challenges." The court approved the request on October 17.

Kabila's opponents—largely united in a coalition called Le Rassemblement—accused the president and his government of purposefully delaying the election and circumventing the democratic process to allow Kabila to remain in power. The government continually denied these claims, stating alternately that the country needed more money or more time to prepare for the election. "We have decided to delay the elections to avoid locking out a huge number of people—most of them young voters," Kabila told reporters in early October. "As many as 10 million unregistered voters could miss out on the chance to vote if we proceed with the elections." Kabila also denied that the DRC was in a political crisis, describing what was happening in the country as "just some political tension ahead of elections, which is a normal thing in many parts of Africa."

Some also claimed that Kabila's administration was attempting to undermine the president's political opponents. In May, popular former governor and wealthy businessman Moïse Katumbi declared his candidacy for president. The same week, the Ministry of Justice and Human Rights announced that the government had "documented proof" that Katumbi had hired mercenaries to help devise a plot against the government, charges that Katumbi said were "grotesque lies." Katumbi was later found guilty of separate charges involving an illegal real estate sale and was sentenced in absentia to thirty-six months in prison. (Katumbi had gone into exile in Belgium before the verdict was reached.)

PROTESTS IN KINSHASA

During various demonstrations in the capital of Kinshasa and other sites around the country, thousands of Congolese joined the opposition in calling for Kabila to step down. Tens of thousands of people attended a rally in the capital on July 31, demanding an election take place in November. "We are attached to our constitution, and it says that the president cannot go beyond two mandates," Tshisekedi said while addressing the crowd, adding that if the electoral commission did not convene the electorate, "we will talk of high treason."

Another major protest took place September 19–21 in Kinshasa, following the electoral commission's request to postpone the election. Protesters clashed with security forces, who used water cannons, tear gas, and live fire to disperse participants, and the headquarters of three opposition parties were set on fire. According to a report by the UN Joint Human Rights Office (UNJHRO), at least 53 people were killed and another 143 persons were injured during the protests. More than 299 people were unlawfully arrested and detained. All told, UNJHRO said it documented "over 422 victims of human rights violations in Kinshasa" and that the national police, soldiers, and Republic Guard were the main perpetrators of these violations. The UNJHRO said that these counts were not final, because their team was still trying to confirm some reports. They also noted that officials had denied their team access to some detention centers and records from some of the country's morgues and public hospitals. The government blamed the violence on the opposition and banned all future protests.

On October 17, Kabila's People's Party for Reconstruction and Democracy and its allies signed an agreement with opposition fringe groups, pushing the election to April 2018 and allowing Kabila to stay in power until the new president took office. Le Rassemblement boycotted the negotiations and called for a general strike on October 19 to continue pressuring Kabila to step down in December. Streets were quiet and most stores were closed in the capital the day of the strike, although the DRC's second-largest city, Lubumbashi, remained active.

Kabila declined to step down on December 19 and in fact announced the formation of a new government that evening. Prime Minister Augustin Matata Ponyo and his cabinet resigned in November per the agreement signed in October. According to Human Rights Watch, at least thirty-four people were killed by violence during protests that continued after Kabila's announcement.

INTERNATIONAL SANCTIONS IMPOSED

In response to the government's postponing of the election and treatment of the opposition, the United States and the EU imposed sanctions on several Congolese officials on December 12. The U.S. Treasury Department named Deputy Prime Minister and Minister of the Interior and Security Évariste Boshab and General Administrator for the National Intelligence Agency Kalev Mutondo as sanctioned individuals for engaging in actions or policies that undermined democratic processes or institutions in the country. Under the sanctions, Boshab and Mutondo's assets within U.S. jurisdictions were frozen and U.S. citizens were prohibited from conducting transactions with them.

The European Council implemented travel restrictions and an asset freeze against seven other individuals "who hold positions of authority in the chain of command over the Congolese security forces which have exercised a disproportionate use of force." In announcing the sanctions, the council noted that Kabila's constitutional mandate was quickly coming to an end and that "the date approaches fraught with risk and uncertainty after the recent crackdowns and violations of fundamental rights. Any new government in place after that date must ground its legitimacy in a clearly and inclusively defined political framework, otherwise the country's relations with the European Union will suffer."

COMPROMISE AGREEMENT REACHED

Many feared that the country would return to a period of civil war if an agreement for a peaceful transition of power could not be reached. The African Union attempted to organize negotiations between Kabila's party and the opposition with Edem Kodjo, a former Togolese premier, appointed as mediator. However, the opposition refused to work with Kodjo, accusing him of being biased toward Kabila.

On December 8, the National Episcopal Conference of Congo (CENCO) initiated talks between the ruling coalition and Le Rassemblement to reach a compromise and establish a transitional authority until the next presidential election could be held. No agreement was reached by the December 16 deadline set by CENCO negotiators. "The ruling majority is sitting on its positions and refuses to offer any concessions on matters that require a political response," said Marc Kabund, secretary-general of the UDPS.

Talks resumed on December 20, with a Christmas deadline for a final agreement, but negotiations reached another stalemate and did not resume until December 29. Issues of contention during the negotiations included the opposition's desire to restructure the electoral commission and Constitutional Court, which they claim are partisan to Kabila. The opposition also sought the release of political prisoners and wanted the charges against Katumbi dropped. Additionally, there was disagreement between the two sides over who would serve as the prime minister until the election was held. Kabila had appointed Samy Badibanga, a UDPS member who had participated in the October negotiations, but Le Rassemblement wanted someone in the position who represented the main opposition coalition.

On December 31, the ruling and opposition parties signed an agreement to hold an election by the end of 2017. Kabila would remain in power until that time, and an opposition party politician would serve as his prime minister. A transitional government would be in place by March 2017. The agreement prevents Kabila from seeking an amendment to the constitution that would enable him to run for a third term, establishes a commission to consider the release of political prisoners on a case-by-case basis, and calls for CENCO to examine Katumbi's case. Archbishop Marcel Utembi, the leader of CENCO, acknowledged that while a deal had been reached, the country faced a difficult road ahead. "It's one thing to have a political compromise but putting it into place is another," he said.

If the agreement is implemented, it will mark the DRC's first peaceful transfer of power.

—Linda Fecteau Grimm

Following is the UN Joint Human Rights Office's preliminary report on human rights violations and violence during the Kinshasha demonstrations, released October 7, 2016; a press release from the U.S. Treasury Department from December 12, 2016, announcing sanctions against two Congolese officials; a press release from the European Council from December 12, 2016, announcing travel restrictions and asset freezes on select Congolese officials; and the text of the European Council's restrictions, released December 12, 2016.

UN Report on Human Rights Violations during Kinshasa Demonstrations

DOCUMENT

October 7, 2016

[Footnotes have been omitted.]

SUMMARY

This report of the United Nations Joint Human Rights Office (UNJHRO) addresses human rights violations and abuses committed between 19 and 21 September 2016 in Kinshasa and other circumstances relevant to understand the overall environment of the demonstrations organized by the opposition platform *Rassemblement des forces politiques et sociales acquises au changement*, calling for the respect of constitutional timelines for holding national elections.

Between 19 and 21 September 2016, the UNJHRO documented over 422 victims of human rights violations in Kinshasa by State agents. In total, the UNJHRO was able to confirm that at least 53 persons, including seven women, two children, and four police agents, were killed. Forty-eight were killed by State actors, while the rest of the perpetrators were not clearly identified. One hundred and forty-three persons, including 13 women and 11 children were injured, of which 75 by State actors and 68 by unidentified perpetrators; and more than 299 people were unlawfully arrested and detained. Violations of the right to freedom of the press, including the arrest of eight journalists, as well as destruction of property including premises belonging to political parties, police stations and shops, have also been documented. These violations resulted in further restricting the enjoyment of civil and political rights in the country.

The figures presented in this report are not final, as the UNJHRO has received numerous allegations that are pending confirmation due to access restrictions. Notably, UNJHRO teams have been denied access to some detention centres on the instructions of senior officials as well as to official records of some morgues and public hospitals, from 21 September to date.

The report concludes with a series of recommendations taking fully into account the State's obligations under international human rights law and the Congolese constitution. The implementation of these recommendations by the Congolese authorities, all political actors, the media and the international community, is essential to ensure respect for fundamental freedoms, including guaranteeing an open democratic space that allows inclusive, credible and transparent electoral process and national dialogue.

I. INTRODUCTION

1. As the Democratic Republic of Congo (DRC) enters its critical electoral cycle, the United Nations Joint Human Rights Office (UNJHRO) has documented a significant deterioration of the situation of civil and political rights across the country since January 2015. This manifested itself in the violence which characterised the events which took place in Kinshasa from 19 to 21 September 2016. This report presents the preliminary findings of ongoing investigations by the UNJHRO on human rights violations and abuses perpetrated during and after the demonstrations of 19 September 2016 in Kinshasa.

2. Although a significant number of allegations remain unconfirmed, the UNJHRO has documented significant instances of human rights violations allegedly perpetrated by defence and security forces, and, to a lesser extent, violence by demonstrators. Notably, the number of persons killed attributable to State agents exceeds those documented by the UNJHRO during the whole 2011 electoral process. The actual number could be much higher, as the UNJHRO faced several restrictions during its investigations, including denials of access to places of detention and sources of information.

3. The information collected shows that agents of the *Police Nationale Congolaise* (PNC), together with soldiers of the *Forces armées de la République démocratique du Congo* (FARDC) and the Republican Guard (GR) were the main perpetrators of the human rights violations documented by the UNJHRO. Notably, these included violations of the right to life by excessive use of force and widespread use of lethal weapons in crowd control. Defence and security forces were used to cordon demonstrators.

4. The UNJHRO also documented violence, ransacking and destruction of property, including those of pro-government parties and police stations, and the killing of four police agents attributable to unidentified demonstrators.

5. This report does not claim to be exhaustive by documenting all relevant incidents that occurred before, during and after the demonstrations. Nevertheless, the UNJHRO considers that the report illustrates the main patterns of violations perpetrated by State agents and criminal acts by others.

II. METHODOLOGY AND CONSTRAINTS

6. From 19 September 2016 onwards, the UNJHRO conducted investigations in various neighbourhoods of Kinshasa, including the communes of Lemba, Limete, Ndjili, Ngaliema, Funa, Lingwala, Ma Campagne, Kimbanseke, Nsele, Maluku, Bandalungwa, Gombe, Kasa-Vubu, Kisenso, Makala, Mungafula, Ngiri-Ngiri, Selembao, Masina and Kalamu. In the scope of the 2011 electoral cycle, the UNJHRO had documented at least 41 victims of arbitrary killings, over 168 victims of violations to the right of physical integrity and over 400 victims of violations to the right of liberty and security of the person. The main perpetrators were agents of the Congolese national police and of the Presidential Guard. To date, no progress was registered in the investigation open by the Congolese authorities in this respect.

7. Based on the standard methodology of the Office of the High-Commissioner for Human Rights (OHCHR), the UNJHRO adopted an inclusive approach to collecting and corroborating information. Information-gathering methods included: (a) interviews with more than 112 victims, witnesses and other sources, among which 11 women; (b) site-visits to specific locations where incidents had occurred; (c) *in situ* visits of 26 hospitals and health centres to consult medical reports on killed and injured persons admitted during those days and in relation to those events; d) reviews of reports from various sources and partners; (e) at least 29 meetings with various State authorities, including representatives of *Etat-Major des renseignements militaires*—former DEMIAP—(EMRM), *Agence nationale de renseignements* (ANR), FARDC, PNC, as well as judiciary and penitentiary authorities.

8. UNJHRO findings rely primarily on first-hand information collected by its human rights officers. Information from other sources, including publications, reports and other communications, was only used as means of secondary corroboration.

9. Investigations and access to information were hindered by several restrictions. Movements of UNJHRO teams were limited due to the security situation on 19 and 20 September 2016. In addition, UNJHRO teams were denied access to detention facilities upon instructions from senior Ministry of Defence officials, arguing the teams needed to seek an authorisation prior to the visit. This was notably the case of ANR detention cells as well as FARDC Kokolo Camp, where access has been denied since 21 September 2016. Most of the people arrested during the 19 September 2016 demonstrations, as well as bodies of those killed and injured victims, were reportedly taken to that camp.

10. Denial of access has therefore significantly hindered UNJHRO's work and access to information, in violation of the memorandum of understanding signed between the national authorities and OHCHR. UNJHRO teams were also denied access to official records of other morgues and public hospitals. As an illustration, on several occasions, the UNJHRO received reports that an undetermined number of victims injured by bullets were thrown into the Ndjili River by the defence and security forces. Similarly, there have been allegations of mass graves in the commune of Masina. Again, although military trucks carrying bodies were seen in the neighbourhood, difficulties in accessing morgues prevented the UNJHRO from confirming them.

11. Moreover, on 19 September 2016, on the first day of the demonstrations, security and defence forces prevented two UN vehicles from accessing the location of the events. At 11 a.m., a PNC agent shot tear gas at a UN vehicle. A few minutes later, on Avenue Sendwe, a sniper on top of an anti-riot PNC truck shot twice at a UN vehicle but missed its target. In the second case, it has not been possible to determine whether live ammunition or blank bullets were used. In both incidents, no material damage was reported. Investigations by MONUSCO into the incidents are underway.

12. Besides, the UNJHRO received several concordant reports about the distribution by authorities of machetes and money to approximately one hundred

young men, with a view to disturbing the demonstration. Similar allegations had already been reported during previous demonstrations. These men were allegedly paid to attack the private homes of members and supporters of the ruling party, the *Parti du peuple pour la reconstruction et la démocratie* (PPRD), with a view to then shift the responsibility to the supporters of the opposition. The UNJHRO was however not able to corroborate this plan of targeted attacks.

III. Legal framework

13. The right to peaceful assembly and freedom of demonstration are both guaranteed by the DRC Constitution, which does not require permission nor justification prior to demonstrations. Indeed, Article 26 of the Constitution only requires that organisers of a demonstration planned to take place on public roads or in open air inform the competent authority in writing. However, in practice, the system of prior authorisation in application of law n°196 of 29 July 1999 remains in force.

14. The notification required according to Article 26 of the Constitution is envisaged to allow competent authorities to take all necessary measures to facilitate holding of demonstrations and to protect demonstrators, therefore ensuring their role in maintaining law and order. However, since January 2015, in Kinshasa, Government officials and security forces have often banned private and public meetings of political opposition parties and/or civil society organizations, arguing that they constituted threats against State security. State agents have frequently prevented opposition leaders from moving freely, fired tear gas—and sometimes even live ammunition—against peaceful protestors, and have arbitrarily arrested and detained some of them, in violation of the rights guaranteed in the DRC Constitution. In contrast, gatherings organised by the Presidential majority have largely taken place without any disruption from the authorities.

15. Moreover, the Constitution states that no one is obliged to implement an order that is manifestly illegal or contrary to human rights and fundamental freedoms.

16. Organic laws on the organisation and functioning of the PNC7 and Armed Forces provide that defence and security forces shall use force only in cases of absolute necessity and solely to achieve a legitimate goal. In accordance with international standards, the use of force and firearms should be exceptional, and when unavoidable, must be proportionate. If the use of force is necessary for maintaining law and order, it must respect the above-mentioned principles.

17. Finally, the DRC is party to many international human rights instruments guaranteeing freedom of association and the right to peaceful assembly, including the International Covenant on Civil and Political Rights (ICCPR) and the International Covenant on Economic, Social and Cultural Rights (ICESCR). National authorities are therefore obliged to respect, protect and fulfil those rights and to prevent their violations. Any allegation of human rights violations or abuses must be promptly, thoroughly, impartially and independently investigated and those found responsible must be brought to justice.

IV. CONTEXT

18. Prior to the demonstrations, in Kinshasa, leaders of the main opposition parties, namely *Forces novatrices pour l'union et la solidarité* (FONUS) and *Union pour la Démocratie et le Progrès Social* (UDPS), as well as representatives of the civil society organization *Association Africaine des Droits de l'Homme* (ASADHO), mobilised the population, with calls for the organization of national elections and for respect of the Constitution.

19. Leaders of the political platform *Rassemblement des forces politiques et sociales acquises au changement* ("Rassemblement")—organisers of the 19 September demonstration—held three meetings with the Governor of Kinshasa to agree on an itinerary for those demonstrations. Organisers and authorities agreed that the event would start from *Echangeur* of Limete and that, in the afternoon, a delegation of 35 members of the *Rassemblement* would file a memorandum to CENI, in the Gombe commune.

20. In the evening of 18 September, the night before the demonstration, radio and television programs, including State-controlled media, broadcast erroneous information on the approved itinerary. This may have contributed to subsequent mismanagement of the demonstration the next day. The PNC Spokesperson also informed the media of a different route from that agreed upon by the competent authorities. Around 6 p.m., on 18 September, the same Spokesperson stated that the PNC would closely monitor one of the demonstration's assembly points, between *Avenue de l'enseignement and Stade des Martyrs*. Furthermore, media channels such as *Radio-télévision nationale congolaise* (RTNC), *Télé* 50 and *RTNC* 2, broadcast messages from the main majority party, the PPRD, calling pro-Kabila supporters to defend the President's mandate and to support the national dialogue. Reports indicate that flyers in Lingala were distributed to the population with the writing: "*Ekoyinda le 19 Septembre 2016*" ("It will blow out on 19 September 2016").

21. A National Operations Center, as a central command, was activated for managing temporary incidents. The Center was integrated by commanding officers of EMRM, FARDC, ANR and PNC.

22. Also, from 14 to 18 September 2016, in several districts of Kinshasa, PNC agents conducted a major operation, reportedly to prevent any political meeting from taking place, during which they arrested in various circumstances, leaders and organisers of political and advocacy activities. On 15 September 2016, 15 people who had participated in a sensitization meeting on the involvement of youth in the electoral process were arrested without warrant by PNC and ANR agents. On 16 September 2016, at approximately 4 a.m., PNC and ANR agents surrounded the house of the President of the NGO *Union des Jeunes Congolais pour le Changement* (UJCC), arrested him without a warrant and took him to ANR facilities, where he is allegedly still being held at the time of writing this report.

23. On 15 September 2016, PNC agents conducted a cordon-search operation in Mombele, Limete commune, which is known as a UDPS stronghold. According to the PNC, the operation was launched following allegations that ammunition,

firearms (AK-47 and pistols), machetes, Molotov cocktails and other craft weapons hidden by the population were being distributed in order to be used during the demonstrations. According to information made available to the UNJHRO, during that operation no weapon has been seized. During this operation, PNC agents arrested more than 23 people, including six minors.

V. HUMAN RIGHTS VIOLATIONS AND OTHER FINDINGS

24. The UNJHRO documented cases of more than 422 victims of human rights violations attributable to the State during the events related to the opposition demonstration of 19 September 2016 in Kinshasa. In total, the UNJHRO was able to confirm that at least 53 persons, including seven women, two children, and four police agents, were killed. Forty-eight were killed by State actors, while the rest of the perpetrators were not clearly identified. One hundred and forty-three persons, including 13 women and 11 children were injured, of which 75 by State actors and 68 by unidentified perpetrators; and more than 299 people were unlawfully arrested and detained. Violations of the rights to life, to physical integrity and to the liberty and security of the person were committed with an aim to further restrict the freedom of expression and right to peaceful assembly, raising concerns about significant restrictions of the democratic space.

i. Freedom of peaceful assembly

25. The first violations of the right to peaceful assembly took place in the morning of 19 September 2016, around 7.30 a.m., when PNC agents started to disperse gatherings with tear gas and arrested eight people in the Lemba commune. PNC agents also blocked protestors and attempted to disperse them while they were heading towards assembly points in Tchangu (Kimbanseke commune), Kinkole (Maluku commune), Funa (Makala commune) and the Moulaert roundabout (Bandalungwa commune), as per the route agreed upon the day before. Around 9.30 a.m. the National Operations Centre reportedly decided to prohibit the demonstrations without informing the organisers, and military reinforcement composed of FARDC and GR soldiers were called upon.

26. Between 11 a.m. and 3 p.m., the anti-riot police built barricades and cordoned the area between *Lumumba* and *Sendwe Boulevards*, and between *Boulevard Triomphal* and *Avenue de l'Enseignement*. FARDC and GR soldiers were positioned at several strategic points, and shots were fired at demonstrators, both tear gas and live ammunition. Moreover, from 3 p.m. onwards, military elements of GR and FARDC and PNC agents restricted movements in certain areas, including for ambulances and medical personnel trying to evacuate the wounded.

27. All the violations of human rights by defence and security forces from 19 to 21 September 2016, either the killings, people injured or people arrested, are the result of the violation of the freedom of peaceful assembly. Indeed, those violations were committed with the aim and/or with the consequence that the victims were impeded from peacefully exercising their freedom of assembly and demonstration.

ii. Right to life

28. The UNJHRO documented the killing of at least 53 persons, including seven women and two children. At least 48 of those individuals were killed by State agents, including at least 18 by PNC agents, 10 by GR soldiers and eight by FARDC soldiers. For the other 12 victims, all shot dead, the UNJHRO could not determine accurately which specific State agents were responsible because they were killed during operations involving different forces that acted jointly. In most cases, the deaths were caused by an excessive use of force against the protestors not in a way that can be assessed as "strictly unavoidable in order to protect life".

29. Among the victims, 38 were killed by bullet, including 16 by PNC agents, eight by FARDC soldiers and two by GR soldiers. At least 11 victims were hit by bullet on the upper parts of the body, namely in the head, chest and back, including a five-year old girl. The first victim to be killed received two bullets in the chest shot by an unidentified State agent around 9.30 a.m. on 19 September on *Avenue de l'Université* in the commune of Limete. He died on the spot.

30. Seven people whose body were burned were killed by GR soldiers including during an attack against UDPS headquarters, and one woman was killed with a machete by GR soldiers. Moreover, it should be noted that several bodies of victims of GR soldiers showed signs of injuries caused by machetes.

31. Information collected shows that PNC agents beat a man to death and stabbed to death another man in Limete commune.

32. A forty-ninth victim was documented, but information is not available to the UNJHRO as to the identity of the perpetrator. The victim, a 33 year-old woman, was in a TRANSCO bus when an altercation between PNC agents and protestors broke outside. According to several sources, stones were thrown from both sides, one of them hitting the woman on the head and causing her death.

33. In addition, the killings of four PNC agents on 19 September were documented. One PNC officer was killed in the commune of Limete. Protesters reportedly beat him before burning him alive and grabbing his service weapon. Another one was beaten to death in front of Kisenso police station. Two others, including a woman police officer, were also beaten to death in commune of Kimbanseke.

34. Finally, the UNJHRO documented several cases in which by-standers were indirectly affected by the violence, the demonstrations and the road blockades limiting the movements of ambulances. For example, on 20 September 2016, a pregnant woman died right upon arrival at the hospital. She had reportedly tried to reach Malamu, but could not get there on time because the road was blocked.

iii. Right to physical integrity

35. The UNJHRO documented at least 143 persons, including 13 women and 11 children, who were injured during the violence of 19, 20 and 21 September 2016. At least 75 persons, including 10 women and 11 children, were injured by State agents. For 16 of them, the UNJHRO was able to identify the perpetrators: 10 by PNC agents and six by soldiers (including three by FARDC and three

by GR soldiers). Other 59 people (out of the 75 by State agents) were also victims of State agents, but the UNJHRO could not accurately determine which, as different groups of State agents were acting together. For the remaining 68, the UNJHRO was not able to determine the identity of the alleged perpetrators (either State agents or not).

36.   Out of the 75 victims of State agents, a total of 61 people, including nine women and nine children, were injured by bullets. In most cases, the injuries were the result of excessive use of force against demonstrators during joint operations and not carried out in self-defence. In the cases of 57 persons out of the 61 injured by bullets, the UNJHRO could not accurately determine which State agents had shot them. The UNJHRO could however verify that one man was injured by a PNC officer, another man by a GR soldier, and two persons—including a child—by FARDC soldiers. Among those injured by bullets, six were hit on the upper part of their body, including the head, the chest and the back.

37.   With regard to the remaining 14 victims out of the 75 injured by State agents, ten suffered injuries resulting from the use of tear gas fired against the crowd by State agents. Among them, nine were directly hit in the abdomen or chest, including eight by PNC agents. Finally, two people were burned in the second and third degrees by GR soldiers, one victim was injured by machete by a PNC officer, and one woman was hit on the head with a rifle butt by a FARDC soldier.

38.   Furthermore, the UNJHRO has also documented 68 other individuals injured, including 41 by bullet and 27 by stones thrown at them. The UNJHRO could however not verify information about the perpetrators. Indeed, it should be noted that a large number of those wounded by bullet were directly transferred to the FARDC Kokolo Camp hospital, where access has been denied to the UNJHRO since 21 September 2016.

39.   The road blockades prevented the evacuation of the wounded to hospitals. For example, on 20 September 2016, MONUSCO had to escort an ambulance transporting a five-year old child shot and wounded in the back. The ambulance had been blocked in the commune of Lemba by PNC agents, but was later able to reach the hospital thanks to MONUSCO's escort.

iv. Right to liberty and security of person

40.   At least 299 people, including at least six children and two women, were arrested between 19 and 21 September 2016 during the demonstrations in Kinshasa. On 19 September 2016, hundreds of people were arrested and taken to various police sub-stations, before being transferred to the FARDC Kokolo Camp, on the orders of the National Operations Centre, also ordering that all so-called "political cases" (those concerning the representatives of political parties and other public figures) were in turn transferred to the ANR.

41.   Moreover, in violation to the freedom of the press, journalists covering the events *in situ* were targeted by security forces, arbitrarily arrested between 11.30 a.m. and 4 p.m. and unlawfully detained with the aim to prevent them from informing on events on the ground. PNC agents harassed and arrested

those using video cameras, photo cameras or other recording devices such as mobile phones during the demonstrations. Eight journalists and other workers from international media such as *Radio France Internationale* (RFI), *Agence France Presse* (AFP), TV 5, as well as from national media such as *Canal Télévision Congo* (CCTV), the daily newspaper *La prospérité*, and the magazine *Takomi Wapi*, were harassed and arbitrarily detained by security forces during the demonstrations. The eight journalists were harassed, robbed, beaten and detained for several hours before being released. Three of them were taken to FARDC Kokolo Camp and released following the intervention of the UNJHRO and others.

42.   On 20 and 21 September 2016, PNC agents and GR soldiers conducted raids including at night in several districts of the city, such as Limete, Lemba, Matete, Ndjili and Masina, in targeted search of opposition sympathisers previously identified in a list, and broke into houses with no judicial warrants.

43.   On 29 September 2016, 103 individual cases concerning those arrested were transferred to different *Parquets*. The judicial authorities issued 53 judgments and other decisions in *flagrante delicto* hearings. In total, 25 people were sentenced to prison terms ranging from one month to two years for conspiracy, rebellion, malicious destruction and/or voluntary arson. In addition, 20 people were acquitted for lack of evidence. In eight cases, the courts declined to hear the cases, either because of territorial (five cases) or personal (three children) lack of jurisdiction. Those three cases were referred to the Juvenile Court of Ndjili. Furthermore, according to information received by the UNJHRO from the tribunal, 50 cases still remain pending.

v. Destruction, looting of property and attacks against political parties' premises and public and private properties

44.   On 20 September 2016, the UNJHRO documented cases of destruction of property, including attacks against the headquarters of five opposition political parties, UDPS, FONUS, *Mouvement lumumbiste progressiste* (MLP), *Parti démocrate chrétien* (PDC), and *Mouvement des Démocrates Congolais* (MDCO), allegedly attributable to State agents either directly (by being themselves the perpetrators of the violation) or indirectly (by being present at the scene without intervening and/or denying access to people trying to extinguish the fire or to rescue victims). All those headquarters of opposition political parties, located in the commune of Limete, were set on fire.

45.   The headquarter of the human rights NGO *Gouvernance plus*, which is near the MLP headquarters, was also attacked and burned on the same day. The UNJHRO could however not determine whether it was a targeted attack or collateral damage.

46.   The attacks described in paragraph 44 were allegedly perpetrated following a similar *modus operandi* from 2 to 4 a.m. They have been carried out by a group of twenty men, some of whom were dressed in GR uniforms, some in civilian clothes and others partially in military uniforms. The men arrived on board of two pickup-type white jeeps. Most of them were hooded and all were speaking in various languages possibly English, Swahili and Lingala.

47. The FONUS headquarter was attacked at around 4 a.m. Men in civilian attire reportedly arrived in two above-mentioned white jeeps and tried to force the entrance gate. FONUS activists, who had remained in the office for the night, retaliated with stones. Then, GR soldiers allegedly threw a grenade at the FONUS headquarters, forcing activists to escape to neighbouring plots by climbing the fence walls. The GR soldiers reportedly managed to enter the headquarters, where they opened the doors, broke the building's windows and poured gasoline before exiting. Then, five GR soldiers allegedly set the building ablaze. The soldiers then went back to the two vehicles and drove away. Allegedly, when FONUS activists and neighbours tried to extinguish the fire, PNC agents in three vehicles blocked the road and chased them.

48. Around 3.30 a.m., two jeeps arrived at the UDPS headquarter. Persons wearing civilian clothes and other persons wearing GR uniforms tried to break in. Then, they reportedly pulled away and threw tear gas grenades inside the compound. More than twenty UDPS activists were inside at the time. While some activists managed to escape by climbing the walls, others were attacked with machetes by the perpetrators. In addition, five UDPS members were forcibly detained and beaten by alleged GR soldiers. The attackers set the building on fire using petrol, and threw these five UDPS members inside the flames, before fleeing the area. At the time of the attack, PNC agents were reportedly near the scene and did not intervene. They cordoned off the area shortly after the fire was set, preventing also the arrival of ambulances and the evacuation of the wounded. A total of five people were killed, fifteen wounded, including by machetes, and nine missing, all as a result of the incident.

49. In addition to the attacks against party headquarters, several private goods were also seized by State agents. For example, 40 motorcycles were confiscated by PNC agents on 19 September 2016 in Matete. This incident reportedly triggered violence, with demonstrators setting three buildings on fire before recovering the motorcycles. PNC agents were also involved in looting. An agency of the *Banque internationale pour l'Afrique au Congo* (BIAC) was looted by PNC agents, including a PNC major who was subsequently arrested for those acts.

50. Finally, cases of extortion were reported. On 20 September 2016, an unknown number of people were arbitrarily arrested by PNC agents in the areas of Mokali, Pascal and Kimbanseke, and taken to the commune of Ndjili, where policemen allegedly demanded payment of 100,000 Congolese Francs per person for their release.

vi. Victims' profiles

51. As a result of excessive and disproportionate use of force by State agents as well as the violence used by demonstrators, victims come from different groups. They include opposition sympathisers, police agents as well as by-standers notably women and children. Additionally, international and national journalists and human rights defenders were targeted. Health workers and human rights defenders continued to be threatened for reporting on the events.

VI. Alleged perpetrators

52. The majority of the documented human rights violations were perpetrated by PNC agents and FARDC and GR soldiers. Thus, at least 422 individuals were victims of human rights violations perpetrated by State agents. Information collected by the UNJHRO shows that PNC agents were responsible for the extrajudicial killings of at least 18 persons, including 16 shot dead, the wounding of at least 10 others, as well as the majority of the 299 unlawful and/or arbitrary arrests. FARDC soldiers are responsible for the death of at least eight individuals and for violations of the right to physical integrity of three others. Moreover, they were involved in the unlawful detention of the majority of those arrested in the Kokolo military camp. GR soldiers are responsible for at least 10 summary executions, including seven people burned, and three violations of the right to physical integrity.

53. Furthermore, in several documented cases, information collected shows that persons in civilian clothing acted jointly with defence and security forces, or with their acquiescence or complicity, to perpetrate human rights violations. This was for example the case during the attack against UDPS headquarter.

54. Reportedly, bodies of the deceased victims, as well as several wounded persons, were taken away by the authorities, often rapidly and sometimes by force and against the will of the victims' families. The UNJHRO got reports of military and police trucks retrieving corpses of demonstrators shot on 19 September in various communes of the city.

55. Finally, as of the morning of 19 September 2016, a National Operations Centre was used as a central command centre. This integrated cell was jointly managed by senior FARDC, PNC and ANR agents. On 19 September 2016, at around 9:30 am, it was reportedly this cell that decided to prohibit the event without informing the organisers. It also reportedly radioed orders to PNC agents, asking them to put an end to the demonstration and informing them of the imminent arrival of military reinforcements. The National Operations Centre reportedly authorized the use of force including fire arms against demonstrators.

VII. Violence by demonstrators

56. The UNJHRO, during its investigation, was informed of many cases of violence by demonstrators. The killings of four PNC agents on 19 September were documented. One PNC agent was killed in the commune of Limete. Protesters reportedly beat him before burning him alive and grabbing his service weapon. Another one was beaten to death in front of Kisenso police station. Two others, including a woman police officer, were also beaten to death in [the] commune of Kimbanseke. The DRC Government declared that four PNC agents were killed during the demonstrations.

57. Demonstrators also erected barricades, including by burning tires, during the day of 19 September 2016, reportedly. During clashes with defence and security forces, they allegedly threw stones and also destroyed and looted the headquarters of three political parties linked to the presidential majority, namely the

PPRD, the *Alliance des travaillistes congolais pour le développement* (ATCD) and the *Convention nationale congolaise* (CNC).

58. Authorities reported that demonstrators were responsible for the destruction and looting of many public buildings and other facilities. According to information received by the UNJHRO, 28 police stations, substations and antennas as well as various tribunals were sacked and burned by demonstrators. Also, 30 long rifles with ammunitions were stolen, three have been recovered so far.

59. Finally, on 27 September 2016, during the presentation of the report of the United Nations High Commissioner for Human Rights at the 33rd session of the Human Rights Council, the Minister of Justice and Human Rights of DRC referred in his statement to the gang rape of an eight-year old girl, as well as to cases of beheadings and emasculations perpetrated by demonstrators. Despite seeking information from police stations, hospitals and networks combatting sexual violence as well as exchanges with other partners, the UNJHRO was unable to verify these allegations.

VIII. ACTIONS UNDERTAKEN BY CONGOLESE AUTHORITIES

60. As the events unfolded, the Government announced laying charges against the organisers of the demonstration, those involved in the violence and "the intellectual authors". The announcement also stated that the organisers would be prevented from traveling abroad, which is a restriction on the freedom of movement. On 22 September 2016, defence and security forces conducted a cordon and search operation around military camps Kokolo and Kabila aiming at retreating goods looted by Kulunas and State actors. In addition, 25 people, who were arrested during the demonstrations between 19 and 21 September 2016, were sentenced to prison terms ranging from one month to two years for conspiracy, rebellion, malicious destruction and/or arson.

61. On 21 September 2016, during a press conference, the President of the National Human Rights Commission announced the opening of an independent inquiry into the public demonstrations of 19 and 20 September in Kinshasa. The inquiry is mandated to collect information on cases of human rights violations documented during those events, and possibly, as part of the Commission's mandate, to file complaints on behalf of the victims.

62. Finally, on 22 September 2016, the Governor of Kinshasa decided to prohibit all public demonstrations until further notice. Therefore, a demonstration organised by the Presidential Majority the week after was banned to prevent further violence.

IX. CONCLUSION AND RECOMMENDATIONS

63. From 19 to 21 September 2016 in Kinshasa, the UNJHRO recorded serious human rights violations as a result of a disproportionate and excessive use of force, including lethal force, by the Congolese authorities in reaction to the demonstration organized by opposition members.

64. The UNJHRO has been able to verify that at least 53 persons were shot, burned, hacked with machetes, beaten or stoned, including at least 48 by the defence and security forces. In addition, at least 143 civilians were injured, including at least 75 by State agents, mainly PNC agents and FARDC and GR soldiers.

65. The UNJHRO also documented violence, criminal acts and destruction of property by the demonstrators including the killing of four police agents, which is contrary to principles of peaceful assembly and should be promptly, thoroughly, independently and impartially investigated and those responsible prosecuted in compliance with the DRC law.

66. At least 299 people, including members of political parties, journalists and human rights activists, were arrested by PNC agents and GR soldiers. As of 29 September 2016, the judicial authorities have convicted during *flagrante delicto* hearings 25 persons to prison sentences ranging from one month to two years for conspiracy, rebellion, malicious destruction and/or arson.

67. The headquarters of political parties, of one human rights NGO and other public and private properties were attacked by men affiliated with defence and security forces as well as by demonstrators.

68. The conclusions presented in this report only relate to the preliminary findings of the investigation by the UNJHRO. Given that a large number of allegations await verification, the information presented cannot be considered to be an exhaustive list of all human rights violations and abuses perpetrated during the Kinshasa events. Further, the UNJHRO regrets that its investigations and access to information were hindered by restrictions imposed by Congolese authorities, including access to ANR cells and to the FARDC Kokolo Camp.

69. In addition to the recommendations made in its previous reports, the UNJHRO urges:

    A. *The Congolese authorities*

    - to conduct prompt, independent, thorough, credible, transparent and impartial investigations into allegations of human rights violations committed by State agents and those affiliated with the State agents in the context of the crackdown on demonstrations in Kinshasa and the rest of the country between 19 and 21 September 2016; to bring those responsible to justice, irrespective of their rank or position;

    - in addition, to adopt disciplinary measures against all State agents who abused their authority;

    - to conduct prompt, independent, thorough, credible, transparent and impartial investigations, in accordance with international standards, to determine those responsible for the violence during demonstrations, and unconditionally release all those arbitrarily or unlawfully arrested or against whom no charge has been retained;

    - to ensure the full exercise of the right to peaceful assembly and protest, in accordance with the DRC Constitution and international obligations;

and to use all appropriate means to ensure that these rights can be exercised freely and securely, including by making sure that the safety of demonstrators is guaranteed;

- to equip PNC units with adequate material means to manage situations where they must maintain or re-establish public order, to remove lethal weapons and to authorise the use the force [sic] only as a last resort and in compliance with the principles of necessity, proportionality and legality, in accordance with international standards;

- to ensure the protection of the human rights and fundamental freedoms of all persons, such as political opponents, journalists, other civil society actors, women and children; and to ensure that any restrictions on those freedoms respect the principles of legality, necessity and proportionality;

- to prevent human rights violations from being committed at future events by providing training to defence and security forces on respecting human rights norms and standards, especially in relation to the use of force;

- for the Parliament to urgently adopt the draft law setting out measures to ensure the freedom to hold demonstrations including a prior notification system for demonstrations and ensure the law's full compliance with international standards;

- for the Parliament to urgently adopt the draft law on protection of human rights defenders;

- to ensure full access of UN personnel and other international monitors to the victims of the demonstrations and detention centres, especially ANR cells and the FARDC Kokolo Camp;

B. *Political actors and media in the DRC*

- Political actors to publically [sic] promote the rights guaranteed in the Constitution and other national laws as well as international human rights norms and standards, and abide by principles of nonviolence;

- Political actors to abide by the provisions of the Code of Conduct for political parties;

- to firmly condemn the use of violence by members of political parties, and to take appropriate measures to prevent and end it;

C. *The international community*

- to call upon the Congolese authorities to promptly, thoroughly, independently and impartially conduct investigation into human rights allegations perpetrated in the context of the repression of the demonstrations and prosecute those responsible;

- to call upon the Congolese authorities to take preventive measures to ensure that these human rights violations will not reoccur, and to monitor measures taken by the Government in response to these violations;

- to call upon political actors to carry out their activities through peaceful means and in strict compliance with the legislation of the DRC.

SOURCE: United Nations Human Rights Office of the High Commissioner. "UNITED NATIONS JOINT HUMAN RIGHTS OFFICE (UNJHRO) MONUSCO-OHCHR: Preliminary investigation report on human rights violations and violence perpetrated during demonstrations in Kinshasa between 19 and 21 September 2016." October 7, 2016. http://www.ohchr.org/Documents/Countries/CD/UNJHROSeptember2016_en.pdf.

U.S. Treasury Sanctions Two Congolese Government Officials

DOCUMENT

December 12, 2016

Today, the U.S. Department of the Treasury's Office of Foreign Assets Control (OFAC) sanctioned two Democratic Republic of the Congo (DRC) government officials pursuant to Executive Order (E.O.) 13413, as amended by E.O. 13671, as the Government of the DRC continues to suppress political opposition and delay political progress in the country, often through violent means. Specifically, OFAC designated Evariste Boshab and Kalev Mutondo for engaging in actions or policies that undermine democratic processes or institutions in the DRC. As a result of today's actions, all of the designated individuals' assets within U.S. jurisdiction are frozen, and U.S. persons are generally prohibited from engaging in transactions with them.

"The Congolese government continues to undermine democratic processes in the DRC and repress the political rights and freedoms of the Congolese people, putting the long-term stability and prosperity of the country at risk," said Adam Szubin, Acting Under Secretary for Terrorism and Financial Intelligence at the U.S. Department of the Treasury. "Today's designation is intended to alter the behavior of the targeted individuals with the aim of fostering a better and more stable future for the DRC and the Congolese people."

The United Nations Joint Human Rights Office has reported that since the beginning of 2015, DRC state agents have increasingly violated human rights, political rights and public freedoms of Congolese people, including the freedoms of expression speech and peaceful assembly. In late June 2016, the United Nations Security Council expressed concern over the arrest of political opposition members in the DRC and urged the president to hold elections by the end of the year, as required by the constitution.

The Government has conducted extra-constitutional arrests and detentions, used torture as a tool of political oppression, has reportedly committed closed media outlets, and prevented the holding of peaceful protests. In several provinces, defense and security forces have violently repressed peaceful demonstrations organized to oppose a new draft electoral law that many fear would allow President Kabila to run for a third term, an action that is currently prohibited under the constitution. The Government of the DRC has also barred human rights-focused researchers from a number of non-governmental organizations, including the Congo Research Group, Global Witness, and Human Rights Watch.

EVARISTE BOSHAB, DEPUTY PRIME MINISTER AND MINISTER OF INTERIOR AND SECURITY

Evariste Boshab (Boshab) is a key player in leading DRC President Kabila's strategy to remain in power after December 19, 2016, when President Kabila's constitutional term officially ends. In January 2015, Boshab introduced a bill before the DRC National Assembly to amend the electoral law in a manner that would delay elections and prolong President Kabila's term beyond its constitutional limit. Boshab has also offered to pay National Assembly members for their votes. In December 2015, Boshab overstepped his authority by appointing commissioners for newly-created provinces in the DRC without holding elections. In addition, Boshab has told officials that they should leave their posts if they supported the opposition and he has supported the neutralization of opposition demonstrations.

KALEV MUTONDO, GENERAL ADMINISTRATOR OF THE NATIONAL INTELLIGENCE AGENCY

Kalev Mutondo (Kalev) has ordered officials to ensure that the DRC's electoral process favored President Kabila's Presidential Majority or "MP" political coalition. He has ordered surveillance of the opposition and supported the neutralization of opposition demonstrations and the extrajudicial arrest and detainment of opposition members, many of whom were reportedly tortured. Kalev has been accused of pressuring DRC authorities to act outside the scope of the law to thwart the political opposition. Kalev directed support for President Kabila's "MP" political coalition using violent intimidation and government resources. Additionally, Kalev may be linked to the illegal export of minerals from the DRC.

SOURCE: U.S. Treasury Department. "Treasury Sanctions Two Congolese Government Officials." December 12, 2016. http://www.treasury.gov/press-center/press-releases/Pages/jl0682.aspx.

EU Declaration on the Situation in the Democratic Republic of the Congo

December 12, 2016

The Council has adopted travel restrictions and an asset freeze in respect of seven individuals occupying **positions of authority in the chain of command over perpetrators of violence,** with immediate effect. Meeting within the Council of the European Union, foreign affairs ministers discussed the latest developments in the country. Member states agreed on a declaration on the situation in the DRC.

"The European Union and its Member States are deeply concerned about the political situation in the Democratic Republic of the Congo. The constitutional mandate of President Kabila will come to an end on 19 December, and the date approaches fraught with risk and uncertainty after the recent crackdowns and violations of fundamental rights. Any new government in place after that date must ground its legitimacy in a clearly and inclusively defined political framework, otherwise the country's relations with the European Union will suffer.

Efforts have been made to reconcile positions and to reach an inclusive agreement on a transition which will allow the country to hold peaceful, credible elections as soon as possible, in accordance with the Constitution of the DRC and UN Security Council Resolution 2277 (2016).

The European Union has supported these initiatives, in particular the ongoing mediation efforts of the DRC Catholic Bishops' Conference. It invites all political stakeholders, from both the government and the opposition, to heed its call to assume responsibility, show good will, and make full use of their good offices. It commends the constructive role that regional organisations and other countries in the region, in particular Angola and the Republic of the Congo, have played in attempting to find a peaceful solution.

With the 19 December deadline fast approaching, the European Union calls upon the Congolese people to show restraint and to promote dialogue by rejecting violence.

The acts of violence which caused the death of at least 50 people on 19 and 20 September in Kinshasa constitute serious violations of human rights and fundamental freedoms, attested to by several observers, including the UN Joint Human Rights Office. In the Council Conclusions of 23 May and again on 17 October, the European Union pledged to adopt restrictive measures against those responsible for that violence and those who are allegedly trying to obstruct a peaceful and consensual solution to the crisis in the DRC.

Therefore, the EU Foreign Affairs Council have today taken the decision to impose restrictive measures against the seven individuals who hold positions of authority in the chain of command over the Congolese security forces which have exercised a disproportionate use of force.

The European Union calls upon the Government of the DRC to cooperate with a transparent and independent investigation with the goal of bringing to justice those responsible for the acts of violence. It also calls for full compliance with fundamental rights, including freedom of expression, freedom of assembly and freedom of the press.

The European Union will be monitoring the crucial political developments taking place in the DRC during the coming weeks with increased attention. In this context, additional restrictive measures may be considered in the event of further violence or the political process being impeded.

The Candidate Countries the former Yugoslav Republic of Macedonia*, Montenegro* and Albania*, the country of the Stabilisation and Association Process and potential candidate Bosnia and Herzegovina, and the EFTA countries Iceland and Liechtenstein, members of the European Economic Area, as well as Ukraine and the Republic of Moldova align themselves with this Declaration.

*The former Yugoslav Republic of Macedonia, Montenegro, and Albania continue to be part of the Stabilisation and Association Process."

* * *

The individuals subject to a travel ban and an asset freeze include:

- four members of the Congolese republican guard, army or police force, who contributed to acts constituting serious violations of human rights in the DRC, by planning, directing or carrying out those acts;

- three senior figures and influential persons trying to obstruct a consensual and peaceful solution to the crisis as regards the holding of elections in the DRC, in particular through acts of violence, repression or incitement to violence, or actions that undermine the rule of law;

The names of the individuals concerned and the reasons why the Council has listed them appear in the Official Journal of 12 December 2016. The restrictive measures take effect immediately.

SOURCE: Council of the European Union. "Democratic Republic of the Congo (DRC): EU Adopts Sanctions against 7 Individuals Responsible for Violence." December 12, 2016. © European Union, 2016. http://www.consilium.europa.eu/en/press/press-releases/2016/12/12-drc-sanctions.

European Council Amends
Restrictive Actions against the DRC

December 12, 2016

THE COUNCIL OF THE EUROPEAN UNION,
  Having regard to the Treaty on European Union, and in particular Article 29 thereof,
  Having regard to the proposal of the High Representative of the Union for Foreign Affairs and Security Policy,
  Whereas:

(1) On 20 December 2010, the Council adopted Decision 2010/788/CFSP (1).

(2) On 17 October 2016, the Council adopted conclusions expressing deep concern at the political situation in the Democratic Republic of the Congo (DRC). In particular it strongly condemned the acts of extreme violence that took place on 19 and 20 September in Kinshasa, noting that those acts further exacerbated the deadlock in the country due to the failure to call the presidential elections by the constitutional deadline of 20 December 2016.

(3) The Council stressed that, in order to create a climate conducive to dialogue and the holding of elections, the Government of the DRC must clearly commit to ensuring that human rights and the rule of law are respected and must cease all use of the justice system as a political tool. It also called on all stakeholders to reject the use of violence.

(4) The Council also indicated its readiness to use all the means at its disposal, including restrictive measures against those responsible for serious human rights violations, those who promote violence and those who try to obstruct a consensual and peaceful solution to the crisis which respects the aspiration of the people of the DRC to elect their representatives.

(5) Decision 2010/788/CFSP should therefore be amended accordingly.

(6) Further action by the Union is needed in order to implement certain measures,

HAS ADOPTED THIS DECISION:

Article 1

Decision 2010/788/CFSP is amended as follows:

(1) Article 3 is replaced by the following:

'Article 3

1. Restrictive measures as provided for in Articles 4(1) and 5(1) and (2) shall be imposed against persons and entities designated by the Sanctions Committee for engaging in or providing support for acts that undermine the peace, stability or security of the DRC. Such acts include:

    (a) acting in violation of the arms embargo and related measures as referred to in Article 1;

    (b) being political and military leaders of foreign armed groups operating in the DRC who impede the disarmament and the voluntary repatriation or resettlement of combatants belonging to those groups;

    (c) being political and military leaders of Congolese militias, including those receiving support from outside the DRC, who impede the participation of their combatants in disarmament, demobilisation and reintegration processes;

    (d) recruiting or using children in armed conflict in the DRC in violation of applicable international law;

    (e) being involved in planning, directing, or committing acts in the DRC that constitute human rights violations or abuses or violations of international humanitarian law, as applicable, including those acts involving the targeting of civilians, including killing and maiming, rape and other sexual violence, abduction, forced displacement, and attacks on schools and hospitals;

    (f) obstructing the access to or the distribution of humanitarian assistance in the DRC;

    (g) supporting persons or entities, including armed groups or criminal networks, involved in destabilising activities in the DRC through the illicit exploitation of or trade in natural resources, including gold, or wildlife or wildlife products;

    (h) acting on behalf of or at the direction of a designated person or entity, or acting on behalf of or at the direction of an entity owned or controlled by a designated person or entity;

    (i) planning, directing, sponsoring or participating in attacks against MONUSCO peacekeepers or United Nations personnel;

    (j) providing financial, material, or technological support for, or goods or services to a designated person or entity.

The relevant persons and entities covered by this paragraph are listed in Annex I.

2. Restrictive measures as provided for in Articles 4(1) and 5(1) and (2) shall be imposed against persons and entities:

   (a) obstructing a consensual and peaceful solution towards elections in DRC, including by acts of violence, repression or inciting violence, or by undermining the rule of law;

   (b) involved in planning, directing or committing acts that constitute serious human rights violations or abuses in DRC;

   (c) associated with those referred to in points (a) and (b);

as listed in Annex II.';

(2) Article 4 is replaced by the following:

'Article 4

1. Member States shall take the necessary measures to prevent the entry into or transit through their territories of the persons referred to in Article 3.

2. Paragraph 1 shall not oblige a Member State to refuse its own nationals entry into its territory. . . .

(3) Article 5 is replaced by the following:

'Article 5

1. All funds, other financial assets and economic resources owned or controlled directly or indirectly by the persons or entities referred to in Article 3 or held by entities owned or controlled directly or indirectly by them or by any persons or entities acting on their behalf or at their direction, as identified in Annex I and II, shall be frozen.

2. No funds, other financial assets or economic resources shall be made available, directly or indirectly, to or for the benefit of the persons or entities referred to in paragraph 1.

3. With regard to persons and entities referred to in Article 3(1), Member States may allow for exemptions from the measures referred to in paragraphs 1 and 2 in respect of funds, other financial assets and economic resources which are:

   (a) necessary for basic expenses, including payments for foodstuffs, rent or mortgage, medicines and medical treatment, taxes, insurance premiums, and public utility charges;

   (b) intended exclusively for the payment of reasonable professional fees and reimbursement of incurred expenses associated with the provision of legal services;

   (c) intended exclusively for the payment of fees or service charges, in accordance with national laws, for routine holding or maintenance of frozen funds, or other financial assets and economic resources;

(d) necessary for extraordinary expenses, after notification by the Member State concerned to, and approval by, the Sanctions Committee; or

(e) the subject of a judicial, administrative or arbitral lien or judgment, in which case the funds, other financial assets and economic resources may be used to satisfy that lien or judgment provided that the lien or judgment was entered before designation by the Sanctions Committee of the person or entity concerned, and is not for the benefit of a person or entity referred to in Article 3, after notification by the Member State concerned to the Sanctions Committee.

4.   The exemptions referred to in points (a), (b) and (c) of paragraph 3 may be made after notification to the Sanctions Committee by the Member State concerned of its intention to authorise, where appropriate, access to such funds, other financial assets and economic resources, and in the absence of a negative decision by the Sanctions Committee within four working days of such notification.

5.   With regard to persons and entities referred to in Article 3(2), the competent authority of a Member State may authorise the release of certain frozen funds or economic resources, or the making available of certain funds or economic resources, under such conditions as it deems appropriate, after having determined that the funds or economic resources concerned are:

(a) necessary to satisfy the basic needs of the persons and entities and dependent family members of such natural persons, including payments for foodstuffs, rent or mortgage, medicines and medical treatment, taxes, insurance premiums, and public utility charges;

(b) intended exclusively for the payment of reasonable professional fees and the reimbursement of incurred expenses associated with the provision of legal services;

(c) intended exclusively for the payment of fees or service charges for the routine holding or maintenance of frozen funds or economic resources; or

(d) necessary for extraordinary expenses, provided that the competent authority has notified the competent authorities of the other Member States and the Commission of the grounds on which it considers that a specific authorisation should be granted, at least two weeks prior to the authorisation.

The Member State concerned shall inform the other Member States and the Commission of any authorisation granted under this paragraph. . . . '

(4) Article 6 is replaced by the following:

'Article 6

1.   The Council shall amend the list contained in Annex I on the basis of the determinations made by the United Nations Security Council or by the Sanctions Committee.

2.   The Council, acting upon a proposal from a Member State or from the High Representative of the Union for Foreign Affairs and Security Policy, shall establish and amend the list in Annex II.'; . . .

[Articles 7–8 have been omitted.]

(7) Article 9 is replaced by the following:

'Article 9

1. This Decision shall be reviewed, amended or repealed as appropriate, in particular in the light of relevant decisions by the United Nations Security Council.

2. The measures referred to in Article 3(2) shall apply until 12 December 2017. They shall be renewed, or amended as appropriate, if the Council deems that their objectives have not been met.';

(8) The Annex to Decision 2010/788/CFSP is renamed Annex I and the headings in that Annex are replaced by the following '(a) List of persons referred to in Article 3(1)' and '(b) List of entities referred to in Article 3(1)';

Article 2

This Decision shall enter into force on the day of its publication in the *Official Journal of the European Union*.

[The president's signature and Annex have been omitted.]

SOURCE: *Official Journal of the European Union*. "COUNCIL DECISION (CFSP) 2016/2231 of 12 December 2016 amending Decision 2010/788/CFSP concerning restrictive measures against the Democratic Republic of the Congo." December 12, 2016. © European Union, 2016. http://eur-lex.europa .eu/legal-content/EN/TXT/?uri=uriserv:OJ.L1.2016.336.01.0007.01.ENG&toc=OJ:L:2016:336I:TOC.

OTHER HISTORIC DOCUMENTS OF INTEREST

FROM PREVIOUS *HISTORIC DOCUMENTS*

Clinton and Trump Meet in Second Presidential Debate

The second presidential debate for the 2016 General Election took place at Washington University in St. Louis on Sunday, October 9. It featured the Democratic nominee, former secretary of state Hillary Clinton, and Republican nominee, businessman Donald Trump, and was presented in a town hall format, with half the questions coming from uncommitted voters selected by the Gallup Organization. Moderators Martha Raddatz of ABC and Anderson Cooper of CNN asked the remainder of the questions. Ahead of the town hall, the Commission on Presidential Debates announced that it would accept suggestions for questions for the moderators to ask the candidates, separate from those asked by the town hall participants. These questions were then voted on by the American public, and CNN and ABC agreed to consider the thirty most popular submissions during debate planning. Topics raised during the debate ranged from scandals plaguing the two candidates to energy, health care, taxation, and foreign policy. A CNN/ORC poll taken after the end of the debate found that 57 percent of respondents thought Clinton won the debate, while 34 percent thought Trump was victorious.

CLINTON AND TRUMP SCANDALS HEADLINE THE DEBATE

Following a heated first debate on September 26, and charged rhetoric out of each campaign about the opposition since that time, it was unsurprising, although unusual, that when the candidates met on stage on October 9 they did not shake hands as is customary. Neither candidate was given the opportunity to make an opening statement; instead the moderators went straight to the first question from a town hall member about whether the candidates felt that they model appropriate behavior for America's youth. This was followed by two separate question-and-answer segments between the candidates and moderators relating to recent scandals.

Only two days before the debate, the *Washington Post* had released a video from 2005 in which Trump could be heard making lewd comments to then–*Access Hollywood* host Billy Bush about how Trump treats women because he is famous. The comments earned quick rebukes from the Republican National Committee (RNC) and congressional Republicans. When asked about the comments during the debate, Trump responded, "No, I didn't say that at all" and claimed that the comments were "locker room talk." The candidate added, "I'm not proud of it. I apologize to my family; I apologize to the American people. Certainly I'm not proud of it, but this is locker room talk." Trump went on to say that he was embarrassed by the release of the tape and that while "[n]obody has more respect for women than I do," those comments were "just words."

Clinton was given the opportunity to respond to the query about the video and remarked, "What we all saw and heard on Friday was Donald talking about women—what he thinks about women, what he does to women." She added, "It's not only women and it's not only this video that raises questions about his fitness to be president." Clinton then went on to describe times when, in her view, Trump had acted in a manner unbecoming of the presidency. This included a campaign speech when Trump appeared to mock a disabled reporter, disparaging remarks made about the weight of a former Miss Universe contestant, the questioning of the ability of a judge of Mexican heritage to fairly rule in a case against Trump University, and apparently promising to ban Muslims from the country. "This is not who we are," Clinton said.

Trump took the opportunity to turn the spotlight onto Clinton's husband, former president Bill Clinton, who was in the debate audience with their daughter, Chelsea. During his two terms as president, a number of women alleged that they had been sexually assaulted by the president. Clinton admitted to extramarital affairs with only two of the women, former White House intern Monica Lewinsky and actress and model Gennifer Flowers. "If you look at Bill Clinton. . . . Mine were words and his was action. There has never been anyone in the history of politics who has been so abusive to women," Trump said. "Hillary Clinton has attacked those same women and attacked them viciously," he added of Clinton's past remarks defending her husband. As his guests at the debate, Trump invited three of Clinton's accusers—Juanita Broaddrick, Paula Jones, and Kathleen Wiley—as well as a woman named Kathy Shelton, who alleged she had been raped in 1975 at age twelve by a man Clinton defended against those charges in court during her time as a public defender. Trump held a predebate press conference with the four women during which Shelton said, "Hillary put me through something that you would never put a 12-year-old through. And she says she is for women and children." Broaddrick said that "Trump may have said some bad words" but that Bill Clinton's actions were far worse. When asked about the decision to invite the women, RNC chair Reince Priebus said, "I wasn't involved, and it's a campaign decision."

The moderators also brought up the scandal surrounding the 33,000 e-mail messages deleted from Clinton's private e-mail server during her time as secretary of state and allegations that she had lied under oath during her testimony before Congress regarding whether any e-mail handled on her private server were labeled classified. Clinton said what she had done was a "mistake," adding that she takes responsibility for her actions. "I'm not making any excuses," she said, while reminding the audience that there was no evidence that her e-mail had been hacked or that national security was ever in jeopardy. Trump said that if he was elected president, he would "instruct my attorney general to get a special prosecutor to look into your situation, because there has never been so many lies, so much deception." Clinton responded that it was "good that someone with the temperament of Donald Trump is not in charge of the law in our country," to which Trump stated, "You'd be in jail."

HEALTH INSURANCE

Eight questions were asked by members of the town hall audience during the October 9 debate, including one from Ken Karpowitz, who asked, "The Affordable Care Act known as Obamacare, it is not affordable. Premiums have gone up, deductibles have gone up, copays have gone up, prescriptions have gone up. And the coverage has gone down. What will you do to bring the cost down and make coverage better?"

Clinton was given the first chance to respond and touted the Affordable Care Act's (ACA) benefits, including eliminating the ability of health insurance companies to deny coverage due to preexisting conditions, allowing individuals up to age twenty-six to remain on their parents' health insurance plans, the end of lifetime caps on coverage, and equal charges for men and women. But, Clinton said, reining in the cost of health insurance "has to be the highest priority for the next president." Clinton proposed that she would "save what works and is good about the Affordable Care Act" while working to "get costs down" and "provide additional help to small businesses" to afford coverage for their employees. Clinton cautioned against repealing the ACA, as Trump has proposed, noting that "all of those benefits I just mentioned are lost to everybody, not just people who get their health insurance on the exchange. And then we would have to start all over again." Cooper asked Clinton about a comment her husband had made just one week earlier about the ACA, in which he called it "the craziest thing in the world" because premiums have gone up while coverage has gone down. Clinton defended those comments by returning to her central theme that starting all over by repealing Obamacare would be more difficult and overall worse for the country than simply fixing what is broken.

Trump called the ACA "a disaster." He continued, "You know it. We all know it. It's going up at numbers that nobody's ever seen worldwide. Nobody's ever seen numbers like this for health care." Trump said that the plans offered under the ACA are expensive for both the individual and the country and that it must be repealed and replaced with something less expensive. Trump's plan, for which he did not provide many specifics, would eliminate a current ACA provision that does not allow individuals to seek coverage from insurance providers outside of their own states. Eliminating this, Trump said, would increase competition and lower costs. Trump went on to criticize Clinton for wanting a single-payer health insurance program in the United States and for simply attempting to seek new solutions for the ACA. Trump did not respond to repeated questioning by Cooper on whether he would require Americans to have health insurance, as the ACA does, but said that if he were elected, Americans would "have the finest health care plan there is."

U.S. Policy in Syria

Raddatz read a question received on social media, asking, "If you were president, what would you do about Syria and the humanitarian crisis in Aleppo? Isn't it a lot like the Holocaust when the U.S. waited too long before we helped?" In her response, Clinton drew heavily on her time as secretary of state, saying that she advocated for, and continues to advocate for, a no-fly zone to be implemented in Aleppo to stop the government of Bashar Al-Assad and his supporters. She also criticized the Russian government for siding with Assad and the Iranians, who have provided support to the Syrian government, which has been killing its citizens. "The situation in Syria is catastrophic," Clinton said. "Every day that goes by, we see the results of the regime by Assad in partnership with the Iranians on the ground, the Russians in the air, bombarding places, in particular Aleppo . . . and there is a determined effort by the Russian air force to destroy Aleppo in order to eliminate the last of the Syrian rebels who are really holding out against the Assad regime." Clinton acknowledged that when the United States can partner with Russia, "That's fine," but that they must be held accountable, along with the Syrians, for war crimes committed against Syrian civilians. Clinton also stated that she would not send American ground troops into Syria, but would continue the Obama administration's tactics of providing training and counterintelligence assistance. Clinton would also consider arming the Kurds and would specifically target al Qaeda leader Abu Bakr al-Baghdadi to eliminate some of the leadership in the terrorist cells operating in and around Syria.

Trump was highly critical of Clinton's foreign policy experience and her comments on Russia. "The fact is," Trump said, "almost everything she's done in foreign policy has been a mistake and it's been a disaster." Trump said that Russia made progress against the Islamic State of Iraq and the Levant (ISIL), alternately known as the Islamic State of Iraq and Syria (ISIS), while the United States has been weak on foreign policy in the region. Raddatz brought up comments made by Indiana Governor Mike Pence, Trump's running mate, on Syria, that if Syrian and Russian missions continue to target civilians, the United States must "use military force to strike the military targets of the Assad regime." Trump admitted that he had not spoken to Pence about the issue but that he disagreed with Pence's stance. Trump went on to state that before the United States could worry about the humanitarian crisis in Syria, it must first eliminate ISIL. To do this, Trump said he would conduct "a sneak attack, and after the attack is made, inform the American public that we've knocked out the leaders, we've had a tremendous success." Trump criticized current efforts in the region, notably the operation to retake Mosul, Iraq, from ISIL control, because there is too much public advance notice provided ahead of these operations. "How stupid is our country?" Trump asked. Raddatz suggested that there are reasons for making these plans public, such as giving civilians the time to escape, but Trump went on to say, "General George Patton, General Douglas MacArthur are spinning in their grave at the stupidity of what we're doing in the Middle East."

Environmental Policy

The penultimate question of the evening was asked by Ken Bone, who became an overnight Internet sensation for his appearance and demeanor at the town hall. Bone asked the candidates, "What steps will your energy policy take to meet our energy needs, while at the same time remaining environmentally friendly and minimizing job loss for fossil power plant workers?" Trump was given the first chance to respond, and he came out criticizing the Obama administration and the Environmental Protection Agency (EPA) for crushing the energy sector with regulations implemented in a drive toward more renewable sources of energy. "We are killing—absolutely killing our energy business in this country. Now, I'm all for alternative forms of energy, including wind, including solar, et cetera. But we need much more than wind and solar." Trump, who had been receiving heavy support in coal-mining states, such as West Virginia and Kentucky, throughout his campaign, also spoke about the need to ensure these individuals maintain their livelihoods. "Hillary Clinton wants to put all the miners out of business. There is a thing called clean coal," Trump said. He added, "Now we have natural gas and so many other things because of technology. . . . We have found over the last seven years, we have found tremendous wealth right under our feet," which Trump insinuated could be used to pay off the national debt. Trump promised to bring energy companies back to America and put in place policies that would allow them to compete. Right now, Trump said, "we are putting our energy companies out of business. We have to bring back our workers."

Clinton focused instead on America's energy independence. "We are not dependent upon the Middle East," she said, adding that the United States has been "producing a lot of natural gas, which serves as a bridge to more renewable fuels. And I think that's an important transition." Clinton said as president it would be her goal to maintain America's energy independence while also supporting twenty-first-century energy projects that focus on clean, renewable energy. On the campaign trail Clinton had promised that those individuals who work in energy sector jobs that are eliminated by the switch to cleaner fuels would be provided training to obtain a higher-paying job in new energy sectors. She echoed these promises during the debate, saying she wanted "to be sure that we don't leave people behind. That's why I'm the only candidate from the very beginning of this campaign who had a plan to help us revitalize coal country. . . . I don't want to walk away from them. So we've got to do something for them." But, Clinton cautioned, because the price of coal has fallen around the world, America's energy strategies must be viewed in a more comprehensive way than simply putting these individuals back to work in the mines.

SECOND PRESIDENTIAL DEBATE ANALYSIS

Mainstream media outlets appeared to agree that Clinton had won the debate, and polling data after the event reflected this belief, but Clinton was panned by some for not approaching the debate with the biting criticism against Trump with which she came to the first debate. Some argued that this was to enable Trump's campaign to implode on its own following the release of the *Access Hollywood* tape, but it also gave Trump a chance to land more blows against Clinton than he had during the first debate, specifically about her e-mail and her husband's alleged sexual misconduct. Fact checkers found that Trump had misstated more facts than Clinton, but that it only served to strengthen his support within his base rather than widening his appeal with independent and swing state voters, which Mike Dawidziak, a former consultant to George H. W. Bush, said would be essential for a victory. For example, the *Washington Post* reported that Trump pulled his allegation that Clinton wants to put coal miners out of business from a speech she gave with her running mate, Sen. Tim Kaine, D-Va., but that she went on to say that she would ensure that those individuals who lose their jobs are not forgotten. Similarly, the *Post* took issue with Clinton's assertion that the United States is energy independent for the first time, because the United States is still a net importer of crude oil and refined petroleum products. Dawidziak called the second debate "pretty much a mud fight" and said that Clinton missed a prime opportunity to hit back at Trump over his assertion that she should be jailed.

—Heather Kerrigan

Following is the edited transcript of the October 9, 2016, debate between Donald Trump and former secretary of state Hillary Clinton.

Transcript of the Second 2016 Presidential Debate

October 9, 2016

[Due to its length, the transcript of the second presidential debate has been excerpted to include only those sections pertaining to the topics addressed in the headnote.]

RADDATZ: Ladies and gentlemen the Republican nominee for president, Donald J. Trump, and the Democratic nominee for president, Hillary Clinton. *[applause]*

COOPER: Thank you very much for being here. We're going to begin with a question from one of the members in our town hall. Each of you will have two minutes to respond to this question. Secretary Clinton, you won the coin toss, so you'll go first. . . .

[A question from a town hall participant about whether the candidates feel they are modeling appropriate behavior for America's youth, as well as questions and answers regarding videotaped comments made by Trump and Clinton's private e-mail server, have been omitted.]

QUESTION: Thank you. Affordable Care Act, known as Obamacare, it is not affordable. Premiums have gone up. Deductibles have gone up. Copays have gone up. Prescriptions have gone up. And the coverage has gone down. What will you do to bring the cost down and make coverage better?

. . . CLINTON: Well, I think Donald was about to say he's going to solve it by repealing it and getting rid of the Affordable Care Act. And I'm going to fix it, because I agree with you. Premiums have gotten too high. Copays, deductibles, prescription drug costs, and I've laid out a series of actions that we can take to try to get those costs down.

But here's what I don't want people to forget when we're talking about reining in the costs, which has to be the highest priority of the next president, when the Affordable Care Act passed, it wasn't just that 20 million got insurance who didn't have it before. But that in and of itself was a good thing. I meet these people all the time, and they tell me what a difference having that insurance meant to them and their families.

But everybody else, the 170 million of us who get health insurance through our employees big benefits. Number one, insurance companies can't deny you coverage because of a pre-existing condition. Number two, no lifetime limits, which is a big deal if you have serious health problems.

Number three, women can't be charged more than men for our health insurance, which is the way it used to be before the Affordable Care Act. Number four, if you're under 26, and your parents have a policy, you can be on that policy until the age of 26, something that didn't happen before.

So I want very much to save what works and is good about the Affordable Care Act. But we've got to get costs down. We've got to provide additional help to small businesses so that they can afford to provide health insurance. But if we repeal it, as Donald has proposed, and start over again, all of those benefits I just mentioned are lost to everybody, not just people who get their health insurance on the exchange. And then we would have to start all over again.

Right now, we are at 90 percent health insurance coverage. That's the highest we've ever been in our country. . . .

TRUMP: It is such a great question and it's maybe the question I get almost more than anything else, outside of defense. Obamacare is a disaster. You know it. We all know it. It's going up at numbers that nobody's ever seen worldwide. Nobody's ever seen numbers like this for health care.

It's only getting worse. In '17, it implodes by itself. Their method of fixing it is to go back and ask Congress for more money, more and more money. We have right now almost $20 trillion in debt.

Obamacare will never work. It's very bad, very bad health insurance. Far too expensive. And not only expensive for the person that has it, unbelievably expensive for our country. It's going to be one of the biggest line items very shortly.

We have to repeal it and replace it with something absolutely much less expensive and something that works, where your plan can actually be tailored. We have to get rid of the lines around the state, artificial lines, where we stop insurance companies from coming in and competing, because they want—and President Obama and whoever was working on it—they want to leave those lines, because that gives the insurance companies essentially monopolies. We want competition.

You will have the finest health care plan there is. She wants to go to a single-payer plan, which would be a disaster, somewhat similar to Canada. And if you haven't noticed the Canadians, when they need a big operation, when something happens, they come into the United States in many cases because their system is so slow. It's catastrophic in certain ways.

But she wants to go to single payer, which means the government basically rules everything. Hillary Clinton has been after this for years. Obamacare was the first step. Obamacare is a total disaster. And not only are your rates going up by numbers that nobody's ever believed, but your deductibles are going up, so that unless you get hit by a truck, you're never going to be able to use it. . . .

TRUMP: It is a disastrous plan, and it has to be repealed and replaced.

COOPER: Secretary Clinton, let me follow up with you. Your husband called Obamacare, quote, "the craziest thing in the world," saying that small-business owners are getting killed as premiums double, coverage is cut in half. Was he mistaken or was the mistake simply telling the truth?

CLINTON: No, I mean, he clarified what he meant. And it's very clear. Look, we are in a situation in our country where if we were to start all over again, we might come up with a different system. But we have an employer-based system. That's where the vast majority of people get their health care.

And the Affordable Care Act was meant to try to fill the gap between people who were too poor and couldn't put together any resources to afford health care, namely people on Medicaid. Obviously, Medicare, which is a single-payer system, which takes care of our elderly and does a great job doing it, by the way, and then all of the people who were employed, but people who were working but didn't have the money to afford insurance and didn't have anybody, an employer or anybody else, to help them.

That was the slot that the Obamacare approach was to take. And like I say, 20 million people now have health insurance. So if we just rip it up and throw it away, what Donald's not telling you is we just turn it back to the insurance companies the way it used to be, and that means the insurance companies . . . get to do pretty much whatever they want, including saying, look, I'm sorry, you've got diabetes, you had cancer, your child has asthma . . . you may not be able to have insurance because you can't afford it. So let's fix what's broken about it, but let's not throw it away and give it all back to the insurance companies and the drug companies. That's not going to work. . . .

TRUMP: Well, I just want—just one thing. First of all, Hillary, everything's broken about it. Everything. Number two, Bernie Sanders said that Hillary Clinton has very bad judgment. This is a perfect example of it, trying to save Obamacare, which is a disaster. . . .

COOPER: You've said you want to end Obamacare. You've also said you want to make coverage accessible for people with pre-existing conditions. How do you force insurance companies to do that if you're no longer mandating that every American get insurance?

TRUMP: We're going to be able to. You're going to have plans . . .

COOPER: What does that mean?

TRUMP: Well, I'll tell you what it means. You're going to have plans that are so good, because we're going to have so much competition in the insurance industry. Once we break out—once we break out the lines and allow the competition to come . . .

COOPER: Are you going—are you going to have a mandate that Americans have to have health insurance?

TRUMP: President Obama—Anderson, excuse me. President Obama, by keeping those lines, the boundary lines around each state, it was almost gone until just very toward the end of the passage of Obamacare, which, by the way, was a fraud. You know that, because Jonathan Gruber, the architect of Obamacare, was said—he said it was a great lie, it was a big lie. President Obama said you keep your doctor, you keep your plan. The whole thing was a fraud, and it doesn't work.

But when we get rid of those lines, you will have competition, and we will be able to keep pre-existing, we'll also be able to help people that can't get—don't have money because we are going to have people protected.

And Republicans feel this way, believe it or not, and strongly this way. We're going to block grant into the states. We're going to block grant into Medicaid into the states . . .

COOPER: Thank you, Mr. Trump.

TRUMP: . . . so that we will be able to take care of people without the necessary funds to take care of themselves. . . .

[Questions about Islamophobia in America, Clinton's paid speeches, and each candidate's tax plan have been omitted.]

RADDATZ: Mr. Trump, we're going to move on. The heart-breaking video of a 5-year-old Syrian boy named Omran sitting in an ambulance after being pulled from the rubble after an air strike in Aleppo focused the world's attention on the horrors of the war in Syria, with 136 million views on Facebook alone.

But there are much worse images coming out of Aleppo every day now, where in the past few weeks alone, 400 people have been killed, at least 100 of them children. Just days ago, the State Department called for a war crimes investigation of the Syrian regime of Bashar al-Assad and its ally, Russia, for their bombardment of Aleppo.

So this next question comes through social media through Facebook. Diane from Pennsylvania asks, if you were president, what would you do about Syria and the humanitarian crisis in Aleppo? Isn't it a lot like the Holocaust when the U.S. waited too long before we helped? Secretary Clinton, we will begin with your two minutes.

CLINTON: Well, the situation in Syria is catastrophic. And every day that goes by, we see the results of the regime by Assad in partnership with the Iranians on the ground, the Russians in the air, bombarding places, in particular Aleppo, where there are hundreds of thousands of people, probably about 250,000 still left. And there is a determined effort by the Russian air force to destroy Aleppo in order to eliminate the last of the Syrian rebels who are really holding out against the Assad regime.

Russia hasn't paid any attention to ISIS. They're interested in keeping Assad in power. So I, when I was secretary of state, advocated and I advocate today a no-fly zone and safe zones. We need some leverage with the Russians, because they are not going to come to the negotiating table for a diplomatic resolution, unless there is some leverage over them. And we have to work more closely with our partners and allies on the ground.

But I want to emphasize that what is at stake here is the ambitions and the aggressiveness of Russia. Russia has decided that it's all in, in Syria. And they've also decided who they want to see become president of the United States, too, and it's not me. I've stood up to Russia. I've taken on Putin and others, and I would do that as president.

I think wherever we can cooperate with Russia, that's fine. And I did as secretary of state. That's how we got a treaty reducing nuclear weapons. It's how we got the sanctions on Iran that put a lid on the Iranian nuclear program without firing a single shot. So I would go to the negotiating table with more leverage than we have now. But I do support the effort to investigate for crimes, war crimes committed by the Syrians and the Russians and try to hold them accountable.

RADDATZ: Thank you, Secretary Clinton. Mr. Trump?

TRUMP: First of all, she was there as secretary of state with the so-called line in the sand, which . . .

CLINTON: No, I wasn't. I was gone. I hate to interrupt you, but at some point . . .

TRUMP: OK. But you were in contact—excuse me. You were . . .

CLINTON: At some point, we need to do some fact-checking here.

TRUMP: You were in total contact with the White House, and perhaps, sadly, Obama probably still listened to you. I don't think he would be listening to you very much anymore.

Obama draws the line in the sand. It was laughed at all over the world what happened.

Now, with that being said, she talks tough against Russia. But our nuclear program has fallen way behind, and they've gone wild with their nuclear program. Not good. Our government shouldn't have allowed that to happen. Russia is new in terms of nuclear. We are old. We're tired. We're exhausted in terms of nuclear. A very bad thing.

Now, she talks tough, she talks really tough against Putin and against Assad. She talks in favor of the rebels. She doesn't even know who the rebels are. You know, every time we take rebels, whether it's in Iraq or anywhere else, we're arming people. And you know what happens? They end up being worse than the people.

Look at what she did in Libya with Gadhafi. Gadhafi's out. It's a mess. And, by the way, ISIS has a good chunk of their oil. I'm sure you probably have heard that. It was a disaster. Because the fact is, almost everything she's done in foreign policy has been a mistake and it's been a disaster.

But if you look at Russia, just take a look at Russia, and look at what they did this week, where I agree, she wasn't there, but possibly she's consulted. We sign a peace treaty. Everyone's all excited. Well, what Russia did with Assad and, by the way, with Iran, who you made very powerful with the dumbest deal perhaps I've ever seen in the history of deal-making, the Iran deal, with the $150 billion, with the $1.7 billion in cash, which is enough to fill up this room.

But look at that deal. Iran now and Russia are now against us. So she wants to fight. She wants to fight for rebels. There's only one problem. You don't even know who the rebels are. So what's the purpose?

... TRUMP: I don't like Assad at all, but Assad is killing ISIS. Russia is killing ISIS. And Iran is killing ISIS. And those three have now lined up because of our weak foreign policy.

RADDATZ: Mr. Trump, let me repeat the question. If you were president ... *[laughter]* ... what would you do about Syria and the humanitarian crisis in Aleppo? And I want to remind you what your running mate said. He said provocations by Russia need to be met with American strength and that if Russia continues to be involved in air strikes along with the Syrian government forces of Assad, the United States of America should be prepared to use military force to strike the military targets of the Assad regime.

TRUMP: OK. He and I haven't spoken, and I disagree. I disagree.

RADDATZ: You disagree with your running mate?

TRUMP: I think you have to knock out ISIS. Right now, Syria is fighting ISIS. We have people that want to fight both at the same time. But Syria is no longer Syria. Syria is Russia and it's Iran, who she made strong and Kerry and Obama made into a very powerful nation and a very rich nation, very, very quickly, very, very quickly.

I believe we have to get ISIS. We have to worry about ISIS before we can get too much more involved. She had a chance to do something with Syria. They had a chance. And that was the line. And she didn't.

RADDATZ: What do you think will happen if Aleppo falls?

TRUMP: I think Aleppo is a disaster, humanitarian-wise.

RADDATZ: What do you think will happen if it falls?

TRUMP: I think that it basically has fallen. OK? It basically has fallen. Let me tell you something. You take a look at Mosul. The biggest problem I have with the stupidity of our foreign policy, we have Mosul. They think a lot of the ISIS leaders are in Mosul. So we have announcements coming out of Washington and coming out of Iraq, we will be attacking Mosul in three weeks or four weeks.

Well, all of these bad leaders from ISIS are leaving Mosul. Why can't they do it quietly? Why can't they do the attack, make it a sneak attack, and after the attack is made, inform the American public that we've knocked out the leaders, we've had a tremendous success? People leave. Why do they have to say we're going to be attacking Mosul within the next four to six weeks, which is what they're saying? How stupid is our country?

RADDATZ: There are sometimes reasons the military does that. Psychological warfare.

TRUMP: I can't think of any. I can't think of any. And I'm pretty good at it.

RADDATZ: It might be to help get civilians out.

TRUMP: And we have General Flynn. And we have—look, I have 200 generals and admirals who endorsed me. I have 21 Congressional Medal of Honor recipients who endorsed me. We talk about it all the time. They understand, why can't they do something secretively, where they go in and they knock out the leadership? How—why would these people stay there? I've been reading now . . .

RADDATZ: Tell me what your strategy is.

TRUMP: . . . for weeks—I've been reading now for weeks about Mosul, that it's the harbor of where—you know, between Raqqa and Mosul, this is where they think the ISIS leaders are. Why would they be saying—they're not staying there anymore. They're gone. Because everybody's talking about how Iraq, which is us with our leadership, goes in to fight Mosul.

Now, with these 200 admirals and generals, they can't believe it. All I say is this. General George Patton, General Douglas MacArthur are spinning in their grave at the stupidity of what we're doing in the Middle East.

RADDATZ: I'm going to go to Secretary Clinton. Secretary Clinton, you want Assad to go. You advocated arming rebels, but it looks like that may be too late for Aleppo. You talk about diplomatic efforts. Those have failed. Cease-fires have failed. Would you introduce the threat of U.S. military force beyond a no-fly zone against the Assad regime to back up diplomacy?

CLINTON: I would not use American ground forces in Syria. I think that would be a very serious mistake. I don't think American troops should be holding territory, which is what they would have to do as an occupying force. I don't think that is a smart strategy.

I do think the use of special forces, which we're using, the use of enablers and trainers in Iraq, which has had some positive effects, are very much in our interests, and so I do support what is happening, but let me just . . .

RADDATZ: But what would you do differently than President Obama is doing?

CLINTON: Well, Martha, I hope that by the time I—if I'm fortunate . . .

TRUMP: Everything.

CLINTON: I hope by the time I am president that we will have pushed ISIS out of Iraq. I do think that there is a good chance that we can take Mosul. And, you know, Donald says he knows more about ISIS than the generals. No, he doesn't.

There are a lot of very important planning going on, and some of it is to signal to the Sunnis in the area, as well as Kurdish Peshmerga fighters, that we all need to be in this. And that takes a lot of planning and preparation.

I would go after Baghdadi. I would specifically target Baghdadi, because I think our targeting of Al Qaida leaders—and I was involved in a lot of those operations, highly classified ones—made a difference. So I think that could help.

I would also consider arming the Kurds. The Kurds have been our best partners in Syria, as well as Iraq. And I know there's a lot of concern about that in some circles, but I think they should have the equipment they need so that Kurdish and Arab fighters on the ground are the principal way that we take Raqqa after pushing ISIS out of Iraq. . . .

[Questions about whether the candidates would represent all Americans, and appointments to the Supreme Court, have been omitted.]

QUESTION: What steps will your energy policy take to meet our energy needs, while at the same time remaining environmentally friendly and minimizing job loss for fossil power plant workers?

COOPER: Mr. Trump, two minutes?

TRUMP: Absolutely. I think it's such a great question, because energy is under siege by the Obama administration. Under absolutely siege. The EPA, Environmental Protection Agency, is killing these energy companies. And foreign companies are now coming in buying our—buying so many of our different plants and then re-jiggering the plant so that they can take care of their oil.

We are killing—absolutely killing our energy business in this country. Now, I'm all for alternative forms of energy, including wind, including solar, et cetera. But we need much more than wind and solar.

And you look at our miners. Hillary Clinton wants to put all the miners out of business. There is a thing called clean coal. Coal will last for 1,000 years in this country. Now we have natural gas and so many other things because of technology. We have unbelievable—we have found over the last seven years, we have found tremendous wealth right under our feet. So good. Especially when you have $20 trillion in debt.

I will bring our energy companies back. They'll be able to compete. They'll make money. They'll pay off our national debt. They'll pay off our tremendous budget deficits, which are tremendous. But we are putting our energy companies out of business. We have to bring back our workers.

You take a look at what's happening to steel and the cost of steel and China dumping vast amounts of steel all over the United States, which essentially is killing our steelworkers and our steel companies. We have to guard our energy companies. We have to make it possible.

The EPA is so restrictive that they are putting our energy companies out of business. And all you have to do is go to a great place like West Virginia or places like Ohio, which is phenomenal, or places like Pennsylvania and you see what they're doing to the people, miners and others in the energy business. It's a disgrace. . . .

TRUMP: It's an absolute disgrace.

COOPER: Secretary Clinton, two minutes.

CLINTON: And actually—well, that was very interesting. First of all, China is illegally dumping steel in the United States and Donald Trump is buying it to build his buildings, putting steelworkers and American steel plants out of business. That's something that I fought against as a senator and that I would have a trade prosecutor to make sure that we don't get taken advantage of by China on steel or anything else.

You know, because it sounds like you're in the business or you're aware of people in the business—you know that we are now for the first time ever energy-independent. We are not dependent upon the Middle East. But the Middle East still controls a lot of the prices. So the price of oil has been way down. And that has had a damaging effect on a lot of the oil companies, right? We are, however, producing a lot of natural gas, which serves as a bridge to more renewable fuels. And I think that's an important transition.

We've got to remain energy-independent. It gives us much more power and freedom than to be worried about what goes on in the Middle East. We have enough worries over there without having to worry about that.

So I have a comprehensive energy policy, but it really does include fighting climate change, because I think that is a serious problem. And I support moving toward more clean, renewable energy as quickly as we can, because I think we can be the 21st century clean energy superpower and create millions of new jobs and businesses.

But I also want to be sure that we don't leave people behind. That's why I'm the only candidate from the very beginning of this campaign who had a plan to help us revitalize coal country, because those coal miners and their fathers and their grandfathers, they dug that coal out. A lot of them lost their lives. They were injured, but they turned the lights on and they powered their factories. I don't want to walk away from them. So we've got to do something for them. . . .

CLINTON: But the price of coal is down worldwide. So we have to look at this comprehensively. . . .

[The final question of the debate, asking each candidate to say something positive about his or her opponent, has been omitted.]

Source: The American Presidency Project. "Presidential Debate at Washington University in St. Louis, Missouri." October 9, 2016. Online by Gerhard Peters and John T. Woolley, *The American Presidency Project.* http://www.presidency.ucsb.edu/ws/?pid=119038.

Other Historic Documents of Interest

From this volume

From previous *Historic Documents*

Yemeni Rebels Fire on U.S. Ship; New Rebel Government Established

---

OCTOBER 12 AND 31, 2016

For the first time since the civil war began in Yemen in 2015, the United States became militarily involved after one of its naval vessels was fired upon. The United States retaliated with missile strikes that destroyed radar targets in a Houthi-controlled area of the country, and there was no further action from Yemen. Shortly after the strike, anti-government groups announced that they had formed their own government in opposition to the internationally recognized government of President Abdu Rabbu Mansour Hadi. The United Nations (UN) and governments around the world refused to recognize the opposition government led by the Houthis, who are backed by the Shiites and Iran, believing that the move runs counter to the efforts toward finalizing a peace deal between the warring factions.

YEMEN'S UNSTABLE GOVERNMENT

Since the Arab Spring movement shook the Middle East and North Africa in 2011, the Yemeni government has been relatively unstable. Hadi took control of the country in February 2012, after Ali Abdullah Saleh was ousted from power. In 2015, Saleh aligned with the opposition group, the Houthis, which had been trying to seize control of the country from Hadi's internationally recognized government. The alignment sparked a civil war that forced President Hadi and most of his government to move to Riyadh, Saudi Arabia, where they have ruled in self-imposed exile since March 2015. Since that time, Saudi Arabia has led a coalition intended to root out Houthi rebels, protect civilians, and restore peace in the country. However, many questions have been raised about the effectiveness of Saudi Arabia's strategies, because, according to the UN, more than 10,000 civilians have been killed since March 2015, and millions have been displaced. Many Saudi airstrikes have hit civilian areas.

Since Hadi's government left, the Houthis have been able to gain control of significant portions of the country, including the capital city of Sana'a, along with weapons and military vehicles. The ongoing civil war resulted in a level-three humanitarian crisis, the highest UN designation. According to the international body, hospitals do not have staff, supplies, or fuel for treatment; civilians lack adequate access to food; and public servant wages have not been paid since August 2016. As of December 31, the UN Office for the Coordination of Humanitarian Affairs had received only 60 percent of the $1.63 billion it requested for its 2016 Yemen humanitarian response plan.

Houthi Rebels Fire on U.S. Ship

During two separate instances in the second week of October, the USS *Mason*, which was stationed off the coast of Yemen in the Bab al-Mandab Strait, one of the busiest shipping routes in the world, was targeted by missiles from a Houthi-controlled area of Yemen while conducting routine operations. The ship responded with defensive fire, and neither missile attack reached the ship. The Houthis denied any involvement in the strike.

In response to the missile attack, the USS *Nitze*, a Navy destroyer, fired Tomahawk cruise missiles at three radar installations located near the area from where the missiles were thought to have been launched. According to the Pentagon, which authorized the strikes with the permission of President Barak Obama, the targets were destroyed. "These limited self-defense strikes were conducted to protect our personnel, our ships, and our freedom of navigation in this important maritime passageway," the Pentagon said in a statement, adding, "The United States will respond to any further threat to our ships and commercial traffic."

The attack on the radar installations marked the first time the United States had become militarily involved in Yemen's civil war. The strike on the USS *Mason* was thought to be in retaliation to a Saudi-led strike against funeral-goers gathered in Sana'a on October 8, where more than 100 civilians were killed. This was not the first civilian-targeting incident undertaken by the Saudi-led coalition, and it raised questions in the United States about whether the White House would continue to support the Saudis' efforts. To this point, the role of the United States in the civil war has primarily been to provide aircraft refueling assistance, planning, and intelligence. The United States has also provided billions in arms to Saudi Arabia, despite Senate attempts to overturn such agreements based primarily on concerns regarding whether the Saudis are intentionally targeting heavily civilian-populated areas during their airstrikes. While the White House continued to wrangle with its ongoing support of Saudi Arabia, in December, the Obama administration canceled a $350 million arms deal between Raytheon and Saudi Arabia because of the ongoing high civilian death toll.

Yemen Government Rejects Peace Roadmap

In late October, UN special envoy to Yemen Ismail Ould Cheikh Ahmed submitted for consideration a peace roadmap for ending the fighting between the Houthis and their supporters, and Hadi's government. The agreement would require Hadi to step down after a new transition government was installed, while the Houthis and Saleh's forces would be required to withdraw from seized territory and give all their medium and heavy weapons to UN arms inspectors.

Shortly after the release of the roadmap, Saleh's allied forces and the Houthi movement announced that they had formed a Government of National Salvation (GNS). Houthi spokesperson Mohammed al Bukhaiti said the new government had been derived from "all walks of the political spectrum who are anti-aggression" and noted that the GNS was "not an alternative to a future unity government that would include members of those who are pro-aggression." The GNS, led by Abdul Aziz Habtoor, a former member of Hadi's government who joined the Houthi coalition in 2015, was granted a vote of confidence in the nation's parliament on December 12. Hadi spokesperson Rajeh Badi said the formation of a new government showed a "disregard not just for the Yemeni people but also for the international community."

Despite the vote in parliament, the GNS was, as of the close of 2016, unable to gain international recognition as the rightful government of Yemen. Ahmed called the formation of a new government "an obstacle" to ending the nation's civil war and installing a peace agreement. Similarly, U.S. State Department spokesperson John Kirby said that GNS was "clearly not conducive to achieving a lasting and comprehensive settlement to the conflict in Yemen, which will require political negotiation and consensus among all parties."

While the Houthis announced on November 16 that they would accept the UN roadmap toward peace, in December, Hadi formally refused to agree with the plan to end the twenty-month civil war, and instead outlined for the UN demands of his own for any future agreement. Hadi said the proposal made by Ahmed contradicts current UN Security Council resolutions and international agreements and called it a "free incentive to the Houthi–Saleh rebels, legitimizing their rebellion, their agenda, and the establishment of a new phase of the bloody conflict." Hadi asked that any future peace agreement require "all those included in the Security Council sanctions regime, and all those with proven involvement in the coup or have committed crimes against civilians, must leave political life and leave the country with their families into self-imposed exile for a period of at least ten years, as well as the implementation of international sanctions against them."

—Heather Kerrigan

Following are two October 12, 2016, statements from the Pentagon regarding the missile attack on the USS Mason *and U.S. military response; and the text of an October 31, 2016, briefing delivered to the UN Security Council regarding the ongoing crisis in Yemen.*

Pentagon Statement on Yemen Missile Attack

October 12, 2016

For the second time in four days, USS Mason responded to an incoming missile threat while conducting routine operations in international waters off the Red Sea coast of Yemen. At about 6 p.m. local time today (11 a.m. EDT), the ship detected at least one missile that we assess originated from Houthi-controlled territory near Al Hudaydah, Yemen. The ship employed defensive countermeasures, and the missile did not reach USS Mason. There was no damage to the ship or its crew. USS Mason will continue its operations. Those who threaten our forces should know that U.S. commanders retain the right to defend their ships, and we will respond to this threat at the appropriate time and in the appropriate manner.

SOURCE: U.S. Defense Department. "Statement by Pentagon Press Secretary Peter Cook on USS Mason." Release No: NR-363-16. October 12, 2016. http://www.defense.gov/News/News-Releases/News-Release-View/Article/971834/statement-by-pentagon-press-secretary-peter-cook-on-uss-mason.

U.S. Military Strikes Radar Sites in Yemen

October 12, 2016

Early this morning local time, the U.S. military struck three radar sites in Houthi-controlled territory on Yemen's Red Sea coast. Initial assessments show the sites were destroyed. The strikes—authorized by President Obama at the recommendation of Secretary of Defense Ash Carter and Chairman of the Joint Chiefs General Joseph Dunford—targeted radar sites involved in the recent missile launches threatening USS Mason and other vessels operating in international waters in the Red Sea and the Bab al-Mandeb. These limited self-defense strikes were conducted to protect our personnel, our ships, and our freedom of navigation in this important maritime passageway. The United States will respond to any further threat to our ships and commercial traffic, as appropriate, and will continue to maintain our freedom of navigation in the Red Sea, the Bab al-Mandeb, and elsewhere around the world.

SOURCE: U.S. Defense Department. "Statement by Pentagon Press Secretary Peter Cook on U.S. Military Strikes Against Radar Sites in Yemen." Release No: NR-365-16. October 12, 2016. http://www.defense .gov/News/News-Releases/News-Release-View/Article/972169/statement-by-pentagon-press-secretary- peter-cook-on-us-military-strikes-against.

UN Security Council Briefing on Yemen

October 31, 2016

Mr. President,

Thank you for this opportunity to update the Council on the latest developments in Yemen and challenges facing efforts to ensure the country's return to peace and stability.

What Yemen is witnessing today contravenes the commitments made by the parties to the United Nations to peace. The security situation is dire, and the humanitarian situation continues to deteriorate despite the efforts of the humanitarian agencies.

With regards to security, the Grand Hall in Sana'a witnessed a tragic attack on 8 October, where nearly one thousand Yemenis were gathered to pay their condolences at a funeral, left more than 140 dead and 550 injured. I visited the site of the attack several days ago together with family members of the victims, and saw for myself the shocking scale of destruction. The Mayor of Sanaa, Abdel Kader Hilal, a seasoned politician known for his bravery and commitment to peace until his last day, and two members of the De-escalation and Coordination Committee (DCC) were among the victims of the attack. The bombing of a funeral is contrary to all Yemeni norms and traditions and the perpetrators must be held accountable. I extend, once again, my deepest condolences to the families of the victims and wish a speedy recovery to those who were wounded in this attack.

I commend the statements by the families of the victims, which called for restraint and thorough investigation of the incident. This is a clear demonstration of their sense of nationalism and their commitment to peace.

The Arab Coalition has taken responsibility for the attack and its Joint Incidents Assessment Team conducted a rapid preliminary investigation, which recommended action against those involved and a revision of the Coalition's rules of engagement. It will be very important to complete the investigations and to ensure accountability of those involved.

Mr. President,

Sadly, the 8 October attack was not the only incident where civilians and civilian infrastructure were targeted in the past weeks. On 3 October, shelling of Bir Basha district of Taiz, from areas controlled by the Houthi-GPC forces, resulted in nine civilian deaths including three children. Indiscriminate attacks on residential areas of Taiz have been ongoing for many months. They have caused great damage to the city and its population and must stop. These incidents are a horrific reminder of the consequences of war, a war that has blighted the country during the last eighteen months of conflict.

Mr. President,

The conduct of the parties on the ground is contrary to the commitments they made previously to engage fully and constructively in the UN-mediated peace process. I called on the parties to recommit to the April 10 Terms and Conditions for the Cessation of Hostilities. Although I would have preferred an open-ended Cessation of Hostilities, I was able to gain agreement on 72-hour pause which entered into force on 19 October. I regret to report that both sides were involved in significant violations of the Cessation of Hostilities from its first day. I am deeply concerned by the escalation of hostilities, which has continued at an alarming rate in the past few weeks. Fighting has escalated in Taiz, Maarib, al-Jawf, Hajjah and on the border with Saudi Arabia, where ballistic missile attacks have increased in both frequency and range. Targeting the area of Mecca al-Mukarrama was a dangerous development, which affects the course of the war and the feelings of more than 1.5 billion Muslims worldwide.

I am also concerned that international vessels travelling off the coast of Yemen have come under fire from Houthi-controlled territories in recent weeks. A UAE vessel was targeted in the Strait of Bab al-Mandab. US destroyers travelling through international waters were reportedly targeted by direct missile attacks, and responded by reportedly firing on Houthi radar sites. These incidents risk a more acute escalation of the conflict, and threaten the security of international maritime movement. I thank the Council for its call on 4 October, for "such attacks to cease immediately".

In southern Yemen, al-Qaeda in the Arabian Peninsula (AQAP) and the so-called "Islamic State" (IS) continue attacks on state institutions and civilian targets. In Aden, on 1 October a suicide bomber killed one civilian and injured three others, and on 29 and 30 September, gunmen affiliated with IS assassinated a retired intelligence officer and a security officer. As part of their counter-terrorism efforts, Yemeni security forces raided the house of a prominent IS leader and confiscated a variety of weapons and explosives. In Abyan, counter-terrorism forces killed three militants, including a high-ranking AQAP affiliate and arrested two others.

Mr. President,

The escalating military situation continues to worsen a very dire *[sic]* the humanitarian situation which requires far greater attention from the international community. Local authorities are unable to provide basic social services for the population. This is particularly prevalent in the health sector, where only 45 per cent of facilities are functional. In addition to the growing difficulty for Yemenis to obtain medical treatment at home, many Yemenis are also unable to seek treatment abroad due to the prohibition of commercial flights from Sana'a. I call for the immediate resumption of commercial flights to and from Sana'a. I also call on the Houthis and the GPC to ensure that access for humanitarian agencies are free from bureaucratic impediments and intimidation. My colleagues Stephen O'Brien, Under-Secretary-General for Humanitarian Affairs and Emergency Relief Coordinator, and Mohannad Hadi, Regional Director of the World Food Programme for the MENA region, will provide you with a more detailed briefing of the humanitarian situation and the UN's efforts to provide assistance.

I should add that the worsening economic situation threatens to create a far greater humanitarian crisis in the coming months if urgent action is not taken. Salary payments for most civil servants have already ceased. This was a primary source of income for much of the population. Unless they are continued quickly, many more Yemenis will face destitution and be forced to rely on humanitarian aid to survive. There should be a commitment from all parties, including the Government of Yemen, the Houthis and GPC to collaborate to ensure the continued functioning of the Central Bank and a rapid resumption of salaries throughout the country.

Mr. President,

Despite the International Community's calls for the Yemeni parties to fully commit to the peace process, the parties continued to embark on unilateral actions, which risk undermining the prospects for peace. On 2 October, the High Political Council established by the Houthis and GPC, asked the former Governor of Aden to form a new government. President Hadi's decision to replace the Governor of the Central Bank and relocate the Bank to Aden has created further economic uncertainty at a time when urgent measures to save the economy are necessary. Prime Minister Ahmed bin Dagher announced via social media plans to convene the National Body to ratify the draft constitution. I urge the parties to refrain from taking any further measures, which will only complicate reaching a negotiated settlement to put Yemen on the path to peace.

I conducted extensive consultations with the Yemeni parties and members of the international community over the last few weeks, and presented the parties with a comprehensive and detailed roadmap to end the conflict. The roadmap is consistent with Security Council resolution 2216 (2015) and other relevant resolutions, the GCC Initiative and its Implementation Mechanism, and the Outcomes of the National Dialogue Conference. The Roadmap contains a set of sequenced political and security steps, conducted in parallel, which would help Yemen return to a peace and orderly political transition.

The Roadmap foresees the creation of military and security committees, which would supervise withdrawals and the handover of weapons in Sanaa, Hodeida and Taiz. The committees would also be tasked with ensuring the complete end of military violence and the safety and security of the population and state institutions. The Roadmap also lays out interim political arrangements including the appointment of a new Vice President and the formation of Government of National Unity which would lead Yemen's transition process and oversee the resumption of political dialogue, completion of the constitutional process and ultimately elections. I was informed, unofficially, that the parties have rejected the Roadmap. This demonstrates that the political elite in Yemen remains unable to overcome their differences and prioritize national, public interest over personal interests. It is time for the parties to realize that there can be no peace without concessions, and no security without agreement. They should base their positions on the question of how to ensure security and stability for the Yemeni people.

I will return to the region immediately following this briefing to start consultations with both parties in Sana'a and Riyadh with the aim of reaching a detailed agreement based on the Roadmap. It is now the responsibility of the delegations to prioritize peace, rather than partisan agendas. The Roadmap and the agreements discussed in Kuwait should allow process towards a comprehensive settlement in the coming weeks if the parties engage in good faith and demonstrate a sense of political and national awareness.

I am grateful for the International Community's continued support to my proposal for a comprehensive agreement and calls for a Cessation of Hostilities. The quadrilateral meetings of the Foreign Ministers of the United States, United Kingdom, Saudi Arabia and the United Arab Emirates in Jeddah, New York and in London have supported these efforts along with their counterparts from the remaining members of the Gulf Cooperation Council. These calls were echoed in other meetings with the Foreign Ministers of the Sultanate of Oman, France, Egypt, Kuwait, Qatar, Bahrain and the deputy Foreign Minister of Russia. I am grateful to the Council Members for their unwavering support of the efforts to restore peace in Yemen.

Mr. President,

After 18 months of horrific fighting, thousands of deaths, injuries and unspeakable human suffering, we all need to ask how long will Yemenis remain hostages to personal and reckless political decisions? What are the parties waiting for to sign a political agreement? Have they not understood that there are no winners in wars?

The Roadmap I have proposed to the parties is widely supported by the International Community because it provides a comprehensive solution, and includes guarantees for the political representation all political groupings.

I would like to ask the Council for its full support of the peace plan, and for an immediate cessation of hostilities and a release of detainees. And to the Yemenis I say, the dawn of peace could be near, in case those responsible decide to prioritize national interest and start working on rebuilding a stable state, which guarantees the rights of all of its people without discrimination.

Thank you.

SOURCE: United Nations Department of Political Affairs. "31 October 2016, Security Council briefing on the situation in the Middle East, Special Envoy of the Secretary-General for Yemen, Ismail Ould Cheikh Ahmed." October 31, 2016. http://www.un.org/undpa/en/speeches-statements/31102016/Middle-East.

OTHER HISTORIC DOCUMENTS OF INTEREST

FROM PREVIOUS *HISTORIC DOCUMENTS*

Google and Facebook Crack Down on Fake News

OCTOBER 13 AND DECEMBER 15, 2016

The 2016 presidential campaign was marred by a rash of a deceptive and false news articles that misled readers with half-truths or lies and fueled conspiracy theories. When the U.S. government charged Russia with orchestrating a sophisticated misinformation campaign using bots, "trolls," and fake social media accounts to undermine trust in American democracy and promote Republican candidate Donald Trump over Democrat Hillary Clinton, the issue of misinformation—also known as "fake news"—came to the forefront of the national conversation. Following months of public and private outcry, two of the world's leading technology companies—Google, the largest search engine in the world, and Facebook, the largest social media network—announced new steps to curb the influence and spread of fake news. Google empowered independent fact-checking websites by labeling certain articles as "fact checks" on their prominent Google News vertical. Two months later, Facebook rolled out a suite of tools that allowed users to flag false or misleading stories for removal, empowered fact checkers, and removed financial incentives for spammers and deceptive websites by curtailing their ad revenue.

GROWTH OF FAKE NEWS AND MISINFORMATION

The year 2016 saw an unprecedented presidential election marked by accusations from both Republicans and Democrats that their rivals were promoting or amplifying damaging fake news articles. Throughout the election, misleading or false news articles spread across the Internet, with their publishers relying on social media networks and search engines to reach and influence millions of Americans. These articles offered conspiracy theories and misleading or false information, usually behind a flashy headline meant to be shared with friends, family, and likeminded supporters.

This increase in fake news was spurred on, experts later alleged, by a sophisticated Russian misinformation campaign meant to affect the outcome of the 2016 presidential election. U.S. officials and independent researchers claimed that state-sanctioned operatives created fake news outlets and articles to sow distrust in the U.S. election system, undermine faith in American democracy, punish Clinton, and boost Trump. The Russian propaganda campaign relied on thousands of "bots," paid human "trolls," and networks of fake social media accounts and websites to boost right-wing conspiracies about Clinton and to amplify the appearance of international tensions with Russia.

For the first time, many leading technology companies found themselves at the center of this fight. In particular, Google and Facebook faced mounting pressure from the public, the U.S. government, and outside groups to implement new measures to root out false or misleading information sources. While each tried to downplay their overall role in combating the issue, arguing that it was not their responsibility to verify or discredit information sources, pressure continued to mount. Finally, the companies acted in late 2016, implementing new tools and partnerships to help verify the information that sped across their domains.

GOOGLE EMPOWERS FACT CHECKERS

A decade before fake news entered the national conversation, Google released a new advertising-supported news aggregator to collect and compile articles from various news websites. The service, Google News, grew to cover more than more than 25,000 publishers and became a major offering for the Internet giant. Three years after the service's introduction, the Mountain View, California, company rolled out new labels to categorize various articles and sources. What started as a tool for quickly discerning between a blog and a news article has since grown to include labels such as In-Depth, Opinion, Wikipedia, and more.

With public and private pressure to combat fake news continuing to grow, Google sought to expand these labels to empower fact-checking organizations and websites. In a blog post published on October 13, 2016, by Richard Gingras, head of news at Google, the company described how the growth of fact checking provided new avenues for ensuring that users are receiving factual information. Furthermore, the company outlined what steps it would take to make it easier for users to quickly find fact-checked articles through Google News.

"Over the last several years, fact checking has come into its own," Gingras wrote. "Led by organizations like the International Fact-Checking Network, rigorous fact checks are now conducted by more than 100 active sites, according to the Duke University Reporter's Lab. They collectively produce many thousands of fact-checks a year, examining claims around urban legends, politics, health, and the media itself." Gingras argued that this growing professionalism and sophistication offered the company a new tool to further refine labels in Google News. "Today, we're adding another new tag, 'Fact check,' to help readers find fact checking in large news stories." The tagged articles would now appear on the Google News' webpage as well as iOS and Android apps.

Google's labeling process relied on language inserted into articles' code to gauge whether they contained fact checks. "Google News determines whether an article might contain fact checks in part by looking for the schema.org ClaimReview markup," according to the company. Schema.org is a collaborative community established to create, maintain, and promote outlines or plans for structured data on the Internet; its ClaimReview markup allows developers to add standardized language to a webpage's code to indicate whether statements or conclusions in an article had been fact checked. Google uses this ClaimReview process to determine via an algorithm whether a fact check is relevant to the story and highlights sources that "follow the commonly accepted criteria for fact checks," the blog post explained. "We're excited to see the growth of the Fact Check community and to shine a light on its efforts to divine fact from fiction, wisdom from spin," Gingras added.

Google's announcement was largely applauded as an important first step to combat fake news and misinformation. The timing was also significant, because the new label arrived less than a month before the conclusion of the contentious presidential election. Finally, the measure underscored the search giant's new understanding that its role has evolved within the Internet community. While many companies argued that they merely aggregated articles or offered users the ability to share them—and therefore should not be responsible for debunking false claims—Google signaled that it understood its broader responsibility as a source of information. Others would soon follow.

Facebook Unveils Tools to Address Hoaxes, Scammers

Like Google, Facebook faced mounting pressure and sharp criticism during the 2016 presidential campaign for doing little to curb the spread of false or misleading articles across its platform. The Silicon Valley giant largely argued that it was a social media network, not a publisher responsible for fact checking information. As one Facebook employee told National Public Radio, "We started out of a college dorm. I mean, c'mon, we're Facebook. We never wanted to deal with this."

Facebook's view of itself largely rang hollow, however. Research released by the Reuters Institute for the Study of Journalism in June 2016 found that social media was the primary source of news for eighteen- to twenty-four-year-olds. In 2016, more than one billion people logged on to Facebook every day to share and read news articles. As hoaxes and conspiracy theories spread across the social media network fueled real world attacks, including a man's assault on a pizza restaurant in Washington, D.C., from which Clinton was allegedly running a human trafficking operation, pressure mounted for Facebook to more accurately address its role as a source of and platform from which to spread information.

Two months after Google's announcement, and one month after Facebook CEO Mark Zuckerberg acknowledged that his company had "much more work" to do in how it handles false stories, the company unveiled a new suite of tools designed to curb the spread and influence of fake news. In an update from Adam Mosseri, Facebook's vice president in charge of its News Feed feature, the company announced steps it would take to better allow users to flag for removal of false or misleading stories and to remove the financial incentives for spammers and deceptive websites. "We believe in giving people a voice and that we cannot become arbiters of truth ourselves, so we're approaching this problem carefully," Mosseri wrote. "We've focused our efforts on the worst of the worst, on the clear hoaxes spread by spammers for their own gain, and on engaging both our community and third party organizations."

First, the social media giant empowered its users to help it identify hoaxes and fake news by streamlining the process of reporting fake stories. The company also tweaked how its algorithm would score articles that few users shared. "We've found that if reading an article makes people significantly less likely to share it, that may be a sign that a story has misled people in some way," Mosseri wrote. "We're going to test incorporating this signal into ranking, specifically for articles that are outliers, where people who read the article are significantly less likely to share it." Both tweaks, the company hoped, would allow it to tap into its user base of more than a billion people to stem the spread of misleading information.

Second, Facebook established partnerships with nonprofit organizations to better identify fake news. "We've started a program to work with third-party fact checking organizations that are signatories of Poynter's International Fact Checking Code of Principles," the blog read. "We'll use the reports from our community, along with other signals, to send stories to these organizations. If the fact checking organizations identify a story as fake, it will get flagged as disputed and there will be a link to the corresponding article explaining why." Users could still share these stories, but a warning would appear stating that the story is disputed by third-party fact checkers.

Finally, Facebook sought to cut off ad revenue to spammers who are financially motivated to spread fake, often sensational, stories. "Spammers make money by masquerading as well-known news organizations, and posting hoaxes that get people to visit to their sites, which are often mostly ads," Mosseri explained. "On the buying side we've eliminated the ability to spoof domains, which will reduce the prevalence of sites that pretend to be real publications. On the publisher side, we are analyzing publisher sites to detect where policy enforcement actions might be necessary." By removing the financial incentive, the company hoped fewer people would attempt to create and spread fake news.

While Facebook's announcement was met with a welcome response from most, many conservative commentators cried censorship. Even before the labels appeared, popular conservative news aggregator *The Drudge Report* proclaimed in a headline, "RISE OF TRUTH POLICE!" The headline linked to an article on far-right-wing host Alex Jones's conspiracy website *Infowars*, which predicted that the company might "use the new feature to blacklist information that runs contrary to any mainstream media narratives." Others worried that the company might overextend itself in the future, rightly deleting fake news now but covering up conservative viewpoints or opinions in the future. Despite this outcry, most saw the measures as a sign that Facebook was starting to take responsible ownership of its growing role as source of information.

Ongoing Fight to Combat Hoaxes and Fake News

In the months following their respective announcements, Google and Facebook continued to roll out new measures, tweaks, and tools to stamp out hoaxes and misleading stories. Following Facebook's lead of going after spammers' financial incentives, Google permanently banned nearly 200 publishers from its AdSense advertising network. Facebook announced changes to its controversial "Trending Topics" feature, which many saw as a key avenue for false information to spread to millions of people, to better promote reliable news articles. The additional measures underscored how the fight against fake news remains a work in progress, one that technology companies, and even governments, will likely continue to address.

—Robert Howard

Following is a blog post by Google head of news Richard Gingras from October 13, 2016, announcing new "Fact Check" labels for Google News; and a blog post from Facebook vice president for news feed Adam Mosseri, announcing new tools to combat fake news, on December 15, 2016.

Google Announces Fact Check Labels for Google News

DOCUMENT

October 13, 2016

Over the last several years, fact checking has come into its own. Led by organizations like the International Fact-Checking Network, rigorous fact checks are now conducted by more than 100 active sites, according to the Duke University Reporter's Lab. They collectively produce many thousands of fact-checks a year, examining claims around urban legends, politics, health, and the media itself.

In the seven years since we started labeling types of articles in Google News (e.g., In-Depth, Opinion, Wikipedia), we've heard that many readers enjoy having easy access to a diverse range of content types. Earlier this year, we added a "Local Source" Tag to highlight local coverage of major stories. Today, we're adding another new tag, "Fact check," to help readers find fact checking in large news stories. You'll see the tagged articles in the expanded story box on news.google.com and in the Google News & Weather iOS and Android apps, starting with the U.S. and the U.K.

Google News determines whether an article might contain fact checks in part by looking for the schema.org ClaimReview markup. We also look for sites that follow the commonly accepted criteria for fact checks. Publishers who create fact-checks and would like to see it appear with the "Fact check" tag should use that markup in fact-check articles. For more information, head on over to our help center.

We're excited to see the growth of the Fact Check community and to shine a light on its efforts to divine fact from fiction, wisdom from spin.

SOURCE: Google Blog. "Labeling fact-check articles in Google News." October 13, 2016. https://blog .google/topics/journalism-news/labeling-fact-check-articles-google-news.

Facebook Blog Post Addressing Hoaxes and Fake News

December 15, 2016

A few weeks ago we previewed some of the things we're working on to address the issue of fake news and hoaxes. We're committed to doing our part and today we'd like to share some updates we're testing and starting to roll out.

We believe in giving people a voice and that we cannot become arbiters of truth ourselves, so we're approaching this problem carefully. We've focused our efforts on the worst of the worst, on the clear hoaxes spread by spammers for their own gain, and on engaging both our community and third party organizations.

The work falls into the following four areas. These are just some of the first steps we're taking to improve the experience for people on Facebook. We'll learn from these tests, and iterate and extend them over time.

EASIER REPORTING

We're testing several ways to make it easier to report a hoax if you see one on Facebook, which you can do by clicking the upper right hand corner of a post. We've relied heavily on our community for help on this issue, and this can help us detect more fake news.

FLAGGING STORIES AS DISPUTED

We believe providing more context can help people decide for themselves what to trust and what to share. We've started a program to work with third-party fact checking organizations that are signatories of Poynter's International Fact Checking Code of Principles. We'll use the reports from our community, along with other signals, to send stories to these organizations. If the fact checking organizations identify a story as fake, it will get flagged as disputed and there will be a link to the corresponding article explaining why. Stories that have been disputed may also appear lower in News Feed.

It will still be possible to share these stories, but you will see a warning that the story has been disputed as you share.

Once a story is flagged, it can't be made into an ad and promoted, either.

INFORMED SHARING

We're always looking to improve News Feed by listening to what the community is telling us. We've found that if reading an article makes people significantly less likely to share it, that may be a sign that a story has misled people in some way. We're going to test incorporating this signal into ranking, specifically for articles that are outliers, where people who read the article are significantly less likely to share it.

DISRUPTING FINANCIAL INCENTIVES FOR SPAMMERS

We've found that a lot of fake news is financially motivated. Spammers make money by masquerading as well-known news organizations, and posting hoaxes that get people to visit to their sites, which are often mostly ads. So we're doing several things to reduce the financial incentives. On the buying side we've eliminated the ability to spoof domains, which will reduce the prevalence of sites that pretend to be real publications. On the publisher side, we are analyzing publisher sites to detect where policy enforcement actions might be necessary.

It's important to us that the stories you see on Facebook are authentic and meaningful. We're excited about this progress, but we know there's more to be done. We're going to keep working on this problem for as long as it takes to get it right.

SOURCE: Facebook. "News Feed FYI: Addressing Hoaxes and Fake News." December 15, 2016. http://newsroom.fb.com/news/2016/12/news-feed-fyi-addressing-hoaxes-and-fake-news.

OTHER HISTORIC DOCUMENTS OF INTEREST

FROM THIS VOLUME

U.S. and Coalition Partners Recommit Troops to Iraq; Retake Control of Mosul

OCTOBER 15, 16, AND 17, AND DECEMBER 11, 2016

Throughout 2014, the Islamic State of Iraq and the Levant (ISIL) (also known as the Islamic State, the Islamic State of Iraq and Syria, and Daesh) took control of a number of the largest cities in Iraq, including Fallujah, Ramadi, and Mosul. The Iraqi military and its coalition partners—led by North Atlantic Treaty Organization (NATO) members including the United States—were able to retake Ramadi in February 2016 and Fallujah in June 2016, but efforts to return Mosul to Iraqi control were largely unsuccessful. Following mid-year commitments by the United States to provide additional intelligence and logistical troop support to the Iraqi forces, the Battle of Mosul began in October 2016 with strong ground and air efforts that experienced halting success. It was not until the start of 2017 that the coalition declared that after three months of fighting it had officially taken control of the eastern portion of the city and would begin to move west.

OBAMA COMMITS ADDITIONAL TROOPS TO IRAQ

Fulfilling a campaign promise, President Barack Obama pulled all U.S. combat troops out of Iraq in 2011. Since that time, the United States had maintained approximately 5,000 soldiers in the country to provide training to Iraqi forces, as well as counterterrorism, logistical, and intelligence support. In July 2016, the Department of Defense announced the tenth troop increase since 2011, agreeing to send 560 additional American troops to Iraq to provide operational support. White House press secretary Josh Earnest called the deployment "an effort to reinforce our support for Iraqi forces that are enjoying some success in driving ISIL out of strategic, important areas in Iraq, that can put them in a position to succeed on a much bigger goal: driving ISIL out of Iraq's second largest city." Obama echoed those remarks, adding that "as ISIL loses territory and the fraud of the caliphate becomes more obvious, they are going to start resorting to more traditional terrorist tactics. . . . They can't govern. They can't deliver anything meaningful to the people whose territory they can control. The one thing they know how to do is kill," making American support crucial to the success of the mission.

The July deployment followed an April announcement that 217 troops would be sent to Iraq to add to the mission and was followed in September by a 615-troop increase to support the Battle of Mosul. "These are military forces that will be deployed to intensify the strategy that's in place, to support Iraqi forces as they prepare for an offensive," said Earnest. In each troop increase throughout 2016, the president stuck to his promise that he would not deploy American ground troops back into the region. Iraq's Prime Minister Haider al-Abadi emphasized in a statement that the role of American troops "is not combat, but for training and consultation only," adding, "It is our troops who will liberate the land."

Effort to Retake Mosul Begins

Mosul, Iraq's second-largest city, fell to ISIL control in June 2014 after six months of battles between Iraqi security forces, tribal militias, and ISIL fighters. A plan to retake the city had been in the works since that time, and previous efforts to reclaim the city, most recently in early 2016, were unsuccessful. The October coalition effort to remove ISIL fighters from the city was thought to be the best attempt at victory thus far, but U.S. Lt. Gen. Stephen Townsend, commander of the NATO coalition, noted that "Mosul would be a tough fight for any army in the world." It was estimated that 25,000 Iraqi, Kurdish, Sunni, and Shia troops would take part in the mission, outnumbering ISIL fighters ten to one. This imbalance raised concerns that ISIL fighters might attempt to use the city's 1.5 million civilians as human shields; so, in an attempt to remove as many citizens as possible ahead of the invasion, the Iraqi military dropped leaflets across Mosul, warning residents about the immediate need to vacate the city and seek safety elsewhere.

On October 16, the Battle of Mosul, alternately known as "Operation We Are Coming, Nineveh," named for a city on the eastern bank of the Tigris River, began on the eastern outskirts of Mosul. The Iraqi government troops were joined on the ground by Kurdish Peshmerga forces, Sunni fighters backed by Turkey, and Shia militia groups known as the Popular Mobilization Forces, while NATO coalition forces provided air support. Abadi said of the operation, "The hour has come and the moment of great victory is near." Secretary of Defense Ash Carter lent his support to the coalition effort, stating, "The United States and the rest of the international coalition stand ready to support Iraqi Security Forces, Peshmerga fighters and the people of Iraq in the difficult fight ahead. We are confident our Iraqi partners will prevail against our common enemy and free Mosul and the rest of Iraq from ISIL's hatred and brutality." Similarly, the president of Iraqi Kurdistan, Masoud Barzani, expressed his "sincere hope that this operation will be successful and that we will collectively liberate the people of Mosul from the tyranny of the terrorists of the Islamic State."

The operation yielded quick results, with dozens of towns and villages liberated on the outskirts of the city within the first couple weeks of the operation. However, efforts slowed on November 1 when the coalition forces officially entered Mosul from the east and were met with heavy resistance. Media reports from the front lines were largely unreliable for determining the success of the mission, and the Iraqi government attempted to control the information that was disseminated to reflect only positive progress. The Iraqi media had declared many neighborhoods in eastern Mosul liberated throughout November, despite ongoing heavy fighting and many locations ultimately remaining under ISIL control. On December 1, the United Nations Assistance Mission for Iraq (UNAMI) reported that nearly 2,000 Iraqi security forces had been killed across Iraq since October, which included "police engaged in combat functions" and "Peshmerga, SWAT, and militias fighting alongside the Iraqi Army." The special representative of the United Nations secretary-general for Iraq, Ján Kubiš, went on to add that civilians had been heavily impacted by the fighting taking place in Mosul, and that ISIL "has been employing the most vicious tactics, using civilian homes as firing positions as well as abducting and forcibly moving civilians, effectively using them as human shields."

The Iraqi military responded to the UNAMI statements, calling the number of troops killed "not accurate and much exaggerated," and warned that "the dissemination of false and fabricated news" would only serve ISIL's mission. UNAMI agreed that it would no longer publish army casualty numbers unless they could be better verified. According to UNAMI, "Owing to the fact that places where conflict is taking place, and where military casualties are likely to arise, are inaccessible and there are few reliable, independent sources available by which statistics can be verified, UNAMI has been relying on a variety of sources, including open sources, to compile military casualty statistics." UNAMI said it had requested casualty statistics from the Iraqi government, but that those requests went unfulfilled.

By December, an estimated 75 percent of Mosul was still under ISIL control. Troops were forced to move through the city house-by-house, building-by-building, leaving soldiers behind to patrol each cleared area. Because many of the streets are narrow, troops often moved on foot rather than utilizing tanks and other heavy-duty vehicles, exposing them to ISIL suicide bombings. Despite the slow progress, Prime Minister Abdi announced in December after meeting with Secretary Carter that "the battle of liberating al-Mosul is going smoothly from all axes and our forces are committed to protect the civilians." His office said that a "military victory" against ISIL was becoming "close."

2017 Breakthrough

In mid-January, Iraqi special forces, the Counter-Terrorism Service (CTS), declared that they had taken control of Mosul University, considered a major accomplishment in the fight against ISIL. At the same time, Iraqi troops reached the Tigris River, which bisects Mosul, and had taken control of most of the eastern half of the city. On February 18, forces began their efforts to retake the more heavily populated, though geographically smaller, western half of the city. Ahead of the effort, the region was covered with leaflets from the military calling for ISIL to surrender. "To those of you who were intrigued by the ISIS ideology, this is your last opportunity to quit your work with ISIS and to leave those foreigners who are in your homeland. Stay at home, raising the white flags as the force approaches." The United Nations also prepared a heavy humanitarian response, believing that there were an estimated 750,000 to 800,000 Iraqi civilians living in the western half of Mosul ahead of the invasion and that food, fuel, and necessary goods were sparse. "We don't know what will happen during the military campaign but we have to be ready for all scenarios. Tens of thousands of people may flee or be forced to leave the city. Hundreds of thousands of civilians might be trapped—maybe for weeks, maybe for months," said Lise Grande, UN humanitarian coordinator for Iraq.

In anticipation of the assault, ISIL rendered the Mosul airport useless by carving deep trenches in all the runways. Air support also struggled in its effectiveness because ISIL had a network of tunnels carved throughout the eastern and western portion of the city, which allowed its fighters to move about undetected by drones or aircraft surveillance. Iraqi forces and their coalition partners made some small gains in the first few days of the effort, taking control of a handful of neighborhoods before progress slowed.

—Heather Kerrigan

Following is an October 15, 2016, statement from the Kurdish president on the Iraqi coalition operation to take control of Mosul from ISIL; an October 16, 2016, statement from the Pentagon on the start of Mosul efforts; an October 17, 2016, article from the Department of Defense regarding activities in the battle for Mosul; and a December 11, 2016, press release from the Iraqi prime minister on the progress made thus far in retaking Mosul from ISIL fighters.

Kurdish President on Military Operations to Retake Mosul

October 15, 2016

For a considerable amount of time, local and international media outlets have been reporting on the preparation for the Mosul operation which would drastically weaken the structure of the terrorists of the Islamic State. Indeed the Mosul operation is of enormous significance to the Kurdistan Region and it has been, among the top priorities of the Kurdistan Region.

It is therefore necessary to announce that the preparation for the operation to liberate Mosul have been completed and have paved the way to begin the Mosul operation. The preparations were reached after an agreement between the Peshmerga forces and the Iraqi military forces. The military tasks and responsibilities were distributed in accordance to that agreement. We thereby would like to reassure all the concerned parties that all of the Peshmerga forces of the Kurdistan Region shall remain committed to meticulously abide by the agreement. Additionally there is complete coordination between the Peshmerga forces and the Iraqi military forces in pursuit of preventing all undesired events.

Baghdad and Erbil have also agreed to establish a joint higher political committee whose task would be to supervise the affairs of Mosul after the liberation.

It is my sincere hope that this operation will be successful and that we will collectively liberate the people of Mosul from the tyranny of the terrorists of the Islamic State. Furthermore, I hope for the safe return of the IDPs to the province of Nineveh.

SOURCE: Kurdistan Region Presidency. "A Statement from President Barzani on the Liberation of Mosul." October 15, 2016. http://www.presidency.krd/english/articledisplay.aspx?id=q+oIpBh7BG4=.

Secretary Carter on Iraqi Mosul Operations

October 16, 2016

Tonight Iraqi Prime Minister Haider al-Abadi announced the start of Iraqi operations to liberate Mosul from ISIL. This is a decisive moment in the campaign to deliver ISIL a lasting defeat. The United States and the rest of the international coalition stand ready to support Iraqi Security Forces, Peshmerga fighters and the people of Iraq in the difficult fight ahead. We are confident our Iraqi partners will prevail against our common enemy and free Mosul and the rest of Iraq from ISIL's hatred and brutality.

SOURCE: U.S. Defense Department. "Statement by Secretary of Defense Ash Carter on Iraqi Announcement Regarding Mosul." Release No: NR-370-16. October 16, 2016. http://www.defense.gov/News/News-Releases/News-Release-View/Article/975156/statement-by-secretary-of-defense-ash-carter-on-iraqi-announcement-regarding-mo.

Iraqi Forces Begin Effort to Retake Mosul

October 17, 2016

Iraqi forces launched their counterattack yesterday to liberate Mosul from the Islamic State of Iraq and the Levant, according to a statement released by Combined Joint Task Force Operation Inherent Resolve officials.

"The United States and the rest of the international coalition stand ready to support Iraqi security forces, peshmerga fighters and the people of Iraq in the difficult fight ahead," Defense Secretary Ash Carter said in a separate statement. "We are confident our Iraqi partners will prevail against our common enemy and free Mosul and the rest of Iraq from ISIL's hatred and brutality."

Lt. Gen. Stephen Townsend, OIR commander, said the operation to regain control of Mosul will likely continue for weeks and possibly longer. But it comes after more than two years of ISIL oppression in Mosul, "during which they committed horrible atrocities [and] brutalized the people" after declaring the city to be one of their twin capitals, the general said in the statement.

The coalition can't predict how long it will take for the Iraqi forces to retake the city, Townsend said, "but we know they will succeed—just as they did in Beiji, in Ramadi, in Fallujah and, more recently in Qayyarah and Sharqat."

Mosul, Iraq's second-largest city, is still home to more than a million people—despite hundreds of thousands reportedly having fled the city since 2014—according to United Nations estimates.

WIDE-RANGING, PRECISE SUPPORT

The OIR coalition will provide "air support, artillery, intelligence, advisors and forward air controllers," Townsend said in the statement, adding that the supporting forces "will continue to use precision to accurately attack the enemy and to minimize any impact on innocent civilians."

During the past two years of ISIL control in Mosul, OIR efforts have expanded to include a coalition of more than 60 countries, which have combined to conduct tens of thousands of precision strikes to support Iraqi operations, and trained and equipped more than 54,000 Iraqi forces, the general said.

"But to be clear, the thousands of ground combat forces who will liberate Mosul are all Iraqis," Townsend said in the statement.

Carter, in his statement, called it a "decisive moment" in the campaign. Townsend said it's not just a fight for the future of Iraq, but also "to ensure the security of all of our nations."

SOURCE: U.S. Defense Department. DoD News, Defense Media Activity. "Iraqi Forces Begin Battle for Mosul." October 17, 2016. http://www.defense.gov/News/Article/Article/975239/iraqi-security-forces-begin-battle-for-mosul.

Iraqi Prime Minister Discusses Ongoing Mosul Operations

DOCUMENT

December 11, 2016

H.E. Prime Minister Dr. Haider Al-Abadi received in his office today Sunday the U.S. Minister of Defense Mr. Ashton Carter and the accompanying delegation.

The meeting discussed the operation of "we are coming Nineveh" and the victories achieved by our brave forces in the battle in addition to the stabilization of the liberated areas and arming the Iraqi forces.

H.E. Dr. Al-Abadi confirmed that "the battle of liberating al-Mosul is going smoothly from all axes and our forces are committed to protect the civilians", indicating that the military victory against Da'esh became close.

On his part, Mr. Carter blessed the achieved victories in Mosul, and commended the professionalism and courage of the Iraqi forces including the army, police, and public mobilization and their commitment in the battle.

Mr. Carter renewed the support of his country and the international community to Iraq in its war against terrorism in addition to the continuation of the U.S. support to the stabilization of the liberated areas.

SOURCE: Prime Minister of Iraq. "H.E. PM Haider Al-Abadi Receives U.S. Minister of Defense." December 11, 2016. http://www.pmo.iq/pme/press2016en/11-12-201601en.htm.

OTHER HISTORIC DOCUMENTS OF INTEREST

FROM PREVIOUS *HISTORIC DOCUMENTS*

Russia and African States Revoke Support for International Criminal Court

OCTOBER 18, 25, AND 27, AND
NOVEMBER 11, 16, AND 30, 2016

In late 2016, the International Criminal Court (ICC), a tribunal based in The Hague that prosecutes genocide, war crimes, and crimes against humanity, faced one of the most serious challenges in its fourteen-year existence. Three African nations, Burundi, Gambia, and South Africa, announced plans to withdraw participation in the Court. Shortly afterward, Russian President Vladimir Putin adopted a decree that was highly critical of the Court. While each of the four nations had specific grievances, they shared a common thread: they were all being investigated by the ICC—Burundi and Russia for actions in foreign conflicts, Gambia for repressing internal dissent, and South Africa for refusing to arrest an indicted individual. These moves came in a context of a global decline in support for multilateral institutions such as the ICC, which coincided with a strengthening of nationalism and populism.

ICC Gets Strong Mandate but far from Universal Acceptance

The ICC was conceived in the 1990s, a time in history when there was strong momentum toward building multilateral institutions to address global challenges. Two wars—in Rwanda in 1993 and Bosnia from 1992 to 1995—where widespread massacres were documented, including genocide, further cemented support for creating a permanent, independent tribunal to prosecute the perpetrators of war crimes. Previously, tribunals had been set up with temporary mandates to prosecute crimes committed during a particular conflict, usually modeled along the lines of the Nuremberg trials, which convicted many Nazi war criminals after World War II.

The Court's founding treaty, known as the Rome Statute, was adopted in 1998. The ICC's core mission was to end impunity, meaning that no war criminal should escape punishment for their crimes. The Rome Statute made the ICC a "court of last resort" intended to complement, rather than to replace, national courts, which remained primarily responsible for prosecuting war criminals. On July 1, 2002, the Court became operational, having reached the necessary sixty states to ratify the Rome Statute. The ICC was given authority to investigate crimes committed on or after this date.

The Court's strongest supporters were European and Latin American countries, nearly all of whose governments ratified the Rome Statute. There were some notable exceptions, however, even among these nations. For example, Russia signed but never ratified the Statute, and Cuba never signed. Further undermining the Court's authority, three of the world's largest nations—China, India, and the United States—did not ratify the Rome Statute. Among the three, the United States was the only one to have signed the Rome Statute, under President Bill Clinton. Clinton's successor, George W. Bush, revoked that signature out of fear that the Court would unfairly target American citizens. In Africa, thirty-four governments, more than half, ratified the Rome Statute. Most Middle Eastern countries declined to ratify, and about half of Asian-Pacific nations became party to the Statute.

By 2016, there were 124 countries that had ratified the Statute. The Court had a staff of 800, six official languages (English, French, Arabic, Chinese, Russian, and Spanish) and two working languages (English and French), and an annual budget that year of €139.5 million. By the end of that year, the ICC had heard twenty-three cases since its inception.

AFRICAN REVOCATIONS SPUR FEARS OF DOMINO EFFECT

On October 12, 2016, the parliament of the small, central African state of Burundi voted to withdraw the country's participation in the ICC. The decision came six months after the ICC had launched an investigation into allegations of human rights abuses by the Burundi government, including killings of antigovernment protesters. Responding to the Burundi parliament's decision, the president of the Assembly of States Parties to the Rome Statute, Sidiki Kaba, said, "The withdrawal from the Statute by a State Party would represent a setback in the fight against impunity and the efforts towards the objective of universality of the Statute." Holding out hope that Burundi might have a change of heart, Kaba invited it "to engage in a dialogue."

On October 19, 2016, the government of South Africa announced its intention to withdraw. In June 2015, South Africa had refused to execute an arrest warrant issued by the ICC against Sudan's President Omar al-Bashir. The warrant was issued for war crimes and genocide charges stemming from the conflict in Darfur in the early 2000s. Al-Bashir had been visiting South Africa at the time, and the arrest warrant caused the South African government embarrassment. The ICC's mandate allows it to indict any individual covered by the Rome Statute, including serving heads of state. South Africa's government maintained that indicting serving leaders was overreach.

On October 25, 2016, the government of Gambia, a small West African country, announced that it, like Burundi and South Africa, would withdraw from the Rome Statute. While the ICC had not opened an investigation into the Gambian government, the human rights group Amnesty International had accused the nation's government of torturing detainees. Justifying the withdrawal, Gambia's Information Minister Sheriff Bojang derisively dubbed the ICC the "International Caucasian Court," claiming it only persecuted people of color, especially African leaders, ignoring many war crimes committed by Western nations.

This succession of African withdrawals from the ICC shone a spotlight on the tribunal. The Court's critics pointed out that every individual to have been put on trial thus far by the ICC has been African. They have included former Congolese Vice President Jean-Pierre Bemba, who was found guilty in March 2016 of war crimes and crimes against humanity committed during military incursions into the neighboring Central African Republic. Of the ten ongoing ICC investigations, nine are Africa-focused. The one non-African investigation is focused on Georgia.

RUSSIA FOLLOWS AFRICAN NATIONS IN CRITICIZING COURT

On November 16, 2016, Russian President Putin signed a decree in which he stated his intention not to become party to the Rome Statute. In September 2000, at the start of his presidency, Putin signed the Rome Statute, but since then he has not taken action to have the Statute ratified. In his new decree, Putin said that the ICC "inspired high hopes of the international community in the fight against impunity . . . unfortunately the Court failed to meet the expectations to become a truly independent, authoritative international tribunal." He noted that in fourteen years of operating, the Court had handed down only a handful of sentences, despite having spent more than $1 billion.

Putin criticized the Court for having leveled accusations of wrongdoing against Russian forces and pro-Russian militia in South Ossetia, a separatist enclave in Georgia, stemming from the August 2008 conflict between Russia and Georgia over the enclave. Noting that the Court had failed to investigate the actions and orders of Georgian officials, Putin said, "We can hardly trust the ICC."

Russia was also irritated by the Court's release of a report that accused Russian forces of committing war crimes during Russia's annexation of Crimea, a province of Ukraine, in the spring of 2014. The ICC accused Russian forces of occupying Crimea without the consent of Ukraine. Russia continued to maintain that its annexation of Crimea was legal and cited as evidence the March 2014 referendum in which Crimean voters overwhelmingly backed becoming part of Russia. The Court also investigated the July 2014 downing of a Malaysia Airlines passenger plane in an attack that killed all 298 people aboard. The plane was destroyed by a missile launched from a pro-Russian separatist enclave in Ukraine.

ICC OFFICIALS AND SUPPORTERS TRY TO STEADY THE SHIP

The big question these developments triggered was whether they would cause a domino effect leading to more withdrawals from the Rome Statute. Since its founding, the Court has contended with two ever-present countervailing currents: first, assertions of state sovereignty, and second, peace processes to end conflicts that favor peace over justice. While both currents remain, the reassertion of state sovereignty was an especially potent force in 2016, while populist political movements gained traction across the globe. This has had a negative impact on international organizations, including the ICC, which have supranational authority and jurisdiction.

U.S. State Department spokesperson John Kirby said of the African withdrawals: "I don't want to get ahead of events, and I don't think we're at the point now where we can call it a trend," adding, "We do think that the ICC has made valuable contributions." The United States has had a complicated and shifting relationship with the ICC. President Bush's revocation of the Rome Statute was in turn followed by President Barack Obama's policy of cooperating with the ICC despite not being party to the Rome Statute. According to the State Department, "the Obama administration has been prepared to support the court's prosecutions and provide assistance in response to specific requests from the ICC prosecutor and other court officials, consistent with U.S. law, when it is in U.S. national interest to do so."

Other African nations were reported to be considering withdrawing support, including Kenya, Namibia, and Uganda. On the other side, the Court still has supporters in Africa, including Botswana, Gabon, and Nigeria. The African Union, a regional integration organization with fifty-five member states, has taken a step toward setting up an alternative court by adopting the Malabo Protocol in June 2014. This court's mandate would differ somewhat, particularly excluding the possibility of prosecuting a sitting head of state. The court has yet to come into existence because no country has ratified the Protocol so far.

Despite the withdrawals, the ICC is continuing its work and has clocked up some successes. It secured convictions against a militant jihadist in Mali for destroying antiquities and against a warlord from the Democratic Republic of the Congo for using rape as a weapon of war. In December 2016, it opened the trial of Dominic Ongwen, a leader of the Lord's Resistance Army, a Ugandan militia group that committed atrocities in several central African countries. In February 2017, the Court received some welcome news from the newly elected government in Gambia, which announced it would not withdraw from the Rome Statute after all, reversing the previous government's policy. Similarly, in March 2017, South Africa announced its intent to remain party to the Rome Statute.

—Brian Beary

Following is an October 18, 2016, statement from the International Criminal Court (ICC) on the decision of the Republic of Burundi to withdraw its membership from the Court; a declaratory statement from South Africa to the United Nations on October 25, 2016, regarding its status within the ICC; the October 27, 2016, official notification from Burundi to the United Nations regarding its intent to withdraw; the November 11, 2016, notification from Gambia on its intent to withdraw from the Rome Statute; a November 16, 2016, statement from the Russian Foreign Ministry on President Vladimir Putin's decision not to ratify the Rome Statute; and the official Russian communication to the United Nations on its decision not to ratify the Rome Statute, dated November 30, 2016.

 *ICC Announces Burundi's Intent to Leave the Tribunal*

DOCUMENT

October 18, 2016

On 12 October 2016, the Parliament of the Republic of Burundi voted in support for a plan to withdraw its country from the Rome Statute ("Statute"), the founding treaty of the International Criminal Court ("ICC").

Taking note of this decision, the President of the Assembly of States Parties to the Rome Statute of the International Criminal Court, H.E. Mr. Sidiki Kaba, expressed concern about this development. "The withdrawal from the Statute by a State Party would represent a setback in the fight against impunity and the efforts towards the objective of universality of the Statute," indicated President Kaba. "I remind that all States Parties have the opportunity to share their concerns before the Assembly of States Parties in accordance with the Statute and invite the Burundian authorities to engage in a dialogue."

The International Criminal Court is the first international permanent jurisdiction in charge of prosecuting genocide, crimes against humanity and war crimes. The Rome Statute of the ICC entered into force on 1 July 2002 and has 124 States Parties to date.

SOURCE: International Criminal Court. "Statement of the President of the Assembly of States Parties on the process of withdrawal from the Rome Statute by Burundi." ICC-CPI-20161014-PRI244. October 18, 2016. http://www.icc-cpi.int/Pages/item.aspx?name=pr1244.

South Africa Issues Declaratory
Statement Regarding the Rome Statute

October 25, 2016

[A footnote has been omitted.]

Reference: C.N.786.2016.TREATIES-XVIII.10 (Depositary Notification)

ROME STATUTE OF THE INTERNATIONAL CRIMINAL COURT
ROME, 17 JULY 1998

SOUTH AFRICA: WITHDRAWAL

The Secretary-General of the United Nations, acting in his capacity as depositary, communicates the following:
    The above action was effected on 19 October 2016, with:

(Original: English)

"Declaratory statement by the Republic of South Africa on the decision to withdraw from the Rome Statute of the International Criminal Court

South Africa is committed to protection of human rights and the fight against impunity which commitment was forged in the struggle for liberation against the inhumanity of colonialism and apartheid. We condemn in the strongest terms human rights violations and international crimes wherever they may occur and we call for the accountability of those responsible. This commitment is reflected in significant role that South Africa played in the international negotiations on the establishment of the International Criminal Court (ICC) and was one of the first signatories to the Rome Statute of the International Court (the Rome Statute). The Rome Statute was domesticated in South Africa with the adoption of the Implementation of the Rome Statute of the International Criminal Court Act, No. 27 of 2002, thus reaffirming South Africa's commitment to a system of international justice.
    South Africa is also a proud member of the African Union that was established in 2001 with its strong focus on promoting human security, peace and stability on the continent and codifying in its Constitutive Act the principle of humanitarian intervention against war crimes, genocide and crimes against humanity.
    South Africa does not view the ICC in isolation, but as an important element in a new system of international law and governance and in the context of the need for the fundamental reform of the system of global governance. Questions on the credibility of

the ICC will persist so long as three of the five permanent members of the Security Council are not State Parties to the Statute. The Security Council has also not played its part in terms of Article 16 of the Rome Statute where the involvement of the ICC will pose a threat to peace and security on the African continent. There is also perceptions of inequality and unfairness in the practice of the ICC that do not only emanate from the Court's relationship with the Security Council, but also by the perceived focus of the ICC on African states, notwithstanding clear evidence of violations by others.

South Africa, from its own experience has always expressed the view that to keep peace one must first make peace. Thus, South Africa is involved in international peace-keeping missions in Africa and is diplomatically involved in inter-related peace processes on a bilateral basis as well as part of AU mandates.

In complex and multi-faceted peace negotiations and sensitive post-conflict situations, peace and justice must be viewed as complementary and not mutually exclusive. The reality is that in an imperfect world we cannot apply international law in an idealistic view that strives for justice and accountability and thus competing with the immediate objectives peace, security and stability.

In 2015, South Africa found itself in the unenviable position where it was faced with conflicting international law obligations which had to be interpreted within the realm of hard diplomatic realities and overlapping mandates when South Africa hosted the 30th Ordinary Session of the Permanent Representatives Committee, the 27th Ordinary Session of the Executive Council and the 25th Ordinary Session of the Assembly of the African Union ('the AU Summit'), from 7 to 15 June 2015. South Africa was faced with the conflicting obligation to arrest President Al Bashir under the Rome Statute, the obligation to the AU to grant immunity in terms of the Host Agreement, and the General Convention on the Privileges and Immunities of the Organization of African Unity of 1965 as well as the obligation under customary international law which recognises the immunity of sitting heads of state. Furthermore, there are no clarity on the nature and scope of the provisions of Article 98 of the Rome Statute and its relationship with Article 27, which is reflected by the inconsistencies in the findings of the Pre-Trail Chambers in the Malawi and Chad cases, on the one hand, and the DRC case on the other hand. Article 27 and Article 98 represent the intersection of the law on immunities applying to Heads of State and Government, and the cooperation obligation of States Parties to the Rome Statute. The relationship between State Parties and non-State Parties continue to be governed by customary international law that bestows on a Head of State immunity ratione personae. Arrest of such a person by a State Party pursuant to its Rome Statute obligations, may therefore result in a violation of its customary international law obligations.

In order to address this untenable position, South Africa used the mechanism of consultation available under Article 97 of the Rome Statute, the first State Party to do so, but to no avail. There are no procedures to guide Article 97 consultations, and South Africa is disappointed that the process, that in our view should clearly have been a diplomatic process was turned into a judicial process. As a result of the lack of clarity in the Rome Statutes and in the Rules of Procedure and Evidence, the experience with the ICC left South Africa with the sense that a violation of its fundamental right to be heard was violated.

This is the background against which South Africa has requested the Assembly of State Parties to develop Rules and Procedures relating to Article 97 consultations in order for Parties that find themselves in a similar position in future, to have the confidence that they can do so on the basis of agreed procedures. South Africa also requested that Assembly of State Parties to clarify the nature and scope of the provisions of Article 98 of the Rome Statu[t]e and its relationship with Article 27. It is disconcerting that there was opposition to this proposal as there are fundamental differences on the issue of immunities of Heads of State.

Under these circumstances South Africa is of the view that to continue to be a State Party to the Rome Statute will compromise its efforts to promote peace and security on the African Continent. Also, there is an urgent need to assess whether the ICC is still reflective of the principles and values which guided its creation and its envisaged role as set out in the Rome Statute. The credibility and acceptability of the ICC to become the universally accepted institution for justice that will ensure the ideal of universality and equality before the law has not been realised and is under threat.

In withdrawing from the ICC, South Africa wishes to reiterate its commitment to human rights and the fight against impunity. Its history of fighting and defeating colonialism and apartheid affirms its commitment to continue to fight against any form of impunity for atrocities perpetrated anywhere in the world. Our commitment to justice and accountability remains unwavering, based on the foundational values of the South African nation, namely human rights, freedom and dignity enshrined in our Constitution."

*****

The action shall take effect for South Africa on 19 October 2017 in accordance with article 127 (1) which reads as follows:

"A State Party may, by written notification addressed to the Secretary-General of the United Nations, withdraw from this Statute. The withdrawal shall take effect one year after the date of receipt of the notification, unless the notification specifies a later date."

SOURCE: United Nations Treaties. "South Africa: Withdrawal." October 25, 2016. https://treaties.un.org/doc/Publication/CN/2016/CN.786.2016-Eng.pdf.

Burundi Submits Formal Intent of Withdrawal from the Rome Statute

October 27, 2016

[The footnote has been omitted.]

Reference: C.N.805.2016.TREATIES-XVIII.10 (Depositary Notification)

ROME STATUTE OF THE INTERNATIONAL CRIMINAL COURT
ROME, 17 JULY 1998

BURUNDI: WITHDRAWAL

The Secretary-General of the United Nations, acting in his capacity as depositary, communicates the following:

The above action was effected on 27 October 2016.

The action shall take effect for Burundi on 27 October 2017 in accordance with article 127 (1) which reads as follows:

"A State Party may, by written notification addressed to the Secretary-General of the United Nations, withdraw from this Statute. The withdrawal shall take effect one year after the date of receipt of the notification, unless the notification specifies a later date."

SOURCE: United Nations Treaties. "Burundi: Withdrawal." October 27, 2016. https://treaties.un.org/doc/Publication/CN/2016/CN.805.2016-Eng.pdf.

Notice Regarding Gambia's Withdrawal from the Rome Statute

November 11, 2016

[The footnote has been omitted.]

Reference: C.N.862.2016.TREATIES-XVIII.10 (Depositary Notification)

ROME STATUTE OF THE INTERNATIONAL CRIMINAL COURT
ROME, 17 JULY 1998

GAMBIA: WITHDRAWAL

The Secretary-General of the United Nations, acting in his capacity as depositary, communicates the following:

The above action was effected on 10 November 2016.

The action shall take effect for the Gambia on 10 November 2017 in accordance with article 127 (1) which reads as follows:

"A State Party may, by written notification addressed to the Secretary-General of the United Nations, withdraw from this Statute. The withdrawal shall take effect one year after the date of receipt of the notification, unless the notification specifies a later date."

SOURCE: United Nations Treaties. "Gambia: Withdrawal." November 11, 2016. https://treaties.un.org/doc/Publication/CN/2016/CN.862.2016-Eng.pdf.

Russian Announcement Regarding the Rome Statute

November 16, 2016

On November 16, the President of the Russian Federation signed the Decree «On the intention not to become a party to the Rome Statute of the International Criminal Court». The notification will be delivered to the Depository shortly.

Russia has been consistently advocating prosecuting those responsible for the most serious international crimes. Our country was at the origins of the Nuremberg and Tokyo tribunals, participated in the development of the basic documents on the fight against genocide, crimes against humanity and war crimes. These were the reasons why Russia voted for the adoption of the Rome Statute and signed it on September 13, 2000.

The ICC as the first permanent body of international criminal justice inspired high hopes of the international community in the fight against impunity in the context of common efforts to maintain international peace and security, to settle ongoing conflicts and to prevent new tensions.

Unfortunately the Court failed to meet the expectations to become a truly independent, authoritative international tribunal. The work of the Court is characterized in a principled way as ineffective and one-sided in different fora, including the United Nations General Assembly and the Security Council. It is worth noting that during the 14 years of the Court's work it passed only four sentences having spent over a billion dollars.

In this regard the demarche of the African Union which has decided to develop measures on a coordinated withdrawal of African States from the Rome Statute is understandable. Some of these States are already conducting such procedures.

The Russian Federation cannot be indifferent to the Court's attitude vis-a-vis the situation of August 2008. The Saakashvili regime's attack on peaceful Tshinval, the assassination of the Russian peacekeepers resulted in the Court's accusations against South-ossetian militia and Russian soldiers. Eventual investigation of actions and orders of Georgian officials was left to the discretion of the Georgian justice and remains outside of the focus of the ICC Prosecutor's office attention. This development speaks for itself. We can hardly trust the ICC in such a situation.

The decision of the Russian Federation not to become a party to the Rome Statute (to withdraw its signature from the Statute) entails legal consequences provided for by the Vienna Convention on the Law of Treaties of 1969.

SOURCE: Ministry of Foreign Affairs of the Russian Federation. "Statement by the Russian Foreign Ministry." November 16, 2016. http://www.mid.ru/en/foreign_policy/news/-/asset_publisher/cKNonkJE02Bw/content/id/2523566.

Russia Submits Formal Notice to UN Regarding the Rome Statute

DOCUMENT

November 30, 2016

Reference: C.N.886.2016.TREATIES-XVIII.10 (Depositary Notification)

ROME STATUTE OF THE INTERNATIONAL CRIMINAL COURT
ROME, 17 JULY 1998
RUSSIAN FEDERATION: COMMUNICATION

The Secretary-General of the United Nations, acting in his capacity as depositary, communicates the following:

The above action, which was effected on 30 November 2016, reads as follows:

(Original: Russian)

I have the honour to inform you about the intention of the Russian Federation not to become a party to the Rome Statute of the International Criminal Court, which was adopted in Rome on 17 July 1998 and signed on behalf of the Russian Federation on 13 September 2000.

I would kindly ask you, Mr. Secretary-General, to consider this instrument as an official notification of the Russian Federation in accordance with paragraph (a) of Article 18 of the Vienna Convention on the Law of Treaties of 1969.

30 November 2016

SOURCE: United Nations Treaties. "Russian Federation: Communication." November 30, 2016. https://treaties.un.org/doc/Publication/CN/2016/CN.886.2016-Eng.pdf.

OTHER HISTORIC DOCUMENTS OF INTEREST

FROM PREVIOUS *HISTORIC DOCUMENTS*

Presidential Recall Referendum Suspended in Venezuela

OCTOBER 20 AND 22, 2016

In 2016, opponents of Venezuelan President Nicolas Maduro initiated a recall referendum against him, seeking to remove the president from office before the end of the year. Maduro's opponents blamed him and his socialist government for the country's ongoing economic crisis, which caused severe shortages of food and medicine and sent inflation skyrocketing. Frustrations with the crisis and with electoral officials' decision to suspend the referendum effort led to widespread protests by opposition supporters throughout the year.

VENEZUELA IN CRISIS

The effort to recall Maduro took place amid a staggering economic crisis that left countless Venezuelans without access to or unable to afford necessary goods and services. The crisis was widely attributed to mismanagement and corruption within the Socialist government that had controlled Venezuela since the late president Hugo Chavez was elected in 1998. The oil-rich country had generated more than $1 trillion in revenue from oil sales in the past seventeen years, yet was often short on funds and continually printed more money to cover its costs, which in turn caused ballooning inflation. The International Monetary Fund projected that Venezuela's inflation would reach 720 percent in 2016 and may grow as high as 2,200 percent in 2017, compared to 275 percent inflation in 2015.

Observers note that poor policy decisions have also fueled the ongoing crisis. For example, Chavez implemented price controls on basic goods in 2003 to help curb inflation and ensure the poor could afford them. These controls were expanded in 2012, and continued into Maduro's first term. The problem with price controls was that they often set prices below goods' production or import costs, which meant that sellers could afford to keep those goods stocked, and ultimately led to shortages. Chronic shortages of food, medicine, and basic items such as toilet paper have plagued Venezuela for years. According to a poll published by *Venebarometro* in April 2016, some 13 percent of Venezuelans said their households eat only once a day. Venezuelans wait for hours—sometimes an entire day—outside of supermarkets in hopes of securing basics such as milk and rice and have increasingly resorted to looting and rioting when shelves are bare. Thousands crossed into Colombia in July 2016 to buy goods during a brief opening in that neighboring country's border. The shortages also gave rise to a lucrative black market, where goods were sold at prices far above the government's set rates. The government attempted to crack down on smuggling and looting by deploying armed guards to supermarkets and troops to seize contraband at the Colombian border. Frustrated by the shortages, Venezuelans protested the government in greater numbers. The Venezuelan Observatory of Social Conflict reported 500 protests over food shortages and fifty-six looting incidents in the first six months of 2015. By comparison, the group reported more than 1,000 such protests and 64 looting incidents in the first two months of 2016.

These challenges were exacerbated by a severe drought early in 2016 that dramatically reduced water levels at Venezuela's main hydroelectric dam. The resulting energy crisis prompted the government to declare in April that schools would be closed on Fridays for two months and cut the public-sector work week to two days. Venezuela's water utilities also implemented strict rationing programs, with some neighborhoods going for days without piped-in water.

Maduro's government took several actions to stem the crisis, but none were successful. He devalued Venezuela's currency, increased public transportation prices, cut public spending, increased the minimum wage, and raised the price of oil (from one cent to sixty cents per gallon). The government also briefly experimented with a food rationing program in 2015, under which Venezuelans were only allowed to go to state-owned supermarkets on certain days of the week, as determined by their personal identification numbers. In January 2016, Maduro declared a sixty-day economic emergency that allowed the government to seize private companies' assets to obtain needed food supplies and other goods.

The Democratic Unity Roundtable (MUD), a coalition of political parties that formed the primary opposition to Maduro's Socialist Party, blamed Maduro for the continuing crisis. Maduro claimed that the crisis was an "economic war" waged against the country by capitalists and right-wing conspirators trying to destabilize his government with the assistance of the United States. Maduro even declared a three-month state of emergency in May 2016 to face "threats from abroad" that the president did not specify but suggested involved a conspiracy to overthrow the government, to which the United States was allegedly a party.

Opposition Pursues a Recall Referendum

After winning a supermajority in the National Assembly during the December 2015 elections, MUD began pursuing actions to remove Maduro from office. The coalition first attempted to pass constitutional reform reducing the president's term from six years to four, but this effort was dismissed by the Supreme Court, which is controlled by Maduro supporters. MUD then began a recall referendum campaign against Maduro. Per Venezuela's constitution, those seeking to call a referendum must follow a three-stage process, which begins with collecting signatures from 1 percent of voters in each of the country's twenty-four states, or approximately 200,000 people. In stage two, signatures must be gathered from 20 percent of the voters in each state—about four million people—within a three-day period to trigger the referendum. The referendum must receive more votes in favor of the president's removal than the total number of votes the president received during his last election. MUD wanted the referendum to take place in 2016 because a vote to recall Maduro would have triggered a new presidential election in the same year; an election poll showed that the opposition would likely win. If the referendum took place in 2017, the vice president would finish out Maduro's term instead.

MUD submitted approximately 1.8 million signatures to the National Electoral Council on May 2, 2016. The council was supposed to meet in June, and then in July, to rule on whether the opposition had submitted enough valid signatures for the referendum process to continue but delayed these meetings, prompting demonstrations in the capital.

The council eventually certified 400,000 of the submitted signatures on August 1, but did not state whether stage two of the referendum process could begin. Frustrated by the delays in the council's deliberations, Venezuelans gathered to protest in Caracas on September 1 in a demonstration the opposition dubbed the "Taking of Caracas." The opposition stated that more than one million people participated in the protest, while state-run news reported that about 30,000 people participated. On September 22, the council ruled that the recall could not take place in 2016, but could be held "halfway through the first quarter of 2017" if enough signatures were collected during a three-day window set for October 26 to 28. The council also said that MUD must meet stage two's 20 percent threshold in each state and approved the placement of 5,932 voting machines around the country for Venezuelans to use to register their signatures. MUD had requested that the 20 percent threshold be applied at the national level (some states have a greater rural population, making signature-gathering more difficult in those locations) and requested the use of 19,500 voting machines. Opposition leaders pushed back on the council's decisions. "We reject the anti-constitutional elements of this announcement by the election board," said Jesús Torrealba, the leader of MUD.

REFERENDUM EFFORT SUSPENDED, VENEZUELANS PROTEST

Just a few days before MUD was to begin collecting stage two signatures, the National Electoral Council suspended the referendum effort. The council's October 20 decision followed rulings issued by four lower courts in different states that same day, which declared that a few thousand of the signatures collected in the opposition's preliminary petition were fraudulent. The governors of these states, who also belonged to the Socialist Party, had requested injunctions from the courts.

Torrealba claimed that the government was trying to push the opposition either to give up or respond with violence. "It wins with both," he said. "We cannot fall into a violent response because that's what they want. But we also cannot docilely accept what is happening." Organization of American States secretary general Luis Amalgro said the council's decision violated the rights of the Venezuelan people and called for other countries in the region to help defend its democracy. "Only dictatorships deprive their citizens of rights, ignore the legislature, and hold political prisoners," he said, adding, "Today we are more convinced than ever of the breakdown of the democratic system. It is time to take concrete actions." By contrast, government officials called for law enforcement action against those involved in collecting the fraudulent signatures. "We hope that those responsible [for fraud] will be found, will be detained, and will go to prison for what they have done," said Vice President Diosdado Cabello. A poll released by Datanalisis in October showed that a clear majority of Venezuelans were aligned with MUD. Ninety percent of those surveyed said they thought the country was going in the wrong direction and 76 percent said they wanted Maduro to leave office in 2016.

With the referendum stalled, the National Assembly held a special session on October 23 during which they approved several measures aimed at ousting Maduro, Supreme Court justices who had been approved without the Assembly's input, and some members of the National Electoral Council. Specifically, the Assembly agreed to present a case against Supreme Court justices and council members to the International Criminal Court, attempt to replace the justices and council members, ask the military not to follow Maduro's orders, and schedule a debate for October 25 to discuss the constitutionality of Maduro's presidency. Assembly members declared that, with the suspension of the referendum, "there has been a breakdown of constitutional order and a continued state of coup led from the highest level of government by President Nicolás Maduro." In response to the Assembly's deliberations, government supporters stormed the Assembly building in protest, stealing lawmakers' cell phones, punching lawmakers, and vandalizing the building. Progovernment lawmakers ultimately persuaded the protesters to leave.

During its October 25 meeting, the Assembly agreed to open an impeachment trial against Maduro and voted to summon the president to testify before the Assembly the following week so they could determine whether to recommend he be removed from office. Speaking to government supporters who gathered at a rally in Caracas the same day, Maduro claimed lawmakers were attempting to wage a "parliamentary coup" and alleged that the opposition's "attacks" were being orchestrated by the Obama administration. The military also affirmed its support of Maduro. Defense Minister Vladimir Padrino López said the opposition was trying to create "chaos and anarchy" in order to overthrow Maduro, "to whom we reiterate our unconditional loyalty and unbreakable commitment."

An impeachment trial is not expected to gain traction because the Socialist Party controls much of the government, including the courts. Maduro also worked with the Supreme Court to take away many of the Assembly's powers, including through a March 2016 law that stripped the Assembly of its oversight of judicial, electoral, and civil authorities. The Assembly also does not have the power to impeach a president; only the Supreme Court can.

While the Assembly deliberated, MUD called on its supporters to protest the National Electoral Council's decision. On October 26, hundreds of thousands of Venezuelans protested at fifty different sites across the country. The government set up roadblocks and closed some subway stations ahead of the protests, leading the opposition to accuse officials of trying to impede them. Clashes between security forces and protesters were reported in several locations outside of Caracas. Some protesters reportedly threw rocks and petrol bombs at police, and protesters were shot in a few locations. The human rights organization Penal Forum reported that more than 208 people were arrested and that 119 of them were still being held as of the end of the day. Government supporters held a smaller countermarch in downtown Caracas.

Following the protest, MUD called for a general strike and threatened to march on the presidential palace on November 3 if officials did not lift the referendum suspension. The strike did occur on October 28, with many schools, shops, and other businesses closing, but it was not widespread. Those in poorer regions of the country, especially, declined to strike. Maduro had warned companies that they could be seized by the government if they joined the strike, and later declared that the strike had failed. The day of the strike, Maduro announced that the government would raise the minimum wage by 20 percent, effective November 1, and that public-sector workers would also receive a 20 percent pay increase. He further pledged to increase food subsidies. Many viewed the announcement as an effort to stem the tide of protests.

The November 3 march on the presidential palace was canceled by the Assembly president.

VATICAN-MEDIATED TALKS BEGIN

Amid the protests and Assembly actions, Torrealba announced on October 24 that MUD would participate in Vatican-mediated talks with the government. This came as a surprise to other members of the opposition, who were displeased with the decision and thought the opposition should not participate in talks until the referendum could proceed. Torrealba defended his decision. "We need to act with the responsibility the situation demands," he said. "The situation is extremely delicate and any mistake won't just cost votes and positions. A mistake now could cost lives." Talks began on October 30, and also involved the Union of South American Nations.

On November 23, Torrealba declared that talks were "frozen" after government officials did not attend two meetings. The opposition claimed the government decided not to participate in the meetings after the previous day's Assembly session, during which lawmakers had sharply criticized Maduro for his family's involvement in an attempted multimillion-dollar drug deal. On December 6, MUD declined to attend a meeting with the government, stating that officials had failed to keep their promises. The two sides had tentative agreements in place on several issues, including on allowing foreign donors to provide food and medicine and working toward replacing directors of the National Electoral Council. MUD also wanted the government to release more than 100 imprisoned activists. A few of these activists had been released, but opponents said it was not enough. Torrealba said the opposition would continue to meet with the talks' facilitators but that "[w]e'll only sit down with the government again once they meet what was agreed on." Vatican envoy Claudio Maria Celli said that both sides would have technical meetings until January 13, at which point he hoped to return to a joint dialogue. However, on December 27, MUD said it would not resume talks with the government. "Conditions do not exist for the return to direct dialogue between the parties on January 13," said Torrealba. The talks remain suspended at the time of writing.

—Linda Fecteau Grimm

Following is the text of the National Electoral Council's decision from October 20, 2016, to suspend the recall referendum; a statement issued by the Democratic Unity Roundtable (MUD) on October 20, 2016, in response to the council's decision; and a statement released by the Organization of American States on October 22, 2016, in response to the referendum suspension.

National Electoral Council on
Suspending the Recall Referendum

October 20, 2016

The process collecting 20% of expressions of intent is postponed until further judicial instruction

The Electoral Power informs the country that it has been notified, by courts of the Republic, of precautionary measures that order the postponement of any act generated by the collection of 1% of expressions of intent required to validate the mediation of the MUD political organization.

The measures decided on this Thursday, October 20th, by the criminal courts of first instance in control functions in Valencia; of third of control in San Fernando de Apure; of first instance in function of third in control in Aragua, and of first instance in control functions in Bolivar, were decided after the admission of criminal complaints of the crimes of false testimony before a public official, profit from false acts, and providing false data to the Electoral Power.

Consequently, these decisions have halted, until further judicial instruction, the process of collecting 20% of the expressions of intent, which was scheduled for October 26, 27, and 28, and on which the National Electoral Council had been working after the completion of the first stage of a petition made by the MUD party last April.

In accordance with the constitutional framework, the CNE complies with the orders given by the courts and has given instructions to postpone the collection process until further judicial instruction.

The Electoral Power reiterates its call for national dialogue as a democratic formula *par excellence* to preserve the peace and stability of the Republic, and is available to politicians and national institutions to assist in the search for the best conditions to make this meeting fruitful.

SOURCE: Bolivarian Republic of Venezuela. National Electoral Council. "Electoral Power accepts precautionary measures ordered by courts of the Republic." Translated by SAGE Publishing. October 20, 2016. http://www.cne.gov.ve/web/sala_prensa/noticia_detallada.php?id=3483.

DOCUMENT   *MUD Responds to the Recall Decision*

October 20, 2016

After 8:00 p.m. this Thursday, leaders of the Mesa De La Unidad Democratica reacted to the refusal of the National Electoral Council to convene and celebrate the constitutional right to recall referendum. The rejection is unanimous.

Henrique Capriles, of the Justice First party, announced that "in the next few hours we will talk to the Venezuelan people and to the international community about the grave fait accompli against the Constitution. The Venezuelan people and international community should be assured of the actions taken in defense of constitutional rights."

For her part, Radical Cause parliamentarian Mariela Magallanes questioned the pressure some of the governors of the PSUV imposed to stop the recall. "The most malicious governors, among them Tareck El Aissami, announced their own fraud before the electoral shakedown. A lot of fear, a lot of dread."

For Juan Andres Mejia, parliamentarian of the Popular Will party, "with the announcement from the CNE, the regime ends up burying democracy and declaring dictatorship in Venezuela. We knew this could happen with this regime. Together we have advanced and overcome obstacles, and this time will not be any different," Mejia said.

SOURCE: Democratic Unity Roundtable. "Unidad leaders reject the CNE's recall decision." Translated by SAGE Publishing. October 20, 2016. http://www.unidadvenezuela.org/2016/10/dirigentes-de-la-unidad-rechazan-decision-del-cne-sobre-el-revocatorio.

OAS Secretary General Statement on Venezuela Recall Referendum

October 22, 2016

The Secretary General of the Organization of American States (OAS), Luis Almagro, today called on the countries of the region to take "concrete actions to defend democracy in Venezuela" after the Venezuelan National Electoral Council (CNE) suspended the process of the collection of signatures to convene a recall referendum, an action he regarded as an inflection point and a breakdown of the democratic system.

The Secretary General underlined that "only dictatorships deprive their citizens of rights, ignore the legislature, and hold political prisoners," and added: "Today we are more convinced than ever of the breakdown of the democratic system. It is time to take concrete actions."

He explained that the denial by the CNE of the constitutional right of the people of Venezuela to hold the recall referendum violates their rights and violates popular sovereignty.

Almagro said the President of Venezuela, Nicolas Maduro, lost "all of his legitimacy of origin after leaving the people of Venezuela without electoral rights" and that therefore the political instability created will be his responsibility.

The OAS leader called on the countries of the Americas to act in the framework of article 20 of the Inter-American Democratic Charter, which "imposes the obligation of concrete results," and urged the use of mediators that have "the trust of everyone."

In this context, the OAS Secretary General referred to the dialogue initiative led by the former Presidents José Luis Rodríguez Zapatero, Martín Torrijos y Leonel Fernández: "it has failed to prevent institutional breakdown; on the contrary whatever its intentions it has aided the string of obstacles placed before the realization of the recall referendum."

Therefore—concluded Almagro—is essential that "there be a new mediation effort that gives moral force to the solutions needed by the Venezuelan people."

SOURCE: Organization of American States. "OAS Secretary General: 'To Deny the Recall Referendum in Venezuela in 2016 Is an Inflection Point.'" October 22, 2016. http://www.oas.org/en/media_center/press_release.asp?sCodigo=E-116/16.

OTHER HISTORIC DOCUMENTS OF INTEREST

FROM PREVIOUS HISTORIC DOCUMENTS

November

China Invalidates Seats of Hong Kong Legislators

NOVEMBER 7 AND 30, 2016

The terms of Hong Kong's semiautonomous existence have been a source of contention since the former British colony was returned to Chinese sovereignty on July 1, 1997. Ambiguity and repeated reinterpretations of the city's charter have stirred ideological strife between pro-democracy factions and those loyal to China. Ideals of self-determination and independence were previously dismissed but have gained currency within the city in recent years as a younger, politically outspoken generation brought the issue to the center of political discourse. The election on September 4, 2016, carried some of that animosity into Hong Kong's legislature, when incoming pro-democracy lawmakers used their oaths of office as a platform to demonstrate contempt toward the central government of China. The resulting unrest pushed the city and its constitution into a precedent-setting predicament. The defiance exhibited by elected officials at their swearing-in, and the Chinese government's response, sparked protests both for and against Chinese involvement in the city's social and political affairs.

CONTENTIOUS OATHS OF OFFICE

Yau Wai-ching and Sixtus "Baggio" Leung Chung-hang, both of the newly formed Youngspiration party, were two of the seventy representatives who were elected to Hong Kong's Legislative Council in September. On October 12, while taking their oaths of office, they pledged allegiance to a "Hong Kong Nation" and each displayed a banner that read "Hong Kong is not China." Both pronounced the name China as *Shee-na*, a term widely considered derogatory since it was first used by the Japanese during their occupation of China during World War II. Yau also included a profanity in "People's Republic of China" during her recitation. Due to these deviations from the prescribed oath, the legislature's head clerk declared their swearing-in to be invalid, and a second swearing-in session was scheduled to take place a week later. Outraged at such behavior, the Hong Kong government condemned the crude demonstration, denouncing unnamed members who "spoke or acted in an offensive manner that harmed the feelings of our compatriots." Hong Kong chief executive Leung Chun-ying also attempted, unsuccessfully, to obtain an injunction barring Yau and Leung from taking a second oath. On October 19, as Yau and Leung were about to retake their oaths, dozens of pro-China lawmakers left the council chamber, placing Chinese and Hong Kong flags in their seats as they exited. This action effectively ended the proceedings by preventing the necessary quorum.

Public response to the new legislators' defiance was mixed. The enraged pro-establishment called the pair "Chinese traitors." While many pro-democracy allies supported the sentiment underlying Yau and Leung's actions, they were critical of the offensive language, calling the stunt "inappropriate" and "not constructive." China's legislature requested an apology but received none.

CHINA INTERVENES

The question of whether Leung and Yau had the right to retake their oath was brought before Hong Kong's High Court, where the Hong Kong government asserted that the pair should be disqualified because they had essentially rejected the first oath. A provision of Hong Kong's Basic Law holds that any person "who declines or neglects to take an oath duly requested" becomes ineligible to take office. The law also states that legislators are required to swear their allegiance to the People's Republic of China. Their replacement of "China" with the disparaging substitute, as well as Yau's use of obscenity, was seen as a refusal to do so. Rather than wait for the Court to complete its judicial review, the Standing Committee of the National People's Congress (NPCSC), a committee within the Chinese legislature that is controlled by the Communist Party, preemptively intervened to issue its own interpretation of the law, citing national unity and territorial integrity as justification. In a ruling welcomed by the Hong Kong government, NPCSC said that oaths should be "solemn, accurate, and complete" the first time, and that second chances should not be given to legislators who fail to comply. A clarification published by HKSAR's Secretary for Constitutional and Mainland Affairs, Raymond Tam, noted that the interpretation by the NPCSC simply reiterates Article 104's meaning and does not "change . . . the content . . . or the legislative intent of the Article." This intervention marked the first time that the Chinese government has involved itself in an issue that was being actively deliberated by a Hong Kong court.

The Basic Law gives Beijing the authority to issue interpretations, as it has done four times previously, but this time critics say that China amended the law rather than simply clarify its terms. China's unsolicited involvement stirred fears among democratic advocacy groups that Hong Kong's judicial system would no longer be fully independent, with many wary the intervention would set a troubling precedent enabling democratically elected opposition lawmakers to be prevented from taking office. The Hong Kong Bar Association warned that intervention by China could inflict a "severe blow" to the judicial autonomy Hong Kong was promised when the United Kingdom (UK) ceded the territory back to China in 1997.

ONE COUNTRY, TWO SYSTEMS

Per the Sino-British Joint Declaration signed by the UK and China before the Hong Kong handover, China is to govern the territory under a principle of "one country, two systems" until 2047. This meant that China's socialist system and policies would not be applied to what became the Hong Kong Special Administrative Region (HKSAR), allowing the territory to preserve its capitalist system. Hong Kong retained a substantial amount of executive, legislative, and judicial independence as well as its currency under the agreement, and the Basic Law grants citizens the freedoms of speech, assembly, and press.

While China has controlled the HKSAR for nearly twenty years, many of Hong Kong's residents identify more strongly with the culture fostered during more than 150 years of British rule than that of China. According to a poll released by Hong Kong University in December 2016, nearly 35 percent of citizens surveyed identify solely as Hong Konger rather than Chinese (among a gradient of options). Socioeconomic factors, particularly economic inequality and immigration from mainland China, have sown discontent and aggravated political divisions. However, China loyalists still dominate the political sphere, giving the central government in Beijing significant, if indirect, leverage over the territory.

A perpetual and growing point of dispute is the NPCSC's multiple reinterpretations of Basic Law. This issue has been attributed to ambiguity within the document itself. For example, Article 45 states that Hong Kong's chief executive "shall be selected by election or through consultations held locally and be appointed by the Central People's Government" and that "the ultimate aim is the selection of the chief executive by universal suffrage upon nomination by a broadly representative nominating committee in accordance with democratic procedures." Yet the steps to be taken to ensure universal suffrage—and when that goal should be achieved—have been left unclear. In 2007, NPCSC ruled that the first election by universal suffrage could occur in 2017. Then in August of 2014, the ruling was retracted, and it was decided that instead of an open election, the next chief executive would be selected from a pool of vetted candidates approved by a largely pro-China screening committee. Just two months earlier, China had released a white paper asserting its "comprehensive jurisdiction" over the city, stressing that Hong Kong's autonomy comes "solely from the authorization by the central government." Pro-democracy activists argue that such procedural barriers give China the ability to eliminate any candidates it disapproves of and maintain its political leverage over the city, which they say shows China's reluctance to allow democratic development. It also highlights concerns among China's central authorities that concessions to Hong Kong would incite liberalization demands on the mainland. Li Fei, chair of the NPCSC Basic Law Committee, said that China is "determined to firmly confront the pro-independence forces without any ambiguity."

The Umbrella Movement: Setting the Stage for a New Political Force

When China reneged on its 2007 promise of greater public participation in selecting a leader, a young generation of activists, many of them high school and university students, took to the streets in protest. The massive demonstrations lasted for seventy-nine days and ultimately gave rise to a new political movement seeking greater self-determination if not outright independence for the territory. It became known as the "Umbrella Movement," a reference to demonstrators' use of umbrellas to protect themselves from attacks by proponents of the Chinese Communist Party and the tear gas used by police to try to disperse the crowds. Police actions during the protests further fueled sentiment among those participating in the movement that China's increasingly strong oversight has abraded the freedoms the Basic Law promises.

Hong Kong's first legislative election since the emergence of the Umbrella Movement saw a record voter turnout. The candidacy of several young political activists, including Yau and Leung, was buoyed by the momentum. Leung founded the youth-centered Youngspiration party to counter China's influence; Yau became the youngest woman to be elected to Hong Kong's Legislative Council. Yau said she felt compelled to get involved in government after seeing the students protest, stating in an interview with *The Guardian* that "adults like us should take more of a part." Leung and Yau were the first open advocates of independence to be elected to the legislature, and like many of their allies, they did not see how Hong Kong could maintain its promised civil liberties under the current circumstances.

An Uncertain Future

Leung and Yau's seats have been declared vacant until by-elections can be held to fill them, though both have expressed intentions to seek an injunction against the by-election and appeal the ruling. Yau has defended her actions by stating, "This is just what China must do to maintain their dictatorship, so we don't think it is our fault." While public opinion on democratic reform in Hong Kong remains divided, China's intervention could lead to more and deeper political disagreements between the territory and the mainland, particularly as the youth movement that supported Leung and Yau continues to strengthen.

—Megan Howes

Following is the interpretation by the Standing Committee of the National People's Congress on Basic Law Article 104, announced on November 7, 2016; and clarification provided by Hong Kong's secretary for constitutional and mainland affairs regarding the interpretation, on November 30, 2016.

NPCSC *Interpretation of* Basic Law Article 104

November 7, 2016

(Adopted by the Standing Committee of the Twelfth National People's Congress at its twenty-fourth Session on 7 November 2016)

The Standing Committee of the Twelfth National people's Congress examined at its Twenty-fourth Session the motion regarding the request for examination of the Draft Interpretation of Article 104 of the Basic Law of the Hong Kong Special Administrative Region of the People's Republic of China submitted by the Council of Chairmen. Having consulted the Committee for the Basic Law of the Hong Kong Special Administrative Region under the Standing Committee of the National People's Congress, the Standing Committee of the National People's Congress has decided to make, under the provisions of Article 67(4) of the Constitution of the People's Republic of China and Article 158(1) of the Basic Law of the Hong Kong Special Administrative Region of the People's Republic of China, an interpretation of the provisions of Article 104 of the Basic Law of the Hong Kong Special Administrative Region of the People's Republic of China regarding "When assuming office, the Chief Executive, principal officials, members of the Executive Council and of the Legislative Council, judges of the courts at all levels and other members of the judiciary in the Hong Kong Special Administrative Region must, in accordance with law, swear to uphold the Basic Law of the Hong Kong Special Administrative Region of the People's Republic of China and swear allegiance to the Hong Kong Special Administrative Region of the People's Republic of China" as follows:

1. "To uphold the Basic Law of the Hong Kong Special Administrative Region of the People's Republic of China" and to bear "allegiance to the Hong Kong Special Administrative Region of the People's Republic of China" as stipulated in Article 104 of the Basic Law of the Hong Kong Special Administrative Region of the People's Republic of China, are not only the legal content which must be included in the oath prescribed by the Article, but also the legal requirements and preconditions for standing for election in respect of or taking up the public office specified in the Article.

2. The provisions in Article 104 of the Basic Law of the Hong Kong Special Administrative Region of the People's Republic of China that "When assuming office", the relevant public officers "must, in accordance with law, swear" bear the following meaning:

    (1) Oath taking is the legal prerequisite and required procedure for public officers specified in the Article to assume office. No public office shall be assumed, no corresponding powers and functions shall be exercised, and no corresponding entitlements shall be enjoyed by anyone who fails to lawfully and validly take the oath or who declines to take the oath.

    (2) Oath taking must comply with the legal requirements in respect of its form and content. An oath taker must take the oath sincerely and solemnly, and must accurately, completely and solemnly read out the oath prescribed by law, the content of which includes "will uphold the Basic Law of the Hong Kong Special Administrative Region of the People's Republic of China, bear allegiance to the Hong Kong Special Administrative Region of the People's Republic of China."

    (3) An oath taker is disqualified forthwith from assuming the public office specified in the Article if he or she declines to take the oath. An oath taker who intentionally reads out words which do not accord with the wording of the oath prescribed by law, or takes the oath in a manner which is not sincere or not solemn, shall be treated as declining to take the oath. The oath so taken is invalid and the oath taker is disqualified forthwith from assuming the public office specified in the Article.

    (4) The oath must be taken before the person authorized by law to administer the oath. The person administering the oath has the duty to ensure that the oath is taken in a lawful manner. He or she shall determine that an oath taken in compliance with this Interpretation and the requirements under the laws of the Hong Kong Special Administrative Region is valid, and that an oath which is not taken in compliance with this Interpretation and the requirements under the laws of the Hong Kong Special Administrative Region is invalid. If the oath taken is determined as invalid, no arrangement shall be made for retaking the oath.

3. The taking of the oath stipulated by Article 104 of the Basic Law of the Hong Kong Special Administrative Region of the People's Republic of China is a legal pledge made by the public officers specified in the Article to the People's Republic of China and its Hong Kong Special Administrative Region, and is legally binding. The oath taker must sincerely believe in and strictly abide by the relevant oath prescribed by law. An oath taker who makes a false oath, or, who, after taking the oath, engages in conduct in breach of the oath, shall bear legal responsibility in accordance with law.

This Interpretation is hereby announced.

SOURCE: National People's Congress Standing Committee. "Interpretation of Article 104 of the Basic Law of the Hong Kong Special Administrative Region of the People's Republic of China by the Standing Committee of the National People's Congress." November 7, 2016.

Hong Kong Offers Clarification on Article 104 Interpretation

November 30, 2016

Following is a question by the Hon Claudia Mo and a reply by the Secretary for Constitutional and Mainland Affairs, Mr Raymond Tam, in the Legislative Council today (November 30):

Question:

At its Twenty-fourth Session on the 7th of this month, the Standing Committee of the Twelfth National People's Congress made an interpretation of Article 104 of the Basic Law (BL) (the NPCSC Interpretation). In this connection, will the Government inform this Council:

(1) as Article 104 stipulates that when assuming office, the public officers specified in the Article (namely the Chief Executive, principal officials, members of the Executive Council and of the Legislative Council, judges of the courts at all levels and other members of the judiciary) must, in accordance with law, swear allegiance to the "Hong Kong Special Administrative Region of the People's Republic of China" (SAR) (i.e. the only party to whom they swear allegiance is SAR), but the NPCSC Interpretation states that "[t]he taking of the oath stipulated by Article 104 . . . is a legal pledge made by the public officers specified in the Article to the People's Republic of China and its Hong Kong Special Administrative Region" (i.e. there are two parties to whom they make the legal pledge, namely the People's Republic of China (China) and SAR), whether China, apart from SAR, is also a party to whom the aforesaid public officers swear allegiance when they take the oath upon assumption of office; if so, whether the authorities have assessed if Members' expression of support for "vindicating the 4 June incident" or "putting an end to the one-party dictatorship of the Communist Party" when they address this Council at its meetings will fall within the meaning of "engag[ing] in conduct in breach of the oath" in the NPCSC Interpretation and they therefore must "bear legal responsibility in accordance with law"; if they have assessed, of the details; if not, the reasons for that; and

(2) given that Article 67 of BL stipulates that permanent residents of SAR who are not of Chinese nationality may also be elected members of the Legislative Council and Article 92 of BL stipulates that judges and other members of the judiciary may be recruited from other common law jurisdictions, whether the authorities have assessed if the public officers who are not of Chinese nationality must also swear allegiance to China when they take the oath pursuant to Article 104 upon assumption of office; if they have assessed and the outcome is in the affirmative, of the justifications; if not, the reasons for that?

Reply:

President,

Article 104 of the Basic Law provides that "[w]hen assuming office, the Chief Executive, principal officials, members of the Executive Council and of the Legislative Council, judges of the courts at all levels and other members of the judiciary in the Hong Kong Special Administrative Region (HKSAR) must, in accordance with law, swear to uphold the Basic Law of the HKSAR of the People's Republic of China (PRC) and swear allegiance to the HKSAR of the PRC."

On November 7, the Standing Committee of the National People's Congress (NPCSC) adopted the interpretation of Article 104 of the Basic Law (the Interpretation). Article 1 of the Interpretation points out that "[t]o uphold the Basic Law of the HKSAR of the PRC" and to bear "allegiance to the HKSAR of the PRC" as stipulated in Article 104 of the Basic Law are the legal content which must be included in the oath concerned; while Article 3 of the Interpretation explains that the taking of the oath stipulated by Article 104 of the Basic Law "is a legal pledge made by the public officers specified in the Article to the PRC and its HKSAR, and is legally binding."

Having consulted the Department of Justice, our reply to each part of the question is as follows:

(1) The Interpretation aims to reiterate and explain clearly the meaning of Article 104 of the Basic Law. No change has been made to the content (including the oath content stipulated in the Article) or the legislative intent of the Article.

The Basic Law is enacted in accordance with Article 31 of the Constitution of the PRC. The aims of which are to provide a legal basis for the establishment of the HKSAR and implementation of the basic policy of "one country, two systems" in the HKSAR. The Basic Law is not only a national law but also a piece of constitutional legal document devised for the implementation of "one country, two systems" in the HKSAR. It is plainly obvious that the basic policy of "one country, two systems" and its implementation involve not only the HKSAR but also the PRC at the same time.

The Basic Law contains not only provisions related to the HKSAR, but also provisions regarding the affairs within the responsibility of the Central Authorities and regarding the relationship between the Central Authorities and the HKSAR. Moreover, Article 2 of the Basic Law provides that the executive, legislative and independent judicial powers, including that of final adjudication, enjoyed by the HKSAR are all authorised by the National People's Congress; and the powers exercised by public officers specified in Article 104 of the Basic Law after assuming office are exactly the powers authorised by the National People's Congress stipulated in Article 2 of the Basic Law. Therefore, it is impossible that upholding the Basic Law refers to only upholding those parts related to the HKSAR.

In view of the analysis above, it is impossible that the party to whom the oath is made under the legal pledge stipulated in Article 104 of the Basic Law on upholding the Basic Law is only limited to the HKSAR. Article 3 of the Interpretation only explains clearly that relevant public officers, in swearing to uphold the Basic Law and to bear allegiance to the HKSAR of the PRC, are making a legal pledge to both the PRC and its HKSAR. The Interpretation (including Article 3 of the Interpretation) does not change the oath content stipulated in Article 104 of the Basic Law. Hence, there is no question of "whether the party to whom the public officers swear allegiance is expanded", and there is no change to the legal rights and responsibilities of the relevant public officers arising from Article 3 of the Interpretation before or after the NPCSC adopted the Interpretation.

(2) In future, oath taking by public officers specified in Article 104 of the Basic Law (including those not of Chinese nationality) when assuming office will continue to be conducted in accordance with Article 104 of the Basic Law and the provisions of the Oaths and Declarations Ordinance.

SOURCE: Government of Hong Kong Special Administrative Region. "LCQ4: Interpretation of Article 104 of the Basic Law." November 30, 2016. http://www.info.gov.hk/gia/general/201611/30/P2016113000464.htm.

OTHER HISTORIC DOCUMENTS OF INTEREST

FROM PREVIOUS *HISTORIC DOCUMENTS*

Indian Government Declares
High-Value Banknotes Invalid

NOVEMBER 8 AND 12, 2016

On November 8, without warning, Indian Prime Minister Narendra Modi declared that at midnight, all Rs 500 and Rs 1,000 rupee notes would become invalid. The overarching intent, according to the government, was to crack down on the shadow economy by bringing illegally held money back into the economy and stop production of counterfeit bills. Indian economists believe that much of the money funding terrorism and corruption inside and outside the country, as well as the large sums held by rich Indians who are attempting to evade paying taxes, are kept in Rs 500 and Rs 1,000 denominations. By declaring these bills illegal, if individuals hiding this tender wanted to keep their money, they would need to declare it, thus bringing it back into the economy, where the government could tax it and reap the benefits. However, in a nation where an estimated 90 percent of all transactions are conducted in cash, and 56 percent of the economy is driven by consumer spending, the decision had a much wider-ranging impact that disproportionately affected poorer, rural residents and slowed overall economic growth.

MODI DEMONETIZES 500 AND 1,000 RUPEE NOTES

For years, economic experts have believed that vast amounts of India's gross domestic product (GDP) is held outside the financial system either in foreign banks or in large sums of high-value banknotes. The World Bank estimated in 2010 that a so-called shadow economy likely comprises one-quarter of the country's GDP. Such undeclared black money, as it is known, allows wealthy Indians to avoid paying taxes on their income. According to an estimate by Global Financial Integrity, India lost $344 billion in black money outflows from 2002 to 2011, which has a major impact on the government's ability to provide services for the nation's 1.2 billion people.

To bring some of this black money back into the economy, and increase the nation's tax base (only 1 to 2 percent of Indians currently pay taxes) on November 8, Prime Minister Modi announced that the Rs 500 and Rs 1,000 notes (approximately $7 and $15) would no longer be considered legal tender. These two denominations were the most valuable notes at the time, and made up 86 percent of the cash in circulation. Growth in the circulation of these two bills had soared during the past five years, causing government speculation that these notes were the most likely to be used in illegal activity. Growth in circulation of the Rs 500 note grew 76 percent from 2011 to 2016, while the Rs 1,000 note circulation increased 109 percent during the same timeframe. "For years, this country has felt that corruption, black money and terrorism are festering sores, holding us back in the race toward development," Modi said in his announcement, adding that "[b]lack money and corruption are the biggest obstacles in eradicating poverty."

Bringing black money back into the economy was a promise made by Modi's Bharatiya Janata Party prior to its election in 2014, but when the prime minister made his announcement in November 8, he gave the nation only four hours of warning. His government argued that providing any advance notice would have allowed those holding black money to find a way to trade in their high-value notes or move more money into offshore accounts. "The decision has not been taken in haste, but after detailed deliberations," said Urjit Patel, Reserve Bank of India chief. "High secrecy had to be maintained."

Ability to Exchange Money

Banks were closed on November 9 to allow the government time to get more money to the outlets for exchange, and ATMs were closed on both November 9 and 10. At the time of his announcement, Modi said that citizens would be given until December 30 to deposit their Rs 500 and Rs 1,000 notes into a bank account or change up to Rs 4,500 for new tender, but on November 24, the government banned cash exchanges, except at a handful of Reserve Bank of India locations. At those locations, citizens would only be able to exchange Rs 2,000 in cash and were required to have a government-issued identification to do so. Any amount above Rs 2,000, or anyone without a government-issued identification, would be required to place their money in a bank account. The identification and bank account requirement made it even more difficult for Indians to exchange their money, because more than 300 million citizens do not have government identification and more than 50 percent do not have a bank account because they distrust the nation's financial system.

To encourage those holding black money to exchange their demonetized notes, the government announced that it would not require Reserve Bank of India locations to declare to them any deposits under Rs 250,000. Individuals depositing more than Rs 250,000, however, would be required to provide a written explanation of why they have so much cash and proof that they have paid taxes on it. If the individual could not produce the latter, fines of up to 200 percent of the tax owed could be levied. The government also offered an amnesty program for black market cash holders, in which the government would accept the notes at a 50 percent tax. When the government was tipped off that some who held large sums of cash paid other Indians to exchange their money for them in smaller sums to avoid the Rs 2,000 cap and Rs 250,000 reporting limit, on November 15, to maintain the cap, a program was implemented in which indelible ink would be used to mark the finger of each individual who exchanged cash.

Public Reaction

On November 10 and 11, Indians began lining up at banks and ATMs across the country to change their money, and cash shortages were rampant. The government had announced that it would introduce new Rs 500 notes into circulation and would create a new Rs 2,000 note; however, not enough was printed ahead of the announcement to prevent banks and ATMs from quickly running out of cash. In response to public criticism, which came primarily from Modi's opposition parties and low-income earners who depend on cash payments, Modi's government said ramping up cash printing operations could have tipped off the public that a demonetization plan was about to be put in place. When citizens were able to find Rs 2,000 notes in exchange for their Rs 500 and Rs 1,000 notes, they reported having difficulty spending it because few merchants had

enough cash to provide change, making it difficult for the citizenry to purchase essentials. This was especially true for the two-thirds of India's population who live in rural areas. Because of this, the government did concede that hospitals, gas stations, and pharmacies would be allowed to accept Rs 500 and Rs 1,000 notes until December 15, to allow Indians to access these vital services.

Opponents of the move, including members of the nation's parliament, called on the prime minister to issue an apology and provide additional time for citizens to trade in their high-value bills. Protests were planned across the nation for November 28 in what was billed as a "Day of Rage." "We are protesting against the undeclared financial emergency imposed by the government and the hardships people across the country are facing because of this illegal decision," said Manish Tewari of the Congress Party. "The decision to demonetize high-value currency was done without any authority and legislation and is clearly illegal," he added. The gatherings ended up being the largest in those states that were already ruled by parties opposed to Modi's government.

For his part, Modi called for calm from the citizenry, noting that the demonetization was just one part of a larger financial plan to improve the nation's economy that would take time to come to fruition. A portion of this plan was intended to encourage more Indians to rely on digital transactions and more merchants to accept credit and debit card payments. "Time has come for everyone, particularly my young friends, to embrace e-banking, mobile banking & more such technology," the prime minister said on Twitter. The Reserve Bank of India did note a slight uptick in mobile banking usage from October to November.

OUTCOME OF THE DEMONETIZATION

In the first four days after the ban was announced, according to Indian Finance Minister Arun Jaitley, the government had received 3 trillion rupees in cash ($44.4 billion). By early December, the Reserve Bank of India reported that 14 trillion rupees worth of banned notes had been returned, but that it had only 4 trillion in replacement supply. The bank said that the large gap between what had been returned and what was available "may drag down growth this year" from an estimated 7.6 percent to 7.1 percent. That estimate was echoed by economists around the world, who said that the decision to pull the Rs 500 and Rs 1,000 notes from circulation would likely slow economic growth, at least in the short term. Brokerage Ambit Capital said the contraction could be far more than the Reserve Bank of India had estimated, noting that it could drop by as much as 4.1 percentage points. However, according to Jonathan Schiessl, chief investment officer at Ashburton Investments, "This initiative . . . will yield significant benefits in the medium to long term as corruption is cut and the ease of doing business improves, as more of the economy moves into the formal sector."

In early January 2017, Fitch Ratings downgraded its growth estimate outlook to 6.9 percent for 2016 to 2017, saying that the decision to demonetize the two notes had "some potential benefits, but the positive effects are unlikely to be strong or last long enough to make a significant difference to government finances or medium-term growth prospects." That view was shared by those who criticized the government's plan and argued that those operating in the shadow economy often hold their cash in gold, silver, real estate, and offshore bank accounts that would not be touched by Modi's proposal, while disproportionately affecting average Indians. "The policy is poorly implemented and has a high cost for those who are least able to bear it," said Rohini Pande, a Harvard Kennedy School

economist, adding that even if the government could reduce corruption "you have to balance that against costs or other ways of reducing black money."

—Heather Kerrigan

Following is an announcement from the Indian Ministry of Finance on November 8, 2016, announcing the cancellation of all 500 and 1,000 rupee notes; and a November 12, 2016, press release, also from the Ministry of Finance, on the availability of cash in the country.

Indian Government Announces Bank Note Cancellation

November 8, 2016

With a view to curbing financing of terrorism through the proceeds of Fake Indian Currency Notes (FICN) and use of such funds for subversive activities such as espionage, smuggling of arms, drugs and other contrabands into India, and for eliminating Black Money which casts a long shadow of parallel economy on our real economy, it has been decided to cancel the legal tender character of the High Denomination bank notes of Rs.500 and Rs.1000 denominations issued by RBI till now. This will take effect from the expiry of the 8th November, 2016.

2.   Fake Indian Currency Notes (FICN) in circulation in these denominations are comparatively larger as compared to those in other denominations. For a common person, the fake notes look similar to genuine notes. Use of FICN facilitates financing of terrorism and drug trafficking. Use of high denomination notes for storage of unaccounted wealth has been evident from cash recoveries made by law enforcement agencies from time to time. High denomination notes are known to facilitate generation of black money. In this connection, it may be noted that while the total number of bank notes in circulation rose by 40% between 2011 and 2016, the increase in number of notes of Rs.500/- denomination was 76% and for Rs.1,000/- denomination was 109% during this period. New Series bank notes of Rs.500/- and Rs.2,000/- denominations will be introduced for circulation from 10th November, 2016. Infusion of Rs.2,000/- bank notes will be monitored and regulated by RBI. Introduction of new series of banknotes which will be distinctly different from the current ones in terms of look, design, size and colour has been planned.

3.   The World Bank in July, 2010 estimated the size of the shadow economy for India at 20.7% of the GDP in 1999 and rising to 23.2% in 2007. There are similar estimates made by other Indian and international agencies. A parallel shadow economy corrodes and eats into the vitals of the country's economy. It generates inflation which adversely affects the poor and the middle classes more than others. It deprives Government of its legitimate revenues which could have been otherwise used for welfare and development activities.

4. In the last two years, the Government has taken a number of steps to curb the menace of black money in the economy including setting up of a Special Investigation Team (SIT); enacting a law regarding undisclosed foreign income and assets; amending the Double Taxation Avoidance Agreement between India and Mauritius and India and Cyprus; reaching an understanding with Switzerland for getting information on Bank accounts held by Indians with HSBC; encouraging the use of non-cash and digital payments; amending the Benami Transactions Act; and implementing the Income Declaration Scheme 2016.

5. In order to implement the above decisions of the Government and keeping inview the need to minimise inconvenience to the public, the following operational guidelines have been issued:-

(i) Old High Denomination Bank Notes may be deposited by individuals/persons into their bank accounts and/or exchanged in bank branches or Issue Offices of RBI till the close of business hours on 30th December, 2016.

(ii) Old High Denomination Bank Notes of aggregate value of Rs.4,000/-only or below held by a person can be exchanged by him/her at any bank branch or Issue Office of Reserve Bank of India for any denomination of bank notes having legal tender character, provided a Requisition Slip as per format to be specified by RBI is presented with proof of identity and along with the Old High Denomination Bank Notes. Similar facilities will also be made available in Post Offices.

(iii) The limit of Rs.4,000/- for exchanging Old High Denomination Bank Notes at bank branches or at issue offices of Reserve Bank of India will be reviewed after 15 days and appropriate notification issued, as may be necessary.

(iv) There will not be any limit on the quantity or value of Old High Denomination Bank Notes to be credited to the account of the tenderer maintained with the bank, where the Old High Denomination Bank Notes are tendered. However, in accounts where compliance with extant Know Your Customer (KYC) norms is not complete, a maximum value of Rs.50,000/- of Old High Denomination Bank Notes can be deposited.

(v) The equivalent value of the Old High Denomination Bank Notes tendered can be credited to an account maintained by the tenderer at any bank in accordance with standard banking procedure and on production of valid proof of Identity.

(vi) The equivalent value of the Old High Denomination Bank Notes tendered can be credited to a third party account, provided specific authorisation therefor accorded by the said account holder is presented to the bank, following standard banking procedure and on production of valid proof of Identity of the person actually tendering.

(vii) Cash withdrawal from a bank account, over the counter will be restricted to Rs.10,000/- subject to an overall limit of Rs. 20,000/- in a week for the first fortnight, i.e., until the end of business hours on November 24, 2016.

(viii) There will be no restriction on the use of any non-cash method of operating the account which will include cheques, demand drafts, credit/debit cards, mobile wallets and electronic fund transfer mechanisms.

(ix) Withdrawal from ATMs would be restricted to Rs.2,000 per day per card up to November 18, 2016. The limit will be raised to Rs.4,000 per day per card from November 19, 2016 onwards.

(x) For those who are unable to exchange their Old High Denomination Bank Notes or deposit the same in their bank accounts on or before December 30, 2016, an opportunity will be given to them to do so at specified offices of the RBI on later dates along with necessary documentation as may be specified by the Reserve Bank of India.

(xi) Instruction is also being issued for closure of banks and Government Treasuries, on 9th November, 2016.

(xii) In addition, all ATMs, Cash Deposit Machines, Cash Recyclers and any other machine used for receipt and payment of cash will remain shut on 9th and 10th November, 2016.

(xiii) The bank branches and Government Treasuries will function from 10th November, 2016.

(xiv) To avoid inconvenience to the public for the first 72 Hours, Old High Denomination Bank Notes will continue to be accepted at Government Hospitals and pharmacies in these hospitals/Railway ticketing counters/ ticket counters of Government/Public Sector Undertaking buses and airline ticketing counters at airports; for purchases at consumer co-operative societies, at milk booths, at crematoria/burial grounds, at petrol/diesel/ gas stations of Public Sector Oil Marketing Companies and for arriving and departing passengers at international airports and for foreign tourists to exchange foreign currency at airports up to a specified amount.

6. The relevant Notifications are available in the website of Finance Ministry (http:// finmin.nic.in/). Further details including Frequently Asked Questions (FAQs) are available on the website of the Reserve Bank of India (https://www.rbi.org.in/).

SOURCE: Government of India Ministry of Finance. "Press Release." November 8, 2016. http://www .finmin.nic.in/press_room/2016/press_cancellation_high_denomination_notes.pdf.

Ministry of Finance Addresses Cash Availability

November 12, 2016

Today (12th November, 2016) Ministry of Finance has reviewed and taken stock of the cash availability and issuance to members of public. Reserve Bank of India (RBI), Indian Banks Association (IBA) and a few major banks participated in the review meeting.

A total of over 7 crore transactions have taken place from 9th November upto *[sic]* mid-day of 12th November (i.e. in the last two and a half days) for deposit, exchange of old notes and withdrawal from ATM and over the counter. Old notes of Rs.500 and 1000 denominations amounting to about Rs. 2 lakh crores have been deposited to banks.

Out of 2 lakh ATMs, about 1.2 lakh are operational. Presently only Rs.100/- notes are being disbursed from the ATMs. Recalibration (requires both software and hardware changes) of ATMs is going on, which will be completed by end of this month. The process of disbursement of Rs.2000/- notes in ATMs will begin next week onwards.

There is sufficient cash available with RBI and Banks. They were advised to step up the supply of cash to the public.

The availability of cash and issuance of cash to bank branches and Post Offices on a daily basis is being constantly monitored and necessary rebalancing being done for more efficient allocation of banknotes of requisite denominations between different areas. To cater to the requirement of rural areas, Banks were advised to supply notes of smaller denominations (Rs. 100 and less) as well as Rs. 10 coins.

SOURCE: Government of India Ministry of Finance. "Availability of cash with bank branches and Post Offices." November 12, 2016. http://finmin.nic.in/press_room/2016/PressReleaseR12112016.pdf.

OTHER HISTORIC DOCUMENTS OF INTEREST

FROM PREVIOUS *HISTORIC DOCUMENTS*

- Secretary Kerry and Prime Minister Modi Remark on Historic Indian Election, *2014*, p. 195

Donald Trump Elected U.S. President

NOVEMBER 9 AND DECEMBER 19, 2016

On November 8, 2016, Americans went to the polls to elect the forty-fifth president of the United States. The election pitted businessman Donald Trump and his running mate, Indiana Governor Mike Pence, against former secretary of state Hillary Clinton and her running mate, Sen. Tim Kaine of Virginia, and the race to the White House was characterized as one of the most divisive in U.S. history. Rhetoric on both sides of the campaign painted unbecoming images of different sects of Americans, the two candidates were widely unpopular even in their own parties, and each had significant scandals that dominated the news cycle. Ultimately, Trump was declared the victor with 304 Electoral College votes to Clinton's 227. Trump became the fifth person in U.S. history to become president despite losing the popular vote—he earned 45.9 percent to Clinton's 48 percent—and he was also the first president without any experience in public service or the military.

Clinton and Trump on the Issues

Clinton officially entered the 2016 presidential race on April 12, 2015, and received the nomination of her party on July 26, 2016, at the Democratic National Convention. Clinton had spent most of her career in public service and most recently served as a U.S. senator for the state of New York and then as secretary of state from 2009 to 2013 under President Barack Obama. Clinton previously sought the Democratic Party's nomination for president in 2008, but lost to then-Senator Obama. Clinton announced her 2016 bid in a video message, saying, "Everyday Americans need a champion. And I want to be that champion." In closing Clinton said she was "hitting the road to earn your vote—because it's your time. And I hope you'll join me on this journey."

Trump, the chair of the Trump Organization, an author, and a real estate developer, declared his candidacy on June 16, 2015, at Trump Tower in New York. "We need somebody that literally will take this country and make it great again. We can do that," Trump told supporters. Despite a long and bitter Republican primary season that began with nineteen candidates, Trump won the Republican Party's nomination at its convention on July 19, 2016. Since entering the public spotlight in the 1980s, Trump was asked multiple times if he'd ever consider running for office. Perhaps his most notable foray into the national political debate came in 2011 when he questioned the citizenship of President Obama and demanded that he produce a birth certificate. Trump even threatened to send his own team of investigators to Hawaii, Obama's birthplace. According to Trump at the time, the investigation could uncover "one of the greatest cons in the history of politics and beyond." In response, the White House released the president's long-form birth certificate in April of that year. Trump was considered a longshot candidate throughout much of 2015 and even into 2016, but his campaign focal points and slogan

"Make American Great Again" resonated with voters who felt that they had been left behind by the political elite.

Trump's campaign strategy rested heavily on nationalist, populist proposals, such as being tough on immigration, renegotiating or leaving trade deals and international organizations, a more aggressive approach to foreign policy (especially in the Middle East), ending government regulations, and lowering taxes. Some of the candidate's most popular promises among his supporters—and those that garnered him the heaviest news coverage—included building a border wall with Mexico, for which the candidate insisted he would force the Mexicans to pay, repealing the Affordable Care Act (ACA), creating a database of Muslims in the country, and scaling back the size of the government. Although mainstream Republicans spoke out against the Muslim registry and border wall, they threw their support behind repealing the ACA, something congressional Republicans had promised to do either through legislation or through the courts since its passage in 2010. Trump said on November 1 that if elected he would "ask Congress to convene a special session so we can repeal and replace. And it will be such an honor for me, for you, and for everybody in this country because Obamacare has to be replaced. And we will do it and we will do it very, very quickly. It is a catastrophe." The candidate promised, however, that his replacement plan would ensure coverage for more Americans, at lower prices, and would be driven by the free market.

Clinton stuck to traditionally Democratic issues throughout her campaign, which she exhaustively outlined point-by-point at events and in her stump speech. Many of Clinton's proposals expanded on work done during the Obama administration. Clinton proposed free college tuition at in-state public institutions for families earning less than $125,000 per year, a change from her preconvention promise to provide two years of free community college, and a nod to supporters of her primary opponent, Independent Vermont senator Bernie Sanders. Like Trump, Clinton also proposed comprehensive immigration reform, but said she would expand on Obama's Deferred Action for Childhood Arrivals program and create a legal path to citizenship for those already in the country. Clinton also said she would continue to build on the ACA, including creating a single-payer, government-managed insurance plan, increase the federal minimum wage to $12 per hour, ensure equal pay for women, expand background checks on gun sales, and make "the biggest investment in new, good-paying jobs since World War II." Clinton also frequently attacked her opponent for accusing her of using her status as the first female nominee of a major political party to gain votes. "If fighting for women's health care and paid family leave and equal pay is playing the woman card, then deal me in," Clinton regularly remarked.

While the Trump campaign website contained just seven pages worth of policy proposals, Clinton's website contained forty pages, many of which linked to separate fact sheets. In a criticism of Trump's more closeted strategy, Clinton said, "I have this old-fashioned idea: If you're running for president, you should say what you want to do and how you will get it done." Where they both had extensive policy proposals, however, was in the area of taxation. Trump said he would drastically simplify the tax code, creating only three brackets—12 percent, 25 percent, and 33 percent—down from the seven currently in place, and would increase the standard deduction for single filers from $6,300 per person to $15,000. Clinton promised tax cuts for those making less than $250,000 per year; her plan also focused on high-income earners. Clinton planned to reduce the number of allowable write-offs for those making $250,000 or more, and said that to ensure everyone pays their "fair share," she would increase taxes on the top 1 percent of households—those earning more than $730,000 per year—and increase the capital gains and estate taxes. The nonpartisan Tax Policy Center estimated that Clinton's plan would result in a tax revenue increase for the government of approximately $1.4 trillion over the next decade, while Trump's would result in a tax revenue decrease of $6.2 trillion.

CANDIDATES PERFORM POORLY IN THE POLLS

Even within their own parties, Clinton and Trump were viewed negatively. The Real Clear Politics average from October 28 to November 7, taking into account favorability polling data from major polling outlets, placed Clinton with a 54.4 percent unfavorable rating and a 41.8 percent favorable rating. Trump had a larger spread, with a 58.5 percent unfavorable rating and a 37.5 percent favorable rating. These low favorability ratings were exacerbated by around the clock media coverage of the scandals within both campaigns.

Clinton, for example, came under fire in 2015 for using her own private e-mail server and e-mail address when she was secretary of state. While use of a private e-mail account that does not pass through State Department servers has not been uncommon among recent secretaries of state, criticism of Clinton's use of a private server abounded. When called to testify before Congress in October 2015, members of Congress speculated about whether Clinton's server was vulnerable to hacking, debated whether she had violated any federal laws when she deleted some 33,000 e-mail messages from the server, and asked if anything sent through her private server was marked classified. The Federal Bureau of Investigation (FBI) concluded on July 5, 2016, that it had found no evidence indicating that there was reason to bring charges against the former secretary of state in relation to the use of her e-mail server. Just five days later, Republicans in Congress asked the Justice Department to open a criminal investigation into Clinton to determine whether she had lied during her testimony about handling classified information on her private server; the Justice Department declined to do so. However, in a surprising turn of events, on October 28, eleven days ahead of the election, FBI director James Comey issued a letter to Congress stating that the FBI was in the process of analyzing more e-mail from Clinton's server that it had come across while investigating an unrelated case involving former New York Congressman Anthony Weiner, the estranged husband of Clinton's top aide, Huma Abedin. Federal investigators from the Justice Department subsequently obtained a warrant to review these e-mail messages on October 30. On November 6, Comey said that these e-mail would not change the FBI's recommendation not to pursue charges against Clinton; however, the Comey letter was seen as a major turning point in the election, and polling data marked a decline for Clinton from October 28. House Minority Leader Nancy Pelosi, D-Calif., called Comey "the leading Republican political operative in the country, wittingly or unwittingly."

Trump's favorability was brought into question throughout his campaign due to the violence committed by supporters at some of his rallies. A protester in Tucson, Arizona, was sucker punched by a Trump supporter; an African American woman was surrounded by white Trump supporters and shoved in Louisville, Kentucky; and in Las Vegas, Trump supporters yelled "Sieg Heil!" as an African American protester was carried out and encouraged security to light the protester on fire. Scuffles outside of Trump rallies between pro- and anti-Trump groups were frequent, and Trump supporters reported that they had been similarly attacked by Clinton backers. In his rhetoric, Trump appeared to encourage the violence, saying he would like to punch protesters in the face and promising to pay the legal fees of any of his supporters who did so. Often, the violence at Trump rallies was directed at nonwhite Americans. This led Clinton, on September 9, to say that "half of

Trump's supporters" could be put into "the basket of deplorables. They're racist, sexist, homophobic, xenophobic, Islamaphobic—you name it." The Trump campaign ran with the "basket of deplorables" remark as a rallying cry for his supporters and accused the Clinton campaign of paying protesters to disrupt his events. Clinton apologized for her remarks on September 10, but frequently revisited the idea in her public remarks that Trump had a large following of racist supporters.

Perhaps the biggest Trump scandal to break late in the campaign occurred on October 7 when a video was released by the *Washington Post* in which Trump could be heard talking to *Access Hollywood*'s then-host Billy Bush in 2005, suggesting that he could sexually assault women because he is famous. "When you're a star," Trump was heard saying, "they let you do it. You can do anything." The release of the video was met by calls from some Republicans that the candidate should step aside and rumors that the Republican National Committee (RNC) might pull its funding from the Trump campaign. "No woman should ever be described in these terms or talked about in this manner. Ever," said RNC chair Reince Priebus. Speaker of the House Paul Ryan, R-Wis., even announced that Trump would not be attending an event Ryan was hosting in Wisconsin. "Women are to be championed and revered, not objectified. I hope Mr. Trump treats this situation with the seriousness it deserves and works to demonstrate to the country that he has greater respect for women than this clip suggests," Ryan said. Trump defended his remarks as "locker room talk" during an October 9 presidential debate and released an apology video on October 8 where he explained, "I've said and done things I regret, and the words released today on this more-than-a-decade-old video are one of them."

TRUMP VICTORY SPURS RECOUNT EFFORTS

Heading into Election Day, the polls still favored a Clinton victory, although by a smaller margin than in the preceding months. As the polls closed across the country on the evening of November 8, it quickly became apparent that Clinton would have the uphill battle as Trump handily won a number of states. In the early morning of November 9, after Wisconsin was called for Trump, pushing him past the 270 electoral votes needed to win, Clinton called her opponent to concede, and Trump delivered his victory speech. In his remarks, Trump thanked his opponent for her service to the country and congratulated her on a hard-fought campaign. "I mean that very sincerely," Trump said. "Now it is time for America to bind the wounds of division, have to get together. To all Republicans and Democrats and independents across this nation, I say it is time for us to come together as one united people." Trump pledged to "be President for all Americans" and called on his opponents to provide "guidance" and "help so that we can work together and unify our great country."

Trump received 304 electoral votes to Clinton's 227. Clinton, however, came out well ahead in the popular vote, garnering 65,853,625 votes to Trump's 62,985,106. Only four other candidates in U.S. history have won the electoral vote without winning the popular vote—George W. Bush in 2000, William Henry Harrison in 1888, Rutherford B. Hayes in 1876, and John Quincy Adams in 1824. Clinton did not deliver her concession speech until the afternoon of November 9. "This is not the outcome we wanted or we worked so hard for and I'm sorry that we did not win this election for the values we share and the vision we hold for our country," Clinton told supporters. Like Trump, Clinton called for the healing of America. "We have seen that our nation is more deeply divided than we thought. But I still believe in America and I always will. And if you do, then we must accept this result and then look to the future. Donald Trump is going to be our president.

We owe him an open mind and the chance to lead." Clinton said it was the responsibility of all Americans "to keep doing our part to build that better, stronger, fairer America we seek." By the time Clinton spoke, protests had already broken out across the country. While Trump backers celebrated, his opponents alternately called for the end of the Electoral College and for its delegates to cast their ballots in opposition to the outcome of their home state's vote.

In an effort to heal the nation, President Obama spoke on November 9 about the election outcome, promised Americans that the nation would continue to move forward no matter who is in charge, and pledged that his office would do everything in its power to ensure a smooth transition. The president also urged Americans to offer the new president a chance to lead. "We're not Democrats first. We're not Republicans first. We are Americans first. We're patriots first. We all want what's best for this country. That's what I heard in Mr. Trump's remarks last night . . . I was heartened by that. That's what the country needs: a sense of unity; a sense of inclusion; a respect for our institutions, our way of life, rule of law; and a respect for each other. I hope that he maintains that spirit throughout this transition, and I certainly hope that's how his Presidency has a chance to begin."

The Clinton campaign was urged to submit recount petitions in the swing states of Wisconsin, Michigan, and Pennsylvania where Trump had won narrowly, and where there was some evidence of a discrepancy between the paper ballot and electronic tallies, indicating that someone may have hacked into the electronic voting machines. Green Party candidate Jill Stein, who earned 1 percent of the popular vote and no electoral votes on November 8, began a fundraiser to pay for recounts in these three swing states. A recount petition was filed by Stein in Wisconsin on November 25, and the Clinton campaign agreed to join the effort. The Pennsylvania petition was filed three days later, and a Michigan request was filed on November 30. The Republican Party and President-elect Trump asked the courts to stop the recount effort. The Michigan recount was halted on December 7 after U.S. district judge Mark Goldsmith ruled that there was not enough evidence presented by Stein to indicate tampering with the voting machines. The Pennsylvania recount never began, and a district judge rejected Stein's petition to force a recount. The Wisconsin recount proceeded without incident, but changed the vote in such a minor way that it did not flip the state for Clinton. The White House said on November 26 that "the federal government did not observe any increased level of malicious cyber activity aimed at disrupting" the election.

ELECTORAL COLLEGE UPROAR

The Electoral College was set to convene on December 19 to formally elect a president and vice president. In the lead up to the vote, there were intense lobbying campaigns of Republican electors, encouraging them to vote against the outcome in their state. (To stop a Trump presidency, thirty-seven electors would have been required to change their votes.) Some members of the Electoral College even encouraged their counterparts to "vote their conscience." The issue of whether electors were able to unbind themselves from the outcome in their own states was tied to each individual state's law. While there is no constitutional requirement or federal law stating that electors must vote based on the outcome in their states, some states require their electors to cast their votes in line with the state's popular vote outcome or risk penalty or replacement. To date, however, no elector had ever been prosecuted for voting against the state's popular vote outcome. A number of lawsuits were filed in 2016 to unbind electors in states with such requirements, but none were successful.

Ahead of the vote, forty electors requested an intelligence briefing from the Director of National Intelligence on potential Russian interference in the election, which may have helped Trump to victory. The request was rejected, and when the Electoral College convened on December 19, seven so-called faithless electors cast their ballots in opposition to their states' votes, higher than the previous record of six set in 1808. Three Clinton delegates from Washington State voted for Colin Powell, while one voted for Faith Spotted Eagle, one Hawaii Clinton elector voted for Bernie Sanders, one Texas Trump elector voted for Ron Paul, and another Texas Trump elector voted for John Kasich. Two electors—from Georgia and Texas—resigned instead of voting for Trump and were replaced by alternates, and three Clinton electors—from Minnesota, Colorado, and Maine—did not cast their ballots for Clinton and were replaced by alternates who did cast their ballot for the Democratic candidate. There were also a number of faithless electors who voted against their states' pledged vice presidential candidate. Trump said of the Electoral College vote that his "election represents a movement that millions of hard working men and women all across the country stood behind and made possible" and again promised "to unite our country and be the President of all Americans."

Ultimately, on January 6, 2017, the final results of the election were certified by Congress, and Trump officially became the president elect and Pence became the vice president elect. Trump and Pence were sworn into office on January 20, 2017.

—Heather Kerrigan

Following is a November 9, 2016, statement from President-elect Donald Trump on his election victory; a statement by President Barack Obama, also on November 9, 2016, on Trump's election; and a December 19, 2016, statement by President-elect Trump on the outcome of the Electoral College vote.

DOCUMENT

Trump Remarks on Election Victory

November 9, 2016

They said we could never do it.

But last night you showed the world that America will once again be a country of, for, and by the PEOPLE.

You fought like a winner, you defied all odds, and history will forever remember the role you played in taking our country back.

I never could've done it without you. Your contributions, your sacrifices, and your unyielding commitment to our movement made last night possible!

Last night we learned that America is still a beacon of hope where the impossible is possible.

For far too long, we've heard Washington politicians give the excuse that "it can't be done." They say we can't balance the budget, we can't stop corruption, we can't control the border, we can't bring jobs back to our country.

I REFUSE to accept that it can't be done. This is the country that declared its independence, won two world wars, and landed a man on the moon. This is America. We can and we WILL get it done.

Now it's time to start uniting our country and binding the wounds of our divided nation. I promise to be a president for ALL Americans. I will work for you. I will fight for you. And I will win for you.

You will soon remember what it's like to win as an American.

Thank you and God bless you,

Donald J. Trump

SOURCE: Republican National Committee. "We Did It!" November 9, 2016. https://gop.com/we-did-it.

President Obama Responds to Election Outcome

November 9, 2016

Good afternoon, everybody. Yesterday, before votes were tallied, I shot a video that some of you may have seen in which I said to the American people: Regardless of which side you were on in the election, regardless of whether your candidate won or lost, the Sun would come up in the morning.

And that is one bit of prognosticating that actually came true. The Sun is up. And I know everybody had a long night. I did as well. I had a chance to talk to President-elect Trump last night—about 3:30 in the morning, I think it was—to congratulate him on winning the election. And I had a chance to invite him to come to the White House tomorrow to talk about making sure that there is a successful transition between our Presidencies.

Now, it is no secret that the President-elect and I have some pretty significant differences. But remember, 8 years ago, President Bush and I had some pretty significant differences. But President Bush's team could not have been more professional or more gracious in making sure we had a smooth transition so that we could hit the ground running. And one thing you realize quickly in this job is that the Presidency—and the Vice Presidency—is bigger than any of us.

So I have instructed my team to follow the example that President Bush's team set 8 years ago and work as hard as we can to make sure that this is a successful transition for the President-elect, because we are now all rooting for his success in uniting and leading the country. The peaceful transition of power is one of the hallmarks of our democracy. And over the next few months, we are going to show that to the world.

I also had a chance last night to speak with Secretary Clinton, and I just had a chance to hear her remarks. I could not be prouder of her. She has lived an extraordinary life of public service. She was a great First Lady. She was an outstanding Senator for the State of New York. And she could not have been a better Secretary of State. I'm proud of her. A lot of Americans look up to her. Her candidacy and nomination was historic and sends a message to our daughters all across the country that they can achieve at the highest levels of politics. And I am absolutely confident that she and President Clinton will continue to do great work for people here in the United States and all around the world.

Now, everybody is sad when their side loses an election. But the day after, we have to remember that we're actually all on one team. This is an intramural scrimmage. We're not Democrats first. We're not Republicans first. We are Americans first. We're patriots first. We all want what's best for this country. That's what I heard in Mr. Trump's remarks last night. That's what I heard when I spoke to him directly. And I was heartened by that. That's what the country needs: a sense of unity; a sense of inclusion; a respect for our institutions, our way of life, rule of law; and a respect for each other. I hope that he maintains that spirit throughout this transition, and I certainly hope that's how his Presidency has a chance to begin.

I also told my team today to keep their heads up, because the remarkable work that they have done day in, day out—often without a lot of fanfare, often with a lot of attention—work in agencies, work in obscure areas of policy that make Government run better and make it more responsive and make it more efficient and make it more service friendly so that it's actually helping more people, that remarkable work has left the next President with a stronger, better country than the one that existed 8 years ago.

So win or lose in this election, that was always our mission. That was our mission from day one. And everyone on my team should be extraordinarily proud of everything that they have done, and so should all the Americans that I've had a chance to meet all across this country who do the hard work of building on that progress every single day: teachers in schools; doctors in ER clinic; small businesses putting their all into starting something up, making sure they're treating their employees well; all the important work that's done by moms and dads and families and congregations in every State—the work of perfecting this Union.

So this was a long and hard-fought campaign. A lot of our fellow Americans are exultant today. A lot of Americans are less so. But that's the nature of campaigns. That's the nature of democracy. It is hard and sometimes contentious and noisy, and it's not always inspiring.

But to the young people who got into politics for the first time and may be disappointed by the results, I just want you to know, you have to stay encouraged. Don't get cynical. Don't ever think you can't make a difference. As Secretary Clinton said this morning, fighting for what is right is worth it.

Sometimes, you lose an argument. Sometimes, you lose an election. The path that this country has taken has never been a straight line. We zig and zag, and sometimes, we move in ways that some people think is forward and others think is moving back. And that's okay. I've lost elections before. Joe hasn't. *[Laughter]* But you know—*[laughter]*.

[At this point, Vice President Joe Biden made the sign of the cross.]

The President. So I've been sort of——

Vice President Biden. Remember, you beat me badly. *[Laughter]*

The President. That's the way politics works sometimes. We try really hard to persuade people that we're right. And then, people vote. And then, if we lose, we learn from our mistakes, we do some reflection, we lick our wounds, we brush ourselves off, we get back in the arena. We go at it. We try even harder the next time.

The point, though, is, is that we all go forward, with a presumption of good faith in our fellow citizens, because that presumption of good faith is essential to a vibrant and functioning democracy. That's how this country has moved forward for 240 years. It's how we've pushed boundaries and promoted freedom around the world. That's how we've expanded the rights of our founding to reach all of our citizens. It's how we have come this far.

And that's why I'm confident that this incredible journey that we're on as Americans will go on. And I am looking forward to doing everything that I can to make sure that the next President is successful in that. I have said before, I think of this job as being a relay runner. You take the baton, you run your best race, and hopefully, by the time you hand it off, you're a little further ahead; you've made a little progress. And I can say that we've done that, and I want to make sure that handoff is well executed, because ultimately, we're all on the same team.

All right? Thank you very much, everybody.

SOURCE: Executive Office of the President. "Remarks on the 2016 Presidential Election." November 9, 2016. *Compilation of Presidential Documents* 2016, no. 00765 (November 9, 2016). http://www.gpo.gov/fdsys/pkg/DCPD-201600765/pdf/DCPD-201600765.pdf.

DOCUMENT

President-Elect Trump on Electoral College Victory

December 19, 2016

Today marks a historic electoral landslide victory in our nation's democracy. I thank the American people for their overwhelming vote to elect me as their next President of the United States. The official votes cast by the Electoral College exceeded the 270 required to secure the presidency by a very large margin, far greater than ever anticipated by the media. This election represents a movement that millions of hard working men and women all across the country stood behind and made possible. With this historic step we can look forward to the bright future ahead. I will work hard to unite our country and be the President of all Americans. Together, we will make America great again.

SOURCE: Office of the President-Elect and of the Vice President-Elect. "Statement from President-Elect Donald J. Trump." December 19, 2016. https://greatagain.gov/statement-from-president-elect-donald-j-trump-a924712a0322#.n0lo6opx6.

OTHER HISTORIC DOCUMENTS OF INTEREST

FROM THIS VOLUME

FROM PREVIOUS *HISTORIC DOCUMENTS*

2016 U.S. State and Local Elections

In addition to selecting a president on November 8, voters across the country were also choosing all 435 members of the House of Representatives, 34 members of the Senate, members of 86 of 99 state legislatures, and 11 governors (plus a special election in Oregon to replace Gov. John Kitzhaber, who resigned in February 2015). Democrats failed to retake control of either chamber of Congress, and also took a hit at the state and local level. Citizens were also voting on 154 statewide ballot measures and hundreds of local referenda, the most popular issues among them being marijuana, minimum wage, the death penalty, health care, tobacco taxes, and gun ownership.

HOUSE AND SENATE REMAIN IN REPUBLICAN CONTROL

Down-ballot races tend to ride the coattails of the party that wins the presidency, and that was true in 2016, despite some predictions that Democrats might be able to take back control of the Senate, which they lost in 2014, needing a net gain of five seats. Taking the House was far less likely, with Democrats requiring a thirty-seat pickup.

A total of thirty-four Senate seats were up for grabs in 2016, and twenty-four of those were held by Republicans in the last Congress. The Democratic candidates picked up momentum in early fall as Clinton's lead expanded over Trump. But when the polls tightened at the top of the ticket in late October, so too did House and Senate races. Democrats had expected to pick up a seat in Wisconsin, where polling indicated that former senator Russ Feingold would likely defeat incumbent senator Ron Johnson. But Johnson came out victorious, 50 percent to 47 percent, and the state swung for a Republican president for the first time since Ronald Reagan was elected in 1984. Sen. John McCain, R-Ariz., was able to withhold a strong challenge from Anne Kirkpatrick, and Sen. Pat Toomey, R-Pa., defeated Katie McGinty in what became the most expensive race in Senate history. (Pennsylvania also went for Trump, voting Republican for the first time since 1988.) Democrats narrowly managed to hold onto the seat being vacated by retiring Senate minority leader Harry Reid, D-Nev., and the victor, Catherine Cortez Masto, would be the first Latina in the Senate. New Hampshire Governor Maggie Hassan, a Democrat, defeated incumbent senator Kelly Ayotte by slightly more than 1,000 votes, but Democrats could not pick up a seat in Louisiana, which held a runoff in December because no candidate won more than 50 percent of the vote in November.

Democrats were able to flip a seat in Illinois, where Rep. Tammy Duckworth, an Iraq war veteran who lost both of her legs in combat, defeated incumbent senator Mark Kirk. Kirk's campaign suffered a significant blow when, in response to a statement by Duckworth at a debate on October 27 regarding the military service of her family going back to the Revolutionary War, Kirk responded, "I had forgotten that your parents came all the way from Thailand to serve George Washington." Duckworth's mother is Thai, while her father is American; Kirk was quickly labeled a racist. In a statement celebrating her victory,

Duckworth said, "Just as I try every day to live up to the sacrifice my buddies made to carry me off that battlefield, I will go to work in the Senate looking to honor the sacrifice and quiet dignity of all those Illinoisans who are facing challenges of their own. After all, this nation didn't give up on me when I was at my most vulnerable, needing the most help. I believe in an America that doesn't give up on anyone who hasn't given up on themselves."

Democrats failed to take control of either the House or the Senate. After all results were in, Republicans held the Senate 52–46–2 (the two Independent senators typically caucus with the Democrats), while the House margin was 241–194 in favor of the Republicans. National Republican Congressional Committee executive director Rob Simms said the victory "was the result of years of hard work." Noting that preparation for the 2016 election began following the 2014 midterms, Simms said, "While Democrats ran a one-size-fits-all national campaign, our members and candidates ran strong races, focused on the issues important to local constituents. These efforts were recognized and rewarded by the voters."

Republicans Gain Ground in State Elections

In November, forty-four states held legislative elections to choose members of eighty-six of the nation's ninety-nine chambers. Republicans flipped 138 seats, while Democrats flipped ninety-five. As a result of the election, seven of the ninety-nine chambers switched party control. Democrats took control of the Nevada House and Senate, and New Mexico House, while Republicans gained a majority in the Kentucky House, Iowa Senate, and Minnesota Senate. Republicans also came out ahead in the gubernatorial elections, and their 2016 victories put more Republicans in the governors' mansions than at any time since 1922. With the result in the gubernatorial and state legislative elections, Republicans now have a trifecta in twenty-five states, where the governor's seat and both chambers of the legislature are controlled by Republicans, while Democrats had a trifecta in only six states.

Perhaps the most notable of the statewide elections in 2016 was in North Carolina, where incumbent Governor Pat McCrory was pitted against Attorney General Roy Cooper. McCrory came into the national spotlight in March 2016 when he signed what became known as the "bathroom bill," which banned transgender individuals from using the restroom that corresponded to the gender with which they identify rather than their gender at birth. McCrory said the measure was necessary to protect women and children against sexual predators in public restrooms and changing facilities. Cooper, in his role as attorney general, refused to defend the law against any legal challenges brought against it. It was not until two months after the governor signed the bill that Cooper even decided to enter the race, and, along with jobs and the economy, the bathroom bill was a key campaign issue.

The race was close on election night, but Cooper issued a victory statement shortly before midnight, despite the fact that he was ahead by only 4,000 votes with an estimated 100,000 provisional and absentee ballots left to count. "We have won this race for governor of North Carolina," Cooper said. "It has been a long, long journey to get to this point, and I know that people waited in long lines to vote and to allow their voice to be heard. I am humbled by that." Cooper's declaration did not sit well with Republicans. "Despite Roy Cooper's rude and grossly premature declaration of victory, under the laws of the state of North Carolina, this election is not over and will not be over for some considerable amount of time," said state Republican Party chair Robin Hayes. On November 23, McCrory's campaign officially requested a recount, and suggested that some ballots cast for Cooper may have been done so fraudulently. It was not until December 5 that McCrory finally conceded the race. Democratic Governors Association Chair Dan Malloy of Connecticut said the North Carolina governor's race was the marquee event of the 2016 election season. Malloy added, "Democrats held all of our incumbents while winning governorships in three states that Donald Trump won. This election proves that strong Democratic candidates can win anywhere in the country."

BALLOT MEASURES

Nationwide, voters cast their ballots on referendums ranging from minimum wage, marijuana, and gun control to the death penalty, LGBTQ rights, law enforcement, and fracking. Of the 154 statewide ballot issues put before voters on November 8, a record 76 were citizen initiatives, likely due to a decline in many states in the number of signatures required to place an issue on the ballot.

Marijuana use was on the ballot in nine states and dozens of municipalities and dealt with medical use, recreational use, cultivation, and sales. In California, the first state to legalize medical marijuana in 1996, voters approved Proposition 64, which would allow for legal recreational use of marijuana by those aged twenty-one and older, 57 percent to 43 percent. Arizona, Maine, Massachusetts, and Nevada had similar measures on their ballots, with Nevada's including the establishment of a 15 percent excise tax on wholesale marijuana sales. Voters approved the legalization measures in each state except Arizona. Voters in Arkansas, Florida, Montana, and North Dakota chose to allow for the legalization of medical marijuana.

Three states—California, Maine, and Nevada—considered whether background checks should be expanded prior to a gun sale being completed. In California, voter-approved Proposition 63 legalized a background check prior to the purchase of ammunition. In Nevada, voters approved a measure to make it illegal for individuals to sell or transfer firearms without a licensed dealer conducting a background check first, but in Maine, citizens voted down Question 3, which would have mandated background checks for those purchasing or transferring firearms from nonlicensed dealers. In Washington, Initiative No. 1491 posed a different question to voters: whether the courts should be allowed to issue a temporary order to stop those with mental illness or violent or criminal behavior from accessing guns if such an order is requested by family, household members, and police, and there is a reasonable suspicion to believe that the person may harm himself or herself or others. Voters approved this measure 69 percent to 31 percent.

Raising the minimum wage was a question put before voters in five states and major cities, including Cincinnati, Los Angeles, San Diego, San Francisco, and Washington, D.C. In Arizona, Colorado, and Maine, the question before voters was whether to raise the state minimum wage to $12 per hour by 2020, and voters in all three states approved the measure. In Washington State, voters chose to pass Initiative 1433, which would increase the minimum wage from $9.47 to $13.50 by 2020. In South Dakota, voters rejected by wide margins a bill that would have lowered the minimum wage for workers under age eighteen from $8.50 per hour to $7.50 per hour.

Taxes on cigarettes and soda were also popular across the country. Colorado, Missouri, and North Dakota citizens all voted down measures that would have increased the tax on each pack of cigarettes, while in California, voters overwhelmingly approved Proposition 56, which would raise cigarette taxes by $2 per pack. The state estimated that the tax would increase California revenue by $1 billion from 2017 to 2018, and that money would be redirected to health care and tobacco control programs. San Francisco, Oakland, and

Albany, California, along with Boulder, Colorado, all approved taxes on sugar-sweetened drinks, aimed at reducing the obesity rate among citizens.

California, Nebraska, and Oklahoma put before voters four different questions about the death penalty. Oklahoma was in the news in 2015 when a case came before the Supreme Court on the state's use of a new drug cocktail during a botched execution. The state had long struggled to obtain the typical drugs used for lethal injection, so in November 2016, it asked voters whether the state should be allowed to use any method for execution so long as it isn't prohibited by the U.S. Constitution. Voters approved the measure, 66 percent to 34 percent. In Nebraska, the state legislature passed a bill in May 2015 repealing the death penalty, and Referendum No. 426 asked voters if they wanted to overturn or maintain the legislature's decision. Ultimately, voters chose to overturn the legislation and maintain the death penalty option. And in California, voters considered two separate measures. Proposition 62, which was not approved, would have repealed the death penalty, but voters did affirm a referendum to speed up the timeframe from conviction to execution.

Given the debate at the federal level surrounding the Affordable Care Act, its effectiveness, and ongoing promises from congressional Republicans to repeal it, health care was a central issue in two states, California and Colorado. Most notably, in Colorado, Amendment 69 would have established a state-run health insurance system known as ColoradoCare. Voters, however, overwhelmingly rejected the measure, 79 percent to 21 percent.

—Heather Kerrigan

Following is a November 10, 2016, memo from Republican Governors Association (RGA) executive director Paul Bennecke on the 2016 gubernatorial results; a memo from the executive director of the National Republican Congressional Committee, also from November 10, 2016, on the House of Representatives remaining in Republican control; and a December 5, 2016, statement by Gov. Dan Malloy, chair of the Democratic Governors Association (DGA), on Roy Cooper's victory in North Carolina.

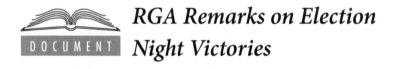

RGA Remarks on Election Night Victories

November 10, 2016

From: Paul Bennecke, RGA Executive Director

To: Interested Parties

RE: 2016 Gubernatorial Election Results: Republicans Achieve What Hasn't Been Done In 94 Years

Date: 11/9/2016

2016 RESULTS: REPUBLICANS CEMENT THEIR DOMINANCE OF GOVERNORSHIPS

After the RGA's successful 2014 results, Republicans entered 2016 with 31 Governors to the Democrat's [sic] 18. With 12 gubernatorial elections this year, the RGA was tasked with defending two incumbents in North Carolina and Utah, and two open seats in North Dakota and Indiana. Democrats were faced with defending three incumbents in Montana, Washington and Oregon, and five open seats in Delaware, Missouri, New Hampshire, Vermont and West Virginia. The RGA went on offense early in the year, investing significant resources in six gubernatorial elections: Vermont, New Hampshire, Missouri, Indiana, West Virginia and North Carolina. Republicans have won four of those six governorships so far, with North Carolina still listed as too close to call.

As the RGA entered Election Day, internal polling showed Republicans leading or effectively tied in those six gubernatorial races. 2016 gubernatorial elections were always a unique opportunity for Republicans to gain seats on Election Day. While it was a very successful night for Republicans at all levels, including Donald Trump winning the White House and both Houses of Congress retaining majorities, Republican governors have added a net gain of at least 2 seats, and that number could increase to a net gain of 3. Republicans will hold at least 33 governorships in 2017, something that hasn't happened in 94 years. TIME Magazine noted that even with a large influx of cash from Democratic groups, Republicans "cemented their dominance of the nation's governors' mansions in elections Tuesday."

VERMONT

The Vermont governor's race was an election no one expected the GOP to be competitive in at the beginning of 2016. After Lt. Gov. Phil Scott won the gubernatorial primary on August 9, the RGA immediately went up on television August 10, and stayed on TV through Election Day. The first six weeks made the crucial difference, as the RGA ran positive TV ads highlighting Scott's record as a pragmatic leader. When the Democrats finally decided to jump in, the race had already been defined on our terms. Even in a deep blue state, trying to catch up is a hard task. All the way until Election Day, the RGA ran positive TV ads for Phil Scott, while also defining Sue Minter, running dual track messages at the same time. On top of our TV advertisement strategy, the RGA also ran a targeted direct mail and digital effort, concentrating on independent swing voters and soft Democrats. Without a doubt, the quality of a candidate matters, even more so in a deep blue state like Vermont. Phil Scott proved that he was ready to lead, and RGA was thrilled to help get him across the finish line.

Days before Election Day, many admitted Phil Scott might get a plurality, but they believed he would likely not reach 50%, thereby handing the election to the Democratic legislature to decide. But instead, Phil Scott easily won the governor's office, defeating Democrat Sue Minter by nearly 10 points, 53%–44%.

The RGA spent over $3 million to elect Phil Scott as governor, including 13 statewide TV ads, 2 statewide radio ads, 500,000 pieces of direct mail, and a targeted digital campaign which had over 5 million impressions.

NEW HAMPSHIRE

While the New Hampshire primary was the final gubernatorial primary in the country on September 13, the RGA always believed that we could win. We proved that by being the first political organization in the country to reserve a television ad buy in the last six weeks of the election, and did so in April. By the time Chris Sununu was our nominee, the U.S. Senate and Presidential races were already in full swing, TV rates had escalated to unprecedented levels, and so the RGA had to answer the question: How do we spend our resources efficiently to impact the race and help Chris Sununu cross the finish line?

Rather than using our remaining resources to increase TV impressions in an expensive and cluttered market, the RGA decided to go into New Hampshire with a highly targeted, relentless digital and mail program in the final five weeks, delivering over 22 million digital impressions and 2 million direct mail pieces. Specific universes were identified, and different messages were sent to different segments. While it's true the Democrats outspent the RGA on broadcast TV, Democrats were outmaneuvered via digital and direct mail, and didn't even know it. Of the over $5.5 million the RGA spent in New Hampshire, one-third was spent on digital and direct mail, targeting key voting groups. Sununu became the first GOP Governor-Elect of New Hampshire in more than a decade. As the RGA has done in other states, and in other years, it put a specific plan of action into place that supplemented normal TV activity. For five weeks, we had a 1-on-1 conversation with targeted voters via their mobile phones, tablets & laptops, and their mailboxes (on top of the television advertisements we were also running).

Democrats outspent the RGA 2–1 on broadcast television, but the RGA spent considerably more on cable, in order to reach those voting groups that we were also targeting via direct mail and digital. As a result, Sununu defeated Democrat Colin Van Ostern 49%–46%.

The RGA spent over $5.5 million in the effort to elect Chris Sununu as governor, including a multi-million dollar TV statewide ad campaign, over 2 million pieces of direct mail, and a targeted digital ad campaign which had over 22 million impressions. The RGA targeted Van Ostern in 4 TV ads, highlighting his record as a Big Government liberal favoring the Washington way, not the New Hampshire way.

MISSOURI

Early in 2016, Democrats consolidated behind Attorney General Chris Koster, giving him the opportunity to build up a $10 million war chest. At the same time, four Republicans were running in a very competitive gubernatorial primary that occurred late in the year on August 2.

One week before the gubernatorial primary, the Democratic Governors Association spent $1 million on television attacking Eric Greitens in an attempt to damage him politically, hoping it would lead to him losing the primary—but it failed. Koster went up on television the day of the primary, thinking his $10 million war chest would put the race out of reach for any Republican nominee.

On August 3, the RGA immediately went up on TV in Missouri, matching Chris Koster's ad buy, and targeting him as a self-serving politician and political opportunist. The RGA then began providing direct contributions to the Greitens campaign, which totaled over $13 million when all was said and done.

This was a state where the RGA viewed field operations, GOTV and a rich data mining operation were vitally important, and helped fund these campaign efforts. Chris Koster had every early advantage in this race. But true to form, a Navy SEAL always finds a way to complete the mission. The RGA was proud to partner with the Greitens campaign and eliminate Koster's $10 million war chest advantage. Greitens soundly defeated Koster 51%–45%.

The RGA spent over $13.5 million on the effort to elect Eric Greitens as governor, including $13 million in direct donations to his campaign, a statewide TV ad campaign, and a targeted digital ad campaign. The RGA TV ad targeted Democrat Chris Koster as just another self-serving politician who puts himself first.

INDIANA

After his selection as the GOP gubernatorial nominee after Governor Mike Pence was chosen as the Vice Presidential Nominee, Eric Holcomb had less than 100 days to run in a race that Democrat John Gregg had been running for five years.

The RGA made an early decision in January 2016, first through the Pence campaign and ultimately through the Holcomb campaign, to help design and fund a robust field program that knocked on over 1.7 million doors and made 5.6 million volunteer phone calls.

Within 24 hours of Eric Holcomb being selected as the nominee, the RGA was on TV defining Democrat John Gregg while Holcomb built his campaign's infrastructure and fundraising operation. Once that infrastructure was in place, due to cost efficiency, the RGA began making direct contributions to Holcomb's campaign for TV ad blitzes and message definition.

When Labor Unions pumped several million dollars late into the race in support of John Gregg, the RGA stepped up and matched them and helped Holcomb defeat Gregg 51%–45%.

The RGA spent over $10 million on the effort to elect Eric Holcomb as governor, including $6.75 million in contributions directly to his campaign, a multi-million dollar TV ad campaign statewide, 2.5 million pieces of direct mail, and a targeted digital campaign which had over 10 million impressions. The RGA ran 4 TV ads targeting Democrat John Gregg as a wasteful spending, tax loving former lobbyist who chose Hillary over Hoosiers.

UTAH

Governor Gary Herbert won a commanding re-election victory over Democratic opponent Mike Weinholtz, 69% to 29%. Over the past six years in office, Governor Herbert built a reputation as a pro-jobs governor focused on positioning Utah for success now and in the future, guiding Utah to over 250,000 new jobs, historic low unemployment, and key investments in education. The RGA contributed $350,000 directly to Governor Herbert's 2016 campaign.

NORTH DAKOTA

In North Dakota, Republican Doug Burgum easily won election in a resounding victory, defeating Democratic opponent Marvin Nelson by 57 points, 76% to 19%. The DGA publicly tried to recruit U.S. Senator Heidi Heitkamp to run for the open seat, but she took a pass. As an innovator, leader, and high-tech businessman, Burgum ran as a new leader for a changing economy, and operated a campaign based on reinventing state government, smart budgeting, and ensuring taxpayers are treated as the customers they are. The RGA invested $100,000 to support Burgum in the general election, contributing directly to his campaign.

CONCLUSION

The one common theme in all of these victories was having the best candidate in the race. Whether it was in a traditionally red state like North Dakota, or a deep blue state like Vermont, or even a state that hadn't elected a GOP governor in 14 years like New Hampshire, RGA invested in these races because we had superior candidates.

The RGA's decision to play early, and even bigger in the closing days, ensured our candidates would get their message to the voters. Committing major portions of our budget to run highly targeted and sophisticated digital efforts allowed RGA to maximize efficiency, talk to specific voters, and do it under the radar.

Placing early base TV buys down before other races dominated the markets or utilizing individual state laws in places like Indiana and Missouri to get candidate rates saved RGA millions of dollars and gave us a distinct advantage over other competing outside groups when they spent more "TV dollars" than we did.

As a result, America now has more Republican Governors than at any time since 1922.

SOURCE: Republican Governors Association. "RGA Memo: 2016 Gubernatorial Election Results." November 10, 2016. http://www.rga.org/rga-memo-2016-gubernatorial-election-results.

National Republican Congressional Committee on House Majority

November 10, 2016

TO: INTERESTED PARTIES

FROM: ROB SIMMS, NRCC EXECUTIVE DIRECTOR

DATE: NOVEMBER 10, 2016

SUBJECT: HOUSE REPUBLICANS MAINTAIN MAJORITY

Last night's election results represented a resounding victory for House Republicans, as voters once again send a strong Republican majority to represent them in Congress. Victories like last night are no accident. They are the culmination of years of hard work and dedication by our Republican members, as well as the NRCC staff.

Early Preparation

Preparations for our victory last night began immediately following the 2014 election. The NRCC identified those new and returning members of the House Republican Conference likely to face close races in 2016, and worked with them through our Patriot Program to begin building the infrastructure needed to ensure victory. Those members went to work on the issues important to their districts, passing legislation aimed at making their constituents' lives better.

At the same time, through our Young Guns program, the NRCC worked to identify and provide support to strong candidates for Open and Democrat-held seats. Our Young

Guns program had another successful cycle, adding at least nine new Republican members to our Conference.

Fundraising

The NRCC shattered fundraising records this cycle, eclipsing $150 million, a $7 million increase from the 2014 and 2012 cycles.

Key to our fundraising efforts was the leadership of Speaker Paul Ryan, who transferred a record $42,662,370 to the committee, and NRCC Chairman Greg Walden, who raised and transferred over $4 million during the 2016 cycle. Beyond his financial contributions, Chairman Walden was relentless in his efforts for the committee, traveling 254,000 miles in his four years heading the committee, the equivalent of ten trips around the world, spending 281 nights on the road and hitting 40 states.

Our traditional fundraising was supplemented by an extremely robust digital operation. The NRCC's Digital Department raised $12 million for 2016, an improvement of more than 60% over last cycle.

Our record-breaking fundraising allowed us to spend $90.3 million in direct support of our candidates, including $85.8 million from September 1 through Election Day. This spending included 145 unique television ads aired by our Independent Expenditure Unit across nearly 30 congressional districts.

Data-Driven Campaign

The committee invested early in our data operation, doubling our data infrastructure compared to 2014. This investment paid dividends as it enabled us to give campaigns the information needed to engage voters, which was vital to win their races in both the persuasion and Get Out the Vote phases of the campaign. In all, our team made nearly 2.7 million voter engagements across 33 congressional districts.

Our data operation was boosted by information provided by the NRCC Polling Department, which spent $5 million in 30+ congressional districts, conducting 292 surveys and focus groups. These surveys proved to be among the most accurate in the country in this unpredictable election, enabling us to respond to movement in the polls, and focus our resources on those congressional districts where the results would be closest.

Local Campaigns

While Democrats ran a one-size-fits-all national campaign, our members and candidates ran strong races, focused on the issues important to local constituents. These efforts were recognized and rewarded by voters who returned a strong Republican majority to the House in 2017.

Republicans were successful in districts across the country, in both red and blue states, including winning in 21 districts that voted for Barack Obama in 2012.

Conclusion

House Republicans' successful 2016 cycle was the result of years of hard work. From record setting fundraising, to a strong, data-driven campaign, the NRCC helped our members and candidates to position themselves to win.

SOURCE: National Republican Congressional Committee. "House Republicans Maintain Majority." November 10, 2016. http://www.nrcc.org/2016/11/10/house-republicans-maintain-majority.

DGA Congratulates North Carolina Governor-Elect Roy Cooper

December 5, 2016

Today, Connecticut Gov. Dan Malloy, Chair of the Democratic Governors Association, issued the following statement on Governor-elect Roy Cooper's victory in North Carolina's gubernatorial race:

"Congratulations to Governor-elect Roy Cooper on a major win in North Carolina's gubernatorial election," said Gov. Malloy. "This election is a strong endorsement of Roy Cooper's correct priorities, and a sharp rebuke of Gov. Pat McCrory's agenda of raising taxes on the middle class, gutting education and passing the discriminatory House Bill 2 into law. In Roy Cooper, North Carolina will have a governor who can build an economy inclusive to all people; a governor who will invest in the state's public schools and teachers; and a governor who can restore the state's reputation as a business leader.

"Democratic governors won the marquee race of 2016, and the biggest state on the map. Democrats held all of our incumbents while winning governorships in three states that Donald Trump won. This election proves that strong Democratic candidates can win anywhere in the country."

SOURCE: Democratic Governors Association. "Malloy Statement on Roy Cooper's Victory in North Carolina." December 5, 2016. https://democraticgovernors.org/malloy-statement-on-roy-coopers-victory-in-north-carolina.

OTHER HISTORIC DOCUMENTS OF INTEREST

FROM THIS VOLUME

- North Carolina Governor Signs Bathroom Bill into Law, p. 179
- Donald Trump Elected U.S. President, p. 612

FROM PREVIOUS *HISTORIC DOCUMENTS*

- Response to 2014 Ballot Initiatives, *2014*, p. 523

President-Elect Donald Trump Forms Transition Team; Nominates Senior Administration Officials

NOVEMBER 13 AND 18, 2016

From the beginning, the transition of President-elect Donald Trump into office was the subject of intense interest. Reports of internal turmoil and transition team staffing changes led to early concerns that Trump would not be sufficiently prepared to take office on January 20, despite his assurances that the transition was progressing smoothly. Speculation about who Trump would nominate to fill key cabinet and White House leadership positions was rampant, and while a number of Trump's selections were controversial, many were confirmed by February 2017.

TRUMP SHAKES UP TRANSITION TEAM, FILLS SENIOR WHITE HOUSE POSITIONS

Concerns about the stability and preparedness of Trump's team were raised early in the transition process, because several significant changes to transition team staffing were made just days after the election. Vice President-elect Mike Pence replaced New Jersey Governor Chris Christie as head of the transition team, with Christie demoted to a vice chair position. Commentators speculated that the change could be due to the recent convictions of two former Christie aides in the George Washington Bridge scandal, Christie's failure to defend Trump at several points during the campaign, or an internal feud between Christie and Trump's son-in-law Jared Kushner. Trump's daughter Ivanka and sons Eric and Donald Jr. were named to top posts in the transition team, which prompted concerns about potential conflicts of interest, since Trump lawyers had indicated that the president-elect's children would take charge of their father's assets while he was in office. Several other transition team members were dismissed in the following days, including Rep. Mike Rogers, R-Mich., who served as the team's senior national security adviser; Richard Bagger, Christie's former chief of staff, who served as the transition's executive director; William Paltucci, who served as general counsel; and Kevin O'Connor, who was overseeing the Department of Justice transition. Most of these men were Christie allies, and their dismissal led to speculation that Trump was limiting his inner circle to those who demonstrated the most loyalty to him during the campaign.

Amid these changes in transition team staffing, Trump began announcing who would fill key senior positions in his White House. On November 13, Trump named former Republican National Committee (RNC) chair Reince Priebus as his chief of staff and Stephen Bannon, the Trump campaign's CEO and former executive chair of *Breitbart News*, as chief strategist and senior counselor to the president. While Priebus was largely viewed favorably by Washington insiders as part of the political establishment and someone who could help smooth relations between Trump and Congress, Bannon's appointment drew a harsh reaction from civil rights groups, Democrats, and some Republican strategists who argued that Bannon would bring anti-Semitic and racist views to the White House. "In his roles as editor of the Breitbart website and as a strategist in the Trump campaign, Mr. Bannon was responsible for the advancement of ideologies antithetical to our nation, including anti-Semitism, misogyny, racism and Islamophobia," said Rabbi Jonah Dov Pesner, director of the Religious Action Center of Reform Judaism. "There should be no place for such views in the White House."

On December 22, Trump named campaign manager Kellyanne Conway as counselor to the president, former RNC communications director Sean Spicer as press secretary, and campaign spokesperson Jason Miller as communications director. Miller's tenure as communications director was incredibly brief—he announced his resignation on December 24, stating that his priority needed to be spending time with his family. His resignation followed allegations that Miller had an affair with another member of the transition team. A. J. Delgado, a Trump campaign surrogate and transition aide, had called for Miller to resign, referring to him as "the baby-daddy" and "the 2016 version of John Edwards" on Twitter. Delgado's Twitter account was deleted following Miller's resignation, and it was reported that Spicer would also fill the communications director role until a replacement was found.

In addition to concerns over these staffing changes, some expressed reservations about Trump's decision not to receive daily intelligence briefings. Reuters reported in early December that Trump was receiving an average of one intelligence briefing per week. Appearing on *Fox News Sunday* on December 11, Trump explained that he did not believe he needed the daily briefings because they were repetitive. "I don't have to be told the same thing in the same words every single day for the next eight years. But I do say, 'If something should change, let us know.'" Trump also noted that Pence and his national security team received regular briefings.

CABINET, NATIONAL SECURITY OFFICIALS APPOINTED

Given Trump's lack of government experience, there was intense interest in whom he would choose to fill cabinet and cabinet-level positions, since his selections were expected to provide a clearer sense of how he planned to govern. Trump went public with his first picks on November 18, nominating Sen. Jeff Sessions, R-Ala., as attorney general, Rep. Mike Pompeo, R-Kans., as director of the Central Intelligence Agency, and Lt. Gen. Michel Flynn as national security adviser. Additional nominations were announced on a rolling basis, including ExxonMobil CEO Rex Tillerson for secretary of state; retired general James Mattis for secretary of defense; former hedge fund manager and Goldman Sachs banker Steve Mnuchin for Treasury secretary; Rep. Ryan Zinke, R-Mont., for secretary of the interior; billionaire investor Wilbur Ross for secretary of commerce; Rep. Tom Price, R-Ga., for health and human services secretary; former neurosurgeon Ben Carson for secretary of housing and urban development; former labor secretary Elaine Chao for transportation secretary; former Texas Governor Rick Perry for energy secretary; Michigan businesswoman and philanthropist Betsy DeVos for education secretary; retired general John Kelly for secretary of homeland security; David Shulkin, former undersecretary of health for the Department of Veterans Affairs (VA), for VA secretary; former Georgia Governor Sonny Perdue for agriculture secretary; and CKE Restaurants CEO Andrew Puzder as labor secretary.

Some media outlets described Trump's nominees as a "conservative dream team" and said the nominees signaled the president-elect's interest in deregulation. Reports also indicated that if confirmed, Trump's cabinet would be the wealthiest in U.S. history. According to the *Washington Post*, President George W. Bush's first cabinet had an inflation-adjusted net worth of approximately $250 million. By contrast, Ross alone had a personal fortune of $2.5 billion. Pew Research Center also observed that Trump's nominees would comprise "one of the most heavily business-oriented Cabinets in U.S. history," reporting that five of the fifteen individuals nominated as of January 19, 2017, had "spent all or nearly all their careers in the business world, with no significant public office or senior military service."

Several of Trump's nominees were particularly controversial. For example, critics raised concerns over the foreign ties Tillerson fostered while at the helm of ExxonMobil, especially with Russia. The company had entered into a $500 billion joint drilling and shale development venture with Russia, for which Tillerson received the Russian Order of Friendship Prize from President Vladimir Putin in 2013. The planned projects were stalled in 2014 when the United States and other countries imposed sanctions on Russia for its actions in Ukraine and Crimea. Some reports also suggested that an ExxonMobil subsidiary conducted business with Iran, Syria, and Sudan at a time when those countries faced sanctions as state sponsors of terrorism. Sessions faced allegations of racism, with critics noting that he had been passed up for a federal judgeship due to racial comments he made in the past. Sessions had reportedly joked that he used to think the Ku Klux Klan was okay until he found out members smoked marijuana, was accused of calling a black assistant U.S. attorney "boy" and telling him to be careful how he spoke to "white folks," and allegedly called the National Association for the Advancement of Colored People "un-American" and "communist-inspired." Sessions declared that such allegations were "damnably false" during his confirmation hearing.

Some nominees had been critical of or seemed to be at odds with the missions of the agencies they were selected to lead. Scott Pruitt, Oklahoma's attorney general and Trump's pick to lead the Environmental Protection Agency, has questioned the science behind climate change and promised to roll back Obama administration emissions limits on power plants. Pruitt also oversaw several lawsuits filed by the state of Oklahoma against the Obama administration's environmental policies, particularly the Clean Power Plan. Perry listed the Department of Energy as one of three agencies he would eliminate if elected during his failed 2012 presidential campaign. DeVos had argued for closing public schools in Detroit and replacing them with a system of charter schools and a voucher program that would help families pay for private schools.

The wealth of some nominees also became a flashpoint for criticism, particularly as they began to complete and submit the financial disclosures required during the confirmation process. Mnuchin, for example, came under fire from lawmakers for failing to disclose $95 million in real estate assets on his ethics questionnaire. He also failed to disclose that he was the director of an investment fund incorporated in the Cayman Islands, a known offshore tax haven. Puzder withdrew his nomination on February 15, 2017, following reports that he had employed an undocumented immigrant as a housekeeper and had not paid employer taxes, as well as allegations that he had abused his ex-wife. Puzder had also been fined by the U.S. Labor Department for workplace safety and wage violations. Trump nominated Alexander Acosta, dean of the Florida International University College of Law, in Puzder's stead. Some commentators also raised concerns with the number of former military personnel being named to senior positions, given the American principle of maintaining civilian control of the military. Mattis's nomination posed a unique challenge because the National Defense Authorization Act requires that defense secretary nominees be civilians for at least seven years before assuming the post; Mattis had been retired for three. Both the House of Representatives and the Senate had to pass a measure waiving the rule to allow Mattis to serve, which they did in mid-January.

Confirmation hearings for the nominees were set to begin the week of January 9, 2017. In a letter written to Senate Minority Leader Chuck Schumer, D-N.Y., and Sen. Elizabeth Warren, D-Mass., and released publicly on January 6, Office of Government Ethics Director Walter Shaub said that the confirmation schedule was "of great concern" because some of the nominees had not yet completed their ethics review. Nominees are required to submit a plan for resolving and avoiding financial conflicts of interest to the Office of Government Ethics before they can assume a cabinet position. This information, along with financial disclosures, is then shared with the Senate committee that will conduct the nominee's confirmation hearing. Shaub wrote that the hearing schedule "created undue pressure on OGE's staff and agency ethics officials to rush through these important reviews," adding that "it has left some of the nominees with potentially unknown or unresolved ethics issues shortly before their scheduled hearings." Some nominees' FBI background checks were reportedly also in progress. Democrats called for the hearings to be delayed until all required paperwork was complete. Senate Majority Leader Mitch McConnell, R-Ky., responded that the Democrats were simply trying to disrupt the confirmation process because they were "frustrated that they lost the election" and said the hearings would continue. Democrats in turn accused McConnell of hypocrisy, noting that he had written to then–senate Majority Leader Harry Reid, D-Nev., in 2009 to ask that all of President Barack Obama's cabinet nominees complete their financial disclosure forms before hearings were scheduled.

As of writing, thirteen of Trump's fifteen cabinet nominees have been confirmed. Pompeo and Pruitt were also confirmed, as were UN ambassador Nikki Haley and Office of Management and Budget director Mick Mulvaney. Flynn, whose appointment as national security adviser did not require Senate confirmation, resigned in February 2017 following revelations that he discussed a possible easing of sanctions with the Russian ambassador after the election and did not fully disclose the nature of his conversation.

Trump Outlines Plan to Avoid Conflicts of Interest

In addition to his cabinet selections, Trump's announcement of a plan for avoiding conflicts of interest stemming from his vast business holdings was highly anticipated. Many observers questioned whether Trump's eventual plan would be sufficient to avoid violations of the emoluments clause, which restricts U.S. officials from accepting gifts or payments from foreign governments, noting that foreign officials may choose to stay at Trump-owned hotels and resorts in an attempt to curry favor with the president. The Trump Organization also owes hundreds of millions of dollars to foreign countries. Additionally, the president is charged with appointing leaders of agencies that have jurisdiction over issues relevant to the operation and success of his business.

On January 11, Trump and his lawyer Sheri Dillon unveiled their plan to avoid conflicts of interest. The president will continue to own the Trump Organization but resigned from all positions held within the company and transferred all his assets into a trust to be managed by his sons. Ivanka also stepped down from her roles within the company. All pending foreign deals were terminated, and the company would not enter into any new foreign deals while Trump is in office. New domestic agreements would be allowed but must be vetted by an ethics adviser who would be hired to help oversee the trust. All profits generated at Trump hotels by foreign governments will be donated to the U.S. Treasury, and all debts will remain in place and be paid down during the regular course of business. Both Dillon and Trump said the president's access to information about his businesses would be severely limited. Additionally, they said the Trump Organization would create a new position of chief compliance counsel to ensure that the company is "operating at the highest level of integrity and not taking any actions that could be perceived as exploiting the office of the presidency." While many had called for Trump to completely divest from his businesses or establish a blind trust, Dillon said it would be unrealistic to do either. "President-elect Trump should not be expected to destroy the company he built," she said. Trump and Dillon further insisted that the emoluments clause did not apply to him and that he was not required to take such actions.

Shaub was among the critics who claimed that Trump's plan was insufficient. "Stepping back from running his positions is meaningless from a conflicts of interest perspective," he said. "Nothing short of divestiture will resolve these conflicts." Rep. Jason Chaffetz, R-Utah, chair of the House Oversight Committee, summoned Shaub to Capitol Hill to answer questions about these comments, writing in a letter that his office's mission was "to provide clear ethics guidance, not engage in public relations." Democrats claimed that Chaffetz was attempting to intimidate Shaub. Chaffetz and Shaub met privately on January 23, with both describing the conversation as "very productive."

—Linda Fecteau Grimm

Following are press releases issued by the Trump transition team on November 13 and November 18, 2016, announcing the president-elect's appointments to senior White House positions, as well as his nominees for attorney general, national security adviser, and CIA director.

Trump Announces Senior White House Leadership Team

November 13, 2016

President-elect Donald J. Trump today announced that Trump for President CEO Stephen K. Bannon will serve as Chief Strategist and Senior Counselor to the President, and Republican National Committee Chairman Reince Priebus will serve as White House Chief of Staff.

Bannon and Priebus will continue the effective leadership team they formed during the campaign, working as equal partners to transform the federal government, making it much more efficient, effective and productive. Bannon and Priebus will also work together with Vice President-elect Mike Pence to help lead the transition process in the run-up to Inauguration Day.

"I am thrilled to have my very successful team continue with me in leading our country," said President-elect Trump. "Steve and Reince are highly qualified leaders who worked well together on our campaign and led us to a historic victory. Now I will have them both with me in the White House as we work to make America great again."

"I want to thank President-elect Trump for the opportunity to work with Reince in driving the agenda of the Trump Administration," noted Bannon. "We had a very successful partnership on the campaign, one that led to victory. We will have that same partnership in working to help President-elect Trump achieve his agenda."

"It is truly an honor to join President-elect Trump in the White House as his Chief of Staff," added Priebus. "I am very grateful to the President-elect for this opportunity to serve him and this nation as we work to create an economy that works for everyone, secure our borders, repeal and replace Obamacare and destroy radical Islamic terrorism. He will be a great President for all Americans."

SOURCE: Office of the President-Elect and of the Vice President-Elect. "President-Elect Donald J. Trump Announces Senior White House Leadership Team." November 13, 2016. https://greatagain.gov/president-elect-donald-j-trump-announces-senior-white-house-leadership-team-3dcbe0a37b8#.sf6n5jtcn.

Trump Announces Nominees for Attorney General, National Security Adviser, and CIA Director

DOCUMENT

November 18, 2016

President-elect Donald J. Trump today announced that he intends to nominate U.S. Senator Jeff Sessions to serve as Attorney General and U.S. Rep. Mike Pompeo as Director of the Central Intelligence Agency. Lt. Gen. Michael Flynn has been selected to be the Assistant to the President for National Security Affairs.

U.S. Senator Jeff Sessions has dedicated his life to public service. He has a distinguished legal career and has served as both the U.S. Attorney for the Southern District of Alabama and Alabama Attorney General prior to his service in the U.S. Senate. He has been one of President-elect Trump's trusted advisors on the campaign and will now continue his service as our nation's chief law enforcement officer.

"It is an honor to nominate U.S. Senator Jeff Sessions to serve as Attorney General of the United States," said President-elect Trump. "Jeff has been a highly respected member of the U.S. Senate for 20 years. He is a world-class legal mind and considered a truly great Attorney General and U.S. Attorney in the state of Alabama. Jeff is greatly admired by legal scholars and virtually everyone who knows him."

"I am humbled to have been asked by President-elect Trump to serve as Attorney General of the United States," said U.S. Senator Sessions. "My previous 15 years working in the Department of Justice were extraordinarily fulfilling. I love the Department, its people and its mission. I can think of no greater honor than to lead them. With the support of my Senate colleagues, I will give all my strength to advance the Department's highest ideals. I enthusiastically embrace President-elect Trump's vision for 'one America,' and his commitment to equal justice under law. I look forward to fulfilling my duties with an unwavering dedication to fairness and impartiality."

Lt. Gen. Michael Flynn, a retired United States Army Lieutenant General and former director of the Defense Intelligence Agency, assumes the position of National Security Advisor with a decorated career of more than 35 years in service to our nation. He served as President-elect Trump's top military advisor during the campaign and will now continue providing expert advice and support to the President-elect as his National Security Advisor.

"I am pleased that Lieutenant General Michael Flynn will be by my side as we work to defeat radical Islamic terrorism, navigate geopolitical challenges and keep Americans safe at home and abroad," said President-elect Trump. "General Flynn is one of the country's foremost experts on military and intelligence matters and he will be an invaluable asset to me and my administration."

"I am deeply humbled and honored to accept the position as National Security Advisor to serve both our country and our nation's next President, Donald J. Trump," said Lieutenant General Flynn.

Congressman Mike Pompeo, representing Kansas' Fourth Congressional District, is a former active duty cavalry officer in the U.S. Army, graduated first in his class from the U.S. Military Academy at West Point, received his J.D. from Harvard Law School and was an editor of the Harvard Law Review. He currently serves on the House Intelligence Committee, which oversees America's intelligence-gathering efforts.

"I am proud to nominate Congressman Mike Pompeo as Director of the Central Intelligence Agency," said President-elect Trump. "He has served our country with honor and spent his life fighting for the security of our citizens. Mike graduated number one in his class at West Point and is a graduate of Harvard Law School where he served as an editor of the Harvard Law Review. He will be a brilliant and unrelenting leader for our intelligence community to ensure the safety of Americans and our allies."

"I am honored to have been given this opportunity to serve and to work alongside President-elect Donald J. Trump to keep America safe. I also look forward to working with America's intelligence warriors, who do so much to protect Americans each and every day," said Congressman Pompeo.

SOURCE: Office of the President-Elect and of the Vice President-Elect. "President-Elect Donald J. Trump Selects U.S. Senator Jeff Sessions for Attorney General, Lt. Gen. Michael Flynn as Assistant to the President for National Security Affairs and U.S. Rep. Mike Pompeo as Director of the Central Intelligence Agency." November 18, 2016. https://greatagain.gov/president-elect-donald-j-3e652b8d0d07#.pnjaofjis.

OTHER HISTORIC DOCUMENTS OF INTEREST

FROM THIS VOLUME

December

United Nations and European Union Respond to Ongoing Refugee Crisis

DECEMBER 5 AND 8, 2016

Throughout 2016, hundreds of thousands of refugees and economic migrants continued to risk their lives by crossing the Mediterranean Sea into Europe in search of a safer, better life. More than 5,000 lost their lives during their journey. Over the course of the year, the main route they took shifted from the Eastern Mediterranean to the Southern Mediterranean. The change came in response to a tightening of border controls between Turkey (which lies outside the European Union [EU]) and neighboring Greece (which is inside the EU). The tightening was done to stem the tide of refugees who had been streaming into Greece from Turkey since the summer of 2015.

Economic migrants made up a larger share of the individuals arriving than they had in 2015 when it was refugees fleeing the war in Syria who comprised the majority. The general public's feeling about the migrant influxes evolved from being generally sympathetic to their plight to one of growing anxiety about what their arrival might bring. This anxiety was heightened by deadly Islamic terrorist attacks in Belgium, France, and Germany. Popular support for anti-immigrant political parties and movements increased and political leaders came under intense pressure to restrict further immigration.

Southern Mediterranean Route Resumes

The number of migrants who drowned in the Mediterranean in 2016 topped 5,000—the highest annual fatality rate ever recorded. Previously, 2015 had been the deadliest year, with 3,771 drownings recorded. Most of the drownings occurred in the Southern Mediterranean. Human smuggling groups packed dozens of passengers onto flimsy rubber dinghies, causing some vessels to collapse from overcrowding, tipping those aboard into the sea. Thousands more were plucked alive from the sea by authorities and humanitarian groups. The boats mainly departed from North Africa and attempted to reach the coastline of Italy, an EU member state. The United Nations High Commission for Refugees (UNHCR) reported that smugglers increasingly resorted to lower-quality vessels to transport the migrants. In an effort to evade capture by border control ships that were patrolling the seas, smugglers often sent out several vessels simultaneously.

The migrants who arrived on Europe's shores were fleeing a combination of conflict, political instability, failed states, and severe human rights abuses. They came from an array of countries, including Afghanistan, Iraq, Libya, Somalia, South Sudan, Syria, and Yemen. Vast refugees came from Syria due to the civil war that raged in that country since 2011, which morphed into a complex, multisided conflict with external proxy powers helping various sides. Because the UN Security Council failed to forge a lasting ceasefire in Syria, the conditions causing the exodus persisted. By the end of 2016, around five million people were estimated to have fled the country since the civil war began.

In 2014 and early 2015, the Southern Mediterranean was the primary point of departure for migrants to try to reach Europe. This area was temporarily supplanted by the Eastern Mediterranean as the dominant transit route from the summer of 2015, when a trickle of refugees traveling from Turkey to Greece and on to other European countries became a flood. Many of these migrants were living in camps in Turkey. In November 2015, the European Union concluded a deal with Turkey aimed at stopping this flow. The deal was initiated by Germany, the EU's largest member state, which had received the greatest share of refugees, with several hundred thousand arriving in the latter half of 2015.

Under the deal, the EU agreed to provide Turkey with €3 billion in humanitarian aid destined for some two million refugees living in Turkey. By the end of 2016, the European Commission had disbursed €677 million of the promised aid. In return, Turkey stepped up border controls, stopping refugees boarding vessels destined for Greek islands just a few miles away. By March 2016, the deal had greatly reduced the numbers arriving in Europe via that route. However, there soon followed a resurgence of migrants arriving in Europe via the North Africa–Italy route. Another part of the deal was the EU's pledge to grant Turkish citizens visa-free travel to the EU. By early 2017, that pledge had yet to be fulfilled because Turkey failed to meet some of the stipulated human rights standards, having notably enacted draconian antiterrorist legislation following a failed coup in the country in July 2016.

Greece and Italy had been the two frontline EU countries where migrants arrive, almost always by sea. The migrants' intended final destination, however, tended to be other EU countries, especially Austria, Germany, and Sweden. Mindful of these intentions, authorities in Greece and Italy allowed many migrants to pass through their territories. Greece and Italy are part of the EU's Schengen free travel area, where there are usually no border controls between member countries, although checks can be reintroduced temporarily for security reasons.

EUROPEAN NATIONS TORN OVER APPROACH

Some EU countries criticized Italy and Greece for not requiring the migrants to remain in their territories. Under EU law, the first EU country that an asylum applicant enters is supposed to be the one where they stay until their claim is processed. Greece and Italy were, in addition, threatened with legal action by the European Commission for failing to systemically fingerprint all asylum applicants, as required by EU law. Fingerprinting upon arrival makes it possible to establish which country is responsible for hosting the asylum applicant and processing their claim.

Germany also received criticism from some of its EU partners. In August 2016, without consulting her EU counterparts, German chancellor Angela Merkel announced that Germany would receive asylum claims from Syrians even if they had first arrived in the EU via a different country. Merkel's action came in response to the surge in Syrian refugees who traveled from Turkey to the EU. Her critics said she was flouting EU rules with this unilateral action and, moreover, had increased the flow of migrants by giving them an incentive to travel to Germany. Hungary was criticized too by some of its EU partners, in its case for being too inhospitable to the refugees. While Germany had received more refugees than any other EU country in raw numbers, as a share of its population, Hungary faced the heaviest burden. Media outlets showed footage of Hungarian law enforcement officers beating migrants transiting the country and stopping some from boarding trains bound for Austria. Hungary also constructed a fence to stop migrants entering Hungary from neighboring Balkan countries, notably Serbia, whose authorities were allowing migrants to transit.

In the summer of 2015, with the goal of sharing the burden of receiving refugees more evenly, most EU member states (Hungary was among those that refused to participate) approved a new EU-wide mechanism. Crafted by the European Commission, it provided for relocating 160,000 asylum-seekers, already present in the EU, to other EU countries that had so far not received so many. But by the end of 2016, only very modest progress had been made in implementing this relocation plan. The Commission reported that between January and November 2016, some 8,162 people had been relocated, 6,212 from Greece and 1,950 from Italy. The goal for 2017 was to increase that rate to about 3,000 a month from Greece and 1,500 from Italy, the Commission said.

The UNHCR urged the EU to fully implement the relocation mechanism. It also urged EU countries to proceed with more resettlement programs, where officials go into refugee camps located in other (non-EU) countries and arrange to transfer some refugees to their own country. An agreement was forged among EU countries in summer 2015 to better coordinate these resettlement programs. By December 2016, some 13,887 refugees had been relocated to EU countries under the mechanism, mostly taken from refugee camps in Jordan, Lebanon, and Turkey.

In late 2016, the EU Commission dropped its lawsuit against Italy and Greece over failing to fingerprint all asylum applicants because both countries by then had resumed comprehensive fingerprinting. The number of new arrivals in Greece had decreased enough to allow asylum-seekers who transited Greece en route to other EU countries to be transferred back to Greece, as of March 2017. Such transfers, required under EU rules on responsibility for processing asylum claims, were suspended when Greece became overwhelmed with asylum applicants.

While European authorities made progress in strengthening border controls and sharing the burden of receiving refugees more evenly, the public became increasingly anxious by these migrant flows. A survey by the Pew Research Center published in September 2016 found that many Europeans—both in countries receiving a lot of refugees, such as Germany and Hungary, and ones such as Poland that received relatively few—were afraid that the influx would trigger an increase in Islamic terrorism. The migrant influx had also generated increasingly negative views of Muslims, the survey found. In a keynote speech given in the EU capital, Brussels, on December 5, United Nations High Commissioner for Refugees Filippo Grandi described how the European mood had changed over the course of the year. "I was struck by how much Europe seemed to distance itself from those fundamental values [of cooperation between European states], as solidarity faltered and the responses of European states fragmented," he said.

TERRORIST ATTACKS EXACERBATE FEARS

Fears across EU member states were exacerbated by several major terrorist attacks perpetrated by individuals either from Middle Eastern countries or of Middle Eastern ancestry. On November 13, 2015, a group of gunmen affiliated with the Islamic State of Iraq and the Levant (ISIL) terrorist group carried out a shooting rampage on civilians in Paris, killing 130 people. At least one of the killers is believed to have slipped into Europe by mingling with arriving refugees. On March 22, 2016, suicide bombings (also claimed by ISIL) targeting Brussels Airport and a Brussels metro station left thirty-two civilians dead. On July 14, 2016, a French resident of Tunisian nationality killed eighty-six people at a beach in Nice by ploughing them down with a truck. On December 19, 2016, a Tunisian man whose asylum claim had been rejected killed twelve people at a Christmas market in Berlin by driving his truck through the crowd.

The uptick in immigration, combined with the terrorist attacks, generated a spike in support for anti-immigrant political parties. In the United Kingdom, the refugee crisis featured prominently in the June 23, 2016, referendum on continued EU membership, the so-called Brexit vote. Leaders of the campaign to leave the EU cited the migration flows as one of the main reasons why Britain would be better off outside the bloc. The referendum result was that 52 percent of voters opted for the UK to leave the EU, setting the country on a course to exit the bloc it joined in 1973.

The refugee and migration situation was also a central issue in political debates in France, Germany, and the Netherlands. All three countries were gearing up for elections for 2017. In France, the National Front party's leader, Marine Le Pen, was expected to be competitive in the spring presidential elections. In the Netherlands, the Party for Freedom led by Geert Wilders saw its support grow, as did Germany's Alternative for Germany party, which strongly opposes the refugee influx.

Acknowledging the shift in public mood, UN high commissioner Grandi said that EU leaders needed to take into account the interests and concerns of their citizens about safety and security, access to jobs, and identity and values. "Perceptions vary significantly, but negativity prevails," he said. "There is a deepening gap between those who see globalisation as rich in opportunities, and those for whom those opportunities have not been realized," with refugees "the flash point around which fear and uncertainty have converged," he said.

—Brian Beary

Following is the text of a speech delivered on December 5, 2016, by Filippo Grandi, the United Nations High Commissioner for Refugees (UNHCR), on the response to the refugee crisis in Europe; and a report from the European Commission released on December 8, 2016, on the progress made on the EU's plan for refugee resettlement.

UN High Commissioner for Refugees
DOCUMENT # on EU Efforts to Resettle Migrants

December 5, 2016

Mr Van Rompuy,

Ladies and gentlemen,

A year has passed since the peak of what has been called—though I am not sure the terminology is correct—the "European refugee crisis". A year in which this "crisis" has become a significant factor in key political and electoral processes, in Europe and beyond; and has had a profound impact on how refugee responses are managed globally, and on the policy debate surrounding them.

As a European, I myself grew up as part of a generation that benefited—socially and economically—from the practical application of the values of cooperation between

European states. It was a Europe also committed to sharing responsibility for meeting common challenges; a model for the world to come. As I watched the events of last year unfold, I was struck by how much Europe seemed to distance itself from those fundamental values, as solidarity faltered and the responses of European states fragmented.

This has serious implications for refugee protection, in Europe and globally. My aim—and I am grateful to the European Policy Centre for giving me this opportunity—is to share perspectives on how that fragmentation might be overcome, and confidence restored in Europe's ability to address refugee crises without creating anxiety, fear or rejection among its citizens. These are elaborated in a set of practical proposals that we have shared with EU Member States and the European Commission, and which aim to inform the important discussions currently taking place regarding the future directions of the European Union's refugee policies.

This is not an abstract debate; after the arrival of more than a million people last year, increased EU–Turkey cooperation and the closure of borders along the Balkans route have applied a brake to the flow of arrivals through the Eastern Mediterranean for the time being. But the challenges have by no means passed. The number of people arriving by sea in Italy this October was the highest in a single month for the last four years, and three times the figure for October last year. And deaths at sea in the Mediterranean have reached record levels, getting close to five thousand this year. That number would have been significantly higher had it not been for the search and rescue operations carried out by EU member states, coastguards and merchant ships, volunteers and NGOs.

The arrival of refugees in Europe, alongside migrants on the move, forms just one dimension of a broader global picture of heightened human mobility. Its refugee component is driven by conflict, instability, state failure and severe human rights violations.

We now live in a world in which power, and the power to harm, is more diffuse and dangerous than ever before. The paralysis of the Security Council—not least over Syria—is a significant symptom of an international peacemaking crisis. Long-standing crises in countries like Somalia and Afghanistan have become entrenched, and a long list of major conflicts—including devastating ones in Syria, Iraq, Libya, Yemen and South Sudan—have emerged or reignited in the last five years. We are watching with apprehension developments in fragile states such as the Central African Republic and the Democratic Republic of Congo.

We continue to struggle with immediate responses: as a consequence, refugees and countries hosting most of them are left without adequate resources. Funding for international humanitarian assistance in 2015 was the largest amount ever recorded, at USD 28 billion, including USD 6.2 billion from private donors. But the shortfall was also the largest in history—with just 55% of the needs identified by the humanitarian appeals process actually funded.

The arrival of some 500,000 Syrians in Europe—the driving factor and the bulk of last year's influx—was determined largely by these two causes: one, lack of prospects for a political resolution of the war and two, a dramatic process of impoverishment, including amongst Syrian refugees in the Middle East affected by cuts in the provision of food assistance. Other refugee populations were similarly affected by overstretched humanitarian resources and in some cases, a weakening of hospitality in terms of rights and support. The absence of alternative pathways for some of them to move to Europe and other destinations through regular, managed arrangements resulted in a chaotic and irregular flow of people, for which Europe was manifestly unprepared.

The vast majority of people arriving in 2015 and early 2016 through the Eastern Mediterranean came from the world's top ten refugee-producing countries—Syria, Iraq, Afghanistan and others.

While these movements also included economic migrants, this was predominantly a refugee flow. Today, the profile of those arriving through the Southern Mediterranean route has become more mixed, with a stronger migratory component, calling for a differentiated response for the categories of people arriving. It is nonetheless critical not to lose sight of the strong refugee dimension of the arrivals, and to ensure that Europe's discourse and policy responses reflect this reality.

Events in Europe last year placed the plight of refugees back on the international agenda. As I have repeated many times, this is not, primarily, a European crisis. Of the 65 million people forcibly displaced worldwide, almost two thirds are inside their own countries, and of those that have fled as refugees, 86% remain in developing countries in their own regions.

And this, perhaps, should not be called a crisis at all: one million people arriving in the course of a year is a large number; but it represents just 0.2% of the population of the European Union—a modest proportion when compared, for example, to Lebanon, where one in four people is a refugee. Uganda, a country of 38 million people with a GDP per capita of USD 675, has received on average 3,500 refugees per day for the past three months—that's more than 300,000 people—and has not closed its borders. And European states themselves, in the past, have demonstrated their ability to respond effectively to large-scale refugee movements—including from Hungary in 1956, and the former Yugoslavia in the 1990s.

The situation in 2015 was certainly challenging, but not unmanageable. However, measures aimed at forging a collective response, including through relocation, were not implemented to any meaningful degree. This left a small number of states—Greece and Italy, as the receiving countries, and Germany, Sweden and Austria, as the countries which 70% of asylum-seekers spontaneously moved to—bearing a grossly uneven share of the responsibility for addressing the situation. Reception at Europe's borders was haphazard and inadequate, leaving people who had survived traumatic journeys in terrible conditions. Now is the time to draw lessons from that experience—and to chart a new course.

We must be realistic. Conflict and instability—including in Europe's neighbourhood—are sadly set to stay for the time being, as are the broader drivers of migration today. Refugee movements to Europe (as part of mixed migratory flows) will unavoidably continue for the foreseeable future. As such, it is important that responses span the entire spectrum of displacement, from internal displacement, to host and transit countries, to asylum in the EU. Even if greater political and economic investments succeed in bringing about a level of stabilisation at the origin, arrivals in Europe will continue to occur, and therefore responses aimed at ensuring a fair, efficient and humane system for receiving and responding to them have to remain in place and have to be improved.

We must also be principled. The same experiences and values that shaped the European identity and institutions after the Second World War are at the heart of the international refugee protection regime. The 1951 Refugee Convention was adopted to ensure the protection of rights by reconciling the interests of refugees with those of the states and communities receiving them, and in parallel, the right to seek asylum was firmly embedded within the system of human rights that shaped post-war Europe, and was incorporated in the Charter of Fundamental Rights.

Europe has been one of the key players in the development of international systems for refugee protection, and the European Union and its member states represent the largest humanitarian donor, including to refugees globally. As such, refugee protection is a critical aspect of the identity of post-war Europe and its foundational values—and Europe has played a key role in transmitting and embedding those values at a global level. The failure to implement a humane, organised, collective response to the large-scale arrivals in 2015, and the resort to policies of containment rather than shared responsibility, with even the relevance of the 1951 Convention being called into question by some, has already set a negative example—there is certainly a link between recent policies by industrialised states and more restrictive refugee policies in the developing world.

This situation is already having a concrete impact on how states globally manage refugees. The decision to allocate three billion euros to Turkey, for example, is useful and important in helping Turkey host the biggest current refugee population of any country. But it has also created a complex precedent, raising questions from other governments hosting large numbers of refugees elsewhere.

More directly, the narrowing of access to Europe has coincided with measures restricting entry by Syrians, for example, to neighbouring countries, leaving them displaced and trapped inside Syria as conflict intensifies. As a result, the right to seek asylum is no longer available to the majority of those affected by the largest and most deadly conflict in the world today. We all express horror at daily images of destruction in Aleppo. But for a Syrian trying to flee Aleppo today, the only way out of the country—if this is even possible—is very dangerous and involves large payments, often to criminal networks.

We must also take charge. Mixed migration, by its nature, demands a transnational response. When the responses of governments are fragmented and inconsistent, the management of mixed migratory flows is assumed by smugglers, traffickers and transnational criminal networks.

The impression that governments are not in control—as it indeed appeared to many when the failure to implement a collective, managed response led to scenes of chaos at borders—also leads to a breakdown in trust, and plays into the hands of those who challenge the legitimacy of those governments and seek to turn refugees into scapegoats. It is important that European governments show, through collective action, that they are just as capable of responding effectively to refugee movements as in the past.

A final, all-important consideration, concerns the citizens of the European Union. Scanning social media, listening to the rhetoric of some politicians, analysing electoral results show that it is imperative to demonstrate—much more clearly than we have done so far—that their interests, the interests of the citizens, are being taken into account in the response to refugee arrivals and mixed migratory flows. Many people have genuine concerns about the impact on key aspects of their lives: their safety and security; their economic prosperity and in particular access to jobs; and their own identity and values—perceptions vary significantly, but negativity prevails. These reactions are not new—the same concerns were voiced, for example, regarding refugees from Hungary in 1956. But there is a deepening gap between those who see globalisation as rich in opportunities, and those for whom those opportunities have not been realised. In that context, refugees and migrants have become the flash point around which fear and uncertainty have converged.

It is important that we work together to engage with these concerns, to develop the evidence base to counter those narratives. Research carried out among recently arrived refugees in Germany demonstrated that they share the same values of democracy, freedom, and commitment to gender equality as German citizens. The OECD points out that the medium and long term effects of migration on public finance, economic growth and the labour market are generally positive.

Analysis of the impact of last year's refugee arrivals in Sweden showed that they provided a boost to the job market through increased public spending. It is important to actively demonstrate that the measures taken to provide protection to refugees are also designed to address the concerns I have just mentioned—and that the social contract between refugees and the States that host them, which incorporates both rights and obligations, is properly established. Like anyone else, refugees must comply with the laws of their host countries and respect their values.

Of course, there is also a strong countervailing trend in Europe—based on the values of compassion, multiculturalism and human rights that are part of the modern European identity. In my experience, the most powerful advocates for refugees are people who have been directly exposed to them and have shared, even momentarily, the reality of their experiences. This is a powerful force to be nurtured, which has the potential to shape public opinion, and to form a bridge between refugees and communities. I very much welcome President Juncker's announcement of the formation of a European Solidarity Corps, to enable young people across Europe to volunteer their help, including for refugees.

Ladies and gentlemen,

The paper we are launching today is aimed at building a system that works for refugees, governments and the people of Europe. This is not an aspirational vision, but a set of very concrete and pragmatic proposals for cooperation, most of which can be implemented through existing financial resources and without new legislation. Let me highlight a few points that have the potential to make a real difference.

The common element running through all of our proposals is that of solidarity—the principle that drove the adoption of the New York Declaration for Refugees and Migrants last September.

Solidarity is indispensable for Europe to move from the short-term tactics of control and rejection to a proper strategy to address refugee flows. This is the core message developed by our paper. Exercised in practical ways, solidarity is based on a genuine commitment to shouldering a common responsibility, and not deflecting that responsibility onto others. This applies both to external solidarity—between the EU and the states outside its borders affected by refugee outflows; and internal solidarity, between EU member states. The two dimensions are not mutually exclusive but must be part of a comprehensive approach to restore European leadership in refugee responses.

First, external solidarity. The European Union is already strongly engaged beyond its borders, including in refugee crises. Globally, however, that engagement must become much more specifically tailored to address the factors driving forced displacement and onward movement. Plans being made to invest large sums for this purpose, in Valletta and subsequent initiatives, could have an enormous impact in preventing and stabilizing refugee flows, but must be more decisively implemented.

Resolving forced displacement is also unavoidably linked to conflict resolution. The European Union has often played an important role in this regard in the past. This role, let me be frank, appears to be in decline, and I would encourage member states to reinforce their efforts in this respect. Targeted investments that help strengthen protection and enable solutions for internally displaced people within their countries can complement conflict resolution initiatives at the political level.

Investment in refugee hosting countries is another critical pillar. There is—finally—an emerging consensus around the key role of substantial and targeted development action in addressing refugee outflows. Thanks to the leadership of the World Bank, this is finally being translated into financial instruments aimed at supporting opportunities for refugees and host communities—with a particular focus on education, jobs and infrastructure. It is crucial that international financial institutions—with the support, encouragement and resources of EU Member States—do more to become predictable and engaged partners.

The EU is already playing an important role—including, for example, through innovative approaches that bundle trade, humanitarian and development support, as in the Jordan Compact that emerged from the London Conference on aid to Syrians in February, but this engagement must be stepped up much faster and further. Other pledges are producing results: primary school enrolment amongst Syrian children in Turkey for example, rose from 37% in September this year to 59% currently. This enhances the prospects for children, but also for their parents, who are less likely to think about moving on. Investments in transit countries—particularly in building asylum systems and strengthening access to protection and opportunities—can also play an important role.

But I would like to offer one word of caution here. Support to host and transit countries should be driven by solidarity, not strict conditionality, and by a commitment to responsibility sharing, in the spirit of the 1951 Convention and the New York Declaration. Caution should be exercised in linking financial aid to other benefits and migration controls. This sets precedents and raises expectations that may not always be met and can ultimately even allow host governments to use population movements as a pressure point or even a threat.

Another key proposal is for a substantial reinforcement and expansion of safe pathways for refugees to move to Europe and other destinations. To provide a sufficiently meaningful alternative to irregular migration routes, and divert refugees from trafficking and smuggling networks, these need to reach a critical mass substantially above current levels.

In particular, we are proposing a robust expansion of the scope of family reunification, and practical measures to make existing programmes more accessible. Increasing opportunities for joining family members through regular channels would avert the need for people to risk unsafe journeys. One very concrete step would be to accord the same rights to family reunification to those granted subsidiary forms of protection as are given to refugees.

We are also calling for a significant expansion of resettlement programmes. Last year, some 81,000 of the most vulnerable refugees were resettled globally to third countries with UNHCR's assistance. This represents fewer than 1% of refugees worldwide and, while it is helpful for those who benefit, it does not yet provide a really meaningful alternative solution. Data related to EU are even less impressive: resettlement averaged 5,700 persons a year between 2011 and 2015—frankly, an irrelevant figure, just 7% of the global resettlement total, although with recent new commitments by 27 member states, the pace is slowly and hesitantly picking up.

This is why we very much welcome the recent Commission proposal for a European Union Resettlement Framework. This must be scaled up quickly and boldly—in a way that is strategic and responsive to global needs, and sets much more ambitious numerical targets. For 2017, we estimate that 1.2 million refugees will be in need of resettlement globally, of whom 40% are Syrian. To make a real (not a symbolic) impact, resettlement and other forms of humanitarian admission to the EU would need to reach a six-digit figure annually.

We welcome the initiative of some EU Member States to complement resettlement, by making other pathways, including scholarships, available to Syrian refugees—hopefully this can be expanded and made available to refugees of other nationalities, together with private sponsorship programmes and labour mobility opportunities. Managed migration programmes for potential migrants who are not refugees can also play a useful role—in contributing to their countries' development, in providing potential answers to the challenges presented by aging populations in Europe, and having the immediate effect of alleviating the pressure on asylum systems caused by unfounded refugee claims made by migrants in the absence of other options.

Let me turn now to the more controversial issue of internal solidarity. Solidarity within the EU is essential for a revitalised and well-managed common asylum system. It is needed from a protection, security, humanitarian and common sense perspective. But there is no consensus among member states on how to share responsibility for asylum-seekers and refugees within Europe.

Our paper sets out some elements that can help reshape the common asylum system and hopefully move towards an agreement at the political level—drawing on the lessons of 2015 and 2016, and building on the Commission's proposals currently on the table. The paper is detailed in this respect. Let me give you five quick examples.

First, we are calling for a common registration system—to make sure that all those who arrive are registered using the same system, that people are directed into the right procedures and those in need of protection have access to it quickly. We have seen how trust in asylum systems has been shaken by images of people moving across Europe without proper registration and screening. Our proposal would improve security screening and data sharing between states, and eliminate costly duplication. Registration databases would be directly linked to the case processing system in each member state, to ensure swift access to asylum procedures. Efforts should also be made to develop compatible systems in EU candidate countries, with appropriate data protection safeguards.

Second, we are issuing an urgent call for action with regard to unaccompanied and separated children. Record numbers applied for asylum throughout the EU last year; 24,000 have arrived in Italy by sea already in 2016. Most have been exposed to appalling risks—separated from their families, detained, exposed to sexual violence, exploitation, trafficking and severe physical and psychological harm.

Later this week, I will be hosting a high level dialogue on "children on the move" in Geneva. We have consulted widely to develop a roadmap to inform better practice, and a number of initiatives are already being undertaken by the EU and Member States. We do not need new guidelines, new legal frameworks, but to come together and secure concrete results.

Children need to be treated as children first. We must end the detention of children. It is never acceptable. We must move away from the immediate channeling of children into asylum systems. Instead, we must ensure a common age assessment methodology across Europe and that children have immediate access to a guardian to help them find a solution that is in their best interest. Then, the right decisions can be made about family tracing, about whether an asylum application should be made and how to ensure that the child is protected and adequately supported.

Third, our proposals include practical suggestions with regard to relocation—the mechanism for distributing responsibility for asylum seekers that the European Commission has proposed, based on experience with schemes established last year. The numbers relocated remain unacceptably low, but the pace of implementation has been picking up and the ideas underlying relocation are good. Getting relocation to work efficiently and at scale will be a central component of solidarity in action.

We believe that the key is a rational system that incorporates clear incentives for Member States and asylum-seekers to comply. We know—for example—that asylum-seekers often move on to join family members, so why not facilitate family reunion at the earliest possible stage—thereby minimising the incentive for irregular movement? For asylum seekers with manifestly unfounded claims, why not apply an accelerated procedure for return, rather than complicating matters by distributing them to another member state? And we have also made a number of concrete suggestions to speed up and simplify the procedures for asylum determination, and to facilitate return for those who are found not to be in need of international protection—an important element of a well-functioning asylum system.

Fourth, we are also urging Europe to invest in preparing for new influxes. While the events of 2015 were certainly exceptional, significant surges in the arrivals of refugees and migrants will certainly feature in the months and years ahead, and it is critical that the scenes of 2015 are not repeated. It is essential that early warning mechanisms, contingency plans, clear coordination structures and standby capacities are established. The civil protection agencies of EU member states have experience and expertise in preparing and responding to emergencies that can be brought to bear. UNHCR stands ready to provide support.

Fifth, we are urging substantial, early investment in integration programmes, including through a mandatory requirement that 30% of the financial support provided through the EU Asylum, Migration and Integration Fund is used for this purpose by Member States on an annual basis. The current system, in which some states do not spend one euro on integration, fosters secondary movements and generates huge disparities. Evidence demonstrates the importance of access to the labour market in facilitating integration and avoiding the creation of an underclass, which contributes to social divisions, intolerance and xenophobia. Under our proposal, targeted investments would be made in employment, housing and language training, and refugee skills and qualifications would be recognised.

Integration is an opportunity, for both refugees and the communities in which they settle, and there are many powerful examples of positive initiatives the engagement of volunteers who give language courses, clothes, toys, food and shelter; the role of the private sector in providing jobs, shaping policies and influencing perceptions; and the involvement of influential sectors of society such as football teams in promoting positive attitudes in hard-to-reach constituencies.

Ladies and gentlemen,

This is indeed a complex moment in Europe's history. On the refugee front, we need prompt and robust action to avert a 'race to the bottom' in which some countries renounce a common approach, believing that only national solutions can work. This does not solve the problem. It generates restrictive measures, hate speech and a drive to deflect refugees to other Member States through hostility and deterrent measures. If Europe does not rise to the challenge of collectively managing mixed flows of refugees and migrants, through both external engagement and internal measures, this will almost certainly lead to more fences, the reestablishment of internal border controls, the end of Schengen and the abolition of one of the European Union's four fundamental freedoms.

Instead—I believe—Europe must lead responses; starting from displacement in conflict, to support to host countries, to an asylum system based on practical and innovative measures that work for refugees, communities in Europe and Member States. History has demonstrated that Europe is stronger when it addresses its challenges together. This is the moment for a new vision for Europe's collective engagement with refugees—drawing on its history of tolerance, openness, and based on protection principles, but also on a pragmatic and practical approach to addressing refugee flows.

SOURCE: United Nations Human Rights Office of the High Commissioner. "Protecting refugees in Europe and beyond: Can the EU rise to the challenge?" December 5, 2016. http://www.unhcr.org/admin/hcspeeches/58456ec34/protecting-refugees-europe-beyond-eu-rise-challenge.html.

European Commission on Refugee Resettlement Efforts

December 8, 2016

The Commission is today reporting on progress made in the implementation of the EU–Turkey Statement and on the EU's relocation and resettlement schemes.

The Commission also adopted a fourth Recommendation today that takes stock of the **progress achieved by Greece to put in place a fully functioning asylum system** and sets out a process for the gradual resumption of Dublin transfers to Greece.

European Commission First Vice-President Frans **Timmermans** said: *"Our comprehensive European approach on migration is showing positive results. We can see this in the continued implementation of the EU–Turkey Statement and the dramatic decrease in the number of irregular migrants arriving in Greece. We also see it in the progress made by the Greek authorities in rectifying deficiencies in the country's asylum system, which has allowed us to recommend the gradual resumption of Dublin transfers to Greece as of 15 March 2017. This will provide further disincentives against irregular entry and secondary movements, and is an important step for the return to a normally functionally Dublin and Schengen system."*

Commissioner for Migration, Home Affairs and Citizenship, Dimitris **Avramopoulos** said: *"Both Italy and Greece have made herculean efforts in recent months in managing the refugee crisis. The fact that today we close the infringement cases on the fingerprinting and registration of migrants is proof of that. This November was a record month for relocation with over 1,400 persons transferred, and Member States must build on this progress by further intensifying and sustaining their efforts. Our aim is to relocate all those in Italy and Greece who are eligible for relocation within the next year. These efforts, together with a lasting reduction in arrivals from Turkey thanks to the EU–Turkey Statement, are necessary building blocks for a gradual return to the Dublin system for Greece."*

STEADY PROGRESS MADE IN THE IMPLEMENTATION OF THE EU–TURKEY STATEMENT

The implementation of the EU–Turkey Statement has confirmed the trend of a steady delivery of results, albeit in the face of many challenges. Numbers of irregular crossings of the Aegean during the reporting period remained dramatically lower than before the EU–Turkey Statement. Since March, arrivals have averaged 90 per day, compared to 10,000 in a single day in October last year. **Return operations** have continued to be carried out with an additional 170 persons returned since the Third Report, bringing the total number of persons returned under the Statement or the Greece–Turkey bilateral readmission protocol to 1,187. However, important shortfalls remain, notably as regards the still too slow pace of returns from Greece to Turkey which has led to additional pressure on the Greek islands. The situation deserves not only careful monitoring but, more importantly, additional efforts to help improve the situation on the Greek islands. It is therefore essential that sufficient resources are provided to ensure the effective processing of asylum applications and that Member States respond in full to calls from the European Asylum Support Office. To ensure full implementation of EU actions under the EU–Turkey Statement and to alleviate the pressure on the islands, the EU Coordinator Maarten Verwey has today published a Joint Action Plan elaborated with the Greek authorities.

As regards the implementation of the **Visa Liberalisation Roadmap**, seven benchmarks remain to be met by Turkey. The Commission encourages Turkey's efforts to complete the delivery of all outstanding benchmarks as soon as possible. The Commission and Turkey have continued their dialogue to find solutions, including on the legislative and procedural changes needed to meet the outstanding benchmarks.

The Commission has continued to accelerate the delivery of funding under the **Facility for Refugees in Turkey**, having already allocated a total of €2.2 billion out of the €3 billion foreseen for 2016–2017 to address the most urgent needs of refugees and host communities in Turkey. The amounts contracted have increased to €1.3 billion. The Commission is making all necessary efforts to ensure an acceleration of disbursements under the Facility, the sum of which has now reached €677 million.

Dublin transfers to Greece to be gradually resumed

Today, the Commission adopted its Fourth Recommendation on the resumption of Dublin transfers to Greece as a step towards a normal functioning of the rules of the Dublin system. The Commission finds that Greece has made significant progress in putting in place the essential institutional and legal structures for a properly functioning asylum system. However, the resumption has to take account of the fact that Greece is still facing high migratory pressure and that deficiencies in the Greek asylum system remain, in particular as regards reception conditions, the treatment of vulnerable applicants and the speed with which asylum applications are registered, lodged and examined.

The Commission therefore recommends that transfers to Greece should be resumed gradually, on the basis of individual assurances from the Greek authorities for each returnee, guaranteeing they will be received in dignity. In order to avoid that an unsustainable burden is placed on Greece, the resumption of transfers will not be applied retroactively and will only concern asylum applicants who have entered Greece irregularly from 15 March 2017 onwards or for whom Greece is responsible from 15 March 2017 under other Dublin criteria. To support the efforts of Greece, the Commission calls on all Member States to fully comply with their relocation obligations and to ensure sufficient deployment of asylum experts to Greece.

Applicants should only be transferred if the Greek authorities give individual assurances in each case that the applicant will be treated in accordance with EU law. Vulnerable asylum applicants, including unaccompanied minors, should not be transferred to Greece for the time being. An EASO team of experts from Member States should be set up to support the cooperation between Member States and to report on whether the persons transferred back to Greece are treated in accordance with the assurances provided by the Greek authorities. The Commission will regularly report on the progress made in the implementation of the Recommendation and update its recommendations if necessary.

PROGRESS ON RELOCATION AND RESETTLEMENT

November saw **1,406** relocations, the highest monthly number so far, confirming a continuous positive trend, with relocation from Greece stabilising around 1,000 per month and relocation from Italy having increased significantly. In total, **8,162** persons have been relocated so far, **6,212** from Greece and **1,950** from Italy.

The Commission considers that it should now be feasible to transfer all eligible relocation applicants in Greece and Italy to other Member States by September 2017. To achieve this goal, Member States should from now on carry out **at least 2,000 relocations per month from Greece and 1,000 from Italy**. As of April 2017, the monthly number of relocations from Greece should be at least 3,000 and from Italy 1,500.

The Commission has continued to work closely with the Greek and Italian authorities as well as Member States to remove obstacles to speedier relocation on the ground. Today, the Commission decided to **close infringement procedures** against Italy and Greece for non-implementation of the Eurodac regulation because in both Member States, there is now a fingerprinting rate of close to 100% of third-country nationals liable to be fingerprinted who entered the EU irregularly at their external borders.

Member States have also continued to increase their efforts on resettlement—offering legal and safe pathways to **13,887** people so far out of the 22,504 agreed under the July 2015 scheme. Since the previous report a record monthly number of 2,035 people have been resettled mainly from Turkey, Jordan and Lebanon. An additional **544** Syrian refugees have been resettled from Turkey, bringing the total number of resettlements from Turkey under the EU–Turkey Statement to **2,761**.

SOURCE: European Commission. "Commission reports on progress made under the European Agenda on Migration." December 8, 2016. © European Union. http://europa.eu/rapid/press-release_IP-16-4281_en.htm.

OTHER HISTORIC DOCUMENTS OF INTEREST

FROM THIS VOLUME

FROM PREVIOUS *HISTORIC DOCUMENTS*

Aleppo Returned to Syrian Government Control; Russia Backs New Trilateral Talks

DECEMBER 7, 14, 20, AND 29, 2016

Late in 2016, the Syrian government of President Bashar al-Assad intensified its efforts to retake the opposition-held eastern portion of Aleppo amid the country's ongoing civil war. As the government advanced on the rebels, the growing humanitarian crisis in the besieged city drew international attention and calls for an agreement to permit aid deliveries and safe passage out of Aleppo for civilians and fighters. Amid a breakdown of multilateral talks and the United States' shrinking involvement in diplomatic efforts to resolve the crisis, Russia and Turkey stepped in to negotiate the evacuation of eastern Aleppo, allowing the Syrian government to retake the city. Russia and Turkey also led efforts to negotiate another ceasefire in the conflict and restart peace talks, despite the assassination of a Russian envoy to Turkey.

BATTLE FOR ALEPPO

Aleppo, Syria's largest city and commercial center before the war began, was divided between the government-controlled west and the opposition-held east since August 2012. The city was subject to repeated bombardments by the Syrian government as it sought to retake control of the city and by rebel groups trying to defend their position. The Syrian government had been supported by Russia in its fight against the opposition, including in and around Aleppo, which began conducting air strikes in Syria in September 2015. While Russia claimed that its airstrikes target terrorist organizations fighting alongside the rebels, such as the Nusra Front, U.S. and other officials have repeatedly accused Russia of indiscriminately attacking Western-backed rebel groups and targeting medical facilities.

Various offensives were conducted in the roughly four-year period in which Aleppo remained divided, with both sides of the conflict periodically losing and recapturing territory. The Syrian government intensified its campaign against the rebels in 2016 and, with Russian support, succeeded in severing the last supply line to eastern Aleppo in July. The government continued to advance on rebel-held territory through the fall, with a final major offensive beginning in mid-November. The government steadily gained ground, pushing the rebels and civilians into a smaller and smaller area. By early December, it was estimated that rebels controlled only a quarter of eastern Aleppo.

While tens of thousands of civilians fled eastern Aleppo as the government advanced, an estimated 100,000 Syrians remained trapped by the offensive, with severely limited and dwindling supplies of food, clean water, fuel, and medical supplies. A December report on the situation in Syria compiled by United Nations (UN) Secretary-General Ban Ki-moon concluded that continued fighting in Aleppo, particularly after November 15, resulted "in the deaths of hundreds and the displacement of tens of thousands of people by the end of the month." The report spoke of "indiscriminate attacks against civilians and civilian infrastructure, especially against medical personnel and facilities and against schools, educational staff, and school children" occurring in November and cited credible reports of twenty-six attacks against medical facilities, twelve of which were located in Aleppo. Photos, videos, and social media posts from the besieged city prompted an international outcry over the growing humanitarian crisis and led to protests at the UN headquarters and in cities including London, Paris, Istanbul, Sarajevo, and Amman. Jens Laerke, a spokesperson for the UN Office for the Coordination of Humanitarian Affairs, described "a complete meltdown of humanity" in Aleppo.

Efforts by UN Security Council members to secure a new seven-day ceasefire to allow humanitarian aid to be delivered to those trapped in the city failed on December 5, when both China and Russia vetoed the ceasefire resolution. The vote marked the fifth and sixth times, respectively, that these two countries had vetoed Syria-related resolutions. Russian officials claimed the resolution was a "bad tactic" because U.S. Secretary of State John Kerry and Russian Foreign Minister Sergey Lavrov were engaged in discussions about, and making progress toward, an agreement that would move the rebels from eastern Aleppo and provide humanitarian aid. The United States and Russia had announced these conversations were ongoing two days prior to the Security Council vote.

Despite Russia's claims, leaders from Canada, France, Germany, Italy, the United Kingdom, and the United States issued a joint statement on December 7 to "condemn the actions of the Syrian regime and its foreign backers, especially Russia, for their obstruction of humanitarian aid, and strongly condemn the Syrian regime's attacks that have devastated civilians and medical facilities and use of barrel bombs and chemical weapons." The statement accused Russia of blocking Security Council action and called for an immediate ceasefire to allow the UN to deliver humanitarian assistance. U.S. President Barack Obama later provided his own sharp criticism of the Syrian government, stating, "We have seen a deliberate strategy of surrounding, besieging, and starving innocent civilians." He added, "Responsibility for this brutality lies in one place alone: the Assad regime and its allies Russia and Iran. The blood for these atrocities are on their hands."

ALEPPO EVACUATED, GOVERNMENT REGAINS CONTROL

Following the breakdown of multilateral peace negotiations, and the United States' withdrawal from bilateral negotiations with Russia, Turkey and Russia worked with the Syrian opposition to develop a ceasefire agreement and a deal under which all remaining fighters would be evacuated to rebel-held territory elsewhere in the country and civilians would be given the option to leave with the fighters or move to government-held areas. The deal was announced on December 13, and evacuations were set to begin at 5:00 a.m. on December 14. The ability to leave and relocate was critical to the rebels, since opposition fighters and the medical and humanitarian workers who helped them had previously been punished by the government as terrorists. Despite the seeming breakthrough, some observers expressed concern about how the agreement would be implemented. The UN said it had received reports of Syrian troops or allied militias killing an estimated eighty-two civilians execution-style in apartments or on the streets. Also, residents reported that a convoy attempting to carry about seventy wounded people out of Aleppo was turned back by progovernment militants and told they could not leave until later in the day. Furthermore, Syrian officials said they had no knowledge of the deal. Iran, another strong ally of the Syrian government, was reportedly also excluded from the negotiation process.

Implementation of the deal was delayed due to reports the morning of December 14 that progovernment forces, including Iranian-backed militias, had resumed their attacks on eastern Aleppo. Rebel groups stationed outside the city in turn resumed shelling government-held areas of the city. Meanwhile, civilians issued pleas for help and called on the international community to exert pressure on the government and its allies to reinstate the agreement. The deal was subsequently modified to include the evacuation of government supporters from two Shiite villages that had been surrounded by Sunni rebels. Evacuations officially began on December 15. An estimated 9,000 people left Aleppo before evacuations were suspended the next day. According to Aleppo Media Center reports, Iranian militias supporting the Syrian government were firing on the road out of eastern Aleppo. Syrian state news claimed that some of the evacuees were violating the terms of the agreement by bringing weapons and advanced communications devices with them. The agreement was revised yet again to allow safe passage for those loyal to the government out of two additional rebel-held cities, and evacuations resumed on December 18. Four days later, the International Committee of the Red Cross reported that the evacuation of eastern Aleppo had been completed, and the Syrian government declared that it had retaken full control of the city. The government now controls Syria's four major cities.

An estimated 31,000 people were killed in Aleppo since the city was divided in 2012, out of roughly 400,000 people killed to date in the Syrian Civil War. While viewed as a turning point in the conflict, the retaking of Aleppo does not mean the war is over. Rebel groups still control the provincial capital of Idlib, where those from eastern Aleppo were relocated, as well as some stretches of rural territory in the northern and southern parts of the country. Kurdish militias and the Islamic State in the Levant (ISIL) control large areas of eastern Syria. Clashes have continued outside of Aleppo, particularly around the capital, Damascus. There is also some concern that by essentially concentrating rebel groups in Idlib, an opportunity for a second Aleppo is being created. "I don't know what will happen in Idlib, but if there is no ceasefire or political accord, then it will become the next Aleppo," said Staffan de Mistura, the UN special envoy for Syria.

Russian Ambassador to Turkey Assassinated

On December 19, while Aleppo was being evacuated, Andrey Karlov, the Russian ambassador to Turkey, was assassinated in the Turkish capital of Ankara while speaking at an art exhibit opening. The gunman was identified as twenty-two-year-old Turkish police officer Mevlut Mert Alintas, who reportedly shouted, "Don't forget Aleppo, don't forget Syria!" after the attack. Alintas was killed in a shootout with Turkish special forces.

Russia and Turkey called the assassination a terrorist attack. Russian President Vladimir Putin said that Karlov had been "despicably killed" to sabotage the country's relationship with Turkey and undermine the peace process in Syria. "The only response we should offer to this murder is stepping up our fight against terror, and the criminals will feel the heat," he said. Turkish President Recep Tayyip Erdoğan shared a similar message. "We know that this is a provocation aiming to destroy the normalization process of Turkey–Russia relations," he said. "But the Russian government and the Turkish republic have the will to not fall into that provocation." Putin and Erdoğan agreed to coordinate on an investigation into the killing and efforts to combat terrorism.

The assassination underscored the Syrian Civil War's impact beyond the country's borders and the anger many felt over the ongoing conflict. In the days preceding the shooting, thousands of Turks had protested Russia's support for the Syrian government and its involvement in the killing and destruction in Aleppo. A protest also took place at the Russian consulate in Ankara the same evening as the shooting. However, observers did not believe that the assassination would lead to a crisis between Russia and Turkey, given officials' shared messages of cooperation and because both countries needed each other to advance their disparate interests in Syria and did not want to risk destabilizing their relations.

Relations between the two countries had previously been strained by Russia's involvement in the war. Turkey provided support to the Syrian opposition early in the war and opened its border to allow the transport of weapons and antigovernment fighters into the country. In supporting the Syrian government, Russia had bombed Turkish-backed rebels and had flown its planes close to the Turkish–Syrian border. (Turkey alleges that some planes also flew across the border.) Relations reached an all-time low when Turkey shot down a Russian jet near the Syrian border in November 2015, and Russia issued sanctions against Turkey in response. Tensions abated in 2016 once Erdoğan apologized for the incident, and he and Putin met in St. Petersburg to discuss the situation in Syria. Turkey later shifted its focus from pushing Assad out of office to preventing Kurdish groups from amassing territory along its border. One of the Kurdish groups involved in the conflict is the People's Protection Units (YPG), which Turkey has designated as a terrorist group. Turkey believes the YPG is linked to the Kurdistan Workers' Party in Turkey, which has also been named a terrorist group and outlawed. Turkey fears that a buildup of Kurds along its border could provide momentum for Kurdish separatists to declare an independent Kurdish state that would claim some of Turkey's land. Observers speculated that Russia and Turkey had arrived at an unofficial agreement in which Turkey would stop supporting certain rebel groups who were a threat to Russian interests in Syria and in return Russia would stop supporting Syrian Kurdish groups. Turkey has also continued its efforts to fight the emergence of ISIL in Syria, seemingly with Russia's tacit support.

Russia, Turkey Lead New Ceasefire and Peace Talks

The day after Karlov's assassination, Lavrov, Turkish foreign minister Mevlüt Çavuşoğlu, and Iranian foreign minister Mohammad Javad Zarif met in Moscow to discuss Syria. They agreed on a joint statement declaring that the crisis in Syria could not be solved militarily and outlining the principles to which a potential political agreement should adhere. Speaking at a joint press conference following the meeting, Lavrov explained that "the disastrous situation in eastern Aleppo, the plight of the people in that part of the city and the need to minimise possible casualties, losses, as well as the need to reduce the number of militants" had spurred the three countries to start their own talks. "We are confident that, while implementation of the [UN Security Council] resolutions is at a standstill, the initiative taken by our three countries can help to overcome the stagnation in efforts to achieve a settlement in Syria," he said.

On December 29, the Turkish Foreign Ministry announced that Turkey and Russia had prepared a ceasefire agreement for Syria, which was signed by the Syrian government and rebel groups, taking effect on December 30. Both Turkey and Russia committed to jointly monitoring the ceasefire, and the Turkish Foreign Ministry called for "the support of the countries with influence on parties on the ground."

Russia then organized indirect talks between the Syrian government and rebel groups. Held in Astana, Kazakhstan, on January 23 and 24, 2017, the talks were also sponsored by

Turkey and Iran and were conducted separately from the UN's peace process. The United States, European Union, and Saudi Arabia were not included in the discussions. By the end of the talks, Iran, Russia, and Turkey had agreed to enforce a partial ceasefire. The countries also agreed to establish a monitoring and enforcement mechanism for the ceasefire but did not outline what that mechanism should look like. There was no discussion of political issues or Assad's future during the talks, although the parties affirmed that "there is no military solution to the Syrian conflict and that it can only be solved through a political process." The countries also reiterated that they would fight jointly against ISIL and the Nusra Front and promised to "separate" them from armed opposition groups.

Notably, neither the Syrian government nor the rebel groups signed the ceasefire agreement. In fact, the government said it would continue its offensive against the opposition in the region northwest of Damascus, which the rebels said was a major violation of the ceasefire. UN-mediated peace talks are scheduled to resume in late February 2017.

—Linda Fecteau Grimm

Following is a joint statement from officials in Canada, France, Germany, Italy, the United Kingdom, and the United States from December 7, 2016, condemning the Syrian government's actions in Aleppo; a report by UN Secretary-General Ban Ki-moon from December 14, 2016, highlighting humanitarian concerns and the UN's efforts to provide aid in Syria; the partial transcript of a joint news conference on December 20, 2016, during which the Russian, Iranian, and Turkish foreign ministers discussed their trilateral talks; and a press release issued by the Turkish Foreign Ministry on December 29, 2016, announcing a new ceasefire agreement in Syria.

DOCUMENT

Joint Statement by International Leaders on the Situation in Aleppo

December 7, 2016

A humanitarian disaster is taking place before our very eyes. Some 200,000 civilians, including many children, in eastern Aleppo are cut off from food and medicine supplies. Aleppo is being subjected to daily bombings and artillery attacks by the Syrian regime, supported by Russia and Iran. Hospitals and schools have not been spared. Rather, they appear to be the targets of attack in an attempt to wear people down. The images of dying children are heart breaking. We condemn the actions of the Syrian regime and its foreign backers, especially Russia, for their obstruction of humanitarian aid, and strongly condemn the Syrian regime's attacks that have devastated civilians and medical facilities and use of barrel bombs and chemical weapons.

The urgent need now is for an immediate ceasefire to allow the United Nations to get humanitarian assistance to people in eastern Aleppo and to provide humanitarian relief to those who have fled eastern Aleppo. The opposition have agreed the UN's four point plan for Aleppo. The regime needs to agree to the plan too. We call on the Syrian regime to do this urgently to alleviate the dire situation in Aleppo; and call on Russia and Iran to use their influence to help make this happen.

We urge all parties in Syria to adhere to international humanitarian law, including the Geneva Conventions. UN SG Ban Ki-moon has spoken about war crimes being committed in Syria. There must not be impunity for those responsible. We call on the UN to investigate respective reports and gather evidence to hold the perpetrators of war crimes to account. We are ready to consider additional restrictive measures against individuals and entities that act for or on behalf of the Syrian regime.

At the same time, Russia is blocking the UN Security Council, which is therefore unable to do its work and put an end to the atrocities. The regime's refusal to engage in a serious political process also highlights the unwillingness of both Russia and Iran to work for a political solution despite their assurances to the contrary. We support the efforts of the UN Special Envoy de Mistura to resume the political process through negotiations. Only a political settlement can bring peace for people in Syria.

SOURCE: The White House. "Canada, France, Germany, Italy, United Kingdom and United States Leaders' Statement on the situation in Aleppo." December 7, 2016. https://obamawhitehouse.archives.gov/the-press-office/2016/12/07/canada-france-germany-italy-united-kingdom-and-united-states-leaders.

UN Secretary-General's Report on the Situation in Syria

DOCUMENT

December 14, 2016

[Tables, figures, boxes, and footnotes have been omitted.]

I. INTRODUCTION

1. The present report is the thirty-fourth submitted pursuant to paragraph 17 of Security Council resolution 2139 (2014), paragraph 10 of Council resolution 2165 (2014), paragraph 5 of Council resolution 2191 (2014) and paragraph 5 of Council resolution 2258 (2015), in which the Council requested the Secretary-General to report, every 30 days, on the implementation of the resolutions by all parties to the conflict in the Syrian Arab Republic.

2. The information contained herein is based on the data available to United Nations agencies on the ground, from the Government of the Syrian Arab Republic, other Syrian sources and open sources. Data from United Nations agencies on their humanitarian deliveries have been reported for the period from 1 to 30 November 2016.

II. MAJOR DEVELOPMENTS

3. November saw a notable military escalation in the Syrian Arab Republic compared with previous months, which resulted in the death and injury of civilians and the destruction of civilian infrastructure. Hospitals and schools continued to be attacked regularly. Insecurity from the fighting remained a major factor limiting the ability of United Nations agencies and their partners to deliver much-needed humanitarian assistance. Heavy fighting

continued nationwide, including in Aleppo, Damascus, Dayr al-Zawr, Hama, Idlib and Rif Dimashq governorates.

4. Aleppo remained a particular focus for humanitarians. Early in November, the United Nations developed a four-point plan to provide humanitarian assistance to besieged eastern Aleppo. The plan envisaged: (a) critical medical evacuations; (b) the provision of health and medical supplies; (c) the provision of food and other essential relief items; and (d) the rotation of medical personnel. Notwithstanding tireless efforts by all parties, verbal approval from the Russian Federation and a preliminary written agreement from the non-State armed opposition groups, it was not possible to reach simultaneous agreement with all parties on the implementation of the plan. The Russian Federation and the Government of the Syrian Arab Republic also unilaterally declared a 10-hour cessation of hostilities on 4 November and on 25 November, when crossing points were opened for civilians and fighters from non-State armed opposition groups to evacuate from eastern Aleppo. There were no reports of the crossing points being used during those periods.

5. The need for humanitarian assistance increased during the reporting period, with the last World Food Programme (WFP) food basket (prepositioned before the besiegement of eastern Aleppo in July) being distributed on 13 November. On 15 November, a major offensive was announced by the Russian Federation, resulting in renewed bombing in eastern Aleppo. The ensuing ground and aerial offensive reportedly killed and injured hundreds and displaced an estimated 30,500 people over five days. Some 18,500 people have been displaced to government-controlled areas, 8,000 moved to Kurdish-controlled Shaykh Maqsud and thousands moved to other parts of eastern Aleppo. Reports of the detention of people crossing into government-controlled areas on 28 and 29 November have emerged, and at least 45 civilians, including at least 15 children, were reportedly killed and dozens more injured by shelling on 30 November as they sought to cross into western Aleppo. Fighting continued to escalate throughout November and, by the end of the month, an area representing 40 per cent of besieged eastern Aleppo had been taken by the Government.

6. The situation in western Aleppo also deteriorated throughout the month as shelling increased, with hundreds of mortars killing scores of people. Significant displacement also constituted a major challenge for western Aleppo. The 18,500 newly displaced individuals from the east joined another 24,000 people displaced by the shelling in the west in the final quarter of November. The newly arrived brought the total estimated number of displaced persons in western Aleppo to 400,000 since the beginning of the conflict in 2011, with an estimated 77,000 residing in unfinished buildings or collective shelters.

7. On 22 November, the United Nations resumed life-saving humanitarian assistance at the berm on the Jordanian–Syrian border. Food and essential items were delivered on 22, 23 and 28 November. Following a brief suspension owing to insecurity and crowd control issues, delivery resumed on 30 November. In total, more than 7,000 people in the Rukban community received assistance in preparation for the winter months. The deliveries are being channelled through a newly constructed distribution point. In addition, a new service facility that includes a health clinic, water tanks and a water-pumping station is being constructed.

8. North of Aleppo city, a number of parties to the conflict advanced to within kilometres of the ISIL-controlled city of Bab, with the fighting resulting in further displacement of civilians. From 23 to 25 November, fighting on the outskirts of the city between the Free Syrian Army and ISIL is reported to have displaced an estimated 6,000 people, many of whom moved towards the nearby districts of Manbij and I'zaz. Syrian government forces and Syrian Democratic Forces are also moving closer to the city of Bab, with the possibility of further humanitarian need among the various parties. There are an estimated 150,000 people in Bab district, including 23,000 in the city itself, some 110,000 of whom have been assessed to be in need of humanitarian assistance.

9. Anti-ISIL operations also resumed north of the city of Raqqah on 6 November, resulting in the displacement of thousands. An estimated 5,000 people are currently displaced into territory around Ayn Isa, with the Syrian Democratic Forces having moved to within 20 km of the city of Raqqah. Following the fighting, some 3,000 people were able to return to their homes. There are also unconfirmed reports of people moving within ISIL-controlled areas. There are reportedly serious health and protection concerns for those escaping from ISIL-controlled areas, in particular women and children. More than 400,000 people are estimated to be in need in the city of Raqqah and the surrounding district.

10. After a number of local agreements were reached in October, the parties continued discussions in November with a view to reaching additional agreements. An agreement between the local committee in the besieged location of Khan al-Shih and the Government resulted in the evacuation of some 3,000 people to Idlib on 28 and 30 November. Serious health, protection and food security issues were reported to the United Nations Relief and Works Agency for Palestine Refugees in the Near East (UNRWA), although humanitarian access continued to be denied to the United Nations. According to the Office of the United Nations High Commissioner for Human Rights (OHCHR), the agreement reportedly included the movement of all civilians to hosting centres near Khan al-Shih. Following a resumption of aerial bombardment in Wa'r, a five-day truce was reportedly reached on 29 November. In addition, discussions continued in Qadsayya and Tall.

Protection

11. The protection of civilians has been consistently identified as a significant area of concern in all governorates, with some 13.5 million people in need of protection and assistance. Indiscriminate attacks against civilians and civilian infrastructure, especially against medical personnel and facilities and against schools, educational staff and school children, continued to be reported in November (see paras. 14–16). Threats from explosive ordnance and against women and the most vulnerable civilians, such as children, older persons or persons with disabilities, as well as other violations and human rights abuses, were also reported.

12. On the basis of information received by OHCHR, the killing of civilians and other abuses and violations of international human rights law and international humanitarian law continued throughout the reporting period. Violence occurred in, inter alia, Aleppo, Raqqah, Damascus and Rif Dimashq, Dar'a, Dayr al-Zawr and Idlib governorates (see table 1). OHCHR documented attacks by all parties to the conflict, including government forces, non-State armed opposition groups and designated terrorist groups. In addition to the violations documented by OHCHR, the Government continued to provide OHCHR with information on alleged violations. In a note verbale dated 23 November, the Permanent Mission of the Syrian Arab Republic provided OHCHR with a list of incidents that allegedly occurred in the period from 7 to 20 November in Aleppo, Damascus, Rif Dimashq, Dar'a, Dayr al-Zawr, Hama, Homs and Qunaytirah governorates. A total of 52 civilians were reportedly killed and more than 72, including women and children, were injured. Casualties resulting from mortars, rocket fire, sniper fire and improvised explosive devices were reported.

13. The United States Department of Defense publicly confirmed that in November, the United States-led coalition carried out at least 321 strikes against ISIL targets in Aleppo, Dayr al-Zawr, Hasakah, Homs Idlib and Raqqah governorates. The Ministry of Defence of the Russian Federation reported having conducted military operations in support of the Government of the Syrian Arab Republic, stressing that it had not carried out strikes within 10 km of the city of Aleppo since 18 October.

14. Primary, secondary and tertiary health-care services continued to experience severe gaps in performance and service delivery, owing to the extensive damage caused to health-care facilities, the rapid turnover in health staff and the lack of qualified professionals in specialized medical fields. Paediatric and maternal health-care services, including routine vaccinations, remained negatively affected, especially in Aleppo, Dar'a, Hama and Homs governorates and in the besieged areas of Rif Dimashq governorate.

15. In blatant disregard for the protected status of medical facilities under international humanitarian law, as further articulated by the Security Council in its resolution 2286 (2016), such facilities continued to be damaged or destroyed by fighting. The United Nations and health partners received credible reports of 26 attacks against medical facilities from 1 to 29 November. Hospitals were the most affected: 10 in Aleppo, 2 in Idlib, 1 in Hama and 2 in Rif Dimashq. Two primary health-care centres in Homs, a health-care centre in eastern Aleppo and an ambulatory service in western Aleppo were also struck. In addition, a medical warehouse in eastern Aleppo and three ambulances in eastern Ghutah, Hama and Kafr Batna were struck. The attacks resulted in multiple civilian casualties, including the deaths of at least 5 health workers and the injury of 15 health workers.

16. Educational facilities continued to be the subject of a number of attacks, with four verified attacks reported by the United Nations during the reporting period. . . .

17. On 22 November, a Kurdish journalist was reportedly abducted and beaten by members of Yekîneyên Parastina Gel (YPG) military intelligence in Hasakah city. The victim managed to escape from the abductors while they were arguing and reached the nearby village of Khama'a.

Humanitarian access

18. The delivery of humanitarian assistance to people in need of assistance in the Syrian Arab Republic remained extremely challenging in many areas of the country as a result of active conflict, shifting conflict lines and deliberate restrictions on the movement of people and goods by the parties to the conflict.

19. Access to the millions of people living in besieged and hard-to-reach locations remained of critical concern. Throughout November, as a result of delays in the issuance of facilitation letters, requirements for additional security approvals above and beyond the two steps agreed with the Government in April, a lack of adherence to agreed protocols at checkpoints and insecurity, only four inter-agency convoys reached a total of 167,500 people in five besieged and hard-to-reach locations (see table 5). This total constitutes about 19 per cent of the total of 904,500 people to whom access had been requested under the plan. In addition, the United Nations provided assistance to some of these areas through single-agency convoys. Moreover, non-governmental organizations continued to provide medical, educational and protection services, as well as some support in other sectors, in hard-to-reach locations, under extremely challenging circumstances.

20. Six inter-agency convoys could not proceed in November, despite having prior approval from the Syrian authorities. These include Wadi Barada on 9 November, Duma on 17 November, Rastan on 20 November and Madaya, Zabadani and Fu'ah/Kafraya on 27 November. For example, on 17 November, a convoy for 70,000 people to Duma, Rif Dimashq governorate, was aborted owing to the absence of approval at the last government checkpoint to proceed without dog searches and the unsealing of the trucks. The convoy had originally been planned for 15 November, but loading could not begin owing to the lack of the requisite facilitation letters from the Government. On 9 November, a convoy to the Wadi Barada area of Rif Dimashq governorate for 30,000 people was aborted after being unable to proceed past a government checkpoint. Convoys to other locations were held up for various reasons, including insecurity, lack of agreement on the routes to be taken or the estimates of the number of people in need and a lack of final green lights from the relevant authorities. In Madaya, two people died owing t o a lack of available medical care.

21. Deliberate interference and restrictions by the parties to the conflict continued to hamper aid delivery. WFP continues to be unable to gain access to populations in need in ISIL-controlled areas of the country, given that all plans to deliver assistance to those areas have been suspended because of the inability to work independently and monitor activities. This is preventing WFP from reaching Raqqah governorate and most of Dayr al-Zawr governorate, as well as pockets of northern rural Aleppo governorate, southern

rural Hasakah governorate and north-western rural Hama governorate. Meanwhile, in Hasakah governorate, WFP continued to face difficulties in obtaining dispatch approvals for some of the partners, which delayed the implementation of planned activities. Negotiations are ongoing with the relevant counterparts to overcome the remaining bottlenecks. Meanwhile, owing to security concerns on the ground, UNRWA has been unable to return to Yalda/Yarmouk since 25 May 2016.

22. The removal of life-saving medicines and medical supplies from humanitarian aid convoys continued throughout November. Life-saving and life-sustaining medical items sufficient for 22,284 treatments were removed from an inter-agency convoy to Rastan and a single-agency World Health Organization (WHO) convoy to Qadsayya. The treatments and supplies removed from convoys in November are shown in table 3. In addition, four inter-agency convoys could not proceed in November, preventing some 120,000 medical treatments from being delivered as planned. In addition, approval for 29 requests by WHO to deliver health supplies remains pending.

23. Under the United Nations inter-agency convoy plan for November, access was requested to 25 locations, including all besieged locations, with the aim of reaching 904,500 people. In its response on 27 October, the Syrian authorities approved access to 623,000 of the requested beneficiaries (68.9 per cent). A total of 281,500 beneficiaries (31.1 per cent) requested under the plan were rejected or not included in the approved number of beneficiaries. The authorities also requested that 20 other locations should be reached in November outside the plan.

24. On 17 November, the United Nations submitted to the Ministry of Foreign Affairs the inter-agency convoy plan for December, which comprised 21 requests to reach 930,250 people in need in besieged, hard-to-reach and priority cross-line areas. A response was expected by 29 November, in line with the agreed two-step approval procedures, but was received on 1 December. All requested locations were either fully or partially approved. In total, 798,200 of the 930,250 requested beneficiaries (85.8 per cent) were approved, while 132,050 beneficiaries (14.2 per cent) were not included in the approved number of beneficiaries. Of the 28 requested locations, 13 were approved in full (46.4 per cent) and 15 were approved with a lower number of beneficiaries (53.6 per cent). The authorities also requested that 38 other locations should be reached in December outside the plan.

25. The Nusaybin/Qamishli crossing in Hasakah governorate has been temporarily closed by the Turkish authorities because of security concerns since 27 December 2015. The governorate also remains largely inaccessible by road for United Nations agencies from within the Syrian Arab Republic owing to insecurity and the presence of ISIL members along the routes. The United Nations continues airlifts from Damascus to Qamishli airport to deliver multisectoral assistance, with some 190,000 people having been reached in November.

Humanitarian response

26. In November, United Nations humanitarian agencies and partners continued to reach millions of people in need through all modalities from within the Syrian Arab Republic and across borders (see table 4). In addition to the United Nations and its partners, non-governmental organizations continued to deliver valuable assistance to people in need in line with previous months. The Government continued to provide basic services to those areas under its control and in many areas beyond its control.

27. Cross-border deliveries continued from Turkey and Jordan into the Syrian Arab Republic under the terms of resolutions 2165 (2014), 2191 (2014) and 2258 (2015) (see fig. III). In line with those resolutions, the United Nations notified the Syrian authorities in advance of each shipment, including its content, destination and number of beneficiaries. The United Nations Monitoring Mechanism for the Syrian Arab Republic continued its operations, monitoring 643 trucks used in 24 convoys in November, confirming the humanitarian nature of each and notifying the Syrian authorities after each shipment. The Mechanism continued to benefit from excellent cooperation with the Governments of Jordan and Turkey.

28. The inter-agency convoys to the besieged and hard-to-reach locations listed in table 5 were completed in November. Moreover, between 10 April and the end of November, the United Nations completed 156 airdrops of food commodities and humanitarian assistance over the city of Dayr al-Zawr. In addition, the logistics cluster continued airlifts to Qamishli from Damascus, with more than 194 airlift rotations having been completed between 9 July and the end of November. During the reporting period, United Nations agencies also undertook single-agency deliveries to cross-line and hard-to-reach locations or reached those locations through their regular programmes.

29. In November, a polio immunization and multi-antigen campaign was conducted from within the Syrian Arab Republic in all governorates. The campaign targeted 977,853 children under 5 years of five, mainly in hard-to-reach and besieged areas. The besieged areas of Fu'ah, Kafraya, Madaya, Mu'addamiyah al-Sham and the Yarmouk camp were reached with vaccines. Both Idlib and Raqqah (except Tall Abyad in Raqqah) could not be reached owing to the refusal of the local authorities. In addition, parts of Aleppo, Qunaytirah and Rif Damashq, governorates could not be reached because of the security situation. Overall results from the campaign are still pending. Separately, some 350,000 children were vaccinated through cross-border operations in November 2016. The antigens used were bivalent oral polio, pentavalent and measles and rubella vaccines. For the cross-border component, parts of Aleppo, Dayr al-Zawr and Raqqah governorates could not be reached owing to insecurity and fighting, affecting the vaccination of some 780,000 children in total. . . .

Safety and security of humanitarian personnel and premises

33. On 13 November, UNRWA tragically lost its seventeenth staff member as a result of the conflict since 2012. Reports indicate that, along with the UNRWA staff

member, two people were killed in the same air strike, which struck a mosque during morning prayers in the Khan al-Shih Palestine refugee camp.

34. On 17 November, intense shelling continued to strike the Khan al-Shih camp. Beira school, an UNRWA school within the premises of the camp, sustained major damage as a result. The school was empty, however, and no casualties were reported.

35. A total of 27 United Nations staff members, 26 of whom are UNRWA staff and 1 of whom is from the United Nations Development Programme, are still detained or missing. Since the beginning of the conflict, dozens of humanitarian workers have been killed, including 20 staff members of the United Nations, 54 staff members and volunteers of the Syrian Arab Red Crescent and 8 staff members and volunteers of the Palestine Red Crescent Society. In addition, many staff members of international and national non-governmental organizations are reported to have been killed

III. Observations

36. The humanitarian situation continues to deteriorate throughout the Syrian Arab Republic. The continuing conflict poses an immediate threat to millions of civilians every day, especially those under attack and those who cannot be reached. As I have previously stated, the conflict has also created a longer-term crisis, given that the bombing of schools, hospitals and other civilian installations by all parties to the conflict will continue to have a negative impact on the population for years to come. These developments are unfolding while the world watches, seemingly helpless to staunch the suffering. I call upon all parties to the conflict to consider where this will lead, as the deepening humanitarian tragedy only pushes the political solution that all have agreed is necessary further out of reach.

37. November witnessed an undeniable military acceleration and, in parallel, a serious deterioration of security for civilians. Nationwide, the Government of the Syrian Arab Republic has gained momentum as it seeks to retake areas, either through military force, as has been the case in eastern Aleppo, or through local agreements with communities, especially in Rif Damashq governorate. The humanitarian impact of such developments has been well documented. It is important, however, that military gains not be mistaken for the attainment of a so-called military solution. In no way will gains on the battlefield obviate the need for an inclusive and negotiated political settlement to the crisis in the Syrian Arab Republic. The only sustainable gains are those that are achieved through a settlement that addresses the legitimate grievances of the population.

38. It is for this reason that I continue to express my firm belief that there is no alternative to political accommodation between the parties to the conflict. Without such steps, tragedy will continue to prevail in the Syrian Arab Republic, with human, political, economic and social consequences in the country and beyond for generations to come. I and my Special Envoy will continue to engage with those actors with influence on the Syrian parties until the very last day of my

tenure as Secretary-General in order to alleviate the suffering and seek an end to the conflict. Although the unfortunate reality may be that a resolution to the Syrian conflict may not occur before I leave office, the groundwork for a political solution has long been laid. It is now up to the parties to the conflict, the Member States that support them and the Security Council to take the appropriate steps necessary to finally end the suffering of the Syrian people.

[The Annex has been omitted.]

SOURCE: United Nations Security Council. "Implementation of Security Council resolutions 2139 (2014), 2165 (2014), 2191 (2014) and 2258 (2015)." December 14, 2016. http://www.securitycouncilreport.org/atf/cf/%7B65BFCF9B-6D27-4E9C-8CD3-CF6E4FF96FF9%7D/s_2016_1057.pdf.

Russian Foreign Minister Remarks at Joint News Conference with Turkish and Iranian Foreign Ministers

December 20, 2016

Ladies and gentlemen,

We have just finished our meeting of the foreign ministers of Russia, Iran and Turkey. In parallel, contacts between our defence ministers took place in different formats in Moscow. The developments in Syria were the focus.

We all agree that it is necessary to fully respect Syria's sovereignty, territorial integrity and unity, and that there is no military solution to the Syrian crisis. We believe there is no alternative to a political and diplomatic settlement of this conflict. Needless to say, the main task is to stop the suffering of completely innocent people, resolve humanitarian issues and wage a relentless fight against terrorism.

We have coordinated a joint statement of the ministers of foreign affairs of the Islamic Republic of Iran, the Russian Federation and the Republic of Turkey on agreed upon measures to step up the political process with a view to ending the Syrian conflict. As I have already said, this is a joint statement of three foreign ministers, but the defence ministers who held parallel meetings also made their contribution. The statement reaffirms our respect for the sovereignty, independence, unity and territorial integrity of the Syrian Arab Republic as a multiethnic, multi-religious, democratic and secular state.

Iran, Russia and Turkey are convinced that there is no military solution to the Syrian conflict. They recognise the important role of the UN in the efforts to resolve this crisis in line with UN Security Council Resolution 2254.

The ministers also take note of the decisions of the International Syria Support Group (ISSG). They are urging all members of the international community to maintain good-faith cooperation in order to remove obstacles in the way of implementing the agreements contained in the aforementioned documents.

Iran, Russia and Turkey welcome the joint efforts in east Aleppo on the voluntary evacuation of civilians and organised withdrawal of the armed opposition. The ministers also welcome the partial evacuation of civilians from Al-Fu'ah, Kafrai, Al-Zabadani and Madaya. They are committed to ensuring the continuous, safe and reliable completion of this process.

The ministers agree on the importance of extending the ceasefire, unhindered access to humanitarian aid, and civilians' free travel in Syria. Iran, Russia and Turkey are ready to help forge the agreement that is the subject of talks between the Syrian Government and the opposition. They are willing to act as its guarantors. They have called on all the countries that have influence on the ground to do the same.

Our nations are profoundly confident that this agreement will give the necessary impetus to resume the political process in Syria in compliance with UN Security Council Resolution 2254—I mean the agreement which the Syrian Government and the opposition are working toward.

The ministers have taken into consideration the Kazakhstani President's kind invitation to meet for the talks in Astana.

In conclusion, Iran, Russia and Turkey confirm their resolve to fight ISIS and Jabhat al-Nusra together, and draw a line between them and the armed opposition groups.

We are satisfied with the results achieved. We are confident that, while implementation of the UNSC resolutions is at a standstill, the initiative taken by our three countries can help to overcome the stagnation in efforts to achieve a settlement in Syria on the basis of these resolutions and advance efforts to put an end to the violence, deliver humanitarian aid and provide conditions for an effective and inclusive political process.

I heartily thank my colleagues. We did good and very useful work together. We have agreed to structure our further interaction around the joint statement approved today.

Question: There are several parallel formats for Syria talks—Russia-Iran-Turkey, Russia-USA, and the Geneva consultations under UN aegis. . . . Which format of talks do you find the most effective and how do they compare?

Sergey Lavrov: I think the format you see now is the most effective. Not that I mean to tarnish the efforts of all our other partners as we seek progress toward a settlement in Syria. I am merely stating a fact. Today, the trilateral format of Iran-Russia-Turkey has proved that there is a need for it with practical efforts. . . .

All those present here have tried to work in broader formats on a collective basis. However, the disastrous situation in eastern Aleppo, the plight of the people in that part of the city and the need to minimise possible casualties, losses, as well as the need to reduce the number of militants, did not allow us to adopt a wait and see position. Over the past few days, our capitals have been actively considering the possibility of using the levers that each of our countries has to influence the opposing sides in Syria to resolve the crisis in eastern Aleppo. These intensive discussions have led to this meeting and the adoption of the document that will be distributed today.

At the same time we were not simply preparing to adopt the document. In reality, in practice, over the past several days and weeks we coordinated measures that made it possible to evacuate the greater part of civilians from eastern Aleppo problem-free with help from the International Red Cross Committee and WHO officers. Our agreements on precisely how to influence the opposing sides played their role here. Apart from the evacuation of civilians, our cooperation has ensured the orderly withdrawal from eastern Aleppo of most groups of armed opposition fighters along coordinated directions to coordinated areas. The evacuation is now in its final stages and we hope it will be completed in one or two days at the most.

Among other things, this shows the effectiveness of the format involving states that at present are probably better prepared than others to contribute to the settlement of the Syria crisis with real actions, not just words. As you will be able to see from our joint statement, we will continue this cooperation. We are not closing ourselves off from contact with all other countries, but on the contrary, are inviting them to join the processes that, in our view, have positive potential and that we recorded today in our joint agreement.

Question (addressed to all three ministers): One of the most important issues is the termination of outside support to terrorist groups. Did today's meeting focus on this issue? . . .

Sergey Lavrov (speaking last): For my part, I will point out that the fight against terrorism does not abide double standards. This is clearly stated in UN Security Council resolutions. This fight should be conducted relentlessly without any ambiguous action. To reiterate, the principle that there can be no dealings with terrorists is enshrined in UN Security Council resolutions, in particular Resolution 2254. . . .

An analysis of the situation shows that no country can, in one way or another, be involved in the Syria conflict or in the efforts to resolve it and fence itself off completely from the terrorist threat. Recently, all countries present here, other Syrian neighbours, European states and the US have suffered terrorist attacks, primarily on the part of ISIS, as well as Jabhat al-Nusra. . . .

Today, Jabhat al-Nusra, a branch of Al Qaeda, is a generally recognised terrorist organisation that has been put on corresponding lists by the UN, Russia, the US and many other countries and, together with ISIS, has been outlawed. All the efforts that we are taking to resolve the Syria crisis, ensure the cessation of hostilities and extend the ceasefire across Syria's entire territory absolutely exclude Jabhat al-Nusra, ISIS and affiliated groups from these arrangements. This is the decision of the UN Security Council and this is what we should be guided by.

Question (addressed to all three ministers): Will Turkey stop Operation Euphrates Shield in Syria, against which the Syrian government has protested? Were you able to overcome major differences in your countries' positions on Syria?

Sergey Lavrov (speaking last): The situation in Syria is tremendously complicated. There are many religious, ethnic and political groups that are joining forces or fighting each other there. Plus there is the overall crisis in relations between Sunni and Shia Muslims. Besides, Syria has been at the crossroads of many countries' interests for ages, both neighbouring countries and those that do not border Syria. All these states have their own interests in Syria, such as compatriot support, security interests and many other issues. When a crisis developed as part of the so-called Arab Spring, many external parties attempted to use it to their own advantage and in their own interests. As you remember, some countries declared the goal of changing the government in Syria.

But gradually, as many colleagues have told me, they came to see the threat of terrorism, the threat of ISIS seizing this ancient country that is so important for the Middle East, and this awareness dominated their thoughts about what they should do in Syria. They are coming to see that the top priority should not be government change but the liquidation of the terrorist threat. The three countries that are represented here share this understanding. We have a common stand on this issue.

As for the groups and countries that are present in Syria, there are those that have been invited by the Syrian government, UN member states, and those who entered Syria without an invitation. As I said, the objective of our presence there is to fight terrorism. This is the objective of the US-led coalition and Turkey's Operation Euphrates Shield. All those who are in Syria by invitation and without it have reaffirmed their respect for Syria's sovereignty, territorial integrity, unity and independence.

We are convinced that by enhancing our coordination . . . we will be able to more consistently and effectively focus our attention on ISIS, Jabhat al-Nusra and associated groups. I am convinced that as we increase our achievements in the fight against terrorism and help Syrians launch a political process, we will be able to formulate common approaches, which will clearly rely on our proclaimed goals—to defeat terrorism and restore Syria's territorial integrity, sovereignty, independence and unity. We are united on this. All this has been sealed in our joint statement. We will work to achieve the objectives set out in this statement.

Source: Ministry of Foreign Affairs of the Russian Federation. "Foreign Minister Sergey Lavrov's remarks and answers to media questions at a joint news conference following trilateral talks with Iranian Foreign Minister Mohammad Javad Zarif and Turkish Foreign Minister Mevlut Cavusoglu, Moscow, December 20, 2016." December 20, 2016. http://www.mid.ru/en/foreign_policy/news/-/asset_publisher/cKNonkJE02Bw/content/id/2574870.

Turkey Announces Ceasefire Agreement

December 29, 2016

Turkey has been undertaking intensive efforts to end the violence and begin the flow of humanitarian aid in Syria and for the resumption of talks between the regime and the opposition for a comprehensive political solution of the Syrian conflict.

As a result of our efforts, the warring parties in Syria reached an understanding on a country-wide ceasefire that will go into effect at 00:00, on December 30, 2016. We welcome this development.

Terrorist organizations designated by the UN Security Council as such are excluded from this ceasefire.

Turkey and the Russian Federation support this understanding as guarantors.

The parties, with this understanding, committed to cease all armed, including aerial, attacks and refrain from expanding the territories under their control at the expense of one another.

Adherence of all parties to this ceasefire is crucial. Turkey and Russia strongly support and will jointly monitor the ceasefire.

The support of the countries with influence on parties on the ground, in sustaining the ceasefire will also be vital.

Turkey played the decisive role in completion of humanitarian evacuations in Aleppo a few days ago and in ensuring the entry of force of the country-wide ceasefire as of tomorrow.

Hopeful that, with full observance of the ceasefire, to realize a genuine political transition based on the Geneva Communique and the UNSCR 2254, the regime and the opposition will soon meet in Astana with the presence of the guarantor countries, to take concrete steps towards revitalizing the UN-led political process, Turkey will continue her efforts to that end incessantly.

SOURCE: Turkish Ministry of Foreign Affairs. "No: 333, 29 December 2016, Press Release Regarding the Announcement of Country-wide Ceasefire Between the Warring Parties in Syria." December 29, 2016. http://www.mfa.gov.tr/no_-333_-29-december-2016_-press-release-regarding-the-announcement-of-country_wide-ceasefire-between-the-conflicting_warring-parties-in-syria.en.mfa.

OTHER HISTORIC DOCUMENTS OF INTEREST

FROM THIS VOLUME

FROM PREVIOUS *HISTORIC DOCUMENTS*

Colombian President Awarded
Nobel Peace Prize

DECEMBER 10, 2016

The Nobel Peace Prize has been awarded ninety-seven times to 130 laureates since 1901. In his will establishing the prize, Alfred Nobel outlined three types of peace work that could qualify for the award: contributions to fraternity between nations, to the abolition or reduction of standing armies, or to the holding and promotion of peace congresses. On December 10, 2016, Colombian President Juan Manuel Santos accepted the Nobel Peace Prize for his work negotiating a peace agreement with the Revolutionary Armed Forces of Colombia (FARC) that had for half a century been engaged in a deadly war with the government. The announcement of the award in October came less than one week after Colombian voters rejected the deal that would have put an end to a fifty-year civil war and was met with mixed reactions. Some argued that the prize should have been awarded to those engaged in civilian rescue operations in Syria or those responding to the refugee crisis in Europe. However, many agreed, and the Nobel Committee ultimately confirmed, that the prize was awarded in an effort to encourage further negotiations between the Colombian government and FARC guerilla group.

Historic Number of Nominations

The Norwegian Nobel Committee keeps secret the names of those who are nominated for the annual Peace Prize for fifty years, but it did release that it received a record 376 nominations in 2016, of which 228 were for individuals and 148 for organizations. Speculation about who may have been nominated for the award is typically driven by two sources. At times, nominating organizations will announce that they have submitted a nomination, but more often, speculation is based on bookmaker's odds. In 2016, the most likely potential victors included a group of Greek islanders who aided refugees received on the island of Lesbos, German chancellor Angela Merkel, and Pope Francis. Denis Mukwege, a name that has been raised as a possible awardee for a number of years, was also thought to be a contender in 2016 for his work as a gynecologist in the Congo helping those recovering from sexual violence. A group widely believed to receive the award was the Syrian Civil Defense, known alternately as the White Helmets for the headgear they wear, a volunteer organization that has helped rescue and care for Syrians in need during the nation's long-running civil war.

Although Santos and FARC leader Rodrigo Londoño Echeverri were considered possible contenders for their brokering of an historic peace deal, they were not among the frontrunners in media speculation. Ultimately, on October 7, 2016, Kaci Kullman Five, the chair of the Nobel Committee, announced that Santos would be the sole recipient of the award "for resolute efforts to bring the country's more than 50-year-long civil war to an end, a war that has cost the lives of at least 220,000 Colombians and displaced close to six million people." Kullman added, "The award should also be seen as a tribute to the Colombian people who, despite great hardships and abuses, have not given up hope of a just peace, and to all parties who have contributed to the peace process."

COLOMBIAN PEACE DEAL

The peace deal for which Santos was awarded was built on years of attempts made by previous governments to engage and disarm the FARC rebels. Prior to the 2016 peace deal, three separate efforts were made to encourage the guerilla group to lay down its arms, most recently in 1998 and 2002, but all failed. Under President Santos, exploratory peace talks began in 2011, and were followed by formal negotiations that started in October 2012. Over the course of four years, the two sides conducted thirty rounds of talks before reaching a final agreement on August 24, 2016.

Under the agreement, the FARC agreed to abandon its camps for specific areas set up around the country and was also required, within six months of the agreement going into effect, to surrender its weapons to United Nations arms inspectors. The FARC was also invited to become a national political party and would be guaranteed a minimum of five seats in the nation's Congress. Those FARC fighters accused and convicted of low-level crimes would be given immunity from punishment, so long as they agreed not to reoffend; those convicted of war crimes, crimes against humanity, genocide, or other serious offenses would still be sentenced. Furthermore, reparations would be provided to the victims of FARC-led violence. A ceasefire went into effect five days after the agreement was reached.

The agreement was officially signed on September 26, and, as promised by Santos, was presented as a referendum to the voters on October 1. Although polling data suggested otherwise, the referendum failed by a narrow margin—50.2 percent to 49.8 percent. The opposition to the agreement was led by Santos's predecessor, Álvaro Uribe, who believed that FARC fighters should face greater consequences for any crimes committed.

SANTOS LEARNS OF PRIZE, CONTINUES EFFORTS TOWARD PEACE

When announcing the award, Five addressed concerns that the peace deal had been rejected, but argued that it was due to the specifics outlined in the document, not an overall disagreement with the necessity for peace. "The committee hopes that the peace prize will give [Santos] strength to succeed in this demanding task. Further, it is the committee's hope that in the years to come, the Colombian people will reap the fruits of the reconciliation process." She added that the negotiations that had already taken place "brought the bloody conflict significantly closer to a peaceful solution" and that "the president's endeavours to promote peace demonstrate the spirit of Alfred Nobel's will." The committee was also questioned about why the award was not also given to Londoño, but Five said she would not comment on those who did not win the award, but noted that Santos was the "keeper of the project."

Santos was unaware of the award for many hours, due to the time difference between Colombia and Norway, and his guards reportedly refused to wake him when news of the award broke. When he heard of the announcement, the president said he accepted "not on my behalf but on behalf of all Colombians, especially the millions of victims of this conflict which we have suffered for more than 50 years." Santos called on those across the country to come together to instill a lasting peace and finalize a revised peace agreement. "I receive this recognition with great humility and as a mandate to continue to work without rest for peace for all Colombians. I will dedicate all my efforts to this cause for the rest of my days," Santos said. Londoño responded to the award on Twitter, saying, "The only award we want is peace with social justice for Colombia without paramilitarism, without retaliation or lies."

Santos and Londoño quickly resumed their work on a new peace deal, inviting into the negotiations those who had rejected the initial version, which they signed on November 24. The new agreement, which did not require the approval of the voters but only needed to pass the nation's Congress, was meant to appease opponents who felt that the FARC was afforded too many concessions. More than fifty changes were made to the original agreement, including a requirement that the FARC declare and hand over all assets, which would then be used to compensate victims, changes that would allow more FARC fighters to face criminal prosecution, and a ban on FARC members running for office in former conflict zones. Colombia's Congress approved the new agreement on November 30, and will be required to approve various pieces of legislation to fully implement the agreement.

Five and Santos Speak on Successful Negotiations

In presenting the award to Santos, Five again addressed the criticism surrounding the timing of the award. "Many observers felt that it would be premature to award you the Nobel Peace Prize this year," she said. "They recommended that the Norwegian Nobel Committee wait another year to see whether the peace process would eventually succeed in bringing about true peace." According to Five, the Committee felt that by awarding Santos in 2016, it would reinvigorate the work toward peace and give critical international backing to the plan. "Developments in the weeks since the announcement of this year's Peace Prize have in no way weakened our conviction in this respect," Five said.

Five found three key principles in Colombia's work toward securing a peace deal not only helped the government and the FARC overcome the referendum results, but could also be replicated by other nations seeking peace. First, Five said, was the willingness of the government to "face up to unpleasant, painful facts in order to lay the foundation for national reconciliation." This included the establishment of a National Center of Historic Memory meant to collect and document the atrocities of the fifty-year war. Second, throughout the various meetings and discussions held about the peace deal, the government invited victims of the FARC's actions to share their stories, and the FARC representatives agreed to listen. This was in part inspired by the reconciliation process in South Africa following the apartheid, and Five commended Londoño "for so clearly, and unreservedly, expressing regret for the suffering that the FARC has inflicted on the civilian population and asking the Colombian people for forgiveness." Finally, Five spoke about the willingness of both the government and the FARC to invite into the discussion critics of the ongoing process, something she noted was of utmost importance after the referendum was rejected by voters.

Before turning to Santos, Five reminded the audience that the work in Colombia was not yet done, but that it was the hope of the Committee that this award would provide the momentum to continue moving forward. "The more than 50-year armed conflict in Colombia is complex, and the country faces a magnitude of problems that must be solved. This will take time, making it even more important to get to work quickly," she said.

In his award lecture, Santos said that reaching a peace agreement, for many in Colombia, "seemed an impossible dream—and for good reason. Very few of us—hardly anybody—could recall a memory of a country at peace." Santos spoke at the outset about the "completely unexpected" outcome of the public referendum on the peace agreement and said it helped him recommit himself to understanding why citizens opposed the agreement and what changes would help reach a consensus moving forward. He added that word of the Nobel Peace Prize came at an important moment. "I must confess to you that this news came as if it were a gift from heaven. At a time when our ship felt adrift, the Nobel Prize was the tailwind that helped us to reach our destination: the port of peace!"

Santos devoted the bulk of his lecture to not only thanking the Colombian and international partners who helped secure the peace agreement, but also to how dialogue among warring factions can be used around the world. "We can now ask the bold question: if war can come to an end in one hemisphere, why not one day in both hemispheres? Perhaps more than ever before, we can now dare to imagine a world without war," Santos said. Santos spoke about the necessity of asking for forgiveness when attempting to instill a lasting peace, studying failure in other peace processes, having the courage to make unpopular decisions when you believe they are for the best of the nation, and listening to those around you with whom you may not agree. "In my case," Santos said, "this meant reaching out to the governments of neighbouring countries with whom I had and continue to have deep ideological differences."

OTHER NOBEL AWARDEES

The Nobel Prize is given out in four other categories: Physiology or Medicine, Physics, Chemistry, and Literature. A separate prize was established by Sweden's central bank in 1968 to recognize achievements in Economic Sciences. In the Literature category, American songwriter Bob Dylan was awarded "for having created new poetic expressions within the great American song tradition." Yoshinori Ohsumi, a Japanese scientist, was presented the award for Physiology or Medicine for identifying cell processes in the 1990s that led to greater understanding of how cells recycle their components, which was key in understanding mutations that cause certain diseases. In the physics category, one half of the prize was awarded to David J. Thouless, while F. Duncan M. Haldane and J. Michael Kosterlitz jointly shared the other half for their study of states of matter, while Jean-Pierre Sauvage, Sir J. Fraser Stoddart, and Bernard L. Feringa were named chemistry laureates "for the design and synthesis of molecular machines."

—Heather Kerrigan

Following is the text of a speech delivered by Norwegian Nobel Committee chair Kaci Kullman Five on December 10, 2016, awarding the 2016 Nobel Peace Prize to Colombian President Juan Manuel Santos; and the Nobel Peace Prize acceptance speech delivered on December 10, 2016, by President Santos.

Nobel Committee Awards 2016
Peace Prize

DOCUMENT

December 10, 2016

Your Majesties, Your Royal Highnesses, Mr. President, Your Excellencies, Distinguished Guests, Ladies and Gentlemen,

The Norwegian Nobel Committee has decided to award the Nobel Peace Prize for 2016 to Colombia's President Juan Manuel Santos for his resolute and courageous efforts to bring to an end the country's more than 50-year-long civil war. The award has been made to President Santos alone. But it is also intended as a tribute to the Colombian people—a people who despite great hardships and countless injustices have never given up hope of a just peace. Many groups and individuals have contributed to the peace process and deserve our thanks and tribute today, including tireless negotiators, facilitators, diplomats, politicians and, of course, leaders from the government and the FARC guerrillas. Our tribute is paid, not least, to the representatives of the civil war's victims, several of whom are present here today. They carry their own painful stories, yet manage to represent other victims as well. We salute all these strong, fearless individuals, and offer them our respectful gratitude.

The armed conflict between the Colombian authorities, the FARC and ELN revolutionary guerrilla groups and various paramilitary groups is the longest civil war in our time. The human and material cost of the conflict is almost inconceivable and very difficult to measure. Numbers give only a vague, albeit horrifying, impression of the extent of the suffering and the war's impact on daily life for several generations of Colombians.

Since the first military confrontations in May 1964 and until the mutual ceasefire entered into force this summer, more than 222 000 Colombians have lost their lives as a direct consequence of the conflict. Four of every five persons killed were civilian non-combatants. In addition, somewhere between five and seven million Colombians were forced to flee their homes. Many have lived ever since as displaced persons in their own country.

In 2013, an investigative report was presented by the Colombian National Center for Historical Memory. The report shows that nearly 2 000 massacres of civilians have taken place in Colombia since the early 1980s. Allegedly, more than 1 000 of these mass killings were carried out by paramilitary groups who fought the rebels, almost 350 by FARC or ELN guerrillas, and close to 300 by Colombian security forces. The rebel guerrillas, for their part, were responsible for a majority of the many kidnappings that terrorised the Colombian people from 1995 to 2005. In that decade an average of one kidnapping took place every eight hours. The guerrillas used the kidnappings and the ever-expanding drug trade to finance their warfare. Colombia has long been the world's biggest producer of cocaine. The social and health effects of drug trafficking is a tragedy in its own right, with consequences far beyond Colombia's borders.

Now, at last, it looks as though this terrible conflict will soon be history.

Mr. President, you initiated the negotiations that culminated in the peace accord between the Colombian government and the FARC guerrillas earlier this autumn. This was an initiative that required considerable political courage and great perseverance. The initiative was grounded in a conviction that negotiations were the only path to creating a better future for your people. After a narrow majority of voters opposed the accord in the referendum held on 2 October, you made it clear that you would in no way give up, but would pursue your efforts to end the civil war with undiminished vigour. Like many others, you realised that the Colombian people had not voted "No" to peace, but to the accord submitted to them. In this critical situation, you issued an invitation to participate in a broad-based national dialogue with a view to reaching an agreement that could also win the support of its critics. The accord has now been renegotiated. While the second agreement has also been subject to criticism, several contentious points in the first accord have been amended and the groundwork has been laid for a historic national compromise. You have been a driving force throughout this peace process.

Mr. President, when the referendum results were announced, many observers felt that it would be premature to award you the Nobel Peace Prize this year. They recommended that the Norwegian Nobel Committee wait another year to see whether the peace process would eventually succeed in bringing about true peace. The Committee, however, saw things differently. In our view, there was no time to lose. On the contrary, the peace process was in danger of collapsing and needed all the international support it could get. Moreover, we were deeply convinced that you Mr. President, as Colombia's head of state, were the one to continue to move the peace process forward. Developments in the weeks since the announcement of this year's Peace Prize have in no way weakened our conviction in this respect.

In awarding the Nobel Peace Prize for 2016 to President Juan Manuel Santos the Norwegian Nobel Committee sought to encourage him and all those working to achieve peace, reconciliation and justice in Colombia not to give up. Political compromises seldom strike a perfect balance. Peace accords are especially hard to balance. Nonetheless, it is our sincere hope that the renegotiated accord that has now been signed by the parties and ratified by the Congress is a solution that can ensure the Colombian people peace and positive development.

Mr. President, after the referendum you emphasised that you would continue to work for peace until your very last day in office, "because that's the way to leave a better country to our children". Children under the age of 15 account for 23 per cent of Colombia's population, or more than 11 million people. Kindling a spark of hope in the eyes of these 11 million children and their loved ones is the best possible investment towards a peaceful future for your people.

Ladies and gentlemen, the history of the Nobel Peace Prize shows that there are many roads to peace. By awarding this year's Peace Prize to President Juan Manuel Santos, the Norwegian Nobel Committee wishes to honour him and all those who have helped stake out what can be called the Colombian road to peace.

This road has three distinctive features that can serve to inspire similar processes in other countries.

One is the will to face up to unpleasant, painful facts in order to lay the foundation for national reconciliation. For too long, victims' memories of abuses, killings and other crimes were either a taboo—or a source of continuing conflict and enmity between the parties. The population's growing desire for peace could never have been satisfied without breaking this vicious cycle. Two important steps in the right direction were taken with the establishment of Colombia's National Center of Historical Memory and the publication in 2013 of the centre's investigative report "Basta Ya!"—"Enough Already!"—which documented in detail the magnitude of the civil war's atrocities.

When you, Mr President, was presented with the report, you stated that it represented "a first window towards the truth that we owe to the victims of this country".

The second distinctive feature of the Colombian road to peace is the participation of the victims and their representatives. The negotiations between the government and the FARC were ground-breaking because they gave the victims' representatives the opportunity to testify about their dreadful experiences in the presence of the parties concerned—and to confront perpetrators on all sides of the conflict. Inspired in part by South Africa's peace and reconciliation process, the parties have recognised that a lasting peace arrangement must safeguard the rights and dignity of the victims while ensuring that the truth becomes known and that the perpetrators are held accountable and admit their guilt.

In this connection, I wish to commend FARC guerrilla leader Rodrigo Londoño for so clearly, and unreservedly, expressing regret for the suffering that the FARC has inflicted on the civilian population and asking the Colombian people for forgiveness. This is an example to be followed.

The third distinctive feature of this peace process is the fact that the parties have engaged critics of the process by inviting them to join in a broad-based national dialogue. This was particularly the case after the referendum, when President Santos reached out to those who had voted "No". Simultaneously, the leader of the FARC gave assurance that the organisation would continue negotiating and "use only words as weapons to build towards the future".

I venture to believe that this means the national reconciliation process is already well underway. There is still, however, a long way to go. After more than 50 years of bitter conflict, true reconciliation does not happen overnight. Overcoming deep-seated distrust and a sense of exclusion is a huge task. We therefore encourage all sides in Colombia to carry on the national dialogue and continue on the road to reconciliation.

Ladies and gentlemen, Alfred Nobel's will refers to three different types of peace work that qualify for the Nobel Peace Prize: contributions to fraternity between nations, to the abolition or reduction of standing armies, or to the holding and promotion of peace congresses. All these forms of peace work are represented in this year's Peace Prize.

The peace process has already helped to foster fraternity between different parts of the population in Colombia. The civil war has also been a source of tension between Colombia and other countries in the region. Ending the civil war once and for all could strengthen fraternity not only in Colombia but also across national borders in the Americas.

This year's Peace Prize also pertains greatly to the abolition or reduction of standing armies—meaning disarmament and arms control. Around 7 000 FARC soldiers are to be disarmed. The surrender and destruction of the weapons will be overseen by the United Nations. Hopefully, a similar negotiated disarmament agreement with the ELN guerrilla will soon be in place as well. Even though the obtained disarmament so far applies primarily to the FARC guerrillas, it is the Committee's hope that the peace accord will also enable the government to reduce its military expenditure and thereby release funds that can be spent on building peace and welfare in Colombia.

And lastly, the long and intense talks that the Colombian government has held with the FARC guerrillas and the victims' representatives, assisted by international facilitators such as Cuba and Norway, have in many ways served as a continual national peace congress.

The award of the Peace Prize to President Santos thus absolutely fulfils the criteria and the spirit of Alfred Nobel's will.

The more than 50-year armed conflict in Colombia is complex, and the country faces a magnitude of problems that must be solved. This will take time, making it even more important to get to work quickly. Only when peace has been restored will it be possible to give priority to education and other important services to assure positive, sustainable development. It is the Norwegian Nobel Committee's hope that, in the years to come, the Colombian people will be able to reap the benefits of the ongoing peace and reconciliation process so that the country can effectively address major challenges such as poverty, social injustice and drug-related crime.

Mr. President, by awarding you this year's Peace Prize, the Norwegian Nobel Committee wished to commend you on the results already achieved in the peace process. But it also sought to strengthen you and those around you in the difficult situation that arose after the referendum. It is with relief and satisfaction that we now note that your stated ambition of travelling to Oslo with a new peace accord in hand has been fulfilled. Perhaps the Nobel Peace Prize has contributed positively by giving you and the peace process a little push forward in these critical weeks. It is the Committee's hope that it will also serve as an inspiration to all Colombians, as they now begin implementing the accord and building a just and lasting peace.

Ladies and gentlemen, seeking forgiveness for atrocities and suffering on the scale we have seen in Colombia is asking a great deal. No one can demand that a victim forgive his or her assailant. But by opening up memories, by having victims and perpetrators alike tell their stories, a foundation is also laid for reconciliation. This is what philosophers have called "the work of memory". It is a painful process, yet at the same time it is a process that makes it possible to leave the pain behind and join forces in building a better future. This year's Peace Prize diploma, which is reproduced in the programme in front of you, addresses this very issue: "The motif may look like a kiss," the artist Willibald Storn has said, "but for me this picture is about forgiveness."

In closing, I would like to quote another Nobel Peace Prize laureate, Archbishop Desmond Tutu, whose words bear direct relevance to the current situation in Colombia: "Forgiving and being reconciled to our enemies or our loved ones are not about pretending that things are other than they are. . . . True reconciliation exposes the awfulness, the abuse, the hurt, the truth. . . . It is a risky undertaking but in the end it is worthwhile, because in the end only an honest confrontation with reality can bring real healing."

SOURCE: The Nobel Foundation. "Award Ceremony Speech." December 10, 2016. © The Nobel Foundation 2016. http://www.nobelprize.org/nobel_prizes/peace/laureates/2016/presentation-speech.html.

President Santos Accepts Nobel Peace Prize

DOCUMENT

December 10, 2016

Your Majesties; Your Royal Highnesses; distinguished members of the Norwegian Nobel Committee; dear fellow citizens of Colombia; citizens of the world; ladies and gentlemen,

Six years ago, it was hard for we Colombians to imagine an end to a war that had lasted half a century. To the great majority of us, peace seemed an impossible dream—and for good reason. Very few of us—hardly anybody—could recall a memory of a country at peace.

Today, after six years of serious and often intense, difficult negotiations, I stand before you and the world and announce with deep humility and gratitude that the Colombian people, with assistance from our friends around the world, are turning the impossible into the possible.

A war that has brought so much suffering and despair to communities all across our beautiful land has finally come to an end.

Like life itself, peace is a process with many surprises. Just two months ago, people in Colombia and indeed in the whole world, were shocked to learn that, in a plebiscite called to ratify the peace agreement with the FARC guerrillas, there were slightly more "No" votes than "Yes" votes.

This outcome was completely unexpected.

A flame of hope had been lit in Cartagena a week earlier, when we signed the agreement in the presence of world leaders, and now that flame appeared to be suddenly snuffed out.

Many of us in Colombia recalled a passage from One Hundred Years of Solitude, the great masterpiece of our Nobel Prize laureate Gabriel García Márquez, which seemed to illustrate the moment we were living:

"It was as if God had decided to put to the test every capacity for surprise and was keeping the inhabitants of Macondo in a permanent alteration between excitement and disappointment, doubt and revelation, to such an extreme that no one knew for certain where the limits of reality lay."

We felt that we ourselves were inhabitants of Macondo, a place that was not only magical but also contradictory.

As Head of State, I sought to understand the significance of this unexpected setback and called at once for a broad national dialogue to seek unity and reconciliation.

I was determined to turn this setback into a chance to develop the widest possible consensus for reaching a new agreement.

I devoted myself to listening to the concerns and recommendations of those who had voted "No", of those who had voted "Yes", and of the majority who did not vote at all—with the aim of achieving a new and improved agreement, an agreement that all of Colombia could stand behind.

Not even four days had passed after the surprising plebiscite when the Norwegian Committee announced an equally surprising award of the Nobel Peace Prize.

I must confess to you that this news came as if it were a gift from heaven. At a time when our ship felt adrift, the Nobel Prize was the tailwind that helped us to reach our destination: the port of peace!

Thank you; thank you very much for this vote of confidence and faith in the future of my country.

Today, distinguished members of the Norwegian Nobel Committee, I come to tell you—and, through you, the international community—that we achieved our goal. We reached our port.

Today, we have a new agreement for ending the armed conflict with the FARC, which incorporates the majority of the proposals we received.

This new agreement was signed two weeks ago, and it was endorsed last week by our Congress, by an overwhelming majority, so that it can be incorporated into our laws. The long-awaited process of implementation has begun, with the invaluable support of the United Nations.

With this new agreement, the oldest and last armed conflict in the Western Hemisphere has ended.

This agreement—as set forth by Alfred Nobel in his will—marks the beginning of the dismantling of an army—this time, an irregular army—and its conversion into a legal political movement.

With this agreement, we can say that the American continent—from Alaska to Patagonia—is a land in peace.

And we can now ask the bold question: if war can come to an end in one hemisphere, why not one day in both hemispheres? Perhaps more than ever before, we can now dare to imagine a world without war.

The impossible is becoming possible.

*****

Alfred Nobel, the great visionary whose legacy gathers us here today on the 120th anniversary of his death, once wrote that war is "the horror of horrors, the greatest of all crimes."

War must never be considered, under any circumstance, an end in itself. It is merely a means, but a means that we must always strive to avert.

I have served as a leader in times of war—to defend the freedom and the rights of the Colombian people—and I have served as a leader in times of making peace.

Allow me to tell you, from my own experience, that it is much harder to make peace than to wage war.

When it is absolutely necessary, we must be prepared to fight, and it was my duty—as Defence Minister and as President—to fight illegal armed groups in my country.

When the roads to peace were closed, I fought these groups with effectiveness and determination[.]

But it is foolish to believe that the end of any conflict must be the elimination of the enemy.

A final victory through force, when nonviolent alternatives exist, is none other than the defeat of the human spirit.

Seeking victory through force alone, pursuing the utter destruction of the enemy, waging war to the last breath, means failing to recognize your opponent as a human being like yourself, someone with whom you can hold a dialogue with.

Dialogue . . . based on respect for the dignity of all. That was our recourse in Colombia. And that is why I have the honour to be here today, sharing what we have learned through our hard-won experience.

Our first and most vital step was to cease thinking of the guerrillas as our bitter enemies, and to see them instead simply as adversaries.

General Álvaro Valencia Tovar—a former Commander of the Colombian Army, a historian and humanist—taught me this distinction.

He said that the word "enemy" gives a sense of a passionate struggle and a connotation of hate, unfit for military honour.

Humanizing war does not just mean limiting its cruelty but also recognizing your opponent as an equal, as a human being.

Historians estimate that up to 187 million people died during the 20th century alone because of war. 187 million! Each one of them a precious human life, loved by their families and dear ones. Tragically, the death toll keeps climbing in this new century.

It is time to remember the haunting question sung by my fellow Nobel laureate Bob Dylan that touched so many youthful hearts in the Sixties, including mine:

"How many deaths will it take 'till he knows that too many people have died? The answer, my friend, is blowin' in the wind".

*****

When people asked me whether I aspired to win the Nobel Peace Prize, I always answered that, for me, the actual prize was peace in Colombia. Because that is the real prize: peace for my country!

And that peace does not belong to a president or a government, but to all the Colombian people, because we must build it together.

That is why I receive this prize on behalf of nearly 50 million Colombians—my fellow countrymen and women—who finally see the end of more than a half-century nightmare that has only brought pain, misery and backwardness to our country.

And I receive this prize—above all—on behalf of the victims, the more than 8 million victims and displaced people whose lives have been devastated by the armed conflict, and the more than 220,000 women, men and children who, to our shame, have been killed in this war.

I am told by scholars that the Colombian peace process is the first in the world that has placed the victims and their rights at the center of the solution.

This negotiation has been conducted with a heavy emphasis on human rights. And that is something that makes us feel truly proud.

Victims want justice, but most of all they want to know the truth, and they—in a spirit of generosity—desire that no new victims should suffer as they did.

Professor Ronald Heifetz, founder of the Center for Public Leadership at the Kennedy School of Government at Harvard University, from which I graduated, once gave me a wise piece of advice:

"Whenever you feel discouraged, tired, pessimistic, talk with the victims. They will give you the push and strength to keep you going."

And it has been just this way. Whenever I had the chance, I listened to the victims of this war and heard their heartbreaking stories. Some of them are here with us today, reminding us why it is so important to build a stable and lasting peace.

Leyner Palacios is one of them. On May 2, 2002, a homemade mortar launched by the FARC, in the middle of a combat with the paramilitaries, landed on the church in his town, Bojayá, where its inhabitants had sought refuge.

Nearly eighty women, men and children—most of the victims were children!—died. In a matter of seconds, Leyner lost 32 relatives, including his parents and three younger brothers.

The FARC has asked for forgiveness for this atrocity, and Leyner, who is now a community leader, has forgiven them.

That is the great paradox I have found: while many who have not suffered the conflict in their own flesh are reluctant to accept peace, the victims are the ones who are most willing to forgive, to reconcile, and to face the future with a heart free of hate.

This peace prize belongs as well to those men and women who, with enormous patience and endurance, negotiated during all these years in Havana. They have reached an agreement that can be offered today as a model for the resolution of armed conflicts that have yet to be resolved around the world.

And here I am referring not only to the Government negotiators but also to the FARC negotiators—my adversaries—, who have demonstrated a great will for peace. I want to praise their willingness to embrace peace, to reach peace, because without it, the process would have failed.

In the same spirit, I dedicate this prize to the heroes of the Colombian Armed Forces, who have never ceased to protect the Colombian people, and who truly understood that the actual victory of any soldier or any police officer is peace itself.

And I wish to include a special acknowledgment—with all the gratitude in my heart—for my family: for my wife and my children, whose support and love throughout this task helped lessen the burden.

Finally, I also share this prize with the international community who, with generosity and unanimous enthusiasm, backed this peace process from the very beginning.

Let me also take this opportunity to convey my very special thanks to the people of Norway for your peaceful character and your extraordinary spirit of solidarity. It was because of these virtues that you were entrusted by Alfred Nobel to promote peace in the world. I must say you have done your job with great effectiveness for my country.

Norway and Cuba, in their role as guarantors; Chile and Venezuela, as witnesses; the United States and the European Union, with their special envoys; all the countries in Latin America and the Caribbean; even China and Russia . . . they all have reasons to take pride in this achievement.

The Kroc Institute for International Peace Studies at the University of Notre Dame in the United States has concluded, based on careful studies of the 34 agreements signed in the world to end armed conflicts in the past three decades, that this peace agreement in Colombia is the most complete and comprehensive ever reached.

As such, the Colombian peace agreement is a ray of hope in a world troubled by so many conflicts and so much intolerance.

It proves that what, at first, seems impossible, through perseverance may become possible even in Syria or Yemen or South Sudan.

The key, in the words of the English poet Tennyson, is "to strive, to seek, to find, and not to yield."

*****

A few lessons can be learned from Colombia's peace process and I would like to share them with the world:

You must properly prepare yourself and seek advice, studying the failures of peace attempts in your own country and learning from other peace processes, their successes and their problems.

The agenda for the negotiation should be focussed and specific, aimed at solving the issues directly related to the armed conflict, rather than attempting to address all the problems faced by the nation.

Negotiations should be carried out with discretion and confidentiality in order to prevent them from turning into a media circus.

Sometimes it is necessary to both fight and talk at the same time if you want to arrive at—a lesson I took from another Nobel laureate, Yitzhak Rabin.

You must also be willing to make difficult, bold and oftentimes unpopular decisions in order to reach your final goal.

In my case, this meant reaching out to the governments of neighbouring countries with whom I had and continue to have deep ideological differences.

Regional support is indispensable in the political resolution of any asymmetric war. Fortunately, today all the countries in the region are allies in the search for peace, the noblest purpose any society can have.

We also achieved a very important objective: agreement on a model of transitional justice that enables us to secure a maximum of justice without sacrificing peace.

I have no doubt this model will be one of the greatest legacies of the Colombian peace process. . . .

*****

Dear friends,

In a world where citizens are making the most crucial decisions—for themselves and for their nations—out of fear and despair, we must make the certainty of hope possible.

In a world where wars and conflicts are fuelled by hatred and prejudice, we must find the path of forgiveness and reconciliation.

In a world where borders are increasingly closed to immigrants, where minorities are attacked and people deemed different are excluded, we must be able to coexist with diversity and appreciate the way it can enrich our societies.

We are human beings after all. For those of us who are believers, we are all God's children. We are part of this magnificent adventure of being alive and populating this planet.

At our core, there are no inherent differences: not the colour of our skin; nor our religious beliefs; nor our political ideologies, nor our sexual preferences. All these are simply facets of humanity's diversity.

Let's awaken the creative capacity for goodness, for building peace, that live within each soul.

In the end, we are one people and one race; of every colour, of every belief, of every preference.

The name of this one people is the world. The name of this one race is humanity.

If we truly understand this, if we make it part of our individual and collective awareness, then we will cut the very root of conflicts and wars.

In 1982—34 years ago—the efforts to find peace through dialogue began in Colombia.

That same year, in Stockholm, Gabriel García Márquez, who was my ally in the pursuit of peace, received the Nobel Prize in Literature, and spoke about "a new and sweeping utopia of life, (. . .) where the races condemned to one hundred years of solitude will have, at last and forever, a second opportunity on earth."

Today, Colombia—my beloved country—is living that second opportunity; and I thank you, members of the Norwegian Nobel Committee, because, on this occasion, you have not only awarded a prize to peace: you helped make it possible!

The sun of peace finally shines in the heavens of Colombia.

May its light shine upon the whole world!

SOURCE: The Nobel Foundation. "Juan Manuel Santos—Nobel Lecture." December 10, 2016. © The Nobel Foundation 2016. http://www.nobelprize.org/nobel_prizes/peace/laureates/2016/santos-lecture_en.html.

OTHER HISTORIC DOCUMENTS OF INTEREST

FROM THIS VOLUME

FROM PREVIOUS *HISTORIC DOCUMENTS*

Obama Issues Order Barring Offshore Drilling in Areas of the Arctic and Atlantic Oceans

DECEMBER 20, 2016

President Barack Obama staked a part of his legacy on environmental issues, striving to balance economic objectives with natural resource conservation. His administration increased the area of federally protected waters by a factor of four and made similar strides in preservation of public lands. In December 2016, as his presidency drew to a close, Obama partnered with Canada to announce a series of measures aimed at protecting vulnerable ocean areas, including his announcement of a ban on future oil and gas drilling across nearly 120 million acres of the Arctic and Atlantic Oceans. Obama also named nine new national monuments and expanded an eighth in 2016, extending federal environmental protections to an historic amount of land and water acreage.

ENVIRONMENTAL DIPLOMACY

As a major player in global policy, and a top emitter of carbon dioxide, the United States plays a prominent role in setting the tone of international dialogue surrounding environmental conservation. In 2015, Obama asserted that protection of the Arctic region is in the national interest due to its economic, strategic, ecological, and cultural value. He also emphasized the importance of improving understanding of the effects of climate change for science-based management. A few months later, the United States assumed a two-year chairmanship of the Arctic Council, an international forum for sustainable development of the Arctic region.

Ratification of the 2016 Paris Agreement on climate change was a milestone in global environmental diplomacy, prompting efforts to frame economic development regarding sustainability. On March 10, 2016, Obama and Canadian Prime Minister Justin Trudeau issued a joint statement resolving that the two countries should be international leaders in sustainable development. Recognizing the serious impact of climate change on the polar regions, and the threat to life and property it poses, the two heads of state reaffirmed their shared vision of resilient and sustainable Arctic communities. In the following months, both countries engaged a variety of stakeholders to discuss future community and ecological resilience in the changing Arctic landscape.

THE ARCTIC DRILLING BAN

A month before leaving the White House, Obama designated the majority of federal waters in the Arctic Ocean as off-limits to future oil and gas exploration. The designated area comprised approximately 115 million acres of water under U.S. jurisdiction, including all the Chukchi Sea and most of the Beaufort Sea. The ruling excluded a portion of near-shore federal waters adjacent to existing infrastructure between Kaktovik and Utqiaġvik, Alaska. Additionally, Obama announced the protection of another 3.8 million acres of the Atlantic Ocean that span ecologically significant coral canyons.

Both regions are part of the Outer Continental Shelf, an area defined by the 1953 Outer Continental Shelf Lands Act as all submerged land within the U.S. Exclusive Economic Zone, which begins where the states' jurisdiction ends and extends to the international water boundary (approximately 200 nautical miles offshore). The act also governs how the executive branch can use and lease federal waters for oil and gas activities. Typically, the act has been used to establish five-year plans for lease distribution. However, Obama employed the less commonly used second provision of the act, which grants the president authority to remove from leasing consideration federally owned waters without specifying a timeframe, effectively preventing any future oil or gas exploration, development, or production in the specified areas. The act was first established to encourage development of fossil fuel resources in response to what President Harry Truman called a "long-range worldwide need" for energy. Obama invoked the rule with a new global imperative in mind, one of equally profound economic and geopolitical implications: climate research has definitively shown that to limit global temperature rise to the accepted safe 2°C, no Arctic oil or gas can be exploited.

Obama's designations were part of a coordinated effort between Canada and the United States, as called for in their March agreement. Trudeau concurrently announced that Canada will, for the time being, also cease oil and gas operations in its Arctic waters. Canada's ruling, however, will be reviewed every five years through an evaluation process based in climate and marine science. "These actions, and Canada's parallel actions, protect a sensitive and unique ecosystem that is unlike any other region on earth," said Obama. "They reflect the scientific assessment that even with the high safety standards that both our countries have put in place, the risks of an oil spill in this region are significant and our ability to clean up from a spill in the region's harsh conditions is limited."

In addition to the drilling ban, the United States and Canada jointly announced a series of other initiatives the partners would engage in to further protect the Artic region. The United States launched an interagency Economic Development Assessment Team in Alaska's Nome region that is charged with identifying future investment opportunities in the area, while Canada committed to collaborating with territorial and provincial governments and Native peoples to establish a new Arctic Policy Framework that guides future education, infrastructure, and economic development in the region. The United States and Canada also pledged to continue working together to establish low-impact shipping corridors, limit the use of heavy fuel oil by their respective Coast Guards, and develop an agreement preventing the opening of unregulated fisheries. Additionally, the Arctic Funders Collaborative announced that it would provide an estimated $27 million in resources or programs across the Arctic in the next three years.

A UNIQUE AND VULNERABLE ECOSYSTEM

There are risks associated with all offshore drilling operations, but especially so in the remote, harsh Arctic environment. The infrastructure and response capacity to deal with a disaster related to Arctic oil drilling does not exist. Response, mitigation, and restoration would be very difficult, and the results detrimental to wildlife and human communities. The expanses of unique marine habitat and wildlife migration routes support many endangered and iconic species such as the polar bear, bowhead whale, and walrus. The well-being of Native Alaskan communities is intrinsically connected to the health of the Arctic environment, since the region's biological productivity has provided subsistence resources to native peoples for millennia. In the past half-century, climate change has caused the polar regions to warm at about twice the rate of the rest of the planet, fundamentally altering the landscape and natural systems. Efforts to limit potential threats posed by oil and gas activity, as well as preclude carbon emissions from that particular reservoir of fossil fuel energy, generally seek to mitigate the further disruption of human and ecological communities of the region.

AN INDEFINITE BAN AND AN UNCERTAIN FUTURE

Because it was put forth so late in Obama's second term, the ban was seen by some as an eleventh-hour effort by a lame-duck president to solidify his environmental legacy. It was criticized as heavy-handed and restrictive by Alaska's congressional delegation, who argued that the federal government was overstepping its bounds to regulate energy extraction in a resource-oriented state. Many of their constituents disagreed: a group of Alaska Native communities issued a statement thanking the president for protecting subsistence resources, and environmental groups also voiced their support.

Offshore mineral exploration in the Arctic is extremely limited, and the oil and gas industry has demonstrated declining interest. The move to withdraw such a large stretch of the Arctic from drilling was construed as largely symbolic, since only a tiny amount (0.1%) of federal offshore crude production occurred there. Since 1979, only forty-three wells have been drilled in the now protected area, most of which were for exploration rather than development. Federal offshore leases declined over 90 percent during 2016, and while Obama's designation does not affect remaining leases, which still cover 205,000 acres in total, most of these will expire in 2017. Several companies that had previously held leases in U.S. waters discontinued exploratory operations by 2015, citing disappointing and cost-prohibitive results. It also would take about fifty years to establish sufficient infrastructure for substantial drilling to occur. For this reason, the White House asserted that there was no real risk of drilling for decades, and this time scale would be incongruent with the need to actively reduce emissions.

Sen. Ted Cruz, R-Tex, joined the president's critics, complaining in a tweet that this was "yet another Obama abuse of power" and suggesting that it would soon be overturned by the incoming administration. President-elect Donald Trump, who has described climate change as "a hoax," has pledged to reverse much of Obama's progress in environmental regulation and, in keeping with his goal to expand American oil and gas production, has appointed longtime proponents of the industry to key cabinet positions. Whether the drilling ban can easily be undone is not entirely clear. Past administrations, Democratic and Republican alike, have used the law to protect smaller areas for a specified duration of time. With the unprecedented geographic scope of protections described by the White House as indefinite, Obama's declaration has taken the rule into uncharted waters.

OBAMA SETS RECORD FOR DESIGNATING, EXPANDING NATIONAL MONUMENTS

Obama followed the Arctic drilling ban with the announcement of two new national monuments on December 28: Bears Ears National Monument in southeast Utah and Gold Butte National Monument in southwest Nevada. The designations extend federal protections against future development to approximately 1.35 million acres and 300,000 acres of land, respectively, in these locations. Bears Ears is to be comanaged by the federal government and Native peoples who have ancestral ties to the region; these groups will still be able to access the land for tribal ceremonies and traditional activities. Both the Bears Ears and Gold Butte designations were controversial because there had been intense debates over who should manage the land, and the issue of land rights was a major point of contention between the federal government and state officials in Nevada and Utah. Rep. Jason Chaffetz, R-Utah, described the announcement as "a slap in the face to the people of Utah, attempting to silence the voices of those who will bear the heavy burden it imposes." He added, "We will work to repeal this top-down decision and replace it with one that garners local support and creates a balanced, win-win solution."

Obama previously announced seven other new national monuments in 2016 and expanded an eighth, the Papahānaumokuākea Marine National Monument near the Northwest Hawaiian Islands. Five of the new monuments also protected vast swaths of land, including the Katahdin Woods and Waters Monument, which protected more than 87,000 acres of Maine's northern woodland, and the Mojave Trails National Monument in California, which applied protections to 1.6 million acres. In January 2017, Obama brought the total number of national monuments he had designated or expanded to thirty-four, announcing the expansion of the California Coastal National Monument and Cascade-Siskiyou National Monument, and the creation of three new monuments honoring the country's civil rights history in Alabama and South Carolina. In total, Obama has acted to protect more than 550 million acres during his two terms in office—more than any other president.

Some political observers question whether Obama's pursuit of a strong conservation agenda, particularly his decisions surrounding national monuments, will prompt the next administration and Republican-controlled Congress to repeal or otherwise limit the scope of the Antiquities Act, which gives the president the authority to create national monuments.

—Megan Howes

Following is a joint statement from President Barack Obama and Canadian Prime Minister Justin Trudeau from December 20, 2016, announcing a new partnership for responsible sustainable development of Arctic communities; and a statement from Obama on December 20, 2016, explaining his decision to prevent future oil and gas leasing in areas of the Arctic.

DOCUMENT

U.S.–Canada Joint Statement on Arctic Partnership

December 20, 2016

[Footnotes have been omitted.]

In March, President Obama and Prime Minister Trudeau announced a new partnership to embrace opportunities and confront challenges in the changing Arctic, with Indigenous and Northern partnerships, and responsible, science-based leadership. Over the past year, both countries have engaged a range of partners and stakeholders, including Indigenous peoples and Northern communities, state, provincial and territorial governments, non-governmental organizations and businesses. Those consulted have expressed a strong desire for real and long-term opportunities to build strong families, communities, and robust economies. Today, President Obama and Prime Minister Trudeau are proud to launch actions ensuring a strong, sustainable and viable Arctic economy and ecosystem, with low-impact shipping, science based management of marine resources, and free from the future risks of offshore oil and gas activity. Together, these actions set the stage for deeper partnerships with other Arctic nations, including through the Arctic Council.

Science-based approach to oil and gas:

In March, the United States and Canada committed that commercial activities will occur only if the highest safety and environmental standards are met, and if they are consistent with national and global climate and environmental goals. Today—due to the important, irreplaceable values of its Arctic waters for Indigenous, Alaska Native and local communities' subsistence and cultures, wildlife and wildlife habitat, and scientific research; the vulnerability of these ecosystems to an oil spill; and the unique logistical, operational, safety, and scientific challenges and risks of oil extraction and spill response in Arctic waters—the United States is designating the vast majority of U.S. waters in the Chukchi and Beaufort Seas as indefinitely off limits to offshore oil and gas leasing, and Canada will designate all Arctic Canadian waters as indefinitely off limits to future offshore Arctic oil and gas licensing, to be reviewed every five years through a climate and marine science-based life-cycle assessment.

Supporting strong Arctic communities:

In March, both countries committed to defining new approaches and exchanging best practices to strengthen the resilience of Arctic communities and continuing to support the well-being of Arctic residents, in particular respecting the rights and territory of Indigenous peoples.

Recently, in direct response to requests from Alaska Native communities, President Obama created the Northern Bering Sea Climate Resilience Area protecting the cultural and subsistence resources of over 80 tribes as well as one of the largest seasonal migrations of marine mammals in the world of bowhead and beluga whales, walrus, ice seals, and sea birds. The United States also launched an interagency Economic Development Assessment Team in the Nome region of Alaska to identify future investment opportunities, with other regions to follow. In addition, the Arctic Funders Collaborative (AFC), a group of 11 U.S., Canadian, and international philanthropic foundations, announced the coordination and mobilization of an estimated $27 million in resources for programs across the Arctic over the next three years.

Today, for its part, Canada is committing to co-develop a new Arctic Policy Framework, with Northerners, territorial and Provincial governments, and First Nations, Inuit, and Métis People that will replace Canada's Northern Strategy. The Framework will include priority areas identified by the Minister of Indigenous and Northern Affairs' Special Representative, such as education, infrastructure, and economic development. The Framework will include an Inuit-specific component, created in partnership with Inuit, as

Inuit Nunangat comprises over a third of Canada's land mass and over half of Canada's coast line, and as Inuit modern treaties govern this jurisdictional space. In parallel, Canada is reducing the reliance of Northern communities on diesel, by deploying energy efficiency and renewable power. Canada will also, with Indigenous and Northern partners, explore how to support and protect the future of the Arctic Ocean's "last ice area" where summer ice remains each year.

Low impact shipping corridors:

In March, the United States and Canada committed to working together to establish consistent policies for ships operating in the region. Today, both countries are launching the first processes ever to identify sustainable shipping lanes throughout their connected Arctic waters, in collaboration with Northern and Indigenous partners. The U.S. Coast Guard is launching a Port Access Route Study (PARS) in the Beaufort and Chukchi Seas. Results from this analysis may be used to establish vessel routing measures including traffic separation schemes, recommended routes, Areas To Be Avoided, or other instruments such as fairways where no structures may be erected. The Canadian Coast Guard and Transport Canada is implementing Northern Marine Transportation Corridors, determining what infrastructure and navigational and emergency response services are needed. Canada is also launching a new program to support training curriculum for Northerners, particularly Indigenous peoples, to join the marine field, as well as programming to support marine infrastructure and safety equipment for communities.

In addition, the U.S. Coast Guard, in consultation with industry, Indigenous communities, and the State of Alaska, has begun a strategy to phase down the use of Heavy Fuel Oil (HFO) in the Arctic. The Canadian Coast Guard is conducting similar outreach and consultations to develop proposals to phase down the use of HFO in 2017. The United States and Canada will each, or jointly, propose a plan for consideration at the International Maritime Organization's spring 2017 meeting.

Science-based management of Arctic fisheries:

In March, the United States and Canada called for a binding international agreement to prevent the opening of unregulated fisheries in the Central Arctic Ocean and to build on a precautionary, science-based approach to commercial fishing that both countries have put in place in their Arctic waters. Today, the United States commits to supporting and strengthening existing commercial fishing closures in the Beaufort and Chukchi Seas, and to conducting scientific research to improve our understanding of the Arctic. Canada commits to working with Northern and Indigenous communities to build world-leading and abundant Arctic fisheries—based on science—that firstly benefit Northern communities. Together, the United States' and Canada's actions will create the largest contiguous area of well-regulated fisheries in the world.

Both countries reaffirm their commitment to a legally binding agreement to prevent unregulated commercial fisheries in the Arctic High Seas until an internationally recognized Regional Fishery Management Organization is in place to provide effective management. Both countries are working towards such an agreement in the coming months.

Source: Executive Office of the President. "Joint Statement—United States–Canada Joint Arctic Leaders' Statement." December 20, 2016. Compilation of Presidential Documents 2016, no. 00859 (December 20, 2016). http://www.gpo.gov/fdsys/pkg/DCPD-201600859/pdf/DCPD-201600859.pdf.

Obama Statement on the Withdrawal of Certain Areas in Arctic and Atlantic Oceans from Mineral Leasing

December 20, 2016

Today, in partnership with our neighbors and allies in Canada, the United States is taking historic steps to build a strong Arctic economy, preserve a healthy Arctic ecosystem, and protect our fragile Arctic waters, including designating the bulk of our Arctic water and certain areas in the Atlantic Ocean as indefinitely off limits to future oil and gas leasing.

These actions, and Canada's parallel actions, protect a sensitive and unique ecosystem that is unlike any other region on Earth. They reflect the scientific assessment that, even with the high safety standards that both our countries have put in place, the risks of an oil spill in this region are significant, and our ability to clean up from a spill in the region's harsh conditions is limited. By contrast, it would take decades to fully develop the production infrastructure necessary for any large-scale oil and gas leasing production in the region, at a time when we need to continue to move decisively away from fossil fuels.

In 2015, just 0.1 percent of U.S. Federal offshore crude production came from the Arctic, and Department of Interior analysis shows that, at current oil prices, significant production in the Arctic will not occur. That's why looking forward, we must continue to focus on economic empowerment for Arctic communities beyond this one sector. My administration has proposed and directed unprecedented Federal investments in the region, but more must be done—by the Federal Government, the private sector, and philanthropy—to enhance infrastructure and our collective security, such as the acquisition of additional icebreaking capacity, and to lay the groundwork for economic growth in the industries of the future.

SOURCE: Executive Office of the President. "Statement on the Withdrawal of Certain Areas in the Arctic and Atlantic Oceans on the Outer Continental Shelf from Mineral Leasing." December 20, 2016. Compilation of Presidential Documents 2016, no. 00858 (December 20, 2016). http://www.gpo.gov/fdsys/pkg/DCPD-201600858/pdf/DCPD-201600858.pdf.

OTHER HISTORIC DOCUMENTS OF INTEREST

FROM THIS VOLUME

FROM PREVIOUS *HISTORIC DOCUMENTS*

South Korean President Impeached

DECEMBER 21 AND 23, 2016

Since the democratization of South Korea in 1987, abuses of power for political and financial gain have been persistent. Every democratically elected president has been implicated in some form of corruption, and, as demonstrated by the scandal absorbing President Park Geun-hye, fraudulence and misappropriation of influence continue to plague Korean politics. While corruption and influence-peddling scandals have been relatively common occurrences while South Korea's democracy has matured, the most recent case involving Park is historically exceptional due to the sheer scale of allegations—over a dozen constitutional and legal offenses—as well as extent and effect of the public reaction. Her refusal to resign all but paralyzed the government and sustained a series of weekly peaceful civilian protests of unprecedented size. The significance of the political turmoil extended beyond the immediate consequences for her administration, because legal proceedings have exposed particularly unscrupulous cases of close government–business relationships and elite privilege.

Family Ties and "Choi-gate"

Park is the daughter of a former South Korean military strongman, Park Chung-hee, who came to power in 1961. His eighteen-year reign was characterized by unsparing repression of dissent, but also rapid economic development and industrialization that pulled much of the country out of poverty. The legacy of her father was a major factor in Park Geun-hye's election as Korea's first woman president and contributed to Park's popularity early in her term. She was backed by older Koreans who had anticipated a contemporary, democratic version of the senior Park's leadership. She was perceived to have her father's political skill, but with citizens' interests at heart. The Parks' conservative ideology prioritizing economic growth made Korea the developed nation it is today, but government-sponsored industrialization also created the conditions that fostered the kind of corruption that plagued each democratically elected administration.

Park Chung-hee supported the creation of corporate giants such as Samsung and Hyundai, which were later embroiled along with others in Park Geun-hye's scandal. Korean business conglomerates, or chaebols, as they are called, were instrumental in economic reconstruction after the Korean War. Strong links between business and government were largely tolerated at the time and remained a central component of the economic and political landscape today. One of the allegations facing Park was that she favored these major companies while they funded the personal interests of her close friend and long-time associate Choi Soon-sil.

In late October 2016, South Korea's National Assembly accused Park of enabling Choi to leverage their relationship for personal gain. "Choi-gate," as the scandal was called, began with revelations that Choi had embezzled almost $70 million in corporate donations from fifty-three companies through the lobby group Federation of Korean Industries.

According to prosecutors, the companies felt compelled to donate the money, or risk unfair treatment by the government. The donations were ostensibly meant for two charitable foundations established by Choi that support presidential initiatives, but she siphoned off much of the funds for personal gain. Some of Park's former aides who were complicit in the scheme were also detained and investigated for their role in pressuring companies to donate.

Additionally, Choi used her influence and proximity to power to wrest admission for her nineteen-year-old daughter, Chung Yoo-ra, to Ewha Womans University, one of Korea's top academic institutions, because Chung lacked the academic record needed to gain admission on her own. This revelation was particularly infuriating to many young Koreans who find it difficult to advance in their careers despite hard work. Chung was soon after expelled, and the university leader resigned.

Choi, called the "shadow president," is suspected to have exerted a considerable amount of undue influence on Park, using her leverage to sway the president's actions. Choi is the daughter of a minor cult leader, who exercised remarkable influence over a young Park following her father's assassination. Many believed that Choi wielded a similar, cult-like influence over the president. Park was accused of allowing Choi to become involved with state affairs despite her having no official capacity and no security clearance. Through documents leaked by an aide, it became apparent that Choi was privy to classified information such as appointments of key officials and was involved in activities ranging from editing speeches to distributing the culture ministry's $150 million budget. Choi pleaded not guilty to charges of extortion, coercion, and fraud. She was arrested, and Park was considered an accomplice due to incriminating instructions from the president regarding raising funds for the two foundations. The prosecution team concluded that Park "played a large role" in the embezzlement scheme, but she could not be indicted as long as she remained president.

Exposure of Park's relationship with Choi was a major source of public distrust and outrage, but was also representative of larger endemic and festering problems between her administration and the public. Over her four-year presidency, Park developed a reputation for being aloof and out of touch with the concerns of her constituents. She has been dogged by accusations of negligence since April 2014, when she failed to effectively respond to the Sewol ferry disaster that killed more than 300 passengers, most of them teenage students on a school trip. The "missing seven hours" often cited as evidence of incompetence refers to her unknown whereabouts between 9:53 a.m. when the incident was first reported, and 5:15 p.m. when she called an emergency meeting. Despite criticism and rampant speculation, she never adequately explained what she had been doing in the interim, when she was sequestered in her official residence. It later came to light that Park had spent part of that time getting her hair styled while the ferry sank, reinforcing the public sentiment that their president was not just withdrawn, but dangerously out of touch.

WIDESPREAD PUBLIC UNREST

Revelations about the extent of Choi's influence on the federal government despite her obvious lack of credibility were infuriating to citizens. This combination of deceit, corruption, and cronyism made Park the country's least popular leader in the thirty years since South Korea became a democracy, with approval ratings at a historically low 4 percent. According to the opinion research firm Hankook Research, 70 percent of the population wanted Park to step down amid the scandal, a sentiment on prominent display during massive weekly candlelight demonstrations of citizens calling for her resignation if not outright impeachment. Each Saturday, crowds of consistently more than one million people gathered in Seoul to demand Park's removal from office. These protests were peaceful, and ultimately achieved their objective without a single arrest. On December 3, 2016, the two opposition parties submitted a joint motion to impeach Park, accusing her of "extensive and serious violations of the Constitution and law" and citing her alleged abuse of power, coercion, bribery, and dereliction of duty during the Sewol ferry disaster.

THE IMPEACHMENT PROCESS

Throughout the impeachment proceedings, Park refused to answer questions, insisting on her innocence. Her attorneys maintained that the allegations were baseless and in any case not serious enough to warrant impeachment. Park did soften her defiant tone in an effort to assuage public furor and apologized for carelessness in her ties to Choi; but misjudging the public mood, her expression of contrition did little to calm the strife. Then in a calculated move that attempted to transfer the conflict to within the National Assembly, Park offered to abdicate her presidency if the legislature could agree on a way for her to leave office. Some lawmakers had been hesitant to start impeachment proceedings because of the extensive timeline, given that Park's term would end in February 2018. Some members of Park's Saenuri Party suggested amending the constitution to allow a president to serve two four-year terms rather than a single five-year term, which would enable Park to leave office more gracefully. However, Park's persistent refusal to answer questions and the public's unrelenting protests ultimately prodded lawmakers to push for impeachment.

A two-thirds majority is needed to pass a motion through the National Assembly. Together, South Korea's two opposition parties held a majority of the 300 seats, but fewer than the 200 required to pass a motion. Yet the motion for impeachment passed the National Assembly by a large margin—234 votes in favor—on December 9. The vote was anonymous, but results signify that nearly half of Saenuri Party lawmakers joined the opposition to support impeachment. Prime Minister Hwang Kyo-Ahn, a Park appointee, became acting president when the motion passed, suspending Park, and he would oversee the administrative functions of government.

PROCEEDINGS CONTINUE

Under South Korean law, impeachment by the National Assembly initiates a presidential trial before the Constitutional Court. Only the court has the power to officially impeach a president and has 180 days from the date that an impeachment motion is passed to consider the evidence against the president and issue a final ruling. Until that time, Park would retain her title and residence in the Blue House (South Korea's executive offices and official residence) during her suspension, but charges could be pressed against her when she no longer holds the title. She will either be removed from office or reinstated once the court rules.

A two-thirds majority of the court's nine justices must find in favor of impeachment for Park to be removed from office. Six of the current justices are conservative and two were set to retire in March 2017. One retired ahead of the ruling, and on March 10, the court's remaining eight justices voted unanimously for impeachment, noting that Park had "betrayed the trust of the people." Because the court voted to remove Park from office, South Korea's constitution requires that a presidential election be held sixty days later to identify a successor to serve a full five-year term.

Whether the scandal can bring about a new era of political transparency in South Korea or not remains to be seen. In anticipation of the upcoming election, as potential candidates vie for a position to run, partisan scrambling will take precedence over political reform. There has been talk of Park's predicament creating a "Trump effect" in South Korea, fueled by public ire toward the political establishment. For many, the ongoing impeachment proceedings represent more than just the transgressions of Park and Choi. Citizens are hopeful that the scandal will provide an impetus to overcome old ways of thought, address corruption, and strengthen checks on presidential power.

—Megan Howes

Following is a press release issued by the National Assembly of the Republic of South Korea on December 21, 2016, announcing a joint meeting between the prosecuting team and legal representatives to discuss plans for President Park Geun-hye's impeachment trial; and a second National Assembly press release from December 23, 2016, announcing the prosecuting team's submission of a written opinion to the Constitutional Court on the impeachment matter.

DOCUMENT

Impeachment Prosecuting Team to Hold Joint Meeting with Legal Representatives

December 21, 2016

A group of National Assembly Members prosecuting the impeachment of President Park Geun-hye announced on December 16 that they will hold a joint meeting with their legal representatives on December 18 at the National Assembly.

The prosecuting team and their representatives will meet once a week to discuss actions and strategies to pursue at the trial, they said.

At their first meeting, they will thoroughly review their overall plan, including their strategy for the trial, selection of legal representatives, and preparation of written opinion.

The prosecuting team comprises nine Assemblymen: Kweon Seong-dong, Chang Je-won and Yoon Han-hong (Saenuri Party); three Members of the Minjoo Party of Korea (not decided); Kim Kwan-young and Son Kum-ju (People's Party); and Lee Jeong-mi (Justice Party).

Their legal representatives will number no more than 20 persons. The negotiating parties are consulting about specific appointments, taking into account candidates' career history and specialties.

SOURCE: National Assembly of the Republic of Korea. "Impeachment prosecuting team to hold joint meeting with legal representatives." December 21, 2016. http://korea.assembly.go.kr/wha/pre_list .jsp?boardid=1000000028.

Prosecuting Team Submits Written Opinion to Constitutional Court

December 23, 2016

The legal representatives of the National Assembly's prosecuting team for the impeachment of President Park Geun-hye on December 19 submitted to the Constitutional Court a written opinion on the procedures of the impeachment trial. The court had requested on December 14 that the prosecuting team submit its opinion on preparatory procedures before the trial begins.

The representatives' opinion is as follows:

1. On whether the preparatory procedures and preparation are needed, the prosecuting team and their representatives will respect the court's decision.

2. As the commissioned justice ordered the prosecuting team to submit "a substantiation plan and list of evidence" by December 21, 2016, the team and their representatives request the court to select the preparatory dates the day after necessary preliminary documents are submitted.

SOURCE: National Assembly of the Republic of Korea. "Prosecuting team submits written opinion to Constitutional Court." December 23, 2016. http://korea.assembly.go.kr/wha/pre_list.jsp?boardid= 1000000028.

OTHER HISTORIC DOCUMENTS OF INTEREST

FROM PREVIOUS *HISTORIC DOCUMENTS*

■ South Korea Elects First Female President, 2012, p. 637

United Nations Issues Resolution on Israeli Settlements

DECEMBER 23, 2016

The long-simmering Israeli–Palestinian conflict made global headlines in December 2016 following the United Nations (UN) Security Council's adoption of a resolution condemning Israeli settlements in Palestinian territories as illegal. The international community has long opposed Israel's settlement-building activities, asserting that they violate international law and undermine efforts to secure peace in the region, while Israel maintains the legality of its settlements and argues that the future of those communities should be determined through peace negotiations. Notably, the United States abstained from the Security Council vote, breaking with its history of vetoing similar measures and serving as Israel's primary defender on the global stage. Israeli officials quickly rejected the Security Council resolution and characterized the United States' abstention as a betrayal while taking actions to limit relations with countries that supported the resolution and pledging to continue settlement construction.

ISRAELI SETTLEMENTS AND THE ISRAELI–PALESTINIAN CONFLICT

At its core, the Israeli–Palestinian conflict is a territorial dispute in which both Israel and Palestine have laid historical, political, and religious claims to the same land. Israelis seek to establish a secure home for Jewish people on the site of their ancient homeland, while Palestinians believe the Jews, with Western assistance, have usurped their rightful homeland. Palestinians want to secure statehood in the West Bank and Gaza Strip regions of Israel, with a capital in East Jerusalem.

The conflict can be traced back at least to the end of World War I, when the League of Nations gave Britain a mandate to oversee the land known as Palestine. British officials pledged support for an independent Arab state in the region, but also expressed support for a Jewish "national home" in the territory. Since 1929, Arabs and Jews have continually clashed in violent territorial disputes. Shortly before the British mandate ended, the UN passed a resolution that divided the land between Arabs and Jews, but Arabs objected to the partition because it designated more land for the Jews. With the British withdrawal in 1948, Israel declared itself an independent state. Several countries launched an invasion into the newly declared state, but ultimately lost much of the land set aside by the UN for the Arab people. At the end of the conflict, Jordan controlled the West Bank and Jerusalem's holy sites, Egypt controlled the Gaza Strip, and Israel controlled the remaining territory. Israel later seized the West Bank and East Jerusalem from Jordan, the Golan Heights from Syria, and the Gaza Strip and Sinai Peninsula from Egypt during the 1967 Arab–Israeli War. The UN passed a resolution following the war calling for the Arab lands to be returned, but Israel declined to do so and instead began to expand Jewish settlements in these territories in the late 1970s. (Israeli troops and settlers withdrew from the Gaza Strip in 2005, a concession to help diminish attacks on Israel.)

Amid ongoing violence in the region, the international community has repeatedly attempted to broker a peace agreement between the Israelis and the Palestinians, with a focus on reaching a two-state solution. Negotiations have achieved some results, including the 1993 Oslo Accords and 1995 Oslo II, which established the Palestinian Authority and designated areas of the West Bank and Gaza under full Palestinian control, while placing others under shared Israel–Palestine control or complete Israeli control. However, the peace process has largely been on hold since the last round of American-mediated negotiations collapsed in the spring of 2014. Peace efforts have been complicated by a weak and fractured Palestinian leadership, some elements of which—namely the militant group Hamas—refuse to recognize Israel.

Talks have also been impacted by the Israeli government's shift to the far-right and adoption of an increasingly pro-settlement stance since Prime Minister Benjamin Netanyahu regained office in 2009. By the end of 2016, an estimated 430,000 Israeli settlers were living in the West Bank with another 200,000 living in East Jerusalem. Their settlements range in size from a few dozen people to the 20,000 Israelis living in the community of Ariel, which is in the heart of the West Bank and has its own university. Thousands of Palestinians' homes have been destroyed in the process of constructing these settlements, fomenting further distrust and anger between the two sides.

UN SECURITY COUNCIL DECLARES SETTLEMENTS VIOLATE INTERNATIONAL LAW

On December 23, 2016, the UN Security Council voted to adopt a resolution reaffirming that "the establishment by Israel of settlements in the Palestinian territory occupied since 1967, including East Jerusalem, has no legal validity and constitutes a flagrant violation under international law and a major obstacle to the achievement of the two-State solution and a just, lasting and comprehensive peace." The resolution demanded that Israel "immediately and completely cease all settlement activities in the occupied Palestinian territory" and called for the acceleration of peace efforts. Furthermore, the resolution stated that the UN would not recognize any changes to the territorial lines agreed to in June 1967, including any changes in Jerusalem, unless said changes had been agreed to by both Israel and Palestine through negotiations. The vote was unanimous, with the United States abstaining, and marked the first time in nearly forty years that the Security Council had passed a resolution criticizing Israeli settlements. However, it is a nonbinding resolution, meaning that it does not include any enforcement mechanisms and is largely a political statement intended to show an international consensus that Israel's settlement-building is wrong.

Prior to the vote, the resolution had been the subject of aggressive lobbying by both the Israelis and the Palestinians. A Palestinian delegation traveled to Washington, D.C., to speak with members of President Barack Obama's administration, and Netanyahu appealed to Egyptian President Abdel Fatal al-Sisi and U.S. President-elect Donald Trump to get involved in support of Israel. (Trump had previously pledged to move the U.S. embassy from Tel Aviv to Jerusalem—something U.S. governments have historically declined to do given the ongoing dispute over Jerusalem territory—and selected a pro-settlement ambassador to Israel.) In fact, the resolution had originally been sponsored by Egypt and was scheduled for a vote on December 22, but Egypt postponed the vote indefinitely under intense pressure from Israel and following a call from Trump—an unprecedented intervention by an incoming president—to withdraw the resolution. Frustrated by Egypt's decision, delegates from Malaysia, New Zealand, Senegal, and Venezuela responsored the resolution.

Given the widespread support for the resolution among other Security Council members, the United States' decision to abstain from the vote effectively ensured the resolution would pass. A Security Council resolution requires nine votes in favor and no vetoes by China, Britain, France, Russia, or the United States to be adopted. The abstention was also a major break with the United States' routine vetoing of similar measures and traditional efforts to protect Israel from such condemnations. In a statement before the council, U.S. Ambassador Samantha Power explained that the United States did not vote for the resolution because of a seeming bias against Israel in the UN, noting that eighteen resolutions condemning Israel had been adopted by the UN General Assembly and Human Rights Council in 2016, but that she did not vote against it because it included important provisions calling on parties to the conflict to prevent acts of terrorism or incitement of violence. Power also explained that the accelerated pace of settlement construction and the stalled peace process had influenced the United States' decision not to veto the resolution. Power reiterated the United States' long-standing position that Israeli settlements jeopardize a two-state solution, which she described as the only possible path to peace. "The United States has been sending a message that settlements must stop privately and publicly for nearly five decades," she said. "One cannot simultaneously champion expanding Israeli settlements and champion a viable two-state solution that would end the conflict. One had to make a choice between settlements and separation." Power added that the vote "does not in any way diminish the United States' steadfast and unparalleled commitment to the security of Israel."

Palestinian officials welcomed the vote and suggested they may leverage the resolution to challenge Israel on other fronts, such as by boycotting the settlements and the companies that work with them. Officials also raised the possibility of prosecuting Israeli leaders before the International Criminal Court, filing lawsuits on behalf of displaced Palestinians, and pressing international authorities to assess whether Israel is violating the Geneva Conventions.

Netanyahu quickly and forcefully rejected what he called a "shameful anti-Israel resolution" and said the country would not abide by its terms. "At a time when the Security Council does nothing to stop the slaughter of half a million people in Syria, it disgracefully gangs up on the one true democracy in the Middle East, Israel," he said. Netanyahu also claimed that Israel had evidence that the Obama administration had initiated and was directly involved in the drafting of the resolution, a charge that U.S. officials denied. In addition to his sharp criticisms, Netanyahu ordered Israel's ambassadors to New Zealand and Senegal to return home and summoned the U.S. ambassador and ambassadors from ten other countries that voted for the resolution and have embassies in Israel to Jerusalem to lodge a personal protest. He canceled a visit by Senegal's foreign minister to Israel as well as meetings he had scheduled with the Ukrainian and British prime ministers and instructed the Foreign Ministry to suspend any other diplomatic trips to countries that supported the resolution. Netanyahu further pledged that Israel would reevaluate its ties to the UN, including the funding it provides to UN entities. "I have already instructed to stop about 30 million shekels ($7.8 million) in funding to five U.N. institutions, five bodies, that are especially hostile to Israel . . . and there is more to come," he said.

Trump was also critical of the Obama administration's decision to abstain from the vote rather than veto the resolution. "As the United States has long maintained, peace between the Israelis and the Palestinians will only come through direct negotiations between the parties and not through the imposition of terms by the United Nations," he said. "This puts Israel in a very poor negotiating position and is extremely unfair to all Israelis." Trump also tweeted that "things will be different after Jan. 20th," a reference to his inauguration day. Several members of Congress also voiced their opposition to the United States' abstention. "It is extremely frustrating, disappointing and confounding that the administration has failed to veto this resolution," said Sen. Chuck Schumer, D-N.Y. Sen. Lindsey Graham, R-S.C., threatened that Congress could take steps to "suspend or significantly reduce" U.S. funding for the UN.

ISRAEL PUSHES FORWARD WITH NEW SETTLEMENTS

True to Netanyahu's word, Israel showed no intention to halt settlement development, despite the resolution's passage. Three days after the vote, on December 26, the Israeli government announced that it planned to approve construction of approximately 6,000 new homes in East Jerusalem. Building permits for 566 of those new housing units were approved on January 22 by the Jerusalem Planning and Building Committee. On January 24, Israel's Ministry of Defense announced that 2,500 new housing units would be built in the West Bank, most of which would be constructed in "settlement blocs" (areas of the West Bank that Israel intends to keep under any potential peace agreement). The Ministry of Defense stated that it would begin soliciting bids for the first 900 homes, while the rest of the units went through further planning phases. In addition, the ministry said it intended to present a plan to the Israeli cabinet for building a large industrial zone in the West Bank to help create jobs for Palestinians.

Observers speculated that Israel was pressing for new settlements in anticipation of warmer and more supportive relations with the incoming Trump administration. Trump, who continually pledged his support for Israel during his campaign, even suggested he would be open to a one-state solution, instead of the long-favored two-state solution, during a joint press conference with Netanyahu on February 15. "I'm looking at two-state and at one-state and I like the one that both parties like," he said. "I can live with either one."

—Linda Fecteau Grimm

Following is a press release issued by the UN Security Council on December 23, 2016, after its adoption of a resolution condemning Israeli settlements, which includes the full text of the resolution.

UN Security Council Resolution on Israeli Settlements

December 23, 2016

The Security Council reaffirmed this afternoon that Israel's establishment of settlements in Palestinian territory occupied since 1967, including East Jerusalem, had no legal validity, constituting a flagrant violation under international law and a major obstacle to the vision of two States living side-by-side in peace and security, within internationally recognized borders.

Adopting resolution 2334 (2016) by 14 votes, with the United States abstaining, the Council reiterated its demand that Israel immediately and completely cease all settlement activities in the occupied Palestinian territory, including East Jerusalem. It underlined that it would not recognize any changes to the 4 June 1967 lines, including with regard to Jerusalem, other than those agreed by the two sides through negotiations.

The Council called for immediate steps to prevent all acts of violence against civilians, including acts of terror, as well as all acts of provocation and destruction. It further called for the strengthening of ongoing efforts to combat terrorism, including through existing security coordination, and to clearly condemn all acts of terrorism. The Council called on both sides to observe calm and restraint, and to refrain from provocative actions, incitement and inflammatory rhetoric in order to de-escalate the situation on the ground and rebuild trust and confidence.

Also by the text, the Council called on all parties to continue to exert collective efforts to launch credible negotiations on all final-status issues in the Middle East peace process, and within the time frame specified by the Middle East Quartet (European Union, Russian Federation, United Nations, United States) in its statement of 21 September 2010. It called upon all States to distinguish, in their relevant dealings, between the territory of the State of Israel and the territories occupied since 1967.

Explaining her delegation's abstention, the representative of the United States said it had been a long-standing position of her country that settlements undermined Israel's security and eroded prospects for peace and stability. She emphasized, however, that her vote today had not been straightforward. Explaining that Israel had been treated differently from other States for as long as it had been a member of the United Nations, she noted that during the course of 2016, 18 resolutions adopted in the General Assembly and others in the Human Rights Council had all condemned Israel. It was because of that bias that the United States had not voted in favour of the resolution, she said, emphasizing that her delegation would not have let the resolution pass had it not addressed terrorism and incitement to violence.

Malaysia's representative said effective Council action must be taken without further delay to reverse dangerous trends on the ground that were threatening any possibility of a two-State solution. Settlement activity constituted the single biggest threat to peace, and had led to settler violence, home demolitions and denial of development. Decades of human rights violations had frustrated those with nothing to lose, leading to acts of violence, she said, adding that the resolution could give hope to the people of Palestine and Israel, the majority of whom still wanted peace and a two-State solution.

Israel's representative said those who had voted "yes" to the resolution had voted "no" to negotiations, to progress and to a chance for better lives for both Israelis and Palestinians, and to the possibility of peace. The resolution would continue to provide excuses for the Palestinians to avoid recognizing Israel's right to exist, he said, adding that the Council had voted to condemn the State of Israel and the Jewish people for building homes in the land of Israel, and to deny "our eternal rights" in Jerusalem. "We will continue to be a democratic State based on the rule of law and full civil and human rights for all our citizens," he declared. "And we will continue to be a Jewish State proudly reclaiming the land of our forefathers."

The Permanent Observer of the State of Palestine said the Council's action, while long-overdue, was timely, necessary and important. The resolution required vigilant follow-up if it was to be meaningful and salvage a two-State solution from relegation to history's archives. Israel's illegal settlements and its wall had undermined the contiguity of Palestinian land and isolated East Jerusalem. To claims of bias, he said the only bias was against law, reason and the vision of two States as the most viable solution.

Egypt's representative said the text expressed the painful reality of illegitimate settlements and confiscation of Palestinian land. Noting that his delegation had been compelled to withdraw its own draft resolution, he emphasized that it was unacceptable for some Council members to have warned Egypt, recalling that his country had been the first to make peace with Israel. . . .

[Summaries of statements offered by the delegates from Malaysia, New Zealand, Venezuela, and Egypt have been omitted.]

SAMANTHA POWER (United States) said the immediate adoption of a freeze on settlements could create confidence, adding that further settlement activities were not necessary for Israel's security. President Ronald Reagan had said that in 1982, she recalled, noting that his words underscored her country's commitment to a lasting peace between Israelis and Palestinians and highlighted its position that settlements undermined Israel's security and eroded prospects for peace and stability.

She said that while her vote today was in line with her country's bipartisan tradition, the vote itself had not been straightforward. Explaining that Israel had been treated differently from other States for as long as it had been a member of the United Nations, she pointed out that in the course of 2016, 18 resolutions had been adopted in the General Assembly and others in the Human Rights Council, all condemning Israel. Because of that bias, and some factors not included in the resolution, the United States had not voted in favour of the resolution, she said, explaining that her delegation would not have let it pass had it not addressed acts of terrorism and incitement to violence.

The issue of settlements was now putting a two-State solution at risk too, she continued. The number of settlers had increased dramatically, and legislation now before the Knesset would legalize most of their outposts. Emphasizing that one must make a choice between settlements and separation, she said her delegation had not supported the resolution because it was focused too narrowly on settlements.

She went on to stress that Palestinian leaders must recognize that incitement for violence eroded prospects for peace. There had been hundreds of attacks, but rather than being condemned, the attackers were upheld as heroes. Israel faced threats in a difficult neighbourhood, and the United States would not waver in its commitment to its security, she said, underlining that a two-State solution was the only path to peace for the people of Israel and Palestine. It was up to them to choose that path.

Statements

[Summaries of statements offered by the delegates from France, Venezuela, China, the United Kingdom, Uruguay, the Russian Federations, Japan, Malaysia, Angola, New Zealand, Senegal and Spain have been omitted.]

DANNY DANON (Israel) described today as a bad day for his country and the peak of hypocrisy. The Council had wasted time to condemn Israel for building homes in the Jewish people's historic homeland. Those who had voted yes had voted no to negotiations, to progress and to a chance for better lives for both Israelis and Palestinians, he said, adding that they had voted no to the possibility of peace. The resolution would continue to provide excuses for the Palestinians to avoid recognizing Israel's right to exist, he said. There had been a disproportionate number of resolutions condemning Israel and today's text would be added to that shameful list.

He went on to call upon the Council to turn a new page and end the bias against Israel. Today it had voted to condemn the State of Israel and to condemn the Jewish people for building homes in the Land of Israel. Asking every voting member who had given them the right to issue such a decree, denying "our eternal rights in Jerusalem", he expressed full confidence in the justice of Israel's cause and the righteousness of its path. "We will continue to be a democratic State based on the rule of law and full civil and human rights for all our citizens," he emphasized. "And we will continue to be a Jewish State proudly reclaiming the land of our forefathers."

RIYAD MANSOUR, Permanent Observer for the State of Palestine, said that the Council's action, while long overdue, was timely, necessary and important. Over the years, the delegation of the State of Palestine had made countless appeals for the Council to uphold its Charter duties, insisting on the need to confront Israel's oppression of Palestinians and its relentless colonization of their land under a half-century of foreign occupation. Those appeals had been calls for the Council to contribute to the cause of peace—for Palestine, Israel, the Middle East and the world, he said.

The resolution would require vigilant follow-up if it was to be meaningful and if it would salvage the two-State solution from relegation to history's archives, he said. Urgent efforts would be needed to reverse the dangerous, negative trends on the ground and to advance collective efforts to end the occupation that had begun in 1967. For five decades, the occupation had persisted with full force, its illegal settlements and wall having undermined the contiguity of Palestinian lands and isolated East Jerusalem. In response to claims of bias, he said the only bias taking place was bias against law, reason and the vision of two States as the most viable solution.

Urging the Security Council to stand firm by its decision, he expressed hope that the global call for an end to Israel's settlement activities and violations would compel its compliance with the law, de-escalate tensions and bring an end to violence. That would be vital for salvaging the prospects for peace and should be led by responsible Council action, including follow-up to the reports requested of the Secretary-General in relation to implementation of today's resolution. Recognizing the efforts of Arab States in the context of the Arab Peace Initiative, as well as those of France, the Quartet, Egypt and the Russian Federation, he called for intensified international and regional efforts to end Israel's occupation and build a just and lasting peace in an independent, sovereign and contiguous State of Palestine, side by side with Israel and within secure and recognized borders.

Resolution

The full text of resolution 2334 (2016) reads as follows:

"*The Security Council*,

"*Reaffirming* its relevant resolutions, including resolutions 242 (1967), 338 (1973), 446 (1979), 452 (1979), 465 (1980), 476 (1980), 478 (1980), 1397 (2002), 1515 (2003), and 1850 (2008),

"*Guided* by the purposes and principles of the Charter of the United Nations, and reaffirming, *inter alia*, the inadmissibility of the acquisition of territory by force,

"*Reaffirming* the obligation of Israel, the occupying Power, to abide scrupulously by its legal obligations and responsibilities under the Fourth Geneva Convention relative to the Protection of Civilian Persons in Time of War, of 12 August 1949, and *recalling* the advisory opinion rendered on 9 July 2004 by the International Court of Justice,

"*Condemning* all measures aimed at altering the demographic composition, character and status of the Palestinian Territory occupied since 1967, including East Jerusalem, including, *inter alia*, the construction and expansion of settlements, transfer of Israeli settlers, confiscation of land, demolition of homes and displacement of Palestinian civilians, in violation of international humanitarian law and relevant resolutions,

"*Expressing* grave concern that continuing Israeli settlement activities are dangerously imperilling the viability of the two-State solution based on the 1967 lines,

"*Recalling* the obligation under the Quartet Roadmap, endorsed by its resolution 1515 (2003), for a freeze by Israel of all settlement activity, including "natural growth", and the dismantlement of all settlement outposts erected since March 2001,

"*Recalling* also the obligation under the Quartet roadmap for the Palestinian Authority Security Forces to maintain effective operations aimed at confronting all those engaged in terror and dismantling terrorist capabilities, including the confiscation of illegal weapons,

"*Condemning* all acts of violence against civilians, including acts of terror, as well as all acts of provocation, incitement and destruction,

"*Reiterating* its vision of a region where two democratic States, Israel and Palestine, live side by side in peace within secure and recognized borders,

"*Stressing* that the status quo is not sustainable and that significant steps, consistent with the transition contemplated by prior agreements, are urgently needed in order to (i) stabilize the situation and to reverse negative trends on the ground, which are steadily eroding the two-State solution and entrenching a one-State reality, and (ii) to create the conditions for successful final status negotiations and for advancing the two-State solution through those negotiations and on the ground,

"1. *Reaffirms* that the establishment by Israel of settlements in the Palestinian territory occupied since 1967, including East Jerusalem, has no legal validity and constitutes a flagrant violation under international law and a major obstacle to the achievement of the two-State solution and a just, lasting and comprehensive peace;

"2. *Reiterates* its demand that Israel immediately and completely cease all settlement activities in the occupied Palestinian territory, including East Jerusalem, and that it fully respect all of its legal obligations in this regard;

"3. *Underlines* that it will not recognize any changes to the 4 June 1967 lines, including with regard to Jerusalem, other than those agreed by the parties through negotiations;

"4. *Stresses* that the cessation of all Israeli settlement activities is essential for salvaging the two-State solution, and calls for affirmative steps to be taken immediately to reverse the negative trends on the ground that are imperilling the two-State solution;

"5. *Calls* upon all States, bearing in mind paragraph 1 of this resolution, to distinguish, in their relevant dealings, between the territory of the State of Israel and the territories occupied since 1967;

"6. *Calls* for immediate steps to prevent all acts of violence against civilians, including acts of terror, as well as all acts of provocation and destruction, calls for accountability in this regard, and calls for compliance with obligations under international law for the strengthening of ongoing efforts to combat terrorism, including through existing security coordination, and to clearly condemn all acts of terrorism;

"7. *Calls upon* both parties to act on the basis of international law, including international humanitarian law, and their previous agreements and obligations, to observe calm and restraint, and to refrain from provocative actions, incitement and inflammatory rhetoric, with the aim, *inter alia*, of de-escalating the situation on the ground, rebuilding trust and confidence, demonstrating through policies and actions a genuine commitment to the two-State solution, and creating the conditions necessary for promoting peace;

"8. *Calls upon* all parties to continue, in the interest of the promotion of peace and security, to exert collective efforts to launch credible negotiations on all final status issues in the Middle East peace process and within the time frame specified by the Quartet in its statement of 21 September 2010;

"9. *Urges in this regard* the intensification and acceleration of international and regional diplomatic efforts and support aimed at achieving, without delay a comprehensive, just and lasting peace in the Middle East on the basis of the relevant United Nations resolutions, the Madrid terms of reference, including the principle of land for peace, the Arab Peace Initiative and the Quartet Roadmap and an end to the Israeli occupation that began in 1967; and *underscores* in this regard the importance of the ongoing efforts to advance the Arab Peace Initiative, the initiative of France for the convening of an international peace conference, the recent efforts of the Quartet, as well as the efforts of Egypt and the Russian Federation;

"10. *Confirms its determination* to support the parties throughout the negotiations and in the implementation of an agreement;

"11. *Reaffirms* its determination to examine practical ways and means to secure the full implementation of its relevant resolutions;

"12. *Requests* the Secretary-General to report to the Council every three months on the implementation of the provisions of the present resolution;

"13. *Decides* to remain seized of the matter."

SOURCE: United Nations. "Israel's Settlements Have No Legal Validity, Constitute Flagrant Violation of International Law, Security Council Reaffirms." December 23, 2016. www.un.org/press/en/2016/sc12657.doc.htm.

OTHER HISTORIC DOCUMENTS OF INTEREST

FROM PREVIOUS *HISTORIC DOCUMENTS*

Index